NOVEL & SHORT STORY WRITER'S MARKET
2016

includes a one-year online subscription to **Novel & Short Story Writer's Market** on

WritersMarket.com

Where & How to Sell What You Write

THE ULTIMATE MARKET RESEARCH TOOL FOR WRITERS

To register your *Novel & Short Story Writer's Market 2016* book and **start your one-year online genre-only subscription**, scratch off the block below to reveal your activation code, then go to www.WritersMarket.com. Find the box that says "Purchased a Deluxe Edition?" then click on "Activate Your Account" and enter the activation code. It's that easy!

UPDATED MARKET LISTINGS FOR YOUR INTEREST AREA
EASY-TO-USE SEARCHABLE DATABASE • RECORD-KEEPING TOOLS
PROFESSIONAL TIPS & ADVICE • INDUSTRY NEWS

Your purchase of *Novel & Short Story Writer's Market* gives you access to updated listings related to this genre of writing (valid through 12/31/16). For just $9.99, you can upgrade your subscription and get access to listings from all of our best-selling Market Books. Visit **www.WritersMarket.com** for more information.

WritersMarket.com

Where & How to Sell What You Write

Activate your WritersMarket.com subscription
to get instant access to:

- **UPDATED LISTINGS IN YOUR WRITING GENRE:** Find additional listings that didn't make it into the book, updated contact information, and more. WritersMarket.com provides the most comprehensive database of verified markets available anywhere.

- **EASY-TO-USE SEARCHABLE DATABASE:** Looking for a specific magazine or book publisher? Just type in its name. Or widen your prospects with the Advanced Search. You can also search for listings that have been recently updated!

- **PERSONALIZED TOOLS:** Store your best-bet markets, and use our popular recording-keeping tools to track your submissions. Plus, get new and updated market listings, query reminders, and more—every time you log in!

- **PROFESSIONAL TIPS & ADVICE:** From pay-rate charts to sample query letters, and from how-to articles to Q&As with literary agents, we have the resources writers need.

YOU'LL GET ALL OF THIS WITH YOUR INCLUDED SUBSCRIPTION TO

WritersMarket.com

Where & How to Sell What You Write

35th ANNUAL EDITION

NOVEL & SHORT STORY WRITER'S MARKET

2016

Rachel Randall, Editor

WRITER'S DIGEST
BOOKS

WritersDigest.com
Cincinnati, Ohio

Publisher: Phil Sexton

Writer's Market website: www.writersmarket.com

Writer's Digest website: www.writersdigest.com

Distributed in Canada by Fraser Direct
100 Armstrong Avenue
Georgetown, Ontario, Canada L7G 5S4
Tel: (905) 877-4411

Distributed in the U.K. and Europe by F&W Media International
Brunel House, Newton Abbot, Devon, TQ12 4PU, England
Tel: (+44) 1626-323200, Fax: (+44) 1626-323319
E-mail: postmaster@davidandcharles.co.uk

Distributed in Australia by Capricorn Link
P.O. Box 704, Windsor, NSW 2756 Australia
Tel: (02) 4577-3555

ISSN: 0897-9812
ISBN-13: 978-1-59963-938-3
ISBN-10: 1-59963-938-6

Attention Booksellers: This is an annual directory of F+W Media, Inc.
Return deadline for this edition is December 31, 2016.

Edited by: Rachel Randall
Cover designed by: Alexis Brown
Designed by: Claudean Wheeler
Production coordinated by: Debbie Thomas

CONTENTS

THE BUSINESS OF FICTION WRITING

MARKETS

RESOURCES

INDEX

FROM THE EDITOR

Lately I've been thinking a lot about brains.

Not the cow brain you dissected in high school—chilled, reeking of formaldehyde, plopped on a stainless steel table—nor the kind often seen on the menu in an episode of *The Walking Dead*. No, we're fiction writers here, so I'm waxing metaphoric. I'm talking about my creative brain and my editing brain.

When I think of my creative brain, I think of the whimsical nature of storytelling. As a child I adored making things up: spinning characters, narratives, dialogue, and scenes from nothing. It was magical; it was euphoric. It was the reason I started writing.

My editing brain was a late bloomer. After college I discovered I had a knack for revision, for snipping and cutting and sometimes hacking away at my work. But my creative brain struggled with this. For years I wrestled with how to satisfy both—to write untethered and uninhibited while my editing brain prodded me in the back with a sharp elbow: *No, you can't write that; it's stupid.* Often I'd settle into a debilitating paralysis, unable to write the next word, let alone the next chapter.

But over time I (we?) realized that I needed both the loose, carefree nature of my creative brain and the more rigid, structured viewpoint of my editing persona to write successfully. The trick was in balancing them, of letting them thrive in parallel.

Novel & Short Story Writer's Market 2016 is filled with ways to help you achieve that balance. You'll find in-depth discussions on crafting stronger dialogue, strengthening your voice, and revising your work until it gleams. You'll read the inspiring thoughts of best-selling authors like Chris Bohjalian, Lisa Scottoline, John Sandford, and more. You'll gain exclusive access to a webinar from fiction instructor K.M. Weiland on the overlooked but essential elements of story structure. (You can find it here: www.writersmarket.com/nsswm16-webinar.) And, in the listings sections, you'll find comprehensive information for seeking the best venues for publishing your work.

Balancing the creative brain with the editing brain is a challenge I suspect many writers face. But when you succeed in melding the indigenous spark of inspiration with the tenants of solid writing craft, you'll be ready to write and publish your best work.

Rachel Randall
Managing Editor, Writer's Market

HOW TO USE *NSSWM*

To make the most of *Novel & Short Story Writer's Market*, you need to know how to use it. And with more than five hundred pages of fiction publishing markets and resources, a writer could easily get lost amid the information. This quick-start guide will help you navigate through the pages of *Novel & Short Story Writer's Market*—as well as the fiction-publishing process—and accomplish your dream of seeing your work in print.

1. READ, READ, READ. Read numerous magazines, fiction collections, and novels to determine if your fiction compares favorably with work currently being published. If your fiction is at least the same caliber as what you're reading, then move on to step two. If not, postpone submitting your work and spend your time polishing your fiction. Reading the work of others is one of the best ways to improve your craft.

You'll find advice and inspiration from best-selling authors and seasoned writers in the articles found in the first few sections of this book (**Craft & Technique, Interviews,** and **The Business of Fiction Writing**). *Novel & Short Story Writer's Market* also includes listings for **Literary Agents** who accept fiction submissions, **Book Publishers** and **Magazines** that publish fiction in a variety of genres, **Contests & Awards** to enter, and **Conferences & Workshops** where you can meet fellow writers and attend instructive sessions to hone your skills.

2. ANALYZE YOUR FICTION. Determine the type of fiction you write to target markets most suitable for your work. Do you write literary, genre, mainstream, or one of many other categories of fiction? For definitions and explanations of genres and subgenres, check out the **Glossary** and the **Genre Glossary** in the **Resources** section of the book. Many magazines and presses are currently seeking specialized work in each of these areas as well as numerous others.

For editors and publishers with specialized interests, see the **Category Index** in the back of the book.

3. LEARN ABOUT THE MARKET. Read *Writer's Digest* magazine (F+W Media, Inc.); *Publishers Weekly*, the trade magazine of the publishing industry; and *Independent Publisher*, which contains information about small- to medium-sized independent presses. And don't forget the Internet. The number of sites for writers seems to grow daily, and among them you'll find www.writers market.com and www.writersdigest.com.

4. FIND MARKETS FOR YOUR WORK. There are a variety of ways to locate markets for fiction. The periodical section in bookstores and libraries is a great place to discover new journals and magazines that might be open to your type of short stories. Read writing-related magazines and newsletters for information about new markets and publications seeking fiction submissions. Also, frequently browse bookstore shelves to see what novels and short story collections are being published and by whom. Check acknowledgment pages for names of editors and agents, too. Online journals often have links to the websites of other journals that may publish fiction. And last, but certainly not least, read the listings found here in *Novel & Short Story Writer's Market*.

5. SEND FOR GUIDELINES. In the listings in this book, we try to include as much submission information as we can get from editors and publishers. Over the course of the year, however, editors' expectations and needs may change. Therefore, it is best to request submission guidelines by sending a self-addressed, stamped envelope (SASE). You can also check each magazine's and press's website—they usually contain a page with guideline information. For an even more comprehensive and continually updated online markets list, access your one-year subscription to the fiction-related listings on www.writers market.com; you'll find the access code on the first page of this book.

6. BEGIN YOUR PUBLISHING EFFORTS WITH JOURNALS AND CONTESTS OPEN TO BEGINNERS. If this is your first attempt at publishing your work, your best bet is to begin with local publications or those you know are open to beginning writers. After you have built a publication history, you can try submitting to the more prestigious and nationally distributed magazines. For markets most open to beginners, look for the O symbol preceding listing titles. Also look for the ◑ symbol that identifies markets open to exceptional work from beginners as well as work from experienced, previously published writers.

7. SUBMIT YOUR FICTION IN A PROFESSIONAL MANNER. Take the time to show editors that you care about your work and are serious about publishing. By following a publication's or book publisher's submission guidelines and practicing standard submission etiquette, you can increase your chances that an editor will want to take the time to read your work and consider it for publication. Remember: First impressions matter. A carelessly assembled submission packet can jeopardize your chances before your story or novel manuscript has had a chance to speak for itself.

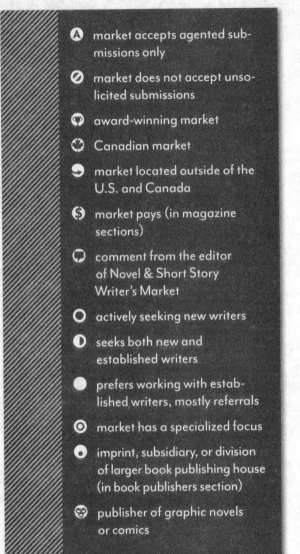

A market accepts agented submissions only

⊘ market does not accept unsolicited submissions

🏆 award-winning market

🍁 Canadian market

🌐 market located outside of the U.S. and Canada

$ market pays (in magazine sections)

💬 comment from the editor of Novel & Short Story Writer's Market

○ actively seeking new writers

◑ seeks both new and established writers

● prefers working with established writers, mostly referrals

◉ market has a specialized focus

⦿ imprint, subsidiary, or division of larger book publishing house (in book publishers section)

😼 publisher of graphic novels or comics

8. KEEP TRACK OF YOUR SUBMISSIONS. Know when and where you have sent fiction and how long you need to wait before expecting a reply. If an editor does not respond in the time indicated in his or her market listing or guidelines, wait a few more months, and then follow up with a letter (and SASE) asking when the editor anticipates making a decision. If you still do not receive a reply from the editor within a month or two, send a letter withdrawing your work from consideration and move on to the next market on your list.

9. LEARN FROM REJECTION. Rejection is the hardest part of the publication process. Unfortunately rejection happens to every writer, and every writer needs to learn to deal with the negativity involved. On the other hand, rejection can be valuable when used as a teaching tool rather than a reason to doubt yourself and your work. If an editor offers suggestions with his or her rejection slip, take those comments into consideration. You don't have to agree with an editor's opinion of your work. It may be that the editor has a different perspective on the piece than you do. Or you may find that the editor's suggestions give you new insight into your work and help you improve your craft.

10. DON'T GIVE UP. The best advice we can offer you as you try to get published is to be persistent and to always believe in yourself and your work. By continually reading other writers' work, constantly working on the craft of fiction writing, and relentlessly submitting your work, you will eventually find that magazine or book publisher that's the perfect match for your fiction. *Novel & Short Story Writer's Market* will be here to help you every step of the way.

GUIDE TO LISTING FEATURES

Below is an example of the market listings contained in *Novel & Short Story Writer's Market*, with callouts identifying the various format features of the listings. (For an explanation of the icons used, see the sidebar on the opposite page.)

EASY-TO-USE REFERENCE ICONS

E-MAIL AND WEBSITE INFORMATION

SPECIFIC CONTACT NAMES

DETAILED SUBMISSION GUIDELINES

EDITOR'S COMMENTS

◑⑤✆ THE SOUTHERN REVIEW

Old President's House, Louisiana State University, Baton Rouge, LA 70803-5001. (225)578-5108. Fax: (225)578-5098. E-mail: southernreview@lsu.edu. **Website:** www.lsu.edu/thesouthern review.

Contact Cara Blue Adams, editor. Magazine: 6¼ × 10; 240 pages; 50 lb. Glatfelter paper; 65 lb. #1 grade cover stock. Quarterly. Circ. 3,000.

• Several stories published in *The Southern Review* were Pushcart Prize selections

NEEDS Literary. "We select fiction that conveys a unique and compelling voice and vision." Receives approximately 300 unsolicited mss/month. Accepts 4-6 mss/issue. Reading period: September-June. Publishes ms 6 months after acceptance. Agented fiction 1%. Publishes 10-12 new writers/year. Recently published work by Jack Driscoll, Don Lee, Peter Levine, and Debbie Urbanski. Also publishes literary essays, literary criticism, poetry, and book reviews.

HOW TO CONTACT Mail hard copy of ms with cover letter and SASE. No queries. ("Prefer brief letters giving author's professional information, including recent or notable publications. Biographical info not necessary." Responds in 10 weeks to mss. Sample copy for $8. Writer's guidelines online. Reviews fiction, poetry.

PAYMENT/TERMS Pays $30/page. Pays on publication for first North American serial rights. Sends page proof to author via e-mail. Sponsors awards/contests.

TIPS "Careful attention to craftsmanship and technique combined with a developed sense of the creation of story will always make us pay attention."

THE INS AND OUTS OF OUTLINES

....

Jennifer D. Foster

Behind every successful novel or short story is an outline, right? Maybe. Some authors swear by a detailed plan (they're known as "plotters"), while others, namely those fly-by-the-seat-of-your-pants writers (known as "pantsers" or "SOPs"), despise outlines. *New York Times* best-selling author Joseph Finder, for example, believes that "writing without an outline is like doing a high-wire act without a net. Some people can do it, but wouldn't you really rather have a net? I would." *New York Times* best-selling author J.A. Jance, however, says she "met outlining in Mrs. Watkin's sixth-grade geography class in Bisbee, Arizona. I hated outlining then; I hate it now. I do *not* outline."

What exactly causes this great divide? By examining this question of process via authors who do and don't outline—and why—and via key insights from a selection of those working directly in the world of publishing, including authors, agents, writing instructors, editors, and publishers, we'll get front-row seats to this age-old debate. For those looking for practical how-tos, tips on creating an effective outline will help send you on your writerly way.

PLOTTERS VERSUS PANTSERS: THE GREAT DEBATE

Plotters: The Benefits of Outlines

Elizabeth Sims, Florida-based author of the award-winning Lillian Byrd crime series, says her favorite method is to "jot down some basic ideas for a plot, focusing on what I call 'heart-clutching moments,' then work out the rest as I write the book. Beyond that, I'll often look ahead two or three chapters and write a paragraph for each one that simply says what has to happen in that chapter." And she prefers to use the term *story map*, disliking the word *outline*. "The term *outline* seems to connote rules and distasteful work. *Story map* brings to mind discovery, adventure, and getting somewhere," emphasizes Sims, who's also a contributing editor for *Writer's Digest*. Lynn Wiese Sneyd, owner of LWS Literary Services in Tuscon, Arizona, refers to outlines as "tracks," and Mary Lou

"Once I've mapped everything out scene by scene, I know where I want to introduce a love scene, a confrontation, some mystery, or a funny bit, just to keep them wanting more. I get a feel for whether it's all going to work to my satisfaction."
—MARY LOU GEORGE

George, a Toronto, Ontario-based mainstream romance novelist, likens them to a "road map," stressing that her willingness to "prepare them is the only thing that separates me from the animal kingdom."

Regardless of what they're called, outlines, for those who prefer them, are a godsend. "For me, the outline is crucial," says George. "A good outline helps me plot and pace the work. It can keep me on track and help me identify weaknesses in my story. I can see where I'm going to run into trouble before I start writing, and I can structure the story accordingly." How does an outline help her? "I map out what's going to happen in each chapter. If my story involves a mystery that needs to be solved, I highlight the clues, misdirection, etc., just to keep track. I list each scene. That way, I can get a feel for high-tension points in the story and pace accordingly. Once I've mapped everything out scene by scene, I know where I want to introduce a love scene, a confrontation, some mystery, or a funny bit, just to keep them wanting more. I get a feel for whether it's all going to work to my satisfaction."

Sims feels that "an outline is well worth the trouble when writing a mystery." So does Kathryn Mockler, Toronto, Ontario-based publisher of *The Rusty Toque* (an online literary, film, and art journal); senior editor at the literary magazine *Joyland: A Hub for Short Fiction* (Toronto); and creative writing lecturer at Western University in London, Ontario. "If you are writing genre fiction or screenplays, you pretty much have to have a tight structure, and outlining can be helpful for that." Nita Pronovost, editorial director at Simon & Schuster Canada and a former senior editor at Penguin Random House in Toronto, Ontario, agrees, adding: "Often, genre writers have more practice using the outline as a technique and tool that guides their creative process rather than stifles it." Jennifer MacKinnon, a freelance editor in Newcastle, Ontario, and a former editor at Scholastic Canada, concurs. "Mystery novels need to have very specific events happen for the story to work in the end, [and that's why] it may help writers work out some plot holes and structural and pacing issues beforehand, which would mean less editorial revisions later." Finder feels the same holds true for his novels. "Thrillers have too many moving parts. They're all about plot. They're almost always too complex to write without doing some sort of outline in advance." For his novel *Power Play*, he took his writer friend Lee Child's advice and "brazened" his way through it, sans outline, which "wound up taking me several months longer than usual, simply because I wasted a lot of time on plot and on characters that I ended up cutting out."

Unleashing Creativity

No one knows how long the controversy over outlining has been around, but it's a bristly debate with deep roots. One thorn of disagreement stems from the notion of creativity: Plotters feel outlining is advantageous and part of the whole process, boosting creativity. Pantsers feel outlining squelches their creative flow. "If you feel like you need an outline in order to write or feel that an outline releases your creativity, then you should use an outline," says Wiese Sneyd. MacKinnon believes that "even with an outline, the author has thought creatively about the story and the plotting and the characters." And Toronto, Ontario-based award-winning author and freelance editor Janice Weaver stresses that new writers should be mindful not to "adopt the mind-set that the outline is somehow the enemy of creativity." George agrees, adding that an outline is "there to help me, to enhance my creativity. That's its reason for living. I don't look at my outline as written in stone. I created it; it's mine to morph into whatever I choose. It's as adaptable as I want to make it."

Sims says, for her, the greatest benefit of a story map is "anxiety reduction. You get up and grab your materials, and you can start that next chapter knowing at least basically what you have to get done in it." Wiese Sneyd concurs. "As you venture into the storytelling and the manuscript, an outline can ease the anxiety of creating that which has never been created: unique characters acting within a unique story. It can shed light on a writing process that otherwise takes place in total darkness." Philadelphia-based non-outliner Robin Black, author of the novel *Life Drawing* and the short story collection *If I Loved You, I Would Tell You This*, expands on this notion. For her, one of the downsides of not outlining is that "it is definitely a less secure process—emotionally, I mean. When I wrote my fully outlined novel, I knew what I was doing every day. … I enjoyed the lack of panic that nothing will occur to me next, or that I'll take some giant wrong turn."

Taking Control of the Process

Another benefit of outlines, according to plotters, is being in the driver's seat. "It partly has to do with control. It feels good

> "As you venture into the storytelling and the manuscript, an outline can ease the anxiety of creating that which has never been created: unique characters acting within a unique story. It can shed light on a writing process that otherwise takes place in total darkness." —LYNN WIESE SNEYD

to know ahead of time where the story is going and how it ends. The blank page can feel very unsettling," says Wiese Sneyd. "I've heard some authors say that their outline consists of a beginning and an ending. Their job is then to fill in the middle." For Wilmington, North Carolina-based Wiley Cash, *New York Times* best-selling author of *A Land More Kind Than Home* and *This Dark Road to Mercy*, "the greatest benefit is that it offers you the chance to see the totality of your idea. I'll typically outline a novel once I know who the main characters are, so that I can get a sense of how I see their lives unfolding and how their lives will flow with and against the narrative." His rationale? "Each character has a tiny plot evolving inside him or her, and it's important to keep that in mind before you try to develop the arc of the broader narrative." Cash says he won't look at the outline for months while he's writing, "but it will always be there in the back of my mind. It's like the map in the glove box that you're hesitant to get out and unfold because you think you may recognize a landmark around the next bend in the road. But the map definitely gives you some peace. It's there if you need it. For me, outlines are the same."

Pronovost also agrees with the outline-as-map benefit. "The initial outline is a kind of map. I can sometimes spot narrative problems right from the outline, which means that the author is saved the aggravation and time of falling into a potential black hole in the story." For her, outlines provide "clarity of thought, organization, direction ... an architecture to a story, and it helps the author

(and editor) retain a kind of muscle memory of the framework long after the outline has been put aside and the work on scenes and chapters begins." And, she says, "what an outline can do, especially for new writers, is save them from becoming too involved in the journey and becoming lost in the maze of superfluous narrative." Weaver concurs: "Outlines are especially important for new writers, because those are the people who sometimes lack the discipline or the critical distance needed to see the problems with their manuscripts." Pronovost also stresses that "the outline provides a way for the author to think from the point of view of the creator and from the point of view of the readership." How, exactly? "The outline creates awareness in the writer of the techniques they are using to tell the story: what each chapter covers, what the main actions are, how each segment opens and closes, where the major turning points occur, and so on. That's taking care of the reader's experience, something an author should always consider."

Treating the Outline as a First Draft

Scottsbluff, Nebraska-based K.M. Weiland, author of *Outlining Your Novel*, *Structuring Your Novel*, and the fantasy novel *Outlander*, has an interesting theory about the pros of outlining. "Many authors who don't use an outline are actually using their *first drafts* as an outline of sorts—from which they then figure out the story's problems and use it as a template to write a better second draft." So, she says, "outlines are my rough draft. And then when I actually go to write the first draft, it's actually the second draft. Since I already know what's going to happen, it's where I get to fine-tune those ideas, smooth them out, and explore them further." For Weiland, "outliners do most of the major revising in the predraft process, which allows for much faster (and, dare I say, more fun?) first drafts and much less revision time afterward."

Karen Wiesner, genre author of more than one hundred novels and of *First Draft in 30 Days* and *From First Draft to Finished Novel*, agrees. She used to be a pantser, but after writing sometimes twelve drafts of a novel to finally get it right, she decided to give outlines a try. "With the right preparation, you can create an outline so complete, it actually qualifies as the first draft of your book and includes every single scene of your book. You can see your entire novel from start to finish in one condensed place. An outline like this ... contains every single one of your plot threads, unfurled with the correct pacing and the necessary tension, culmination, and resolution from beginning to end." For Wiesner, the outline is "the place to work out your story settings, plot conflicts, and in-depth characterization before starting the actual book. This allows you to focus on scenes that work cohesively together and advance all of these. Additionally, tension, foreshadowing, dialogue, introspection, action, descriptions, etc. can best be done within the outline, building strength while adding texture and complexity." The best part? "Creating an outline like this puts the hard work of writing where it belongs—at the beginning of a project. If you work out the kinks in the story in the outline, you ensure that the writing and revising are the easy parts." Wiesner's analogy cements her argument: "When I write a book based

on a 'first draft' outline, pure magic happens because I watch the skeleton—the framework of the book contained in my outline—putting on flesh, becoming a walking, talking, *breathing* story."

Like Weiland, Pronovost, and Wiesner, Weaver believes an outline can save a writer both time and frustration. "Ideally, it will force you to think through the events of your novel before you ever put pen to paper, and in doing so, it can reveal potential pitfalls, uncover creative opportunities you hadn't considered, and give you a broader perspective. An outline can condense that process and minimize the wrong turns, and that makes it more likely that you'll finish what you started." Sally Cooper, Hamilton, Ontario-based author of *Love Object* and *Tell Everything* and creative writing professor at Humber College in Toronto, Ontario, agrees with Weaver's thoughts. "A good outline helps me think through the story ahead of time, so I avoid writing myself into an unresolvable corner. Outlines also create direction, signposts, or goals to look forward to and meet."

Kathy Lowinger, Toronto, Ontario-based author and former publisher of Tundra Books, says that, "oddly enough, a detailed outline can be of most use to those who write beautifully. For them, it is easy to write a great sentence or paragraph or even several pages without benefit of a good skeletal structure. Eventually it becomes apparent that the plot isn't well thought out, but good writing can hide the plot flaws for a long time." She also believes that for writers who claim to be smothered by an outline, "I always think that they don't understand what an outline is. It can be changed if it isn't working, but," she cautions, "the author has to understand that a single change should be looked at in the context of the whole work."

Speaking of the whole work, Weaver has a fitting metaphor regarding outlines. She likes to compare a manuscript to a jigsaw puzzle. "Your job as the writer is to make all the pieces fit together to form a complete and pleasing picture in the end. The outline is the photograph on the puzzle box—it's a guide to remind you what picture you're ultimately trying to create. Sometimes you're contending with a puzzle that comes with extra pieces that don't quite fit. A big challenge for most writers, in my experience, is recognizing that those extra pieces don't belong, and having the courage to let them go. An outline can relieve you of some of those decisions by making it clear when something doesn't fit."

A WORD TO THE WISE FOR PLOTTERS

Even pro-outliners caution against following an outline blindly. "If you get extremely detailed and rigid about the outline process, you can rob yourself of the chance to stumble upon something awesome," says Sims. "An outline can and should be fluid. Be okay with throwing an outline away and starting over or slicing and dicing and adding in new stuff—even if you're halfway through your book. If you get a gut feeling you ought to try something drastically different, give it a go." MacKinnon concurs. "The outline is just a written guideline. Most authors I know would never let an outline get in the way of a good story. If inspiration hits in the middle of writing, and the characters or story seems to be going in a different direction, they follow their instincts and go with the story rather than the outline." Cash holds the same theory, stressing that "the greatest drawback is that there's always the risk of being shackled to your outline. Trust me, you won't disturb the universe if you don't follow it."

Pronovost feels the same. "Just because a writer has a plan doesn't mean she has to dogmatically stick to it. There is always room for creativity in any structure, including in an outline. A rough, flexible, dynamic outline—one where change can occur throughout the drafting process—is a very practical tool." Kevin Morgan Watson, publisher at Press 53 in Winston-Salem, North Carolina, agrees. "An outline should be, to borrow a phrase from the movie *Ghostbusters*, 'more of a guideline than a rule.' A writer should always be open to new ideas that present themselves during the writing process. When that little voice says, 'What if my character does this or goes there instead of following the outline; I wonder what would happen?' I think writers should listen to that voice and take the detour." He cites the "wise words" from American poet Robert Frost as further evidence: "No surprise in the writer, no surprise in the reader."

Shaping the Story

For Sam Hiyate, literary agent, president, and co-founder of The Rights Factory in Toronto, Ontario, "outlines are essential for helping shape a story. You wouldn't start building a house without blueprints. Why start a novel without one?" For Hiyate, who's also a creative writing instructor at the University of Toronto and a publishing instructor at Ryerson University, "the most important thing is to write an outline at the level of detail that makes you comfortable. Some writers might have one [outline] that is two pages, whereas some might want ten to fifteen pages. If you have it in bullet points to start, you can still enter a chapter or scene with a lot of possibility, as long as you know where it will quickly go." For him, it's all about "writing with the level of detail that will keep your writing spontaneous and fresh."

For number one *New York Times* bestselling author John Grisham, outlines are the Holy Grail of productivity and structure. "The books are carefully outlined before I ever start. Chapter by chapter, from beginning to end. And usually tedious and boring and even painful—but it's the only way to make sure the story's going to work. Usually the outline is fifty pages long. And the longer the outline, the easier the book is to write. I have started several books and put them aside—and a couple of times I've gone back and been able to finish them." This level of planning for an outline on the part of the author could be an example of what novelist and short story author Terence M. Green refers to as "the micro-manager, who plans the whole story out in advance before the actual writing. I think it's fair to say that the writer who benefits the most from the micro-planning is the one most concerned with plot, and plot intricacies and twists."

George sees an outline as a life-enhancing literary safety net. "If you run into trouble, it's never too late to create an outline to help you along. It can be as detailed or as sketchy as you'd like. Sometimes, when I'm having a crisis of confidence, I will hone the outline in order get reassurance that my story has merit. That, alone, can get me writing again." And George stresses that the outline may be for the writer's eyes only. "Remember that no one else needs to see the outline.

"The more detailed I got while outlining, the more frustrating the process, because my natural inclination is to figure out a lot along the way. Things come to me, answers to difficult plot questions appear as I write chapter after chapter. And, of course, as I develop characters, I get to know them better and better, and they themselves suggest action, plot points, resolutions, and so on."
—ELIZABETH SIMS

"Part of the joy in writing fiction is the surprise of it, the discovery of things I hadn't known were in me or that I wanted to say, or, more likely, the way those things chose to be said."
—ELIZABETH BERG

It doesn't have to be perfect. You don't have to update it or stay faithful to it—it's so unlike a spouse in that way. In fact, my relationship with my outline is probably the best I've ever known."

Pantsers: The Cons of Outlines

For those who love to hate outlines, the writing process is viewed as more organic and free-flowing. Weiland believes many authors are "so talented and so able to hold the entire novel in their heads. They simply don't need the tools that help the rest of us achieve that same end product." Key West, Florida-based Meg Cabot, a number one *New York Times* best-selling author, is one such writer. "Because writing a book, to me, is like taking a trip. I know in my head where I want to go. I just don't write out an elaborately detailed itinerary. Because the fun part—to me—is figuring out how I'm going to get there, and checking out the interesting sites I see along the way." Author Harlan Coben is another *New York Times* best-selling writer with a similar mind-set. "I don't outline. I usually know the ending before I start. I know very little about what happens in between. It's like driving from New Jersey to California. I may go Route 80, I may go via the Straits of Magellan, or stopover in Tokyo … but I'll end up in California," he says. In an interview for the U.K.'s

The Telegraph, he clarifies further: "E.L. Doctorow has a wonderful quote on writing where he says that it is like driving at night in the fog with your headlights on. You can only see a little bit ahead of you, but you can make the whole journey that way. I concur, except that I know, in the end, where I'm going." And, interestingly enough, for Coben, "there is no 'why' I don't [outline]—you just do what works for you as a writer." Sims believes that memory plays a role in why some writers, like Coben, don't outline— they can hold seemingly endless amounts of material in their heads before turning it into a book. But she muses on the impact time may have. "I sure wouldn't tell him to change, but I wonder how that method will work as he gets older and the brain cells get a little less efficient!"

Pronovost looks at it this way: "Instinctive writers sometimes hold a book's architecture in their mind—essentially, the outline for them is something private, maybe even sacred, and speaking it out loud or committing it to paper can feel counterintuitive or even rigid." Deborah Grabien, author and editor at Plus One Press in San Francisco, California, is in full agreement. "As both a writer (eighteen published novels and music journalism) and an editor of other peoples' work (two anthologies of short fiction), I loathe outlines. I find working with an outline the functional equivalent of trying to dance in a straitjacket or having sex while wearing a suit of armor. My mantra is, 'A writer writes, period; just tell the damned story.' An outline is rigid and, for me, unworkable."

Embracing the Serendipity

Many writers simply love the serendipity and unpredictability of writing that comes without an outline. They don't like what Finder calls being "constricted by the steel girdle of an outline." Hiyate agrees. "The biggest flaw is, you can write yourself into a corner, and the characters are fighting where you want to go with them. Or, because you've planned too much, some of the spontaneity—and suspense—might be lost." Cabot concedes: "Story ideas don't come along often, and when they do, you have to treat them with care. Outlining them too thoroughly—even *talking* about them too much over coffee with a friend—can actually ruin them, because it can make you feel as if the story is already told. And when that happens, if you're like me, you're dead."

MacKinnon explains it this way: "Some authors might be less inspired to start writing if they think they have the story all figured out. They find the story as they write it. Maybe they need the excitement of finding the characters' motivations and the plot as it unfolds to them as well." J.A. Jance is such an author. "I start with someone dead or dying and spend the rest of the book trying to find out who did it and how come. Knowing what the end will be would make it impossible for me to write the middle," she says. "I think if I knew what the ending would be,

my motivation to write would disappear, as would the sense of discovery. I write for the same reason people read—to find out what happens—and I have *never* read the end of a book first." Her reasoning? "This way, I discover the answers at the same time the characters do. This morning, at 60 percent of a book, I just found out that a character I thought was dead isn't. If I had written an outline, would that even have happened?" Finder, a big fan of outlines, agrees in this case: "That's just the kind of unpredictable twist you want, because if *you* didn't expect it, your reader won't either." And that's exactly why, says Cooper, "the biggest hazard of outlining comes to those who refuse to deviate from their meticulously plotted course. The story may have decreased energy or mystery or sense of surprise—for the reader and for the writer. Writing without an outline or with only a loose outline ideally allows the story to unfold like a movie as it's being written."

Sims, who has worked on both sides of the outlining fence, can relate to Jance, Finder, and Cooper. With her Rita Farmer mystery series, she's had to put together a very detailed outline for each book for her agent. But, she says, "the more detailed I got while outlining, the more frustrating the process, because my natural inclination is to figure out a lot along the way. Things come to me, answers to difficult plot questions appear as I write chapter after chapter. And, of course, as I develop characters, I get to know them better and better, and they themselves suggest action, plot points, resolutions, and so on."

Remaining Surprised

For Black, despite her attempt, outlines do not work. While she's not against them and "envies" people for whom they do work, for her "they are a little deadening," and here's why: "With the first novel I wrote—one I wrote, sold, and then withdrew because I saw its failings all too well—I used a pretty detailed outline. But I found that my 'knowing' what was going to happen took out some element of something like a romantic, if rocky, relationship with the book. I wasn't intrigued by it. The process was a bit like paint-by-numbers for me, and finally I realized that the product was a bit that way as well." So for Black, spontaneity and what she calls "openness" are imperative. "One of the great benefits of winging it—or making it up as I go along—is that I feel fluid not only about such things as what is going to happen but also about the deeper meaning of the story. I like being a little stupid about my own work as it's in process, so I don't fight too hard against its natural process of evolution."

Green, a creative writing professor at Western University, cautions against outlines in terms of their relationship to the organic processes of change and revelation inherent in writing. "If one is a micromanager in terms of adhering to the outline, the pleasure of discovering that your character is going to do something that you didn't know he or she was going to do (like a real human being, your character is unpredictable) seldom happens, and formula fiction often rears its head this way. If writing is discovery (and often self-discovery), the fully outlined and adhered-to story can become a 'product'—albeit a professional one." When it comes to writing, Green has "found it more valuable to keep a charted summary of each segment or chapter after it's completed than to try to chart it in advance (like a journal of the novel; Steinbeck did this)." The purpose? The summary "lets me review it each morning and see clearly what has gone before and what I should be addressing next. Then comes the actual writing that day, and often (in best case) the sense of wonder at what has been created at day's end. And repeat the next day. And the next. In that sense, it's a kind of reverse outlining and progression, tied into what has come before."

In her book *Escaping into the Open: The Art of Writing True,* Chicago, Illinois-based, *New York Times* best-selling, and award-

> "I'm not a fan of obsessively outlining every scene because, for me, it kills my desire to write the story. Writing is a process of discovery, and you can miss great nuggets and details if everything is pre-planned. Too much focus on the structure and not enough on the characters and details and themes can make the writing seem formulaic and flat." — **KATHRYN MOCKLER**

winning author Elizabeth Berg says, "there are two kinds of writers: those who start with a plot and those who end up with one. I am one of the latter." Berg says the few times she tried to plot a novel, "it was as though the book rebelled—it went another way entirely, and then all those notes I'd taken to follow the ever-so-neat sequence of events I'd planned were in vain." Like Jance, Black, Sims, and Green, for Berg "part of the joy in writing fiction is the surprise of it, the discovery of things I hadn't known were in me or that I wanted to say, or, more likely, the way those things chose to be said." Berg starts her novels only with a strong feeling of something she wants to say and/or understand, and the novel helps her do it. "I find almost nothing more enjoyable than to be working on a novel and wake up not having any idea what's going to happen that day. It keeps me interested. It keeps me excited. If I had to write what the plot told me was 'up' next, I'd be bored—it would feel too much like homework." Like other pantsers, for Berg "the magic in writing fiction comes from taking that free fall into the unknown and, rather than making things happen, letting them."

Mockler, who outlines depending on the project, shares Berg's overall sentiments: "I'm not a fan of obsessively outlining every scene because, for me, it kills my desire to write the story. Writing is a process of discovery, and you can miss great nuggets and details if everything is pre-planned. Too much focus on the structure and not enough on the characters and details and themes can make the writing seem formulaic and flat."

FINAL FOOD FOR THOUGHT

The reasons why some writers outline and some don't are as vast and varied as the creators themselves. Bottom line? Use whatever structure, or lack thereof, works best for you, without judgment. "Explore and experiment, and figure out what best unleashes *your* creativity," says Weiland. Writing is a highly individual and personal process, a journey of finding balance and what works best. And the tools and techniques that work best for each writer are always based on "personalities, backgrounds, and circumstances," emphasizes Weiland. If you choose to go the outline route, then remember, she says, that outlines are "about discovering your story and organizing it, so you will then have an accurate road map to follow when writing your first draft." But, stresses Wiese Sneyd, remember not to become too attached to your outline. "Outlines need not be written in stone, but in sand. And don't buy into the idea that an outline is essential to writing. It's not," she stresses. "I know many writers who sit down every day and write into the dark, so to speak. They allow the story and the characters to carry them rather than relying on an outline to do so."

Regardless of your path to the finished product, keep this quote in mind, from Stephen King's *On Writing: A Memoir of the Craft*, for inspiration: "Writing is magic, as much the water of life as any other creative art. The water is free. So drink. Drink and be filled up."

BEST TIPS OF THE TRADE

Looking for some writerly inspiration not only to create but also to nail an effective outline? Our industry experts weigh in with these helpful tips.

"If your book were divided in pieces, what would they be called? How many pieces (acts or parts) would there be? What would happen in each segment? Summarize in only a few sentences, not in a thousand pages. Does your outline have a climax? If not, why not? Does your outline have a clear beginning, middle, and end?" —**NITA PRONOVOST**, editorial director at Simon & Schuster Canada, former senior editor at Penguin Random House

"Don't confuse your outline with a summary of your novel. Keep your outline brief. It doesn't even have to be comprised of complete sentences. Don't be afraid to change it or move things around, and consider putting it away once it's completed." —**WILEY CASH**, *New York Times* best-selling author

"Know your characters. Think in terms of scenes, like a filmmaker. Include thematic and symbolic beats, not just plot points, and be open to throwing the outline out the window if the story takes a promising turn." —**SALLY COOPER**, author and creative writing professor at Humber College

"Outlines are a great way to think through a story, to envision a story, much like a drive across the country or a family vacation: You can plan it down to the hour of every day, but it's in the detours along the way where the better story, the better adventure, may be hiding. And what's the harm in taking a detour to see what is there? If you work from an outline, make it a loose guideline. Give yourself permission to veer off course and explore." —**KEVIN MORGAN WATSON**, publisher, Press 53

"The outline is simply a tool; don't let it intimidate you. Use it as an aid to pace your novel well. Read it over from time to time. Your outline can help you identify slow points in your story. It can remind you that you've forgotten something and, if so, then how necessary is that something? Or maybe it was key, and you can't neglect it. The outline will help you make decisions."—**MARY LOU GEORGE**, romance novelist

"Be flexible. Think of an outline as a collection of puzzle pieces. At first you think a piece might fit well here, but then you see it fits better there. Keep moving the pieces around. Don't be afraid to toss some and add new ones." —**LYNN WIESE SNEYD**, owner of LWS Literary Services

"Think of your outline as the bird's-eye view of your manuscript. It's meant to show you the best path to take—and to reveal any roadblocks long before you get to them—but it shouldn't prevent you from taking the odd side road on your way to your destination. An outline can take many different forms, and if one technique is too restrictive or makes you feel too constrained, try another. One bad experience with outlining doesn't mean all outlines are bad." —**JANICE WEAVER**, award-winning author and freelance editor

"Don't be afraid to make a mess. Writing is like life: glorious, unpredictable, full of passion, woe, and joy. Be okay with ambiguity as you map your story; you'll figure it out. And be open to making parts of your outline rough and other parts very detailed. Don't worry about following any particular form."—**ELIZABETH SIMS**, award-winning author and contributing editor for *Writer's Digest*

"Start out with what your central quest is; give your protagonist a series of trials of various flavors (by that I mean level of difficulty, mood, etc.) to overcome; and put the resolution in the protagonist's hands. And make sure that the protagonist is marked by each trial in some way. This holds for almost every novel, whether the quest is something intangible like acceptance or tangible like the Holy Grail." —**KATHY LOWINGER**, author and former publisher of Tundra Books

"Use the outlining phase as an opportunity to build story structure. The single most important factor of a story's success and salability will be the strength of its structure. The outline is the place to start figuring that out so you will be able to place the important plot points and other structural moments at exactly the right place to allow them to achieve their utmost power." —**K.M. WEILAND**, author

"When writing a short story, I've found it useful to take a sheet of paper and divide it into three (usually Intro, Body, and Conclusion, the Body being the substantial part of the page). By filling in these sections with ideas and details, the story can come to life in a general way. The actual writing of the story is where it can come to life in its particulars. For a new writer of fiction: Know the ending of your story. If one has this in mind, the goal is clear, the path straightens itself." —**TERENCE M. GREEN**, creative writing professor at Western University, novelist, and short story author

Jennifer D. Foster is a Toronto, Canada-based freelance writer, editor, and content strategist, who specializes in book and custom publishing, magazines, and marketing and communications through her company, Planet Word. She lives with her husband, their tween son, and their retired racing greyhound, Aquaman. Jennifer is a mentor to novice editors and writers, and loves kidlit, yoga, Scrabble, yard sales, gardening, and all things Japanese. She can be reached via her website, www.lifeonplanetword.wordpress.com.

THE JOURNALIST'S PERSPECTIVE

Revamping Your Fiction
Using Journalistic Techniques

....

Heather Villa

A journalist knows that thoroughly investigated inquiries provide the foundation for a narrative. Alongside the answers a story emerges, complete with characters, setting, tension, and a voice that captures the mood. For an author of fiction, these elements are sometimes elusive. But they don't need to be.

When a fiction writer applies the techniques of a journalist, an engrossing and entertaining story is within reach. Consider how a journalist takes hold of a story in motion. There are places to go, people to meet, and questions to ask about circumstances likely laced with drama. Descriptive details and words become visible, available to a journalist.

When assigned to write about a neighborhood pharmacy for a business journal, I discovered a sixty-year-old story linked to a presidential campaign. I ran with it. Do you see how real life is orchestrated? There are unexpected discoveries stuck right in the middle of the ordinary. Fiction should be no different.

If you're a fiction writer, think like a journalist to reinvigorate your fiction. Here's how.

WRITE ABOUT WHAT YOU DON'T KNOW

Perhaps you've been told to write about what you know. While the advice is sensible, it's limiting. Award-winning screenwriter Randy LaBarge, whose experience includes journalism and fiction, concurs. "But if we only write what we know, we will quickly exhaust the number of topics each of us can write about."

Journalists often are unfamiliar with the topic when they begin an assignment. But they know how to research a topic to uncover answers. Fiction writers can take the same approach.

LaBarge suggests that writing what we don't know creates a sense of wonder that translates to the reader. A writer who sees the Grand Canyon for the first time, he says,

Journalists often are unfamiliar with the topic when they begin an assignment. But they know how to research a topic to uncover answers. Fiction writers can take the same approach.

versus a writer who has written about the canyon dozens of times, may write about details not previously considered.

Within a new perspective is where voice can materialize. LaBarge describes the essence of voice like this: "Simply put, I believe it's how we tell the story. And how each of us tells a story is the result of our individual life experiences. ..."

LISTEN TO WHAT YOUR CHARACTERS SAY

You'll find the answers to your questions when you listen to what your characters are really trying to say by finding out who they are.

Ann Streetman, adult and children's author, describes her approach to writing fiction. "My training as a journalist helps me create a detailed backstory for the main characters and some of the minor, but nevertheless significant, ones," she says. "I study what was going on in their hometowns and in the world during their teenage years, college years, early adulthood, and beyond, as their ages dictate."

A firm grasp of characterization helps an author of fiction capture believable dialogue. Quotes in any journalistic piece sound real because they are real. Fictional conversations should be similarly structured.

Spend time with your characters; they will surprise you. "I have experienced the joy of trusting my characters well enough toward the end to let them take steps that I had not anticipated," Streetman says.

GO TO UNFAMILIAR PLACES

The steps characters take often lead us to unfamiliar places. Jessica McCann, debut historical novelist of *All Different Kinds of Free*, explains it this way: "I actually prefer to write about unfamiliar places and people. That forces me to do a lot of research to fully understand my subject. That research does more than just add authenticity to my story," she says. "It fuels my creativity and generates ideas for characters, scenes, and events for my novel that otherwise may never have come to me. And, of course, all of that adds up to create a distinctive voice for the story."

LaBarge points out how the unfamiliar benefits writers. "Had we not explored the hidden terrain of our topic, we may never have found the next story, may never have ignited a new passion that could lead us to places we never thought we'd ever go."

SET ASIDE BIASES

It's in those unfamiliar places where biases must be set aside. Journalists know to probe both sides of an issue to ensure substance.

"My writing career began with journalism," McCann says. "When I started seriously studying and pursuing a career as a novelist,

I was surprised to learn how many parallels there are between writing fiction and non-fiction. Hemingway said it better than I can: 'As a writer, you should not judge, you should understand.'" She also explains that when fiction writers set aside biases, readers come away with opinions all their own.

LaBarge offers related advice. "Does the story I've told support the facts and data as I understand them? Being able to honestly answer this question, in spite of our personal biases," he says, "leads us to what might be called 'The True Story,' and this is the story that deserves to be told."

A true story is one in which a writer can find the right voice because a revelation is the core focus.

VERIFY DETAILS TO ENSURE AUTHENTICITY

If you want your readers to believe your story, the details must be accurate. Streetman understands this. "Because I often write about characters from diverse cultural backgrounds and different religions, I do detailed research so that I can capture nuances of specific cultures and religious faiths."

"Are the facts I'm being given verifiable?" is a question LaBarge suggests fiction writers ask from the perspective of a journalist.

Furthermore, organization of information is vital. Streetman knows to manage her research to ensure accuracy. "Over the years, I have learned to store all my research for a specific book in digital file folders so I can access the facts to keep checking myself when I write particular passages."

As for the presidential campaign I mentioned earlier, the pharmacist led me past the "smoking room," where politicians once gathered, to the back of the pharmacy and showed me a faded Harry Truman campaign poster still tacked to the side of a bookshelf.

OWN THE STORY

A journalist pulls from the most concrete and eye-catching details to create an engaging hook, and so should a fiction writer. A journalist doesn't include every researched point in a final story. Streetman makes this point clear. "I know that I will never reveal parts of the backstory in dialogue, but having all of it securely in mind informs my characterizations in subtle ways."

After you've chased a story like a journalist, do what only writers of fiction get to do—bend the truth, embellish the details, and exaggerate the tension. Writer Clyde Blakely, whose work is published in several anthologies, says about fiction: "Write about nonfiction, and lie about it." Make a story completely yours. As a result, the fictional piece will be one of substance.

Heather Villa told visual stories as a cartographer before she became a freelance writer in 2011. She writes fiction and nonfiction. Her byline has appeared in *The Writer*, *National Catholic Reporter*, and *Appleseeds*, among others. She recently completed her first middle-grade novel. She lives with her husband and daughter in Oregon. To learn more about her work, visit HeatherVillaWrites.com.

A DRIVING FORCE

Unlocking Character Motives

....

Leslie Lee Sanders

The importance of motive in a story is critical to the conflict. Motive is essentially the driving force behind the entire plot. Without a clear and relevant reason for your characters to move from point A to point B, your story won't tap into readers' emotions and may fail to reach its full potential.

Motive is the character's need that moves a story forward, but it also encompasses every facet of writing fiction, including plot, characterization, dialogue, point of view, and scenes. Read on to explore how motive builds all parts of a story and how you can successfully incorporate it to enhance your novel.

CHARACTER AND MOTIVE

A character's primary goal influences every aspect of a story from start to end, but before you incorporate his motive you must first identify it.

What Is Motive?

Your character's motive is his drive to succeed, his need, and his determination to get the thing he wants most. It's usually fueled by an inner conflict he battles, a character flaw he must overcome, a secret, or some other emotional or mental turmoil like the pursuit of love, victory, revenge, and so on.

Your character's motive will often be revealed to the reader through his thoughts, words, actions, and personality. For readers to understand and identify your character's motive, the character needs to know where he's headed in your story and why. Once established, this helps you convey the motive to your readers. To determine your character's motive, you must be able to answer at least one of these questions.

1. What does the character need to succeed? Why?
2. What does victory mean for the character? Why?
3. What does failing mean for the character? Why?
4. What is the character trying to accomplish? Why?
5. By the end of the book, how will the character change?

Your character's motive will often be revealed to the reader through his thoughts, words, actions, and personality. For readers to understand and identify your character's motive, the character needs to know where he's headed in your story and why.

The motive is the answer to these questions. The way to successfully incorporate it throughout your story lies in the answer to *why*.

Here are some example answers from the 2012 animated tale *Dr. Seuss' The Lorax.*

Q. What does the character need to succeed? Why?

A. Ted needs a Truffula tree **because** he wants to impress a girl.

Q. What does victory mean for the character? Why?

A. Victory means getting a real live Truffula tree **because** Ted will win the girl's affection.

Q. What does failing mean for the character? Why?

A. Failure means losing the last Truffula tree seed **because** Ted won't impress the girl or improve the air quality.

Q. What is the character trying to accomplish? Why?

A. Ted is trying to plant a Truffula seed **because** Truffula trees produce free oxygen.

Q. By the end of the book, how will the character change?

A. Ted will understand the importance of Truffula trees to mankind.

In short, Ted's motive for the entire story is **to get a Truffula tree**. There are many reasons why—one reason sets him off on his journey, and his reasons change over the course of the story—however, the main goal remains the same. That goal is your character's motive.

Secondary Character Motives

Think of your fictional world as a vast ocean and the conflict and chaos as the crashing waves. Your main character is the fearsome shark, swimming his way through the harshness of the dark waters, determined to get to wherever he needs to be. Every character in your story should pursue something, otherwise they are equivalent to planks of wood floating atop the waves of the roaring sea. What's their purpose? Do they help or hinder the protagonist, or are they just there?

Even secondary characters have a purpose for being. If your characters refuse to bring anything to the table, get rid of them. If they don't have a purpose that mirrors, counters, or enhances your main character's goal, delete them from your prose or rewrite them to better fit.

A character with a reason to do what she does makes her more three-dimensional, more believable. It brings her and the story to life.

Secondary character motives are best when interwoven with the main characters' motive. For example:

- Ted's motive is to get a Truffula tree to please Audrey.
- The Once-ler's motive is to put the last Truffula seed into the hands of someone who cares for the trees.
- Audrey, being an environmentalist, wants to see a real live Truffula tree.
- And Mr. O'Hare wants to destroy Truffula trees since they compromise his bottled oxygen business.

Some motives are stronger than others, but every character in this story has a specific goal, and their reasons intertwine with the protagonist's and help to move the story toward the climactic ending, where we find out if the main character gets what he was after.

PLOT AND MOTIVE

The plot is the character's journey from the opening sentence, through conflict, twists and turns, and finally the resolution. Remember the vast ocean metaphor? Plot is the ocean the protagonist swims through, and obstacles are the crashing waves. They go hand in hand.

How Does a Character's Motive Link to the Story Plot?

In the 1997 movie *Titanic*, Rose's motive is freedom from her controlling mother and fiancé. The plot exists around Jack helping her achieve this freedom. Sure, a huge, unsinkable ship is a major part of the storyline, and it serves as the setting and a complication, but the meat of the plot revolves around the inner conflict of the main characters, Rose and Jack. Rose officially meets Jack when he talks her out of escaping her mental and physical restraint by jumping from the ship to her death.

DIALOGUE AND MOTIVE

Not only should what your characters say be entertaining, memorable, and believable, but how they say it should relate directly to the story's goal and help build tension around it.

Regardless of the type of story, it's important to build suspense for the reader. Make the reader wonder if the character will meet his goal or not. A good way to incorporate suspense is to take us inside the character's mind. One of the best ways to enter the mind and see and feel what the protagonist thinks, feels, aspires to, and so forth is through the words he says and the ways he says them. Who he speaks with and even what he doesn't say are all telling.

The character's goal will always be on his mind or at least in the back of his mind. Either way, it's a key focus of his speech, even if subconsciously. Dialogue is a good way to remind the reader what's important and build suspense along the journey to the end.

Secondary characters are part of the protagonist's life and serve to make his existence more real and relatable, but they can also provide a great way to judge the protagonist's characteristics and his fears and wants. How the people who populate your story treat each other, communicate, and react and respond to one another is a great way to expose the protagonist's motive and its importance.

Below are ways to add dialogue, important information, and character traits to your story to build suspense and keep the readers guessing if the character will succeed or fail.

When Talking to Others
We tend to be cautious when talking to others to lessen judgment or emotional pain. We feel truly open and comfortable only around a close circle of people. For instance, what we say to our lover might be different than what we tell our boss.

How would your protagonist speak to the people in her life to reveal more about her motivations?

- Friends or relatives
- Lovers
- Strangers
- Co-workers or employers
- Behind a pseudonym on social media
- Publicly (to the masses)

When Talking to One's Self
We're more honest when no one is around to judge us. What would your protagonist reveal about himself when he's alone?

- Monologue and true thoughts
- Talking to animals or pets
- Writing in journals or jotting down notes
- Secrets, aspirations, dreams

- Denial, regrets, guilt, grievances
- Fears, flaws, weaknesses

How It's Said (or Not Said)
What your protagonist represses, refuses to say, or rephrases can be used to hint at motive, especially an ulterior motive. Use this device with a narrator or the point-of-view character.

SCENE AND MOTIVE

Questions about whether the character gets what she's searching for should be introduced throughout the entire story and through each scene. Questions aren't necessarily literal, but her environment and the world around her should help or hinder her progression toward her goal.

For example, in *Titanic*, the ship itself is one of the many obstacles preventing Rose from fulfilling her goal of obtaining freedom. How free can you really be if you're confined to a ship floating (or sinking) in a remote area of harsh open waters?

USING MOTIVE SUCCESSFULLY
Write Freely
This advice is meant particularly for write-by-the-seat-of-your-pants writers. Get the story down first. Don't dwell on the small things in the first draft, including the motive and whether it fits every part of the story's structure. Wait until the rewrite to incorporate motive throughout the story. Sometimes you'll come to know your characters better as you write, which can help shed light on their true goals.

Outline Your Story

This advice is meant particularly for writers who prefer to plan their stories in advance. Plan how you'd use motive in every segment of your storytelling before you even begin your story. This angle helps you write a perfect opening sentence, twists, dialogue, etc., and introduce motive early and thoroughly.

Know How It Ends

Will your character find what he's looking for? Will he succeed in his quest? Know from the beginning how things will conclude, and then sprinkle clues throughout the story. Your conclusion can or may come as a surprise to your readers, but it should still make sense when they look back over the story.

Be Subtle

Don't hit your readers over the head with motive by repeating it or reminding them often. By leaving minute hints and clues throughout the story, you foreshadow intent, actions, beliefs, and other parts of the character that make up the reasons she does what she does. Not every sentence, every scene, nor every line of dialogue needs to drip with motive, but by spreading out the details and properly placing information (or letting it fall where it feels natural), you can write a well-motivated character successfully.

Leslie Lee Sanders is the author of more than twenty fiction titles. Her work has been included in *2014 Guide to Self-Publishing* and *2015 Guide to Self-Publishing* (published by Writer's Digest Books) and the blog *Be a Freelance Blogger*. Her blog was shortlisted in Goodreads' 2012 Independent Book Blogger Awards in the Publishing Industry category. She has also been shortlisted or the winner of several online short story competitions, including the Electronic Publishing Industry Coalition (EPIC) awards and the Booktrack flash fiction competition. Leslie blogs about the writing craft at www.LeslieLeeSanders.com.

NOT JUST SECOND CLASS

Writing Secondary Characters in Fiction

....

Jack Smith

When you're writing a short story or novel, you naturally give most of your attention to your protagonist. You focus on your main character's arc, doing everything you can to weed out material that detracts from it. But what about secondary characters? What parts do they play? What parts *should* they play? How developed should they be? As you work and rework your protagonist's trajectory, you need to think about all of the characters who interact with your main character and the impact they will have on your protagonist's growth and overall development.

DISCOVERING THE FUNCTIONS OF SECONDARY CHARACTERS

Secondary characters can aid in both characterization and character development. They can function as mirrors in two different ways, says Catherine Ryan Hyde, author of the highly acclaimed *Pay It Forward* and twenty-four other novels. "They can be mirrors in which your protagonist sees

things he might not otherwise see. Or they can be mirrors that allow the readers to see things that still aren't getting through to your lead character." This second function is especially valuable, states Hyde. "As authors we're told 'show, don't tell,' and that's always sticky and challenging, but especially so when we're supposed to show something about our viewpoint character that he doesn't recognize himself. The author can bounce these things off secondary characters, bringing them into the light."

Anthony Varallo, award-winning author of three short story collections, also emphasizes the characterization function of secondary characters. "Secondary characters are useful in the exact degree that they throw a light upon the primary characters. That is, they are another means of characterization, right up there with physical detail, speech, actions, habits, and the like." Varallo makes adept use of a secondary character as an expository device in "Time Apart Together," from *Think of Me and I'll Know*. Brad, the protagonist, meets with his professor about a college paper he's struggling to finish, largely, says Varallo, because "his thesis statement is abstract and meaningless." Note how the professor draws Brad out.

> Professor Thompson read through to the second page, and then began flipping through my paper as if it were a magazine. He stopped every now and then to read a sentence aloud, but didn't say whether this was because the sentence was good or bad. After a while, he put my paper on his desk, facedown. "It never ceases to amaze me," he said, "the lengths a student will go to make everything fit his or her argument." He gave a little laugh. "By hook or by crook."
>
> This seemed a fair assessment of nearly every paper I'd ever written. "I never believe a thing I'm saying," I said. "When I'm writing a paper. Not one word. The whole time I'm typing, I'm thinking, *What a bunch of lies.*"
>
> Professor Thompson looked at me with a wry smile. "The truth is what we make it," he said.
>
> "I see."

Professor Thompson's comments reveal Brad's limitation as an academic. In his interchange with the professor, Brad makes an unabashed admission of his scholarly ineptness. Varallo could have revealed this information about Brad directly through first-person exposition, but he chose the dramatic method instead. "In this instance," Varallo says, "I needed a secondary character to draw out that layer of characterization, indirectly, through dialogue." As Hyde points out, secondary characters can provide a valuable dramatic function, an alternative to the protagonist's internal exposition, turning this "into real scenes, scenes readers can see vividly in their heads."

Beyond their function in characterization, secondary characters can also spark conflict. In fact they must do so, says Varallo, "no matter how small, to earn their narrative keep. The best secondary characters make the primary characters feel uneasy, doubtful, or on edge." For Walter Cummins, longtime editor of *The Literary Review* and author of several story collections, "just about every short story needs at least one secondary character to serve as a source of tension with the protagonist." The secondary character can be an antagonist "in some form of overt competition with the protagonist," says Cummins, or even be "unaware that he or she is an obstacle to the protagonist." A secondary character need not have a physical presence in the story's present time frame, says Cummins, "but could enter as a memory in the protagonist's mind."

Character conflict drives action, which drives plot. Cummins distinguishes between two types of secondary characters: functionary and functional. "The functionary," he notes, "serves at tables, collects tickets, etc." He helps "reveal the protagonist," but does not drive the plot. The functional type, says Cummins, "plays roles that move the plot along and help reveal the main character's dramatic dilemma."

It's the interaction with functional secondary characters that allows your protagonist to "grow, stretch, and change," says Elizabeth Stuckey-French, author of several comic novels. She lays out various possible scenarios: "A secondary character, let's call him Jim, can aid your protagonist, Jenny, or hinder her in her quest. He could even do both. Jim's appearance in the novel should make Jenny's life, and the novel, more complicated. He may have only a walk-on role, or his own subplot, which touches the primary plot, echoing, enriching, and enlarging it along the way. It's best if Jim is connected to Jenny in some important way—for instance, he might be related to her or to someone she loves, he might work with her, be her neighbor, be an old beau reappearing from her past, or perhaps they share a secret. This connection makes him harder for Jenny and the reader to dismiss."

Consider the following excerpt from Stuckey-French's *The Revenge of the Radioactive Lady*. By a chance meeting at a neighborhood roller skating rink, protagonist Vic meets Gigi, whom he knew back in graduate school. Gigi reveals to Vic that she's just been hired to work with him at Florida Testing Company.

> "You'll be my boss. Can you handle it?" She swung her crossed leg, silver high-heeled sandal dangling from her narrow foot.
>
> It would make everything more fun to have someone he actually knew and liked working with him. "You can help me train the language arts scorers." He made this statement without thinking about it first. As soon as he said it, he knew he shouldn't have. But for the first time in forever, he felt a bit reckless. He was aware that he was willing to risk pissing off his boss because he wanted Gigi's company, but what was wrong with that? Why was he arguing with himself?
>
> "Don't you have to be, like, a permanent employee to train scorers?" Gigi asked him. "I mean, it's not that I don't want to …"
>
> She was right. Temps weren't supposed to train people. "I can assign you any job I want to," Vic said. "That's why I make the big bucks!"

We can see an obvious complication arriving with Gigi. Note the suggestive sexual imagery in her swinging her crossed leg, her sandal dangling. More is at stake for Vic, apparently, than the fact of having someone to work with that he "knew and liked." He abruptly breaks with company policy in asking Gigi to help train the language arts scorers. He knows he's being "a bit reckless," but then he doubles down, declaring with bravado that he's in charge, the man making "the big bucks." Clearly from this passage, Gigi is a secondary character who is likely to have an impact on Vic's life. And she does: He comes close to having an affair with her and ruining his marriage.

DEVELOPING SECONDARY CHARACTERS

"Secondary characters receive less page space and, as a result, demand less of the reader's attention," says Varallo. But what's the right amount of space to give them? Where do you draw the line?

To determine how much secondary characters need to be developed, "Initial attention should be given to the role of a secondary character," says Cummins. "Once the writer is clear on that role, the story needs just enough of the character to fulfill his or her purpose." But this doesn't mean secondary characters can't be complex. According to Varallo, "your secondary characters can be as fully imagined and as fully complex as your primary ones. That's actually a lot of fun, to imagine their whole lives." And, for Stuckey-French, it's very important to do so. "I've found that in order to present Jim, my secondary character, in a convincing and engaging manner, I need to know as much about him as I do about Jenny, my protagonist. When drafting a novel I will do a lot of writing and musing in a notebook outside the story, mapping out Jim's life and how it connects to Jenny's, sometimes even keeping a journal or diary in Jim's voice. Not much of it will end up in the novel, but hopefully, as Hemingway's iceberg theory goes, the reader will feel all of Jim's life there under the surface."

Do keep in mind, cautions Hyde, that to achieve depth, you need not go into great detail—which, if you do, can put undue emphasis on the secondary character and his or her role. "A few sentences," says Hyde, "can create a memorable complexity."

Note the economy of detail in the following excerpt from Hyde's novel *The Language of Hoofbeats*. We have just enough to fill in a picture of Dennis Portman, the sheriff's deputy. He shows up to file a report when the main character's foster daughter steals the neighbor's horse. He speaks to Jackie, one of the foster moms of the girl who stole the horse. Portman speaks first.

"Mind if I tell you a little story before we get started?"

"Um … no. Of course not."

"Okay, good. I got a brother, quite a bit older than me. He was a teenager when I was born. So of course I idolize him, and always did. But, truth is, he's just a really good guy, and it's not my imagination. Everybody thinks so. Has three kids. He and his wife Marie, you couldn't find a better set of parents. Like two people you'd read about in a book on parenting, but the story might seem too good to be true. Then last Christmas, his older boy, Jake, goes and steals a car with two friends and takes it for a joy ride. And I have to go out to the house and arrest him. You catch my drift here?"

"Um … no. Sorry. I don't think I do."

"Kids do stupid things. Even kids with good parents do stupid things. They're kids. No matter how you raise them, they're going to take a cruise through Stupid Land."

Notice how Hyde humanizes her secondary character. Portman isn't just the sheriff's deputy, a stock figure charged with carrying out his duty; he's a person with his own sad stories of the human lot—in this case, an older brother he's always idolized, whose son went afoul of the law, and he, the uncle, just had to be the one to arrest him. What else is behind this little anecdote Portman shares? We know there's plenty because from what we've seen, he's fully human.

OVERSHADOWING PROTAGONISTS

Perhaps in the process of writing your story or novel, you realize that a secondary character is becoming more interesting than the protagonist. An alarm bell goes off. Is this a fatal flaw?

According to Varallo, "I think you just let that happen and see where it leads you, really. It's sort of like that old driver's ed wisdom about turning in the direction of a skid: You just keep exploring the character and see what you find. You can still tell a story where the secondary characters eclipse the primary ones. Fagin steals every scene from Oliver Twist."

For Cummins, as long as the protagonist is interesting, there's no problem if the secondary character is more interesting. "The protagonist's relation to and interaction with such a character may be what the story is all about. For example, Gatsby is inherently more interesting than Nick Carraway, yet many readers consider the novel to really be about Nick, because Nick is the one who changes because of the relationship." Yet what if, in the process of writing your short story or novel, you see that your secondary character is completely overshadowing your protagonist, stealing his thunder entirely? If this is the case you do need to make a decision, says Cummins. Either you are "getting off-track," or you should assign a "greater role for this character"—perhaps even making the character the protagonist. Or, perhaps, says Stuckey-French, you should go for two protagonists: "If Jim becomes very intriguing to me, then I will write a section of the novel in his point of view, and, depending on how that works out, he might get cast as a major character along with Jenny. It's fun when this happens!"

But let's go back. It *is* possible, of course, for a protagonist to be completely overshadowed by a secondary character who's not only more interesting but also doesn't allow the protagonist much of a role at all. This usually happens, says Cummins, in "first-person stories in which the teller is an observer of others and, as a result, remains indistinct." If the first-person observer is *also* a participant, like Nick Carraway, you've nailed it. But if the observer is *only* an observer, a "peripheral" character, that's a problem, as Janet Burroway suggests in *Writing Fiction: A Guide to Narrative Craft.*

Cummins's story "Kaiser-Frazer," which first appeared in *West Branch*, demonstrates how to avoid the problem of a secondary character totally stealing the show and reducing the first-person narrator to a merely peripheral character. His protagonist is a first-person narrator who is both observer *and* participant. Cummins performs a fine balancing act in this story: His secondary character is quite compelling and threatens to overshadow the protagonist, and yet as impressive as this secondary character is, he functions instead to help develop the protagonist.

Cummins's protagonist is Bobby, a ten-year-old boy, in the period shortly after the end of World War II. He is sad and alone: his father dead, his mother in the hospital, his older twin sisters working in the city. He wanders his small town until, one day, he happens on a teenager, Tom Maxville, who is staggering down an alley by an abandoned store, "trying to balance a ladder under one arm and carry a bucket of paint and wide brush in his free hand." Note how Tom Maxville, a secondary character, immediately engages the reader's attention.

A DIFFERENT PERSPECTIVE ON "SECONDARY"

Ben Fountain, whose recent novel *Billy Lynn's Long Halftime Walk* was a National Book Award Finalist, offers a 180-degree perspective on the matter of "secondary" characters. Are they really, in fact, *secondary*?

According to Fountain, "When dealing with secondary characters, the notion I try to keep in mind is this: In each character's mind, he or she is the most important person in the story. So, within the world of the secondary character, that character isn't secondary at all; he or she doesn't exist merely to serve the story, or to prompt or react off of the main characters, but is pursuing his or her own agenda."

Fountain calls to mind as an example Hemingway's "A Sea Change," where a couple breaks up as they're sitting at a bar. "These two main characters are beautifully drawn: The woman is distraught, regretful, gentle; the man is bitter and heartbroken. There is, however, a third player in this drama, the bartender who serves them drinks. He's not paying the slightest attention to the drama unfolding beneath his nose but instead is thinking about the horse he's placed a bet on for a race that afternoon. He's got his own reality going, completely apart from that of the main characters, and Hemingway plays that dynamic to pitch-perfect ironic effect."

By many readers' lights, the bartender is surely a secondary character, set apart from the main action of marital break-up. But *is* the main action the marital break-up? Not for the bartender, says Fountain, whose mind is preoccupied with his afternoon's bet. Taking this point further, if we consider that no one individual character's story is more important than another's, then we must say that all characters are protagonists of their own story, and the distinction between protagonist and secondary is a false one.

As further support for his position, Fountain offers an example from *Billy Lynn's Long Halftime Walk*. Note the role that Pastor Rick plays.

> A couple of follow-up phone calls yielded similar uselessness, but now Pastor Rick won't let him go. He keeps calling, texting, sending e-mails and links. Billy gets what's in it for Pastor Rick; it's cool for the reverend to have a "pastoral relationship" with a soldier in the field, it gives him cred, shows a stylish commitment to the issues of the day. Billy can hear the good pastor of a Sunday morning kick-starting his homily with a piece of Billy's soul. "I was communicating the other day with one of our fine young soldiers who's serving in Iraq, and we were discussing blah, blah, blah ..."

Fountain doesn't think of Pastor Rick as a secondary character. He states, "Pastor Rick is in it not so much for what he can do for Billy but for what Billy can do for Pastor Rick's street cred and self-image." Like the bartender's story, Pastor Rick's story is one distinct plot and thematic thread among many in this novel, which portrays the way different people process the war in Iraq—and what they get out of it.

Untended brown curls spilled over his ears and forehead, down the back of his neck. The clothing flapped about his scrawny frame, a tee shirt and dungarees smeared with grease, splotched with yellow paint. With his large head puffed out even more top-heavy by all the hair, he looked like he might snap in two.

As he swayed back and forth, his face scrunched into such an exaggerated grimace I would have laughed if he fell. But when he set down paint and ladder, he met my eyes and grinned so hard I forgot my usual shyness with teenagers and returned his "Hi!" I peered to see through the streaks of whitewash on the inside of the windows. For all the years I could remember the store had contained nothing but a dusty counter and broken boxes.

"What's going on here?" I asked him.

"The future!" he proclaimed.

Tom is speaking of automobiles—"the newest and the best," Kaisers and Frazers—hence the story's title. Tom, with his clownish appearance, his excited vision of the future, and his unrelenting optimism, could easily overshadow Bobby, making him vacuous in comparison, but by story's end, Bobby fully absorbs Tom's infectious enthusiasm, grows, and becomes a participant in his own psychological recovery. We're not stuck with a mere observer of a vivacious or vibrant secondary character.

SUMMING UP

Whether you view secondary characters in the traditional manner or take Fountain's alternative view (see the sidebar on the opposite page), one thing is certain: You must define the role each character plays in your story or novel and how large that role will be. How much development will you give each character? Whose story is it? Is it basically one story, several, or many? Answering these questions will aid in developing secondary characters that refuse to be considered second-class citizens, that function as mirrors to the protagonist, as sources of conflict, and as fully realized individuals in your fiction.

Jack Smith's most current work of fiction is *Icon*, published by Serving House Books in 2014. His satirical novel *Hog to Hog* won the 2007 George Garrett Fiction Prize and was published by Texas Review Press in 2008. He has published stories in a number of literary magazines, including *Southern Review*, *North American Review*, *Texas Review*, *X-Connect*, *In Posse Review*, and *Night Train*. His reviews have appeared widely in such publications as *Ploughshares*, *Georgia Review*, *American Book Review*, *Prairie Schooner*, *Mid-American Review*, *Pleiades*, *The Missouri Review*, and *Environment* magazine. He has published a few dozen articles in *Novel & Short Story Writer's Market* and close to that in *The Writer* magazine. His creative writing book, *Write and Revise for Publication: A 6-Month Plan for Crafting an Exceptional Novel and Other Works of Fiction*, was published in 2013 by Writer's Digest Books. His co-authored nonfiction environmental book, *Killing Me Softly*, was published by Monthly Review Press in 2002. Besides his writing, Smith co-edits *The Green Hills Literary Lantern*, an online literary magazine published by Truman State University.

10 WAYS TO SCREW UP A QUERY LETTER

....

Donna Paris

Even if your focus is on writing fiction, chances are you're supplementing your career with freelance work. That means writing queries—and writing them well.

When I worked as an editor for a national magazine, I received hundreds of query letters—some addressed to the previous editor in my position, some with an incorrect title, some with typos strewn throughout. Some had ideas so broad they were simply topics. Others were queries for ideas like graphic sex quizzes that would have been better directed to a magazine like *Cosmopolitan*, for instance.

As I read these queries, I was thinking this: If someone doesn't have a clue about the publication or can't get basic information right or doesn't bother to proofread, how can I trust this writer? I'll be honest: These queries were often tossed in the trash.

"Think of the query as a tool to market yourself and not just the story," says Margaret Webb, a journalism instructor at Ryerson University in Toronto and the author of *Older, Faster, Stronger: What Women Runners Can Teach Us All About Living Younger, Longer.* Trust me, the query letter is a big deal.

Here, I share the top ten ways writers can screw up their query letters. Don't doom your own queries by committing the same gaffes.

1. IGNORE NAMES AND TITLES; NOBODY CARES.

"Actually, everyone cares," says Cheryl Embrett, a Toronto-based freelance writer. "Nobody likes to see their name misspelled or associated with the wrong title." And with business tools like LinkedIn, it's even easier to do the research.

"Don't pitch to a generic 'Dear Editor' or 'Sir/Madam,'" says Kathy Ullyott, assistant program head of media studies at University of Guelph-Humber in Toronto. "Always take the time to get the name of the person to whom you're talking." And don't forget to include the title of the person you're addressing as well.

2. DON'T WORRY ABOUT SPELLING, GRAMMATICAL, OR FACTUAL ERRORS.

In the case of query letters, you do need to sweat the small stuff. Grammatical errors and typos can cause a quick loss of credibility. "You would think this would be basic, but you'd be surprised how many writers send error-riddled queries," says Ullyott.

And if you have a blog where you post regularly, proof it before posting. Sometimes people are lulled into thinking that just because it isn't in a printed publication, it's okay, even a little bit hipster, to publish a blog post filled with errors. "But when something is online, it lives forever—it's not like a newspaper that people recycle the next day," says Embrett.

3. SKIP THE RESEARCH.

Here's a big tip: Not researching is never a good idea. You want to show the editor that you know the publication. Start by asking for writing guidelines from the publication, if available. "Read at least the last six issues of the magazine you're pitching," says Ullyott. "You can do this at Issuu.com, Zinio, or, of course, old school, at the library." Don't pitch anything remotely close to a feature the magazine has run within the last year.

"When writers pitch me stories, I always appreciate it when they say, 'I checked out your section on the website, and I noticed you don't have any stories about XYZ. Here's why I think you need the XYZ story, and here's how I can help,'" says Simone

Castello, Web editor at canadianliving.com. A simple Google or site search goes a long way. And remember, if a print publication turns you down, pitch the idea to the online staff; it's usually a different staff.

4. SEND IN A LONGER QUERY—IT'S MORE IMPRESSIVE!

Um, no. Editorial departments are struggling with shrinking budgets, so editors are handling a lot of work. It's your job to draw the editor in and grab his interest as soon as possible. "Get to the point of what you're pitching right off the top," says Miriam Osborne, associate managing editor of life and entertainment at *Metro News Canada*. "Too often paragraphs are wasted on who you are and where you've been published previously. These things matter, but they don't matter nearly as much as what your story is about."

5. TREAT QUERIES LIKE FAST FOOD—THEY'RE ALL THE SAME.

Definitely not. Personalizing a query letter makes an editor feel like you want to work exclusively with her. "I've had writers pitch stories to me that they've obviously also pitched to other publications at the same time. In fact, in many instances I'll get an auto-fill meant for someone else," says Castello.

6. FORGET ABOUT TONE.

Get familiar with the tone of a publication. "Write your query letter in the tone that you plan on writing the piece," says Osborne. "I have been sent some query letters that are so formal and stiff that I knew the writer wasn't sure about how *Metro* writes." Even an in-depth health article on cardiovascular disease, for instance, needs to reflect the voice of the publication. Most publications are interested in readable matter, so work toward making your writing sound like you're talking, and ease your way through the information. Make it clear and consistent: easy for the editor and, ultimately, for the reader.

7. WRITE PITCHES IN A FUN, WILLY-NILLY STYLE.

Nope. If you are all over the place in a pitch, it's an indication that your story will be, too. For example, don't pitch an article on diabetes but then move on to discuss another disease and then throw in something about mental health to cover all your bases. "Start your query as you might the actual article, with a strong scene or anecdote, followed by a 'nut-graph' (thesis paragraph) outlining why the story is timely now (news hook) and how you will write the story," says Webb.

Write the pitch in the same manner as you plan to write the article. If the article is meant to be funny, the query should be, too. "A narrative lead or a descriptive lead or an analytical lead or a fact-laden lead tells the reader what the article will be like, or rather, it should," writes Peter P. Jacobi in *The Magazine Article: How to Think It, Plan It, Write It* (Writer's Digest Books).

8. JUST TELL; DON'T BOTHER SHOWING.

It's easier to simply tell a story, but showing is captivating. Ullyott suggests complet-ing this sentence in your query: "My story will show that ..." In other words, a story *about* the link between first responders and suicide doesn't tell the editor anything beyond the basics. A story *showing* that a fire department is implementing a new psychological services program to prevent suicide in first responders is much more engrossing. Likewise, a story showing a mom talking about her child who was diagnosed with cancer will be much more readable than stats about cancer rates in children.

9. IF YOU'RE NOT AN EXPERT, STAY AWAY FROM THE TOPIC.

Wrong again. For instance, more newspapers and magazines are including technology articles focused for less techy readers. "Think of technology [articles] as lifestyle ideas that fit into most aspects of a publication," says Osborne. In one section, *Metro* newspapers ran an article on technology gadgets for the fashionista. "We've run stories about health apps in our wellness section and online streaming in our television and movie pages." Similarly, you don't have to be a doctor to write a health article. But you must be able to land good sources, such as health professionals, for example, whom you can interview to get the information you need.

10. THINK OF YOURSELF AS A WRITER, NOT A SALESPERSON.

Getting a story published starts with marketing an idea. You *are*, in fact, selling your story—as a sales pitch. What should a query letter include?

SOCIAL MEDIA? C'MON, IT'S JUST A FAD!

Social media is a good tool to use for pitching ideas. One freelance writer follows editors on Twitter, makes a connection, and then sometimes asks if she can send those editors a query based on something they have tweeted. "A lot of writers follow me on social media, and I like interacting with them," says Castello. Beware, however, of hounding people on social media. "It's an easy way to stay in contact, but it's also easy to overdo it," adds Castello. "If you send me a query and don't hear from me in a week or two, send one follow-up. If you don't hear after that, consider moving on: Web content moves fairly quickly, so our turnaround times are shorter than print."

- **AN INTRODUCTION:** Let's say you are suggesting a story about why people aren't vaccinating their children. Tell the editor why this is a good idea; i.e., if you are pitching to a parenting magazine, for instance, let the editor know why this is a timely topic. Add a few stats about children who aren't getting vaccinated, and explain why readers will find a story about the repercussions of a child getting measles pertinent.

- **THE ANGLE OF THE STORY:** Your job is to sell *this* idea to this *particular* publication. Your query should answer these questions: *What makes the focus of this story timely? Why is this story a good idea for this publication? What makes it well suited for this audience?*

- **INTERVIEW SUBJECTS:** Tell the editor what makes these sources so valuable. Perhaps they are experts in their field, or perhaps they have discovered something new. Perhaps they have differing views and a fresh perspective on an old topic.

As well, every query should include a proposed word count, your biography and contact information, and a closing. "If you write a strong query, an editor might pass on the story for any number of reasons, but he will keep you in mind as a writer of note to assign other stories," says Webb.

Donna Paris is a former senior editor at *Canadian Living* magazine. Now a freelance writer and editor, she is working on a book of short stories—and getting a taste of what life is like on the other side.

VOICE LESSONS

....

Olivia Markham

Most editors would probably say that the writing voice can't be learned, that it must be found. That is true, but since your voice is found within you, the writer, then with some effort it can be developed, be brought out.

Singers undergo voice lessons that include learning how to control the breath, project the voice, sing from the diaphragm, and avoid singing through the nose. They also learn how to develop the sound they have and bring originality to their style. The singer's voice is her instrument. Without proper training and development, the raw material of a "good" voice will probably not garner the desired success.

The same is true of a writer's voice. Without training and development—with just raw talent—the writer will probably not succeed as he or she would like. To undergo writing voice lessons, you must develop the "instrument" that is within you, the part of you that writes, that draws on your unique self. Like the singer, that means achieving control of the craft while also learning to let go.

But first, what is voice?

Defining voice can be complicated— that's why many writers are both confused and concerned about it. Voice is not point of view (POV), and it's not just the character's voice.

To start, think of a writer's voice as encompassing three levels: the **primary voice**, which is present in original, fresh expression; the **secondary voice**, which manifests through character voices; and the **tertiary voice**, which comes through in the style of writing—the rhythm, imagery, and so on.

- **PRIMARY VOICE:** Voice is you, the writer, expressed on the page. It's your originality, your freshness, your honesty. But what does this really mean? Originality comes from your true self, from your subconscious. It is your distinct way of looking at the world. And this outlook is formed on the page by your unresolved conflicts; by the themes that resonate with you; by the subjects that interest or excite you; by the books you like (romances, thrillers, mysteries,

Just like reading the novel for clarity, logic, storytelling, and flow, you have to know how readers will "hear" your voice.

comedies); by what is important to you in life; and by what you want to express. Ask yourself what is different and original about your worldview. How do you see the world differently from others?

- **SECONDARY VOICE:** As expressed in every book or story, voice is how characters appear on the page: what they say, their personalities, how they say what they say, their attitudes, their choices.

- **TERTIARY VOICE:** Voice is much more than an issue of style, but style plays a part in what we call voice. Think of a writer's style as the words the author uses and how they're used—the music of the language—and how the author varies punctuation, as well as the length of sentences and paragraphs. It's the rhythm of the writing and the imagery employed. Style is also how an author perceives truths, experiences, and the world, and captures these with pithy, original, potent language. It's how the reader experiences the story, the unique way that the plot, characters, narrative, pacing, subplots, and backstory are expressed and come to life. Voice is something that is sensed, seen, but also felt, intuited. It plays in the readers' subconscious.

Voice is also expressed through theme—the reason you're writing your novel or short story. Your choice of theme is drawn from your originality, from what you, as a writer and as a unique individual, want to write. It's also the heart and core and soul of your expression. In *The Godfather*, the theme is "family loyalty leads to a lifetime of crime." In Flaubert's *Madame Bovary*, it's "illicit love leads to death." Other themes might be "love leads to happiness," "sin leads to redemption," or "love conquers all." Theme is about conflicting values. What themes are important to you?

Some examples of great voice include Michael Ondaatje's *The English Patient*, Sherman Alexie's *The Absolutely True Diary of a Part-Time Indian*, Linda Howard's *To Die For* and *Drop Dead Gorgeous*, Boston Teran's *Giv: The Story of a Dog and America*, Janet Evanovich's Stephanie Plum series, and Rebecca Wells' *Divine Secrets of the Ya-Ya Sisterhood*.

So how do you develop your voice? Try my seven-lesson approach—"practicing" all of these lessons at the same time.

1. EVALUATE WHO YOU ARE AS A WRITER.

Identify what you're doing in your writing now: Pay attention to your gut feelings. What are the standout qualities of your writing? On the other hand, is there anything that seems to be slightly "off key" to

STRETCH YOUR VOICE

These writing exercises will help you explore the various levels of your writing voice.

1. Select a paragraph or a page from a novel that has a very different voice from yours, and rewrite it in your own voice. Compare the two, and note what was changed.

2. Choose a page from a novel and rewrite it in several ways, from different perspectives. Which one seems to come the most naturally?

3. Visit a place you haven't visited before, where you can also write. Immerse yourself in the place. Take at least two hours and try to come up with a short story inspired by your surroundings. The genre is up to you.

4. Choose a page or a scene from your novel or short story and rewrite it in a different POV—another character, an animal, an inanimate object. Compare the two and notice what was changed.

5. Select a scene from your novel or short story and assign each of the characters a different voice from the one they currently have. How do the changed voices affect the scene?

6. Read a passage from a novel you admire, and then try to write briefly in the same style, with the same voice. What is it that defines that style? That voice?

you? What isn't fresh or original in your prose? Learn to recognize the correlations and patterns in your own writing. How could your writing improve if you just let loose, if you thought more creatively about your art?

Pay attention to feedback from fellow authors and from editors, readers, and friends. What do others say they like about your writing, your stories, your books? What strikes a chord in them? Then closely examine your writing once more, and ask yourself if those impressions are accurate. Again, listen to your gut. Not everyone's opinion will be accurate or totally correct.

Read your work out loud to a trusted friend, or have the friend read it aloud to you. Authors reread a novel for clarity, logic, storytelling, and flow, but also for how readers will "hear" their voice.

2. LEARN THE CRAFT.

Just like the singer must learn to control his breath or pitch or posture, the writer must learn the craft. Be assured that even seasoned writers continue to learn about craft, even after publishing twenty or more books. So apply yourself to acquiring new knowledge; don't rest on what you already know. Develop more tools for expressing what you want to say and how you want to say it in order to tell the story you want to tell. In any pursuit, it's the fine-tuning that makes a writer excellent, and for writers, that means reading fiction, nonfiction, and books on the writing craft; attending talks hosted by other writers; participating in group critiques; and taking workshops.

3. GATHER MATERIAL FROM LIFE.

Become a close observer of life and yourself. This means experiencing life and people and analyzing new thoughts and ideas. It also means embarking on self-discovery (but don't let it become a preoccupation that keeps you from your writing).

4. REMAIN OPEN TO INSPIRATION.

We tend to be most original when we have just been touched by strong emotion, be it happiness, sadness, or inspiration, from an inner or outer source. For example, when you experience something good or bad for the first time or feel renewed after a long talk with a friend, it's like a well inside you opens up and deepens. Try to write when those feelings of strong emotion or inspiration are at the forefront; this is when you are at your most original. Notice what you are thinking and feeling, and write down anything that bubbles up from that well.

5. KNOW YOURSELF.

By this I mean not who you aspire to be or who you feel you *must be*, but who you really are. Value that real self, and don't be afraid of it—that's important for fulfilling your writing dream. Recognize that you're not just one facet of yourself, bad or good, but a complicated, interwoven personality and character, which means being balanced within yourself but also having real passion for your work. Recognize, too, that you're in the process of "becoming," just like your fictional characters.

In the same way that you may have identified what types of books you should be writing, identify your voice by looking inward and recognizing what resonates with you. How would you describe yourself? How do you see yourself, beyond all the expectations, beyond the things you feel you should be or want to be? Who is your integral self? What are your favorite books, and who are your favorite authors? Why do you particularly like them? How are these books and authors similar? If you enjoy reading a certain type of book, then perhaps you desire to emulate this type of writing in some way, though not necessarily within that particular genre. Rather than copying those authors outright, become aware of what resonates with you, and therefore, what your voice may ultimately be.

6. HARNESS YOUR ORIGINALITY.

Give yourself the freedom to express that original, unique self on the page. This takes courage. One way to do this is to keep a writer's journal. In it, write for just yourself, without the editor in your head. Write without a goal, and don't worry about what someone else will think. You're not planning to show anyone this writing, so let loose, write freely, and treat it as a private space where you can truly be you. Your journal is a space where you can explore thoughts, emotions, ideas, analysis, and insights about people and life and self, as well as short stories and character sketches. It is a space where you don't have to think about whether you're writing something that's not as good as you think it should be.

Use this journal as a tool: It shouldn't be a diary of your emotions or what you did today, unless these topics are inspiring or will have some particular use for your writing. The musings in your journal can eventually serve as the raw material for your fiction and can be great incubators for self-discovery, unearthing characters and writing ideas, and honing your voice.

7. READ, AND READ SOME MORE.

But first, take a small hiatus from reading and focus on your own voice by following the previous steps. One of the problems with continuously reading and observing other authors' work is that our minds are inundated with other characters and stories, and our writing may become an accumulation or composite of them. But note that any writer—in fact, anyone in any arena—builds on the work, methods, and tools that have been used and created previously in their field.

When you do read, read a variety of authors and genres. That will give you a better idea of what you like and allow you to experience a greater assortment of stories and voices. Reading a variety will also keep you from inadvertently copying a favorite author's style or voice. However, if your style *is* similar to a favorite author's, then you'll need to be certain you've made your writing distinct from theirs in other ways—through plot, characterization, setting, and so on.

Reading broadly, especially the writing of experienced best-selling authors, will feed your intuitive self and will also add to your tool kit of how to write well. Notice that on TV cooking contests, participants are often asked to copy a famous recipe by taste, and then the host and judges ask them to whip up something original—they learn what flavors go together, in the right combinations, and can then come up with something wonderful. You can take a similar approach by first sampling and emulating the voices of various bestsellers and then working to develop a voice that is truly unique—and truly yours.

Like the singer who must practice her craft, applying voice lessons to develop her talent and potential, you must apply these writing voice lessons to develop your voice, realize your dream, and achieve the highest degree of success.

Olivia Markham is a freelance writer with five years of experience. She's also a freelance editor with ten years of experience and a master's degree in writing. She edits short stories and novels, and offers classes and workshops at conferences and elsewhere, to writers at all levels. She is a member of the NW Independent Editor's Guild and networks on Twitter, Facebook, and LinkedIn. Her website is www.OliviaMarkham-Editing.com.

HE SAID, SHE SAID

Writing Strong Dialogue

....

Jack Smith

To write great fiction, you must be able to create complex, memorable characters, engaging plots, and vivid settings. You must also be able to create scenes that move, ones that aren't labored or dull. Unless you're writing narrative scenes, this means handling dialogue—and handling it well. When dialogue is rich with energy, characters come alive on the page. The various complexities of the human being are made manifest in what is stated, as well as what is left unsaid—and in the apparent motives behind both speech and silence. It takes some doing to pull all of this off, but that's what it takes to write great dialogue.

THE PROCESS OF WRITING DIALOGUE

Like every other aspect of fiction writing, crafting strong dialogue calls for a process. For T.C. Boyle, award-winning author of fifteen novels and ten short story collections, this process is mostly an unconscious one. He doesn't intentionally set out to energize his dialogue."It just happens in its own energetic way," he says. "Usually it rides along with me in the way that narration does. It all happens in the unconscious spell that overtakes a writer in the flow of composition." Novelist Amanda Filipacchi reports the same experience in drafting her dialogue. "It's something that comes naturally to me and requires very little conscious effort or calculation."

Of course, plenty of authors prepare to write dialogue by doing some field work. Virgil Suárez, author of several novels and story collections, regularly attunes himself to the various ways people speak. "I like to eavesdrop on conversations, and there are plenty of contemporary places where you can go and do exactly that and no one would notice you sitting there taking it all in." But when it comes to the actual writing, for Suárez this is largely intuitive: "It comes in a variety of ways, sometimes even in sleep. I also hear it as I am writing. The lines that come to me often evolve out of a character's need to speak, to be heard. It also comes from watching characters move from scene to scene. What would they say to themselves?"

All this is nonrational, a matter of feel. And yet Suárez has noticed a set of consistent features that energize his dialogue. Banter is an important one. "I am a big believer in banter between characters … as it is a way to create dynamic tension through the way the characters speak." Suárez also plays with the margins between silence and sound. "Always present is the idea that silence is often much better for drama than dialogue itself. I like to punctuate my scenes with lots of quiet banter and have plenty of second-level (daily life noise) action going on in the background. My characters never speak in a vacuum; there's always something going on either in their minds or in their setting."

Notice the repartee in Suárez's short story "Blown," from his collection *The Soviet Circus Comes to Havana.*

> "I bet you didn't know I was in Vietnam," you say.
>
> "A Cuban in Vietnam?"
>
> You notice how her fingers shake as she takes a cigarette out of the YSL Ritz pack.

> "When the time came, everybody went," you say.
>
> "Not everybody."
>
> "You were here?" you ask.
>
> "Cuba," she says and looks at the man playing the electric piano. He jumps up and down as he starts his solo.
>
> "Like I said, I went."
>
> "All right," she says. "How many did you kill?"
>
> "I got there at the end. Before I knew it I was back."
>
> "That's anti-climactic."
>
> "So what?"

Clipped, playful dialogue. Note the man about to gyrate on the electric piano. Banter, silence, sound—these elements tend to pattern Suárez's dialogue, elements ingrained after years of writing, modulated to meet the needs of each new story or novel. It's his stamp of originality.

Originality is also important to Filipacchi, and for her, this means avoiding the predictable. "Dialogue that foils readers' expectations, even in small and subtle ways, can arouse your readers' curiosity and make them pay closer attention. Misunderstandings and misinterpretations between

---

"Dialogue that foils readers' expectations, even in small and subtle ways, can arouse your readers' curiosity and make them pay closer attention. Misunderstandings and misinterpretations between characters can bring entertainment and stress to the reader—two forms of beneficial energy in fiction."
—AMANDA FILIPACCHI

characters can bring entertainment and stress to the reader—two forms of beneficial energy in fiction."

The more you write dialogue, the more you just let it happen, *listening* to your characters speak, you will probably discover your own distinctive approach: energized by the beat or rhythm of your characters' words, their utterances as well as silences, their back-and-forth, their complex, rich voices. Let loose your imagination, your intuitive side. Don't engineer your dialogue. If you force anything, it will come off as fake and inauthentic.

And yet there is always revision. Rethinking, redoing. Like every other element in fiction, you must, at some point, turn a critical eye to your dialogue and demand more of it. Does it reveal character? Does it reveal conflict? Will it keep the reader's interest?

For award-winning short story writer Laura van den Berg, revision strategies come down to several key questions: "Where is the tension? Where is the arc? What is happening underneath the surface?" As she reviews her dialogue, van den Berg pays special attention to this latter issue. "It's crucial to think about what's crackling beneath the surface—where is the subtext? The layers? What is the end game for this conversation for the narrator? What does she want in this moment? These under-layers are a huge part of what brings energy to dialogue."

Notice what's "crackling beneath the surface" in van den Berg's story "I Looked for You, I Called Your Name," from her collection *The Isle of Youth*. Here the narrator, on a honeymoon in Patagonia, is plagued by a series of disasters—for starters a broken nose when their plane makes an emergency landing. You can't help but sense an "under-layer" in the honeymooning couple's conversation with another newly married couple. The narrator replies to a comment about being just recently married.

"Yes," I said. "I suppose we are." I felt as though I was hovering just above the ground. I hooked myself around my husband's elbow. "But doesn't it feel like it's been ages?" I said. "Ages and ages and ages?"

He pulled away from me and leaned toward the Meyer-Stewards. "She broke her nose," he whispered. "During the emergency landing."

Patrick sipped his drink; Susannah sucked on her crab leg.

"You broke it," I said, tapping my cheekbone. "My husband broke my nose."

"What was that?" Patrick asked, rattling the ice around in his glass.

"My husband broke my nose." I felt like signing those words to the entire room. "He broke it with his elbow."

"She doesn't know what she's talking about," my husband said. "It was an accident."

Here, already, on their honeymoon, the narrator feels an unsettling disharmony in her marriage, a potentially broken marriage, symbolized by her broken nose. The spoken, as well as the unspoken, energizes this dialogue. We wonder: What is really going on? What fatal flaw in this marriage has caused the wife to accuse her husband of breaking her nose? The dialogue intrigues the reader to discover the undercurrents, the subtext.

CONSISTENCY OF TONE AND CHARACTER

To zero in on tone, you must capture the core of who your character *is*, his or her sensibility, and so forth. Capturing your character's essential nature takes an imagination that grasps what it's like to be another human being. It requires the writer to get outside herself—to experience empathy. John Keats called it negative capability.

Filipacchi says that, like an actor, you must imagine yourself "in the skin" of your character. You must be aware of both personality and mood. "What kinds of remarks would that personality, in its current mood, utter at that moment? How would that personality and mood react to what has just been said to him or her?" As she writes, Filipacchi automatically asks these questions about all of her characters.

If you haven't pegged the right tone for your character in your initial drafts, do so in the revision stages. For Suárez, getting the tone just right ultimately calls for careful analysis. He tries to match behavior and mannerisms with language—is it a good fit? Additionally, says Suárez, character speech should reflect age, time, place, and thoughts and concerns. "The best trick is always to read the line out loud, play pretend. Block the scene the way a playwright might do it." As she revises, van den Berg also analyzes tone with several criteria in mind. "I think a lot about tics and patterns and habits of speech—is this a polite voice? A voice that curses a lot or is partial to clichés or puns or bad jokes? This can be a way of getting a feel for a voice and distinguishing character."

T.C. Boyle states, "I don't typically work with accents or speech patterns, so it's just a matter of imagining what a developing character might sound like in a given situation." He cites as an example the narrator of *The Inner Circle*, John Milk, an acolyte of Alfred C. Kinsey, the sex researcher. Milk, Boyle notes, "speaks and writes formally, a function of his shyness and uncertainty." The following excerpt, from a scene early in the novel, sets the tone for Boyle's protagonist. A co-ed at IU approaches Milk.

> "Listen," she said, "I just wanted to know if you'd mind getting engaged to me—"
>
> Her words hung there between us, closing out everything else—the chatter of the group of freshmen materializing suddenly from the men's room, the sound of an automobile horn out on the street—and I can only imagine the look I must have given her in response. This was long before Prok taught me to tuck all the loose strands of my emotions behind a mask of impassivity, and everything I was thinking routinely rushed to my face along with the blood that settled in my cheeks like a barometer of confusion.
>
> "John, you're not blushing, are you?"
>
> "No," I said, "not at all. I'm just—"
>
> She held my eyes, enjoying the moment. "Just what?"
>
> I shrugged. "We were out in the sun—yesterday it was, yesterday afternoon. Moving furniture. So, I guess, well—"

It's a "pretend" engagement for a college course, as the young woman soon clarifies. We can see in John's stumbling language here, including his "well—," a hesitancy, a sense of unease, which characterizes his speech throughout the novel. Milk's

> "I think a lot about tics and patterns and habits of speech—is this a polite voice? A voice that curses a lot or is partial to clichés or puns or bad jokes? This can be a way of getting a feel for a voice and distinguishing character." —LAURA VAN DEN BERG

formality is established in his thoughts, his interior language.

BREAKING WITH DIALOGUE CONVENTION

If you break with the traditional method of handling dialogue (double quotation marks), you need a purpose for doing so—don't break convention merely to be fashionable or trendy. As Boyle points out, "The trend lately has been to dispense with quotation marks, but trends by their very nature tend to give way to other trends, which inevitably loop back to standard procedure. Another way to look at it: Each story, each novel, finds its own mode of expression, which may or may not be reflected formally."

"Sometimes," says Boyle, "I dispense with quotation marks as a way (ask old Bill Faulkner) of total immersion, but generally I do use them for the sake of clarity." Most of the time Suárez sticks with quotation marks, too, though he did find reason to break with the standard method in his second novel, *Latin Jazz*. "I had a whole cast of characters to worry about, so I used different punctuation marks for the dialogue to signal which character was speaking."

Van den Berg follows convention, but, she says, "I can think of many stories in which breaking the traditional standards is very effective—when you're trying to dissolve the barrier between thought and speech, for example."

And this is exactly what Filipacchi did in her first novel, *Nude Men*. "I wanted my main character to have imaginary conversations with his cat. I had to decide whether or not to use quotation marks for those conversations. I decided against it, in order to convey that those conversations are taking place in his head." Note the "conversation" between the first-person narrator and his cat, Minou.

> At home, Minou is sitting in a corner of the apartment. That's unusual for her; she usually runs to greet me at the door. I hang up my coat, drink some orange juice, go to the bathroom.
>
> How's the weather outside? asks Minou from her corner.
>
> Fine. Why are you sitting in that corner? I ask.
>
> Because I like it. Did you see any cats more beautiful than I in the pet store window?
>
> No. Only vulgar Himalayans. Are you feeling okay? I've never seen you sit in that corner before.
>
> I'm feeling fine.
>
> Aren't you even going to leave your corner to say hello to me?
>
> I said hello.
>
> First of all, no, you did not say hello, you asked me how the weather was. Second of all,

I want one of your usual warm welcomes, I say, walking toward her.

No, she says, cringing farther into the corner.

As we see in this comic exchange, thought and speech are not distinguished by the standard quotation marks because speech is occurring in the narrator's head. We hear the narrator speak; we hear the cat speak. This is dialogue, but it's imaginary dialogue. Dropping the double quotation marks makes sense here: It has a purpose. It's not willy-nilly, and it's not employed merely to latch onto a trend.

TYPICAL DIALOGUE PROBLEMS

Few writers create polished work the first time around. Probably as you revise, you will discover some problems with your dialogue. These issues can fall into one of several categories.

Giving Away Too Much

"Most obvious," says Boyle, "is giving away too much by way of dialogue exposition. We see this in poorly devised sci-fi movies but never, never, never in quality literary fiction. I'm not given to assigning long speeches to characters either, but obviously other writers really run with this (Dostoevsky, anyone?)."

Inauthentic-Sounding Speech

For Suárez, there is a distinct difference between character thought and speech. The former isn't a good fit for dialogue. "I prefer to always split the narrative into what the character is thinking and what the character is

actually saying. It's a nice, quick way of getting to know my character right away. It's very true to real life. Ninety-nine percent of the things we think about are never spoken."

Dialogue That Goes Nowhere

"Often I have dialogue in early drafts that is just blather," says van den Berg. "There's language being exchanged, but it's lacking energy and weight and momentum. In revision, I think hard about the role of the exchange in the story—what is being revealed here? Why does this matter?"

Repetition

"A common mistake a writer can make in an early draft," says Filipacchi, "is to make dialogue too long, not only in the back-and-forth between characters but in each individual utterance by each character. Cutting down the nonessential and repetitive portions is the easiest way of energizing dialogue. Ask yourself if the information delivered in that dialogue is crucial. If yes, are there other ways of dispensing that information throughout the novel in a less tedious way?"

SUMMING UP

When dialogue fails, it's because the language of your character seems contrived and doesn't sound real or authentic. It lacks energy. Given your particular character, the tone is off. Powerful dialogue makes us see and hear characters in their own voices, not the author's. It's high octane. It fuels character conflict, and it has an ultimate destination.

TIPS FROM THE PROS

"Follow your instincts. You create and absorb a billion bits of dialogue in your life off-screen. Ask yourself if what you've put in the mouths of your characters sounds real—i.e., as if someone would actually say those words and use those expressions in the very particular situation in which you've put them. I like to set my socks on fire once in a while just to see what sort of expression will emerge from my own vocal apparatus when the flames reach my ankles." —**T.C. BOYLE**

"Listen. And then listen some more. Crisp, real dialogue comes from watching carefully how people behave, move, and punctuate with gestures. Silence is extremely dramatic and should be reverted to as often as possible. I like to listen to people talk; I like to watch their expressions. Nervous tics and mannerisms are golden. Realistic dialogue is *never* spoken in complete sentences. Fragmented dialogue sounds real, timely, urgent." —**VIRGIL SUÁREZ:**

"Dialogue is more than speech. It's about what's passing between two people. Condense as much as possible. Be as precise as possible. Think about what the characters want and need and fear and love and hate." —**LAURA VAN DEN BERG**

"Add tension and energy. Pique your reader's interest by paying close attention to what a character chooses to divulge to another character. How truthful will the information be? How tactful will a character be? How carefully will she choose her wording? Will the character exercise self-restraint or blurt things he will regret later? Playing with these elements can add tension and energy to dialogue." —**AMANDA FILIPACCHI**

POST-PRODUCTION

Polish Your Completed Novel or Short Story Before Submitting It

....

Fred White

You've just typed "THE END" to the story you've spent the past month, six months, or year slaving over, and you are rightfully proud of your accomplishment. Your gut tells you it's a good story, and with a little bit o' luck it'll get published somewhere. In fact, you're so jazzed about its quality that you're compelled to send it off *right now* to one of the top fiction markets. And with nearly every agent, small publisher, and periodical accepting electronic submissions these days, it's as easy as a few mouse clicks to pick a market and hit Send. (Okay, you'll run it through the spell-checker and *then* send it off.)

My advice: Whoa, not so fast!

Filmmaking has a phase called "post-production," during which the completed movie undergoes a thorough, time-consuming editing process. Scenes are shortened, lengthened, deleted, rearranged; settings are altered for optimal effect; the soundtrack is refined. Sometimes new scenes are written, filmed, edited, and re-edited. Post-production often takes longer than the initial filming itself. I suggest that you think of your newly completed short story or novel the way a director thinks of his newly completed movie: ready for post-production, but not yet ready for audience consumption. If you want to improve your chances of having your literary labor of love stand out from the fierce competition—on average, only one out of every two hundred unsolicited manuscripts is selected for publication—then you must approach your "post-production" phase with care.

The first step is to set your completed manuscript aside for a while, at least for a couple of days. Start another writing project; it will help you distance yourself from the newly completed manuscript and gain a fresh perspective so that you can become your own toughest critic. While you were drafting, you were in the throes of creativity, too preoccupied with telling your story to think about revision issues. Now your goal is to make it the best story it can be, first by acquiring the perspective of a reader, or better yet, an editor. Get ready to scrutinize every

word, sentence, paragraph, and segment—
but not everything at once, or you might
overlook things. Again, patience is the su-
preme virtue for conducting post-production work on your short story or novel.

CHOOSING A POST-PRODUCTION PROCEDURE

To ensure success during the post-production phase, decide on a procedure. Write it
out and tape it to your desk or bookshelf
so you don't lose sight of it. The procedure
I recommend below works for me, but you
may want to adjust it to suit your own work
habits. For example, I begin with content-
related issues because I find these the most
challenging (and therefore the most worrisome) and want to resolve them first. You,
on the other hand, may prefer to deal with
surface errors first because you find grammar more worrisome.

Be that as it may, I see literary quality control as a four-step intensive review process:

1. Review for content.
2. Review for structural integrity.
3. Review for style.
4. Proofread.

REVIEWING FOR CONTENT

Problems with story content are the main
cause of rejection. Probing the depths of your
"completed" story or novel requires full concentration and takes time. Avoid the tempta-
tion to gloss over the manuscript or to assume
that an editor or agent will point out problems
(they rarely do; they're just too busy).

To begin, read through your story, imagining that you are your ideal reader, eager to
enter your fictional world. As this reader, you
would be deeply disappointed if you encountered any gaffes that broke the spell of experiencing that world vicariously. As you're reading, ask yourself these questions:

Is the story compelling enough not just to keep reading but to be unable to stop reading?

Think of what keeps you turning the pages of your favorite novels, even thousand-
page sagas. The overriding question the story should generate is *What is going to happen?* (or variations thereof, such as *How
will this situation be resolved?*) The protagonist of Stephen King's *11/22/63* goes back
in time in an effort to keep Lee Harvey
Oswald from changing history. Will he succeed? What will be the consequences if he
does? The unexpected obstacles he faces
only make us turn the pages even faster.

Is the story milieu sufficiently developed?

A storyteller creates an alternate reality with
vivid sensory details that make that fictional world seem authentic. Notice in *Girl with
a Pearl Earring* how author Tracy Chevalier,
through the eyes of her young protagonist,
Griet, depicts the studio of the seventeenth-
century Dutch painter Vermeer, in whose
house she works as a maid.

> It was a large, square space, not as long as
> the great hall downstairs. With the windows
> open it was bright and airy, with white-
> washed walls, and grey and white marble

tiles on the floor, the darker tiles set in a pattern of square crosses. A row of Delft tiles painted with cupids lined the bottom of the walls to protect the whitewash from our mops.

For 233 pages, Chevalier immerses her readers in the milieu of seventeenth-century Holland, conveying not just the conventional depictions of landscapes and interiors but painterly descriptions of these sites immortalized by Western Europe's most gifted painters.

Does the story possess elements of surprise in addition to the climax or epiphany?

If Stephen King's protagonist prevents Oswald from assassinating the President, what are the unexpected consequences of his attempt to change history? What are the unexpected consequences resulting from Vermeer's painterly obsession with the sixteen-year-old servant in his household? Anticipation needs to be compounded by elements of surprise (even shock) for readers to experience lasting satisfaction from your story or novel.

Do the characters come across as real people?

The underlying question here is *What do you mean by "real"?* Answer: Characters seem real when they remind us of people we've encountered but are distinctive at the same time. Do your characters behave in ways that make them stand out as individuals, either positively or negatively? Do their actions stem plausibly from their temperaments, their stations in society, or the predicaments you've placed them in? Your characters must be rendered in enough detail to be easily visualized. Look over the way you've described your characters' behavioral characteristics: Is there enough detail to enable your readers to distinguish them from the other characters? Do they each speak in their own distinctive way, or do they all sound similar?

Dialogue is an especially powerful means of conveying individual personality traits. Mystery novelist Robert B. Parker uses dialogue in *Double Deuce* (1992) not only to capture the personalities of his two principal characters, the tough and witty P.I. Spenser and his formidable yet admirable friend Hawk, but also to establish the conflict situation, investigating the drive-by murder of a teenager and her infant daughter at a ghetto housing project. In this passage, Spenser is speaking to Hawk.

> "What do they [the Boston police] want done?"
>
> "They want the murderer of the kid and her baby brought to, ah, justice. And they want the gangs out of the project."
>
> "You got a plan?" I said.
>
> "Figure you and me go talk with the minister and the church folks, and then we work one out."
>
> The traffic was just starting to accumulate on Storrow Drive and the first of the young female joggers had appeared. Colorful tights stretched smoothly over tight backsides.
>
> "The gangs don't scare us?" I said.
>
> "I a brother," Hawk said.

With just a few choice brushstrokes, Parker conveys Hawk's and Spenser's personalities through their manner of speech, using the speech content to alert the reader to the challenge that lies ahead. Note, too, how the brief narrative interlude (the description of "The traffic …") hints at Spenser's amusingly keen interest in people-watching, especially people of the opposite sex.

REVIEWING FOR STRUCTURAL INTEGRITY

Content influences structure and vice versa; everything should sooner or later coalesce as a unified whole. But just as in real life, an event in your story's present can trigger flashbacks in which effects are traced back to events that came before. A well-structured story does not necessarily mean one that unfolds chronologically, but it does mean that the reader can follow temporal movement, whether forward or backward.

To examine the structural integrity of your story, ask these questions:

Does the opening propel your readers into the story and keep them there?

Study the way a master storyteller like Ambrose Bierce establishes scene and situation with just a few deft sentences in "An Occurrence at Owl Creek Bridge," his Civil War story of a man about to be hanged.

> A man stood upon a railroad bridge in northern Alabama, looking down into the swift water twenty feet below. The man's hands were behind his back, the wrists bound with a cord. A rope closely encircled his neck.

Just three short sentences and Bierce establishes setting, character, situation, and dramatic immediacy. Whether you're writing a novel or flash fiction, the opening lines must pull your readers into the story and fully immerse them in your fictional world.

Does suspense or intrigue increase as the story unfolds?

What terrible event will the compounding clues in one of Dan Brown's Robert Langdon novels (*The Da Vinci Code, Angels and Demons, The Lost Symbol, Inferno*) finally reveal? Each clue adds to the final revelation. Does your story intensify reader curiosity as it progresses? Check carefully for slack spots that could break the spell of intrigue.

Is the climax or epiphany satisfying, or does it fall flat?

Readers feel cheated if you do not deliver a satisfying climactic moment or revelation. Your protagonist need not achieve the intended goal—but there must be something to compensate for that failure. Alternatively, even if the protagonist does succeed, that success needs to be tempered by some kind of sacrifice. In a satisfying story, although success ultimately is achieved one way or another, that success carries a price.

Have you included sufficient backstory to clarify the present situation, and are the movements from past to present clearly presented?

A fine example of this kind of structuring is in Gillian Flynn's *Dark Places*, in which the narrator struggles to find out who really butchered her family one horrifying night when she was seven years old. Flynn takes us from present day in one chapter to that fateful day in the following chapter, and each chapter introduces new potential revelations for both time periods.

REVIEW FOR STYLE

Style is a slippery concept because it is many things intertwined. Every writer possesses a stylistic signature, as distinctive as a literal signature but even more intricate. How you express a thought, depict action, build mood, or shape your sentences and paragraphs will contribute to your style. The terms *voice* and *style* are sometimes used interchangeably, but *voice*, as the word suggests, is usually limited to the narrator's particular way of telling the story. Mark Twain, for example, establishes his narrator Huck Finn's voice at the very outset of *The Adventures of Huckleberry Finn*.

> You don't know about me, without you have read a book by the name of "The Adventures of Tom Sawyer," but that ain't no matter.

Of course, a voice does not have to be colloquial like Huck's to be distinctive. Notice how Stephen Crane's narrator, in his famous short story "The Open Boat," captures the feeling of disorientation caused by being capsized at sea.

> None of them knew the color of the sky. Their eyes glanced level, and were fastened upon the waves that swept toward them. These waves were of the hue of slate, save for the tops, which were of foaming white, and all of the men knew the colors of the sea. The horizon narrowed and widened, and dipped and rose, and at all times its edge was jagged with waves that seemed thrust up in points like rocks.

As you reread your story for style, pay attention to the holding power of your narrator's voice: Does it project a distinctive state of mind, or an attitude toward the world, rather than a voice that sounds artificial or disconnected from the story you're telling?

PROOFREAD

We say that one *revises* content and style but one *corrects* grammar, spelling, punctuation, wordiness, and the like. It is the easiest of the post-production tasks to tend to—but don't let that fool you. It is every bit as important as the others. Why is that? Whether justified or not, surface errors signal a lack of professionalism. Blemishes, alas, do matter; that makes proofreading as important as revising for content.

The first thing to learn about proofreading is that it is not the same as regular reading. You're not reading in the conventional sense but combing the manuscript line by line for mistakes. I hasten to point out that although your computer's grammar and spell-checker is a good place to start, it would be a mistake to let it replace your own proofreading. Grammar checkers are lousy at detecting redundancies like unnecessary intensifiers ("very shocking"); sluggish sentence openers ("There was a sudden silence that filled the room" rather than "A sudden silence filled the room"); weak verbs ("Sue was the winner of the race" instead of "Sue won the race"); typos that happen to resemble correct words (not just homonyms like "whether" vs. "weather" but "tail" when you meant to write "trail"). Not only that, when you proofread the old-fashioned way—on a printed copy—you are likely to catch other issues like dangling modifiers ("Switching on my computer, the power went out," instead of "As soon as I switched on my computer, the power went out"); choppy or incomplete sentences; or overuse of a particular word or phrase.

Checking for usage errors is another important proofreading step you don't want to overlook. Did you accidentally use the contraction *it's* ("It's a fine day") for the possessive pronoun *its* ("The dog buried its bone")? Many do—and an editor or agent would likely assume you didn't know the difference and stop reading your story then and there. Other common usage errors include mistaking *lay* for *lie* ("I like to lie [present tense] on the couch" vs. "They lay [past tense] in the sun all day"). Compare that with *lay* (present tense), meaning to set down: "Lay the book on the table." Er-

rors in usage could instantly mark you as an unschooled amateur.

One last pointer before hitting Send: Solicit an objective reader's response. No matter how carefully you copyedit and proofread, you can benefit from another person's critique—assuming, of course, that your chosen reader is willing to be forthright.

CONCLUDING THOUGHTS

One of the most important lessons I've learned as a writer is that it always pays not only to check your completed opus for the many easily overlooked details I've just described, but to double, triple, and quadruple check them—and to do so in widely spaced intervals rather than back to back. You need a certain amount of time and distance from your hot-off-the-press creations. Sure, it takes a lot of patience and resolve—but you'll always thank yourself for not having been hasty with the short story or novel you have already devoted so much time to creating.

Fred White (Ph.D., University of Iowa) is professor of English Emeritus at Santa Clara University, where he taught courses in writing and literature for more than thirty years. In 1997 he received the Louis and Dorina Brutocao Award for teaching excellence. His essays, short stories, and plays have appeared in many periodicals and anthologies, including *Atticus Review*, *The Chronicle of Higher Education*, *College Literature*, *Confrontation*, *Pleiades*, *Rathalla Review*, *Southwest Review*, and *Writer's Digest*. His most recent books are *The Writer's Idea Thesaurus* and *Where Do You Get Your Ideas?* (both published by Writer's Digest Books). He lives with his wife, Terry, an attorney, near Sacramento, CA.

LAURA DRAKE

Telling the Perfect Truth

....

Janice Gable Bashman

Four hundred and seventeen rejections over fifteen years. Three books written starting at age forty-three. One agent who took a chance on an unknown author. Nine months later a three-book series sold to Grand Central, and four more books sold to Harlequin's Superromance line. Incredible, right? Wait. That's not all. Her first pub-lished book, *The Sweet Spot*, was named the 2014 Romance Writers of America RITA winner in the Best First Book category. So who is this author who persevered for so long trying to fulfill her dream of becoming published? She's the amazing Laura Drake.

Laura says she kept writing because "it's about wanting something. It's just as hard and simple as that. It's not for the struggle or the accolades (awesome as they are). It's for the joy of writing—getting down that one perfect sentence that describes *just* how something feels. Something that matters deeply. My goal has always been to give others the experience I've had so many times in my life; to read something, stop, and think, that's *just* how that feels, and I've never heard it described that way, but it's true. One perfect sentence, telling the perfect truth."

Laura is a city girl who never grew out of her tomboy ways or a serious cowboy crush. She writes both women's fiction and romances. She recently realized a lifelong dream of becoming a Texan and is currently working on her accent. She gave up the corporate CFO gig to write full time. She's a wife, grandmother, and motorcycle chick in her remaining waking hours.

You received a lot of rejections over many years before achieving success as a novelist. Why is perseverance so important in the publishing business?

Because this is *hard*! I compare it to learning to play golf—while riding a bicycle.

There are two very different skill sets involved in being published. First, there's the right-brain side—the creativity you need to write a novel. World building, storycraft, character development, timing, grammar, voice, point of view, conflict, backstory. … The learning curve is much longer than I realized, and much longer than most writers expect. Ultimately you can't just be good at all of this; you need a breakout novel to sell for the first time.

Then there's the business side, the left-brain side: submissions, marketing, social media, networking, and branding to name only a few. This involves a completely different skill set and another learning curve! I was lucky enough to have a leg up here. My career as a corporate CFO made the business side easier for me.

Everyone will be stronger with one side or the other, but both sides are critical to become a published author today, whether you go the traditional route or self-publish. So if you add

those two time lines together … that's where persistence comes in.

What was the process like for you in attempting to achieve your dream of becoming a published fiction author?

Before I learned to ride my own motorcycle, I rode a hundred thousand miles on the back of my husband's. I'd prop a book on his back and read during the boring stretches. One day, outside Kernville, California, a dog ran in front of the bike. After a gut-clenching scare, he trotted back the way he came. But it gave me a germ of an idea for a story that wouldn't leave me alone.

I debated for over a year. Who was I to write a book? Authors were way smarter than I. One day, while staring at a blank Word doc, I looked down. Hey, I had a "delete" key! I could write the book, and no one would ever have to see it. So that's what I did.

But a year and a half later, when I finished, I had a new goal. I wanted to hold a book in my hand with my name on the cover.

So I sent queries to agents—170 of them. I had a few requests for full manuscripts, but ultimately everyone turned me down.

So I started writing another book and finished it nine months later. I sent out 132 queries. There was more interest this time but still no takers.

So I wrote another book. Even *I* felt this one was good. My critique group told me it would be sure to sell. So I sent 120 queries (some agents had gone

> "It's impossible to know what you don't know when you don't know it. All you can do is work hard, do your best, and keep at it."

out of business). I entered contests, and even won four of them, but *still* the rejections poured in.

I belong to a local writers group and had volunteered to be their treasurer that year. We had an editor coming to town to speak, and since my office was close to the airport, I offered to pick her up. Friday afternoon traffic in Southern California is brutal, but that day a tanker truck spill meant that poor woman had to sit in a massive traffic jam with an aspiring author for two-and-a-half hours. She eventually asked me what I wrote, so I pitched my story. When she asked me to send her a partial, I reached in the back seat and handed it to her. (I had a goal—not pride!) She was a bit taken aback but promised to read it on the plane on the way home.

She was as good as her word. She called me Monday and said, "The first thing we need to do is get you an agent." Yeah, like I hadn't thought of *that*. She introduced me to my perfect agent, Nalini Akolekar of Spencerhill Associates.

What did you find most challenging about the publishing process, and how did you overcome it?

My own lack of objectivity. When I submitted my first book, I believed it was good enough to be published. I learned a lot, then I wrote my second book, which

I also thought was good enough. Both of those books were eventually published, but not without lots of blood, rewriting, sweat, and editing. It's impossible to know what you don't know when you don't know it. All you can do is work hard, do your best, and keep at it.

When you felt like giving up, what did you do to motivate yourself?

I reminded myself why I began writing to begin with, and it had nothing to do with being published. It was about the love of writing. To convey on paper what is perfect in my head. I never tire of that challenge; to create one perfect sentence. Over and over.

You stated you "try to write real characters, in could-be-real situations." Why is this so important in your work?

Because that's what I like to read. I have a low threshold for suspending disbelief. If the characters aren't fully rounded and "real," I'll put the book down. My books have been published as romance, but half the editors considered them women's fiction. I'll always give a hopeful ending, but my books have explored tough subjects:

- *The Sweet Spot*: loss of a child, divorce, addiction to pills
- *Nothing Sweeter*: questionable morals, felony conviction, and prison time

- *Sweet on You*: PTSD, survivor's guilt
- *Her Road Home*: childhood sexual abuse

They are romances and all end with, if not a happily-ever-after, at least a happy-for-now and a realistic resolution to the protagonist's issues. I guess I want to remind people who are going through real-life hard times that there is hope and things won't always be as bad as they may seem right now.

You have said that writing is about telling the perfect truth. What does that mean, and how do you accomplish this in your novels?

It takes me six to nine months to write a novel. To commit to and stay interested in a story for that long, the theme has to be one that resonates with me. I think that all fiction is, to some extent, autobiographical. Authors return to the themes that fascinate them. Stephen King, for example, explores good vs. evil and the innocence of childhood in almost every book. Pat Conroy returns to issues of discipline and coming of age in the South. Anne Rice writes about passion in its many forms—good and bad. I tend to write about guilt and forgiveness. I'm fascinated by people's choices: how good people can make very bad decisions and how they can grow past huge mistakes in their pasts.

For example, my book *Her Road Home* is about a woman who rides a motorcycle cross-country, never stay-ing in one place long, running from memories of past sexual abuse. The story is what happens when she stops running and turns to face her fears. In *The Sweet Spot*, the protagonist struggles to move past a dependence on depressants to forgive her ex and, ultimately, herself for the accident that took her young son's life.

Why is it worth it to tell the perfect truth?

Once you pass a certain age, you're more aware of time. When you realize that you have less time ahead than behind, you don't waste time on things that are not important to you. And if you choose a deep theme, you'll not only never run out of things to write, you'll have lots of readers waiting for your next book. Because themes are universal for a reason; they are over-arching problems that everyone understands. Not everyone has lost a child (and thank God, I haven't), but we all can relate to grief and loss and the damage it can do in our lives.

What happens if you find yourself struggling to tell the perfect truth?

If I'm struggling, it's always because I'm afraid. The fear of failure. Fear of not being good enough. But under all that is the fear of exposing myself—showing the really deep stuff that we'd all rather keep hidden.

To get past it, I think about my all-time favorite books. The ones that touched me. Changed me. Without exception, the authors exposed themselves in the writing.

I'd love for one of my books to touch a reader that deeply. I've spent a total of seventeen years of my life in this endeavor—why, if I'm going to let fear keep me from telling that perfect truth?

That fear is waiting for me, every single day I sit down to write. So how do I make myself do it, day after day, year after year?

Because I have a larger fear; the fear of wasted potential. If I sit down one day and chicken out by either not writing at all, or not writing the hard stuff, I'll know. Maybe no one else will, but that doesn't really matter, because I'll have let myself down.

That's what haunts me: to grow old and sit in a rocker on a porch somewhere, sorting through regrets. I believe the worst regrets aren't the mistakes you made—they're the things you wanted to do but didn't because you were afraid.

I think fear is at the bottom of why many writers find other things to do rather than finish that novel. The fear of writing my truth can make cleaning barroom toilets sound like a better alternative.

But to be an author, you have to face and surmount that fear every day.

What advice can you give to other writers about pursuing their dream to become published authors?

I love quotes. I saw one the other day [from an unknown source] that says it better than I could: "Never give up on something that you can't go a day without thinking about."

If you need my advice to keep you motivated, publishing isn't for you. It has to be something you can't *not* do. And if writing isn't it, go find what is, because everyone should experience the wonder of something *that* important in their lives.

See, that's the trap. By the time I finished that first book, I was hooked. I'd still be writing, even if I hadn't published. Because capturing that truth and putting it on the page is the always-just-beyond-my-fingertips goal. I haven't captured it yet. I doubt I ever will. But maybe, the next idea, the *next* book …. .

Writing is the hardest thing I've ever accomplished.

But it's the thing I'm the most proud of.

Janice Gable Bashman is a Bram Stoker Award-nominated author of *Predator* and *Wanted Undead or Alive*. She is the editor of *The Big Thrill*, the International Thriller Writers' magazine. Visit Janice at janicegablebashman.com.

CHRIS BOHJALIAN

Writing the World

....

Jessica Strawser

PHOTO CREDIT © VICTORIA BLEWER

Chris Bohjalian moves through the world as a writer. His honest answer to that quintessential question *Where do you get your ideas?* could be summed up in one word: *everywhere.* His novels have been born from a dinner party, a wartime diary, a homeless man's photography, and more than one fortuitous bike ride, though it's not unusual for those ideas to percolate for years before they start to take form. And just as he might not have a defining moment when a story begins, he doesn't keep the world at bay once he starts writing, either. In fact, he invites it in—often stopping midscene to go in search of new inspiration through hands-on research.

He acknowledges that some writers might find this an unstructured way to work. But to say it works for Bohjalian is an understatement. His sixteen novels span a decades-long career and multiple genres—often combining touches of thriller, romance, and history. Oprah may have made his name known with her selection of his 1997 novel *Midwives* at the height of her book club's popularity, but Bohjalian has kept it a bestseller list staple with his dramatic explorations of such difficult and broad-reaching topics as the homeless epidemic (*The Double Bind*), domestic violence (*Secrets of Eden*), the Armenian Genocide (*The Sandcastle Girls*), and the

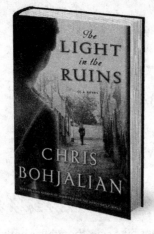

I know in my case I have to be passionately interested in a topic. The reality is that a novel [usually] takes years to write, and if you're not emotionally invested in the subject, it just becomes work. And I *never* want writing a novel to be work. My sense is that if I'm not having fun when I'm writing the book, readers aren't going to enjoy reading it. Certainly not everything I write in my books is fun—my books are pretty dark, that's the reality—but still, there has to be a real spark for me to want to invest so much of my life in one story.

German retreat from Italy during World War II (*The Light in the Ruins*). Readers love him for his open approach to social media, his standing invitation to Skype with groups, and his clear passion for the craft—he even writes a column for his local paper, the *Burlington Free Press*. In short, he walks the walk so well it's become his natural stride.

But there have been hurdles: discouraging writing professors, rejections by the hundreds, even a random life-threatening encounter in a New York City taxi that inspired his move away from the city to small-town Vermont—where, as it turned out, he'd find his voice. Bohjalian's life, in fact, reads like the story of a writer—and as this candid and comfortable conversation reveals, that's just as it should be.

Even before you delved into historicals, most of your fiction was inspired by something in life. Do you feel the most powerful fiction is born from a grain of truth?

Given your affinity for drawing inspiration in that way, did it at some point seem as if historical fiction was an inevitable next step for you?

I never thought I was going to write historical fiction—I never thought that was my sweet spot. The first time I wrote historical fiction was *Skeletons at the Feast*, my 2008 novel, and that is a book that ended up gestating for a lot of years before I started writing it. It actually had its origins when a friend of mine [asked if I'd] have any interest in taking a look at his grandmother's diary. His mother had just translated it from German. The diary was incredibly interesting, and his grandmother when she was fifteen years old [during WWII] was spectacularly heroic, but it never crossed my mind that there was a novel in this—instead, I sent the diary to publishers to see if they wanted a memoir, and nothing became of that. It would be at least five or six years later that I happened to read a history of the last year of the war in Germany, and I kept seeing echoes of this diary. And that's when it clicked that that diary was the kernel for a *novel*.

So that was the first time I wrote historical fiction, and obviously [*The Light in the Ruins* and *The Sandcastle Girls* are] historical [as well]. But my [most recent] book, [*Close Your Eyes, Hold Hands*,] is set in contemporary Vermont. The book I'm anticipating will follow is probably going to be set in the present Adirondacks. That doesn't mean I won't write more historical fiction, but I tend to write whatever interests me at the moment. And I never, *ever* want to write the same book twice—that is so important to me. I don't want to be sitting down with readers and have them tell me that my new book is too reminiscent of my previous novel.

[But] to go back to something you were getting at earlier, even *The Light in the Ruins* began with a deeply personal moment. I was watching a production of *West Side Story*, and my daughter was one of the Shark girlfriends, which meant I saw that production a lot. And I realized that I loved [that idea of] reimagining *Romeo and Juliet*, and I wanted to tell my own. But I had no idea where it would be set and when, so I just sort of squirreled away that idea. Then, two summers later I was biking with a friend of mine in Tuscany. He pointed out [Montisi's] fouteenth-century granary tower, and he said, "You know, don't you, that that used to go up fifteen feet higher? The Nazis blew it up when they were retreating." And then he sort of shrugged and smiled and said, "They tried to blow the whole thing up, but they couldn't. Man, we built things to last seven hundred years ago."

And the minute he told me that story I realized, this is where I wanted to set my *Romeo and Juliet*. ... I hadn't realized until that moment how violent Tuscany was in 1944. And so that's why I decided to write my *Romeo and Juliet* as historical fiction when it very well could have been set, if I had a Baz Luhrmann sensibility [laughing], in Miami in the present. Those events just married nicely.

You've said that researching your books is a process of discovery, where you don't know what will trigger a scene or a character until you stumble upon it. How much of a story do you typically know at the start?

When I begin a book, I have only the vaguest premise of what it's about. I know that a lot of novelists think that's a really bad way to work. But I really do depend on my characters to take me by the hand and lead me through the dark of the story. So when I begin, all I have to know is, (1) Is it third person or is it first person? And if it's first person, who is the narrator, and why is this voice appropriate? And (2) A *vague* premise of what the book is going to be about.

"I always had fun writing. ... Not everyone who picks up a tennis racket is going to wind up at Wimbledon, but that doesn't mean they shouldn't play tennis."

For example, *Midwives* didn't begin as a dark novel about a mother dying in a home birth and a midwife on trial for manslaughter. It began as a gently comic novel narrated by a midwife's daughter who is having a lot of fun at the expense of her hippy-dippy midwife mom. And if you look at the first chapter and the lion's share of the second chapter, you will see nothing in there that suggests this is going to be a devastating book.

But about 5,000 words in, my mother was diagnosed with lung cancer, and it was clearly going to be terminal. And so this book took this unexpected turn, and suddenly the young girl is coming of age as her mother is on trial for manslaughter. Most of my books have changes *that* dramatic at some point in the first draft.

Even *The Light in the Ruins* changed dramatically. Originally the book was going to be set entirely in the last year of [WWII] in Italy. There was going to be no moving back in forth in time between 1955 and the end of the war, [the way the chapters alternate now]. I was writing a scene where I was killing off a very minor character, Serafina. But that morning I couldn't bring myself to kill her because I liked her so much. So instead I simply scarred her—physically,

emotionally. And when I broke for lunch, I was really excited, because I had before me my own *Girl with the Dragon Tattoo*. And the book morphed, because where is Serafina ten years later? Well, she's the first woman in the Firenzi homicide squad.

Are your stories often inspired by a character that way?

They usually begin with a premise and a voice. I hesitate to say a character because with a book like *The Sandcastle Girls*, it was [all] about the premise: I wanted desperately to tell the story of the Armenian Genocide to the millions of people in this world who can't even find Armenia on a map. ...

In writing a book like that, where does the research stop and the writing begin? Or do the processes overlap?

They definitely overlap. Before I start a book, I might spend between a week and three weeks researching the plausibility of the premise. ... Once I start writing, I research simultaneously. I know a lot of writers think the Internet is satanic when it comes to creativity. I actually find the Internet *incredibly* helpful, principally via things such as Google Images.

I've also found that when I have writer's block, it isn't precisely writer's block so much as it's the reality that I've failed to do sufficient homework. So I will often stop writing a scene and interview whoever I need to interview to learn more.

Close Your Eyes, Hold Hands is narrated by a [teenage] girl in Vermont who is trying to keep it together on the streets in the wake of a nuclear plant meltdown. There were a number of people who, when a scene wasn't working, I'd meet with to learn more. A perfect example is a terrific therapist who works with homeless teens. I'd want to know, "OK, how is Emily going to get a shower?" And it isn't necessarily that [she'd] solve the scene by saying, "She'd take a shower at the Y, she'd get a day pass." She might say something else about, who knows, shoplifting, that would trigger a whole new scene.

I was astounded to read that for *Midwives* you interviewed sixty-five people. I was going to ask: What makes you keep digging? But it sounds like the story leads you.

That's really true. To go back to *Midwives*, the scene where Sybil performs the cesarean is the heart of the novel, and I wanted that scene to be emotionally devastating. I can remember thinking, *This might take three full days to write*. Well, it ended up taking closer to three weeks—[in part] because I ended up spending two days following around the medical examiner for the state, because I needed to understand exactly how much blood would be in

the cavity [to make the arguments in the story's resulting manslaughter trial plausible]. I also [talked] to an OB-GYN about, "What does the uterine wall feel like when you're pulling it aside in a cesarean?" I wanted to know what it would feel like to Sybil.

Early in your career, did you find that people were open to sharing those experiences? I think aspiring writers can be intimidated by that kind of research.

In my experience, we're all a little narcissistic about our professions and *love* sharing information. That doesn't mean that a writer *shouldn't* be a little intimidated, maybe, but I would encourage writers—even if they haven't published yet, even if it's just for a short story—to approach even professional strangers with their questions. More times than not people will enjoy talking about their work, and will elevate the writing in unexpected ways. ... When my books work, I think they're filled with those unexpected wonderful tidbits.

How much of a responsibility do you feel novelists have to be historically or factually accurate? Is there a philosophy you have in deciding what liberties to take?

What's more important to me than anything, whether it's historical or contemporary fiction, is not having something so implausible that it wakes the reader from the fictional dream—that's a great term from John Gardner,

I think, in *The Art of Fiction*. He was really onto something. You don't ever want to violate your reader's trust by playing so fast and loose with either history or contemporary plausibility that you lose your reader.

You've written so many different kinds of books. Is there a lesson there for other writers? So many publishers seem eager to brand their authors. Have you had to resist pressure to stick with one genre?

I never had to resist it because Knopf Doubleday is amazing. In the two decades I've been with them, they have been relentlessly supportive of my work. ...

Now, that doesn't mean that if you're a young writer, you shouldn't find your niche and live there happily. Book marketing has changed since my first novel was published in 1988. And there's a comfort level to know you're always in the same genre. It might be a lot easier to build a career [that way] in 2015. I think the most important lesson isn't necessarily to try and write a different book every time, or to try and brand yourself, [but] to write the kind of books you love to read. Because first of all, you're *doing something you love*. Second, you're working in your comfort zone, and third, even if this particular book doesn't work, it's going to be a lot more pleasant an experience.

Following that rule, you must love a little of everything.

[Laughs.] I really do! I probably have the only Sirius radio in the world that has as the two presets the NFL Network and Broadway. The truth is I do read a lot of [different genres]—the only things I really don't read a lot of are short stories and poetry. And I think that's because I'm a terrible poet, and I'm terrible at writing short stories.

Here's a true story: I amassed 250 rejection slips before I sold a single word, and all of those were for short stories I was writing in my late teens and early to mid-twenties. And when I finally sold a short story and it was published, I started hearing from agents, and they all were asking the same thing: "Do you have a novel?" And I didn't. And this lightbulb went off in my head. I had not tried to write a novel because I was intimidated by it, and because I wanted the immediate gratification of short stories—and you get *no* immediate gratification from a novel. You might get no gratification *ever* from a novel. But the truth is, when I had been in college, I had never been one of those young writers sitting at the feet of the short story gurus. I always loved *doorstops*. I loved *War and Peace*, I loved *Anna Karenina*, I loved *Les Misérables*. So I wrote my first novel. I wasted a lot of years writing short stories when I clearly should have been writing novels because *that's what I loved*.

Did you sell that first novel?

I did. And it sold quickly; it went out to three houses and got two offers. Just for the record, however, that novel is the single worst first novel ever published, bar none. If you go to my website you won't see anything about my first three published books. In some ways that's the sort of apprentice fiction that should never have been published, but for better or worse it was.

How would you describe your path of finding your way as a writer from that point, then? Was it a straight path, or were there a lot of turns?

Part of it is finding my voice. And writers talk with an agonizing amount of hubris about how they found their voice, but the reality is that I found my voice when my wife and I moved to Vermont. I wrote my first books when I was still living in New York City. And I love New York City. But it was when I came to Vermont that I wrote books like *Water Witches* and *Midwives* that are first-person, vaguely new-age-y books about women and men on the social margins. Narrators like [those] I think are where I found my voice. In subsequent years I'd get more comfortable with third person, with omniscient and historical fiction, but I am really grateful to Vermont. ... So while it feels like a linear path, it certainly had its ups and downs.

Here's a story I've never shared with *anyone*: In 1990, my wife and I sold all the furniture in our living room to pay the bills and make sure we had health insurance. To do what I wanted to do certainly took not simply unbeliev-

able persistence—250 rejection slips—unbelievable hubris, selling the furniture, and unbelievable commitment. I mean, here's another reality: I wrote my first three novels while employed full time at ad agencies. So I wrote fiction from 5–7 A.M. every day of the week, then Monday and Tuesday nights when I came home from work.

You've often told a horrific story about a novelist you admired leading a writing workshop you applied for when you were in college, and advising you to become a banker. And that was before the 250 rejections. What was it that made you keep writing all those years?

The short answer is: I always had fun writing. Even when people really close to me were saying, "Maybe it's time to give up this dream," it never crossed my mind to stop—because I've just always loved telling stories, I've always loved crafting sentences. And there was always that immense satisfaction when I would stop that I'd written even *one sentence* that I really liked. Or one scene that I felt was really moving. And I love that experience. I don't want to liken it necessarily to being a weekend tennis player versus Rafael Nadal—*but*, the truth is, not everyone who picks up a tennis racket is going to wind up at Wimbledon, but that doesn't mean they shouldn't play tennis.

You have one desk where you write and another where you revise. Is that symbolic of how you view the process?

No, I wish it were—it's not as poetic as that. It's because of the size of my desks. [Laughs.] The way the process works for me is that I write on a computer, and every forty or fifty pages I print out what I have and spend three or four or five days editing those pages by hand, with a fountain pen, because fountain pens are messy, so you have to move more slowly—you're really thinking about the right word. I'll input those changes, and write another forty or fifty pages, and then I'll print out one hundred pages and spend a week or ten days editing those pages. And since my books tend to be roughly 100,000 words, I will do that seven to ten times before I have a first draft.

The other important part of the process, though, is that often somewhere between pages 100 and 200, the book will change dramatically when I figure something out, such as my revelation about what I wanted to do with Sera-fina [in *The Light in the Ruins*]. When I have those revelations I go all the way back to page 1 and I simply start rewriting from the very beginning, even if I'm just retyping what I wrote.

In the first draft there's resemblance to the final draft, but you might say they are no more than cousins, not even siblings, because I will make copious changes between the first and the fifth or sixth draft based on my own instincts about what's working and what is not working, what my editor suggests, what my wife suggests, and based on what expert readers think—people who are in the field [that I'm writing about].

So you're not afraid to start over when you're revising.

[I do it] *all the time*. Was it Gabriel García Márquez who said, "The only reason writers publish is to stop rewriting"? Yeah!

Jessica Strawser is the editorial director of *Writer's Digest*.

JOHN SANDFORD

Just the Facts

....

Adrienne Crezo

Few journalists find the level of success that earns a Pulitzer Prize, and few authors can brag that every novel they've written has landed on *The New York Times* bestseller list. Even fewer writers can claim both—but John Sandford can.

Before he began a decades-long career at the top of the thriller charts, the writ-er born John Roswell Camp was a success-ful journalist. His career included stints at *Southeast Missourian* and the *Miami Herald*, a place on the Pulitzer shortlist in 1980, and the Distinguished Writing Award of the American Society of Newspaper Editors in 1985. In 1986, Camp was awarded a Pulitzer for Non-Deadline Feature Writing for his *St. Paul Pioneer Press* article series chronicling the life and work of a Minnesota farm fam-ily (johnsandford.org/farm.html). Around that time, he tried his hand at long-form nonfiction with two books, one about the paintings of John Stuart Ingle and anoth-er about plastic surgery. "Neither," he says, "will ever be a bestseller."

In 1989, he wrote and published his first two novels—*Rules of Prey* and *The Fool's Run*. Each would spawn a successful series: Prey, featuring his iconic Lucas Davenport character, a loner detective with a woman-izing streak, and the Kidd series, which fol-lows a computer genius who doesn't mind taking sketchy hacking jobs—as long as the money is good. In 2007, he launched yet

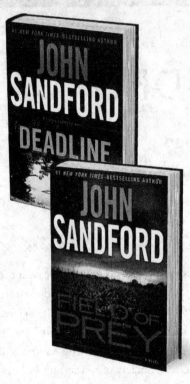

in New York for ThrillerFest 2014 falls in the midst of the tour for *Uncaged*. In one week, he and Cook have been to an event in Houston, held a signing at a New York bookstore, hosted MasterCraft classes at ThrillerFest, and are on their way to another series of events in St. Louis. His career is one of strict writing schedules (he averages two books per year), aggressive book tours, and the dogged pursuit of far-flung hobbies in between: He is the primary financial supporter of the Beth-Shean Valley Archaeological Project in Israel, and he writes songs "as a kind of side hobby."

So it's not surprising at all that he feels a bit weathered. Despite this, Sandford is funny, well spoken, and smart. And fortunately, he wasn't too worn out to talk at length about how he works, why he writes mostly fiction now, and why his work is still "a struggle all the way through."

another wildly popular series, Virgil Flowers, about a rough-around-the-edges cop who only does "the hard stuff." To date, Sandford has sold more than 10 million copies of nearly forty best-selling crime thrillers. In 2015 alone, Sandford released three titles: the twenty-fourth Davenport book, *Field of Prey*; the eighth Virgil Flowers installment, *Deadline*; and his first young adult thriller, *Uncaged*, the start of The Singular Menace series co-authored with his wife, fellow journalist-turned-author Michele Cook.

When I lead John to our reserved meeting room, he tells me he's tired. "Just beat up," he says as he runs his hands over his face. And it's understandable; this stop

You've had two distinct and successful careers in writing, first as a journalist and now as a thriller author. Is your nonfiction background helpful in writing your novels?

The major benefit of working in journalism is the stuff you get to see. I think a lot of writers—young writers—don't know enough. It's simply that they haven't been around long enough. They just don't have enough references in their head yet. One thing that journalism does is it gives you all that stuff in a hurry, so that if you're a general assignment reporter like I was for most of my career ... you'll see crime scenes, you'll do feature stories on all kinds of

> "Most awful crimes are committed by really stupid people, and really stupid people are not much of a challenge for your character. So you've got to have a smart person who is committing really ugly crimes. You have to depart from the reality that I experienced as a reporter."

things. I must have done several dozen stories on medicine and surgeries. I spent a month in a prison interviewing killers once. I spent a lot of time doing stories with farmers. You pack all this stuff into your head.

So it really does come down to writing what you know. Are most aspects of your books based on your experience or research?

I tend not to want to write about things I don't [already] know about. But some things I have done [additional] research on. I actually have a pretty extensive knowledge of guns because I grew up in the countryside in Iowa and I first shot a gun when I was probably four or five years old. But I bought a bunch of pistols specifically to do research with. And that's why my characters always use Berettas or Colts or Smith & Wessons. I have one of each of those weapons. I can take them out and look at them. I've fired them all. I know how to take them apart and put them back together. So I do that kind of research, and I will also do location research, like people do for movies, because I want the locations to be correct.

What you want is a specific kind of location because all places have idiosyncrasies, and putting the idiosyncrasies in the book makes the scene more tactile and real. So I do that kind of research, too. …

The characters are not based on anybody that I know. There are no cops like Lucas Davenport. He's a cross between a cop and a movie star. … Lucas [and his wife] have this real relationship in which she doesn't like some of the things he does, and she'll give him a hard time about them but is basically supportive, and he basically supports her. It's a wonderful thing. The reason I don't really base it on real people is that real people are much more inflected than that, and you don't have time really in a thriller—especially in a thriller in which the velocity is seriously important—to deal with all that stuff, so you have ways of indicating it. …

The events hardly ever resemble anything I covered [as a journalist] because real events are often too ugly. As ugly as some of my books have been, I've backed away from things I've actually seen because what you actually see is often too ugly, and also too pedestrian.

Most awful crimes are committed by really stupid people, and really stupid people are not much of a challenge for your character. So you've got to have a smart person who is committing really ugly crimes. You have to depart from the reality that I experienced as a reporter. ... I might look at some kind of killer, the BTK killer or someone like that, and then put it in the book in a different fashion.

I imagine you've researched so many murderers now that the crimes all sort of run together.

[The Minnesota prison system] had a system where [inmates] were allowed to start a company in the prison. Most of the money from the companies went to victims' funds and families. ... So they had one company that did computer work, and it was the most boring kind of programming in the world, the kind that nobody wanted to do. They [trained] lifers to work at the company because they were in there long enough to learn how to program. I talked to all these killers who were smart enough to learn programming, and it really gave me a lot of information about how their brains worked. I had long, intimate conversations with these guys—and not about their crimes, but about the way they thought about things. And virtually none of them took any responsibility for the murders whatsoever, even when they admitted doing it. That was enormously useful.

Do other imprisoned killers ever reach out to you, unsolicited, to talk about their crimes?

It's happened three or four times. And every once in awhile my website will get a letter from a guy in prison who's killed somebody, and he'll say he really enjoyed my books. What do you say to that?

You're not secretive about your pseudonym. Why did you choose to write as John Sandford instead of publishing under your real name, John Camp?

The pseudonym is an accident, actually. I was publishing two different books with two different companies at the same time. And Putnam, which was paying me much more money, said, *You know, you're publishing a series of books for [another publisher], and we really don't want them riding on our publicity. Can you use a pseudonym?* And that's why I use a pseudonym. ...

[But] I prefer anonymity. I really do. I don't like people looking at *me* because *I* like to look at *people*. ... I was a newspaper columnist for a while, and I had my picture at the top of the column and people would talk to me in the street and it just always scared the hell out of me. Someone says, *Hey, John!* and you realize you don't know this person and it startles you.

You were awarded a Pulitzer—that's a career pinnacle for most journalists. Did you move to fiction hoping to achieve a similar kind of success?

What happened was this: I wrote the series and I won the Pulitzer, and the [editor] called me into the office and they gave me a $50 a week raise. And I went home and I sat down, and I realized that with this raise—working for a metropolitan newspaper, in Minnesota, big circulation and all that—I [still] couldn't afford to send my kids to the state college. And that sort of changed my attitude toward writing. I realized that, to some extent, I wanted the money. This is the one life I've got, and journalism wasn't giving me the kind of range I wanted. I can't do much on fifty bucks a week. ... If I hadn't become a best-selling writer, I was going to stop.

So the first book was a bestseller?

I thought that I would get to be a bestseller. ... The thing is that it took awhile. It takes awhile to become established, and so you can't be discouraged if just one or two books don't sell. But if I had written, say, ten books, and they didn't sell well ... I would've done something else entirely.

Do you keep a strict schedule?

I write virtually every day. Every day when I'm not traveling. And when I am traveling, I take a computer with me and I will often write. I would like to be able to write 3,000 words tonight. ... I suspect I probably work 350 days a year. The last time I went [on vacation] to Paris I probably wrote 10,000 words while I was there—I was working every

day. ... I think a lot of people do that. You write almost compulsively.

I think many people would balk at working 350 days per year. That's very strenuous.

Stephen King has written more than I have, he writes more than I do, and so I think he *must* work every day. I publish twice a year, and he publishes as often as I do and his books are twice as big. ... And Stephen King is not exactly a hero of mine, but he's a guy I pay attention to because he's really smart and he knows what he's doing. And his writing book, *On Writing*, is the best writing book I've ever encountered. ... One of the things he says early on in the book is that you've got to know grammar. I think that most good writers really know grammar. They may not know the formal structural grammar, but they know when to use bad grammar and when to use good grammar, they know how words fit together, and they listen to people talk. He uses all kinds of different structures and all kinds of different language, and he's able to do that because he understands the basics.

Do you write many drafts, or do you edit as you go?

I will write a chapter, and because I don't outline, I won't necessarily know what's coming up. So I write a chapter, and then I write the next chapter, and then to make the first chapter fit with the second chapter, I'll go back and re-edit the first chapter. ... So after that, I just kind of struggle through it until I get to about 80,000 words. I then will often outline to the end because I want the end to be *extremely* fast. I want people not to be able to stop reading it. So everything then comes *bang bang bang bang bang*, it comes in a very fast, hard sequence. ...

By the time I get to the end of the book, I may have looked at the first page ten or fifteen times. Then I go back and spend probably a month working over the book. Working *really* hard. I can read [a chapter] in about ten minutes, but I will spend several hours working over each one, trying to untangle sentences and get the right word in the right place. Which I am not always successful with, but you know, I try. And then after I do that basic rewrite, I go back and look at the first and last chapters especially to make sure that they're really smooth.

Some writers say they can't start until they know the ending. Is that true for you, being that you don't outline?

That may be true in the details, but if you're writing a thriller book like mine, they have an arc to the novel. You know that there's going to be a crime to set things off, because there has to be— I'm writing about a cop. And so then the cop gets involved, and at the end of the novel the cop is going to either win or tie. He's not going to lose. By "tie" I mean that the bad guy's going to get away with it, but he's going to pay some kind of price. ... And [recognizing that arc] is important, because then you know what the general shape of the book is going to be in the back of your head very solidly before you start.

Does having that "general shape" make it easier?

It's not easy. It's a struggle all the way through. Actually, the hardest parts are the ideas and the scenes. The writing process itself, if you tell me what the scene is going to be, I can write it. I have no problem writing very smooth, idiosyncratic, nicely curved scenes, but I've got to know what the idea is, and that's the hard part.

Adrienne Crezo is the managing editor of *Writer's Digest*.

LISA SCOTTOLINE

An Original Voice

....

Jessica Strawser

PHOTO CREDIT © RYAN COLLERD

Lisa Scottoline doesn't like labels. But she does classify herself as a People Person—and about thirty seconds into any conversation with her, it's easy to see why. Just as the bestseller's twenty-two novels are cross-shelved as Crime Fiction, Legal Thrillers,

and Women's Fiction, she herself could be cross-categorized as both a Readers Person and a Writers Person. She opens her home to hundreds of book club members every year; she has served as president of the Mystery Writers of America; she exudes gratitude for her success, having begun her keynote at the 2014 Erma Bombeck Writers' Workshop by calling *thank you* "the two most important words in the English language." All of which is to say that if she isn't already one of your favorite authors, she probably will be if you ever meet her.

It didn't take long after her 1993 debut, *Everywhere That Mary Went*, for Scottoline to be dubbed "the female John Grisham," as the lawyer-turned-author made her own name writing a series of legal thrillers centered on an all-female law firm, Rosato & Associates. (The thirteenth installment, *Betrayed*, was published in 2014.) Yet as she has expanded her body of work to include stand-alone bestsellers—including her April 2014 release *Keep Quiet*, about a suburban father who makes a split-second

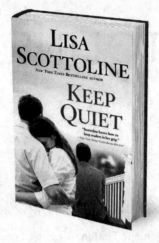

uated magna cum laude in three years with a concentration in Contemporary American Fiction before going on to law school at her alma mater, where in recent years she developed and taught a course called "Justice and Fiction." She has 25 million books in print, in more than thirty countries.

I first met Scottoline at ThrillerFest several years ago, where she told a riveted audience that with her writing, she still follows a rule she learned in law school: "Milk the facts." The *facts* of your story, she says, will yield incredible possibilities if you let them. Here are the facts of hers.

decision to leave the scene of a fatal hit-and-run car accident after letting his teenage son take the wheel—her books have become known above all for their emotionality and real, down-to-earth characters (yes, even the lawyers!) facing moral and ethical questions.

The quick-witted author also pens a *Philadelphia Inquirer* humor column with her daughter, Francesca Serritella. Their essays have been collected in several books, the latest of which, *Have a Nice Guilt Trip*, hit shelves in July 2014.

If you're keeping track, that's three new books out in 2014 alone—a pace she has no intention of slowing. Her work ethic is a product of a writing career that began when she was an in-debt, newly divorced mom struggling to provide for the infant Francesca. Scottoline has won awards ranging from the Edgar for excellence in crime fiction to the Fun Fearless Female title from *Cosmopolitan*. She studied under Philip Roth at the University of Pennsylvania, where she grad-

Your books make people ask themselves hard questions about what they'd do in impossibly tough situations. Is that something you set out to do—is that part of what compels you to write a particular story?

You look at your work from the inside out. So to a certain extent you're not even sure why you're doing something, or *that* you are doing it. For sixteen to seventeen years, I was writing a certain kind of story: Rosato. And what I started to really like was the dilemma it always posed—the disconnect between law and justice. I always thought that drama arose out of a *choice*. That's the thing about law: There's always a choice.

And I'll be straight with you: I started to find that I didn't like being categorized as a legal thriller writer. They [called me] "the female John Grisham," and I was like, *I'm cross-dressing, it's strange.* As flattered as I was by the comparison, it didn't feel like what I was doing from the inside out.

I said to myself, *Look at what you're doing that is making that happen.* You can't keep secretly complaining about writing legal thrillers when every main character is a lawyer. And then it occurred to me that issues of right and wrong and justice happen all the time, and not just to lawyers—in fact, probably rarest to lawyers! [Laughs.] So that's when I said, "If you love writing about these issues, you're really writing about an *emotional justice.* Do it, try it. …"

It was a huge gamble. I was writing this successful series, it had gotten me very far. To sort of just ditch it—I mean, I did. The first [stand-alone novel] was *Look Again*, and that [protagonist] was a journalist. This woman gets this card in the mail, and it says "Missing/Abducted Child," and the kid is her kid, who's adopted. And the readers know right away, something's wrong with her adoption; she didn't know. What is she going to do? Is she going to tell the truth and lose her child, or is she going to keep the truth to herself?

So that was a very happy thing, when the book did so well—and all the following stand-alones. They come out [every] April, and that's where I get to kind of run around—write about justice but not in a legal context. And it got me out of a corner I'd painted myself into.

[But eventually] I actually missed those Rosato characters. And those readers, they didn't desert, but they still said, "When are you going to write about Rosato?" When I figured out how to get better control … I [decided to continue the Rosato series] *and* the other stories *and* [the nonfiction humor] books with Francesca, about family life.

People say, "Where do you find the time for that?" Well, you get really ruthless. You really cut back socially. And who needs to wash your hair—who needs contacts? [Laughs.]

I think it was Stephen King who said you can choose to be an author or a writer, and that's a paraphrase, but the idea makes sense to me. It's really cool to be an author and swan around, and, you know, people clap, but if you do too much of that, you can't write. At least, I can't. And so that's how you can do three books a year, and not go crazy—in fact, feel the happiest and the luckiest you've ever, ever felt.

Some writers don't like to talk about branding, but your early books looked like what you'd expect a thriller to look like. Now, they even look more character driven.

You're right, and you're right to notice it, and I think it's important to talk about. Everybody has to think about it, whether you're self-published or published by legacy publishers. That stuff really matters.

It was a change when I changed publishers. And we *still* work on the covers. I have a wonderful editor, and she said, you know what, these distinctions we're

> "You have to believe [your writing dream] actually can happen, and nobody tells you that. It can happen!"

making [between the stand-alones and the Rosato books] are not really meaningful ones. People are coming to you for a family story and a crime story. Whether one is the plot or the subplot—lawyers say it's a "distinction without a difference." So Rosato is going to start to look more like the stand-alones, because to me, I'm writing stories about people. I think character and voice and plot are all the same thing.

It *is* about branding, and it helps the book find its audience—conversely, it also makes sure you put a book in somebody's hands and it's what they expect. … I've been very lucky to be very involved [with the publisher's marketing decisions]. And it seems like it's really working.

It sounds like you've really been embraced by book clubs.

Right! It always bothered me with Rosato—why don't book clubs read these? So I started to ask them, and they go, "Well, we don't read 'books like that.' They're crime fiction." So eight years ago, I [started my own] book club on Facebook. All you have to do is show me a picture of your book club, everybody holding a book, and you will be invited to a big party at my house. At my actual house where I actually live. People couldn't believe it.

They were like, "Isn't that kind of personal?" And I said, "Wait a minute. If you read a novel of mine, you know my soul. Do you really think it matters if you see my couch?"

We put a tent up, I buy all the food, I do a little talk, they ask questions, and it ends up being an amazing personal experience just to meet these people.

Now, other authors have faster trajectories. But in my career, it's built on good books, delivered at regular intervals. And at the book club, you meet people who've read you for ten or fifteen years, and you get to say to them, "You know how much you matter to me?" … It's all mixed up in what's great about books. You can't even match that experience.

You mentioned you've come to feel character and plot are the same thing. Could you talk more about that?

The example I always think of is if everybody is in a room, and all of a sudden a bad guy comes in and starts shooting. Everybody is going to react, and by definition they're going to react in character. Some people are going to jump in front of the children. Some people are going to call 911. Some people are going to try to attack him. And some people are going to run and hide. *Action reveals character.* I've learned, really just from my life: *We are what we do.*

Now, if your characters are what they do, it also drives the plot. As soon as you make that decision—actions are choices, they're just quick choices—that tells you what happens next. So the guy in *Keep Quiet,* he makes the choice [to leave] the scene. You know why he makes the choice: He wants to protect his son. He's completely off balance, blind-sided, a time when the best choices don't get made.

And the coolest thing is that not only does it reveal character but it *forms* character. There's a lot of slipperiness in the world. So you tell a little lie, and you think that's OK, or you get away with it, and then you start to become a liar. Because as soon as he decides he's not going to tell, he's got to go home, and he's got to keep his secret, and he's got to make his kid keep a secret, which is going to be really hard. So [character and plot] become the same thing. It is a distinction without a difference.

You've said you don't know in advance how your stories "middle," let alone finish. Yet you're known for plot twists. Do you have any strategies for pulling those off?

This is going to sound a little bit woo-woo—and I don't want to say the characters write the books, I never think that—but I do think you have to be open to the character behaving the way the character would behave. *Keep Quiet* turned out to be pretty twisty, and

it's because of getting out of the character's way, and going, *What would this guy really do?* If you don't have an outline that you need to overlay, you're not going to force anybody into a box. They're going to do something that is going to hand you something really interesting, and you need to let that happen, and not be afraid.

When I wanted to be a writer—and I always did—I always thought, *Wow, the writing is the hard part.* The writing isn't the hard part. The figuring out what comes next is the hard part! And it really matters at the end. I happen to think that a lot of novels fall down at the end, and I try not to make that happen. The main character can't fold up the tent. You've got to go forward. We all have difficulties, we all get plot twists; we just have to win in the end.

Do you ever write yourself into a corner?

No—because if you have a really logical narrative flow, honestly I think it's the best thing you can ever have for a page-turner. The reader is always following the character, they know why the character does things, because I didn't construct it out of thin air.

So I never get to a point where I lose two hundred pages. Sometimes I get to a point where I don't how this book is going to end, and I'm worried that it's going to be unsatisfying. … The weird thing—and I hope other authors feel this way—is there's a point, and usually for me it's about midway, where it gets *real.* It's a *real problem.* Everything in *Keep Quiet* can happen. So then you go, well, if this happened to a guy, he's going to *have* to figure a way out of it. And that's what makes him a hero. Not that he's true blue, not that he has superpowers—I don't write that person. I write every man, and every woman, in trouble, sometimes of their own devising. I think that's my life. [Laughs.] So you've got to figure it out.

Francesca has said that the most valuable thing you taught her was to give herself permission to take her writing seriously. Why do you think that can be so hard?

The world is really tough on people who want to be writers, and there's precious little support for it. And if you're a good person, and most people are, you have a lot of responsibilities. We're so good that we put them first, and lose ourselves.

I think it's a bit about [being] an adult who has a dream. Like, little kids, when you go, "What do you want to be when you grow up?" you think that when you're thirty, you should have answered that and you should be it already. But that's really not fair. In my case, it didn't work out. I was a lawyer, and when I got divorced and my daughter was born, I wanted to be something else. You have to nurture this dream.

I visualize it as a candle. You're the person in the movie walking around in the dark scary house, and you have the candle in the little dish, and you have to protect it with your hand. It can blow out very easily. And the world is not going to help you hold the candle.

You've *got to protect the candle.* You've got to go, "No, I can't come into work on the weekends—[that's] when I work on my novel." … People deserve those dreams, and they have to fight for them. You don't want to be at the end of your life and go, "Oh, I met all the obligations people had for me."

You have to believe that it actually can happen, and nobody tells you that. It can happen! I had five years of rejection. I had the worst rejection letter ever. But it happened to me, it can happen to you. But you have to give yourself permission, say to yourself, "I'm not foolish for wanting this."

All writers have to fight the same fight. I have to write 2,000 words today, no matter what. That's my discipline, and that's me protecting the work.

As the former "female John Grisham," do you imagine the day a writer is dubbed "a male Lisa Scottoline?"

[Laughs.] I would not wish that on anyone! You know, you love writing, I love writing. We all want to be known as an original voice.

THE BUSINESS OF FICTION WRITING

It's true there are no substitutes for talent and hard work. A writer's first concern must always be attention to craft. No matter how well presented, a poorly written story or novel has little chance of being published. On the other hand, a well-written piece may be equally hard to sell in today's competitive publishing market. Talent alone is just not enough.

To be successful, writers need to study the field and pay careful attention to finding the right market. While the hours spent perfecting your writing are usually hours spent alone, you're not alone when it comes to developing your marketing plan. *Novel & Short Story Writer's Market* provides you with detailed listings containing the essential information you'll need to locate and contact the markets most suitable for your work.

Once you've determined where to send your work, you must turn your attention to presentation. We can help here, too. We've included the basics of manuscript preparation, along with information on submission procedures and how to approach markets. We also include tips on promoting your work. No matter where you're from or what level of experience you have, you'll find useful information here on everything from presentation to mailing to selling rights to promoting your work—the "business" of fiction.

APPROACHING MAGAZINE MARKETS

A query letter by itself is usually not required by most magazine fiction editors. If you are approaching a magazine to find out if fiction is accepted, a query is fine, but editors looking for short fiction want to see the actual piece. A cover letter can be useful as a letter of introduction, but the key here is brevity. A successful cover letter is no more than one page (20-lb. bond paper). It should be single-spaced with a double space between paragraphs, proofread carefully, and neatly typed in a standard typeface (not script or italic). The writer's name, address, phone number, and e-mail address must appear at the top, and the letter should be addressed, ideally, to a specific editor. (If the editor's name is unavailable, use "Fiction Editor.")

The body of a successful cover letter contains the name and word count of the story, a brief list of previous publications, if you have any, and the reason you are submitting to this particular publication. Mention that you have enclosed a self-addressed, stamped envelope for reply. Also, let the editor know if you are sending a disposable manuscript (not to be returned; more and more editors prefer disposable manuscripts that save them time and save you postage). Finally, don't forget to thank the editor for considering your story.

Note that more and more publications prefer to receive electronic submissions, both as e-mail attachments and through online submission forms. See individual listings for specific information on electronic submission requirements, and always visit magazines' websites for up-to-date guidelines.

APPROACHING BOOK PUBLISHERS

Some book publishers do ask for queries first, but most want a query plus sample chapters or an outline or, occasionally, the complete manuscript. Again, make your letter brief. Include the essentials about yourself: name, address, phone number, e-mail address, and publishing experience. Include a three- or four-sentence "pitch" and only the personal information related to your story. Show that you have researched the market with a few sentences about why you chose this publisher.

BOOK PROPOSALS

A book proposal is a package sent to a publisher that includes a cover letter and one or more of the following: sample chapters, outline, synopsis, author bio, publications list. When asked to send sample chapters, send up to three consecutive chapters. An outline covers the highlights of your book chapter by chapter. Be sure to include details on main characters, the plot, and subplots. Outlines can run up to thirty pages, depending on the length of your novel. The object is to tell what happens in a concise but clear manner. A synopsis is a shorter summary of your novel, written in a way that expresses the emotion of the story in addition to just explaining the essential points. Evan Marshall, literary agent and author of *The Marshall Plan for Getting Your Novel Published* (Writer's Digest Books), suggests you aim for a page of synopsis for every twenty-five pages of manuscript. Marshall also advises you write the synopsis as one unified narrative, without section heads, subheads, or chapters to break up the text. The terms *synopsis* and *outline* are sometimes used interchangeably, so be sure to find out exactly what each publisher wants.

A FEW WORDS ABOUT AGENTS

Agents are not usually needed for short fiction and most do not handle it unless they already have a working relationship with you. For novels, you may want to consider working with an agent, especially if you intend to market your book to publishers who do not look at unsolicited submissions. For more on approaching agents and to read listings of agents willing to work with beginning and established writers, see our **Literary Agents** section. You can also refer to this year's edition of *Guide to Literary Agents*, edited by Chuck Sambuchino.

MANUSCRIPT MECHANICS

A professionally presented manuscript will not guarantee publication. But a sloppy, hard-to-read manuscript will not be read—publishers simply do not have the time. Here's a list of suggested submission techniques for polished manuscript presentation:

- For a short story manuscript, your first page should include your name, address, phone number, and e-mail address (single spaced) in the upper left corner. In the upper right, indicate an approximate word count. Center the name of your story about one-third of the way down the page, skip a line, and center your byline (the byline is optional). Skip four lines and begin your story. On subsequent pages, put your last name and page number in the upper right corner.
- For book manuscripts, use a separate title page. Put your name, address, phone number, and e-mail address in the lower right corner and word count in the upper right. If you have representation, list your agent's name and address in the lower right. (This bumps your name and contact information to the upper left corner.) Center your title and byline about halfway down the page. Start your first chapter on the next page. Center the chapter number and title (if there is one) one-third of the way down the page. Include your last name and the novel's title in all caps in the upper left header, and put the page number in the upper right header of this page and each page to follow. Start each chapter with a new page.
- Proofread carefully. Keep a dictionary, thesaurus, and stylebook handy and use the spell-check function on your computer.
- Include a word count. Your word processing program can likely give you a word count.
- Suggest art where applicable. Most publishers do not expect you to provide artwork and some insist on selecting their own illustrators, but if you have suggestions, let them know. Magazine publishers work in a very visual field and are usually open to ideas.
- Keep accurate records. This can be done in a number of ways, but be sure to keep track of where your stories are and when you sent them out. Write down submission dates. If you do not hear about your submission for a long time—about one to two months longer than the reporting time stated in the listing—you may want to contact the publisher. When you do, you will need an accurate record for reference.

ABOUT OUR POLICIES

We occasionally receive letters asking why a certain magazine, publisher, or contest is not in the book. Sometimes when we contact listings, the editors do not want to be listed because they:

- do not use very much fiction.
- are overwhelmed with submissions.
- are having financial difficulty or have been recently sold.
- use only solicited material.
- accept work from a select group of writers only.
- do not have the staff or time for the many unsolicited submissions a listing may bring.

Some of the listings do not appear because we have chosen not to list them. We investigate complaints of unprofessional conduct in editors' dealings with writers and misrepresentation of information provided to us by editors and publishers. If we find these reports to be true, after a thorough investigation we will delete the listing from future editions.

There is no charge to the companies that list in this book. Listings appearing in *Novel & Short Story Writer's Market* are compiled from detailed questionnaires, phone interviews, and information provided by editors, publishers, and directors of awards and conferences. The publishing industry is volatile, and changes of address, editor, policies, and needs happen frequently. To keep up with the changes between editions of the book, we suggest you check the market information on the Writer's Market website at www.writersmarket.com. Many magazine and book publishers offer updated information for writers on their websites. Check individual listings for those website addresses.

Organization newsletters and small magazines devoted to helping writers also list market information. Several offer online bulletin boards, message centers, and chat lines with up-to-the-minute changes and happenings in the writing community.

We rely on our readers, as well, for new markets and information about market conditions. E-mail us if you have any new information or if you have suggestions on how to improve our listings to better suit your writing needs.

Electronic Submissions

- If sending electronic submissions via e-mail or online submission form, check the publisher's website first for specific information and follow the directions carefully.

Hard-Copy Submissions

- Use white 8½" × 11" bond paper, preferably 16- or 20-lb. weight. The paper must be heavy enough not to show pages underneath and strong enough to take handling by several people.

> Some people are under the mistaken impression that copyright is something they have to send away for.

- Type your manuscript on a computer and print it out using a laser or ink-jet printer (or, if you must, use a typewriter with a new ribbon).
- An occasional spot of white-out is okay, but don't send a marked-up manuscript with many typos.
- Always double-space and leave a 1" margin on all sides of the page.
- Don't forget word count. If you are using a typewriter, there are several ways to count the number of words in your piece. One way is to count the words in five lines and divide that number by five to find an average. Then count the number of lines and multiply to find the total words. For long pieces, you may want to count the words in the first three pages, divide by three, and multiply by the number of pages you have.
- Always keep a copy. Manuscripts do get lost. To avoid expensive mailing costs, send only what is required. If you are including artwork or photos but you are not positive they will be used, send photocopies. Artwork is hard to replace.
- Enclose a self-addressed, stamped envelope (SASE) if you want a reply or if you want your manuscript returned. For most letters, a business-size (#10) envelope will do. Avoid using any envelope too small for an 8½" × 11" sheet of paper. For manuscripts, be sure to include enough postage and an envelope large enough to contain it. If you are requesting a sample copy of a magazine or a book publisher's catalog, send an appropriately sized envelope.
- Consider sending a disposable manuscript that saves editors time (this will also save you money).

RIGHTS

The Copyright Law states that writers are selling one-time rights (in almost all cases) unless they and the publisher have agreed otherwise. A list of various rights follows. Be sure you know exactly what rights you are selling before you agree to the sale.

Copyright is the legal right to exclusive publication, sale, or distribution of a literary work. As the writer or creator of a written work, you need simply to include your name, date, and the copyright symbol © on your piece in order to copyright it. Be aware, however, that most editors today consider placing the copyright symbol on your work the sign of an amateur and many are even offended by it.

To get specific answers to questions about copyright (but not legal advice), you can call the Copyright Public Information Office at (202)707-3000 weekdays between 8:30 A.M. and 5 P.M. EST. Publications listed in *Novel & Short Story Writer's Market* are copyrighted unless otherwise stated. In the case of magazines that are not copyrighted, be sure to keep a copy of your manuscript with your notice printed on it. For more information on copyrighting your work, see *The Copyright Handbook: What Every Writer Needs to Know, 11th edition*, by Stephen Fishman (Nolo Press, 2011).

Some people are under the mistaken impression that copyright is something they have to send away for and that their writing is not properly protected until they have "received" their copyright from the government. The fact is, you don't have to register your work with the Copyright Office in order for your work to be copyrighted; all writing is copyrighted the moment it is put to paper.

Although it is generally unnecessary, registration is a matter of filling out an application form (for writers, that's Form TX). The Copyright Office now recommends filing an online claim at www.copyright.gov/forms. The online service carries a basic claim fee of $35. If you opt for snail mail, send the completed form, a nonreturnable copy of the work in question, and a check for $65 to the Library of Congress, Copyright Office-TX, 101 Independence Ave. SE, Washington, DC 20559-6000. If the thought of paying $65 each to register every piece you write does not appeal to you, you can cut costs by registering a group of your works with one form, under one title, for one $65 fee.

Most magazines are registered with the Copyright Office as single collective entities themselves; that is, the individual works that make up the magazine are not copyrighted individually in the names of the authors. You'll need to register your article yourself if you wish to have the additional protection of copyright registration.

For more information, visit the U.S. Copyright Office online at www.copyright.gov.

First Serial Rights

This means the writer offers a newspaper or magazine the right to publish the article, story, or poem for the first time in a particular periodical. All other rights to the material remain with the writer. The qualifier "North American" is often added to this phrase to specify a geographical limit to the license.

When material is excerpted from a book scheduled to be published and it appears in a magazine or newspaper prior to book publication, this is also called first serial rights.

One-Time Rights

A periodical that licenses one-time rights to a work (also known as simultaneous rights) buys the nonexclusive right to publish the work once. That is, there is nothing to stop the author from selling the work to other publications at the same time. Simultaneous sales would typically be to periodicals with different audiences.

Second Serial (Reprint) Rights

This gives a newspaper or magazine the opportunity to print an article, poem, or story after it has already appeared in another newspaper or magazine. Second serial rights are nonexclusive; that is, they can be licensed to more than one market.

All Rights

This is just what it sounds like. All rights means a publisher may use the manuscript anywhere and in any form, including movie and book club sales, without further payment to the writer (although such a transfer, or assignment, of rights will terminate after thirty-five years). If you think you'll want to use the material more than once, you must avoid submitting to such markets or refuse payment and withdraw your material. Ask the editor whether he is willing to buy first rights instead of all rights before you agree to an assignment or sale. Some editors will reassign rights to a writer after a given period, such as one year. It's worth an inquiry in writing.

Subsidiary Rights

These are the rights, other than book publication rights, that should be covered in a book contract. These may include various serial rights; movie, television, audiotape, and other electronic rights; translation rights, etc. The book contract should specify who controls these rights (author or publisher) and what percentage of sales from the licensing of these subrights goes to the author.

Dramatic, Television, and Motion Picture Rights

This means the writer is selling his material for use on the stage, in television, or in the movies. Often a one-year option to buy such rights is offered (generally for 10 percent of the total price). The interested party then tries to sell the idea to actors, directors, studios, or television networks. Some properties are optioned over and over again, but most fail to become dramatic productions. In such cases, the writer can sell his rights again and again—as long as there is interest in the material.

Electronic Rights

These rights cover usage in a broad range of electronic media, from online magazines and databases to interactive games. The editor should state in writing the specific electronic rights he is requesting. The presumption is that the writer keeps unspecified rights.

Compensation for electronic rights is a major source of conflict between writers and publishers, as many book publishers seek control of them and many magazines routinely include electronic rights in the purchase of print rights, often with no additional payment. Writers can suggest an alternative way of handling this issue by asking for an additional 15 percent to purchase first rights and a royalty system based on the number of times an article is accessed from an electronic database.

MARKETING AND PROMOTION

Everyone agrees writing is hard work whether you are published or not. Yet once you achieve publication, the work changes. Now not only do you continue writing and revising your next project, you must also concern yourself with getting your book into the hands of readers. It's time to switch hats from artist to salesperson.

While even best-selling authors whose publishers have committed big bucks to marketing are asked to help promote their books, new authors may have to take it upon themselves to plan and initiate some of their own promotion, usually dipping into their own pockets. While this does not mean that every author is expected to go on tour, sometimes at their own expense, it does mean authors should be prepared to offer suggestions for promoting their books.

Depending on the time, money, and personal preferences of the author and publisher, a promotional campaign could mean anything from mailing out press releases to setting up book signings to hitting the talk-show circuit. Most writers can contribute to their own promotion by providing contact names—reviewers, hometown newspapers, civic groups, organizations—that might have a special interest in the book or the writer.

Above all, when it comes to promotion, be creative. What is your book about? Try to capitalize on it. Focus on your potential audiences and how you can help them connect with your book.

IMPORTANT LISTING INFORMATION

- Listings are not advertisements. Although the information here is as accurate as possible, the listings are not endorsed or guaranteed by the editors of *Novel & Short Story Writer's Market.*
- *Novel & Short Story Writer's Market* reserves the right to exclude any listing that does not meet its requirements.

SHORT IS THE NEW LONG

Write Bite-Size Fiction to Enhance Your Career

....

Anne R. Allen

I thought short stories stopped being relevant for professional writers decades ago, when mainstream magazines such as *The Saturday Evening Post* stopped publishing fiction; I equated short fiction with those finger exercises piano students do before they graduate to real music. If you're serious about a career in fiction, you write novels … right?

Wrong. Short stories are having a revival in the digital age. As book marketing guru Penny C. Sansevieri wrote in *The Huffington Post*, "Short is the new long. Thanks to consumers who want quick bites of information and things like Kindle Singles, consumers love short." It seems the short story is back—on an iPhone near you.

Here are nine factors working in favor of a short story renaissance.

1. Small, portable screens are changing the way we read.

"The single-serving quality of a short narrative is the perfect art form for the digital age. … Stories are models of concision, can be read in one sitting, and are infinitely downloadable and easily consumed on screens," bestselling short story writer Amber Dermont told *The New York Times*.

Cal Morgan of Harper Perennial agrees. "The Internet has made people a lot more open to reading story forms that are different from the novel," he says.

In 2011, when Amazon launched its Kindle Singles program—which publishes works of fiction or creative nonfiction of 5,000–30,000 words—it sold more than 2 million short titles in fourteen months. Today, it's further promoting short fiction with a Short Reads section—where customers can choose stories from the Singles library by the length of time required to read them—and *Day One* magazine, which showcases short fiction from new authors. (Find submission guidelines at tinyurl. com/pwc2lrj.)

2. Anthologies are hot.

Multi-author anthologies are a great sales tool, and they've been reborn in the e-book space, where they're inexpensive to put

> Years ago, placing stories was tough. ... Now, most journals are available online. They have larger readerships, and you don't have to pay a fortune to read them to find out what the editors want. More publications focus on genre or flash fiction, not just literary work.

together and provide wide visibility. While digital-only anthologies usually don't pay and often donate proceeds to a charity, if you can get a story featured alongside well-known authors in your genre, you'll be paid in publicity that would be hard to buy at any price.

Print anthologies are also a fantastic way for newer authors to break onto bookshelves; there are still plenty of staples, such as the Chicken Soup series, being stocked in stores in droves. Multi-author collections vary in prestige—the venerable Best American Short Stories is a solid bestseller every year, packed with the top names in literary fiction—but getting your work into any anthology vetted by an editor and chosen through a submission process will look great in your bio and draw fans to your other work. You can find calls for submissions to anthologies on sites such as Duotrope (duotrope.com) and Writer's Relief (writersrelief.com) in the classified sections of magazines such as *Writer's Digest*, and through simple Internet searches.

3. Publication identifies you as a professional.

If you're on a career track, you need to show agents, publishers, and reviewers you're serious. Placing stories in respected literary journals will do that. Years ago, placing stories was tough. Fiction had vanished from most mainstream magazines. Even no-pay literary journals were fiercely competitive and expensive to buy. Now, most journals are available online. They have larger readerships, and you don't have to pay a fortune to read them to find out what the editors want. More publications focus on genre or flash fiction, not just literary work. And there are showcases for short fiction where you can start building a fan base before you publish a novel, including Wattpad (wattpad.com), which allows all users to upload their stories, free for other users to read, and Readwave (readwave.com), which shares "3-minute stories" written by users.

4. Networking with short fiction editors can further your career.

Editors at small magazines often have connections in the publishing world. I found my first publisher because one of its editors volunteered for a digital literary magazine that accepted one of my stories. The litzine went under before my story appeared, but the editor asked if I had any novels he could take to the small publishing house where he worked. Two months later, I had my first publishing contract.

5. Filmmakers buy rights to short stories.

Just as indies are re-invigorating publishing, they are also the lifeblood of the film industry. While big studios concentrate on huge comic book spectacles, many emotionally rich, award-winning films are coming from small-budget indies, such as Larry Yust's adaptation of Shirley Jackson's "The Lottery," Chandler Tuttle's *2081*, based on Kurt Vonnegut's "Harrison Bergeron," and Steph Green's on-screen retelling of Roddy Doyle's "New Boy."

6. Online retailers favor authors with more titles.

The more titles you have in an online bookstore, the more visible you are. Most writers can't turn out more than a couple of books a year, but they can write and publish short stories and novellas in between.

7. Short fiction contests can build your bio.

Contests are easy to find and enter in the Internet era. C. Hope Clark's Funds for Writers (fundsforwriters.com) and Winning Writers (winningwriters.com) are good free sources for vetted and free contests, and established publications often sponsor competitions that provide opportunities for authors in all genres. A win or even honorable mention looks great in a query or bio. Some of the biggest awards in literature are still for short fiction, sometimes offering a prize as high as a standard novel advance, as do the Pushcart and O. Henry Prizes.

8. Shorts keep fans engaged and draw new ones.

Forward-looking agents encourage authors to self-publish short stories—especially when writing a series. Shorts keep fans interested while they're waiting for the next book, and a free story in between is a great marketing tool. Consider writing a couple of shorts about your main characters while you're working on the novel. It may get you through a tricky spot in the big work and give you a salable product for later. (Also, many great novels started as shorts. A story about a minor character may expand into a novel of its own.)

9. Today's short stories make money and hold their value.

Per word, a story can make more money than a novel. Not only does it take less time to write, a Kindle Single often sells for the same price as a novel-length e-book, and it can be repurposed many times. Some large magazines still publish short fiction, and publications such as *Asimov's*, *Ellery Queen*, and *Woman's World* still pay top dollar for genre stories.

Short stories are great for practice, too. Learning to write short can keep your prose from getting flabby. You shouldn't give up on your *magnum opus*, but try a few ideas out in short stories. You'll be grateful you have inventory when opportunity comes knocking.

....

Anne R. Allen is the author of seven comic mysteries and co-author of *How to Be a Writer in the E-Age: A Self-Help Guide*, written with Catherine Ryan Hyde.

....

THE EVOLVING AGENT

*How Progressive Literary Agencies Are
Redefining the Traditional Role of the Agent*

....

Jane Friedman

Claire Cook is living the dream. She wrote her first novel at forty-five, and five years later, she walked the red carpet at the Hollywood premiere of the adaptation of her second novel, *Must Love Dogs*. She's the *USA Today* best-selling author of eleven novels, and her books have been translated into fourteen languages.

And she no longer has an agent.

Cook recently broke with her long-standing agency when they reached an impasse over how to handle her indie work. She says that while she loved the support of being agented, she didn't want to be pressured to sell her new work to traditional publishers and would prefer an agent willing to allow her the freedom to pursue alternatives. As she considers her next steps, she says, "I decided to write the book I'd wanted to write for years that nobody on my former publishing team felt fit my novelist brand."

Cook's story illustrates a larger shift in the industry, where authors' needs and long-term career trajectories are no longer auto-matically defined by selling their next book to a big publisher. Self-publishing and digi-tal publishing now can serve as important (and lucrative) building blocks for growing a readership, and more authors are choos-ing a hybrid model of publishing, where they decide how and where to publish on a project-by-project basis.

So agents' guidance and support may be as critical as ever, but flexibility is needed, too—which has led to a reassessment and re-envisioning for many agencies in how they support their clients. The difficulty is that, traditionally speaking, the only ac-ceptable way for agents to earn money is through commission on authors' sales, typ-ically starting at 15 percent. The Associa-tion of Authors' Representatives—the pro-fessional organization for literary agents—explicitly prohibits its members from acting as publishers given the potential conflict of interest that can arise from representing an author to traditional publishers while also publishing his work. Therefore, most agents have begun assisting with self-publishing only on a commission basis, taking their standard 15 percent on sales.

"We make sure there is … no incentive for us to recommend to our authors that they pursue one avenue or another," says Laura Rennert, senior agent with Andrea Brown Literary Agency. "We advise our authors based on an objective weighing of the authors' business and artistic interests and a consideration of what is most important to them." Rennert points to *The New York Times* bestseller Catherine Ryan Hyde as a success story in terms of how her agency works. Hyde, who had made her name years before with the novel-turned-movie-turned-movement *Pay It Forward*, was the first client who Rennert later helped self-publish to supplement her traditional deals. "We offer representation selectively, as we always have, and make what we hope is a long-term commitment to our clients."

THE VALUE OF AGENT-ASSISTED SELF-PUBLISHING

In the self-publishing community, some authors bridle at the thought of agents taking a 15 percent commission on their work. But it's important to make a distinction between (1) agents who take a commission on specific projects where they provide assistance, administration, and/or marketing support, and (2) agents who take a commission on every work their client produces, regardless of the agency's support.

The first scenario raises an important question: Does an author benefit from having an agent assist with self-publishing? Arguably it depends on the personality of the author, her existing skills and resources, and how much time she can spend on the self-publishing process. Some authors are well equipped to be publishing entrepreneurs, while others prefer the experience and resources of someone in the industry they trust.

Forward-thinking agents see long-term benefit in assisting their clients but point out that it's not an insignificant extension of the work they do. "It's very time intensive … . The bookkeeping is horrendously expensive (and we don't charge for our time here)," says Liza Dawson, of Liza Dawson Associates. "But it's also fun. I've just retitled and repackaged my client Tom Stone's book. It was originally published by Bloomsbury. And finally we figured out who the book's audience is, how to package it, and what the right title is."

The agents who are engaged and invested in their clients' self-published work don't click "upload" and walk away. They help in a strategic manner, in many ways doing the same work a publisher would, with ongoing marketing support and insight. "It's not just, 'Let's toss this one thing out here, hurl this other over here, and hope something works,'" The Knight Agency's Deidre Knight says. "We look at the author, what type of writer she is, and … see how doing a particular work or series in digital self-pub might enhance a broader picture."

Several years ago, when agents began assisting clients with self-publishing, some offered a one-size-fits-all model, which usually meant a 15 percent commission on sales, with the author paying freelance costs, such as copyediting, cover design, and e-book formatting.

Today, some have moved to tiers of service or customizable arrangements to take into account the unique needs of each client. The agent may earn a higher commission for providing hands-on marketing support, which can involve advertising placements, blog tours, advance galleys, Goodreads campaigns, and more—if the author wants.

WHEN AGENTS USE THIRD PARTIES TO ASSIST

None of the agents mentioned in this article obligate their clients to self-publish with them; it's strictly optional, and authors are free to self-publish on their own with no financial obligation to the agent. This is an important detail, because some agencies demand a 15 percent commission on *all* of an author's work, which means, in practical terms, the author must work through the agency to self-publish (as was the situation Claire Cook found herself in).

Agencies that demand you publish your indie work through them may use distributors such as Argo Navis to provide the service, which can be financially disadvantageous for the author. For example, for a $10 e-book, this would be the financial breakdown for a single unit sold through Amazon using Argo Navis:

- Amazon takes 30 percent ($3), leaving $7
- Argo Navis takes 30 percent of the $7, leaving $4.90
- The agent takes 15 percent of $4.90, leaving $4.17 for the author

The author earns less than if the agent were distributing directly on her behalf, plus the agent receives 15 percent even though Argo Navis does the work. Furthermore, distributors such as Argo Navis do not cover freelance costs; those are borne by the author.

Argo Navis's services are available to authors only through a literary agent. Another program available only through an agent is the Amazon White Glove program, which might be considered as competing against Argo Navis.

You won't find a complete list of agencies involved in White Glove, nor will you find mention of this program on Amazon's site, but the basic outline is this: The agent assists the author in self-publishing exclusively with Amazon for 6 to 12 percent (taking his customary commission), and in return, Amazon offers thirty days of promotion on its website, in rotation with other titles in the program. Before going down this path, it's important to ask your agent what happens after the exclusivity period is over, which brings us to the larger issue of contract terms for agent-assisted arrangements.

WHAT YOU SHOULD ASK

Before self-publishing with an agent's assistance, ask the following questions:

- Who covers the costs associated with self-publishing? In most cases, the author covers the cost, but sometimes the agent will cover expenses and deduct them from the author's earnings.

- Who controls rights to the self-published work? (It should be the author.)
- How long must you commit to giving the agent 15 percent of sales on the work? (It shouldn't be indefinitely.)
- How/when can the agreement be terminated?

When an agency assists clients directly (without a distributor such as Argo Navis), it generally sets up distribution accounts for its clients (e.g., at Amazon), administers those accounts, and pays the authors after taking its commission. Ideally, the author has access to those distribution accounts—which means access to pricing, files, and reporting—and those accounts are turned over to the author if the agreement with the agent is terminated. That way the author doesn't risk later having to re-upload the book as if it were an entirely new product, losing sales rankings and reviews in the process.

If you seek an agent who would support a hybrid approach to your publishing career, look for those who already have a track record with hybrid clients. Query your project on its own merit, and if representation is offered, tell the agent about your publishing goals, and ask:

- How does the agency assist with self-published work, if at all? What arrangements are most common or acceptable?
- What happens if you self-publish without the agency's assistance?

The overriding goal for most agents, especially in representing unpublished clients, is to sell the authors' work to traditional publishers. Don't expect to receive a response to your initial submission with an offer to help you self-publish; that conversation typically happens only after months of trying the traditional route, and by mutual agreement. For established clients, agents may assist in getting their backlists on sale again and helping release digital shorts in between larger book releases (a strategy more and more authors are using to keep readers engaged and to earn extra money in the process).

SELECT AGENCIES THAT ASSIST WITH SELF-PUBLISHING

The following agencies (listed in alphabetical order) offer a supportive environment to assist clients in digitally self-publishing their work. Authors retain their rights but may be asked to commit to a set term of agreement, such as six months, a year, or longer. Note that some of these agents have broken with AAR, but that isn't necessarily the red flag it once was. As agents forego working on a commission-only basis, and act more like talent managers or even publishers, they will be working outside of AAR's current guidelines. Still, as always, read contracts carefully before signing.

Andrea Brown Literary Agency
www.andreabrownlit.com

Author covers all costs; once the author recoups all expenses through sales, then the agency earns its standard commission. No set term of agreement.

April Eberhardt Literary
aprileberhardt.com

Helps authors evaluate potential publishing partners and models, identify and vet free-lancers, and find supplemental resources as needed, based on the authors' goals and skill sets. Works on either a commission or fee-for-service basis.

Curtis Brown (UK)

curtisbrown.co.uk

Exclusively distributes through Amazon White Glove. Offers a sliding scale of commissions, conditional on the work required. Deals are flexible and meant to suit the author's needs at that time, with no terms or fixed periods.

Dystel & Goderich Literary Management

www.dystel.com

Author covers all freelance costs; authors can terminate the relationship with sixty days' written notice.

Levine Greenberg Rostan Literary Agency

lgrliterary.com/ebooks

Works with Argo Navis, Amazon White Glove, and many other partners. Terms vary by author and partner.

Liza Dawson Associates

lizadawsonassociates.com

Deducts freelance costs from the authors' earnings. No standardized model for hybrid authors; every arrangement is based on the client's needs.

NLA Digital

nladigitalbooks.com

Established by agent Kristin Nelson to offer clients two self-publishing options: full service and distribution-only. With full service, NLA assists clients with cover art, copyediting, file conversion, and distribution. With distribution-only, clients use NLA Digital to get access to venues they can't reach on their own, such as library markets. In spring 2014, NLA Digital opened its distribution-only services to guest authors who are not clients of NLA.

CONTRACT TERMS: For full-service, NLA Digital requires a two-year agreement and fronts all costs. The author reimburses NLA Digital for half of those costs via royalties earned. There is no commitment or cost involved for distribution-only. In either scenario, NLA Digital takes its standard agency commission.

The Knight Agency

knightagency.net

Offers several tiers of service and takes a customized, dynamic approach when working with clients on a project.

Trident Media Group

tridentmediagroup.com/contact-us/ebook-submissions

Accepts submissions from authors who would like to self-publish original e-book titles or have Trident represent their foreign or audio rights. Works with Amazon White Glove, among others.

It's important to make a distinction between (1) agents who take a commission on specific self-published projects where they provide assistance, and (2) agents who take a commission on every work their client produces, regardless of the agency's support.

DIGITAL IMPRINTS ESTABLISHED BY AGENTS

Did you know the oldest independent digital publisher was founded by an agent? Richard Curtis launched E-Reads in 1999 to create an e-book market for authors and had more than 1,200 titles available when it was acquired in spring 2014 by another digital publisher, Open Road Media.

Many more agents have now started publishing companies; a selection is listed below. While each one is a distinct company operating separately from the agencies (to avoid conflicts of interest), some are focused on incubating projects arising from the agency's client base. Others have very little crossover; their only connection to agenting is the fact they were founded by an agent.

When working with any of these publishers, the same rules apply as when considering a traditional deal. Read the contract carefully and understand all of the terms, especially how and when rights revert to you.

BEYOND THE PAGE PUBLISHING
Agent-founder: Jessica Faust, BookEnds LLC
beyondthepagepub.com
In addition to traditional agenting, BookEnds offers agent-assisted self-publishing services for clients only, where the agency takes a 15 percent commission. Separately, the agency has also established Beyond the Page Publishing, which acts as a digital publisher. The author enters into an agreement for a set term; advances and royalties are confidential and specific to each author.

SHORT FUSE
Agent-founder: Laurie McLean, Fuse Literary
www.fuseliterary.com/short-fuse
Short Fuse publishes shorter works, such as short stories, novellas, flash fiction, poetry, and short nonfiction. Editorial director Gordon Warnock says, "We consider Short Fuse to be in between traditional concepts of 'assisted self-publishing' and 'independent publisher.'" Although Short Fuse is open to submissions from other agencies and publishers, its

main focus is to offer comprehensive, multi-track career growth for authors represented by Fuse. The contract is royalty based; it pays no advance and charges no fees. Authors retain all rights, and agreements have a set term.

REPUTATION BOOKS
Agent-founder: Kimberley Cameron
reputationbooksonline.com
Reputation Books aims to fully service the clients of Kimberley Cameron & Associates. It publishes both backlist and original works.

RIVERDALE AVENUE BOOKS
Agent-founder: Lori Perkins
riverdaleavebooks.com
Riverdale Avenue Books (RAB) publishes e-books as well as audio books under five imprints covering pop culture; LGBT; horror, science fiction, and fantasy; erotica; and sports and gaming. They consider previously published material and are open to all authors. Contracts are royalty based; they pay no advances and charge no fees.

Jane Friedman, former publisher of *Writer's Digest*, teaches digital media at the University of Virginia. Find her at janefriedman.com.

BOOK TRAILER BASICS

Cindy Callaghan

In recent years, authors and publishers have taken a tip from Hollywood and begun creating video "trailers" to promote their books. At first, most book trailers were little more than jazzy PowerPoint presentations, but the quality and content now range from quirky DIY videos to productions with full blockbuster glitz. Read on to learn how to create a promo of your own, and what to do with it once you have it.

CHOOSING AN APPROACH

Options for your video book trailer's style and content are as limitless as your imagination. But if you're looking for tried-and-true approaches, here are three to consider.

1. The Hybrid

Award-winning mystery author and investigative reporter Hank Phillippi Ryan utilized an interesting customer insight when developing the trailer for her crime thriller *The Other Woman*. She'd found in her promotional efforts that "readers respond most enthusiastically to a face-to-face meeting with an author," Ryan explains. So, her trailer spotlights the storyteller as well as the story. This is known as the hybrid trailer. Her video toggles from book synopsis to author interview. "I tried to re-create the experience of a conversation, chatting with readers about my work and my books, answering their questions."

The result? "When I place the video on my Facebook (facebook.com/HankPhillippiRyanAuthorPage) or Twitter (@hank_phillippi) pages, I get an automatic influx of e-mail. This tells me it resonates. I have no doubt that the video has made a difference for *The Other Woman* in terms of sales, attention, and readership," Ryan says.

For another example of the hybrid trailer, check out the promotional video for James Patterson's middle-grade novel *Middle School: Get Me Out of Here*. In the trailer, Patterson interviews an animated version of the protagonist, Rafe Khatchadorian. Through this discussion we get to know both Patterson and Rafe.

At first, most book trailers were little more than jazzy PowerPoint presentations, but the quality and content now range from quirky DIY videos to productions with full blockbuster glitz.

2. Clever, Low-Tech DIY

When it comes to making a video all on your own, don't be intimidated by technology. It isn't always the production quality that counts—sometimes a unique do-it-yourself angle can attract a following on a shoestring budget.

Max Barry, author of *Jennifer Government* and *Syrup*, took a clever approach to the trailer for his sci-fi thriller *Machine Man*. First, Barry explains to his audience that he must have a trailer because that's what authors are expected to do. He runs through a few boring ideas and then quotes his publisher's suggestion: "Act out a scene from the book." Because the book is about a man who amputates his own limbs and replaces them with homemade parts, Barry has only one real choice. It's low-budget and simple in execution but memorable and effective as well.

3. Bonus Content

For the launch of my latest middle-grade book, *Lost in London*, I've created a video piece that's not exactly a trailer. It splices together video clips presented as actual footage captured by the book's main characters during their escapades in London. A montage of the characters' personal pictures and videos not only teases would-be readers to buy but also engages readers who've already enjoyed the book.

DELIVERING THE GOODS

No matter what form your book trailer takes, the key to making it an effective tool is in distribution. A successful video trailer must first reach its target audience. For that to happen, an author must be strategic and creative.

1. Strategic Distribution

You might be surprised to learn that video trailers are not just for online use. "For a teen and tween audience, online distribution makes sense," explains Julie Schoerke of JKS Communications. "For those less responsive to online videos, we've been successful with offline channels." Schoerke recently worked with a mystery author whose video ran in New York City taxis during the large Book Expo America conference and thus was delivered directly to those traveling to the event. "It's a surprisingly economical way to generate quality coverage," Schoerke says.

Kate Klise, author of the humorous children's mystery series 43 Old Cemetery Road and Three-Ring Rascals, says librarians use her trailers to prepare students for her school visits. "Trailers are a fun way to introduce young readers to authors." Klise adds that she often hears from children who discovered her trailers *after* reading her books—further demonstrating that strategic distribution of a trailer engages enthusiastic readers at all stages and encourages them to look for more information about favorite books and authors.

2. Sponsorships

Publicist Dana Kaye negotiated a sponsorship for client Jamie Freveletti's first novel, *Running from the Devil*, which involved an ultramarathon runner. For this project, Sugoi Running Apparel provided Freveletti with clothes to wear in the video. "Sugoi wrote a review on their consumer website and provided signed books to their top accounts," Kaye says. "This distribution quadrupled views and reached an audience we wouldn't have reached otherwise."

3. Video Press Releases

According to Mary Ann Zissimos, former HarperCollins senior publicist, the video trailer can be an efficient, nontext way to get your book in front of website editors and book reviewers who might otherwise disregard yet another press release. E-mailing a video trailer is an attention grabber. "I get more responses from media to whom I've sent a link to a trailer," Zissimos says. "Even if they tell me they aren't running a story, they respond, so I know they've looked at the pitch. They like it because it's different, fast, and catchy."

Whether online or offline, built by a pro or a creative novice, an effective video trailer breaks through the clutter with innovative content and a targeted distribution strategy. As Paul Fireman, owner of video and content development agency Fireman Creative, says, "It's an exciting time for authors to have a video trailer. They have excellent options to get their story in front of billions of eyeballs. Social media makes an author's video piece highly accessible to a wide variety of potential customers."

Cindy Callaghan is the author of the middle-grade novels *Just Add Magic*, *Lost in London*, and *Lucky Me*. Watch *Lost in London*'s trailer at cindycallaghan.com.

GET THE MOST OUT OF YOUR PR DOLLARS

How to Market Your Novel for Publication

·····································

Mari Passananti

Congratulations on the impending publication of your novel—one of hundreds of thousands of titles to hit the shelves this year!

With more novels competing for ever-shrinking review space, how can yours stand out in the overcrowded marketplace? Four prominent book publicity and marketing professionals share their best tips and insights on how to get the most buzz for your buck.

UNDERSTAND YOUR PUBLISHER'S PLANS FOR YOUR NOVEL. "Too many authors don't understand their publisher's marketing and publicity plans," says M.J. Rose, founder of the marketing service AuthorBuzz and co-author of *What to Do Before Your Book Launch*. "It's critical that authors and their agents know who is responsible for what aspects of the book launch." Read all contracts, and ask questions before and during the marketing campaign.

APPROACH PR AS AN INVESTMENT. As an author, it's a good idea to spend the necessary funds to build your brand, no matter the uncertainty. "The correlation between reviews and sales is unpredictable at best," says Sharon Bially of BookSavvy PR. "The true value of media exposure is comparable to building a résumé or an art portfolio, which will always be part of an author's identity and cachet going forward."

But Rose cautions that many authors focus heavily on publicity—a gamble—but give short shrift to marketing, which guarantees coverage through ads. "The purpose of a paid campaign is to get conversations going," she says. "Nothing sells a book like word of mouth."

HIRE BOOK SPECIALISTS. Fauzia Burke of the book marketing firm FSB Associates says a solid track record matters. Novelists should seek out professionals who have run successful campaigns *for* novels. "Hire an experienced book publicist who has years invested in media relationships," she says. Specialists help authors cast a wide net within a strategically defined media segment—not target every existing outlet.

"There's no shame in being a solid midlist writer who keeps getting contracts. Authors do themselves a disservice by having their eye on the golden ring—being among the 1 percent who become bestsellers. You've won by getting on the merry-go-round." —M.J. ROSE

TIME EVERYTHING CAREFULLY. An author should focus on buzz at least three to six months before her novel launches. But if you miss that window, you can still invest in targeted advertising, especially on sites or in publications that draw self-identified readers. "Because of the Internet, no book dies anymore," says Rose. "A book is new to any reader who's never heard of it before."

PARTICIPATE. Don't let your publicist or marketer do all the dirty work. Take initiative in a variety of promotion, from being a guest blogger on a website to getting a byline in a magazine. "Be as involved as possible," says Jocelyn Kelley of Kelley & Hall Book Publicity. "Come up with ideas, angles, [and] areas of interest [to help promote your book]."

Burke advises her clients to have their "digital houses"—website and social media presence—in place before launching a book campaign. "Every time you create and share content, you shape your professional brand," she says. "Today, publicity serves to amplify—not launch—an author's brand."

EMBRACE TRENDS. Kelley says many novelists worry that their books will appear too much like other books already on shelves, a fear she calls unfounded. "Books with similar storylines can actually help bring your book to the attention of editors and reviewers," she says. "They are always looking for trends."

EXPECT ENTHUSIASM, PROFESSIONALISM, AND COMMUNICATION. "The publicist should be excited and eager to spread the word about your book," Kelley says. "The publicist should have read your book. He or she should be generating unique angles to help spark interest from editors and reviewers."

A publicist should also provide a detailed work plan, including a list of outlets they intend to pitch. "The author should see the pitch before the professional uses it to make sure [everyone is] on the same page," says Rose.

UNDERSTAND COSTS. Most marketing firms work on monthly retainers (standard fees). Many set minimum lengths for campaigns—two or three months is typical—though some charge on a project basis. "The average monthly retainer for a respected firm is $3,000–7,000," says Burke.

Don't dismiss the "small guys." It's rash to ignore little-known media places. Many book blogs and similar smaller venues have dedicated followings of readers who love to talk about books—exactly the readers novelists want to reach. So market your work accordingly. "Authors sometimes look at smaller media outlets as a waste of time," says Kelley. "Some feel that if it isn't Oprah, it isn't worth the time or effort to write a guest post or answer interview questions. [But] you never know who is following a particular website."

USE SOCIAL NETWORKING SITES WISELY. "With social media, it has never been easier to find and interact with readers, and to create long-term engagement with the community," says Burke, recommending that authors set aside time daily for updating their social media accounts, including Twitter, Facebook, and author blogs.

BE REALISTIC. No matter what steps you take in marketing your work, know the road to publishing success is long and that the outcome you yearn for might not transpire. "It's very hard to make your book a bestseller if your house doesn't want it to be a bestseller," says Rose. "There's no shame in being a solid midlist writer who keeps getting contracts. Authors do themselves a disservice by having their eye on the golden ring—being among the 1 percent who become bestsellers. You've won by getting on the merry-go-round."

Mari Passananti is the author of *The K Street Affair* and *The Hazards of Hunting While Heartbroken*. She is currently working on her third novel.

LITERARY AGENTS

Many publishers are willing to look at unsolicited submissions, but most feel having an agent is in the writer's best interest. In this section we include agents who specialize in or represent fiction.

The commercial fiction field is intensely competitive. Many publishers have small staffs and little time. For that reason, many book publishers rely on agents for new talent. Some publishers even rely on agents as "first readers" who must wade through the deluge of submissions from writers to find the very best. For writers a good agent can be a foot in the door—someone willing to do the necessary work to put your manuscript in the right editor's hands.

It would seem today that finding a good agent is as hard as finding a good publisher. Yet those writers who have agents say they are invaluable. Not only can a good agent help you make your work more marketable, an agent also acts as your business manager

and adviser, protecting your interests during and after contract negotiations.

Still, finding an agent can be very difficult for a new writer. If you are already published in magazines, you have a better chance than someone with no publishing credits. (Some agents read periodicals searching for new writers.) Although many agents do read queries and manuscripts from unpublished authors without introduction, referrals from their writer clients can be a big help. If you don't know any published authors with agents, attending a conference is a good way to meet agents. Some agents even set aside time at conferences to meet new writers.

Almost all the agents listed here have said they are open to working with new, previously unpublished writers as well as published writers. They do not charge a fee to cover the time and effort involved in reviewing a manuscript or a synopsis and chapters, but their time is still extremely valuable.

Only send an agent your work when you feel it is as complete and polished as possible.

USING THE LISTINGS

It is especially important that you read individual listings carefully before contacting these busy agents. The first information after the company name includes the address and phone, fax, e-mail address (when available), and website. **Member Agents** gives the names of individual agents working at that company. (Specific types of fiction an agent handles are indicated in parentheses after that agent's name). The **Represents** section lists the types of fiction the agency works with. Reading the **Recent Sales** gives you the names of writers an agent is currently working with and, very important, publishers the agent has placed manuscripts with. **Tips** presents advice directly from the agent to authors.

Also, look closely at the openness to submissions icon that precedes most listings. It indicates how willing an agency is to take on new writers.

THE AHEARN AGENCY, INC.

2021 Pine St., New Orleans LA 70118. (504)861-8395. **Fax:** (504)866-6434. **E-mail:** pahearn@aol.com. **Website:** www.ahearnagency.com. **Contact:** Pamela G. Ahearn. Other memberships include MWA, RWA, ITW. Represents 35 clients. 20% of clients are new/unpublished writers.

○ Prior to opening her agency, Ms. Ahearn was an agent for 8 years and an editor with Bantam Books.

REPRESENTS Considers these fiction areas: romance, suspense, thriller, women's.

�➤ Handles women's fiction and suspense fiction only. Does not want to receive category romance, science fiction or fantasy.

HOW TO CONTACT Query with SASE or via e-mail. Please send a one-page query letter stating the type of book you're writing, word length, where you feel your book fits into the current market, and any writing credentials you may possess. Please do not send ms pages or synopses if they haven't been previously requested. If you're querying via e-mail, send no attachments. Accepts simultaneous submissions. Responds in 2-3 months to queries and mss. Obtains most new clients through recommendations from others, solicitations, conferences.

TERMS Agent receives 15% commission on domestic sales. Agent receives 20% commission on foreign sales. Offers written contract, binding for 1 year; renewable by mutual consent.

RECENT SALES *Black-Eyed Susans* by Julia Heaberlin; *The Art of Sinning* by Sabrina Jeffries; *The Comfort of Black* by Carter Wilson; *Flirting with Felicity* by Gerri Russell; *The Iris Fan* by Laura Joh Rowland.

TIPS "Be professional! Always send in exactly what an agent/editor asks for—no more, no less. Keep query letters brief and to the point, giving your writing credentials and a very brief summary of your book. If 1 agent rejects you, keep trying—there are a lot of us out there!"

●○ AITKEN ALEXANDER ASSOCIATES

18-21 Cavaye Place, London England SW10 9PT United Kingdom. (020)7373-8672. **Fax:** (020)7373-6002. **E-mail:** reception@aitkenalexander.co.uk; reception@aitkenalexander.com. **Website:** www.aitkenalexander.co.uk. Estab. 1976.

MEMBER AGENTS Gillon Aitken; Clare Alexander (literary, commercial, memoir, narrative nonfiction); **Matthew Hamilton** (literary fiction, memoir, music, politics and sports); **Gillie Russell** (middle-grade, young adult); **Anna Stein O'Sullivan**; **Imogen Pelham** (literary, commercial, serious narrative nonfiction, short stories); **Mary Pachnos**; **Anthony Sheil**; **Lucy Luck** (quality fiction and nonfiction); **Lesley Thorne**; **Matias Lopez Portillo** (high-end commercial thrillers and literary fiction [with a particular focus on Latin America]); **Shruti Debi**.

REPRESENTS nonfiction books, novels. **Considers these fiction areas:** commercial, literary, mainstream, middle-grade, thriller, young adult.

�➤ "We specialize in literary fiction and nonfiction." Does not represent illustrated children's books, poetry, or screenplays.

HOW TO CONTACT "If you would like to submit your work to us, please e-mail your covering letter with a short synopsis and the first 30 pages (as a Word document) to submissions@aitkenalexander.co.uk indicating if there is a specific agent who you would like to consider your work. Submissions for the attention of the U.S. Office should be sent to reception@aitkenalexander.com. Please note that the Indian Office does not accept unsolicited submissions." Accepts simultaneous submissions. Obtains most new clients through recommendations from others, solicitations.

TERMS Agent receives 15% commission on domestic sales. Agent receives 20% commission on foreign sales. Offers written contract; 28-day notice must be given to terminate contract. Charges for photocopying and postage.

RECENT SALES Sold 50 titles in the last year. *My Life with George* by Judith Summers (Voice); *The Separate Heart* by Simon Robinson (Bloomsbury); *The Fall of the House of Wittgenstein* by Alexander Waugh (Bloomsbury); *Shakespeare's Life* by Germane Greer (Picador); *Occupational Hazards* by Rory Stewart.

TIPS "Before submitting to us, we advise you to look at our existing client list to establish whether your work will be of interest. Equally, you should consider whether the material you have written is ready to submit to a literary agency. If you feel your work qualifies, then send us a letter introducing yourself. Keep it relevant to your writing (e.g., tell us about any previously published work, be it a short story or journalism; you may be studying or have completed a post graduate qualification in creative writing; when it comes to nonfiction, we would want to know what qualifies you to write about the subject)."

⊘⊙ ALIVE COMMUNICATIONS, INC.

7680 Goddard St., Suite 200, Colorado Springs CO 80920. (719)260-7080. **Fax:** (719)260-8223. **E-mail:** submissions@alivecom.com. **Website:** www.alivecom.com. **Contact:** Rick Christian. Member of AAR. Other memberships include Authors Guild.

MEMBER AGENTS **Rick Christian**, president (blockbusters, bestsellers); Lee Hough (popular/commercial nonfiction and fiction, thoughtful spirituality, children's); **Andrea Heinecke** (thoughtful/inspirational nonfiction, women's fiction/nonfiction, popular/commercial nonfiction and fiction); **Bryan Norman**; **Lisa Jackson**.

REPRESENTS nonfiction books, novels, short story collections, novellas. **Considers these fiction areas:** adventure, contemporary issues, crime, family saga, historical, humor, inspirational, literary, mainstream, mystery, police, religious, satire, suspense, thriller.

8—⚡ This agency specializes in fiction, Christian living, how-to and commercial nonfiction. Actively seeking inspirational, literary, and mainstream fiction, and work from authors with established track records and platforms. Does not want to receive poetry, scripts or dark themes.

HOW TO CONTACT "Because all our agents have full client loads, they are only considering queries from authors referred by clients and close contacts." New clients come through recommendations from others.

TERMS Agent receives 15% commission on domestic sales. Offers written contract; two-month notice must be given to terminate contract.

TIPS Rewrite and polish until the words on the page shine. Endorsements and great connections may help, provided you can write with power and passion. Network with publishing professionals by making contacts, joining critique groups, and attending writers' conferences in order to make personal connections and to get feedback. Alive Communications, Inc., has established itself as a premiere literary agency. We serve an elite group of authors who are critically acclaimed and commercially successful in both Christian and general markets.

⊙ AMBASSADOR LITERARY AGENCY & SPEAKERS BUREAU

P.O. Box 50358, Nashville TN 37205. (615)370-4700. **Website:** www.ambassadoragency.com. **Contact:** Wes Yoder. Represents 25-30 clients. 10% of clients are new/unpublished writers. Currently handles nonfiction books (95%), novels (5%).

○ Prior to becoming an agent, Mr. Yoder founded a music artist agency in 1973; he established a speakers bureau division of the company in 1984.

REPRESENTS nonfiction books, novels.

8—⚡ "This agency specializes in religious market publishing dealing primarily with A-level publishers." Actively seeking popular nonfiction themes, including the following: practical living, Christian spirituality, literary fiction. Does not want to receive short stories, children's books, screenplays, or poetry.

HOW TO CONTACT Authors should e-mail a short description of their ms with a request to submit their work for review. Official submission guidelines will be sent if we agree to review a ms. Speakers should submit a bio, headshot, and speaking demo. Direct all inquiries and submissions to info@ambassador-speakers.com. Accepts simultaneous submissions. Obtains most new clients through recommendations from others.

TERMS Agent receives 15% commission on domestic sales. Agent receives 20% commission on foreign sales. Offers written contract.

⊙ BETSY AMSTER LITERARY ENTERPRISES

6312 SW Capitol Hwy #503, Portland OR 97239. **Website:** www.amsterlit.com. **Contact:** Betsy Amster (adult); Mary Cummings (children's and YA). Estab. 1992. Member of AAR. Represents more than 65 clients. 35% of clients are new/unpublished writers. Currently handles nonfiction books (65%), novels (35%).

○ Prior to opening her agency, Ms. Amster was an editor at Pantheon and Vintage for 10 years, and served as editorial director for the Globe Pequot Press for 2 years.

REPRESENTS nonfiction books, novels. **Considers these fiction areas:** ethnic, literary, women's, high quality.

8—⚡ "Actively seeking strong narrative nonfiction, particularly by journalists; outstanding literary fiction (the next Jennifer Haigh or Jess Walter); witty, intelligent commerical women's fiction (the next Elinor Lipman); mysteries that open new worlds to us; and high-profile self-help and psychology, preferably research based." Does not want to receive poetry, children's books, romances, western, science fiction, action/adventure, screenplays, fantasy, techno-thrillers, spy capers, apocalyptic scenarios, or political or religious arguments.

HOW TO CONTACT For adult titles: b.amster. assistant@gmail.com. "For fiction or memoirs, please embed the first 3 pages in the body of your e-mail. For nonfiction, please embed your proposal." For children's and YA: b.amster.kidsbooks@gmail.com. See submission requirements online at website. "For picture books, please embed the entire text in the body of your e-mail. For novels, please embed the first 3 pages." Accepts simultaneous submissions. Responds in 1 month to queries. Responds in 2 months to mss. Obtains most new clients through recommendations from others, solicitations, conferences.

TERMS Agent receives 15% commission on domestic sales. Agent receives 20% commission on foreign sales. Offers written contract, binding for 1 year; three-month notice must be given to terminate contract. Charges for photocopying, postage, messengers, galleys/books used in submissions to foreign and film agents and to magazines for first serial rights.

○ THE AXELROD AGENCY

55 Main St., P.O. Box 357, Chatham NY 12037. (518)392-2100. **E-mail:** steve@axelrodagency.com. **Website:** www.axelrodagency.com. **Contact:** Steven Axelrod. Member of AAR. Represents 15-20 clients. Currently handles novels (95%).

○ Prior to becoming an agent, Mr. Axelrod was a book club editor.

REPRESENTS novels. **Considers these fiction areas:** crime, mystery, new adult, romance, women's.

☙—☛ This agency specializes in women's fiction and romance.

HOW TO CONTACT Query. Accepts simultaneous submissions. Obtains most new clients through recommendations from others.

TERMS Agent receives 15% commission on domestic sales. Agent receives 20% commission on foreign sales. No written contract.

WRITERS CONFERENCES RWA National Conference.

◑ AZANTIAN LITERARY AGENCY

E-mail: queries@azantianlitagency.com. **Website:** www.azantianlitagency.com. Estab. 2014.

○ Prior to her current position, Ms. Azantian was with Sandra Dijkstra Literary Agency.

☙—☛ Actively seeking fantasy, science fiction and psychological horror for adult, young adult, and middle-grade readers. Does not want to receive nonfiction or picture books.

HOW TO CONTACT To submit, send your query letter, one- to two-page synopsis, and first 10-15 pages all pasted in an e-mail (no attachments) to queries@ azantianlitagency.com. Please note in the e-mail subject line if your work was requested at a conference, is an exclusive submission, or if your work was referred by a current client. Accepts simultaneous submissions. Responds within 6 weeks. Check the website before submitting to make sure Jennifer is currently open to queries.

BARONE LITERARY AGENCY

385 North St., Batavia OH 45103. (513)732-6740. **Fax:** (513)297-7208. **E-mail:** baroneliteraryagency@roadrunner.com. **Website:** www.baroneliteraryagency. com. **Contact:** Denise Barone. Estab. 2010. RWA

REPRESENTS Considers these fiction areas: action, adventure, cartoon, comic books, commercial, confession, contemporary issues, crime, detective, erotica, ethnic, experimental, family saga, fantasy, feminist, frontier, gay, glitz, hi-lo, historical, horror, humor, inspirational, juvenile, lesbian, literary, mainstream, metaphysical, military, multicultural, multimedia, mystery, New Age, occult, plays, psychic, regional, religious, romance, science fiction, sports, thriller, women's, young adult.

☙—☛ Actively seeking adult contemporary romance. Does not want textbooks.

HOW TO CONTACT "We are no longer accepting snail mail submissions; send a query letter via e-mail. If I like your query letter, I will ask for the first 3 chapters and a synopsis as attachments." Accepts simultaneous submissions. Obtains new clients by queries/submissions, Facebook, recommendations from others.

TERMS 15% commission on domestic sales, 20% on foreign sales. Offers written contract.

RECENT SALES *All The Glittering Bones* by Anna Snow (Entangled Publishing); *Melody Massacre to the Rescue* by Anna Snow (Entangled Publishing); *A Taste of Terror* by Anna Snow (Entangled Publishing); *Devon's Choice* by Cathy Bennett (Astraea Press); *In Deep* by Laurie Albano (Solstice Publishing); *Tread-*

ing on Dandelions by Jennifer Petersen Fraser (Solstice Publishing); *Fire and Ice* by Michele Barrow-Belisle (Astraea Press).

TIPS "In the immortal words of Sir Winston Churchill, if you want to get published, you must never give up!"

BARRON'S LITERARY MANAGEMENT

4615 Rockland Dr., Arlington TX 76016. **E-mail:** barronsliterary@sbcglobal.net. **Contact:** Adele Brooks, president.

Barron's Literary Management is a small Dallas/Fort Worth-based agency with good publishing contacts. Seeks tightly written, fast moving fiction and nonfiction authors with a significant platform or subject area expertise. Considers legal, crime, techno or medical thrillers. Considers all romance. Considers nonfiction: business, cooking, health, investing, psychology and true crime.

HOW TO CONTACT Contact by e-mail initially. Send bio and a brief synopsis of story (fiction) or a nonfiction book proposal. Obtains most new clients through e-mail submissions.

TIPS "Have your book tightly edited, polished and ready to be seen before contacting agents. I respond quickly and if interested may request an electronic or hard copy mailing."

LORELLA BELLI LITERARY AGENCY (LBLA)

54 Hartford House, 35 Tavistock Crescent, Notting Hill, London England W11 1AY United Kingdom. (44)(207)727-8547. **Fax:** (44)(870)787-4194. **E-mail:** info@lorellabelliagency.com. **Website:** www.lorellabelliagency.com. **Contact:** Lorella Belli. Membership includes AAA, Crime Writers' Association, Romantic Novelists Association.

This agency handles adult fiction, adult nonfiction, YA. Does not want to receive children's picture books, fantasy, science fiction, screenplays, short stories, poetry, academic or specialist books.

HOW TO CONTACT E-query. Do not send a proposal or ms before it's requested.

TERMS Agent receives 15% commission on domestic sales. Agent receives 20% commission on foreign sales.

THE BENT AGENCY

Bent Agency, The, 159 20th St., #2B, Brooklyn NY 11232. **E-mail:** info@thebentagency.com. **Website:** www.thebentagency.com. **Contact:** Jenny Bent, Susan Hawk, Molly Ker Hawn, Gemma Cooper, Louise Fury, Brooks Sherman, Beth Phelan, Victoria Lowes, Heather Flaherty. Estab. 2009.

Prior to forming her own agency, Ms. Bent was an agent and vice president at Trident Media.

MEMBER AGENTS Jenny Bent (adult fiction including women's fiction, romance and crime/suspense, she particularly likes novels with magical or fantasy elements that fall outside of genre fiction; young adult and middle-grade fiction; memoir; humor); **Susan Hawk** (young adult and middle-grade and picture books; within the realm of kids' stories, she likes contemporary, mystery fantasy, science fiction, and historical fiction); **Molly Ker Hawn** (young adult and middle-grade books, including contemporary, historical science fiction, fantasy, thrillers, mystery); **Gemma Cooper** (all ages of children's and young adult books, including picture books, likes historical, contemporary, thrillers, mystery, humor, and science fiction); **Louise Fury** (picture books, literary middle-grade, all young adult, speculative fiction, suspense/thriller, commercial fiction, all subgenres of romance including erotic, nonfiction: cookbooks, pop culture); **Brooks Sherman** (speculative and literary adult fiction, select narrative nonfiction; all ages of children's and young adult books, including picture books; likes historical, contemporary, thrillers, humor, fantasy, and horror); **Beth Phelan** (young adult, thrillers, suspense and mystery, romance and women's fiction, literary and general fiction, cookbooks, lifestyle and pets/animals); **Victoria Lowes** (romance and women's fiction, thrillers and mystery, and young adult); **Heather Flaherty** (young adult [fiction and nonfiction], middle-grade [fiction and nonfiction]; in her juvenile stories, she likes contemporary, humor, horror, historical, sci-fi, fantasy and thrillers; select pop culture and humor nonfiction).

REPRESENTS Considers these fiction areas: commercial, crime, fantasy, historical, horror, literary, mystery, picture books, romance, suspense, thriller, women's, young adult.

HOW TO CONTACT For Jenny Bent, e-mail: queries@thebentagency.com; for Susan Hawk, e-mail: kidsqueries@thebentagency.com; for Molly Ker Hawn, e-mail: hawnqueries@thebentagency.com; for Gemma Cooper, e-mail: cooperqueries@thebentagency.com.; for Louise Fury, e-mail: furyqueries@thebentagency.com; for Brooks Sherman, e-mail:

shermanqueries@thebentagency.com; for Beth Phelan, e-mail: phelanagencies@thebentagency.com; for Victoria Lowes, e-mail: lowesqueries@thebentagency.com; for Heather Flaherty, e-mail flahertyqueries@thebentagency.com. "Tell us briefly who you are, what your book is, and why you're the one to write it. Then include the first 10 pages of your material in the body of your e-mail. We respond to all queries; please re-send your query if you haven't had a response within 4 weeks." Accepts simultaneous submissions.

RECENT SALES *The Pocket Wife* by Susan Crawford (Morrow); *The Smell of Other Peoples Houses* by Bonnie-Sue Hitchcock (Wendy Lamb Books); *The Graham Cracker Plot* by Shelley Tougas (Roaring Brook); *Murder Is Bad Manners* by Robin Stevens (Simon & Schuster); *The Inside Out Series* by Lisa Renee Jones (Simon & Schuster); *True North* by Liora Blake (Pocket Star).

BOOKENDS, LLC

Website: www.bookends-inc.com. **Contact:** Jessica Faust, Kim Lionetti, Jessica Alvarez, Beth Campbell. Member of AAR. RWA, MWA Represents 50+ clients. 10% of clients are new/unpublished writers. Currently handles nonfiction books (50%), novels (50%).

MEMBER AGENTS Jessica Faust, JFaust@bookends-inc.com (fiction: women's fiction, mysteries, suspense; all other genres accepted by referral only); **Kim Lionetti**, klionetti@bookends-inc.com (only currently considering contemporary romance, women's fiction, cozies, new adult, and contemporary young adult); **Jessica Alvarez** (romance, women's fiction, erotica, romantic suspense); **Beth Campbell** (urban fantasy, science fiction, YA, suspense, romantic suspense, mystery).

REPRESENTS nonfiction books, novels. **Considers these fiction areas:** mainstream, mystery, romance, women's.

"BookEnds is currently accepting queries from published and unpublished writers in the areas of romance (and all its subgenres), erotica, mystery, suspense, women's fiction, and literary fiction." BookEnds does not want to receive children's books, screenplays, poetry, or technical/military thrillers.

HOW TO CONTACT Review website for guidelines, as they change. BookEnds is no longer accepting unsolicited proposal packages or snail mail queries. Send query in the body of e-mail to only 1 agent. No attachments.

BOOKS & SUCH LITERARY AGENCY

52 Mission Circle, Suite 122, PMB 170, Santa Rosa CA 95409. **E-mail:** representation@booksandsuch.com. **Website:** www.booksandsuch.com. **Contact:** Janet Kobobel Grant, Wendy Lawton, Rachel Kent, Mary Keeley, Rachelle Gardner. Member of AAR. Member of CBA (associate), American Christian Fiction Writers. Currently handles nonfiction books (50%), novels (50%).

Prior to becoming an agent, Ms. Grant was an editor for Zondervan and managing editor for *Focus on the Family*; Ms. Lawton was an author, sculptor, and designer of porcelein dolls. Ms. Keeley accepts both nonfiction and adult fiction. She previously was an acquisition editor for Tyndale publishers.

REPRESENTS nonfiction books, novels. **Considers these fiction areas:** historical, literary, mainstream, new adult, religious, romance, young adult.

This agency specializes in general and inspirational fiction, romance, and in the Christian booksellers market. Actively seeking well-crafted material that presents Judeo-Christian values, if only subtly.

HOW TO CONTACT Query via e-mail only; no attachments. Accepts simultaneous submissions. Responds in 1 month to queries. "If you don't hear from us asking to see more of your writing within 30 days after you have sent your e-mail, please know that we have read and considered your submission but determined that it would not be a good fit for us." Obtains most new clients through recommendations from others, conferences.

TERMS Agent receives 15% commission on domestic sales. Agent receives 20% commission on foreign sales. Offers written contract; two-month notice must be given to terminate contract. No additional charges.

RECENT SALES A full list of this agency's clients (and the awards they have won) is on the agency website.

WRITERS CONFERENCES Mount Hermon Christian Writers Conference; Writing for the Soul; American Christian Fiction Writers Conference; San Francisco Writers Conference.

TIPS "Our agency highlights personal attention to individual clients that includes coaching on how to thrive in a rapidly changing publishing climate, grow a career, and get the best publishing offers possible."

BRADFORD LITERARY AGENCY

5694 Mission Center Rd., #347, San Diego CA 92108. (619)521-1201. **E-mail:** queries@bradfordlit.com. **Website:** www.bradfordlit.com. **Contact:** Laura Bradford, Natalie Lakosil, Sarah LaPolla. Estab. 2001. Member of AAR. RWA, SCBWI, ALA Represents 50 clients. 20% of clients are new/unpublished writers.Currently handles nonfiction books (5%), novels (95%).

REPRESENTS Considers these fiction areas: erotica, middle-grade, mystery, paranormal, picture books, romance, thriller, women's, young adult.

☛ Actively seeking many types of romance (historical, romantic suspense, paranormal, category, contemporary, erotic). Does not want to receive poetry, screenplays, short stories, westerns, horror, new age, religion, crafts, cookbooks, gift books.

HOW TO CONTACT Accepts e-mail queries only; send to queries@bradfordlit.com (or sarah@bradfordlit if contacting Sarah LaPolla). The entire submission must appear in the body of the e-mail and not as an attachment. The subject line should begin as follows: QUERY: (the title of the ms or any short message that is important should follow). For fiction: e-mail a query letter along with the first chapter of ms and a synopsis. Include the genre and word count in cover letter. Nonfiction: e-mail full nonfiction proposal including a query letter and a sample chapter. Accepts simultaneous submissions. Responds in 2-4 weeks to queries. Responds in 10 weeks to mss. Obtains most new clients through solicitations.

TERMS Agent receives 15% commission on domestic sales. Agent receives 20% commission on foreign sales. Offers written contract. Charges for extra copies of books for foreign submissions.

RECENT SALES Sold 93 titles in the last year. *The Sweetness of Honey* by Alison Kent (Montlake); *Weave of Absence* by Carol Ann Martin (NAL); *Pushing the Limit* by Emmy Curtis (Forever Yours); *Voyage of the Heart* by Soraya Lane (Amazon); *The Last Cowboy in Texas* by Katie Lane (Grand Central); *Broken Open* by Lauren Dane (HQN); *Lovely Wild* by Megan Hart (Mira).

WRITERS CONFERENCES RWA National Conference; Romantic Times Booklovers Convention.

ANDREA BROWN LITERARY AGENCY, INC.

1076 Eagle Dr., Salinas CA 93905. (831)422-5925. **E-mail:** andrea@andreabrownlit.com; caryn@andre-abrownlit.com; lauraqueries@gmail.com; jennifer@andreabrownlit.com; kelly@andreabrownlit.com; jennL@andreabrownlit.com; jamie@andreabrownlit.com; jmatt@andreabrownlit.com; lara@andreabrownlit.com. **Website:** www.andreabrownlit.com. Member of AAR. 10% of clients are new/unpublished writers.

💬 Prior to opening her agency, Ms. Brown served as an editorial assistant at Random House and Dell Publishing and as an editor with Knopf.

MEMBER AGENTS Andrea Brown (President); Laura Rennert (Senior Agent); Caryn Wiseman (Senior Agent); Kelly Sonnack (Agent); Jennifer Rofé (Agent); Jennifer Laughran (Agent); Jamie Weiss Chilton (Agent); Jennifer Mattson (Associate Agent); Lara Perkins (Associate Agent, Digital Manager).

REPRESENTS nonfiction, fiction, juvenile books. **Considers these fiction areas:** juvenile, literary, picture books, women's, young adult middle-grade, all juvenile genres.

☛ Specializes in "all kinds of children's books—illustrators and authors." 98% juvenile books. Considers: nonfiction, fiction, picture books, young adult.

HOW TO CONTACT For picture books, submit complete ms. For fiction, submit query letter, first 10 pages. For nonfiction, submit proposal, first 10 pages. Illustrators: submit a query letter and 2-3 illustration samples (in jpeg format), link to online portfolio, and text of picture book, if applicable. "We only accept queries via e-mail. No attachments, with the exception of .jpeg illustrations from illustrators." Visit the agents' bios on our website and choose only *1* agent to whom you will submit your e-query. Send a short e-mail query letter to that agent with QUERY in the subject field. Accepts simultaneous submissions. If we are interested in your work, we will certainly follow up by e-mail or by phone. However, if you haven't heard from us within 6-8 weeks, please assume that we are passing on your project. Obtains most new clients through referrals from editors, clients and agents. Check website for guidelines and information.

TERMS Agent receives 15% commission on domestic sales. Agent receives 25% commission on foreign sales. Offers written contract.

RECENT SALES *The Scorpio Races* by Maggie Stiefvater (Scholastic); *The Raven Boys* by Maggie Stiefvater (Scholastic); Wolves of Mercy Falls series by Maggie Stiefvater (Scholastic); *The Future of Us* by Jay Asher; *Triangles* by Ellen Hopkins (Atria); *Crank* by Ellen Hopkins (McElderry/S&S); *Burned* by Ellen Hopkins (McElderry/S&S); *Impulse* by Ellen Hopkins (McElderry/S&S); *Glass* by Ellen Hopkins (McElderry/S&S); *Tricks* by Ellen Hopkins (McElderry/S&S); *Fallout* by Ellen Hopkins (McElderry/S&S); *Perfect* by Ellen Hopkins (McElderry/S&S); *The Strange Case of Origami Yoda* by Tom Angleberger (Amulet/Abrams); *Darth Paper Strikes Back* by Tom Angleberger (Amulet/Abrams); *Becoming Chloe* by Catherine Ryan Hyde (Knopf); Sasha Cohen autobiography (HarperCollins); *The Five Ancestors* by Jeff Stone (Random House); *Thirteen Reasons Why* by Jay Asher (Penguin); *Identical* by Ellen Hopkins (S&S).

WRITERS CONFERENCES SCBWI; Asilomar; Maui Writers Conference; Southwest Writers Conference; San Diego State University Writers Conference; Big Sur Children's Writing Workshop; William Saroyan Writers Conference; Columbus Writers Conference; Willamette Writers Conference; La Jolla Writers Conference; San Francisco Writers Conference; Hilton Head Writers Conference; Pacific Northwest Conference; Pikes Peak Conference.

TRACY BROWN LITERARY AGENCY

P.O. Box 772, Nyack NY 10960. (914)400-4147. **Fax:** (914)931-1746. **E-mail:** tracy@brownlit.com. **Contact:** Tracy Brown. Represents 35 clients. Currently handles nonfiction books (90%), novels (10%).

○ Prior to becoming an agent, Mr. Brown was a book editor for 25 years.

REPRESENTS Considers these fiction areas: literary.

○→ Specializes in thorough involvement with clients' books at every stage of the process from writing to proposals to publication. Actively seeking serious nonfiction and fiction. Does not want to receive YA, sci-fi, or romance.

HOW TO CONTACT Submit outline/proposal, synopsis, author bio. Accepts simultaneous submissions. Responds in 2 weeks to queries. Obtains most new clients through referrals.

TERMS Agent receives 15% commission on domestic sales. Agent receives 20% commission on foreign sales. Offers written contract.

RECENT SALES *Why Have Kids?* by Jessica Valenti (HarperCollins); *Tapdancing to Work* by Carol J. Loomis (Portfolio); *Mating in Captivity* by Esther Perel.

SHEREE BYKOFSKY ASSOCIATES, INC.

PO Box 706, Brigantine NJ 08203. **E-mail:** shereebee@aol.com. **E-mail:** submitbee@aol.com. **Website:** www.shereebee.com. **Contact:** Sheree Bykofsky. Member of AAR. Memberships include Author's Guild, Atlantic City Chamber of Commerce, WNBA. Currently handles nonfiction books (80%), novels (20%).

○ Prior to opening her agency, Ms. Bykofsky served as executive editor of the Stonesong Press and managing editor of Chiron Press. She is also the author or coauthor of more than 20 books, including *The Complete Idiot's Guide to Getting Published.* As an adjunct professor, Ms. Bykofsky teaches publishing at Rosemont College, NYU, and SEAK, Inc.

MEMBER AGENTS Janet Rosen, associate; Thomas V. Hartmann, associate.

REPRESENTS nonfiction, novels. **Considers these fiction areas:** contemporary issues, literary, mainstream, mystery, suspense.

○→ This agency specializes in popular reference nonfiction, commercial fiction with a literary quality, and mysteries. "I have wide-ranging interests, but it really depends on quality of writing, originality, and how a particular project appeals to me (or not). I take on fiction when I completely love it—it doesn't matter what area or genre." Does not want to receive poetry, material for children, screenplays, westerns, horror, science fiction, or fantasy.

HOW TO CONTACT "We only accept e-queries now and will only respond to those in which we are interested. E-mail short queries to submitbee@aol.com. Please, no attachments, snail mail, or phone calls. One-page query, one-page synopsis, and first page of ms in the body of the e-mail. **Nonfiction:** One-page query in the body of the e-mail. We cannot open attached Word files or any other types of attached files. These will be deleted." Accepts simultaneous submissions. Responds in 1 month to requested mss. Obtains most new clients through recommendations from others.

TERMS Agent receives 15% commission on domestic sales. Agent receives 15% commission on foreign sales, plus international co-agent receives another 10%. Offers written contract, binding for 1 year. Charges for postage, photocopying, fax.

RECENT SALES *ADHD Does Not Exist* by Dr. Richard Saul (Harper Collins); *Be Bold and Win the Sale* by Jeff Shore (McGraw-Hill); *Idea to Invention* by Patricia Nolan-Brown (Amacom); *The Hour of Lead* by Bruce Holbert (Counterpoint); *Slimed! An Oral His-*

tory of *Nickelodeon's Golden Age* by Matthew Klickstein (Plume); *Bang the Keys: Four Steps to a Lifelong Writing Practice* by Jill Dearman (Alpha, Penguin); *Signed, Your Student: Celebrities on the Teachers Who Made Them Who They Are Today* by Holly Holbert (Kaplan); *The Five Ways We Grieve* by Susan Berger (Trumpeter/Shambhala).

WRITERS CONFERENCES Truckee Meadow Community College, Keynote; ASJA Writers Conference; Asilomar; Florida Suncoast Writers Conference; Whidbey Island Writers Conference; Florida First Coast Writers' Festival; Agents and Editors Conference; Columbus Writers Conference; Southwest Writers Conference; Willamette Writers Conference; Dorothy Canfield Fisher Conference; Maui Writers Conference; Pacific Northwest Writers Conference; IWWG.

TIPS "Read the agent listing carefully and comply with guidelines."

KIMBERLEY CAMERON & ASSOCIATES
1550 Tiburon Blvd., #704, Tiburon CA 94920. **Fax:** (415)789-9191. **Website:** www.kimberleycameron.com. **Contact:** Kimberley Cameron. Member of AAR.

Kimberley Cameron & Associates (formerly The Reece Halsey Agency) has had an illustrious client list of established writers, including the estate of Aldous Huxley, and has represented Upton Sinclair, William Faulkner, and Henry Miller.

MEMBER AGENTS Kimberley Cameron; Elizabeth Kracht, liz@kimberleycameron.com (literary, commercial, women's, thrillers, mysteries, and YA with crossover appeal); Pooja Menon, pooja@kimberleycameron.com (international stories, literary, historical, commercial, fantasy and high-end women's fiction; in nonfiction, she's looking for adventure and travel memoirs, journalism and human-interest stories, and self-help books addressing relationships and the human psychology from a fresh perspective); Amy Cloughley, amyc@kimberleycameron.com (literary and upmarket fiction, women's, mystery, narrative nonfiction); Mary C. Moore (literary fiction; she also loves a good commercial book; commercially she is looking for unusual fantasy, grounded science fiction, and atypical romance; strong female characters and unique cultures especially catch her eye).

REPRESENTS **Considers these fiction areas:** commercial, fantasy, historical, literary, mystery, romance, science fiction, thriller, women's, young adult.

"We are looking for a unique and heartfelt voice that conveys a universal truth."

HOW TO CONTACT "We accept e-mail queries only. Please address all queries to 1 agent only. Please send a query letter in the body of the e-mail, written in a professional manner and clearly addressed to the agent of your choice. Attach a one-page synopsis and the first 50 pages of your ms as separate Word or PDF documents. We have difficulties opening other file formats. Include 'Author Submission' in the subject line. If submitting nonfiction, attach a nonfiction proposal." Obtains new clients through recommendations from others, solicitations.

TERMS Agent receives 15% on domestic sales; 10% on film sales. Offers written contract, binding for 1 year.

TIPS "Please consult our submission guidelines and send a polite, well-written query to our e-mail address."

MARIA CARVAINIS AGENCY, INC.
Rockefeller Center, 1270 Avenue of the Americas, Suite 2320, New York NY 10020. (212)245-6365. **Fax:** (212)245-7196. **E-mail:** mca@mariacarvainisagency.com. **Website:** mariacarvainisagency.com. Estab. 1977. Member of AAR. Signatory of WGA. Other memberships include Authors Guild, Women's Media Group, ABA, MWA, RWA. Represents 75 clients.

Prior to opening her agency, Ms. Carvainis spent more than 10 years in the publishing industry as a senior editor with Macmillan Publishing, Basic Books, Avon Books, and Crown Publishers. Ms. Carvainis has served as a member of the AAR Board of Directors and AAR Treasurer, as well as serving as chair of the AAR Contracts Committee. She presently serves on the AAR Royalty Committee.

MEMBER AGENTS Maria Carvainis, president/literary agent.

REPRESENTS nonfiction books, novels. **Considers these fiction areas:** historical, literary, mainstream, middle-grade, mystery, suspense, thriller, women's, young adult.

The agency does not represent screenplays, children's picture books, science fiction, or poetry.

HOW TO CONTACT You can query via e-mail or snail mail. If by snail mail, send your submission "ATTN: Query Department." Please send a query letter, a synopsis of the work, 2 sample chapters, and note any writing credentials. Obtains most new clients through recommendations from others, conferences, query letters.

TERMS Agent receives 15% commission on domestic sales. Agent receives 20% commission on foreign sales. Offers written contract. Charges clients for foreign postage and bulk copying.

RECENT SALES *A Secret Affair* by Mary Balogh (Delacorte); *Tough Customer* by Sandra Brown (Simon & Schuster); *A Lady Never Tells* by Candace Camp (Pocket Books); *The King James Conspiracy* by Phillip Depoy (St. Martin's Press).

CASTIGLIA LITERARY AGENCY

P.O. Box 1094, Sumerland CA 93067. **E-mail:** castigliaagency-query@yahoo.com. **Website:** www.castigliaagency.com. Member of AAR. Other memberships include PEN. Represents 65 clients. Currently handles nonfiction books (55%), novels (45%).

MEMBER AGENTS Julie Castiglia (not accepting queries at this time); Win Golden (fiction: thrillers, mystery, crime, science fiction, YA, commercial/literary fiction; nonfiction: narrative nonfiction, current events, science, journalism).

REPRESENTS nonfiction books, novels. **Considers these fiction areas:** commercial, crime, literary, mystery, science fiction, thriller, young adult.

8—⚓ "We'd particularly like to hear from you if you are a journalist or published writer in magazines." Does not want to receive horror, screenplays, poetry, or academic nonfiction.

HOW TO CONTACT Query via e-mail to CastigliaAgency-query@yahoo.com. Send no materials via first contact besides a one-page query. No snail mail submissions accepted. Obtains most new clients through recommendations from others, solicitations, conferences.

TERMS Agent receives 15% commission on domestic sales. Agent receives 25% commission on foreign sales. Offers written contract; 6-week notice must be given to terminate contract.

WRITERS CONFERENCES Santa Barbara Writers Conference; Southern California Writers Conference; Surrey International Writers Conference; San Diego State University Writers Conference; Willamette Writers Conference.

TIPS "Be professional with submissions. Attend workshops and conferences before you approach an agent."

JANE CHELIUS LITERARY AGENCY

548 Second St., Brooklyn NY 11215. (718)499-0236. **Fax:** (718)832-7335. **E-mail:** jane@janechelius.com.

E-mail: queries@janechelius.com. **Website:** www.janechelius.com. Member of AAR.

MEMBER AGENTS Jane Chelius, Mark Chelius.

REPRESENTS nonfiction books, novels. **Considers these fiction areas:** literary, mystery, suspense, women's.

8—⚓ Does not want to receive children's books, fantasy, science fiction, children's books, stage plays, screenplays, or poetry.

HOW TO CONTACT E-query. Does not consider e-mail queries with attachments. No unsolicited sample chapters or mss. Responds if interested. Responds in 3-4 weeks.

ELYSE CHENEY LITERARY ASSOCIATES, LLC

78 Fifth Avenue, 3rd Floor, New York NY 10011. (212)277-8007. **Fax:** (212)614-0728. **E-mail:** elyse@cheneyliterary.com. **E-mail:** submissions@cheneyliterary.com. **Website:** www.cheneyliterary.com. **Contact:** Elyse Cheney; Adam Eaglin; Alex Jacobs.

Prior to her current position, Ms. Cheney was an agent with Sanford J. Greenburger Associates.

MEMBER AGENTS Elyse Cheney; Adam Eaglin (literary fiction and nonfiction, including history, politics, current events, narrative reportage, biography, memoir, and popular science); Alexander Jacobs (narrative nonfiction [particularly in the areas of history, science, politics, and culture], literary fiction, crime, and memoir); Sam Freilich (literary fiction, crime, biography, narrative nonfiction, and anything about Los Angeles).

REPRESENTS nonfiction, novels. **Considers these fiction areas:** commercial, family saga, historical, literary, short story collections, suspense, women's.

HOW TO CONTACT Query by e-mail or snail mail. For a snail mail responses, include a SASE. If e-query, feel free to paste up to 3 chapters of your work in the e-mail below your query. Do not query more than 1 agent.

RECENT SALES *Moonwalking with Einstein: The Art and Science of Remembering Everything* by Joshua Foer; *The Possessed: Adventures with Russian Books and the People Who Read Them* by Elif Batuman (Farrar, Strauss & Giroux); *The Coldest Winter Ever* by Sister Souljah (Atria); *A Heartbreaking Work of Staggering Genius* by Dave Eggers (Simon and Schuster); *No Easy Day* by Mark Owen; *Malcom X: A Life of Reinvention* by Manning Marable.

⊘⊙ COMPASS TALENT

6 East 32nd Street, 6th Floor, New York NY 10016. (646)376-7718. **E-mail:** query@compasstalent.com. **Website:** www.compasstalent.com. **Contact:** Heather Schroder.

REPRESENTS Considers these fiction areas: commercial, juvenile, literary, mainstream.

HOW TO CONTACT This agency is currently closed to unsolicited submissions.

RECENT SALES A full list of agency clients is available on the website.

⊙ DON CONGDON ASSOCIATES INC.

110 William St., Suite 2202, New York NY 10038. (212)645-1229. **Fax:** (212)727-2688. **E-mail:** dca@doncongdon.com. **Website:** doncongdon.com. **Contact:** Michael Congdon, Susan Ramer, Cristina Concepcion, Maura Kye Casella, Katie Kotchman, Katie Grimm. Member of AAR. Represents 100 clients.

REPRESENTS Considers these fiction areas: action, adventure, contemporary issues, crime, detective, literary, mainstream, middle-grade, mystery, police, short story collections, suspense, thriller, women's, young adult.

☛ Especially interested in narrative nonfiction and literary fiction.

HOW TO CONTACT "For queries via e-mail, you must include the word 'Query' and the agent's full name in your subject heading. Please also include your query and sample chapter in the body of the e-mail, as we do not open attachments for security reasons. Please query only 1 agent within the agency at a time." Responds in 3 weeks to queries. Responds in 1 month to mss. Obtains most new clients through recommendations from other authors.

TERMS Agent receives 15% commission on domestic sales. Agent receives 20% commission on foreign sales. Charges client for extra shipping costs, photocopying, copyright fees, book purchases.

RECENT SALES This agency represents many bestselling clients such as David Sedaris and Kathryn Stockett.

TIPS "Writing a query letter with an SASE is a must. We cannot guarantee replies to foreign queries via standard mail. No phone calls. We never download attachments to e-mail queries for security reasons, so please copy and paste material into your e-mail."

◖ THE DOE COOVER AGENCY

P.O. Box 668, Winchester MA 01890. (781)721-6000. **E-mail:** info@doecooveragency.com. **Website:** www.doecooveragency.com. Represents 150+ clients. Currently handles nonfiction books (80%), novels (20%).

MEMBER AGENTS Doe Coover (general nonfiction, including business, cooking/food writing, health and science); **Colleen Mohyde** (literary and commercial fiction, general nonfiction); associate **Frances Kennedy**.

☛ The agency specializes in narrative nonfiction, particularly biography, business, cooking and food writing, health, history, popular science, social issues, gardening, and humor; literary and commercial fiction. The agency does not represent poetry, screenplays, romance, fantasy, science fiction or unsolicited children's books.

HOW TO CONTACT Accepts queries by e-mail only. Check website for submission guidelines. No unsolicited mss. Accepts simultaneous submissions. Responds within 4-6 weeks, only if additional material is required. Obtains most new clients through solicitation and recommendation.

TERMS Agent receives 15% commission on domestic sales, 10% of original advance commission on foreign sales. No reading fees.

RECENT SALES *Vegetable Literacy* by Deborah Madison (Ten Speed Press); *L.A. Son: My Life, My City, My Food* by Roy Choi (Anthony Bourdain/Ecco); *The Big-Flavor Grill* by Chris Schlesinger and John Willoughby (Ten Speed Press); *The Shape Of The Eye: A Memoir* by George Estreich (Tarcher). *Frontera: Margaritas, Guacamoles, and Snacks* by Rick Bayless and Deann Groen Bayless (W.W. Norton); *The Essay* by Robin Yocum (Arcade Publishing); *The Flower of Empire* by Tatiana Holway (Oxford University Press); Dulcie Schwartz mystery series by Clea Simon (Severn House U.K.). Other clients include: WGBH, New England Aquarium, Duke University, Cheryl and Bill Jamison, Blue Balliett, David Allen, Jacques Pepin, Cindy Pawlcyn, Joann Weir, Suzanne Berne, Paula Poundstone, Anita Silvey, Marjorie Sandor, Tracy Daugherty, Carl Rollyson, and Joel Magnuson.

◖ CORVISIERO LITERARY AGENCY

MEMBER AGENTS Marisa A. Corvisiero, senior agent and literary attorney (nonfiction, picture books, middle-grade, new adult, young adult, romance, thrillers, adventure, paranormal, fantasy, science fiction, and Christmas themes; **Saritza Hernandez**, senior agent (all kinds of romance, GLBT young adult, erotica); **Sarah Negovetich** (young adult, middle-grade); **Doreen McDonald** (do not query); **Cate Hart** (YA, MG, historical romance, erotica, LGBTQ, romance, steampunk, clockpunk, candlepunk); **Samantha Bremekamp** (children's, middle-grade, young adult, and new adult); **Ella Kennen** (picture books, MG, YA, some nonfiction).

REPRESENTS Considers these fiction areas: adventure, commercial, erotica, fantasy, gay, historical, lesbian, middle-grade, multicultural, mystery, new adult, paranormal, picture books, science fiction, thriller, urban fantasy, young adult.

HOW TO CONTACT Accepts submissions via e-mail only. Include 5 pages of complete and polished ms pasted into the body of an e-mail, and a one- to two-page synopsis. For nonfiction, include a proposal instead of the synopsis. Put "Query for [Agent]" in the e-mail subject line.

TIPS "For tips and discussions on what we look for in query letters and submissions, please take a look at Marisa A. Corvisiero's blog: Thoughts From A Literary Agent."

⊘ CRICHTON & ASSOCIATES

6940 Carroll Ave., Takoma Park MD 20912. (301)495-9663. Fax: (202)318-0050. **E-mail:** query@crichton-associates.com. **Website:** www.crichton-associates.com. **Contact:** Sha-Shana Crichton. 90% of clients are new/unpublished writers. Currently handles nonfiction books 50%, fiction 50%.

○ Prior to becoming an agent, Ms. Crichton did commercial litigation for a major law firm.

REPRESENTS nonfiction books, novels. **Considers these fiction areas:** ethnic, feminist, inspirational, literary, mainstream, mystery, religious, romance, suspense chick lit.

⊶ Actively seeking women's fiction, romance, and chick lit. Looking also for multicultural fiction and nonfiction. Does not want to receive poetry, children's, YA, science fiction, or screenplays.

HOW TO CONTACT "In the subject line of e-mail, please indicate whether your project is fiction or nonfiction. Please do not send attachments. Your query letter should include a description of the project and your biography. If you wish to send your query via snail mail, please include your telephone number and e-mail address. We will respond to you via e-mail.

For fiction, include short synopsis and first 3 chapters with query. For nonfiction, send a book proposal." Responds in 3-5 weeks to queries.

TERMS Agent receives 15% commission on domestic sales. Agent receives 20% commission on foreign sales. Offers written contract, binding for 45 days. Only charges fees for postage and photocopying.

RECENT SALES *The African American Entrepreneur* by W. Sherman Rogers (Praeger); *The Diversity Code* by Michelle Johnson (Amacom); *Secret & Lies* by Rhonda McKnight (Urban Books); *Love on the Rocks* by Pamela Yaye (Harlequin). Other clients include Kimberley White, Beverley Long, Jessica Trap, Altonya Washington, Cheris Hodges.

WRITERS CONFERENCES Silicon Valley RWA; BookExpo America.

CURTIS BROWN, LTD.

10 Astor Place, New York NY 10003-6935. (212)473-5400. **Website:** www.curtisbrown.com. **Contact:** Ginger Knowlton. Alternate address: Peter Ginsberg, president at CBSF, 1750 Montgomery St., San Francisco CA 94111; (415)954-8566. Member of AAR. Signatory of WGA.

MEMBER AGENTS Ginger Clark (science fiction, fantasy, paranormal romance, literary horror, and young adult and middle-grade fiction); **Katherine Fausset** (adult fiction and nonfiction, including literary and commercial fiction, journalism, memoir, lifestyle, prescriptive and narrative nonfiction); **Holly Frederick**; **Peter Ginsberg**, president; **Elizabeth Harding**, vice president (represents authors and illustrators of juvenile, middle-grade and young adult fiction); **Steve Kasdin** (commercial fiction, including mysteries/thrillers, romantic suspense—emphasis on the suspense, and historical fiction; narrative nonfiction, including biography, history and current affairs; and young adult fiction, particularly if it has adult crossover appeal); **Ginger Knowlton**, executive vice president (authors and illustrators of children's books in all genres); **Timothy Knowlton**, chief executive officer; **Jonathan Lyons** (biographies, history, science, pop culture, sports, general narrative nonfiction, mysteries, thrillers, science fiction and fantasy, and young adult fiction); **Laura Blake Peterson**, Vice President (memoir and biography, natural history, literary fiction, mystery, suspense, women's fiction, health and fitness, children's and young adult, faith issues and popular culture); **Maureen Walters**, Senior Vice

President (working primarily in women's fiction and nonfiction projects on subjects as eclectic as parenting and child care, popular psychology, inspirational/motivational volumes as well as a few medical/nutritional book); **Mitchell Waters** (literary and commercial fiction and nonfiction, including mystery, history, biography, memoir, young adult, cookbooks, self-help and popular culture); **Kerry D'Agostino** (a wide range of literary and commercial fiction, as well as narrative nonfiction and memoir); **Noah Ballard** (literary debuts, upmarket thrillers and narrative nonfiction, and he is always on the look-out for honest and provocative new writers).

REPRESENTS nonfiction books, novels, short story collections, juvenile. **Considers these fiction areas:** adventure, confession, detective, erotica, ethnic, experimental, fantasy, feminist, gay, historical, horror, humor, juvenile, literary, mainstream, middle-grade, military, multicultural, multimedia, mystery, New Age, occult, picture books, regional, religious, romance, spiritual, sports, thriller, translation, women's, young adult.

HOW TO CONTACT "Send us a query letter, a synopsis of the work, a sample chapter and a brief resume. Illustrators should send 1-2 samples of published work, along with 6-8 color copies (no original art). Please send all book queries to our address, Attn: Query Department. Please enclose a SASE for our response and return postage if you wish to have your materials returned to you. We typically respond to queries within 6 to 8 weeks." Note that some agents list their e-mail on the agency website and are fine with e-mail submissions. Note in your submission if the query is being considered elsewhere. Responds in 3 weeks to queries; 5 weeks to mss. Obtains most new clients through recommendations from others, solicitations, conferences.

TERMS Agent receives 15% commission on domestic sales; 20% on foreign sales. Offers written contract. 75-day notice must be given to terminate contract. Offers written contract. Charges for some postage (overseas, etc.).

RECENT SALES This agency prefers not to share information on specific sales.

D4EO LITERARY AGENCY

7 Indian Valley Rd., Weston CT 06883. (203)544-7180. **Fax:** (203)544-7160. **Website:** www.d4eoliteraryagency.com. **Contact:** Bob Diforio.

○ Prior to opening his agency, Mr. Diforio was a publisher.

MEMBER AGENTS **Bob Diforio** (prefers referrals); **Mandy Hubbard** (middle-grade, young adult, and genre romance); **Kristin Miller** (closed to queries); **Bree Odgen** (children's, young adult, juvenile nonfiction, graphic novels, pop culture, art books, genre horror, noir, genre romance, historical, hard sci-fi); **Joyce Holland**; **Pam van Hycklama Vlieg**.

REPRESENTS nonfiction books, novels. **Considers these fiction areas:** adventure, detective, erotica, historical, horror, humor, juvenile, literary, mainstream, middle-grade, mystery, picture books, romance, sports, thriller.

HOW TO CONTACT Each of these agents has a different submission e-mail and different tastes regarding how they review material. See all on their individual agent pages on the agency website. Responds in 1 week to queries if interested. Obtains most new clients through recommendations from others.

TERMS Offers written contract, binding for 2 years; automatic renewal unless 60 days notice given prior to renewal date. Charges for photocopying and submission postage.

DANIEL LITERARY GROUP

1701 Kingsbury Dr., Suite 100, Nashville TN 37215. (615)730-8207. **E-mail:** submissions@danielliterarygroup.com. **Website:** www.danielliterarygroup.com. **Contact:** Greg Daniel. Represents 45 clients. 30% of clients are new/unpublished writers.

○ Prior to becoming an agent, Mr. Daniel spent 10 years in publishing—6 at the executive level at Thomas Nelson Publishers.

REPRESENTS nonfiction.

○— "We take pride in our ability to come alongside our authors and help strategize about where they want their writing to take them in both the near and long term. Forging close relationships with our authors, we help them with such critical factors as editorial refinement, branding, audience, and marketing." The agency is open to submissions in almost every popular category of nonfiction, especially if authors are recognized experts in their fields. No fiction, screenplays, poetry, science fiction/fantasy, romance, children's, or short stories.

HOW TO CONTACT Query via e-mail only. Submit publishing history, author bio, key selling points; no attachments. Check Submissions Guidelines before querying or submitting. Please do not query via telephone. Responds in 2-3 weeks to queries.

◯ DARHANSOFF & VERRILL LITERARY AGENTS

133 West 72nd St., Room 304, New York NY 10023. (917)305-1300. **Fax:** (917)305-1400. **E-mail:** submissions@dvagency.com. **Website:** www.dvagency.com. Member of AAR.

MEMBER AGENTS Liz Darhansoff; Chuck Verrill; Michele Mortimer; Catherine Luttinger (science fiction, fantasy, historical fiction, thrillers, mysteries).

REPRESENTS Considers these fiction areas: fantasy, historical, literary, mystery, science fiction, suspense, thriller.

HOW TO CONTACT Send queries via e-mail (submissions@dvagency.com) or by snail mail with SASE. Obtains most new clients through recommendations from others.

RECENT SALES A full list of clients is available on their website.

◑ LIZA DAWSON ASSOCIATES

350 Seventh Ave., Suite 2003, New York NY 10001. (212)465-9071. **Website:** www.lizadawsonassociates. com. **Contact:** Caitie Flum. Member of AAR. Other memberships include MWA, Women's Media Group. Represents 50+ clients. 30% of clients are new/unpublished writers.

◔ Prior to becoming an agent, Ms. Dawson was an editor for 20 years, spending 11 years at William Morrow as vice president and 2 years at Putnam as executive editor. Ms. Blasdell was a senior editor at HarperCollins and Avon.

MEMBER AGENTS Liza Dawson, queryliza@ lizadawsonassociates.com (plot-driven literary and popular fiction, historicals, thrillers, suspense, history,psychology [both popular and clinical], politics, narrative nonfiction and memoirs); **Caitlin Blasdell**, querycaitlin@lizadawsonassociates.com (science fiction, fantasy [both adult and young adult], parenting, business, thrillers and women's fiction; **Hannah Bowman**, queryhannah@lizadawsonassociates.com; (commercial fiction—especially science fiction and fantasy, women's fiction, cozy mysteries, romance, young adult, also nonfiction in the areas of mathematics, science, and spirituality); **Monica Odom**, querymonica@lizadawsonassociates.com (literary fiction, women's fiction, voice-driven memoir, nonfiction in

the areas of pop culture, food and cooking, history, politics, and current affairs); **Caitie Flum**, querycaitie@lizadawsonassociates.com (commercial fiction, especially historical, women's fiction, mysteries, new adult and young adult, nonfiction in the areas of theater, memoir, current affairs and pop culture).

⚲ This agency specializes in readable literary fiction, thrillers, mainstream historicals, women's fiction, academics, historians, journalists, and psychology.

HOW TO CONTACT Query by e-mail only. No phone calls. Each of these agents has their own specific submission requirements, which you can find online at their website. Responds in 4 weeks to queries; 8 weeks to mss. Obtains most new clients through recommendations from others, conferences.

TERMS Agent receives 15% commission on domestic sales. Agent receives 20% commission on foreign sales. Offers written contract.

◑ THE JENNIFER DECHIARA LITERARY AGENCY

31 East 32nd St., Suite 300, New York NY 10016. (212)481-8484. **Fax:** (212)481-9582. **Website:** www. jdlit.com.

MEMBER AGENTS Jennifer DeChiara, jenndec@ aol.com (literary, commercial, women's fiction (no bodice-rippers, please), chick-lit, mysteries, suspense, thrillers, funny/quirky picture books, middle-grade and young adult; for nonfiction: celebrity memoirs and biographies, GLBTQ, memoirs, books about the arts and performing arts, behind-the-scenes-type books, and books about popular culture); **Stephen Fraser**, fraserstephena@gmail.com (one-of-a-kind picture books; strong chapter book series; whimsical, dramatic, or humorous middle-grade; dramatic or high-concept young adult; powerful and unusual nonfiction; nonfiction with a broad audience on topics as far reaching as art history, theater, film, literature, and travel); **Marie Lamba**, marie.jdlit@gmail. com (young adult and middle-grade fiction, along with general and women's fiction and some memoir; interested in established illustrators and picture book authors); **Linda Epstein**, linda.p.epstein@gmail.com (young adult, middle-grade, literary fiction, quality upscale commercial fiction, vibrant narrative nonfiction, compelling memoirs, health and parenting books, cookbooks); **Roseanne Wells**, queryroseanne@gmail.com (literary fiction, YA, middle-grade, narrative nonfiction, select memoir, science (popular or trade, not academic), history, religion (not inspirational), travel, humor, food/cooking, and similar subjects); **Victoria Selvaggio**, vselvaggio@windstream.net (lyrical picture books, middle-grade and young adult fiction, mysteries, suspense, thrillers, paranormal, fantasy, narrative nonfiction).

REPRESENTS nonfiction books, novels, juvenile. **Considers these fiction areas:** commercial, literary, middle-grade, mystery, picture books, suspense, thriller, women's, young adult.

HOW TO CONTACT Each agent has their own e-mail submission address and submission instructions. Accepts simultaneous submissions. Obtains most new clients through recommendations from others, conferences, query letters.

TERMS Agent receives 15% commission on domestic sales. Agent receives 20% commission on foreign sales. Offers written contract.

① DEFIORE & CO.

47 E. 19th St., 3rd Floor, New York NY 10003. (212)925-7744. **Fax:** (212)925-9803. **E-mail:** brian@defliterary.com. **E-mail:** info@defliterary.com; submissions@defliterary.com. **Website:** www.defioreandco.com. Member of AAR.

Prior to becoming an agent, Mr. DeFiore was publisher of Villard Books (1997-1998), editor in chief of Hyperion (1992-1997), and editorial director of Delacorte Press (1988-1992).

MEMBER AGENTS Brian DeFiore (popular nonfiction, business, pop culture, parenting, commercial fiction); Laurie Abkemeier (memoir, parenting, business, how-to/self-help, popular science); Kate Garrick (literary fiction, memoir, popular nonfiction); Matthew Elblonk (young adult, popular culture, narrative nonfiction); Caryn Karmatz-Rudy (popular fiction, self-help, narrative nonfiction); Adam Schear (commercial fiction, humor, YA, smart thrillers, historical fiction, and quirky debut literary novels. For nonfiction: popular science, politics, popular culture, and current events); Meredith Kaffel (smart upmarket women's fiction, literary fiction [especially debut] and literary thrillers, narrative nonfiction, nonfiction about science and tech, sophisticated pop culture/humor books); Rebecca Strauss (literary and commercial fiction, women's fiction, urban fantasy, romance, mystery, YA, memoir, pop culture, and select nonfiction); Debra Goldstein (nonfiction books on how to live better).

REPRESENTS nonfiction books, novels. **Considers these fiction areas:** ethnic, literary, mainstream, middle-grade, mystery, paranormal, romance, short story collections, suspense, thriller, women's, young adult.

☛ "Please be advised that we are not considering poetry, adult science fiction and fantasy, or dramatic projects at this time."

HOW TO CONTACT Query with SASE or e-mail to submissions@defliterary.com. "Please include the word 'Query' in the subject line. All attachments will be deleted; please insert all text in the body of the e-mail. For more information about our agents, their individual interests, and their query guidelines, please visit our 'About Us' page on our website." There is more information (details, sales) for each agent on the agency website. Accepts simultaneous submissions. Obtains most new clients through recommendations from others.

TERMS Agent receives 15% commission on domestic sales. Agent receives 20% commission on foreign sales. Offers written contract; ten-day notice must be given to terminate contract. Charges clients for photocopying and overnight delivery (deducted only after a sale is made).

○ JOELLE DELBOURGO ASSOCIATES, INC.

101 Park St., 3rd Floor, Montclair NJ 07042. (973)773-0836. **Fax:** (973)783-6802. **E-mail:** joelle@delbourgo.com. **E-mail:** submissions@delbourgo.com. **Website:** www.delbourgo.com. Represents more than 100 clients. Currently handles nonfiction books (75%), novels (25%).

Prior to becoming an agent, Ms. Delbourgo was an editor and senior publishing executive at HarperCollins and Random House.

MEMBER AGENTS Joelle Delbourgo; Jacqueline Flynn; Carrie Cantor.

REPRESENTS nonfiction books, novels. **Considers these fiction areas:** fantasy, literary, mainstream, middle-grade, science fiction, thriller, women's, young adult.

☛ "We are former publishers and editors with deep knowledge and an insider perspective. We have a reputation for individualized attention to clients, strategic management of authors' careers, and creating strong partnerships with publishers for our clients."

HOW TO CONTACT It's preferable if you submit via e-mail to a specific agent. Query 1 agent only. No attachments. Put the word "Query" in the subject line. "While we do our best to respond to each query, if you have not received a response in 60 days you may consider that a pass. Please do not send us copies of self-published books unless requested. Let us know if you are sending your query to us exclusively or if this is a multiple submission.For nonfiction, let us know if a proposal and sample chapters are available. If not, you should probably wait to send your query when you have a completed proposal. For fiction and memoir, embed the FIRST 10 pages of ms into the e-mail after your query letter. Please no attachments. If we like your first pages, we may ask to see your synopsis and more ms. Both should be completed before you query us." Accepts simultaneous submissions.

TERMS Agent receives 15% commission on domestic sales. Agent receives 20% commission on foreign sales. Offers written contract. Charges clients for postage and photocopying.

RECENT SALES *Alexander the Great* by Philip Freeman; *The Big Book of Parenting Solutions* by Dr. Michele Borba; *The Secret Life of Ms. Finkelman* by Ben H. Wintners; *Not Quite Adults* by Richard Settersten Jr. and Barbara Ray; *Tabloid Medicine* by Robert Goldberg, PhD; *Table of Contents* by Judy Gerlman and Vicky Levi Krupp.

TIPS "Do your homework. Do not cold call. Read and follow submission guidelines before contacting us. Do not call to find out if we received your material. No e-mail queries. Treat agents with respect, as you would any other professional, such as a doctor, lawyer or financial advisor."

◑ SANDRA DIJKSTRA LITERARY AGENCY

1155 Camino del Mar, PMB 515, Del Mar CA 92014. (858)755-3115. **Fax:** (858)794-2822. **E-mail:** elise@dijkstraagency.com. **Website:** www.dijkstraagency.com. Member of AAR. Other memberships include Authors Guild, PEN West, PEN USA, Organization of American Historians, Poets and Editors, MWA. Represents 100+ clients. 30% of clients are new/unpublished writers.

MEMBER AGENTS Sandra Dijkstra, president (adult only). Acquiring Sub-agents: **Elise Capron** (adult only), **Jill Marr** (adult only), **Thao Le** (adult and YA), **Roz Foster** (adult and YA), **Jessica Watterson** (subgenres of adult and new adult romance, and women's fiction).

REPRESENTS nonfiction books, novels. **Considers these fiction areas:** commercial, horror, literary, middle-grade, new adult, romance, science fiction, suspense, thriller, women's, young adult.

HOW TO CONTACT "Please see guidelines on our website, and note that we only accept e-mail submissions. Due to the large number of unsolicited submissions we receive, we are only able to respond those submissions in which we are interested." Accepts simultaneous submissions. Responds to queries of interest within 6 weeks.

TERMS Works in conjunction with foreign and film agents. Agent receives 15% commission on domestic sales and 20% commission on foreign sales. Offers written contract. No reading fee.

TIPS "Remember that publishing is a business. Do your research and present your project in as professional a way as possible. Only submit your work when you are confident that it is polished and ready for prime-time. Make yourself a part of the active writing community by getting stories and articles published, networking with other writers, and getting a good sense of where your work fits in the market."

DONAGHY LITERARY GROUP

(647)527-4353. **E-mail:** query@donaghyliterary.com. **Website:** www.donaghyliterary.com.

MEMBER AGENTS Stacey Donaghy (romantic suspense, LGBT stories, stand-alone or series, mystery of all kinds, contemporary romance, erotica; Stacey also seeks nonfiction—authorized biographies, compelling stories written by celebrities, music industry professionals, pop culture, film/television, Canadian/international content; she is not seeking general nonfiction or memoirs unless you are a rock icon or celebrity); **Valerie Noble** (science fiction and fantasy [think Kristin Cashore and Suzanne Collins] for young adults and adults).

REPRESENTS Considers these fiction areas: erotica, fantasy, mystery, romance, science fiction, young adult.

HOW TO CONTACT Check the website, because the agency can close to submissions at any time.

◑◐ JIM DONOVAN LITERARY

5635 SMU Blvd., Suite 201, Dallas TX 75206. **E-mail:** jdliterary@sbcglobal.net. **Contact:** Melissa Shultz, agent.

MEMBER AGENTS Jim Donovan (history—particularly American, military and Western; biography; sports; popular reference; popular culture; fiction—

literary, thrillers and mystery); **Melissa Shultz** (all subjects listed above [like Jim], along with parenting and women's issues).

8—⚷ This agency specializes in commercial fiction and nonfiction. "Does not want to receive poetry, children's, sci-fi, fantasy, short stories, inspirational or anything else not listed above."

HOW TO CONTACT "For nonfiction, I need a well thought out query letter telling me about the book: What it does, how it does it, why it's needed now, why it's better or different than what's out there on the subject, and why the author is the perfect writer for it. For fiction, the novel has to be finished, of course; a short (two- to five-page) synopsis—not a teaser, but a summary of all the action, from first page to last—and the first 30-50 pages is enough. This material should be polished to as close to perfection as possible." Accepts simultaneous submissions. Responds in 2 weeks to queries; in 1 month to mss. Obtains most new clients through recommendations from others.

TERMS Agent receives 15% commission on domestic sales. Agent receives 20% commission on foreign sales. Offers written contract, binding for 1 year; 30-day notice must be given to terminate contract. This agency charges for things such as overnight delivery and ms copying. Charges are discussed beforehand.

RECENT SALES *Manson* by Jeff Guinn (S&S); *The Last Outlaws* by Thom Hatch (NAL); *Rough Riders* by Mark Lee Gardner (Morrow); *James Monroe* by Tim McGrath (NAL); *What Lurks Beneath* by Ryan Lockwood (Kensington); *Battle for Hell's Island* by Stephen Moore (NAL); *Powerless* by Tim Washburn (Kensington).

TIPS "Get published in short form—magazine reviews, journals, etc.—first. This will increase your credibility considerably, and make it much easier to sell a full-length book."

⊙ DOYEN LITERARY SERVICES, INC.

1931-660th St., Newell IA 50568-7613. **E-mail:** bestseller@barbaradoyen.com. **Website:** www.barbaradoyen.com. **Contact:** (Ms.) B.J. Doyen, president. Currently handles nonfiction books (100%).

⊙ Prior to opening her agency, Ms. Doyen worked as a published author, teacher, guest speaker, and wrote and appeared in her own weekly TV show airing in 7 states. She is also the coauthor of *The Everything Guide to Writing a Book Proposal* (Adams 2005) and *The Everything Guide to Getting Published* (Adams 2006).

REPRESENTS nonfiction for adults, no children's.

8—⚷ This agency specializes in nonfiction. Actively seeking business, health, science, how-to, self-help—all kinds of adult nonfiction suitable for the major trade publishers. Does not want to receive pornography, screenplays, children's books, fiction, or poetry.

HOW TO CONTACT Send a **query letter** initially. "Do not send us any attachments. Your text must be in the body of the e-mail. Please read the website before submitting a query. Include your background information in a bio. Send no unsolicited attachments." Accepts simultaneous submissions. Responds immediately to queries; in 3 weeks to mss.

TERMS Agent receives 15% commission on domestic sales. Agent receives 20% commission on foreign sales. Offers written contract, binding for 2 years.

TIPS "Our authors receive personalized attention. We market aggressively, undeterred by rejection. We get the best possible publishing contracts. We are very interested in nonfiction book ideas at this time and will consider most topics. Many writers come to us from referrals, but we also get quite a few who initially approach us with query letters. Do not call us regarding queries. It is best if you do not collect editorial rejections prior to seeking an agent, but if you do, be upfront and honest about it. Do not submit your ms to more than 1 agent at a time—querying first can save you (and us) much time. We're open to established or beginning writers—just send us a terrific letter!"

➊ DUNHAM LITERARY, INC.

110 William St., Suite 2202, New York NY 10038. (212)929-0994. **E-mail:** query@dunhamlit.com. **Website:** www.dunhamlit.com. **Contact:** Jennie Dunham. Member of AAR, SCBWI. Represents 50 clients. 15% of clients are new/unpublished writers. Currently handles nonfiction books (25%), novels (25%), juvenile books (50%).

💬 Prior to opening her agency, Ms. Dunham worked as a literary agent for Russell & Volkening. The Rhoda Weyr Agency is now a division of Dunham Literary, Inc.

REPRESENTS Considers these fiction areas: ethnic, juvenile, literary, mainstream, picture books, young adult.

HOW TO CONTACT Query with SASE. Responds in 3 weeks to queries; 2 months to mss. Obtains most new clients through recommendations from others, solicitations.

TERMS Agent receives 15% commission on domestic sales. Agent receives 20% commission on foreign sales.
RECENT SALES Sales include The Bad Kitty Series by Nick Bruel (Macmillan); *The Little Mermaid* by Robert Sabuda (Simon & Schuster); *The Gollywhopper Games* and Sequels by Jody Feldman (HarperCollins); *Learning Not to Drown* by Anna Shinoda (Simon & Schuster); *The Things You Kiss Goodbye* by Leslie Connor (HarperCollins); *Gangsterland* by Tod Goldberg (Counterpoint); *Ancestors and Others* by Fred Chappell (Macmillan), *Forward from Here* by Reeve Lindbergh (Simon & Schuster).

○ DUNOW, CARLSON, & LERNER AGENCY

27 W. 20th St., Suite 1107, New York NY 10011. (212)645-7606. **E-mail:** betsy@dclagency.com; jennifer@dclagency.com. **E-mail:** mail@dclagency.com. **Website:** www.dclagency.com. Member: AAR.
MEMBER AGENTS Jennifer Carlson (narrative nonfiction writers and journalists covering current events and ideas and cultural history, as well as literary and upmarket commercial novelists); **Henry Dunow** (quality fiction—literary, historical, strongly written commercial—and with voice-driven nonfiction across a range of areas—narrative history, biography, memoir, current affairs, cultural trends and criticism, science, sports); **Erin Hosier** (nonfiction: popular culture, music, sociology and memoir); **Betsy Lerner** (nonfiction writers in the areas of psychology, history, cultural studies, biography, current events, business; fiction: literary, dark, funny, voice driven); **Yishai Seidman** (broad range of fiction: literary, postmodern, and thrillers; nonfiction: sports, music, and pop culture); **Amy Hughes** (nonfiction in the areas of history, cultural studies, memoir, current events, wellness, health, food, pop culture, and biography; also literary fiction); **Eleanor Jackson** (literary, commercial, memoir, art, food, science and history); **Julia Kenny** (fiction—adult, middle-grade, and YA—and is especially interested in dark, literary thrillers and suspense); **Edward Necarsulmer IV** (strong new voices in teen and middle-grade as well as picture books).
REPRESENTS nonfiction books, novels, juvenile. **Considers these fiction areas:** commercial, literary, mainstream, middle-grade, mystery, picture books, thriller, young adult.
HOW TO CONTACT Query via snail mail with SASE, or by e-mail. No attachments. Responds if interested.

RECENT SALES A full list of agency clients is on the website.

⊘ DUPREE/MILLER AND ASSOCIATES INC.

100 Highland Park Village, Suite 350, Dallas TX 75205. (214)559-BOOK. **Fax:** (214)559-PAGE. **E-mail:** editorial@dupreemiller.com. **Website:** www.dupreemiller.com. Member of ABA. Represents 200 clients. 20% of clients are new/unpublished writers. Currently handles nonfiction books (90%), novels (10%).
MEMBER AGENTS Jan Miller, founder/CEO; Shannon Miser-Marven, president; Nena Madonia, senior lead agent; Lacy Lynch, senior lead agent; Dabney Rice, foreign rights director.
REPRESENTS nonfiction books, novels, scholarly, syndicated religious.inspirational/spirituality. **Considers these fiction areas:** action, adventure, crime, detective, ethnic, experimental, family saga, feminist, glitz, historical, humor, inspirational, literary, mainstream, mystery, picture books, police, psychic, religious, satire, sports, supernatural, suspense, thriller.
☞ This agency specializes in commercial fiction and nonfiction.
HOW TO CONTACT This agency does not request unsolicited submissions, and meets their new clients through referrals or face-to-face events. Obtains all new clients through recommendations from current clients.
TERMS Agent receives 15% commission on domestic sales. Offers written contract.
WRITERS CONFERENCES Aspen Summer Words Literary Festival.

○ EAST/WEST LITERARY AGENCY, LLC

1158 26th St., Suite 462, Santa Monica CA 90403. (310)573-9303. **Fax:** (310)453-9008. **E-mail:** dwarren@eastwestliteraryagency.com. **Contact:** Deborah Warren. Estab. 2000. Currently handles juvenile books (90%), adult books 10%.
MEMBER AGENTS Deborah Warren, founder.
REPRESENTS Considers these fiction areas: middle-grade, picture books, young adult.
HOW TO CONTACT By referral only. Submit proposal and first 3 sample chapters, table of contents (2 pages or fewer), synopsis (1 page). For picture books, submit entire ms. Requested submissions should be sent by mail as a Word document in Courier, 12-pt., double-spaced with 1.20-inch margin on left, ragged right text, 25 lines per page, continuously paginated,

with all your contact info on the first page. Only responds if interested, no need for SASE. Responds in 60 days. Obtains new clients through recommendations from others.

TERMS Agent receives 15% commission on domestic sales. Agent receives 25% commission on foreign sales. Offers written contract; 30-day notice must be given to terminate contract. Charges for out-of-pocket expenses, such as postage and copying.

ETHAN ELLENBERG LITERARY AGENCY

155 Suffolk St., No. 2R, New York NY 10002. (212)431-4554. **E-mail:** agent@ethanellenberg.com. **Website:** ethanellenberg.com. **Contact:** Ethan Ellenberg. Estab. 1984.

○ Prior to opening his agency, Mr. Ellenberg was contracts manager of Berkley/Jove and associate contracts manager for Bantam.

MEMBER AGENTS Evan Gregory, senior agent; **Bibi Lewis**, associate agent.

⚷ "We specialize in commercial fiction and children's books. In commercial fiction we want to see science fiction, fantasy, romance, mystery, thriller, women's fiction; all genres welcome. In children's books, we want to see everything: picture books, early reader, middle-grade, and young adult. We do some nonfiction: history, biography, military, popular science, and cutting-edge books about any subject. Does not want to receive poetry, short stories, or screenplays.

HOW TO CONTACT Query by e-mail. Paste the query, synopsis, and first 50 pages (or 3 chapters) into the e-mail. For nonfiction, paste the proposal. For picture books, paste the entire text. Accepts simultaneous submissions. Responds in 2 weeks to queries (no attachments); 4-6 weeks to mss.

TERMS Agent receives 15% commission on domestic sales. Agent receives 10% commission on foreign sales. Offers written contract. Charges clients (with their consent) for direct expenses limited to photocopying and postage.

WRITERS CONFERENCES RWA National Conference; Novelists, Inc.; and other regional conferences.

THE ELAINE P. ENGLISH LITERARY AGENCY

4710 41st St. NW, Suite D, Washington DC 20016. (202)362-5190. **Fax:** (202)362-5192. **Website:** www.elaineenglish.com/. **Contact:** Elaine English. Member of AAR.

○ Ms. English has been working in publishing for more than 20 years. She is also an attorney specializing in media and publishing law.

MEMBER AGENTS Elaine English (novels).

REPRESENTS novels. **Considers these fiction areas:** historical, multicultural, mystery, suspense, thriller, women's romance (single title, historical, contemporary, romantic, suspense, chick lit, erotic), general women's fiction. The agency is slowly but steadily acquiring in all mentioned areas.

⚷ Actively seeking women's fiction, including single-title romances. Does not want to receive any science fiction, time travel, or picture books.

HOW TO CONTACT Not accepting queries as of 2015. Keep checking the website for further information and updates. Responds in 1-2 months to queries; 3 months to requested submissions. Obtains most new clients through recommendations from others, conferences, submissions.

TERMS Agent receives 15% commission on domestic sales. Agent receives 20% commission on foreign sales. Offers written contract; 30-day notice must be given to terminate contract. Charges only for shipping expenses; generally taken from proceeds.

RECENT SALES Have been to Sourcebooks, Tor, Harlequin.

WRITERS CONFERENCES RWA National Conference; Novelists, Inc.; Malice Domestic; Washington Romance Writers Retreat, among others.

JUDITH EHRLICH LITERARY MANAGEMENT, LLC

880 Third Ave., 8th Floor, New York NY 10022. (646)505-1570. **Fax:** (646)505-1570. **Website:** www.judithehrlichliterary.com. Member of the Author's Guild and the American Society of Journalists and Authors.

○ Prior to her current position, Ms. Ehrlich was a senior associate at the Linda Chester Agency and is an award-winning journalist; she is the co-author of *The New Crowd: The Changing of the Jewish Guard on Wall Street* (Little, Brown).

MEMBER AGENTS Judith Ehrlich, jehrlich@judithehrlichliterary.com (nonfiction—narrative, women's, business, prescriptive); **Sophia Seidner**: sseidner@judithehrlichliterary.com (upmarket fiction and nonfiction including prescriptive, narrative nonfiction, memoir, and biography; areas of special interest include medical and health-related topics, science [popular, political, and social], animal welfare, current events, politics, law, history, ethics, parody and humor, sports, and business self-help).

REPRESENTS Considers these fiction areas: commercial, literary. Also seeks prescriptive books offering fresh information and advice.

⚬━ Does not want to receive novellas, poetry, textbooks, plays, or screenplays.

HOW TO CONTACT E-query, with a synopsis and some sample pages. The agency will respond only if interested.

RECENT SALES *Power Branding: Leveraging the Success of the World's Best Brands* by Steve McKee (Palgrave Macmillan); *What was the Underground Railroad?* by Yona Zeldis McDonough (Grosset & Dunlap); *Confessions of a Sociopath: A Life Spent Hiding in Plain Sight* by M.E. Thomas (Crown); *The Last Kiss* by Leslie Brody (TitleTown); *Love, Loss, and Laughter: Seeing Alzheimer's Differently* (Lyons Press); *Luck and Circumstance: A Coming of Age in New York, Hollywood, and Points Beyond* by Michael Lindsay-Hogg (Knopf); *Paris Under Water: How the City of Light Survived the Great Flood of 1910* by Jeffrey H. Jackson (Palgrave Macmillan). Fiction titles: *Two of a Kind* by Yona Zeldis McDonough (NAL, September 2013); *Once We Were* by Kat Zhang (HarperCollins, September 2013).

◑ FELICIA ETH LITERARY REPRESENTATION

555 Bryant St., Suite 350, Palo Alto CA 94301-1700. **E-mail:** feliciaeth.literary@gmail.com. **Website:** eth-literary.com. **Contact:** Felicia Eth. Member of AAR. Represents 25-35 clients. Currently handles nonfiction books (75%), novels (25% adult).

REPRESENTS nonfiction books, novels. **Considers these fiction areas:** literary, mainstream.

⚬━ This agency specializes in high-quality fiction (preferably mainstream/contemporary) and provocative, intelligent, and thoughtful nonfiction on a wide array of commercial subjects.

HOW TO CONTACT Query with SASE. Accepts simultaneous submissions. Responds in 3 weeks to queries; in 4-6 weeks to mss.

TERMS Agent receives 15% commission on domestic sales. Agent receives 20% commission on foreign sales. Agent receives 20% commission on film sales. Charges clients for photocopying and express mail service.

RECENT SALES *Bumper Sticker Philosophy* by Jack Bowen (Random House); *Boys Adrift* by Leonard Sax (Basic Books; *The Memory Thief* by Emily Colin (Bal-

lantine Books); *The World is a Carpet* by Anna Badkhen (Riverhead).

WRITERS CONFERENCES "Wide array—from Squaw Valley to Mills College."

TIPS "For nonfiction, established expertise is certainly a plus—as is magazine publication—though not a prerequisite. I am highly dedicated to those projects I represent, but highly selective in what I choose."

◑ FAIRBANK LITERARY REPRESENTATION

P.O. Box 6, Hudson NY 12534-0006. (617)576-0030. **Fax:** (617)576-0030. **E-mail:** queries@fairbankliterary.com. **Website:** www.fairbankliterary.com. **Contact:** Sorche Fairbank. Member of AAR.

MEMBER AGENTS Sorche Fairbank (narrative nonfiction, commercial and literary fiction, memoir, food and wine); **Matthew Frederick**, matt@fairbankliterary.com (sports nonfiction, architecture, design).

REPRESENTS nonfiction books, novels, short story collections. **Considers these fiction areas:** action, adventure, feminist, gay, lesbian, literary, mainstream, mystery, sports, suspense, thriller, women's Southern voices.

⚬━ "I tend to gravitate toward literary fiction and narrative nonfiction, with a strong interest in women's issues and women's voices, international voices, class and race issues, and projects that simply teach me something new about the greater world and society around us. We have a good reputation for working closely and developmentally with our authors and love what we do." Actively seeking literary fiction, international and culturally diverse voices, narrative nonfiction, topical subjects (politics, current affairs), history, sports, architecture/design, and pop culture. Does not want to receive romance, poetry, science fiction, pirates, vampire, young adult, or children's works.

HOW TO CONTACT Query with SASE. Submit author bio. Accepts simultaneous submissions. Obtains most new clients through recommendations from others, solicitations, conferences, ideas generated in-house.

TERMS Agent receives 15% commission on domestic sales. Agent receives 20% commission on foreign sales. Offers written contract, binding for 12 months; 45-day notice must be given to terminate contract.

RECENT SALES *When Clowns Attack* by Chuck Sambuchino (Running Press); 101 Things I Learned in School series by Matthew Fredericks; all recent sales available on website.

TIPS "Be professional from the very first contact. There shouldn't be a single typo or grammatical flub in your query. Have a reason for contacting me about your project other than I was the next name listed on some website. Please do not use form query software! Believe me, we can get a dozen or so a day that look identical—we know when you are using a form. Show me that you know your audience—and your competition. Have the writing and/or proposal at the very, very best it can be before starting the querying process. Don't assume that if someone likes it enough they'll 'fix' it. The biggest mistake new writers make is starting the querying process before they—and the work—are ready. Take your time and do it right."

DIANA FINCH LITERARY AGENCY

116 W. 23rd St., Suite 500, New York NY 10011. (917)544-4470. **E-mail:** diana.finch@verizon.net. **Website:** dianafinchliteraryagency.blogspot.com. **Contact:** Diana Finch. Member of AAR.

> Seeking to represent books that change lives. Prior to opening her agency in 2003, Ms. Finch worked at Ellen Levine Literary Agency for 18 years.

REPRESENTS nonfiction books, novels, scholarly. **Considers these fiction areas:** action, adventure, crime, detective, ethnic, historical, literary, mainstream, police, thriller, young adult.

> "Does not want romance, mysteries, or children's picture books."

HOW TO CONTACT This agency prefers submissions via its online form: https://dianafinchliterary-agency.submittable.com/submit. Accepts simultaneous submissions. Obtains most new clients through recommendations from others.

TERMS Agent receives 15% commission on domestic sales. Agent receives 20% commission on foreign sales. Offers written contract. "I charge for overseas postage, galleys, and books purchased, and try to recoup these costs from earnings received for a client, rather than charging outright."

TIPS "Do as much research as you can on agents before you query. Have someone critique your query letter before you send it. It should be only 1 page and describe your book clearly—and why you are writing it—but also demonstrate creativity and a sense of your writing style."

FINEPRINT LITERARY MANAGEMENT

115 W. 29th, 3rd Floor, New York NY 10001. (212)279-1282. **Website:** www.fineprintlit.com. Member of AAR.

MEMBER AGENTS Peter Rubie, CEO, peter@fineprintlit.com (nonfiction interests include narrative nonfiction, popular science, spirituality, history, biography, pop culture, business, technology, parenting, health, self-help, music, and food; fiction interests include literate thrillers, crime fiction, science fiction and fantasy, military fiction and literary fiction, middle-grade and YA fiction, and nonfiction for boys); Stephany Evans, stephany@fineprintlit.com (nonfiction: health and wellness, especially women's health; spirituality, environment/sustainability, food and wine, memoir, and narrative nonfiction; fiction interests include stories with a strong and interesting female protagonist, both literary and upmarket commercial/book club fiction, romance [all subgenres], mysteries); Janet Reid (crime fiction and narrative nonfiction); Laura Wood, laura@fineprintlit.com (serious nonfiction, especially in the areas of science and nature, along with substantial titles in business, history, religion, and other areas by academics, experienced professionals, and journalists); June Clark (see juneclark.com).

REPRESENTS **Considers these fiction areas:** commercial, crime, fantasy, middle-grade, military, mystery, romance, science fiction, suspense, thriller, women's, young adult.

HOW TO CONTACT E-query. For fiction, send a query, synopsis, bio, and 30 pages pasted into the e-mail. No attachments. For nonfiction, send a query only; proposal requested later if the agent is interested. Obtains most new clients through recommendations from others, solicitations.

TERMS Agent receives 15% commission on domestic sales. Agent receives 20% commission on foreign sales.

FLANNERY LITERARY

1140 Wickfield Ct., Naperville IL 60563. (630)428-2682. **E-mail:** jennifer@flanneryliterary.com. **Contact:** Jennifer Flannery. Represents 40 clients. 50% of clients are new/unpublished writers. Currently handles juvenile books (100%).

REPRESENTS **Considers these fiction areas:** juvenile, middle-grade, young adult.

This agency specializes in children's and young adult fiction and nonfiction. It also accepts picture books. 100% juvenile books.

HOW TO CONTACT Query by mail with SASE. "Multiple queries are fine, but please inform us. Mail that requires a signature will be returned to sender, as we are not always available to sign for mail." Responds in 2 weeks to queries; 1 month to mss. Obtains new clients through referrals and queries.

TERMS Agent receives 15% commission on domestic sales. Agent receives 20% commission on foreign sales. Offers written contract, binding for life of book in print.

TIPS "Write an engrossing, succinct query describing your work. We are always looking for a fresh new voice."

FOLIO LITERARY MANAGEMENT, LLC

The Film Center Building, 630 Ninth Ave., Suite 1101, New York NY 10036. (212)400-1494. **Fax:** (212)967-0977. **Website:** www.foliolit.com. Member of AAR. Represents 100+ clients.

Prior to creating Folio Literary Management, Mr. Hoffman worked for several years at another agency; Mr. Kleinman was an agent at Graybill & English.

MEMBER AGENTS Claudia Cross, Scott Hoffman, Jeff Kleinman, Frank Weimann, Michelle Brower, Michael Harriot, Erin Harris, Molly Jaffa, Katherine Latshaw, Erin Niumata, Ruth Pomerance, Marcy Posner, Jeff Silberman, Michael Sterling, Steve Troha, Emily van Beek, Melissa Sarver White.

REPRESENTS nonfiction books, novels, short story collections. **Considers these fiction areas:** commercial, erotica, fantasy, horror, literary, middle-grade, mystery, picture books, religious, romance, thriller, women's, young adult.

No poetry, stage plays, or screenplays.

HOW TO CONTACT Query via e-mail only (no attachments). Read agent bios online for specific submission guidelines and e-mail addresses.

TIPS "Please do not submit simultaneously to more than 1 agent at Folio. If you're not sure which of us is exactly right for your book, don't worry. We work closely as a team, and if one of our agents gets a query that might be more appropriate for someone else, we'll always pass it along. It's important that you check each agent's bio page for clear directions as to how to submit, as well as when to expect feedback."

FOUNDRY LITERARY + MEDIA

33 West 17th St., PH, New York NY 10011. (212)929-5064. **Fax:** (212)929-5471. **Website:** www.foundrymedia.com.

MEMBER AGENTS Peter McGuigan, pmsubmissions@foundrymedia.com; Yfat Reiss Gendell, yrgsubmissions@foundrymedia.com (practical nonfiction projects in the areas of health and wellness, diet, lifestyle, how-to, and parenting and a broad range of narrative nonfiction that includes humor, memoir, history, science, pop culture, psychology, and adventure/travel stories); Mollie Glick, mgsubmissions@foundrymedia.com (literary fiction, young adult fiction, narrative nonfiction, and a bit of practical nonfiction in the areas of popular science, medicine, psychology, cultural history, memoir and current events); Chris Park, cpsubmissions@foundrymedia.com (memoirs, narrative nonfiction, sports books, Christian nonfiction and character-driven fiction); Hannah Brown Gordon, hbgsubmissions@foundrymedia.com (stories and narratives that blend genres, including thriller, suspense, historical, literary, speculative, memoir, pop-science, psychology, humor, and pop culture); Brandi Bowles, bbsubmissions@foundrymedia.com (literary and commercial fiction, especially high-concept novels that feature strong female bonds and psychological or scientific themes); Kirsten Neuhaus, knsubmissions@foundrymedia.com (platform-driven narrative nonfiction, in the areas of lifestyle (beauty/fashion/relationships), memoir, business, current events, history and stories with strong female voices, as well as smart, upmarket, and commercial fiction); Jessica Regel, jrsubmissions@foundrymedia.com (young adult and middle-grade books, as well as a select list of adult general fiction, women's fiction, and adult nonfiction); Anthony Mattero, amsubmissions@foundrymedia.com (smart, platform-driven nonfiction particularly in the genres of pop-culture, humor, music, sports, and pop-business); Matt Wise, mwsubmissions@foundrymedia.com (a wide array of projects, from controversial narrative nonfiction to literary fiction to art and design projects); Peter Steinberg, pssubmissions@foundrymedia.com (narrative nonfiction, commercial and literary fiction, memoir, health, history, lifestyle, humor, sports and young adult); Roger Freet, rfsubmissions@foundrymedia.com (narrative and idea-driven nonfiction clients in the areas of religion, spirituality, memoir, and cultural issues by leading scholars, pastors, historians, activists and musicians).

REPRESENTS Considers these fiction areas: commercial, historical, humor, literary, middle-grade, suspense, thriller, women's, young adult.

HOW TO CONTACT Target 1 agent only. Send queries to the specific submission e-mail of the agent. For fiction: send query, synopsis, author bio, first 3 chapters—all pasted in the e-mail. For nonfiction, send query, sample chapters, table of contents, author bio (all pasted).

RECENT SALES *Tell the Wolves I'm Home* by Carol Rifka Blunt; *The Rathbones* by Janice Clark; *This is Your Captain Speaking* by Jon Methven; *The War Against the Assholes* and *The November Criminals* by Sam Munson; *Ready Player One* by Ernest Cline.

TIPS "Consult website for each agent's submission instructions."

FOX LITERARY

110 W. 40th St., Suite 410, New York NY 10018. **E-mail:** submissions@foxliterary.com. **Website:** www.publishersmarketplace.com/members/fox/.

REPRESENTS Considers these fiction areas: fantasy, historical, literary, mainstream, romance, science fiction, thriller, young adult graphic novels.

⌘━ Does not want to receive screenplays, poetry, category westerns, horror, Christian/inspirational, or children's picture books.

HOW TO CONTACT E-mail query and first 5 pages in body of e-mail. E-mail queries preferred. For snail mail queries, must include an e-mail address for response, and no response means NO. Do not send SASE. No e-mail attachments.

RECENT SALES *Black Ships* by Jo Graham (Orbit); Evernight series by Claudia Gray (HarperCollins); October Daye series by Seanan McGuire (DAW); *Salt and Silver* by Anna Katherine (Tor); *Alcestis* by Katharine Beutner (Soho Press); *Shadows Cast Bby Stars* by Catherine Knutsson (Atheneum); *Saving June* and *Speechless* by Hannah Harrington (Harlequin Teen); Spellcaster trilogy by Claudia Gray (HarperCollins).

○ LYNN C. FRANKLIN ASSOCIATES, LTD.

1350 Broadway, Suite 2015, New York NY 10018. (212)868-6311. **Fax:** (212)868-6312. **E-mail:** agency@franklinandsiegal.com. **Website:** www.publishersmarketplace.com/members/LynnCFranklin. **Contact:** Lynn Franklin, president; Claudia Nys, foreign rights. Other memberships include PEN America.

REPRESENTS nonfiction books, novels.

⌘━ Primary interest lies in nonfiction (memoir, biography, current affairs, spirituality, psychology/self-help, alternative medicine, etc.).

HOW TO CONTACT Query via e-mail to agency@franklinandsiegal.com. No unsolicited mss. No attachments. For nonfiction, query letter with short outline and synopsis. For fiction, query letter with short synopsis and a maximum of 10 sample pages (in the body of the e-mail). Please indicate "query adult" or "query children's" in the subject line. Accepts simultaneous submissions. Obtains most new clients through recommendations from others, solicitations.

TERMS Agent receives 15% commission on domestic sales. Agent receives 20% commission on foreign sales. Offers written contract.

RECENT SALES *The Wahls Protocol: How I Beat Progressive MS Using Paleo Principles And Functional Medicine* by Terry Wahls, M.D. (Avery/Penguin); *The Book Of Forgiving: The Four-Fold Path To Healing For Ourselves And Our World* by Archbishop Desmond Tutu and Reverend Mpho Tutu (U.S.: HarperOne, U.K.: Collins); *The Customer Rules: 39 Essential Practices For Delivering Sensational Service* by Lee Cockerell (Crown Business/Random House); *My Name Is Jody Williams* by Jody Williams (University of California Press-Berkeley); *Everybody Matters: A Memoir* by Mary Robinson (U.S.: Bloomsbury, U.K. and Ireland: Hodder).

○ SARAH JANE FREYMANN LITERARY AGENCY

59 W. 71st St., Suite 9B, New York NY 10023. (212)362-9277. **E-mail:** sarah@sarahjanefreymann.com; Submissions@SarahJaneFreymann.com. **Website:** www.sarahjanefreymann.com. **Contact:** Sarah Jane Freymann, Steve Schwartz.

MEMBER AGENTS Sarah Jane Freymann (nonfiction books, novels, illustrated books); Jessica Sinsheimer, jessica@sarahjanefreymann.com (young adult fiction); Steven Schwartz, steve@sarahjanefreymann.com; Katharine Sands.

REPRESENTS Considers these fiction areas: ethnic, literary, mainstream, young adult.

HOW TO CONTACT Query. Responds in 2 weeks to queries; in 6 weeks to mss. Obtains most new clients through recommendations from others.

TERMS Agent receives 15% commission on domestic sales. Agent receives 20% commission on foreign sales. Offers written contract. Charges clients for long distance, overseas postage, photocopying. 100% of business is derived from commissions on ms sales.

RECENT SALES *How to Make Love to a Plastic Cup: And Other Things I Learned While Trying to Knock Up My Wife* by Greg Wolfe (Harper Collins); *I Want to Be Left Behind: Rapture Here on Earth* by Brenda Peterson (a Merloyd Lawrence Book); *That Bird Has My Name: The Autobiography of an Innocent Man on Death Row* by Jarvis Jay Masters with an Introduction by Pema Chodrun (HarperOne); *Perfect One-Dish Meals* by Pam Anderson (Houghton Mifflin); *Birdology* by Sy Montgomery (Simon & Schuster); *Emptying the Nest: Launching Your Reluctant Young Adult* by Dr. Brad Sachs (Macmillan); *Tossed & Found* by Linda and John Meyers (Steward, Tabori & Chang); *32 Candles* by Ernessa Carter; *God and Dog* by Wendy Francisco.

TIPS "I love fresh, new, passionate works by authors who love what they are doing and have both natural talent and carefully honed skill."

FREDRICA S. FRIEDMAN AND CO., INC.

136 E. 57th St., 14th Floor, New York NY 10022. (212)829-9600. **Fax:** (212)829-9669. **E-mail:** submissions@fredricafriedman.com. **Website:** www.fredricafriedman.com. **Contact:** Ms. Chandler Smith.

Prior to establishing her own literary management firm, Ms. Friedman was the Editorial Director, Associate Publisher and Vice President of Little, Brown & Co., a division of Time Warner, and the first woman to hold those positions.

REPRESENTS nonfiction books, novels anthologies. **Considers these fiction areas:** literary.

"We represent a select group of outstanding nonfiction and fiction writers. We are particularly interested in helping writers expand their readership and develop their careers." Does not want poetry, plays, screenplays, children's books, sci-fi/fantasy, or horror.

HOW TO CONTACT Submit e-query, synopsis; be concise, and include any pertinent author information, including relevant writing history. If you are a fiction writer, we also request a one-page sample from your ms to provide its voice. We ask that you keep all material in the body of the e-mail. Accepts simultaneous submissions. Responds in 4-6 weeks to queries; in 4-6 weeks to mss. Obtains most new clients through recommendations from others.

TERMS Agent receives 15% commission on domestic sales. Agent receives 25% commission on foreign sales. Offers written contract. Charges for photocopying and messenger/shipping fees for proposals.

TIPS "Spell the agent's name correctly on your query letter."

REBECCA FRIEDMAN LITERARY AGENCY

E-mail: Abby@rfliterary.com. **Website:** www.rfliterary.com/. Estab. 2013.

Prior to opening her own agency in 2013, Ms. Friedman was with Sterling Lord Literistic from 2006 to 2011, then with Frederick Hill Bonnie Nadell.

MEMBER AGENTS Rebecca Friedman, brandie@rfliterary.com (literary novels of suspense, women's fiction, contemporary romance, and young adult, as well as journalistic nonfiction and memoir); **Kimberly Brower**, kimberly@rfliterary.com (commercial and literary fiction, with an emphasis in women's fiction, contemporary romance, mysteries/thrillers, new adult, and young adult, as well as certain areas of nonfiction, including business, diet, and fitness); **Rachel Marks,** rachel@rfliterary.com (young adult, fantasy, science fiction, new adult, and romance).

REPRESENTS **Considers these fiction areas:** commercial, fantasy, literary, new adult, romance, science fiction, suspense, women's, young adult.

The agency is interested in commercial and literary fiction with a focus on literary novels of suspense, women's fiction, contemporary romance, and young adult, as well as journalistic nonfiction and memoir. Most of all, we are looking for great stories told in strong voices.

HOW TO CONTACT Please submit your query letter and first chapter (no more than 15 pages, double-spaced). If querying Kimberly, paste a synopsis and the book's first 50 pages into the e-mail submission.

RECENT SALES *So Much Pretty* by Cara Hoffman; *The Black Nile* by Dan Morrison; *Maybe One Day* by Melissa Kantor; *Devoured* by Emily Snow. A complete list of agency authors is available online.

FULL CIRCLE LITERARY, LLC

7676 Hazard Center Dr., Suite 500, San Diego CA 92108. **E-mail:** submissions@fullcircleliterary.com. **Website:** www.fullcircleliterary.com. **Contact:** Stefanie Von Borstel. Member of AAR. Represents 55 clients. 60% of clients are new/unpublished writers.

MEMBER AGENTS Lilly Ghahremani; Stefanie Von Borstel; Adriana Dominguez; Taylor Martindale (multicultural voices).

REPRESENTS nonfiction books, juvenile. **Considers these fiction areas:** literary, middle-grade, picture books, women's, young adult.

⚷ "Our full-service boutique agency, representing a range of nonfiction and children's books (limited fiction), provides a one-stop resource for authors. Our extensive experience in the realms of law and marketing provide Full Circle clients with a unique edge." Actively seeking nonfiction by authors with a unique and strong platform, projects that offer new and diverse viewpoints, and literature with a global or multicultural perspective. We are particularly interested in books with a Latino or Middle Eastern angle and books related to pop culture.

HOW TO CONTACT Agency accepts e-queries. Put "Query for [Agent]" in the subject line. Send a one-page query letter (in the body of the e-mail) including a description of your book, writing credentials and author highlights. Following your query, please include the first 10 pages or complete picture book ms text within the body of the e-mail. For nonfiction, include a proposal with 1 sample chapter. Accepts simultaneous submissions. Obtains most new clients through recommendations from others, solicitations, conferences.

TERMS Agent receives 15% commission on domestic sales. Agent receives 20% commission on foreign sales. Offers written contract; up to 30-day notice must be given to terminate contract. Charges for copying and postage.

TIPS "Put your best foot forward. Contact us when you simply can't make your project any better on your own, and please be sure your work fits with what the agent you're approaching represents. Little things count, so copyedit your work. Join a writing group and attend conferences to get objective and constructive feedback before submitting. Be active about building your platform as an author before, during, and after publication. Remember this is a business and your agent is a business partner."

◎ NANCY GALLT LITERARY AGENCY

273 Charlton Ave., South Orange NJ 07079. (973)761-6358. **Website:** www.nancygallt.com. **Contact:** Nancy Gallt, Marietta Zacker. Represents 40 clients. 30% of clients are new/unpublished writers.

💬 Prior to opening her agency, Ms. Gallt was subsidiary rights director of the children's book division at Morrow, Harper and Viking.

MEMBER AGENTS Nancy Gallt; Marietta Zacker.

REPRESENTS juvenile. **Considers these fiction areas:** juvenile, middle-grade, picture books, young adult.

⚷ "We only handle children's books." Actively seeking picture books, middle-grade, and young adult novels.

HOW TO CONTACT Submit through online submission for on agency website. No e-mail queries, please. Accepts simultaneous submissions. Obtains new clients through recommendations from others.

TERMS Agent receives 15% commission on domestic sales. Agent receives 20% commission on foreign sales. Offers written contract; 30-day notice must be given to terminate contract.

RECENT SALES *Toya* by Randi Revill; Rick Riordan's Books (Hyperion); *Something Extraordinary* by Ben Clanton (Simon & Schuster); *The Baby Tree* by Sophie Blackall (Nancy Paulsen Books/Penguin); *Fenway And Hattie* by Victoria J Coe (Putnam/Penguin); *The Meaning Of Maggie* by Megan Jean Sovern (Chronicle); *The Misadventures Of The Family Fletcher* by Dana Alison Levy (Random House); *Abrakapow!* by Isaiah Campbell (Simon & Schuster); *Subway Love* by Nora Raleigh Baskin (Candlewick).

TIPS "Writing and illustrations stand on their own, so submissions should tell the most compelling stories possible—whether visually, in words, or both."

❶ GELFMAN SCHNEIDER/ICM PARTNERS

850 7th Ave., Suite 903, New York NY 10019. (212)245-1993. **Fax:** (212)245-8678. **E-mail:** mail@gelfmanschneider.com. **Website:** www.gelfmanschneider.com. **Contact:** Jane Gelfman, Deborah Schneider. Member of AAR. Represents 300+ clients. 10% of clients are new/unpublished writers.

MEMBER AGENTS Deborah Schneider, Jane Gelfman, Victoria Marini, Heather Mitchell.

REPRESENTS fiction and nonfiction books. **Considers these fiction areas:** historical, literary, mainstream, middle-grade, mystery, science fiction, suspense, westerns, women's, young adult.

⚷ Does not want to receive romance or illustrated children's books.

HOW TO CONTACT Query. Send queries via snail mail only. No unsolicited mss. Please send a query letter, a synopsis, and a SAMPLE CHAPTER ONLY. Consult website for each agent's submission requirements. Note that Ms. Marini is the only agent at this agency who accepts e-queries: victoria.gsliterary@gmail.com. If querying Marini, put "Query" in the subject line and paste all materials (query, 1-3 sample chapters) in the body of the e-mail. Responds in 1 month to queries; in 2 months to mss.

TERMS Agent receives 15% commission on domestic sales. Agent receives 20% commission on foreign sales. Agent receives 15% commission on film sales. Offers written contract. Charges clients for photocopying and messengers/couriers.

GLASS LITERARY MANAGEMENT

138 West 25th St., 10th Floor, New York NY 10001. (646)237-4881. **E-mail:** submissions@glassliterary.com. **Website:** www.glassliterary.com. Estab. 2014. Member of AAR.

HOW TO CONTACT "Please send your query letter in the body of an e-mail and if we are interested, we will respond and ask for the complete ms or proposal. No attachments."

RECENT SALES *So That Happened: A Memoir* by Jon Cryer; *Lawless* by Matt Bondurant; *Bad Kid* by David Crabb.

❶ THE SUSAN GOLOMB LITERARY AGENCY

540 President St., 3rd Floor, Brooklyn NY 11215. **Fax:** (212)239-9503. **E-mail:** queries@sgolombagency.com. **Contact:** Susan Golomb; Krista Ingebretson.

MEMBER AGENTS Susan Golomb (accepts queries); **Krista Ingebretson** (accepts queries); **Soumeya Bendimerad** (literary fiction, upmarket/book club fiction, and select young adult and middle-grade; in nonfiction, she is seeking topics in popular culture, music and art history, unconventional business, politics, narrative nonfiction, sociology, cooking, travel, memoir).

REPRESENTS novels, short story collections. **Considers these fiction areas:** ethnic, historical, humor, literary, mainstream, middle-grade, satire, thriller, women's, young adult.

⌐ "We specialize in literary and upmarket fiction and nonfiction that is original, vibrant and of excellent quality and craft. Nonfiction should be edifying, paradigm-shifting, fresh and entertaining." Actively seeking writers with strong voices.

HOW TO CONTACT Query by e-mail. Will respond if interested. Obtains most new clients through recommendations from others, solicitations, and unsolicited queries.

TERMS Offers written contract.

❶ IRENE GOODMAN LITERARY AGENCY

27 W. 24th St., Suite 700B, New York NY 10010. **Website:** www.irenegoodman.com. Member of AAR.

MEMBER AGENTS Irene Goodman (her fiction list includes upmarket women's fiction, middle-grade, young adult, thrillers, historical fiction, and mysteries; her nonfiction list includes pop culture, science, Francophilia, and lifestyle); **Beth Vesel** (narrative nonfiction, cultural criticism, psychology, science and memoir; **Miriam Kriss** (commercial fiction, and she represents everything from hardcover historical mysteries to all subgenres of romance, from young adult fiction to kick ass urban fantasies, and everything in between); **Barbara Poelle** (thrillers, literary suspense, young adult and upmarket fiction); **Rachel Ekstrom** (young adult, women's fiction, new adult, mysteries, thrillers, romance, and the occasional quirky work of nonfiction).

REPRESENTS nonfiction, novels. **Considers these fiction areas:** crime, detective, historical, mystery, romance, thriller, women's, young adult.

⌐ "Specializes in the finest in commercial fiction and nonfiction. We have a strong background in women's voices, including mysteries, romance, women's fiction, thrillers, suspense. Historical fiction is one of Irene's particular passions and Miriam is fanatical about modern urban fantasies. In nonfiction, Irene is looking for topics on narrative history, social issues and trends, education, Judaica, Francophilia, Anglophilia, other cultures, animals, food, crafts, and memoir." Barbara is looking for commercial thrillers with strong female protagonists; Miriam is looking for urban fantasy and edgy sci-fi/young adult. No children's picture books, screenplays, poetry, or inspirational fiction.

HOW TO CONTACT Query. Submit synopsis, first 10 pages. E-mail queries only! See the website submission page. No e-mail attachments. Query 1 agent only. Responds in 2 months to queries. Consult website for each agent's submission guidelines.

RECENT SALES *The Ark* by Boyd Morrison; *Isolation* by C.J. Lyons; *The Sleepwalkers* by Paul Grossman;

Dead Man's Moon by Devon Monk; *Becoming Marie Antoinette* by Juliet Grey; *What's Up Down There* by Lissa Rankin; *Beg for Mercy* by Toni Andrews; *The Devil Inside* by Jenna Black.

TIPS "We are receiving an unprecedented amount of e-mail queries. If you find that the mailbox is full, please try again in 2 weeks. E-mail queries to our personal addresses will not be answered. E-mails to our personal inboxes will be deleted."

○ ASHLEY GRAYSON LITERARY AGENCY

1342 W. 18th St., San Pedro CA 90732. **E-mail:** graysonagent@earthlink.net. **Website:** www.publishersmarketplace.com/members/CGrayson/. Estab. 1976. Member of AAR.

MEMBER AGENTS Ashley Grayson (fantasy, mystery, thrillers, young adult); Carolyn Grayson (chick lit, mystery, children's, nonfiction, women's fiction, romance, thrillers); Lois Winston (women's fiction, chick lit, mystery).

REPRESENTS nonfiction books, novels. **Considers these fiction areas:** fantasy, juvenile, middle-grade, multicultural, mystery, romance, science fiction, suspense, women's, young adult.

☛ "We represent literary and commercial fiction, as well as nonfiction for adults (self-help, parenting, pop culture, mind/body/spirit, true crime, business, science). We also represent fiction for younger readers (chapter books through YA). We are seeking more mysteries and thrillers." Actively seeking previously published fiction authors.

HOW TO CONTACT The agency is temporarily closed to queries from fiction writers who are not previously published at book length (self published or print-on-demand do not count). There are only 3 exceptions to this policy: (1) Unpublished authors who have received an offer from a reputable publisher, who need an agent before beginning contract negotiations; (2) Authors who are recommended by a published author, editor or agent who has read the work in question; (3) Authors whom we have met at conferences and from whom we have requested submissions. Nonfiction authors who are recognized within their field or area may still query with proposals. Note: We cannot review self-published, subsidy-published, and POD-published works to evaluate moving them to mainstream publishers.

TERMS Agent receives 15% commission on domestic sales. Agent receives 20% commission on foreign sales.

TIPS "We do request revisions as they are required. We are long-time agents, professional and known in the business. We perform professionally for our clients and we ask the same of them."

○ SANFORD J. GREENBURGER ASSOCIATES, INC.

55 Fifth Ave., New York NY 10003. (212)206-5600. **Fax:** (212)463-8718. **Website:** www.greenburger.com. Member of AAR. Represents 500 clients.

MEMBER AGENTS Matt Bialer, LRibar@sjga.com (fantasy, science fiction, thrillers, and mysteries as well as a select group of literary writers, and also loves smart narrative nonfiction including books about current events, popular culture, biography, history, music, race, and sports); Brenda Bowen, querybb@sjga.com (literary fiction, writers and illustrators of picture books, chapter books, and middle-grade and teen fiction); Lisa Gallagher, lgsubmissions@sjga.com (accessible literary fiction, quality commercial women's fiction, crime fiction, lively narrative nonfiction); Faith Hamlin, fhamlin@sjga.com (receives submissions by referral); Heide Lange, queryHL@sjga.com; Daniel Mandel, querydm@sjga.com (literary and commercial fiction, as well as memoirs and nonfiction about business, art, history, politics, sports, and popular culture); Courtney Miller-Callihan, cmiller@sjga.com (YA, middle-grade, women's fiction, romance, and historical novels, as well as nonfiction projects on unusual topics, humor, pop culture, and lifestyle books); Nicholas Ellison, nellison@sjga.com; Chelsea Lindman, clindman@sjga.com (playful literary fiction, upmarket crime fiction, and forward thinking or boundary-pushing nonfiction); Rachael Dillon Fried, rfried@sjga.com (both fiction and nonfiction authors, with a keen interest in unique literary voices, women's fiction, narrative nonfiction, memoir, and comedy); Lindsay Ribar, co-agents with Matt Bailer (young adult and middle-grade fiction); Thomas Miller (primarily nonfiction projects in the areas of wellness and health, popular culture, psychology and self-help, business, diet, spirituality, cooking, and narrative nonfiction).

REPRESENTS nonfiction books and novels. **Considers these fiction areas:** crime, fantasy, historical, literary, middle-grade, mystery, picture books, romance, science fiction, thriller, women's, young adult.

☛ No Westerns. No screenplays.

HOW TO CONTACT E-query. "Please look at each agent's profile page for current information about what each agent is looking for and for the correct e-mail address to use for queries to that agent. Please be sure to use the correct query e-mail address for each agent." Accepts simultaneous submissions. Responds in 2 months to queries and mss. Obtains most new clients through recommendations from others.

TERMS Agent receives 15% commission on domestic sales. Agent receives 20% commission on foreign sales. Charges for photocopying and books for foreign and subsidiary rights submissions.

RECENT SALES *Inferno* by Dan Brown; *Hidden Order* by Brad Thor; *The Chalice* by Nancy Bilveau; *Horns* by Joe Hill.

THE GREENHOUSE LITERARY AGENCY

4035 Ridge Top Road, Suite 550, Fairfax VA 22030. **E-mail:** submissions@greenhouseliterary.com. **Website:** www.greenhouseliterary.com. Member of AAR. Other memberships include SCBWI. Represents 20 clients. 100% of clients are new/unpublished writers. Currently handles juvenile books (100%).

Sarah Davies has had an editorial and management career in children's publishing spanning 25 years; for 5 years prior to launching the Greenhouse she was Publishing Director of Macmillan Children's Books in London, and publishing leading authors from both sides of the Atlantic.

MEMBER AGENTS Sarah Davies, vice president (middle-grade and young adult); **John M. Cusick**, agent (picture books, chapter books, middle-grade, YA); **Polly Nolan**, agent (fiction by U.K., Irish, Commonwealth—including Australia, NZ and India—authors, from picture books to young fiction series, through middle-grade and young adult).

REPRESENTS juvenile. **Considers these fiction areas:** juvenile, middle-grade, picture books, young adult.

"We exclusively represent authors writing fiction for children and teens. The agency has offices in both the U.S. and U.K., and Sarah Davies (who is British) personally represents authors to both markets. The agency's commission structure reflects this—taking 15% for sales to both U.S. and U.K., thus treating both as 'domestic' market.'" All genres of children's and YA fiction—ages 5+. Does not want to receive nonfiction, poetry, picture books (text or illustration) or work aimed at adults; short stories,

educational or religious/inspirational work, preschool/novelty material, or screenplays.

HOW TO CONTACT Query 1 agent only. Put the target agent's name in the subject line. Paste the first 5 pages of your story (or your complete picture book) after the query. Obtains most new clients through recommendations from others, solicitations, conferences.

TERMS Agent receives 15% commission on domestic sales. Agent receives 25% commission on foreign sales. Offers written contract. This agency occasionally charges for submission copies to film agents or foreign publishers.

RECENT SALES *Vengeance* by Megan Miranda (Bloomsbury); *Fiendish* by Brenna Yovanoff (Razorbill); *The Very Nearly Honorable League Of Pirates* by Caroline Carlson (Harpercollins); *We All Looked Up* by Tommy Wallach (Simon & Schuster); *Shutter* by Courtney Alameda (Feiwel/Macmillan); *Can't Look Away* by Donna Cooner (Scholastic); *Moonpenny Island* by Tricia Springstubb (Harpercollins); *The Chapel Wars* by Lindsey Leavitt (Bloomsbury); *The Third Twin* by C.J.Omololu (Delacorte).

WRITERS CONFERENCES Bologna Children's Book Fair, ALA and SCBWI conferences, BookExpo America.

TIPS "Before submitting material, authors should read the Greenhouse's 'Top 10 Tips for Authors of Children's Fiction' and carefully follow our submission guidelines which can be found on the website."

KATHRYN GREEN LITERARY AGENCY, LLC

250 West 57th St., Suite 2302, New York NY 10107. (212)245-4225. **Fax:** (212)245-4042. **E-mail:** query@kgreenagency.com. **Contact:** Kathy Green. Other memberships include Women's Media Group. Represents approximately 20 clients. 50% of clients are new/unpublished writers.

Prior to becoming an agent, Ms. Green was a book and magazine editor.

REPRESENTS **Considers these fiction areas:** crime, detective, family saga, historical, humor, juvenile, literary, mainstream, middle-grade, mystery, police, romance, satire, suspense, thriller, women's, young adult.

Keeping the client list small means that writers receive my full attention throughout the process of getting their project published. Does not want to receive science fiction or fantasy.

HOW TO CONTACT Query to query@kgreenagency.com. Send no samples unless requested. Accepts simultaneous submissions. Responds in 1-2 months to mss. Obtains most new clients through recommendations from others, solicitations, conferences.

TERMS Agent receives 15% commission on domestic sales. Agent receives 20% commission on foreign sales.

🌑🛈 GREGORY & COMPANY AUTHORS' AGENTS

3 Barb Mews, Hammersmith, London W6 7PA England. (44)(207)610-4676. **Fax:** (44)(207)610-4686. **E-mail:** info@gregoryandcompany.co.uk. **Website:** www.gregoryandcompany.co.uk. Other memberships include AAA.

MEMBER AGENTS Jane Gregory, Stephanie Glencross, Claire Morris.

REPRESENTS Considers these fiction areas: crime, detective, historical, literary, thriller, women's.

�━◄ As a British agency, we do not generally take on American authors. Actively seeking well-written, accessible novels. Does not want to receive horror, science fiction, fantasy, mind/body/spirit, children's books, screenplays, plays, short stories or poetry.

HOW TO CONTACT Query with SASE. Submit outline, first 10 pages by e-mail or post, publishing history, author bio. Send submissions to Mary Jones, submissions editor: maryjones@gregoryandcompany. co.uk. Accepts simultaneous submissions. Returns materials only with SASE. Obtains most new clients through recommendations from others, conferences.

TERMS Agent receives 15% commission on domestic sales. Agent receives 20% commission on foreign sales. Offers written contract; one-month notice must be given to terminate contract. Charges clients for photocopying of whole typescripts and copies of book for submissions.

🛈 JILL GRINBERG LITERARY AGENCY

392 Vanderbilt Ave., Brooklyn NY 11238. (212)620-5883. **Fax:** (212)627-4725. **E-mail:** info@jillgrinbergliterary.com. **Website:** www.jillgrinbergliterary.com. Estab. 1999.

💬 Prior to her current position, Ms. Grinberg was at Anderson Grinberg Literary Management.

MEMBER AGENTS Jill Grinberg, jill@jillgrinbergliterary.com; **Cheryl Pientka**, cheryl@jillgrinbergliterary.com; **Katelyn Detweiler**, katelyn@jillgrinbergliterary.com.

REPRESENTS nonfiction books, novels. **Considers these fiction areas:** fantasy, juvenile, literary, mainstream, romance, science fiction, young adult.

HOW TO CONTACT Please send your query letter to info@jillgrinbergliterary.com and attach the first 50 pages (fiction) or proposal (nonfiction) as a Word doc file. All submissions will be read, but electronic mail is preferred.

RECENT SALES *Cinder*, Marissa Meyer; *The Hero's Guide to Saving Your Kingdom*, Christopher Healy; *Kiss and Make Up*, Katie Anderson; *i*, T.J. Stiles; *Eon and Eona*, Alison Goodman; *American Nations*, Colin Woodard; *HALO Trilogy*, Alexandra Adornetto; *Babymouse*, Jennifer and Matthew Holm; Uglies/Leviathan Trilogy, Scott Westerfeld; *Liar*, Justine Larbalestier; *Turtle in Paradise*, Jennifer Holm; *Wisdom's Kiss* and *Dairy Queen*, Catherine Gilbert Murdock.

TIPS "We prefer submissions by mail."

🛈 JILL GROSJEAN LITERARY AGENCY

1390 Millstone Rd., Sag Harbor NY 11963. (631)725-7419. **E-mail:** JillLit310@aol.com. **Contact:** Jill Grosjean. Estab. 1999. No No

💬 Prior to becoming an agent, Ms. Grosjean managed an independent bookstore. She also worked in publishing and advertising.

REPRESENTS Considers these fiction areas: literary, mainstream, mystery.

�━◄ Actively seeking literary novels and mysteries.

HOW TO CONTACT E-mail queries preferred, no attachments. No cold calls, please. Accepts simultaneous submissions, though when ms requested, requires exclusive reading time. Accepts simultaneous submissions. Responds in 1 week to queries; 1 month to mss. Obtains most new clients through recommendations and solicitations.

TERMS Agent receives 15% commission on domestic sales; 20% commission on foreign and film sales.

RECENT SALES *A Spark of Death*, *Fatal Induction*, and *Capacity for Murder* by Bernadette Pajer (Poison Pen Press); *Neutral Ground* by Greg Garrett (Bondfire Books); *Threading the Needle* by Marie Bostwick (Kensington Publishing); *Tim Cratchit's Christmas Carol: A Novel of Scrooge's Legacy* by Jim Piecuch (Simon & Schuster).

WRITERS CONFERENCES Thrillerfest; Texas Writer's League; Book Passage Mystery's Writer's Conference.

🛈 LAURA GROSS LITERARY AGENCY

P.O. Box 610326, Newton Highlands MA 02461. (617)964-2977. **E-mail:** query@lg-la.com. **Website:** www.lg-la.com. Estab. 1988. Represents 30 clients.

💬 Prior to becoming an agent, Ms. Gross was an editor and ran a reading series.

REPRESENTS nonfiction books, novels.

🔑 Actively seeking high-quality fiction—including mystery and suspense—as well as biography, books on cultural, social issues, currently affairs, history. Does not want romance, erotica, how-to, children's, screenplays.

HOW TO CONTACT Queries accepted online via online form on LGLA website. No e-mail queries. Responds in several days to queries.

TERMS Agent receives 15% commission on domestic sales. Agent receives 20% commission on foreign sales. Offers written contract.

⭕ HARTLINE LITERARY AGENCY

123 Queenston Dr., Pittsburgh PA 15235-5429. (412)829-2483. **Fax:** (412)829-2432. **E-mail:** joyce@hartlineliterary.com. **Website:** www.hartlineliterary.com. **Contact:** Joyce A. Hart. Represents 40 clients. 20% of clients are new/unpublished writers. Currently handles nonfiction books (40%), novels (60%).

MEMBER AGENTS Joyce A. Hart, principal agent (no unsolicited queries); **Jim Hart**, jim@hartlineliterary.com; **Terry Burns**: terry@hartlineliterary.com (some YA and middle-grade along with his other interests); **Diana Flegal**: diana@hartlineliterary.com; **Linda Glaz**, linda@hartlineliterary.com; **Andy Scheer**, andy@hartlineliterary.com.

REPRESENTS nonfiction books, novels.

🔑 "This agency specializes in the Christian bookseller market." Actively seeking adult fiction, self-help, nutritional books, Christian living, devotional, and business. Does not want to receive erotica, gay/lesbian, fantasy, horror, etc.

HOW TO CONTACT E-query only. Target 1 agent only. "All e-mail submissions sent to Hartline Agents should be sent as a MS Word doc (or in rich text file format from another word processing program) attached to an e-mail with "submission: title, authors name and word count" in the subject line. A proposal is a single document, not a collection of files. Place the query letter in the e-mail itself. Do not send the entire proposal in the body of the e-mail or send PDF files." Further guidelines online. Accepts simultaneous submissions. Responds in 2 months to queries; in 3 months to mss. Obtains most new clients through recommendations from others.

TERMS Agent receives 15% commission on domestic sales. Offers written contract.

⭕ JOHN HAWKINS & ASSOCIATES, INC.

80 Maiden Lane, Suite 1503, New York NY 10038. (212)807-7040. **Fax:** (212)807-9555. **E-mail:** jha@jhalit.com. **Website:** www.jhalit.com. **Contact:** Moses Cardona (rights and translations); Liz Free (permissions); Warren Frazier, literary agent; Anne Hawkins, literary agent. Member of AAR. Represents 100+ clients. 5-10% of clients are new/unpublished writers. Currently handles nonfiction books (40%), novels (40%), juvenile books (20%).

MEMBER AGENTS Moses Cardona, moses@jhalit.com (commercial fiction, suspense, business, science, and multicultural fiction); **Warren Frazier**, frazier@jhalit.com (nonfiction—technology, history, world affairs and foreign policy); **Anne Hawkins** ahawkins@jhalit.com (thrillers to literary fiction to serious nonfiction; she also has particular interests in science, history, public policy, medicine and women's issues).

REPRESENTS nonfiction books, novels. **Considers these fiction areas:** commercial, historical, literary, multicultural, suspense, thriller.

HOW TO CONTACT Query. Include the word "Query" in the subject line. For fiction, include 1-3 chapters of your book as a single Word attachment. For nonfiction, include your proposal as a single attachment. E-mail a particular agent directly if you are targeting one. Accepts simultaneous submissions. Responds in 1 month to queries. Obtains most new clients through recommendations from others.

TERMS Agent receives 15% commission on domestic sales. Agent receives 20% commission on foreign sales. Charges clients for photocopying.

RECENT SALES *Publishing* by Gail Godwin; *Interesting Facts: Stories* by Adam Johnson; *The Sacrifice* by Joyce Carol Oates; *Thin Air* by Ann Cleeves; *The Dead Student* by John Katzenbach; *The Catch* by Taylor Stevens.

⭕ HEACOCK HILL LITERARY AGENCY, INC.

West Coast Office, 1020 Hollywood Way, #439, Burbank CA 91505. (818)951-6788. **E-mail:** agent@heacockhill.com. **Website:** www.heacockhill.com. **Contact:** Catt LeBaigue or Tom Dark. Estab. 2009. Member of AAR. Other memberships include SCBWI.

◑ Prior to becoming an agent, Ms. LeBaigue spent 18 years with Sony Pictures and Warner Bros.

MEMBER AGENTS Tom Dark (adult fiction, nonfiction); **Catt LeBaigue** (juvenile fiction, adult nonfiction including arts, crafts, anthropology, astronomy, nature studies, ecology, body/mind/spirit, humanities, self-help).

REPRESENTS nonfiction, fiction. **Considers these fiction areas:** juvenile, middle-grade, picture books, young adult.

☞ Not presently accepting new clients for adult fiction. Please check the website for updates.

HOW TO CONTACT E-mail queries only. No unsolicited mss. No e-mail attachments. Responds in 1 week to queries. Obtains most new clients through recommendations from others, solicitations.

TERMS Offers written contract.

TIPS "Write an informative original e-query expressing your book idea, your qualifications, and short excerpts of the work. No unfinished work, please."

ⓘ RICHARD HENSHAW GROUP

145 W. 28th St., 12th Floor, New York NY 10001. (212)414-1172. **E-mail:** submissions@henshaw.com. **Website:** www.richardhenshawgroup.com. **Contact:** Rich Henshaw. Member of AAR.

○ Prior to opening his agency, Mr. Henshaw served as an agent with Richard Curtis Associates, Inc.

MEMBER AGENTS Richard Henshaw; Susannah Taylor.

REPRESENTS nonfiction books, novels. **Considers these fiction areas:** crime, detective, fantasy, historical, horror, literary, mainstream, mystery, police, science fiction, supernatural, suspense, thriller, young adult.

☞ This agency specializes in thrillers, mysteries, science fiction, fantasy and horror. "We only consider works between 65,000-150,000 words." "We do not represent children's books, screenplays, short fiction, poetry, textbooks, scholarly works, or coffee-table books."

HOW TO CONTACT "Please feel free to submit a query letter in the form of an e-mail of fewer than 250 words to submissions@henshaw.com address." No snail mail queries. Responds in 3 weeks to queries; in 6 weeks to mss. Obtains most new clients through recommendations from others, solicitations, conferences.

TERMS Agent receives 15% commission on domestic sales. Agent receives 20% commission on foreign sales. No written contract. Charges clients for photocopying and book orders.

RECENT SALES *Though Not Dead* by Dana Stabenow; *The Perfect Suspect* by Margaret Coel; *City of Ruins* by Kristine Kathryn Rusch; *A Dead Man's Tale*

by James D. Doss, *Wickedly Charming* by Kristine Grayson, History of the World series by Susan Wise Bauer; *Notorious Pleasures* by Elizabeth Hoyt.

TIPS "While we do not have any reason to believe that our submission guidelines will change in the near future, writers can find up-to-date submission policy information on our website. Always include a SASE with correct return postage."

ⓘ HIDDEN VALUE GROUP

27758 Santa Margarita Pkwy., #361, Mission Viejo CA 92691. **E-mail:** bookquery@hiddenvaluegroup. com. **Website:** www.hiddenvaluegroup.com. **Contact:** Nancy Jernigan. Represents 55 clients. 10% of clients are new/unpublished writers.

MEMBER AGENTS Jeff Jernigan, jjernigan@hiddenvaluegroup.com (men's nonfiction, fiction, Bible studies/curriculum, marriage and family); Nancy Jernigan, njernigan@hiddenvaluegroup.com (nonfiction, women's issues, inspiration, marriage and family, fiction).

REPRESENTS nonfiction books and adult fiction; no poetry.

☞ We are currently interested in receiving proposals in a variety of genres such as family/parenting/marriage, inspirational, self-help, men's and women's issues, business and fiction. No poetry or short stories. Actively seeking established fiction authors, and authors who are focusing on women's issues. Does not want to receive poetry or short stories.

HOW TO CONTACT Query with SASE. Submit synopsis, 2 sample chapters, author bio, and marketing and speaking summary. Accepts queries to bookquery@hiddenvaluegroup.com. No fax queries. Responds in 1 month to queries; in 1 month to mss. Obtains most new clients through recommendations from others, solicitations.

TERMS Agent receives 15% commission on domestic sales. Agent receives 15% commission on foreign sales. Offers written contract.

WRITERS CONFERENCES Glorieta Christian Writers Conference; CLASS Publishing Conference.

HOPKINS LITERARY ASSOCIATES

2117 Buffalo Rd., Suite 327, Rochester NY 14624-1507. (585)352-6268. **Contact:** Pam Hopkins. Member of AAR. Other memberships include RWA.

REPRESENTS novels. **Considers these fiction areas:** romance, women's.

☞ This agency specializes in women's fiction, particularly historical, contemporary, and category romance, as well as mainstream work.

HOW TO CONTACT Regular mail with synopsis, 3 sample chapters (or first 50 pages), SASE. Accepts simultaneous submissions. Obtains most new clients through recommendations from others, solicitations, conferences.

TERMS Agent receives 15% commission on domestic sales. Agent receives 20% commission on foreign sales. No written contract.

WRITERS CONFERENCES RWA National Conference.

⦿ ANDREA HURST & ASSOCIATES

P.O. Box 1467, Coupeville WA 98239. **E-mail:** andrea@andreahurst.com. **Website:** www.andreahurst.com/literary-management/. **Contact:** Andrea Hurst. Represents 100+ clients. 50% of clients are new/unpublished writers.

○ Prior to becoming an agent, Ms. Hurst was an acquisitions editor as well as a freelance editor and published writer.

MEMBER AGENTS Andrea Hurst, queryandrea@andreahurst.com (adult fiction, women's fiction, nonfiction, including personal growth, health and wellness, science, business, parenting, relationships, women's issues, animals, spirituality, women's issues, metaphysical, psychological, cookbooks, and self-help); **Katie Reed**, querykate@andreahurst.com, (represents YA fiction and nonfiction and adult nonfiction); **Genevieve Nine**, querygenevieve@andreahurst.com (young adult, middle-grade, mystery, thriller, historical, romantic comedy, magical realism, food memoir, travel memoir); **Amberly Finarelli** (not accepting new queries).

REPRESENTS nonfiction, novels, juvenile books. **Considers these fiction areas:** fantasy, historical, literary, mainstream, mystery, romance, science fiction, suspense, thriller, women's, young adult.

☞ "We work directly with our signed authors to help them polish their work and their platform for optimum marketability. Our staff is always available to answer phone calls and e-mails from our authors and we stay with a project until we have exhausted all publishing avenues." Actively seeking "well written nonfiction by authors with a strong platform; superbly crafted fiction with depth that touches the mind and heart and all of our listed subjects." Does not want to receive horror, Western, poetry, or screenplays.

HOW TO CONTACT E-mail query with SASE. Submit outline/proposal, synopsis, 2 sample chapters, author bio. Query a specific agent after reviewing website. Use (agentfirstname)@andreahurst.com. Accepts simultaneous submissions. Obtains most new clients through recommendations from others, solicitations, conferences.

TERMS Agent receives 15% commission on domestic sales. Agent receives 20% commission on foreign sales. Offers written contract, binding for 6-12 months; 30-day notice must be given to terminate contract. This agency charges for postage. No reading fees.

RECENT SALES *Art of Healing* by Bernie Siegel; *Truly, Madly, Deadly* by Hannah Jayne; *Ultimate Poultry Cookbook* by Chef John Ash; *The Guestbook* by Andrea Hurst; *No Buddy Left Behind* by Terrir Crisp and Cindy Hurn, Lyons Press; *A Year of Miracles* Dr. Bernie Siegel, NWL; *Selling Your Crafts on Etsy* (St. Martin's); *The Underground Detective Agency* (Kensington); *Alaskan Seafood Cookbook* (Globe Pequot); *Faith, Hope and Healing* by Dr. Bernie Siegel (Rodale); *Code Name: Polar Ice* by Jean-Michel Cousteau and James Fraioli (Gibbs Smith); *How to Host a Killer Party* by Penny Warner (Berkley/Penguin).

WRITERS CONFERENCES San Francisco Writers Conference; Willamette Writers Conference; PNWA; Whidbey Island Writers Conference.

TIPS "Do your homework and submit a professional package. Get to know the agent you are submitting to by researching their website or meeting them at a conference. Perfect your craft: Write well and edit ruthlessly over and over again before submitting to an agent. Be realistic: Understand that publishing is a business and be prepared to prove why your book is marketable and how you will market it on your own. Be persistent! Andrea Hurst is no longer accepting unsolicited query letters. Unless you have been referred by one of our authors, an agent or publisher, please check our website for another appropriate agent. www.andreahurst.com."

INKLINGS LITERARY AGENCY

8363 Highgate Drive, Jacksonville FL 32216. (904)527-1686. **Fax:** (904)758-5440. **Website:** www.inklingsliterary.com. Estab. 2013.

MEMBER AGENTS Michelle Johnson, michelle@inklingsliterary.com (in fiction, contemporary, suspense, thriller, mystery, horror, fantasy—including paranormal and supernatural elements within those genres), romance of every level, nonfiction in the areas of memoir and true crime); **Dr. Jamie Bodnar Drowley**, jamie@inklingsliterary.com (new adult fiction in the areas of romance [all subgenres], fantasy [urban fantasy, light sci-fi, steampunk], mystery and thrillers—as well as young adult [all subgenres] and middle-grade stories); **Margaret Bail**, margaret@inklingsliterary.com (romance, science fiction, mystery, thrillers, action adventure, historical fiction, Western, some fantasy, memoir, cookbooks, true crime); **Naomi Davis**, naomi@inklingsliterary.com (romance of any variety—including paranormal, fresh urban fantasy, general fantasy, new adult, and light sci-fi; young adult in any of those same genres; memoirs about living with disabilities, facing criticism, and mental illness); **Whitley Abell**, whitley@inklingsliterary.com (young adult, middle-grade, and select upmarket women's fiction); **Alex Barba**, alex@inklingsliterary.com (YA fiction).

HOW TO CONTACT E-queries only. To query, type "Query (Agent Name)" plus the title of your novel in the subject line, then please send the following pasted into the body of the e-mail to query@inklingsliterary.com. Check the agency website to make sure that your targeted agent is currently open to submissions.

◐ INKWELL MANAGEMENT, LLC

521 Fifth Ave., 26th Floor, New York NY 10175. (212)922-3500. **Fax:** (212)922-0535. **E-mail:** submissions@inkwellmanagement.com. **Website:** www.inkwellmanagement.com. Represents 500 clients.

MEMBER AGENTS Stephen Barbara (select adult fiction and nonfiction); **Lizz Blaise** (literary fiction, women's and young adult fiction, suspense, and psychological thriller); **William Callahan** (nonfiction of all stripes, especially American history and memoir, pop culture and illustrated books, as well as voice-driven fiction that stands out from the crowd); **Michael V Carlisle**; **Catherine Drayton** (best-selling authors of books for children, young adults and women readers); **David Forrer** (literary, commercial, historical and crime fiction to suspense/thriller, humorous nonfiction and popular history); **Alexis Hurley** (literary and commercial fiction, memoir, narrative nonfiction and more); **Nathaniel Jacks** (memoir, narrative nonfiction, social sciences, health, current affairs, business, religion, and popular history, as well

as fiction—literary and commercial, women's, young adult, historical, short story, among others); **Alyssa Mozdzen**; **Jacqueline Murphy**; (fiction, children's books, graphic novels and illustrated works, and compelling narrative nonfiction); **Richard Pine**; **Eliza Rothstein** (literary and commercial fiction, narrative nonfiction, memoir, popular science, and food writing); **Emma Schlee** (literary fiction, the occasional thriller, travel and adventure books, and popular culture and philosophy books); **Hannah Schwartz**; **David Hale Smith**; **Lauren Smythe** (smart narrative nonfiction [narrative journalism, modern history, biography, cultural criticism, personal essay, humor], personality-driven practical nonfiction [cookbooks, fashion and style], and contemporary literary fiction); **Kimberly Witherspoon**; **Monika Woods** (literary and commercial fiction, young adult, memoir, and compelling nonfiction in popular culture, science, and current affairs); **Lena Yarbrough** (literary fiction, upmarket commercial fiction, memoir, narrative nonfiction, history, investigative journalism, and cultural criticism).

REPRESENTS nonfiction books, novels. **Considers these fiction areas:** commercial, crime, historical, literary, middle-grade, picture books, romance, short story collections, suspense, thriller, women's, young adult.

HOW TO CONTACT In the body of your e-mail, please include a query letter and a short writing sample (1-2 chapters). We currently accept submissions in all genres except screenplays. Due to the volume of queries we receive, our response time may take up to 2 months. Feel free to put "Query for [Agent Name]: [Your Book Title]" in the e-mail subject line. Obtains most new clients through recommendations from others.

TERMS Agent receives 15% commission on domestic sales. Agent receives 20% commission on foreign sales. Offers written contract.

TIPS "We will not read mss before receiving a letter of inquiry."

⊘ ◉ ICM PARTNERS

730 Fifth Ave., New York NY 10019. (212)556-5600. **Website:** www.icmtalent.com. **Contact:** Literary Department. Member of AAR. Signatory of WGA.

REPRESENTS nonfiction, fiction, novels, juvenile books.

✂━ *"We do not accept unsolicited submissions."*

HOW TO CONTACT This agency is generally not open to unsolicited submissions. However, some agents do attend conferences and meet writers then. The agents take referrals, as well. Obtains most new clients through recommendations from others.

TERMS Agent receives 15% commission on domestic sales. Agent receives 20% commission on foreign sales.

⊘ INTERNATIONAL TRANSACTIONS, INC.

P.O. Box 97, Gila NM 88038-0097. (845)373-9696. **Fax:** (480)393-5162. **E-mail:** submission-nonfiction@ intltrans.com; submission-fiction@intltrans.com. **Website:** www.intltrans.com. **Contact:** Peter Riva.

MEMBER AGENTS Peter Riva (nonfiction, fiction, illustrated; television and movie rights placement); Sandra Riva (fiction, juvenile, biographies); JoAnn Collins (fiction, women's fiction, medical fiction).

REPRESENTS nonfiction books, novels, short story collections, juvenile, scholarly illustrated books, anthologies. **Considers these fiction areas:** action, adventure, crime, detective, erotica, experimental, family saga, feminist, gay, historical, humor, lesbian, literary, mainstream, mystery, police, satire, spiritual, sports, suspense, thriller, women's, young adult chick lit.

⊶ "We specialize in large and small projects, helping qualified authors perfect material for publication." Actively seeking intelligent, well-written innovative material that breaks new ground. Does not want to receive material influenced by TV (too much dialogue); a rehash of previous successful novels' themes, or poorly prepared material.

HOW TO CONTACT First, e-query with an outline or synopsis. E-queries only. Put "Query: [Title]" in the e-mail subject line. Responds in 3 weeks to queries. Responds in 5 weeks to mss. Obtains most new clients through recommendations from others, solicitations.

TERMS Agent receives 15% (25% on illustrated books) commission on domestic sales. Agent receives 20% commission on foreign sales. Offers written contract; 120-day notice must be given to terminate contract.

TIPS "'Book'—a published work of literature. That last word is the key. Not a string of words, not a book of (TV or film) 'scenes,' and never a stream of consciousness unfathomable by anyone outside of the writer's coterie. A writer should only begin to get 'interested in getting an agent' if the work is polished, literate and ready to be presented to a publishing house. Anything less is either asking for a quick rejection or is a thinly disguised plea for creative assistance—which is often given but never fiscally sound for the agents involved. Writers, even published authors, have difficulty in being objective about their own work. Friends and family are of no assistance in that process either. Writers should attempt to get their work read by the most unlikely and stern critic as part of the editing process, months before any agent is approached. In another matter: the economics of our job have changed as well. As the publishing world goes through the transition to e-books (much as the music industry went through the change to downloadable music)—a transition we expect to see at 95% within 10 years—everyone is nervous and wants 'assured bestsellers' from which to eke out a living until they know what the new e-world will bring. This makes the sales rate and, especially, the advance royalty rates, plummet. Hence, our ability to take risks and take on new clients' work is increasingly perilous financially for us and all agents."

◑ JABBERWOCKY LITERARY AGENCY

49 West 45th St., New York NY 10036. (718)392-5985. **Website:** www.awfulagent.com. **Contact:** Joshua Bilmes. Other memberships include SFWA. Represents 40 clients. 15% of clients are new/unpublished writers. Currently handles nonfiction books (15%), novels (75%), scholarly books (5%), other (5% other).

MEMBER AGENTS Joshua Bilmes; Eddie Schneider; Lisa Rodgers; Sam Morgan.

REPRESENTS novels. **Considers these fiction areas:** action, adventure, contemporary issues, crime, detective, ethnic, family saga, fantasy, gay, glitz, historical, horror, humor, lesbian, literary, mainstream, middle-grade, police, psychic, regional, satire, science fiction, sports, supernatural, thriller, young adult.

⊶ This agency represents quite a lot of genre fiction and is actively seeking to increase the amount of nonfiction projects. It does not handle children's or picture books. Book-length material only—no poetry, articles, or short fiction.

HOW TO CONTACT "We are currently open to unsolicited queries. No e-mail, phone, or fax queries, please. Query with SASE. Please check our website, as there may be times during the year when we are not accepting queries. Query letter only; no ms material unless requested." Accepts simultaneous submissions. Responds in 3 weeks to queries. Obtains most new clients through solicitations, recommendation by current clients.

TERMS Agent receives 15% commission on domestic sales. Agent receives 20% commission on foreign sales. Offers written contract, binding for 1 year. Charges clients for book purchases, photocopying, international book/ms mailing.

RECENT SALES 188 individual deals done in 2014: 60 domestic and 128 foreign. *Alcatraz #5* by Brandon Sanderson; *Aurora Teagarden* by Charlaine Harris; *The Unnoticeables* by Robert Brockway; *Messenger's Legacy* by Peter V. Brett; *Slotter Key* by Elizabeth Moon. Other clients include Tanya Huff, Simon Green, Jack Campbell, Myke Cole, Marie Brennan, Daniel Jose Older, Jim Hines, Mark Hodder, Toni Kelner, Ari Marmell, Ellery Queen, Erin Tettensor, and Walter Jon Williams.

TIPS "In approaching with a query, the most important things to us are your credits and your biographical background to the extent it's relevant to your work. I (and most agents) will ignore the adjectives you may choose to describe your own work."

J DE S ASSOCIATES, INC.

9 Shagbark Road, Wilson Point, South Norwalk CT 06854. (203)838-7571. **E-mail:** jdespoel@aol.com. **Website:** www.jdesassociates.com. **Contact:** Jacques de Spoelberch.

Prior to opening his agency, Mr. de Spoelberch was an editor with Houghton Mifflin.

REPRESENTS nonfiction books, novels. **Considers these fiction areas:** crime, detective, frontier, historical, juvenile, literary, mainstream, mystery, New Age, police, suspense, westerns, young adult.

HOW TO CONTACT "Brief queries by regular mail and e-mail are welcomed for fiction and nonfiction, but kindly do not include sample proposals or other material unless specifically requested to do so." Responds in 2 months to queries. Obtains most new clients through recommendations from authors and other clients.

TERMS Agent receives 15% commission on domestic sales. Agent receives 20% commission on foreign sales. Charges clients for foreign postage and photocopying.

RECENT SALES Joshilyn Jackson's new novel *A Grown-Up Kind of Pretty* (Grand Central), Margaret George's final Tudor historical *Elizabeth I* (Penguin), the fifth in Leighton Gage's series of Brazilian thrillers *A Vine in the Blood* (Soho), Genevieve Graham's romance *Under the Same Sky* (Berkley Sensation), Hilary Holladay's biography of the early Beat Herbert Huncke, *American Hipster* (Magnus), Ron Rozelle's *My Boys and Girls Are In There: The 1937 New London School Explosion* (Texas A&M), the concluding novel in Dom Testa's YA science fiction series, *The Galahad Legacy* (Tor), and Bruce Coston's new collection of animal stories *The Gift of Pets* (St. Martin's Press).

JET LITERARY ASSOCIATES

941 Calle Mejia, #507, Santa Fe NM 87501. (505)780-0721. **E-mail:** etp@jetliterary.com. **Website:** www.jetliterary.com. **Contact:** Liz Trupin-Pulli. Represents 75 clients. 35% of clients are new/unpublished writers.

MEMBER AGENTS Liz Trupin-Pulli (adult fiction/nonfiction; romance, mysteries, parenting); **Jim Trupin** (adult fiction/nonfiction, military history, pop culture).

REPRESENTS nonfiction books, novels, short story collections.

"JET was founded in New York in 1975, so we bring a wealth of knowledge and contacts, as well as quite a bit of expertise to our representation of writers." JET represents the full range of adult fiction and nonfiction, including humor and cookbooks. Does not want to receive YA, sci-fi, fantasy, horror, poetry, children's, or religious books.

HOW TO CONTACT An e-query only is accepted. Responds in 1 week to queries. Responds in 8 weeks to mss. Obtains most new clients through recommendations from others, solicitations, conferences.

TERMS Agent receives 15% commission on domestic sales. Agent receives 10% commission on foreign sales, while foreign agent receives 10%. Offers written agency contract, binding for 3 years. This agency charges for reimbursement of mailing and any photocopying.

TIPS "Do not write cute queries; stick to a straightforward message that includes the title and what your book is about, why you are suited to write this particular book, and what you have written in the past (if anything), along with a bit of a bio."

VIRGINIA KIDD LITERARY AGENCY, INC.

P.O. Box 278, Milford PA 18337. (570)296-6205. **Fax:** (570)296-7266. **Website:** www.vk-agency.com. Other memberships include SFWA, SFRA. Represents 80 clients.

REPRESENTS novels. **Considers these fiction areas:** fantasy, science fiction, speculative.

This agency specializes in science fiction and fantasy. "The Virginia Kidd Literary Agency is one of the longest established, science fiction specialized literary agencies in the world—with almost half a century of rich experience in the science fiction and fantasy genres. Our client list reads like a top notch 'who's-who' of science fiction: Beth Bernobich, Gene Wolfe, Anne McCaffrey, Ted Chiang, Alan Dean Foster and others set the bar very high indeed. Our authors have won Hugos, Nebulas, World Fantasy, Tiptree, National Book Award, PEN Malamud, SFWA Grandmaster, Gandalf, Locus Award, Margaret Edwards Award, IAMTW Lifetime Achievement Award (Grand Master), Rhysling Award, Author Emeritus SFWA, BSFA Award—and more. The point is, we represent the best of the best. We welcome queries from prospective and published authors."

HOW TO CONTACT Snail mail queries only.

TERMS Agent receives 15% commission on domestic sales. Agent receives 20-25% commission on foreign sales. Agent receives 20% commission on film sales. Offers written contract; two-month notice must be given to terminate contract. Charges clients occasionally for extraordinary expenses.

RECENT SALES *Sagramanda* by Alan Dean Foster (Pyr); *Incredible Good Fortune* by Ursula K. Le Guin (Shambhala); *The Wizard and Soldier of Sidon* by Gene Wolfe (Tor); *Voices and Powers* by Ursula K. Le Guin (Harcourt); *Galileo's Children* by Gardner Dozois (Pyr); *The Light Years Beneath My Feet* and *Running From the Deity* by Alan Dean Foster (Del Ray); *Chasing Fire* by Michelle Welch. Other clients include Eleanor Arnason, Ted Chiang, Jack Skillingstead, Daryl Gregory, Patricia Briggs, and the estates for James Tiptree, Jr., Murray Leinster, E.E. "Doc" Smith, R.A. Lafferty.

TIPS "If you have a completed novel that is of extraordinary quality, please send us a query."

HARVEY KLINGER, INC.

300 W. 55th St., Suite 11V, New York NY 10019. (212)581-7068. **E-mail:** queries@harveyklinger.com. **Website:** www.harveyklinger.com. **Contact:** Harvey Klinger. Member of AAR. Represents 100 clients. 25% of clients are new/unpublished writers. Currently handles nonfiction books (50%), novels (50%).

MEMBER AGENTS Harvey Kliinger; David Dunton (popular culture, music-related books, literary fiction, young adult, fiction, and memoirs); **Sara Crowe** (children's and young adult authors, adult fiction and nonfiction, foreign rights sales); **Andrea Somberg** (literary fiction, commercial fiction, romance, sci-fi/fantasy, mysteries/thrillers, young adult, middle-grade, quality narrative nonfiction, popular culture, how-to, self-help, humor, interior design, cookbooks, health/fitness).

REPRESENTS nonfiction books, novels. **Considers these fiction areas:** action, adventure, crime, detective, family saga, glitz, literary, mainstream, mystery, police, suspense, thriller.

This agency specializes in big, mainstream, contemporary fiction and nonfiction.

HOW TO CONTACT Use online e-mail submission form on the website, or query with SASE via snail mail. No phone or fax queries. Don't send unsolicited mss or e-mail attachments. Make submission letter to the point and as brief as possible. Responds in 2-4 weeks to queries, if interested. Obtains most new clients through recommendations from others.

TERMS Agent receives 15% commission on domestic sales. Agent receives 25% commission on foreign sales. Offers written contract. Charges for photocopying mss and overseas postage for mss.

RECENT SALES *Rainbows on the Moon* by Barbara Wood; *I Am Not a Serial Killer* by Dan Wells; *Me, Myself and Us* by Brian Little; *The Secret of Magic* by Deborah Johnson; *Children of the Mist*; by Paula Quinn. Other clients include: George Taber, Terry Kay, Scott Mebus, Jacqueline Kolosov, Jonathan Maberry, Tara Altebrando, Alex McAuley, Eva Nagorski, Greg Kot, Justine Musk, Michael Northrup, Nina LaCour, Ashley Kahn, Barbara De Angelis.

KNEERIM, WILLIAMS & BLOOM

90 Canal St., Boston MA 02114. **Website:** www.kw-blit.com. Also located in New York and Washington D.C. Estab. 1990.

Prior to becoming an agent, Mr. Williams was a lawyer; Ms. Kneerim was a publisher and editor; Mr. Wasserman was an editor and journalist; Ms. Bloom worked in magazines; Ms. Flynn worked in academia.

MEMBER AGENTS Brettne Bloom, bloom@kw-blit.com (memoir, history, current events, biography, travel, adventure, science, parenting, popular culture, cooking and food narratives, personal growth and women's issues, adult commercial and literary fiction and young adult fiction); **Katherine Flynn**, flynn@kwblit.com (history, biography, politics, current affairs, adventure, nature, pop culture, science, and psychology for nonfiction and particularly loves exciting narrative nonfiction; literary and commercial fiction with urban or foreign locales, crime novels, insight into women's lives, biting wit, and historical settings); **Jill Kneerim**, jill@kwblit.com (narrative history; sociology; psychology and anthropology; biography; women's issues; and good writing); **Ike Williams**, jtwilliams@kwblit.com (biography, history, politics, natural science, and anthropology); **Carol Franco**, carolfranco@comcast.net (business; nonfiction; distinguished self-help/how-to); **Gerald Gross**, ggreens336@comcast.net (array of nonfiction, serious history, and memoir).

⌒➻ Actively seeking distinguished authors, experts, professionals, intellectuals, and serious writers.

HOW TO CONTACT E-query an individual agent. Send no attachments. Put "Query" in the subject line. Accepts simultaneous submissions. Obtains most new clients through recommendations from others.

◑ KRAAS LITERARY AGENCY

E-mail: ikraas@yahoo.com. **Website:** www.kraasliteraryagency.com. **Contact:** Irene Kraas. Estab. 1990.
MEMBER AGENTS Irene Kraas, principal.
REPRESENTS **Considers these fiction areas:** mystery, thriller.

⌒➻ This agency is interested in working with published writers, but that does not mean self-published writers. Does not want to receive short stories, plays, or poetry. This agency no longer represents adult fantasy or science fiction.

HOW TO CONTACT Query and e-mail the first 10 pages of a completed ms. Requires exclusive read on mss. Attachments aren't accepted. Accepts simultaneous submissions.

TERMS Offers written contract.

TIPS "I am interested in material—in any genre—that is truly, truly unique."

◑ STUART KRICHEVSKY LITERARY AGENCY, INC.

381 Park Ave. S., Suite 428, New York NY 10016. (212)725-5288. **Fax:** (212)725-5275. **Website:** www.skagency.com. Member of AAR.

MEMBER AGENTS Stuart Krichevsky, query@skagency.com (emphasis on narrative nonfiction, literary journalism and literary and commercial fiction); **Allison Hunter**, AHquery@skagency.com (literary and commercial fiction, memoir, narrative nonfiction, cultural studies and pop culture; she is always looking for funny female writers, great love stories, family epics, and for nonfiction projects that speak to the current cultural climate); **Ross Harris**, RHquery@skagency.com (voice-driven humor and memoir, books on popular culture and our society, narrative nonfiction and literary fiction); **David Patterson**, dp@skagency.com (writers of upmarket narrative nonfiction and literary fiction, historians, journalists and thought leaders); **Shana Cohen**.

REPRESENTS nonfiction books, novels. **Considers these fiction areas:** commercial, contemporary issues, literary.

HOW TO CONTACT Please send a query letter and the first few (up to 10) pages of your ms or proposal in the body of an e-mail (not an attachment) to one of the e-mail addresses. No attachments. Responds if interested. Obtains most new clients through recommendations from others, solicitations.

EDITE KROLL LITERARY AGENCY, INC.

20 Cross St., Saco ME 04072. (207)283-8797. **Fax:** (207)283-8799. **E-mail:** ekroll@maine.rr.com. **Contact:** Edite Kroll. Represents 45 clients. 20% of clients are new/unpublished writers.

◗ Prior to opening her agency, Ms. Kroll served as a book editor and translator.

⌒➻ "We represent writers and writer-artists of both adult and children's books. We have a special focus on international feminist writers, women writers of nonfiction, and artists who write their own books (including children's and humor books)." Actively seeking artists who write their own books and international feminists who write in English. Does not represent genre fiction (mysteries, thrillers, diet, cookery, etc.), photography books, coffee table books, romance, or commercial fiction.

HOW TO CONTACT Query with SASE or by e-mail. Submit outline/proposal, synopsis, 1-2 sample chapters, author bio, entire ms (or dummy) if sending picture book. No phone queries. Responds in 2-4 weeks to queries; in 1-2 months to mss. Obtains most new clients through recommendations from others.

TERMS Agent receives 15% commission on domestic sales. Agent receives 20% commission on foreign sales. Offers written contract; 30-day notice must be given to terminate contract. Charges clients for photocopying and legal fees with prior approval from writer.

RECENT SALES Sold 12 domestic and 30 foreign titles in the last year. Clients include Shel Silverstein and Charlotte Zolotow estates.

TIPS "Please do your research so you won't send me books/proposals I specifically excluded."

KT LITERARY, LLC

9249 S. Broadway, #200-543, Highlands Ranch CO 80129. (720)344-4728. **Fax:** (720)344-4728. **E-mail:** queries@ktliterary.com. **Website:** ktliterary.com. **Contact:** Kate Schafer Testerman. Member of AAR. Other memberships include SCBWI. Represents 20 clients. 60% of clients are new/unpublished writers.

Prior to her current position, Ms. Schafer was an agent with Janklow & Nesbit.

MEMBER AGENTS Kate Schafer (middle-grade and young adult); **Renee Nyen** (middle-grade and young adult); **Sara Megibow**, saraquery@ktliterary.com (middle-grade, young adult, new adult, romance, erotica, science fiction and fantasy; LGBTQ and diversity friendly).

REPRESENTS Considers these fiction areas: middle-grade, young adult.

"We're thrilled to be actively seeking new clients writing brilliant, funny, original middle-grade and young adult fiction, both literary and commercial." Does not want picture books, serious nonfiction, and adult literary fiction.

HOW TO CONTACT "To submit to kt literary, please e-mail us a query letter with the first 3 pages of your ms in the body of the e-mail. The subject line of your e-mail should include the word 'Query' along with the title of your ms. Queries should not contain attachments. Attachments will not be read, and queries containing attachments will be deleted unread. We aim to reply to all queries within 2 weeks of receipt. No snail mail queries." Responds in 2 weeks to queries; in 2 months to mss. Obtains most new clients through recommendations from others, solicitations, conferences.

TERMS Agent receives 15% commission on domestic sales. Agent receives 20% commission on foreign sales. Offers written contract; 30-day notice must be given to terminate contract.

RECENT SALES *Albatross* by Julie Bloss; *The Last Good Place of Lily Odilon* by Sara Beitia; *Texting the Underworld* by Ellen Booraem. A full list of clients is available on the agency website.

WRITERS CONFERENCES Various SCBWI conferences, BookExpo.

TIPS "If we like your query, we'll ask for (more). Continuing advice is offered regularly on my blog 'Ask Daphne,' which can be accessed from my website."

THE LA LITERARY AGENCY

P.O. Box 46370, Los Angeles CA 90046. (323)654-5288. **E-mail:** ann@laliteraryagency.com; mail@laliteraryagency.com. **Website:** www.laliteraryagency.com. **Contact:** Ann Cashman.

Prior to becoming an agent, Eric Lasher worked in broadcasting and publishing in New York and Los Angeles. Prior to opening the agency, Maureen Lasher worked in New York at Prentice-Hall, Liveright, and Random House.

MEMBER AGENTS Ann Cashman, Eric Lasher, Maureen Lasher.

REPRESENTS nonfiction books, novels. **Considers these fiction areas:** commercial, literary.

HOW TO CONTACT Prefers submissions by mail, but welcomes e-mail submissions as well. Nonfiction: query letter and book proposal. Fiction: Query with outline and first 50 pages as an attachment, 1 sample chapter. Please visit the agency website for more info. Accepts simultaneous submissions.

RECENT SALES *The Fourth Trimester* by Susan Brink (University of California Press); *Rebels in Paradise* by Hunter Drohojowska-Philp (Holt); *La Cucina Mexicana* by Marilyn Tausend (UC Press); *The Orpheus Clock* by Simon Goodman (Scribner).

PETER LAMPACK AGENCY, INC.

The Empire State Building, 350 Fifth Ave., Suite 5300, New York NY 10118. (212)687-9106. **Fax:** (212)687-9109. **E-mail:** andrew@peterlampackagency.com. **Website:** www.peterlampackagency.com. **Contact:** Andrew Lampack.

REPRESENTS nonfiction books, novels. **Considers these fiction areas:** action, adventure, commercial, crime, detective, family saga, literary, mainstream, mystery, police, suspense, thriller.

"This agency specializes in commercial fiction, and nonfiction by recognized experts." Actively seeking literary and commercial fiction in the following categories: adventure, action, thrillers, mysteries, suspense, and psychological thrillers. Does not want to receive horror, romance, science fiction, westerns, historical literary fiction or academic material.

HOW TO CONTACT The Peter Lampack Agency no longer accepts material through conventional mail. E-queries only. When submitting, you should include a cover letter, author biography and a one- or two-page synopsis. Please do not send more than 1 sample chapter of your ms at a time. Due to the extremely high volume of submissions,we ask that you allow 4-6 weeks for a response. Accepts simultaneous submissions. Obtains most new clients through referrals made by clients.

TERMS Agent receives 15% commission on domestic sales. Agent receives 20% commission on foreign sales.

RECENT SALES *The Assassin by* Clive Cussler And Justin Scott; *The Solomon Curse* by Clive Cussler and Russell Blake; *Patriot* by Ted Bell; *The Good Story* by J.M. Coetzee And Arabella Kurtz; *Police State: How America's Cops Get Away With Murder* by Gerry Spence.

WRITERS CONFERENCES BookExpo America; Mystery Writers of America.

TIPS "Submit only your best work for consideration. Have a very specific agenda of goals you wish your prospective agent to accomplish for you. Provide the agent with a comprehensive statement of your credentials—educational and professional accomplishments."

❶ LAURA LANGLIE, LITERARY AGENT

147-149 Green St., Hudson NY 12534. (518)828-4708. **Fax:** (518)828-4787. **E-mail:** laura@lauralanglie.com. **Contact:** Laura Langlie. Represents 25 clients. 50% of clients are new/unpublished writers.

Prior to opening her agency, Ms. Langlie worked in publishing for 7 years and as an agent at Kidde, Hoyt & Picard for 6 years.

REPRESENTS Considers these fiction areas: crime, detective, ethnic, feminist, historical, humor, juvenile, literary, mainstream, mystery, police, suspense, thriller, young adult mainstream.

"I'm very involved with and committed to my clients. Most of my clients come to me via recommendations from other agents, clients and editors. I've met very few at conferences. I've often sought out writers for projects, and I still find new clients via the traditional query letter." Does not want to receive how-to, chil-

dren's picture books, hardcore science fiction, poetry, men's adventure, or erotica.

HOW TO CONTACT Query with SASE. Accepts queries via fax. Accepts simultaneous submissions. Responds in 1 week to queries. Responds in 1 month to mss. Obtains most new clients through recommendations, submissions.

TERMS Agent receives 15% commission on domestic sales. Agent receives 20% commission on foreign and dramatic sales. No written contract.

RECENT SALES Sold 15 titles in the last year. *The Evening Spider* by Emily Arsenault (William Morrow); *The Swans of 5th Avenue* by Melanie Benjamin (Delacorte Press).

TIPS "Be complete, forthright and clear in your communications. Do your research as to what a particular agent represents."

⊘ MICHAEL LARSEN/ELIZABETH POMADA, LITERARY AGENTS

1029 Jones St., San Francisco CA 94109. (415)673-0939. **E-mail:** larsenpoma@aol.com. **Website:** www.larsen-pomada.com. **Contact:** Mike Larsen, Elizabeth Pomada. Member of AAR. Other memberships include Authors Guild, ASJA, WNBA, California Writers Club, National Speakers Association. Represents 100 clients. 40-45% of clients are new/unpublished writers. Currently handles nonfiction books (70%), novels (30%).

Prior to opening their agency, Mr. Larsen and Ms. Pomada were promotion executives for major publishing houses. Mr. Larsen worked for Morrow, Bantam, and Pyramid (now part of Berkley); Ms. Pomada worked at Holt, David McKay and Dial Press. Mr. Larsen is the author of the 4th edition of *How to Write a Book Proposal* and *How to Get a Literary Agent* as well as the coauthor of *Guerilla Marketing for Writers: 100 Weapons for Selling Your Work*, which was republished in September 2009.

MEMBER AGENTS Michael Larsen (nonfiction); Elizabeth Pomada (fiction and narrative nonfiction).

REPRESENTS Considers these fiction areas: action, adventure, contemporary issues, crime, detective, ethnic, experimental, family saga, feminist, gay, glitz, historical, humor, inspirational, lesbian, literary, mainstream, mystery, police, religious, romance, satire, suspense.

We have diverse tastes. We look for fresh voices and new ideas. We handle literary, commercial and genre fiction, and the full range of non-fiction books. Actively seeking commercial, genre, and literary fiction. Does not want to receive children's books, plays, short stories, screenplays, pornography, poetry, or stories of abuse.

HOW TO CONTACT As of early 2015, this agency is closed to submissions for some time. Responds in 8 weeks to pages or submissions.

TERMS Agent receives 15% commission on domestic sales. Agent receives 20% (30% for Asia) commission on foreign sales. May charge for printing, postage for multiple submissions, foreign mail, foreign phone calls, galleys, books, legal fees.

WRITERS CONFERENCES This agency organizes the annual San Francisco Writers Conference (www.sfwriters.org).

TIPS "We love helping writers get the rewards and recognition they deserve. If you can write books that meet the needs of the marketplace and you can promote your books, now is the best time ever to be a writer. We must find new writers to make a living, so we are very eager to hear from new writers whose work will interest large houses, and nonfiction writers who can promote their books. For a list of recent sales, helpful info, and 3 ways to make yourself irresistible to any publisher, please visit our website."

THE STEVE LAUBE AGENCY

5025 N. Central Ave., #635, Phoenix AZ 85012. (602)336-8910. **Website:** www.stevelaube.com. Other memberships include CBA. Represents 60+ clients. 5% of clients are new/unpublished writers.

Prior to becoming an agent, Mr. Laube worked 11 years as a Christian bookseller and 11 years as editorial director of nonfiction with Bethany House Publishers. Mrs. Murray was an accomplished novelist and agent. Mrs. Ball was an executive editor with Tyndale, Multnomah, Zondervan, and B&H. Mr. Balow was marketing director for the Left Behind series at Tyndale.

MEMBER AGENTS Steve Laube, president, Tamela Hancock Murray, Karen Ball, or Dan Balow.

REPRESENTS nonfiction books, novels. **Considers these fiction areas:** inspirational, religious.

Primarily serves the Christian market (CBA). Actively seeking Christian fiction and religious nonfiction. Does not want to receive children's picture books, poetry, or cookbooks.

HOW TO CONTACT Submit proposal package, outline, 3 sample chapters, SASE. For e-mail submissions, attach as Word doc or PDF. Consult website for guidelines, because queries are sent to assistants, and the assistants' e-mail addresses must change. Accepts simultaneous submissions. Responds in 6-8 weeks to queries. Obtains most new clients through recommendations from others, solicitations, conferences.

TERMS Agent receives 15% commission on domestic sales. Agent receives 20% commission on foreign sales. Offers written contract; 30-day notice must be given to terminate contract.

RECENT SALES Sold 200 titles in the last year. Other clients include Deborah Raney, Allison Bottke, H. Norman Wright, Ellie Kay, Jack Cavanaugh, Karen Ball, Susan May Warren, Lisa Bergren, Cindy Woodsmall, Karol Ladd, Judith Pella, Margaret Daley, William Lane Craig, Ginny Aiken, Kim Vogel Sawyer, Mesu Andrews, Mary Hunt, Hugh Ross, Bill and Pam Farrel, Ronie Kendig.

WRITERS CONFERENCES Mount Hermon Christian Writers Conference; American Christian Fiction Writers Conference; ACFW.

ROBERT LECKER AGENCY

4055 Melrose Ave., Montreal QC H4A 2S5 Canada. **E-mail:** robert.lecker@gmail.com. **Website:** www.leckeragency.com. **Contact:** Robert Lecker. Represents 20 clients. 20% of clients are new/unpublished writers. Currently handles nonfiction books (80%), novels (10%), scholarly books (10%).

Prior to becoming an agent, Mr. Lecker was the cofounder and publisher of ECW Press and professor of English literature at McGill University. He has 30 years of experience in book and magazine publishing.

MEMBER AGENTS Robert Lecker (popular culture, music); Mary Williams (travel, food, popular science).

REPRESENTS nonfiction books, novels, scholarly syndicated material. **Considers these fiction areas:** action, adventure, crime, detective, erotica, literary, mainstream, mystery, police, suspense, thriller.

"RLA specializes in books about popular culture, popular science, music, entertainment, food, and travel. The agency responds to articulate, innovative proposals within 2 weeks. We do not represent children's literature, screenplays, poetry, self-help books, or spiritual guides."

HOW TO CONTACT E-query. In the subject line, write: "New Submission QUERY." Accepts simultaneous submissions. Responds in 2 weeks to queries. Responds in 1 month to mss. Obtains most new clients through recommendations from others, conferences, interest in website.

TERMS Agent receives 15% commission on domestic sales. Agent receives 15-20% commission on foreign sales. Offers written contract, binding for 1 year; 6-month notice must be given to terminate contract.

LEVINE GREENBERG ROSTAN LITERARY AGENCY, INC.

307 Seventh Ave., Suite 2407, New York NY 10001. (212)337-0934. **Fax:** (212)337-0948. **E-mail:** submit@levinegreenberg.com. **Website:** www.levinegreenberg.com. Member of AAR. Represents 250 clients. 33% of clients are new/unpublished writers. Currently handles nonfiction books (70%), novels (30%).

○ Prior to opening his agency, Mr. Levine served as vice president of the Bank Street College of Education.

MEMBER AGENTS Jim Levine; Stephanie Rostan (adult fiction, nonfiction, YA); Melissa Rowland; **Daniel Greenberg** (literary fiction; nonfiction: popular culture, narrative nonfiction, memoir, and humor); **Victoria Skurnick; Danielle Svetcov; Elizabeth Fisher; Lindsay Edgecombe** (narrative nonfiction, memoir, lifestyle and health, illustrated books, as well as literary fiction); **Monika Verma** (nonfiction: humor, pop culture, memoir, narrative nonfiction and style and fashion titles; some young adult fiction); **Kerry Sparks** (young adult and middle-grade); **Tim Wojcik** (quirky adventures, as-yet-untold oral histories, smart humor, anything sports, music and food-related, thrillers, mysteries, and literary fiction); **Arielle Eckstut** (no queries); **Kirsten Wolf** (adult and children's literature).

REPRESENTS nonfiction books, novels. **Considers these fiction areas:** literary, mainstream, middle-grade, mystery, thriller, women's, young adult.

➤ This agency specializes in business, psychology, parenting, health/medicine, narrative nonfiction, spirituality, religion, women's issues, and commercial fiction.

HOW TO CONTACT E-query, or online submission form. Do not submit directly to agents. Prefers electronic submissions. Cannot respond to submissions by mail. Do not attach more than 50 pages. Obtains most new clients through recommendations from others.

TERMS Agent receives 15% commission on domestic sales. Agent receives 20% commission on foreign sales. Offers written contract. Charges clients for out-of-pocket expenses—telephone, fax, postage, photocopying—directly connected to the project.

RECENT SALES *Gone Girl* by Gillian Flynn; *Hyperbole and a Half* by Allie Brosh; *Our Dumb Century* by editors of the The Onion; *Predictably Irrational* by Dan Ariely.

WRITERS CONFERENCES ASJA Writers Conference.

TIPS "We focus on editorial development, business representation, and publicity and marketing strategy."

◑ PAUL S. LEVINE LITERARY AGENCY

1054 Superba Ave., Venice CA 90291. (310)450-6711. **Fax:** (310)450-0181. **E-mail:** paul@paulslevinelit.com. **Website:** www.paulslevinelit.com. **Contact:** Paul S. Levine. Other memberships include the State Bar of California. Represents over 100 clients. 75% of clients are new/unpublished writers. Currently handles nonfiction books (60%), novels (10%), movie scripts (10%), TV scripts (5%), juvenile books (5%).

MEMBER AGENTS Paul S. Levine (children's and young adult fiction and nonfiction, adult fiction and nonfiction except sci-fi, fantasy, and horror); Loren R. Grossman (archaeology, art/photography/architecture, gardening, education, health, medicine, science).

REPRESENTS nonfiction books, novels, episodic drama, movie, TV, movie scripts, feature film, TV movie of the week, sitcom, animation, documentary, miniseries syndicated material, reality show. **Considers these fiction areas:** action, adventure, comic books, confession, crime, detective, erotica, ethnic, experimental, family saga, feminist, frontier, gay, glitz, historical, humor, inspirational, lesbian, literary, mainstream, mystery, police, regional, religious, romance, satire, sports, suspense, thriller, westerns.

➤ Does not want to receive science fiction, fantasy, or horror.

HOW TO CONTACT Query with SASE. Accepts simultaneous submissions. Responds in 1 day to queries. Responds in 6-8 weeks to mss. Obtains most new clients through conferences, referrals, listings on various websites and in directories.

TERMS Agent receives 15% commission on domestic sales. Offers written contract. Charges for postage and actual, out-of-pocket costs only.

RECENT SALES Sold 8 books in the last year.
WRITERS CONFERENCES Willamette Writers Conference; San Francisco Writers Conference; Santa Barbara Writers Conference; and many others.
TIPS "Write good, sellable books."

⬤ LIPPINCOTT MASSIE MCQUILKIN

27 West 20th Street, Suite 305, New York NY 10011. **Fax:** (212)352-2059. **E-mail:** info@lmqlit.com. **Website:** www.lmqlit.com.
MEMBER AGENTS Shannon O'Neill, shannon@lmqlit.com (narrative nonfiction and nonfiction in the areas of popular science, current affairs, history, and memoir; she is also interested in literary and upmarket commercial fiction); **Laney Katz Becker**, laney@lmqlit.com (book club fiction, smart thrillers and suspense, memoir and nonfiction from platform-heavy authors); **Kent Wolf**, kent@lmqlit.com (literary and commercial fiction, including young adult and select middle-grade, narrative nonfiction, memoir, essays, and pop culture); **Ethan Bassoff**, ethan@lmqlit.com (literary fiction, crime fiction, and narrative nonfiction in the areas of history, sports writing, journalism, science writing, pop culture, humor, and food writing); **Jason Anthony**, jason@lmqlit.com (commercial fiction of all types, including young adult, and nonfiction in the areas of memoir, pop culture, true crime, and general psychology and sociology); **Will Lippincott**, will@lmqlit.com (narrative nonfiction and nonfiction in the areas of politics, history, biography, foreign affairs, and health. He is not looking for fiction at this time); **Maria Massie**, maria@lmqlit.com (literary and upmarket commercial fiction [including select young adult and middle-grade], memoir, and narrative nonfiction); **Rob McQuilkin**, rob@lmqlit.com (literary fiction as well as narrative nonfiction and nonfiction in the areas of memoir, history, biography, art history, cultural criticism, and popular sociology and psychology); **Amanda Panitch**, amanda@lmqlit.com (young adult and middle-grade); **Rayhane Sanders**, rayhane@lmqlit.com (literary fiction, historical fiction, upmarket commercial fiction [including select YA], narrative nonfiction [including essays], and select memoir).
REPRESENTS nonfiction books, novels, short story collections, scholarly graphic novels. **Considers these fiction areas:** action, adventure, cartoon, comic books, confession, family saga, feminist, gay, historical, humor, lesbian, literary, mainstream, regional, satire.

⊶ "LMQ focuses on bringing new voices in literary and commercial fiction to the market, as well as popularizing the ideas and arguments of scholars in the fields of history, psychology, sociology, political science, and current affairs. Actively seeking fiction writers who already have credits in magazines and quarterlies, as well as nonfiction writers who already have a media platform or some kind of a university affiliation." Does not want to receive romance, genre fiction, or children's material.
HOW TO CONTACT E-query. Include the word 'Query' in the subject line of your e-mail. Review the agency's online page of agent bios (lmqlit.com/contact.html), as some agents want sample pages with their submissions and some no not. If you have not heard back from the agency in 4 weeks, assume they are not interested in seeing more. Accepts simultaneous submissions. Obtains most new clients through recommendations from others, solicitations, conferences.
TERMS Agent receives 15% commission on domestic sales. Agent receives 20% commission on foreign sales. Offers written contract; 30-day notice must be given to terminate contract. Only charges for reasonable business expenses upon successful sale.
RECENT SALES Clients include: Peter Ho Davies, Kim Addonizio, Natasha Trethewey, Anne Carson, David Sirota, Katie Crouch, Uwen Akpan, Lydia Millet, Tom Perrotta, Jonathan Lopez, Chris Hayes, Caroline Weber.

⬤ THE LITERARY GROUP INTERNATIONAL

1357 Broadway,, Suite 316, New York NY 10018. (212)400-1494, ext. 380. **Website:** www.theliterarygroup.com. **Contact:** Frank Weimann. 1900 Ave. of the Stars, 25 Fl., Los Angeles, CA 90067; Tel: (310)282-8961; **Fax:** (310) 282-8903 65% of clients are new/unpublished writers.
MEMBER AGENTS Frank Weimann.
REPRESENTS nonfiction books, novels graphic novels. **Considers these fiction areas:** adventure, contemporary issues, detective, ethnic, experimental, family saga, fantasy, feminist, historical, horror, humor, literary, multicultural, mystery, psychic, regional, romance, sports, thriller, young adult.
⊶ This agency specializes in nonfiction (memoir, military, history, biography, sports, how-to).
HOW TO CONTACT Query. Prefers to read materials exclusively. Only responds if interested. Obtains

most new clients through referrals, writers conferences, query letters.

TERMS Agent receives 15% commission on domestic sales. Agent receives 20% commission on foreign sales. Offers written contract; 30-day notice must be given to terminate contract.

RECENT SALES *As You Wish* by Cary Elwes (Simon and Schuster); *Ginger and Elvis* by Ginger Alden (Berkley); *Indulge* by Kathy Wakile (St. Martin's Press).

WRITERS CONFERENCES San Diego State University Writers Conference; Agents and Editors Conference; NAHJ Convention in Puerto Rico, others.

○ LITERARY MANAGEMENT GROUP, INC.

16970 San Carlos Blvd., Suite 160-100, Fort Myers FL 33908. **E-mail:** brucebarbour@literarymanagementgroup.com; brb@brucebarbour.com. **Website:** literarymanagementgroup.com; www.brucebarbour.com. **Contact:** Bruce Barbour.

⬤ Prior to becoming an agent, Mr. Barbour held executive positions at several publishing houses, including Revell, Barbour Books, Thomas Nelson, and Random House.

REPRESENTS nonfiction books, novels.

⤸ "Although we specialize in the area of Christian publishing from an Evangelical perspective, we have editorial contacts and experience in general interest books as well." Does not want to receive gift books, poetry, children's books, short stories, or juvenile/young adult fiction. No unsolicited mss or proposals from unpublished authors.

HOW TO CONTACT Query with SASE. E-mail proposal as an attachment. Consult website for each agent's submission guidelines.

TERMS Agent receives 15% commission on domestic sales.

○ LOWENSTEIN ASSOCIATES INC.

15 East 23rd St., Floor 4, New York NY 10010. (212)206-1630. **Fax:** (212)727-0280. **E-mail:** assistant@bookhaven.com. **Website:** www.lowensteinassociates.com. **Contact:** Barbara Lowenstein. Member of AAR.

MEMBER AGENTS Barbara Lowenstein, president (nonfiction interests include narrative nonfiction, health, money, finance, travel, multicultural, popular culture, and memoir; fiction interests include literary fiction and women's fiction).

REPRESENTS nonfiction books, novels. **Considers these fiction areas:** commercial, fantasy, literary, middle-grade, science fiction, women's, young adult.

⤸ Barbara Lowenstein is currently looking for writers who have a platform and are leading experts in their field, including business, women's issues, psychology, health, science and social issues, and is particularly interested in strong new voices in fiction and narrative nonfiction. Does not want Westerns, textbooks, children's picture books and books in need of translation.

HOW TO CONTACT "For fiction, please send us a one-page query letter, along with the first 10 pages pasted in the body of the message by e-mail to assistant@bookhaven.com. If nonfiction, please send a one-page query letter, a table of contents, and, if available, a proposal pasted into the body of the e-mail. Please put the word 'QUERY' and the title of your project in the subject field of your e-mail and address it to the agent of your choice. Please do not send an attachment as the message will be deleted without being read and no reply will be sent." Accepts simultaneous submissions. Responds in 6 weeks to queries. Obtains most new clients through recommendations from others, solicitations, conferences.

TERMS Agent receives 15% commission on domestic sales. Agent receives 20% commission on foreign sales. Offers written contract. Charges for large photocopy batches, messenger service, international postage.

TIPS "Know the genre you are working in and read!"

○ DONALD MAASS LITERARY AGENCY

121 W. 27th St., Suite 801, New York NY 10001. (212)727-8383. **Website:** www.maassagency.com. Estab. 1980. Member of AAR. Other memberships include SFWA, MWA, RWA. Represents more than 100 clients. 5% of clients are new/unpublished writers. Currently handles novels (100%).

⬤ Prior to opening his agency, Mr. Maass served as an editor at Dell Publishing (New York) and as a reader at Gollancz (London). He also served as the president of AAR.

MEMBER AGENTS Donald Maass (mainstream, literary, mystery/suspense, science fiction, romance); **Jennifer Jackson** (commercial fiction, romance, science fiction, fantasy, mystery/suspense); **Cameron McClure** (literary, mystery/suspense, urban, fantasy, narrative nonfiction and projects with multicultural, international, and environmental themes, gay/lesbian); **Stacia Decker** (fiction, memoir, narrative nonfiction, pop-culture [cooking, fashion, style, music, art], smart humor, upscale erotica/erotic memoir and multicultural fiction/nonfiction); **Amy Boggs** (fantasy and science fiction, especially urban fantasy, paranormal romance, steampunk, YA/children's, and alternate history. historical fiction, multicultural fiction, westerns); **Katie Shea Boutillier** (women's fiction/book club; edgy/dark, realistic/contemporary YA; commercial-scale literary fiction; and celebrity memoir); **Jennifer Udden** (speculative fiction (both science fiction and fantasy), urban fantasy, and mysteries, as well as historical, erotic, contemporary, and paranormal romance).

REPRESENTS nonfiction, novels. **Considers these fiction areas:** crime, detective, fantasy, historical, horror, literary, mainstream, multicultural, mystery, paranormal, police, psychic, romance, science fiction, supernatural, suspense, thriller, westerns, women's, young adult.

➤ This agency specializes in commercial fiction, especially science fiction, fantasy, mystery and suspense. Actively seeking to expand in literary fiction and women's fiction. We are fiction specialists. All genres are welcome.

HOW TO CONTACT E-query. All the agents have different submission addresses and instructions. See the website and each agent's online profile for exact submission instructions. Accepts simultaneous submissions.

TERMS Agent receives 15% commission on domestic sales. Agent receives 20% commission on foreign sales.

RECENT SALES *Codex Alera 5: Princep's Fury* by Jim Butcher (Ace); *Fonseca 6: Bright Futures* by Stuart Kaimsky (Forge): *Fathom* by Cherie Priest (Tor); *Gospel Grrls 3: Be Strong and Curvaceous* by Shelly Adina (Faith Words); *Ariane 1: Peacekeeper* by Laura Reeve (Roc); *Execution Dock* by Anne Perry (Random House).

WRITERS CONFERENCES Donald Maass: World Science Fiction Convention; Frankfurt Book Fair; Pacific Northwest Writers Conference; Bouchercon. Jennifer Jackson: World Science Fiction Convention; RWA National Conference.

TIPS We are fiction specialists, also noted for our innovative approach to career planning. Few new clients are accepted, but interested authors should query with a SASE. Works with subagents in all principle foreign

countries and Hollywood. No prescriptive nonfiction, picture books, or poetry will be considered.

⊘⊙ MACGREGOR LITERARY INC.

P.O. Box 1316, Manzanita OR 97130. (503)389-4803. **Website:** www.macgregorliterary.com. **Contact:** Chip MacGregor. Signatory of WGA. Represents 40 clients. 10% of clients are new/unpublished writers.Currently handles nonfiction books (40%), novels (60%).

💭 Prior to his current position, Mr. MacGregor was the senior agent with Alive Communications. Most recently, he was associate publisher for Time-Warner Book Group's Faith Division, and helped put together their Center Street imprint.

MEMBER AGENTS Chip MacGregor, Amanda Luedeke; Holly Lorincz; Erin Buterbaugh.

REPRESENTS nonfiction books, novels. **Considers these fiction areas:** crime, detective, historical, inspirational, mainstream, mystery, police, religious, romance, suspense, thriller, women's chick lit.

➤ "My specialty has been in career planning with authors—finding commercial ideas, then helping authors bring them to market, and in the midst of that assisting the authors as they get firmly established in their writing careers. I'm probably best known for my work with Christian books over the years, but I've done a fair amount of general market projects as well." Actively seeking authors with a Christian worldview and a growing platform. Does not want to receive fantasy, sci-fi, children's books, poetry or screenplays.

HOW TO CONTACT Do not query this agency without an invitation or referral. Accepts simultaneous submissions. Responds in 3 weeks to queries. Obtains most new clients through recommendations from others. Not looking to add unpublished authors except through referrals from current clients.

TERMS Agent receives 15% commission on domestic sales. Agent receives 15% commission on foreign sales. Offers written contract; 30-day notice must be given to terminate contract. Charges for exceptional fees after receiving authors' permission.

WRITERS CONFERENCES Blue Ridge Christian Writers Conference; Write to Publish.

TIPS "Seriously consider attending a good Writers Conference. It will give you the chance to be face-to-face with people in the industry. Also, if you're a novelist, consider joining one of the national writers' organizations. The American Christian Fiction Writers (ACFW) is a wonderful group for new as well as established writers. And if you're a Christian writer of any kind, check into The Writer's View, an online writing group. All of these have proven helpful to writers."

CAROL MANN AGENCY

55 Fifth Ave., New York NY 10003. (212)206-5635. **Fax:** (212)675-4809. **E-mail:** submissions@carolmannagency.com. **Website:** www.carolmannagency.com. **Contact:** Lydia Byfield. Member of AAR. Represents roughly 200 clients. 15% of clients are new/unpublished writers.

MEMBER AGENTS Carol Mann (health/medical, religion, spirituality, self-help,parenting, narrative nonfiction, current affairs); **Laura Yorke; Gareth Esersky; Myrsini Stephanides** (nonfiction areas of interest: pop culture and music, humor, narrative nonfiction and memoir, cookbooks; fiction areas of interest: offbeat literary fiction, graphic works, and edgy YA fiction); **Joanne Wyckoff** (nonfiction areas of interest: memoir, narrative nonfiction,personal narrative, psychology, women's issues, education, health and wellness, parenting, serious self-help, natural history; also accepts fiction).

REPRESENTS nonfiction books, novels. **Considers these fiction areas:** commercial, literary, young adult graphic works.

Does not want to receive genre fiction (romance, mystery, etc.).

HOW TO CONTACT Please see website for submission guidelines. Responds in 4 weeks to queries.

TERMS Agent receives 15% commission on domestic sales. Agent receives 20% commission on foreign sales. Offers written contract.

MANSION STREET LITERARY MANAGEMENT

Website: mansionstreet.com. **Contact:** Jean Sagendorph; Michelle Witte.

MEMBER AGENTS Jean Sagendorph, querymansionstreet@gmail.com (pop culture, gift books, cookbooks, general nonfiction, lifestyle, design, brand extensions), **Michelle Witte**, querymichelle@mansionstreet.com (young adult, middle-grade, juvenile nonfiction).

REPRESENTS Considers these fiction areas: juvenile, middle-grade, young adult.

HOW TO CONTACT Send a query letter and no more than the first 10 pages of your ms in the body of an e-mail. Query 1 specific agent at this agency. No attachments. You must list the genre in the subject line. If the genre is not in the subject line, your query will be deleted. Responds in 6 weeks.

RECENT SALES Authors: Paul Thurlby, Steve Ouch, Steve Seabury, Gina Hyams, Sam Pocker, Kim Siebold, Jean Sagendorph, Heidi Antman, Shannon O'Malley, Meg Bartholomy, Dawn Sokol, Hollister Hovey, Porter Hovey, Robb Pearlman.

MANUS & ASSOCIATES LITERARY AGENCY, INC.

425 Sherman Ave., Suite 200, Palo Alto CA 94306. (650)470-5151. **Fax:** (650)470-5159. **Website:** www.manuslit.com. **Contact:** Jillian Manus, Jandy Nelson, Penny Nelson. NYC address: 444 Madison Ave., 29th Floor, New York, NY 10022. Member of AAR.

Prior to becoming an agent, Ms. Manus was associate publisher of 2 national magazines and director of development at Warner Bros. and Universal Studios; she has been a literary agent for 20 years.

MEMBER AGENTS Jandy Nelson (currently not taking on new clients). **Jillian Manus**, jillian@manuslit.com (political, memoirs, self-help, history, sports, women's issues, thrillers); **Penny Nelson,** penny@manuslit.com (memoirs, self-help, sports, nonfiction).

REPRESENTS nonfiction books, novels. **Considers these fiction areas:** thriller.

"Our agency is unique in the way that we not only sell the material, but we edit, develop concepts, and participate in the marketing effort. We specialize in large, conceptual fiction and nonfiction, and always value a project that can be sold in the TV/feature film market." Actively seeking high-concept thrillers, commercial literary fiction, women's fiction, celebrity biographies, memoirs, multicultural fiction, popular health, women's empowerment and mysteries. No horror, romance, science fiction, fantasy, western, young adult, children's, poetry, cookbooks, or magazine articles.

HOW TO CONTACT Snail mail submissions welcome. E-queries also accepted. For nonfiction, send a full proposal via snail mail. For fiction, send a query letter and 30 pages (unbound) if submitting via snail mail. Send only an e-query if submitting fiction via e-mail. If querying by e-mail, submit directly to one of the agents. Accepts simultaneous submissions. Responds in 3 months to queries and mss. Obtains most new clients through recommendations from others, solicitations, conferences.

TERMS Agent receives 15% commission on domestic sales. Agent receives 20-25% commission on foreign sales. Offers written contract, binding for 2 years; 60-day notice must be given to terminate contract. Charges for photocopying and postage/UPS.

RECENT SALES *Nothing Down for the 2000s* and *Multiple Streams of Income for the 2000s* by Robert Allen; *Missed Fortune 101* by Doug Andrew; *Cracking the Millionaire Code* by Mark Victor Hansen and Robert Allen; *Stress Free for Good* by Dr. Fred Luskin and Dr. Ken Pelletier; *The Mercy of Thin Air* by Ronlyn Domangue; *The Fine Art of Small Talk* by Debra Fine; *Bone Men of Bonares* by Terry Tamoff.

WRITERS CONFERENCES Maui Writers Conference; San Diego State University Writers Conference; Willamette Writers Conference; BookExpo America; MEGA Book Marketing University.

TIPS "Research agents using a variety of sources."

○ THE EVAN MARSHALL AGENCY

07068-1121, Roseland NJ 07068-1121. (973)287-6216. **Fax:** (973)488-7910. **E-mail:** evan@evanmarshallagency.com. **Contact:** Evan Marshall. Member of AAR. Currently handles novels (100%).

REPRESENTS novels. **Considers these fiction areas:** action, adventure, erotica, ethnic, frontier, historical, horror, humor, inspirational, literary, mainstream, mystery, religious, satire, science fiction, suspense, western romance (contemporary, gothic, historical, regency).

HOW TO CONTACT Do not query. Currently accepting clients only by referral from editors and our own clients. Responds in 1 week to queries. Responds in 1 month to mss. Obtains most new clients through recommendations from others.

TERMS Agent receives 15% commission on domestic sales. Agent receives 20% commission on foreign sales. Offers written contract.

RECENT SALES *My Very Best Friend* by Cathy Lamb (Kensington); *Johanna's Bridegroom* by Emma Miller (Love Inspired); *If He's Noble* by Hannah Howell (Kensington); *Meet Me at the Beach* by V. K. Sykes (Grand Central Forever; *Killing Cupid* by Laura Levine (Kensington).

○ THE MARTELL AGENCY

1350 Avenue of the Americas, Suite 1205, New York NY 10019. **Fax:** (212)317-2676. **E-mail:** submissions@themartellagency.com. **Website:** www.themartellagency.com. **Contact:** Alice Martell.

REPRESENTS nonfiction, novels.

⚭ Seeks the following subjects in fiction: literary and commercial, including mystery, suspense and thrillers. Does not want to receive romance, genre mysteries, genre historical fiction, or children's books.

HOW TO CONTACT E-query Alice Martell. This should include a summary of the project and a short biography and any information, if appropriate, as to why you are qualified to write on the subject of your book, including any publishing credits. Send to submissions@themartellagency.com.

RECENT SALES *New York Times* bestseller *Defending Jacob* by William Landay; Pulitzer Finalist *The Forest Unseen: A Year's Watch in Nature* by David Haskell; *How Paris Became Paris: The Birth Of The Modern City* by Joan Dejean; National Book Award Winner *Waiting for Snow in Havana* by Carlos Eire; National Book Award Finalist *The Boy Kings of Texas* by Domingo Martinez.

◐ MARGRET MCBRIDE LITERARY AGENCY

P.O. Box 9128, La Jolla CA 92038. (858)454-1550. **Fax:** (858)454-2156. **E-mail:** staff@mcbridelit.com. **Website:** www.mcbrideliterary.com. **Contact:** Michael Daley, submissions manager. Member of AAR. Other memberships include Authors Guild.

◌ Prior to opening her agency, Ms. McBride worked at Random House, Ballantine Books, and Warner Books.

MEMBER AGENTS Margret McBride; Faye Atchinson.

REPRESENTS nonfiction books, novels. **Considers these fiction areas:** action, adventure, crime, detective, historical, humor, literary, mainstream, mystery, police, satire, suspense, thriller.

⚭ This agency specializes in mainstream fiction and nonfiction. Actively seeking commercial fiction and nonfiction, business, health, self-help. Please do not send screenplays, romance, poetry, or children's.

HOW TO CONTACT "Submit a query letter to us via e-mail (staff@mcbridelit.com) or snail mail. In your letter, please provide a brief synopsis of your work, as well as any pertinent information about yourself." There are detailed nonfiction proposal guidelines online. Accepts simultaneous submissions. Responds in 8 weeks to queries and mss.

TERMS Agent receives 15% commission on domestic sales. Agent receives 25% commission on foreign sales. Charges for overnight delivery and photocopying.

RECENT SALES *Value Tales Treasure: Stories for Growing Good People* by Spencer Johnson, MD. (Simon & Schuster Children's); *The 6 Reasons You'll Get the Job: What Employers Really Want—Whether They Know It or Not* by Debra MacDougall and Elisabeth Harney Sanders-Park (Tarcher); *The Solution: Conquer Your Fear, Control Your Future* by Lucinda Bassett (Sterling).

TIPS "Our office does not accept e-mail queries!"

THE MCCARTHY AGENCY, LLC

456 Ninth St., No. 28, Hoboken NJ 07030. **E-mail:** McCarthylit@aol.com. **Contact:** Shawna McCarthy. Member of AAR.

MEMBER AGENTS Shawna McCarthy.

REPRESENTS nonfiction books, novels. **Considers these fiction areas:** fantasy, middle-grade, mystery, new adult, science fiction, women's, young adult.

&—☛ This agency represents mostly novels. No picture books.

HOW TO CONTACT E-queries only. Accepts simultaneous submissions.

MCCARTHY CREATIVE SERVICES

625 Main St., Suite 834, New York NY 10044-0035. (212)832-3428. **Fax:** (212)829-9610. **E-mail:** paulmccarthy@mccarthycreative.com. **Website:** www.mccarthycreative.com. **Contact:** Paul D. McCarthy. Other memberships include the Authors Guild, American Society of Journalists & Authors, National Book Critics Circle, Authors League of America. Represents 5 clients. No clients are new/unpublished writers. Currently handles nonfiction books (95%), novels (5%).

○ Prior to his current position, Mr. McCarthy was a professional writer, literary agent at the Scott Meredith Literary Agency, senior editor at publishing companies (Simon & Schuster, HarperCollins and Doubleday) and a public speaker. Learn much more about Mr. McCarthy by visiting his website.

MEMBER AGENTS Paul D. McCarthy.

REPRESENTS nonfiction books, novels. **Considers these fiction areas:** glitz, adventure, confession, detective, erotica, ethnic, family, fantasy, feminist, gay, historical, horror, humor, literary, mainstream, mystery, regional, romance, science, sports, thriller, western, young, women's.

&—☛ "I deliberately founded my company to be unlimited in its range. That's what I offer, and the world has responded. My agency was founded so that I could maximize and build on the value of my combined experience for my authors and other clients, in all of my capacities and more. I think it's *very* important for authors to know that because I'm so exclusive as an agent, I may not be able to offer representation on the basis of the ms they submit. However, if they decide to invest in their book and lifetime career as authors by engaging my professional, near-unique editorial services, there is the possibility that at the end of the process, when they've achieved the very best, most salable and competitive book they can write, I may see sufficient potential in the book and their next books, that I do offer to be their agent. Representation is never guaranteed." Established authors of serious and popular nonfiction, who want the value of being one of MCS's very exclusive authors who receive special attention, and of being represented by a literary agent who brings such a rich diversity and depth of publishing/creative/professorial experience, and distinguished reputation. No first novels. "Novels by established novelists will be considered very selectively."

HOW TO CONTACT Submit outline, 1 chapter (either first or best). Queries and submissions by e-mail only. Send as e-mail attachment. Responds in 3-4 weeks to queries. Obtains most new clients through recommendations from others.

TERMS Agent receives 15% commission on domestic sales. Agent receives 20% commission on foreign sales. Offers written contract; 30-day notice must be given to terminate contract. "All reading done in deciding whether or not to offer representation is free. Editorial services are available. Mailing and postage expenses that incurred on the author's behalf are always approved by them in advance."

TIPS "Always keep in mind that your query letter/proposal is only one of hundreds and thousands that are competing for the agent's attention. Therefore, your presentation of your book and yourself as author has to be immediate, intense, compelling, and concise. Make the query letter one-page, and after short, introductory paragraph, write a 150-word KEYNOTE description of your ms."

● THE MCGILL AGENCY, INC.

10000 N. Central Expressway, Suite 400, Dallas TX 75231. (214)390-5970. **E-mail:** info.mcgillagency@gmail.com. **Contact:** Jack Bollinger. Estab. 2009. Represents 10 clients. 50% of clients are new/unpublished writers.

MEMBER AGENTS Jack Bollinger (eclectic tastes in nonfiction and fiction); Amy Cohn (nonfiction interests include women's issues, gay/lesbian, ethnic/cultural, memoirs, true crime; fiction interests include mystery, suspense and thriller).

REPRESENTS Considers these fiction areas: historical, mainstream, mystery, romance, thriller.

HOW TO CONTACT Query via e-mail. Responds in 2 weeks to queries; in 6 weeks to mss. Obtains new clients through conferences.

TERMS Agent receives 15% commission.

○ MENDEL MEDIA GROUP, LLC

115 W. 30th St., Suite 800, New York NY 10001. (646)239-9896. **Fax:** (212)685-4717. **E-mail:** scott@mendelmedia.com. **Website:** www.mendelmedia.com. Member of AAR. Represents 40-60 clients.

Prior to becoming an agent, Mr. Mendel was an academic. "I taught American literature, Yiddish, Jewish studies, and literary theory at the University of Chicago and the University of Illinois at Chicago while working on my PhD in English. I also worked as a freelance technical writer and as the managing editor of a healthcare magazine. In 1998, I began working for the late Jane Jordan Browne, a long-time agent in the book publishing world."

REPRESENTS nonfiction books, novels, scholarly, with potential for broad/popular appeal. **Considers these fiction areas:** action, adventure, contemporary issues, crime, detective, erotica, ethnic, feminist, gay, glitz, historical, humor, inspirational, juvenile, lesbian, literary, mainstream, mystery, picture books, police, religious, romance, satire, sports, thriller, young adult Jewish fiction.

"I am interested in major works of history, current affairs, biography, business, politics, economics, science, major memoirs, narrative nonfiction, and other sorts of general nonfiction."

Actively seeking new, major or definitive work on a subject of broad interest, or a controversial, but authoritative, new book on a subject that affects many people's lives. I also represent more light-hearted nonfiction projects, such as gift or novelty books, when they suit the market particularly well." Does not want "queries about projects written years ago that were unsuccessfully shopped to a long list of trade publishers by either the author or another agent. I am specifically not interested in reading short, category romances (regency, time travel, paranormal, etc.), horror novels, supernatural stories, poetry, original plays, or film scripts."

HOW TO CONTACT Query with SASE. Do not e-mail or fax queries. For nonfiction, include a complete, fully edited book proposal with sample chapters. For fiction, include a complete synopsis and no more than 20 pages of sample text. Responds in 2 weeks to queries; in 4-6 weeks to mss. Obtains most new clients through recommendations from others.

TERMS Agent receives 15% commission on domestic sales. Agent receives 20% commission on foreign sales.

WRITERS CONFERENCES BookExpo America; Frankfurt Book Fair; London Book Fair; RWA National Conference; Modern Language Association Convention; Jerusalem Book Fair.

TIPS "While I am not interested in being flattered by a prospective client, it does matter to me that she knows why she is writing to me in the first place. Is one of my clients a colleague of hers? Has she read a book by one of my clients that led her to believe I might be interested in her work? Authors of descriptive nonfiction should have real credentials and expertise in their subject areas, either as academics, journalists, or policy experts, and authors of prescriptive nonfiction should have legitimate expertise and considerable experience communicating their ideas in seminars and workshops, in a successful business, through the media, etc."

● MOVEABLE TYPE MANAGEMENT

244 Madison Ave., Suite 334, New York NY 10016. (646)431-6134. **Website:** www.mtmgmt.net.

MEMBER AGENTS Adam Chromy.

REPRESENTS Considers these fiction areas: commercial, literary, mainstream, romance, women's, young adult.

Mr. Chromy is a generalist, meaning that he accepts fiction submissions of virtually any kind (except juvenile books aimed for middle-grade and younger) as well as nonfiction. He has sold books in the following categories: new adult, women's, romance, memoir, pop culture, young adult, lifestyle, horror, how-to, and general fiction.

HOW TO CONTACT E-queries only. Responds if interested. For nonfiction: Send a query letter in the body of an e-mail that precisely introduces your topic and approach, and includes a descriptive bio. For journalists and academics, please also feel free to include a CV. Fiction: Send your query letter and the first 10 pages of your novel in the body of an e-mail. Your subject line needs to contain the word "Query" or your message will not reach the agency. No attachments and no snail mail.

RECENT SALES *The Gin Lovers* by Jamie Brenner (St. Martin's Press); *Miss Chatterley* by Logan Belle (Pocket/S&S); *Sons Of Zeus* by Noble Smith (Thomas Dunne Books); *World Made By Hand And Too Much Magic* by James Howard Kunstler (Grove/Atlantic Press); *Dirty Rocker Boys* by Bobbie Brown (Gallery/S&S).

DEE MURA LITERARY

P.O. Box 131, Massapequa NY 11762. (516)795-1616. **Fax:** (516)795-8797. **E-mail:** query@deemuraliterary.com. **Website:** www.deemuraliterary.com. **Contact:** Dee Mura. 50% of clients are new/unpublished writers.

Prior to opening her agency, Mura was a public relations executive with a roster of film and entertainment clients. She is the president and CEO of both Dee Mura Literary and Dee Mura Entertainment.

MEMBER AGENTS Dee Mura, Kimiko Nakamura, Kaylee Davis.

REPRESENTS Considers these fiction areas: adventure, commercial, contemporary issues, crime, erotica, family saga, fantasy, historical, literary, middle-grade, mystery, new adult, paranormal, romance, satire, science fiction, suspense, thriller, women's, young adult espionage, magical realism, speculative fiction.

Fiction with crossover film potential. No screenplays, poetry, or children's picture books.

HOW TO CONTACT Query with SASE or e-mail query@deemuraliterary.com (e-mail queries are preferred). Please include the first 25 pages in the body of the e-mail as well as a short author bio and synopsis of the work. Responds in 3-4 weeks to queries; in 2 months to mss. Obtains new clients through recommendations, solicitation, and conferences Accepts simultaneous submissions. Obtains new clients through recommendations, solicitation, and conferences.

TERMS Agent receives 15% commission on domestic sales. Agent receives 20% commission on foreign sales. Offers written contract.

RECENT SALES *An Infinite Number of Parallel Universes* by Randy Ribay; *The Number 7* by Jessica Lidh.

WRITERS CONFERENCES Alaska Writers Guild Conference, BookExpo America, Hampton Roads Writers Conference, NESCBWI Regional Conference, San Francisco Writers Conference, Books Alive! Conference, Writer's Digest Conference East, LVW's Writers Meet Agents Conference

JEAN V. NAGGAR LITERARY AGENCY, INC.

216 E. 75th St., Suite 1E, New York NY 10021. (212)794-1082. **E-mail:** jweltz@jvnla.com; atasman@jvnla.com. **Website:** www.jvnla.com. **Contact:** Jean Naggar. Member of AAR. Other memberships include Women's Media Group, SCBWI, Pace University's Masters in Publishing Board Member. Represents 450 clients. 20% of clients are new/unpublished writers.

Ms. Naggar has served as president of AAR.

MEMBER AGENTS Jennifer Weltz (well researched and original historicals, thrillers with a unique voice, wry dark humor, and magical realism; enthralling narrative nonfiction; young adult, middle-grade); **Jean Naggar** (taking no new clients); **Alice Tasman** (literary, commercial, YA, middle-grade, and nonfiction in the categories of narrative, biography, music or pop culture); **Elizabeth Evans** (narrative nonfiction [travel/adventure], memoir, current affairs, pop science, journalism, health and wellness, psychology, history, pop culture, cookbooks and humor); **Laura Biagi** (literary fiction, magical realism, psychological thrillers, young adult novels, middle-grade novels, and picture books).

REPRESENTS nonfiction books, novels. **Considers these fiction areas:** commercial, fantasy, literary, middle-grade, picture books, thriller, young adult.

This agency specializes in mainstream fiction and nonfiction and literary fiction with commercial potential. Does not want to receive screenplays.

HOW TO CONTACT "Visit our website, www.jvnla.com, for complete, up-to-date submission guidelines.

Please be advised that Jean Naggar is no longer accepting new clients." Accepts simultaneous submissions.

TERMS Agent receives 15% commission on domestic sales. Agent receives 20% commission on foreign sales. Offers written contract. Charges for overseas mailing, messenger services, book purchases, long-distance telephone, photocopying—all deductible from royalties received.

RECENT SALES *Mort(e)* by Robert Repino; *The Paying Guests* by Sarah Waters; *Woman with a Gun* by Phillip Margolin; *An Unseemly Wife* by E.B. Moore; *The Man Who Walked Away* by Maud Casey; *A Lige in Men* by Gina Frangello; *The Tudor Vendetta* by C.W. Gortner; *Prototype* by M.D. Waters.

TIPS "We recommend courage, fortitude, and patience: the courage to be true to your own vision, the fortitude to finish a novel and polish it again and again before sending it out, and the patience to accept rejection gracefully and wait for the stars to align themselves appropriately for success."

NELSON LITERARY AGENCY

1732 Wazee St., Suite 207, Denver CO 80202. (303)292-2805. **Website:** www.nelsonagency.com. **Contact:** Kristin Nelson, president. Estab. 2002. Member of AAR, RWA, SCBWI, SFWA.

- Prior to opening her own agency, Ms. Nelson worked as a literary scout and subrights agent for agent Jody Rein.

REPRESENTS Considers these fiction areas: commercial, fantasy, literary, mainstream, middle-grade, romance, science fiction, women's, young adult.

- NLA specializes in representing commercial fiction and high-caliber literary fiction. They represent many pop genre categories, including things like historical romance, steampunk, and all subgenres of YA. Does not want short story collections, mysteries, thrillers, Christian, horror, children's picture books, or screenplays.

HOW TO CONTACT Query by e-mail. Put the word "Query" in the e-mail subject line. No attachments; querykristin@nelsonagency.com. Responds in 1 month.

RECENT SALES *Champion* by Marie Lu (young adult); *Wool* by Hugh Howey (science fiction); *The Whatnot* by Stefan Bachmann (middle-grade); *Catching Jordan* by Miranda Kenneally (young adult); *Broken Like This* by Monica Trasandes (debut literary fiction); *The Darwin Elevator* by Jason Hough (debut science fiction). A full list of clients is available online.

NEW LEAF LITERARY & MEDIA, INC.

110 W. 40th St., Suite 410, New York NY 10018. (646)248-7989. **Fax:** (646)861-4654. **E-mail:** query@newleafliterary.com. Member of AAR.

MEMBER AGENTS Joanna Volpe (women's fiction, thriller, horror, speculative fiction, literary fiction and historical fiction, young adult, middle-grade, art-focused picture books); **Kathleen Ortiz**, Director of Subsidiary Rights and literary agent (new voices in YA nd animator/illustrator talent); **Suzie Townsend** (new adult, young adult, middle-grade, romance [all subgenres], fantasy [urban fantasy, science fiction, steampunk, epic fantasy] and crime fiction [mysteries, thrillers]); **Pouya Shahbazian**, Director of Film and Television; **Mackenzie Brady** (her taste in nonfiction extends beyond science books to memoirs, lost histories, epic sports narratives, true crime and gift/lifestyle books; she represents select adult and YA fiction projects, as well).

REPRESENTS Considers these fiction areas: crime, fantasy, historical, horror, literary, mainstream, middle-grade, mystery, new adult, paranormal, picture books, romance, thriller, women's, young adult.

HOW TO CONTACT "Only query us when your ms is complete. Do not query more than 1 agent at New Leaf Literary & Media, Inc. Put the word 'Query' in the subject line along with the target agent's name. No attachments. Responds if interested."

RECENT SALES *Four* by Veronica Roth (HarperCollins); *The Little World of Liz Climo* by Liz Climo (Running Press); *Ruin and Risin,g* by Leigh Bardugo (Henry Holt); *A Snicker of Magic* by Natalie Lloyd (Scholastic).

PARK LITERARY GROUP, LLC

270 Lafayette St., Suite 1504, New York NY 10012. (212)691-3500. **Fax:** (212)691-3540. **E-mail:** queries@parkliterary.com. **Website:** www.parkliterary.com. Estab. 2005.

MEMBER AGENTS Theresa Park (plot-driven fiction and serious nonfiction); **Abigail Koons** (popular science, history, politics, current affairs and art, and women's fiction); **Peter Knapp** (middle-grade and young adult fiction).

REPRESENTS nonfiction books, novels. **Considers these fiction areas:** middle-grade, suspense, thriller, women's, young adult.

The Park Literary Group represents fiction and nonfiction with a boutique approach: an emphasis on servicing a relatively small number of clients, with the highest professional standards and focused personal attention. Does not want to receive poetry or screenplays.

HOW TO CONTACT Please specify the first and last name of the agent to whom you are submitting in the subject line of the e-mail and send your query letter and accompanying material to queries@parkliterary. com. All materials must be in the body of the e-mail. Responds if interested. For fiction submissions to Abigail Koons or Theresa Park, please include a query letter with short synopsis and the first 3 chapters of your work. For middle-grade and young adult submissions to Peter Knapp, please include a query letter and the first 3 chapters of your novel (no synopsis necessary). For nonfiction submissions, please send a query letter, proposal, and sample chapter(s).

RECENT SALES This agency's client list is on their website. It includes bestsellers Nicholas Sparks, Soman Chainani, Emily Giffin, and Debbie Macomber.

L. PERKINS AGENCY

5800 Arlington Ave., Riverdale NY 10471. (718)543-5344. **Fax:** (718)543-5354. **E-mail:** submissions@lperkinsagency.com. **Website:** lperkinsagency.com. Member of AAR. Represents 90 clients. 10% of clients are new/unpublished writers.

Ms. Perkins has been an agent for 20 years. She is also the author of *The Insider's Guide to Getting an Agent* (Writer's Digest Books), as well as 3 other nonfiction books. She has also edited 12 erotic anthologies, and is also the editorial director of Ravenousromance.com, an e-publisher.

MEMBER AGENTS Tish Beaty, ePub agent (erotic romance – including paranormal, historical, gay/lesbian/bisexual, and light-BDSM fiction; also, she seeks new adult and YA); **Sandy Lu**, sandy@lperkinsagency.com (fiction: she is looking for dark literary and commercial fiction, mystery, thriller, psychological horror, paranormal/urban fantasy, historical fiction, YA, historical thrillers or mysteries set in Victorian times; nonfiction: narrative nonfiction, history, biography, pop science, pop psychology, pop culture [music/theatre/film], humor, and food writing); **Lori Perkins** (not currently taking new clients); **Leon Husock** (science fiction and fantasy, as well as young adult and middle-grade); **Rachel Brooks** (picture books, all genres of young adult and new adult fiction, as well as adult romance—especially romantic suspense).

REPRESENTS nonfiction books, novels. **Considers these fiction areas:** commercial, erotica, fantasy, gay, historical, horror, lesbian, middle-grade, mystery, new adult, paranormal, picture books, science fiction, thriller, urban fantasy, young adult.

"Most of my clients write both fiction and nonfiction. This combination keeps my clients publishing for years. I am also a published author, so I know what it takes to write a good book."

HOW TO CONTACT E-queries only. Include your query, a one-page synopsis, and the first 5 pages from your novel pasted into the e-mail. No attachments. Submit to only 1 agent at the agency. No snail mail queries. "If you are submitting to one of our agents, please be sure to check the submission status of the agent by visiting their social media accounts listed [on the agency website]." Accepts simultaneous submissions. Obtains most new clients through recommendations from others, solicitations, conferences.

TERMS Agent receives 15% commission on domestic sales. Agent receives 20% commission on foreign sales. No written contract. Charges clients for photocopying.

WRITERS CONFERENCES NECON; Killercon; BookExpo America; World Fantasy Convention, RWA, Romantic Times.

TIPS "Research your field and contact professional writers' organizations to see who is looking for what. Finish your novel before querying agents. Read my book, *An Insider's Guide to Getting an Agent*, to get a sense of how agents operate. Read agent blogs-agentinthemiddle.blogspot.com and ravenousromance. blogspot.com."

LINN PRENTIS LITERARY

155 East 116th St., #2F, New York NY 10029. **Fax:** (212)875-5565. **Website:** www.linnprentis.com. **Contact:** Amy Hayden, acquisitions; Linn Prentis, agent. Represents 18-20 clients. 25% of clients are new/unpublished writers. Currently handles nonfiction books (5%), novels (65%), story collections (7%), novella (10%), juvenile books (10%), scholarly books (3%).

Prior to becoming an agent, Ms. Prentis was a nonfiction writer and editor, primarily in magazines. She also worked in book promotion in New York. Ms. Prentis then worked for and later ran the Virginia Kidd Agency. She is known particularly for her assistance with ms development.

REPRESENTS Considers these fiction areas: adventure, ethnic, fantasy, gay, glitz, historical, horror, humor, lesbian, literary, mainstream, thriller.

8—➤ "Because of the Virginia Kidd connection and the clients I brought with me at the start, I have a special interest in sci-fi and fantasy, but, really, fiction is what interests me. As for nonfiction projects, they are books I just couldn't resist." Actively seeking hard science fiction, family saga, mystery, memoir, mainstream, literary, women's. Does not want to "receive books for little kids."

HOW TO CONTACT Query. No phone or fax queries. No snail mail. E-mail queries to ahayden@linnprentis. com. Include first 10 pages and synopsis as either attachment or as text in the e-mail. Accepts simultaneous submissions. Obtains most new clients through recommendations from others, solicitations.

TERMS Agent receives 15% commission on domestic sales. Agent and partners take 20% commission on foreign sales. Offers written contract; 60-day notice must be given to terminate contract.

RECENT SALES Sales include *Vienna* for new author William Kirby; *Hunting Ground, Frost Burned* and *Night Broken* titles in 2 series for *New York Times* best-selling author Patricia Briggs (as well as a graphic novel *Homecoming*) and a story collection; with more coming; a duology of novels for A.M. Dellamonica whose first book, *Indigo Springs*, won Canada's annual award for best fantasy, as well as several books abroad for client Tachyon Publications.

TIPS "Consider query letters and synopses as writing assignments. Spell names correctly."

✪ P.S LITERARY AGENCY

20033 - 520 Kerr St., Oakville ON L6K 3C7 Canada. **E-mail:** query@psliterary.com. **Website:** www.psliterary.com. **Contact:** Curtis Russell, principal agent; Carly Watters, agent; Maria Vicente, associate agent. Estab. 2005. Currently handles nonfiction books (50%), novels (50%).

MEMBER AGENTS Curtis Russell (young adult and middle-grade books); **Carly Watters** (young adult, book club fiction, commercial fiction, women's fiction, contemporary romance, cookbooks, unique memoirs, pop science and psychology, literary thrill-

ers and mysteries, platform-heavy nonfiction); **Maria Vicente** (young adult, middle-grade and illustrated picture books); **Kurestin Armada** (particular affection for science fiction and fantasy, especially books that recognize and subvert typical tropes of genre fiction).

REPRESENTS nonfiction, novels, juvenile books. **Considers these fiction areas:** action, adventure, detective, erotica, ethnic, family saga, historical, horror, humor, juvenile, literary, mainstream, middle-grade, mystery, new adult, picture books, romance, sports, thriller, women's, young adult biography/autobiography, business, child guidance/parenting, cooking/food/nutrition, current affairs, government/politics/law, health/medicine, history, how-to, humor, memoirs, military/war, money/finance/economics, nature/environment, popular culture, science/technology, self-help/personal improvement, sports, true crime/investigative, women's issues/women's studies.

8—➤ "What makes our agency distinct: We take on a small number of clients per year in order to provide focused, hands-on representation. We pride ourselves in providing industry-leading client service." Actively seeking both fiction and nonfiction. Seeking both new and established writers. Does not want to receive poetry or screenplays.

HOW TO CONTACT Queries by e-mail only. Submit query letter and bio. "Please limit your query to 1 page." Accepts simultaneous submissions. Responds in 6 weeks to queries/proposals; mss 8 weeks. Obtains most new clients through solicitations.

TERMS Agent receives 15% commission on domestic sales. Agent receives 25% commission on foreign sales. We offer a written contract, with 30-days notice terminate. Fees for postage/messenger services only if project is sold. "This agency charges for postage/messenger services only if a project is sold."

TIPS "Please review our website for the most up-to-date submission guidelines. We do not charge reading fees. We do not offer a critique service."

◑ REES LITERARY AGENCY

14 Beacon St., Suite 710, Boston MA 02108. (617)227-9014. **Fax:** (617)227-8762. **Website:** reesagency.com. Estab. 1983. Member of AAR. Represents more than 100 clients. 50% of clients are new/unpublished writers. **MEMBER AGENTS** Ann Collette, Agent10702@aol. com (literary, mystery, thrillers, suspense, vampire,

and women's fiction; in nonfiction, she prefers true crime, narrative nonfiction, military and war, work to do with race and class, and work set in or about Southeast Asia); **Lorin Rees**, lorin@reesagency.com (literary fiction, memoirs, business books, self-help, science, history, psychology, and narrative nonfiction); **Rebecca Podos**, rebecca@reesagency.com (young adult fiction of all kinds, including contemporary, emotionally driven stories, mystery, romance, urban and historical fantasy, horror and sci-fi; occasionally, she considers literary and commercial adult fiction, new adult, and narrative nonfiction).

REPRESENTS nonfiction books, novels. **Considers these fiction areas:** commercial, historical, horror, literary, mystery, new adult, romance, science fiction, suspense, thriller, urban fantasy, women's, young adult.

HOW TO CONTACT Consult website for each agent's submission guidelines and e-mail addresses, as they differ. Obtains most new clients through recommendations from others, conferences, submissions.

TERMS Agent receives 15% commission on domestic sales. Agent receives 20% commission on foreign sales.

RECENT SALES Recent titles include: *The Art Forger* by B.A. Shapiro; *Busy Monsters* by William Giraldi; *Pitch Dark* by Steven Sidor; *You Know When the Men Are Gone* by Siobhan Fallon; and *Death Drops* by Chrystle Fieldler. Other titles include: *Get Your Ship Together* by Capt. D. Michael Abrashoff; *Overpromise and Overdeliver* by Rick Berrara; *Opacity* by Joel Kurtzman; *America the Broke* by Gerald Swanson; *Murder at the B-School* by Jeffrey Cruikshank; *Bone Factory* by Steven Sidor; *Father Said* by Hal Sirowitz; *Winning* by Jack Welch; *The Case for Israel* by Alan Dershowitz; *As the Future Catches You* by Juan Enriquez; *Blood Makes the Grass Grow Green* by Johnny Rico; *DVD Movie Guide* by Mick Martin and Marsha Porter; *Words That Work* by Frank Luntz; *Stirring It Up* by Gary Hirshberg; *Hot Spots* by Martin Fletcher; *Andy Grove: The Life and Times of an American* by Richard Tedlow; *Girls Most Likely To* by Poonam Sharma.

REGAL LITERARY AGENCY

236 W. 26th St., #801, New York NY 10001. (212)684-7900. **Fax:** (212)684-7906. **E-mail:** submissions@regal-literary.com. **Website:** www.regal-literary.com. London Office: 36 Gloucester Ave., Primrose Hill, London NW1 7BB, United Kingdom, uk@regal-literary.com Estab. 2002. Member of AAR. Represents 70 clients. 20% of clients are new/unpublished writers.

MEMBER AGENTS Michelle Andelman (all categories of children's books); **Claire Anderson-Wheeler**; **Markus Hoffmann** (international and literary fiction, crime, [pop] cultural studies, current affairs, economics, history, music, popular science, and travel literature); **Joseph Regal** (literary fiction, international thrillers, history, science, photography, music, culture, and whimsy).

REPRESENTS Considers these fiction areas: literary, middle-grade, picture books, thriller, women's, young adult.

Actively seeking literary fiction and narrative nonfiction. "We do not consider romance, science fiction, poetry, or screenplays."

HOW TO CONTACT "Query with SASE or via e-mail. No phone calls. Submissions should consist of a one-page query letter detailing the book in question, as well as the qualifications of the author. For fiction, submissions may also include the first 10 pages of the novel or 1 short story from a collection." Responds if interested. Accepts simultaneous submissions. Responds in 1-2 months.

TERMS Agent receives 15% commission on domestic sales. Agent receives 20% commission on foreign sales. "We charge no reading fees."

RECENT SALES Audrey Niffenegger's *The Time Traveler's Wife* (Mariner) and *Her Fearful Symmetry* (Scribner), Gregory David Roberts' *Shantaram* (St. Martin's), Josh Bazell's *Beat the Reaper* (Little, Brown), John Twelve Hawks' *The Fourth Realm Trilogy* (Doubleday), James Reston, Jr.'s *The Conviction of Richard Nixon* (Three Rivers) and *Defenders of the Faith* (Penguin), Michael Psilakis' *How to Roast a Lamb: New Greek Classic Cooking* (Little, Brown), Colman Andrews' *Country Cooking of Ireland* (Chronicle) and *Reinventing Food: Ferran Adria and How He Changed the Way We Eat* (Phaidon).

TIPS "We are deeply committed to every aspect of our clients' careers, and are engaged in everything from the editorial work of developing a great book proposal or line editing a fiction ms to negotiating state-of-the-art book deals and working to promote and publicize the book when it's published. We are at the forefront of the effort to increase authors' rights in publishing contracts in a rapidly changing commercial environment. We deal directly with co-agents and publishers in every foreign territory and also work directly and with co-agents for feature film and television rights, with extraordinary success in both arenas. Many of our clients' works have sold in dozens of translation markets, and a high proportion of our books have been sold in Hollywood. We have strong relationships with speaking agents, who can assist in arranging author tours and other corporate and college speaking opportunities when appropriate. We also have a staff publicist and marketer to help promote our clients and their work."

✪ THE RIGHTS FACTORY

P.O. Box 499, Station C, Toronto ON M6J 3P6 Canada. (416)966-5367. **Website:** www.therightsfactory.com. Estab. 2004.

MEMBER AGENTS Sam Hiyate, Ali McDonald (children's literature of all kinds); **Haskell Nussbaum; Drea Cohane** (fiction, memoir, crime, nonfiction and YA; her roster consists of British, American, and Canadian clients; international talent is welcome); **Olga Filina** (commercial and historical fiction, great genre fiction in the area of romance and mystery, nonfiction in the field of business, wellness, lifestyle and memoir; and young adult and middle-grade novels with memorable characters); **Lydia Moed** (science fiction and fantasy, though she also enjoys magic realism, historical fiction and stories inspired by folklore from around the world; for nonfiction, she is interested in narrative nonfiction on a wide variety of topics, including history, popular science, biography, and memoir).

REPRESENTS Considers these fiction areas: commercial, crime, fantasy, historical, literary, mainstream, middle-grade, mystery, picture books, romance, science fiction, young adult.

HOW TO CONTACT There is a submission form on this agency's website. You can also query via snail mail.

⬤ ANN RITTENBERG LITERARY AGENCY, INC.

15 Maiden Lane, Suite 206, New York NY 10038. **Website:** www.rittlit.com. **Contact:** Ann Rittenberg, president. Member of AAR. Currently handles fiction (75%), nonfiction (25%).

➣ This agent specializes in specific fiction genres—upmarket thrillers, literary fiction and literary nonfiction. Does not want to receive screenplays, straight genre fiction, poetry, self-help.

HOW TO CONTACT Query with SASE. Submit outline, 3 sample chapters, SASE. Query via postal mail or e-mail to info@rittlit.com. Accepts simultaneous submissions. Responds in 6 weeks to queries; in 2 months to mss. Obtains most new clients through referrals from established writers and editors.

TERMS Agent receives 15% commission on domestic sales. Agent receives 20% commission on foreign sales. Offers written contract. This agency charges clients for photocopying only.

RECENT SALES *World Gone By* by Dennis Lehane; *Leaving Haven* by Kathleen McCleary; *The Bone Orchard* by Paul Doiron; *Endangered* by C.J. Box.

◑ RLR ASSOCIATES, LTD.

Literary Department, 7 W. 51st St., New York NY 10019. (212)541-8641. **Fax:** (212)262-7084. **E-mail:** sgould@rlrassociates.net. **Website:** www.rlrassociates.net. **Contact:** Scott Gould. Member of AAR. Represents 50 clients. 25% of clients are new/unpublished writers. Currently handles nonfiction books (70%), novels (25%), story collections (5%).

REPRESENTS nonfiction books, novels, short-story collections, scholarly. **Considers these fiction areas:** commercial, literary, mainstream, middle-grade, picture books, romance, women's, young adult.

➣ "We provide a lot of editorial assistance to our clients and have connections." Actively seeking fiction, current affairs, history, art, popular culture, health and business. Does not want to receive screenplays.

HOW TO CONTACT Query by either e-mail or snail mail. For fiction, send a query and 1-3 chapters (pasted). For nonfiction, send query or proposal. Accepts simultaneous submissions. "If you do not hear from us within 3 months, please assume that your work is out of active consideration." Obtains most new clients through recommendations from others.

TERMS Agent receives 15% commission on domestic sales. Agent receives 20% commission on foreign sales. Offers written contract.

RECENT SALES Clients include Shelby Foote, The Grief Recovery Institute, Don Wade, Don Zimmer, The Knot.com, David Plowden, PGA of America, Danny Peary, George Kalinsky, Peter Hyman, Daniel Parker, Lee Miller, Elise Miller, Nina Planck, Karyn Bosnak, Christopher Pike, Gerald Carbone, Jason Lethcoe, Andy Crouch.

TIPS "Please check out our website for more details on our agency."

◑ B.J. ROBBINS LITERARY AGENCY

5130 Bellaire Ave., North Hollywood CA 91607-2908. **E-mail:** Robbinsliterary@gmail.com. **Website:** www.publishersmarketplace.com/members/bjrobbins.

Contact: (Ms.) B.J. Robbins, or Amy Maldonado. Estab. 1992. Member of AAR.

REPRESENTS nonfiction books, novels. **Considers these fiction areas:** crime, detective, ethnic, literary, mainstream, mystery, police, sports, suspense, thriller.

☞ "We do not represent screenplays, plays, poetry, science fiction, horror, westerns, romance, techno-thrillers, religious tracts, dating books or anything with the word 'unicorn' in the title."

HOW TO CONTACT E-query with no attachments. Accepts simultaneous submissions. Only responds to projects if interested. Obtains most new clients through conferences, referrals.

TERMS Agent receives 15% commission on domestic sales. Agent receives 20% commission on foreign sales. Offers written contract; three-month notice must be given to terminate contract.

① THE ROSENBERG GROUP

23 Lincoln Ave., Marblehead MA 01945. (781)990-1341. **Fax:** (781)990-1344. **Website:** www.rosenberggroup.com. **Contact:** Barbara Collins Rosenberg. Estab. 1998. Member of AAR. Recognized agent of the RWA. Represents 25 clients. 15% of clients are new/unpublished writers.Currently handles nonfiction books (30%), novels (30%), scholarly books (10%), (30% college textbooks).

○ Prior to becoming an agent, Ms. Rosenberg was a senior editor for Harcourt.

REPRESENTS nonfiction books, novels, textbooks, college textbooks only. **Considers these fiction areas:** romance, women's chick lit.

☞ Ms. Rosenberg is well-versed in the romance market (both category and single title). She is a frequent speaker at romance conferences. The Rosenberg Group is accepting new clients working in romance fiction (please see my Areas of Interest for specific romance subgenres); women's fiction and chick lit. Does not want to receive inspirational, time travel, futuristic or paranormal.

HOW TO CONTACT Query via snail mail. Your query letter should not exceed 1 page in length. It should include the title of your work, the genre and/or subgenre; the ms's word count; and a brief description of the work. If you are writing category romance, please be certain to let her know the line for which your work

is intended. Responds in 2 weeks to queries. Responds in 6 weeks to mss. Obtains most new clients through recommendations from others, solicitations, conferences.

TERMS Agent receives 15% commission on domestic sales. Agent receives 15% commission on foreign sales. Offers written contract; one-month notice must be given to terminate contract. Charges maximum of $350/year for postage and photocopying.

RECENT SALES Sold 27 titles in the last year.

WRITERS CONFERENCES RWA National Conference; BookExpo America.

○ JANE ROTROSEN AGENCY LLC

318 E. 51st St., New York NY 10022. (212)593-4330. **Fax:** (212)935-6985. **Website:** www.janerotrosen.com. Estab. 1974. Member of AAR. Other memberships include Authors Guild. Represents more than 100 clients.

MEMBER AGENTS Jane Rotrosen Berkey (not taking on clients); **Andrea Cirillo**, acirillo@janerotrosen.com (suspense and women's fiction); **Annelise Robey**, arobey@janerotrosen.com (women's fiction, suspense, mystery, literary fiction and the occasional nonfiction project); **Meg Ruley**, mruley@janerotrosen.com (women's fiction as well as suspense, thrillers, and mystery); **Christina Hogrebe**, chogrebe@janerotrosen.com (young adult, contemporary romance and new adult, women's fiction, historical fiction, mystery, fanfiction); **Amy Tannenbaum**, atannenbaum@janerotrosen.com (contemporary romance and new adult; Amy is particularly interested in those areas, as well as women's fiction that falls into that sweet spot between literary and commercial); **Rebecca Scherer** (women's fiction, mystery, suspense/thriller, romance, upmarket fiction at the cross between commercial and literary).

REPRESENTS nonfiction books, novels. **Considers these fiction areas:** literary, mystery, new adult, romance, suspense, thriller, women's.

HOW TO CONTACT Agent submission e-mail addresses are different. Send a query letter, a brief synopsis, and up to 3 chapters of your novel or the proposal for nonfiction. No attachments. Responds in 2 weeks to writers who have been referred by a client or colleague. Responds in 2 months to mss. Obtains most new clients through recommendations from others.

TERMS Agent receives 15% commission on domestic sales. Agent receives 20% commission on foreign sales. Offers written contract, binding for 3 years; two-month notice must be given to terminate contract. Charges clients for photocopying, express mail, overseas postage, book purchase.

● VICTORIA SANDERS & ASSOCIATES

40 Buck Rd., Stone Ridge NY 12484. (212)633-8811. **Fax:** (212)633-0525. **E-mail:** queriesvsa@gmail.com. **Website:** www.victoriasanders.com. **Contact:** Victoria Sanders. Estab. 1992. Member of AAR. Signatory of WGA. Represents 135 clients. 25% of clients are new/unpublished writers.

MEMBER AGENTS Victoria Sanders, Chris Kepner, Bernadette Baker-Baughman.

REPRESENTS nonfiction books, novels. **Considers these fiction areas:** action, adventure, contemporary issues, crime, ethnic, family saga, feminist, lesbian, literary, mainstream, mystery, new adult, picture books, thriller, young adult.

HOW TO CONTACT Query by e-mail only. "We will not respond to e-mails with attachments or attached files."

TERMS Agent receives 15% commission on domestic sales. Agent receives 20% commission on foreign/film sales. Offers written contract. Charges for photocopying, messenger, express mail. If in excess of $100, client approval is required.

RECENT SALES Sold 20+ titles in the last year.

TIPS "Limit query to letter (no calls) and give it your best shot. A good query is going to get a good response."

◐ SCHIAVONE LITERARY AGENCY, INC.

236 Trails End, West Palm Beach FL 33413-2135. (561)966-9294. **Fax:** (561)966-9294. **E-mail:** profschia@aol.com. **Website:** www.publishersmarketplace.com/members/profschia; blog site: www.schiavoneliteraryagencyinc.blogspot.com. **Contact:** Dr. James Schiavone, CEO, corporate offices in Florida; Jennifer DuVall, president, New York office; Francine Edelman, senior executive VP. Other memberships include National Education Association.

◔ Prior to opening his agency, Dr. Schiavone was a full professor of developmental skills at the City University of New York and author of 5 trade books and 3 textbooks. Jennifer DuVall has many years of experience in office management and agenting.

MEMBER AGENTS James Schiavone, profschia@aol.com; Jennifer DuVall, jendu77@aol.com; Kevin McAdams, kvn.mcadams@yahoo.com.

REPRESENTS Considers these fiction areas: fantasy, literary, mainstream, middle-grade, mystery, romance, science fiction, suspense, thriller, young adult.

⌖ This agency specializes in celebrity biography and autobiography and memoirs. Does not want to receive poetry.

HOW TO CONTACT "One-page e-mail queries only. Absolutely no attachments. Postal queries are not accepted. No phone calls. We do not consider poetry, short stories, anthologies or children's books. No scripts or screen plays. We handle dramatic, film and TV rights, options, and screen plays for books we have agented. We are NOT interested in work previously published in any format (e.g., self-published; online; ebooks; Print On Demand). E-mail queries may be addressed to any of the agency's agents." Accepts simultaneous submissions. Responds in 2 weeks to queries. Responds in 6 weeks to mss. Obtains most new clients through recommendations from others, solicitations, conferences.

TERMS Agent receives 15% commission on domestic sales. Agent receives 20% commission on foreign sales. Offers written contract. Charges clients for postage only.

WRITERS CONFERENCES Key West Literary Seminar; South Florida Writers Conference; Tallahassee Writers Conference, Million Dollar Writers Conference; Alaska Writers Conference.

TIPS "We prefer to work with established authors published by major houses in New York. We will consider marketable proposals from new/previously unpublished writers."

●◐ SUSAN SCHULMAN LITERARY AGENCY

454 W. 44th St., New York NY 10036. (212)713-1633. **Fax:** (212)581-8830. **E-mail:** Susan@Schulmanagency.com. **Website:** www.publishersmarketplace.com/members/Schulman/. **Contact:** Susan Schulman. Estab. 1980. Member of AAR. Signatory of WGA. Other memberships include Dramatists Guild. 10% of clients are new/unpublished writers. Currently handles nonfiction books (50%), novels (25%), juvenile books (15%), stage plays (10%).

REPRESENTS Considers these fiction areas: juvenile, literary, mainstream, women's.

⌖ "We specialize in books for, by, and about women and women's issues including nonfiction self-help books, fiction and theater projects. We also handle the film, television and allied rights for several agencies as well as foreign rights for several publishing houses." Actively seeking new nonfiction. Considers plays. Does not want to receive poetry, television scripts or concepts for television.

HOW TO CONTACT "For fiction: query letter with outline and 3 sample chapters, resume and SASE. For nonfiction: query letter with complete description of subject, at least 1 chapter, resume and SASE. Queries may be sent via regular mail or e-mail. Please do not submit queries via UPS or Federal Express. Please do not send attachments with e-mail queries." Accepts simultaneous submissions. Responds in 6 weeks to queries/mss. Obtains most new clients through recommendations from others, solicitations, conferences.

TERMS Agent receives 15% commission on domestic sales. Agent receives 20% commission on foreign sales. Offers written contract; 30-day notice must be given to terminate contract.

RECENT SALES Sold 50 titles in the last year; hundred of subsidiary rights deals.

WRITERS CONFERENCES Geneva Writers Conference (Switzerland); Columbus Writers Conference; Skidmore Conference of the Independent Women's Writers Group.

TIPS "Keep writing!" Schulman describes her agency as "professional boutique, long-standing, eclectic."

⬤ SCRIBE AGENCY, LLC

5508 Joylynne Dr., Madison WI 53716. **E-mail:** whattheshizzle@scribeagency.com. **E-mail:** submissions@scribeagency.com. **Website:** www.scribeagency.com. **Contact:** Kristopher O'Higgins. Represents 11 clients. 18% of clients are new/unpublished writers.Currently handles novels (98%), story collections (2%).

○ "With more than 15 years experience in publishing, with time spent on both the agency and editorial sides, with marketing experience to boot, Scribe Agency is a full-service literary agency, working hands-on with its authors on their projects. Check the website (scribeagency.com) to make sure your work matches the Scribe aesthetic."

MEMBER AGENTS Kristopher O'Higgins.

REPRESENTS novels anthologies. **Considers these fiction areas:** experimental, fantasy, feminist, horror, literary, mainstream, science fiction, thriller.

⟞ Actively seeking excellent writers with ideas and stories to tell.

HOW TO CONTACT E-queries only: submissions@scribeagency.com. See the website for submission info, as it may change. Responds in 3-4 weeks to queries. Responds in 5 months to mss.

TERMS Agent receives 15% commission on domestic sales. Agent receives 20% commission on foreign sales. Offers written contract. Charges for postage and photocopying.

WRITERS CONFERENCES BookExpo America; WisCon; Wisconsin Book Festival; World Fantasy Convention; WorldCon.

SECRET AGENT MAN

P.O. Box 1078, Lake Forest CA 92609. (949)698-6987. **E-mail:** query@secretagentman.net. **Website:** www.secretagentman.net. **Contact:** Scott Mortenson.

⟞ Selective mystery, thriller, suspense and detective fiction. Does not want to receive scripts or screenplays.

HOW TO CONTACT Query via e-mail only; include sample chapter(s), synopsis and/or outline. Prefers to read the real thing rather than a description of it. Obtains most new clients through recommendations from others.

LYNN SELIGMAN, LITERARY AGENT

400 Highland Ave., Upper Montclair NJ 07043. (973)783-3631. **Contact:** Lynn Seligman.

○ Prior to opening her agency, Ms. Seligman worked in the subsidiary rights department of Doubleday and Simon & Schuster, and served as an agent with Julian Bach Literary Agency (which became IMG Literary Agency). Foreign rights are represented by Books Crossing Borders, Inc.

REPRESENTS nonfiction books, novels. **Considers these fiction areas:** detective, ethnic, fantasy, feminist, historical, horror, humor, literary, mainstream, mystery, romance, contemporary, gothic, historical, regency, science fiction.

⟞ "This agency specializes in general nonfiction and fiction. I also do illustrated and photography books and have represented several photographers for books."

HOW TO CONTACT Query with SASE. Prefers to read materials exclusively. Accepts simultaneous submissions. Responds in 2 weeks to queries. Responds in 2 months to mss. Obtains most new clients through referrals from other writers and editors.

TERMS Agent receives 15% commission on domestic sales. Agent receives 25% commission on foreign sales. Charges clients for photocopying, unusual postage, express mail, telephone expenses (checks with author first).

RECENT SALES Sold 15 titles in the last year. Lords of Vice series by Barbara Pierce; Untitled series by Deborah Leblanc.

SERENDIPITY LITERARY AGENCY, LLC

305 Gates Ave., Brooklyn NY 11216. (718)230-7689. **Fax:** (718)230-7829. **E-mail:** rbrooks@serendipitylit.com; info@serendipitylit.com. **Website:** www.serendipitylit.com; facebook.com/serendipitylit. **Contact:** Regina Brooks. Represents 50 clients. 50% of clients are new/unpublished writers.Currently handles nonfiction books (50%), other (50% fiction).

Prior to becoming an agent, Ms. Brooks was an acquisitions editor for John Wiley & Sons, Inc. and McGraw-Hill Companies.

MEMBER AGENTS Regina Brooks; Dawn Michelle Hardy (sports, pop culture, blog and trend, music, lifestyle and social science), Karen Thomas (narrative nonfiction, celebrity, pop culture, memoir, general fiction, women's fiction, romance, mystery, self-help, inspirational, Christian based fiction and nonfiction including Evangelical), John Weber (unique YA and middle-grade); Folade Bell (literary and commercial women's fiction, YA, literary mysteries and thrillers, historical fiction, African-American issues, gay/lesbian, Christian fiction, humor and books that deeply explore other cultures); Nadeen Gayle (romance, memoir, pop culture, inspirational/ religious, women's fiction, parenting young adult, mystery and political thrillers, and all forms of nonfiction).

REPRESENTS Considers these fiction areas: commercial, gay, historical, humor, lesbian, literary, middle-grade, mystery, romance, thriller, women's, young adult.

African-American nonfiction, commercial fiction, young adult novels, and juvenile books. No stage plays, screenplays or poetry.

HOW TO CONTACT Check the website, as there are online submission forms for fiction, nonfiction and juvenile. Accepts simultaneous submissions. Obtains most new clients through conferences, referrals.

TERMS Agent receives 15% commission on domestic sales. Agent receives 20% commission on foreign sales. Offers written contract; two-month notice must be given to terminate contract. Charges clients for office fees, which are taken from any advance.

RECENT SALES *How I Discovered Poetry* by Marilyn Nelson; *Cooking Allergy Free* by Jenna Short; *Cleo Edi-*

son Oliver by Sundee Frazier; *Flight Of The Seahawks* by Jerry Brewer; *It's Not A Game* by Kent Babb; *Drop The Act: It's Exhausting* by Beth Thomas Cohen; *College, Quicker: The Fast-Track To a More Affordable College Degree* by Katherine Stephens; *Every Closed Eye Ain't Sleep* by Marita Teague Tips "

TIPS "See the books *Writing Great Books For Young Adults* and *You Should Really Write A Book: How To Write Sell And Market Your Memoir*. We are looking for high concept ideas with big hooks. If you get writer's block try possibiliteas.co; it's a muse in a cup."

THE SEYMOUR AGENCY

475 Miner St., Canton NY 13617. (315)386-1831. **E-mail:** marysue@twcny.rr.com; nicole@theseymouragency.com; julie@theseymouragency.com; lane@theseymouragency.com. **Website:** www.theseymouragency.com. Member of AAR. Signatory of WGA. Other memberships include RWA, Authors Guild.

Ms. Seymour is a retired New York State certified teacher. Ms. Resciniti was recently named "Agent of the Year" by the ACFW.

MEMBER AGENTS Mary Sue Seymour (accepts queries in Christian, inspirational, romance, and nonfiction); Nicole Resciniti (accepts all genres of romance, young adult, middle-grade, new adult, suspense, thriller, mystery, sci-fi, fantasy); Julie Gwinn (Christian and inspirational fiction and nonfiction, women's fiction [contemporary and historical], new adult, Southern fiction, literary fiction and young adult); Lane Heymont (science fiction, fantasy, nonfiction).

REPRESENTS nonfiction books, novels. **Considers these fiction areas:** action, fantasy, inspirational, middle-grade, mystery, new adult, religious, romance, science fiction, suspense, thriller, young adult.

HOW TO CONTACT For Mary Sue: E-query with synopsis, first 50 pages for romance. Accepts e-mail queries. For Nicole and Julie: E-mail the query plus first 5 pages of the ms pasted into the e-mail. Accepts simultaneous submissions. Responds in 1 month to queries. Responds in 3 months to mss.

TERMS Agent receives 12-15% commission on domestic sales.

KEN SHERMAN & ASSOCIATES

1275 N. Hayworth, Ste. 103, Los Angeles CA 90046. (310)273-8840. **Fax:** (310)271-2875. **Website:** www.kenshermanassociates.com. **Contact:** Ken Sherman.

Prior to opening his agency, Mr. Sherman was with The William Morris Agency, The Lantz

Office and Paul Kohner, Inc. He has taught The Business of Writing For Film and Television and The Book Worlds at UCLA and USC. He also lectures extensively at writer's conferences and film festivals around the U.S. He is currently a Commissioner of Arts and Cultural Affairs in the City of West Hollywood and is on the International Advisory Board of the Christopher Isherwood Foundation.

REPRESENTS nonfiction books, novels, movie, tv, not episodic drama teleplays, life rights, film/TV rights to books and life rights. **Considers these fiction areas:** glitz, newage, psychic, adventure, comic, confession, detective, erotica, ethnic, experimental, family, fantasy, feminist, gay, gothic, hi lo, historical, horror, humor, literary, mainstream, military, multicultural, multimedia, mystery, occult, picture books, plays, poetry, poetry translation, regional, religious, romance, science, short, spiritual, sports, thriller, translation, western, young adult.

HOW TO CONTACT Contact by referral only. Reports in approximately 1 month to mss. Obtains most new clients through recommendations from others.

TERMS Agent receives 15% commission on domestic sales. Agent receives 15% commission on foreign sales. Agent receives 10-15% commission on film sales. Offers written contract. Charges clients for reasonable office expenses (postage, photocopying, etc.)

RECENT SALES Sold more than 20 scripts in the last year. *Back Roads* by Tawni O'Dell with Adrian Lyne set to direct; *Priscilla Salyers Story*, produced by Andrea Baynes (ABC); *Toys of Glass* by Martin Booth (ABC/Saban Entertainment); *Brazil* by John Updike (film rights to Glaucia Carmagos); *Fifth Sacred Thing* by Starhawk (Bantam), with Starhawk adapting her book into a screenplay; *Questions From Dad* by Dwight Twilly (Tuttle); *Snow Falling on Cedars* by David Guterson (Universal Pictures); *The Witches of Eastwick—The Musical* by John Updike (Cameron Macintosh, Ltd.); *Rabbit/HBO-1-Hr Series*, John Updike.

WRITERS CONFERENCES Maui Writers Conference; Squaw Valley Writers' Workshop; Santa Barbara Writers Conference; Screenwriting Conference in Santa Fe; Aspen Summer Words Literary Festival (The Aspen Institute and the San Francisco Writers Conference). San Francisco Writers Conference, Chautauqua Writers Conference.

WENDY SHERMAN ASSOCIATES, INC.

27 W. 24th St., Suite 700B, New York NY 10010. (212)279-9027. **E-mail:** submissions@wsherman.com. **Website:** www.wsherman.com. **Contact:** Wendy Sherman; Kim Perel. Member of AAR.

○ Prior to opening the agency, Ms. Sherman served as vice president, executive director, associate publisher, subsidiary rights director, and sales and marketing director for major publishers.

MEMBER AGENTS Wendy Sherman (women's fiction that hits that sweet spot between literary and mainstream, Southern voices, historical dramas, suspense with a well-developed protagonist, and writing that illuminates the multicultural experience); **Kim Perel** (illustrated lifestyle books in the areas of fashion, home décor and food; she also loves unique memoir that reads like fiction, in-depth journalistic no-fiction, "big idea" books about why we think, live or process thoughts the way we do, and fiction that straddles literary and commercial with a strong story and beautifully-crafted prose).

REPRESENTS Considers these fiction areas: mainstream Mainstream fiction that hits the sweet spot between literary and commercial.

☛ "We specialize in developing new writers, as well as working with more established writers. My experience as a publisher has proven to be a great asset to my clients."

HOW TO CONTACT Query via e-mail only. "We ask that you include your last name, title, and the name of the agent you are submitting to in the subject line. For fiction, please include a query letter and your first 10 pages copied and pasted in the body of the e-mail. We will not open attachments unless they have been requested. For nonfiction, please include your query letter and author bio. Due to the large number of e-mail submissions that we receive, we can only reply to e-mail queries in the affirmative. We respectfully ask that you do not send queries to our individual e-mail addresses." Accepts simultaneous submissions. Obtains most new clients through recommendations from other writers.

TERMS Agent receives standard 15% commission. Offers written contract.

RECENT SALES *Z, A Novel of Zelda Fitzgerald* by Therese Anne Fowler; *The Silence of Bonaventure Arrow* by Rita Leganski; *Together Tea* by Marjan Kamali; *A Long Long Time Ago and Essentially True* by Brigid Pasulka; *Illuminations* by Mary Sharratt; *The Ac-*

counting by William Lashner; *Lunch in Paris* by Elizabeth Bard; *The Rules of Inheritance* by Claire Bidwell Smith; *Love in Ninety Days* by Dr. Diana Kirschner; *The Wow Factor* by Jacqui Stafford; *Humor Memoirs* by Wade Rouse.

TIPS "The bottom line is: Do your homework. Be as well prepared as possible. Read the books that will help you present yourself and your work with polish. You want your submission to stand out."

☽◑ JEFFREY SIMMONS LITERARY AGENCY

15 Penn House, Mallory St., London NW8 8SX England. (44)(207)224-8917. **E-mail:** jasimmons@unicombox. co.uk. **Contact:** Jeffrey Simmons. Represents 43 clients. 40% of clients are new/unpublished writers.Currently handles nonfiction books (65%), novels (35%).

○ Prior to becoming an agent, Mr. Simmons was a publisher. He is also an author.

REPRESENTS nonfiction books, novels. **Considers these fiction areas:** action, adventure, confession, crime, detective, family saga, literary, mainstream, mystery, police, suspense, thriller.

⊶ "This agency seeks to handle good books and promising young writers. My long experience in publishing and as an author and ghostwriter means I can offer an excellent service all around, especially in terms of editorial experience where appropriate." Actively seeking quality fiction, biography, autobiography, showbiz, personality books, law, crime, politics, and world affairs. Does not want to receive science fiction, horror, fantasy, juvenile, academic books, or specialist subjects (e.g., cooking, gardening, religious).

HOW TO CONTACT Submit sample chapter, outline/proposal, SASE (IRCs if necessary).Prefers to read materials exclusively. Responds in 1 week to queries. Responds in 1 month to mss. Obtains most new clients through recommendations from others, solicitations.

TERMS Agent receives 10-15% commission on domestic sales. Agent receives 15% commission on foreign sales. Offers written contract, binding for lifetime of book in question or until it becomes out of print.

TIPS "When contacting us with an outline/proposal, include a brief biographical note (listing any previous publications, with publishers and dates). Preferably tell us if the book has already been offered elsewhere."

○○ BEVERLEY SLOPEN LITERARY AGENCY

131 Bloor St. W., Suite 711, Toronto ON M5S 1S3 Canada. (416)964-9598. **E-mail:** beverly@slopenagency.ca. **Website:** www.slopenagency.ca. **Contact:** Beverley Slopen. Represents 70 clients. 20% of clients are new/unpublished writers.

○ Prior to opening her agency, Ms. Slopen worked in publishing and as a journalist.

REPRESENTS nonfiction books, novels, scholarly. **Considers these fiction areas:** commercial, literary, mystery, suspense.

⊶ "This agency has a strong bent toward Canadian writers." Actively seeking serious nonfiction that is accessible and appealing to the general reader. Does not want to receive fantasy, science fiction, or children's books.

HOW TO CONTACT Query by e-mail. Returns materials only with SASE (Canadian postage only). To submit a work for consideration, e-mail a short query letter and a few sample pages. Submit only 1 work at a time. If we want to see more, we will contact the writer by phone or e-mail. Accepts simultaneous submissions. Responds in 2 months to queries.

TERMS Agent receives 15% commission on domestic sales. Agent receives 10% commission on foreign sales. Offers written contract, binding for 2 years; three-month notice must be given to terminate contract.

RECENT SALES *Solar Dance* by Modris Eksteins (Knopf Canada, Harvard University Press.U.S.); *The Novels* by Terry Fallis; *God's Brain* by Lionel Tiger and Michael McGuire (Prometheus Books); *What They Wanted* by Donna Morrissey (Penguin Canada, Premium/DTV Germany); *The Age of Persuasion* by Terry O'Reilly and Mike Tennant (Knopf Canada, Counterpoint U.S.); *Prisoner of Tehran* by Marina Nemat (Penguin Canada, Free Press U.S., John Murray U.K.); *Race to the Polar Sea* by Ken McGoogan (HarperCollins Canada, Counterpoint U.S.); *Transgression* by James Nichol (HarperCollins U.S., McArthur Canada, Goldmann Germany); *Midwife of Venice* and *The Harem Midwife* by Roberta Rich; *Vermeer's Hat* by Timothy Brook (HarperCollins Canada, Bloomsbury U.S.); *Distantly Related to Freud* by Ann Charney (Cormorant).

TIPS "Please, no unsolicited mss."

◑ SPECTRUM LITERARY AGENCY

320 Central Park W., Suite 1-D, New York NY 10025. **Fax:** (212)362-4562. **Website:** www.spectrumliterary-

agency.com. **Contact:** Eleanor Wood, president. Estab. 1976. SFWA Represents 90 clients. Currently handles nonfiction books (10%), novels (90%).

MEMBER AGENTS Eleanor Wood (referrals only), **Justin Bell** (science fiction, mysteries, nonfiction). **REPRESENTS** nonfiction books, novels. **Considers these fiction areas:** mystery, science fiction.

HOW TO CONTACT Snail mail query with SASE. Submit author bio, publishing credits. No unsolicited mss will be read. Responds in 1-3 months to queries. Obtains most new clients through recommendations from authors.

TERMS Agent receives 15% commission on domestic sales. Deducts for photocopying and book orders.

TIPS "Spectrum's policy is to read only book-length mss that we have specifically asked to see. Unsolicited mss are not accepted. The letter should describe your book briefly and include publishing credits and background information or qualifications relating to your work, if any."

SPENCERHILL ASSOCIATES

8131 Lakewood Main St., Building M, Suite 2015, Lakewood Ranch FL 34202. (518)392-9293. **Fax:** (518)392-9554. **E-mail:** submissions@spencerhillassociates.com. **Website:** www.spencerhillassociates.com. **Contact:** Karen Solem, Nalini Akolekar or Amanda Leuck. Member of AAR. Represents 96 clients. 10% of clients are new/unpublished writers.

Prior to becoming an agent, Ms. Solem was editor in chief at HarperCollins and an associate publisher.

MEMBER AGENTS Karen Solem; Nalini Akolekar; Amanda Leuck.

REPRESENTS novels. **Considers these fiction areas:** commercial, erotica, literary, mainstream, mystery, paranormal, romance, thriller.

"We handle mostly commercial women's fiction, historical novels, romance (historical, contemporary, paranormal, urban fantasy), thrillers, and mysteries. We also represent Christian fiction only—no nonfiction." No nonfiction, poetry, science fiction, children's picture books, or scripts.

HOW TO CONTACT "We accept electronic submissions and are no longer accepting paper queries. Please send us a query letter in the body of an e-mail, pitch us your project and tell us about yourself: Do you have prior publishing credits? Attach the first 3 chapters and synopsis preferably in .doc, .rtf or .txt format to your e-mail. Send all queries to submission@spencerhillassociates.com. We do not have a preference for exclusive submissions, but do appreciate knowing if the submission is simultaneous. We receive thousands of submissions a year and each query receives our attention. Unfortunately, we are unable to respond to each query individually. If we are interested in your work, we will contact you within 8 weeks." Accepts simultaneous submissions.

TERMS Agent receives 15% commission on domestic sales. Agent receives 20% commission on foreign sales. Offers written contract; three-month notice must be given to terminate contract.

RECENT SALES A full list of sales and clients is available on the agency website.

THE SPIELER AGENCY

27 W. 20 St., Suite 305, New York NY 10011. **E-mail:** thespieleragency@gmail.com. **Contact:** Joe Spieler. Represents 160 clients. 2% of clients are new/unpublished writers.

Prior to opening his agency, Mr. Spieler was a magazine editor.

MEMBER AGENTS Eric Myers, eric@thespieleragency.com (pop culture, memoir, history, thrillers, young adult, middle-grade, new adult, and picture books [text only]); **Victoria Shoemaker**, victoria@thespieleragency.com (environment and natural history, popular culture, memoir, photography and film, literary fiction and poetry, and books on food and cooking); **John Thornton**, john@thespieleragency.com (nonfiction); **Joe Spieler**, joe@thespieleragency.com (nonfiction and fiction and books for children and young adults).

REPRESENTS novels, juvenile books. **Considers these fiction areas:** literary, middle-grade, New Age, picture books, thriller, young adult.

HOW TO CONTACT "Before submitting projects to the Spieler Agency, check the listings of our individual agents and see if any particular agent shows a general interest in your subject (e.g., history, memoir, YA, etc.). Please send all queries either by e-mail or regular mail. If you query us by regular mail, we can only reply to you if you include a self-addressed, stamped envelope." Accepts simultaneous submissions. Cannot guarantee a personal response to all queries. Obtains most new clients through recommendations, listing in *Guide to Literary Agents*.

TERMS Agent receives 15% commission on domestic sales. Charges clients for messenger bills, photocopying, postage.

WRITERS CONFERENCES London Book Fair.

TIPS "Check www.publishersmarketplace.com/members/spielerlit/."

○ NANCY STAUFFER ASSOCIATES

P.O. Box 1203, Darien CT 06820. (203)202-2500. E-mail: nancy@staufferliterary.com. **Website:** www.publishersmarketplace.com/members/nstauffer. **Contact:** Nancy Stauffer Cahoon. Other memberships include Authors Guild. Currently handles nonfiction books (10%), novels (90%).

"Over the course of my more than 20 year career, I've held positions in the editorial, marketing, business, and rights departments of *The New York Times*, McGraw-Hill, and Doubleday. Before founding Nancy Stauffer Associates, I was Director of Foreign and Performing Rights then Director, Subsidiary Rights, for Doubleday, where I was honored to have worked with a diverse range of internationally known and best-selling authors of all genres."

HOW TO CONTACT Accepts simultaneous submissions. Obtains most new clients through referrals from existing clients.

TERMS Agent receives 15% commission on domestic sales. Agent receives 20% commission on foreign sales.

RECENT SALES *Blasphemy* by Sherman Alexie; *Benediction* by Kent Haruf; *Bone Fire* by Mark Spragg; *The Carry Home* by Gary Ferguson.

◑ STEELE-PERKINS LITERARY AGENCY

26 Island Ln., Canandaigua NY 14424. (585)396-9290. **Fax:** (585)396-3579. **E-mail:** pattiesp@aol.com. **Contact:** Pattie Steele-Perkins. Member of AAR. Other memberships include RWA. Currently handles novels (100%).

REPRESENTS novels. **Considers these fiction areas:** romance, women's category romance, romantic suspense, historical, contemporary, multi-cultural, and inspirational.

HOW TO CONTACT Submit query along with synopsis and 1 chapter via e-mail (no attachments) or snail mail. Snail mail submissions require SASE. Accepts simultaneous submissions. Obtains most new clients through recommendations from others, queries/solicitations.

TERMS Agent receives 15% commission on domestic sales. Offers written contract, binding for 1 year; one-month notice must be given to terminate contract.

RECENT SALES Sold 130 titles last year. This agency prefers not to share specific sales information.

TIPS "Be patient. E-mail rather than call. Make sure what you are sending is the best it can be."

○ STERNIG & BYRNE LITERARY AGENCY

2370 S. 107th St., Apt. #4, Milwaukee WI 53227. (414)328-8034. **Fax:** (414)328-8034. **E-mail:** jackbyrne@hotmail.com. **Website:** www.sff.net/people/jackbyrne. **Contact:** Jack Byrne. Other memberships include SFWA, MWA.

REPRESENTS nonfiction books, novels, juvenile. **Considers these fiction areas:** fantasy, horror, mystery, science fiction, suspense.

"Our client list is comfortably full, and our current needs are therefore quite limited." Actively seeking science fiction/fantasy and mystery by established writers. Does not want to receive romance, poetry, textbooks, or highly specialized nonfiction.

HOW TO CONTACT Query with SASE. Prefers e-mail queries (no attachments); hard copy queries also acceptable.

TIPS "Don't send first drafts, have a professional presentation (including cover letter), and know your field. Read what's been done—good and bad."

○ THE STROTHMAN AGENCY, LLC

63 East 9th St., 10X, New York NY 10003. **E-mail:** info@strothmanagency.com. **Website:** www.strothmanagency.com. **Contact:** Wendy Strothman, Lauren MacLeod. Member of AAR. Other memberships include Authors' Guild. Represents 50 clients.

Prior to becoming an agent, Ms. Strothman was head of Beacon Press (1983-1995) and executive vice president of Houghton Mifflin's Trade and Reference Division (1996-2002).

MEMBER AGENTS Wendy Strothman; Lauren MacLeod.

REPRESENTS nonfiction, juvenile books. **Considers these fiction areas:** literary, middle-grade, young adult.

"Because we are highly selective in the clients we represent, we increase the value publishers place on our properties. We specialize in narrative nonfiction, memoir, history, science and nature, arts and culture, literary travel, current affairs, young adult, middle-grade, and some business." The Strothman Agency seeks out scholars, journalists, and other acknowledged and emerging experts in their fields. We are now actively looking for authors of well-written young-adult fiction and nonfiction. Browse the Latest News to get an idea of the types of books that we represent. For more about what we're looking for, read Pitching an Agent: The Strothman Agency on the publishing website www.strothmanagency.com." Does not want to receive adult fiction or self-help.

HOW TO CONTACT Accepts queries only via e-mail at strothmanagency@gmail.com. See submission guidelines online. Accepts simultaneous submissions. Responds in 4 weeks to queries. Responds in 8 weeks to mss. Obtains most new clients through recommendations from others.

TERMS Agent receives 15% commission on domestic sales. Agent receives 20% commission on foreign sales. Offers written contract; 30-day notice must be given to terminate contract.

EMMA SWEENEY AGENCY, LLC

245 E 80th St., Suite 7E, New York NY 10075. **E-mail:** queries@emmasweeneyagency.com. **Website:** www. emmasweeneyagency.com. Member of AAR. Other memberships include Women's Media Group. Represents 80 clients. 5% of clients are new/unpublished writers.Currently handles nonfiction books (50%), novels (50%).

Prior to becoming an agent, Ms. Sweeney was director of subsidiary rights at Grove Press. Since 1990, she has been a literary agent.

MEMBER AGENTS Emma Sweeney, president.

REPRESENTS nonfiction books, novels. **Considers these fiction areas:** literary, mainstream, mystery.

Does not want to receive romance, Westerns or screenplays.

HOW TO CONTACT "We accept only electronic queries, and ask that all queries be sent to queries@ emmasweeneyagency.com rather than to any agent directly. Please begin your query with a succinct (and hopefully catchy) description of your plot or proposal. Always include a brief cover letter telling us how you heard about ESA, your previous writing credits, and a few lines about yourself. We cannot open any attachments unless specifically requested, and ask that you paste the first 10 pages of your proposal or novel into the text of your e-mail."

TERMS Agent receives 15% commission on domestic sales. Agent receives 10% commission on foreign sales.

TALCOTT NOTCH LITERARY

2 Broad St., Second Floor, Suite 10, Milford CT 06460. (203)876-4959. **Fax:** (203)876-9517. **E-mail:** editori-al@talcottnotch.net. **Website:** www.talcottnotch.net. **Contact:** Gina Panettieri, President. Represents 35 clients. 25% of clients are new/unpublished writers.

Prior to becoming an agent, Ms. Panettieri was a freelance writer and editor.

MEMBER AGENTS Gina Panettieri, gpanettieri@ talcottnotch.net (history, business, self-help, science, gardening, cookbooks, crafts, parenting, memoir, true crime and travel, women's fiction, paranormal, urban fantasy, horror, science fiction, historical, mystery, thrillers and suspense); **Paula Munier**, pmunier@talcottnotch.net (mystery/thriller, SF/fantasy, romance, YA, memoir, humor, pop culture, health and wellness, cooking, self-help, pop psych, New Age, inspirational, technology, science, and writing); **Rachael Dugas**, rdugas@talcottnotch.net (young adult, middle-grade, romance, and women's fiction); **Jessica Negron**, jnegron@talcottnotch.net (commercial fiction, sci fi and fantasy (and all the little sub genres), psychological thrillers, cozy mysteries, romance, erotic romance, YA); **Suba Sulaiman**, ssulaiman@ talcottnotch.net (upmarket literary and commercial fiction, romance [all subgenres except paranormal], character-driven psychological thrillers, cozy mysteries, memoir, young adult [except paranormal and sci-fi], middle-grade, and nonfiction humor).

REPRESENTS Considers these fiction areas: commercial, fantasy, historical, horror, literary, mainstream, middle-grade, mystery, New Age, paranormal, romance, science fiction, suspense, thriller, urban fantasy, women's, young adult.

HOW TO CONTACT Query via e-mail (preferred) with first 10 pages of the ms pasted within the body of the e-mail, not as an attachment. Accepts simultaneous submissions. Responds in 1 week to queries. Responds in 4-6 weeks to mss.

TERMS Agent receives 15% commission on domestic sales. Agent receives 20% commission on foreign sales. Offers written contract, binding for 1 year.

RECENT SALES Sold 36 titles in the last year. *Delivered From Evil* by Ron Franscell (Fairwinds) and *Sourtoe* (Globe Pequot Press); *Hellforged* by Nancy Holzner (Berkley Ace Science Fiction); *Welcoming Kitchen; 200 Allergen- and Gluten-Free Vegan Recipes* by Kim Lutz and Megan Hart (Sterling); *Dr. Seteh's Love Prescription* by Dr. Seth Meyers (Adams Media); *The Book of Ancient Bastards* by Brian Thornton (Adams Media); *Hope in Courage* by Beth Fehlbaum (Westside Books) and more.

TIPS "Know your market and how to reach them. A strong platform is essential in your book proposal. Can you effectively use social media/Are you a strong networker: Are you familiar with the book bloggers in your genre? Are you involved with the interest-specific groups that can help you? What can you do to break through the 'noise' and help present your book to your readers? Check our website for more tips and information on this topic."

TRANSATLANTIC LITERARY AGENCY

2 Bloor St., Suite 3500, Toronto ON M4W 1A8 Canada. (416)488-9214. **E-mail:** info@transatlanticagency.com. **Website:** transatlanticagency.com.

MEMBER AGENTS **Trena White** (nonfiction); **Amy Tompkins** (fiction, nonfiction, juvenile); **Stephanie Sinclair** (fiction, nonfiction); **Fiona Kenshole** (juvenile, illustrators); **Samantha Haywood** (fiction, nonfiction, graphic novels); **Jesse Finkelstein** (nonfiction); **Marie Campbell** (middle-grade fiction); **Shaun Bradley** (referrals only); **Sandra Bishop** (fiction, nonfiction, serious narratives to inspirational romance); **Barb Miller**; **Lynn Bennett**; **David Bennett**.

REPRESENTS nonfiction books, novels, juvenile.

"In both children's and adult literature, we market directly into the U.S., the United Kingdom and Canada." Actively seeking literary children's and adult fiction, nonfiction. Does not want to receive picture books, poetry, screenplays or stage plays.

HOW TO CONTACT Always refer to the website, as guidelines will change, and only various agents are open to new clients at any given time. Obtains most new clients through recommendations from others.

TERMS Agent receives 15% commission on domestic sales. Agent receives 20% commission on foreign sales. Offers written contract; 45-day notice must be given to terminate contract. This agency charges for photocopying and postage when it exceeds $100.

RECENT SALES Sold 250 titles in the last year.

TRIADA U.S. LITERARY AGENCY, INC.

P.O. Box 561, Sewickley PA 15143. (412)401-3376. **E-mail:** uwe@triadaus.com; brent@triadaus.com; laura@triadaus.com. **Website:** www.triadaus.com. **Contact:** Dr. Uwe Stender. Member of AAR.

MEMBER AGENTS **Uwe Stender**; **Brent Taylor** (middle-grade, young adult, new adult, and select mystery/crime and women's fiction); **Laura Crockett**.

REPRESENTS fiction, nonfiction. **Considers these fiction areas:** action, adventure, crime, detective, ethnic, historical, horror, juvenile, literary, mainstream, middle-grade, mystery, new adult, occult, police, romance, women's, young adult.

"We are looking for great writing and story platforms. Our response time is fairly unique. We recognize that neither we nor the authors have time to waste, so we guarantee a 5-day response time. We usually respond within 24 hours. "Actively looking for both fiction and nonfiction in all areas.

HOW TO CONTACT E-mail queries preferred. Accepts simultaneous submissions. Obtains most new clients through recommendations from others, conferences.

TERMS Agent receives 15% commission on domestic sales. Agent receives 20% commission on foreign sales. Offers written contract; 30-day notice must be given to terminate contract.

RECENT SALES *The Man Whisperer* by Samantha Brett and Donna Sozio (Adams Media); *Whatever Happened to Pudding Pops* by Gael Fashingbauer Cooper and Brian Bellmont (Penguin/Perigee); *86'd* by Dan Fante (Harper Perennial); *Hating Olivia* by Mark SaFranko (Harper Perennial); *Everything I'm Not Made Me Everything I Am* by Jeff Johnson (Smiley Books).

TIPS "I comment on all requested mss that I reject."

TRIDENT MEDIA GROUP

41 Madison Ave., 36th Floor, New York NY 10010. (212)333-1511. **Website:** www.tridentmediagroup.com. **Contact:** Ellen Levine. Member of AAR.

MEMBER AGENTS **Kimberly Whalen**, ws.assistant@tridentmediagroup (commercial fiction and nonfiction, women's fiction, suspense, paranormal, and pop culture); **Scott Miller**, smiller@tridentmediagroup.com (thrillers, crime fiction, women's and book club fiction, and a wide variety of nonfiction, such as military, celebrity and pop culture, narrative, sports, prescriptive, and current events); **Melissa Flashman**, mflashman@tridentmediagroup.com (pop culture, memoir, wellness, popular science, business and economics, and technology—also fiction in the genres of mystery, suspense or YA); **Alyssa Eisner Henkin**, ahenkin@tridentmediagroup.com (juvenile, children's, young adult); **Don Fehr**, dfehr@tridentmediagroup.com (literary and commercial fiction, narrative nonfiction, memoirs, travel, science, and health); **John Silbersack**, silbersack.

assistant@tridentmediagroup.com (commercial and literary fiction, science fiction and fantasy, narrative nonfiction, young adult, thrillers); **Erica Spellman-Silverman**; **Ellen Levine**, levine.assistant@tridentmediagroup.com (popular commercial fiction and compelling nonfiction—memoir, popular culture, narrative nonfiction, history, politics, biography, science, and the odd quirky book); **MacKenzie Fraser-Bub**, MFraserBub@tridentmediagroup.com (many genres of fiction—specializing in women's fiction); **Mark Gottlieb** (science fiction, fantasy, young adult, comics, graphic novels, historical, history, horror, literary, middle-grade, mystery, thrillers and new adult; in nonfiction, he seeks arts, cinema, photography, biography, memoir, self-help, sports, travel, world cultures, true crime, mind/body/spirit, narrative nonfiction, politics, current affairs, pop culture, entertainment, relationships, family, science, technology); **Alexander Slater**, aslater@tridentmdiagroup.com (children's, middle-grade, and young adult fiction and nonfiction, from new and established authors).

REPRESENTS Considers these fiction areas: commercial, crime, fantasy, juvenile, literary, middle-grade, mystery, paranormal, science fiction, suspense, thriller, women's, young adult.

8— Actively seeking new or established authors in a variety of fiction and nonfiction genres.

HOW TO CONTACT While some agents are open to e-queries, all seem open to submissions through the agency's online submission form on the agency website. Query only 1 agent at a time. If you e-query, include no attachments.

RECENT SALES Recent sales include: *Sacred River* by Syl Cheney-Coker; *Saving Quinton* by Jessica Sorensen; *The Secret History of Las Vegas* by Chris Abani; *The Summer Wind* by Mary Alice Munroe.

TIPS "If you have any questions, please check FAQ page before e-mailing us."

THE UNTER AGENCY

23 W. 73rd St., Suite 100, New York NY 10023. (212)401-4068. **E-mail:** Jennifer@theunteragency.com. **Website:** www.theunteragency.com. **Contact:** Jennifer Unter. Estab. 2008.

Ms. Unter began her book publishing career in the editorial department at Henry Holt & Co. She later worked at the Karpfinger Agency while she attended law school. She then became an associate at the entertainment firm of Cowan, DeBaets, Abrahams & Sheppard LLP where she practiced primarily in the areas of publishing and copyright law.

REPRESENTS Considers these fiction areas: commercial, mainstream, middle-grade, picture books, young adult.

8— This agency specializes in children's and nonfiction, but does take quality fiction.

HOW TO CONTACT Send an e-query. There is also an online submission form. If you do not hear back from this agency within 3 months, consider that a no.

RECENT SALES A full list of recent sales/titles is available on the agency website.

UPSTART CROW LITERARY

244 Fifth Avenue, 11th Floor, New York NY 10001. **E-mail:** danielle.submission@gmail.com. **Website:** www.upstartcrowliterary.com. **Contact:** Danielle Chiotti, Alexandra Penfold. Estab. 2009.

MEMBER AGENTS Michael Stearns (not accepting submissions); **Danielle Chiotti** (young adult, middle-grade, adult upmarket commercial that explores deep emotional relationships in an interesting or unusual way, and nonfiction in the areas of narrative/memoir, lifestyle, relationships, humor, current events, food, wine, and cooking); **Ted Malawer** (accepting queries only through conference submissions and client referrals); **Alexandra Penfold** (not accepting submissions).

REPRESENTS Considers these fiction areas: middle-grade, picture books, women's, young adult.

HOW TO CONTACT Submit a query and 20 pages pasted into an e-mail.

VENTURE LITERARY

2683 Via de la Valle, G-714, Del Mar CA 92014. (619)807-1887. **Fax:** (772)365-8321. **E-mail:** submissions@ventureliterary.com. **Website:** www.ventureliterary.com. **Contact:** Frank R. Scatoni.

Prior to becoming an agent, Mr. Scatoni worked as an editor at Simon & Schuster.

MEMBER AGENTS Frank R. Scatoni (general nonfiction, biography, memoir, narrative nonfiction, sports, serious nonfiction, graphic novels, narratives).

REPRESENTS nonfiction books, novels graphic novels, narratives. **Considers these fiction areas:** action, adventure, crime, detective, literary, mainstream, mystery, police, sports, suspense, thriller, women's.

HOW TO CONTACT Considers e-mail queries only. *No unsolicited mss* and no snail mail whatsoever. See website for complete submission guidelines. Obtains most new clients through recommendations from others.

TERMS Agent receives 15% commission on domestic sales. Agent receives 20% commission on foreign sales. Offers written contract.

CHERRY WEINER LITERARY AGENCY

925 Oak Bluff Ct., Dacula GA 30019. (732)446-2096. **Fax:** (732)792-0506. **E-mail:** cherry8486@aol.com. **Contact:** Cherry Weiner. Represents 40 clients. 10% of clients are new/unpublished writers.

REPRESENTS novels. **Considers these fiction areas:** action, adventure, contemporary issues, crime, detective, family saga, fantasy, frontier, historical, mainstream, mystery, police, psychic, romance, science fiction, supernatural, thriller, westerns.

☛ *This agency is currently not accepting new clients except by referral or by personal contact at writers' conferences.* Specializes in fantasy, science fiction, westerns, mysteries (both contemporary and historical), historical novels, Native-American works, mainstream, and all genre romances.

HOW TO CONTACT Accepts e-queries only. Only wishes to receive submissions from referrals and from writers she has met at conferences/events. Responds in 1 week to queries. Responds in 2 months to mss that I have asked for.

TERMS Agent receives 15% commission on domestic sales. Agent receives 15% commission on foreign sales. Offers written contract. Charges clients for extra copies of mss, first-class postage for author's copies of books, express mail for important documents/mss.

RECENT SALES Sold 65 titles in the last year. This agency prefers not to share information on specific sales.

TIPS "Meet agents and publishers at conferences. Establish a relationship, then get in touch with them and remind them of the meeting and conference."

THE WEINGEL-FIDEL AGENCY

310 E. 46th St., 21E, New York NY 10017. (212)599-2959. **Contact:** Loretta Weingel-Fidel. Currently handles nonfiction books (75%), novels (25%).

Prior to opening her agency, Ms. Weingel-Fidel was a psychoeducational diagnostician.

REPRESENTS nonfiction books, novels. **Considers these fiction areas:** literary, mainstream.

☛ This agency specializes in commercial and literary fiction and nonfiction. Actively seeking investigative journalism. Does not want to receive genre fiction, self-help, science fiction, or fantasy.

HOW TO CONTACT Accepts writers by referral only. *No unsolicited mss.*

TERMS Agent receives 15% commission on domestic sales. Agent receives 20% commission on foreign sales. Offers written contract, binding for 1 year with automatic renewal. Bills sent back to clients are all reasonable expenses, such as UPS, express mail, photocopying, etc.

TIPS "A very small, selective list enables me to work very closely with my clients to develop and nurture talent. I only take on projects and writers about which I am extremely enthusiastic."

LARRY WEISSMAN LITERARY, LLC

526 8th St., #2R, Brooklyn NY 11215. **E-mail:** lwsubmissions@gmail.com. **Contact:** Larry Weissman.

REPRESENTS nonfiction books, novels, short story collections. **Considers these fiction areas:** literary.

☛ "Very interested in established journalists with bold voices. Interested in anything to do with food. Fiction has to feel 'vital' and short stories are accepted, but only if you can sell us on an idea for a novel as well." Nonfiction, including food and lifestyle, politics, pop culture, narrative, cultural/social issues, journalism. No genre fiction, poetry or children's.

HOW TO CONTACT "Send e-queries only. If you don't hear back, your project was not right for our list."

TERMS Agent receives 15% commission on domestic sales. Agent receives 20% commission on foreign sales.

WELLS ARMS LITERARY

E-mail: info@wellsarms.com. **Website:** www.wellsarms.com. **Contact:** Victoria Wells Arms. Estab. 2013.

Prior to opening her agency, Victoria was a children's book editor for Dial Books.

REPRESENTS **Considers these fiction areas:** juvenile, middle-grade, picture books, young adult.

☛ We focus on books for readers of all ages, and we particularly love board books, picture books, readers, chapter books, middle-grade, and young adult fiction—both authors and illustrators. We do not represent to the textbook, magazine, adult romance or fine art markets.

HOW TO CONTACT E-query. Put "Query" in your e-mail subject line. No attachments.

○ WHIMSY LITERARY AGENCY, LLC

49 North 8th St., G6, Brooklyn NY 11249. (212)674-7162. **E-mail:** whimsynyc@aol.com. **Website:** whimsyliteraryagency.com/. **Contact:** Jackie Meyer. Other memberships include Center for Independent Publishing Advisory Board. Represents 30 clients. 20% of clients are new/unpublished writers.

○ Prior to becoming an agent, Ms. Meyer was with Warner Books for 19 years.

MEMBER AGENTS Jackie Meyer; Lenore Skomal.

REPRESENTS nonfiction books. **Considers these fiction areas:** mainstream.

8—π "Whimsy looks for projects that are concept- and platform-driven. We seek books that educate, inspire and entertain." Actively seeking experts in their fields with good platforms.

HOW TO CONTACT Send a query letter via e-mail. Send a synopsis, bio, platform, and proposal. No snail mail submissions. Responds "quickly, but only if interested" to queries. *Does not accept unsolicited mss.* Obtains most new clients through recommendations from others, solicitations.

TERMS Agent receives 15% commission on domestic sales. Agent receives 20% commission on foreign sales. Offers written contract.

○ WM CLARK ASSOCIATES

186 Fifth Ave., Second Floor, New York NY 10010. (212)675-2784. **Fax:** (347)-649-9262. **E-mail:** wmclark@wmclark.com. **E-mail:** general@wmclark.com. **Website:** www.wmclark.com. Estab. 1997. Member of AAR. 50% of clients are new/unpublished writers.Currently handles nonfiction books (50%), novels (50%).

○ Prior to opening WCA, Mr. Clark was an agent at the William Morris Agency.

REPRESENTS nonfiction books, novels. **Considers these fiction areas:** contemporary issues, ethnic, historical, literary, mainstream Southern fiction.

8—π William Clark represents a wide range of titles across all formats to the publishing, motion picture, television, and new media fields on behalf of authors of first fiction and award-winning, best-selling narrative nonfiction, international authors in translation, chefs, musicians, and artists. Offering individual focus and a global presence, the agency undertakes to discover, develop, and market today's most interesting content and the talent that create it, and forge sophisticated and innovative plans for self-promotion, reliable revenue streams, and an enduring creative

career. Referral partners are available to provide services including editorial consultation, media training, lecture booking, marketing support, and public relations. Agency does not respond to screenplays or screenplay pitches. It is advised that before querying you become familiar with the kinds of books we handle by browsing our Book List, which is available on our website.

HOW TO CONTACT Accepts queries via online form only. "We respond to all queries submitted via this form." Responds in 1-2 months to queries.

TERMS Agent receives 15% commission on domestic sales. Agent receives 20% commission on foreign sales. Offers written contract.

TIPS "WCA works on a reciprocal basis with Ed Victor, Ltd. (U.K.) in representing select properties to the U.S. market and vice versa. Translation rights are sold directly in the German, Italian, Spanish, Portuguese, Latin American, French, Dutch, and Scandinavian territories in association with Andrew Nurnberg Associates Ltd. (U.K.); through offices in China, Bulgaria, Czech Republic, Latvia, Poland, Hungary, and Russia; and through corresponding agents in Japan, Greece, Israel, Turkey, Korea, Taiwan, and Thailand."

WOLF LITERARY SERVICES, LLC

Website: wolflit.com. Estab. 2008.

MEMBER AGENTS Kirsten Wolf (no queries); Adriann Ranta (all genres for all age groups with a penchant for edgy, dark, quirky voices, unique settings, and everyman stories told with a new spin; she loves gritty, realistic, true-to-life stories with conflicts based in the real world; women's fiction and nonfiction; accessible, pop nonfiction in science, history, and craft; and smart, fresh, genre-bending works for children); Kate Johnson (literary fiction, particularly character-driven stories, psychological investigations, modern-day fables, and the occasional high-concept plot; she also represents memoir, cultural history and narrative nonfiction, and loves working with journalists); Allison Devereux (literary and upmarket commercial fiction, everyman characters in unlikely situations, debut voices, and psychologically adept narratives with a surreal bent; she loves narrative nonfiction, examinations of contemporary culture, pop science, cultural history, illustrated/graphic memoir, humor, and blog-to-book).

REPRESENTS Considers these fiction areas: literary, women's, young adult magical realism.

HOW TO CONTACT To submit a project, please send a query letter along with a 50-page writing sample (for fiction) or a detailed proposal (for nonfiction) to queries@wolflit.com. Samples may be submitted as an attachment or embedded in the body of the e-mail. **RECENT SALES** *Hoodoo* by Ronald Smith (Clarion); *Binary Star* by Sarah Gerard (Two Dollar Radio); *Conviction* by Kelly Loy Gilbert (Hyperion); *The Empire Striketh Back* by Ian Doescher (Quirk Books).

WOLFSON LITERARY AGENCY

P.O. Box 266, New York NY 10276. **E-mail:** query@wolfsonliterary.com. **Website:** www.wolfsonliterary.com. **Contact:** Michelle Wolfson. Estab. 2007. Adheres to AAR canon of ethics.

Prior to forming her own agency in December 2007, Ms. Wolfson spent 2 years with Artists & Artisans, Inc. and 2 years with Ralph Vicinanza, Ltd.

Actively seeking commercial fiction: young adult, mainstream, mysteries, thrillers, suspense, women's fiction, romance, practical or narrative nonfiction (particularly of interest to women).

HOW TO CONTACT E-queries only. Accepts simultaneous submissions. Responds only if interested. Positive response is generally given within 2-4 weeks. Responds in 3 months to mss. Obtains most new clients through queries or recommendations from others.

TERMS Agent receives 15% commission on domestic sales. Agent receives 25% commission on foreign sales. Offers written contract; 30-day notice must be given to terminate contract.

TIPS "Be persistent."

WRITERS' REPRESENTATIVES, LLC

116 W. 14th St., 11th Floor, New York NY 10011-7305. **E-mail:** transom@writersreps.com. **Website:** www.writersreps.com. Represents 100 clients. Currently handles nonfiction books (90%), novels (10%).

Prior to becoming an agent, Ms. Chu was a lawyer; Mr. Hartley worked at Simon & Schuster, Harper & Row and Cornell University Press.

MEMBER AGENTS Lynn Chu, Glen Hartley.

REPRESENTS nonfiction books, novels. **Considers these fiction areas:** literary.

Serious nonfiction and quality fiction. No motion picture or television screenplays.

HOW TO CONTACT Query with SASE. Prefers to read materials exclusively. Considers simultaneous queries, but must be informed at time of submission. Consult website section "FAQ" for detailed submission guidelines.

TERMS Agent receives 15% commission on domestic sales. Agent receives 20% commission on foreign sales.

TIPS "Always include a SASE; it will ensure a response from the agent and the return of your submitted material."

YATES & YATES

1551 N. Tustin Ave, Suite 710, Santa Ana CA 92705. (714)480-4000. **Fax:** (714)480-4001. **E-mail:** submissions@yates2.com. **E-mail:** email@yates2.com. **Website:** www.yates2.com. Represents 60 clients.

REPRESENTS nonfiction books.

RECENT SALES *No More Mondays* by Dan Miller (Doubleday Currency).

HELEN ZIMMERMANN LITERARY AGENCY

New Paltz NY 12561. **E-mail:** submit@ZimmAgency.com. **Website:** www.zimmermannliterary.com. **Contact:** Helen Zimmermann. Estab. 2003. Currently handles nonfiction books (80%), other (20% fiction).

Prior to opening her agency, Ms. Zimmermann was the director of advertising and promotion at Random House and the events coordinator at an independent bookstore.

REPRESENTS Considers these fiction areas: literary.

"As an agent who has experience at both a publishing house and a bookstore, I have a keen insight for viable projects. This experience also helps me ensure every client gets published well, through the whole process." Actively seeking memoirs, pop culture, women's issues, and accessible literary fiction. Does not want to receive horror, science fiction, poetry or romance.

HOW TO CONTACT Accepts e-mail queries only. E-mail should include a short description of project and bio, whether it be fiction or nonfiction. Accepts simultaneous submissions. Responds in 2 weeks to queries. Responds in 1 month to mss. Obtains most new clients through recommendations from others, solicitations.

TERMS Agent receives 15% commission on domestic sales. Offers written contract; 30-day notice must be given to terminate contract.

WRITERS CONFERENCES BEA/Writer's Digest Books Writers Conference; Portland, ME Writers Conference; Berkshire Writers and Readers Conference; La Jolla Writers Conference; The New School Writers Conference; Vermont Writers Conference; ASJA Conference; Books Alive! Conference; Southeast Writers Conference; Kansas Writers Conference.

MAGAZINES

This section contains magazine listings that fall into one of several categories: literary, consumer, small circulation, and online. Our decision to combine magazines under one section was two-fold: All of these magazines represent markets specifically for short fiction, and many magazines now publish both print and online versions, making them more difficult to subcategorize. Below, we outline specifics for literary, online, consumer, and small circulation magazines.

LITERARY MAGAZINES

Although definitions of what constitutes literary writing vary, editors of literary journals agree they want to publish the best fiction they can acquire. Qualities they look for in fiction include fully developed characters, strong and unique narrative voice, flawless mechanics, and careful attention to detail in content and manuscript preparation. Most of the authors writing such fiction are well read and well educated, and many are students or graduates of university creative writing programs.

Stepping Stones to Recognition

Some well-established literary journals pay several hundred or even several thousand dollars for a short story. Most, though, can only pay with contributor's copies or a subscription to their publication. However, being published in literary journals offers the important benefits of experience, exposure, and prestige. Agents and major book publishers regularly read literary magazines in search of new writers. Work from these journals is also selected for inclusion in annual prize anthologies.

You'll find most of the well-known prestigious literary journals listed here. Many, including *The Southern Review* and *Ploughshares*, are associated with universities, while others like *The Paris Review* are independently published.

Selecting the Right Literary Magazine

Once you have browsed through this section and have a list of journals you might like to submit to, read those listings again carefully. Remember, this is information editors provide to help you submit work that fits their needs. Note that you will find some magazines that do not read submissions all year long. Whether limited reading periods are tied to a university schedule or meant to accommodate the capabilities of a very small staff, those periods are noted within listings (when the editors notify us). The staffs of university journals are usually made up of student editors and a managing editor who is also a faculty member. These staffs often change every year. Whenever possible, we indicate this in listings and give the name of the current editor and the length of that editor's term. Also be aware that the schedule of a university journal usually coincides with that university's academic year, meaning that the editors of most university publications are difficult or impossible to reach during the summer.

Furthering Your Search

It cannot be stressed enough that reading the listings for literary journals is only the first part of developing your marketing plan. The second part, equally important, is to obtain fiction guidelines and to read with great care the actual journal you'd like to submit to. Reading copies of these journals helps you determine the fine points of each magazine's publishing style and sensibility. There is no substitute for this type of hands-on research.

Unlike commercial periodicals available at most newsstands and bookstores, it requires a little more effort to obtain some of the literary magazines listed. The super-chain bookstores are doing a better job these days of stocking literaries, and you can find some in independent and college bookstores, especially those published in your area. The Internet is an invaluable resource for submission guidelines, as more and more journals establish an online presence. You may, however, need to send for a sample copy. We include sample copy prices in the listings whenever possible. In addition to reading your sample copies, pay close attention to the **Tips** section of each listing. There you'll often find a very specific description of the style of fiction the editors at that publication prefer.

Another way to find out more about literary magazines is to check out the various prize anthologies and take note of journals whose fiction is being selected for publication in them. Studying prize anthologies not only lets you know which magazines are publishing award-winning work, but it also provides a valuable overview of what is considered to be the best fiction published today. Those anthologies include:

- *Best American Short Stories*, published by Houghton Mifflin
- *New Stories from the South: The Year's Best*, published by Algonquin Books of Chapel Hill
- *The O. Henry Prize Stories*, published by Doubleday/Anchor
- *Pushcart Prize: Best of the Small Presses,* published by Pushcart Press

CONSUMER MAGAZINES

Consumer magazines are publications that reach a broad readership. Many have circulations in the hundreds of thousands or millions. And among the oldest magazines listed in this section are ones not only familiar to us, but also to our parents, grandparents, and even great-grandparents: *The Atlantic Monthly* (1857), *Esquire* (1933), and *Ellery Queen's Mystery Magazine* (1941).

Consumer periodicals make excellent markets for fiction in terms of exposure, prestige, and payment. Because these magazines are well known, however, competition is great. Even the largest consumer publications buy only one or two stories an issue, yet thousands of writers submit to these popular magazines.

Despite the odds, it is possible for talented new writers to break into consumer magazines. Your keys to breaking into these markets include careful research, professional presentation, and, of course, top-quality fiction.

SMALL-CIRCULATION MAGAZINES

Small-circulation magazines include general interest, special interest, regional, and genre magazines with circulations under ten thousand. Although these magazines vary greatly in size, theme, format, and management, the editors are all looking for short stories. Their specific fiction needs present writers of all degrees of expertise and interests with an abundance of publishing opportunities. Among the diverse publications in this section are magazines devoted to almost every topic, every level of writing, and every type of writer. Some of these markets publish fiction about a particular geographic area or by authors who live in that locale.

Although not as high-paying as the large-circulation consumer magazines, you'll find some of the publications listed here do pay writers 10–50¢/word or more. Also, unlike the big consumer magazines, these markets are very open to new writers and relatively easy to break into. Their only criterion is that your story be well written, well presented, and suitable for their particular readership.

ONLINE MARKETS

As production and distribution costs go up and the number of subscribers falls, more and more magazines are giving up print publication and moving online. Relatively inexpensive to maintain and quicker to accept and post submissions, online fiction sites are growing fast in numbers and legitimacy. The benefit for writers is that your stories can get more attention in online journals than in small literary journals. Small journals have small print runs—five hundred to one thousand copies—so there's a limit on how many people will read your work. There is no limit when your work appears online.

There is also no limit to the types of online journals being published, offering outlets for a rich and diverse community of voices. These include genre sites, particularly those for science fiction, fantasy, and horror, and mainstream short fiction markets. Online literary journals range from the traditional to those with a decidedly quirkier bent. Writers will also find online outlets for more highly experimental and multimedia work.

While the medium of online publication is different, the traditional rules of publishing apply to submissions. Writers should research the site and archives carefully, looking for a match in sensibility for their work. Follow submission guidelines exactly and submit courteously. True, these sites aren't bound by traditional print schedules, so your work theoretically may be published more quickly. But that doesn't mean online journals have larger staffs, so exercise patience with editors considering your manuscript.

A final note about online publication: Like literary journals, the majority of these markets are either nonpaying or very low paying. In addition, writers will not receive print copies of the publications because of the medium. So in most cases, do not expect to be paid for your exposure.

SELECTING THE RIGHT MARKET

First, zero in on those markets most likely to be interested in your work. Begin by looking at the Category Index. If your work is more general—or conversely, very specialized—you may wish to browse through the listings, perhaps looking up those magazines published in your state or region.

In addition to browsing through the listings and using the Category Index, check the openness icons at the beginning of listings to find those most likely to be receptive to your work. This is especially true for beginning writers, who should look for magazines that say they are especially open to new writers O and for those giving equal weight to both new and established writers ◑. For more explanation about these icons, see the inside back cover of this book.

Once you have a list of magazines you might like to try, read their listings carefully. Much of the material within each listing carries clues that tell you more about the magazine. "How to Use *NSSWM*" describes in detail the listing information common to all the markets in this book.

The physical description appearing near the beginning of the listings can give you clues about the size and financial commitment to the publication. This is not always an indication of quality, but chances are a publication with expensive paper and four-color artwork on the cover has more prestige than a photocopied publication featuring a clip-art cover.

FURTHERING YOUR SEARCH

Most of the magazines listed here are published in the U.S. You will also find some English-speaking markets from around the world. These foreign publications are denoted with a ◉ symbol at the beginning of listings. To make it easier to find Canadian markets, we include a ◎ symbol at the start of those listings.

5-TROPE

Website: www.5trope.com. **Contact:** Doren Robbins, editor. Estab. 1999. "Our intention is to seek out guest editors who will solicit excellent experimental work from their colleagues, which we will then publish; and in this way each issue will become the fruit of a single editor's labour and guidance, a thematically united work of Internet art in its own right. Let us call this *5_trope*'s overarching experiment: to discover what happens when editorship and authorship collide. We welcome applications for guest editorship, but please be aware that applications will not be considered from novice writers and that we may not be able to respond to every person we do not select. Applications may be sent to: editor.5trope@gmail.com. Give us your best pitch."

580 SPLIT, A JOURNAL OF ARTS AND LETTERS

Mills College, P.O. Box 9982, Oakland CA 94613-0982. **E-mail:** five80split@gmail.com. **Website:** www.mills.edu/academics/graduate/eng/about/580_split.php. "*580 Split* is an annual journal of arts and literature published by graduate students of the English Department at Mills College. This national literary journal includes innovative and risk-taking fiction, creative nonfiction, poetry, and art and is one of the few literary journals carried by the Oakland Public Library. *580 Split* is also distributed in well-known Bay Area bookstores."

HOW TO CONTACT Submit via online submissions manager.

PAYMENT/TERMS Pays 1 contributor's copy.

TIPS "Get a hold of a past issue, read through it, find out what we are about. Check the website for most recent information."

ABLE MUSE

467 Saratoga Ave., #602, San Jose CA 95129-1326. **Website:** www.ablemuse.com. **Contact:** Alex Pepple, editor. Estab. 1999. "*Able Muse: A Review of Poetry, Prose & Art* published twice/year, predominantly publishes metrical poetry complemented by art and photography, fiction, and nonfiction including essays, book reviews, and interviews with a focus on metrical and formal poetry. We are looking for well-crafted poems of any length or subject that employ skillful and imaginative use of meter and rhyme, executed in a contemporary idiom, that reads as naturally as your free-verse poems."

Considers poetry by teens. "High levels of craft still required even for teen writers." Also sponsors 2 annual contests: The Able Muse Write Prize for Poetry & Fiction, and The Able Muse Book Award for Poetry (in collaboration with Able Muse Press at www.ablemusepress.com). See website for details.

ACM (ANOTHER CHICAGO MAGAZINE)

P.O. Box 408439, Chicago IL 60640. **E-mail:** editors@anotherchicagomagazine.net. **Website:** www.anotherchicagomagazine.net. **Contact:** Jacob S. Knabb, editor in chief; Caroline Eick, managing editor. Estab. 1977. "*Another Chicago Magazine* is a biannual literary magazine that publishes work by both new and established writers. We look for work that goes beyond the artistic and academic to include and address the larger world. The editors read submissions in fiction, poetry, and creative nonfiction year round. The best way to know what we publish is to read what we publish. If you haven't read *ACM* before, order a sample copy to know if your work is appropriate." Sends prepublication galleys.

Work published in *ACM* has been included frequently in *The Best American Poetry* and *The Pushcart Prize*.

NEEDS Length: 15-20 pages or less.

HOW TO CONTACT Submit short stories and novel excerpts.

TIPS "Support literary publishing by subscribing to at least one literary journal—if not ours, another. Get used to rejection slips, and don't get discouraged. Keep introductory letters short. Make sure ms has name and address on every page, and that it is clean, neat, and proofread. We are looking for stories with freshness and originality in subject angle and style and work that encounters the world."

THE ADIRONDACK REVIEW

Black Lawrence Press, 8405 Bay Parkway, Apt C8, Brooklyn NY 11214. **E-mail:** editors@theadirondackreview.com. **Website:** www.adirondackreview.homestead.com. **Contact:** Angela Leroux-Lindsey, editor; Amanda Himmelmann, fiction editor; Nicholas Samaras, poetry editor. Estab. 2000. *The Adirondack Review*, published quarterly online, is a literary journal dedicated to quality free verse poetry and short fiction as well as book and film reviews, art, photography, and interviews. "We are open to both new and established writers. Our only requirement is excellence. We would like to publish more French and German poetry translations as well as original poems in these languages. We publish an eclectic mix of voices and styles, but all poems should show attention to craft. We are open to beginners who demonstrate talent, as well as established voices. The work should speak for itself."

NEEDS "We like modern tales with a quality of timelessness: stories with realistic, powerful dialogue and dynamic characters." Length: up to 4,000 words.

HOW TO CONTACT Submit via online submissions manager.

TIPS "*The Adirondack Review* accepts submissions all year long, so send us your poetry, fiction, nonfiction, translation, reviews, interviews, and art and photography."

ADVOCATE, PKA'S PUBLICATION

1881 Little Westkill Rd., Prattsville NY 12468. (518)299-3103. **Website:** advocatepka.weebly.com; www.facebook.com/Advocate/PKAPublications; www.facebook.com/GaitedHorseAssociation. **Contact:** Patricia Keller, publisher. Estab. 1987. *Advocate, PKA's Publication*, published bimonthly, is an advertiser-supported tabloid using "original, previously unpublished works, such as feature stories, essays, 'think' pieces, letters to the editor, profiles, humor, fiction, poetry, puzzles, cartoons, or line drawings. Advocates for good writers and quality writings. We publish art, fiction, photos and poetry. *Advocate*'s submitters are talented people of all ages who do not earn their livings as writers. We wish to promote the arts and to give those we publish the opportunity to be published."

○ "This publication has a strong horse orientation." Includes Gaited Horse Association newsletter. Horse-oriented stories, poetry, art and photos are currently needed.

NEEDS Looks for "well-written, entertaining work, whether fiction or nonfiction." Wants to see more humorous material, nature/environment, and romantic comedy. "Nothing religious, pornographic, violent, erotic, pro-drug, or anti-enviroment." Length: up to 1,500 words.

HOW TO CONTACT Send complete ms.

PAYMENT/TERMS Pays contributor copies.

TIPS "Please, no simultaneous submissions, work that has appeared on the Internet, pornography, overt religiosity, anti-environmentalism, or gratuitous violence. Artists and photographers should keep in mind that we are a b&w paper. Please do not send postcards. Use envelope with SASE."

AFRICAN VOICES

African Voices Communications, Inc., 270 W. 96th St., New York NY 10025. (212)865-2982. **Fax:** (212)316-3335. **E-mail:** info@africanvoices.com. **Website:** www.africanvoices.com. **Contact:** Maitefa Angaza, managing editor; Mariahadessa Ekere Tallie, poetry editor. Estab. 1992. *African Voices*, published quarterly, is an "art and literary magazine that highlights the work of people of color. We publish ethnic literature and poetry on any subject. We also consider all themes and styles: avant-garde, free verse, haiku, light verse, and traditional. We do not wish to limit the reader or author."

○ *African Voices* is about 48 pages, magazine-sized, professionally printed, saddle-stapled, with paper cover. Receives about 100 submissions/year, accepts about 30%. Press run is 20,000.

NEEDS Length: 500-2,500 words.

HOW TO CONTACT Send complete ms. Include short bio. Accepts submissions by e-mail (in text box), by fax, and by postal mail. Send SASE for return of ms.

PAYMENT/TERMS Pays $25-50.

TIPS "A ms stands out if it is neatly typed with a well-written and interesting storyline or plot. Originality is encouraged. We are interested in more horror, erotic, and drama pieces. *AV* wants to highlight the diversity in our culture. Stories must touch the humanity in us all. We strongly encourage new writers/poets to send in their work. Accepted contributors are encouraged to subscribe."

A GATHERING OF THE TRIBES

P.O. Box 20693, Tompkins Square Station, New York NY 10009. (212)777-2038. **E-mail:** gatheringofthetribes@gmail.com. **E-mail:** tribes.editor@gmail.com. **Website:** www.tribes.org. **Contact:** Steve Cannon. Estab. 1992. "*A Gathering of the Tribes* is a multicultural and multigenerational publication featuring poetry, fiction, interviews, essays, visual art, and musical scores. Audience is anyone interested in the arts from a diverse perspective."

○ Magazine: 8.5x10; 130 pages; glossy paper and cover; illustrations; photos. Receives 20 unsolicited mss/month. Publishes 40% new writers/year. Has published work by Carl Watson, Ishle Park, Wang Pang, and Hanif Kureishi. Sponsors awards/contests.

NEEDS "Would like to see more satire/humor. We are open to all; just no poor writing/grammar/syntax." Length: 2,500-5,000 words.

HOW TO CONTACT Send complete ms by postal mail or e-mail.

PAYMENT/TERMS Pays 1 contributor's copy.

TIPS "Make sure your work has substance."

AGNI

Creative Writing Program, Boston University, 236 Bay State Rd., Boston MA 02215. (617)353-7135. **Fax:** (617)353-7134. **E-mail:** agni@bu.edu. **Website:** www.agnimagazine.org. **Contact:** Sven Birkerts, editor. Estab. 1972. "Eclectic literary magazine publishing first-rate poems, essays, translations, and stories."

Reading period is September 1-May 31 only. Online magazine carries original content not found in print edition. All submissions are considered for both. Founding editor Askold Melnyczuk won the 2001 Nora Magid Award for Magazine Editing. Work from *AGNI* has been included and cited regularly in the *Pushcart Prize* and *Best American* anthologies.

NEEDS Buys stories, prose poems. "No science fiction or romance."

HOW TO CONTACT Query by mail.

PAYMENT/TERMS Pays $10/page up to $150; a one-year subscription; and, for print publication, 2 contributor's copies and 4 gift copies.

TIPS "We're also looking for extraordinary translations from little-translated languages. It is important to read work published in *AGNI* before submitting, to see if your own might be compatible."

ALASKA QUARTERLY REVIEW

University of Alaska Anchorage, 3211 Providence Dr. (ESH 208), Anchorage AK 99508. **Fax:** 907-786-6916. **E-mail:** aqr@uaa.alaska.edu. **Website:** www.uaa.alaska.edu/aqr. **Contact:** Ronald Spatz, editor in chief. Estab. 1982. *"Alaska Quarterly Review* is a literary journal devoted to contemporary literary art, publishing fiction, short plays, poetry, photo essays, and literary nonfiction in traditional and experimental styles. The editors encourage new and emerging writers, while continuing to publish award-winning and established writers."

Magazine: 6×9; 232-300 pages; 60 lb. Glatfelter paper; 12 pt. C15 black ink or 4-color; varnish cover stock; photos on cover and photo essays. Reads mss August 15-May 15.

NEEDS "Works in *AQR* have certain characteristics: freshness, honesty, and a compelling subject. The voice of the piece must be strong—idiosyncratic enough to create a unique persona. We look for craft, putting it in a form where it becomes emotionally and intellectually complex. Many pieces in *AQR* concern everyday life. We're not asking our writers to go outside themselves and their experiences to the absolute exotic to catch our interest. We look for the experiential and revelatory qualities of the work. We will champion a piece that may be less polished or stylistically sophisticated if it engages me, surprises me, and resonates for me. The joy in reading such a work is in discovering something true. Moreover, in keeping with our mission to publish new writers, we are looking for voices our readers do not know, voices that may not always be reflected in the dominant culture and that, in all instances, have something important to convey." No romance, children's, or inspirational/religious. Length: up to 50 pages.

HOW TO CONTACT Submit complete ms by postal mail. Include cover letter with contact information and SASE for return of ms.

PAYMENT/TERMS Pays contributor's copies and honoraria when funding is available.

TIPS "Although we respond to e-mail queries, we cannot review electronic submissions."

ALBEDO ONE

8 Bachelor's Walk, Dublin 1 Ireland. (353)1 8730 177. **E-mail:** bobn@yellowbrickroad.ie. **Website:** www.albedo1.com. **Contact:** Bob Nielson. Estab. 1993. "We hope to publish interesting and unusual fiction by new and established writers. We will consider anything, as long as it is well written and entertaining, though our definitions of both may not be exactly mainstream. We like stories with plot and characters that live on the page. Most of our audience are probably committed genre fans, but we try to appeal to a broad spectrum of readers."

NEEDS Length: 2,000-8,000 words.

PAYMENT/TERMS Pays €6 per 1,000 words, to a maximum of 8,000 words, and 1 contributor's copy.

TIPS "We look for good writing, good plot, good characters. Read the magazine, and don't give up."

ALBERTA VIEWS

Alberta Views, Ltd., Suite 208, 320 23rd Ave. SW, Calgary AB T2S 0J2 Canada. (403)243-5334; (877)212-5334. **Fax:** (403)243-8599. **E-mail:** queries@albertaviews.ab.ca. **Website:** www.albertaviews.ab.ca. **Contact:** Evan Osenton, editor. Estab. 1997. "We are a regional magazine providing thoughtful commentary and background information on issues of concern to Albertans. Most of our writers are Albertans."

No phone queries.

NEEDS Only fiction by Alberta writers via the annual *Alberta Views* fiction contest. Length: 2,500-4,000 words.

HOW TO CONTACT Send complete ms.

PAYMENT/TERMS Pays up to $1,000.

THE ALEMBIC

Providence College, English Dept., Attn: The Alembic Editors, 1 Cunningham Square, Providence RI 02918-0001. **Website:** www.providence.edu/english/creative-writing/Pages/alembic.aspx. **Contact:** Magazine has revolving editor. Editorial term: 1 year. Estab. 1940. "*The Alembic* is an international literary journal featuring the work of both established and student writers and photographers. It is published each April by Providence College in Providence, Rhode Island."

Magazine: 6×9, 80 pages. Contains illustrations, photographs.

NEEDS "We are open to all styles of fiction." Does not read December 1-July 31. Published Bruce Smith, Robin Behn, Rane Arroyo, Sharon Dolin, Jeff Friedman, and Khalid Mattawa. Length: up to 6,000 words.

HOW TO CONTACT Send complete ms with cover letter. Include brief bio. Send SASE (or IRC) for return of ms. Does not accept online submissions.

PAYMENT/TERMS Pays 2 contributor's copies.

TIPS "We're looking for stories that are wise, memorable, grammatical, economical, poetic in the right places, and end strongly. Take Heraclitus' claim that 'character is fate' to heart and study the strategies, styles, and craft of such masters as Anton Chekov, J. Cheever, Flannery O'Connor, John Updike, Rick Bass, Phillip Roth, Joyce Carol Oates, William Treavor, Lorrie Moore, and Ethan Canin."

ALIMENTUM, THE LITERATURE OF FOOD

P.O. Box 210028, Nashville TN 37221. **E-mail:** editor@alimentumjournal.com. **Website:** www.alimentumjournal.com. **Contact:** Peter Selgin, fiction and nonfiction editor; Cortney Davis, poetry editor. Estab. 2005. "*Alimentum* celebrates the literature and art of food. We welcome work from like-minded writers, musicians, and artists."

Semiannual. *Alimentum* is 128 pages, perfect-bound, with matte coated cover with 4-color art, interior b&w illustration, includes ads. Contains illustrations. Essays appearing in *Alimentium* have appeared in *Best American Essays* and *Best Food Writing*.

NEEDS Published Mark Kurlansky, Oliver Sacks, Dick Allen, Ann Hood, and Carly Sachs. Publishes short shorts. Also publishes literary essays, poetry, spot illustrations. Rarely comments on/critiques rejected mss. Length: up to 2,000 words.

HOW TO CONTACT Send complete ms with cover letter (snail mail only). Send either SASE (or IRC) for return of ms or disposable copy of ms and #10 SASE for reply only.

PAYMENT/TERMS Pays 1 contributor's copy.

TIPS "No e-mail submissions, only snail mail. Mark outside envelope to the attention of Poetry, Fiction, or Nonfiction Editor."

ALL DUE RESPECT

All Due Respect Books, 2976 W. 100 S., Greenfield IN 46140. **E-mail:** allduerespect@outlook.com. **Website:** allduerespectbooks.com. **Contact:** Chris Rhatigan, editor; Mike Monson, managing editor. Estab. 2010. *All Due Respect* is a quarterly digital and hard copy magazine featuring fiction. Works with publisher All Due Respect Books.

NEEDS Length: up to 8,000 words.

HOW TO CONTACT Submit complete ms via e-mail. Before submission, format your story in the following manner: double-spaced; first line of paragraphs indented .25"; use 3 asterisks, centered, to indicate scene breaks; and save the file as: last name_title of story.doc (or .docx, .rtf).

PAYMENT/TERMS Pays $25 for fiction.

ALLEGORY

P.O .Box 2714, Cherry Hill NJ 08034. **E-mail:** submissions@allegoryezine.com. **Website:** www.allegoryezine.com. **Contact:** Ty Drago, editor. Estab. 1998. "We are an e-zine by writers for writers. Our articles focus on the art, craft, and business of writing. Our links and editorial policy all focus on the needs of fiction authors."

Allegory (as Peridot Books) won the Page One Award for Literary Contribution.

NEEDS Receives 150 unsolicited mss/month. Accepts 8 mss/issue; 24 mss/year. Agented fiction 5%. Publishes 10 new writers/year. Also publishes literary essays, literary criticism. Often comments on rejected mss. "No media tie-ins (*Star Trek*, *Star Wars*, etc., or space opera, vampires)." Length: 1,500-7,500 words; average length: 4,500 words.

HOW TO CONTACT "All submissions should be sent by e-mail (no letters or telephone calls) in either text or .rtf format. Please place 'Submission [Title]-[first and last name]' in the subject line. Include the following in both the body of the e-mail and the attachment: your name, name to use on the story (byline) if different, your preferred e-mail address, your mailing address, the story's title, and the story's word count."

PAYMENT/TERMS $15/story-article.

TIPS "Give us something original, preferably with a twist. Avoid gratuitous sex or violence. Funny always scores points. Be clever and imaginative, but be able to tell a story with proper mood and characterization. Put your name and e-mail address in the body of the story. Read the site and get a feel for it before submitting."

ⓘ ALLIGATOR JUNIPER

Prescott College, 220 Grove Ave., Prescott AZ 86301. (928)350-2012. **Website:** alligatorjuniper.wordpress.com. "*Alligator Juniper* features contemporary poetry, fiction, creative nonfiction, and b&w photography. We encourage submissions from writers and photographers at all levels: emerging, early career, and established." Annual magazine comprised of the winners and finalists of national contests. "All entrants pay an $18 submission fee and receive a complementary copy of that year's issue in the spring. First-place winning writers in each genre recieve a $1,000 prize. The first-place winner in photography receives a $500 award. Finalists in writing and images are published and paid in contributor copies. There is currently no avenue for submissions other than the annual contest."

NEEDS "No children's literature or genre work." Length: up to 30 pages.

HOW TO CONTACT Accepts submissions only through annual contest. Submit via online submission form or regular mail. If submitting by regular mail, include $18 entry fee payable to *Alligator Juniper* for each story. Include cover letter with name, address, phone number, and e-mail. Mss should be typed with numbered pages, double-spaced, 12-point font, and 1" margins. Include author's name on first page. "Double-sided submissions are encouraged." No e-mail submissions.

ⓘ AMERICAN LITERARY REVIEW

University of North Texas, P.O. Box 311307, Denton TX 76203-1307. (940)565-2755. **E-mail:** americanliteraryreview@gmail.com. **Website:** www.americanliteraryreview.com. **Contact:** Bonnie Friedman, editor in chief. Estab. 1990. "The *American Literary Review* publishes "excellent poetry, fiction, and nonfiction by writers at all stages of their careers." Beginning in fall 2013, *ALR* became an online publication."

Reading period is from October 1-May 1.

NEEDS "We would like to see more short shorts and stylistically innovative and risk-taking fiction. We like to see stories that illuminate the various layers of characters and their situations with great artistry. Give us distinctive character-driven stories that explore the complexities of human existence." Looks for "the small moments that contain more than at first possible, that surprise us with more truth than we thought we had a right to expect." Has published work by Marylee MacDonald, Michael Isaac Shokrian, Arthur Brown, Roy Bentley, Julie Marie Wade, and Karin Forfota Poklen. No genre works. Length: up to 8,000 words.

HOW TO CONTACT Submit 1 complete ms online through submission manager for a fee of $3. Does not accept submissions via e-mail or postal mail.

TIPS "We encourage writers and artists to examine our journal."

ⓘⓢ AMERICAN SHORT FICTION

Badgerdog Literary Publishing, P.O. Box 301209, Austin TX 78703. (512) 538-1305. **Fax:** (512) 538-1306. **E-mail:** editors@americanshortfiction.org. **Website:** www.americanshortfiction.org. **Contact:** Rebecca Markovits and Adeena Reitberger, editors. Estab. 1991. "Issued triannually, *American Short Fiction* publishes work by emerging and established voices: stories that dive into the wreck, that stretch the reader between recognition and surprise, that conjure a particular world with delicate expertise—stories that take a different way home."

Stories published by *American Short Fiction* are anthologized in *Best American Short Stories*, *Best American Non-Required Reading*, *The O. Henry Prize Stories*, *The Pushcart Prize: Best of the Small Presses*, and elsewhere.

NEEDS "Open to publishing mystery or speculative fiction if we feel it has literary value." Does not want young adult or genre fiction. Length: open.

HOW TO CONTACT *American Short Fiction* seeks "short fiction by some of the finest writers working in contemporary literature, whether they are established, new, or lesser-known authors." Also publishes stories under 2,000 words online. Submit 1 story at a time via online submissions manager ($3 fee). No paper submissions.

PAYMENT/TERMS Writers receive $250-500, 2 contributor's copies, free subscription to the magazine. Additional copies $5.

TIPS "We publish fiction that speaks to us emotionally, uses evocative and precise language, and takes risks in subject matter and/or form. Try to read an issue or two of *American Short Fiction* to get a sense of what we like. Also, to be concise is a great virtue."

❶❷🎧⑤ ANALOG SCIENCE FICTION & FACT

Dell Magazines, 44 Wall St., Suite 904, New York NY 10005-2401. **E-mail:** analog@dellmagazines.com. **Website:** www.analogsf.com. **Contact:** Trevor Quachri, editor. Estab. 1930. *Analog* seeks "solidly entertaining stories exploring solidly thought-out speculative ideas. But the ideas, and consequently the stories, are always new. Real science and technology have always been important in *ASF,* not only as the foundation of its fiction but as the subject of articles about real research with big implications for the future."

◐ Fiction published in *Analog* has won numerous Nebula and Hugo Awards.

NEEDS "Basically, we publish science fiction stories. That is, stories in which some aspect of future science or technology is so integral to the plot that, if that aspect were removed, the story would collapse. The science can be physical, sociological, psychological. The technology can be anything from electronic engineering to biogenetic engineering. But the stories must be strong and realistic, with believable people (who needn't be human) doing believable things—no matter how fantastic the background might be." No fantasy or stories in which the scientific background is implausible or plays no essential role. Length: 2,000-7,000 words for short stories, 10,000-20,000 words for novelettes and novellas, and 40,000-80,000 for serials.

HOW TO CONTACT Send complete ms via online submissions manager (preferred) or postal mail. Does not accept e-mail submissions.

PAYMENT/TERMS Analog pays 8-10¢/word for short stories up to 7,500 words, 8-8.5¢ for longer material, 6¢/word for serials.

TIPS "I'm looking for irresistibly entertaining stories that make me think about things in ways I've never done before. Read several issues to get a broad feel for our tastes, but don't try to imitate what you read."

❶❷❸⑤ ANCIENT PATHS

E-mail: skylarburris@yahoo.com. **Website:** www.editorskylar.com/magazine/table.html. **Contact:** Skylar H. Burris, Editor. Estab. 1998. *Ancient Paths* provides "a forum for quality Christian poetry and flash fiction. All works should have a spiritual theme.

The theme may be explicitly Christian or broadly religious. Works published in *Ancient Paths* explore themes such as redemption, sin, forgiveness, doubt, faith, gratitude for the ordinary blessings of life, spiritual struggle, and spiritual growth. Please, no overly didactic works. Subtlety is preferred."

◐ New issues of *Ancient Paths* are no longer being produced in print. *Ancient Paths* online is published as a regularly updated Facebook page.

NEEDS E-mail submissions only. Paste flash fiction directly in e-mail message. Use the subject heading "AP Online Submission (title of your work)." Include name and e-mail address at top of e-mail. Previously published works accepted, provided they are not currently available online. Please indicate if your work has been published elsewhere." Length: no more than 900 words.

PAYMENT/TERMS Pays $1.25 per work published. Published authors also receive discount code for $3 off 2 past printed issues.

TIPS "Read the great religious poets: John Donne, George Herbert, T.S. Eliot, Lord Tennyson. Remember not to preach. This is a literary magazine, not a pulpit. This does not mean you do not communicate morals or celebrate God. It means you are not overbearing or simplistic when you do so."

ANDROIDS2 MAGAZINE

Man's Story 2 Publishing Co., 1321 Snapfinger Rd., Decatur GA 30032. **E-mail:** mansstory2@aol.com. **Website:** www.androids2.com. Estab. 2001. *"Androids 2 Magazine* strives to re-create the pulp fiction that was published in the magazines of the 1920s through the 1970s with strong emphasis on 3D graphic art."

◐ Online e-zine. Story subjects tend to slant toward the "damsel in distress."

NEEDS Length: 10,000 words minimum (word count can be made up of several stories).

HOW TO CONTACT Send complete ms as Word doc attachment.

PAYMENT/TERMS Pays $50.

TIPS "We suggest interested writers visit our website. Then, read the 1960s-style pulp fiction stories posted in our online mini-magazine and/or read one of our magazines, or find an old pulp fiction magazine that was published in the 1960s. If all else fails, e-mail us."

◐⑤ THE ANTIGONISH REVIEW

St. Francis Xavier University, P.O. Box 5000, Antigonish NS B2G 2W5 Canada. (902)867-3962. **Fax:** (902)867-5563. **E-mail:** tar@stfx.ca. **Website:** www.

antigonishreview.com. **Contact:** Bonnie McIsaac, office manager. Estab. 1970. *The Antigonish Review,* published quarterly, tries "to produce the kind of literary and visual mosaic that the modern sensibility requires or would respond to."

NEEDS Send complete ms. Accepts submissions by fax. Accepts electronic (disk compatible with Word-Perfect/IBM and Windows) submissions. Prefers hard copy. No erotica. Length: 500-5,000 words.

HOW TO CONTACT Send complete ms.

PAYMENT/TERMS Pays $50 and 2 contributor's copies for stories.

TIPS "Send for guidelines and/or sample copy. Send ms with cover letter and SASE with submission."

◑Ⓢ ANTIOCH REVIEW

P.O. Box 148, Yellow Springs OH 45387-0148. **E-mail:** mkeyes@antiochreview.org. **Website:** www.antiochreview.org. **Contact:** Robert S. Fogarty, editor; Judith Hall, poetry editor. Estab. 1941. Literary and cultural review of contemporary issues and literature for general readership. *The Antioch Review* "is an independent quarterly of critical and creative thought. For well over 70 years, creative authors, poets, and thinkers have found a friendly reception—regardless of formal reputation. We get far more poetry than we can possibly accept, and the competition is keen. Here, where form and content are so inseparable and reaction is so personal, it is difficult to state requirements or limitations. Studying recent issues of *The Antioch Review* should be helpful."

Work published in *The Antioch Review* has been included frequently in *The Best American Stories, Best American Essays,* and *The Best American Poetry.* Finalist for National Magazine Award for essays in 2009 and 2011, and for fiction in 2010.

NEEDS Quality fiction only, distinctive in style with fresh insights into the human condition. No science fiction, fantasy, or confessions. Length: generally under 8,000 words.

HOW TO CONTACT Send complete ms with SASE, preferably mailed flat. Fiction submissions are not accepted between June 1-September 1.

PAYMENT/TERMS Pays $20/printed page, plus 2 contributor's copies.

◐ APALACHEE REVIEW

Apalachee Press, P.O. Box 10469, Tallahassee FL 32302. (850)644-9114. **E-mail:** arsubmissions@ gmail.com (for queries outside the U.S.). **Website:** apalacheereview.org. **Contact:** Michael Trammell, editor; Kathleen Laufenberg, nonfiction editor; Mary Jane Ryals, fiction editor; Jay Snodgrass and Dominika Wrozynski, poetry editors. Estab. 1976. "At *Apalachee Review,* we are interested in outstanding literary fiction, but we especially like poetry, fiction, and nonfiction that addresses intercultural issues in a domestic or international setting/context." Annual.

Apalachee Review is 120 pages, digest-sized, professionally printed, perfect-bound, with card cover. Press run is 400-500. Includes photographs. Member CLMP.

NEEDS Receives 60-100 mss/month. Accepts 5-10 mss/issue. Agented fiction: 0.5%. Publishes 1-2 new writers/year. Has published Lu Vickers, Joe Clark, Joe Taylor, Jane Arrowsmith Edwards, Vivian Lawry, Linda Frysh, Charles Harper Webb, Reno Raymond Gwaltney. Also publishes short shorts. Does not want cliché-filled, genre-oriented fiction. Length: 600-5,500 words; average length: 3,500 words. Average length of short shorts: 250 words.

HOW TO CONTACT Send complete ms with cover letter. Include brief bio, list of publications. Send either SASE (international authors should see website for "international" guidelines: no IRCs, please) for return of ms or disposable copy of ms and #10 SASE for reply only.

PAYMENT/TERMS Pays 2 contributor's copies.

◑Ⓢ APEX MAGAZINE

Apex Publications, LLC, P.O. Box 24323, Lexington KY 40524. (859)312-3974. **E-mail:** jason@apexbookcompany.com. **Website:** www.apexbookcompany.com. **Contact:** Lesley Conner, managing editor. Estab. 2004. "An elite repository for new and seasoned authors with an other-worldly interest in the unquestioned and slightly bizarre parts of the universe."

"We want science fiction, fantasy, horror, and mash-ups of all three of the dark, weird stuff down at the bottom of your little literary heart." Monthly e-zine publishing dark speculative fiction.

NEEDS Length: 100-7,500 words.

HOW TO CONTACT Send complete ms.

PAYMENT/TERMS Pays 6¢/word.

◐ APPALACHIAN HERITAGE

CPO 2166, Berea KY 40404. (859)985-3699. **Fax:** (859)985-3903. **E-mail:** appalachianheritage@berea.

edu. **Website:** pub.berea.edu/appalachian-heritage. **Contact:** George Brosi. Estab. 1973. "We are seeking poetry, short fiction, literary criticism and biography, book reviews, and creative nonfiction, including memoirs, opinion pieces, and historical sketches. Unless you request not to be considered, all poems, stories, and articles published in *Appalachian Heritage* are eligible for our annual Plattner Award. All honorees are rewarded with a sliding bookrack with an attached commemorative plaque from Berea College Crafts, and First Place winners receive an additional stipend of $200."

🜕 Submission period: August 1-February 27.

NEEDS "We do not want to see fiction that has no ties to Southern Appalachia." Length: up to 7,500 words.

HOW TO CONTACT Submit complete ms. Send SASE for reply, return of ms.

PAYMENT/TERMS Pays 3 contributor's copies.

TIPS "Sure, we are *Appalachian Heritage* and we do appreciate the past, but we are a forward-looking contemporary literary quarterly, and, frankly, we receive too many nostalgic submissions. Please spare us the 'Papaw Was Perfect' poetry and the 'Mamaw Moved Mountains' mss and give us some hard-hitting prose, some innovative poetry, some inventive photography, and some original art. Help us be the ground-breaking, stimulating kind of quarterly we aspire to be."

❶ APPARATUS MAGAZINE

Chicago IL **E-mail:** submissions@apparatusmagazine.com; editor@apparatusmagazine.com. **Website:** www.apparatusmagazine.com. **Contact:** Adam W. Hart, publisher/editor. Estab. 2009. "*Apparatus Magazine* strives to bring readers poetry and fiction from around the world that explores the mythos of 'man (or woman) vs. machine,' that conjures up words from the inner machine, and more. Each issue features work from around the world, bringing the reader literary updates from the *internal machine*."

NEEDS No restrictions as to genre or style. Prefers work that opens the form up to new directions. No overtly inspirational fiction, fiction aimed at children, or confessional. Avoid work that is overtly sexist, racist, violent, homophobic, discriminatory, pornographic, or otherwise in questionable taste. Length: up to 500 words.

HOW TO CONTACT Submit up to 3 pieces at a time via e-mail; no postal submissions. Send complete ms with a cover letter including estimated word count,

brief bio, list of publications. Label subject line with "fiction submission."

TIPS "Be sure to read the guidelines as posted. Submit more than just 1 poem, so I can get a feel for your work. Be sure to read back issues of the magazine. The journal tends to select work that focuses on specific themes and usually tries to pick work that will complement/contrast with other pieces selected for the issue. Send your best work, and don't be afraid of trying again. I often suggest other publications/markets if a piece is not a good match for the journal. Do not submit additional new material until you've heard back from us, though."

🜕🜕🜕 APPLE VALLEY REVIEW: A JOURNAL OF CONTEMPORARY LITERATURE

88 South 3rd St., Suite 336, San Jose CA 95113. **E-mail:** editor@leahbrowning.net. **Website:** www.applevalleyreview.com. **Contact:** Leah Browning, editor. Estab. 2005. *Apple Valley Review: A Journal of Contemporary Literature,* published semiannually online, features "beautifully crafted poetry, short fiction, and essays."

NEEDS Receives 100+ mss/month. Accepts 1-4 mss/issue; 2-8 mss/year. Published Glen Pourciau, Robert Radin, Jessica Rafalko, Thomas Andrew Green, Inderjeet Mani, and Lisa Robertson. Also publishes short shorts. Does not want strict genre fiction, erotica, work containing explicit language, or anything "extremely violent or depressing." Length: 100-4,000+ words. Average length: 2,000 words. Average length of short shorts: 800 words.

HOW TO CONTACT Send complete ms with cover letter.

❶ ARIES: A JOURNAL OF CREATIVE EXPRESSION

c/o Dr. Price McMurray, General Editor, School of Aries and Letters, 1201 Wesleyan St., Fort Worth TX 76105. **E-mail:** aries@txwes.edu; ariesjournal1@gmail.com. **Website:** ariesjournal.wix.com/aries. **Contact:** Rolandra West, managing editor; Price McMurray, general editor. Estab. 1985. *Aries: A Journal of Creative Expression,* is published annually by the Department of Languages and Literature at Texas Wesleyan University. Accepting poetry, short fiction, creative nonfiction, short plays, and b&w photography. Reads submissions August 15-December 15.

NEEDS Submit ms by mail or e-mail. Include cover letter and SASE. Do not include name or contact info on ms. Length: up to 4,000 words.

TIPS *"Aries* is open to a wide variety of perspectives, ideas, and theoretical approaches; however, at the heart of all editorial decisions is the overall quality of the work submitted."

ARKANSAS REVIEW: A JOURNAL OF DELTA STUDIES

Department of English and Philosophy, P.O. Box 1890, Office: Wilson Hall, State University AR 72467-1890. (870) 972-3043; (870)972-2210. **Fax:** (870)972-3045. **E-mail:** mtribbet@astate.edu. **E-mail:** jcollins@astate.edu; arkansasreview@astate.edu. **Website:** al-tweb.astate.edu/arkreview. **Contact:** Dr. Marcus Tribbett, general editor. Estab. 1998. "All material, creative and scholarly, published in the *Arkansas Review* must evoke or respond to the natural and/or cultural experience of the Mississippi River Delta region."

Arkansas Review is 92 pages, magazine-sized, photo offset-printed, saddle-stapled, with 4-color cover. Press run is 600; 50 distributed free to contributors.

NEEDS Receives 30-50 unsolicited mss/month. Accepts 2-3 mss/issue; 5-7 mss/year. Agented fiction 1%. Publishes 3-4 new writers/year. Has published work by Susan Henderson, George Singleton, Scott Ely, and Pia Erhart. "No genre fiction. Must have a Delta focus." Length: up to 10,000 words.

HOW TO CONTACT Send complete ms.

PAYMENT/TERMS Pays 3 contributor's copies.

TIPS "Immerse yourself in the literature of the Delta, but provide us with a fresh and original take on its land, its people, its culture. Surprise us. Amuse us. Recognize what makes this region particular as well as universal, and take risks. Help us shape a new Delta literature."

ARTFUL DODGE

Dept. of English, College of Wooster, Wooster OH 44691. (330)263-2577. **E-mail:** artfuldodge@wooster.edu. **Website:** www.wooster.edu/artfuldodge. **Contact:** Daniel Bourne, editor in chief; Karin Lin-Greenberg, fiction editor; Marcy Campbell, associate fiction editor; Carolyne Wright, translation editor. Estab. 1979. *Artful Dodge* is an Ohio-based literary magazine that publishes "work with a strong sense of place and cultural landscape. Besides new American fiction, poetry, and narrative essay, we're also interested in contemporary translation—from all over the globe. There is no theme in this magazine, except literary power. We also have an ongoing interest in translations from Central/Eastern Europe and elsewhere."

NEEDS "We judge by literary quality, not by genre. We are especially interested in fine English translations of significant prose writers. Translations should be submitted with original texts."

PAYMENT/TERMS Pays at least 2 contributor's copies.

TIPS "Poets may send books for review consideration; however, there is no guarantee we can review them."

ARTS & LETTERS JOURNAL OF CONTEMPORARY CULTURE

Georgia College & State University, Milledgeville GA 31061. (478)445-1289. **E-mail:** al.journal@gcsu.edu. **Website:** al.gcsu.edu. Estab. 1999. *Arts & Letters Journal of Contemporary Culture*, published semiannually, is devoted to contemporary arts and literature, featuring ongoing series such as The World Poetry Translation Series and The Mentors Interview Series. Wants work that is of the highest literary and artistic quality.

Work published in *Arts & Letters Journal* has received the Pushcart Prize.

NEEDS No genre fiction. Length: up to 25 pages typed and double-spaced.

PAYMENT/TERMS Pays $10 per printed page (minimum payment: $50) and 1 contributor's copy.

ART TIMES

A Literary Journal and Resource for All the Arts, P.O. Box 730, Mount Marion NY 12456. (845)246-6944. **Fax:** (845)246-6944. **E-mail:** info@ArtTimesJournal.com. **Website:** www.arttimesjournal.com. **Contact:** Raymond J. Steiner, editor. Estab. 1984. *"Art Times* covers the art fields and is distributed in locations most frequented by those enjoying the arts. Our copies are distributed throughout the lower part of the northeast as well as the metropolitan New York area; locations include theaters, galleries, museums, schools, art clubs, cultural centers, and the like. Our readers are mostly over 40, affluent, art-conscious and sophisticated. Subscribers are located across U.S. and abroad (Italy, France, Germany, Greece, Russia, etc.)."

NEEDS Looks for quality short fiction that aspires to be literary. Publishes 1 story each issue. "Nothing violent, sexist, erotic, juvenile, racist, romantic, political, off-beat, or related to sports or juvenile fiction." Length: up to 1,500 words.

HOW TO CONTACT Send complete ms.

PAYMENT/TERMS Pays $25 and a one-year subscription.

TIPS "Competition is greater (more submissions received), but keep trying. We print new as well as published writers. Be advised that we are presently on an approximate three-year lead for short stories, two-year lead for poetry. We are now receiving 300-400 poems and 40-50 short stories per month. Be familiar with *Art Times* and its special audience."

⚙○ ASCENT ASPIRATIONS

1560 Arbutus Dr., Nanoose Bay BC C9P 9C8 Canada. **E-mail:** ascentaspirations@shaw.ca. **Website:** www.ascentaspirations.ca. **Contact:** David Fraser, editor. Estab. 1997. "*Ascent Aspirations* magazine publishes monthly online and once in print. The print issues are operated as contests. Please refer to current guidelines before submitting. *Ascent Aspirations* is a quality electronic publication dedicated to the promotion and encouragement of aspiring writers of any genre. The focus, however, is toward interesting experimental writing in dark mainstream, literary, science fiction, fantasy, and horror. Poetry can be on any theme. Essays need to be unique, current, and have social, philosophical commentary."

○ Magazine: 40 electronic pages; illustrations; photos. Receives 100-200 unsolicited mss/month. Accepts 40 mss/issue; 240 mss/year. Publishes ms 3 months after acceptance. Publishes 10-50 new writers/year. Has published work by Taylor Graham, Janet Buck, Jim Manton, Steve Cartwright, Don Stockard, Penn Kemp, Sam Vargo, Vernon Waring, Margaret Karmazin, Bill Hughes, and recently spoken-word artists Sheri-D Wilson, Missy Peters, Ian Ferrier, Cathy Petch, and Bob Holdman.

NEEDS Length: up to 1,000 words. Publishes short shorts.

HOW TO CONTACT Query by e-mail with Word attachment. Include estimated word count, brief bio, and list of publications. "If you have to submit by mail because it is your only avenue, provide a SASE with either International Coupons or Canadian stamps only."

PAYMENT/TERMS "No payment at this time."

TIPS "Short fiction should first of all tell a good story, take the reader to new and interesting imaginary or real places. Short fiction should use language lyrically and effectively, be experimental in either form or content, and take the reader into realms where they can analyze and think about the human condition. Write with passion for your material, be concise and economical, and let the reader work to unravel your story. In terms of editing, always proofread to the point where what you submit is the best it possibly can be. Never be discouraged if your work is not accepted; it may just not be the right fit for a current publication."

❶⚙⑤ ASIMOV'S SCIENCE FICTION

Dell Magazines, 44 Wall St., Suite 904, New York NY 10005. **E-mail:** asimovs@dellmagazines.com. **Website:** www.asimovs.com. **Contact:** Sheila Williams, editor; Victoria Green, senior art director. Estab. 1977. "Magazine consists of science fiction and fantasy stories for adults and young adults. Publishes the best short science fiction available."

○ Named for a science fiction "legend," *Asimov's* regularly receives Hugo and Nebula Awards.

NEEDS Wants "science fiction primarily. Some fantasy and humor. It is best to read a great deal of material in the genre to avoid the use of some very old ideas." Submit ms via online submissions manager or postal mail; no e-mail submissions. No horror or psychic/supernatural, sword and sorcery, explicit sex or violence that isn't integral to the story. Would like to see more hard science fiction. Length: 750-15,000 words.

PAYMENT/TERMS Pays 8-10¢/word for short stories up to 7,500 words; 8-8.5¢/word for longer material. Works between 7,500-10,000 words by authors who make more than 8¢/word for short stories will receive a flat rate that will be no less than the payment would be for a shorter story.

TIPS "In general, we're looking for 'character-oriented' stories, those in which the characters, rather than the science, provide the main focus for the reader's interest. Serious, thoughtful, yet accessible fiction will constitute the majority of our purchases, but there's always room for the humorous as well."

❶⑤ THE ATLANTIC MONTHLY

The Watergate, 600 New Hampshire Ave., NW, Washington DC 20037. **E-mail:** submissions@theatlantic.com; pitches@theatlantic.com. **Website:** www.theatlantic.com. **Contact:** Scott Stossel, magazine editor; Ann Hulbert, literary editor. Estab. 1857. General magazine for an educated readership with broad cultural and public-affairs interests. "*The Atlantic* considers unsolicited mss, either fiction or nonfiction. A general familiarity with what we have published in the past is the best guide to our needs and preferences."

NEEDS "Seeks fiction that is clear, tightly written with strong sense of 'story' and well-defined characters." No longer publishes fiction in the regular magazine. Instead, it will appear in a special newsstand-only fiction issue. Receives 1,000 unsolicited mss/month. Accepts 7-8 mss/year. **Publishes 3-4 new writers/year.** Preferred length: 2,000-6,000 words.

HOW TO CONTACT Submit via e-mail with Word document attachment to submissions@theatlantic. com. Mss submitted via postal mail must be typewritten and double-spaced.

PAYMENT/TERMS Payment varies.

TIPS "Writers should be aware that this is not a market for beginner's work (nonfiction and fiction), nor is it truly for intermediate work. Study this magazine before sending only your best, most professional work. When making first contact, cover letters are sometimes helpful, particularly if they cite prior publications or involvement in writing programs. Common mistakes: melodrama, inconclusiveness, lack of development, unpersuasive characters and/or dialogue."

THE AVALON LITERARY REVIEW

CCI Publishing, P.O. Box 780696, Orlando FL 32878. (407)574-7355. **E-mail:** submissions@avalonliteraryreview.com. **Website:** www.avalonliteraryreview.com. **Contact:** Valerie Rubino, managing editor. Estab. 2011. "*The Avalon Literary Review* welcomes work from both published and unpublished writers and poets. We accept submissions of poetry, short fiction, and personal essays. While we appreciate the genres of fantasy, historical romance, science fiction, and horror, our magazine is not the forum for such work." Quarterly magazine.

NEEDS No erotica, science fiction, or horror. Length: 250-2,500.

HOW TO CONTACT Submit complete ms. Only accepts electronic submissions.

PAYMENT/TERMS Pays 5 contributor's copies.

TIPS "The author's voice and point of view should be unique and clear. We seek pieces which spring from the author's life and experiences. Fiction submissions which explore both the sweet and bitter of life, with a touch of humor, and poetry with vivid imagery, are a good fit for our review."

BABEL: THE MULTILINGUAL, MULTICULTURAL ONLINE JOURNAL AND COMMUNITY OF ARTS AND IDEAS

E-mail: submissions@towerofbabel.com. **Website:** towerofbabel.com. **Contact:** Malcolm Lawrence, editor in chief. Estab. 1996. *Babel* publishes regional reports from international stringers all over the planet, as well as features, round-table discussions, fiction, columns, poetry, erotica, travelogues, and reviews of all the arts and editorials. "Our bloggers include James Schwartz, the first out gay poet raised in the Old Order Amish community in Southwestern Michigan and author of the book *The Literary Party*; Susanna Zaraysky, author of the book *Language Is Music: Making People Multilingual*; James Rovira, Assistant Professor of English and Program Chair of Humanities at Tiffin University and author of the book *Blake & Kierkegaard: Creation and Anxiety*; and Paul B. Miller, Assistant Professor Department of French and Italian at Vanderbilt University. We're interested in fiction, nonfiction, and poetry from all over the world, including multicultural or multilingual work." Cover letter is required. Reviews books/chapbooks of poetry and other magazines, single- and multibook format. Open to unsolicited reviews. Send materials for review consideration.

Babel is recognized by the U.N. as one of the most important social and human sciences online periodicals.

NEEDS "We are currently looking for WordPress bloggers in the following languages: Arabic, Bulgarian, Bengali, Catalan, Czech, Welsh, Danish, German, English, Esperanto, Spanish, Persian, Finnish, Faroese, French, Hebrew, Croatian, Indonesian, Italian, Japanese, Korean, Latvian, Malay, Dutch, Polish, Portuguese, Russian, Albanian, Serbian, Swedish, Tamil, Thai, Ukrainian, Urdu, Uzbek, Vietnamese and Chinese."

HOW TO CONTACT Send queries/mss by e-mail. "Please send submissions with a résumé/cover letter or biography attached to the e-mail."

TIPS "We would like to see more fiction with first-person male characters written by female authors, as well as more fiction first-person female characters written by male authors. We would also like to see that dynamic in action when it comes to other languages, cultures, races, classes, sexual orientations, and ages. Know what you are writing about, and write passionately about it."

BACKROADS

P.O. Box 317, Branchville NJ 07826. (973)948-4176. **Fax:** (973)948-0823. **E-mail:** editor@backroadsusa.com. **Website:** www.backroadsusa.com. Estab. 1995. "*Backroads* is a motorcycle tour magazine geared toward getting motorcyclists on the road and traveling. We provide interesting destinations, unique roadside attractions and eateries, plus Rip & Ride Route Sheets. We cater to all brands. Although *Backroads* is geared towards the motorcycling population, it is not by any means limited to just motorcycle riders. Nonmotorcyclists enjoy great destinations, too. As time has gone by, *Backroads* has developed more and more into a cutting-edge touring publication. We like to see submissions that give the reader the distinct impression of being part of the ride they're reading. Words describing the feelings and emotions brought on by partaking in this great and exciting lifestyle are encouraged."

THE BALTIMORE REVIEW

6514 Maplewood Rd., Baltimore MD 21212. **E-mail:** editor@baltimorereview.org. **Website:** www.baltimorereview.org. **Contact:** Barbara Westwood Diehl, senior editor; Kathleen Hellen, senior editor. Estab. 1996. *The Baltimore Review* publishes poetry, fiction, and creative nonfiction from Baltimore and beyond. Submission periods are August 1-November 30 and February 1-May 31.

In 2012, *The Baltimore Review* began its new life as a quarterly, online literary. Also prints annual anthology.

NEEDS Length: 100-6,000 words.

HOW TO CONTACT Send complete ms using online submission form. Publishes 16-20 mss per online issue. Work published online also published in annual anthology.

PAYMENT/TERMS Pays in contributor's copies.

TIPS "See editor preferences on staff page of website."

THE BANGALORE REVIEW

The Purple Patch Foundation, No. 149, 2nd Floor, 4th Cross, Kasturi Nagar, Bangalore Karnataka India. **E-mail:** info@bangalorereview.com. **E-mail:** submissions@bangalorereview.com. **Website:** www.bangalorereview.com. **Contact:** Arvind Radhakrishnan, editor; Suhail Rasheed, managing editor. Estab. 2013. *The Bangalore Review* is a monthly online magazine aimed at promoting literature, arts, culture, criticism, and philosophy at a deeper level. Strives to inculcate the habit of not just reading but the reading of good literature in the youth of today while also aspiring to be an unbiased, nonrestrictive platform for young and promising independent writers. The editorial team seeks to strike a balance between the old and the young, the published and the unpublished, the known and the unknown, and the mainstream and the unconventional, while curating the articles for each edition.

NEEDS Does not want erotica. Length: 250-5,000.

HOW TO CONTACT Query with complete ms.

PAYMENT/TERMS Does not offer payment.

BARBARIC YAWP

BoneWorld Publishing, 3700 County Route 24, Russell NY 13684-3198. (315)347-2609. **Website:** www.boneworldpublishing.com. Estab. 1997. "We publish what we like. Fiction should include some bounce and surprise. Our publication is intended for the intelligent, open-minded reader."

Barbaric Yawp, published quarterly, is digest-sized; 44 pages; matte cover stock.

NEEDS "We don't want any pornography, gratuitous violence, or whining."

HOW TO CONTACT Send SASE for reply and return of ms, or send a disposable copy of ms. Accepts simultaneous, multiple submissions and reprints.

PAYMENT/TERMS Pays 1 contributor's copy; additional copies $3.

TIPS "Don't give up. Read much, write much, submit much. Observe closely the world around you. Don't borrow ideas from TV or films. Revision is often necessary—grit your teeth and do it. Never fear rejection."

THE BARCELONA REVIEW

Correu Vell 12-2, Barcelona 08002 Spain. (00 34) 93 319 15 96. **E-mail:** editor@barcelonareview.com. **Website:** www.barcelonareview.com. **Contact:** Jill Adams, editor. Estab. 1997. *The Barcelona Review* is "the Web's first multilingual review of international, contemporary, cutting-edge fiction. *TBR* is actually 3 separate reviews—English, Spanish, and Catalan—with occasional translations from one language to another. Original texts of other languages are presented along with English and Spanish translations as available."

NEEDS Length: up to 4,500 words.

HOW TO CONTACT Submit 1 story at a time. To submit via e-mail, send an attached document. Do not send in the body of an e-mail. Include "Submission/ Author Name" in the subject box. Accepts hard copies, but they will not be returned. Double-space ms.

PAYMENT/TERMS "We cannot offer money to contributors, but in lieu of pay we can sometimes offer an excellent Spanish translation (worth quite a bit of money in itself). Work is showcased along with 2 or more known authors in a high-quality literary review with an international readership."

TIPS "Send top drawer material that has been drafted 2, 3, 4 times—whatever it takes. Then sit on it for a while and look at it afresh. Keep the text tight. Grab the reader in the first paragraph and don't let go. Keep in mind that a perfectly crafted story that lacks a punch of some sort won't cut it. Make it new, make it different. Surprise the reader in some way. Read the best of the short fiction available in your area of writing to see how yours measures up. Don't send anything off until you feel it's ready, and then familiarize yourself with the content of the review/magazine to which you are submitting."

ⓞ BATEAU

P.O. Box 1584, Northampton MA 01061. (413)586-2494. **E-mail:** jgrin@mac.com. **Website:** www.bateaupress.org. **Contact:** James Grinwis, editor. Estab. 2007. "*Bateau*, published annually, subscribes to no trend but serves to represent as wide a cross-section of contemporary writing as possible. For this reason, readers will most likely love and hate at least something in each issue. We consider this a good thing. To us, it means *Bateau* is eclectic, open-ended, and not mired in a particular strain."

⚫   *Bateau* is around 80 pages, digest-sized, offset print, perfect-bound, with a 100% recycled letterpress cover. Press run is 250.

HOW TO CONTACT Submit via online submission form. Cover letter not needed.

PAYMENT/TERMS Pays in contributor's copies.

ⓞ BAYOU

Dept. of English, University of New Orleans, 2000 Lakeshore Dr., New Orleans LA 70148. (504)280-5423. **E-mail:** bayou@uno.edu. **Website:** bayoumagazine.org. **Contact:** Joanna Leake, editor in chief. Estab. 2002. "A nonprofit journal for the arts, each issue of *Bayou* contains beautiful fiction, nonfiction, and poetry. From quirky shorts to more traditional stories, we are committed to publishing solid work. Regardless of style, at *Bayou* we are always interested first in a well-told tale. Our poetry and prose are filled with memorable characters observing their world, acknowledging both the mundane and the sublime, often at once, and always with an eye toward beauty. *Bayou* is packed with a range of material from established, award-winning authors as well as new

voices on the rise. Recent contributors include Eric Trethewey, Virgil Suarez, Marilyn Hacker, Sean Beaudoin, Tom Whalen, Mark Doty, Philip Cioffari, Lyn Lifshin, Timothy Liu, and Gaylord Brewer. In 1 issue every year, *Bayou* features the winner of the annual Tennessee Williams/New Orleans Literary Festival One-Act Play Competition."

⚫   Does not accept e-mail submissions. Reads submissions from September 1-June 1.

NEEDS "Flash fiction and short-shorts are welcome. No novel excerpts, please, unless they can stand alone as short stories." No horror, gothic, or juvenile fiction. Length: up to 7,500 words.

HOW TO CONTACT Send complete ms via online submission system or postal mail.

PAYMENT/TERMS Pays 2 contributor's copies.

TIPS "Do not submit in more than 1 genre at a time. Don't send a second submission until you receive a response to the first."

ⓞ ⓖ THE BEAR DELUXE MAGAZINE

Orlo, 240 N. Broadway, #112, Portland OR 97227. **E-mail:** bear@orlo.org. **Website:** www.orlo.org. **Contact:** Tom Webb, editor in chief; Kristin Rogers Brown, art director. Estab. 1993. "*The Bear Deluxe Magazine* is a national independent environmental arts magazine publishing significant works of reporting, creative nonfiction, literature, visual art, and design. Based in the Pacific Northwest, it reaches across cultural and political divides to engage readers on vital issues effecting the environment. Published twice per year, *The Bear Deluxe* includes a wider array and a higher percentage of visual artwork and design than many other publications. Artwork is included both as editorial support and as standalone or independent art. It has included nationally recognized artists as well as emerging artists. As with any publication, artists are encouraged to review a sample copy for a clearer understanding of the magazine's approach. Unsolicited submissions and samples are accepted and encouraged."

NEEDS "We are most excited by high-quality writing that furthers the magazine's goal of engaging new and divergent readers. We appreciate strong aspects of storytelling and are open to new formats, though we wouldn't call ourselves publishers of 'experimental fiction.'" No traditional sci-fi, horror, romance, or crime/action. Length: up to 4,000 words.

HOW TO CONTACT Query or send complete ms. Prefers postal mail submissions.

PAYMENT/TERMS Pays free subscription to the magazine, contributor's copies, and $25-400, depending on piece; additional copies for postage.

TIPS "Offer to be a stringer for future ideas. Get a copy of the magazine and guidelines, and query us with specific nonfiction ideas and clips. We're looking for original, magazine-style stories, not fluff or PR. Fiction, essay, and poetry writers should know we have an open and blind review policy and they should keep sending their best work even if rejected once. Be as specific as possible in queries."

BEGINNINGS PUBLISHING INC.

P.O. Box 2534, Sag Harbor NY 11963. **Website:** www.literarybeginnings.org. **Contact:** Jenine Boisits, fiction editor; Colleen Little, poetry editor. Estab. 1999. "*Beginnings* serves as a forum exclusively for the new writer, as well as a launching pad for their literary creations."

Beginnings was selected as one of the top 30 fiction markets in 2002 and 2003 by *Writer's Digest*.

NEEDS "No pornography, sex, or obscenities (within reason) and no content that is racist or otherwise extremely offensive or abusive to others." Length: up to 3,500 words.

HOW TO CONTACT Send complete ms via postal mail; no e-mail submissions. Include cover letter with short bio.

BELLEVUE LITERARY REVIEW

NYU Langone Medical Center, Department of Medicine, 550 First Ave., OBV-A612, New York NY 10016. (212)263-3973. **E-mail:** info@BLReview.org. **E-mail:** stacy.bodziak@nyumc.org. **Website:** www.blreview.org. **Contact:** Stacy Bodziak, managing editor. Estab. 2001. *Bellevue Literary Review*, published semiannually, prints "works of fiction, nonfiction, and poetry that touch upon relationships to the human body, illness, health, and healing."

Work published in *Bellevue Literary Review* has appeared in *The Pushcart Prize* and *Best American Short Stories*. Recently published work by Linda Pastan, Rachel Hadas, and Tom Sleigh.

NEEDS Agented fiction 1%. **Publishes 3-6 new writers/year.** Publishes short shorts. Sometimes comments on rejected mss. No genre fiction. Length: 5,000 words. Average length: 2,500 words.

HOW TO CONTACT Receives 100-200 unsolicited mss/month. Accepts 10-12 mss/issue; 24 mss/year. Submit online at www.blreview.org (preferred). Also accepts mss via postal mail. Send complete ms. Send SASE (or IRC) for return of ms or disposable copy of the ms and #10 SASE for reply only.

PAYMENT/TERMS Pays 2 contributor's copies, one-year subscription, and one-year gift subscription; additional copies $6.

BELLINGHAM REVIEW

Mail Stop 9053, Western Washington University, Bellingham WA 98225. (360)650-4863. **E-mail:** bellingham.review@wwu.edu. **Website:** wwww.bhreview.org. **Contact:** Brenda Miller, editor in chief; Kaitlyn Teer, managing editor. Estab. 1977. Nonprofit magazine published once/year in the spring. Seeks "literature of palpable quality: poems, stories, and essays so beguiling they invite us to touch their essence. *Bellingham Review* hungers for a kind of writing that nudges the limits of form or executes traditional forms exquisitely."

The editors are actively seeking submissions of creative nonfiction, as well as stories that push the boundaries of the form. Open submission period is from September 15-December 1.

NEEDS Does not want anything nonliterary. Length: up to 6,000 words.

HOW TO CONTACT Submit complete ms via online submissions manager.

PAYMENT/TERMS Pays as funds allow, plus contributor's copies.

TIPS "The *Bellingham Review* holds 3 annual contests: the 49th Parallel Award for poetry, the Annie Dillard Award for Nonfiction, and the Tobias Wolff Award for Fiction. See the individual listings for these contests under Contests & Awards for full details."

BELOIT FICTION JOURNAL

Box 11, Beloit College, 700 College St., Beloit WI 53511. (608)363-2079. **E-mail:** bfj@beloit.edu. **Website:** https://www.beloit.edu/bfj. **Contact:** Chris Fink, editor in chief. Estab. 1985. "*The Beloit Fiction Journal* publishes the best in contemporary short fiction. Traditional and experimental narratives find a home in our pages. We publish new writers alongside established writers. Our fiction-only format allows us to consider very long as well as very short stories. We occasionally publish excerpts."

Reading period: August 1-December 1. Work first appearing in *Beloit Fiction Journal* has been reprinted in award-winning collections, including the Flannery O'Connor and the Milkweed Fiction Prize collections, and has won the Iowa Short Fiction award. Has published work by Dennis Lehane, Silas House, and David Harris Ebenbach.

NEEDS Receives 200 unsolicited mss/month. Accepts 14 mss/year. Publishes ms 9 months after acceptance. **Publishes new writers every year.** Sometimes comments on rejected mss. Wants more experimental and short shorts. Would like to see more "stories with a focus on both language and plot, unusual metaphors and vivid characters." No pornography, religious dogma, science fiction, horror, political propaganda or genre fiction.

HOW TO CONTACT No fax, e-mail, or disk submissions. Accepts simultaneous submissions if identified as such. Please send 1 story at a time. Always include SASE.

PAYMENT/TERMS Pays contributor copies.

TIPS "Many of our contributors are writers whose work we had previously rejected. Don't let 1 rejection slip turn you away from our—or any—magazine."

BERKELEY FICTION REVIEW

102 Hearst Gym MC #4500, University of California, Berkeley, Berkeley CA 94720. (510)642-2892. **E-mail:** berkeleyfictionreview@gmail.com. **Website:** bfictionreview.wordpress.com. Estab. 1981. "The *Berkeley Fiction Review* is a UC Berkeley undergraduate, student-run publication. We look for innovative short fiction that plays with form and content, as well as traditionally constructed stories with fresh voices and original ideas."

BFR nominates to O.Henry, *Best American Short Stories* and *Pushcart* prizes. Sponsored by the ASUC.

NEEDS Length: no more than 25 pages.

HOW TO CONTACT Submit via e-mail with "Submission: Name, Title" in subject line. Include cover letter in body of e-mail, with story as an attachment.

PAYMENT/TERMS Pays 1 contributor's copy.

TIPS "Our criteria is fiction that resonates. Voices that are strong and move a reader. Clear, powerful prose (either voice or rendering of subject) with a point. Unique ways of telling stories—these capture the editors. Work hard, don't give up. Ask an honest person to point out your writing weaknesses, and then work on them. We look forward to reading fresh new voices."

BEYOND CENTAURI

White Cat Publications, LLC, 33080 Industrial Rd., Suite 101, Livonia MI 48150. **E-mail:** beyondcentauri@whitecatpublications.com. **Website:** www.whitecatpub-

lications.com/guidelines/beyond-centauri. Estab. 2003. *Beyond Centauri*, published quarterly, contains fantasy, science fiction, sword and sorcery, very mild horror short stories, poetry, and illustrations for readers ages 10 and up.

Beyond Centauri is 44 pages, magazine-sized, offset printed, perfect-bound, with paper cover for color art, includes ads. Receives about 200 poems/year, accepts about 50 (25%). Press run is 100; 5 distributed free to reviewers.

NEEDS Looks for themes of science fiction or fantasy. "Science fiction and especially stories that take place in outer space will find great favor with us." Length: up to 2,500 words.

HOW TO CONTACT Submit in the body of an e-mail, or as an RTF attachment.

PAYMENT/TERMS Pays $6/story, $3/reprints, and $2/flash fiction (under 1,000 words), plus 1 contributor's copy.

BIG BRIDGE

Big Bridge Press, P.O. Box 870, Guerniville CA 95446. **E-mail:** walterblue@bigbridge.org. **Website:** www.bigbridge.org. **Contact:** Michael Rothenberg and Terri Carrion, editors. "*Big Bridge* is a webzine of poetry and everything else. If we like it, we'll publish it. We're interested in poetry, fiction, nonfiction essays, journalism, and art (photos, line drawings, performance, installations, siteworks, comics, graphics)."

HOW TO CONTACT Only accepts electronic submissions. Submit via e-mail.

TIPS "We are guided by whimsy and passion and urgency. Each issue will feature an online chapbook."

BIG MUDDY: A JOURNAL OF THE MISSISSIPPI RIVER VALLEY

Southeast Missouri State University Press, One University Plaza, MS 2650, Cape Girardeau MO 63701. (573)651-2044. **Website:** www6.semo.edu/universitypress/bigmuddy. **Contact:** Susan Swartwout, publisher/editor. Estab. 2000. "*Big Muddy* explores multidisciplinary, multicultural issues, people, and events mainly concerning, but not limited to, the 10-state area that borders the Mississippi River. We publish fiction, poetry, historical essays, creative nonfiction, environmental essays, biography, regional events, photography, art, etc."

NEEDS No romance, fantasy, or children's.

HOW TO CONTACT Receives 50 unsolicited mss/month. Accepts 20-25 mss/issue. Accepts multiple submissions.

PAYMENT/TERMS Pays 2 contributor's copies; additional copies $5.

TIPS "We look for clear language, avoidance of clichés except in necessary dialogue, a fresh vision of the theme or issue. Find some excellent and honest readers to comment on your work-in-progress and final draft. Consider their viewpoints carefully. Revise if needed."

BIG PULP

Exter Press, P.O. Box 92, Cumberland MD 21501. **E-mail:** editors@bigpulp.com. **Website:** www.bigpulp.com. **Contact:** Bill Olver, editor. *Big Pulp* defines "pulp fiction" very broadly: It's lively, challenging, thought-provoking, thrilling, and fun, regardless of how many or how few genre elements are packed in. Doesn't subscribe to the theory that genre fiction is disposable; a great deal of literary fiction could easily fall under one of their general categories. Places a higher value on character and story than genre elements.

Currently accepting submissions for themed collections only. See website for details on current needs. Submissions are only accepted during certain reading periods; check website to see if magazine is currently open.

NEEDS Does not want generic slice-of-life, memoirs, inspirational, political, pastoral odes. Length: up to 10,000 words.

HOW TO CONTACT Submit complete ms.

PAYMENT/TERMS Pays $5-25.

TIPS "We like to be surprised, and we have few boundaries. Fantasy writers may focus on the mundane aspects of a fantastical creature's life or the magic that can happen in everyday life. Romances do not have to be requited or have happy endings, and the object of one's obsession may not be a person. Mysteries need not focus on 'whodunit?' We're always interested in science or speculative fiction focusing on societal issues, but writers should avoid being partisan or shrill. We also like fiction that crosses genre; for example, a science fiction romance or a fantasy crime story. We have an online archive for fiction and poetry and encourage writers to check it out. That said, *Big Pulp* has a strong editorial bias in favor of stories with monkeys. Especially talking monkeys."

BILINGUAL REVIEW

Arizona State University, Hispanic Research Center, P.O. Box 875303, Tempe AZ 85287-5303. (480)965-3867. **Fax:** (480)965-0315. **E-mail:** brp@asu.edu. **Web-**site: www.asu.edu/brp/submit. **Contact:** Gary Francisco Keller, publisher. Estab. 1974. *Bilingual Review* is "committed to publishing high-quality writing by both established and emerging writers."

Magazine: 7×10; 96 pages; 55 lb. acid-free paper; coated cover stock.

NEEDS Receives 50 unsolicited mss/month. Accepts 3 mss/issue; 9 mss/year. "We do not publish literature about tourists in Latin America and their perceptions of the 'native culture.' We do not publish fiction about Latin America unless there is a clear tie to the U.S."

HOW TO CONTACT Submit via postal mail. Send 2 copies of complete ms with SAE and loose stamps. Does not usually accept e-mail submissions except through special circumstance/prior arrangement.

PAYMENT/TERMS Pays 2 contributor's copies; 30% discount for additional copies. Acquires 50% of reprint permission fee given to author as matter of policy rights.

THE BINNACLE

University of Maine at Machias, 116 O'Brien Ave., Machias ME 04654. **E-mail:** ummbinnacle@maine.edu. **Website:** www.umm.maine.edu/binnacle. Estab. 1957. "We are interested in fresh voices, not Raymond Carver's, and not the Iowa Workshop's. We want the peculiar and the idiosyncratic. We want playful and experimental but understandable. Please see our website for details on our Annual Ultra-Short Competition. (Prize of a minimum of $300.) We accept submissions for the Fall Ultra-Short Edition from December 1-March 15 and report to writers in early June. We accept submissions for the Spring Edition from September 1-November 30 and report to writers between February 1-March 1."

Does not accept paper submissions. Electronic/e-mail submissions only.

NEEDS No extreme erotica, fantasy, horror, or religious, but any genre attuned to a general audience can work. Length: up to 2,500 words.

HOW TO CONTACT Send complete ms via e-mail only.

TIPS "We want fiction, poetry, and images that speak to real people, people who have lives, people who have troubles, people who laugh, too."

THE BITTER OLEANDER

4983 Tall Oaks Dr., Fayetteville NY 13066. **Fax:** (315)637-5056. **E-mail:** info@bitteroleander.com. **Website:** www.bitteroleander.com. **Contact:** Paul B. Roth, editor and publisher. "We're reading to find a language uncommitted to the commonplace and more integrated with the natural world. A language that helps define the same particulars in nature that exist in us but have not been socialized out of us."

⬤ *The Bitter Oleander* is 6×9, 128 pages, 55 lb. paper, 12 pt. CIS cover stock, contains photos. Biannual.

NEEDS Receives 300 unsolicited mss/month. Accepts 4-5 mss/issue; 8-10 mss/year. Does not read in July. Recently published work by Kristiina Ehin (Estonia), Norberto Luis Romero (Spain), Anders Benson, Martín Camps, and Jane Arnold. Publishes short shorts. Also publishes literary essays, poetry. Always comments on rejected mss. Does not want family stories with moralistic plots or fantasy that involves hyper-reality of any sort. Length: 300-2,500 words.

HOW TO CONTACT Query. Send mss by mail with SASE for response. Whether you live in the U.S. or outside, we accept e-mail submissions or postal mail submissions if SASE is enclosed.

PAYMENT/TERMS Pays contributor's copies.

TIPS "If you are writing poems or short fiction in the tradition of 98% of all journals publishing in this country, then your work will usually not fit for us. If within the first 400 words my mind drifts, the rest rarely makes it. Be yourself, and listen to no one but yourself."

⬤ BLACKBIRD

Virginia Commonwealth University Department of English, P.O. Box 843082, Richmond VA 23284. (804)827-4729. **E-mail:** blackbird@vcu.edu. **Website:** www.blackbird.vcu.edu. Estab. 2001. *Blackbird* is published twice a year.

NEEDS "We primarily look for short stories, but novel excerpts are acceptable if self-contained."

HOW TO CONTACT Submit using online submissions manager or by postal mail. Online submission is preferred.

TIPS "We like a story that invites us into its world, that engages our senses, soul, and mind. We are able to publish long works in all genres, but query *Blackbird* before you send a prose piece over 8,000 words or a poem exceeding 10 pages."

⬤ ⬤ BLACK LACE

P.O. Box 83912, Los Angeles CA 90083. (310)410-0808. **Fax:** (310)410-9250. **E-mail:** newsroom@blk.com. **Website:** www.blacklace.org. Estab. 1991. "*Black Lace* seeks stories, articles, photography, models, illustration, and a very limited amount of poetry all related to black women unclothed or in erotic situations."

NEEDS Length: 2,000-4,000 words.

HOW TO CONTACT Submit via postal mail (include SASE if you want your work returned), fax, or e-mail.

TIPS "*Black Lace* seeks erotic material of the highest quality, but it need not be written by professional writers. The most important thing is that the work be erotic and that it feature black women in the life or ITL themes. We are not interested in stories that demean black women or place them in stereotypical situations."

⬤ ⬤ ⬤ BLACK WARRIOR REVIEW

P.O. Box 862936, Tuscaloosa AL 35486. (205)348-4518. **E-mail:** interns.bwr@gmail.com. **Website:** www.bwr.ua.edu. **Contact:** Kirby Johnson, editor. Estab. 1974. "We publish contemporary fiction, poetry, reviews, essays, and art for a literary audience. We publish the freshest work we can find."

⬤ Work that appeared in the *Black Warrior Review* has been included in the *Pushcart Prize* anthology, *Harper's Magazine, Best American Short Stories, Best American Poetry,* and *New Stories from the South.*

NEEDS "We are open to good experimental writing and short-short fiction. No genre fiction please." Publishes novel excerpts if under contract to be published. Length: no more than 7,000 words.

HOW TO CONTACT One story/chapter per envelope. Wants work that is conscious of form and well-crafted.

PAYMENT/TERMS "*BWR* pays a one-year subscription and a nominal lump-sum fee for all works published."

TIPS "We look for attention to language, freshness, honesty, a convincing and sharp voice. Send us a clean, well-printed, proofread ms. Become familiar with the magazine prior to submission."

⬤ ⬤ BLOOD LOTUS

Wales. **E-mail:** bloodlotusjournal@gmail.com. **Website:** www.bloodlotusjournal.com. **Contact:** Bethany Brownholtz, art director and co-editor. *Blood Lotus*, published quarterly online, publishes "poetry, fiction, and anything in between!" Wants "fresh language, memorable characters, strong images, and vivid artwork." Will not open attachments. Reads submissions year round.

NEEDS Send "1-3 polished, self-contained short shorts or flash fiction pieces, e-mailed to bloodlotusfiction@gmail.com." No attachments.

TIPS "Don't be boring."

⬤ BLUELINE

120 Morey Hall, Dept. of English and Communication, Postdam NY 13676. (315)267-2044. **E-mail:** blue-

line@potsdam.edu. **Website:** bluelinemagadk.com. **Contact:** Donald McNutt, editor; Caroline Downing, art editor; Donald McNutt, nonfiction editor; Stephanie Coyne-Deghett, fiction editor; Rebecca Lehmann, poetry editor. Estab. 1979. "*Blueline* seeks poems, stories, and essays relating to the Adirondacks and regions similar in geography and spirit, or focusing on the shaping influence of nature. Submission period is July-November. *Blueline* welcomes electronic submissions as Word document (.doc or .docx) attachments. Please identify genre in subject line. Please avoid using compression software."

○ "Proofread all submissions. It is difficult for our editors to get excited about work containing typographical and syntactic errors."

NEEDS Receives 8-10 unsolicited mss/month. Accepts 2-3 mss/issue. Does not read January-June. Publishes 2 new writers/year. Recently published work by Jim Meirose, T. Stores, Gail Gilliland, Lou Gaglia, Roger Sheffer, and Mason Smith. No urban stories or erotica. Length: 500-3,000 words. Average length: 2,500 words.

PAYMENT/TERMS Pays 1 contributor's copy; charges $9 each for 3 or more copies.

TIPS "We look for concise, clear, concrete prose that tells a story and touches upon a universal theme or situation. We prefer realism to romanticism but will consider nostalgia if well done. Pay attention to grammar and syntax. Avoid murky language, sentimentality, cuteness, or folkiness. We would like to see more good, creative nonfiction centered on the literature and/or culture of the Adirondacks, Northern New York, New England, or Eastern Canada. If ms has potential, we work with author to improve and reconsider for publication. Our readers prefer fiction to poetry (in general) or reviews. Write from your own experience, be specific and factual (within the bounds of your story), and if you write about universal features such as love, death, change, etc., write about them in a fresh way. You'll catch our attention if your writing is interesting, vigorous, and polished."

BLUE MESA REVIEW

700 Lomas NE, Suite 108, Albuquerque NM 87102. **E-mail:** bmreditr@unm.edu. **Website:** bluemesareview. org. **Contact:** Has rotating editorial board; see website for current masthead. Estab. 1989. "Originally founded by Rudolfo Anaya, Gene Frumkin, David Johnson, Patricia Clark Smith, and Lee Bartlette in 1989, the *Blue Mesa Review* emerged as a source of innovative

writing produced in the Southwest. Over the years the magazine's nuance has changed, sometimes shifting towards more craft-oriented work, other times realigning with its original roots."

○ Open for submissions from September 30-March 31. Contest: June 1-August 31. Only accepts submissions through online submissions manager, available through website.

NEEDS Length: up to 6,000 words.

HOW TO CONTACT Submit via online submissions manager.

TIPS "In general, we are seeking strong voices and lively, compelling narrative with a fine eye for craft. We look forward to reading your best work!"

◐ BLUESTEM

English Deptartment, Eastern Illinois University, **E-mail:** info@bluestemmagazine.com. **Website:** www. bluestemmagazine.com. **Contact:** Lania Knight, editor. Estab. 1966. *Bluestem*, formerly known as *Karamu*, produces a quarterly online issue (December, March, June, September) and an annual print issue. Submissions are accepted September 1-May 1. There is no compensation for online contributors but we will promote your work enthusiastically and widely. Past issues have included themes such as: The Humor Issue, The Music Issue, The Millennium. Produced by the English Department at Eastern Illinois University.

○ Only accepts submissions through online submissions manager.

NEEDS Length: no more than 5,000 words.

HOW TO CONTACT Submit only 1 short story at a time. Include bio (less than 100 words) with submission. Query if longer than 5,000 words.

PAYMENT/TERMS Pays 1 contributor's copy and discount for additional copies.

◑⑤ BOMB MAGAZINE

New Arts Publications, 80 Hanson Place, Suite 703, Brooklyn NY 11217. (718)636-9100. **Fax:** (718)636-9200. **E-mail:** generalinquiries@bombsite.com. **Website:** www.bombmagazine.com. **Contact:** Mónica de la Torre, senior editor. Estab. 1981. "Written, edited, and produced by industry professionals and funded by those interested in the arts, *BOMB Magazine* publishes work which is unconventional and contains an edge, whether it be in style or subject matter."

NEEDS No genre fiction: romance, science fiction, horror, western. Length: up to 25 pages.

HOW TO CONTACT *BOMB Magazine* accepts unsolicited poetry and prose submissions for our literary supplement *First Proof* by online submission manager in January and August. Submissions sent outside these months will not be read. Submit complete ms via online submission manager. E-mailed submissions will not be considered.

PAYMENT/TERMS Pays $100 and contributor's copies.

TIPS "Mss should be typed, double-spaced, and proofread, and should be final drafts. Purchase a sample issue before submitting work."

◐◑⑨ BOSTON REVIEW

PO Box 425786, Cambridge MA 02142. (617)324-1360. **Fax:** (617)452-3356. **E-mail:** review@bostonreview.net. **Website:** www.bostonreview.net. Estab. 1975. "The editors are committed to a society and culture that foster human diversity and a democracy in which we seek common grounds of principle amidst our many differences. In the hope of advancing these ideals, the *Review* acts as a forum that seeks to enrich the language of public debate."

◐ *Boston Review* is a recipient of the Pushcart Prize in Poetry.

NEEDS Looking for "stories that are emotionally and intellectually substantive and also interesting on the level of language. Things that are shocking, dark, lewd, comic, or even insane are fine so long as the fiction is *controlled* and purposeful in a masterly way. Subtlety, delicacy, and lyricism are attractive, too. Simultaneous submissions are fine as long as we are notified of the fact." No romance, erotica, genre fiction. Length: 1,200-5,000 words. Average length: 2,000 words.

HOW TO CONTACT Send complete ms.

PAYMENT/TERMS Pays $25-300 and contributor's copies.

TIPS "The best way to get a sense of the kind of material *Boston Review* is looking for is to read the magazine. "

◐◑⑨ BOULEVARD

Opojaz, Inc., 6614 Clayton Rd., Box 325, Richmond Heights MO 63117. (314)324-3351. **Fax:** (314)862-2982. **E-mail:** richardburgin@netzero.com; jessicarogen@boulevardmagazine.org. **E-mail:** https://boulevard.submittable.com/submit. **Website:** www.boulevard-magazine.org. **Contact:** Richard Burgin, editor; Jessica Rogen, managing editor. Estab. 1985. The Short Fiction Contest for Emerging Writers: $1,500 and publication in *Boulevard*. Postmarked deadline is December 31. Entry fee is $15 for each individual story, with no limit per author. Entry fee includes a one-year subscription to *Boulevard* (1 per author). Make

check payable to *Boulevard*. For contests, make check payable to *Boulevard* or submit online at https://boulevard.submittable.com/submit. "*Boulevard* is a diverse literary magazine presenting original creative work by well-known authors, as well as by writers of exciting promise." Triannual magazine featuring fiction, poetry, and essays.Sometimes comments on rejected mss. *Boulevard* has been called 'one of the half-dozen best literary journals' by Poet Laureate Daniel Hoffman in *The Philadelphia Inquirer*. We strive to publish the finest in poetry, fiction, and nonfiction. We frequently publish writers with previous credits, we are very interested in publishing less experienced or unpublished writers with exceptional promise. We've published everything from John Ashbery to Donald Hall to a wide variety of styles from new or lesser known poets. We're eclectic. We are interested in original, moving poetry written from the head as well as the heart. It can be about any topic."

◐ *Boulevard* is 175-250 pages, digest-sized, flat-spined, with glossy card cover. Receives over 600 unsolicited mss/month. Accepts about 10 mss/issue. Publishes 10 new writers/year. Recently published work by Joyce Carol Oates, Floyd Skloot, John Barth, Stephen Dixon, David Guterson, Albert Goldbarth, Molly Peacock, Bob Hicok, Alice Friman, Dick Allen, and Tom Disch.

NEEDS "We do not want erotica, science fiction, romance, western, horror, or children's stories." Length: up to 8,000 words.

PAYMENT/TERMS Pays $50-500 (sometimes higher) for accepted work.

TIPS "Read the magazine first. The work *Boulevard* publishes is generally recognized as among the finest in the country. We continue to seek more good literary or cultural essays. Send only your best work."

◐◑ BRAIN, CHILD

Erielle Media, LLC, 341 Newtown Turnpike, Wilton CT 06897. (203)563-9149. **E-mail:** submissions@brainchildmag.com. **Website:** www.brainchildmag.com. **Contact:** Marcelle Soviero, editor in chief. Estab. 2000. "*Brain, Child: The Magazine for Thinking Mothers,* reflects modern motherhood—the way it really is. It is the largest print literary magazine devoted to motherhood. *Brain, Child* as a community for and by mothers who like to think about what raising kids does for (and to) the mind and soul. *Brain, Child* isn't your typical parenting magazine. We couldn't cupcake-decorate our way out of a paper bag. We are more 'literary' than 'how-to,' more *New Yorker* than *Parents*. We shy away from expert advice on childrearing in favor of first-hand reflections by great writers (Jane Smiley, Barbara Ehrenreich, Anne Tyler) on life as a mother. Each quarterly issue is full of essays, features, humor, reviews, fiction, art, cartoons, and our readers' own stories. Our philosophy is pretty simple: Motherhood is worthy of literature. And there are a lot of ways to mother, all of them interesting. We're proud to be publishing articles and essays that are smart, down to earth, sometimes funny, and sometimes poignant."

NEEDS "We publish fiction that has a strong motherhood theme." No genre fiction. Length: 800-5,000 words.

HOW TO CONTACT Send complete ms.

PAYMENT/TERMS Payment varies.

TIPS Prefers e-mail submissions. No attachments.

THE BRIAR CLIFF REVIEW

3303 Rebecca St., Sioux City IA 51104. (712)279-5477. **E-mail:** tricia.currans-sheehan@briarcliff.edu (editor); jeanne.emmons@briarcliff.edu (poetry). **Website:** bcreview.org. **Contact:** Tricia Currans-Sheehan, Jeanne Emmons, Phil Hey, Paul Weber, editors. Estab. 1989. *The Briar Cliff Review*, published annually in April, is "an attractive, eclectic literary/art magazine." It focuses on (but is not limited to) "Siouxland writers and subjects. We are happy to proclaim ourselves a regional publication. It doesn't diminish us; it enhances us."

Magazine: 8.5×11; 125 pages; 70 lb. 100# Altima Satin Text; illustrations; photos; perfect-bound, with 4-color cover on dull stock. Member: CLMP, Humanities International Complete. Reads submissions August 1-November 1 only.

NEEDS Accepts 5 mss/year. **Publishes 10-14 new writers/year.** Publishes ms 3-4 months after acceptance. Recently published work by Leslie Barnard, Daryl Murphy, Patrick Hicks, Siobhan Fallon, Shelley Scaletta, Jenna Blum, Brian Bedard, Rebecca Tuch, Scott H. Andrews, and Josip Novakovich. "No romance, horror, or alien stories." Length: 2,500-5,000 words; average length: 3,000 words.

HOW TO CONTACT Submit by postal mail (send SASE for return of ms) or via Submittable. Does not accept e-mail submissions (unless from overseas). Seldom comments on rejected mss.

PAYMENT/TERMS Pays 2 contributor's copies; additional copies available for $12.

TIPS "So many stories are just telling. We want some action. It has to move. We prefer stories in which there is no gimmick, no mechanical turn of events, no moral except the one we would draw privately."

BRILLIANT CORNERS: A JOURNAL OF JAZZ & LITERATURE

Lycoming College, 700 College Place, Williamsport PA 17701. **Website:** www.lycoming.edu/brilliantcorners. **Contact:** Sascha Feinstein. Estab. 1996. "We publish jazz-related literature—fiction, poetry, and nonfiction. We are open as to length and form." Semiannual.

Does not read mss May 15-September 1.

NEEDS Receives 10-15 unsolicited mss/month. Accepts 1-2 mss/issue; 2-3 mss/year.

HOW TO CONTACT Submit with SASE for return of ms, or send disposable copy of ms. Accepts unpublished work only. No e-mail or fax submissions. Cover letter is preferred.

TIPS "We look for clear, moving prose that demostrates a love of both writing and jazz. We primarily publish established writers, but we read all submissions carefully and welcome work by outstanding young writers."

BROKEN PENCIL

P.O. Box 203, Station P, Toronto ON M5S 2S7 Canada. **E-mail:** editor@brokenpencil.com. **Website:** www.brokenpencil.com. Estab. 1995. "*Broken Pencil* is one of the few magazines in the world devoted exclusively to underground culture and the independent arts. We are a great resource and a lively read! *Broken Pencil* reviews the best zines, books, websites, videos, and artworks from the underground and reprints the best articles from the alternative press. From the hilarious to the perverse, *Broken Pencil* challenges conformity and demands attention."

NEEDS "We're particularly interested in work from emerging writers." Reads fiction submissions only between February 1 and September 15. Length: 50-3,000 words.

HOW TO CONTACT Submit using online submissions manager.

PAYMENT/TERMS Pays $30-300.

TIPS "Remember, we are a guide to alternative and independent culture. We don't want your thoughts on Hollywood movies or your touching tale about coming of age on the prairies! Make sure you have some sense of the kind of work we use before getting in touch. Never send us something if you haven't at least read *Broken Pencil*. Always include your address, phone number, and e-mail, so we know where to find you, and a little something about yourself, so we know who you are."

BRYANT LITERARY REVIEW

Faculty Suite F, Bryant University, 1150 Douglas Pike, Smithfield RI 02917. **E-mail:** blr@bryant.edu. **Website:** bryantliteraryreview.org. **Contact:** Tom Chandler, editor; Kimberly Keyes, managing editor; Jeff Cabusao, fiction editor; Lucie Koretsky, associate editor. Estab. 2000. *Bryant Literary Review* is an international magazine of poetry and fiction published annually in May. Features poetry, fiction, photography, and art. "Our only standard is quality."

○ *Bryant Literary Review* is 125 pages, digest-sized, offset-printed, perfect-bound, with 4-color cover with art or photo. Has published poetry by Michael S. Harper, Mary Crow, Denise Duhamel, and Baron Wormser. Reading period: September 1-December 1.

NEEDS Length: up to 5,000 words.

HOW TO CONTACT Submit 1 ms at a time; include SASE.

PAYMENT/TERMS Pays contributor's copies.

TIPS "We expect readers of the *Bryant Literary Review* to be sophisticated, educated, and familiar with the conventions of contemporary literature. We see our purpose to be the cultivation of an active and growing connection between our community and the larger literary culture. Our production values are of the highest caliber, and our roster of published authors includes major award and fellowship winners. The *BLR* provides a respected venue for creative writing of every kind from around the world. Our only standard is quality. No abstract expressionist poems, please. We prefer accessible work of depth and quality."

BURNSIDE REVIEW

P.O. Box 1782, Portland OR 97207. **E-mail:** sid@burnsidereview.org. **Website:** www.burnsidereview.org. **Contact:** Sid Miller, founder and editor; Dan Kaplan, managing editor. Estab. 2004. *Burnside Review,* published every 9 months, prints "the best poetry and short fiction we can get our hands on." Each issue includes 1 featured poet with an interview and new poems. "We tend to publish writing that finds beauty in truly unexpected places; that combines urban and natural imagery; that breaks the heart."

○ *Burnside Review* is 80 pages, 6x6, professionally printed, perfect-bound. Charges a $3 submission fee to cover printing costs.

NEEDS "Send anything from a group of flash-fiction pieces to a traditional short story, so long as the word count doesn't exceed 5,000 words. We like story. We like character. We don't like hobgoblins. Barthelme, Munro, Carver, and Bender are some of the folks whose work we love."

HOW TO CONTACT Submit 1 short story at a time. Accepts submissions through online submission manager only.

PAYMENT/TERMS Pays $25 plus 1 contributor's copy.

TIPS "*Burnside Review* accepts submissions of poetry and fiction. If you have something else that you think would be a perfect fit for our journal, please query the editor before submitting. We like work that breaks the heart. That leaves us in a place that we don't expect to be. We like the lyric. We like the narrative. We like when the two merge. We like whiskey. We like hourglass figures. We like crying over past mistakes. We like to be surprised. Surprise us. Read a past issue and try to understand our tastes. At least please read the sample poems we have linked from our prior issues."

BUTTON

P.O. Box 77, Westminster MA 01473. **E-mail:** sally@moonsigns.net. **Website:** www.moonsigns.net. Estab. 1993. "*Button* is New England's tiniest magazine of poetry, fiction, and gracious living, published once a year. As 'gracious living' is on the cover, we like wit, brevity, cleverly-conceived essays/recipes, poetry that isn't sentimental, or song lyrics. I started *Button* so that a century from now, when people read it in landfills or, preferably, libraries, they'll say, 'Gee, what a great time to have lived. I wish I lived back then.'"

○ Receives 20-40 unsolicited mss/month. Accepts 3-6 mss/issue; 3-6mss/year. *Button* is 16-24 pages, saddle-stapled, with cardstock offset cover with illustrations that incorporate 1 or more buttons. Has published poetry by Amanda Powell, Brendan Galvin, Jean Monahan, Mary Campbell, KevinMcGrath, and Ed Conti.

NEEDS Seeks quality fiction. No genre fiction, science fiction, techno-thriller. "Wants more of anything Herman Melville, Henry James, or Betty MacDonald would like to read." Length: 300-2,000 words.

HOW TO CONTACT Send complete ms with bio, list of publications, and explain how you found the magazine. Include SASE.

PAYMENT/TERMS Pays honorarium and subscriptions.

TIPS *"Button* writers have been widely published elsewhere, in virtually all the major national magazines. They include Ralph Lombreglia, Lawrence Millman, They Might Be Giants, Combustible Edison, Sven Birkerts, Stephen McCauley, Amanda Powell, Wayne Wilson, David Barber, Romayne Dawnay, Brendan Galvin, and Diana DerHovanessian. Follow the guidelines, make sure you read your work aloud, and don't inflate or deflate your publications and experience. We've published plenty of new folks, but on the merits of the work."

❶❷❸ CADET QUEST MAGAZINE

P.O. Box 7259, Grand Rapids MI 49510-7259. (616)241-5616. **Fax:** (616)241-5558. **E-mail:** submissions@calvinistcadets.org. **Website:** www.calvinistcadets.org. **Contact:** G. Richard Broene, editor. Estab. 1958. *Cadet Quest Magazine* shows boys 9-14 how God is at work in their lives and in the world around them.

NEEDS "Fast-moving, entertaining stories that appeal to a boy's sense of adventure or to his sense of humor are welcomed. Stories must present Christian life realistically and help boys relate Christian values to their own lives. Stories must have action without long dialogues. Favorite topics for boys include sports and athletes, humor, adventure, mystery, friends, etc. They must also fit the theme of that issue of *Cadet Quest*. Stories with preachiness and/or clichés are not of interest to us." No fantasy, science fiction, fashion, horror, or erotica. Length: 1,000-1,300 words.

HOW TO CONTACT Send complete ms by postal mail or e-mail (in body of e-mail; no attachments).

PAYMENT/TERMS Pays 5¢/word and 1 contributor's copy.

TIPS "The best time to submit stories/articles is early in the year (January-April). Also remember readers are boys ages 9-14. Stories must reflect or add to the theme of the issue and be from a Christian perspective."

❶❷❸ THE CAFE IRREAL

E-mail: editors@cafeirreal.com. **Website:** www.cafeirreal.com. **Contact:** G.S. Evans, Alice Whittenburg, coeditors. Estab. 1998. "Our audience is composed of people who read or write literary fiction with fantastic themes, similar to the work of Franz Kafka, Kobo Abe, or Clarice Lispector. This is a type of fiction (ir-real) that has difficulty finding its way into print in the English-speaking world and defies many of the conventions of American literature especially. As a result ours is a fairly specialized literary publication, and we would strongly recommend that prospective writers look at our current issue and guidelines carefully."

Recently published work by Vanessa Gebbie, Vicente Luis Mora, Marianne Villanueva, Peter Cherches, Amélie Olai, and JP Briggs.

NEEDS Accepts 6-8 mss/issue; 24-32 mss/year. No horror or 'slice-of-life' stories; no genre or mainstream science fiction or fantasy. Length: up to 2,000 words.

HOW TO CONTACT Accepts submissions by e-mail. No attachments; include submission in body of e-mail. Include estimated word count.

PAYMENT/TERMS Pays 1¢/word, $2 minimum.

TIPS "Forget formulas. Write about what you don't know, take me places I couldn't possibly go, don't try to make me care about the characters. Read short fiction by writers such as Franz Kafka, Jorge Luis Borges, Donald Barthelme, Magnus Mills, Ana Maria Shua, and Stanislaw Lem. Also read our website and guidelines."

CAKETRAIN

P.O. Box 82588, Pittsburgh PA 15218. **E-mail:** editors@caketrain.org. **Website:** www.caketrain.org. **Contact:** Amanda Raczkowski and Joseph Reed, editors. Estab. 2003.

NEEDS Submit via e-mail; no postal submissions. Include cover letter with titles of pieces and brief bio. Please do not submit any additional work until a decision has been made regarding your current submission.

PAYMENT/TERMS Pays 1 contributor's copy.

❶ CALLALOO: A JOURNAL OF AFRICAN DIASPORA ARTS & LETTERS

Texas A&M University, 249 Blocker Hall, College Station TX 77843-4227. (979)458-3108. **Fax:** (979)458-3275. **E-mail:** callaloo@tamu.edu. **Website:** callaloo.tamu.edu. Estab. 1976. *Callaloo: A Journal of African Diaspora Arts & Letters*, published quarterly, is devoted to poetry dealing with the African Diaspora, including North America, Europe, Africa, Latin and Central America, South America, and the Caribbean. Features about 15-20 poems (all forms and styles) in each issue along with short fiction, interviews, literary criticism, and concise critical book reviews.

NEEDS Would like to see more experimental fiction, science fiction, and well-crafted literary fiction particularly dealing with the black middle class, immigrant communities and/or the black South. Accepts 3-5 mss/issue; 10-20 mss/year. **Publishes 5-10 new writers/year.** Recently published work by Charles Johnson, Edwidge Danticat, Thomas Glave, Nallo Hopkinson, John Edgar Wideman, Jamaica Kincaid, Percival Everett, and Patricia Powell. Also publishes poetry. No romance, confessional. Length: up to 10,000 words.

TIPS "We look for freshness of both writing and plot, strength of characterization, plausibility of plot. Read what's being written and published, especially in journals such as *Callaloo*."

CALLIOPE

30 Grove St., Suite C, Peterborough NH 03458-1454. (603)924-7209. **Fax:** (603)924-7380. **E-mail:** customerservice@caruspub.com. **Website:** www.cobblestonepub.com. **Contact:** Rosalie Baker and Charles Baker, co-editors; Lou Waryncia, editorial director; Ann Dillon, art director. Estab. 1990.

Articles must relate to the issue's theme. Lively, original approaches to the subject are the primary concerns of the editors in choosing material.

NEEDS Material must relate to forthcoming themes. Length: no more than 800 words.

HOW TO CONTACT Query with cover letter, one-page outline, bibliography, SASE.

PAYMENT/TERMS Pays 20-25¢/word.

CALYX

Calyx, Inc., P.O. Box B, Corvallis OR 97339. (541)753-9384. **Fax:** (541)753-0515. **E-mail:** info@calyxpress.org; editor@calyxpress.org. **Website:** www.calyxpress.org. **Contact:** Brenna Crotty, senior editor. Estab. 1976. "*CALYX* exists to publish fine literature and art by women and is committed to publishing the work of all women, including women of color, older women, working-class women and other voices that need to be heard. We are committed to discovering and nurturing developing writers."

Annual open submission period is October 1-December 31.

NEEDS Length: no more than 5,000 words.

HOW TO CONTACT All submissions should include author's name on each page and be accompanied by a brief (50-word or less) biographical statement, phone number, and e-mail address. Submit using online submissions manager.

PAYMENT/TERMS Pays in contributor's copies and one-volume subscription.

TIPS "A forum for women's creative work—including work by women of color, lesbian and queer women, young women, old women—*CALYX* breaks new ground.

Each issue is packed with new poetry, short stories, full-color artwork, photography, essays, and reviews."

CANADIAN WRITER'S JOURNAL

Box 1178, New Liskeard ON P0J 1P0 Canada. (705)647-5424. **Fax:** (705)647-8366. **E-mail:** cwj@cwj.ca. **Website:** www.cwj.ca. **Contact:** Deborah Ranchuk, editor. Estab. 1984. Digest-size magazine for writers emphasizing short "how-to" articles, which convey easily understood information useful to both apprentice and professional writers. General policy and postal subsidies require that the magazine must carry a substantial Canadian content. "We try for about 90% Canadian content but prefer good material over country of origin or how well you're known. Writers may query, but unsolicited mss are welcome."

NEEDS Fiction is published only through annual short fiction contest with April 30 deadline. Send SASE for rules, or see guidelines on website. Does not want to see gratuitous violence or sex.

HOW TO CONTACT Accepts submissions by e-mail.

TIPS "We prefer short, tightly written, informative how-to articles. U.S. writers: note that U.S. postage cannot be used to mail from Canada. Obtain Canadian stamps, use IRCs, or send small amounts in cash."

THE CAPILANO REVIEW

2055 Purcell Way, North Vancouver BC V7J 3H5 Canada. (604)984-1712. **E-mail:** tcr@capilanou.ca. **Website:** www.thecapilanoreview.ca. **Contact:** Todd Nickel, managing editor. Estab. 1972. Triannual visual and literary arts magazine that "publishes only what the editors consider to be the very best fiction, poetry, drama, or visual art being produced. *TCR* editors are interested in fresh, original work that stimulates and challenges readers. Over the years, the magazine has developed a reputation for pushing beyond the boundaries of traditional art and writing. We are interested in work that is new in concept and in execution."

NEEDS No traditional, conventional fiction. Wants to see more innovative, genre-blurring work. Length: up to 5,000 words

HOW TO CONTACT Send complete ms with SASE and Canadian postage or IRCs. Does not accept submissions through e-mail or on disks.

PAYMENT/TERMS Pays $50-300.

ORSON SCOTT CARD'S INTERGALACTIC MEDICINE SHOW

Hatrack River Publications, P.O. Box 18184, Greensboro NC 27419. **Website:** intergalacticmedicineshow.

com; oscigms.com. **Contact:** Edmund R. Schubert, editor. Estab. 2005. *"Orson Scott Card's InterGalactic Medicine Show* is an online fantasy and science fiction magazine. We are a bimonthly publication featuring content from both established as well as talented new authors. In addition to our bimonthly issues, we offer weekly columns and reviews on books, movies, video games, and writing advice."

NEEDS "We like to see well-developed milieus and believable, engaging characters. We also look for clear, unaffected writing." Length: up to 17,000 words.

HOW TO CONTACT Submit via online submission form. Submit only 1 story at a time. Include estimated word count, e-mail address.

PAYMENT/TERMS Pays 6¢/word.

TIPS "Please note: *IGMS* is a PG-13 magazine and website. That means that while stories can deal with intense and adult themes, we will not accept stories with explicit or detailed sex of the sort that would earn a movie rating more restrictive than PG-13; nor will there be language of the sort that earns an R rating."

◯ THE CARIBBEAN WRITER

University of the Virgin Islands, RR 1, P.O. Box 10,000, Kingshill, St. Croix USVI 00850. (340)692-4152. **Fax:** (340)692-4026. **E-mail:** info@thecaribbeanwriter.org. **E-mail:** submit@thecaribbeanwriter.org. **Website:** www.thecaribbeanwriter.org. **Contact:** Alscess Lewis-Brown, editor. Estab. 1987. *"The Caribbean Writer* features new and exciting voices from the region and beyond that explore the diverse and multi-ethnic culture in poetry, short fiction, personal essays, creative nonfiction, and plays. Social, cultural, economic and sometimes controversial issues are also explored, employing a wide array of literary devices."

◖ Poetry published in *The Caribbean Writer* has appeared in *The Pushcart Prize. The Caribbean Writer* is 300+ pages, digest-sized, handsomely printed on heavy stock, perfect-bound, with glossy card cover. Press run is 1,200.

NEEDS Submit complete ms. E-mail as attachment; no fax submissions. Name, address, phone number, e-mail address, and title of ms should appear in cover letter along with brief bio. Title only on ms. Guidelines available by e-mail or on website. Length: up to 3,500 words or 10 pages.

◑ CAVEAT LECTOR

400 Hyde St., #606, San Francisco CA 94109. (415)928-7431. **Fax:** (415)928-7431. **E-mail:** editors@caveat-lec-tor.org. **E-mail:** caveatlectormagazine@gmail.com. **Website:** www.caveat-lector.org. **Contact:** Christopher Bernard, co-editor. Estab. 1989. *Caveat Lector,* published 2 times/year, is devoted to the arts and cultural and philosophical commentary. As well as literary work, they publish art, photography, music, streaming audio of selected literary pieces, and short films. Poetry, fiction, artwork, music, and short films are posted on website. "Don't let those examples limit your submissions. Send what you feel is your strongest work, in any style and on any subject."

◖ All submissions should be sent with a brief bio and SASE, or submitted electronically (poetry submissions only accepted through postal mail). Reads poetry submissions February 1-June 30; reads all other submissions year round.

NEEDS Accepts prose submissions (short stories, excerpts from longer works) throughout the year. Submit complete ms by e-mail or postal mail.

PAYMENT/TERMS Pays contributor's copies.

◯ CC&D: CHILDREN, CHURCHES & DADDIES: THE UNRELIGIOUS, NON-FAMILY-ORIENTED LITERARY AND ART MAGAZINE

Scars Publications and Design, 829 Brian Court, Gurnee IL 60031. (847)281-9070. **E-mail:** ccandd96@scars.tv. **Website:** scars.tv/ccd. **Contact:** Janet Kuypers. Estab. 1993. "Our biases are works that relate to issues such as politics, sexism, society, and the like, but are definitely not limited to such. We publish good work that makes you think, that makes you feel like you've lived through a scene instead of merely reading it. If it relates to how the world fits into a person's life (political story, a day in the life, coping with issues people face), it will probably win us over faster. We have received comments from readers and other editors saying that they thought some of our stories really happened. They didn't, but it was nice to know they were so concrete, so believable that people thought they were nonfiction. Do that to our readers." Publishes every other month online and in print; issues sold via Amazon.com throughout the U.S., U.K., and continental Europe. Publishes short shorts, essays, and stories. Also publishes poetry. Always comments on/critiques rejected mss if asked.

◖ Has published Mel Waldman, Kenneth DiMaggio, Linda Webb Aceto, Brian Looney, Joseph Hart, Fritz Hamilton, G.A. Scheinoha, and Ken Dean.

NEEDS Does not want religious, rhyming, or family-oriented material. Average length: 1,000 words. "Contact us if you are interested in submitting very long stories or parts of a novel. (If you are accepted, it would appear in parts in multiple issues.)"

HOW TO CONTACT Send complete ms with cover letter, or query with clips of published work. Prefers submissions by e-mail. "If you have e-mail and send us a snail-mail submission, we will accept writing only if you e-mail it to us. 99.5% of all submissions are via e-mail only, so if you do not have electronic access, there is a strong chance you will not be considered. We recommend you e-mail submissions to us, either as an attachment (.txt, .rtf, .doc, or .docx, but not .pdf) or by placing it directly in the e-mail letter). Send either SASE (or IRC) for return of ms or disposable copy of ms and #10 SASE for reply only, but if you have e-mail please send us an electronic submission instead. (If we accept your writing, we'll only ask for you to e-mail it to us anyway.)" Reviews fiction, essays, journals, editorials, short fiction.

CEMETERY MOON

Fortress Publishing, Inc., 3704 Hartzdale Dr., Camp Hill PA 17011. **E-mail:** cemeterymoon@yahoo.com. **Website:** www.fortresspublishinginc.com. *Cemetery Moon* is a magazine filled with short stories and poetry devoted to horror, suspense, and Gothic. This magazine brings to light what lurks in the darkness.

NEEDS Length: up to 5,000 words.

HOW TO CONTACT Send complete ms with cover letter by e-mail only.

TIPS "We want compelling stories—if we stop reading your story, so will the reader. We don't care about trick or twist endings; we're more concerned about how you take us there. Don't try to reinvent the wheel. Listen to advice with an open mind. Read your story, reread it, then read it again before you send it anywhere."

CHA

Hong Kong **E-mail:** editors@asiancha.com; j@asiancha.com. **E-mail:** submissions@asiancha.com. **Website:** www.asiancha.com. **Contact:** Tammy Ho Lai-Ming, founding co-editor; Jeff Zroback, founding co-editor; Eddie Tay, reviews editor. Estab. 2007. *Cha* is the first Hong Kong-based English online literary journal; it is dedicated to publishing quality poetry, fiction, creative nonfiction, reviews, photography & art. *Cha* has a strong focus on Asian-themed creative work and work done by Asian writers and artists. It also publishes established and emerging writers/artists from around the world. *Cha* is an affiliated organisation of the Asia-Pacific Writing Partnership and it is catalogued in the School of Oriental and African Studies (SOAS) Library, among other universities. *Cha* was named Best New Online Magazine of 2008. "At this time, we can only accept work in English or translated into English. If you want to review a book for *Cha*, please also write for further information."

NEEDS Length: 100-5,000 words.

HOW TO CONTACT Submit via e-mail.

TIPS "Please read the guidelines on our website carefully before you submit work to us. Do not send attachments in your e-mail. Include all writing in the body of e-mail. Include a brief biography (100 words)."

CHAFFIN JOURNAL

English Department, Eastern Kentucky University, Richmond KY 40475-3102. (859)622-3080. **E-mail:** robert.witt@eku.edu. **Website:** www.english.eku.edu/chaffin_journal. **Contact:** Robert Witt, editor. Estab. 1998. *The Chaffin Journal*, published annually in December, prints quality short fiction and poetry by new and established writers/poets. "We publish fiction on any subject; our only consideration is the quality."

Receives 20 unsolicited mss/month. Accepts 6-8 mss/year. Does not read mss October 1-May 31. Publishes 2-3 new writers/year. Has published work by Meridith Sue Willis, Marie Manilla, Raymond Abbott, Marjorie Bixler, Chris Helvey.

NEEDS No erotica, fantasy. Length: 10,000 words per submission period; average length: 5,000 words.

PAYMENT/TERMS Pays 1 contributor's copy.

TIPS "All mss submitted are considered."

THE CHARITON REVIEW

Truman State University Press, 100 E Normal Ave., Kirksville MO 63501. (660)785-8336. **E-mail:** chariton@truman.edu. **Website:** tsup.truman.edu/aboutChariton.asp. **Contact:** James D'Agostino, editor; Barbara Smith-Mandell and Jen Creer, managing editors. Estab. 1975. *The Chariton Review* is an international literary journal publishing the best in short fiction, essays, poetry, and translations in 2 issues each year.

THE CHATTAHOOCHEE REVIEW: EXPORTING THE SOUTH, IMPORTING THE WORLD

555 N. Indian Creek Dr., Clarkston GA 30021. **E-mail:** gpccr@gpc.edu. **Website:** thechattahoocheereview.

gpc.edu. **Contact:** Lydia Ship, managing editor. Estab. 1980. *The Chattahoochee Review,* published quarterly, prints poetry, short fiction, essays, reviews, and interviews. "We publish a number of Southern writers, but *The Chattahoochee Review* is not by design a regional magazine. All themes, forms, and styles are considered as long as they impact the whole person: heart, mind, intuition, and imagination."

⚬ Has recently published work by George Garrett, Jim Daniels, Jack Pendarvis, Ignacio Padilla, and Kevin Canty. *The Chattahoochee Review* is 160 pages, digest-sized, professionally printed, flat-spined, with four-color silk-matte card cover. Press run is 1,250; 300 are complimentary copies sent to editors and "miscellaneous VIPs." No e-mail submissions.

NEEDS Length: 500-1,000 words for short shorts; up to 6,000 words for short stories and novellas.

HOW TO CONTACT "*TCR* publishes high-quality literary fiction characterized by interest in language, development of distinctive settings, compelling conflict, and complex, unique characters." Submit 1 story or up to 3 short shorts via online submissions manager.

PAYMENT/TERMS Pays 2 contributor's copies.

◑ CHAUTAUQUA LITERARY JOURNAL

Dept. of Creative Writing, University of North Carolina at Wilmington, 601 S. College Rd., Wilmington NC 28403. **E-mail:** clj@uncw.edu. **Website:** www.ciweb.org/literary-journal. **Contact:** Jill Gerard and Philip Gerard, editors. Estab. 2003. *Chautauqua,* published annually in June, prints poetry, short fiction, and creative nonfiction. The editors actively solicit writing that expresses the values of Chautauqua Institution broadly construed: a sense of inquiry into questions of personal, social, political, spiritual, and aesthetic importance, regardless of genre. Considers the work of any writer, whether or not affiliated with Chautauqua Institution. Looking for a mastery of craft, attention to vivid and accurate language, a true lyric "ear," an original and compelling vision, and strong narrative instinct. Above all, it values work that is intensely personal, yet somehow implicitly comments on larger public concerns, like work that answers every reader's most urgent question: Why are you telling me this?

⚬ Reads submissions February 15-April 15 and August 15-November 15.

NEEDS *Chautauqua* short stories, self-contained novel excerpts, or flash fiction demonstrate a sound storytelling instinct, using suspense in the best sense, creating a compulsion in the reader to continue reading. Wants to engage readers' deep interest in the characters and their actions, unsettled issues of action or theme, or in some cases simple delight at the language itself. A superior story will exhibit the writer's attention to language—both in style and content—and should reveal a masterful control of diction and syntax. Length: up to 25 double-spaced pages or 7,000 words.

HOW TO CONTACT Submit online through submissions manager or postal mail (include SASE).

PAYMENT/TERMS Pays 2 contributor's copies.

◑ CHICAGO QUARTERLY REVIEW

517 Sherman Ave., Evanston IL 60202. **Website:** www.chicagoquarterlyreview.com. **Contact:** Syed Afzal Haider and Elizabeth McKenzie, editors. Estab. 1994. "The *Chicago Quarterly Review* is a nonprofit, independent literary journal publishing the finest short stories, poems, translations, and essays by both emerging and established writers. We hope to stimulate, entertain, and inspire."

⚬ The *Chicago Quarterly Review* is 6x9; 225 pages; illustrations; photos. Receives 250 unsolicited mss/month. Accepts 10-15 mss/issue; 20-30 mss/year. Publishes ms 6 months-1 year after acceptance. Agented fiction 5%. **Publishes 8-10 new writers/year.**

NEEDS Length: up to 5,000 words; average length: 2,500 words.

HOW TO CONTACT Submit through online submissions manager only.

PAYMENT/TERMS Pays 2 contributor's copies; additional copies $14.

TIPS "The writer's voice ought to be clear and unique and should explain something of what it means to be human. We want well-written stories that reflect an appreciation for the rhythm and music of language, work that shows passion and commitment to the art of writing."

◑ CHICAGO REVIEW

Taft House, 935 E. 60th St., Chicago IL 60637. **E-mail:** chicago-review@uchicago.edu. **Website:** chicagoreview.org. **Contact:** Nicholas Y.H. Wong, managing editor. Estab. 1946.

NEEDS "We will consider work in any literary style but are typically less interested in traditional narrative approaches." Length: no more than 5,000 words.

HOW TO CONTACT Submit 1 short story or up to 5 short short stories submitted in 1 file. Submit via online submissions manager, Submittable. Prefers electronic submissions.

PAYMENT/TERMS Pays in contributor's copies.

TIPS "We strongly recommend that authors familiarize themselves with recent issues of *Chicago Review* before submitting. Submissions that demonstrate familiarity with the journal tend to receive more attention than those that appear to be part of a carpet-bombing campaign."

● CHIRON REVIEW

522 E. South Ave., St. John KS 67576. **E-mail:** editor@chironreview.com. **Website:** chironreview.com. **Contact:** Michael Hathaway, editor. Estab. 1982 as *The Kindred Spirit*. *Chiron Review*, published quarterly, presents the widest possible range of contemporary creative writing—fiction and nonfiction, traditional and off-beat—in an attractive, perfect-bound digest, including artwork and photographs. No taboos. Has published poetry by Charles Bukowski, Charles Harper Webb, Edward Field, Wanda Coleman, and Marge Piercy. Press run is about 1,000.

NEEDS Submit up to 3 flash fictions or 1 short story at a time. Only submit 4 times a year. Accepts e-mail and postal mail submissions. "Send all pieces in ONE MS Word or translatable attachment. Complete postal address must accompany every single submission regardless of how many times you have submitted in the past. It helps if you put your name and genre of submission in subject line." Include SASE via postal mail.

PAYMENT/TERMS Pays 1 contributor's copy.

TIPS "Please visit our website for updates."

● CIMARRON REVIEW

205 Morrill Hall, English Department, Oklahoma State University, Stillwater OK 74078. **E-mail:** cimarronreview@okstate.edu. **Website:** cimarronreview.com. **Contact:** Toni Graham, editor; Lisa Lewis, poetry editor. Estab. 1967. "We want strong literary writing. We are partial to fiction in the modern realist tradition and distinctive poetry—lyrical, narrative, etc."

○   *Cimarron Review* is 6.5×8.5; 110 pages. Accepts 3-5 mss/issue; 12-15 mss/year. Publishes 2-4 new writers/year. Eager to receive mss from both established and less experienced writers "who intrigue us with their unusual perspective, language, imagery, and character." Has published work by Molly Giles, Gary Fincke, David Galef, Nona Caspers, Robin Beeman, Edward J. Delaney, William Stafford, John

Ashbery, Grace Schulman, Barbara Hamby, Patricia Fargnoli, Phillip Dacey, Holly Prado, and Kim Addonizio.

NEEDS No juvenile or genre fiction. Length: up to 25 pages.

HOW TO CONTACT Send complete ms with SASE or submit online through submission manager; include cover letter.

PAYMENT/TERMS Pays 2 contributor's copies.

TIPS "All postal submissions must come with SASE. A cover letter is encouraged. No e-mail submissions from authors living in North America. Query first and follow guidelines. In order to get a feel for the kind of work we publish, please read an issue or two before submitting."

○ ⊕ THE CINCINNATI REVIEW

P.O. Box 210069, Cincinnati OH 45221-0069. (513)556-3954. **E-mail:** editors@cincinnatireview.com. **Website:** www.cincinnatireview.com. **Contact:** Michael Griffith, fiction editor; Don Bogen, poetry editor. Estab. 2003. A journal devoted to publishing the best new literary fiction, creative nonfiction, and poetry, as well as book reviews, essays, and interviews.

○   *The Cincinnati Review* is 180-200 pages, digest-sized, perfect-bound, with matte paperback cover with full-color art. Press run is 1,000.

NEEDS Does not want genre fiction. Length: 125-10,000 words.

HOW TO CONTACT Send complete mss with SASE. Does not consider e-mail submissions; accepts electronic submissions through submission manager at cincinnatireview.com/submissions. Accepts simultaneous submissions with notice.

PAYMENT/TERMS Pays $25/page and 2 contributor's copies.

TIPS "Each issue includes a translation feature. For more information on translations, please see our website."

○ THE CLAREMONT REVIEW

Suite 101, 1581-H Hillside Ave., Victoria V8T 2C1 B.C. (250)216-4248. **E-mail:** claremontreview@gmail.com. **Website:** www.theclaremontreview.ca. **Contact:** Jody Carrow, editor in chief. "We publish anything from traditional to postmodern but with a preference for works that reveal something of the human condition. By this we mean stories that explore real characters in modern settings. Who are we, what are we doing to the planet, what is our relationship to one another, the earth, or God? Also, reading samples on the website or from past issues will give you a clearer indication of what we are looking for."

NEEDS Does not want science fiction, fantasy, or romance. Length: 5,000 maximum.

HOW TO CONTACT Send complete ms; should be double-spaced. Include SASE.

TIPS "Read guidelines before submitting."

CLARK STREET REVIEW

P.O. Box 1377, Berthoud CO 80513. **E-mail:** clarkreview@earthlink.net. **Contact:** Ray Foreman, editor. Estab. 1998. *Clark Street Review*, published 6 times/year, uses narrative poetry and short shorts. Tries "to give writers and poets cause to keep writing by publishing their best work." Press run is 200.

○ "Editor reads everything with a critical eye of 30 years of experience in writing and publishing small-press work."

NEEDS Wants short shorts. Include SASE for reply. No cover letter. No limit on submissions. Length: up to 1,200 words.

CLOUD RODEO

E-mail: editors@cloudrodeo.org. **E-mail:** submit@cloudrodeo.org. **Website:** cloudrodeo.org. "We want your problems deploying a term liek nonelen. We want your isolated photographs of immense locomotives slogged down by the delirium of drunken yet pristine jungles. We want the one eye you caught on fire doing alchemy. The world you collapsed playing architect. We want what you think is too. We want you to anesthetize this aesthetic. Your Enfer, your Ciel, your Qu'importe. We want all your to to sound out."

HOW TO CONTACT Submit 1 prose piece via e-mail as a .doc or .docx attachment.

TIPS "Let's get weird."

○ COAL CITY REVIEW

Coal City Press, English Department, University of Kansas, Lawrence KS 66045. **E-mail:** briandal@ku.edu. **Website:** coalcitypress.wordpress.com. **Contact:** Brian Daldorph, editor. "*Coal City Review*, published annually, usually late in the year, publishes poetry, short stories, reviews: "The best material I can find."

NEEDS Accepts mainly mainstream fiction: " Please don't send 'experimental' work our way."

PAYMENT/TERMS Pays in contributor's copies.

○ COLD MOUNTAIN REVIEW

Department of English, Appalachian State University, ASU Box 32052, Boone NC 28608. **E-mail:** coldmoun-

tain@appstate.edu. **Website:** www.coldmountain.appstate.edu. **Contact:** Betty Miller Conway, managing editor. *Cold Mountain Review*, published twice/year (Spring and Fall), features poetry, interviews with poets, poetry book reviews, and b&w graphic art. Has published poetry by Sarah Kennedy, Robert Morgan, Susan Ludvigson, Aleida Rodríguez, R.T. Smith, and Virgil Suaárez.

○ *Cold Mountain Review* is about 72 pages, digest-sized, neatly printed with 1 poem/page (or 2-page spread), perfect-bound, with light cardstock cover. Publishes only 10-12 poems/issue; "hence, we are extremely competitive: send only your best." Reading period is August-May.

NEEDS Considers novel excerpts if the submissions is "an exemplary stand-alone piece." Length: up to 6,000 words.

PAYMENT/TERMS Pays in contributor's copies.

⑤ COLORADO REVIEW

Center for Literary Publishing, Colorado State University, 9105 Campus Delivery, Fort Collins CO 80523. (970)491-5449. **E-mail:** creview@colostate.edu. **Website:** coloradoreview.colostate.edu. **Contact:** Stephanie G'Schwind, editor in chief and nonfiction editor; Steven Schwartz, fiction editor; Don Revell, Sasha Steensen, and Matthew Cooperman, poetry editors; Dan Beachy-Quick, book review editor. Literary magazine published 3 times/year.

○ Work published in *Colorado Review* has been included in *Best American Poetry*, *Best New American Voices*, *Best Travel Writing*, *Best Food Writing*, and the *Pushcart Prize Anthology*.

NEEDS No genre fiction. Length: under 30 ms pages.

HOW TO CONTACT Send complete ms. Fiction mss are read August 1-April 30. Mss received May 1-July 31 will be returned unread. Send no more than 1 story at a time.

PAYMENT/TERMS Pays $200 for short stories.

① COLUMBIA: A JOURNAL OF LITERATURE AND ART

Columbia University, New York NY 10027. **E-mail:** columbia.editor@gmail.com. **Website:** columbiajournal.org. **Contact:** Mary Jean Murphy, managing editor. Estab. 1977. "*Columbia: A Journal of Literature and Art* is an annual publication that features the very best in poetry, fiction, nonfiction, and art. We were founded in 1977 and continue to be one of the few national literary journals entirely edited, designed, and produced by students. You'll find that our minds are open, our interests diverse. We solicit mss from writers we love and select the most exciting finds from our virtual submission box. Above all, our commitment is to our readers—to producing a collection that informs, surprises, challenges, and inspires."

Reads submissions March 1-September 15.

HOW TO CONTACT Submit complete ms via online submissions manager.

COMMON GROUND REVIEW

Western New England University, H-5132, Western New England University, 1215 Wilbraham Rd., Springfield MA 01119. **E-mail:** editors@cgreview.org. **Website:** cgreview.org. **Contact:** Janet Bowdan, editor. Estab. 1999. *Common Ground Review*, published semiannually (Spring/Summer, Fall/Winter), prints poetry and 1 short nonfiction piece in the Fall issue and 1 short fiction piece in the Spring issue. "This is the official literary journal of Western New England."

NEEDS Length: up to 12 pages double-spaced.

PAYMENT/TERMS Pays 1 contributor's copy.

TIPS "For poems, use a few good images to convey ideas. Poems should be condensed and concise, free from words that do not contribute. The subject matter should be worthy of the reader's time and should appeal to a wide range of readers. Sometimes the editors may suggest possible revisions."

CONCEIT MAGAZINE

P.O. Box 884223, San Francisco CA 94188-4223. (510479-5408. **E-mail:** conceitmagazine2007@yahoo.com. **Website:** https://sites.google.com/site/conceit-magazine. **Contact:** Perry Terrell, editor. Estab. 2007.

Magazine publishing poetry, short stories, articles, and essays. "Very few guidelines—let me see your creative work."

NEEDS List of upcoming themes available for SASE and on website. Receives 60-70 mss/month. Accepts 20-22 mss/issue; up to 264 mss/year. Ms published 3-10 months after acceptance. Publishes 150 new writers/year. Published D. Neil Simmers, Tamara Fey Turner, Eve J. Blohm, Barbara Hantman, David Body, Milton Kerr, and Juanita Torrence-Thompson. Does not want profanity, porn, gruesomeness. Length: 100 words (min)-3,000 words (max). Average length: 1,500-2,000 words. Publishes short shorts. Average length of short shorts: 50-500 words.

HOW TO CONTACT Will read and review your books. "Send review copies to Perry Terrell." Query

first or send complete ms with cover letter. Accepts submissions by e-mail and snail mail. Include estimated word count, brief bio, list of publications.

PAYMENT/TERMS Pays 1 contributor's copy. Additional copies $4.50. PayPal to conceitmagazine@yahoo.com. Pays writers through contests. "Occasionally sponsors contests. Send SASE or check blog on website for details."

TIPS "Uniqueness and creativity make a ms stand out. Be brave and confident. Let me see what you created."

CONCHO RIVER REVIEW

Angelo State University, ASU Station #10894, San Angelo TX 76909. (325)486-6137. **E-mail:** crr@angelo.edu. **Website:** conchoriverreview.org. **Contact:** R. Mark Jackson, general editor. "CRR aims to provide its readers with escape, insight, laughter, and inspiration for many years to come. We urge authors to submit to the journal and readers to subscribe to our publication."

NEEDS "Editors tend to publish traditional stories with a strong sense of conflict, finely drawn characters, and crisp dialogue." Length: 1,500-5,000 words.

HOW TO CONTACT Submit only 1 ms at a time. Electronic submissions preferred. See website for appropriate section editor.

PAYMENT/TERMS Pays 1 contributor's copy.

CONFRONTATION

English Department, LIU Post, Brookville NY 11548. (516)299-2720. **E-mail:** confrontationmag@gmail.com. **Website:** www.confrontationmagazine.org. **Contact:** Jonna Semeiks, editor in chief; Belinda Kremer, poetry editor. Estab. 1968. "*Confrontation* has been in continuous publication since 1968. Our taste and our magazine is eclectic, but we always look for excellence in style, an important theme, a memorable voice. We enjoy discovering and fostering new talent. Each issue contains work by both well-established and new writers. We read August 16-April 15. Do not send mss or e-mail submissions between April 16 and August 15."

Confrontation has garnered a long list of awards and honors, including the Editor's Award for Distinguished Achievement from CLMP (given to Martin Tucker, the founding editor of the magazine) and NEA grants. Work from the magazine has appeared in numerous anthologies, including the *Pushcart Prize*, *Best Short Stories*, and *The O. Henry Prize Stories*.

NEEDS "We judge on quality of writing and thought or imagination, so we will accept genre fiction. However, it must have literary merit or must transcend or challenge genre." No "proselytizing" literature or conventional genre fiction. Length: Up to 7,200 words.

HOW TO CONTACT Send complete ms.

PAYMENT/TERMS Pays $175-250; more for commissioned work.

TIPS "We look for literary merit. Keep honing your skills and keep trying."

CONGRUENT SPACES

820 Taylor St. #5, Medford OR 97504. **E-mail:** congruentspacesmag@gmail.com. **Website:** www.congruentspaces.com. **Contact:** Michael Camarata. Estab. 2011. *"Congruent Spaces* was developed as a common ground for a diverse variety of voices and writing styles within the writing community. In keeping with this sense of community, all submissions are posted directly to the slush pile in our Writer's Lair, where our community of writers and readers come together to read and rate these submissions. For each issue we then select from the top-rated submissions which stories and poems appear within the pages of our magazine. Our magazine covers fantasy, horror, literary/mainstream fiction, poetry, and science fiction."

NEEDS No erotic/pornographic material. Length: up to 2,500 words.

PAYMENT/TERMS Pays contributor's copies.

TIPS "Don't submit your work unless you truly believe it is ready for publication. Be sure to proof your formatting for readability before posting the ms for our ratings process. The most common error is failing to adequately separate paragraphs after copying and pasting the submission in the submission form. The easier it is to read your ms, the better your chances of receiving a quality rating and being published."

❶❷❸ CONTRARY

PO Box 806363, Chicago IL 60616-3299 (no submissions). **E-mail:** chicago@contrarymagazine.com (no submissions). **Website:** www.contrarymagazine.com. **Contact:** Jeff McMahon, editor; Frances Badgett, fiction editor; Shaindel Beers, poetry editor. Estab. 2003. *Contrary* publishes fiction, poetry, and literary commentary, and prefers work that combines the virtues of all those categories. Founded at the University of Chicago, it now operates independently and not-for-profit on the South Side of Chicago. "We like work that is not only contrary in content, but contrary in its evasion of the expectations established by its genre. Our fiction defies traditional story form. For example, a story may bring us to closure without ever delivering an ending. We don't insist on the ending, but we do insist on the closure. And we value fiction as poetic as any poem." Quarterly. Member CLMP.

NEEDS Receives 650 mss/month. Accepts 6 mss/issue; 24 mss/year. Publishes 1 new writer/year. Has published Sherman Alexie, Andrew Coburn, Amy Reed, Clare Kirwan, Stephanie Johnson, Laurence Davies, and Edward McWhinney. Length: 2,000 words (maximum); average length: 750 words. Publishes short shorts. Average length of short shorts: 750 words.

HOW TO CONTACT Accepts submissions through website only: www.contrarymagazine.com/Contrary/Submissions.html. Include estimated word count, brief bio, list of publications. Considers simultaneous submissions.

PAYMENT/TERMS Pays $20-60.

TIPS "Beautiful writing catches our eye first. If we realize we're in the presence of unanticipated meaning, that's what clinches the deal. Also, we're not fond of expository fiction. We prefer to be seduced by beauty, profundity, and mystery than to be presented with the obvious. We look for fiction that entrances, that stays the reader's finger above the mouse button. That is, in part, why we favor microfiction, flash fiction, and short shorts. Also, we hope writers will remember that most editors are looking for very particular species of work. We try to describe our particular species in our mission statement and our submission guidelines, but those descriptions don't always convey nuance. That's why many editors urge writers to read the publication itself, in the hope that they will intuit an understanding of its particularities. If you happen to write that particular species of work we favor, your submission may find a happy home with us. If you don't, it does not necessarily reflect on your quality or your ability. It usually just means that your work has a happier home somewhere else."

❶ CONVERGENCE: AN ONLINE JOURNAL OF POETRY AND ART

An Online Journal of Poetry and Art, **E-mail:** clinville@csus.edu. **Website:** www.convergence-journal.com. **Contact:** Cynthia Linville, managing editor. Estab. 2003. *Convergence* seeks to unify the literary and visual arts and draw new interpretations of the written word by pairing poems and flash fiction with complementary art. Quarterly. Estab. 2003. Circ. 200. "We look for well-crafted work with fresh images and a strong voice. Work from a series or with a common theme has a greater chance of being accepted. Seasonally-themed work is appreciated (spring and summer for the January deadline, fall and winter for the June deadline). Please include a 75-word bio with your work (bios may be edited for length and clarity). A cover letter is not needed. Absolutely no simultaneous or previously published submissions."

○ Deadlines are January 5 and June 5.

NEEDS Accepts 5 mss/issue. Publishes ms 1-6 months after acceptance. Recently published work by Oliver Rice, Simon Perchik, Mary Ocher. Publishes short shorts. Also publishes poetry.

HOW TO CONTACT Send complete ms. E-mail submissions only with "Convergence" in subject line. No simultaneous submissions. Responds in less than a week to queries; 6 months to mss. Writer's guidelines online. Submit no more than 5 fiction pieces, no longer than 1000 words each.

PAYMENT/TERMS Acquires first rights.

TIPS "We look for freshness and originality and a mastery of the craft of flash fiction. Working with a common theme has a greater chance of being accepted."

THE COPPERFIELD REVIEW

E-mail: copperreview@aol.com. **Website:** www.copperfieldreview.com. **Contact:** Meredith Allard, executive editor. Estab. 2000. "We are a quarterly online literary journal that publishes historical fiction, reviews, and interviews related to historical fiction. We believe that by understanding the lessons of the past through historical fiction, we can gain better insight into the nature of our society today, as well as a better understanding of ourselves."

○ Needs essays, literary, literary criticism.

NEEDS "We will consider submissions in most fiction categories, but the setting must be historical in nature. We don't want to see anything not related to historical fiction." Receives 30 unsolicited mss/month. Accepts 7-10 mss/issue; 28-40 mss/year. Publishes 30-40% new writers/year. Publishes short shorts. Length: 500-3,000 words.

HOW TO CONTACT Send complete ms. Name and e-mail address should appear on the first page of the submission. Accepts submissions by e-mail or online submission. "Queries are not required. Send the complete ms according to our guidelines. Please submit online using our e-submissions manager or our Submission Guidelines page."

TIPS "We wish to showcase the very best in literary historical fiction. Stories that use historical periods and details to illuminate universal truths will immediately stand out. We are thrilled to receive thoughtful work that is polished, poised, and written from the heart. Be professional, and only submit your very best work. Be certain to adhere to a publication's submission guidelines, and always treat your e-mail submissions with the same care you would use with a traditional publisher. Above all, be strong and true to your calling as a writer. It is a difficult, frustrating, but wonderful journey. It is important for writers to review our online submission guidelines prior to submitting."

◑ COTTONWOOD

Room 400 Kansas Union, 1301 Jayhawk Blvd., University of Kansas, Lawrence KS 66045. **E-mail:** tlorenz@ku.edu. **Website:** www2.ku.edu/~englishmfa/cottonwood. **Contact:** Tom Lorenz, fiction editor. Estab. 1965. "Established in the 1960s, *Cottonwood* is the nationally circulated literary review of the University of Kansas. We publish high-quality literary work in poetry, fiction, and creative nonfiction. Over the years authors such as William Stafford, Rita Dove, Connie May Fowler, Virgil Suarez, and Cris Mazza have appeared in the pages of *Cottonwood*, and recent issues have featured the work of Kim Chinquee, Quinn Dalton, Carol Lee Lorenzo, Jesse Kercheval, Joanne Lowery, and Oliver Rice. We welcome submissions from new and established writers. New issues appear once yearly, in the fall."

NEEDS Length: no more than 8,500 words.

HOW TO CONTACT Submit with SASE.

PAYMENT/TERMS Pays in contributor's copies.

TIPS "We're looking for depth and originality of subject matter, engaging voice and style, emotional honesty, command of the material and the structure. *Cottonwood* publishes high-quality literary fiction, but we are very open to the work of talented new writers. Write something honest and that you care about, and write it as well as you can. Don't hesitate to keep trying us. We sometimes take a piece from a writer we've rejected a number of times. We generally don't like clever, gimmicky writing. The style should be engaging but not claim all the the attention itself."

CRAB CREEK REVIEW

7315 34th Ave. NW, Seattle WA 98117. **E-mail:** crabcreekreview@gmail.com. **Website:** www.crabcreekreview.org. **Contact:** Sayantani Dasgupta, nonfiction editor; Martha Silano, poetry editor. *Crab Creek Review* is an 80- to 120-page, perfect-bound paperback. "We are an international journal based in the Pacific Northwest that is looking for poems, stories, and essays that pay attention to craft while still surprising us in positive ways with detail and content. We publish well-known and emerging writers."

Nominates for the Pushcart Prize and offers annual *Crab Creek Review* Editors' Prize of $100 for the best poem, essay, or short story published in the previous year. Annual *Crab Creek Review* poetry prize: $500.

NEEDS Accepts only the strongest fiction. Prefers shorter work. Has published fiction by Shann Ray and Daniel Homan. Length: 3,500 words.

HOW TO CONTACT Send complete ms.

PAYMENT/TERMS Pays 1 contributor's copy.

CRAB ORCHARD REVIEW

Dept. of English, Southern Illinois University Carbondale, Faner Hall 2380, Mail Code 4503, 1000 Faner Dr., Carbondale IL 62901. (618)453-6833. **Fax:** (618)453-8224. **Website:** www.craborchardreview.siu.edu. **Contact:** Jon Tribble, managing editor. Estab. 1995. "We are a general-interest literary journal published twice/year. We strive to be a journal that writers admire and readers enjoy. We publish fiction, poetry, creative nonfiction, fiction translations, interviews, and reviews."

Reads submissions February 15-April 1(Winter/Spring issue) and October-November 15 (special Summer/Fall issue).

NEEDS No science fiction, romance, western, horror, gothic, or children's. Wants more novel excerpts that also stand alone as pieces. Length: up to 25 pages double-spaced.

HOW TO CONTACT Send SASE for reply, return of ms.

PAYMENT/TERMS Pays $25/published magazine page, $100 minimum, 2 contributor's copies and 1-year subscription.

CRAZYHORSE

College of Charleston, Department of English, 66 George St., Charleston SC 29424. (843)953-4470. **E-mail:** crazyhorse@cofc.edu. **Website:** crazyhorse.cofc.edu. **Contact:** Jonathan Bohr Heinen, managing editor; Emily Rosko, poetry editor; Anthony Varallo, fiction editor; Bret Lott, nonfiction editor. Estab. 1960. "We like to print a mix of writing regardless of its form, genre, school, or politics. We're especially on the lookout for original writing that doesn't fit the categories and that engages in the work of honest communication."

Reads submissions September 1-May 31.

NEEDS Accepts all fiction of fine quality, including short shorts and literary essays. Length: 2,500-8,500 words.

PAYMENT/TERMS Pays 2 contributor's copies and $20 per page ($200 maximum).

TIPS "Write to explore subjects you care about. The subject should be one in which something is at stake. Before sending, ask, 'What's reckoned with that's important for other people to read?'"

CREATIVE WITH WORDS PUBLICATIONS

P.O. Box 223226, Carmel CA 93922. **Fax:** (831)655-8627. **E-mail:** geltrich@mbay.net. **Website:** creativewithwords.tripod.com. **Contact:** Brigitta Gisella Geltrich-Ludgate, publisher and editor. Estab. 1975. *Creative With Words* publishes "poetry, prose, illustrations, photos by all ages."

NEEDS No violence or erotica, overly religious fiction, or sensationalism.

HOW TO CONTACT Submit complete ms by mail or e-mail. Always include SASE and legitimate address with postal submissions. Cover letter preferred.

TIPS "We offer a great variety of themes. We look for clean family-type fiction/poetry. Also, we ask the writer to look at the world from a different perspective, research topic thoroughly, be creative, apply brevity, tell the story from a character's viewpoint, tighten dialogue, be less descriptive, proofread before submitting, and be patient. We will not publish every ms we receive. It has to be in standard English, well written, proofread. We do not appreciate receiving mss where we have to do the proofreading and correct the grammar."

CRUCIBLE

Barton College, Wilson NC 27893. **E-mail:** crucible@barton.edu. **Website:** www.barton.edu/crucible. Estab. 1964. *Crucible*, published annually in the fall, publishes poetry and fiction as part of its Poetry and Fiction Contest run each year. Deadline for submissions: May 1.

○ *Crucible* is under 100 pages, digest-sized, professionally printed on high-quality paper, with matte card cover. Press run is 500.

NEEDS Length: up to 8,000 words.

HOW TO CONTACT Submit ms by e-mail. Ms accepted only through May 1. Do not include name on ms. Include separate bio.

PAYMENT/TERMS Pays $150 for 1st prize, $100 for 2nd prize, contributor's copies.

CURA: A LITERARY MAGAZINE OF ART AND ACTION

441 E. Fordham Rd., English Department, Dealy 541W, Bronx NY 10548. **E-mail:** curamag@fordham. edu. **Website:** www.curamag.com. **Contact:** Sarah Gambito, managing editor. Estab. 2011. *CURA: A Literary Magazine of Art and Action* is a multi-media initiative based at Fordham University committed to integrating the arts and social justice. Featuring creative writing, visual art, new media and video in response to current news, we seek to enable an artistic process that is rigorously engaged with the world at the present moment. *CURA* is taken from the Ignatian educational principle of "cura personalis," care for the whole person. On its own, the word "cura" is defined as guardianship, solicitude, and significantly, written work.

○ Reading period: October 1-March 15.

NEEDS Length: no more than 6,000 words.

HOW TO CONTACT Submit complete ms.

PAYMENT/TERMS Pays 1 contributor's copy.

○◐ CURRENT ACCOUNTS

Current Accounts, Apt. 2D, Bradshaw Hall, Hardcastle Gardens, Bolton BL2 4NZ U.K. **E-mail:** bswscribe@gmail.com. **E-mail:** fjameshartnell@aol. com. **Website:** for Bank Street Writers: sites.google. com/site/bankstreetwriters. **Contact:** Rod Riesco. Estab. 1994. *Current Accounts*, an online publication, prints poetry, drama, fiction, and nonfiction by members of Bank Street Writers, and other contributors.

○ Receives about 200 poems and stories/plays per year; accepts about 5%.

NEEDS Length: no longer than 1,500 words, and preferably under 1,000 words for short stories. Plays should be 1 act and no longer than 4 minutes read aloud.

HOW TO CONTACT E-mail submissions only. "Stories need to be well-constructed with good believable characters, an awareness of 'show, don't tell' dialogue that is real, a plot that moves along and an ending

that is neither obvious nor ridiculously far-fetched. Too many stories are overwritten and leave nothing unexplained for the reader to work out and enjoy. All genres (within the word length) are acceptable. We don't get enough plays."

PAYMENT/TERMS Pays 1 contributor's copy.

TIPS Bank Street Writers meets once/month and offers workshops, guest speakers, and other activities. E-mail for details. "We like originality of ideas, images, and use of language. No inspirational or religious verse unless it's also good in poetic terms."

CUTTHROAT, A JOURNAL OF THE ARTS

P.O. Box 2414, Durango CO 81302. (970)903-7914. **E-mail:** cutthroatmag@gmail.com. **Website:** www. cutthroatmag.com. **Contact:** William Luvaas, fiction editor; William Pitt Root, poetry editor. Estab. 2005. "Sponsors the Rick DeMarinis Short Fiction Prize ($1,250 first prize). See separate listing and website for more information." "We publish only high-quality fiction and poetry. We are looking for the cutting edge, the endangered word, fiction with wit, heart, soul, and meaning." *CUTTHROAT* is a literary magazine/journal and "one separate online edition of poetry, translations, short fiction and book reviews yearly."

○ Member CCLMP.

NEEDS Send review copies to Pamela Uschuk. List of upcoming themes available on website. Receives 100+ mss/month. Accepts 6 mss/issue; 10-12 mss/year. Does not read from October 1-March 1 and from June 1-July 15. **Publishes 5-8 new writers/year.** Published Michael Schiavone, Rusty Harris, Timothy Rien, Summer Wood, Peter Christopher, Jamey Genna, Doug Frelke, Sally Bellerose, and Marc Levy. Publishes short shorts and book reviews. Does not want romance, horror, historical, fantasy, religious, teen, orjuvenile. Length: 500 words-5,000 words.

HOW TO CONTACT "We prefer online submissions through our submission manager! If submitting by mail, please include cover letter and SASE for response only; mss are recycled."

PAYMENT/TERMS Pays in contributor copies. Additional copies $10.

TIPS "Read our magazine and see what types of work we've published. The piece must have heart and soul, excellence in craft. "

◐◑ THE DALHOUSIE REVIEW

Dalhousie University, Halifax NS B3H 4R2 Canada. **E-mail:** dalhousie.review@dal.ca. **Website:** dalhousiereview.dal.ca. **Contact:** Carrie Dawson, editor.

Estab. 1921. *Dalhousie Review*, published 3 times/year, is a journal of criticism publishing poetry and fiction. Considers poetry from both new and established writers.

○ *Dalhousie Review* is 144 pages, digest-sized. Accepts about 5% of poems received. Press run is 500.

NEEDS Length: up to 5,000 words.

HOW TO CONTACT Submit via postal mail only. Writers are encouraged "to follow whatever canons of usage might govern the particular work in question and to be inventive with language, ideas, and form."

PAYMENT/TERMS Pays 2 contributor's copies and 10 offprints.

○⊘ DARGONZINE

E-mail: dargon@dargonzine.org. **Website:** dargonzine.org. **Contact:** Jon Evans, editor. "*DargonZine* is an e-zine that prints original fantasy fiction by aspiring fantasy writers. The Dargon Project is a shared world anthology whose goal is to provide a way for aspiring fantasy writers to meet and improve their writing skills through mutual contact and collaboration as well as through contact with a live readership via the Internet. Our goal is to write fantasy fiction that is mature, emotionally compelling, and professional. Membership in the Dargon Project is a requirement for publication."

○ Publishes 1-3 new writers/year.

PAYMENT/TERMS "As a strictly noncommercial magazine, our writers' only compensation is their growth and membership in a lively writing community.

TIPS "The Readers and Writers FAQs on our website provide much more detailed information about our mission, writing philosophy, and the value of writing for *DargonZine*."

⑤ THE DARK

311 Fairbanks Ave., Northfield NJ 08225. **E-mail:** thedarkmagazine@gmail.com. **Website:** www.thedarkmagazine.com. **Contact:** Jack Fisher and Sean Wallace, editors. Estab. 2013.

NEEDS Does not want blatant horror, fantasy, or science fiction. All fiction must have a dark and strange blend. Length: 1,000-5,000 words.

HOW TO CONTACT Send complete ms by e-mail attached in Microsoft Word doc only. Accepts electronic submissions at thedarkmagazine@gmail.com. Accepts simultaneous submissions with notice.

PAYMENT/TERMS Pays $25-150.

TIPS "All fiction must have a dark, surreal, fantastical bend to it. It should be out of the ordinary and/or experimental. Can also be contemporary."

⚫①⑤ DARK TALES

Dark Tales, 7 Offley Street, Worcester WR3 8BH United Kingdom. **E-mail:** sean@darktales.co.uk. **Website:** www.darktales.co.uk. **Contact:** Sean Jeffery, editor. Estab. 2003. Has occasional contests; see website for details. "We publish horror and speculative short fiction from anybody, anywhere, and the publication is professionally illustrated throughout."

NEEDS Receives 25+ mss/month. Accepts 10-15 mss/issue; 25-40 mss/year. Ms published 6 months after acceptance. **Publishes 20 new writers/year.** Has published Davin Ireland, Niall McMahon, David Robertson, Valerie Robson, K.S. Dearsley, and Mark Cowley. Length: 500-3,500 words. Average length: 2,500 words. Publishes short shorts. Average length of short shorts: 500 words.

HOW TO CONTACT Send complete ms with cover letter. Include estimated word count, list of publications. Send disposable copy of ms and #10 SASE for reply only.

PAYMENT/TERMS Pays $5 per 1,000 words. Additional copies $7.10.

TIPS "Have a believable but inspiring plot, sympathetic characters, an original premise, and a human heart no matter how technical or disturbing a story. Read a copy of the magazine! Make sure you get your writing basics spot-on. Don't rehash old ideas—if you must go down the werewolf/vampire route, put a spin on it."

○① THE DEAD MULE SCHOOL OF SOUTHERN LITERATURE

NC **E-mail:** deadmule@gmail.com. **E-mail:** submit.mule@gmail.com. **Website:** www.deadmule.com. **Contact:** Valerie MacEwan, publisher and editor. The *Mule* sponsors flash-fiction contests with no entry fees. See the site for specifics. Chapbooks published by invitation, also short fiction compilations. "No good southern fiction is complete without a dead mule." The *Dead Mule* is one of the oldest, if not *the* oldest, continuously published online literary journals alive today. Publisher and editor Valerie MacEwan welcomes submissions. *The Dead Mule School of Southern Literature* wants flash fiction, visual poetry, essays, and creative nonfiction. "We usually publish new work on the 1st and 15th of the month, depending on whims, obligations, and mule jumping contest dates."

○ "*The Dead Mule School of Southern Literature* Institutional Alumni Association recruits year round. Want to join the freshman class of 2018? Submit today."

NEEDS "We welcome the ingenue and the established writer. It's mostly about you entertaining us and capturing our interest. Everyone is South of Somewhere; go ahead, check us out."

HOW TO CONTACT All submissions must be accompanied by a "Southern legitimacy statement," details of which can be seen within each page on *The Dead Mule* and within the submishmash entrypage.

PAYMENT/TERMS Pays sporadically "whenever CafePress/*Dead Mule* sales reach an agreeable amount."

TIPS "Read the site to get a feel for what we're looking to publish. Read the guidelines. We look forward to hearing from you. We are nothing if not for our writers. *The Dead Mule* strives to deliver quality writing in every issue. It is in this way that we pay tribute to our authors. Send us something original."

○ ○ DENVER QUARTERLY

University of Denver, 2000 E. Asbury, Denver CO 80208. (303)871-2892. **E-mail:** denverquarterly@gmail.com. **Website:** www.du.edu/denverquarterly/. **Contact:** Laird Hunt, editor. Estab. 1965. Publishes fiction, articles, and poetry for a generally well-educated audience, primarily interested in literature and the literary experience. Audience reads *DQ* to find something a little different from a stictly academic quarterly or a creative writing outlet. Quarterly. Reads between September 15 and May 15.

○ *Denver Quarterly* received an Honorable Mention for Content from the American Literary Magazine Awards and selections have been anthologized in the *Pushcart Prize* anthologies.

NEEDS "We are interested in experimental fiction (minimalism, magic realism, etc.) as well as in realistic fiction and in writing about fiction. No sentimental, science fiction, romance, or spy thrillers." Length: up to 15 pages.

HOW TO CONTACT Submit ms by mail, include SASE.

PAYMENT/TERMS Pays $5/page for fiction and poetry and 2 contributor's copies.

TIPS "We look for serious, realistic, and experimental fiction; stories which appeal to intelligent, demanding readers who are not themselves fiction writers. Nothing so quickly disqualifies a ms as sloppy proofreading

and mechanics. Read the magazine before submitting to it. We try to remain eclectic, but the odds for beginners are bound to be small considering the fact that we receive nearly 10,000 mss per year and publish only about 10 short stories."

○ DESCANT

P.O. Box 314, Station P, Toronto ON M5S 2S8 Canada. (416)593-2557. **Fax:** (416)593-9362. **E-mail:** info@descant.ca. **E-mail:** submit@descant.ca; managingeditor@descant.ca. **Website:** www.descant.ca. **Contact:** Karen Mulhallen, editor in chief; Vera DeWaard, managing editor. Estab. 1970. *Descant* is a quarterly journal publishing new and established contemporary writers and visual artists from Canada and around the world. *Descant* is devoted to the discovery and development of new writers, and to placing their work in the company of celebrated writers.

○ Pays $100 honorarium, plus 1-year's subscription for accepted submissions of any kind.

NEEDS Short stories or book excerpts. Maximum length 6,000 words; 3,000 words or less preferred. No erotica, fantasy, gothic, horror, religious, romance, beat.

HOW TO CONTACT Send complete ms with cover letter. Include estimated word count and brief bio.

PAYMENT/TERMS Pays $100 (Canadian).

TIPS "Familiarize yourself with our magazine before submitting."

○ ○ DESCANT: FORT WORTH'S JOURNAL OF POETRY AND FICTION

TCU Department of English, Box 297270, Ft. Worth TX 76129. (817)257-5907. **Fax:** (817)257-6239. **E-mail:** descant@tcu.edu; m.pitt@tcu.edu. **Website:** www.descant.tcu.edu. **Contact:** Matt Pitt, editor in chief. Estab. 1956. "*descant* seeks high-quality poems and stories in both traditional and innovative form." Member CLMP. Magazine: 6×9; 120-150 pages; acid-free paper; paper cover.

○ Reading period: Septmeber 1-April 1. Offers 4 cash awards: The $500 Frank O'Connor Award for the best story in an issue; the $250 Gary Wilson Award for an outstanding story in an issue; the $500 Betsy Colquitt Award for the best poem in an issue; and the $250 Baskerville Publishers Award for outstanding poem in an issue. Several stories first published by *descant* have appeared in *Best American Short Stories*.

NEEDS Receives 20-30 unsolicited mss/month. Accepts 25-35 mss/year. Publishes ms 1 year after acceptance. Publishes 50% new writers/year. Recently published work by William Harrison, Annette Sanford, Miller Williams, Patricia Chao, Vonesca Stroud, and Walt McDonald. No horror, romance, fantasy, erotica. Length: 1,000-5,000 words; average length: 2,500 words.

HOW TO CONTACT Send complete ms with cover letter. Include estimated word count and brief bio.

TIPS "We look for character and quality of prose. Send your best short work."

DIAGRAM

Department of English, University of Arizona, P.O. Box 210067, Tucson AZ 85721-0067. **E-mail:** editor@thediagram.com. **Website:** www.thediagram.com. **Contact:** Ander Monson, editor; T. Fleischmann and Nicole Walker, nonfiction editors; Sarah Blackman and Lauren Slaughter, fiction editors; Heidi Gotz and E.A. Ramey, poetry editors. "*DIAGRAM* is an electronic journal of text and art, found and created. We're interested in representations, naming, indicating, schematics, labeling and taxonomy of things; in poems that masquerade as stories; in stories that disguise themselves as indices or obituaries. We specialize in work that pushes the boundaries of traditional genre or work that is in some way schematic. We do publish traditional fiction and poetry, too, but hybrid forms (short stories, prose poems, indexes, tables of contents, etc.) are particularly welcome! We also publish diagrams and schematics (original and found)."

Publishes 6 new writers/year. Bimonthly. Member CLMP. "We sponsor yearly contests for unpublished hybrid essays and innovative fiction. Guidelines on website."

NEEDS Receives 100 unsolicited mss/month. Accepts 2-3 mss/issue; 15 mss/year. "We don't publish genre fiction unless it's exceptional and transcends the genre boundaries." Average length: 250-2,000 words.

HOW TO CONTACT Send complete ms. Accepts submissions by online submissions manager; no e-mail. If sending by snail mail, send SASE for return of the ms or send disposable copy of the ms and #10 SASE for reply only.

PAYMENT/TERMS Acquires first, serial, electronic rights.

TIPS "Submit interesting text, images, sound, and new media. We value the insides of things, vivisection, urgency, risk, elegance, flamboyance, work that moves us, language that does something new, or does

something old—well. We like iteration and reiteration. Ruins and ghosts. Mechanical, moving parts, balloons, and frenzy. We want art and writing that demonstrates interaction; the processes of things; how functions are accomplished; how things become or expire, move or stand. We'll consider anything."

THE DOS PASSOS REVIEW

Briery Creek Press, Longwood University, Department of English and Modern Languages, 201 High St., Farmville VA 23909. **E-mail:** dospassosreview@gmail.com. **Website:** brierycreekpress.wordpress.com/the-dos-passos-review. "We are looking for writing that demonstrates characteristics found in the work of John Dos Passos, such as an intense and original exploration of specifically American themes; an innovative quality; and a range of literary forms, especially in the genres of fiction and creative nonfiction. We are not interested in genre fiction, or prose that is experiment for the sake of experiment. We are also not interested in nonfiction that is scholarly or critical in nature. Send us your best unpublished literary prose or poetry."

NEEDS Length: up to 3,000 words for short stories; up to 1,000 for flash fiction.

HOW TO CONTACT Stories or essays should be typed, double-spaced, and paginated, with your name, address, phone number, and e-mail on the first page, title on subsequent pages. "We are unable to read entire mss, novellas, or submissions of more than 1 story at a time. We do not accept novel excerpts. If submitting flash fiction, you may submit up to 3 pieces." Reading periods vary: April 1-July 31 for Fall Issue, February 1-May 31 for Spring Issue. Submissions postmarked outside these reading periods will be returned unread.

PAYMENT/TERMS Pays 2 contributor's copies.

DOWN IN THE DIRT

829 Brian Court, Gurnee IL 60031-3155. (847)281-9070. **E-mail:** dirt@scars.tv. **Website:** www.scars.tv/dirt. **Contact:** Janet Kuypers, editor. Estab. 2000. *Down in the Dirt*, published every other month online and in print issues sold via Amazon.com throughout the U.S., U.K., and continental Europe, prints "good work that makes you think, that makes you feel like you've lived through a scene instead of merely read it." Also considers poems. *Down in the Dirt* is published "electronically as well as in print, either as printed magazines sold through our printer over the Inter-

net, on the Web (Internet web pages), or sold through our printer."

⬭ Literary magazine/journal. Has published work by Mel Waldman, Ken Dean, Jon Brunette, John Ragusa, and Liam Spencer.

NEEDS No religious, rhyming, or family-oriented material. Average length: 1,000 words. "Contact us if you are interested in submitting very long stories or parts of a novel (if accepted, it would appear in parts in multiple issues)."

HOW TO CONTACT Query editor with e-mail submission. "99.5% of all submissions are via e-mail only, so if you do not have electronic access, there is a strong chance you will not be considered. We recommend you e-mail submissions to us, either as an attachment (.txt, .rtf, .doc, or .docx files, but not .pdf) or by placing it directly in the e-mail letter). For samples of what we've printed in the past, visit our website."

PAYMENT/TERMS No payment.

TIPS Scars Publications sponsors a contest "where accepted writing appears in a collection book. Write or e-mail (dirt@scars.tv) for information." Also able to publish electronic chapbooks. Write for more information.

DOWNSTATE STORY

1825 Maple Ridge, Peoria IL 61614. (309)688-1409. E-mail: ehopkins7@prodigy.net. **Website:** www.wiu. edu/users/mfgeh/dss; www.downstatestory.com. Estab. 1992.

NEEDS Does not want porn. Length: 300-2,000 words.

HOW TO CONTACT Submit complete ms with cover letter and SASE. Submit via postal mail.

TIPS "We want more political fiction. We also publish short shorts and literary essays."

DRAMATICS MAGAZINE

Educational Theatre Association, 2343 Auburn Ave., Cincinnati OH 45219. (513)421-3900. **E-mail:** dcorathers@schooltheatre.org. **Website:** schooltheatre.org. **Contact:** Don Corathers, editor. Estab. 1929. *Dramatics* is for students (mainly high school age) and teachers of theater. Mix includes how-to (tech theater, acting, directing, etc.), informational, interview, photo feature, humorous, profile, technical. *Dramatics* wants student readers to grow as theater artists and become a more discerning and appreciative audience. Material is directed to both theater students and their teachers, with strong student slant. Tries to portray the theater community in all its diversity.

NEEDS Young adults: drama (one-act and full-length plays). "We prefer unpublished scripts that have been produced at least once." Does not want to see plays that show no understanding of the conventions of the theater. No plays for children, no Christmas or didactic "message" plays. Length: 10 minutes to full length.

HOW TO CONTACT Submit complete ms. Buys 5-9 plays/year. Emerging playwrights have better chances with résumé of credits.

PAYMENT/TERMS Pays $100-500 for plays.

TIPS "Obtain our writer's guidelines and look at recent back issues. The best way to break in is to know our audience—drama students, teachers, and others interested in theater—and write for them. Writers who have some practical experience in theater, especially in technical areas, have an advantage, but we'll work with anybody who has a good idea. Some freelancers have become regular contributors."

⬭ DUCTS

P.O. Box 3203, Grand Central Station, New York NY 10163. **E-mail:** vents@ducts.org. **Website:** www.ducts. org. **Contact:** Jonathan Kravetz, editor in chief. Estab. 1999. *DUCTS* is a semi-annual webzine of personal stories, fiction, essays, memoirs, poetry, humor, profiles, reviews and art. "*DUCTS* was founded in 1999 with the intent of giving emerging writers a venue to regularly publish their compelling, personal stories. The site has been expanded to include art and creative works of all genres. We believe that these genres must and do overlap. *DUCTS* publishes the best, most compelling stories and we hope to attract readers who are drawn to work that rises above."

HOW TO CONTACT Submit to fiction@ducts.org.

TIPS "We prefer writing that tells a compelling story with a strong narrative drive."

ECHO INK REVIEW

E.I. Publishing Services, Published by Sildona Creative, 5920 Nall Ave., Suite 301, Mission KS 66202. **Website:** www.echoinkreview.com. **Contact:** Don Balch, managing editor. Estab. 1997. "*Echo Ink Review* seeks well-crafted mss from beginning or established writers."

NEEDS "Ultimately, we select mss that work, meaning we look for those mss that achieve the highest degree of unity between elements. Mss that also involve some element of surprise, irony, or understatement are appreciated." Has published Marie Manilla, William J. Cobb, Gina Frangello, Kelli Allen, and others. Length: 250-2,500 words for flash fiction; 2,501-10,000 words for short fiction.

HOW TO CONTACT Submit using online submission manager.

ECLECTICA

E-mail: editors@eclectica.org. **Website:** www.eclectica.org. **Contact:** Tom Dooley, managing editor. Estab. 1996. "A sterling-quality literary magazine on the World Wide Web. Not bound by formula or genre, harnessing technology to further the reading experience and dynamic and interesting in content. *Eclectica* is a quarterly online journal devoted to showcasing the best writing on the Web, regardless of genre. 'Literary' and 'genre' work appear side-by-side in each issue, along with pieces that blur the distinctions between such categories. Pushcart Prize, National Poetry Series, and Pulitzer Prize winners, as well as Nebula Award nominees, have shared issues with previously unpublished authors."

Submission deadlines: December 1 for January/February issue, and March 1 for April/May issue.

NEEDS Needs "high-quality work in any genre." Accepts short stories and novellas. Length: up to 20,000 words for short fiction; longer novella-length pieces accepted.

HOW TO CONTACT Submit via online submissions manager.

TIPS "We pride ourselves on giving everyone (high schoolers, convicts, movie executives, etc.) an equal shot at publication, based solely on the quality of their work. Because we like eclecticism, we tend to favor the varied perspectives that often characterize the work of international authors, people of color, women, alternative lifestylists—but others who don't fit into these categories often surprise us."

ECOTONE

Department of Creative Writing, University of North Carolina Wilmington, 601 S. College Rd., Wilmington NC 28403. (910)962-2547. **Fax:** (910)962-7461. **E-mail:** info@ecotonejournal.com. **Website:** www.ecotonejournal.com. **Contact:** Kate O'Reilly, managing editor; Peter Kusnic, nonfiction editor; Ryan Kaune, fiction editor; Laurel Jones, poetry editor. "*Ecotone* is a literary journal of place that seeks to publish creative works about the environment and the natural world while avoiding the hushed tones and clichés of much of so-called nature writing.

Reading period is August 15-April 15."

NEEDS Length: up to 30 pages double-spaced.

HOW TO CONTACT Send complete ms via postal mail or online submission manager.

ECOTONE, REIMAGINING PLACE

UNCW Dept. of Creative Writing, 601 S. College Rd., Wilmington NC 28403. **E-mail:** info@ecotonejournal.com. **Website:** www.ecotonejournal.com. Estab. 2005. "*Ecotone* is a literary journal of place seeking to publish creative work that illuminates the edges between science and literature, the urban and rural, and the personal and biological." Semiannual.

Literary magazine/journal: 6×9. Reading period: August 15-April 15. "*Ecotone* charges a small fee for electronic submissions. If you are unable to pay this fee, please submit by postal mail."

NEEDS Also publishes literary essays, poetry. Has published Kevin Brockmeier, Michael Branch, Brock Clarke, Daniel Orozco, and Steve Almond, and Pattiann Rogers. Does not want genre (fantasy, horror, sci-fi, etc.) or young adult fiction. Length: up to 30 pages. "We are now considering shorter prose works (under 2,500 words) as well."

HOW TO CONTACT Submit via online submissions manager. Include brief cover letter, listing both the title of the piece and the word count. Do not include identifying information on or within the ms itself.

ELLERY QUEEN'S MYSTERY MAGAZINE

Dell Magazines, 267 Broadway, 4th Floor, New York NY 10017. (212)686-7188. **Fax:** (212)686-7414. **E-mail:** elleryqueenmm@dellmagazines.com. **Website:** www.themysteryplace.com/eqmm. **Contact:** Jackie Sherbow, assistant editor. Estab. 1941. "*Ellery Queen's Mystery Magazine* welcomes submissions from both new and established writers. We publish every kind of mystery short story: the psychological suspense tale, the deductive puzzle, the private eye case—the gamut of crime and detection from the realistic (including the policeman's lot and stories of police procedure) to the more imaginative (including 'locked rooms' and 'impossible crimes'). We look for strong writing, an original and exciting plot, and professional craftsmanship. We encourage writers whose work meets these general criteria to read an issue of *EQMM* before making a submission."

⊙ Magazine: 5⅞×8⅝, 112 pages with special 192-page combined March/April and September/October issues.

NEEDS "We always need detective stories. Special consideration given to anything timely and original." Publishes ms 6-12 months after acceptance. Agented fiction 50%. **Publishes 10 new writers/year.** Recently published work by Jeffery Deaver, Joyce Carol Oates, and Margaret Maron. Sometimes comments on rejected mss. No explicit sex or violence, no gore or horror. Seldom publishes parodies or pastiches. "We do not want true detective or crime stories." Length: 2,500-8,000 words, but occasionally accepts longer and shorter submissions—including minute mysteries of 250 words, stories up to 12,000 words, and novellas of up to 20,000 words from established authors

HOW TO CONTACT *"EQMM uses an online submission system (eqmm.magazinesubmissions.com) that has been designed to streamline our process and improve communication with authors. We ask that all submissions be made electronically, using this system, rather than on paper. All stories should be in standard ms format and submitted in .doc format. We cannot accept .docx, .rtf, or .txt files at this time. For detailed submission instructions, see eqmm.magazinesubmissions.com or our writers guidelines page (www.themysteryplace.com/eqmm/guidelines).*

PAYMENT/TERMS Pays 5-8¢/word; occasionally higher for established authors

TIPS "We have a Department of First Stories to encourage writers whose fiction has never before been in print. We publish an average of 10 first stories every year. Mark subject line Attn: Dept. of First Stories."

⊙⑤ ELLIPSIS MAGAZINE

Westminster College of Salt Lake City, 1840 S. 1300 East, Salt Lake City UT 84105. (801)832-2321. **E-mail:** ellipsis@westminstercollege.edu. **Website:** www.westminstercollege.edu/ellipsis. Estab. 1965. *Ellipsis,* published annually in April, needs good literary poetry, fiction, essays, plays, and visual art. Has published poetry by Allison Joseph, Molly McQuade, Virgil Suaárez, Maurice Kilwein-Guevara, Richard Cecil, and Ron Carlson.

⊙ Reads submissions August 1-November 1. Staff changes from year to year. Check website for an updated list of editors. *Ellipsis* is 120 pages, digest-sized, perfect-bound, with color cover. Accepts about 5% of submissions received. Press run is 2,000; most distributed free through college.

NEEDS Receives 110 unsolicited mss/month. Accepts 4 mss/issue. Does not read mss November 1-July 31. Publishes ms 3 months after acceptance. **Publishes 2 new writers/year.** Length: 6,000 words; average length: 4,000 words. Also publishes poetry. Rarely comments on rejected mss. Needs good literary fiction and plays. Length: 6,000 words.

HOW TO CONTACT Send complete ms. Send SASE (or IRC) for return of ms or send disposable copy of the ms and #10 SASE for reply only. Responds in 6 months to mss. Accepts simultaneous submissions. Sample copy for $7.50. Writer's guidelines online. Send complete ms. Submit through Submittable.

PAYMENT/TERMS Pays $50 per story and 2 contributor's copy; additional copies $3.50. Pays on publication for first North American serial rights. Not copyrighted. Pays $50 per story and 1 contributor's copy; additional copies $3.50

EPOCH

251 Goldwin Smith Hall, Cornell University, Ithaca NY 14853-3201. (607)255-3385. **Fax:** (607)255-6661. **Website:** english.arts.cornell.edu/publications/epoch. **Contact:** Michael Koch, editor; Heidi E. Marschner, managing editor. Estab. 1947. Looking for well-written literary fiction, poetry, personal essays. Newcomers welcome. Open to mainstream and avant-garde writing.

⊙ Magazine: 6×9; 128 pages; good quality paper; good cover stock. Receives 500 unsolicited mss/month. Accepts 15-20 mss/issue. Reads submissions September 15-April 15. Publishes 3-4 new writers/year. Has published work by Antonya Nelson, Doris Betts, Heidi Jon Schmidt.

NEEDS No genre fiction. Would like to see more Southern fiction (Southern U.S).

HOW TO CONTACT Send complete ms. Considers fiction in all forms, short short to novella length.

PAYMENT/TERMS Pays $5 and up/printed page (maximum of $150/story).

TIPS "Tell your story, speak your poem, straight from the heart. We are attracted to language and to good writing, but we are most interested in what the good writing leads us to, or where."

⊙ ESSAYS & FICTIONS

(914)572-7351. **E-mail:** essaysandfictions@gmail.com. **Website:** essaysandfictions.com. **Contact:** David Pollock and Danielle Winterton, co-founding editors. Estab. 2007. "*Essays & Fictions* publishes fictional essay, reflective essay, academic rhetorical essay, literary narrative essay, lyric essay, linear fiction, nonlinear fiction, essayistic fiction, fictionalized memoir, questionable histories, false historical accounts, botched accounts, cultural analysis, criticism or commentary, compositional analysis, criticism or commentary, or any blend thereof. We do not differentiate between essay and fiction in the table of contents because we consciously challenge the validity of genre boundaries and definitions. We believe language is not fixed and neither is truth. As art, forms of literature have varying degrees of truth value. Many writers have recently chosen to compose works that blend or subvert the genres of short fiction and essay. We are particularly interested in publishing these kinds of writers. We encourage writers to experiment with hybrid forms that lead to literary transcendence." Semiannual.

NEEDS Receives 10-20 mss/month, accepts approx 3/month, 6/year. Reading periods are February 1-May 31 for October issue, and September 1-December 31 for May issue. **Publishes 3-4 new writers each year.** Authors published: Veronica Vela, Charles Lowe, John Taylor, Philippe Jaccottet, Myronn Hardy, Joseph Michaels, Paul Stubbs, Veroniki Dalakoura, Margot Berwin, William Luvaas, Greg Sanders, Danielle Winterton, David Pollock, Karl Parker, and Lee Matthew Goldberg. Does not want "genre writing, American Realism, or straight, formulaic reflective memoir." Length: up to 10,000 words. Average length: 3,000 words.

HOW TO CONTACT Send complete ms with cover letter.

PAYMENT/TERMS Contributors get 1 free copy and 15% off additional copies of the issue in which they are published.

TIPS "We look for confident work that uses form/structure and voice in interesting ways without sounding overly self-conscious or deliberate. We encourage rigorous excellence of complex craft in our submissions and discourage bland reproductions of reality. Read the journal. Be familiar with the *Essays & Fictions* aesthetic. We are particularly interested in writers who read theory and/or have multiple intellectual and artistic interests, and who set high intellectual standards for themselves and their work."

⬤⬤○ EUROPEAN JUDAISM

LBC, The Sternberg Centre, 80 East End Rd., London N3 2SY England. **E-mail:** european.judaism@lbc.ac.uk.

Website: www.journals.berghahnbooks.com/ej. **Contact:** managing editor. Estab. 1966. "For over 40 years, *European Judaism* has provided a voice for the postwar Jewish world in Europe. It has reflected the different realities of each country and helped to rebuild Jewish consciousness after the Holocaust. It is a peer-reviewed journal with emphasis on European Jewish theology, philosophy, literature, and history. Each issue includes a poetry and book reviews section."

⬤ EVANGEL

Light and Life Communications, 770 N. High School Rd., Indianapolis IN 46214. (317)244-3660. **Contact:** Julie Innes, editor. Estab. 1897 by Free Methodist denomination. *Evangel,* published quarterly, is an adult Sunday School paper. "Devotional in nature, it lifts up Christ as the source of salvation and hope. The mission of *Evangel* is to increase the reader's understanding of the nature and character of God and the nature of a life lived for Christ. Material fitting this mission and not longer than 1,200 words will be considered." Press run is less than 10,000.

NEEDS Fiction involves people coping with everyday crises, making decisions that show spiritual growth. Accepts 3-4 mss/issue; 156-200 mss/year. "No fiction without any semblance of Christian message or where the message clobbers the reader. Looking for devotional-style short pieces, 500 words or less."

HOW TO CONTACT Send complete ms. Accepts multiple submissions.

PAYMENT/TERMS Pays 5¢/word and 2 contributor's copies.

TIPS Desires concise, tight writing that supports a solid thesis and fits the mission expressed in the guidelines.

⬤ EVANSVILLE REVIEW

University of Evansville Creative Writing Deptartment, 1800 Lincoln Ave., Evansville IN 47722. (812)488-1042. **E-mail:** evansvillereview@evansville.edu. **Website:** evansvillereview.evansville.edu. **Contact:** Jessica Ingle, editor in chief. Estab. 1990. *The Evansville Review* is an annual literary journal published at the University of Evansville. Past contributors include Arthur Miller, Joseph Brodsky, John Updike, Rita Dove, Willis Barnstone, W.D. Snodgrass, Edward Albee, Dana Gioia, and Marjorie Agosin.

◔ Reading period: September 1-December 1.

NEEDS "We're open to all creativity. No discrimination. All fiction, screenplays, nonfiction, poetry, interviews, and anything in between." Does not want erotica, fantasy, experimental or children's fiction. Length: no more than 10,000 words.

HOW TO CONTACT Submit through postal mail. Include a brief bio.

PAYMENT/TERMS Pays in contributor's copies.

TIPS "Because editorial staff rolls over every 1-2 years, the journal always has a new flavor."

EVENING STREET REVIEW

Evening Street Press, Inc., 7652 Sawmill Rd. #352, Dublin OH 43016. **E-mail:** editor@eveningstreetpress.com. **Website:** www.eveningstreetpress.com. Estab. 2007. "Intended for a general audience, *Evening Street Press* is centered on Elizabeth Cady Stanton's 1848 revision of the Declaration of Independence: 'that all men and women are created equal,' with equal rights to 'life, liberty, and the pursuit of happiness.' It focuses on the realities of experience, personal and historical, from the most gritty to the most dreamlike, including awareness of the personal and social forces that block or develop the possibilities of this new culture."

HOW TO CONTACT Send complete ms. E-mail submissions preferred.

PAYMENT/TERMS Pays 1 contributor's copy.

TIPS "Does not want to see male chauvinism. Mss are read year round. See website for chapbook and book competitions."

EXOTIC MAGAZINE

X Publishing Inc., 818 SW 3rd Ave., Suite 1324, Portland OR 97204. (503)241-4317. **Fax:** (503)914-0439. **E-mail:** editorial@xmag.com; info@xmag.com. **Website:** www.xmag.com. **Contact:** John R. Voge, editor. Estab. 1993. "*Exotic* is pro-sex, informative, amusing, mature, and intelligent. Our readers rent and/or buy adult videos, visit strip clubs, and are interested in topics related to the adult entertainment industry and sexuality/culture. Don't talk down to them or fire too far over their heads. Many readers are computer literate and well-traveled. We're also interested in insightful fetish material. We are not a 'hard core' publication."

NEEDS "We are currently overwhelmed with fiction submissions. Please only send fiction if it's really amazing." Length: 1,000-1,800 words.

HOW TO CONTACT Send complete ms.

PAYMENT/TERMS Pays 10¢/word, up to $150.

TIPS "Read adult publications, spend time in the clubs doing more than just tipping and drinking. Look for new insights in adult topics. For the industry to continue to improve, those who cover it must also be educated consumers and affiliates. Please type, spell-check and be realistic about how much time the editor can take 'fixing' your ms."

FAILBETTER.COM

2022 Grove Ave., Richmond VA 23221. **E-mail:** submissions@failbetter.com. **Website:** www.failbetter.com. **Contact:** Thom Didato, editor. Estab. 2000. "We are a quarterly online magazine published in the spirit of a traditional literary journal—dedicated to publishing quality fiction, poetry, and artwork. While the Web plays host to hundreds, if not thousands, of genre-related sites (many of which have merit), we are not one of them."

Member CLMP.

NEEDS "If you're sending a short story or novel excerpt, send only one at a time. Wait to hear from us before sending another."

HOW TO CONTACT Submit work by pasting it into the body of an e-mail. Must put "Submission" in e-mail's subject line. Do not send attachments. Also accepts postal mail submissions.

TIPS "Read an issue. Read our guidelines! We place a high degree of importance on originality, believing that even in this age of trends it is still possible. We are not looking for what is current or momentary. We are not concerned with length: One good sentence may find a home here, as the bulk of mediocrity will not. Most importantly, know that what you are saying could only come from you. When you are sure of this, please feel free to submit."

FAULTLINE

University of California at Irvine, Dept. of English, 435 Humanities Instructional Building, Irvine CA 92697. (949)824-1573. **E-mail:** faultline@uci.edu. **Website:** faultline.sites.uci.edu. Estab. 1992.

Reading period is August 15-January 15. Submissions sent at any other time will not be read. Editors change in September of each year.

NEEDS Length: up to 20 pages.

HOW TO CONTACT Submit complete ms via online submissions manager or postal mail. "While simultaneous submissions are accepted, multiple submissions are not accepted. Please restrict your submissions to one story at a time, regardless of length."

PAYMENT/TERMS Pays contributor copies.

TIPS "Our commitment is to publish the best work possible from well-known and emerging authors with vivid and varied voices."

FEMINIST STUDIES

0103 Taliaferro Hall, University of Maryland, College Park MD 20742. (301)405-7415. **Fax:** (301)405-8395. **E-mail:** info@feministstudies.org; atambe@umd. edu. **E-mail:** kmantilla@feministstudies.org. **Website:** www.feministstudies.org. **Contact:** Ashwini Tambe, editorial director; Karla Mantilla, managing editor. Estab. 1974. Over the years, *Feminist Studies* has been a reliable source of significant writings on issues that are important to all classes and races of women. Those familiar with the literature on women's studies are well aware of the importance and vitality of the journal and the frequency with which articles first published in *Feminist Studies* are cited and/or reprinted elsewhere. Indeed, no less than 4 anthologies have been created from articles originally published in *Feminist Studies*: *Clio's Consciousness Raised: New Perspectives on the History of Women*; *Sex and Class in Women's History*; *U.S. Women in Struggle: A Feminist Studies Anthology*; and *Lesbian Subjects: A Feminist Studies Reader.*"

"*Feminist Studies* is committed to publishing an interdisciplinary body of feminist knowledge that sees intersections of gender with racial identity, sexual orientation, economic means, geographical location, and physical ability as the touchstone for our politics and our intellectual analysis. Whether work is drawn from the complex past or the shifting present, the articles and essays that appear in *Feminist Studies* address social and political issues that intimately and significantly affect women and men in the United States and around the world."

NEEDS "We are interested in work that addresses questions of interest to the *Feminist Studies* audience, particularly work that pushes past the boundaries of what has been done before." Length: up to 15 pages or 5,500 words.

HOW TO CONTACT Submit May 1-December 1. Submit complete ms by mail or e-mail (creative@feministstudies.org). Has published Meena Alexander, Nicole Brossard, Jayne Cortez, Toi Derricotte, Diane Glancy, Marilyn Hacker, Lyn Hejinian, June Jordan, Audre Lorde, Cherrie Moraga, Sharon Olds, Grace Paley, Ruth Stone, and Mitsuye Yamada.

FICKLE MUSES

2820 Utah Street NE, Albuquerque NM 87110. **E-mail:** editor@ficklemuses.com. **Website:** www.fickl-

emuses.com. "*Fickle Muses* is an online journal of poetry and fiction engaged with myth and legend. A poet or fiction writer is featured each week, with new selections posted on Sundays. Art is updated monthly."

HOW TO CONTACT Submit complete ms through online submissions manager. Query via e-mail. Submissions are accepted year round.

TIPS Seeks "originality. An innovative look at an old story. I'm looking to be swept away. Get a feel from our website."

FICTION

Dept. of English, The City College of New York, 138th St. & Covenant Ave., New York NY 10031. **Website:** www.fictioninc.com. **Contact:** Mark J. Mirsky, editor. Estab. 1972. "As the name implies, we publish only fiction; we are looking for the best new writing available, leaning toward the unconventional. *Fiction* has traditionally attempted to make accessible the inaccessible, to bring the experimental to a broader audience." Reading period for unsolicited mss is September 15-May 15.

Stories first published in *Fiction* have been selected for the *Pushcart Prize: Best of the Small Presses*, *O. Henry Prize Stories*, and *Best American Short Stories*.

NEEDS No romance, science fiction, etc. Length: up to 5,000 words.

HOW TO CONTACT Submit complete ms via online submissions manager.

TIPS "The guiding principle of *Fiction* has always been to go to terra incognita in the writing of the imagination and to ask that modern fiction set itself serious questions, if often in absurd and comedic voices, interrogating the nature of the real and the fantastic. It represents no particular school of fiction, except the innovative. Its pages have often been a harbor for writers at odds with each other. As a result of its willingness to publish the difficult, experimental, and unusual, while not excluding the well known, *Fiction* has a unique reputation in the U.S. and abroad as a journal of future directions."

FICTION TERRIFICA

17 9th Ave. NW, Suite C, Glen Burnie MD 21061. (443)985-7874. **E-mail:** dschaff@fictionterrifica.com; inquiries@fictionterrifica.com. **E-mail:** submissions@fictionterrifica.com. **Website:** www.fictionterrifica.com. **Contact:** Dana Schaff, managing editor. Estab. 2014. *Fiction Terrifica* is a website/bimonthly

e-zine dedicated to helping small press writers and previously unpublished writers gain exposure on the Internet. "We promote writers on Facebook and Twitter, along with any works they may have currently for sale. Our only requirement for acceptance is that the work be horror or dark fiction related. We also publish book reviews and publishing related articles along with interviews. We host links to our authors works available at other sites. We also offer Kindle publishing on a royalty basis."

NEEDS Length: 1,500-10,000 words.

HOW TO CONTACT Query before submitting.

TIPS "The best advice I can give is to write a good story, article, or personal experience publishing piece and submit it. We are always looking to promote new and upcoming writers. Have your piece polished and ready for publication."

✪◑🆂 THE FIDDLEHEAD

University of New Brunswick, Campus House, 11 Garland Court, Box 4400, Fredericton NB E3B 5A3 Canada. (506)453-3501. **Fax:** (506) 453-5069. **E-mail:** fiddlehd@unb.ca. **Website:** www.thefiddle-head.ca. **Contact:** Kathryn Taglia, managing editor. Estab. 1945. "Canada's longest living literary journal, *The Fiddlehead* is published 4 times/year at the University of New Brunswick, with the generous assistance of the University of New Brunswick, the Canada Council for the Arts, and the Province of New Brunswick. It is experienced, wise enough to recognize excellence, and always looking for freshness and surprise. *The Fiddlehead* publishes short stories, poems, book reviews, and a small number of personal essays. Our full-color covers have become collectors' items and feature work by New Brunswick artists and from New Brunswick museums and art galleries. The journal is open to good writing in English from all over the world, looking always for freshness and surprise. Our editors are always happy to see new unsolicited works in fiction and poetry. Work is read on an ongoing basis; the acceptance rate is around 1-2%. Apart from our annual contest, we have no deadlines for submissions."

🌓 "No criteria for publication except quality. For a general audience, including many poets and writers." Has published work by George Elliott Clarke, Kayla Czaga, Daniel Woodrell, and Clea Young. *The Fiddlehead* also sponsors an annual writing contest.

NEEDS Receives 100-150 unsolicited mss/month. Accepts 4-5 mss/issue; 20-40 mss/year. Agented fiction: small percentage. Publishes high percentage of new writers/year. Length: up to 6,000 words. Also publishes short shorts.

HOW TO CONTACT Send SASE and *Canadian* stamps or IRCs for return of mss. No e-mail, fax, or disc submissions. Simultaneous submissions only if stated on cover letter; must contact immediately if accepted elsewhere.

PAYMENT/TERMS Pays up to $40 (Canadian)/published page and 2 contributor's copies.

TIPS "If you are serious about submitting to *The Fiddlehead*, you should subscribe or read several issues to get a sense of the journal. Contact us if you would like to order sample back issues ($10-15 plus postage)."

✪◑🆂 THE FIFTH DI ...

P.O. Box 782, Cedar Rapids IO 52406-0782. **E-mail:** thefifthdi@yahoo.com. **Website:** www.nomadicdelir-iumpress.com/fifth.htm. Estab. 1994. *The Fifth Di ...*, published quarterly online, features fiction from the science fiction and fantasy genres.

NEEDS Open to most forms, but all submissions must be science fiction or fantasy. Does not want horror, or anything that is not science fiction or fantasy. Length: up to 7,500 words.

HOW TO CONTACT Submit by e-mail with .rtf attachment only; no .doc or .docx submissions. Include the word "Submission" in subject line.

PAYMENT/TERMS Pays $10 per story.

✪◑ FILLING STATION

P.O. Box 22135, Bankers Hall, Calgary AB T2P 4J5 Canada. **E-mail:** mgmt@fillingstation.ca; poetry@fillingstation.ca; fiction@fillingstation.ca; nonfiction@fillingstation.ca. **Website:** www.fillingstation.ca. **Contact:** Paul Zits, managing editor. Estab. 1993. *filling Station*, published 3 times/year, prints contemporary poetry, fiction, visual art, interviews, reviews, and articles. "We are looking for all forms of contemporary writing, but especially that which is original and/or experimental."

🌓 Has published poetry by Fred Wah, Larissa Lai, Margaret Christakos, Robert Kroetsch, Ron Silliman, Susan Holbrook, and many more. *filling Station* is 64 pages, 8.5×11, perfect-bound, with card cover, includes photos and artwork. Receives about 100 submissions for each issue, accepts approximately 10%. Press run is 700. Subscription: $20/3 issues; $36 for 6 issues.

HOW TO CONTACT E-mail up to 10 pages to fiction@fillingstation.ca. "We receive any of the following fiction, or a combination thereof: flash fiction, postcard fiction, short fiction, experimental fiction, or a novel excerpt that can stand alone. A submission lacking mailing address and/or bio will be considered incomplete."

TIPS "*filling Station* accepts singular or simultaneous submissions of previously unpublished poetry, fiction, creative nonfiction, nonfiction, or art. We are always on the hunt for great writing!"

⑤ THE FIRST LINE

Blue Cubicle Press, LLC, P.O. Box 250382, Plano TX 75025. (972)824-0646. **E-mail:** submission@thefirstline.com. **Website:** www.thefirstline.com. **Contact:** Robin LaBounty, ms coordinator. Estab. 1999. "*The First Line* is an exercise in creativity for writers and a chance for readers to see how many different directions we can take when we start from the same place. The purpose of *The First Line* is to jumpstart the imagination—to help writers break through the block that is the blank page. Each issue contains short stories that stem from a common first line; it also provides a forum for discussing favorite first lines in literature."

NEEDS "We only publish stories that start with the first line provided. We are a collection of tales—of different directions writers can take when they start from the same place. " Length: 300-5,000 words.

HOW TO CONTACT Submit complete ms.

PAYMENT/TERMS Pays $25-50.

TIPS "Don't just write the first story that comes to mind after you read the sentence. If it is obvious, chances are other people are writing about the same thing. Don't try so hard. Be willing to accept criticism."

① FLINT HILLS REVIEW

Dept. of English, Modern Languages, and Journalist (Box 4019), Emporia State University, 1200 Commercial St., Emporia KS 66801. **Website:** www.emporia.edu/fhr. **Contact:** Kevin Rabas. Estab. 1996. *Flint Hills Review*, published annually in December, is "a regionally focused journal presenting writers of national distinction alongside new authors. *FHR* seeks work informed by a strong sense of place or region, especially Kansas and the Great Plains region. We seek to provide a publishing venue for writers of the Great Plains and Kansas while also publishing authors whose work evidences a strong sense of place, writing of literary quality, and accomplished use of language and depth of character development."

○ Magazine: 9×6; 120-200 pages; perfect-bound; 60 lb. paper; glossy cover; illustrations; photos. Has published work by Elizabeth Dodds, Kim Stafford, and Brian Daldorph. Reads mss January to mid-March.

NEEDS "No religious, inspirational, children's." Want to see more "writing of literary quality with a strong sense of place." Publishes short shorts. Also publishes literary essays, literary criticism, poetry. Length: 1-3 pages for short shorts; 7-25 pages for short stories.

HOW TO CONTACT Submit complete ms by mail; include SASE.

PAYMENT/TERMS Pays 1 contributor's copy; additional copies at discounted price.

TIPS Submit writing that has "strong imagery and voice, writing that is informed by place or region, writing of literary quality with depth of character development. Hone the language down to the most literary depiction possible in the shortest space that still provides depth of development without excess length."

① THE FLORIDA REVIEW

Department of English, University of Central Florida, P.O. Box 161346, Orlando FL 32816. **E-mail:** flreview@mail.ucf.edu. **Website:** floridareview.cah.ucf.edu/. **Contact:** Jocelyn Bartkevicius, editor. Estab. 1972. "We publish fiction and essays of high 'literary' quality—stories that delight, instruct, and take risks. Our audience consists of avid readers of fiction, poetry, graphic narrative, and creative nonfiction."

○ Recently published work by Gerald Vizenor, Billy Collins, Sherwin Bitsui, Kelly Clancy, Denise Duhamel, Tony Hoagland, Baron Wormser, Marcia Aldrich, and Patricia Foster.

NEEDS No genre fiction. Length: no limit. "We prefer prose that is between 3-25 ms pages."

HOW TO CONTACT Send complete ms through postal mail or electronically on website.

TIPS "We're looking for writers with fresh voices and original stories. We like risk."

FLOYD COUNTY MOONSHINE

720 Christiansburg Pike, Floyd VA 24091. (540)745-5150. **E-mail:** floydshine@gmail.com. **Website:** www.floydcountymoonshine.org. **Contact:** Aaron Lee Moore, editor in chief. Estab. 2008. *Floyd County*

Moonshine, published biannually, is a "literary and arts magazine in Floyd, Virginia, and the New River Valley. We accept poetry, short stories, and essays addressing all manner of themes; however, preference is given to those works of a rural or Appalachian nature. *Floyd County Moonshine* publishes a variety of home-grown Appalachian writers in addition to writers from across the country. The mission of *Floyd County Moonshine* is to publish thought-provoking, well-crafted, free-thinking, uncensored prose and poetry. Our literature explores the dark and Gothic as well as the bright and pleasant in order to give an honest portrayal of the human condition. We aspire to publish quality literature in the local color genre, specifically writing that relates to Floyd, Virginia, and the New River Valley. Floyd and local Appalachian authors are given priority consideration; however, to stay versatile we also aspire to publish some writers from all around the country in every issue. We publish both well-established and beginning writers."

Wants "literature addressing rural or Appalachian themes." Has published poetry by Steve Kistulentz, Louis Gallo, Ernie Wormwood, R.T. Smith, Chelsea Adams, and Justin Askins.

TIPS "If we favor your work, it may appear in several issues, so prior contributors are also encouraged to resubmit. Every year we choose at least 1 featured author for an issue. We also nominate for *Pushcart* prizes, and we will do book reviews if you mail us the book."

FLYLEAF

Flyleaf, LLC, 6627 Old Oaks Blvd., Pearland TX 77584. **E-mail:** info@flyleafjournal.com. **E-mail:** submissions@flyleafjournal.com. **Website:** www.flyleaf.journal.com. **Contact:** Matthew Jankiewicz, editor; Parker Stockman, managing editor. Estab. 2014. *Flyleaf Journal* is a literary periodical that publishes one short story every month. Each story is produced as a two-sided, four-panel gatefold that opens up to reveal a literary and graphic landscape. Each story is integrated with the photographs and illustrations of a graphic collaborator, designed exclusively for that story.

NEEDS Length: 500-2,000 words.

HOW TO CONTACT Send complete ms.

PAYMENT/TERMS Pays $50 per story.

TIPS "We love to read unique and memorable voices in fiction. We want to receive stories written out of love, passion, or anger. If it doesn't move the writer, we will most likely not be moved as well. Our fiction celebrates the short memories in life that make the biggest impact on us."

FLYWAY

Department of English, 206 Ross Hall, Iowa State University, Ames IA 50011-1201. **E-mail:** flywayjournal@gmail.com; flyway@iastate.edu. **Website:** www.flyway.org. **Contact:** Elizabeth A. Giorgi, managing editor. Estab. 1995. Based out of Iowa State University, *Flyway: Journal of Writing and Environment* publishes poetry, fiction, nonfiction, and visual art exploring the many complicated facets of the word environment—at once rural, urban, and suburban—and its social and political implications. Also open to all different interpretations of environment.

Reading period is September 15-May 15. Has published work by Rick Bass, Jacob M. Appel, Madison Smartt Bell, Jane Smiley. Also sponsors the annual fall "Notes from the Field" nonfiction contest, and the spring "Sweet Corn Prize in Fiction" short story contest. Details on website.

NEEDS Length: up to 5,000 words. Average length: 3,000 words. Also publishes short shorts of up to 1,000 words. Average length: 500 words.

HOW TO CONTACT Submit mss only via online submission manager. Receives 50-100 mss monthly. Accepts 3-5 stories per issue; up to 10 per year. Also reviews novels and short-story collections. Submit 1 short story or up to 3 short shorts.

PAYMENT/TERMS Pays one-year subscription to *Flyway.*

TIPS "For *Flyway*, there should be tension between the environment or setting of the story and the characters in it. A well-known place should appear new, even alien and strange through the eyes and actions of the characters. We want to see an active environment, too—a setting that influences actions, triggers it's one events."

FOGGED CLARITY

Fogged Clarity and Nicotine Heart Press, P.O. Box 1016, Muskegon MI 49443-1016. (231)670-7033. **E-mail:** editor@foggedclarity.com. **E-mail:** submissions@foggedclarity.com. **Website:** www.foggedclarity.com. **Contact:** Editors. Estab. 2008. "*Fogged Clarity* is an arts review that accepts submissions of poetry, fiction, nonfiction, music, visual art, and reviews of work in all mediums. We seek art that is stabbingly eloquent. Our print edition is released once every year, while new issues of our online journal come out at the beginning of every month. Artists maintain the copyrights to their work until they are monetarily compensated for said work. If your work is selected for our print edition and you consent to its publication, you will be compensated."

"By incorporating music and the visual arts and releasing a new issue monthly, *Fogged Clarity* aims to transcend the conventions of a typical literary journal. Our network is extensive, and our scope is as broad as thought itself; we are, you are, unconstrained. With that spirit in mind, *Fogged Clarity* examines the work of authors, artists, scholars, and musicians, providing a home for exceptional art and thought that warrants exposure."

NEEDS Length: up to 8,000 words.

HOW TO CONTACT Submit 1-2 complete ms by e-mail (submissions@foggedclarity.com) as attached .doc or .docx file. Subject line should be formatted as: "Last Name: Medium of Submission." For example, "Evans: Fiction." Include brief cover letter, complete contact information, and a third-person bio.

TIPS "The editors appreciate artists communicating the intention of their submitted work and the influences behind it in a brief cover letter. Any artists with proposals for features or special projects should feel free to contact Ben Evans directly at editor@fogged-clarity.com."

FOLIATE OAK LITERARY MAGAZINE

University of Arkansas-Monticello, P.O. Box 3460, Monticello AR 71656. (870)460-1247. **E-mail:** foliateoak@uamont.edu. **Website:** www.foliateoak.com. **Contact:** Online submission manager. Estab. 1973. Magazine: 6×9; 80 pages. Monthly.

NEEDS adventure, comics/graphic novels, ethnic/multicultural, experimental, family saga, feminist, gay, historical, humor/satire, lesbian, literary, mainstream, science fiction (soft/sociological). No religious, sexist or homophobic work. Receives 80 unsolicited mss/month. Accepts 20 mss/issue; 160 mss/year. Does not read mss May-August. Publishes ms 1 month after acceptance. Publishes 130 new writers/year. Recently published work by David Barringer, Thom Didato, Joe Taylor, Molly Giles, Patricia Shevlin, and Tony Hoagland. Length: 50-2,500 words; average length: 1,500 words. Publishes short shorts. Also publishes literary essays, literary criticism, poetry. Rarely comments on rejected mss.

HOW TO CONTACT Use our online submission manager to submit work. Postal submissions will not be read. Responds in 4 weeks. Only accepts submissions August through April. Accepts simultaneous submissions and multiple submissions. Please contact ASAP if work is accepted elsewhere. Sample copy with SASE and 6×8 envelope. Read writer's guidelines online. Reviews fiction.

PAYMENT/TERMS Pays 1 contributor's copy if included in the annual print anthology. Acquires electronic rights. Sends galleys to author. Not copyrighted.

TIPS "We're open to honest, experimental, offbeat, realistic and surprising writing, if it has been edited. Limit poems to 5 per submission, and 1 short story or creative nonfiction (less than 2,500 words. You may send up to 3 flash fictions. Please put your flash fiction in 1 attachment. Please don't send more writing until you hear from us regarding your first submission. We are also looking for artwork sent as .jpg or .gif files."

FOLIO, A LITERARY JOURNAL AT AMERICAN UNIVERSITY

Department of Literature, American University, Washington DC 20016. (202)885-2971. **Fax:** (202)885-2938. **E-mail:** folio.editors@gmail.com. **Website:** www.american.edu/cas/literature/folio. Estab. 1984. "*Folio* is a nationally recognized literary journal sponsored by the College of Arts and Sciences at American University in Washington, DC. Since 1984, we have published original creative work by both new and established authors. Past issues have included work by Michael Reid Busk, Billy Collins, William Stafford, and Bruce Weigl, and interviews with Michael Cunningham, Charles Baxter, Amy Bloom, Ann Beattie, and Walter Kirn. We look for well-crafted poetry and prose that is bold and memorable."

Poems and prose are reviewed by editorial staff and senior editors. Press run is 250; 50-60 distributed free to the American University community and contributors. Reads submissions September 1-January 1.

NEEDS Length: up to 5,000 words.

HOW TO CONTACT Submit via online submission form at https://foliolitjournal.submittable.com/submit. "Cover letters must contain all of the following: brief bio, e-mail address, snail mail address, phone number, and title(s) of work enclosed."

PAYMENT/TERMS Pays $50 and 2 contributor's copies.

FOURTEEN HILLS

Dept. of Creative Writing, San Francisco State University, 1600 Holloway Ave., San Francisco CA 94132. **Website:** www.14hills.net. Estab. 1994. "*Fourteen Hills* publishes the highest-quality innovative fiction and poetry for a literary audience." Editors change each year. Always sends prepublication galleys.

○ Semiannual magazine: 6×9; 200 pages; 60 lb. paper; 10-point C15 cover. Reading periods: September 1-December 1 for summer issue; March 1-June 1 for winter issue.

NEEDS Has published work by Susan Straight, Yiyun Li, Alice LaPlante, Terese Svoboda, Peter Rock, Stephen Dixon, and Adam Johnson. Length: up to 25 pages for short stories; up to 10 pages for experimental or cross-genre literature (including graphic stories).

HOW TO CONTACT Submit complete ms via online submissions manager.

PAYMENT/TERMS Pays 2 contributor's copies and discount on additional copies.

TIPS "Please read an issue of *Fourteen Hills* before submitting."

THE FOURTH RIVER

Chatham College, Woodland Rd., Pittsburgh PA 15232. **E-mail:** 4thriver@gmail.com. **Website:** four-thriver.chatham.edu. Estab. 2005. *The Fourth River*, an annual publication of Chatham University's MFA in Creative Writing Programs, features literature that engages and explores the relationship between humans and their environments. Wants writings that are richly situated at the confluence of place, space, and identity, or that reflect upon or make use of landscape and place in new ways.

○ *The Fourth River* is digest-sized, perfect-bound, with full-color cover by various artists. *The Fourth River*'s contributors have been published in *Glimmer Train, Alaska Quarterly Review, The Missouri Review, The Best American Short Stories, The O. Henry Prize Stories*, and *The Best American Travel Writing*.

NEEDS Length: up to 7,000 words.

HOW TO CONTACT Submit complete ms via online submissions manager.

○⑤ FREEFALL MAGAZINE

Freefall Literary Society of Calgary, 922 Ninth Ave. SE, Calgary AB T2G 0S4 Canada. **E-mail:** editors@ freefallmagazine.ca. **Website:** www.freefallmagazine. ca. **Contact:** Ryan Stromquist, managing editor. Estab. 1990. "Magazine published triannually containing fiction, poetry, creative nonfiction, essays on writing, interviews, and reviews. We are looking for exquisite writing with a strong narrative."

NEEDS Length: no more than 4,000 words.

HOW TO CONTACT Submit via website form. Attach submission file (file name format is lastname_firstname_storytitle.doc or .docx or .pdf).

PAYMENT/TERMS Pays $10 per printed page in the magazine, to a maximum of $100, and 1 contributor's copy.

TIPS "Our mission is to encourage the voices of new, emerging, and experienced Canadian writers and provide a platform for their quality work."

●○ FREEXPRESSION

P.O. Box 4, West Hoxton NSW 2171 Australia. **E-mail:** editor@freexpression.com.au. **Website:** www. freexpression.com.au. **Contact:** Peter F. Pike, managing editor. Estab. 1993. *FreeXpresSion*, published monthly, contains "creative writing, how-to articles, short stories, and poetry, including cinquain, haiku, etc., and bush verse." Open to all forms. "Christian themes OK. Humorous material welcome. No gratuitous sex; bad language OK. We don't want to see anything degrading."

○ *FreeXpresSion* also publishes books up to 200 pages through subsidy arrangements with authors. Some poems published throughout the year are used in *Yearbooks* (annual anthologies). *FreeXpresSion* is 32 pages, magazine-sized, offset-printed, saddle-stapled, full color. Receives about 3,500 poems/year, accepts about 30%.

HOW TO CONTACT Submit prose via e-mail.

●○ THE FROGMORE PAPERS

21 Mildmay Rd., Lewes, East Sussex BN7 1PJ England. **Website:** www.frogmorepress.co.uk. **Contact:** Jeremy Page, editor. Estab. 1983. *The Frogmore Papers*, published semiannually, is a literary magazine with emphasis on new poetry and short stories.

○ *The Frogmore Papers* is 46 pages, photocopied in photo-reduced typescript, saddle-stapled, with matte card cover. Accepts 2% of poetry received. Press run is 500. Reading periods: October 1-31 for March issue and April 1-30 for September issue.

NEEDS Length: up to 2,000 words.

HOW TO CONTACT Submit by e-mail or mail (postal submissions only accepted from within the U.K.).

PAYMENT/TERMS Pays 1 contributor's copy.

❶⊕⑤ FUGUE LITERARY MAGAZINE

200 Brink Hall, University of Idaho, P.O. Box 44110, Moscow ID 83844. **E-mail:** fugue@uidaho.edu. **Web-**

site: www.fuguejournal.org. **Contact:** Alexandra Teague, faculty advisor. Estab. 1990. Biannual literary magazine. "Submissions are accepted online only. Poetry, fiction, and nonfiction submissions are accepted September 1-April 1. All material received outside of this period will not be read." $3 submission fee per entry. See website for submission instructions.

○ Work published in *Fugue* has won the Pushcart Prize and has been cited in *Best American Essays*.

HOW TO CONTACT Submit complete ms via online submissions manager. "Please send no more than 2 short shorts or 1 story at a time. Submissions in more than 1 genre should be submitted separately. All multiple submissions will be returned unread. Once you have submitted a piece to us, wait for a response on this piece before submitting again."

PAYMENT/TERMS Pays 2 contributor's copies and additional payment.

TIPS "The best way, of course, to determine what we're looking for is to read the journal. As the name *Fugue* indicates, our goal is to present a wide range of literary perspectives. We like stories that satisfy us both intellectually and emotionally, with fresh language and characters so captivating that they stick with us and invite a second reading. We are also seeking creative literary criticism which illuminates a piece of literature or a specific writer by examining that writer's personal experience."

FUNNY TIMES

Funny Times, Inc., P.O. Box 18530, Cleveland Heights OH 44118. (216)371-8600. **Fax:** (216)371-8696. **E-mail:** info@funnytimes.com. **Website:** www.funnytimes.com. **Contact:** Ray Lesser and Susan Wolpert, editors. Estab. 1985. "*Funny Times* is a monthly review of America's funniest cartoonists and writers. We are the *Reader's Digest* of modern American humor with a progressive/peace-oriented/environmental/politically activist slant."

NEEDS Wants anything funny. Length: 500-700 words.

HOW TO CONTACT Query with published clips.

PAYMENT/TERMS Pays $50-150.

TIPS "Send us a small packet (1-3 items) of only your very funniest stuff. If this makes us laugh, we'll be glad to ask for more. We particularly welcome previously published material that has been well received elsewhere."

GARBANZO LITERARY JOURNAL

Seraphemera Books, 211 Greenwood Ave., Suite 224, Bethel CT 06801. **E-mail:** storyteller@garbanzoliteraryjournal.org. **Website:** www.garbanzoliteraryjournal.org. **Contact:** Marc Moorash and Ava Dawn Heydt, co-editors. Estab. 2010. Limited-edition handmade book, also available at iBookstore. "We are calling out to all who have placed word on page (and even those who still carry all their works in the mind). Stories of up to 1,172 words, poems of up to 43 lines, micro-fiction, macro-fiction, limericks, villanelles, cinquains, couplets, couplings, creative nonfiction, noncreative fictions … and whatever form your moving, thoughtful, memorable tale wishes to take (which means disregard the rules, punk-rock style). In our specific instance, there is always a light that shines through these works, always a redemption that happens in the end. We're whimsical and full of light, even though some of the subject matter and form is dark. If your work is full of sarcasm and cynicism, if your cover letter is full of the same, we're probably not a good fit to work with each other. We somewhat consider each issue of *Garbanzo* to be a moment in infinite space when a group of mostly disparate people wind up in the same room due to some strange space/time glitch. We're not all going to agree on everything, and we probably wouldn't all get along, but we're not going to waste that moment together in complaint … We're going to celebrate each picking up a feather and causing this massive bird to fly …"

NEEDS Length: 1-29,318 words.

HOW TO CONTACT Submit complete ms.

PAYMENT/TERMS Pays contributor's copies.

TIPS "Read our website and the various suggestions therein. We're not much for rules—so surprise us. In that same regard, if you send us certain things it will be immediately obvious that you are sending to us another long list and haven't bothered to learn about us. Those who pay attention to detail are far more interesting to work with—as we're very interactive with our published authors. We want people who want to work and play with our style of publishing as much as we want good writing."

GARBLED TRANSMISSIONS MAGAZINE

5813 NW 20th St., Margate FL 33063. **E-mail:** jamesrobertpayne@yahoo.com. **E-mail:** editor@garbledtransmission.com. **Website:** www.garbledtransmission.com. **Contact:** James Payne, editor in chief.

Estab. 2011. Daily online literary magazine featuring fiction and book, movie, and comic book reviews.

○ "Stories should have a dark/strange/twisted slant to them and should be original ideas, or have such a twist to them that they redefine the genre. We like authors with an original voice. That being said, we like Stephen King, Richard Matheson, Neil Gaiman, A. Lee Martinez, Chuck Palahniuk, and Clive Barker. Movies and TV shows that inspire us include 'Lost,' *The Matrix, Fight Club, 3:10 to Yuma, Dark City, The Sixth Sense,* 'X-Files,' and *Super 8.*"

NEEDS No romance. Length: 500-15,000 words.

HOW TO CONTACT Send complete ms. Submit via e-mail with subject line "Garbled Transmissions Submission."

TIPS "The best way to see what we like is to visit our website and read some of the stories we've published to get a taste of what style we seek."

○ GARGOYLE

Paycock Press, 3819 N. 13th St., Arlington VA 22201. (703)525-9296. **E-mail:** rchrdpeabody9@gmail.com. **E-mail:** gargoyle@gargoylemagazine.com. **Website:** www.gargoylemagazine.com. **Contact:** Richard Peabody, editor, Lucinda Ebersole, co-editor. Estab. 1976. "*Gargoyle* has always been a scallywag magazine, a maverick magazine, a bit too academic for the underground and way too underground for the academics. We are a writer's magazine in that we are read by other writers and have never worried about reaching the masses." Annual.

○ Accepts submissions from February 1 until full; in 2014 that was by February 14. Recently published work by Shane Allison, Rafael Alvarez, Carolyn Banks, Alison Bundy, Sophy Burnham, Valentina Cano, Theodore Carter, James Cervantes, Peter Cherches, Kelly Cherry, Joan Colby, Anne Colwell, Michael Daley, William Virgil Davis, Trevor Dodge, Sarah Einstein, Angela Featherstone, Thalia Field, Gary Fincke, Andy Fogle, Jesse Glass, Myronn Hardy, Lola Haskins, Allison Hedge-Coke, Wayne Karlin, Eurydice Kamvisseli, W.F. Lantry, Nathan Leslie, Melvin E. Lewis, Lyn Lifshin, Adrian C. Louis, Mary Mackey, Nick Mamatas, David McAleavey, Margaret McCarthy, Franetta McMillian, Dora E. McQuaid, Mark Melnicove, Stephen C. Middleton, Roberto Montes, Samina Najmi, Amelie Olaiz, Jose Padua,

Ted Pelton, Deborah Pintonelli, Shelley Puhak, Carol Quinn, Misti Rainwater-Lites, Kit Reed, Doug Rice, Lou Robinson, Stuart Ross, Tomaz Salamun, Lynda Schor, E.M. Schorb, Helen Maryles Shankman, Gregg Shapiro, Rose Solari, Marilyn Stablein, D.E. Steward, Art Taylor, David A. Taylor, An Tran, Michael Waters, Paul West, Tom Whalen, and Paula Whyman.

NEEDS Wants "edgy realism or experimental works. We run both." Wants to see more Canadian, British, Australian, and Third World fiction. Receives 200 unsolicited mss/week during submission period. Accepts 20-50 mss/issue. Agented fiction 5%. **Publishes 2-3 new writers/year.** Publishes 2 titles/year. Format: trade paperback originals. No romance, horror, science fiction. Length: 1,000-4,500 words.

TIPS "We have to fall in love with a particular fiction."

THE GEORGIA REVIEW

The University of Georgia, Main Library, Room 706A, 320 S. Jackson St., Athens GA 30602. (706)542-3481. **Fax:** (706)542-0047. **E-mail:** garev@uga.edu. **Website:** thegeorgiareview.com. **Contact:** Stephen Corey, editor. Estab. 1947. "Our readers are educated, inquisitive people who read a lot of work in the areas we feature, so they expect only the best in our pages. All work submitted should show evidence that the writer is at least as well educated and well read as our readers. Essays should be authoritative but accessible to a range of readers."

○ Electronic submissions available for $3 fee. Reading period: August 15-May 15.

NEEDS "We seek original, excellent writing not bound by type." "Ordinarily we do not publish novel excerpts or works translated into English, and we strongly discourage authors from submitting these."

HOW TO CONTACT Send complete ms via online submissions manager or postal mail.

PAYMENT/TERMS Pays $50/published page.

○ GERTRUDE

P.O. Box 28281, Portland OR 97228. **E-mail:** editor@gertrudepress.org. Estab. 1999. *Gertrude,* the annual literary arts journal of Gertrude Press, is a "publication featuring the voices and visions of the gay, lesbian, bisexual, transgender, and supportive community."

NEEDS Has published work by Carol Guess, Demrie Alonzo, Henry Alley, and Scott Pomfret. Length: up to 3,000 words.

HOW TO CONTACT Submit 1-2 pieces via online submissions manager, double-spaced. Include word count for each piece in cover letter.

TIPS "We look for strong characterization and imagery, and new, unique ways of writing about universal experiences. Follow the construction of your work until the ending. Many stories start out with zest, then flipper and die. Show us, don't tell us."

THE GETTYSBURG REVIEW

Gettysburg College, Gettysburg PA 17325. (717)337-6770. **Fax:** (717)337-6775. **E-mail:** pstitt@gettysburg.edu; mdrew@gettysburg.edu. **Website:** www.gettysburgreview.com. **Contact:** Peter Stitt, editor; Ellen Hathaway, managing editor; Mark Drew, assistant editor. Estab. 1988. Published quarterly, *The Gettysburg Review* considers unsolicited submissions of poetry, fiction, and essays. "Our concern is quality. Mss submitted here should be extremely well written. Reading period September 1-May 31."

NEEDS Wants high-quality literary fiction. "We require that fiction be intelligent and esthetically written." No genre fiction. Length: 2,000-7,000 words.

HOW TO CONTACT Send complete ms with SASE.

PAYMENT/TERMS Pays $30/page and 1 contributor's copy.

GINOSKO LITERARY JOURNAL

P.O. Box 246, Fairfax CA 94978. **E-mail:** editorginosko@aol.com. **Website:** www.ginoskoliteraryjournal.com. **Contact:** Robert Paul Cesaretti, editor. Estab. 2002. *Ginosko* Flash Fiction Contest: Deadline is March 1; $5 entry fee; $250 prize. "*Ginosko* (ghin-océ-koe): To perceive, understand, realize, come to know; knowledge that has an inception, a progress, an attainment. The recognition of truth by experience." Accepting short fiction and poetry, creative nonfiction, interviews, social justice concerns, and literary insights for www.GinoskoLiteraryJournal.com.

○ Reads year round. Length of articles flexible; accepts excerpts. Publishing as semiannual ezine. Check downloadable issues on website for tone and style. Downloads free; accepts donations. Also looking for books, art, and music to post on website, and links to exchange. Member CLMP.

HOW TO CONTACT Submit via postal mail, e-mail (prefers attachments: .wps, .doc, or .rtf), or online submissions manager (https://ginosko.submittable.com/submit).

⑤ GLIMMER TRAIN STORIES

Glimmer Train Press, Inc., P.O. Box 80430, Portland OR 97280. **Fax:** (503)221-0837. **E-mail:** eds@glimmertrain.org. **Website:** www.glimmertrain.org. Estab. 1991. "We are interested in literary short stories, particularly by new and emerging writers."

○ Recently published work by Benjamin Percy, Laura van den Berg, Manuel Muñoz, Claire Vaye Watkins, Abby Geni, Peter Ho Davies, William Trevor, Thisbe Nissen, and Yiyun Li.

NEEDS Length: 1,200-12,000 words.

HOW TO CONTACT Submit via the website at www.glimmertrain.org. "In a pinch, send a hard copy and include SASE for response." Receives 36,000 unsolicited mss/year. Accepts 15 mss/issue; 45 mss/year. Agented fiction 2%. Publishes 20 new writers/year.

PAYMENT/TERMS Pays $700 for standard submissions, up to $2,500 for contest-winning stories.

TIPS "In the last 2 years over half of the first-place stories have been their authors' very first publications. See our contest listings in Contests & Awards section."

GOTHIC CITY PRESS

Sacred City Productions, Ltd., 5781 Springwood Ct., Mentor on the Lake OH 44060. (440)290-9325. **E-mail:** info@gothiccitypress.com. **E-mail:** info@gothiccitypress.com. **Website:** www.gothiccitypress.com. **Contact:** Erin and Colleen Garlock, editors/owners. Estab. 2013. Gothic City Press is a print and online imprint dedicated to creative endeavors using the back drop of all things Gothic or urban as inspiration.

NEEDS Gothic City Press's fiction focus is on dark fiction for publication in short story anthologies. "We tend to favor stories that have dark overtones, though this is not a requirement." Looking for 500-8,000 word stories.

HOW TO CONTACT Send complete ms via online submission form.

PAYMENT/TERMS Pays $10 for stories over 500 words, $20 for stories over 2,000 words. Once royalties earned by the publication equal the total amount paid out to all contributors, the contributors will receive a 50/50 pro-rate share of the anthology's earnings, if any, relevant to the number of contributors. A royalty breakdown sheet will be supplied at the end of a project.

TIPS "We are very interested in submissions from first-time authors and authors with a very limited record."

○○⑤ GRAIN

P.O. Box 67, Saskatoon SK S7K 3K1 Canada. (306)244-2828. **Fax:** (306)565-8554. **E-mail:** grainmag@skwriter.com. **Website:** www.grainmagazine.ca. **Contact:** Rilla Friesen, editor. Estab. 1973. "*Grain, The Journal Of Eclectic Writing* is a literary quarterly that publishes engaging, diverse, and challenging writing and art by some of the best Canadian and international writers and artists. Every issue features superb new writing from both developing and established writers. Each issue also highlights the unique artwork of a different visual artist. *Grain* has garnered national and international recognition for its distinctive, cutting-edge content and design."

○ *Grain* is 112-128 pages, digest-sized, professionally printed. Press run is 1,100. Receives about 3,000 submissions/year. Submissions are read September-May only. Mss postmarked between June 1 and August 31 will not be read.

NEEDS No romance, confession, science fiction, vignettes, mystery. Length: up to 5,000 words. "Stories at the longer end of the word count must be of exceptional quality."

HOW TO CONTACT "Submissions must be typed in readable font (ideally 12 point, Times Roman or Courier), free of typos, printed on 1 side only. No staples. Your name and address must be on every page. Pieces of more than 1 page must be numbered. Cover letter with all contact information, title(s), and genre of work is required." Postal mail submissions only.

PAYMENT/TERMS Pays $50-250 CAD (depending on number of pages) and 2 contributor's copies.

TIPS "Only work of the highest literary quality is accepted. Read several back issues."

● GRASSLIMB

P.O. Box 420816, San Diego CA 92142. **E-mail:** editor@grasslimb.com. **Website:** www.grasslimb.com. **Contact:** Valerie Polichar, editor. Estab. 2002. "*Grasslimb* publishes literary prose, poetry, and art. Fiction is best when it is short and avant-garde or otherwise experimental."

○ *Grasslimb*, published semiannually, is 14×20; 8 pages; 60 lb. white paper; with illustrations.

NEEDS Accepts 2-4 mss/issue; 4-8 mss/year. Publishes ms 3-6 months after acceptance. Publishes 4 new writers/year. Has published work by Kuzhali Manickavel, James Sallis. Publishes short shorts. Reviews fiction. Does not want romance, elder care/aging, children, or religious writings. Length: 500-2,000 words; average length: 1,500 words.

HOW TO CONTACT Send complete ms. Send SASE for return of ms or disposable copy of ms and #10 SASE for reply only. Accepts simultaneous and reprints, multiple submissions.

PAYMENT/TERMS Writers receive $10 minimum; $70 maximum, and 2 contributor's copies; additional copies $3.

TIPS "We publish brief fiction work that can be read in a single sitting over a cup of coffee. Work is generally 'literary' in nature rather than mainstream. Experimental work welcome. Remember to have your work proofread and to send short work. We cannot read over 2,500 words and prefer under 2,000 words. Include word count."

● GREEN HILLS LITERARY LANTERN

Truman State University, Dept. of English, Truman State University, Kirksville MO 63501. **E-mail:** adavis@truman.edu. **Website:** ghll.truman.edu. **Contact:** Adam Brooke Davis, managing editor; Joe Benevento, poetry editor. Estab. 1990. *Green Hills Literary Lantern* is published annually, in June, by Truman State University. Historically, the print publication ran between 200-300 pages, consisting of poetry, fiction, reviews, and interviews. The digital magazine is of similar proportions and artistic standards. Open to the work of new writers, as well as more established writers.

NEEDS "We are interested in stories that demonstrate a strong working knowledge of the craft. Avoid genre fiction or mainstream religious fiction. Otherwise, we are open to short stories of various settings, character conflict, and styles, including experimental. Above all, we demand that work be 'striking.' Language should be complex, with depth, through analogy, metaphor, simile, understatement, irony, etc.—but all this must not be overwrought or self-consciously literary. If style is to be at center stage, it must be interesting and provocative enough for the reader to focus on style alone. 'Overdone' writing surely is not either." No word limit.

HOW TO CONTACT Submit complete ms.

PAYMENT/TERMS No payment provided.

GREEN MOUNTAINS REVIEW

Johnson State College, 337 College Hill, Johnson VT 05656. (802)635-1350. **E-mail:** gmr@jsc.edu. **Website:** greenmountainsreview.com/. **Contact:** Elizabeth Powell, editor. The editors are open to a wide rane of styles and subject matter.

○ Open reading period: September 1-May 15.

NEEDS Adventure, experimental, humor/satire, literary, mainstream, serialized novels, translations. Recently published work by Tracy Daugherty, Terese

Svoboda, Walter Wetherell, T.M. McNally, J. Robert Lennon, Louis B. Jones, and Tom Whalen. Publishes short shorts. Also publishes literary criticism, poetry. Sometimes comments on rejected mss. Length: up to 25 pages, double-spaced.

PAYMENT/TERMS Pays contributor's copies, 1-year subscription and small honorarium, depending on grants.

TIPS "We encourage you to order some of our back issues to acquaint yourself with what has been accepted in the past."

⑩⑪ THE GREENSBORO REVIEW

MFA Writing Program, 3302 HHRA Building, UNC-Greensboro, Greensboro NC 27402. (336)334-5459. **E-mail:** jlclark@uncg.edu. **Website:** tgronline.net. **Contact:** Jim Clark, editor. Estab. 1965. "A local lit mag with an international reputation. We've been 'old school' since 1965."

○ Stories for *the Greensboro Review* have been included in *Best American Short Stories, The O. Henry Awards Prize Stories, New Stories from The South* and *Pushcart Prize*. Does not accept e-mail submissions.

NEEDS Length: up to 7,500 words.

HOW TO CONTACT Submit complete ms via online submission form or postal mail. Include cover letter and estimated word count.

PAYMENT/TERMS Pays in contributor's copies.

TIPS "We want to see the best being written regardless of theme, subject, or style."

THE GRIFFIN

Gwynedd Mercy College, 1325 Sumneytown Pike, P.O. Box 901, Gwynedd Valley PA 19437-0901. (215)641-5518. **Fax:** (215)641-5552. **E-mail:** allego.d@gmercyu. edu. **Website:** www.gmercyu.edu/about-gwynedd-mercy/publications/griffin. **Contact:** Dr. Donna M. Allego, editor. Estab. 1999. Published by Gwynedd Mercy University, *The Griffin* is a literary journal for the creative writer—subscribing to the belief that improving the human condition requires dedication to and respect for the individual and the community. Seeks works which explore universal qualities—truth, justice, integrity, compassion, mercy … Publishes poetry, short stories, short plays, and reflections.

NEEDS All genres considered. No slashers, graphic violence, or sex, however. Length: up to 2,500 words.

HOW TO CONTACT Submit complete ms via e-mail or on disk with a hard copy. Include short author bio.

TIPS "Pay attention to the word length requirements, the mission of the magazine, and how to submit ms as set forth. These constitute the writer's guidelines listed online."

⑩⑪ GUERNICA MAGAZINE

112 W. 27th St., Suite 600, New York NY 10001. **E-mail:** editors@guernicamag.com; art@guernicamag. com; publisher@guernicamag.com. **Website:** www. guernicamag.com. **Contact:** See masthead online for specific editors. Estab. 2005. "*Guernica* is called a 'great online literary magazine' by *Esquire*. *Guernica* contributors come from dozens of countries and write in nearly as many languages."

○ Received Caine Prize for African Writing, Best of the Net.

NEEDS "*Guernica* strongly prefers fiction with a diverse international outlook—or if American, from an underrepresented or alternative perspective. (No stories about American tourists in other countries, please.)" Has published Jesse Ball, Elizabeth Crane, Josh Weil, Justo Arroyo, Sergio Ramírez Mercado, Matthew Derby, E.C. Osondu (Winner of the 2009 Caine Prize for African Writing). No genre fiction or satire. Length: 1,200-4,500 words.

HOW TO CONTACT Submit complete ms via online submissions manager.

TIPS "Please read the magazine first before submitting. Most stories that are rejected simply do not fit our approach. Submission guidelines available online."

⑪ GULF COAST: A JOURNAL OF LITERATURE AND FINE ARTS

4800 Calhoun Road, Houston TX 77204-3013. (713)743-3223. **E-mail:** editors@gulfcoastmag.org. **Website:** www.gulfcoastmag.org. **Contact:** Adrienne Perry, editor; Martin Rock, managing editor; Carlos Hernandez, digital editor; Conor Bracken, Katie Condon, Sam Mansfield, poetry editors; Julia Brown, Laura Jok, Dino Piacentini, fiction editors; Talia Mailman, Steve Sanders, nonfiction editors; Matthew Salesses, online fiction editor; Christopher Murray, online poetry editor; Talia Mailman, online nonfiction editor. Estab. 1986.

○ Magazine: 7x9; approximately 300 pages; stock paper, gloss cover; illustrations; photos.

NEEDS "Please do not send multiple submissions; we will read only 1 submission per author at a given time, except in the case of our annual contests." No children's, genre, religious/inspirational.

HOW TO CONTACT *Gulf Coast* reads general submissions, submitted by post or through the online submissions manager September 1-March 1. Submissions e-mailed directly to the editors or postmarked March 1-September 1 will not be read or responded to. "Please visit our contest page for contest submission guidelines." Receives 500 unsolicited mss/month. Accepts 6-8 mss/issue; 12-16 mss/year. Agented fiction: 5%. Publishes 2-8 new writers/year. Recently published work by Alan Heathcock, Anne Carson, Bret Anthony Johnston, John D'Agata, Lucie Brock-Broido, Clancy Martin, Steve Almond, Sam Lipsyte, Carl Phillips, Dean Young, and Eula Biss. Publishes short shorts.

PAYMENT/TERMS Pays $50/page.

TIPS "Submit only previously unpublished works. Include a cover letter. Online submissions are strongly preferred. Stories or essays should be typed, double-spaced, and paginated with your name, address, and phone number on the first page and the title on subsequent pages. Poems should have your name, address, and phone number on the first page of each." The Annual Gulf Coast Prizes award publication and $1,500 each in poetry, fiction, and nonfiction; opens in December of each year. Honorable mentions in each category will receive a $250 second prize. Postmark/online entry deadline: March 22 of each year. Winners and honorable mentions will be announced in May. **Entry fee:** $23 (includes one-year subscription). Make checks payable to *Gulf Coast*. Guidelines available on website.

🌑 GULF STREAM MAGAZINE

English Department, FIU, Biscayne Bay Campus, 3000 NE 151 St., North Miami FL 33181. **E-mail:** gulfstreamfiu@yahoo.com. **Website:** www.gulfstreamlitmag.com. **Contact:** Paul Christiansen, editor in chief. Estab. 1989. "*Gulf Stream Magazine* has been publishing emerging and established writers of exceptional fiction, nonfiction, and poetry since 1989. We also publish interviews and book reviews. Past contributors include Sherman Alexie, Steve Almond, Jan Beatty, Lee Martin, Robert Wrigley, Dennis Lehane, Liz Robbins, Stuart Dybek, David Kirby, Ann Hood, Ha Jin, B.H. Fairchild, Naomi Shihab Nye, F. Daniel Rzicznek, and Connie May Fowler. *Gulf Stream Magazine* is supported by the Creative Writing Program at Florida International University in Miami, Florida. Each year we publish 2 online issues."

NEEDS Does not want romance, historical, juvenile, or religious work.

HOW TO CONTACT "Submit online only. Please read guidelines on website in full. Submissions that do not conform to our guidelines will be discarded. We do not accept e-mailed or mailed submissions. We read from September 1-November 1 and January 1-March 1."

PAYMENT/TERMS Pays contributor's copies.

TIPS "Looks for fresh, original writing—well-plotted stories with unforgettable characters, fresh poetry, and experimental writing. Usually longer stories do not get accepted. There are exceptions, however."

HADASSAH MAGAZINE

50 W. 58th St., New York NY 10019. (212)688-0227. **Fax:** (212)446-9521. **E-mail:** magazine@hadassah.org. **Website:** www.hadassah.org/magazine. **Contact:** Elizabeth Barnea. Zelda Shluker, managing editor. Jewish general-interest magazine: 7×10.5; 64-80 pages; coated paper; slick, medium weight coated cover; drawings and photos. "*Hadassah* is a general interest Jewish journalistic feature and literary magazine. We speak to our readers on a vast array of subjects ranging from politics to parenting, to midlife crisis to Mideast crisis. Our readers want coverage on social and economic issues, Jewish women's (feminist) issues, the arts, travel and health." Bi-monthly. Circ. 255,000.

NEEDS Ethnic/multicultural (Jewish). No personal memoirs, "schmaltzy" or shelter magazine fiction. Receives 20-25 unsolicited mss/month. Publishes some new writers/year. Recently published work by Jay Neugeboren and Curt Leviant. Short stories with strong plots and positive Jewish values. Length: 1,500-2,000 words.

HOW TO CONTACT Responds in 4 months to mss. Sample copy and writer's guidelines for 9×12 SASE. Stories can also be e-mailed to lbarnea@hadassah.org.

PAYMENT/TERMS Pays $700 minimum. Pays on acceptance for first North American serial, first rights. Pays $500 minimum

TIPS "Stories on a Jewish theme should be neither self-hating nor schmaltzy."

🌑 HAIGHT ASHBURY LITERARY JOURNAL

558 Joost Ave., San Francisco CA 94127. (415)584-8264. **E-mail:** haljeditor@gmail.com. **Website:** haightashburyliteraryjournal.wordpress.com; www.facebook.com/pages/Haight-Ashbury-Literary-Journal/365542018331. **Contact:** Alice Rogoff and Cesar Love, editors. Estab. 1979. *Haight Ashbury Literary*

Journal, publishes "well-written poetry and fiction. *HALJ*'s voices are often of people who have been marginalized, oppressed, or abused. *HALJ* strives to bring literary arts to the general public, to the San Francisco community of writers, to the Haight Ashbury neighborhood, and to people of varying ages, genders, ethnicities, and sexual preferences. The Journal is produced as a tabloid to maintain an accessible price for low-income people."

NEEDS Submit 1-3 short stories or 1 long story. Submit only once every 6 months. No e-mail submissions (unless overseas); postal submissions only. "Put name and address on every page, and include SASE. No bio." Sometimes publishes theme issues (each issue changes its theme and emphasis).

HARDBOILED

Gryphon Publications, P.O. Box 280209, Brooklyn NY 11228. **E-mail:** gryphonbooks@att.net. **Website:** www.gryphonbooks.com. **Contact:** Gary Lovisi, editor. Estab. 1988. "Hard-hitting crime fiction and private-eye stories—the newest and most cutting-edge work and classic reprints."

○   *Hardboiled*, published 1-2 times/year, is 100 pages with color cover.

NEEDS "No pastiches, violence for the sake of violence." Length: 500-3,000 words.

HOW TO CONTACT Query or send complete ms.

PAYMENT/TERMS Pays $5-50.

TIPS "Your best bet for breaking in is short hardcrime fiction filled with authenticity and brevity. Try a subscription to *Hardboiled* to get the perfect idea of what we are after."

HARPER'S MAGAZINE

666 Broadway, 11th Floor, New York NY 10012. (212)420-5720. **Fax:** (212)228-5889. **E-mail:** readings@harpers.org; scg@harpers.org. **Website:** www.harpers.org. **Contact:** Ellen Rosenbush, editor. Estab. 1850. *Harper's Magazine* encourages national discussion on current and significant issues in a format that offers arresting facts and intelligent opinions. By means of its several shorter journalistic forms—Harper's Index, Readings, Forum, and Annotation—as well as with its acclaimed essays, fiction, and reporting, *Harper's* continues the tradition begun with its first issue in 1850: to inform readers across the whole spectrum of political, literary, cultural, and scientific affairs.

○   *Harper's Magazine* will neither consider nor return unsolicited nonfiction mss that have not been preceded by a written query. *Harper's* will consider unsolicited fiction. Unsolicited poetry will not be considered or returned. No queries or mss will be considered unless they are accompanied by a SASE. All submissions and written queries (with the exception of Readings submissions) must be sent by mail to above address.

NEEDS Will consider unsolicited fiction. Has published work by Rebecca Curtis, George Saunders, Haruki Murakami, Margaret Atwood, Allan Gurganus, Evan Connell, and Dave Bezmosgis. Length: 3,000-5,000 words.

HOW TO CONTACT Submit complete ms by postal mail.

PAYMENT/TERMS Generally pays 50¢-$1/word.

TIPS "Some readers expect their magazines to clothe them with opinions in the way that Bloomingdale's dresses them for the opera. The readers of *Harper's Magazine* belong to a different crowd. They strike me as the kind of people who would rather think in their own voices and come to their own conclusions."

HARPUR PALATE

English Department, P.O. Box 6000, Binghamton University, Binghamton NY 13902-6000. **E-mail:** harpur.palate@gmail.com. **Website:** harpurpalate.blogspot.com. **Contact:** Melanie J. Cordova, editor. Estab. 2000. *Harpur Palate*, published biannually, is "dedicated to publishing the best poetry and prose, regardless of style, form, or genre. We have no restrictions on subject matter or form. Quite simply, send us your highest-quality fiction and poetry."

○   Submission periods are September 1-November 15 for the Winter issue and February 1-April 15 for the Summer issue.

NEEDS Receives 400 unsolicited mss/month. Accepts 5-10 mss/issue; 12-20 mss/year. Publishes ms 1-2 months after acceptance. Publishes 5 new writers/year. Has published work by Darryl Crawford and Tim Hedges, Jesse Goolsby, Ivan Faute, and Keith Meatto. Length: 250-6,000 words. Average length: 2,000-4,000 words.

HOW TO CONTACT Send complete ms with a cover letter. Include e-mail address on cover letter. Include estimated word count, brief bio, list of publications. Send a disposable copy of ms and #10 SASE for reply only. No more than 1 submission per envelope.

PAYMENT/TERMS Pays 2 contributor copies.

TIPS "We are interested in high-quality writing of all genres but especially literary poetry and fiction. We also sponsor a fiction contest for the Summer issue and a poetry and nonfiction contest for the Winter issue with $500 prizes."

HARVARD REVIEW

Houghton Library of the Harvard College Library, Lamont Library, Harvard University, Cambridge MA 02138. (617)495-9775. **Fax:** (617)496-3692. **E-mail:** info@harvardreview.org. **Website:** harvardreview.fas.harvard.edu. **Contact:** Christina Thompson, editor; Suzanne Berne, fiction editor; Major Jackson, poetry editor. Estab. 1992. Semiannual magazine covering poetry, fiction, essays, drama, graphics, and reviews in the spring and fall by an eclectic range of international writers. "Previous contributors include John Updike, Alice Hoffman, Joyce Carol Oates, Miranda July, and Jim Crace. We also publish the work of emerging and previously unpublished writers."

◯ Does not accept e-mail submissions. Reading period: September 1-May 31.

NEEDS Length: up to 7,000 words.

HOW TO CONTACT Submit using online submissions manager or by mail.

TIPS "Writers at all stages of their careers are invited to apply, however, we can only publish a very small fraction of the material we receive. We recommend that you familiarize yourself with *Harvard Review* before you submit your work."

◍ HAWAI'I PACIFIC REVIEW

1060 Bishop St., Honolulu HI 96813. (808)544-1108. **Fax:** (808)544-0862. **Website:** hawaiipacificreview.org. **Contact:** Tyler McMahon, editor; Bianca Flores, managing editor. Estab. 1987. "*Hawai'i Pacific Review* is the online literary magazine of Hawai'i Pacific University. It features poetry and prose by authors from Hawai'i, the mainland, and around the world. *HPR* was started as a print annual in 1987. In 2013, it began to publish exclusively online. *HPR* publishes work on a rolling basis. Poems, stories, and essays are posted one piece at a time, several times a month. All contents are archived on the site."

NEEDS Prefers literary work to genre work. Length: up to 6,000 words.

HOW TO CONTACT Submit 1 ms via online submissions manager.

TIPS "We look for the unusual or original plot; prose with the texture and nuance of poetry. Character development or portrayal must be unusual/original; humanity shown in an original insightful way (or characters); sense of humor where applicable. Be sure it's a draft that has gone through substantial changes, with supervision from a more experienced writer, if you're a beginner. Write about intense emotion and feeling, not just about someone's divorce or shaky relationship. No soap-opera-like fiction."

HAWAII REVIEW

University of Hawaii Board of Publications, 2445 Campus Rd., Hemenway Hall 107, Honolulu HI 96822. (808)956-3030. **Fax:** (808)956-3083. **E-mail:** hawaiireview@gmail.com. **Website:** www.kaleo.org/hawaii_review. Estab. 1973. *Hawai'i Review* is a student run biannual literary and visual arts print journal featuring national and international writing and visual art, as well as regional literature and visual art of Hawai'i and the Pacific.

◯ Accepts submissions online through Submittable only. Offers yearly award with $500 prizes in poetry and fiction.

NEEDS Length: up to 7,000 words for short stories, up to 2,500 words for flash fiction.

HOW TO CONTACT Send 1 short story or 2 pieces of flash fiction via online submission manager.

TIPS "Make it new."

◍◍◍ HAYDEN'S FERRY REVIEW

c/o Dept. of English,, Arizona State University, P.O. Box 870302, Tempe AZ 85287. **E-mail:** hfr@asu.edu. **Website:** www.haydensferryreview.org. **Contact:** Editorial staff changes every year; see website for current masthead. Estab. 1986. "*Hayden's Ferry Review* publishes the best quality fiction, poetry, and creative nonfiction from new, emerging, and established writers."

◯ Work from *Hayden's Ferry Review* has been selected for inclusion in *Pushcart Prize* anthologies and *Best Creative Nonfiction*. No longer accepts postal mail submissions.

NEEDS Word length open, but typically does not accept submissions over 25 pages.

HOW TO CONTACT Send complete ms via online submissions manager.

PAYMENT/TERMS Pays 2 contributor's copies and one-year subscription.

◍◍ THE HELIX

Central Connecticut State University English Dept., **E-mail:** helixmagazine@gmail.com. **Website:** helixmagazine.org. **Contact:** See masthead online for current editorial staff. "*The Helix* is a Central Connecticut State University publication, and it puts out an issue every semester. It accepts submissions from all over the globe. The magazine features writing from CCSU students, writing from the Hartford County community, and an array of submissions from all over the world. The magazine publishes multiple genres of literature and art including: poetry, fiction, drama, nonfiction, paintings, photography, watercolor, collage, stencil, and computer-generated artwork. It is a student-run publication, and is funded by the university."

NEEDS Length: up to 3,000 words.

HOW TO CONTACT Submit complete ms by online submissions manager.

TIPS "Please see our website for specific deadlines, as it changes every semester based on a variety of factors, but we typically leave the submission manager open sometime starting in the summer to around the end of October for the Fall issue, and during the winter to late February or mid-March for the Spring issue. Contributions are invited from all members of the campus community, as well as the literary community at large."

HELLOHORROR

Houston TX **E-mail:** info@hellohorror.com. **E-mail:** submissions@hellohorror.com. **Website:** www.hellohorror.com. **Contact:** Brent Armour, editor in chief. Estab. 2012. "*HelloHorror* is an online literary magazine and blog. We are currently in search of literary pieces, photography, and visual art including film from writers and artists that have a special knack for inducing goose bumps and raised hairs. This genre has become, especially in film, noticeably saturated in gore and high shock-value aspects as a crutch to avoid the true challenge of bringing about real, psychological fear to an audience that's persistently more and more numb to its tactics. While we are not opposed to the extreme, blood and guts need bones and cartilage. Otherwise it's just a sloppy mess."

NEEDS "We don't want fiction that can in no way be classified as horror. Some types of dark science fiction are acceptable, depending on the story." Length: 6-8 pages for short stories; up to 1,000 words for flash fiction.

HOW TO CONTACT Submit complete ms via e-mail.

TIPS "We like authors that show consideration for their readers. A great horror story leaves an impression on the reader long after it is finished. The motivation behind creating the site was the current satura-

tion of gore and shock-value horror. A story that gives you goosebumps is a much greater achievement than a story that just grosses you out. We have television for that. Consider your reader and consider yourself. What really scares you as opposed to what's stereotypically supposed to scare you? Bring us and our readers into that place of fear with you."

HOBART

P.O. Box 1658, Ann Arbor MI 48103. **E-mail:** aaron@hobartpulp.com. **Website:** www.hobartpulp.com. **Contact:** Aaron Burch, editor. Also accepts comics submissions; see online examples. "We tend to like quirky stories like truck driving, mathematics, and vagabonding. We like stories with humor (humorous but engaging, literary but not stuffy). We want to get excited about your story and hope you'll send your best work."

All submissions must go through online submissions manager. Only accepting submissions for online journal.

NEEDS "We publish nonstuffy, unpretentious, high-quality fiction that never takes itself too serious and always entertains." Also publishes erotica. Length: up to 2,000 words; prefers submissions of about 1,000 words.

HOW TO CONTACT Submit complete ms via online submissions manager.

TIPS "We'd love to receive fewer run-of-the-mill relationship stories and more stories concerning truck drivers, lumberjacks, carnival workers, and gunslingers. In other words: surprise us. Show us a side of life rarely depicted in literary fiction."

HOME PLANET NEWS

P.O. Box 455, High Falls NY 12440. (845)687-4084. **E-mail:** homeplanetnews@gmail.com. **Website:** www.homeplanetnews.org. **Contact:** Donald Lev, editor. Estab. 1979. Triannual. *Home Planet News* publishes mainly poetry along with some fiction, as well as reviews (books, theater, and art) and articles of literary interest.

HPN has received a small grant from the Puffin Foundation for its focus on AIDS issues. Receives 12 unsolicited mss/month. Accepts 1 mss/issue; 3 mss/year. Has published work by Hugh Fox, Walter Jackman, and Jim Story. "Our spin-off publication, *Home Planet News Online*, can be found at homeplanetnews.org/AOnLine.html. We urge everyone to check it out."

NEEDS No children's or genre stories (except rarely some science fiction). Length: 500-2,500 words; average length: 2,000 words.

HOW TO CONTACT Send complete ms. Send SASE for reply, return of ms, or send a disposable copy of the ms. Publishes special fiction issue or anthology.

PAYMENT/TERMS Pays 3 contributor's copies; additional copies $1.

TIPS "We use very little fiction, and a story we accept just has to grab us. We need short pieces of some complexity, stories about complex people facing situations which resist simple resolutions."

HOMESTEAD REVIEW

Box A-5, 156 Homestead Ave., Hartnell College, Salinas CA 93901. (831)755-6700. **E-mail:** thehomesteadreview@gmail.com. **Website:** old-www.hartnell.edu/homestead_review/. Estab. 1985. *Homestead Review* is published twice a year by the Department of Language Arts, Hartnell College. The spring issue is published in both print and online versions. The fall issue is published online only.

Reading Period: February 1-June 1 for online fall issue, September 1-December 1 for spring online/print issue.

NEEDS Length: 1,000 words or less.

HOW TO CONTACT Submit short fiction via e-mail. Include a biographical sketch, e-mail, and mailing addresses.

HORIZONS

100 Witherspoon St., Louisville KY 40202-1396. (844)797-2872. **E-mail:** yvonne.hileman@pcusa.org. **Website:** www.pcusa.org/horizons. **Contact:** Yvonne Hileman, assistant editor. Estab. 1988. *Horizons* magazine provides information, inspiration, and education from the perspectives of women who are committed to Christ, the church and faithful discipleship. *Horizons* brings current issues dealing with family life, the mission of the church and the challenges of culture and society to its readers. Interviews, feature articles, Bible study resources, and departments offer help and insight for up-to-date, day-to-day concerns of the church and individual Christians.

NEEDS Length: 600-1,800 words.

HOW TO CONTACT Submit queries and/or complete ms by mail, e-mail, or fax. Include contact information.

PAYMENT/TERMS Pays an honorarium of no less than $50 per page printed in the magazine—amount will vary depending on time and research required for writing the article.

HOTEL AMERIKA

Columbia College, English Department, 600 S. Michigan Ave., Chicago IL 60605. (312)369-8175. **E-mail:** editors@hotelamerika.net. **Website:** www.hotelamerika.net. **Contact:** David Lazar, editor; Adam McOmber, managing editor. Estab. 2002. *Hotel Amerika* is a venue for both well-known and emerging writers. Publishes exceptional writing in all forms. Strives to house the most unique and provocative poetry, fiction, and nonfiction available.

Mss will be considered between September 1 and May 1. Materials received after May 1 and before September 1 will be returned unread. Send submissions only via mail, with SASE. Work published in *Hotel Amerika* has been included in *The Pushcart Prize* and *The Best American Poetry* and featured on *Poetry Daily*.

NEEDS Welcomes submissions in all genres of creative writing, generously defined. Does not publish book reviews as such, although considers review-like essays that transcend the specific objects of consideration.

THE HUDSON REVIEW

The Hudson Review, Inc., 684 Park Ave., New York NY 10065. (212)650-0020. **E-mail:** info@hudsonreview.com. **Website:** hudsonreview.com. **Contact:** Paula Deitz, editor. Estab. 1948.

Send with SASE. Mss sent outside accepted reading period will be returned unread if SASE contains sufficient postage.

NEEDS Length: up to 10,000 words.

HOW TO CONTACT Send complete ms by postal mail between **September 1-November 30** only.

TIPS "We do not specialize in publishing any particular 'type' of writing; our sole criterion for accepting unsolicited work is literary quality. The best way for you to get an idea of the range of work we publish is to read a current issue. Unsolicited mss submitted outside of specified reading times will be returned unread. Do not send submissions via e-mail."

HUNGER MOUNTAIN

Vermont College of Fine Arts, 36 College St., Montpelier VT 05602. (802)828-8517. **E-mail:** hungermtn@vcfa.edu. **Website:** www.hungermtn.org. **Contact:** Miciah Bay Gault, editor. Estab. 2002. Accepts high-quality work from unknown, emerging, or successful writers. No genre fiction, drama, or academic articles, please.

○ *Hunger Mountain* is about 200 pages, 7x10, professionally printed, perfect-bound, with full-bleed color artwork on cover. Press run is 1,000; 10,000 visits online monthly. Uses online submissions manager. Member: CLMP.

NEEDS "We look for work that is beautifully crafted and tells a good story, with characters that are alive and kicking, storylines that stay with us long after we've finished reading, and sentences that slay us with their precision." No genre fiction, meaning science fiction, fantasy, horror, erotica, etc. Length: up to 10,000 words.

HOW TO CONTACT Submit ms using online submissions manager.

PAYMENT/TERMS Pays $25-100.

TIPS "Mss must be typed, prose double-spaced. Poets submit at least 3 poems. No multiple genre submissions. Fresh viewpoints and human interest are very important, as is originality. We are committed to publishing an outstanding journal of the arts. Do not send entire novels, mss, or short story collections. Do not send previously published work."

I-70 REVIEW

Writing From the Middle and Beyond, 913 Joseph Dr., Lawrence KS 66044. **E-mail:** i70review@gmail.com. **Website:** www.fieldinfoserv.com. **Contact:** Gary Lechliter, editor; Maryfrances Wagner, editor; Greg Field, editor; Jan Duncan-O'Neal, editor. Estab. 1998. *I-70 Review* is an annual literary magazine. "Our interests lie in writing grounded in fresh language, imagery, and metaphor. We prefer free verse in which the writer pays attention to the sound and rhythm of the language. We appreciate poetry with individual voice and a good lyric or a strong narrative. In fiction, we like short pieces that are surprising and uncommon. We want writing that captures the human spirit with unusual topics or familiar topics with different perspective or approaches. We reject stereotypical and clichéd writing, as well as sentimental work or writing that summarizes and tells instead of shows. We look for writing that pays attention to wrds, sentences, and style. We publish literary writing. We do not publish anything erotic, religious, or political." All submissions should be typed and submitted in a single document via e-mail. See website for complete guidelines. Open submission period is July 1-December 1.

NEEDS Rejects anything over 1,000 words, unless solicited. Not interested in anything political, religious, spiritual, didactic, or erotic. Accepts mainly flash fiction and very short literary fiction. Pays in contributor copies.

ⓘⓈ ICONOCLAST

1675 Amazon Rd., Mohegan Lake NY 10547-1804. **Website:** www.iconoclastliterarymagazine.com. **Contact:** Phil Wagner, editor and publisher. Estab. 1992. *Iconoclast Magazine* seeks and chooses the best new writing and poetry available—of all genres and styles and entertainment levels. Its mission is to provide a serious publishing opportunity for unheralded, unknown but deserving creators, whose work is often overlooked or trampled in the commercial, university, or Internet marketplace.

NEEDS "Subjects and styles are completely open (within the standards of generally accepted taste—though exceptions, as always, can be made for unique and visionary works)." No slice-of-life stories, stories containing alcoholism, incest, and domestic or public violence. Accepts most genres, "with the exception of mysteries."

HOW TO CONTACT Submit by postal mail; include SASE. Cover letter not necessary.

PAYMENT/TERMS Pays 1¢/word and 2 contributor's copies. Contributors get 40% discount on extra copies.

TIPS "Please don't send preliminary drafts—rewriting is half the job. If you're not sure about the story, don't truly believe in it, or are unenthusiastic about the subject (we will not recycle your term papers or thesis), then don't send it. This is not a lottery (luck has nothing to do with it)."

ⓘⓆⓈ THE IDAHO REVIEW

Dept. of English, Boise State University, 1910 University Dr., Boise ID 83725. (208)426-1002. **Fax:** (208)426-4373. **E-mail:** idahoreview@boisestate.edu; mwieland@boisestate.edu. **Website:** idahoreview.org. **Contact:** Mitch Wieland, editor. Estab. 1998. *The Idaho Review* is the literary journal of Boise State University.

○ Recent stories reprinted in *The Best American Short Stories, The O. Henry Prize Stories, The Pushcart Prize,* and *New Stories from The South.*

NEEDS No genre fiction of any type.

HOW TO CONTACT Prefers submissions using online submissions manager, but will accept submissions by postal mail.

PAYMENT/TERMS Pays $100 per story and contributor's copies.

TIPS "We look for strongly crafted work that tells a story that needs to be told. We demand vision and intelligence and mystery in the fiction we publish."

○○⊙ IDEOMANCER

Canada. **E-mail:** query@ideomancer.com. **Website:** www.ideomancer.com. **Contact:** Leah Bobet, publisher and editor. Estab. 2001. "*Ideomancer* publishes speculative fiction and poetry that explores the edges of ideas; stories that subvert, refute, and push the limits. We want unique pieces from authors willing to explore nontraditional narratives and take chances with tone, structure, and execution, balance ideas and character, emotion, and ruthlessness. We also have an eye for more traditional tales told with excellence."

○ Quarterly online magazine. Contains illustrations. Does not read February, May, August, and November.

NEEDS Has published Sarah Monette, Ruth Nestvold, Christopher Barzak, Nicole Kornher-Stace, Tobias Buckell, Yoon Ha Lee, and David Kopaska-Merkel. Also publishes book reviews, poetry. *Requests only* to have a novel or collection reviewed should be sent to the reviews editor. (reviews@ideomancer.com). Does not want fiction without a speculative element. Length: up to 7,000 words. Average length: 4,000 words. Publishes short shorts. Average length of short shorts: 1,000 words.

HOW TO CONTACT Submit by e-mail to fiction@ideomancer.com; .RTF attachment only. Include cover letter with name, story title, genre, and word count.

PAYMENT/TERMS Pays 3¢/word, maximum of $40.

TIPS "Beyond the basics of formatting the fiction as per our guidelines, good writing and intriguing characters and plot, where the writer brings depth to the tale, make a ms stand out. We receive a number of submissions that showcase good writing but lack the details that make them spring to life for us. Visit our website and read some of our fiction to see if we're a good fit. Read our submission guidelines carefully and use .RTF formatting as requested. We're far more interested in your story than your cover letter, so spend your time polishing that."

●○ IDIOM 23

Central Queensland University, Idiom 23 Literary Magazine, Rockhampton QLD 4702 Australia. **E-mail:** idiom@cqu.edu.au. **Website:** www.cqu.edu.au/idi-

om23. **Contact:** *Idiom 23* editorial board. Estab. 1988. *Idiom 23*, published annually, is "named for the Tropic of Capricorn and is dedicated to developing the literary arts throughout the Central Queensland region. Submissions of original short stories, poems, articles, and b&w drawings and photographs are welcomed by the editorial collective. *Idiom 23* is not limited to a particular viewpoint but, on the contrary, hopes to encourage and publish a broad spectrum of writing. The collective seeks out creative work from community groups with as varied backgrounds as possible."

● ILLUMINATIONS

Dept. of English, College of Charleston, 66 George St., Charleston SC 29424-0001. (843)953-4972. **E-mail:** illuminations@cofc.edu. **Website:** illuminations.cofc.edu. **Contact:** Simon Lewis, editor. Estab. 1982. "Over these many years *Illuminations* has remained consistently true to its mission statement to publish new writers alongside some of the world's finest, including Nadine Gordimer, James Merrill, Carol Ann Duffy, Dennis Brutus, Allen Tate, interviews with Tim O'Brien, and letters from Flannery O'Connor and Ezra Pound. A number of new poets whose early work appeared in *Illuminations* have gone on to win prizes and accolades, and we at *Illuminations* sincerely value the chance to promote the work of emerging writers."

HOW TO CONTACT Send SASE for reply, return of ms, or send a disposable copy of ms.

PAYMENT/TERMS Pays 2 contributor's copies of current issue; 1 of subsequent issue.

○ ILLYA'S HONEY

E-mail: dpcer09@gmail.com. **Website:** www.illyas-honey.com. Estab. 1994. *Illya's Honey* is the online literary journal of the Dallas Poet's Community. Its main purpose has always been to publish well-crafted poetry using the best electronic means available.

○ Online magazine published in January, April, July, and October.

●⊙ IMAGE

3307 Third Ave. W., Seattle WA 98119. (206)281-2988. **Fax:** (206)281-2979. **E-mail:** image@imagejournal.org. **Website:** www.imagejournal.org. **Contact:** Gregory Wolfe, publisher and editor in chief. Estab. 1989. "*Image* is a unique forum for the best writing and artwork that is informed by—or grapples with—religious faith. We have never been interested in art that merely regurgitates dogma or falls back on easy answers or didacticism. Instead, our focus has been on writing and visual artwork that embody a spiritual struggle, that seek to strike a balance between tradition and a profound openness to the world. Each issue explores this relationship through outstanding fiction, poetry, painting, sculpture, architecture, film, music, interviews, and dance. *Image* also features 4-color reproductions of visual art."

○ Magazine: 7×10; 136 pages; glossy cover stock; illustrations; photos.

NEEDS "No sentimental, preachy, moralistic, obvious stories, or genre stories (unless they manage to transcend their genre)." Length: up to 6,000 words.

HOW TO CONTACT Send complete ms. Send SASE for reply, return of ms, or send disposable copy of ms. Does not accept e-mail submissions.

PAYMENT/TERMS Pays $10/page ($150 maximum) and 4 contributor's copies.

TIPS "Fiction must grapple with religious faith, though subjects need not be overtly religious."

INDIANA REVIEW

Ballantine Hall 465, 1020 E. Kirkwood, Indiana University, Bloomington IN 47405. (812)855-3439. **E-mail:** inreview@indiana.edu. **Website:** indianareview.org. **Contact:** Britt Ashley, editor; Justin Wolfe, nonfiction editor; Joe Hiland, fiction editor; Michael Mlekoday, poetry editor. Estab. 1976. "*Indiana Review*, a nonprofit organization run by IU graduate students, is a journal of previously unpublished poetry and fiction. Literary interviews and essays are also considered. We publish innovative fiction, nonfiction, and poetry. We're interested in energy, originality, and careful attention to craft. While we publish many well-known writers, we also welcome new and emerging poets and fiction writers."

NEEDS "We look for daring stories which integrate theme, language, character, and form. We like polished writing, humor, and fiction which has consequence beyond the world of its narrator." No genre fiction. Length: up to 8,000 words.

HOW TO CONTACT Submit via online submissions manager.

PAYMENT/TERMS Pays $5/page ($10 minimum), plus 2 contributor's copies

TIPS "We're always looking for nonfiction essays that go beyond merely autobiographical revelation and utilize sophisticated organization and slightly radical narrative strategies. We want essays that are both lyrical and analytical where confession does not mean nostalgia. Read us before you submit. Often reading is slower in summer and holiday months. Only submit work to journals you would proudly subscribe to, then subscribe to a few. Take care to read the latest 2 issues and specifically mention work you identify with and why. Submit work that 'stacks up' with the work we've published. Offers annual poetry, fiction, short short/prose poem prizes. See website for full guidelines."

INTERNATIONAL EXAMINER

622 S. Washington St., Seattle WA 98104. (206)624-3925. **Fax:** (206)624-3046. **E-mail:** editor@iexaminer. org. **Website:** www.iexaminer.org. **Contact:** Travis Quezon, editor in chief. Estab. 1974. "*International Examiner* is about Asian American issues and things of interest to Asian Americans. We do not want stuff about Asian things (stories on your trip to China, Japanese Tea Ceremony, etc. will be rejected). Yes, we are in English."

NEEDS Asian American authored fiction by or about Asian Americans only.

HOW TO CONTACT Query.

TIPS "Write decent, suitable material on a subject of interest to the Asian American community. All submissions are reviewed; all good ones are contacted. It helps to call and run an idea by the editor before or after sending submissions."

THE IOWA REVIEW

308 EPB, The University of Iowa, Iowa City IA 52242. (319)335-0462. **Website:** www.iowareview.org. **Contact:** Harilaos Stecopoulos. Estab. 1970. *The Iowa Review*, published 3 times/year, prints fiction, poetry, essays, reviews, and, occasionally, interviews. Receives about 5,000 submissions/year, accepts up to 100. Press run is 2,900; 1,500 distributed to stores. Subscription: $25. Stories, essays, and poems for a general readership interested in contemporary literature.

○ This magazine uses the help of colleagues and graduate assistants. Its reading period for unsolicited work is September 1-December 1. From January through April, they read entries to their annual Iowa Awards competition. Check the website for further information.

NEEDS "We are open to a range of styles and voices and always hope to be surprised by work we then feel we need." Receives 600 unsolicited mss/month. Accepts 4-6 mss/issue; 12-18 mss/year. Does not read mss January-August. Publishes ms an average of 12-18 months after acceptance. Agented fiction less than 2%. **Publishes some new writers/year.** Recently published work by Johanna Hunting, Bennett Sims, and Pedro Mairal.

HOW TO CONTACT Send complete ms with cover letter. "Don't bother with queries." SASE for return of ms. SASE required. Accepts mss by snail mail and online submission form at https://iowareview.submittable.com/submit; no e-mail submissions.

PAYMENT/TERMS Pays 8¢ per word ($100 minimum), plus 2 contributor's copies.

TIPS "We publish essays, reviews, novel excerpts, stories, poems, and photography. We have no set guidelines as to content or length but strongly recommend that writers read a sample issue before submitting."

ISLAND

P.O. Box 4703, Bathurst St. Post Office, Hobart Tasmania 7000 Australia. **E-mail:** matthew@island-mag.com. **Website:** www.islandmag.com. **Contact:** Matthew Lamb, editorial director and features editor. Estab. 1979. *Island* seeks quality fiction, poetry, and essays. It is "one of Australia's leading literary magazines, tracing the contours of our national, and international culture, while still retaining a uniquely Tasmanian perspective."

Only publishes the work of subscribers; you can submit if you are not currently a subscriber, but if your piece is chosen, the subscription will be taken from the fee paid for the piece.

HOW TO CONTACT Submit 1 piece at a time.
PAYMENT/TERMS Pay varies.

ITALIAN AMERICANA

University of Rhode Island, Alan Shawn Feinstein College of Continuing Education, 80 Washington St., Providence RI 02903. (401)277-5306. **Fax:** (401)277-5100. **E-mail:** it.americana@yahoo.com. **Website:** www.uri.edu/prov/research/italianamericana/italianamericana.html. **Contact:** Carol Bonomo Albright, editor in chief. Estab. 1974. A semi-annual historical and cultural journal devoted to the Italian experience in America. *Italian Americana*, in cooperation with the American Italian Historical Association, is the first and only cultural as well as historical review dedicated to the Italian experience in the New World.

Offers annual prizes: $1,000 John Ciardi Poetry Prize, $500 Massaro Prize for the best critical essay, $250 Bruno Arcudi Short Fiction Award, and $250 A. William Salamone History Award. See website for details.

NEEDS Does not want nostalgia. Length: up to 20 pages double-spaced.

HOW TO CONTACT Send complete ms (in triplicate) with SASE and cover letter. Include 3-5 line bio, list of publications.

PAYMENT/TERMS Pays in contributor's copies.

JABBERWOCK REVIEW

Department of English, Mississippi State University, Drawer E, Mississippi State MS 39762. **E-mail:** jabberwockreview@english.msstate.edu. **Website:** www.jabberwockreview.org.msstate.edu. **Contact:** Becky Hagenston, editor. Estab. 1979. "*Jabberwock Review* is a literary journal published semi-annually by students and faculty of Mississippi State University. The journal consists of art, poetry, fiction, and nonfiction from around the world. Funding is provided by the Office of the Provost, the College of Arts & Sciences, the Shackouls Honors College, the Department of English, fundraisers, and subscriptions."

Submissions will be accepted from August 15-October 20 and January 15-March 15.

NEEDS No science fiction or romance.

HOW TO CONTACT Submit no more than 1 story at a time.

PAYMENT/TERMS Pays in contributor's copies.

TIPS "It might take a few months to get a response from us, but your ms will be read with care. Our editors enjoy reading submissions (really!) and will remember writers who are persistent and committed to getting a story 'right' through revision."

JEWISH CURRENTS

P.O. Box 111, Accord NY 12404. (845)626-2427. **E-mail:** editor@jewishcurrents.org. **Website:** www.jewishcurrents.org. Estab. 1946. *Jewish Currents*, published 4 times/year, is a progressive Jewish bimonthly magazine that carries on the insurgent tradition of the Jewish left through independent journalism, political commentary, and a "countercultural" approach to Jewish arts and literature.

Jewish Currents is 80 pages, magazine-sized, offset-printed, saddle-stapled with a full-color arts section, "Jcultcha & Funny Pages." "Our Winter issue is a 12-month arts calendar."

HOW TO CONTACT Send complete ms with cover letter. "Writers should include brief biographical information."

PAYMENT/TERMS Pays contributor's copies or small honoraria.

🌑❸ JEWISH WOMEN'S LITERARY ANNUAL

Eleanor Leff Jewish Women's Resource Center, 241 W. 72nd St., New York NY 10023. (212)687-5030. **E-mail:** info@ncjwny.org. **Website:** www.ncjwny.org/services_annual.htm. **Contact:** Henny Wenkart, editor. Estab. 1994. *Jewish Women's Literary Annual*, published in April, prints poetry, fiction, and creative nonfiction by Jewish women.

🌑 *Jewish Women's Literary Annual* is 230 pages, digest-sized, perfect-bound, with laminated card cover. Press run is 1,500.

HOW TO CONTACT Submit complete ms by postal mail.

TIPS "Send only your very best. We are looking for humor, as well as other things, but nothing cutesy or smart-aleck. We do no politics and prefer topics other than 'Holocaust'."

🌑 J JOURNAL: NEW WRITING ON JUSTICE

524 West 59th St., 7th Floor, New York NY 10019. (212)237-9697. **E-mail:** jjournal@jjay.cuny.edu. **Website:** www.jjournal.org. **Contact:** Adam Berlin and Jeffrey Heiman, editors. Estab. 2008. "*J Journal* publishes literary fiction, creative nonfiction, and poetry on the justice theme. Subjects often include crime, criminal justice, law, law enforcement, and prison writing. While the theme is specific, it need not dominate the work. We're interested in questions of justice from all perspectives. Tangential connections to justice are often better than direct."

NEEDS Receives 100 mss/month. Accepts 20 mss/issue; 40 mss/year. Length: 750-6,000 words. Average length: 4,000 words.

HOW TO CONTACT Send complete ms with cover letter. Include estimated word count, brief bio, list of publications.

PAYMENT/TERMS Writers receive 2 contributor's copies. Additional copies $10.

TIPS "We're looking for literary fiction/memoir/personal narrative poetry with a connection, direct or tangential, to the theme of justice."

🌑❸ THE JOURNAL

The Ohio State University, 164 W. 17th Ave., Columbus OH 43210. (614)292-6065. **Fax:** (614)292-7816. **E-mail:** managingeditor@thejournalmag.org. **Website:** thejournalmag.org. Estab. 1973. "We are interested in quality fiction, poetry, nonfiction, art, and reviews of new books of poetry, fiction, and nonfiction. We impose no restrictions on category, type, or length of submission for fiction, poetry, and nonfiction. We are happy to consider long stories and self-contained excerpts of novels. Please double-space all prose submissions. Please send 3-5 poems in 1 submission. We only accept online submissions and will not respond to mailed submissions."

🌑 "We're open to all forms; we tend to favor work that gives evidence of a mature and sophisticated sense of the language."

NEEDS No romance, science fiction, or religious/devotional.

HOW TO CONTACT Does not accept queries. Send full ms via online submission system at thejournal.submittable.com. "Mss are rejected because of lack of understanding of the short story form, shallow plots, undeveloped characters. Cure: Read as much well-written fiction as possible. Our readers prefer 'psychological' fiction rather than stories with intricate plots. Take care to present a clean, well-typed submission."

🌑 KAIMANA: LITERARY ARTS HAWAI'I

Hawai'i Literary Arts Council, P.O. Box 11213, Honolulu HI 96828. **E-mail:** reimersa001@hawaii.rr.com. **Website:** www.hawaii.edu/hlac. Estab. 1974. *Kaimana: Literary Arts Hawai'i*, published annually, is the magazine of the Hawai'i Literary Arts Council. Wants submissions with "some Pacific reference—Asia, Polynesia, Hawai'i—but not exclusively."

🌑 *Kaimana* is 64-76 pages, 7.5x10, saddle-stapled, with high-quality printing. Press run is 1,000. "Poets published in *Kaimana* have received the Pushcart Prize, the Hawaii Award for Literature, the Stefan Baciu Award, the Cades Award, and the John Unterecker Award."

HOW TO CONTACT Submit ms with SASE. No e-mail submissions. Cover letter is preferred.

PAYMENT/TERMS Pays 2 contributor's copies.

TIPS "Hawai'i gets a lot of 'travelling regionalists,' visiting writers with inevitably superficial observations. We also get superb visiting observers who are careful craftsmen anywhere. *Kaimana* is interested in the latter, to complement our own best Hawai'i writers."

🌑❷❸ KALEIDOSCOPE

Kaleidoscope, 701 S. Main St., Akron OH 44311-1019. (330)762-9755. **Fax:** (330)762-0912. **E-mail:** kaleidoscope@udsakron.org. **Website:** www.kaleidoscope-online.org. **Contact:** Gail Willmott, editor in chief. Estab. 1979. "*Kaleidoscope* magazine creatively focuses on the experiences of disability through literature and the fine arts. Unique to the field of disability studies, this award-winning publication expresses the diversity of the disablity experience from a variety of perspectives including: individuals, families, friends, caregivers, educators, and healthcare professionals, among others."

○ *Kaleidoscope* has received awards from the Great Lakes Awards Competition and Ohio Public Images; received the Ohioana Award of Editorial Excellence.

NEEDS Short stories with a well-crafted plot and engaging characters. No fiction that is stereotypical, patronizing, sentimental, erotic, or maudlin. No romance, religious or dogmatic fiction; no children's literature. Length: no more than 5,000 words. All rights revert to author upon publication.

HOW TO CONTACT Submit complete ms by website or e-mail. Include cover letter.

PAYMENT/TERMS Pays $10-100.

TIPS "The material chosen for *Kaleidoscope* challenges and overcomes stereotypical, patronizing, and sentimental attitudes about disability. We accept the work of writers with and without disabilities; however the work of a writer without a disability must focus on some aspect of disability. The criteria for good writing apply: effective technique, thought-provoking subject matter, and, in general, a mature grasp of the art of storytelling. Writers should avoid using offensive language and always put the person before the disability."

○○◎ THE KELSEY REVIEW

Liberal Arts Division, Mercer County Community College, P.O. Box 17202, Trenton NJ 08690. **E-mail:** kelsey.review@mccc.edu. **Website:** www.mccc.edu/community_kelsey-review.shtml. **Contact:** Ed Carmien. Estab. 1988. *The Kelsey Review*, published annually online in September by Mercer County Community College, serves as "an outlet for literary talent of people living and working in Mercer County, New Jersey only."

NEEDS Has no specifications as to form, subject matter, or style. Length: up to 4,000 words.

HOW TO CONTACT Deadline is May 15. Submissions are limited to people who live, work, or give literary readings in Mercer County, New Jersey. Decisions on which material will be published are made by the 4-person editorial board in June and July. Contributors will be notified of submission acceptance determination(s) by the second week of August.

TIPS "See *The Kelsey Review* website for current guidelines. Note: We only accept submissions from the Mercer County, New Jersey area."

○○⑤ THE KENYON REVIEW

Finn House, 102 W. Wiggin, Gambier OH 43022. (740)427-5208. **Fax:** (740)427-5417. **E-mail:** kenyonreview@kenyon.edu. **Website:** www.kenyonreview.org. **Contact:** Marlene Landefeld. Estab. 1939. "An international journal of literature, culture, and the arts, dedicated to an inclusive representation of the best in new writing (fiction, poetry, essays, interviews, criticism) from established and emerging writers."

○ *The Kenyon Review* receives about 8,000 submissions/year. Also now publishes *KR Online*, a separate and complementary literary magazine.

NEEDS Receives 800 unsolicited mss/month. Unsolicited mss read September 15-January 15 only. Recently published work by Alice Hoffman, Beth Ann Fennelly, Romulus Linney, John Koethe, Albert Goldbarth, Erin McGraw. Length: 3-15 typeset pages preferred.

HOW TO CONTACT Only accepts mss via online submissions program; visit website for instructions. Do not submit via e-mail or snail mail.

PAYMENT/TERMS Pays $30/page.

TIPS "We no longer accept mailed or e-mailed submissions. Work will only be read if it is submitted through our online program on our website. Reading period is September 15-January 15. We look for strong voice, unusual perspective, and power in the writing."

○◎⑤ LADY CHURCHILL'S ROSEBUD WRISTLET

150 Pleasant St., #306, Easthampton MA 01027. **E-mail:** smallbeerpress@gmail.com. **Website:** www.smallbeerpress.com/lcrw. **Contact:** Gavin Grant, editor. Estab. 1996. *Lady Churchill's Rosebud Wristlet* accepts fiction, nonfiction, poetry, and b&w art. "The fiction we publish tends toward, but is not limited to, the speculative. This does not mean only quietly desperate stories. We will consider items that fall out with regular categories. We do not accept multiple submissions."

○ Semiannual.

NEEDS Receives 100 unsolicited mss/month. Accepts 4-6 mss/issue; 8-12 mss/year. Publishes 2-4 new writers/year. Also publishes literary essays, poetry. Has published work by Ted Chiang, Gwenda Bond, Alissa Nutting, and Charlie Anders. "We do not publish gore, sword and sorcery, or pornography. We can discuss these terms if you like. There are places for them all; this is not one of them." Length: 200-7,000 words; average length: 3,500 words.

HOW TO CONTACT Send complete ms with a cover letter. Include estimated word count. Send SASE (or IRC) for return of ms, or send a disposable copy of ms and #10 SASE for reply only.

PAYMENT/TERMS Pays $25.

TIPS "We recommend you read *Lady Churchill's Rosebud Wristlet* before submitting. You can procure a copy from us or from assorted book shops."

🌑 LA KANCERKLINIKO

162 rue Paradis, P.O. Box 174, 13444 Marseille Cantini Cedex France. (33)2-48-61-81-98. **Fax:** (33)2-48-61-81-98. **E-mail:** lseptier@hotmail.com. **Contact:** Laurent Septier. An Esperanto magazine that appears 4 times annually. Each issue contains 32 pages. *La Kancerkliniko* is a political and cultural magazine. Accepts disk submissions.

🔘 Publishes 2-3 new writers/year. Has published work by Mao Zifu, Manuel de Seabra, Peter Brown. and Aldo de'Giorgi.

PAYMENT/TERMS Pays in contributor's copies.

🌓 LAKE EFFECT: A JOURNAL OF THE LITERARY ARTS

School of Humanities & Social Sciences, Penn State Erie, 4951 College Dr., Erie PA 16563-1501. (814)898-6281. **Fax:** (814)898-6032. **E-mail:** gol1@psu.edu. **Website:** www.pserie.psu.edu/lakeeffect. **Contact:** George Looney, editor in chief. Estab. 1978. *Lake Effect* is a publication of the School of Humanities and Social Sciences at Penn State Erie, The Behrend College.

NEEDS "*Lake Effect* is looking for stories that emerge from character and language as much as from plot. *Lake Effect* does not, in general, publish genre fiction, but literary fiction. *Lake Effect* seeks work from both established and new and emerging writers." Length: up to 15 pages, if longer, query first.

HOW TO CONTACT Submit complete ms with SASE.

🌗 LAKE SUPERIOR MAGAZINE

Lake Superior Port Cities, Inc., P.O. Box 16417, Duluth MN 55816-0417. (218)722-5002. **Fax:** (218)722-4096. E-mail: edit@lakesuperior.com. **Website:** www.lakesuperior.com. **Contact:** Konnie LeMay, editor. Estab. 1979.

NEEDS Must be targeted regionally. Wants stories that are Lake Superior related. Rarely uses fiction stories. Length: 300-2,500 words.

HOW TO CONTACT Query with published clips.

PAYMENT/TERMS Pays $50-125.

TIPS "Well-researched queries are attended to. We actively seek queries from writers in Lake Superior communities. We prefer mss to queries. Provide enough information on why the subject is important to the region and our readers, or why and how something is unique. We want details. The writer must have a thorough knowledge of the subject and how it relates to our region. We prefer a fresh, unused approach to the subject which provides the reader with an emotional involvement. Almost all of our articles feature quality photography, color or b&w. It is a prerequisite of all nonfiction. All submissions should include a *short* biography of author/photographer; mug shot sometimes used. Blanket submissions need not apply."

THE LAND

Free Press Co., P.O. Box 3169, Mankato MN 56002-3169. (507)345-4523. **E-mail:** editor@thelandonline.com. **Website:** www.thelandonline.com. Estab. 1976. "Although we're not tightly focused on any one type of farming, our articles must be of interest to farmers. In other words, will your article topic have an impact on people who live and work in rural areas? Prefers to work with Minnesota or Iowa writers."

TIPS "Be enthused about rural Minnesota and Iowa life and agriculture, and be willing to work with our editors. We try to stress relevance. When sending me a query, convince me the story belongs in a Minnesota farm publication."

🌑 LANDFALL: NEW ZEALAND ARTS AND LETTERS

Otago University Press, P.O. Box 56, Dunedin New Zealand. (64)(3)479-4155. **Fax:** (64)(3)479-8385. **E-mail:** landfall@otago.ac.nz. **Website:** www.otago.ac.nz/press/landfall. Estab. 1947. *Landfall: New Zealand Arts and Letters* contains literary fiction and essays, poetry, extracts from work in progress, commentary on New Zealand arts and culture, work by visual artists including photographers and reviews of local books. (*Landfall* does not accept unsolicited reviews.)

🔘 Deadlines for submissions: January 10 for the May issue, June 10 for the November issue.

NEEDS Length: up to 5,000 words.

HOW TO CONTACT Submit up to 3 pieces at a time. Prefers e-mail submissions. Include cover letter with contact info and bio of about 30 words.

◎⑨ LEADING EDGE

4087 JKB, Provo UT 84602. **E-mail:** editor@leadingedgemagazine.com; fiction@leadingedgemagazine.com; art@leadingedgemagazine.com. **Website:** www.leadingedgemagazine.com. **Contact:** Kenna Blaylock, editor in chief. Estab. 1981. "*Leading Edge* is a magazine dedicated to new and upcoming talent in the fields of science fiction and fantasy. We strive to encourage developing and established talent and provide high-quality speculative fiction to our readers." Does not accept mss with sex, excessive violence, or profanity.

◖　　Accepts unsolicited submissions.

NEEDS Length: 15,000 words maximum.

HOW TO CONTACT Send complete ms with cover letter and SASE. Include estimated word count.

PAYMENT/TERMS Pays 1¢/word; $10 minimum.

TIPS "Buy a sample issue to know what is currently selling in our magazine. Also, make sure to follow the writer's guidelines when submitting."

① LEFT CURVE

P.O. Box 472, Oakland CA 94604-0472. (510)763-7193. **E-mail:** editor@leftcurve.org. **Website:** www.leftcurve.org. **Contact:** Csaba Polony, editor. Estab. 1974. "*Left Curve* is an artist-produced journal addressing the problem(s) of cultural forms emerging from the crises of modernity that strive to be independent from the control of dominant institutions, based on the recognition of the destructiveness of commodity (capitalist) systems to all life." Published irregularly.

◖　　Magazine: 8.5×11; 144 pages; 60 lb. paper; 100 pt. C1S gloss layflat lamination cover; illustrations; photos. Receives 50 unsolicited mss/month. Accepts 3-4 mss/issue. Has published work by Mike Standaert, Ilan Pappe, Terrence Cannon, John Gist.

NEEDS "No topical satire, religion-based pieces, melodrama. We publish critical, open, social/political-conscious writing." Length: 500-5,000 words; average length: 2,500 words. Also publishes short shorts.

HOW TO CONTACT Send complete ms with cover letter. Include "statement of writer's intent, brief bio, and reason for submitting to *Left Curve*. We accept electronic submissions and hard copy, though for accepted work we request e-mail copy, either in body of text or as attachments. For accepted longer work,

we prefer submission of final draft in digital form via disk or e-mail."

PAYMENT/TERMS Pays in contributor's copies.

TIPS "We look for continuity, adequate descriptive passages, endings that are not simply abandoned (in both meanings). Dig deep; no superficial personalisms, no corny satire. Be honest, realistic, and gouge out the truth you wish to say. Understand yourself and the world. Have writing be a means to achieve or realize what is real."

◎⑨⑨ LIGUORIAN

One Liguori Dr., Liguori MO 63057. (636)223-1538. **Fax:** (636)223-1595. **E-mail:** liguorianeditor@liguori.org. **Website:** www.liguorian.org. **Contact:** Elizabeth Herzing, managing editor. Estab. 1913. "Our purpose is to lead our readers to a fuller Christian life by helping them better understand the teachings of the gospel and the church and by illustrating how these teachings apply to life and the problems confronting them as members of families, the church, and society."

NEEDS Length: 1,500-2,200 words.

HOW TO CONTACT Send complete ms.

PAYMENT/TERMS Pays 12-15¢/word and 5 contributor's copies.

TIPS "First read several issues containing short stories. We look for originality and creative input in each story we read. Consideration requires the author studies the target market and presents a carefully polished ms. We publish 1 fiction story per issue. Compare this with the 25 or more we receive over the transom each month. We believe fiction is a highly effective mode for transmitting the Christian message; however, many fiction pieces are written without a specific goal or thrust—an interesting incident that goes nowhere is not a story."

LILITH MAGAZINE: INDEPENDENT, JEWISH & FRANKLY FEMINIST

Attn: Submissions, 250 W. 57th St., Suite 2432, New York NY 10107. (212)757-0818. **Fax:** (212)757-5705. **E-mail:** info@lilith.org; naomi@lilith.org. **Website:** www.lilith.org. **Contact:** Susan Weidman Schneider, editor in chief; Naomi Danis, managing editor. Estab. 1976. *Lilith Magazine: Independent, Jewish & Frankly Feminist*, published quarterly, welcomes submissions of high-quality, lively writing: reportage, opinion pieces, memoirs, fiction, and poetry on subjects of interest to Jewish women.

◖　　*Lilith Magazine* is 48 pages, magazine-sized, with glossy color cover. Press run is about 10,000 (about 6,000 subscribers). Subscription: $26/year. For all submissions: Make sure name and contact information appear on each page of mss. Include a short bio (1-2 sentences), written in third person. Accepts submissions year round.

NEEDS Length: up to 3,000 words.

HOW TO CONTACT Send complete ms via online submissions form or mail.

TIPS "Read a copy of the publication before you submit your work. Please be patient."

THE LISTENING EYE

Kent State University Geauga Campus, 14111 Claridon-Troy Rd., Burton OH 44021. (440)286-3840. **E-mail:** grace_butcher@msn.com. **Contact:** Grace Butcher, editor. Estab. 1970. "We look for powerful, unusual imagery, content, and plot in our short stories. In poetry, we look for tight lines that don't sound like prose, unexpected images or juxtapositions, the unusual use of language, noticeable relationships of sounds, a twist in viewpoint, an ordinary idea in extraordinary language, an amazing and complex idea simply stated, play on words and with words, an obvious love of language. Poets need to read the 'Big Three'—Cummings, Thomas, Hopkins—to see the limits to which language can be taken. Then read the 'Big Two'—Dickinson to see how simultaneously tight, terse, and universal a poem can be, and Whitman to see how sprawling, cosmic, and personal. Then read everything you can find that's being published in literary magazines today, and see how your work compares to all of the above."

Magazine: 5.5×8.5; 60 pages; photographs. "We publish the occasional very short stories (750 words/3 pages double-spaced) in any subject and any style, but the language must be strong, unusual, free from cliché and vagueness. We are a shoestring operation from a small campus, but we publish high-quality work." Reads submissions January 1-April 15 only.

NEEDS "Pretty much anything will be considered except porn." Recently published work by Simon Perchik, Lyn Lifshin, and John Hart. Publishes short shorts. Also publishes poetry. Sometimes comments on rejected mss.

HOW TO CONTACT Send SASE for return of ms or disposable copy of ms with SASE for reply only.

LITERAL LATTÉ

200 E. 10th St., Suite 240, New York NY 10003. (212)260-5532. **E-mail:** litlatte@aol.com. **Website:** www.literal-latte.com. **Contact:** Jenine Gordon Bockman, editor and publisher. Estab. 1994. Bimonthly online publication with an annual print anthology featuring the best of the website. "We want great writing in all styles and subjects. A feast is made of a variety of flavors."

NEEDS Length: no more than 6,000 words.

HOW TO CONTACT Send complete ms via postal mail.

PAYMENT/TERMS Pays minimum of anthology copies and maximum of $1,000.

TIPS "Keeping free thought free and challenging entertainment are not mutually exclusive. Words make a ms stand out, words beautifully woven together in striking and memorable patterns."

LITERARY JUICE

Sammamish WA 98075. **E-mail:** info@literaryjuice.com. **E-mail:** srajan@literaryjuice.com. **Website:** www.literaryjuice.com. **Contact:** Sara Rajan, editor in chief; Andrea O'Connor and Dinesh Rajan, managing editors. Bimonthly online literary magazine. "*Literary Juice* publishes original works of short fiction, flash fiction, and poetry. We do not publish nonfiction material, essays, or interviews, nor do we accept previously published works."

NEEDS "We do not publish works with intense sexual content." Length: 100-2,500 words.

HOW TO CONTACT Submit complete ms.

TIPS "It is crucial that writers read our submission guidelines, which can be found on our website. Most important, send us your very best writing. We are looking for works that are not only thought provoking but venture into unconventional territory as well. For instance, avoid sending mainstream stories and poems (stories about wizards or vampires fall into this category). Instead, take the reader to a new realm that has yet to be explored."

LITERARY MAMA

SC 29843. **E-mail:** lminfo@literarymama.com. **Website:** www.literarymama.com. **Contact:** Maria Scala, editor in chief. Estab. 2003. Website offering writing about the complexities and many faces of motherhood in a variety of genres. "Departments include columns, creative nonfiction, fiction, Literary Reflections, poetry, and Profiles & Reviews. We are interested in reading pieces that are long, complex, ambiguous, deep, raw, irreverent, ironic, and body conscious."

TIPS "We seek top-notch creative writing. We also look for quality literary criticism about mother-centric literature and profiles of mother writers. We publish writing with fresh voices, superior craft, and vivid imagery. Please send submission (copied into e-mail) to appropriate departmental editors. Include a brief cover letter. We tend to like stark revelation (pathos, humor, and joy); clarity; concrete details; strong narrative development; ambiguity; thoughtfulness; delicacy; irreverence; lyricism; sincerity; the elegant. We need the submissions 3 months before the following months: October (Desiring Motherhood); May (Mother's Day Month); and June (Father's Day Month)."

THE LITERARY REVIEW

285 Madison Ave., Madison NJ 07940. (973)443-8564. **Fax:** (973)443-8364. **E-mail:** info@theliteraryreview. org. **Website:** www.theliteraryreview.org. **Contact:** Minna Proctor, editor. Estab. 1957.

Work published in *The Literary Review* has been included in *Editor's Choice, Best American Short Stories* and *Pushcart Prize* anthologies. Uses online submissions manager.

NEEDS Wants works of high literary quality only. Does not want to see "overused subject matter or pat resolutions to conflicts."

HOW TO CONTACT Submit electronically only. Does not accept paper submissions.

PAYMENT/TERMS Pays 2 contributor's copies and a 1-year subscription.

TIPS "We want original dramatic situations with complex moral and intellectual resonance and vivid prose. We don't want versions of familiar plots and relationships. Too much of what we are seeing today is openly derivative in subject, plot, and prose style. We pride ourselves on spotting new writers with fresh insight and approach."

LITTLE PATUXENT REVIEW

P.O. Box 6084, Columbia MD 21045. **E-mail:** editor@littlepatuxentreview.org. **Website:** www.littlepatuxentreview.org. **Contact:** Steven Leyva, editor. Estab. 2006. "*Little Patuxent Review (LPR)* is a community-based, biannual print journal devoted to literature and the arts, primarily in the Mid-Atlantic region. We profile the work of a major poet or fiction writer and a visual artist in each issue. We celebrate the launch of each issue with a series of readings and broadcast highlights on *LPR*'s YouTube channel. All forms and styles considered. Please see our website for the current theme."

LPR is about 120 pages; digest-sized; 100# finch cover; artwork (varies depending on featured artist). Has published poetry by Lucille Clifton,

Martín Espada, Donald Hall, Joy Harjo, Marie Howe, Myra Sklarew, Clarinda Harriss, and Alan King. 2011 Pushcart Prize for "Patronized" by Tara Hart.

NEEDS Length: up to 5,000 words.

HOW TO CONTACT Submit complete ms by online submissions manager; no mail or e-mail submissions. Include word count and 75-word bio.

PAYMENT/TERMS Pays 1 contributor's copy.

TIPS "Please see our website for the current theme. Poetry and prose must exhibit the highest quality to be considered. Please read a sample issue before submitting."

LIVE

Gospel Publishing House, 1445 N. Boonville Ave., Springfield MO 65802-1894. (417)862-1447. **Fax:** (417)862-0416. **E-mail:** rl-live@gph.org. **Website:** www.gospelpublishing.com. Estab. 1928. "*LIVE* is a take-home paper distributed weekly in young adult and adult Sunday school classes. We seek to encourage Christians in living for God through fiction and true stories which apply Biblical principles to everyday problems."

NEEDS No preachy fiction, fiction about Bible characters, or stories that refer to religious myths (e.g., Santa Claus, Easter Bunny, etc.). No science or Bible fiction. No controversial stories about such subjects as feminism, war, or capital punishment. Length: 800-1,200 words.

HOW TO CONTACT Send complete ms.

PAYMENT/TERMS Pays 7-10¢/word.

TIPS "Don't moralize or be preachy. Provide human interest articles with Biblical life application. Stories should consist of action, not just thought-life, interaction, not just insight. Heroes and heroines should rise above failures, take risks for God, prove that scriptural principles meet their needs. Conflict and suspense should increase to a climax! Avoid pious conclusions. Characters should be interesting, believable, and realistic. Avoid stereotypes. Characters should be active, not just pawns to move the plot along. They should confront conflict and change in believable ways. Describe the character's looks and reveal his personality through his actions to such an extent that the reader feels he has met that person. Readers should care about the character enough to finish the story. Feature racial, ethnic, and regional characters in rural and urban settings."

THE LONDON MAGAZINE

11 Queen's Gate, London SW7 5EL England. (44) (0)20 7584 5977. **E-mail:** admin@thelondonmagazine.org. **E-mail:** submissions@thelondonmagazine.org. **Website:** www.thelondonmagazine.org. **Contact:** Steven O'Brien, editor. Estab. 1732. "We publish literary writing of the highest quality. We look for poetry and short fiction that startles and entertains us. Reviews, essays, memoir pieces, and features should be erudite, lucid, and incisive. We are obviously interested in writing that has a London focus, but not exclusively so, since London is a world city with international concerns."

NEEDS "Short fiction should address mature and sophisticated themes. Moreover, it should have an elegance of style, structure and characterization. We do not normally publish science fiction or fantasy writing, or erotica." Length: up to 4,000 words.

HOW TO CONTACT Send complete ms. Submit via online submissions manager, e-mail (as an attachment), or postal mail (enclose SASE).

TIPS "Please look at *The London Magazine* before you submit work so that you can see the type of material we publish."

LONG LIFE

Longevity through Technology, The Immortalist Society, 1437 Pineapple Ave., Melbourne FL 32935. **E-mail:** porter@kih.net. **Website:** www.cryonics.org/resources/long-life-magazine. **Contact:** York Porter, executive editor. Estab. 1968. "*Long Life* magazine is a publication for people who are particularly interested in cryonic suspension: the theory, practice, legal problems, etc. associated with being frozen when you die in the hope of eventual restoration to life and health. Many people who receive the publication have relatives who have undergone cryonic preparation or have made such arrangements for themselves or are seriously considering this option. Readers are also interested in other aspects of life extension such as anti-aging research and food supplements that may slow aging. Articles we publish include speculation on what the future will be like; problems of living in a future world, and science in general, particularly as it may apply to cryonics and life extension."

NEEDS "We occasionally publish short fiction, but cryonics and life extension should be essential to the story. We are not interested in horror, in stories where the future is portrayed as gloom and doom, end-of-the-world stories, or those with an inspirational theme." Length: up to 2,500 words.

PAYMENT/TERMS Pays 1 contributor's copy.

TIPS "We are a small magazine but with a highly intelligent and educated readership which is socially and economically diverse. We currently don't pay for material but are seeking new authors and provide contributors with copies of the magazine with the contributor's published works. Look over a copy of *Long Life*, or talk with the editor to get the tone of the publication. There is an excellent chance that your ms will be accepted if it is well written and 'on theme.' Pictures to accompany the article are always welcome, and we like to publish photos of the authors with their first ms."

THE LONG STORY

18 Eaton St., Lawrence MA 01843. (978)686-7638. **E-mail:** rpburnham@mac.com. **Website:** www.longstorylitmag.com. **Contact:** R.P. Burnham. Estab. 1983. For serious, educated, literary people. We publish high literary quality of any kind but especially look for stories that have difficulty getting published elsewhere: committed fiction, working class settings, left-wing themes, etc."

NEEDS Receives 25-35 unsolicited mss/month. Accepts 6-7 mss/issue. Publishes 90% new writers/year. No science fiction, adventure, romance, etc. Length: 8,000-20,000 words; average length: 8,000-12,000 words.

HOW TO CONTACT Include SASE.

PAYMENT/TERMS Pays 2 contributor's copies; $5 charge for extras.

TIPS "Read us first and make sure submitted material is the kind we're interested in. Send clear, legible mss. We're not interested in commercial success; rather we want to provide a place for long stories, the most difficult literary form to publish in our country."

LOST LAKE FOLK OPERA

Shipwreckt Books Publishing Company, 309 W. Stevens Ave., Rushford MN 55971. **E-mail:** contact@shipwrecktbooks.com. **Website:** www.shipwrecktbooks.com. **Contact:** Tom Driscoll, managing editor. Estab. 2013. *Lost Lake Folk Opera* magazine is the arts heartbeat and journalistic pulse of rural Mid-America. Currently accepting submissions of critical journalism, short fiction, poetry, and graphic art. Published 3 times annually.

NEEDS Length: 250-3,500 words.

HOW TO CONTACT Query with sample.

PAYMENT/TERMS Does not offer payment.

TIPS "Send clean copies of your work. When in doubt, edit and cut."

◑ LOUISIANA LITERATURE

SLU Box 10792, Hammond LA 70402. **E-mail:** lalit@selu.edu. **Website:** www.louisianaliterature.org. **Contact:** Jack B. Bedell, editor. Estab. 1984. "Since 1984, *Louisiana Literature* has featured some of the finest writing published in America. The journal has always striven to spotlight local talent alongside nationally recognized authors. Whether it's work from established writers or from first-time publishers, *Louisiana Literature* is always looking to print the finest poetry and fiction available.

◑ Biannual magazine: 6×9; 150 pages; 70 lb. paper; card cover; illustrations. Receives 100 unsolicited mss/month. May not read mss June-July. Publishes 4 new writers/year. Publishes theme issues. Has published work by Anthony Bukowski, Aaron Gwyn, Robert Phillips, R.T. Smith. Work first published in *Louisiana Literature* is regularly reprinted in collections and is nominated for prizes from the National Book Awards for both genres and the Pulitzer. Recently, stories by Aaron Gwyn and Robert Olen Butler were selected for inclusion in *New Stories from the South*.

NEEDS Reviews fiction. "No sloppy, ungrammatical mss." Length: 1,000-6,000 words; average length: 3,500 words.

HOW TO CONTACT Submit ms via online submissions manager. Ms. should be double-spaced.

PAYMENT/TERMS Pays 2 contributor's copies.

TIPS "Cut out everything that is not a functioning part of the story. Make sure your ms is professionally presented. Use relevant, specific detail in every scene. We love detail, local color, voice, and craft. Any professional ms stands out."

◑ THE LOUISIANA REVIEW

Division of Liberal Arts, Louisiana State University Eunice, P.O. Box 1129, Eunice LA 70535. (337)550-1315. **E-mail:** bfonteno@lsue.edu. **Website:** web.lsue.edu/la-review. **Contact:** Dr. Billy Fontenot, fiction editor; Dr. Jude Meche, poetry editor; Dr. Diane Langlois, art editor. Estab. 1999. *The Louisiana Review*, published annually during the fall or spring semester, offers "Louisiana poets, writers, and artists a place to showcase their most beautiful pieces. Others may submit Louisiana- or Southern-related poetry, stories, and art, as well as interviews with Louisiana writers. We want to publish the highest-quality poetry, fiction, and art." Wants "strong imagery, metaphor, and evidence of craft."

◑ *The Louisiana Review* is 100 pages, digest-sized, professionally printed, perfect-bound. Press run is 300-600.

NEEDS Receives 25 unsolicited mss/month. Accepts 5-7 mss/issue. Reads year round. Has published work by Ronald Frame, Tom Bonner, Laura Cario, and Sheryl St. Germaine. Also publishes short shorts. Length: up to 9,000 words; average length: 2,000 words.

HOW TO CONTACT Send SASE for return of ms. Accepts multiple submissions.

PAYMENT/TERMS Pays 1 contributor's copy.

TIPS "We do like to have fiction play out visually as a film would, rather than bestatic and undramatized. Louisiana or Gulf Coast settings and themes preferred."

LULLWATER REVIEW

Lullwater Review, P.O. Box 122036, Atlanta GA 30322. **E-mail:** emorylullwaterreview@gmail.com. **Website:** www.lullwaterreview.wordpress.com. **Contact:** Aneyn M. O'Grady, editor in chief; Gabriel Unger, managing editor. Estab. 1990. "We're a small, student-run literary magazine published out of Emory University in Atlanta, Georgia with 2 issues yearly—once in the fall and once in the spring. You can find us in the *Index of American Periodical Verse*, the *American Humanities Index* and as a member of the Council of Literary Magazines and Presses. We welcome work that brings a fresh perspective, whether through language or the visual arts."

NEEDS Recently published work by Greg Jenkins, Thomas Juvik, Jimmy Gleacher, Carla Vissers, and Judith Sudnolt. No romance or science fiction, please. 5,000 words maximum.

HOW TO CONTACT Send complete ms via e-mail. *Does not accept postal mail submissions.*

PAYMENT/TERMS Pays 3 contributor's copies.

TIPS "We at the *Lullwater Review* look for clear cogent writing, strong character development and an engaging approach to the story in our fiction submissions. Stories with particularly strong voices and well-developed central themes are especially encouraged. Be sure that your ms is ready before mailing it off to us. Revise, revise, revise! Be original, honest, and of course, keep trying."

LUNGFULL!MAGAZINE

316 23rd St., Brooklyn NY 11215. **E-mail:** editor@lungfull.org. **E-mail:** lungfull@rcn.com. **Website:** lungfull.org. **Contact:** Brendan Lorber, editor/publisher. Estab. 1994. "*LUNGFULL!* Magazine World Headquarters in Brooklyn is home to a team of daredevils who make it their job to bring you only the finest in typos, misspellings, and awkward phrases. That's because *LUNGFULL!magazine* is the only literary and art journal in America that prints the rough drafts of people's work so you can see the creative process as it happens."

○ *LUNGFULL!* was the recipient of a grant from the New York State Council for the Arts.

NEEDS Publishes rough drafts.

HOW TO CONTACT Submit up to 15 pages of prose. Include cover letter.

LYRICAL PASSION POETRY E-ZINE

P.O. Box 17331, Arlington VA 22216. **Website:** lyricalpassionpoetry.yolasite.com. **Contact:** Raquel D. Bailey, founding editor. Estab. 2007. Founded by award-winning poet Raquel D. Bailey, *Lyrical Passion Poetry E-Zine* is an attractive monthly online literary magazine specializing in Japanese short-form poetry. Publishes quality artwork, well-crafted short fiction, and poetry in English by emerging and established writers. Literature of lasting literary value will be considered. Welcomes the traditional to the experimental. Poetry works written in German will be considered if accompanied by translations. Offers annual short-fiction and poetry contests.

HOW TO CONTACT Send complete ms, typed, double-spaced. Cover letter preferred.

THE MACGUFFIN

18600 Haggerty Rd., Livonia MI 48152. (734)462-4400, ext 5327. **E-mail:** macguffin@schoolcraft.edu. **Website:** www.macguffin.org. **Contact:** Steven A. Dolgin, editor; Gordon Krupsky, managing editor;. Estab. 1984. "Our purpose is to encourage, support and enhance the literary arts in the Schoolcraft College community, the region, the state, and the nation. We also sponsor annual literary events and give voice to deserving new writers as well as established writers."

NEEDS Length: 5,000 words.

HOW TO CONTACT Submit 2 stories, maximum. Prose should be typed and double-spaced. Include word count. Send SASE or e-mail.

PAYMENT/TERMS Pays 2 contributor's copies.

MAD HATTERS' REVIEW: EDGY AND ENLIGHTENED ART, LITERATURE AND MUSIC IN THE AGE OF DEMENTIA

Wales. **E-mail:** askalice@madhatarts.com. **Website:** www.madhattersreview.com. **Contact:** Marc Vincenz, publisher and editor in chief. *Mad Hatters' Review* "seeks to foster the work of writers and poets: explosive, lyrical, passionate, deeply wrought voices and aesthetic experiments that stretch the boundaries of language, narrative, and image, vital and enduring literary voices that sing on the page as well as in the mind. The name of our annual reflects our view of the world as essentially demented and nonsensical, too frequently a nightmare or 'nondream' that needs to be exposed to the light for what it is, as well as what it is not. We're particularly interested in risky, thematically broad (i.e., saying something about the world and its creatures), psychologically and philosophically sophisticated works. Humor, satire, irony, magical realism, and surrealism are welcome.We look for originality, surprise, intellectual and emotional strength, lyricism, and rhythm. We love writers who stretch their imaginations to the limits and challenge conventional notions of reality and style; we care little for categories. We also adore collaborative ventures, between/among writers, visual artists, and composers."

○ *Mad Hatters' Review* has received an Artistry Award from Sixty Plus Design, 2006-2007 Web Design Award from Invision Graphics, and a Gold Medal Award of Excellence for 2006-7 from ArtSpace2000.com. Member: CLMP.

NEEDS Submissions are open briefly for each issue: check guidelines periodically for dates. **Publishes 1 new writer/year.** Has published Alastair Gray, Kass Fleisher, Vanessa Place, Harold Jaffe, Andrei Codrescu, Sheila Murphy, Simon Perchik, Terese Svoboda, Niels Hav, Martin, Nakell, and Juan Jose Millas (translated from the Spanish). Does not want mainstream prose/story that doesn't exhibit a love of language and a sophisticated mentality. No religious or inspirational writings, confessionals, boys sowing oats, sentimental and coming-of-age stories. Length: up to 3,000 words. Average length: 1,500-2,500 words. Publishes short shorts. Average length of short shorts: 500-800 words.

HOW TO CONTACT Submit via online submissions manager.

TIPS "Imagination, skill with and appreciation of language, inventiveness, rhythm, sense of humor/

irony/satire, and compelling style make a ms stand out. Read the magazine. Don't necessarily follow the rules you've been taught in the usual MFA program or workshop."

THE MADISON REVIEW

University of Wisconsin, 600 N, Park St., 6193 Helen C. White Hall, Madison WI 53706. **E-mail:** madisonrevw@gmail.com. **Website:** www.english.wisc.edu/madisonreview. **Contact:** Will Conley and Sam Zisser, fiction editors; Mckenna Kohlenberg and Cody Dunn, poetry editors. Estab. 1972. *The Madison Review* is a student-run literary magazine that looks to publish the best available fiction and poetry.

Does not publish unsolicited interviews or genre fiction. Send all submissions through online submissions manager.

NEEDS Wants well-crafted, compelling fiction featuring a wide range of styles and subjects. Does not read May-September. No genre: horror, fantasy, erotica, etc. Length: 500-30,000 words, up to 30 pages.

HOW TO CONTACT Send complete ms.

PAYMENT/TERMS Pays 2 contributor's copies, $5 for additional copies.

TIPS "Our editors have very eclectic tastes, so don't specifically try to cater to us. Above all, we look for original, high-quality work."

THE MAGAZINE OF FANTASY & SCIENCE FICTION

P.O. Box 3447, Hoboken NJ 07030. (201) 876-2551. **E-mail:** fandsf@aol.com. **Website:** www.fandsf.com. **Contact:** C.C. Finlay, editor. Estab. 1949. *"The Magazine of Fantasy and Science Fiction* publishes various types of science fiction and fantasy short stories and novellas, making up about 80% of each issue. The balance of each issue is devoted to articles about science fiction, a science column, book and film reviews, cartoons, and competitions." Bimonthly.

The *Magazine of Fantasy and Science Fiction* won a Nebula Award for Best Novelet for *What We Found* by Geoff Ryman in 2012. Also won the 2012 World Fantasy Award for Best Short Story for *The Paper Menagerie* by Ken Liu.

NEEDS "Prefers character-oriented stories. We receive a lot of fantasy fiction but never enough science fiction." Length: up to 25,000 words.

HOW TO CONTACT No electronic submissions. Send complete ms.

PAYMENT/TERMS Pays 7-10¢/word.

TIPS "Good storytelling makes a submission stand out. Regarding mss, a well-prepared ms (i.e., one that follows the traditional format, like that describted here: www.sfwa.org/writing/vonda/vonda.htm) stands out more than any gimmicks. Read an issue of the magazine before submitting. New writers should keep their submissions under 15,000 words—we rarely publish novellas by new writers."

THE MAGNOLIA QUARTERLY

P.O. Box 10294, Gulfport MS 39505. **E-mail:** writerpllevin@gmail.com. **Website:** www.gcwriters.org. **Contact:** Phil Levin, editor. Estab. 1985. *The Magnolia Quarterly* publishes poetry, fiction, nonfiction, and reviews. **For members of GCWA only.**

The Magnolia Quarterly is 40 pages, pocket-sized, stapled, with glossy cover, includes ads. Editing service offered on all prose.

NEEDS Length: about 700 words.

HOW TO CONTACT E-mail submissions in .doc format as attachments.

PAYMENT/TERMS No payment.

THE MAIN STREET RAG

P.O. Box 690100, Charlotte NC 28227-7001. (704)573-2516. **E-mail:** editor@mainstreetrag.com. **Website:** www.mainstreetrag.com. **Contact:** M. Scott Douglass, editor/publisher. Estab. 1996. *The Main Street Rag*, published quarterly, prints "poetry, short fiction, essays, interviews, reviews, photos, and art. We like publishing good material from people who are interested in more than notching another publishing credit, people who support small independent publishers like ourselves." Will consider "almost anything," but prefers "writing with an edge—either gritty or bitingly humorous. Contributors are advised to visit our website prior to submission to confirm current needs."

The Main Street Rag receives about 5,000 submissions/year; publishes 50+ poems and 3-5 short stories per issue, a featured interview, photos, and an occasional nonfiction piece. Press run is about 500 (250 subscribers, 15 libraries).

NEEDS Length: up to 6,000 words.

HOW TO CONTACT E-mail submissions only. Cover letter is preferred. "No bios or credits—let the work speak for itself."

PAYMENT/TERMS Pays 1 contributor's copy.

THE MALAHAT REVIEW

The University of Victoria, P.O. Box 1700, STN CSC, Victoria BC V8W 2Y2 Canada. (250)721-8524. E-

mail: malahat@uvic.ca (for queries only). **Website:** www.malahatreview.ca. **Contact:** John Barton, editor. Estab. 1967. Quarterly magazine covering poetry, fiction, creative nonfiction, and reviews. "We try to achieve a balance of views and styles in each issue. We strive for a mix of the best writing by both established and new writers."

NEEDS Length: up to 8,000 words.

HOW TO CONTACT Submit via online submissions manager: malahatreview.ca/submission_guidelines.html#submittable.

PAYMENT/TERMS Pays $50/magazine page

TIPS "Please do not send more than 1 submission at a time: 3-5 poems, 1 piece of creative nonfiction, or 1 short story (do not mix poetry and prose in the same submission). See *The Malahat Review*'s Open Season Awards for poetry and short fiction, creative nonfiction, long poem, and novella contests in the Awards section of our website."

MANGROVE

University of Miami, Dept. of English, P.O Box 248145, Coral Gables FL 33124-4632. **E-mail:** mangrovejournal@gmail.com. **Website:** www.as.miami.edu/mangrove. **Contact:** Sarah Ryan, editor in chief; Natash Mijares, managing editor. Estab. 1992. "*Mangrove* is the undergraduate literary journal at the University of Miami, publishing the best undergraduate fiction, poetry, nonfiction, art, and design in the country."

Accepts work from undergraduate students throughout the year, but for submissions to be considered for the spring print journal, submit before January 15.

NEEDS Accepts short stories and micro and flash fiction. Length: up to 20 pages.

HOW TO CONTACT Submit via online submissions manager. Submissions should be double-spaced. Include cover letter with short bio, projected year of graduation, and college/university where currently enrolled.

MANOA

English Dept., University of Hawaii, Honolulu HI 96822. (808)956-3070. **Fax:** (808)956-3083. **E-mail:** mjournal-l@lists.hawaii.edu. **Website:** manoajournal.hawaii.edu. **Contact:** Frank Stewart, editor. Estab. 1989. *Manoa* is seeking "high-quality literary fiction, poetry, essays, and personal narrative. In general, each issue is devoted to new work from Pacific and Asian nations. Our audience is international. U.S. writing need not be confined to Pacific settings

or subjects. Please note that we seldom publish unsolicited work."

Manoa has received numerous awards, and work published in the magazine has been selected for prize anthologies. See website for recently published issues.

NEEDS Query first and/or see website. No Pacific exotica. Length: 1,000-7,500 words.

HOW TO CONTACT Send complete ms.

PAYMENT/TERMS Pays $100-500 normally ($25/printed page).

TIPS "Not accepting unsolicited mss at this time because of commitments to special projects. Please query before sending mss as e-mail attachments."

THE MASSACHUSETTS REVIEW

University of Massachusetts, Photo Lab 309, Amherst MA 01003. (413)545-2689. **E-mail:** massrev@external.umass.edu. **Website:** www.massreview.org. **Contact:** Emily Wojcik, managing editor. Estab. 1959. Seeks a balance between established writers and promising new ones. Interested in material of variety and vitality relevant to the intellectual and aesthetic questions of our time. Aspire to have a broad appeal.

Does not respond to mss without SASE.

NEEDS Wants short stories. Accepts 1 short story per submission. Include name and contact information on the first page. Encourages page numbers. Has published work by Ahdaf Soueif, Elizabeth Denton, and Nicholas Montemarano. Length: up to 30 pages or 8,000 words.

HOW TO CONTACT Send complete ms.

PAYMENT/TERMS Pays $50.

TIPS "No mss are considered May-September. Electronic submission process can be found on website. No fax or e-mail submissions. No simultaneous submissions. Shorter rather than longer stories preferred (up to 28-30 pages)." Looks for works that "stop us in our tracks." Mss that stand out use "unexpected language, idiosyncrasy of outlook, and are the opposite of ordinary."

MERIDIAN

University of Virginia, P.O. Box 400145, Charlottesville VA 22904-4145. **E-mail:** meridianuva@gmail.com; meridianpoetry@gmail.com; meridianfiction@gmail.com. **Website:** www.readmeridian.org. Estab. 1998. *Meridian* Editors' Prize Contest offers annual $1,000 award. Submit online only; see website for formatting details. **Entry fee:** $8.50, includes one-year electronic subscription to *Meridian* for all U.S. entries or 1 copy of the prize issue for all international entries. **Deadline:** December or January; see website for current deadline. *Meridian*, published semiannually, prints poetry, fiction, nonfiction, interviews, and reviews. "*Meridian* is interested in writing that is vibrant, moving, and alive, and welcomes contributions from a variety of aesthetic approaches. Has published such poets as Alexandra Teague, Gregory Pardlo, Sandra Meek, and Bob Hicok, and such fiction writers as Matt Bell, Kate Milliken, and Ron Carlson. Has recently interviewed C. Michael Curtis, Ann Beatty, and Claire Messud, among other luminaries. Also publishes a recurring feature called 'Lost Classic,' which resurrects previously unpublished work by celebrated writers and which has included illustrations from the mss of Jorge Luis Borges, letters written by Elizabeth Bishop, Stephen Crane's deleted chapter from *The Red Badge of Courage*, and a letter written by Flannery O'Connor about her novel *Wise Blood*."

O *Meridian* is 130 pages, digest-sized, offset-printed, perfect-bound, with color cover. Receives about 2,500 poems/year, accepts about 40 (less than 1%). Press run is 1,000 (750 subscribers, 15 libraries, 200 shelf sales); 150 distributed free to writing programs. Work published in *Meridian* has appeared in *The Best American Poetry* and *The Pushcart Prize Anthology*.

NEEDS Submit complete ms via online submissions manager or postal mail. Length: up to 6,500 words.

PAYMENT/TERMS Pays 2 contributor's copies (additional copies available at discount).

O O O MICHIGAN QUARTERLY REVIEW

0576 Rackham Bldg., 915 E. Washington, Ann Arbor MI 48109-1070. (734)764-9265. **E-mail:** mqr@umich.edu. **Website:** www.michiganquarterlyreview.com. **Contact:** Jonathan Freedman, editor; Vicki Lawrence, managing editor. Estab. 1962. *MQR* is an eclectic interdisciplinary journal of arts and culture that seeks to combine the best of poetry, fiction, and creative nonfiction with outstanding critical essays on literary, cultural, social, and political matters. The flagship journal of the University of Michigan, *MQR* draws on lively minds here and elsewhere, seeking to present accessible work of all varieties for sophisticated readers from within and without the academy.

O The Laurence Goldstein Award is a $500 annual award to the best poem published in *MQR*

during the previous year. The Lawrence Foundation Award is a $1,000 annual award to the best short story published in *MQR* during the previous year. The Page Davidson Clayton Award for Emerging Poets is a $500 annual award given to the best poet appearing in *MQR* during the previous year who has not yet published a book.

NEEDS "No restrictions on subject matter or language. We are very selective. We like stories that are unusual in tone and structure, and innovative in language. No genre fiction written for a market. Would like to see more fiction about social, political, cultural matters, not just centered on a love relationship or dysfunctional family." Receives 300 unsolicited mss/month. Accepts 3-4 mss/issue; 12-16 mss/year. Publishes 1-2 new writers/year. Has published work by Rebecca Makkai, Peter Ho Davies, Laura Kasischke, Gerald Shapiro, and Alan Cheuse. Length: 1,500-7,000 words; average length: 5,000 words.

HOW TO CONTACT Send complete ms.

PAYMENT/TERMS Pays $10/published page.

TIPS "Read the journal and assess the range of contents and the level of writing. We have no guidelines to offer or set expectations; every ms is judged on its unique qualities. On essays—query with a very thorough description of the argument and a copy of the first page. Watch for announcements of special issues, which are usually expanded issues and draw upon a lot of freelance writing. Be aware that this is a university quarterly that publishes a limited amount of fiction and poetry and that it is directed at an educated audience, one that has done a great deal of reading in all types of literature."

MICROHORROR: SHORT STORIES. ENDLESS NIGHTMARES

P.O. Box 32259, Pikesville MD 21282-2259. (443) 670-6133. **E-mail:** microhorror@gmail.com. **Website:** www.microhorror.com. **Contact:** Nathan Rosen, editor. Estab. 2006. "*MicroHorror* is not a magazine in the traditional sense. Instead, it is a free online archive for short-short horror fiction. With a strict limit of 666 words, *MicroHorror* showcases the power of short-short horror to convey great emotional impact in only a few brief paragraphs."

O Golden Horror Award from Horrorfind.com in 2007.

NEEDS Length: no more than 666 words.

HOW TO CONTACT Send all submission through online submission form.

TIPS "This is horror. Scare me. Make shivers run down my spine. Make me afraid to look behind the shower curtain. Pack the biggest punch you can into a few well-chosen sentences. Read all the horror you can, and figure out what makes it scary. Trim away all the excess trappings until you get right to the core, and use what you find."

MID-AMERICAN REVIEW

Bowling Green State University, Dept. of English, Bowling Green OH 43403. (419)372-2725. **E-mail:** mar@bgsu.edu. **E-mail:** marsubmissions.bgsu.edu. **Website:** www.bgsu.edu/midamericanreview. **Contact:** Abigail Cloud, editor in chief; Laura Walter, fiction editor. Estab. 1981. "We aim to put the best possible work in front of the biggest possible audience. We publish contemporary fiction, poetry, creative nonfiction, translations, and book reviews."

Contests: The Fineline Competition for Prose Poems, Short Shorts, and Everything In Between (June 1 deadline, $10 per 3 pieces, limit 500 words each); The Sherwood Anderson Fiction Award (November 1 deadline, $10 per piece); and the James Wright Poetry Award (November 1 deadline, $10 per 3 pieces).

NEEDS Publishes traditional, character-oriented, literary, experimental, prose poem, and short-short stories. No genre fiction. Length: 6,000 words maximum.

HOW TO CONTACT Submit ms by post with SASE or with online submission manager. Agented fiction 5%. Recently published work by Mollie Ficek and J. David Stevens.

TIPS "We are seeking translations of contemporary authors from all languages into English; submissions must include the original and proof of permission to translate. We would also like to see more creative nonfiction."

MIDWAY JOURNAL

8 Durham Street #3, Somerville MA 02143. (763)516-7463. **E-mail:** editors@midwayjournal.com. **Website:** www.midwayjournal.com. **Contact:** Ralph Pennel, fiction editor. Estab. 2006. "Just off of I-94 and on the border between St. Paul and Minneapolis, the Midway, like any other state fairgrounds, is alive with a mix of energies and people. Its position as mid-way, as a place of boundary crossing, also reflects our vision for this journal. The work here complicates and questions the boundaries of genre, binary, and aesthetic. It offers surprises and ways of re-seeing, re-thinking, and re-feeling: a veritable banquet of literary fare. Which is why, in each new issue, we are honored to present work by both new and established writers alike."

Midway Journal is a member of Council of Literary Magazines and Presses (CLMP).

HOW TO CONTACT Submit 1 piece of fiction or 2 pieces of flash/sudden fiction via online submissions manager.

TIPS "An interesting story with engaging writing, both in terms of style and voice, make a ms stand out. Round characters are a must. Writers who take chances either with content or with form grab an editor's immediate attention. Spend time with the words on the page. Spend time with the language. The language and voice are not vehicles; they, too, are tools."

MINAS TIRITH EVENING-STAR: JOURNAL OF THE AMERICAN TOLKIEN SOCIETY

American Tolkien Society, P.O. Box 97, Highland MI 48357-0097. **E-mail:** editor@americantolkiensociety.org; americantolkiensociety@yahoo.com. **Website:** www.americantolkiensociety.org. **Contact:** Amalie A. Helms, editor. Estab. 1967. *Minas Tirith Evening-Star: Journal of the American Tolkien Society*, published quarterly, publishes poetry, book reviews, essays, and fan fition. *Minas Tirith Evening-Star* is digest-sized, offset-printed from typescript, with cartoon-like b&w graphics. Press run is 400. Single copy: $3.50; subscription: $12.50. Sample: $3. Make checks payable to American Tolkien Society.

HOW TO CONTACT Submit complete ms by mail or e-mail.

PAYMENT/TERMS Pays 1 contributor's copy.

THE MINNESOTA REVIEW

Virginia Tech, ASPECT, 202 Major Williams Hall (0192), Blacksburg VA 24061. **E-mail:** editors@theminnesotareview.org. **Website:** minnesotareview.wordpress.com. **Contact:** Janell Watson, editor. Estab. 1960. *The Minnesota Review*, published biannually, is a journal featuring creative and critical work from writers on the rise or who are already established. Each issue is about 200 pages, digest-sized, flat-spined, with glossy card cover. Press run is 1,000 (400 subscribers). Also available online. Subscription: $30/2 years for individuals, $60/year for institutions. Sample: $15.

Open to submissions August 1-November 1 and January 1-April 1. Accepts submissions via online submissions manager.

NEEDS Length: 10,000 words for short stories, 1,000 words for flash fiction.

HOW TO CONTACT Limit submissions to 1 short story or 4 flash fiction pieces.

MISSISSIPPI REVIEW

University of Southern Mississippi, 118 College Dr., #5144, Hattiesburg MS 39406-0001. (601)266-4321. **Fax:** (601)266-5757. **E-mail:** msreview@usm.edu. **Website:** www.usm.edu/mississippi-review. **Contact:** Andrew Malan Milward, editor in chief; Caleb Tankersley and Allison Campbell, associate editors. Estab. 1972. *Mississippi Review* "is one of the most respected literary journals in the country. Raymond Carver, an early contributor to the magazine, once said that *Mississippi Review* 'is one of the most remarkable and indispensable literary journals of our time.' Well-known and established writers have appeared in the pages of the magazine, including Pulitzer and Nobel Prize winners, as well as new and emerging writers who have gone on to publish books and to receive awards."

Publishes 25-30 new writers/year. Annual fiction and poetry competition: $1,000 awarded in each category, plus publication of all winners and finalists. Fiction entries: 8,000 words or less. Poetry entries: 1-5 poems; page limit is 10. $15 entry fee includes copy of prize issue. No limit on number of entries. Deadline December 1. No mss returned.

NEEDS No juvenile or genre fiction. Length: 30 pages maximum.

THE MISSOURI REVIEW

357 McReynolds Hall, University of Missouri, Columbia MO 65211. (573)882-4474. **Fax:** (573)884-4671. **E-mail:** question@moreview.com. **Website:** www.missourireview.com. **Contact:** Speer Morgan, editor; Michael Nye, managing editor. Estab. 1978. Publishes contemporary fiction, poetry, interviews, personal essays, cartoons, special features—such as History as Literature series and Found Text series—for the literary and the general reader interested in a wide range of subjects.

NEEDS No genre or flash fiction. Length: 9,000-12,000 words or 2,000 words or less (flash fiction).

HOW TO CONTACT Send complete ms.

PAYMENT/TERMS Pays $40/printed page. Also, The William Peden Prize of $1,000 is awarded annually to the best piece of fiction to have appeared in the previous volume year. The winner is chosen by an outside judge from stories published in TMR. There is no separate application process.

TIPS "Send your best work."

MOBIUS

149 Talmadge, Madison WI 53704. (608)335-9340. **E-mail:** fmschep@charter.net. **Website:** www.mobius-magazine.com. **Contact:** Fred Schepartz, publisher and executive editor. Estab. 1989. *Mobius: The Journal of Social Change* became an online-only journal, published quarterly in March, June, September, and December, in 2009.

NEEDS Wants fiction dealing with themes of social change. "We like social commentary, but mainly we like good writing." "No porn, no racist, sexist or any other kind of -*ist*. No Christian or spirituality proselytizing fiction." Length: up to 5,000 words.

HOW TO CONTACT Submit no more than 1 story at a time via e-mail (preferred). Paste story in body of e-mail or send as an attachment.

TIPS "We like high impact. We like plot- and character-driven stories that function like theater of the mind. We look first and foremost for good writing. Prose must be crisp and polished; the story must pique my interest and make me care due to a certain intellectual, emotional aspect. *Mobius* is about social change. We want stories that make some statement about the society we live in, either on a macro or micro level. Not that your story needs to preach from a soapbox (actually, we prefer that it doesn't), but your story needs to have something to say."

THE MOCHILA REVIEW

Missouri Western State University, 4525 Downs Dr., St. Joseph MO 64507. **E-mail:** mochila@missouri-western.edu. **Website:** www.missouriwestern.edu/orgs/mochila/homepage.htm. **Contact:** Marianne Kunkel, editor. Estab. 2000. "We are looking for writing that has a respect for the sound of language. We value poems that have to be read aloud so your mouth can feel the shape of the words. Send us writing that conveys a sense of urgency, writing that the writer can't *not* write. We crave fresh and daring work."

NEEDS Length: 1 piece of no more than 5,000 words.

HOW TO CONTACT Submit complete ms by postal mail. Include cover letter, contact information, SASE.

PAYMENT/TERMS Pays in contributor's copies.

TIPS "Mss with fresh language, energy, passion, and intelligence stand out. Study the craft and be entertaining and engaging."

⬤◐ MORPHEUS TALES

E-mail: morpheustales@blueyonder.co.uk. **Website:** www.morpheustales.com. **Contact:** Adam Bradley, publisher. Estab. 2008. "We publish the best in horror, science fiction, and fantasy—both fiction and nonfiction."

NEEDS Length: 800-3,000 words.

HOW TO CONTACT Send complete ms.

◐◑ MUZZLE BLASTS

P.O. Box 67, Friendship IN 47021. (812)667-5131. **Fax:** (812)667-5136. **E-mail:** ttrowbridge@nmlra.org. **Website:** www.nmlra.org. Estab. 1939. "Articles must relate to muzzleloading or the muzzleloading era of American history."

NEEDS Must pertain to muzzleloading. Length: 2,500 words.

HOW TO CONTACT Query.

PAYMENT/TERMS Pays $50-300.

◐◑ MYTHIC DELIRIUM

3514 Signal Hill Ave. NW, Roanoke VA 24017-5148. **E-mail:** mythicdelirium@gmail.com. **Website:** www. mythicdelirium.com. **Contact:** Mike Allen, editor. Estab. 1998. "*Mythic Delirium* is an online and e-book venue for fiction and poetry that ranges through science fiction, fantasy, horror, interstitial, and cross-genre territory—we love blurred boundaries and tropes turned on their heads. We are interested in work that demonstrates ambition, that defies traditional approaches to genre, that introduces readers to the legends of other cultures, that re-evaluates the myths of old from a modern perspective, that twists reality in unexpected ways. We are committed to diversity and are open to and encourage submissions from people of every race, gender, nationality, sexual orientation, political affiliation and religious belief. We publish 12 short stories and 24 poems a year. Our quarterly ebooks in PDF, EPUB, and MOBI formats, published in July, October, January, and April, will each contain 3 stories and 6 poems. We will also publish 1 story and 2 poems on our website each month." Reading period: August 1-October 1 annually.

NEEDS "No unsolicited reprints or multiple submissions. Please use the words 'fiction submission' in the e-mail subject line. Stories should be sent in standard ms format as .rtf or .doc attachments." Length: up to 4,000 words (firm).

PAYMENT/TERMS Pays 2¢/word.

TIPS "*Mythic Delirium* isn't easy to get into, but we publish newcomers in every issue. Show us how ambitious you can be, and don't give up."

N+1

The Editors, 68 Jay St., Suite 405, Brooklyn NY 11201. **E-mail:** editors@nplusonemag.com. **E-mail:** submissions@nplusonemag.com. **Website:** www.nplusonemag.com. **Contact:** Nikil Saval and Dayna Tortorici, editors.

NEEDS Submit queries or finished pieces by e-mail.

TIPS "Most of the slots available for a given issue will have been filled many months before publication. If you would like to brave the odds, the best submission guidelines are those implied by the magazine itself. Read an issue or two through to get a sense of whether your piece might fit into *n+1*."

◐◑ NA'AMAT WOMAN

505 Eighth Ave., Suite 1204, New York NY 10018. (212)563-5222. **E-mail:** naamat@naamat.org; judith@naamat.org. **Website:** www.naamat.org. **Contact:** Judith Sokoloff, editor. Estab. 1926. "Magazine covering a wide variety of subjects of interest to the Jewish community—including political and social issues, arts, profiles; many articles about Israel and women's issues. Fiction must have a Jewish theme. Readers are the American Jewish community." Circ. 15,000. "Magazine covering a wide variety of subjects of interest to the Jewish community—including political and social issues, arts, profiles; many articles about Israel and women's issues. Fiction must have a Jewish theme. Readers are the American Jewish community."

NEEDS Ethnic/multicultural, historical, humor/satire, literary, novel excerpts, women-oriented. Receives 10 unsolicited mss/month. Accepts 1-3 mss/year. "We want serious fiction, with insight, reflection and consciousness." "We do not want fiction that is mostly dialogue. No corny Jewish humor. No Holocaust fiction." Length: 2,000-3,000 words.

HOW TO CONTACT Query with published clips or send complete mss. Responds in 6 months to queries; 6 months to mss. Sample copy for 9×11.5 SAE and $2 postage or look online. Sample copy for $2. Writer's guidelines for #10 SASE, or by e-mail. Query with published clips or send complete ms.

PAYMENT/TERMS Pays 10¢/word and 2 contributor's copies. Pays on publication for first North American serial, first, one time, second serial (reprint) rights, makes work-for-hire assignments. Pays 10-20¢/word for assigned articles and for unsolicited articles.

TIPS "No maudlin nostalgia or romance; no hackneyed Jewish humor."

◐ NARRATIVE MAGAZINE

2443 Fillmore St. #214, San Francisco CA 94115. **Website:** www.narrativemagazine.com. **Contact:** Michael Croft, senior editor; Mimi Kusch, managing editor; Michael Wiegers, poetry editor. Estab. 2003. "*Narrative* publishes high-quality contemporary literature in a full range of styles, forms, and lengths. Submit poetry, fiction, and nonfiction, including stories, short shorts, novels, novel excerpts, novellas, personal essays, humor, sketches, memoirs, literary biographies, commentary, reportage, interviews, and short audio recordings of short-short stories and poems. We welcome submissions of previously unpublished mss of all lengths, ranging from short-short stories to complete book-length works for serialization. In addition to submissions for issues of *Narrative* itself, we also encourage submissions for our Story of the Week, literary contests, and Readers' Narratives. Please read our Submission Guidelines for all information on ms formatting, word lengths, author payment, and other policies. We accept submissions only through our electronic submission system. We do not accept submissions through postal services or e-mail. You may send us mss for the following submission categories: General Submissions, Narrative Prize, Story of the Week, Readers' Narrative, iPoem, iStory, Six-Word Story, or a specific Contest. Your ms must be in one of the following file forms: .doc, .rtf, .pdf, .docx, .txt, .wpd, .odf, .mp3, .mp4, .mov, or .flv."

◑ *Narrative* has received recognitions in *New Stories from the South*, *Best American Mystery Stories*, *O. Henry Prize Stories*, *Best American Short Stories*, *Best American Essays*, and the *Pushcart Prize Collection*. In their first quarterly issue of 2010, the National Endowment for the Arts featured an article on the business of books, with *Narrative*'s digital publishing model a key focus. Providing a behind-the-scenes look at the way in which *Narrative* functions and thrives, it is an essential read for anyone looking to learn more about the current state of publishing both in the print and digital arenas.

NEEDS Has published work by Amy Bloom, Tobias Wolff, Marvin Bell, Jane Smiley, Joyce Carol Oates, E.L. Doctorow, Min Jin Lee, and Alice Munro. Publishes new and emerging writers.

HOW TO CONTACT Send complete ms.

PAYMENT/TERMS Pays on publication between $150-1,000, $1,000-5,000 for book length, plus annual prizes of more than $32,000 awarded.

TIPS "Log on and study our magazine online. Narrative fiction, graphic art, and multimedia are selected, first and foremost, for quality."

◐ NASSAU REVIEW

Nassau Community College, State University of New York, English Dept., 1 Education Dr., Garden City NY 11530. **E-mail:** nassaureview@ncc.edu. **Website:** www.ncc.edu/nassaureview. **Contact:** Christina Rau, editor in chief and poetry editor; Beth Beatrice Smith, fiction editor; Emily Hegarty, creative nonfiction editor. Estab. 1964. *The Nassau Review* welcomes submissions of many genres, preferring work that is "innovative, captivating, well-crafted, and unique, work that crosses boundaries of genre and tradition. You may be serious. You may be humorous. You may be somewhere in between. We are looking simply for quality. New and seasoned writers are welcome."

◑ All open submissions are under consideration for the Writer Awards.

NEEDS Accepts simultaneous submissions: "Please let us know they are simultaneous when you submit them." Does not want "children's literature; cliché, unoriginal work; fan fiction." Length: 100-3,000 words.

HOW TO CONTACT Submit via online submissions manager. Include title, word count, and bio of up to 100 words.

PAYMENT/TERMS Pays 1 contributor's copy.

◐ NATURAL BRIDGE

Dept. of English, University of Missouri-St. Louis, One University Blvd., St. Louis MO 63121. (314)516-7327. **E-mail:** natural@umsl.edu. **Website:** www.umsl.edu/~natural. Estab. 1999. *Natural Bridge*, published biannually in May and December, invites submissions of poetry, fiction, personal essays, and translations.

◑ No longer accepts submissions via e-mail. Accepts submissions through online submission form and postal mail only.

NEEDS Literary. Submit year round; however, "we do not read May 1-August 1." Recently published work by Tayari Jones, Steve Stern, Jamie Wriston Colbert, Lex Williford, and Mark Jay Mirsky. Also publishes literary essays, poetry. Sometimes comments on rejected mss.

HOW TO CONTACT Submit 1 ms through online submissions manager ($3 fee for nonsubscribers) or by postal mail (free).

PAYMENT/TERMS Pays 2 contributor's copies and one-year subscription.

NEBO

Arkansas Tech University, Department of English, Russellville AR 72801. (501)968-0256. **E-mail:** nebo@ atu.edu. **Website:** www.atu.edu/worldlanguages/ Nebo.php. **Contact:** Editor. Estab. 1983. "*Nebo* routinely publishes Arkansas Tech students and unpublished writers alongside nationally known writers."

Literary journal: 5x8; 50-60 pages. For general, academic audience. Receives 20-30 unsolicited mss per month. *Nebo* is published in the spring and fall.

NEEDS Accepts all genres. Contact editor for specifics. Submit by mail. Reads mss August 15-January 31. Length: up to 2,000 words.

PAYMENT/TERMS Pays 1 contributor's copy.

TIPS "Avoid pretentiousness. Write something you genuinely care about. Please edit your work for spelling, grammar, cohesiveness, and overall purpose. Many of the mss we receive should be publishable with a little polishing. Mss should never be submitted handwritten or on 'onion skin' or colored paper."

NEON MAGAZINE

U.K. **E-mail:** info@neonmagazine.co.uk. **Website:** www.neonmagazine.co.uk. **Contact:** Krishan Coupland. Quarterly website and print magazine covering alternative work of any form of poetry and prose, short stories, flash fiction, artwork and reviews. "Genre work is welcome. Experimentation is encouraged. We like stark poetry and weird prose. We seek work that is beautiful, shocking, intense, and memorable. Darker pieces are generally favored over humorous ones."

Neon was previously published as *FourVolts Magazine.*

NEEDS "No nonsensical prose; we are not appreciative of sentimentality." No word limit.

PAYMENT/TERMS Pays royalties.

TIPS "Send several poems, 1 or 2 pieces of prose or several images via form e-mail. Include the word 'submission' in your subject line. Include a short bio-graphical note (up to 100 words). Read submission guidelines before submitting your work."

NEW DELTA REVIEW

Department of English, 15 Allen Hall, Louisiana State University, Baton Rouge LA 70803. **E-mail:** editor@ ndrmag.org. **Website:** ndrmag.org. Estab. 1984. "We seek vivid and exciting work from new and established writers. We have published fiction from writers such as National Book Award finalist Patricia Smith, *Pushcart Prize* winner Stacey Richter, and former poet laureate Billy Collins."

Semiannual. Editors change every year; check website. Online only. *New Delta Review* also sponsors the Matt Clark Prizes for fiction and poetry, the annual Ryan Gibbs Awards for short fiction and photography, and an annual chapbook contest. Work from the magazine has been included in the *Pushcart Prize* anthology.

NEEDS Publishes short shorts. Receives 300 unsolicited mss/month. Accepts 15-25 mss/issue; 30-50 mss/ year. Reads year-round. **Publishes 10-15 new writers/ year.** Also publishes poetry. "No Elvis stories, overwrought 'Southern' fiction, or cancer stories." Average length: 1,500-3,000 words for prose submission.

PAYMENT/TERMS No payment, but all published pieces are eligible for yearly editor's prize of $250.

TIPS "Our staff is open-minded and youthful. We base decisions on merit, not reputation. The ms that's most enjoyable to read gets the nod. Be bold, take risks, surprise us."

NEW ENGLAND REVIEW

Middlebury College, Middlebury VT 05753. (802)443-5075. **E-mail:** nereview@middlebury.edu. **Website:** www.nereview.com. **Contact:** Carolyn Kuebler, editor. Estab. 1978. *New England Review* is a prestigious, nationally distributed literary journal. Reads September 1-May 31 (postmarked dates).

New England Review is 200+ pages, 7x10, printed on heavy stock, flat-spined, with glossy cover with art. Receives 3,000-4,000 poetry submissions/year, accepts about 70-80 poems/year. Receives 550 unsolicited mss/month, accepts 6 mss/issue, 24 fiction mss/year. Does not accept mss June-August. Agented fiction less than 5%.

NEEDS Send 1 story at a time, unless it is very short. Serious literary only, novel excerpts. Publishes approximately 10 new writers/year. Has published work by Steve Almond, Christine Sneed, Roy Kesey, Thomas Gough, Norman Lock, Brock Clarke, Carl Phillips, Lucia Perillo, Linda Gregerson, and Natasha Trethewey. Length: not strict on word count.

HOW TO CONTACT Send complete ms via online submission manager or postal mail (with SASE). No e-mail submissions. "Will consider simultaneous submissions, but must be stated as such and you must notify us immediately if the ms accepted for publication elsewhere."

PAYMENT/TERMS Pays $20/page ($20 minimum), and 2 contributor's copies.

TIPS "We consider short fiction, including short shorts, novellas, and self-contained extracts from novels in both traditional and experimental forms. In nonfiction, we consider a variety of general and literary but not narrowly scholarly essays; we also publish long and short poems, screenplays, graphics, translations, critical reassessments, statements by artists working in various media, testimonies, and letters from abroad. We are committed to exploration of all forms of contemporary cultural expression in the U.S. and abroad. With few exceptions, we print only work not published previously elsewhere."

NEW LETTERS

University of Missouri-Kansas City, 5101 Rockhill Rd., Kansas City MO 64110. (816)235-1168. **Fax:** (816)235-2611. **E-mail:** newletters@umkc.edu. **Website:** www.newletters.org. **Contact:** Robert Stewart, editor in chief. Estab. 1934. "*New Letters* continues to seek the best new writing, whether from established writers or those ready and waiting to be discovered. In addition, it supports those writers, readers, and listeners who want to experience the joy of writing that can both surprise and inspire us all."

Submissions are not read May 1-October 1.

NEEDS No genre fiction. Length: up to 5,000 words.

HOW TO CONTACT Send complete ms.

PAYMENT/TERMS Pays $30-75.

TIPS "We aren't interested in essays that are footnoted or essays usually described as scholarly or critical. Our preference is for creative nonfiction or personal essays. We prefer shorter stories and essays to longer ones (an average length is 3,500-4,000 words). We have no rigid preferences as to subject, style, or genre, although commercial efforts tend to put us off. Even so, our only fixed requirement is good writing."

NEW MADRID

Murray State University, Department of English and Philosophy, 7C Faculty Hall, Murray KY 42071-3341.

(270)809-4730. **E-mail:** msu.newmadrid@murray-state.edu. **Website:** newmadridjournal.org. **Contact:** Ann Neelon, editor. "*New Madrid* is the national journal of the low-residency MFA program at Murray State University. It takes its name from the New Madrid seismic zone, which falls within the central Mississippi Valley and extends through western Kentucky."

See website for guidelines and upcoming themes. "We have 2 reading periods, one from August 15-October 15, and one from January 15-March 15." Also publishes poetry and creative nonfiction. Rarely comments on/critiques rejected mss.

NEEDS Length: up to 20 pages double-spaced.

HOW TO CONTACT Accepts submissions by online submissions manager only. Include brief bio, list of publications. Considers multiple submissions.

PAYMENT/TERMS Pays 2 contributor's copies.

TIPS "Quality is the determining factor for breaking into *New Madrid*. We are looking for well-crafted, compelling writing in a range of genres, forms, and styles."

NEW MILLENNIUM WRITINGS

New Messenger Writing and Publishing, P.O. Box 2463, Knoxville TN 37901. (865)428-0389. **Website:** newmillenniumwritings.com. **Contact:** Elizabeth Petty, submissions editor. Estab. 1996. Only accepts general submissions January-April, but holds 4 contests twice each year for all types of fiction, nonfiction, short-short fiction, and poetry.

Annual anthology. 6x9, 204 pages, 50 lb. white paper, glossy 4-color cover. Contains illustrations and photographs.

NEEDS Receives average of 200 mss/month. Accepts 60 mss/year. **Publishes 10 new writers/year.** Rarely comments on/critiques rejected mss. Has published work by Charles Wright, Ted Kooser, Pamela Uschuk, William Pitt Root, Allen Wier, Lucille Clifton, John Updike, and Don Williams. Length: up to 6,000 words; up to 1,000 words for short shorts. Average length: 4,000 words for fiction.

NEW MOON GIRLS

New Moon Girl Media, P.O. Box 161287, Duluth MN 55816. (218)728-5507. **Fax:** (218)728-0314. **E-mail:** submissions@newmoon.com. **Website:** www.newmoon.com. Estab. 1992. "*New Moon Girls* is for every girl who wants her voice heard and her dreams taken seriously. *New Moon* celebrates girls, explores the passage from girl to woman, and builds healthy resistance to gender inequities. The *New Moon* girl is true to herself, and *New Moon Girls* helps her as she pursues her unique path in life, moving confidently into the world."

◯ In general, all material should be pro-girl and feature girls and women as the primary focus.

NEEDS Prefers girl-written material. All girl-centered. Length: 900-1,600 words.

HOW TO CONTACT Send complete ms by e-mail.

PAYMENT/TERMS Pays 6-12¢/word.

TIPS "We'd like to see more girl-written feature articles that relate to a theme. These can be about anything the girl has done personally, or she can write about something she's studied. Please read *New Moon Girls* before submitting to get a sense of our style. Writers and artists who comprehend our goals have the best chance of publication. We love creative articles—both nonfiction and fiction—that are not condescending to our readers. Keep articles to suggested word lengths; avoid stereotypes. Refer to our guidelines and upcoming themes online."

◑ NEW OHIO REVIEW

English Department, 360 Ellis Hall, Ohio University, Athens OH 45701. (740)597-1360. **E-mail:** noreditors@ohio.edu. **Website:** www.ohiou.edu/nor. **Contact:** Jill Allyn Rosser, editor. Estab. 2007. *New Ohio Review*, published biannually in spring and fall, publishes fiction, nonfiction, and poetry.

◯ Member CLMP. Reading period is September 15-December 15 and January 15-April 1.

NEEDS Considers literary short fiction; no novel excerpts.

HOW TO CONTACT Send complete ms.

PAYMENT/TERMS Pays $30 minimum in addition to 2 contributor's copies and one-year subscription.

◑◔◉ NEW ORLEANS REVIEW

Box 195, Loyola University, New Orleans LA 70118. (504)865-2295. **E-mail:** noreview@loyno.edu. **Website:** neworleansreview.org. **Contact:** Heidi Braden, managing editor. Estab. 1968. *New Orleans Review* is a biannual journal of contemporary literature and culture, publishing new poetry, fiction, nonfiction, art, photography, film and book reviews.

◯ The journal has published an eclectic variety of work by established and emerging writers including Walker Percy, Pablo Neruda, Ellen Gilchrist, Nelson Algren, Hunter S. Thompson, John Kennedy Toole, Richard Brautigan, Barry Spacks, James Sallis, Jack Gilbert, Paul Hoover, Rodney Jones, Annie Dillard, Everette Mad-

dox, Julio Cortazar, Gordon Lish, Robert Walser, Mark Halliday, Jack Butler, Robert Olen Butler, Michael Harper, Angela Ball, Joyce Carol Oates, Diane Wakoski, Dermot Bolger, Roddy Doyle, William Kotzwinkle, Alain Robbe-Grillet, Arnost Lustig, Raymond Queneau, Yusef Komunyakaa, Michael Martone, Tess Gallagher, Matthea Harvey, D. A. Powell, Rikki Ducornet, and Ed Skoog.

NEEDS Length: up to 6,500 words.

HOW TO CONTACT "We are now using an online submission system and require a $3 fee." See website for details.

PAYMENT/TERMS Pays $25-50 and 2 contributor's copies.

TIPS "We're looking for dynamic writing that demonstrates attention to the language and a sense of the medium, writing that engages, surprises, moves us. We're not looking for genre fiction or academic articles. We subscribe to the belief that in order to truly write well, one must first master the rudiments: grammar and syntax, punctuation, the sentence, the paragraph, the line, the stanza. We receive about 3,000 mss a year and publish about 3% of them. Check out a recent issue, send us your best, proofread your work, be patient, be persistent."

◑◉ THE NEW QUARTERLY

St. Jerome's University, 290 Westmount Rd. N., Waterloo ON N2L 3G3 Canada. (519)884-8111, ext. 28290. **E-mail:** editor@tnq.ca; info@tnq.ca. **Website:** www.tnq.ca. Estab. 1981. "Emphasis on emerging writers and genres, but we publish more traditional work as well if the language and narrative structure are fresh."

◯ Open to Canadian writers only. Reading periods: March 1-August 31; September 1-February 28.

NEEDS "*Canadian work only*. We are not interested in genre fiction. We are looking for innovative, beautifully crafted, deeply felt literary fiction."

HOW TO CONTACT Send complete ms. Does not accept submissions by e-mail. Accepts simultaneoues submissions if indicated in cover letter.

PAYMENT/TERMS Pays $250/story.

TIPS "Reading us is the best way to get our measure. We don't have preconceived ideas about what we're looking for other than that it must be Canadian work (Canadian writers, not necessarily Canadian content). We want something that's fresh, something that will repay a second reading, something in which the language soars and the feeling is complexly rendered."

NEW SOUTH

English Dept., Georgia State University, P.O Box 3970, Atlanta GA 30302-3970. (404)413-5874. **E-mail:** newsoutheditors@gmail.com. **Website:** www.newsouthjournal.com. Estab. 1980. Semiannual magazine dedicated to finding and publishing the best work from artists around the world. Wants original voices searching to rise above the ordinary. Seeks to publish high-quality work, regardless of genre, form, or regional ties.

New South is 160+ pages. Press run is 2,000; 500 distributed free to students. The *New South* Annual Writing Contest offers $1,000 for the best poem and $1,000 for the best story or essay; one-year subscription to all who submit. Submissions must be unpublished. Submit up to 3 poems, 1 story, or 1 essay on any subject or in any form. Specify "poetry" or "fiction" on outside envelope. Guidelines available by e-mail or on website. Competition receives 300 entries. Past judges include Sharon Olds, Jane Hirschfield, Anthony Hecht, Phillip Levine, and Jake Adam York. Winner will be announced in the Fall issue.

NEEDS Receives 200 unsolicited mss/month. Publishes and welcomes short shorts. Length: up to 9,000 words (short stories); up to 1,000 words (short shorts).

HOW TO CONTACT Submit 1 short story or up to 5 short shorts through Submittable.

PAYMENT/TERMS Pays 2 contributor's copies.

TIPS "We want what's new, what's fresh, and what's different—whether it comes from the Southern United States, the South of India, or the North, East or West of Anywhere."

NEW WELSH REVIEW

P.O. Box 170, Aberystwyth, Ceredigion Wa SY23 1 WZ United Kingdom. 01970-626230. **E-mail:** editor@newwelshreview.com. **E-mail:** submissions@newwelshreview.com. **Website:** www.newwelshreview.com. **Contact:** Gwen Davies, editor. "*NWR*, a literary quarterly ranked in the top 5 of British literary magazines, publishes stories, poems, and critical essays. The best of Welsh writing in English, past and present, is celebrated, discussed, and debated. We seek poems, short stories, reviews, special features/articles, and commentary." Quarterly.

HOW TO CONTACT Send hard copy only with SASE or international money order for return. Outside the U.K., submission by e-mail only.

PAYMENT/TERMS Pays "cheque on publication and 1 free copy."

THE NEW WRITER

1 Vicarage Lane, Stubbington Hampshire PO14 2JU United Kingdom. (44)(158)021-2626. **Website:** newwriteronline.com. Estab. 1996. Hosts *The New Writer* Flash Fiction Award, in which readers vote on the best flash fiction submission. "Now under new management and with a new home online, your favourite writing magazine has undergone a rebirth. We're starting with a free weekly e-newsletter delivering the best writing articles from around the Web to your inbox every Friday. Now we're working on turning *The New Writer Online* into a thriving community—a home for writers on the Web."

Currently accepting submissions of flash fiction, which *The New Writer Online* will publish as e-blasts to their online newsletter subscribers.

NEEDS Only accepting flash fiction submissions. Length: up to 1,000 words.

HOW TO CONTACT Submit via online submissions manager.

THE NEW YORKER

1 World Trade Center, New York NY 10007. **Website:** www.newyorker.com. **Contact:** David Remnick, editor in chief. Estab. 1925. A quality weekly magazine of distinct news stories, articles, essays, and poems for a literate audience.

The New Yorker receives approximately 4,000 submissions per month.

NEEDS Publishes 1 ms/issue.

HOW TO CONTACT Send complete ms by e-mail (as PDF attachment) or mail (address to Fiction Editor).

PAYMENT/TERMS Payment varies.

TIPS "Be lively, original, not overly literary. Write what you want to write, not what you think the editor would like."

NIMROD: INTERNATIONAL JOURNAL OF POETRY AND PROSE

University of Tulsa, 800 S. Tucker Dr., Tulsa OK 74104-3189. (918)631-3080. **Fax:** (918)631-3033. **E-mail:** nimrod@utulsa.edu. **Website:** www.utulsa.edu/nimrod. **Contact:** Eilis O'Neal, editor in chief. Estab. 1956. "*Nimrod*'s mission is the discovery and support of new writing of vigor and quality from this country and abroad. The journal seeks new, unheralded writers; writers from other lands who become accessible to the English-speaking world through translation, and established authors who have vigorous new work to present that has not found a home within the establishment. We believe in a living literature; that it is possible to search for, recognize, and reward contemporary writing of content and vigor, without reliance on a canon."

⬡ Semiannual magazine: 200 pages; perfectbound; 4c cover. Receives 120 unsolicited mss/month. **Publishes 5-10 new writers/year.** Reading period: January 1-November 30. Does not accept submissions by e-mail unless the writer is living outside the U.S. Poetry published in *Nimrod* has been included in *The Best American Poetry.*

NEEDS Wants "vigorous writing, characters that are well developed, dialogue that is realistic without being banal." Length: up to 7,500 words.

HOW TO CONTACT Submit complete ms by mail. Include SASE.

PAYMENT/TERMS Pays 2 contributor's copies.

NINTH LETTER

Department of English, University of Illinois, 608 S. Wright St., Urbana IL 61801. (217)244-3145. **E-mail:** info@ninthletter.com; editor@ninthletter.com. **Website:** www.ninthletter.com. **Contact:** Jodee Stanley, editor. "*Ninth Letter* accepts submissions of fiction, poetry, and essays from September 1-February 28 (postmark dates). *Ninth Letter* is published semiannually at the University of Illinois, Urbana-Champaign. We are interested in prose and poetry that experiment with form, narrative, and nontraditional subject matter, as well as more traditional literary work."

⬡ *Ninth Letter* won Best New Literary Journal 2005 from the Council of Editors of Learned Journals (CELJ) and has had poetry selected for *The Pushcart Prize, Best New Poets,* and *The Year's Best Fantasy and Horror.*

NEEDS Length: up to 8,000 words.

HOW TO CONTACT "Please send only 1 story at a time. All mailed submissions must include an SASE for reply."

PAYMENT/TERMS Pays $25 per printed page and 2 contributor's copies.

NITE-WRITER'S INTERNATIONAL LITERARY ARTS JOURNAL

158 Spencer Ave., Suite 100, Pittsburgh PA 15227. (412)668-0691. **E-mail:** nitewritersliteraryarts@gmail. com. **Website:** nitewritersinternational.webs.com.

Contact: John Thompson. Estab. 1994. *Nite-Writer's International Literary Arts Journal* is an online literary arts journal. "We are 'dedicated to the emotional intellectual' with a creative perception of life."

⬡ Journal is open to beginners as well as professionals.

NEEDS Length: up to 1,200 words.

HOW TO CONTACT All literary works should be in MS Word at 12-point font.

TIPS "Read a lot of what you write—study the market. Don't fear rejection, but use it as a learning tool to strengthen your work before resubmitting."

NON + X: AN EXPERIMENTAL JOURNAL OF BUDDHIST THOUGHT

E-mail: admin@nonplusx.com. **E-mail:** wtompepper@att.net. **Website:** www.nonplusx.com. **Contact:** Tom Pepper, editor. Estab. 2012. "*non + x* is an experimental e-journal dedicated to the critique of Buddhist and other contemporary cultural materials. Our goal 'consists in wresting vital potentialities of humans from the artificial forms and static norms that subjugate them' (Marjorie Gracieuse)."

NEEDS Query.

THE NORMAL SCHOOL

The Press at the California State University - Fresno, 5245 North Backer Ave., M/S PB 98, Fresno CA 93740-8001. **E-mail:** editors@thenormalschool.com. **Website:** thenormalschool.com. **Contact:** Steven Church, editor. Estab. 2008. Semiannual magazine that accepts outstanding work by beginning and established writers.

⬡ Mss are read from September 1 to December 1 and from January 15 to April 15. Address submissions to the appropriate editor. Charges $3 fee for each online submission, due to operational costs.

NEEDS Also publishes short shorts (fewer than 1,500 words). Sponsors The Normal Prizes in Fiction Contest and Creative Nonfiction Contest. Does not want any genre writing. Length: 12,000 words maximum.

HOW TO CONTACT Submit complete ms.

NORTH AMERICAN REVIEW

University of Northern Iowa, 1222 W. 27th St., Cedar Falls IA 50614. (319)273-6455. **Fax:** (319)273-4326. **E-mail:** nar@uni.edu. **Website:** northamericanreview. wordpress.com. **Contact:** Kim Groninga, nonfiction editor. Estab. 1815. "The *NAR* is the oldest literary magazine in America and one of the most respected;

though we have no prejudices about the subject matter of material sent to us, our first concern is quality."

○ This is the oldest literary magazine in the country and one of the most prestigious. Also one of the most entertaining—and a tough market for the young writer.

NEEDS "No flat narrative stories where the inferiority of the character is the paramount concern." Wants to see more "well-crafted literary stories that emphasize family concerns. We'd also like to see more stories engaged with environmental concerns." Reads fiction mss all year. **Publishes 2 new writers/year.** Recently published work by Lee Ann Roripaugh, Dick Allen, Rita Welty Bourke.

HOW TO CONTACT Accepts submissions by USPS mail only. Send complete ms with SASE.

TIPS "We like stories that start quickly and have a strong narrative arc. Poems that are passionate about subject, language, and image are welcome, whether they are traditional or experimental, whether in formal or free verse (closed or open form). Nonfiction should combine art and fact with the finest writing."

⑤ NORTH CAROLINA LITERARY REVIEW

East Carolina University, Mailstop 555 English, Greenville NC 27858-4353. (252)328-1537. **Fax:** (252)328-4889. **E-mail:** nclrsubmissions@ecu.edu. **Website:** www.nclr.ecu.edu. **Contact:** Margaret Bauer. Estab. 1992. "Articles should have a North Carolina slant. Fiction, creative nonfiction, and poetry accepted through yearly contests. First consideration is always for quality of work. Although we treat academic and scholarly subjects, we do not wish to see jargon-laden prose; our readers, we hope, are found as often in bookstores and libraries as in academia. We seek to combine the best elements of a magazine for serious readers with the best of a scholarly journal."

○ Accepts submissions through Submittable.

NEEDS Length: up to 6,000 words.

HOW TO CONTACT Submit fiction for the Doris Betts Fiction Prize competition via Submittable.

PAYMENT/TERMS Published writers paid in copies of the journal. First-place winners of contests receive a prize of $250.

TIPS "By far the easiest way to break in is with special issue sections. We are especially interested in reports on conferences, readings, meetings that involve North Carolina writers, and personal essays or short narratives with a strong sense of place. See back is-

sues for other departments. Interviews are probably the other easiest place to break in; no discussions of poetics/theory, etc., except in reader-friendly (accessible) language. Interviews should be personal, more like conversations, that explore connections between a writer's life and his/her work."

◐ NORTH DAKOTA QUARTERLY

276 Centennial Dr. Stop 7209, Merrifield Hall Room 15, Grand Forks ND 58202. (701)777-3322. **Website:** www.und.edu/org/ndq. **Contact:** Kate Sweney, managing editor. Estab. 1911. "*North Dakota Quarterly* strives to publish the best fiction, poetry, and essays that in our estimation we can. Our tastes and interests are best reflected in what we have been recently publishing, and we suggest that you look at some current issues for guidance."

○ Only reads fiction and poetry between September 1-May 1. Work published in *North Dakota Quarterly* was selected for inclusion in *The O. Henry Prize Stories, The Pushcart Prize Series,* and *Best American Essays*.

NEEDS No length restrictions.

HOW TO CONTACT Submit hard copies only.

◐◑⑤ NOTRE DAME REVIEW

University of Notre Dame, B009C McKenna Hall, Notre Dame IN 46556. **Website:** ndreview.nd.edu. Estab. 1995. "The *Notre Dame Review* is an indepenent, noncommercial magazine of contemporary American and international fiction, poetry, criticism, and art. Especially interested in work that takes on big issues by making the invisible seen, that gives voice to the voiceless. In addition to showcasing celebrated authors like Seamus Heaney and Czelaw Milosz, the *Notre Dame Review* introduces readers to authors they may have never encountered before but who are doing innovative and important work. In conjunction with the *Notre Dame Review*, the online companion to the printed magazine, the *nd[re]view* engages readers as a community centered in literary rather than commercial concerns, a community we reach out to through critique and commentary as well as aesthetic experience."

○ Does not accept e-mail submissions. Only reads hardcopy submissions September-November and January-March.

NEEDS "We're eclectic. Upcoming theme issues planned. List of upcoming themes or editorial calendar available for SASE." No genre fiction. Length: up to 3,000 words.

HOW TO CONTACT Send complete ms with cover letter. Include 4-sentence bio. Send SASE for response, return of ms, or send a disposable copy of ms.

PAYMENT/TERMS Pays $5-25.

TIPS "We're looking for high-quality work that takes on big issues in a literary way. Please read our back issues before submitting."

NOW & THEN: THE APPALACHIAN MAGAZINE

East Tennessee State University, Box 70556, Johnson City TN 37614-1707. (423)439-5348. **Fax:** (423)439-6340. **E-mail:** nowandthen@etsu.edu. **E-mail:** sandersr@etsu.edu. **Website:** www.etsu.edu/cass/nowandthen. **Contact:** Randy Sanders, managing editor; Wayne Winkler, music editor; Charlie Warden, photo editor. Estab. 1984. Literary magazine published twice/year. "*Now & Then* accepts a variety of writing genres: fiction, poetry, nonfiction, essays, interviews, memoirs, and book reviews. All submissions must relate to Appalachia and to the issue's specific theme. Our readership is educated and interested in the region."

◑ *Now & Then* tells the stories of Appalachia and presents a fresh, revealing picture of life in Appalachia, past and present, with engaging articles, personal essays, fiction, poetry, and photography.

NEEDS "Absolutely has to relate to Appalachian theme. Can be about adjustment to new environment, themes of leaving and returning, for instance. Nothing unrelated to region." Accepts 1-2 mss/issue. Publishes ms 4 months after acceptance. Publishes some new writers/year. Length: 1,000-1,500 words.

HOW TO CONTACT Send complete ms. Accepts submissions by mail, e-mail, with a strong preference for e-mail. Include "information we can use for contributor's note." SASE (or IRC). Rarely accepts simultaneous submissions. Reviews fiction.

PAYMENT/TERMS Pays $50 for each accepted article. Pays on publication.

TIPS "Keep in mind that *Now & Then* only publishes material related to the Appalachian region. Plus we only publish fiction that has some plausible connection to a specific issue's themes. We like to offer first-time publication to promising writers."

◑ NTH DEGREE

1219-M Gaskins Rd., Henrico VA 23238. **E-mail:** submissions@nthzine.com. **Website:** www.nthzine.com.

Contact: Michael Pederson. Estab. 2002. Free online fanzine to promote up-and-coming new science fiction and fantasy authors and artists. Also supports the world of fandom and conventions.

◑ No longer accepts hard copy submissions.

NEEDS Length: up to 7,500 words.

HOW TO CONTACT Submit complete ms via e-mail.

PAYMENT/TERMS Pays in contributor's copies.

TIPS "Don't submit anything that you may be ashamed of 10 years later."

◐◑ NTHPOSITION

E-mail: val@nthposition.com. **Website:** www.nthposition.com. **Contact:** Val Stevenson, managing editor. Estab. 2002. *nthposition*, published monthly online, is an eclectic, London-based journal with politics and opinion, travel writing, fiction and poetry, art reviews and interviews, and some high weirdness.

TIPS "Submit as text in the body of an e-mail, along with a brief bio note (2-3 sentences). If your work is accepted, it will be archived into the British Library's permanent collection."

◑ NUTHOUSE

P.O. Box 119, Ellenton FL 34222. **Website:** www.nuthousemagazine.com. *Nuthouse*, published every 3 months, uses humor of all kinds, including homespun and political.

◑ *Nuthouse* is 12 pages, digest-sized, photocopied from desktop-published originals. Receives about 500 poems/year, accepts about 100. Press run is 100. Subscription: $5 for 4 issues.

NEEDS "We publish all genres, from the homespun to the horrific. We don't automatically dismiss crudity or profanity. We're not prudes. Yet we consider such elements cheap and insulting unless essential to the gag. *NuTHOuSe* seeks submissions that are original, tightly written, and laugh-out-loud funny." Length: up to 1,000 words. "The shorter, the better."

HOW TO CONTACT Send complete ms with SASE and cover letter. Include estimated word count, bio (paragraph), and list of publications. No e-mail submissions.

PAYMENT/TERMS Pays 1 contributor's copy.

◑ OBSIDIAN

North Carolina State University, Department of English, Box 8105, Raleigh NC 27695. **E-mail:** obsidianatbrown@gmail.com. **Website:** obsidian-magazine.tumblr.com. **Contact:** Maya Finoh, managing editor.

Estab. 1975. *Obsidian* is a "literary and visual space to showcase the creativity and experiences of black people, specifically at Brown University, formed out of the need for a platform made for us, by us." It is "actively intersectional, safe, and open: a space especially for the stories and voices of black women, black queer and trans people, and black people with disabilities."

NEEDS Length: up to 4,000 words.

HOW TO CONTACT Submit by e-mail. Include brief bio up to 3 sentences.

TIPS "Following proper format is essential. Your title must be intriguing and text clean. Never give up. Some of the writers we publish were rejected many times before we published them."

OHIO TEACHERS WRITE

1209 Heather Run, Wilmington OH 45177. **E-mail:** ohioteacherswrite@octela.org. **Website:** www.octela.org/OTW.html. **Contact:** Eimile Máiréad Green, editor. Estab. 1995. "*Ohio Teachers Write* is a literary magazine published annually by the Ohio Council of Teachers of English Language Arts. This publication seeks to promote both poetry and prose of Ohio teachers and to provide an engaging collection of writing for our readership of educators and other like-minded adults. Invites electronic submissions from both active and retired Ohio educators for our annual literary print magazine."

NEEDS Submissions are limited to Ohio Educators. Length: up to 1,500 words.

HOW TO CONTACT Submit by e-mail.

PAYMENT/TERMS Pays 2 contributor's copies.

TIPS Check website for yearly theme.

ONE STORY

232 3rd St., #A108, Brooklyn NY 11215. **Website:** www.one-story.com. **Contact:** Maribeth Batcha, publisher. Estab. 2002. "*One Story* is a literary magazine that contains, simply, one story. Approximately every 3-4 weeks, subscribers are sent *One Story* in the mail. *One Story* is artfully designed, lightweight, easy to carry, and ready to entertain on buses, in bed, in subways, in cars, in the park, in the bath, in the waiting rooms of doctor's offices, on the couch, or in line at the supermarket. Subscribers also have access to a website where they can learn more about *One Story* authors and hear about *One Story* readings and events. There is always time to read *One Story*."

Reading period: September 1-May 31.

NEEDS *One Story* only accepts short stories. Do not send excerpts. Do not send more than 1 story at a time. Length: 3,000-8,000 words.

HOW TO CONTACT Send complete ms using online submission form.

PAYMENT/TERMS Pays $500 and 25 contributor's copies.

TIPS "*One Story* is looking for stories that are strong enough to stand alone. Therefore they must be very good. We want the best you can give."

ON SPEC

P.O. Box 4727, Station South, Edmonton AB T6E 5G6 Canada. (780)628-7121. **E-mail:** onspec@onspec.ca. **Website:** www.onspec.ca. Estab. 1989. "We publish speculative fiction and poetry by new and established writers, with a strong preference for Canadian-authored works."

See website guidelines for submission announcements. "Please refer to website for information regarding submissions, as we are not open year round."

NEEDS No media tie-in or shaggy-alien stories. No condensed or excerpted novels, religious/inspirational stories, fairy tales. Length: 1,000-6,000 words.

HOW TO CONTACT Send complete ms. Electronic submissions preferred.

TIPS "We want to see stories with plausible characters, a well-constructed, consistent, and vividly described setting, a strong plot, and believable emotions; characters must show us (not tell us) their emotional responses to each other and to the situation and/or challenge they face. Also: Don't send us stories written for television. We don't like media tie-ins, so don't watch TV for inspiration! Read instead! Strong preference given to submissions by Canadians."

ON THE PREMISES: A GOOD PLACE TO START

On the Premises, LLC, 4323 Gingham Court, Alexandria VA 22310. **E-mail:** questions@onthepremises.com. **Website:** www.onthepremises.com. **Contact:** Tarl Roger Kudrick or Bethany Granger, co-publishers. Estab. 2006. "Stories published in *On the Premises* are winning entries in contests that are held every 4 months. Each contest challenges writers to produce a great story based on a broad premise that our editors supply as part of the contest. *On the Premises* aims to promote newer and/or relatively unknown writers who can write what we feel are creative, compelling stories told in effective, uncluttered, and evocative prose. Entrants pay no fees, and winners receive cash prizes in addition to publication."

○ Does not read February, June, and October. Receives 50-125 mss/month. Accepts 3-6 mss/issue; 9-18 mss/year. Has published A'llyn Ettien, Cory Cramer, Mark Tullius, Michael Van Ornum, Ken Liu, and K. Stoddard Hayes. Member Small Press Promotions.

NEEDS Themes are announced the day each contest is launched. List of past and current premises available on website. "All genres considered. All stories must be based on the broad premise supplied as part of the contest. Sample premise, taken from the first issue: 'One or more characters are traveling in a vehicle, and never reach their intended destination. Why not? What happens instead?'" No young adult, children's, or "preachy" fiction. "In general, we don't like stories that were written solely to make a social or political point, especially if the story seems to assume that no intelligent person could possibly disagree with the author. Save the ideology for editorial and opinion pieces, please. But above all, we *never ever* want to see stories that do not use the contest premise! Use the premise, and make it 'clear' and 'obvious' that you are using the premise." Length: 1,000-5,000 words. Average length: 3,500 words.

HOW TO CONTACT Submit stories only via submission form at onthepremises.submittable.com/submit. "We no longer accept e-mailed submissions."

PAYMENT/TERMS Pays $60-220.

TIPS "Make sure you use the premise, not just interpret it. If the premise is 'must contain a real live dog,' then think of a creative, compelling way to use a real dog. Revise your draft, then revise again and again. Remember, we judge blindly, so craftmanship and creativity matter, not how well known you are."

☼ OPEN MINDS QUARTERLY

Northern Initiative for Social Action, 36 Elgin St., 2nd Floor, Sudbury ON P3C 5B4 Canada. (705)675-9193, ext. 8286. **E-mail:** openminds@nisa.on.ca. **Website:** www.openmindsquarterly.com. **Contact:** Dinah Laprairie, editor. Estab. 1997. *Open Minds Quarterly* provides a venue for individuals who have experienced mental illness to express themselves via poetry, short fiction, essays, first-person accounts of living with mental illness, and book/movie reviews. Wants unique, well-written, provocative poetry. Does not want overly graphic or sexual violence.

○ *Open Minds Quarterly* is 24 pages, magazine-sized, saddle-stapled, with 100 lb. stock cover with original artwork, includes ads. Press run is 550; 100 distributed free to potential subscribers, published writers, advertisers, and conferences and events.

HOW TO CONTACT Accepts e-mail and postal submissions. Cover letter is required. Info in cover letter: indication as to "consumer/survivor" of the mental health system status. Reads submissions year round.

☯ ORBIS

17 Greenhow Ave., West Kirby Wirral CH48 5EL U.K. **E-mail:** carolebaldock@hotmail.com. **Website:** www.orbisjournal.com. **Contact:** Carole Baldock, editor; Noel Williams, reviews editor. Estab. 1969. "*Orbis* has long been considered one of the top 20 small-press magazines in the U.K. We are interested in social inclusion projects and encouraging access to the Arts, young people, Under 20s, and 20-somethings. Subjects for discussion: 'day in the life,' technical, topical."

○ Please see guidelines on website before submitting.

NEEDS Length: 1,000 words max.

TIPS "Any publication should be read cover to cover because it's the best way to improve your chances of getting published. Enclose SAE with all correspondence. Overseas: 2 IRCs, 3 if work is to be returned."

◐◑ OXFORD MAGAZINE

Miami University, Oxford OH 45056. **Website:** www.oxfordmagazine.org. Estab. 1984. *Oxford Magazine*, published annually online in May, is open in terms of form, content, and subject matter. "Since our premiere in 1984, our magazine has received Pushcart Prizes for both fiction and poetry and has published authors such as Charles Baxter, William Stafford, Robert Pinsky, Stephen Dixon, Helena Maria Viramontes, Andre Dubus, and Stuart Dybek."

○ Work published in *Oxford Magazine* has been included in the *Pushcart Prize* anthology. Does not read submissions June through August.

NEEDS Length: up to 3,000 words.

HOW TO CONTACT Submit complete ms via online submissions manager.

◑ OYEZ REVIEW

Roosevelt University, Dept. of Literature & Languages, 430 S. Michigan Ave., Chicago IL 60605. **E-mail:** oyezreview@roosevelt.edu. **Website:** oyezreview.

wordpress.com. Estab. 1965. Annual magazine of the Creative Writing Program at Roosevelt University, publishing fiction, creative nonfiction, poetry, and art. There are no restrictions on style, theme, or subject matter.

O   Reading period is August 1-October 1. Each issue has 104 pages: 92 pages of text and an 8-page spread of 1 artist's work (in color or b&w). Work by the issue's featured artist also appears on the front and back cover, totaling 10 pieces. The journal has featured work from such writers as Charles Bukowski, James McManus, Carla Panciera, Michael Onofrey, Tim Foley, John N. Miller, Gary Fincke, and Barry Silesky, and visual artists Vivian Nunley, C. Taylor, Jennifer Troyer, and Frank Spidale. Accepts queries by e-mail.

NEEDS "We publish short stories and flash fiction on their merit as contemporary literature rather than the category within the genre." Length: up to 5,000 words.

HOW TO CONTACT Send complete ms via online submissions manager or postal mail.

PAYMENT/TERMS Pays 2 contributor's copies.

OYSTER BOY REVIEW

P.O. Box 1483, Pacifica CA 94044. **E-mail:** email_2015@oysterboyreview.com. **Website:** www.oysterboyreview.com. **Contact:** Damon Suave, editor/publisher. Estab. 1993. Electronic and print magazine. *Oyster Boy Review*, published annually, is interested in "the underrated, the ignored, the misunderstood, and the varietal. We'll make some mistakes."

NEEDS Wants "fiction that revolves around characters in conflict with themselves or each other; a plot that has a beginning, a middle, and an end; a narrative with a strong moral center (not necessarily 'moralistic'); a story with a satisfying resolution to the conflict; and an ethereal something that contributes to the mystery of a question but does not necessarily seek or contrive to answer it." Submit complete ms by postal mail or e-mail. No genre fiction.

PAYMENT/TERMS Pays 2 contributor's copies.

TIPS "Keep writing, keep submitting, keep revising."

PACIFICA LITERARY REVIEW

E-mail: pacificalitreview@gmail.com. **Website:** www.pacificareview.com. *Pacifica Literary Review* is a small literary arts magazine based in Seattle. Our print editions are published biannually in winter and summer. *PLR* is now accepting submissions of poetry, fiction,

creative nonfiction, author interview, and b&w photography. Submission period: September 15-May 7.

NEEDS Wants literary fiction and flash fiction. Length: up to 6,000 words for literary fiction; 300-1,000 words for flash fiction.

HOW TO CONTACT Submit complete ms.

PACIFIC REVIEW

Dept. of English and Comparative Literature, San Diego State University, 5500 Campanile Dr., MC6020, San Diego CA 92182-6020. **E-mail:** pacrevjournal@gmail.com. **Website:** pacificreview.sdsu.edu. **Contact:** Ryan Kelly, editor in chief. "We welcome submissions of previously published poems, short stories, translations, and creative nonfiction, including essays and reviews." For information on theme issues see website. **Publishes 15 new writers/year.** Recently published work by Ai, Alurista, Susan Daitch, Lawrence Ferlinghetti, and William T. Vollmann.

O   Does not accept e-mail submissions. See website for theme.

NEEDS Length: up to 5,000 words.

HOW TO CONTACT Submit ms via online submissions manager. Include cover letter with name, postal address, e-mail addresss, phone number, and short bio.

PAYMENT/TERMS Pays 2 contributor's copies.

TIPS "We welcome all submissions, especially those created in or in the context of the West Coast/California and the space of our borders."

PACKINGTOWN REVIEW

111 S. Lincoln St., Batavia IL 60510. **E-mail:** editors@packingtownreview.com. **Website:** www.packingtownreview.com. Estab. 2008. *Packingtown Review* publishes imaginative and critical prose and poetry by emerging and established writers. Welcomes submissions of poetry, scholarly articles, drama, creative nonfiction, fiction, and literary translation, as well as genre-bending pieces.

O   Literary magazine/journal. 8.5x11, 250 pages. Press run: 500.

NEEDS Does not want to see uninspired or unrevised work. Wants to avoid fantasy, science fiction, overtly religious, or romantic pieces. Length: up to 4,000 words.

HOW TO CONTACT Send complete ms with cover letter. Include estimated word count, brief bio, SASE.

PAYMENT/TERMS Pays 2 contributor's copies.

TIPS "We are looking for well-crafted prose. We are open to most styles and forms. We are also looking for prose that takes risks and does so successfully. We will consider articles about prose."

⟲➊❻ PAINTED BRIDE QUARTERLY

Drexel University, Department of English and Philosophy, 3141 Chestnut St., Philadelphia PA 19104. **E-mail:** pbq@drexel.edu. **Website:** pbq.drexel.edu. Estab. 1973. *Painted Bride Quarterly* seeks literary fiction (experimental and traditional), poetry, and artwork and photographs.

NEEDS Publishes theme-related work; check website. Holds annual fiction contests. Length: up to 5,000 words.

HOW TO CONTACT Send complete ms.

PAYMENT/TERMS Pays contributor's copy.

TIPS "We look for freshness of idea incorporated with high-quality writing. We receive an awful lot of nicely written work with worn-out plots. We want quality in whatever—we hold experimental work to as strict standards as anything else. Many of our readers write fiction; most of them enjoy a good reading. We hope to be an outlet for quality. A good story gives, first, enjoyment to the reader. We've seen a good many of them lately, and we've published the best of them."

PALABRA

P.O. Box 86146, Los Angeles CA 90086. **E-mail:** info@palabralitmag.com. **Website:** www.palabralitmag.com. Estab. 2006. *"PALABRA* is about exploration, risk, and ganas—the myriad intersections of thought, language, story, and art—*el mas alla of letters*, symbols and spaces into meaning."

⟲   Reading period: September 1-April 30.

NEEDS No genre work, i.e., mystery, romance, suspense, science fiction, etc. Length: up to 4,000 words; up to 750 for flash fiction.

HOW TO CONTACT Send complete ms via postal mail. If submitting in more than one genre submit each one separately. Include brief cover letter and SASE.

PAYMENT/TERMS Pays $25-$40.

PANK

PANK, Department of Humanities, 1400 Townsend Dr., Houghton MI 49931-1200. **Website:** www.pank-magazine.com. **Contact:** M. Bartley Seigel, editor. Estab. 2006. *"PANK* Magazine fosters access to emerging and experimental poetry and prose, publishing the brightest and most promising writers for the most adventurous readers. To the end of the road, up country,

a far shore, the edge of things, to a place of amalgamation and unplumbed depths, where the known is made and unmade, and where unimagined futures are born, a place inhabited by contradictions, a place of quirk and startling anomaly. *PANK*, no soft pink hands allowed."

NEEDS "Bright, new, energetic, passionate writing, writing that pushes our tender little buttons and gets us excited. Push our tender buttons, excite us, and we'll publish you."

HOW TO CONTACT Send complete ms through online submissions manager.

PAYMENT/TERMS Pays $20, a one-year subscription, and a *PANK* t-shirt.

TIPS "To read *PANK* is to know *PANK*. Or, read a lot within the literary magazine and small press universe—there's plenty to choose from. Unfortunately, we see a lot of submissions from writers who have clearly read neither *PANK* nor much else. Serious writers are serious readers. Read. Seriously."

⟲➊ PAPERPLATES

19 Kenwood Ave., Toronto ON M6C 2R8 Canada. (416)651-2551. **E-mail:** magazine@paperplates.org. **Website:** www.paperplates.org. **Contact:** Bernard Kelly, publisher. Estab. 1990. *paperplates* is a literary quarterly published in Toronto. "We make no distinction between veterans and beginners. Some of our contributors have published several books; some have never before published a single line."

⟲   No longer accepts IRCs.

NEEDS Length: no more than 7,500 words.

HOW TO CONTACT Submit by mail or e-mail. "Do not send fiction as an e-mail attachment. Copy the first 300 words or so into the body of your message. If you prefer not to send a fragment, you have the option of using surface mail." Include short bio with submission.

➊❻ THE PARIS REVIEW

544 West 27th St., New York NY 10001. (212)343-1333. **E-mail:** queries@theparisreview.org. **Website:** www.theparisreview.org. **Contact:** Lorin Stein, editor; Robyn Creswell, poetry editor. *The Paris Review* publishes "fiction and poetry of superlative quality, whatever the genre, style, or mode. Our contributors include prominent, as well as less well-known and previously unpublished writers. The Writers at Work interview series includes important contemporary writers discussing their own work and the craft of writing."

Address submissions to proper department. Do not make submissions via e-mail.

NEEDS Study the publication. Annual Plimpton Prize award of $10,000 given to a new voice published in the magazine. Recently published work by Ottessa Moshfegh, John Jeremiah Sullivan, and Lydia Davis. Length: no limit.

HOW TO CONTACT Send complete ms.

PAYMENT/TERMS Pays $1,000-3,000.

PASSAGER

Passager Press, 1420 N. Charles St., Baltimore MD 21201. **E-mail:** editors@passagerbooks.com. **Website:** www.passagerbooks.com. **Contact:** Mary Azrael and Kendra Kopelke, editors. Estab. 1990. "*Passager* has a special focus on older writers. Its mission is to encourage, engage, and strengthen the imagination well into old age and to give mature readers oppertunities that are sometimes closed off to them in our youth-oriented culture. We are dedicated to honoring the creativity that takes hold in later years and to making public the talents of those over the age of 50." Passager publishes 2 issues/year, an Open issue (fall/winter) and a Poetry Contest issue (spring/summer).

Literary magazine/journal. 8.25x8.25, 84 pages, recycled paper.

NEEDS Accepts submissions from writers over 50. Has published Miriam Karme, Lucille Schulberg Warner, Sally Bellerose, and Craig Hartglass. Length: up to 4,000 words.

HOW TO CONTACT Send complete ms with cover letter. Check website for guidelines. Include estimated word count, brief bio, list of publications. Send either SASE (or IRC) for return of ms or disposable copy of ms and #10 SASE for reply only.

PAYMENT/TERMS Pays 1 contributor's copy.

TIPS "Stereotyped images of old age will be rejected immediately. Write humorous, tongue-in-cheek essays. Read the publication, or at least visit the website."

PASSAGES NORTH

English Department, Northern Michigan University, 1401 Presque Isle Ave., Marquette MI 49855. (906)227-1203. **E-mail:** passages@nmu.edu. **Website:** www.passagesnorth.com. **Contact:** Jennifer A. Howard, editor in chief; Matt Weinkam and Robin McCarthy, managing editors; Matthew Gavin Frank, nonfiction editor; Martin Achatz, poetry editor; Timston Johnston, fiction editor. Estab. 1979. *Passages North*, pub-

lished annually in spring, prints poetry, short fiction, creative nonfiction, essays, and interviews.

Magazine: 7×10; 200-300 pgs; 60 lb. paper. Publishes work by established and emerging writers.

NEEDS "Don't be afraid to surprise us." No genre fiction, science fiction, "typical commercial-press work." Length: up to 7,000 words.

HOW TO CONTACT Send 1 short story or as many as 3 short-short stories (paste them all into 1 document).

TIPS "We look for voice, energetic prose, writers who take risks. We look for an engaging story in which the author evokes an emotional response from the reader through carefully rendered scenes, complex characters, and a smart, narrative design. Revise, revise. Read what we publish."

PASSION

Crescent Moon Publishing, P.O. Box 1312, Maidstone Kent ME14 5XU United Kingdom. (44)(162)272-9593. **E-mail:** cresmopub@yahoo.co.uk. **Website:** www.crmoon.com. Estab. 1988. *Passion*, published quarterly, features poetry, fiction, reviews, and essays on feminism, art, philosophy, and the media.

Wants "thought-provoking, incisive, polemical, ironic, lyric, sensual, and hilarious work." Does not want "rubbish, trivia, party politics, sport, etc."

HOW TO CONTACT Submit complete ms by postal mail. Include short bio.

PAYMENT/TERMS Pays 1 contributor's copy.

THE PATERSON LITERARY REVIEW

Passaic County Community College, Cultural Affairs Dept., One College Blvd., Paterson NJ 07505-1179. (973)684-6555. **Fax:** (973)523-6085. **E-mail:** mGillan@pccc.edu. **Website:** www.pccc.edu/poetry. **Contact:** Maria Mazziotti Gillan, editor/executive director. *Paterson Literary Review*, published annually, is produced by the The Poetry Center at Passaic County Community College. Wants poetry of "high quality; clear, direct, powerful work."

Work for *PLR* has been included in the *Pushcart Prize* anthology and *Best American Poetry*.

NEEDS "We are interested in quality short stories, with no taboos on subject matter." Receives 60 unsolicited mss/month. Publishes 5% new writers/year.

HOW TO CONTACT Send SASE for reply or return of ms. "Indicate whether you want story returned."

PAYMENT/TERMS Pays in contributor's copies.

TIPS Looks for "clear, moving, and specific work."

THE PAUMANOK REVIEW

E-mail: editor@paumanokreview.com. **E-mail:** submissions@paumanokreview.com. **Website:** www.paumanokreview.com. Estab. 2000. "*The Paumanok Review* is a quarterly Internet literary magazine dedicated to promoting and publishing the best in contemporary art, music, and literature. *TPR* is published exclusively on the Web and is available free of charge.

NEEDS Length: 1,000-6,000+ words for short stories; 200-1,000 words for short shorts.

HOW TO CONTACT Submit complete ms by e-mail (submissions@paumanokreview.com) with cover letter.

TIPS "*TPR* does not accept multiple submissions. The best statement of *TPR*'s publishing preferences is the magazine itself. Please read at least 1 issue before submitting."

PAVEMENT SAW

Pavement Saw Press, 321 Empire St., Montpelier OH 43543. **E-mail:** editor@pavementsaw.org. **Website:** pavementsaw.org. **Contact:** David Baratier, editor. *Pavement Saw*, published annually in August, wants "letters, short fiction, and poetry on any subject, especially work." Dedicates 15-20 pages of each issue to a featured writer.

Pavement Saw is 88 pages, digest-sized, perfect-bound. Press run is 550.

HOW TO CONTACT No e-mail submissions; postal submissions only. Cover letter is required. "No fancy typefaces."

THE PEDESTAL MAGAZINE

6815 Honors Court, Charlotte NC 28210. **E-mail:** pedmagazine@carolina.rr.com. **Website:** www.the-pedestalmagazine.com. **Contact:** John Amen, editor in chief. Estab. 2000. Committed to promoting diversity and celebrating the voice of the individual.

See website for reading periods for different forms. Member: CLMP.

NEEDS "We are receptive to all sorts of high-quality literary fiction. Genre fiction is encouraged as long as it crosses or comments upon its genre and is both character-driven and psychologically acute. We encourage submissions of short fiction, no more than 3 flash fiction pieces at a time. There is no need to query prior to submitting; please submit via online submission manager—no e-mail to the editor." Length: up to 4,000 words; up to 1,000 words for flash fiction.

PAYMENT/TERMS Pays 3¢/word.

TIPS "If you send us your work, please wait for a response to your first submission before you submit again."

PENNSYLVANIA ENGLISH

Penn State DuBois, College Place, DuBois PA 15801-3199. (814)375-4785. **Fax:** (814)375-4785. **E-mail:** avallone@psu.edu. **Website:** www.english.iup.edu/pcea/publications.htm. **Contact:** Dr. Jess Haggerty, editor; Dr. Michael Cox, nonfiction and fiction editor (mwcox@pitt.edu). Estab. 1985. *Pennsylvania English*, published annually, is "sponsored by the Pennsylvania College English Association. Our philosophy is quality. We publish literary fiction (and poetry and nonfiction). Our intended audience is literate, college-educated people."

Pennsylvania English is 5.25×8.25, up to 200 pages, perfect -bound, full-color cover featuring the artwork of a Pennsylvania artist. Reads mss during the summer. Publishes 4-6 new writers/year. Has published work by Dave Kress, Dan Leone, Paul West, Liz Rosenberg, Walt MacDonald, Amy Pence, Jennifer Richter, and Jeff Schiff.

NEEDS No genre fiction or romance.

HOW TO CONTACT Submit via the online submission manager at https://paenglish.submittable.com/submit. "For all submissions, please include a brief bio for the contributors' page. Be sure to include your name, address, phone number, e-mail address, institutional affiliation (if you have one), the title of your short story, and any other relevant information. We will edit if necessary for space."

PAYMENT/TERMS Pays 1 contributor's copy.

TIPS "Quality of the writing is our only measure. We're not impressed by long-winded cover letters detailing awards and publications we've never heard of. Beginners and professionals have the same chance with us. We receive stacks of competently written but boring fiction. For a story to rise from the rejection pile, it takes more than the basic competence."

PENNSYLVANIA LITERARY JOURNAL

Anaphora Literary Press, 1803 Treehills Parkway, Stone Mountain GA 30088. (520)425-4266. **E-mail:** director@anaphoraliterary.com. **Website:** anaphoraliterary.com. **Contact:** Anna Faktorovich, editor/director. Estab. 2009. "*Pennsylvania Literary Journal* is a printed, peer-reviewed journal that publishes critical essays, book reviews, short stories, interviews, photographs, art, and poetry. Published triannually, most are special issues with room for random projects in a wide variety of different fields. These special issues can be used to present a set of conference papers, so feel free to apply on behalf of a conference you are in charge of, if you think attending writers might be interested in seeing their revised conference papers published."

NEEDS No word limit.

HOW TO CONTACT Send complete ms via e-mail.

PAYMENT/TERMS Does not provide payment.

TIPS "We are just looking for great writing. Send your materials; if they are good and you don't mind working for free, we'll take it."

PENNY DREADFUL: TALES & POEMS OF FANTASTIC TERROR

P.O. Box 719, Radio City Station, Hell's Kitchen NY 10101-0719. **E-mail:** mmpendragon@aol.com. **Website:** www.mpendragon.com. Estab. 1996. *Penny Dreadful: Tales & Poems of Fanastic Terror*, published irregularly (about once a year), features goth-romantic poetry and prose. Publishes poetry, short stories, essays, letters, listings, reviews, and b&w artwork "which celebrate the darker aspects of Man, the World, and their Creator." Wants "literary horror in the tradition of Poe, M.R. James, Shelley, M.P. Shiel, and LeFanu—dark, disquieting tales and verses designed to challenge the reader's perception of human nature, morality, and man's place within the Darkness. Stories and poems should be set prior to 1910 and/or possess a timeless quality." Does not want "references to 20th- and 21st-century personages/events, graphic sex, strong language, excessive gore and shock elements."

> "Works appearing in *Penny Dreadful* have been reprinted in *The Year's Best Fantasy and Horror*." *Penny Dreadful* nominates best tales and poems for Pushcart Prizes. *Penny Dreadful* is over 100 pages, digest-sized, desktop-published, perfect-bound. Press run is 200.

NEEDS Length: up to 5,000 words.

HOW TO CONTACT Submit complete ms by mail or e-mail. "Mss should be submitted in the standard, professional format: typed, double-spaced, name and address on the first page, name and title of work on all subsequent pages, etc. Include SASE for reply. Also include brief cover letter with a brief bio and publication history."

PAYMENT/TERMS Pays 1 contributor's copy.

PENTHOUSE VARIATIONS

FriendFinder Networks, 20 Broad Street, 14th Floor, New York NY 10005. **Website:** penthouse.com. Estab. 1978. A digest-sized print and digital magazine publishing erotic short stories; publishes 12 issues/year.

NEEDS Send complete first-person, past tense ms; no queries. No poetry. No serialized fiction. Length: 3,000-3,500 words.

PAYMENT/TERMS Pays $400 for an accepted ms.

TIPS "*Variations* publishes first-person, sex-positive narratives in which the author fully describes sex scenes squarely focused within one of the magazine's usual categories, in highly explicit erotic detail. To submit material to *Variations* you must be 18 years of age or older."

PEREGRINE

Amherst Writers & Artists Press, P.O. Box 1076, Amherst MA 01004. (413)253-3307. **Fax:** (413)253-7764. **E-mail:** peregrine@amherstwriters.com. **Website:** www.amherstwriters.com. **Contact:** Jan Haag, editor. Estab. 1983. *Peregrine*, published annually, features poetry and fiction. "*Peregrine* has provided a forum for national and international writers since 1983 and is committed to finding excellent work by emerging as well as established writers. We welcome work reflecting diversity of voice. We like to be surprised. We look for writing that is honest, unpretentious, and memorable. All decisions are made by the editors."

> Magazine: 6x9; 100+ pages; 60 lb. white offset paper; glossy cover. Member: CLMP. Reading period: March 15-May 15.

NEEDS Length: up to 750 words.

HOW TO CONTACT Submit via e-mail. Include word count on first page of submissions. "Shorter stories have a better chance."

PAYMENT/TERMS Pays in contributor's copies.

TIPS "Check guidelines before submitting your work. Familiarize yourself with *Peregrine*. We look for heart and soul as well as technical expertise. Trust your own voice."

PERMAFROST: A LITERARY JOURNAL

c/o English Dept., Univ. of Alaska Fairbanks, P.O. Box 755720, Fairbanks AK 99775. **E-mail:** editor@ permafrostmag.com. **Website:** permafrostmag.com. Estab. 1977. *Permafrost: A Literary Journal*, published in May/June, contains poems, short stories, creative nonfiction, b&w drawings, photographs, and prints. "We survive on both new and established writers, hoping and expecting to see the best work out there. We have published work by E. Ethelbert Miller, W. Loran Smith, Peter Orlovsky, Jim Wayne Miller, Allen Ginsberg, and Andy Warhol."

○ *Permafrost* is about 200 pages, digest-sized, professionally printed, flat-spined. Also publishes summer online edition.

NEEDS Length: up to 8,000 words.

HOW TO CONTACT Submit complete ms via online submissions manager at permafrostmag.submittable. com; "e-mail submissions will not be read."

PAYMENT/TERMS Pays 1 contributor's copy. Reduced contributor rate of $5 on additional copies.

○ PERSIMMON TREE: MAGAZINE OF THE ARTS BY WOMEN OVER SIXTY

1534 Campus Dr., Berkeley CA 94708. **E-mail:** editor@persimmontree.org; Submissions@persimmontree.org. **Website:** www.persimmontree.org. **Contact:** Sue Leonard, editor. "*Persimmon Tree*, an online magazine, is a showcase for the creativity and talent of women over sixty. Too often older women's artistic work is ignored or disregarded, and only those few who are already established receive the attention they deserve. Yet many women are at the height of their creative abilities in their later decades and have a great deal to contribute. *Persimmon Tree* is committed to bringing this wealth of fiction, nonfiction, poetry, and art to a broader audience, for the benefit of all."

NEEDS Length: under 3,500 words.

HOW TO CONTACT Submit complete ms via e-mail. "Note: You must be signed onto the e-mail newsletter to be considered for publication."

TIPS "High quality of writing and an interesting or unique point of view make a ms stand out. Make it clear that you're familiar with the magazine. Tell us why the piece would work for our audience."

○ PERSPECTIVES

4500 60th St. SE, Grand Rapids MI 49512. **E-mail:** submissions@perspectivesjournal.org. **Website:** perspectivesjournal.org. "*Perspectives* is a journal of theology in the broad Reformed tradition. We seek to express the Reformed faith theologically; to engage issues that Reformed Christians meet in personal, ecclesiastical, and societal life; and thus to contribute to the mission of the church of Jesus Christ.The editors are interested in submissions that contribute to a contemporary Reformed theological discussion. Our readers tend to be affiliated with the Presbyterian

Church (USA), the Reformed Church in America, and the Christian Reformed Church. Some of our subscribers are academics or pastors, but we also gear our articles to thoughtful, literate laypeople who want to engage in Reformed theological reflection on faith and culture."

○ *Perspectives* is 24 pages, magazine-sized, Web offset-printed, saddle-stapled, with paper cover containing b&w illustration. Receives about 300 poems/year, accepts 6-20. Press run is 3,300.

NEEDS Length: up to 3,000 words.

HOW TO CONTACT Submit complete ms by e-mail.

○ PHILADELPHIA STORIES

Fiction/Art/Poetry of the Delaware Valley, 93 Old York Rd., Suite 1/#1-753, Jenkintown PA 19046. (215) 551-5889. **E-mail:** christine@philadelphiastories.org; info@philadelphiastories.org. **Website:** www.philadelphiastories.org. **Contact:** Christine Weiser, executive director/co-publisher. Estab. 2004. *Philadelphia Stories*, published quarterly, publishes "fiction, poetry, essays, and art written by authors living in, or originally from, Pennsylvania, Delaware, or New Jersey. "*Philadelphia Stories* also hosts 2 national writing contests: The Marguerite McGlinn Short Story Contest ($2,000 first-place prize; $500 second-place prize; $250 third-place prize) and the Sandy Crimmins National Poetry Contest ($1,000 first-place prize, 3 $100 runner-up prizes). Visit our website for details. "*Philadelphia Stories* also launched a "junior" version in 2012 for Philadelphia-area writers ages 18 and younger. Visit www.philadelphiastories.org/junior for details.

○ Literary magazine/journal. 8.5×11; 24 pages; 70# matte text, all 4-color paper; 70# matte text cover. Contains illustrations, photographs. Subscription: "We offer $20 memberships that include home delivery." Make checks payable to *Philadelphia Stories*. Member: CLMP.

NEEDS Receives 45-80 mss/month. Accepts 3-4 mss/issue for print, additional 1-2 online; 12-16 mss/year for print, 4-8 online. Publishes 50% new writers/year. Also publishes book reviews. Send review queries to: info@philadelphiastories.org. "We will consider anything that is well written but are most inclined to publish literary or mainstream fiction. We are *not* particularly interested in most genres (sci fi/fantasy, romance, etc.)." Length: up to 5,000 words. Average length: 4,000 words. Also publishes short shorts; average length: 800 words.

PAYMENT/TERMS Pays 2+ contributor's copies.

TIPS "We look for exceptional, polished prose, a controlled voice, strong characters and place, and interesting subjects. Follow guidelines. We cannot stress this enough. Read every guideline carefully and thoroughly before sending anything out. Send out only polished material. We reject many quality pieces for various reasons; try not to take rejection personally. Just because your piece isn't right for one publication doesn't mean it's bad. Selection is an extremely subjective process."

PHOEBE: A JOURNAL OF LITERATURE AND ART

MSN 2C5, George Mason University, 400 University Dr., Fairfax VA 22030. **E-mail:** phoebeliterature@gmail.com. **Website:** www.phoebejournal.com. Estab. 1972. Publishes poetry, fiction, nonfiction, and visual art. "*Phoebe* prides itself on supporting up-and-coming writers, whose style, form, voice, and subject matter demonstrate a vigorous appeal to the senses, intellect, and emotions of our readers."

NEEDS No romance or erotica. Length: up to 4,000 words.

HOW TO CONTACT Submit 1 fiction submission via online submission manager.

PAYMENT/TERMS Pays 2 contributor's copies.

PILGRIMAGE MAGAZINE

Colorado State University-Pueblo, Dept. of English, 2200 Bonforte Blvd., Pueblo CO 81001. **E-mail:** info@pilgrimagepress.org. **Website:** www.pilgrimagepress.org. **Contact:** Juan Morales, editor. Estab. 1976. Serves an eclectic fellowship of readers, writers, artists, naturalists, contemplatives, activists, seekers, adventurers, and other kindred spirits.

NEEDS Length: up to 6,000 words. "Shorter works are easier to include, due to space constraints."

TIPS "Our interests include wildness in all its forms; inward and outward explorations; home ground, the open road, service, witness, peace, and justice; symbols, story, and myth in contemporary culture; struggle and resilience; insight and transformation; wisdom wherever it is found; and the great mystery of it all. We like good storytellers and a good sense of humor. No e-mail submissions, please."

THE PINCH

English Department, University of Memphis, Memphis TN 38152. (901)678-4591. **E-mail:** editor@pinch-journal.com. **Website:** www.pinchjournal.com. **Contact:** Tim Johnston, editor in chief; Matthew Gallant, managing editor. Estab. 1980. Semiannual literary magazine. "We publish fiction, creative nonfiction, poetry, and art of literary quality by both established and emerging artists."

"The Pinch Literary Awards in Fiction, Poetry, and Nonfiction offer a $1,000 prize and publication. Check our website for details."

NEEDS Wants "character-based" fiction with a "fresh use of language." No genre fiction. Length: up to 5,000 words.

HOW TO CONTACT "We do NOT accept submissions via e-mail. Submissions sent via e-mail will not receive a response. To submit, see guidelines." Submit through mail or via online submissions manager.

TIPS "We have a new look and a new edge. We're soliciting work from writers with a national or international reputation as well as strong, interesting work from emerging writers."

THE PINK CHAMELEON

E-mail: dpfreda@juno.com. **Website:** www.thepink-chameleon.com. **Contact:** Dorothy Paula Freda, editor/publisher. Estab. 2000. *The Pink Chameleon*, published annually online, contains "family-oriented, upbeat poetry, stories, essays, and articles, any genre in good taste that gives hope for the future."

Reading period is January 1-April 30 and September 1-October 31.

NEEDS "No violence for the sake of violence." No novels or novel excerpts. Length: 500-2,500 words; average length: 2,000 words.

HOW TO CONTACT Send complete ms in the body of the e-mail. No attachments. Accepts reprints. Has published work by Deanne F. Purcell, Martin Green, Albert J. Manachino, James W. Collins, Ron Arnold, Sally Kosmalski, Susan Marie Davniero, and Glenn D. Hayes.

PAYMENT/TERMS No payment.

TIPS Wants "simple, honest, evocative emotion; upbeat fiction and nonfiction submissions that give hope for the future; well-paced plots; stories, poetry, articles, essays that speak from the heart. Read guidelines carefully. Use a good, but not ostentatious, opening hook. Stories should have a beginning, middle, and end that make the reader feel the story was worth his or her time. This also applies to articles and essays. In the latter 2, wrap your comments and conclusions in a neatly packaged final paragraph. Turnoffs include violence and bad language. Simple, genuine, and sensitive work does not need to shock with vulgarity to be interesting and enjoyable."

PINYON POETRY

Mesa State College, Languages, Literature and Mass Communications, Mesa State College, Grand Junction CO 81502. **E-mail:** rphillis@mesa5.mesa.colorado.edu. **Website:** org.coloradomesa.edu/~rphillis/. **Contact:** Randy Phillis, editor. Estab. 1995. *Pinyon Poetry*, published annually in June, prints "the best available contemporary American poetry. No restrictions other than excellence. We appreciate a strong voice."

Literary magazine/journal: 8.5×5.5, 120 pages, heavy paper. Contains illustrations and photographs. Press run is 300; 100 distributed free to contributors, friends, etc.

TIPS "Ask yourself if the work is something you would like to read in a publication."

PISGAH REVIEW

Division of Humanities, Brevard College, 1 Brevard College Dr., Brevard NC 28712. (828)577-8324. **E-mail:** tinerjj@brevard.edu. **Website:** www.pisgahreview.com. **Contact:** Jubal Tiner, editor. Estab. 2005. "*Pisgah Review* publishes primarily literary short fiction, creative nonfiction, and poetry. Our only criteria is quality of work; we look for the best."

Has published Ron Rash, Thomas Rain Crowe, Joan Conner, Gary Fincke, Steve Almond, and Fred Bahnson.

NEEDS Receives 85 mss/month. Accepts 6-8 mss/issue; 12-15 mss/year. Publishes 5 new writers/year. Does not want genre fiction or inspirational stories. Length: 2,000-7,500 words. Average length: 4,000 words. Average length of short shorts: 1,000 words.

HOW TO CONTACT "Send complete ms to our submission manager on our website."

PAYMENT/TERMS Writers receive 2 contributor's copies. Additional copies $7.

TIPS "We select work of only the highest quality. Grab us from the beginning and follow through. Engage us with your language and characters. A clean ms goes a long way toward acceptance. Stay true to the vision of your work, revise tirelessly, and submit persistently."

PLANET-THE WELSH INTERNATIONALIST

P.O. Box 44, Aberystwyth Ceredigion SY23 3ZZ United Kingdom. **E-mail:** emily.trahair@planetmagazine.org.uk. **Website:** www.planetmagazine.org.uk. **Contact:** Emily Trahair, editor. Estab. 1970. A literary/cultural/political journal centered on Welsh affairs but with a strong interest in minority cultures in Europe and elsewhere. *Planet: The Welsh Internationalist*, published quarterly, is a cultural magazine "centered on Wales, but with broader interests in arts, sociology, politics, history, and science."

Planet is 128 pages, A5, professionally printed, perfect-bound, with glossy color card cover. Receives about 500 submissions/year, accepts about 5%. Press run is 1,550 (1,500 subscribers, about 10% libraries, 200 shelf sales).

NEEDS Would like to see more inventive, imaginative fiction that pays attention to language and experiments with form. No magical realism, horror, science fiction. Length: 1,500-2,750 words.

HOW TO CONTACT Submit complete ms via mail or e-mail (with attachment). For postal submissions, no submissions returned unless accompanied by an SASE. Writers submitting from abroad should send at least 3 IRCs for return of typescript; 1 IRC for reply only.

PAYMENT/TERMS Pays £50/1,000 words.

TIPS "We do not look for fiction that necessarily has a 'Welsh' connection, which some writers assume from our title. We try to publish a broad range of fiction, and our main criterion is quality. Try to read copies of any magazine you submit to. Don't write out of the blue to a magazine which might be completely inappropriate for your work. Recognize that you are likely to have a high rejection rate, as magazines tend to favor writers from their own countries."

PLEIADES

Pleiades Press, Department of English, University of Central Missouri, Martin 336, Warrensburg MO 64093. (660)543-8106. **E-mail:** pleiades@ucmo.edu. **Website:** www.ucmo.edu/pleiades. **Contact:** Kevin Prufer, editor-at-large. Estab. 1991. "We publish contemporary fiction, poetry, interviews, literary essays, special-interest personal essays, and reviews for a general and literary audience from authors from around the world." Reads August 15-May 15.

NEEDS Reads fiction year-round. No science fiction, fantasy, confession, erotica. Length: 2,000-6,000 words.

HOW TO CONTACT Send complete ms via online submission manager.

PAYMENT/TERMS Pays $10 and contributor's copies.

TIPS "Submit only 1 genre at a time to appropriate editors. Show care for your material and your readers—submit quality work in a professional format. Include cover letter with brief bio and list of publications. Include SASE. Cover art is solicited directly from artists. We accept queries for book reviews."

⚫⚫⚫ PLOUGHSHARES

Emerson College, 120 Boylston St., Boston MA 02116. (617)824-3757. **E-mail:** pshares@pshares.org. **Website:** www.pshares.org. **Contact:** Ladette Randolph, editor in chief/executive director; Andrea Martucci, managing editor. Estab. 1971. *Ploughshares*, published 3 times/year, is "a journal of new writing guest-edited by prominent poets and writers to reflect different and contrasting points of view. Translations are welcome if permission has been granted. Our mission is to present dynamic, contrasting views on what is valid and important in contemporary literature and to discover and advance significant literary talent. Each issue is guest-edited by a different writer. We no longer structure issues around preconceived themes." Editors have included Carolyn Forché, Gerald Stern, Rita Dove, Chase Twichell, and Marilyn Hacker. "We do accept electronic submissions—there is a $3 fee per submission, which is waived if you are a subscriber."

⚫ *Ploughshares* is 200 pages, digest-sized. Receives about 11,000 poetry, fiction, and essay submissions/year. Reads submissions June 1-January 15 (postmark); mss submitted January 16-May 31 will be returned unread.

NEEDS Has published work by ZZ Packer, Antonya Nelson, and Stuart Dybek. "No genre (science fiction, detective, gothic, adventure, etc.), popular formula or commerical fiction whose purpose is to entertain rather than to illuminate." Length: up to 6,000 words

HOW TO CONTACT Submit via online submissions form or by mail.

PAYMENT/TERMS Pays $25/printed page ($50 minimum, $250 maximum); 2 contributor's copies; and one-year subscription.

⚫ PMS POEMMEMOIRSTORY

University of Alabama at Birmingham, HB 217, 1530 3rd Ave. S, Birmingham AL 35294. (205)934-2641. **Fax:** (205)975-8125. **E-mail:** poemmemoirstory@gmail.com. **Website:** pms-journal.org. **Contact:** Kerry Madden, editor in chief. "*PMS poemmemoirstory* appears once a year. We accept unpublished, original submissions of poetry, memoir, and short fiction during our January 1-March 31 reading period. We accept simultaneous submissions; however, we ask that you please contact us immediately if your piece is published elsewhere so we may free up space for other authors. While *PMS* is a journal of exclusively women's writing, the subject field is wide open."

⚫ *PMS* has gone all-digital on Submittable. "There is now a $3 fee, which covers costs associated with our online submissions system. Please send all submissions to https://poemmemoirstory.submittable.com/submit."

NEEDS Length: up to 15 pages or 4,300 words.

HOW TO CONTACT Submit through online submissions manager.

PAYMENT/TERMS Pays 2 contributor's copies.

TIPS "We strongly encourage you to familiarize yourself with *PMS* before submitting. You can find links to some examples of what we publish in the pages of *PMS 8* and *PMS 9*. We look forward to reading your work."

⚫⚫ POCKETS

The Upper Room, P.O. Box 340004, Nashville TN 37203. (615)340-7333. **E-mail:** pockets@upperroom.org. **Website:** pockets.upperroom.org. **Contact:** Lynn W. Gilliam, editor. Estab. 1981. In addition to receiving regular submissions, *Pockets* sponsors a fiction contest each year. Magazine published 11 times/year. "*Pockets* is a Christian devotional magazine for children ages 6-12. All submissions should address the broad theme of the magazine. Each issue is built around a theme with material which can be used by children in a variety of ways. Scripture stories, fiction, poetry, prayers, art, graphics, puzzles and activities are included. Submissions do not need to be overtly religious. They should help children experience a Christian lifestyle that is not always a neatly wrapped moral package but is open to the continuing revelation of God's will. Seasonal material, both secular and liturgical, is desired."

⚫ Does not accept e-mail or fax submissions.

NEEDS "Stories should contain lots of action, use believable dialogue, be simply written, and be relevant to the problems faced by this age group in everyday life." Length: 600-1,000 words.

HOW TO CONTACT Submit complete ms by mail. No e-mail submissions.

TIPS "Theme stories, role models, and retold scripture stories are most open to freelancers. Poetry is also open. It is very helpful if writers read our writers' guidelines and themes on our website."

POETICA MAGAZINE, CONTEMPORARY JEWISH WRITING

P.O. Box 11014, Norfolk VA 23517. **E-mail:** poetica-publishing@aol.com. **Website:** www.poeticamagazine.com. Estab. 2002. *Poetica Magazine, Contemporary Jewish Writing*, published in print 3 times/year, offers "an outlet for the many writers who draw from their Jewish backgrounds and experiences to create poetry/prose/short stories, giving both emerging and recognized writers the opportunity to share their work with the larger community."

○ *Poetica* is 70 pages, perfect-bound, full-color cover, includes some ads. Receives about 500 poems/year, accepts about 60%. Press run is 350.

NEEDS Length: up to 4 pages.

HOW TO CONTACT Submit ms through online submissions manager. Include e-mail, bio, and mailing address.

PAYMENT/TERMS Pays 1 contributor's copy.

TIPS "We publish original, unpublished works by Jewish and non-Jewish writers alike. We are interested in works that have the courage to acknowledge, challenge, and celebrate modern Jewish life beyond distinctions of secular and sacred. We like accessible works that find fresh meaning in old traditions that recognize the challenges of our generation. We evaluate works on several levels, including its skillful use of craft, its ability to hold interest, and layers of meaning."

● POETRY INTERNATIONAL

San Diego State University, 5500 Campanile Dr., San Diego CA 92182-6020. (619)594-1522. **Fax:** (619)594-4998. **E-mail:** poetryintl@gmail.com. **Website:** poetryinternational.sdsu.edu. **Contact:** Jenny Minniti-Shippey, managing editor. Estab. 1997. *Poetry International*, published annually in November, is "an eclectic poetry magazine intended to reflect a wide range of poetry being written today." Wants "a wide range of styles and subject matter. We're particularly interested in translations." Does not want "cliché-ridden, derivative, or obscure poetry." Has published poetry by Adrienne Rich, Robert Bly, Hayden Carruth, Kim Addonizio, Maxine Kumin, and Gary Soto. "We intend to continue to publish poetry that makes a difference in people's lives, and startles us anew with the endless capacity of language to awaken our senses and expand our awareness."

○ *Poetry International* is 200 pages, perfect-bound, with coated cardstock cover. Features the Poetry International Prize ($1,000) for best original poem. Submit up to 3 poems with a $15 entry fee.

HOW TO CONTACT Query.

TIPS "Seeks a wide range of styles and subject matter. We read unsolicited mss only between September 1-December 31 of each year. Mss received any other time will be returned unread."

● POINTED CIRCLE

Portland Community College, Cascade Campus, SC 206, 705 N. Killingsworth Street, Portland OR 97217. **E-mail:** wendy.bourgeois@pcc.edu. **Website:** www.pcc.edu/about/literary-magazines/pointed-circle. **Contact:** Wendy Bourgeois, faculty advisor. Estab. 1980. Publishes "anything of interest to educationally/culturally mixed audience. We will read whatever is sent, but we encourage writers to remember we are a quality literary/arts magazine intended to promote the arts in the community. No pornography, nothing trite. Be mindful of deadlines and length limits." Accepts submissions by e-mail, mail; artwork in high-resolution digital form.

○ Reading period: October 1-February 7. Magazine: 80 pages; b&w illustrations; photos.

NEEDS Length: Up to 3,000 words.

HOW TO CONTACT Submitted materials will not be returned; SASE for notification only. Accepts multiple submissions.

PAYMENT/TERMS Pays 2 contributor's copies.

○ POLYPHONY H.S.

An International Student-Run Literary Magazine for High School Writers and Editors, Polyphony High School, 1514 Elmwood Ave., Suite 2, Evanston IL 60201. (847)910-3221. **E-mail:** info@polyphonyhs.com; billy@polyphonyhs.com. **Website:** www.polyphonyhs.com. **Contact:** Billy Lombardo, co-founder and managing editor. Estab. 2005. "Our mission is to create a high-quality literary magazine written, edited, and published by high school students. We believe that when young writers put precise and powerful language to their lives it helps them better understand their value as human beings. We believe the development of that creative voice depends upon close, careful, and compassionate attention. Helping young editors become proficient at providing thoughtful and informed attention to the work of their peers is essential to our mission. We believe this important exchange between young writers and editors provides each with a better understanding of craft, of the writing process, and of the value of putting words to their own lives while preparing them for participation in the broader literary community. We strive to build respectful, mutually beneficial writer-editor relationships that form a community devoted to improving students' literary skills in the areas of poetry, fiction, and creative nonfiction."

○ Does not accept hard-copy entries; submit only through online submissions form.

NEEDS Length: up to 1,500 words.

HOW TO CONTACT Submit complete ms via online submissions form.

PAYMENT/TERMS Pays 1 contributor's copy.

TIPS "We manage the Claudia Ann Seaman Awards for Young Writers; cash awards for the best poem, best story, best essay. See website for details."

○ PORTLAND REVIEW

Portland State University, P.O. Box 751, Portland OR 97207. **Website:** portlandreview.org. **Contact:** Alex Dannemiller, editor in chief. Estab. 1956. Triannual magazine covering short prose, poetry, photography, and art. Press run is 1,000 for subscribers, libraries, and bookstores nationwide.

NEEDS Publishes 40 mss/year. Length: up to 5,000 words.

HOW TO CONTACT Send complete ms.

PAYMENT/TERMS Pays contributor's copies.

TIPS "View website for current guidelines."

○ POTOMAC REVIEW: A JOURNAL OF ARTS & HUMANITIES

Montgomery College, 51 Mannakee St., MT/212, Rockville MD 20850. (240)567-4100. **E-mail:** PotomacReviewEditor@montgomerycollege.edu. **Website:** www.montgomerycollege.edu/potomacreview. **Contact:** Julie Wakeman-Linn, editor in chief; Kathleen Smith, poetry editor. Estab. 1994. *Potomac Review: A Journal of Arts & Humanities*, published semiannually in August and February, welcomes poetry from across the spectrum, both traditional and nontraditional poetry, free verse and in-form (translations accepted). Essays, fiction, and creative nonfiction are also welcome.

○ Reading period: September 1-May 1. Has published work by David Wagoner, Jacob Appel, Sandra Beasley, and Amy Holman.

NEEDS Length: up to 5,000 words.

HOW TO CONTACT Submit electronically through website.

○○ THE PRAIRIE JOURNAL

P.O. Box 68073, 28 Crowfoot Terrace NW, Calgary AB Y3G 3N8 Canada. **E-mail:** editor@prairiejournal.org (queries only); prairiejournal@yahoo.com. **Website:** www.prairiejournal.org. **Contact:** A.E. Burke, literary editor. Estab. 1983. "The audience is literary, university, library, scholarly, and creative readers/writers."

○ "Use our mailing address for submissions and queries with samples or for clippings."

NEEDS No genre (romance, horror, western—sagebrush or cowboys), erotic, science fiction, or mystery. Length: 100-3,000 words.

HOW TO CONTACT Send complete ms. No e-mail submissions.

PAYMENT/TERMS Pays $10-75.

TIPS "We publish many, many new writers and are always open to unsolicited submissions because we are 100% freelance. Do not send U.S. stamps; always use IRCs. We have poems, interviews, stories, and reviews online (query first)."

○○ PRAIRIE SCHOONER

The University of Nebraska Press, Prairie Schooner, 123 Andrews Hall, University of Nebraska, Lincoln NE 68588. (402)472-0911. **Fax:** (402)472-1817. **E-mail:** PrairieSchooner@unl.edu. **Website:** prairieschooner.unl.edu. **Contact:** Ashley Strosnider, managing editor. Estab. 1926. "We look for the best fiction, poetry, and nonfiction available to publish, and our readers expect to read stories, poems, and essays of extremely high quality. We try to publish a variety of styles, topics, themes, points of view, and writers with a variety of backgrounds in all stages of their careers. We like work that is compelling—intellectually or emotionally—either in form, language, or content."

○ Submissions must be received between September 1 and May 1. Poetry published in *Prairie Schooner* has been selected for inclusion in *The Best American Poetry* and *The Pushcart Prize*.

NEEDS "We try to remain open to a variety of styles, themes, and subject matter. We look for high-quality writing, 3-D characters, well-wrought plots, setting, etc. We are open to realistic and/or experimental fiction."

HOW TO CONTACT Send complete ms with SASE and cover letter listing previous publications (where, when).

PAYMENT/TERMS Pays 3 copies of the issue in which the writer's work is published.

TIPS "Send us your best, most carefully crafted work, and be persistent. Submit again and again. Constantly work on improving your writing. Read widely in literary fiction, nonfiction, and poetry. Read *Prairie Schooner* to know what we publish."

◑○ PREMONITIONS

13 Hazely Combe, Arrenton Isle of Wight PO30 3AJ United Kingdom. **E-mail:** mail@pigasuspress.co.uk. **Website:** www.pigasuspress.co.uk. **Contact:** Tony Lee, editor. "Science fiction and horror stories, plus genre poetry and fantastic artwork."

NEEDS Wants "original, high-quality SF/fantasy. Horror must have a science fiction element and be psychological or scary, rather than simply gory. Cutting-edge SF and experimental writing styles (cross-genre scenarios, slipstream, etc.) are always welcome." "No supernatural fantasy-horror." Length: 500-6,000 words. Send 1 story at a time.

HOW TO CONTACT Submit via mail and include SAE or IRC if you want material returned. "Use a standard ms format: double-spaced text, no right-justify, no staples." Do not send submissions via e-mail, unless by special request from editor. Include personalized cover letter with brief bio and publication credits.

PAYMENT/TERMS Pays minimum $5 or £5 per 1,000 words, plus copy of magazine.

TIPS "Potential contributors are advised to study recent issues of the magazine."

◐◑◉◉ PRISM INTERNATIONAL

Dept. of Creative Writing, Buch E462, 1866 Main Mall, University of British Columbia, Vancouver British Columbia V6T 1Z1 Canada. (604)822-2514. **Fax:** (604)822-3616. **E-mail:** prismcirculation@gmail.com. **Website:** www.prismmagazine.ca. Estab. 1959. A quarterly international journal of contemporary writing—fiction, poetry, drama, creative nonfiction and translation. *PRISM international* is 80 pages, digest-sized, elegantly printed, flat-spined, with original color artwork on a glossy card cover. Readership: public and university libraries, individual subscriptions, bookstores—a world-wide audience concerned with the contemporary in literature. "We have no thematic or stylistic allegiances: Excellence is our main criterion for acceptance of mss." Receives 1,000 submissions/year, accepts about 80. Circulation is for 1,200

subscribers. Subscription: $35/year for Canadian subscriptions, $40/year for U.S. subscriptions, $45/year for international. Sample: $13.

NEEDS Experimental, traditional. New writing that is contemporary and literary. Short stories and self-contained novel excerpts (up to 25 double-spaced pages). Works of translation are eagerly sought and should be accompanied by a copy of the original. Would like to see more translations. "No gothic, confession, religious, romance, pornography, or sci-fi." Also looking for creative nonfiction that is literary, not journalistic, in scope and tone. Receives over 100 unsolicited mss/month. Accepts 70 mss/year. "PRISM publishes both new and established writers; our contributors have included Franz Kafka, Gabriel García Maárquez, Michael Ondaatje, Margaret Laurence, Mark Anthony Jarman, Gail Anderson-Dargatz and Eden Robinson." Publishes ms 4 months after acceptance. **Publishes 7 new writers/year.** Recently published work by Ibi Kaslik, Melanie Little, Mark Anthony Jarman. Publishes short shorts. Also publishes poetry. For Drama: one-acts/excerpts of no more than 1500 words preferred. Also interested in seeing dramatic monologues. "New writing that is contemporary and literary. Short stories and self-contained novel excerpts. Works of translation are eagerly sought and should be accompanied by a copy of the original. Would like to see more translations. No gothic, confession, religious, romance, pornography, or science fiction." 25 pages maximum

HOW TO CONTACT Send complete ms by mail: Department of Creative Writing, Buch E462, 1866 Main Mall, University of British Columbia, Vancouver BC V6T 1Z1 Canada; or submit online through prismmagazine.ca. "Keep it simple. U.S. contributors take note: Do not send SASEs with U.S. stamps, they are not valid in Canada. Send International Reply Coupons instead." Responds in 4 months to queries; 3-6 months to mss. Sample copy for $13 or on website. Writer's guidelines online. Send complete ms.

PAYMENT/TERMS Pays $20/printed page of prose, $40/printed page of poetry, and 2 copies of issue. Pays on publication for first North American serial rights. Selected authors are paid an additional $10/page for digital rights. Cover art pays $300 and 2 copies of issue. Sponsors awards/contests, including annual short fiction, poetry, and nonfiction contests. Pays $20/printed page, and 12 copies of issue

TIPS "We are looking for new and exciting fiction. Excellence is still our No. 1 criterion. As well as poetry, imaginative nonfiction and fiction, we are especially open to translations of all kinds, very short fiction pieces and drama which work well on the page. Translations must come with a copy of the original language work."

A PUBLIC SPACE

323 Dean St., Brooklyn NY 11217. (718)858-8067. **E-mail:** general@apublicspace.org. **Website:** www.apublicspace.org. **Contact:** Brigid Hughes, founding editor; Anne McPeak, managing editor. *A Public Space*, published quarterly, is an independent magazine of literature and culture. "In an era that has relegated literature to the margins, we plan to make fiction and poetry the stars of a new conversation. We believe that stories are how we make sense of our lives and how we learn about other lives. We believe that stories matter."

- Accepts unsolicited submissions from September 15-April 15. Submissions accepted through Submittable or by mail (with SASE).

NEEDS No word limit.

HOW TO CONTACT Submit 1 complete ms via online submissions manager.

○ PUERTO DEL SOL

New Mexico State University, English Dept., P.O. Box 30001, MSC 3E, Las Cruces NM 88003. (505)646-3931. **E-mail:** puertodelsoljournal@gmail.com. **Website:** www.puertodelsol.org. **Contact:** Carmen Giménez Smith, editor in chief and poetry editor; Lily Hoang, prose editor. Estab. 1964. Publishes innovative work from emerging and established writers and artists. Wants poetry, fiction, nonfiction, drama, theory, artwork, interviews, reviews, and interesting combinations thereof.

- *Puerto del Sol* is 150 pages, digest-sized, professionally printed, flat-spined, with matte card cover with art. Press run is 1,250 (300 subscribers, 25-30 libraries). Reading period is September 15-December 1 and January 1-March 1.

NEEDS Accepts 8-12 mss/issue; 16-24 mss/year. Publishes several new writers/year. Has published work by David Trinidad, Molly Gaudry, Ray Gonzalez, Cynthia Cruz, Steve Tomasula, Denise Leto, Rae Bryant, Joshua Cohen, Blake Butler, Trinie Dalton, and Rick Moody.

HOW TO CONTACT Send 1 short story or 2-4 short short stories at a time through online submission manager.

PAYMENT/TERMS Pays 2 contributor's copies.

TIPS "We are especially pleased to publish emerging writers who work to push their art form or field of study in new directions."

◑ QUARTER AFTER EIGHT

Ohio University, 360 Ellis Hall, Athens OH 45701. **Website:** www.quarteraftereight.org. **Contact:** Patrick Swaney and Brad Aaron, editors. "*Quarter After Eight* is an annual literary journal devoted to the exploration of innovative writing. We celebrate work that directly challenges the conventions of language, style, voice, or idea in literary forms. In its aesthetic commitment to diverse forms, *QAE* remains a unique publication among contemporary literary magazines."

- Holds annual short prose (any genre) contest with grand prize of $1,000. Deadline is November 30.

NEEDS Length: no more than 10,000 words.

HOW TO CONTACT Submit through online submissions manager.

PAYMENT/TERMS Pays 2 contributor's copies.

TIPS "We look for prose and poetry that is innovative, exploratory, and—most importantly—well written. Please subscribe to our journal and read what is published to get acquainted with the *QAE* aesthetic."

◑◑⑤ QUARTERLY WEST

University of Utah, 255 S. Central Campus Dr., Room 3500, Salt Lake City UT 84112. **E-mail:** quarterlywest@gmail.com. **Website:** www.quarterlywest.com. **Contact:** Lillian Bertram and Claire Wahmanholm, editors. Estab. 1976. "We publish fiction, poetry, nonfiction, and new media in long and short formats, and will consider experimental as well as traditional works."

- *Quarterly West* was awarded first place for Editorial Content from the American Literary Magazine Awards. Work published in the magazine has been selected for inclusion in the *Pushcart Prize* anthology and *The Best American Short Stories* anthology.

NEEDS No preferred lengths; interested in longer, fuller short stories and short shorts. Accepts 6-10 mss/year. No detective, science fiction, or romance.

HOW TO CONTACT Send complete ms using online submissions manager only.

TIPS "We publish a special section of short shorts every issue, and we also sponsor an annual novella contest. We are open to experimental work—potential contributors should read the magazine! Don't send more than 1 story per submission. Novella competition guidelines available online. We prefer work with interesting language and detail—plot or narrative are less important. We don't do religious work."

☺︎☺︎☺︎ QUEEN'S QUARTERLY

144 Barrie St., Queen's University, Kingston ON K7L 3N6 Canada. (613)533-2667. **Fax:** (613)533-6822. **E-mail:** queens.quarterly@queensu.ca. **Website:** www. queensu.ca/quarterly. **Contact:** Joan Harcourt, literary editor (fiction and poetry); Boris Castel, nonfiction editor (articles, essays and reviews). Estab. 1893. *Queen's Quarterly* is "a general interest intellectual review featuring articles on science, politics, humanities, arts and letters, extensive book reviews, and some poetry and fiction."

◯ Has published work by Gail Anderson-Dargatz, Tim Bowling, Emma Donohue, Viktor Carr, Mark Jarman, Rick Bowers, and Dennis Bock.

NEEDS Length: 2,500-3,000 words. "Submissions over 3,000 words shall not be accepted."

HOW TO CONTACT Send complete ms with SASE and/or IRC. No reply with insufficient postage. Accepts 2 mss/issue; 8 mss/year. Publishes 5 new writers/year.

PAYMENT/TERMS "Payment to new writers will be determined at time of acceptance."

THE RAG

P.O. Box 17463, Portland OR 97217. **E-mail:** submissions@raglitmag.com. **Website:** raglitmag.com. **Contact:** Seth Porter, editor; Dan Reilly, editor. Estab. 2011. *The Rag* focuses on the grittier genres that tend to fall by the wayside at more traditional literary magazines. *The Rag*'s goal is to put the literary magazine back into the entertainment market while rekindling the social and cultural value short fiction once held in North American literature.

◯ Fee to submit online ($3) is waived if you subscribe or purchase a single issue.

NEEDS Accepts all styles and themes. Length: up to 10,000 words.

HOW TO CONTACT Send complete ms.

PAYMENT/TERMS Pays 5¢/word, the average being $250/story.

TIPS "We like gritty material: material that is psychologically believable and that has some humor in it, dark or otherwise. We like subtle themes, original characters, and sharp wit."

☺︎ RAINBOW RUMPUS

P.O. Box 6881, Minneapolis MN 55406. **Website:** www.rainbowrumpus.org. **Contact:** Beth Wallace, editor in chief and fiction editor. Estab. 2005. "*Rainbow Rumpus* is the world's only online literary magazine for children and youth with lesbian, gay, bisexual, and transgender (LGBT) parents. We are creating a new genre of children's and young adult fiction. Please carefully read and observe the guidelines on our website."

NEEDS "Stories should be written from the point of view of children or teens with lesbian, gay, bisexual, or transgender parents or other family members, or who are connected to the LGBT community. Stories featuring families of color, bisexual parents, transgender parents, family members with disabilities, and mixed-race families are particularly welcome." Length: 800-2,500 words for stories for 4- to 12-year-olds; up to 5,000 words for stories for 13- to 18-year-olds.

HOW TO CONTACT Query editor through website's Contact page. Be sure to select the Submissions category.

PAYMENT/TERMS Pays $300/story.

TIPS "Emerging writers encouraged to submit. You do not need to be a member of the LGBT community to participate."

☺︎ RALEIGH REVIEW LITERARY & ARTS MAGAZINE

P.O. Box 6725, Raleigh NC 27628-6725. **E-mail:** info@ raleighreview.org. **Website:** www.raleighreview.org. **Contact:** Rob Greene, editor; Karin Wiberg, managing editor; Craig Lincoln and Landon Houle, fiction editors; Sierra Golden, poetry editor. Estab. 2010. "*Raleigh Review* is a national nonprofit magazine of poetry, short fiction (including flash), and art. We believe that great literature inspires empathy by allowing us to see the world through the eyes of our neighbors, whether across the street or across the globe. Our mission is to foster the creation and availability of accessible yet provocative contemporary literature. We look for work that is emotionally and intellectually complex without being unnecessarily 'difficult.'"

NEEDS "We prefer work that is physically grounded and accessible, though complex and rich in emotional or intellectual power. We delight in stories from unique voices and perspectives. Any fiction that is born from a relatively unknown place grabs our attention. We are not opposed to genre fiction, so long as it has real, human characters and is executed artfully." Length: 250-7,500 words. "While we accept fiction up to 7,500 words, we are more likely to publish work in the 4,500- to 5,000-word range."

HOW TO CONTACT Submit complete ms.

PAYMENT/TERMS Pays $10 maximum.

TIPS "Please be sure to read the guidelines and look at sample work on our website. Every piece is read for its intrinsic value, so new/emerging voices are often published alongside nationally recognized, award-winning authors."

◑⑤ RATTAPALLAX

Rattapallax Press, 217 Thompson St., Suite 353, New York NY 10012. **E-mail:** info@rattapallax.com. **Website:** www.rattapallax.com. **Contact:** Flávia Rocha, editor n chief. Estab. 1999. Receives 15 unsolicited mss/month. Accepts 3 mss/issue; 6 mss/year. Agented fiction 15%. Receives about 5,000 poems/year; accepts 2%. Publishes 3 new writers/year. Has published work by Stuart Dybek, Howard Norman, Molly Giles, Rick Moody, Anthony Hecht, Sharon Olds, Lou Reed, Marilyn Hacker, Billy Collins, and Glyn Maxwell. *Rattapallax*, published semiannually, is named for "Wallace Stevens's word for the sound of thunder. The magazine includes a DVD featuring poetry films and audio files. *Rattapallax* is looking for the extraordinary in modern poetry and prose that reflect the diversity of world cultures. Our goals are to create international dialogue using literature and focus on what is relevant to our society."

○ *Rattapallax* is 112 pages, magazine-sized, off-set-printed, perfect-bound, with 12-pt. CS1 cover; some illustrations; photos. Press run is 2,000 (100 subscribers, 50 libraries, 1,200 shelf sales); 200 distributed free to contributors, reviews, and promos.

NEEDS Length: up to 2,000 words.

HOW TO CONTACT Submit via online submissions manager at rattapallax.submittable.com/submit.

PAYMENT/TERMS Pays 2 contributor's copies.

◑ RATTLING WALL

c/o PEN USA, 269 S. Beverly Dr. #1163, Beverly Hills CA 90212. **E-mail:** michelle@penusa.org. **Website:** therattlingwall.com. **Contact:** Michelle Meyering, editor. Estab. 2010.

○ Magazine: 6x9, square bound.

NEEDS Length: up to 15 pages.

HOW TO CONTACT Submit 1 complete story; no excerpts. Submissions should be double-spaced. In-clude cover letter with contact information, brief bio, writing sample.

PAYMENT/TERMS Pays 2 contributor's copies.

◑⑤ THE RAVEN CHRONICLES

A Journal of Art, Literature, & the Spoken Word, 15528 12th Ave. NE, Shoreline WA 98155. (206)941-2955. **E-mail:** editors@ravenchronicles.org. **Website:** www.ravenchronicles.org. Estab. 1991. "*The Raven Chronicles* publishes work which reflects the cultural diversity of the Pacific Northwest, Canada, and other areas of America. We promote art, literature and the spoken word for an audience that is hip, literate, funny, informed, and lives in a society that has a multicultural sensibility. We publish fiction, talk art/spoken word, poetry, essays, reflective articles, reviews, interviews, and contemporary art. We look for work that reflects the author's experiences, perceptions, and insights."

NEEDS "Experimental work is always of interest." Length: 10-12 pages, 3,500-4,000 words. "Check with us for maximum length. We sometimes print longer pieces."

HOW TO CONTACT Submit complete ms via postal mail with SASE.

TIPS "In 2015 we will be changing to an online submission process. See our website for details."

◐◑ THE READER

The Reader Organisation, Calderstones Mansion, Calderstones Park, Liverpool L18 3JB United Kingdom. **E-mail:** magazine@thereader.org.uk; info@thereader.org.uk. **Website:** www.thereader.org.uk. **Contact:** Philip Davis, editor. Estab. 1997. "*The Reader* is a quarterly literary magazine aimed at the intelligent 'common reader'—from those just beginning to explore serious literary reading to professional teachers, academics, and writers. As well as publishing short fiction and poetry by new writers and established names, the magazine features articles on all aspects of literature, language, and reading; regular features, including a literary quiz and a section on the Reading Revolution, reporting on The Reader Organisation's outreach work; reviews; and readers' recommendations of books that have made a difference to them. *The Reader* is unique among literary magazines in its focus on reading as a creative, important, and pleasurable activity, and in its combination of high-quality material and presentation with a genuine commitment to ordinary but dedicated readers." Also publishes literary essays, literary criticism, poetry.

NEEDS Wants short fiction and (more rarely) novel excerpts. Has published work by Karen King Arbisala, Ray Tallis, Sasha Dugdale, Vicki Seal, David Constantine, Jonathan Meades, and Ramesh Avadhani. Length: 1,000-3,000 words. Average length: 2,300 words. Publishes short shorts. Average length of short shorts: 1,500 words.

HOW TO CONTACT No e-mail submissions. Send complete ms with cover letter. Include estimated word count, brief bio, list of publications.

TIPS "The style or polish of the writing is less important than the deep structure of the story (though, of course, it matters that it's well written). The main persuasive element is whether the story moves us—and that's quite hard to quantify. It's something to do with the force of the idea and the genuine nature of enquiry within the story. When fiction is the writer's natural means of thinking things through, that'll get us. "

READER'S CARNIVAL

317-7185 Hall Rd., Surrey BC V3W4X5 Canada. **E-mail:** info@readerscarnival.ca; readerscarnival@gmail.com. **Website:** www.readerscarnival.ca. **Contact:** Doug Langille, editor; Anisa Irwin, managing editor. Estab. 2014.

◔ Must be an upgraded member of Writer's Carnival to submit to *Reader's Carnival*. Upgraded members can also enter contests on WC. Contests are every second month with $100 prize.

NEEDS Each issue has a different theme. Not interested in erotica, slasher horror (torture, overly gruesome). Length: 25-2,000 words.

HOW TO CONTACT Submit complete ms.

PAYMENT/TERMS Pays 2¢/word (CAD). Flash fiction under 250 words is $5 flat.

TIPS "Be open to writing all kinds of fiction. Call us Doug or Anisa, not 'To whom it may concern.' Writing is serious and fun. Edit your work to the best of your ability and write like you love it."

◑ REAL: REGARDING ARTS & LETTERS

Stephen F. Austin State University, P.O. Box 13007, Nacogdoches TX 75962-3007. **E-mail:** brininsta@sfasu.edu. **Website:** regardingartsandletters.wordpress.com. **Contact:** Andrew Brininstool, editor. "*REAL: Regarding Arts & Letters* was founded in 1968 as an academic journal which occasionally published poetry. Now, it is an international creative magazine dedicated to publishing the best contemporary fiction, poetry, and nonfiction." Features both established and emerging writers.

◔ Magazine:semiannual, 120 pages, perfect-bound.

NEEDS "We're not interested in genre fiction—sci-fi or romance or the like—unless you're doing some cheeky genre-bending. Otherwise, send us your best literary work." Publishes short shorts. Length: up to 8,000 words.

HOW TO CONTACT Submit via online submissions manager. Include cover letter addressed to Andrew Brininstool or John McDermott.

TIPS "We are looking for the best work, whether you are established or not."

◐◑ REALPOETIK

Athens GA **E-mail:** realpoetikblog@gmail.com. **Website:** www.realpoetik.club. **Contact:** Thibault Raoult, editor. Estab. 1996. *RealPoetik* publishes innovative work. Poems are published online and also sent to subscribers via e-mail. "We provide a club/poem atmosphere."

◔ Publishes 20-30 new poets/year.

REDACTIONS: POETRY, POETICS, & PROSE

604 N. 31st Ave., Apt. D-2, Hattiesburg MS 39401. **E-mail:** redactionspoetry@yahoo.com (poetry and essays on poetry); redationsprose@yahoo.com (creative prose). **Website:** www.redactions.com. *Redactions*, released every 9 months, covers poems, reviews of new books of poems, translations, manifestos, interviews, essays concerning poetry, poetics, poetry movements, or concerning a specific poet or a group of poets; and anything dealing with poetry. "We now also publish fiction and creative nonfiction."

TIPS "We only accept submissions by e-mail. We read submissions throughout the year. E-mail us and attach submission into one Word, Wordpad, Notepad, .rtf, or .txt document, or place in the body of an e-mail. Include brief bio and your snail-mail address. Query after 90 days if you haven't heard from us. See website for full guidelines for each genre, including artwork."

◑ THE RED CLAY REVIEW

Dr. Jim Elledge, Director, M. A. in Professional Writing Program, Department of English, Kennesaw State University, 1000 Chastain Rd., #2701, Kennesaw GA 30144. **E-mail:** redclay2013@gmail.com. **Website:** redclayreview.com. **Contact:** Javy Gwaltney, editor in chief. Estab. 2008. *The Red Clay Review* is supported by the Graduate Writers Association of Kennesaw State University. America's only literary magazine to feature exclusively the work of graduate and doctoral students. Publishes poetry, flash fiction, short fiction, creative nonfiction, and one-act/10-minute plays. Accepts new and established authors.

◐ Submission period begins annually in August.

NEEDS Does not have any specific themes or topics. Reads whatever is sent in. "We will publish whatever we deem to be great literary writing. So in essence, every topic is open to submission, and we are all interested in a wide variety of subjects. We do not prohibit any topic or subject matter from being submitted. As long as submissions adhere to our guidelines, we are open to reading them. However, subject matter in any area that is too extreme may be less likely to be published because we want to include a broad collection of literary graduate work, but on the other hand, we cannot morally reject great writing." Length: up to 10 pages.

HOW TO CONTACT Send complete ms with cover letter. A brief bio, list of publications, and an e-mail address must be supplied for the student, as well as the student's advisor's contact information (to verify student status).

PAYMENT/TERMS Pays in contributor's copies.

TIPS "Because the editors of *RCR* are graduate student writers, we are mindful of grammatical proficiency, vocabulary, and the organizational flow of the submissions we receive. We appreciate a heightened level of writing from fellow graduate writing students, but we also hold it to a standard to which we have learned in our graduate writing experience. Have your submission(s) proofread by a fellow student or professor."

REDIVIDER

Department of Writing, Literature, and Publishing, Emerson College, 120 Boylston St., Boston MA 02116. **E-mail:** editor@redividerjournal.org. **Website:** www.redividerjournal.org. Estab. 1986. *Redivider*, a journal of literature and art, is published twice a year by students in the graduate writing, literature, and publishing department of Emerson College. Editors change each year. Prints high-quality poetry, art, fiction, and creative nonfiction.

◐ Every spring, *Redivider* hosts the Beacon Street Prize Writing Contest, awarding a cash prize and publication to the winning submission in fiction, poetry, and nonfiction categories. See www.redividerjournal.org for details.

NEEDS Length: no more than 10,000 words.

HOW TO CONTACT Submit electronically. Include cover letter.

PAYMENT/TERMS Pays 2 contributor's copies.

TIPS "Our deadlines are July 1 for the Fall issue and December 1 for the Spring issue."

◑ RED ROCK REVIEW

College of Southern Nevada, CSN Department of English, J2A, 3200 E. Cheyenne Ave., North Las Vegas NV 89030. (702)651-4094. **Fax:** (702)651-4455. **E-mail:** redrockreview@csn.edu. **Website:** sites.csn.edu/english/redrockreview. **Contact:** Erica Vital-Lazare, senior editor; John Ziebell, fiction editor (john.zeibell@csn.edu);. Estab. 1994. Dedicated to the publication of fine contemporary literature.

◐ Does not accept submissions during June, July, August, or December. Any files sent at this time will be deleted. *Red Rock Review* is about 130 pages, magazine-sized, professionally printed, perfect-bound, with 10-pt. CS1 cover. Accepts about 15% of poems received/year. Press run is 2,350.

NEEDS "We're looking for the very best literature. Stories need to be tightly crafted, strong in character development, built around conflict." Length: up to 5,000 words.

HOW TO CONTACT Send ms as Word, RTF, or PDF file attachment.

PAYMENT/TERMS Pays 2 contributor's copies.

TIPS "Open to short fiction and poetry submissions from September 1-May 31. Include SASE and include brief bio. No general submissions between June 1 and August 31. See guidelines online."

◑ RED WHEELBARROW

De Anza College, 21250 Stevens Creek Blvd., Cupertino CA 95014. **Website:** www.deanza.edu/redwheelbarrow. Estab. 1976 as *Bottomfish*; 2000 as *Red Wheelbarrow*.

◐ "We seek to publish a diverse range of styles and voices from around the country and the world." Publishes a student edition and a national edition.

NEEDS Length: up to 4,000 words.

HOW TO CONTACT Send complete ms by mail (include SASE) or e-mail.

TIPS "Write freely, rewrite carefully. Resist clichés and stereotypes. We are not affiliated with Red Wheelbarrow Press or any similarly named publication.

REED MAGAZINE

San Jose State University, Dept. of English, One Washington Square, San Jose CA 95192. (408)924-4425. **E-mail:** reedmagazinesjsu@gmail.com; cathleen.miller@sjsu.edu. **Website:** www.reedmag.org. **Contact:** Cathleen Miller, editor in chief. Estab. 1944. *Reed Magazine* is the oldest literary journal west of the Mississippi. It publishes works of short fiction, nonfiction, poetry, and art, and offers nearly $4,000 in cash prizes.

Accepts electronic submissions only.

NEEDS Does not want children's, young adult, fantasy, or erotic. Length: up to 5,000 words.

HOW TO CONTACT Submit complete ms via online submissions manager.

PAYMENT/TERMS Contest contributors receive 1 free copy; additional copies $10.

TIPS "Well-writen, original, clean grammatical prose is essential. We are interested in established authors as well as fresh new voices. Keep submitting!"

RHINO

The Poetry Forum, Inc., P.O. Box 591, Evanston IL 60204. **E-mail:** editors@rhinopoetry.org. **Website:** rhinopoetry.org. "This independent, eclectic annual journal of more than 35 years accepts poetry, flash fiction (750 words max), and poetry-in-translation from around the world that experiments, provokes, compels. More than 80 emerging and established poets are showcased." Accepts general submissions April 1-August 31 and Founders' Prize submissions September 1-October 31.

NEEDS Length: no more than 750 words.

PAYMENT/TERMS Pays in contributor's copies.

TIPS "Our diverse group of editors looks for the very best in contemporary writing, and we have created a dynamic process of soliciting and reading new work by local, national, and international writers. We are open to all styles and look for idiosyncratic, rigorous, well-crafted, lively, and passionate work."

RIVER STYX MAGAZINE

Big River Association, 3139A Grand Blvd., Suite 203, St. Louis MO 63118. (314)533-4541. **E-mail:** bigriver@riverstyx.org. **Website:** www.riverstyx.org. **Contact:** Richard Newman, editor. Estab. 1975. Sponsors an annual Microfiction Contest, judged by the editors. Deadline: December 31. Guidelines available for SASE or on website. *"River Styx* publishes the highest-quality fiction, poetry, interviews, essays, and visual art.

We are an internationally distributed multicultural literary magazine. Mss read May-November."

Work published in *River Styx* has been selected for inclusion in past volumes of *New Stories from the South, The Best American Poetry, Best New Poets, New Poetry from the Midwest,* and *The Pushcart Prize Anthology.*

NEEDS Recently published work by George Singleton, Philip Graham, Katherine Min, Richard Burgin, Nancy Zafris, Jacob Appel, and Eric Shade. No genre fiction, less thinly veiled autobiography. Length: no more than 23-30 ms pages.

HOW TO CONTACT Send complete ms with SASE.

PAYMENT/TERMS Pays 2 contributor copies, plus one-year subscription. Cash payment as funds permit.

ROANOKE REVIEW

Roanoke College, 221 College Lane, Salem VA 24153-3794. **E-mail:** review@roanoke.edu. **Website:** roanokereview.wordpress.com. **Contact:** Paul Hanstedt, editor. Estab. 1967. "The *Roanoke Review* is an online literary journal that is dedicated to publishing accessible fiction, nonfiction, and poetry that is smartly written. Humor is encouraged; humility as well."

Has published work by Siobhan Fallon, Jacob M. Appel, and JoeAnn Hart.

NEEDS Receives 150 unsolicited mss/month. Accepts 30 mss/year. Does not read mss February 1-September 1. Publishes 1-5 new writers/year. Length: 1,000-5,000 words. Average length: 3,000 words.

HOW TO CONTACT Submit via Submittable, or send SASE for return of ms, or send a disposable copy of ms and #10 SASE for reply only.

PAYMENT/TERMS Pays $10-50/story (when budget allows).

TIPS "Pay attention to sentence-level writing—verbs, metaphors, concrete images. Don't forget, though, that plot and character keep us reading. We're looking for stuff that breaks the MFA story style. Be real. Know rhythm. Concentrate on strong images."

THE ROCKFORD REVIEW

The Rockford Writers Guild, P.O. Box 858, Rockford IL 61105. **E-mail:** rwg@rockfordwritersguild.com. **Website:** www.rockfordwritersguild.com. **Contact:** Connie Kluntz. Estab. 1947. "Published twice/year. Members only edition in summer-fall and winter-spring edition which is open to all writers. Open season to submit for the winter-spring edition of *The Rockford Review* is August. If pubished in the winter-spring edition of *The Rockford Review*, payment is one copy of magazine and $5 per published piece. Credit line given. Check website for frequent updates. We are also on Facebook under Rockford Writers' Guild."

○ Poetry 50 lines or less, prose 1,300 words or less.

NEEDS "Prose should express fresh insights into the human condition." No sexist, pornographic, or supremacist content. Length: no more than 1,300 words.

TIPS "We're wide open to new and established writers alike—particularly short satire."

◑ ROMANCE FLASH

Romance Flash, 1112 Dakota Street, Watertown WI 53094. **E-mail:** info@romanceflash.com. **E-mail:** submissions@romanceflash.com. **Website:** www.romanceflash.com. **Contact:** Kat de Falla and Rachel Green, editors. Estab. 2010. Monthly online magazine featuring romantic flash fiction stories of 1,000 words or fewer.

NEEDS No heavy erotica. Length: 1,000 words or less.

PAYMENT/TERMS Pays $3 per story (paid via PayPal only).

○◑◉ ROOM

P.O. Box 46160, Station D, Vancouver BC V6J 5G5 Canada. **E-mail:** contactus@roommagazine.com. **Website:** www.roommagazine.com. Estab. 1975. "*Room* is Canada's oldest literary journal by, for, and about women. Published quarterly by a group of volunteers based in Vancouver, *Room* showcases fiction, poetry, reviews, art work, interviews, and profiles about the female experience. Many of our contributors are at the beginning of their writing careers, looking for an opportunity to get published for the first time. Some later go on to great acclaim. *Room* is a space where women can speak, connect, and showcase their creativity. Each quarter we publish original, thought-provoking works that reflect women's strength, sensuality, vulnerability, and wit."

○ *Room* is digest-sized; illustrations, photos. Press run is 1,000 (420 subscribers, 50-100 libraries, 350 shelf sales).

NEEDS Accepts literature that illustrates the female experience—short stories, creative nonfiction, poetry—by, for and about women.

HOW TO CONTACT Submit complete ms via online submissions manager.

PAYMENT/TERMS Pays $50-120 (Canadian), 2 contributor's copies, and a one-year subscription.

◑ ROSEBUD

N3310 Asje Rd., Cambridge WI 53523. (608)423-9780. **Website:** www.rsbd.net. **Contact:** Roderick Clark, publisher/managing editor; John Lehman, founder/editor-at-large. Estab. 1993. *Rosebud*, published 3 times/year in April, August, and December, has presented many of the most prominent voices in the nation and has been listed as among the very best markets for writers.

○ *Rosebud* is elegantly printed with full-color cover. Press run is 10,000.

NEEDS Has published work by Ray Bradbury, XJ Kennedy, and Nikki Giovanni. Publishes short shorts. Also publishes literary essays. Often comments on rejected mss. "No formula pieces."

HOW TO CONTACT Send complete ms. Include SASE for return of ms and $1 handling fee.

TIPS "Each issue has 6 or 7 flexible departments (selected from a total of 16 departments that rotate). We are seeking stories; articles; profiles; and poems of love, alienation, travel, humor, nostalgia and unexpected revelation. Something has to 'happen' in the pieces we choose, but what happens inside characters is much more interesting to us than plot manipulation. We like good storytelling, real emotion, and authentic voice."

SACRED CITY PRODUCTIONS

Sacred City Productions, Ltd., 5781 Springwood Ct., Mentor on the Lake OH 44060. (440)290-9325. **E-mail:** info@sacredcityproductions.com. **E-mail:** info@sacredcityproductions.com. **Website:** sacredcityproductions.com. **Contact:** Erin Garlock, editor/owner. Estab. 2011. Sacred City Productions is dedicated to creative endeavors that promote the ideals of a positive faith life. "We ask people to think about what they believe and to take action on those beliefs. Our own actions reflect our Christian beliefs as we reach out in ministry to extend an uplifting hand to those around us."

NEEDS Sacred City Production's fiction focus is on speculative Christian fiction for publication in short story anthologies. Length: 500-8,000 words.

HOW TO CONTACT Submit completed story via online submission form.

PAYMENT/TERMS Pays $10 for stories over 500 words, $20 for stories over 2,000 words. Once royalties earned by the publication equal the total amount paid out to all contributors, a 50/50 pro-rate share of the anthology's earnings, if any, will be paid as royalties at a ratio, to the aforementioned rates, relevant to the number of contributors. A royalty breakdown sheet will be supplied at the end of a project.

TIPS "We are very interested in submissions from first-time authors and authors with a very limited record."

ⓞⓞ SALMAGUNDI

Skidmore College, 815 North Broadway, Saratoga Springs NY 12866. **Fax:** (518)580-5188. **E-mail:** salmagun@skidmore.edu. **E-mail:** ssubmit@skidmore.edu. **Website:** cms.skidmore.edu/salmagundi. Estab. 1965. Receives 300-500 unsolicited mss/month; "many sent, few accepted." Reads unsolicited mss February 1-April 15 "but from time to time close the doors even during this period because the backlog tends to grow out of control." Agented fiction 10%. "*Salmagundi* publishes an eclectic variety of materials, ranging from short-short fiction to novellas from the surreal to the realistic. Authors include Nadine Gordimer, Russell Banks, Steven Millhauser, Gordon Lish, Clark Blaise, Mary Gordon, Joyce Carol Oates, and Cynthia Ozick. Our audience is a generally literate population of people who read for pleasure."

ⓞ   Magazine: 8x5; illustrations; photos. *Salmagundi* authors are regularly represented in *Pushcart* collections and *Best American Short Story* collections. Reading period: November 1-December 1.

NEEDS Length: up to 12,000 words.

HOW TO CONTACT Submit via e-mail.

PAYMENT/TERMS Pays 6-10 contributor's copies and one-year subscription.

TIPS "I look for excellence and a very unpredictable ability to appeal to the interests and tastes of the editors. Be brave. Don't be discouraged by rejection. Keep stories in circulation. Of course, it goes without saying: Work hard on the writing. Revise tirelessly. Study magazines and send only to those whose sensibility matches yours."

SALT HILL JOURNAL

Creative Writing Program, Syracuse University, English Deptartment, 401 Hall of Languages, Syracuse University, Syracuse NY 13244. **Website:** salthilljournal.net. **Contact:** Emma DeMilta and Jessica Poli, editors. "*Salt Hill* is published through Syracuse University's Creative Writing MFA program. We strive to publish a mix of the best contemporary and emerging talent in poetry, fiction, and nonfiction. Your work, if accepted, would appear in a long tradition of excep-

tional contributors, including Steve Almond, Mary Caponegro, Kim Chinquee, Edwidge Danticat, Denise Duhamel, Brian Evenson, B.H. Fairchild, Mary Gaitskill, Terrance Hayes, Bob Hicok, Laura Kasischke, Etgar Keret, Phil Lamarche, Dorianne Laux, Maurice Manning, Karyna McGlynn, Ander Monson, David Ohle, Lucia Perillo, Tomaž Šalamun, Zachary Schomburg, Christine Schutt, David Shields, Charles Simic, Patricia Smith, Dara Wier, and Raúl Zurita among many others."

ⓞ   Only accepts submissions by online submission form; does not accept unsolicited e-mail submissions.

NEEDS Length: up to 30 pages.

HOW TO CONTACT Submit via online submissions manager; contact fiction editor via e-mail for retractions and queries only.

ⓞ THE SAME

P.O. Box 494, Mount Union PA 17066. **E-mail:** editors@thesamepress.com. **Website:** www.thesamepress.com. **Contact:** Nancy Eldredge, managing editor. Estab. 2000. *The Same*, published biannually, prints nonfiction (essays, reviews, literary criticism), poetry, and short fiction.

ⓞ   *The Same* is 50-100 pages, desktop-published, and perfect-bound.

HOW TO CONTACT Query before submitting.

ⓞ THE SANDY RIVER REVIEW

University of Maine at Farmington, 114 Prescott St., Farmington ME 04938. **E-mail:** srreview@gmail.com. **Website:** sandyriverreview.com. **Contact:** Nicole Byrne, editor. "*The Sandy River Review* seeks prose, poetry, and art submissions twice a year for our Spring and Fall issues. Prose submissions may be either fiction or creative nonfiction and should be a maximum of 3,500 words in length, 12-point, Times New Roman font, and double-spaced. Most of our art is published in b&w and must be submitted as 300-dpi quality, CMYK color mode, and saved as a TIFF file. We publish a wide variety of work from students as well as professional, established writers. Your submission should be polished and imaginative with strongly drawn characters and an interesting, original narrative. The review is the face of the University of Maine at Farmington's venerable BFA Creative Writing program, and we strive for the highest quality prose and poetry standard."

NEEDS "The review is a literary journal—please, no horror, science fiction, romance." Length: max 3,5000 words, no minimum.

HOW TO CONTACT Send complete ms.

PAYMENT/TERMS Pays 3 copies of the published issue.

TIPS "We recommend that you take time with your piece. As with all submissions to a literary journal, submissions should be fully completed, polished final drafts that require minimal to no revision once accepted. Double-check your prose pieces for basic grammatical errors before submitting."

SANSKRIT LITERARY-ARTS MAGAZINE

UNC Charlotte, Student Media, Student Union Rm. 045, 9201 University City Blvd., Charlotte NC 28223. (704)687-7141. **E-mail:** editor@sanskritmagazine. com. **Contact:** Joshua Wood, editor. Estab. 1968. "*Sanskrit* is UNC Charlotte's nationally recognized, award winning literary-arts magazine. It is published once a year in April. *Sanskrit* is a collection of poems, short stories, and art from people all around the world and students just like you. All of the work goes through a selection process that includes our staff and University professors. Finally, each year the magazine has a theme. This theme is completely independent from the work and is chosen by the editor as a design element to unify the magazine. The theme is kept secret until the return of the magazine in April when we have our annual Gallery Showing and Poetry Reading."

Sanskrit has received the Pacemaker, Associated College Press, Gold Crown, and Columbia Scholastic Press awards.

NEEDS Length: up to 3,500 words.

HOW TO CONTACT Submit by mail; include SASE, 30- to 70-word bio. All stories should be typed and double-spaced on 8.5x11 paper.

PAYMENT/TERMS Pays contributor's copies.

SANTA CLARA REVIEW

Santa Clara Review, Santa Clara University, 500 El Camino Real, Box 3212, Santa Clara CA 95053-3212. (408)554-4484. **E-mail:** santaclarareview@gmail. com. **Website:** www.santaclarareview.com. Estab. 1869. "*SCR* is one of the oldest literary publications in the West. Entirely student-run by undergraduates at Santa Clara University, the magazine draws upon submissions from SCU affiliates as well as contributors from around the globe. The magazine is published in February and May each year. In addition to publishing the magazine, the Review staff organizes a writing practicum, open mic nights, and retreats for writers and artists, and hosts guest readers. Our printed magazine is also available to view free online. For contacts, queries, and general info, visit our website. *SCR* accepts submissions year round.

NEEDS Length: up to 5,000 words.

HOW TO CONTACT Submit via online submissions manager or mail (include SASE for return of ms).

SANTA MONICA REVIEW

Santa Monica College, 1900 Pico Blvd., Santa Monica CA 90405. **Website:** www.smc.edu/sm_review. **Contact:** Andrew Tonkovich, editor. Estab. 1988. The *Santa Monica Review*, published twice yearly in fall and spring, is a nationally distributed literary arts journal sponsored by Santa Monica College. It currently features fiction and nonfiction.

NEEDS "No crime and detective, mysogyny, footnotes, TV, dog stories. We want more self-conscious, smart, political, humorous, digressive, meta-fiction."

HOW TO CONTACT Submit complete ms with SASE. No e-mail submissions.

PAYMENT/TERMS Pays in contributor's copies and subscription.

THE SARANAC REVIEW

Dept. of English, Champlain Valley Hall, 101 Broad St., Plattsburgh NY 12901. **Website:** saranacreview. com. **Contact:** J.L. Torres, editor. Estab. 2004. "*The Saranac Review* is committed to dissolving boundaries of all kinds, seeking to publish a diverse array of emerging and established writers from Canada and the U.S. *The Saranac Review* aims to be a textual clearing in which a space is opened for cross-pollination between American and Canadian writers. In this way the magazine reflects the expansive, bright spirit of the etymology of its name, Saranac, meaning 'cluster of stars.'" Published annually.

"*The Saranac Review* is digest-sized, with color photo or painting on cover, includes ads. Publishes both digital and print-on-demand versions. Has published Lawrence Raab, Jacob M. Appel, Marilyn Nelson, Tom Wayman, Colette Inez, Louise Warren, Brian Campbell, Gregory Pardlo, Myfanwy Collins, William Giraldi, Xu Xi, Julia Alvarez, and other fine emerging and established writers.

NEEDS "We're looking for well-crafted fiction that demonstrates respect for and love of language. Fiction that makes us feel and think, that edifies without being didactic or self-indulgent and ultimately connects us to our sense of humanity." No genre material (fantasy, sci-fi, etc.) or light verse. Length: up to 7,000 words.

HOW TO CONTACT Submit complete ms via online submissions manager.

PAYMENT/TERMS Pays 2 contributor's copies and offers discount on additional copies.

○⑤ THE SAVAGE KICK LITERARY MAGAZINE

Murder Slim Press, 29 Alpha Rd., Gorleston Norfolk NR31 0EQ United Kingdom. **E-mail:** moonshine@ murderslim.com. **Website:** www.murderslim.com. Estab. 2005. "*Savage Kick* primarily deals with viewpoints outside the mainstream: honest emotions told in a raw, simplistic way. It is recommended that you are very familiar with the *SK* style before submitting. Ensure you have a distinctive voice and story to tell."

NEEDS "Real-life stories are preferred, unless the work is distinctively extreme within the crime genre. No poetry of any kind, no mainstream fiction, Oprah-style fiction, Internet/chat language, teen issues, excessive Shakespearean language, surrealism, overworked irony, or genre fiction (horror, fantasy, science fiction, western, erotica, etc.)." Length: 500-6,000 words.

HOW TO CONTACT Send complete ms.

PAYMENT/TERMS Pays $35.

SCREAMINMAMAS

Harmoni Productions, LLC, 1911 Cleveland St., Hollywood FL 33020. **E-mail:** screaminmamas@gmail. com. **Website:** www.screaminmamas.com. **Contact:** Darlene Pistocchi, editor; Denise Marie, managing editor. Estab. 2012. "We are the voice of everyday moms. We share their stories, revelations, humorous rants, photos, talent, children, ventures, etc."

NEEDS Does not want vulgar, obscene, derogatory, or negative fiction. Length: 800-3,000 words.

HOW TO CONTACT Send complete ms.

TIPS "Visit our submissions page and themes page on our website."

THE SEATTLE REVIEW

Box 354330, University of Washington, Seattle WA 98195. (206)543-2302. **E-mail:** seaview@uw.edu. **Website:** www.seattlereview.org. **Contact:** Andrew Feld, editor in chief. Estab. 1978. *The Seattle Review* includes poetry, fiction, and creative nonfiction.

○ *The Seattle Review* will only publish long works. Poetry must be 10 pages or longer, and prose must be 40 pages or longer. *The Seattle Review* is 8x10; 175-250 pages. Receives 200 unsolicited mss/month. Accepts 10-15 mss/issue; 20-30 mss/year. Publishes ms 6 months-1 year after acceptance.

NEEDS "Currently, we do not consider, use, or have a place for genre fiction (sci-fi, detective, etc.) or visual art." Length: 500-10,000 words.

HOW TO CONTACT Send complete ms. Accepts electronic submissions only.

TIPS "Know what we publish; no genre fiction. Look at our magazine and decide if your work might be appreciated. Beginners do well in our magazine if they send clean, well-written mss. We've published a lot of 'first stories' from all over the country and take pleasure in discovery."

①⑤ SEEK

8805 Governor's Hill Dr., Suite 400, Cincinnati OH 45239. (513)931-4050, ext. 351. **E-mail:** seek@standardpub.com. **Website:** www.standardpub.com. Estab. 1970. "Inspirational stories of faith-in-action for Christian adults; a Sunday School take-home paper." Quarterly.

○ Magazine: 5.5×8.5; 8 pages; newsprint paper; art and photo in each issue.

NEEDS List of upcoming themes available online. Accepts 150 mss/year. Send complete ms. Prefers submissions by e-mail. "*SEEK* corresponds to the topics of Standard Publishing's adult curriculum line and is designed to further apply these topics to everyday life." Unsolicited mss must be written to a theme list. Does not want poetry.

HOW TO CONTACT Send complete ms. Prefers submissions by e-mail.

PAYMENT/TERMS Pays 7¢/word.

TIPS "Write a credible story with a Christian slant—no preachments; avoid overworked themes such as joy in suffering, generation gaps, etc. Most mss are rejected by us because of irrelevant topic or message, unrealistic story, or poor character and/or plot development. We use fiction stories that are believable."

SEQUESTRUM

Sequestrum Publishing, 1023 Garfield Ave., Ames IA 50014. **E-mail:** sequr.info@gmail.com. **Website:** www.

sequestrum.org. **Contact:** R.M. Cooper, managing editor. Estab. 2014. All publications are cpaired with a unique visual component. Regularly holds contests and features well-known authors, as well as promising new and emerging voices.

NEEDS Will consider genre fiction, but it must move beyond the bounds of its genre. Length: 5,000 words max.

HOW TO CONTACT Submit complete ms via online submissions manager.

PAYMENT/TERMS Pays $10-15/story.

TIPS "Reading a past issue goes a long way; there's little excuse not to: Our entire archive is available online and subscribing is free. Send your best, most interesting work. General submissions are open, though we regularly hold contests and offer awards which are themed."

THE SEWANEE REVIEW

University of the South, 735 University Ave., Sewanee TN 37383-1000. (931)598-1000. **E-mail:** sreview@sewanee.edu. **Website:** review.sewanee.edu. **Contact:** George Core, editor. Estab. 1892. *The Sewanee Review* is America's oldest continuously published literary quarterly. Publishes original fiction, poetry, essays on literary and related subjects, and book reviews for well-educated readers who appreciate good American and English literature. Only erudite work representing depth of knowledge and skill of expression is published. Does not read mss June 1-August 31.

NEEDS No erotica, science fiction, fantasy, or excessively violent or profane material. Length: 3,500-7,500 words. No short-short stories.

HOW TO CONTACT Submit complete ms by mail; no electronic submissions.

PAYMENT/TERMS Pays $10-12/printed page, plus 2 contributor's copies.

SHADOWS & LIGHT

P.O. Box 1171, Clackamas OR 97015. **E-mail:** angelshadow7@msn.com. **Website:** angelshadowauthor.webs.com/shadowslight.htm. **Contact:** Shawna (Angel Shadow), editor. *Shadows & Light*, published as a yearly anthology, features short stories, flash fiction, poetry, nonfiction, memoir, and self-help articles.

NEEDS Does not want porn or heavy sexual content. Length: up to 7,000 words for short stories.

HOW TO CONTACT Submit complete ms by e-mail. Include "Submission" in subject line.

PAYMENT/TERMS Pays 1 contributor's copy.

TIPS "A well-written story makes a ms stand out, as well as good character development. Just submit your story. All stories have the potential of being heard. Keep writing. Don't give up."

SHENANDOAH

Washington and Lee University, Lexington VA 24450. (540)458-8908. **Fax:** (540)458-8461. **E-mail:** shenandoah@wlu.edu. **Website:** shenandoahliterary.org. **Contact:** R.T. Smith, editor. Estab. 1950. Sponsors the Shenandoah Prize for Fiction, awarded annually to the best story published in a volume year of *Shenandoah*, and the Bevel Summers Prize for the Short Short Story, awarded annually to the best short short story of up to 1,000 words. Prizes for both contests are $1,000. For over half a century, *Shenandoah* has been publishing splendid poems, stories, essays, and reviews which display passionate understanding, formal accomplishment, and serious mischief.

NEEDS No sloppy, hasty, slight fiction. Length: up to 20 pages.

HOW TO CONTACT Send complete ms via online submissions manager or postal mail.

PAYMENT/TERMS Pays $25/page ($250 maximum), one-year subscription, and 1 contributor's copy.

SHINE BRIGHTLY

GEMS Girls' Clubs, 1333 Alger St., SE, Grand Rapids MI 49507. (616)241-5616. **Fax:** (616)241-5558. **E-mail:** shinebrightly@gemsgc.org. **Website:** www.gemsgc.org. **Contact:** Kristine Palosaari, executive director; Kelli Gilmore, managing editor. Estab. 1970. "Our purpose is to lead girls into a living relationship with Jesus Christ and to help them see how God is at work in their lives and the world around them. Puzzles, crafts, stories, and articles for girls ages 9-14."

NEEDS Does not want "unrealistic stories and those with trite, easy endings. We are interested in mss that show how girls can change the world." Believable only. Nothing too preachy. Length: 700-900 words.

HOW TO CONTACT Submit complete ms in body of e-mail. No attachments.

PAYMENT/TERMS Pays up to $35, plus 2 copies.

TIPS Writers: "Please check our website before submitting. We have a specific style and theme that deals with how girls can impact the world. The stories should be current, deal with pre-adolescent problems and joys, and help girls see God at work in their lives through humor as well as problem-solving." Prefers not to see anything on the adult level, secular material, or violence. Writers frequently oversimplify the articles and often write with a Pollyanna attitude. An author should be able to see his/her writing style as exciting and appealing to girls ages 9-14. The style can be fun, but also teach a truth. Subjects should be current and important to *SHINE brightly* readers. Use our theme update as a guide. We would like to receive material with a multicultural slant."

SHORT STORY AMERICA

Short Story America, LLC, 2121 Boundary St., Suite 204, Beaufort SC 29902. (843)597-3220. **E-mail:** editors@shortstoryamerica.com. **Website:** www.shortstoryamerica.com. **Contact:** Tim Johnston, editor. Estab. 2010. "Our readers are fans of the short story. Our audience simply wants to enjoy reading great stories."

NEEDS No erotica. Length: 500-12,000 words.

HOW TO CONTACT Submit complete ms via online submissions form.

PAYMENT/TERMS Pays $25-50.

TIPS "We want stories readers will remember and want to read again. If your story entertains from the first page forward, and the pacing and conflict engages the reader's interest from plot, character, and thematic standpoints, then please submit your story today! If the reader genuinely wants to know what eventually happens in your story and is still thinking about it 10 minutes after finishing, then your story works."

⊘ SHORT STUFF

Bowman Publications, 2001 I St., #5, Fairbury NE 68352. (402)587-5003. **E-mail:** shortstf89@aol.com. Estab. 1989. "We are perhaps an enigma in that we publish only clean stories in any genre. We'll tackle any subject but don't allow obscene language or pornographic description. Our magazine is for grown-ups, not X-rated 'adult' fare."

NEEDS Receives 500 unsolicited mss/month. Accepts 9-12 mss/issue; 76 mss/year. Has published work by Bill Hallstead, Dede Hammond, and Skye Gibbons. "We want to see more humor—not essay format—real stories with humor; 1,000-word mysteries, modern lifestyles. The 1,000-word pieces have the best chance of publication. No erotica; nothing morbid or pornographic. Length: 500-1,500 words.

HOW TO CONTACT Send complete ms.

PAYMENT/TERMS Payment varies.

TIPS "We are holiday-oriented; mark on outside of envelope if story is for Easter, Mother's Day, etc. We receive 500 mss each month. This is up about 200%. Because of this, I implore writers to send 1 ms at a time. I would not use stories from the same author

more than once an issue, and this means I might keep the others too long. Please don't e-mail your stories! If you have an e-mail address, please include that with the cover letter so we can contact you. If no SASE, we destroy the ms."

SIERRA NEVADA REVIEW

999 Tahoe Blvd., Incline Village NV 89451. **E-mail:** sncreview@sierranevada.edu. **Website:** www.sierra-nevada.edu/academics/humanities-social-sciences/english/the-sierra-nevada-review. Estab. 1990. "*Sierra Nevada Review*, published annually in May, features poetry, short fiction, and literary nonfiction by new and established writers. Wants "writing that leans toward the unconventional, surprising, and risky."

◔ Reads submissions September 1-February 15 only.

HOW TO CONTACT Prose (fiction and nonfiction) submissions should be 4,000 words or less.

◑ SINISTER WISDOM

P.O. Box 3252, Berkeley CA 94703. **Website:** www.sinisterwisdom.org. Estab. 1976. *Sinister Wisdom* is a quarterly lesbian-feminist journal providing fiction, poetry, drama, essays, journals, and artwork. Past issues include "Lesbians of Color," "Old Lesbians/Dykes," and "Lesbians and Religion."

◔ *Sinister Wisdom* is 5.5x8.5; 128-144 pages; 55 lb. stock; 10 pt. C1S cover; with illustrations, photos.

NEEDS List of upcoming themes available on website. Receives 30 unsolicited mss/month. Accepts 6 mss/issue; 24 mss/year. Recently published work by Jacqueline Miranda, Amanda Esteva, and Sharon Bridgforth. No heterosexual or male-oriented fiction; no '70s amazon adventures; nothing that stereotypes or degrades women. Length: 500-5,000 words; average length: 2,000 words.

HOW TO CONTACT Send complete ms. Strongly prefers submissions through online submissions manager. Publishes short shorts. Also publishes literary essays, literary criticism, poetry. Sometimes comments on rejected mss. Reviews fiction.

PAYMENT/TERMS Pays 1 contributor's copy and one-year subscription.

TIPS *Sinister Wisdom* is "a multicultural lesbian journal reflecting the art, writing, and politics of our communities."

◐ THE SITE OF BIG SHOULDERS

1543 N. Milwaukee Ave., Chicago IL 60622. **E-mail:** info@sobs.org. **E-mail:** submissions@sobs.org. **Web-**

site: sobs.org. Estab. 1996. *"The Site of Big Shoulders* features original content with a connection to the greater Chicago area by virtue of authorship or subject matter. *SOBS* is a 501 (c) (3) not-for-profit organization and a noncommercial community publishing effort that focuses on high editorial quality, aesthetics, and production value without regard to commercial need or mass appeal."

○ This site has won the 2003 Community Arts Assistance Program Grant, the Bronze Trophy for Exceptional Creativity from the Chicago Internet Review (1998); the Artis Hot Site Award (1998); and the Juno Silver Award (1998).

NEEDS Has published work by James Ogle, Jack Lowe, Phil Brody and Li Young-Lee. Length: up to 3,000 words.

HOW TO CONTACT Submit complete ms by e-mail: submissions@sobs.org.

TIPS "We are very open to the idea of publishing hypertext or other experimental fiction. Please submit clean, edited copy."

❶ SLOW TRAINS LITERARY JOURNAL

P.O. 4741, Denver CO 80155. **E-mail:** editor@ slowtrains.com. **Website:** www.slowtrains.com. **Contact:** Susannah Grace Indigo, editor. Estab. 2000. Looking for fiction, essays, and poetry that reflect the spirit of adventure, the exploration of the soul, the energies of imagination, and the experience of Big Fun. Music, travel, sex, humor, love, loss, art, spirituality, childhood/coming of age, baseball, and dreams, but most of all, *Slow Trains* wants to read about the things you are passionate about.

NEEDS Genre writing is not encouraged. No sci-fi, erotica, horror, romance, though elements of those may naturally be included. Length: up to 5,000 words.

HOW TO CONTACT Submit via e-mail only.

❶❸ SNOWY EGRET

The Fair Press, P.O. Box 9265, Terre Haute IN 47808. **Website:** www.snowyegret.net. Estab. 1922. *Snowy Egret,* published in spring and autumn, specializes in work that is nature-oriented. Features fiction, nonfiction, artwork, and poetry.

○ *Snowy Egret* is 60 pages, magazine-sized, offset-printed, saddle-stapled.

NEEDS Publishes works which celebrate the abundance and beauty of nature and examine the variety of ways in which human beings interact with landscapes and living things. Wants nature writing from literary, artistic, psychological, philosophical, and historical perspectives. No genre fiction, e.g., horror, western, romance, etc.

HOW TO CONTACT Send complete ms with SASE. Cover letter optional: do not query.

PAYMENT/TERMS Pays $2/page and 2 contributor's copies.

TIPS Looks for "honest, freshly detailed pieces with plenty of description and/or dialogue which will allow the reader to identify with the characters and step into the setting; fiction in which nature affects character development and the outcome of the story."

○ SNREVIEW

197 Fairchild Ave., Fairfield CT 06825-4856. (203)366-5991. **E-mail:** editor@snreview.org. **Website:** www. snreview.org. **Contact:** Joseph Conlin, editor. Estab. 1999. "We search for material that not only has strong characters and plot but also a devotion to imagery." Quarterly.

○ Also publishes literary essays, poetry. Print and Kindle edition is now available from an on-demand printer.

NEEDS Receives 300 unsolicited mss/month. Accepts 40+ mss/issue; 150 mss/year. Publishes 75 new writers/year. Has published work by Frank X. Walker, Adrian Louis, Barbara Burkhardt, E. Lindsey Balkan, Marie Griffin, and Jonathan Lerner. "No romance, mystery, science fiction, fantasy, or horror genre fiction." Length: 1,000-7,000 words; average length: 4,000 words.

HOW TO CONTACT Submit via e-mail; label the e-mail "SUB: Name of Story." Copy and paste work into the body of the e-mail. Don't send attachments. Include 100-word bio and list of publications.

SOLDIER OF FORTUNE

2135 11th St., Boulder CO 80302. (303)443-0300. **E-mail:** editorsof@aol.com. **Website:** www.sofmag.com. **Contact:** Lt. Col. Robert A. Brown, editor/publisher. Estab. 1975. "We are an action-oriented magazine; we cover combat hot spots around the world. We also provide timely features on state-of-the-art weapons and equipment; elite military and police units; and historical military operations. Readership is primarily active-duty military, veterans, and law enforcement."

TIPS "Submit a professionally prepared, complete package. All artwork with cutlines, double-spaced typed ms with 5.25 or 3.5 IBM-compatible disk, if available, cover letter including synopsis of article, supporting documentation where applicable, etc. Ms must be factual; writers have to do their homework and get all their facts straight. One error means rejection. Vietnam features, if carefully researched and art heavy, will always get a careful look. Combat reports, again, with good art, are No. 1 in our book and stand the best chance of being accepted. Military unit reports from around the world are well received, as are law-enforcement articles (units, police in action). If you write for us, be complete and factual; pros read *Soldier of Fortune*, and are very quick to let us know if we (and the author) err."

SO TO SPEAK

George Mason University, 4400 University Dr., MSN 2C5, Fairfax VA 22030-4444. **E-mail:** sts@gmu.edu (inquiries only). **Website:** sotospeakjournal.org. **Contact:** Jessie Szalay, editor in chief; Alex Ghaly, nonfiction editor; Robert Schuster, fiction editor; A.K. Padovich, poetry editor. Estab. 1993. *So to Speak*, published semiannually, prints "high-quality work relating to feminism, including poetry, fiction, nonfiction (including book reviews and interviews), photography, artwork, collaborations, lyrical essays, and other genre-questioning texts." Wants "work that addresses issues of significance to women's lives and movements for women's equality. Especially interested in pieces that explore issues of race, class, and sexuality in relation to gender." Reads submissions August 20-October 25 for Spring issue and January 1-March 15 for Fall issue.

○ *So to Speak* is 100-128 pages, digest-sized, photo-offset-printed, perfect-bound, with glossy cover; includes ads. Press run is 1,000 (75 subscribers, 100 shelf sales); 500 distributed free to students/contributors.

NEEDS Receives 100 unsolicited mss/month. Accepts 3-5 mss/issue; 6-10 mss/year. **Publishes 7 new writers/year.** Sponsors awards/contests. No science fiction, mystery, genre romance. Length: up to 4,500 words.

HOW TO CONTACT Accepts submissions only via submissions manager on website. Does not accept paper or e-mail submissions. "Fiction submitted during the January 1–March 15 reading period will be considered for our Fall annual fiction contest and must be accompanied by a $15 reading fee. See contest guidelines. Contest entries will not be returned."

PAYMENT/TERMS Pays 2 contributor's copies.

TIPS "Every writer has something they do exceptionally well; do that and it will shine through in the work. We look for quality prose with a definite appeal to a feminist audience. We are trying to move away from strict genre lines. We want high-quality fiction, nonfiction, poetry, art, innovative and risk-taking work."

SOUL FOUNTAIN

90-21 Springfield Blvd., Queens Village NY 11428. **E-mail:** davault@aol.com. **Website:** www.thevault. org. **Contact:** Tone Bellizzi, editor. Estab. 1997. *Soul Fountain*, published 2-3 times/year, is produced by The Vault, a not-for-profit arts project of the Hope for the Children Foundation, committed to empowering young and emerging artists of all disciplines at all levels to develop and share their talents through performance, collaboration, and networking. Prints poetry, art, photography, short fiction, and essays. Open to all. Publishes quality submitted work, and specializes in emerging voices. Favors visionary, challenging, and consciousness-expanding material.

○ *Soul Fountain* is 28 pages, magazine-sized, offset-printed, saddle-stapled.

NEEDS Length: ms must fit on 1 page.

HOW TO CONTACT Submit complete ms by e-mail. No cover letters, please.

PAYMENT/TERMS Pays 1 contributor's copy.

THE SOUTH CAROLINA REVIEW

Center for Electronic and Digital Publishing, Strode Tower Room 611, Box 340522, Clemson SC 29634-0522. (864)656-5399. **Fax:** (864)656-1345. **E-mail:** cwayne@clemson.edu. **Website:** www.clemson.edu/cedp/press/scr/index.htm. **Contact:** Wayne Chapman, editor. Estab. 1967. "Since 1968, *The South Carolina Review* has published fiction, poetry, interviews, unpublished letters and mss, essays, and reviews from well-known and aspiring scholars and writers."

○ *The South Carolina Review* is 6×9; 200 pages; 60 lb. cream white vellum paper; 65 lb. color cover stock. Semiannual. Does not read mss June-August or December. Receives 50-60 unsolicited mss/month.

NEEDS Submit complete ms. Cover letter is preferred. Ms format should be according to new MLA Stylesheet. Do not submit during June, July, August, or December. Recently published work by Thomas E. Kennedy, Ronald Frame, Dennis McFadden, Dulane Upshaw Ponder, and Stephen Jones. Rarely comments on rejected mss.

SOUTH DAKOTA REVIEW

The University of South Dakota, Dept. of English, 414 E. Clark St., Vermillion SD 57069. (605)677-5184. E-mail: sdreview@usd.edu. **Website:** www.usd.edu/sdreview. **Contact:** Lee Ann Roripaugh, editor in chief. Estab. 1963. "*South Dakota Review*, published quarterly, is committed to cultural and aesthetic diversity. First and foremost, we seek to publish exciting and compelling work that reflects the full spectrum of the contemporary literary arts. Since its inception in 1963, *South Dakota Review* has maintained a tradition of supporting work by contemporary writers writing from or about the American West. We hope to retain this unique flavor through particularly welcoming works by American Indian writers, writers addressing the complexities and contradictions of the 'New West,' and writers exploring themes of landscape, place, and/or eco-criticism in surprising and innovative ways. At the same time, we'd like to set these ideas and themes in dialogue with and within the context of larger global literary communities. Single copy: $12; subscription: $40/year, $65/2 years. Sample: $8.

○ Writing from *South Dakota Review* has appeared in *Pushcart* and *Best American Essays* anthologies. Press run is 500-600 (more than 500 subscribers, many of them libraries).

NEEDS "Our aesthetic is eclectic, but we tend to favor deft use of language in both our poetry and prose selections, nuanced characterization in our fiction, and either elegantly or surprisingly executed formal strategies. As part of our unique flavor, a small handful works in each issue will typically engage with aspects of landscape, ecocritical issues, or place (oftentimes with respect to the American West)." Length: up to 6,000 words.

HOW TO CONTACT Submit via online submissions manager. Include cover letter.

PAYMENT/TERMS Pays 2 contributor's copies.

THE SOUTHEAST REVIEW

Florida State University, Tallahassee FL 32306-1036. **Website:** southeastreview.org. **Contact:** Erin Hoover, editor. Estab. 1979. "The mission of *The Southeast Review* is to present emerging writers on the same stage as well-established ones. In each semi-annual issue, we publish literary fiction, creative nonfiction, poetry, interviews, book reviews, and art. With nearly 60 members on our editorial staff who come from throughout the country and the world, we strive to publish work that is representative of our diverse interests and aesthetics, and we celebrate the eclectic mix this produces. We receive approximately 400 submissions per month, and we accept less than 1-2% of them."

○ Publishes 4-6 new writers/year. Has published work by Eduardo J. Astigarraga, Matthew Gavin Frank, Kent Shaw, Charles Harper Webb, and Leslie Wheeler.

NEEDS "We try to respond to submissions within 2-4 months. If after 4 months you have not heard back regarding your submission, you may query the appropriate section editor. *SER* accepts simultaneous submissions, but we request that you withdraw the submission by way of our online submission manager if your piece is accepted elsewhere." Length: up to 7,500 words.

PAYMENT/TERMS Pays 2 contributor's copies.

TIPS "*The Southeast Review* accepts regular submissions for publication consideration year-round exclusively through the online submission manager. **Except in the case of contests, paper submissions sent through regular postal mail will not be read or returned**. Avoid trendy experimentation for its own sake (present-tense narration, observation that isn't also revelation). Fresh stories; moving, interesting characters; and a sensitivity to language are still fiction mainstays. We also publish the winner and runners-up of the World's Best Short Story Contest, Poetry Contest, and Creative Nonfiction Contest."

SOUTHERN CALIFORNIA REVIEW

University of Southern California, Master of Professional Writing Program, 3501 Trousdale Pkwy., Mark Taper Hall of Humanities, THH 355J, Los Angeles CA 90089. **Website:** southerncaliforniareview.wordpress.com. Estab. 1982. The *Southern California Review* encourages new, emerging, and established writers to submit previously unpublished work. Accepts fiction, poetry, nonfiction, comics, and dramatic forms (including one-act plays, scenes, and short films or screenplay excerpts). Different theme for each issue; check website for current/upcoming themes.

○ Unsolicited mss are read September 1-December 1.

NEEDS Genre fiction is discouraged and will be considered only if it transcends the boundaries of its genre. Length: up to 7,000 words.

HOW TO CONTACT Submit complete ms by mail or online submissions manager.

PAYMENT/TERMS Pays 2 contributor's copies.

SOUTHERN HUMANITIES REVIEW

Auburn University, 9088 Haley Center, Auburn University AL 36849. (334)844-9088. **Fax:** (334)844-9027. **E-mail:** shr@auburn.edu. **Website:** www.southernhumanitiesreview.com. **Contact:** Aaron Alford, managing editor. Estab. 1967. *Southern Humanities Review* publishes fiction, nonfiction, and poetry.

THE SOUTHERN REVIEW

338 Johnston Hall, Louisiana State University, Baton Rouge LA 70803. (225)578-5108. **Fax:** (225)578-5098. **E-mail:** southernreview@lsu.edu. **Website:** thesouthernreview.org. **Contact:** Jessica Faust, co-editor and poetry editor; Emily Nemens, co-editor and prose editor. Estab. 1935. "*The Southern Review* is one of the nation's premiere literary journals. Hailed by *Time* as 'superior to any other journal in the English language,' we have made literary history since our founding in 1935. We publish a diverse array of fiction, nonfiction, and poetry by the country's—and the world's—most respected contemporary writers." Reading period: September1-December 1. All mss submitted during outside the reading period will be recycled.

NEEDS Wants short stories of lasting literary merit, with emphasis on style and technique; novel excerpts. "We emphasize style and substantial content. No mystery, fantasy, or religious mss." Length: up to 8,000 words.

HOW TO CONTACT Submit 1 ms at a time by mail. "We rarely publish work that is longer than 8,000 words. We consider novel excerpts if they stand alone."

PAYMENT/TERMS Pays $25/printed page (max $200), 2 contributor's copies, and one-year subscription.

TIPS "Careful attention to craftsmanship and technique combined with a developed sense of the creation of story will always make us pay attention."

⬤ SOUTHWESTERN AMERICAN LITERATURE

Center for the Study of the Southwest, Texas State University, Brazos Hall, 601 University Dr., San Marcos TX 78666-4616. (512)245-2224. **Fax:** (512)245-7462. **E-mail:** swpublications@txstate.edu. **Website:** www.txstate.edu/cssw/publications/sal.html. **Contact:** William Jensen, editor. Estab. 1971. *Southwestern American Literature* is a biannual scholarly journal that includes literary criticism, fiction, poetry, and book reviews concerning the Greater Southwest.

NEEDS Wants "crisp language and an interesting approach to material; a regional approach is desired but not required. We seek stories that probe the relationship between the tradition of Southwestern American literature and the writer's own imagination in creative ways—stories that move beyond stereotype." Length: no more than 6,000 words/25 pages.

HOW TO CONTACT Submit using online submissions manager. Include contact information and brief bio.

PAYMENT/TERMS Pays 2 contributor's copies.

TIPS "We look for crisp language, an interesting approach to material; a regional approach is desired but not required. Read widely, write often, revise carefully. We are looking for stories that probe the relationship between the tradition of Southwestern American literature and the writer's own imagination in creative ways. We seek stories that move beyond stereotype and approach the larger defining elements and also ones that, as William Faulkner noted in his Nobel Prize acceptance speech, treat subjects central to good literature—the old verities of the human heart, such as honor and courage and pity and suffering, fear and humor, love and sorrow."

SOUTHWEST REVIEW

P.O. Box 750374, Dallas TX 75275-0374. (214)768-1037. **Fax:** (214)768-1408. **E-mail:** swr@smu.edu. **Website:** www.smu.edu/southwestreview. **Contact:** Willard Spiegelman, editor in chief. Estab. 1915. The majority of readers are well-read adults who wish to stay abreast of the latest and best in contemporary fiction, poetry, and essays in all but the most specialized disciplines. Published quarterly.

⬤ Has published work by Alice Hoffman, Sabina Murray, Alix Ohlin. The Elizabeth Matchett Stover Memorial Award presents $250 to the author of the best poem or groups of poems (chosen by editors) published in the preceding year. Also offers The Morton Marr Poetry Prize and the David Nathan Meyerson Prize for Fiction.

NEEDS Publishes fiction in widely varying styles. Prefers stories of character development, of psychological penetration, to those depending chiefly on plot. No specific requirements as to subject matter. Length: 3,500-7,000 words preferred.

HOW TO CONTACT Submissions accepted online for a $2 fee. No fee for submissions sent by mail. Submit one story at a time. Reading period: September 1-May 31.

PAYMENT/TERMS Accepted pieces receive nominal payment upon publication and copies of the issue.

TIPS "Despite the title, we are not a regional magazine. Before you submit your work, it's a good idea to take a look at recent issues to familiarize yourself with the magazine. We strongly advise all writers to include a cover letter. Keep your cover letter professional and concise, and don't include extraneous personal information, a story synopsis, or a résumé. When authors ask what we look for in a strong story submission, the answer is simple regardless of graduate degrees in creative writing, workshops, or whom you know: We look for good writing, period."

SOU'WESTER

Department of English, Box 1438, Southern Illinois University Edwardsville, Edwardsville IL 62026. **Website:** souwester.org. **Contact:** Allison Funk poetry editor; Valerie Vogrin, prose editor. Estab. 1960. *Sou'wester* appears biannually in spring and fall. Leans toward poetry with strong imagery, successful association of images, and skillful use of figurative language. Has published poetry by Robert Wrigley, Beckian Fritz Goldberg, Eric Pankey, Betsy Sholl, and Angie Estes.

Uses online submission form. Open to submissions in mid-August for fall and spring issues. Close submissions in winter and early spring. *Sou'wester* has 30-40 pages of poetry in each digest-sized, 100-page issue. *Sou'wester* is professionally printed, flat-spined, with textured matte card cover, press run is 300 for 500 subscribers of which 50 are libraries. Receives 3,000 poems (from 600 poets) each year, accepts 36-40, has a 6-month backlog. Subscription: $15/2 issues.

HOW TO CONTACT Submit 1 piece of prose at a time. Will consider a suite of 2 or 3 flash pieces.

PAYMENT/TERMS Pays 2 contributor's copies and a 1-year subscription.

SPACE AND TIME

458 Elizabeth Ave., Somerset NJ 08873. **Website:** www.spaceandtimemagazine.com. **Contact:** Hildy Silverman, editor in chief. Estab. 1966. "We love stories that blend elements—horror and science fiction, fantasy with SF elements, etc. We challenge writers to try something new and send us their unclassifiable works-what other publications reject because the work doesn't fit in their 'pigeonholes.'"

NEEDS "We are looking for creative blends of science fiction, fantasy, and/or horror." "Do not send children's stories." Length: 1,000-10,000/words. Average length: 6,500 words. Average length of short shorts: 1,000.

HOW TO CONTACT Submit electronically as a Word doc or .rtf attachment.

PAYMENT/TERMS Pays 1¢/word.

SPITBALL: THE LITERARY BASEBALL MAGAZINE

5560 Fox Rd., Cincinnati OH 45239. **E-mail:** spitball5@hotmail.com. **Website:** www.spitballmag.com. **Contact:** Mike Shannon, editor in chief. Estab. 1981. *Spitball: The Literary Baseball Magazine*, published semiannually, is a unique magazine devoted to poetry, fiction, and book reviews exclusively about baseball. Newcomers are very welcome, but they must know the subject. "Perhaps a good place to start for beginners is one's personal reactions to the game, a game, a player, etc., and take it from there." Writers submitting to *Spitball* for the first time must buy a sample copy (waived for subscribers). "This is a one-time-only fee, which we regret, but economic reality dictates that we insist those who wish to be published in *Spitball* help support it, at least at this minimum level."

Spitball is 96 pages, digest-sized, computer-typeset, perfect-bound. Receives about 1,000 submissions/year, accepts about 40. Press run is 1,000. Subscription: $12. Sample: $6.

NEEDS Length: 5-15 pages, double-spaced. Short stories longer than 20 pages must be exceptionally good.

HOW TO CONTACT Submit with a biography and SASE.

TIPS "Take the subject seriously. We do. In other words, get a clue (if you don't already have one) about the subject and about the poetry that has already been done and published about baseball. Learn from it—think about what you can add to the canon that is original and fresh—and don't assume that just anybody with the feeblest of efforts can write a baseball poem worthy of publication. And most importantly, stick with it. Genius seldom happens on the first try."

SPOTLIGHT ON RECOVERY MAGAZINE

R. Graham Publishing Company, 9602 Glenwood Road, #140, Brooklyn NY 11236. (347)831-9373. **E-mail:** rgraham_100@msn.com. **Website:** www.spotlightonrecovery.com. **Contact:** Robin Graham, publisher and editor in chief. Estab. 2001. "This is the premiere outreach and resource magazine in New York. Its goal is to be the catalyst for which the human spirit could heal. Everybody knows somebody who has mental illness, substance abuse issues, parenting problems, educational issues, or someone who is homeless, unemployed, physically ill, or the victim of a crime. Many people suffer in silence. *Spotlight on Recovery* will provide a voice to those who suffer in silence and begin the dialogue of recovery."

TIPS "Send a query and give a reason why you would choose the subject posted to write about."

STAND MAGAZINE

Leeds University, School of English, Leeds LS2 9JT United Kingdom. (44)(113)233-4794. **Fax:** (44)(113)233-2791. **E-mail:** stand@leeds.ac.uk. **Website:** www.standmagazine.org. **Contact:** Jon Glover, managing editor. Estab. 1952. *"Stand Magazine* is concerned with what happens when cultures and literatures meet, with translation in its many guises, with the mechanics of language, with the processes by which the policy receives or disables its cultural makers. *Stand* promotes debate of issues that are of radical concern to the intellectual community worldwide. U.S. submissions can be made through the Virginia office (see separate listing).

Does not accept e-mail submissions.

NEEDS No genre fiction. Length: up to 3,000 words.

ST. ANTHONY MESSENGER

Franciscan Media, 28 W. Liberty St., Cincinnati OH 45202-6498. (513)241-5615. **Fax:** (513)241-0399. **E-mail:** magazineeditors@franciscanmedia.org. **Website:** www.stanthonymessenger.org. **Contact:** John Feister, editor in chief. Estab. 1893. *St. Anthony Messenger* is a Catholic family magazine which aims to help its readers lead more fully human and Christian lives. "We publish articles that report on a changing church and world, opinion pieces written from the perspective of Christian faith and values, personality profiles, and fiction which entertains and informs."

NEEDS "We do not want mawkishly sentimental or preachy fiction. Stories are most often rejected for poor plotting and characterization, bad dialogue (listen to how people talk), and inadequate motivation. Many stories say nothing, are 'happenings' rather than stories. No fetal journals, no rewritten Bible stories." Length: 2,000-2,500 words.

HOW TO CONTACT Send complete ms.

PAYMENT/TERMS Pays 20¢/word maximum and 2 contributor's copies; $1 charge for extras.

TIPS "The freelancer should consider why his or her proposed article would be appropriate for us, rather than for *Redbook* or *Saturday Review*. We treat human problems of all kinds, but from a religious perspective. Articles should reflect Catholic theology, spirituality, and employ a Catholic terminology and vocabulary. We need more articles on prayer, scripture, Catholic worship. Get authoritative information (not merely library research); we want interviews with experts. Write in popular style; use lots of examples, stories, and personal quotes. Word length is an important consideration."

STEAMPUNK MAGAZINE, PUTTING THE PUNK BACK INTO STEAMPUNK

Combustion Books, New York NY **E-mail:** collective@steampunkmagazine.com. **Website:** www.steampunkmagazine.com. Estab. 2007. *"SteamPunk Magazine* is a print-and-web periodical devoted to the genre and burgeoning subculture of steampunk. We pride ourselves on promoting a version of steampunk that does not forget the punk aspects of it—challenging authority, Do-It-Yourself attitudes, and creating our own culture in the face of an alienating and boring mainstream one. We publish fiction set in the Victorian era, set in the far future, and set in fantasy worlds. We have a fairly broad interpretation of what might be considered steampunk, resisting the urge to limit ourselves and create a "pure" definition of the word. We also publish DIY how-to articles, essays on fashion, historical tracts, rants and manifestos ... anything we think will serve the greater steampunk community."

NEEDS "We appreciate well-written, grammatically consistent fiction. That said, we are more interested in representing the underclasses and the exploited, rather than the exploiters." No misogynistic or racist work. Length: "We will work with fiction of nearly any length, although works longer than 6,000 words are less likely to be accepted, as they may have to be split over multiple issues."

HOW TO CONTACT Submit ms as an e-mail attachment. Include word count.

TIPS "Please keep in mind before submitting that we publish under Creative Commons licensing, which means that people will be free to reproduce and alter your work for noncommercial purposes. We are not currently a paying market. Please introduce yourself in your introduction letter: We like to know that we're working with actual people. Surprise us! We're nicer people than we sound!"

○ STEPPING STONES MAGAZINE

First Step Press, P.O. Box 902, Norristown PA 19404-0902. **E-mail:** info@ssmalmia.com. **Website:** ssmalmia.com. **Contact:** Trinae A. Ross, publisher. Estab. 1996. *Stepping Stones Magazine*, a Web publication with a rolling publication date, seeks "poetry as diverse as the authors themselves. Poems should have something to say other than, 'Hi, I'm a poem please publish me.'" Does not want "poems that promote intolerance for race, religion, gender, or sexual preference." Also accepts fiction and nonfiction.

○   Has published poetry by Richard Fenwick, Karlanna Lewis, and Stephanie Kaylor. Receives about 600 poems/year, accepts about 10-15%.

NEEDS Fiction should be able to hold the reader's interest in the first paragraph and sustain that interest throughout the rest of the story. Send no more than 3 stories per submission. Length: up to 4,000 words.

HOW TO CONTACT Submit via e-mail to: fiction@ssmalmia.com.

○ STILL CRAZY

(614)746-0859. **E-mail:** editor@crazylitmag.com. **Website:** www.crazylitmag.com. **Contact:** Barbara Kussow, editor. *Still Crazy*, published biannually in January and July, features poetry, short stories, and essays written by or about people over age 50. The editor is particularly interested in material that challenges the stereotypes of older people and that portrays older people's inner lives as rich and rewarding. Wants writing by people over age 50 and writing by people of any age if the topic is about people over 50.

○   Accepts 3-4 mss/issue; 6-8/year. Reads submissions year round.

NEEDS Publishes short shorts. Ms published 6-12 months after acceptance. Sometimes features a "First Story," a story by an author who has not been published before. Does not want material that is "too sentimental or inspirational, 'Geezer' humor, or anything too grim." Length: up to 3,500 words, but stories fewer than 3,000 words are more likely to be published.

HOW TO CONTACT Upload submissions via submissions manager on website. Include estimated word count, brief bio, age of writer or "Over 50."

PAYMENT/TERMS Pays 1 contributor's copy.

TIPS Looking for "interesting characters and interesting situations that might interest readers of all ages. Humor and lightness welcomed."

○ STIRRING: A LITERARY COLLECTION

c/o Erin Elizabeth Smith, Dept. of English, 301 McClung Tower, University of Tennessee, Knoxville TN 37996. **E-mail:** eesmith81@gmail.com. **E-mail:** stirring.fiction@gmail.com; stirring.poetry@gmail.com; stirring.nonfiction@gmail.com. **Website:** www.sundresspublications.com/stirring. **Contact:** Erin Elizabeth Smith, managing editor. Estab. 1999. "*Stirring* is one of the oldest continually-published literary journals on the web. *Stirring* is a monthly literary magazine that publishes poetry, short fiction, creative nonfiction, and photography by established and emerging writers."

NEEDS Length: up to 5,000 words.

HOW TO CONTACT Submit complete ms by e-mail to stirring.fiction@gmail.com

○○○ STORIE

Via Suor Celestina Donati 13/E, Rome 00167 Italy. (+39)06-454-33670. **Fax:** (+39)06-454-33670. **E-mail:** info@storie.it. **Website:** www.storie.it/english. Estab. 1986. "*Storie* is one of Italy's leading cultural and literary magazines. Committed to a truly crossover vision of writing, the bilingual (Italian/English) review publishes high-quality fiction and poetry, interspersed with the work of alternative wordsmiths such as filmmakers and musicians. Through writings bordering on narratives and interviews with important contemporary writers, it explores the culture and craft of writing."

HOW TO CONTACT "Mss may be submitted directly by regular post without querying first; however, we do not accept unsolicited mss via e-mail. Please query via e-mail first. We only contact writers if their work has been accepted. We also arrange for and oversee a high-quality, professional translation of the piece."

PAYMENT/TERMS Pays $30-600 and 2 contributor's copies.

TIPS "More than erudite references or a virtuoso performance, we're interested in a style merging news writing with literary techniques in the manner of new journalism. *Storie* reserves the right to include a brief review of interesting submissions not selected for publication in a special column of the magazine."

○○ STORY BYTES

E-mail: editor@storybytes.com. **Website:** www.storybytes.com. **Contact:** Mark Stanley Bubein. "A monthly e-zine and weekly electronic mailing list presenting the Internet's (and the world's) shortest stories—fiction ranging from 2 to 2,048 words. Just as eyes, art often provides a window to the soul. *Story Bytes'* very short stories offer a glimpse through this window into brief vignettes of life, often reflecting or revealing those things which make us human."

NEEDS "Story length must fall on a power of 2. That's 2, 4, 8, 16, 32, 64, 128, 256, 512, 1,024, and 2,048 words long. Stories must match one of these lengths exactly." See website for examples. No sexually explicit material. Length: 2-2,048 words.

HOW TO CONTACT Submit story as plain text via e-mail. "The easiest way to do so is to simply copy it from your word processor and paste it into an e-mail message. Specify the word count below the title."

TIPS "In *Story Bytes* the very short stories themselves range in topic. Many explore a brief event—a vignette of something unusual, unique, and at times even commonplace. Some stories can be bizarre, while others quite lucid. Some are based on actual events, while others are entirely fictional. Try to develop conflict early on (in the first sentence if possible!), and illustrate or resolve this conflict through action rather than description."

⊙ STORYSOUTH

5603B W. Friendly Ave., Suite 282, Greensboro NC 27410. **E-mail:** terry@storysouth.com. **Website:** www.storysouth.com. **Contact:** Terry Kennedy, editor; Cynthia Nearman, creative nonfiction editor; Drew Perry, fiction editor; Julie Funderburk, poetry editor. Estab. 2001. "*storySouth* accepts unsolicited submissions of fiction, poetry, and creative nonfiction during 2 submission periods annually: March 15-June 15 and September 15-December 15. Long pieces are encouraged. Please make only 1 submission in a single genre per reading period."

NEEDS No word limit.

HOW TO CONTACT Submit 1 story via online submissions manager.

TIPS "What really makes a story stand out is a strong voice and a sense of urgency—a need for the reader to keep reading the story and not put it down until it is finished."

THE STORYTELLER

2441 Washington Rd., Maynard AR 72444. (870)647-2137. **E-mail:** storytellermag1@yahoo.com. **Website:** www.thestorytellermagazine.com. **Contact:** Regina Williams, editor. Estab. 1996.

NEEDS Does not want pornography, erotica, horror, graphic language or violence, children's stories, or anything deemed racial or biased toward any religion, race, or moral preference.

HOW TO CONTACT Send complete ms with cover letter and SASE.

TIPS "*The Storyteller* is one of the best places you will find to submit your work, especially new writers. Our best advice, be professional. You have one chance to make a good impression. Don't blow it by being unprofessional."

THE STRAND MAGAZINE

P.O. Box 1418, Birmingham MI 48012-1418. (800)300-6652. **Fax:** (248)874-1046. **E-mail:** strandmag@strandmag.com. **Website:** www.strandmag.com. Estab. 1998. "After an absence of nearly half a century, the magazine known to millions for bringing Sir Arthur Conan Doyle's ingenious detective, Sherlock Holmes, to the world has once again appeared on the literary scene. First launched in 1891, *The Strand* included in its pages the works of some of the greatest writers of the 20th century: Agatha Christie, Dorothy Sayers, Margery Allingham, W. Somerset Maugham, Graham Greene, P.G. Wodehouse, H.G. Wells, Aldous Huxley, and many others. In 1950, economic difficulties in England caused a drop in circulation which forced the magazine to cease publication."

NEEDS "We are interested in mysteries, detective stories, tales of terror and the supernatural as well as short stories. Stories can be set in any time or place, provided they are well written, the plots interesting and well thought." Occasionally accepts short shorts and short novellas. We are not interested in submissions with any sexual content. Length: 2,000-6,000 words.

HOW TO CONTACT Submit complete ms by postal mail. Include SASE. No e-mail submissions.

PAYMENT/TERMS Pays $25-150.

TIPS "No gratuitous violence, sexual content, or explicit language, please."

⊙⊙⊙ STRANGE HORIZONS

Strange Horizons, Inc., P.O. Box 1693, Dubuque IA 52004-1693. **E-mail:** editor@strangehorizons.com. **Website:** strangehorizons.com. **Contact:** Niall Harrison, editor in chief. Estab. 2000. **E-mail:** fiction@strangehorizons.com. "*Strange Horizons* is a magazine of and about speculative fiction and related nonfiction. Speculative fiction includes science fiction, fantasy, horror, slipstream, and other flavors of fantastica."

⬤   Work published in *Strange Horizons* has been shortlisted for or won Hugo, Nebula, Rhysling, Theodore Sturgeon, James Tiptree Jr., and World Fantasy Awards.

NEEDS "We love, or are interested in, fiction from or about diverse perspectives and traditionally under-represented groups, settings, and cultures, written from a nonexoticizing and well-researched position; unusual yet readable styles and inventive structures and narratives; stories that address political issues in complex and nuanced ways, resisting oversimplification; and hypertext fiction." No excessive gore. Length: up to 10,000 words (under 5,000 words preferred).

HOW TO CONTACT Submit via online submissions manager; no e-mail or postal submission accepted.

PAYMENT/TERMS Pays 8¢/word, $50 minimum.

⭕ STRAYLIGHT

UW-Parkside, English Department, University of Wisconsin-Parkside, 900 Wood Rd., Kenosha WI 53141. **E-mail:** submissions@straylightmag.com. **Website:** www.straylightmag.com. Estab. 2005. *Straylight*, published biannually, seeks fiction and "poetry of almost any style as long as it's inventive."

⬤   Literary magazine/journal: 6x9, 115 pages, quality paper, uncoated index stock cover. Contains illustrations, photographs.

NEEDS "*Straylight* is interested in publishing high-quality, character-based fiction of any style. We tend not to publish strict genre pieces, though we may query them for future special issues. We do not publish erotica." Publishes short shorts and novellas. Does not read May-August. Agented fiction 10%. Length: 1,000-5,000 words for short stories; under 1,000 words for flash fiction; 17,500-45,000 for novellas. Average length: 1,500-3,000 words.

HOW TO CONTACT Send complete ms with cover letter. Accepts submissions by online submission manager or mail (send either SASE or IRC for return of ms, or disposable copy of ms and #10 SASE for reply only). Include brief bio, list of publications.

PAYMENT/TERMS Pays 2 contributor's copies.

TIPS "We tend to publish character-based and inventive fiction with cutting-edge prose. We are unimpressed with works based on strict plot twists or novelties. Read a sample copy to get a feel for what we publish."

STRAYLIGHT ONLINE

University of Wisconsin-Parkside, English Department, University of Wisconsin-Parkside, 900 Wood Rd., Box 2000, Kenosha WI 53414-2000. (262) 595-2139. **Fax:** (262) 595-2271. **E-mail:** villa@straylight-mag.com. **Website:** straylightmag.com. **Contact:** appropriate genre editor (revolving editors). Estab. 2008. *Straylight Online* is the web counterpart to *Straylight Literary Arts Journal*. It does not mirror the content of the print edition but is dedicated to exploring narrative of all fashion.

NEEDS "We look for stories with a strong sense of place and moments that are character-centered rather than those that rely on plot turns and literary tricks. We welcome submissions that cross genre boundaries as well as those that explore the way visual art, music, and literature combine to produce new manifestations of story and verse." Length: up to 1,000 words for short stories, 17,500-45,000 words for novellas.

HOW TO CONTACT Submit complete ms via online submissions manager. Include brief bio.

⭕ STRUGGLE: A MAGAZINE OF PROLETARIAN REVOLUTIONARY LITERATURE

P.O. Box 28536, Detroit MI 48228. (313)273-9039. **E-mail:** timhall11@yahoo.com. **Website:** www.struggle-magazine.net. **Contact:** Tim Hall, editor. Estab. 1985. "A quarterly magazine featuring African American, Latino and other writers of color, prisoners, disgruntled workers, activists in the anti-war, anti-racist and other mass movements, and many writers discontented with Obama and with the Republicans, their joint austerity campaign against the workers and the poor, and their continuing aggressive wars and drone murders abroad. While we urge literature in the direction of revolutionary working-class politics and a vision of socialism as embodying a genuine workers' power, in distinction to the state-capitalist regimes of the former Soviet Union, present-day China, North Korea, Cuba, etc., we accept a broader range of rebellious viewpoints in order to encourage creativity and dialogue."

NEEDS "Readers would like fiction about anti-globalization, the fight against racism, global militarism including the Afghanistan war, the struggle of immigrants, and the disillusionment with the Obama Administration as it reveals its craven service to the rich billionaires. Would also like to see more fiction that depicts life, work, and struggle of the working class of every background, especially young workers in the struggle for a $15/hour wage and unionization in fast-food and Walmart; also the struggles of the 1930s and '60s illustrated and brought to life." No romance, psychic, mystery, western, erotica, or religious. Length: 4,000 words; average length: 1,000-3,000 words.

HOW TO CONTACT Submit ms via e-mail or postal mail.

PAYMENT/TERMS Pays 1 contributor's copy.

🌐⭘ STUDIO, A JOURNAL OF CHRISTIANS WRITING

727 Peel St., Albury NS 2640 Australia. (61)(2)6021-1135. **E-mail:** studio00@bigpond.net.au. **Contact:** Paul Grover, publisher. Estab. 1980. *Studio, A Journal of Christians Writing*, published quarterly, prints "poetry and prose of literary merit, offering a venue for previously published, new, and aspiring writers and seeking to create a sense of community among Christians writing." Also publishes occasional articles as well as news and reviews of writing, writers, and events of interest to members. People who send material should be comfortable being published under this banner: *Studio, A Journal of Christians Writing*.

⭘ *Studio* is 36 pages, digest-sized, professionally printed on high-quality recycled paper, saddle-stapled, with matte card cover. Press run is 300 (all subscriptions).

NEEDS Cover letter is required. Include brief details of previous publishing history, if any. SAE with IRC required. "Submissions must be typed and double-spaced on 1 side of A4 white paper. Name and address must appear on the reverse side of each page submitted."

PAYMENT/TERMS Pays 1 contributor's copy.

♻🌐⭘⑤ SUBTERRAIN

Strong Words for a Polite Nation, P.O. Box 3008, MPO, Vancouver BC V6B 3X5 Canada. (604)876-8710. **Fax:** (604)879-2667. **E-mail:** subter@portal.ca. **Website:** www.subterrain.ca. **Contact:** Brian Kaufman, editor in chief. Estab. 1988. "*subTerrain* magazine is published 3 times/year from modest offices just off of Main Street in Vancouver, BC. We strive to produce a stimulating fusion of fiction, poetry, photography, and graphic illustration from uprising Canadian, U.S., and international writers and artists."

⭘ Magazine: 8.25×10.75; 72 pages; gloss stock paper; color gloss cover stock; illustrations; photos. "Strong words for a polite nation."

NEEDS Receives 100 unsolicited mss/month. Accepts 4 mss/issue; 10-15 mss/year. Recently published work by J.O. Bruday, Lisa Pike, and Peter Babiak. Does not want genre fiction or children's fiction.

HOW TO CONTACT Send complete ms. Include disposable copy of the ms and SASE for reply only. Accepts multiple submissions.

PAYMENT/TERMS Pays $50/page for prose.

TIPS "Read the magazine first. Get to know what kind of work we publish."

⑤ SUBTROPICS

University of Florida, P.O. Box 112075, 4008 Turlington Hall, Gainesville FL 32611-2075. **E-mail:** subtropics@english.ufl.edu. **Website:** www.english.ufl.edu/subtropics. **Contact:** David Leavitt, editor. Estab. 2005. *Subtropics* seeks to publish the best literary fiction, essays, and poetry being written today, both by established and emerging authors. Will consider works of fiction of any length, from short shorts to novellas and self-contained novel excerpts. Gives the same latitude to essays. Appreciates work in translation and, from time to time, republishes important and compelling stories, essays, and poems that have lapsed out of print by writers no longer living. Member: CLMP.

⭘ Literary magazine/journal: 9x6, 160 pages. Includes photographs. Submissions accepted from September 1-April 15.

NEEDS Does not read May 1-August 31. Agented fiction 33%. **Publishes 1-2 new writers/year.** Has published John Barth, Ariel Dorfman, Tony D'Souza, Allan Gurganus, Frances Hwang, Kuzhali Manickavel, Eileen Pollack, Padgett Powell, Nancy Reisman, Jarret Rosenblatt, Joanna Scott, and Olga Slavnikova. No genre fiction. Length: up to 15,000 words. Average length: 5,000 words. Average length of short shorts: 400 words.

HOW TO CONTACT Submit complete ms via online submissions manager.

PAYMENT/TERMS Pays $500 for short shorts; $1,000 for full stories; 2 contributor's copies.

TIPS "We publish longer works of fiction, including novellas and excerpts from forthcoming novels. Each issue includes a short-short story of about 250 words on the back cover. We are also interested in publishing works in translation for the magazine's English-speaking audience."

SUCCESS STORIES

Franklin Publishing Company, 2723 Steamboat Circle, Arlington TX 76006. (817)548-1124. **E-mail:** ludwigotto@sbcglobal.net. **Website:** www.franklinpub-lishing.net; www.londonpress.us. **Contact:** Dr. Ludwig Otto. Estab. 1983.

HOW TO CONTACT Send complete ms.

◑ THE SUMMERSET REVIEW

25 Summerset Dr., Smithtown NY 11787. **E-mail:** editor@summersetreview.org. **Website:** www.summersetreview.org. **Contact:** Joseph Levens, editor. Estab. 2002. "Our goal is simply to publish the highest-quality literary fiction, nonfiction, and poetry intended for a general audience. This is a simple online literary journal of high-quality material, so simple you can call it unique."

◔   Magazine: illustrations and photographs. Periodically releases print issues. Quarterly.

NEEDS No sci-fi, horror, or graphic erotica. Length: up to 8,000 words; average length: 3,000 words. Publishes short shorts.

HOW TO CONTACT Send complete ms by e-mail as attachment or by postal mail with SASE.

TIPS "Style counts. We prefer innovative or at least very smooth, convincing voices. Even the dullest premises or the complete lack of conflict make for an interesting story if it is told in the right voice and style. We like to find little, interesting facts and/or connections subtly sprinkled throughout the piece. Harsh language should be used only if/when necessary. If we are choosing between light and dark subjects, the light will usually win."

THE SUN

107 N. Roberson St., Chapel Hill NC 27516. (919)942-5282. **Fax:** (919)932-3101. **Website:** www.thesunmagazine.org. **Contact:** Sy Safransky, editor. Estab. 1974. *The Sun* publishes essays, interviews, fiction, and poetry. "We are open to all kinds of writing, though we favor work of a personal nature."

◔   Magazine: 8.5x11; 48 pages; offset paper; glossy cover stock; photos.

NEEDS Open to all fiction. Receives 800 unsolicited mss/month. Accepts 20 short stories/year. Recently published work by Sigrid Nunez, Susan Straight, Lydia Peelle, Stephen Elliott, David James Duncan, Linda McCullough Moore, and Brenda Miller. No science fiction, horror, fantasy, or other genre fiction. "Read an issue before submitting." Length: up to 7,000 words.

HOW TO CONTACT Send complete ms. Accepts reprint submissions.

PAYMENT/TERMS Pays $300-1,500.

TIPS "Do not send queries except for interviews. We're open to unusual work. Read the magazine to get a sense of what we're about. Our submission rate is extremely high. Please be patient after sending us your work and include return postage."

SUSPENSE MAGAZINE

JRSR Ventures, 26500 W. Agoura Rd., Suite 102-474, Calabasas CA 91302. **Fax:** (310)626-9670. **E-mail:** editor@suspensemagazine.com; john@suspensemagazine.com. **E-mail:** stories@suspensemagazine.com. **Website:** www.suspensemagazine.com. **Contact:** John Raab, publisher/CEO/editor in chief. Estab. 2007.

NEEDS No explicit scenes. Length: 1,500-5,000 words.

HOW TO CONTACT Submit story in body of e-mail. "Attachments will not be opened."

TIPS "Unpublished writers are welcome and encouraged to query. Our emphasis is on horror, suspense, thriller, and mystery."

SYCAMORE REVIEW

Purdue University Department of English, 500 Oval Dr., West Lafayette IN 47907. (765) 494-3783. **Fax:** (765) 494-3780. **E-mail:** sycamore@purdue.edu. **Website:** www.sycamorereview.com. **Contact:** Kara Krewer, editor in chief; Bess Cooley, managing editor. *Sycamore Review* is Purdue University's internationally acclaimed literary journal, affiliated with Purdue's College of Liberal Arts and the Dept. of English. Strives to publish the best writing by new and established writers. Looks for well-crafted and engaging work, works that illuminate our lives in the collective human search for meaning. Would like to publish more work that takes a reflective look at national identity and how we are perceived by the world. Looks for diversity of voice, pluralistic worldviews, and political and social context.

◔   Reading period: September 1-March 31.

NEEDS No genre fiction.

HOW TO CONTACT Submit complete ms via online submissions manager.

PAYMENT/TERMS Pays in contributor's copies and $50/short story.

TIPS "We look for originality, brevity, significance, strong dialogue, and vivid detail. We sponsor the Wabash Prize for Poetry (deadline: December 1) and Fiction (deadline: April 17). $1,000 award for each. All contest submissions will be considered for regular inclusion in the *Sycamore Review*."

🐦🚻 TAKAHE

P.O. Box 13-335, Christchurch 8001 New Zealand. (03)359-8133. **E-mail:** admin@takahe.org.nz. **Website:** www.takahe.org.nz/index.php. The Takahē Collective Trust is a nonprofit organization that aims to support emerging and published writers, poets, artists, and cultural commentators. The *Takahē* magazine appears 3 times/year and publishes short stories, poetry, and art by established and emerging writers and artists as well as essays and interviews (by invitation) and book reviews in these related areas.

NEEDS "We look for stories that have something special about them: an original idea, a new perspective, an interesting narrative style or use of language, an ability to evoke character and/or atmosphere. Above all, we like some depth, an extra layer of meaning, an insight—something more than just an anecdote or a straightforward narration of events. Humor of the understated, unforced variety is welcome." Length: 1,500-3,000 words, "although we do occasionally accept shorter work."

HOW TO CONTACT E-mail submissions are preferred (fiction@takahe.org.nz). Include cover letter with contact information and 40-word biography. "**Please note:** U.S. stamps should not be used on SAEs. They do not work in New Zealand. Please enclose IRCs and supply e-mail address."

PAYMENT/TERMS Pays 1 contributor's copy and free one-year subscription.

TIPS "We pay a flat rate to each writer/poet appearing in a particular issue regardless of the number/length of items. Editorials and literary commentaries are by invitation only."

🅾 TALKING RIVER

Division of Literature and Languages, 500 8th Ave., Lewiston ID 83501. (208)792-2189. **Fax:** (208)792-2324. **E-mail:** talkingriver@lcmail.lcsc.edu. **Website:** www.lcsc.edu/talking-river. **Contact:** Kevin Goodan, editorial advisor. Estab. 1994. "We look for new voices with something to say to a discerning general audience." Wants more well-written, character-driven stories that surprise and delight the reader with fresh, arresting yet unselfconscious language, imagery, metaphor, revelation. Reads mss September 1-May 1 only. Recently published work by Chris Dombrowski, Sherwin Bitsui, and Lia Purpura.

🎧   Submission period runs August 1-April 1.

NEEDS No stories that are sexist, racist, homophobic, erotic for shock value; no genre fiction. Length: 4,000 words; average length: 3,000 words.

HOW TO CONTACT Send complete ms with cover letter by postal mail. Include estimated word count, two-sentence bio, and list of publications. Send SASE for reply and return of ms, or send disposable copy of ms.

PAYMENT/TERMS Pays contributor's copies; additional copies $4.

TIPS "We look for the strong, the unique; we reject clichéd images and predictable climaxes."

TAMPA REVIEW

University of Tampa Press, 401 W. Kennedy Blvd., Tampa FL 33606. (813)253-6266. **Fax:** (813)258-7593. **E-mail:** utpress@ut.edu. **Website:** www.ut.edu/tampareview. **Contact:** Richard Mathews, editor; Elizabeth Winston, nonfiction editor; Yuly Restrepo and Andrew Plattner, fiction editors; Erica Dawson, poetry editor. Estab. 1988. An international literary journal publishing art and literature from Florida and Tampa Bay as well as new work and translations from throughout the world.

NEEDS "We are far more interested in quality than in genre. Nothing sentimental as opposed to genuinely moving, nor self-conscious style at the expense of human truth." Length: 200-5,000 words.

HOW TO CONTACT Send complete ms. Include brief bio.

PAYMENT/TERMS Pays $10/printed page.

TIPS "Send a clear cover letter stating previous experience or background. Our editorial staff considers submissions between September and December for publication in the following year."

🅾 TEKKA

134 Main St., Watertown MA 02472. (617)924-9044. **E-mail:** editor@tekka.net; bernstein@eastgate.com. **Website:** www.tekka.net. **Contact:** Mark Bernstein, publisher. Estab. 2003. "*Tekka* takes a close look at serious ideas that intertwingle computing and expression: hypertext, new media, software aesthetics, and the changing world that lies beyond the new economy. *Tekka* is always seeking new writers who can enhance our understanding, tempt our palate, and help explore new worlds and advance the state of the art. We welcome proposals for incisive, original features, reviews, and profiles from freelance writers. Our rates vary by length, department, and editorial requirements

but are generally in line with the best Web magazines. We welcome proposals from scholars as well. We also publish short hypertext fiction, as well as fiction that explores the future of reading, writing, media, and computing. We are probably the best market for Web fiction, but we are extremely selective."

HOW TO CONTACT Query.

PAYMENT/TERMS Pay rates vary.

TELLURIDE MAGAZINE

Big Earth Publishing, Inc., P.O. Box 3488, Telluride CO 81435. (970)728-4245. **Fax:** (866)936-8406. **E-mail:** deb@telluridemagazine.com. **Website:** www.telluridemagazine.com. **Contact:** Deb Dion Kees, editor in chief. Estab. 1982. "*Telluride Magazine* speaks specifically to Telluride and the surrounding mountain environment. Telluride is a resort town supported by the ski industry in winter, festivals in summer, outdoor recreation year round, and the unique lifestyle all of that affords. As a National Historic Landmark District with a colorful mining history, it weaves a tale that readers seek out. The local/visitor interaction is key to Telluride's success in making profiles an important part of the content. Telluriders are an environmentally minded and progressive bunch who appreciate efforts toward sustainability and protecting the natural landscape and wilderness that are the region's number one draw."

NEEDS "Please contact us; we are very specific about what we will accept." Length: 800-1,200 words.

HOW TO CONTACT Query with published clips.

TERRAIN.ORG: A JOURNAL OF THE BUILT + NATURAL ENVIROMENTS

Terrain.org, P.O. Box 19161, Tucson AZ 85731-9161. **E-mail:** contact2@terrain.org. **Website:** www.terrain.org. **Contact:** Simmons B. Buntin, editor in chief. Receives 25 mss/month. Accepts 12-15 mss/year. Agented fiction 5%. **Publishes 1-3 new writers/year.** Published Al Sim, Jacob MacAurthur Mooney, T.R. Healy, Deborah Fries, Andrew Wingfield, Braden Hepner, Chavawn Kelly, Tamara Kaye Sellman. *Terrain.org* is based on, and thus welcomes quality submissions from, new and experienced authors and artists alike. Our online journal accepts only the finest poetry, essays, fiction, articles, artwork, and other contributions' material that reaches deep into the earth's fiery core, or humanity's incalculable core, and brings forth new insights and wisdom. *Terrain.org* is searching for that interface—the integration among the built and natural environments, that might be called the soul of place. The works contained within *Terrain.org* ultimately examine the physical realm around us and how those environments influence us and each other physically, mentally, emotionally, and spiritually."

Beginning March 2014, publication schedule is rolling; we will no longer be issue-based. Sends galleys to author. Publication is copyrighted. Sponsors *Terrain.org* Annual Contest in Poetry, Fiction, and Nonfiction. **Deadline:** August 1. Submit via online submissions manager.

NEEDS Does not want erotica. Length: up to 6,000 words. Average length: 5,000 words. Publishes short shorts. Average length of short shorts: 750 words.

HOW TO CONTACT Accepts submissions online at sub.terrain.org. Include brief bio. Send complete ms with cover letter. Reads September 1-May 30 for regular submissions; contest submissions open year round.

TIPS "We have 3 primary criteria in reviewing fiction: (1) The story is compelling and well crafted. (2) The story provides some element of surprise; whether in content, form, or delivery we are unexpectedly delighted in what we've read. (3) The story meets an upcoming theme, even if only peripherally. Read fiction in the current issue and perhaps some archived work, and if you like what you read—and our overall enviromental slant—then send us your best work. Make sure you follow our submission guidelines (including cover note with bio), and that your mss is as error-free as possible."

TEXAS REVIEW

Texas Review Press, Department of English, Sam Houston State University, Box 2146, Huntsville TX 77341-2146. (936)294-1992. **Fax:** (936)294-3070. **E-mail:** eng_pdr@shsu.edu; cww006@shsu.edu. **Website:** www.shsu.edu/~www_trp. **Contact:** Dr. Paul Ruffin, editor/director; Greg Bottoms, essay editor; Eric Miles Williamson, fiction editor; Nick Lantz, poetry editor. Estab. 1976. "We publish top-quality poetry, fiction, articles, interviews, and reviews for a general audience." Semiannual.

Texas Review is 6×9; 148-190 pages; best quality paper; 70 lb. cover stock; illustrations; photos. Receives 40-60 unsolicited mss/month. Accepts 4 mss/issue; 6 mss/year. Does not read mss May-September. A member of the Texas A&M University Press consortium.

NEEDS "We are eager enough to consider fiction of quality, no matter what its theme or subject matter. No juvenile fiction."

HOW TO CONTACT Send complete ms. No mss accepted via fax. Send disposable copy of ms and #10 SASE for reply only. Accepts multiple submissions.
PAYMENT/TERMS Pays contributor's copies and one-year subscription.

⦾ⓢ THEMA

Thema Literary Society, P.O. Box 8747, Metairie LA 70011-8747. **E-mail:** thema@cox.net. **Website:** themaliterarysociety.com. **Contact:** Gail Howard, poetry editor. Estab. 1988. *"THEMA* is designed to stimulate creative thinking by challenging writers with unusual themes, such as 'The Box Under the Bed' and 'Put It In Your Pocket, Lillian.' Appeals to writers, teachers of creative writing, and general reading audience."

○   *THEMA* is 100 pages, digest-sized professionally printed, with glossy card cover. Receives about 400 poems/year, accepts about 8%. Press run is 400 (230 subscribers, 30 libraries). Subscription: $20 U.S./$30 foreign. Has published poetry by Beverly Boyd, Elizabeth Creith, James Penha and Matthew J. Spireng.

NEEDS No erotica.

HOW TO CONTACT Send complete ms with SASE, cover letter; include "name and address, brief introduction, specifying the intended target issue for the mss." SASE. Accepts simultaneous, multiple submissions, and reprints. Does not accept e-mailed submissions.
PAYMENT/TERMS Pays $10-25.

THIRD COAST

Western Michigan University, English Dept., 1903 W. Michigan Ave., Kalamazoo MI 49008-5331. **Website:** www.thirdcoastmagazine.com. **Contact:** Laurie Ann Cedilnik, editor in chief. Estab. 1995. Sponsors an annual fiction contest. 1st Prize: $1,000 and publication. Guidelines available on website. **Entry fee:** $16, includes one-year subscription to *Third Coast.* "*Third Coast* publishes poetry, fiction (including traditional and experimental fiction, shorts, and novel excerpts, but not genre fiction), creative nonfiction (including reportage, essay, memoir, and fragments), drama, and translations."

○   *Third Coast* is 176 pages, digest-sized, professionally printed, perfect-bound, with 4-color cover with art. Reads mss from September through December of each year.

NEEDS Has published work by Bonnie Jo Campbell, Peter Ho Davies, Robin Romm, Lee Martin, Caitlin Horrocks, and Peter Orner. No genre fiction. Length: up to 8,000 words or 25 pages. Query for longer works.

HOW TO CONTACT Send complete ms via online submissions manager.
PAYMENT/TERMS Pays 2 contributor's copies and one-year subscription.
TIPS "We will consider many different types of fiction and favor those exhibiting a freshness of vision and approach."

⦾ⓢ THIRD WEDNESDAY: A LITERARY ARTS MAGAZINE

174 Greenside Up, Ypsilanti MI 48197. (734) 434-2409. **E-mail:** submissions@thirdwednesday.org; LaurenceWT@aol.com. **Website:** thirdwednesday.org. **Contact:** Laurence Thomas, editor. Estab. 2007. "*Third Wednesday* publishes quality (a subjective term at best) poetry, short fiction, and artwork by experienced writers and artists. We welcome work by established writers/artists, as well as those who are not yet well known but headed for prominence."

NEEDS Receives 5-10 mss/month. Accepts 3-5 mss/issue. Does not want "purely anecdotal accounts of incidents, sentimentality, pointless conclusions, or stories without some characterization or plot development." Length: 1,500 words (maximum); average length: 1,000 words.

HOW TO CONTACT Send complete ms with cover letter. Include estimated word count and brief bio.
PAYMENT/TERMS Pays $3 and 1 contributor's copy.
TIPS "Of course, originality is important, along with skill in writing, deft handling of language, and meaning, which goes hand in hand with beauty—whatever that is. Short fiction is specialized and difficult, so the writer should read extensively in the field."

⦾⦾ 34THPARALLEL MAGAZINE

P.O. Box 4823, Irvine CA 92623. **E-mail:** 34thParallel@gmail.com. **Website:** www.34thparallel.net. **Contact:** Tracey Swan, Martin Chipperfield, editors. *34thParallel Magazine,* published quarterly in digital and print editions, seeks "to promote and publish the exceptional writing of new and emerging writers overlooked by large commercial publishing houses and mainstream presses. Wants work that experiments with and tests boundaries: anything that communicates a sense of wonder, reality, tragedy, fantasy, and brilliance. Does not want historical romance, erotica, Gothic horror, or book reviews."

○   "Milan Kundera wrote that fiction is like a parallel reality (okay, so he didn't say that exactly). But reality and fiction mix up, don't you think?

Our lives exist in words; it's how we make our reality. But maybe the fiction is truer? What if in our writing we reach out beyond the parallels of reality and fiction? Question life, challenge the boundaries, confront our perceptions and misconceptions. Welcome again to the *34thParallel*."

NEEDS Length: 1,500-3,500 words.

PAYMENT/TERMS Pays 1 contributor's copy in PDF format and offers print-edition copy at cost from print-on-demand publisher Lulu.

TIPS "We want it all, but we don't want everything. Take a look at the mag to get a feel for our style."

◐ ⑤ THREE-LOBED BURNING EYE

Portland OR **Website:** www.3lobedmag.com. Estab. 1999. *Three-Lobed Burning Eye* is a speculative fiction magazine published online twice per year (usually spring and fall) and as a print anthology every other year. Each issue features six stories.

NEEDS "We are looking for quality speculative fiction, in the vein of horror and dark fantasy, what you might call magical realism, slipstream, cross genre, or weird fiction. We will consider the occasional science fiction, suspense, or western story, though we prefer that it contain some speculative element. Sword and sorcery, hard SF, space opera, and extreme horror are hard sells. We like voices both literary and pulpy, with unique and flowing but not experimental styles. All labels aside, we want stories that expand genre, that value originality in character, narrative, and plot." Has published work by Gemma Files, DF Lewis, Laird Barron, Brenden Connell, Amy Grech, Neil Ayres, and Tim Waggoner. Does not want fan or franchise tie-in fiction (*Star Trek, Buffy, D&D*, etc.), serial stories, or novel excerpts. No erotica. Length: up to 7,000 for short stories; 500-1,000 words for flash fiction.

HOW TO CONTACT Submit via online submissions manager.

PAYMENT/TERMS Pays 3¢/word, up to $35.

TIPS "Send only your best fiction, distinct and remarkable tales that the reader cannot forget. We encourage diverse authors, characters and points of view, inclusive of all races, cultures, genders, and orientations."

THE THREEPENNY REVIEW

P.O. Box 9131, Berkeley CA 94709. (510)849-4545. **E-mail:** wlesser@threepennyreview.com. **Website:** www.threepennyreview.com. **Contact:** Wendy Lesser, editor. Estab. 1980. "We are a general-interest, na-

tional literary magazine with coverage of politics, the visual arts, and the performing arts." Reading period: January 1-June 30.

NEEDS No fragmentary, sentimental fiction. Length: 800-4,000 words.

HOW TO CONTACT Send complete ms.

PAYMENT/TERMS Pays $400.

TIPS Nonfiction (political articles, memoirs, reviews) is most open to freelancers.

TIMBER JOURNAL

E-mail: timberjournal@gmail.com. **Website:** www.timberjournal.com. *Timber* is a literary journal, run by students in the MFA program at the University of Colorado Boulder, dedicated to the promotion of innovative literature. Publishes work that explores the boundaries of poetry, fiction, creative nonfiction, and digital literatures. Produces both an online journal that explores the potentials of the digital medium and an annual print anthology.

◑ Reading period: August-March (submit just once during this time). Staff changes regularly; see website for current staff members.

NEEDS Length: up to 5,000 words.

HOW TO CONTACT Submit via online submissions manager. Include 30-50 word bio.

PAYMENT/TERMS Pays 1 contributor's copy.

TIPS "We are looking for innovative poetry, fiction, creative nonfiction, and digital lit (screenwriting, digital poetry, multimedia lit, etc.)."

TIN HOUSE

McCormack Communications, P.O. Box 10500, Portland OR 97296. (503)219-0622. **E-mail:** info@tinhouse.com. **Website:** www.tinhouse.com. **Contact:** Cheston Knapp, managing editor; Holly MacArthur, founding editor. Estab. 1999. "We are a general-interest literary quarterly. Our watchword is quality. Our audience includes people interested in literature in all its aspects, from the mundane to the exalted."

◑ Reading period: September 1-May 31.

NEEDS Length up to 10,000 words.

HOW TO CONTACT Submit via online submissions manager or postal mail. Include cover letter with word count.

PAYMENT/TERMS Pays $200-800.

TOAD SUCK REVIEW

Department of Writing, University of Central Arkansas, Conway AR 72035. **E-mail:** toadsuckreview@gmail.com. **Website:** toadsuckreview.org. **Contact:**

Mark Spitzer, editor in chief. Estab. 2011. "The innovative *Toad Suck Review* is a cutting-edge mixture of poetry, fiction, creative nonfiction, translations, reviews, and artwork with a provocative sense of humor and an interest in diverse cultures and politics. No previously published work. 'Previously published' work includes: poetry posted on a public website/blog/forum and poetry posted on a private, password-protected forum. Reads mss in the summer." Prefers submissions from skilled, experienced poets; will consider work from beginning poets.

◯ The journal received a *Library Journal* award for being one of the 10 best lit mags published in 2012. Has published work by Charles Bukowski, Lawrence Ferlinghetti, Edward Abbey, Gary Snyder, Anne Waldman, Ed Sanders, Tyrone Jaeger, Jean Genet, Louis-Ferdinand Céline, Antler, David Gessner, C.D. Wright, and Amiri Baraka.

NEEDS No religious, straight-up realism, or odes to dead dogs. Length: 200-10,000 words; average length: 5,000 words.

HOW TO CONTACT Send reviews of novels and short story collections to editor. Include cover letter with disposable copy of complete ms. Accepts 5 mss/year.

PAYMENT/TERMS Pays contributor's copy.

TIPS "Our guidelines are very open and ambiguous. Don't send us too much, and don't make it too long. If you submit in an e-mail, use Word or RTF. We're easy. If it works, we'll be in touch. It's a brutal world—wear your helmet."

◯ TOASTED CHEESE

E-mail: editors@toasted-cheese.com. **E-mail:** submit@toasted-cheese.com. **Website:** www.toasted-cheese.com. Estab. 2001. "*Toasted Cheese* accepts submissions of previously unpublished fiction, flash fiction, creative nonfiction, poetry, and book reviews. See site for book review requirements and guidelines. Our focus is on quality of work, not quantity. Some issues will therefore contain fewer or more pieces than previous issues. We don't restrict publication based on subject matter. We encourage submissions from innovative writers in all genres."

NEEDS Receives 150 unsolicited mss/month. Accepts 1-10 mss/issue; 5-30 mss/year. Publishes 15 new writers/year. Sponsors awards/contests. "No fan fiction. No chapters or excerpts unless they read as a stand-alone story. No first drafts."

HOW TO CONTACT Send complete ms in body of e-mail; no attachments. Accepts submissions by e-mail.

TIPS "We are looking for clean, professional writing from writers of any level. Accepted stories will be concise and compelling. We are looking for writers who are serious about the craft: tomorrow's literary stars before they're famous. Take your submission seriously, yet remember that levity is appreciated. You are submitting not to traditional 'editors' but to fellow writers who appreciate the efforts of those in the trenches. Follow online submission guidelines."

◯ TRAIL OF INDISCRETION

Fortress Publishing, Inc., Lemoyne PA 17011. **E-mail:** realm.beyond@yahoo.com. **Website:** www.fortress-publishinginc.com. **Contact:** Brian Koscienski, editor. *Trail of Indiscretion* publishes fantasy, science fiction, and horror short stories.

NEEDS No profanity or graphic scenes. Length: up to 5,000 words.

HOW TO CONTACT E-mail Word document.

PAYMENT/TERMS Pays contributor's copies.

TIPS "If it's a story about a 13-year-old girl named Mary coping with the change to womanhood while poignantly reflecting the recent passing of her favorite aunt, Gertrude, we DON'T want it! Now, if Mary is the 13-year-old daughter of a vampire cowboy who stumbles upon a government conspiracy involving aliens and unicorns while investigating, hard-boiled style, the grisly murder of her favorite aunt, Gertrude, then we'll take a look at it."

◐◑ TRANSITION: AN INTERNATIONAL REVIEW

104 Mount Auburn St., 3R, Cambridge MA 02138. (617)496-2845. **Fax:** (617)496-2877. **E-mail:** transition@fas.harvard.edu. **Website:** hutchinscenter.fas.harvard.edu/transition. **Contact:** Sara Bruya, managing editor. Estab. 1961. *Transition Magazine* is a trimestrial international review known for compelling and controversial writing from and about Africa and the Diaspora. This prestigious magazine is edited at the Hutchins Center for African American Research at Harvard University.

◯ Essays first published in a recent issue of *Transition* were selected for inclusion in *Best American Essays 2008*, *Best American Nonrequired Reading 2008*, and *Best African American Writing 2009*. Four-time winner of the Alternative Press Award for international reporting

(2001, 2000, 1999, 1995); finalist in the 2001 National Magazine Award in General Excellence category. Author Tope Folarin, winner of the 2013 Caine Prize for African Writing for story "Miracle," published in *Transition*.

HOW TO CONTACT "For all submissions, please include the following information in your e-mail or cover letter and in the top left corner of the first page of all documents: name, address, e-mail address, word count, date of submission. Please also include a title with each work."

PAYMENT/TERMS Pays 1 contributor's copy.

TIPS "We look for a nonwhite, alternative perspective dealing with issues of race, ethnicity, and identity in an unpredictable, provocative way."

TRIQUARTERLY

School of Continuing Studies, Northwestern University, 339 E. Chicago Ave., Chicago IL 60611. **E-mail:** triquarterly@northwestern.edu. **Website:** www.triquarterly.org. **Contact:** Adrienne Gunn, managing editor. Estab. 1964. *TriQuarterly*, the literary magazine of Northwestern University, welcomes submissions of fiction, creative nonfiction, poetry, short drama, and hybrid work. "We also welcome short-short prose pieces." Reading period: February 16-July 15.

NEEDS Length: up to 3,500 words.

HOW TO CONTACT Submit complete ms via online submissions manager.

PAYMENT/TERMS Pays honoraria.

TIPS "We are especially interested in work that embraces the world and continues, however subtly, the ongoing global conversation about culture and society that *TriQuarterly* pursued from its beginning in 1964."

◑ TRUE CONFESSIONS

105 E. 34th St., Box 141, New York NY 10016. **E-mail:** shazell@truerenditionsllc.com. **Contact:** Samantha Hazell, editor. "*True Confessions* is a women's magazine featuring true-to-life stories about working-class women and their families. The stories must be in first-person and generally deal with family problems, relationship issues, romances, single moms, abuse, and any other realistic issue women face in our society. The stories we look for are true or at least believable. We look for stories that evoke some sort of emotion, be it happiness or sadness, but in the end there needs to be some sort of moral or lesson learned."

NEEDS "Stories should be written in first person and past tense. We generally look for more serious stories.

The underlying theme is overcoming adversities in life. These are supposed to be 'true' stories—or at least stories that could be true!" Length: 3,000-7,000 words.

HOW TO CONTACT E-mail submissions preferred (trueswriters@yahoo.com). Include contact information and brief synopsis of story. To submit by postal mail, include disk saved in Word, a hard copy, and SASE for return of materials.

PAYMENT/TERMS Pays 3¢/word.

◑ TULANE REVIEW

Tulane University, 122 Norman Mayer, New Orleans LA 70118. **E-mail:** tulane.review@gmail.com; litsoc@tulane.edu. **Website:** www.tulane.edu/~litsoc/index.html. Estab. 1988. *Tulane Review*, published biannually, is a national literary journal seeking quality submissions of prose, poetry, and art.

◑ *Tulane Review* is the recipient of an AWP Literary Magazine Design Award. *Tulane Review* is 70 pages, 7x9, perfect-bound, with 100# cover with full-color artwork.

NEEDS Length: up to 4,000 words.

HOW TO CONTACT Submit via online submissions manager. No longer accepts paper and e-mail submissions.

PAYMENT/TERMS Pays 2 contributor's copies.

◉ U.S. CATHOLIC

Claretian Publications, 205 W. Monroe St., Chicago IL 60606. (312)236-7782. **Fax:** (312)236-8207. **E-mail:** editors@uscatholic.org. **E-mail:** submissions@uscatholic.org. **Website:** www.uscatholic.org. Estab. 1935. "*U.S. Catholic* puts faith in the context of everyday life. With a strong focus on social justice, we offer a fresh and balanced take on the issues that matter most in our world, adding a faith perspective to such challenges as poverty, education, family life, the environment, and even pop culture."

◑ Please include SASE with written ms.

NEEDS Accepts short stories. "Topics vary, but unpublished fiction should be no longer than 1,500 words and should include strong characters and cause readers to stop for a moment and consider their relationships with others, the world, and/or God. Specifically religious themes are not required; subject matter is not restricted. E-mail submissions@uscatholic.org." Length: 700-1,500 words.

HOW TO CONTACT Send complete ms.

PAYMENT/TERMS Pays minimum $200.

VAMPIRES 2 MAGAZINE

Man's Story 2 Publishing Co., 1321 Snapfinger Rd., Decatur GA 30032. **E-mail:** vampires2com2@aol.com. **Website:** www.vampires2.us. **Contact:** Carlos Dunn, founder and editor. Estab. 1999. "Online e-zine that strives to re-create vampire romance in the pulp fiction style of the 1920s through the 1970s with strong emphasis on 3D graphic art." Also features illustrated stories, online magazine, online photo galleries, and more.

○ "We publish books, publish online, and operate websites. In 2000 we became one of *Writer's Digest*'s top 100 markets for fiction writers and have since become listed with 20 other outstanding writers organizations."

NEEDS Length: up to 3,500 words or up to 10,000 words (two options offered; see website for details).

HOW TO CONTACT Send complete ms via e-mail as a .doc attachment. Include short summary of story.

TIPS "Your story must come to us edited, error free, and ready to publish. We prefer stories that have a strong romantic angle and a tastefully written lovemaking scene. Your story must have a compelling plot, nonstop action, and a satisfying ending, and you must tell a story well."

●○ VAN GOGH'S EAR: BEST WORLD POETRY & PROSE

French Connection Press, 12 Rue Lamartine, Paris 75009 France. (33)(1)4016-1147. **E-mail:** tinafayeayres@gmail.com. **Website:** www.frenchcx.com; theoriginalvangoghsearanthology.com. Estab. 2002. *Van Gogh's Ear*, published annually in April, is an anthology series "devoted to publishing powerful poetry and prose in English and English translations by major voices and innovative new talents from around the globe."

○ *Van Gogh's Ear* is 280 pages, digest-sized, off-set-printed, perfect-bound, with 4-color matte cover with commissioned artwork. Poetry published in *Van Gogh's Ear* has appeared in *The Best American Poetry.*

NEEDS Length: up to 1,500 words.

HOW TO CONTACT Submit up to 2 prose pieces by e-mail. Cover letter is preferred, along with a brief bio of up to 120 words.

PAYMENT/TERMS Pays 1 contributor's copy.

TIPS "As a 501(c)(3) nonprofit enterprise, *Van Gogh's Ear* needs the support of individual poets, writers, and readers to survive. Any donation, large or small, will help *Van Gogh's Ear* continue to publish the best cross-section of contemporary poetry and prose. Because of being an anglophone publication based in France, *Van Gogh's Ear* is unable to get any grants or funding. Your contribution will be tax-deductible. Make donation checks payable to Committee on Poetry-*VGE*, and mail them (donations **only**) to the Allen Ginsberg Trust, P.O. Box 582, Stuyvesant Station, New York NY 10009."

●❸ VANILLEROTICA LITERARY EZINE

Cleveland OH 44102. (216)799-9775. **E-mail:** talentdripseroticpublishing@yahoo.com. **Website:** eroticatalentdrips.wordpress.com. **Contact:** Kimberly Steele, founder. Estab. 2007. *Vanillerotica*, published monthly online, focuses solely on showcasing new erotic fiction.

NEEDS Length: 5,000-10,000 words.

HOW TO CONTACT Submit short stories by e-mail to talentdripseroticpublishing@yahoo.com. Stories should be pasted into body of message. Reads submissions during publication months only.

PAYMENT/TERMS Pays $15 for each accepted short story.

TIPS "Please read our take on the difference between *erotica* and *pornography*; it's on the website. *Vanillerotica* does not accept pornography. And please keep poetry 30 lines or less."

●○ VERANDAH LITERARY & ART JOURNAL

Faculty of Arts, Deakin University, 221 Burwood Hwy., Burwood, Victoria 3125 Australia. (61)(3)9251-7134. **E-mail:** verandah@deakin.edu.au. **Website:** www.deakin.edu.au/verandah. Estab. 1985. *Verandah*, published annually in August, is a high-quality literary journal edited by professional writing students. It aims to give voice to new and innovative writers and artists.

○ Submission period: February 1-June 5. Has published work by Christos Tsiolka, Dorothy Porter, Seamus Heaney, Les Murray, Ed Burger, and John Muk Muk Burke. *Verandah* is 120 pages, professionally printed on glossy stock, flat-spined, with full-color glossy card cover.

NEEDS Length: 350-2,500 words.

HOW TO CONTACT Submit by mail or e-mail. However, electronic version of work must be available if accepted by *Verandah*. Do not submit work without the required submission form (available for download on website). Reads submissions by June 5 deadline (postmark).

PAYMENT/TERMS Pays 1 contributor's copy, "with prizes awarded accordingly."

VESTAL REVIEW

127 Kilsyth Road, Apt. 3, Brighton MA 02135. **E-mail:** submissions@vestalreview.net. **Website:** www.vestal-review.org. Semi-annual print magazine specializing in flash fiction.

○ *Vestal Review*'s stories have been reprinted in the *Mammoth Book of Miniscule Fiction, Flash Writing, E2Ink Anthologies*, and in the *WW Norton Anthology Flash Fiction Forward*. **Reading periods:** February-May and August-November.

NEEDS No porn, racial slurs, excessive gore, or obscenity. No children's or preachy stories. Length: 50-500 words.

HOW TO CONTACT Publishes flash fiction. "We accept submissions only through our submission manager."

PAYMENT/TERMS Pays 3-10¢/word and 1 contributor's copy; additional copies for $10 (plus postage).

TIPS "We like literary fiction with a plot that doesn't waste words. Don't send jokes masked as stories."

⑤ THE VIRGINIA QUARTERLY REVIEW

P.O. Box 400223, Charlottesville VA 22904. **E-mail:** vqr@vqronline.org. **Website:** www.vqronline.org. **Contact:** W. Ralph Eubanks, editor. Estab. 1925. "*VQR*'s primary mission has been to sustain and strengthen Jefferson's bulwark, long describing itself as 'A National Journal of Literature and Discussion.' And for good reason. From its inception in prohibition, through depression and war, in prosperity and peace, *The Virginia Quarterly Review* has been a haven—and home—for the best essayists, fiction writers, and poets, seeking contributors from every section of the United States and abroad. It has not limited itself to any special field. No topic has been alien: literary, public affairs, the arts, history, the economy. If it could be approached through essay or discussion, poetry or prose, *VQR* has covered it." Press run is 4,000.

NEEDS "We are generally not interested in genre fiction (such as romance, science fiction, or fantasy)." Length: 2,000-10,000 words.

HOW TO CONTACT Accepts online submissions only at virginiaquarterlyreview.submittable.com/submit.

PAYMENT/TERMS Pays $1,000-2,500 for short stories; $1,000-$4,000 for novellas and novel excerpts.

WEST BRANCH

Stadler Center for Poetry, Bucknell University, Lewisburg PA 17837-2029. (570)577-1853. **Fax:** (570)577-1885. **E-mail:** westbranch@bucknell.edu. **Website:** www.bucknell.edu/westbranch. **Contact:** G.C. Waldrep, editor. *West Branch* publishes poetry, fiction, and nonfiction in both traditional and innovative styles.

○ Reading period: August 15-April 1. No more than 3 submissions from a single contributor in a given reading period.

NEEDS No genre fiction. Length: no more than 30 pages.

HOW TO CONTACT Send complete ms.

PAYMENT/TERMS Pays 5¢/word, with a maximum of $100.

TIPS "All submissions must be sent via our online submission manager. Please see website for guidelines. We recommend that you acquaint yourself with the magazine before submitting."

●①⑤ WESTERLY

University of Wester Australia, The Westerly Centre (M202), Crawley WA 6009 Australia. (61)(8)6488-3403. **Fax:** (61)(8)6488-1030. **E-mail:** westerly@uwa.edu.au. **Website:** westerlymag.com.au. **Contact:** Delys Bird and Tony Hughes-D'Aeth, editors. Estab. 1956. *Westerly*, published in July and November, prints quality short fiction, poetry, literary criticism, socio-historical articles, and book reviews with special attention given to Australia, Asia, and the Indian Ocean region. "We assume a reasonably well-read, intelligent audience. Past issues of *Westerly* provide the best guides. Not consciously an academic magazine."

○ *Westerly* is about 200 pages, digest-sized, "electronically printed." Press run is 1,200. Subscription information available on website. Deadline for July edition: March 31; deadline for November edition: August 31.

NEEDS Length: up to 3,500 words.

HOW TO CONTACT Submit complete ms by mail, e-mail, or online submissions form.

PAYMENT/TERMS Pays $150 and contributor's copies.

WESTERN HUMANITIES REVIEW

University of Utah, English Department, 255 S. Central Campus Dr., Salt Lake City UT 84112-0494. (801)581-6070. **Fax:** (801)585-5167. **E-mail:** whr@

mail.hum.utah.edu. **Website:** ourworld.info/whrweb/. **Contact:** Barry Weller, editor; Nate Liederbach, managing editor. Estab. 1947. *Western Humanities Review* is a journal of contemporary literature and culture housed in the University of Utah English Department. Publishes poetry, fiction, nonfiction essays, artwork, and work that resists categorization.

○ Reading period: September 1-April 15. All submissions must be sent through online submissions manager.

NEEDS Does not want genre (romance, sci-fi, etc.). Length: 5,000 words.

HOW TO CONTACT Send complete ms.

PAYMENT/TERMS Pays $5/published page (when funds available).

TIPS "Because of changes in our editorial staff, we urge familiarity with recent issues of the magazine. We do not publish writer's guidelines because we think that the magazine itself conveys an accurate picture of our requirements. Please, no e-mail submissions."

WHISKEY ISLAND MAGAZINE

English Dept., Cleveland State University, Cleveland OH 44115. (216)687-3951. **E-mail:** whiskeyisland@csuohio.edu. **Website:** whiskeyislandmagazine.com. "*Whiskey Island* is a nonprofit literary magazine that has been published in one form or another by students of Cleveland State University for over 30 years."

○ Reading periods: August 15-November 15 and January 15-April 15. Paper and e-mail submissions are not accepted. No multiple submissions.

NEEDS "No translations, please." Length: 1,500-8,000 words for short stories; up to 1,500 words for flash fiction.

HOW TO CONTACT Submit via online submissions manager.

PAYMENT/TERMS Pays 2 contributor's copies.

●◐☺ WHITE FUNGUS: AN EXPERIMENTAL ARTS MAGAZINE

Room 5, Floor 9, 420 Nantun Rd., Section 2, Nantun District, Taichung City Taiwan +886 987 208 516. **E-mail:** mail@whitefungus.com. **Website:** www.whitefungus.com. Estab. 2004. "*White Fungus* is an art magazine based in Taichung City, Taiwan. Founded by brothers Ron and Mark Hanson in Wellington in 2004 as a quasi-political manifesto, copies of the first issue were produced on a photocopier, wrapped in Christmas paper, and hurled anonymously through the entrances of businesses throughout the city. Now

a magazine featuring interviews, writing on art, new music, history, and politics, *White Fungus* takes a dialogical approach to the work it covers. The name of the publication comes from a can of 'white fungus' the Hansons found in their local supermarket in the industrial zone of Taichung City."

HOW TO CONTACT Query.

◐ WICKED ALICE

Dancing Girl Press & Studio, 410 S. Michigan #921, Chicago IL 60605. **E-mail:** wickedalicepoetry@yahoo.com. **Website:** www.sundresspublications.com/wickedalice. **Contact:** Kristy Bowen, editor. Estab. 2001. "*Wicked Alice* is a women-centered poetry journal dedicated to publishing quality work by both sexes, depicting and exploring the female experience." Wants "work that has a strong sense of image and music. Work that is interesting and surprising, with innovative, sometimes unusual, use of language. We love humor when done well, strangeness, wackiness. Hybridity, collage, intertexuality."

NEEDS Length: up to 2,000 words.

HOW TO CONTACT Submit comple ms by e-mail.

◐ WILD VIOLET

P.O. Box 39706, Philadelphia PA 19106. **E-mail:** wildvioletmagazine@yahoo.com. **Website:** www.wildviolet.net. **Contact:** Alyce Wilson, editor. Estab. 2001. *Wild Violet*, published weekly online, aims "to make the arts more accessible, to make a place for the arts in modern life, and to serve as a creative forum for writers and artists. Our audience includes English-speaking readers from all over the world who are interested in both 'high art' and pop culture."

NEEDS Receives 30 unsolicited mss/month. Accepts 3-5 mss/issue; 135 mss/year. **Publishes 70 new writers/year.** Recently published work by Bill Gaythwaite, Jonathan Lowe, and Nancy Christie. Also publishes literary essays, literary criticism, poetry. Sometimes comments on rejected mss. "No stories where sexual or violent content is just used to shock the reader. No racist writings." Length: 500-6,000 words; average length: 3,000 words.

HOW TO CONTACT Send complete ms. Accepts submissions by e-mail and postal mail. Include estimated word count and brief bio. Send SASE for return of ms or send a disposable copy of ms and #10 SASE for reply only. Accepts simultaneous, multiple submissions.

PAYMENT/TERMS Writers receive bio and links on contributor's page. Sponsors awards/contests.

TIPS "We look for stories that are well-paced and show character and plot development. Even short shorts should do more than simply paint a picture. Mss stand out when the author's voice is fresh and engaging. Avoid muddying your story with too many characters, and don't attempt to shock the reader with an ending you have not earned. Experiment with styles and structures, but don't resort to experimentation for its own sake."

WILLARD & MAPLE

163 S. Willard St., Freeman 302, Box 34, Burlington VT 05401. (802)860-2700 ext.2462. **E-mail:** willardandmaple@champlain.edu. **Website:** www.champlain.edu/student-life/campus-life/activities-and-clubs/student-publications/willard-and-maple. Estab. 1994. *Willard & Maple*, published annually in spring, is a student-run literary magazine from Champlain College's Professional Writing Program that considers short fiction, essays, reviews, fine art, and poetry by adults, children, and teens. Wants creative work of the highest quality.

Willard & Maple is 200 pages, digest-sized, digitally printed, perfect-bound. Receives about 500 poems/year, accepts about 20%. Press run is 600 (80 subscribers, 4 libraries); 200 are distributed free to the Champlain College writing community.

HOW TO CONTACT Send complete ms via e-mail or postal mail. Send SASE for return of ms or send disposable copy of mss and #10 SASE for reply only.

PAYMENT/TERMS Pays 2 contributor's copies.

TIPS "The power of imagination makes us infinite."

WILLOW REVIEW

College of Lake County Publications, College of Lake County, 19351 W. Washington St., Grayslake IL 60030-1198. (847)543-2956. **E-mail:** com426@clcillinois.edu. **Website:** www.clcillinois.edu/community/willowreview.asp. **Contact:** Michael Latza, editor. Estab. 1969. Prizes totaling $400 are awarded to the best poetry and short fiction/creative nonfiction in each issue. *Willow Review*, published annually, is interested in poetry, creative nonfiction, and fiction of high quality. "We have no preferences as to form, style, or subject, as long as each piece stands on its own as art and communicates ideas."

The editors award prizes for best poetry and prose in the issue. Prize awards vary contingent on the current year's budget but normally range from $100-400. There is no reading fee or separate application for these prizes. All accepted mss are eligible. "*Willow Review* can be found on EBSCOhost databases, assuring a broader targeted audience for our authors' work. *Willow Review* is a nonprofit journal partially supported by a grant from the Illinois Arts Council (a state agency), College of Lake County Publications, private contributions, and sales."

NEEDS Accepts short fiction. Considers simultaneous submissions "if indicated in the cover letter" and multiple submissions.

HOW TO CONTACT Send complete ms with cover letter. Include estimated word count, brief bio, list of publications. Send either SASE (or IRC) for return of ms or disposable copy of ms and #10 SASE for reply only.

PAYMENT/TERMS Pays 2 contributor's copies.

WILLOW SPRINGS

668 N. Riverpoint Blvd. 2 RPT - #259, Spokane WA 99202. (509)359-7435. **E-mail:** willowspringsewu@gmail.com. **Website:** willowsprings.ewu.edu. **Contact:** Samuel Ligon, editor. Estab. 1977. *Willow Springs* is a semiannual magazine covering poetry, fiction, literary nonfiction and interviews of notable writers. Published twice a year, in spring and fall.

Reading period: September 1-May 31. Reading fee: $3/submission.

NEEDS "We accept any good piece of literary fiction. Buy a sample copy." Does not want to see genre fiction that does not transcend its subject matter. Length: open for short stories; up to 750 words for short shorts.

HOW TO CONTACT Submit via online submissions manager.

PAYMENT/TERMS Pays $100 and 2 contributor's copies for short stories; $40 and 2 contributor's copies for short shorts.

TIPS "While we have no specific length restrictions, we generally publish fiction and nonfiction no longer than 10,000 words and poetry no longer than 120 lines, though those are not strict rules. *Willow Springs* values poems and essays that transcend the merely autobiographical and fiction that conveys a concern for language as well as story."

WINDHOVER

A Journal of Christian Literature, P.O. Box 8008, 900 College St., Belton TX 76513. (254)295-4561. **E-mail:** windhover@umhb.edu. **Website:** undergrad.umhb.edu/english/windhover-journal. **Contact:** Dr. Nathaniel Hansen, editor. Estab. 1997. "*Windhover* is devoted to promoting writers and literature with

Christian perspectives and with a broad definition of those perspectives. We accept poetry, short fiction, nonfiction, and creative nonfiction."

Reading period is February 1-August 1.

NEEDS Receives 30 unsolicited mss/month. Recently published work by Walt McDonald, Cleatus Rattan, Greg Garrett, and Barbara Crooker. No erotica. Length: 1,500-4,000 words. Average length: 3,000 words.

PAYMENT/TERMS Pays 1 contributor's copy.

TIPS "We are looking for writing that avoids the didactic, the melodramatic, the trite, the obvious. Eschew tricks and gimmicks. We want writing that invites rereading."

WISCONSIN REVIEW

University of Wisconsin Oshkosh, 800 Algoma Blvd., Oshkosh WI 54901. (920)424-2267. **E-mail:** wisconsinreview@uwosh.edu. **Website:** www.uwosh.edu/wisconsinreview. Estab. 1966. *Wisconsin Review*, published semiannually, is a "contemporary poetry, prose, and art magazine run by students at the University of Wisconsin Oshkosh."

Wisconsin Review is around 100 pages, digest-sized, perfect-bound, with 4-color glossy coverstock. Receives about 400 poetry submissions/year, accepts about 50; Press run is 1,000. Reading period: May through October for Spring issue; November through April for Fall issue.

NEEDS "Standard or experimental styles will be considered, although we look for outstanding characterization and unique themes." Submit via postal mail (include SASE) or online submission manager. Length: up to 15 pages, double-spaced with 12-point font.

PAYMENT/TERMS Pays with 2 contributor copies.

TIPS "We are open to any poetic form and style, and look for outstanding imagery, new themes, and fresh voices—poetry that induces emotions."

WITCHES AND PAGANS

BBI Media, Inc., P.O. Box 687, Forest Grove OR 97116. (888)724-3966. **E-mail:** editor2@bbimedia.com. **Website:** www.witchesandpagans.com. Estab. 2002. "*Witches and Pagans* is dedicated to witches, wiccans, neo-pagans, and various other earth-based, pre-Christian, shamanic, and magical practitioners. We hope to reach not only those already involved in what we cover but the curious and completely new as well."

"Devoted exclusively to promoting and covering contemporary Pagan culture, *W&P* features exclusive interviews with the teachers, writers, and activists who create and lead our traditions, visits to the sacred places and people who inspire us, and in-depth discussions of our ever-evolving practices. You'll also find practical daily magic, ideas for solitary ritual and devotion, God/dess-friendly craft-projects, Pagan poetry and short fiction, reviews, and much more in every 88-page issue. *W&P* is available in either traditional paper copy sent by postal mail or as a digital PDF e-zine download that is compatible with most computers and readers."

NEEDS Does not want faction (fictionalized retellings of real events). Avoid gratuitous sex, violence, sentimentality, and pagan moralizing. Don't beat our readers with the Rede or the Threefold Law. Length: 1,000-5,000 words.

HOW TO CONTACT Send complete ms.

TIPS "Read the magazine, do your research, write the piece, send it in. That's really the only way to get started as a writer; everything else is window dressing."

THE WORCESTER REVIEW

1 Ekman St., Worcester MA 01607. (508)797-4770. **E-mail:** twr.diane@gmail.com. **Website:** www.theworcesterreview.org. **Contact:** Diane Mulligan, managing editor. Estab. 1972. *The Worcester Review*, published annually by the Worcester County Poetry Association, encourages "critical work with a New England connection; no geographic limitation on poetry and fiction." Wants "work that is crafted, intuitively honest and empathetic. We like high-quality, creative poetry, artwork, and fiction. Critical articles should be connected to New England."

 The Worcester Review is 160 pages, digest-sized, professionally printed in dark type on quality stock, perfect-bound, with matte card cover. Press run is 600.

NEEDS Accepts about 10% unsolicited mss. Agented fiction less than 10%. Recently published work by Robert Pinsky, Marge Piercy, Wes McNair, and Ed Hirsch. Length: 1,000-4,000 words. Average length: 2,000 words.

HOW TO CONTACT Send complete ms. "Send only 1 short story—reading editors do not like to read 2 by the same author at the same time. We will use only 1."

PAYMENT/TERMS Pays 2 contributor's copies and honorarium if possible.

TIPS "We generally look for creative work with a blend of craftsmanship, insight, and empathy. This does not exclude humor. We won't print work that is shoddy in any of these areas."

◐ WORD RIOT

P.O. Box 414, Middletown NJ 07748-3143. (732)706-1272. **Fax:** (732)706-5856. **E-mail:** wr.submissions@gmail.com. **Website:** www.wordriot.org. **Contact:** Jackie Corley, publisher; Kevin O'Cuinn, fiction editor; Doug Paul Case, poetry editor. Estab. 2002. "*Word Riot* publishes the forceful voices of up-and-coming writers and poets. We like edgy. We like challenging. We like unique voices. Each month we provide readers with book reviews, author interviews, and, most importantly, writing from some of the best and brightest making waves on the literary scene."

◖ Online magazine. Member CLMP.

NEEDS Accepts 20-25 mss/issue; 240-300 mss/year. Agented fiction 5%. Publishes 8-10 new writers/year. "No fantasy, science fiction, romance." Length: 1,000-6,500 words.

HOW TO CONTACT Submit via online submissions manager at wordriot.submittable.com/submit. Do not send submissions by mail.

TIPS "We're always looking for something edgy or quirky. We like writers who take risks."

◉ WORKERS WRITE!

Blue Cubicle Press, LLC, P.O. Box 250382, Plano TX 75025. **E-mail:** info@workerswritejournal.com. **Website:** www.workerswritejournal.com. **Contact:** David LaBounty, managing editor. Estab. 2005. "*Workers Write!* is an annual print journal published by Blue Cubicle Press, an independent publisher dedicated to giving voice to writers trapped in the daily grind. Each issue focuses on a particular workplace; check website for details. Submit your stories via e-mail or send a hard copy."

NEEDS "We need your stories about the workplace from our Overtime series. Every 3 months, we'll release a chapbook containing 1 story that centers on work." Length: 500-5,000 words.

HOW TO CONTACT Send complete ms.

PAYMENT/TERMS Payment: $5-$50 (depending on length and rights requested).

THE WRITE PLACE AT THE WRITE TIME

E-mail: submissions@thewriteplaceatthewritetime.org. **Website:** www.thewriteplaceatthewritetime.org. **Contact:** Nicole M. Bouchard, editor in chief. Estab. 2008. Online literary magazine, published 3 times/year. Publishes fiction, personal nonfiction, craft essays by professionals, and poetry that "speaks to the heart and mind."

◖ "Our writers range from previously unpublished to having written for *The New York Times*, *Time* magazine, *The New Yorker*, *The Wall Street Journal*, *Glimmer Train*, *Newsweek*, and *Business Week*, and they come from all over the world. Interview subjects include *NYT* best-selling authors such as Dennis Lehane, Janet Fitch, Alice Hoffman, Joanne Harris, Arthur Golden, Jodi Picoult, and Frances Mayes."

NEEDS Considers literary and most genre fiction if thought-provoking and emotionally evocative. No erotica, explicit horror/gore/violence, political. Length: 3,500 words max. Average length of stories: 3,000 words. Average length of short-shorts: 1,000 words. "If we feel the strength of the submission merits added length, we are happy to consider exceptions."

HOW TO CONTACT Send complete ms with cover letter by e-mail—no attachments. Include estimated word count and brief bio. Accepts multiple submissions, up to 3 stories at a time. Accepts simultaneous submissions if indicated; other publications must be notified immediately upon acceptance. "If accepted elsewhere, we must be notified." Accepts 90-100 mss/year; receives 500-700 mss/year.

TIPS "Through our highly personalized approach to content, feedback, and community, we aim to give a very human visage to the publishing process. We wish to speak deeply of the human condition through pieces that validate the entire spectrum of emotions and the real circumstances of life. Every piece has a unique power and presence that stands on its own; we've had writers write about surviving an illness, losing a child, embracing a foreign land, learning of their parent's suicide, discovering love, finding humor in dark hours, and healing from abuse. Our collective voice, from our aesthetic to our artwork to the words, looks at and highlights aspects of life through a storytelling lens that allows for or promotes a universal understanding."

◐ WRITER'S BLOC

MSC 162, Fore Hall Rm. 110, 700 University Blvd., Texas A&M University-Kingsville, Kingsville TX 78363. (361)593-2514. **E-mail:** octavio.quintanilla@tamuk.edu. **Website:** www.tamuk.edu/artsci/langlit/index4.html. **Contact:** Dr. Octavio Quintanilla. *Writer's Bloc*, published annually, prints poetry, short fiction, flash fiction, one-act plays, interviews, and essays. "About half of our pages are devoted to the works of Texas A&M University-Kingsville students and half to the works of writers and artists from all over the world." Wants quality poetry; no restrictions on content or form.

○ *Writer's Bloc* is 96 pages, digest-sized. Press run is 300. Reading period: February-May.

NEEDS Submit via postal mail. Include cover letter with contact info, short bio. Accepts about 6 mss/year. Publishes short shorts. Also publishes literary essays, poetry. No pornography, genre fiction, or work by children. Length: up to 3,500 words. Average length is 2,500 words.

PAYMENT/TERMS Pays 1 contributor's copy.

THE WRITER'S MONTHLY REVIEW MAGAZINE

Rivercity Today / X-Press, 2413 Bethel Rd., Logansport LA 71049. (318)697-5649. **E-mail:** writersmonthlyreviewmag@gmail.com. **Website:** https://writersmonthlyreview.com. **Contact:** Marcella Simmons, managing editor. Estab. 2015.

○ All mss should be submitted with a cover letter, brief bio, and name and address.

○○ THE WRITING DISORDER

P.O. Box 93613, Los Angeles CA 90093. (323)336-5822. **E-mail:** submit@thewritingdisorder.com. **Website:** www.writingdisorder.com. **Contact:** C.E. Lukather, editor; Paul Garson, managing editor; Julianna Woodhead, poetry editor; Pamela Ramos Langley, fiction editor; C.E. Lukather, nonfiction editor. Estab. 2009. *"The Writing Disorder* is an online literary magazine devoted to literature, art, and culture. The mission of the magazine is to showcase new and emerging writers—particularly those in writing programs—as well as established ones. The magazine also features original artwork, photography, and comic art. Although we strive to publish original and experimental work, *The Writing Disorder* remains rooted in the classic art of storytelling."

NEEDS Does not want to see romance, religious, or fluff. Length: 7,500 words maximum.

HOW TO CONTACT Query.

PAYMENT/TERMS Pays contributor's copies.

TIPS "We are looking for work from new writers, writers in writing programs, and students and faculty of all ages."

XAVIER REVIEW

Xavier University of Louisiana, 1 Drexel Dr., Box 89, New Orleans LA 70125-1098. **Website:** www.xula.edu/review. **Contact:** Ralph Adamo, editor. Estab. 1980. *"Xavier Review* accepts poetry, fiction, translations, creative nonfiction, and critical essays. Content

focuses on African American, Caribbean, and Southern literature, as well as works that touch on issues of religion and spirituality. We do, however, accept quality work on all themes. (Please note: This is not a religious publication.)"

NEEDS Has published work by Andrei Codrescu, Terrance Hayes, Naton Leslie, and Patricia Smith. Also publishes literary essays and literary criticism.

HOW TO CONTACT Send complete ms. Include 2-3 sentence bio and SASE. "We rarely accepts mss over 20 pages."

PAYMENT/TERMS Pays 2 contributor's copies; offers 40% discount on additional copies.

THE YALE REVIEW

Yale University, P.O. Box 208243, New Haven CT 06520-8243. (203)432-0499. **Fax:** (203)432-0510. **Website:** www.yale.edu/yalereview. **Contact:** J.D. McClatchy, editor. Estab. 1911. "Like Yale's schools of music, drama, and architecture, like its libraries and art galleries, *The Yale Review* has helped give the University its leading place in American education. In a land of quick fixes and short view and in a time of increasingly commercial publishing, the journal has an authority that derives from its commitment to bold established writers and promising newcomers, to both challenging literary work and a range of essays and reviews that can explore the connections between academic disciplines and the broader movements in American society, thought, and culture. With independence and boldness, with a concern for issues and ideas, with a respect for the mind's capacity to be surprised by speculation and delighted by elegance, *The Yale Review* proudly continues into its third century."

HOW TO CONTACT Submit complete ms with SASE. All submissions should be sent to the editorial office.

PAYMENT/TERMS Pays $400-500.

THE YALOBUSHA REVIEW

University of Mississippi, P.O. Box 1848, Dept. of English, University MS 38677. (662)915-3175. **E-mail:** yreditors@gmail.com. **Website:** yr.olemiss.edu. **Contact:** Liam Baranauskas and Marty Cain, senior editors. Estab. 1995.

NEEDS Length: up to 5,000 words for short stories; up to 1,000 words for flash fiction.

HOW TO CONTACT Submit 1 short story or up to 3 pieces of flash fiction via online submissions manager.

PAYMENT/TERMS Pays honorarium when funding is available.

◐◑ YEMASSEE

University of South Carolina, Department of English, Columbia SC 29208. (803)777-2085. **Fax:** (803)777-9064. **E-mail:** editor@yemasseejournalonline.org. **Website:** yemasseejournalonline.org. **Contact:** Jennifer Blevins, Brandon Rushton, or Matthew Fogarty, co-editors. Estab. 1993. "*Yemassee* is the University of South Carolina's literary journal. Our readers are interested in high-quality fiction, poetry, drama, and creative nonfiction. We have no editorial slant; quality of work is our only concern. We publish in the fall and spring, printing 5-7 stories, 2-3 essays, and 12-15 poems per issue. We tend to solicit reviews, essays, and interviews but welcome unsolicited queries. We do not favor any particular aesthetic or school of writing."

◐ Stories from *Yemassee* have been published in *New Stories From the South*. As of 2012, only accepts submissions through online submissions manager.

NEEDS "We are open to a variety of subjects and writing styles. We publish primarily fiction and poetry, but we are also interested in one-act plays, brief excerpts of novels, and interviews with literary figures. Our essential consideration for acceptance is the quality of the work." "No romance, religious/inspirational, young adult/teen, children's/juvenile, erotica. Wants more experimental work." Length: up to 5,000 words.

HOW TO CONTACT Send complete ms. "Submissions for all genres should include a cover letter that lists the titles of the pieces included, along with your contact information (including author's name, address, e-mail address, and phone number)." William Richey Short Fiction Contest: $1,000 award. Check website for deadline.

PAYMENT/TERMS Pays 2 contributor's copies.

◐◑ ZEEK: A JEWISH JOURNAL OF THOUGHT AND CULTURE

125 Maiden Ln., 8th Floor, New York NY 10038. (212)453-9435. **E-mail:** zeek@zeek.net. **Website:** www.zeek.net. **Contact:** Erica Brody, editor in chief. Estab. 2001. *ZEEK* "relaunched in late February 2013 as a hub for the domestic Jewish social justice movement, one that showcases the people, ideas, and conversations driving an inclusive and diverse progressive Jewish community. At the same time, we've reaffirmed our commitment to building on *ZEEK*'s reputation for original, ahead-of-the-curve Jewish writing and arts, culture and spirituality content, incubating emerging voices and artists, as well as established ones." *ZEEK* seeks "great writing in a variety of styles and voices, original thinking, and accessible content. That means we're interested in hearing your ideas for first-person essays, reflections and commentary, reporting, profiles, Q&As, analysis, infographics, and more. For the near future, *ZEEK* will focus on domestic issues. Our discourse will be civil."

NEEDS "Calls for fiction submissions are issued periodically. Follow *ZEEK* on Twitter @ZEEKMag for announcements and details."

⑤ ZOETROPE: ALL-STORY

Zoetrope: All-Story, The Sentinel Bldg., 916 Kearny St., San Francisco CA 94133. (415)788-7500. **Website:** www.all-story.com. **Contact:** fiction editor. Estab. 1997. *Zoetrope: All Story* presents a new generation of classic stories.

NEEDS Length: up to 7,000 words. "Excerpts from larger works, screenplays, treatments, and poetry will be returned unread."

HOW TO CONTACT "Writers should submit only 1 story at a time and no more than 2 stories a year. We do not accept artwork or design submissions. We do not accept unsolicited revisions nor respond to writers who don't include an SASE." Send complete ms by mail.

PAYMENT/TERMS Pays up to $1,000.

TIPS "Before submitting, nonsubscribers should read several issues of the magazine to determine if their works fit with *All-Story*. Electronic versions of the magazine are available to read, in part, at the website, and print versions are available for purchase by single-issue order and subscription."

⑤ ZYZZYVA

57 Post St., Suite 604, San Francisco CA 94104. (415)757-0465. **E-mail:** editor@zyzzyva.org. **Website:** www.zyzzyva.org. **Contact:** Laura Cogan, editor; Oscar Villalon, managing editor. Estab. 1985. "Every issue is a vibrant mix of established talents and new voices, providing an elegantly curated overview of contemporary arts and letters with a distinctly San Francisco perspective."

◐ Accepts submissions January 1-May 31 and August 1-November 30. Does not accept online submissions.

NEEDS Length: no limit.

HOW TO CONTACT Send complete ms by mail. Include SASE and contact information.

PAYMENT/TERMS Pays $50.

TIPS "We are not currently seeking work about any particular theme or topic; that said, reading recent issues is perhaps the best way to develop a sense for the length and quality we are looking for in submissions."

BOOK PUBLISHERS

//

In this section, you will find many of the "big name" book publishers. Many of these publishers remain tough markets for new writers or for those whose work might be considered literary or experimental. Indeed, some only accept work from established authors, and then often only through an author's agent. Although having your novel published by one of the big commercial publishers listed in this section is difficult, it is not impossible. The trade magazine *Publishers Weekly* regularly features interviews with writers whose first novels are being released by top publishers. Many editors at large publishing houses find great satisfaction in publishing a writer's first novel.

In the References section, you'll find the publishing industry's "family tree," which maps out each of the large book publishing conglomerates' divisions, subsidiaries, and imprints. Remember, most manuscripts are acquired by imprints, not their parent company, so avoid submitting to the conglomerates themselves. (For example, submit to Dutton or Berkley Books, not to their parent Penguin.)

Also listed here are "small presses," which publish four or more titles annually. Included among them are independent presses, university presses, and other nonprofit publishers. Introducing new writers to the reading public has become an increasingly important role of these smaller presses at a time when the large conglomerates are taking fewer chances on unknown writers. Many of the successful small presses listed in this section have built their reputations and their businesses in this way and have become known for publishing prize-winning fiction.

These smaller presses also tend to keep books in print longer than larger houses. And, since small presses publish a smaller number of books, each title is equally important to the publisher and each is promoted in much the same way and with the same commitment. Editors also stay at small presses longer because they have more of a stake in the business—often they own the business. Many smaller book publishers are writers themselves and know firsthand the importance of a close editor-author or publisher-author relationship.

TYPES OF BOOK PUBLISHERS

Large or small, the publishers in this section publish books "for the trade." That is, unlike textbook, technical, or scholarly publishers, trade publishers publish books to be sold to the general consumer through bookstores, chain stores, or other retail outlets. Within the trade book field, however, there are a number of different types of books.

The easiest way to categorize books is by their physical appearance and the way they are marketed. Hardcover books are the more expensive editions of a book, sold through bookstores and carrying a price tag of around $20 and up. Trade paperbacks are softbound books, also sold mostly in bookstores, but they carry a more modest price tag of usually around $10 to $20. Today a lot of fiction is published in this form because it means a lower financial risk than hardcover.

Mass-market paperbacks are another animal altogether. These are the smaller "pocket-size" books available at bookstores, grocery stores, drugstores, chain retail outlets, etc. Much genre or category fiction is published in this format. This area of the publishing industry is very open to the work of talented new writers who write in specific genres such as science fiction, romance, and mystery.

At one time, publishers could be easily identified and grouped by the type of books they produce. Today, however, the lines between hardcover and paperback books are blurred. Many publishers known for publishing hardcover books also publish trade paperbacks and have paperback imprints. This enables them to offer established authors (and a very few lucky newcomers) hard-soft deals in which their book comes out in both versions. Thanks to the mergers of the past decade, too, the same company may own several hardcover and paperback subsidiaries and imprints, even though their editorial focuses may remain separate.

CHOOSING A BOOK PUBLISHER

In addition to checking the bookstores and libraries for books by publishers that interest you, you may want to refer to the Category Index at the back of this book to find publishers divided by specific subject categories. The subjects listed in the index are general. Read individual listings to find which subcategories interest a publisher. For example, you will find several romance publishers listed, but you should read the listings to find which type of romance is considered: gothic, contemporary, regency, futuristic, and so on.

The icons appearing before the names of the publishers will also help you in selecting a publisher. These codes are especially important in this section, because many of the publishing houses listed here require writers to submit through an agent. The ⬢ symbol indicates that a publisher accepts agented submissions only. A ● icon identifies those that mostly publish established and agented authors, while a ○ points to publishers most open to new writers. See the inside back cover of this book for a complete list and explanations of symbols used in this book.

IN THE LISTINGS

We include several symbols to help you narrow your search. English-speaking foreign markets are denoted by a ☯. The maple leaf symbol ✪ identifies Canadian presses. If you are not a Canadian writer but are interested in a Canadian press, check the listing carefully. Many small presses in Canada receive grants and other funds from their provincial or national government and are, therefore, restricted to publishing Canadian authors.

We also include editorial comments set off by a bullet (○) within listings. This is where we include information about any special requirements or circumstances that will help you know even more about the publisher's needs and policies. The ○ symbol identifies publishers who have recently received honors or awards for their books. The ☺ denotes publishers who produce comics and graphic novels.

Each listing includes a summary of the houses's editorial mission, an overarching principle that ties together what they pub-

lish. Under the heading **Contact** we list one or more editors, often with their specific area of expertise.

Book editors asked us again this year to emphasize the importance of paying close attention to the **Needs** and **How to Contact** subheads of listings for book publishers. Unlike magazine editors, who want to see complete manuscripts of short stories, most of the book publishers listed here ask that writers send a query letter with an outline and/or synopsis and several chapters of their novel. "The Business of Fiction Writing," found earlier in this book, outlines how to prepare work to submit directly to a publisher.

There are no subsidy book publishers listed in *Novel & Short Story Writer's Market*. By subsidy, we mean any arrangement in which the writer is expected to pay all or part of the cost of producing, distributing, and marketing his book. We feel a writer should not be asked to share in any cost of turning his manuscript into a book. All the book publishers listed here told us that they do not charge writers for publishing their work. If any of the publishers listed here ask you to pay any part of publishing or marketing your manuscript, please let us know.

A NOTE ABOUT AGENTS

Some publishers are willing to look at unsolicited submissions, but most feel having an agent is in the writer's best interest. In this section more than any other, you'll find a number of publishers who prefer submissions from agents. That's why we've included a section of agents open to submissions from fiction writers (see the Literary Agents section of the listings). For even more agents, along with a great deal of helpful articles about approaching and working with them, refer to *Guide to Literary Agents*.

If you use the Internet or another resource to find an agent not listed in this book, be wary of any agents who charge large sums of money for reading a manuscript. Reading fees do not guarantee representation. Think of an agent as a potential business partner and feel free to ask tough questions about his or her credentials, experience, and business practices.

⊘ ABBEVILLE FAMILY

Abbeville Press, 137 Varick St., New York NY 10013. (212)366-5585. **Fax:** (212)366-6966. **E-mail:** abbeville@abbeville.com. **Website:** www.abbeville.com. Estab. 1977. "Our list is full for the next several seasons."

○ *Not accepting unsolicited book proposals at this time.*

NEEDS Picture books: animal, anthology, concept, contemporary, fantasy, folktales, health, hi-lo, history, humor, multicultural, nature/environment, poetry, science fiction, special needs, sports, suspense. Average word length 300-1,000 words.

HOW TO CONTACT Please refer to website for submission policy.

ABDO PUBLISHING CO.

8000 W. 78th St., Suite 310, Edina MN 55439. (800)800-1312. **Fax:** (952)831-1632. **E-mail:** nonfiction@abdopublishing.com. **E-mail:** fiction@abdopublishing.com; illustration@abdopublishing.com. **Website:** www.abdopub.com. **Contact:** Paul Abdo, editor in chief. Estab. 1985. ABDO publishes nonfiction children's books (pre-kindergarten to 8th grade) for school and public libraries—mainly history, sports, biography, geography, science, and social studies. "Please specify each submission as either nonfiction, fiction, or illustration." Publishes hardcover originals. Guidelines online.

ABINGDON PRESS

Imprint of The United Methodist Publishing House, 201 Eighth Ave. S., P.O. Box 801, Nashville TN 37202. (615)749-6000. **Fax:** (615)749-6512. **Website:** www.abingdonpress.com. Estab. 1789. "Abingdon Press, America's oldest theological publisher, provides an ecumenical publishing program dedicated to serving the Christian community—clergy, scholars, church leaders, musicians, and general readers—with quality resources in the areas of Bible study, the practice of ministry, theology, devotion, spirituality, inspiration, prayer, music and worship, reference, Christian education, and church supplies." Publishes hardcover and paperback originals. Book catalog available free. Guidelines online.

NEEDS Publishes stories of faith, hope, and love that encourage readers to explore life.

HOW TO CONTACT Agented submissions only for fiction.

TERMS Pays 7.5% royalty on retail price. Responds in 2 months to queries.

⊘ HARRY N. ABRAMS, INC.

115 W. 18th St., 6th Floor, New York NY 10011. (212)206-7715. **Fax:** (212)519-1210. **E-mail:** abrams@abramsbooks.com. **Website:** www.abramsbooks.com. **Contact:** Managing Editor. Estab. 1951. Publishes hardcover and a few paperback originals.

○ Does not accept unsolicited materials.

IMPRINTS Stewart, Tabori & Chang; Abrams Appleseed; Abrams Books for Young Readers; Abrams Image; STC Craft; Amulet Books.

NEEDS Publishes hardcover and "a few" paperback originals. Averages 150 total titles/year.

TIPS "We are one of the few publishers who publish almost exclusively illustrated books. We consider ourselves the leading publishers of art books and high-quality artwork in the U.S. Once the author has signed a contract to write a book for our firm the author must finish the ms to agreed-upon high standards within the schedule agreed upon in the contract."

⊘ ABRAMS BOOKS FOR YOUNG READERS

115 W. 18th St., New York NY 10011. **Website:** www.abramsyoungreaders.com.

○ Abrams no longer accepts unsolicited mss or queries.

ACADEMY CHICAGO PUBLISHERS

814 N. Franklin St., Chicago IL 60610. (312)337-0747. **Fax:** (312)337-5985. **E-mail:** frontdesk@ipgbook.com. **Website:** www.academychicago.com. **Contact:** Anita Miller and Jordan Miller, editors at large. Estab. 1975. "We publish quality fiction and nonfiction. Our audience is literate and discriminating. No novelized biography, history, or science fiction." No electronic submissions. Publishes hardcover and some paperback originals and trade paperback reprints. Book catalog online. Guidelines online.

NEEDS "We look for quality work, but we do not publish experimental, avant garde, horror, science fiction, thrillers novels."

HOW TO CONTACT Submit proposal package, synopsis, 3 sample chapters, and short bio.

TERMS Pays 7-10% royalty on wholesale price. Responds in 3 months.

TIPS "At the moment, we are looking for good nonfiction; we certainly want excellent original fiction, but we are swamped. No fax queries, no disks. No electronic submissions. We are always interested in reprinting good out-of-print books."

AO ACE SCIENCE FICTION AND FANTASY

Imprint of the Berkley Publishing Group, Penguin Group (USA), Inc., 375 Hudson St., New York NY 10014. (212)366-2000. **Website:** www.us.penguingroup. com. Estab. 1953. Ace publishes science fiction and fantasy exclusively. Publishes hardcover, paperback, and trade paperback originals and reprints.

O   As imprint of Penguin, Ace is not open to unsolicited submissions.

NEEDS No other genre accepted. No short stories.

HOW TO CONTACT Due to the high volume of mss received, most Penguin Group (USA) Inc. imprints do not normally accept unsolicited mss.

TERMS Pays royalty. Pays advance.

⊘ ALADDIN

Simon & Schuster, 1230 Avenue of the Americas, 4th Floor, New York NY 10020. (212)698-7000. **Website:** www.simonandschuster.com. **Contact:** Acquisitions Editor. Aladdin publishes picture books, beginning readers, chapter books, middle-grade and tween fiction and nonfiction, and graphic novels and nonfiction in hardcover and paperback, with an emphasis on commercial, kid-friendly titles. Publishes hardcover/paperback originals and imprints of Simon & Schuster Children's Publishing Children's Division.

HOW TO CONTACT Simon & Schuster does not review, retain or return unsolicited materials or artwork. "We suggest prospective authors and illustrators submit their mss through a professional literary agent."

ALGONQUIN BOOKS OF CHAPEL HILL

Workman Publishing, P.O. Box 2225, Chapel Hill NC 27515-2225. (919)967-0108. **Website:** www.algonquin.com. **Contact:** Editorial Department. "Algonquin Books publishes quality literary fiction and literary nonfiction." Publishes hardcover originals. Guidelines online.

IMPRINTS Algonquin Young Readers.

HOW TO CONTACT Query first.

ALONDRA PRESS, LLC

4119 Wildacres Dr., Houston TX 77072. **E-mail:** lark@alondrapress.com. **Website:** www.alondrapress.com. **Contact:** Henry Hollenbaugh, fiction editor; Solomon Tager, nonfiction editor. Estab. 2007. Publishes trade paperback originals and reprints. Guidelines online.

NEEDS "Just send us a few pages in an e-mail attachment, or the entire ms. We will look at it quickly and tell you if it interests us."

TERMS Responds in 1 month to queries/proposals; 3 months to mss.

TIPS "Be sure to read our guidelines before sending a submission. We will not respond to authors who do not observe our simple guidelines. Send your submissions in an e-mail attachment only."

AMERICAN QUILTER'S SOCIETY

5801 Kentucky Dam Rd., Paducah KY 42003. (270)898-7903. **Fax:** (270)898-1173. **E-mail:** editor@aqsquilt.com. **Website:** www.americanquilter.com. **Contact:** Elaine Brelsford, executive book editor (primarily how-to and patterns, but other quilting books sometimes published, including quilt-related fiction). Estab. 1984. "American Quilter's Society publishes how-to and pattern books for quilters (beginners through intermediate skill level). We are not the publisher for nonquilters writing about quilts. We now publish quilt-related craft cozy romance and mystery titles, series only. Humor is good. Graphic depictions and curse words are bad." Publishes trade paperbacks. Guidelines online.

O   Accepts simultaneous nonfiction submissions. Does not accept simultaneous fiction submissions.

HOW TO CONTACT Submit a synopsis and 2 sample chapters, plus an outline of the next 2 books in the series.

TERMS Pays 5% royalty on retail price for both nonfiction and fiction. Responds in 2 months to proposals.

AMG PUBLISHERS

6815 Shallowford Rd., Chattanooga TN 37421-1755. (423)894-6060. **Fax:** (423)894-9511. **E-mail:** ricks@amgpublishers.com. **Website:** www.amgpublishers.com. **Contact:** Rick Steele, product development/acquisitions. Publishes hardcover and trade paperback originals, electronic originals, and audio Bible and book originals. Book catalog and guidelines online.

IMPRINTS Living Ink Books; God and Country.

NEEDS Young Adult (teen and preteen) contemporary and fantasy; historical fiction for adults to expand God and Country imprint. "We are looking for youth/young adult (teen) fantasy that contains spiritual truths. We are also now looking for historical fiction for adults."

TERMS Pays 10-14% royalty on net sales. Responds in 1 month to queries, 4 months to proposals/mss.

TIPS "AMG is open to well-written, niche books that meet immediate needs in the lives of adults and young adults."

AMIRA PRESS

2721 N. Rosedale St., Baltimore MD 21216. (704)858-7533. **E-mail:** submissions@amirapress.com. **Website:** www.amirapress.com. **Contact:** Yvette A. Lynn, CEO (any sub genre). Estab. 2007. "We are a small press which publishes sensual and erotic romance. Our slogan is 'Erotic and Sensual Romance. Immerse Yourself.' Our authors and stories are diverse." Format publishes in paperback originals, e-books, POD printing. Guidelines online.

HOW TO CONTACT Submit complete ms with cover letter by e-mail. "No snail mail." Include estimated word count, heat level, brief bio, list of publishing credits. Accepts unsolicited mss. Sometimes critiques/comments on rejected mss.

TERMS Pays royalties, 8.5% of cover price (print)—30-40% of cover price (e-books). Responds in 3 months.

TIPS "Please read our submission guidelines thoroughly and follow them when submitting. We do not consider a work until we have all the requested information and the work is presented in the format we outline."

AMULET BOOKS

115 W. 18th St., New York NY 10001. **Website:** www.amuletbooks.com. Estab. 2004.

Does not accept unsolicited mss or queries.

NEEDS Middle readers: adventure, contemporary, fantasy, history, science fiction, sports. Young adults/teens: adventure, contemporary, fantasy, history, science fiction, sports, suspense.

ANKERWYCKE

American Bar Association, 321 N. Clark St., Chicago IL 60654. **Website:** www.ababooks.org. **Contact:** Tim Brandhorst, director of new product development. Estab. 1878. "In 1215, the Magna Carta was signed underneath the ancient Ankerwycke Yew tree, starting the process which led to rule by constitutional law—in effect, giving rights and the law to the people. And today, the ABA's Ankerwycke line of books continues to bring the law to the people. With legal fiction, true crime books, popular legal histories, public policy handbooks, and prescriptive guides to current legal and business issues, Ankerwycke is a contemporary and innovative line of books for everyone from a trusted and vested authority." Publishes hardcover and trade paperback originals. Book catalog and ms guidelines online.

NEEDS "We're actively acquiring legal fiction with extreme verisimilitude."

HOW TO CONTACT Query with cover letter; outline or TOC; and CV/bio including other credits. Include e-mail address for response.

TERMS Responds in 1 month to queries and proposals; 3 months to mss.

ANNICK PRESS, LTD.

15 Patricia Ave., Toronto ON M2M 1H9 Canada. (416)221-4802. **Fax:** (416)221-8400. **Website:** www.annickpress.com. **Contact:** The Editors. "Annick Press maintains a commitment to high-quality books that entertain and challenge. Our publications share fantasy and stimulate imagination, while encouraging children to trust their judgment and abilities." *Does not accept unsolicited mss.* Publishes picture books, juvenile and YA fiction and nonfiction; specializes in trade books. Book catalog and guidelines online.

NEEDS Publisher of children's books. Not accepting picture books at this time.

TERMS Pays authors royalty of 5-12% based on retail price. Offers advances (average amount: $3,000). Pays illustrators royalty of 5% minimum.

ANVIL PRESS

P.O. Box 3008 MPO, Vancouver BC V6B 3X5 Canada. (604)876-8710. **Fax:** (604)879-2667. **E-mail:** info@anvilpress.com. **Website:** www.anvilpress.com. Estab. 1988. "Anvil Press publishes contemporary adult fiction, poetry, and drama, giving voice to up-and-coming Canadian writers, exploring all literary genres, discovering, nurturing, and promoting new Canadian literary talent. Currently emphasizing urban/suburban themed fiction and poetry; de-emphasizing historical novels." Canadian authors only. No e-mail submissions. Publishes trade paperback originals. Book catalog for 9x12 SAE with 2 first-class stamps. Guidelines online.

NEEDS Contemporary, modern literature; no formulaic or genre.

HOW TO CONTACT Query with 20-30 pages and SASE.

TERMS Pays advance. Average advance is $500-2,000, depending on the genre. Responds in 2 months to queries; 6 months to mss.

TIPS "Audience is informed, educated, aware, with an opinion, culturally active (films, books, the performing arts). No U.S. authors. Research the appropriate publisher for your work."

ARBORDALE PUBLISHING

612 Johnnie Dodds, Suite A2, Mt. Pleasant SC 29464. (843)971-6722. **Fax:** (843)216-3804. **E-mail:** katie@arbordalepublishing.com. **E-mail:** donna@arbordalelpublishing.com. **Website:** www.arbordalepublishing.com. **Contact:** Donna German and Katie Hall, editors. Estab. 2004. "The picture books we publish are usually, but not always, fictional stories with nonfiction woven into the story that relate to science and math and retellings of traditional cultural folklore with an underlying science theme. All books should subtly convey an educational theme through a warm story that is fun to read and that will grab a child's attention. Each book has a 4-page *For Creative Minds* section to reinforce the educational component. This section will have a craft and/or game as well as 'fun facts' to be shared by the parent, teacher, or other adult. Authors do not need to supply this information. Mss should be less than 1,500 words and meet all of the following 4 criteria: Fun to read—mostly fiction with nonfiction facts woven into the story; National or regional in scope; Must tie into early elementary school curriculum; must be marketable through a niche market such as a zoo, aquarium, or museum gift shop." Publishes hardcover, trade paperback, and electronic originals. Book catalog and guidelines online.

NEEDS Picture books: animal, folktales, nature/environment, math-related. Word length—picture books: no more than 1,500.

HOW TO CONTACT Accepts electronic submissions only. Snail mail submissions are discarded without being opened.

TERMS Pays 6-8% royalty on wholesale price. Pays small advance. Acknowledges receipt of ms submission within 1 month.

TIPS "Please make sure that you have looked at our website to read our complete submission guidelines and to see if we are looking for a particular subject. Mss must meet all 4 of our stated criteria. We look for fairly realistic, bright and colorful art—no cartoons. We want the children excited about the books. We envision the books being used at home and in the classroom."

ARCADE PUBLISHING

Skyhorse Publishing, 307 W. 36th St., 11th Floor, New York NY 10018. (212)643-6816. **Fax:** (212)643-6819. **E-mail:** arcadesubmissions@skyhorsepublishing.com. **Website:** www.arcadepub.com. **Contact:** Acquisitions Editor. Estab. 1988. "Arcade prides itself on publishing top-notch literary nonfiction and fiction, with a significant proportion of foreign writers." Publishes hardcover originals, trade paperback reprints. Book catalog and ms guidelines for #10 SASE.

NEEDS No romance, historical, science fiction.

HOW TO CONTACT Submit proposal with brief query, one- to two-page synopsis, chapter outline, market analysis, sample chapter, bio.

TERMS Pays royalty on retail price and 10 author's copies. Pays advance. Responds in 2 months if interested.

⊕ ARCHAIA

Imprint of Boom! Studios, 1680 N. Vine St., Hollywood CA 90028. **Website:** www.archaia.com. **Contact:** Mark Smylie, chief creative officer. Use online submission form.

NEEDS Looking for graphic novel submissions that include finished art. "Archaia is a multi-award-winning graphic novel publisher with more than 75 renowned publishing brands, including such domestic and international hits as *Artesia, Mouse Guard*, and a line of Jim Henson graphic novels including *Fraggle Rock* and *The Dark Crystal*. Publishes creator-shared comic books and graphic novels in the adventure, fantasy, horror, pulp noir, and science fiction genres that contain idiosyncratic and atypical writing and art. *Archaia does not generally hire freelancers or arrange for freelance work, so submissions should only be for completed book and series proposals.*"

ARCH STREET PRESS

1429 S. 9th St., Philadelphia PA 19147. (877)732-ARCH. **E-mail:** contact@archstreetpress.org. **Website:** www.archstreetpress.org. **Contact:** Managing Editor. Estab. 2010. Publishes hardcover, trade paperback, mass-market paperback, and electronic originals. Book catalog and guidelines online.

HOW TO CONTACT Query with SASE. Submit proposal package, including outline and 3 sample chapters.

TERMS Pays 6-20% royalty on retail price. Responds in 1-2 months.

◑ ARROW PUBLICATIONS, LLC

20411 Sawgrass Dr., Montgomery Village MD 20886. (301)299-9422. **Fax:** (240)632-8477. **E-mail:** arrow_info@arrowpub.com. **Website:** www.arrowpub.com. **Contact:** Tom King, managing editor; Maryan Gibson, acquisition editor. Estab. 1987. Guidelines online.

◐ No graphic novels until further notice.

NEEDS "We are looking for outlines of stories heavy on romance with elements of adventure/intrigue/mystery. We will consider other romance genres such as fantasy, western, inspirational, and historical as long as the romance element is strong."

HOW TO CONTACT Query with outline first with SASE. Consult submission guidelines online before submitting.

TERMS Makes outright purchase of accepted completed scripts. Responds in 2 month to queries; 1 month to mss sent upon request.

TIPS "Our audience is primarily women 18 and older. Send query with outline only."

◯ ARSENAL PULP PRESS

#202-211 East Georgia St., Vancouver BC V6A 1Z6 Canada. (604)687-4233. **Fax:** (604)687-4283. **E-mail:** info@arsenalpulp.com. **Website:** www.arsenalpulp. com. **Contact:** Editorial Board. Estab. 1980. "We are interested in literature that traverses uncharted territories, publishing books that challenge and stimulate and ask probing questions about the world around us." Publishes trade paperback originals, and trade paperback reprints. Book catalog for 9x12 SAE with IRCs or online. Guidelines online.

NEEDS No children's books or genre fiction, i.e., westerns, romance, horror, mystery, etc.

HOW TO CONTACT Submit proposal package, outline, clips, 2-3 sample chapters.

TERMS Responds in 2-4 months.

ARTE PUBLICO PRESS

University of Houston, 4902 Gulf Fwy, Bldg 19, Rm 100, Houston TX 77204-2004. **Fax:** (713)743-2847. **E-mail:** submapp@uh.edu. **Website:** artepublicopress. com. **Contact:** Nicolas Kanellos, editor. Estab. 1979. Arte Publico Press is the oldest and largest publisher of Hispanic literature for children and adults in the United States. "We are a showcase for Hispanic literary creativity, arts and culture. Our endeavor is to provide a national forum for U.S.-Hispanic literature." Publishes hardcover originals, trade paperback originals and reprints. Book catalog available free. Guidelines online.

NEEDS "Written by U.S.-Hispanics."

HOW TO CONTACT Submissions made through online submission form.

TERMS Pays 10% royalty on wholesale price. Provides 20 author's copies; 40% discount on subsequent copies. Pays $1,000-3,000 advance. Responds in 1 month to queries and proposals; 4 months to mss.

TIPS "Include cover letter in which you 'sell' your book—why should we publish the book, who will

want to read it, why does it matter, etc. Use our ms submission online form. Format files accepted are: Word, plain/text, rich/text files. Other formats will not be accepted. Ms files cannot be larger than 5MB. Once editors review your ms, you will receive an e-mail with the decision. Revision process could take up to 4 months."

ASABI PUBLISHING

Asabi Publishing, (813)671-8827. **E-mail:** submissions@asabipublishing.com. **Website:** www.asabi-publishing.com. **Contact:** Tressa Sanders, publisher. Estab. 2004. Publishes hardcover, mass-market and trade paperback originals. Book catalog online. Guidelines online.

IMPRINTS Solomon Publishing Group-Sweden.

HOW TO CONTACT Submit professional query letter.

TERMS Pays 10% royalty on wholesale or list price. Pays up to $500 advance. Responds in 1 month to queries and proposals, 2-6 months to mss.

◯ ◯ ATHENEUM BOOKS FOR YOUNG READERS

Simon & Schuster, 1230 Avenue of the Americas, New York NY 10020. **Website:** kids.simonandschuster.com. Estab. 1961. Publishes hardcover originals. Guidelines for #10 SASE.

NEEDS All in juvenile versions. "We have few specific needs except for books that are fresh, interesting and well written. Fad topics are dangerous, as are works you haven't polished to the best of your ability. We also don't need safety pamphlets, ABC books, coloring books and board books. In writing picture book texts, avoid the coy and 'cutesy,' such as stories about characters with alliterative names." Agented submissions only. No paperback romance-type fiction.

TIPS "Study our titles."

AUTUMN HOUSE PRESS

87½ Westwood St., Pittsburgh PA 15211. (412)381-4261. **E-mail:** info@autumnhouse.org. **Website:** www. autumnhouse.org. **Contact:** Michael Simms, editor in chief (fiction). Estab. 1998. "We are a nonprofit literary press specializing in high-quality poetry, fiction, and nonfiction. Our editions are beautifully designed and printed, and they are distributed nationally. Approximately one-third of our sales are to college literature and creative writing classes." Member CLMP and Academy of American Poets. "We distribute our own titles. We do extensive national promotion through ads, web-marketing, reading tours, bookfairs and conferences. We are open to all genres. The quality of writing concerns us, not the genre." You can also learn about our annual Fiction Prize, Poetry Prize, Nonfiction Prize, and Chapbook Award competitions, as well as our online journal, *Coal Hill Review*. (Please note that Autumn House accepts unsolicited mss *only* through these competitions.) Publishes hardcover, trade paperback, and electronic originals. Format: acid-free paper; offset printing; perfect and casebound (cloth) bound; sometimes contains illustrations. Average print order: 1,000. Debut novel print order: 1,000. Catalog free on request. Guidelines online.

NEEDS Holds competition/award for short stories, novels, story collections, memoirs, nonfiction. *We ask that all submissions from authors new to Autumn House come through one of our annual contests.* See website for official guidelines. Responds to queries in 2 days. Accepts mss only through contest. Never critiques/comments on rejected mss.

HOW TO CONTACT "Submit only through our annual contest. The competition is tough, so submit only your best work!"

TERMS Pays 7% royalty on wholesale price. Pays $0-2,500 advance. Responds in 1-3 days on queries and proposals; 3 months on mss

TIPS "The competition to publish with Autumn House is very tough. Submit only your best work."

AVON ROMANCE

Harper Collins Publishers, 10 E. 53 St., New York NY 10022. **E-mail:** info@avonromance.com. **Website:** www.avonromance.com. Estab. 1941. "Avon has been publishing award-winning books since 1941. It is recognized for having pioneered the historical romance category and continues to bring the best of commercial literature to the broadest possible audience." Publishes paperback and digital originals and reprints.

HOW TO CONTACT Submit a query and ms via the online submission form at www.avonromance.com/impulse.

⊘ AZRO PRESS

PMB 342, 1704 Llano St. B, Santa Fe NM 87505. (505)989-3272. **Fax:** (505)989-3832. **E-mail:** books@azropress.com. **Website:** www.azropress.com. Estab. 1997. Catalog online.

"We like to publish illustrated children's books by Southwestern authors and illustrators. We are always looking for books with a Southwestern look or theme."

NEEDS Picture books: animal, history, humor, nature/environment. Young readers: adventure, animal, hi-lo, history, humor. Average word length: picture books—1,200; young readers—2,000-2,500.

TERMS Pays authors royalty of 5-10% based on wholesale price. Pays illustrators by the project ($2,000) or royalty of 5%. Responds in 3-4 months.

TIPS "We are not currently accepting new mss. Please see our website for acceptance date."

BAEN BOOKS

P.O. Box 1188, Wake Forest NC 27588. (919)570-1640. **E-mail:** info@baen.com. **Website:** www.baen.com. Estab. 1983. "We publish only science fiction and fantasy. Writers familiar with what we have published in the past will know what sort of material we are most likely to publish in the future: powerful plots with solid scientific and philosophical underpinnings are the sine qua non for consideration for science fiction submissions. As for fantasy, any magical system must be both rigorously coherent and integral to the plot, and overall the work must at least strive for originality."

NEEDS "Style: Simple is generally better; in our opinion good style, like good breeding, never calls attention to itself. Length: 100,000-130,000 words Generally we are uncomfortable with mss under 100,000 words, but if your novel is really wonderful send it along regardless of length."

HOW TO CONTACT "Query letters are not necessary. We prefer to see complete mss accompanied by a synopsis. We prefer not to see simultaneous submissions. Electronic submissions are strongly preferred. *We no longer accept submissions by e-mail.* Send ms by using the submission form at: ftp.baen.com/Slush/submit.aspx. No disks unless requested. Attach ms as a Rich Text Format (.rtf) file. Any other format will not be considered."

TERMS Responds to mss within 12-18 months.

BAILIWICK PRESS

309 East Mulberry St., Fort Collins CO 80524. (970)672-4878. **Fax:** (970)672-4731. **E-mail:** info@bailiwickpress.com. **E-mail:** aldozelnick@gmail.com. **Website:** www.bailiwickpress.com. "We're a micro-press that produces books and other products that inspire and tell great stories. Our motto is 'books with something to say.' We are now considering submissions, agented and unagented, for children's and young adult fiction. We're looking for smart, funny,

and layered writing that kids will clamor for. Authors who already have a following have a leg up. We are only looking for humorous children's fiction. Please do not submit work for adults. Illustrated fiction is desired but not required. (Illustrators are also invited to send samples.) Make us laugh out loud, ooh and aah, and cry, 'Eureka!'"

HOW TO CONTACT "Please read the Aldo Zelnick series to determine if we might be on the same page, then fill out our submission form. Please do not send submissions via snail mail or phone calls. You must complete the online submission form to be considered. If, after completing and submitting the form, you also need to send us an e-mail attachment (such as sample illustrations or excerpts of graphics), you may e-mail them to aldozelnick@gmail.com."

TERMS Responds in 6 months.

🅐⊘ BAKER BOOKS

Division of Baker Publishing Group, 6030 East Fulton Rd., Ada MI 49301. (616)676-9185. **Website:** bakerpublishinggroup.com/bakerbooks. Estab. 1939. "We will consider unsolicited work only through one of the following avenues. Materials sent through a literary agent will be considered. In addition, our staff attends various writers' conferences at which prospective authors can develop relationships with those in the publishing industry." Publishes in hardcover and trade paperback originals, and trade paperback reprints. Book catalog for 9.5x12.5 envelope and 3 first-class stamps. Guidelines online.

💭 "Baker Books publishes popular religious nonfiction reference books and professional books for church leaders. Most of our authors and readers are evangelical Christians, and our books are purchased from Christian bookstores, mail-order retailers, and school bookstores. Does not accept unsolicited queries."

TIPS "We are not interested in historical fiction, romances, science fiction, biblical narratives or spiritual warfare novels. Do not call to 'pass by' your idea."

🅐 BALLANTINE BOOKS

Imprint of Random House, Inc., 1745 Broadway, 18th Floor, New York NY 10019. (212)782-9000. **Website:** www.randomhouse.com. Estab. 1952. Ballantine Books publishes a wide variety of nonfiction and fiction. Publishes hardcover, trade paperback, mass-market paperback originals. Guidelines online.

HOW TO CONTACT Agented submissions only.

🅐 BALZER & BRAY

HarperCollins Children's Books, 10 E. 53rd St., New York NY 10022. **Website:** www.harpercollinschildrens.com. Estab. 2008. "We publish bold, creative, groundbreaking picture books and novels that appeal directly to kids in a fresh way."

NEEDS Picture Books, Young Readers: adventure, animal, anthology, concept, contemporary, fantasy, history, humor, multicultural, nature/environment, poetry, science fiction, special needs, sports, suspense. Middle readers, young adults/teens: adventure, animal, anthology, contemporary, fantasy, history, humor, multicultural, nature/environment, poetry, science fiction, special needs, sports, suspense.

HOW TO CONTACT Agented submissions only.

TERMS Offers advances. Pays illustrators by the project.

🅐 BANCROFT PRESS

P.O. Box 65360, Baltimore MD 21209-9945. (410)358-0658. **Fax:** (410)764-1967. **E-mail:** bruceb@bancroftpress.com. **Website:** www.bancroftpress.com. **Contact:** Bruce Bortz, editor/publisher (health, investments, politics, history, humor, literary novels, mystery/thrillers, chick lit, young adult). "Bancroft Press is a general trade publisher. We publish young adult fiction and adult fiction, as well as occasional nonfiction. Our only mandate is 'books that enlighten.'" Publishes hardcover and trade paperback originals. Guidelines online.

NEEDS "Our current focuses are young adult fiction, women's fiction, and literary fiction."

HOW TO CONTACT Submit complete ms.

TERMS Pays 6-8% royalty. Pays various royalties on retail price. Pays $750 advance. Responds in 6-12 months.

TIPS "We advise writers to visit our website and to be familiar with our previous work. Patience is the number one attribute contributors must have. It takes us a very long time to get through submitted material, because we are such a small company. Also, we only publish 4-6 books per year, so it may take a long time for your optioned book to be published. We like to be able to market our books to be used in schools and in libraries. We prefer fiction that bucks trends and moves in a new direction. We are especially interested in mysteries and humor (especially humorous mysteries)."

🅐⊘ BANTAM BOOKS

Imprint of Random House, Inc., 1745 Broadway, New York NY 10019. (212)782-9000. **Website:** www.bantam-dell.atrandom.com. *Not seeking mss at this time.*

Ⓐ BANTAM DELL PUBLISHING GROUP

1745 Broadway, New York NY 10019. **E-mail:** bdpublicity@randomhouse.com. **Website:** www.bantamdell.com. Estab. 1945. Agented submissions only.

BARBARIAN BOOKS

P.O. Box 170881, Boise ID 83716. **E-mail:** submissions@barbarianbooks.com. **Website:** www.barbarianbooks.com. **Contact:** Conda Douglas, e-talent scout; Kathy McIntosh, e-talent scout. Estab. 2011. Barbarian Books believes that quality e-books should be plentiful and affordable. Offers great reads for great readers. By only publishing for digital devices, Barbarian Books believes it can bring more well written stories to more people, faster than ever before. Publishes electronic originals. Catalog available online. Ms guidelines available online.

NEEDS "Strong plots and compelling characters are more important than easily classified genre. A Barbarian Books title is an excellent and often refreshingly different choice for a reader of crime, fantasy, romance, science fiction, westerns, and cross-genre. Our motto is: Great reads for great readers."

HOW TO CONTACT Submit completed ms. Looking for submissions of entire, completed novel-length mss, around 60,000 words.

TERMS Pays authors 70% royalties on retail price. Responds in 2-6 months on mss.

Ⓞ BARBOUR PUBLISHING, INC.

1810 Barbour Dr., P.O. Box 719, Urichsville OH 44683. **E-mail:** editors@barbourbooks.com; aschrock@barbourbooks.com; fictionsubmit@barbourbooks.com. **Website:** www.barbourbooks.com. Estab. 1981. "Barbour Books publishes inspirational/devotional material that is nondenominational and evangelical in nature. We're a Christian evangelical publisher." Specializes in short, easy-to-read Christian bargain books. "Faithfulness to the Bible and Jesus Christ are the bedrock values behind every book Barbour's staff produces."

Ⓞ "We no longer accept unsolicited submissions unless they are submitted through professional literary agencies. For more information, we encourage new fiction authors to join a professional writers organization like American Christian Fiction Writers."

FREDERIC C. BEIL, PUBLISHER, INC.

609 Whitaker St., Savannah GA 31401. (912)233-2446. **Fax:** (912)233-6456. **E-mail:** editor@beil.com. **Web-**

site: www.beil.com. Estab. 1982. Frederic C. Beil publishes in the fields of history, literature, and biography. Publishes hardcover originals and reprints. Book catalog available free.

HOW TO CONTACT Query with SASE.

TERMS Pays 7.5% royalty on retail price. Responds in 1 week to queries.

TIPS "Our objectives are (1) to offer to the reading public carefully selected texts of lasting value; (2) to adhere to high standards in the choice of materials and in bookmaking craftsmanship; (3) to produce books that exemplify good taste in format and design; and (4) to maintain the lowest cost consistent with quality."

BELLEVUE LITERARY PRESS

New York University School of Medicine, Dept. of Medicine, NYU School of Medicine, 550 First Avenue, OBV 612, New York NY 10016. (212)263-7802. **E-mail:** blpsubmissions@gmail.com. **Website:** blpress.org. **Contact:** Erika Goldman, publisher/editorial director. Estab. 2005. "Publishes literary and authoritative fiction and nonfiction at the nexus of the arts and the sciences, with a special focus on medicine. As our authors explore cultural and historical representations of the human body, illness, and health, they address the impact of scientific and medical practice on the individual and society."

HOW TO CONTACT Submit complete ms.

TIPS "We are a project of New York University's School of Medicine and while our standards reflect NYU's excellence in scholarship, humanistic medicine, and science, our authors need not be affiliated with NYU. We are not a university press and do not receive any funding from NYU. Our publishing operations are financed exclusively by foundation grants, private donors, and book sales revenue."

Ⓐ Ⓞ BERKLEY BOOKS

Penguin Group (USA) Inc., 375 Hudson St., New York NY 10014. **Website:** us.penguingroup.com/. **Contact:** Leslie Gelbman, president and publisher. Estab. 1955. The Berkley Publishing Group publishes a variety of general nonfiction and fiction including the traditional categories of romance, mystery and science fiction. Publishes paperback and mass-market originals and reprints.

Ⓞ "Due to the high volume of mss received, most Penguin Group (USA) Inc. imprints do not normally accept unsolicited mss. The preferred and standard method for having mss considered for publication by a major publisher is to submit them through an established literary agent."

IMPRINTS Ace; Jove; Heat; Sensation; Berkley Prime Crime; Berkley Caliber.

NEEDS No occult fiction.

HOW TO CONTACT Prefers agented submissions.

⊘ BETHANY HOUSE PUBLISHERS

Division of Baker Publishing Group, 6030 E. Fulton Rd., Ada MI 49301. (616)676-9185. **Fax:** (616)676-9573. **Website:** bakerpublishinggroup.com/bethanyhouse. Estab. 1956. Bethany House Publishers specializes in books that communicate Biblical truth and assist people in both spiritual and practical areas of life. "While we do not accept unsolicited queries or proposals via telephone or e-mail, we will consider one-page queries sent by fax and directed to adult nonfiction, adult fiction, or young adult/children." *All unsolicited mss returned unopened.* Publishes hardcover and trade paperback originals, mass-market paperback reprints. Book catalog for 9x12 envelope and 5 first-class stamps. Guidelines online.

TERMS Pays royalty on net price. Pays advance. Responds in 3 months to queries.

TIPS "Bethany House Publishers' publishing program relates Biblical truth to all areas of life—whether in the framework of a well-told story, of a challenging book for spiritual growth, or of a Bible reference work. We are seeking high-quality fiction and nonfiction that will inspire and challenge our audience."

BIRCH BOOK PRESS

P.O. Box 81, Delhi NY 13753. **Fax:** (607)746-7453. **E-mail:** birchbrook@copper.net. **Website:** www.birchbrookpress.info. **Contact:** Tom Tolnay, editor/publisher; Leigh Eckmair, art & research editor. Estab. 1982. Birch Brook Press "is a letterpress book printer/typesetter/designer that uses monies from these activities to publish several titles of its own each year with cultural and literary interest." Specializes in literary work, flyfishing, baseball, outdoors, theme anthologies, and books about books. Occasionally publishes trade paperback originals. Book catalog online.

NEEDS "Mostly we do anthologies around a particular theme generated inhouse. We make specific calls for fiction when we are doing an anthology."

HOW TO CONTACT Query with SASE and submit sample chapter(s), synopsis.

TERMS Pays modest royalty on acceptance. Responds in 3-6 months.

TIPS "Write well on subjects of interest to BBP, such as outdoors, flyfishing, baseball, music, literary stories, fine poetry, and occasional novellas, books about books."

BKMK PRESS

University of Missouri - Kansas City, 5101 Rockhill Rd., Kansas City MO 64110-2499. (816)235-2558. **Fax:** (816)235-2611. **E-mail:** bkmk@umkc.edu. **Website:** newletters.org. Estab. 1971. "BkMk Press publishes fine literature. Reading period January-June." Publishes trade paperback originals. Guidelines online.

HOW TO CONTACT Query with SASE.

TERMS Responds in 4-6 months to queries.

TIPS "We skew toward readers of literature, particularly contemporary writing. Because of our limited number of titles published per year, we discourage apprentice writers or 'scattershot' submissions."

BLACK HERON PRESS

P.O. Box 13396, Mill Creek WA 98082. **Website:** www.blackheronpress.com. Estab. 1984. "Black Heron Press publishes primarily literary fiction." Publishes hardcover and trade paperback originals, trade paperback reprints. Catalog available online.

NEEDS "All of our fiction is character driven. We don't want to see fiction written for the mass market. If it sells to the mass market, fine, but we don't see ourselves as a commercial press."

HOW TO CONTACT Submit proposal package, including cover letter and first 40-50 pages pages of your completed novel.

TERMS Pays 8% royalty on retail price. Responds in 6 months.

TIPS "Our Readers love good fiction—they are scattered among all social classes, ethnic groups, and zip code areas. If you can't read our books, at least check out our titles on our website."

⑤ BLACK LAWRENCE PRESS

326 Bigham St., Pittsburgh PA 15211. **E-mail:** editors@blacklawrencepress.com. **Website:** www.blacklawrencepress.com. **Contact:** Diane Goettel, executive editor. Estab. 2003. Black Lawrence press seeks to publish intriguing books of literature—novels, short story collections, poetry collections, chapbooks, anthologies, and creative nonfiction. Will also publish the occasional translation from German. Publishes 15-20 books/year, mostly poetry and fiction. Mss are selected through open submission and competition. Books are 20-400 pages, offset-printed or high-quality POD, perfect-bound, with 4-color cover.

HOW TO CONTACT Submit complete ms.

TERMS Pays royalties. Responds in 6 months to mss.

BLACK LYON PUBLISHING, LLC

P.O. Box 567, Baker City OR 97814. **E-mail:** info@blacklyonpublishing.com. **E-mail:** queries@blacklyonpublishing.com. **Website:** www.blacklyonpublishing.com. **Contact:** The Editors. Estab. 2007. "Black Lyon Publishing is a small, independent publisher. We are very focused on giving new novelists a launching pad into the industry." Publishes paperback and e-book originals. Guidelines online.

HOW TO CONTACT Prefers e-mail queries.

TERMS Responds in 2-3 months to queries.

TIPS "Write a good, solid romance with a setting, premise, character or voice just a little 'different' than what you might usually find on the market. We like unique books—but they still need to be romances."

BLACK VELVET SEDUCTIONS PUBLISHING

E-mail: ric@blackvelvetseductions.com. **Website:** www.blackvelvetseductions.com. **Contact:** Richard Savage, acquisitions editor. Estab. 2005. "We publish 2 types of material: (1) romance novels and short stories and (2) romantic stories involving spanking between consenting adults. We look for well-crafted stories with a high degree of emotional impact. No first person point of view. All material must be in third person point of view." Publishes trade paperback and electronic originals. "We have a high interest in re-publishing backlist titles in electronic and trade paperback formats once rights have reverted to the author." Accepts only complete mss. Query with SASE. Submit complete ms. Publishes trade paperback and electronic originals and reprints. Catalog free or online. Guidelines online.

NEEDS All stories must have a strong romance element. "There are very few sexual taboos in our erotic line. We tend to give our authors the widest latitude. If it is safe, sane, and consensual we will allow our authors latitude to show us the eroticism. However, we will not consider mss with any of the following: bestiality (sex with animals), necrophilia (sex with dead people), pedophillia (sex with children)."

HOW TO CONTACT Only accepts electronic submissions.

TERMS Pays 10% royalty for paperbacks; 50% royalty for electronic books. Responds in 6 months to queries; 8 months to proposals; 8-12 months to mss.

TIPS "We publish romance and erotic romance. We look for books written in very deep point of view. Shallow point of view remains the number one reason we reject mss in which the storyline generally works."

JOHN F. BLAIR, PUBLISHER

1406 Plaza Dr., Winston-Salem NC 27103. (336)768-1374. **Fax:** (336)768-9194. **E-mail:** editorial@blairpub.com. **Website:** www.blairpub.com. **Contact:** Carolyn Sakowski, president. Estab. 1954.

NEEDS "We specialize in regional books, with an emphasis on nonfiction categories such as history, travel, folklore, and biography. We publish only 1 or 2 works of fiction each year. Fiction submitted to us should have some connection with the Southeast. We do not publish children's books, poetry, or category fiction such as romances, science fiction, or spy thrillers. We do not publish collections of short stories, essays, or newspaper columns."

HOW TO CONTACT Accepts unsolicited mss. Any fiction submitted should have some connection with the Southeast, either through setting or author's background. Send a cover letter, giving a synopsis of the book. Include the first 2 chapters (at least 50 pages) of the ms. "You may send the entire ms if you wish. If you choose to send only samples, please include the projected word length of your book and estimated completion date in your cover letter. Send a biography of the author, including publishing credits and credentials."

TERMS Pays royalties. Pays negotiable advance. Responds in 3-6 months.

TIPS "We are primarily interested in nonfiction titles. Most of our titles have a tie-in with North Carolina or the southeastern United States, we do not accept short-story collections. Please enclose a cover letter and outline with the ms. We prefer to review queries before we are sent complete mss. Queries should include an approximate word count."

BLAZEVOX [BOOKS]

131 Euclid Ave., Kenmore NY 14217. **E-mail:** editor@blazevox.org. **Website:** www.blazevox.org. **Contact:** Geoffrey Gatza, editor/publisher. Estab. 2005. "We are a major publishing presence specializing in innovative fictions and wide-ranging fields of innovative forms of poetry and prose. Our goal is to publish works that are challenging, creative, attractive, and yet affordable to individual readers. Articles of submission depend on many criteria, but overall items

submitted must conform to one ethereal trait, your work must not suck. This put plainly, bad art should be punished; we will not promote it. However, all submissions will be reviewed and the author will receive feedback. We are human too." Guidelines online.

NEEDS Submit complete ms via e-mail.

TERMS Pays 10% royalties on fiction and poetry books, based on net receipts. This amount may be split across multiple contributors. "We do not pay advances."

TIPS "We actively contract and support authors who tour, read and perform their work, play an active part of the contemporary literary scene, and seek a readership."

Ⓐ BLOOMSBURY CHILDREN'S BOOKS

Imprint of Bloomsbury USA, 1385 Broadway, 5th Floor, New York NY 10008. **Website:** www.bloomsbury.com/us/childrens. No phone calls or e-mails. *Agented submissions only.* Book catalog online. Guidelines online.

HOW TO CONTACT Agented submissions only.

TERMS Pays royalty. Pays advance. Responds in 6 months.

BOA EDITIONS, LTD.

P.O. Box 30971, Rochester NY 14603. (585)546-3410. **Fax:** (585)546-3913. **E-mail:** contact@boaeditions.org. **Website:** www.boaeditions.org. **Contact:** Peter Conners, publisher; Melissa Hall, development director/office manager. Estab. 1976. "BOA Editions publishes distinguished collections of poetry, fiction and poetry in translation. Our goal is to publish the finest American contemporary poetry, fiction and poetry in translation." Publishes hardcover and trade paperback originals. Book catalog online. Guidelines online.

NEEDS "We now publish literary fiction through our American Reader Series. While aesthetic quality is subjective, our fiction will be by authors more concerned with the artfulness of their writing than the twists and turns of plot. Our strongest current interest is in short story collections (and short-short story collections), although we will consider novels. We strongly advise you to read our first published fiction collections." *Temporarily closed to novel/collection submissions.*

TERMS Negotiates royalties. Pays variable advance. Responds in 1 week to queries; 5 months to mss.

BOLD STROKES BOOKS, INC.

P.O. Box 249, Valley Falls NY 12185. (518)677-5127. **Fax:** (518)677-5291. **E-mail:** sandy.boldstrokes@gmail.com. **E-mail:** submissions@boldstrokesbooks.

com. **Website:** www.boldstrokesbooks.com. **Contact:** Sandy Lowe, senior editor. Publishes trade paperback originals and reprints; electronic originals and reprints. Guidelines online.

IMPRINTS BSB Fiction; Victory Editions Lesbian Fiction; Liberty Editions Gay Fiction; Soliloquy Young Adult; Heat Stroke Erotica.

NEEDS "Submissions should have a gay, lesbian, transgendered, or bisexual focus and should be positive and life-affirming."

HOW TO CONTACT Submit completed ms with bio, cover letter, and synopsis—electronically only.

TERMS Sliding scale based on sales volume and format. Responds in 1 month to queries; 2 months to proposals; 4 months to mss.

TIPS "We are particularly interested in authors who are interested in craft enhancement, technical development, and exploring and expanding traditional genre definitions and boundaries and are looking for a long-term publishing relationship."

🌀 BOOKOUTURE

StoryFire Ltd., 23 Sussex Rd., Ickenham UB10 8P United Kingdom. **E-mail:** questions@bookouture.com. **E-mail:** pitch@bookouture.com. **Website:** www.bookouture.com. **Contact:** Oliver Rhodes, founder and publisher. Estab. 2012. Publishes mass-market paperback and electronic originals and reprints. Book catalog online.

IMPRINTS Imprint of StoryFire Ltd.

NEEDS "We are looking for entertaining fiction targeted at modern women. That can be anything from Steampunk to Erotica, Historicals to thrillers. A distinctive author voice is more important than a particular genre or ms length."

HOW TO CONTACT Submit complete ms.

TERMS Pays 45% royalty on wholesale price. Responds in 1 month.

TIPS "The most important question that we ask of submissions is why would a reader buy the next book? What's distinctive or different about your storytelling that will mean readers will want to come back for more. We look to acquire global English language rights for e-book and Print on Demand."

⊘🌀 BOREALIS PRESS, LTD.

8 Mohawk Crescent, Napean ON K2H 7G6 Canada. (613)829-0150. **Fax:** (613)829-7783. **E-mail:** drt@borealispress.com. **Website:** www.borealispress.com. Estab. 1972. "Our mission is to publish work that will

be of lasting interest in the Canadian book market." Currently emphasizing Canadian fiction, nonfiction, drama, poetry. De-emphasizing children's books. Publishes hardcover and paperback originals and reprints. Book catalog online. Guidelines online.

IMPRINTS Tecumseh Press.

NEEDS Only material Canadian in content and dealing with significant aspects of the human situation.

HOW TO CONTACT Query with SASE. Submit clips, 1-2 sample chapters. *No unsolicited mss.*

TERMS Pays 10% royalty on net receipts; plus 3 free author's copies. Responds in 2 months to queries; 4 months to mss.

◐⊘ BROADWAY BOOKS

The Crown Publishing Group/Random House, 1745 Broadway, New York NY 10019. (212)782-9000. **Fax:** (212)782-9411. **Website:** crownpublishing.com/imprint/broadway-books. Estab. 1995. "Broadway publishes high-quality general interest nonfiction and fiction for adults." Publishes hardcover and trade paperback books.

IMPRINTS Broadway Books; Broadway Business; Doubleday; Doubleday Image; Doubleday Religious Publishing; Main Street Books; Nan A. Talese.

HOW TO CONTACT *Agented submissions only.*

TERMS Pays royalty on retail price. Pays advance.

BRONZE MAN BOOKS

Millikin University, 1184 W. Main, Decatur IL 62522. (217)424-6264. **E-mail:** rbrooks@millikin.edu. **Website:** www.bronzemanbooks.com. **Contact:** Dr. Randy Brooks, editorial board; Edwin Walker, editorial board. Estab. 2006. Publishes hardcover, trade paperback, and mass-market paperback originals.

NEEDS Subjects include art, graphic design, exhibits, general.

HOW TO CONTACT Submit completed ms.

TERMS Outright purchase based on wholesale value of 10% of a press run. Responds in 1-3 months.

TIPS "The art books are intended for serious collectors and scholars of contemporary art, especially of artists from the Midwestern U.S. These books are published in conjunction with art exhibitions at Millikin University or the Decatur Area Arts Council. The children's books have our broadest audience, and the literary chapbooks are intended for readers of contemporary fiction, drama, and poetry."

◑ THE BRUCEDALE PRESS

P.O. Box 2259, Port Elgin ON N0H 2C0 Canada. (519)832-6025. **E-mail:** info@brucedalepress.ca. **Website:** brucedalepress.ca. The Brucedale Press publishes books and other materials of regional interest and merit, as well as literary, historical, and/or pictorial works. Publishes hardcover and trade paperback originals. Book catalog online. Guidelines online.

◐ *Accepts works by Canadian authors only. Book submissions reviewed November to January. Submissions to The Leaf Journal accepted in September and March ONLY.*

TERMS Pays royalty.

TIPS "Our focus is very regional. In reading submissions, I look for quality writing with a strong connection to the Queen's Bush area of Ontario. All authors should visit our website, get a catalog, and read our books before submitting."

BULLITT PUBLISHING

P.O. Box, Austin TX 78729. **E-mail:** bullittpublishing@yahoo.com. **E-mail:** submissions@bullittpublishing.com. **Website:** bullittpublishing.com. **Contact:** Pat Williams, editor. Estab. 2012. "Bullitt Publishing is a royalty-offering publishing house specializing in smart, contemporary romance. We are proud to provide print on demand distribution through the world's most comprehensive distribution channel including Amazon.com and BarnesandNoble.com. Digital distribution is available through the world's largest distibutor of e-books and can be downloaded to reading devices such as the iPhone, iPod Touch, Amazon Kindle, Sony Reader or Barnes & Noble nook. E-books are distributed to the Apple iBookstore, Barnes & Noble, Sony, Kobo and the Diesel eBook Store. Whether this is your first novel or your 101st novel, Bullitt Publishing will treat you with the same amount of professionalism and respect. While we expect well-written entertaining mss from all of our authors, we promise to provide high-quality, professional product in return." Publishes trade paperback and electronic originals.

IMPRINTS Includes imprint Tempo Romance.

◐ BUSTER BOOKS

9 Lion Yard, Tremadoc Rd., London WA SW4 7NQ United Kingdom. (020)7720-8643. **Fax:** (022)7720-8953. **E-mail:** enquiries@mombooks.com. **Website:** www.busterbooks.co.uk. "We are dedicated to providing irresistible and fun books for children of all ages. We typically publish black & white nonfiction for children aged 8-12 novelty titles-including doodle books."

HOW TO CONTACT Submit synopsis and sample text.

TIPS "We do not accept fiction submissions. Please do not send original artwork as we cannot guarantee its safety." Visit website before submitting.

BY LIGHT UNSEEN MEDIA

P.O. Box 1233, Pepperell MA 01463. (978)433-8866. **Fax:** (978)433-8866. **E-mail:** vyrdolak@bylightunseenmedia.com. **Website:** www.bylightunseenmedia.com. **Contact:** Inanna Arthen, owner/editor in chief. Estab. 2006. Publishes hardcover, paperback and electronic originals; trade paperback reprints. Catalog online. Ms guidelines online.

NEEDS "We are a niche small press that *only* publishes fiction relating in some way to vampires. Within that guideline, we're interested in almost any genre that includes a vampire trope, the more creative and innovative, the better. Restrictions are noted in the submission guidelines (no derivative fiction based on other works, such as Dracula, no gore-for-gore's-sake 'splatter' horror, etc.) We do not publish anthologies."

HOW TO CONTACT Submit proposal package including synopsis, 3 sample chapters, brief author bio. *"We encourage electronic submissions."* All unsolicited mss will be returned unopened.

TERMS Pays royalty of 20-50% on net as explicitly defined in contract. Payment quarterly. Pays $200 advance. Responds in 3 months.

TIPS "We strongly urge authors to familiarize themselves with the vampire genre and not imagine that they're doing something new and amazingly different just because they're not imitating the current fad."

⊘ CALAMARI PRESS

Via Titta Scarpetta #28, Rome 00153 Italy. **E-mail:** derek@calamaripress.net. **Website:** www.calamaripress.com. Calamari Press publishes books of literary text and art. Mss are selected by invitation. Occasionally has open submission period—check website. Helps to be published in *SleepingFish* first. Publishes paperback originals. Guidelines online.

HOW TO CONTACT Query with outline/synopsis and 3 sample chapters. Accepts queries by e-mail only. Include brief bio. Send SASE or IRC for return of ms.

TERMS Pays in author's copies. Responds to mss in 2 weeks.

CALKINS CREEK

Boyds Mills Press, 815 Church St., Honesdale PA 18431. **Website:** www.calkinscreekbooks.com. Estab. 2004. "We aim to publish books that are a well-written blend of creative writing and extensive research, which emphasize important events, people, and places in U.S. history." Guidelines online.

HOW TO CONTACT Submit outline/synopsis and 3 sample chapters.

TERMS Pays authors royalty or work purchased outright.

TIPS "Read through our recently published titles and review our catalog. When selecting titles to publish, our emphasis will be on important events, people, and places in U.S. history. Writers are encouraged to submit a detailed bibliography, including secondary and primary sources, and expert reviews with their submissions."

ⒶⓄ CANDLEWICK PRESS

99 Dover St., Somerville MA 02144. (617)661-3330. **Fax:** (617)661-0565. **E-mail:** bigbear@candlewick.com. **Website:** www.candlewick.com. Estab. 1991. "Candlewick Press publishes high-quality, illustrated children's books for ages infant through young adult. We are a truly child-centered publisher." Publishes hardcover and trade paperback originals, and reprints.

Ⓞ *Candlewick Press is not accepting queries or unsolicited mss at this time.*

NEEDS Picture books: animal, concept, contemporary, fantasy, history, humor, multicultural, nature/environment, poetry. Middle readers, young adults: contemporary, fantasy, history, humor, multicultural, poetry, science fiction, sports, suspense/mystery.

HOW TO CONTACT "We currently do not accept unsolicited editorial queries or submissions. If you are an author or illustrator and would like us to consider your work, please read our submissions policy (online) to learn more."

TERMS Pays authors royalty of 2.5-10% based on retail price. Offers advance.

TIPS *"We no longer accept unsolicited mss. See our website for further information about us."*

CANTERBURY HOUSE PUBLISHING, LTD.

4535 Ottawa Trail, Sarasota FL 34233. (941)312-6912. **Website:** www.canterburyhousepublishing.com. **Contact:** Sandra Horton, editor. Estab. 2009. "Our audience is made up of readers looking for wholesome fiction with good southern stories, with elements of mystery, romance, and inspiration and/or are looking for true stories of achievement and triumph over challenging circumstances. We are very strict on our submission guidelines due to our small staff, and our target market of Southern regional settings." Publishes hardcover, trade paperback, and electronic originals. Book catalog online. Guidelines online.

HOW TO CONTACT Query with SASE and through website.

TERMS Pays 10-15% royalty on wholesale price. Responds in 1 month to queries; 3 months to mss.

TIPS "Because of our limited staff, we prefer authors who have good writing credentials and submit edited mss. We also look at authors who are business and marketing savvy and willing to help promote their books."

CARNEGIE MELLON UNIVERSITY PRESS

5032 Forbes Ave., Pittsburgh PA 15289-1021. (412)268-2861. **Fax:** (412)268-8706. **E-mail:** carnegiemellonuniversitypress@gmail.com. **Website:** www.cmu.edu/universitypress/. **Contact:** Cynthia Lamb, senior editor. Estab. 1972. Publishes hardcover and trade paperback originals. Book catalog and guidelines online.

CAROLINA WREN PRESS

120 Morris St., Durham NC 27701. (919)560-2738. **E-mail:** carolinawrenpress@earthlink.net. **Website:** www.carolinawrenpress.org. **Contact:** Andrea Selch, president. Estab. 1976. "We publish poetry, fiction, and memoirs by, and/or about people of color, women, gay/lesbian issues, and work by writers from, living in, or writing about the U.S. South." Guidelines online.

Accepts simultaneous submissions, but "let us know if work has been accepted elsewhere."

NEEDS "We are no longer publishing children's literature of any topic." Books: 6x9 paper; typeset; various bindings; illustrations. Distributes titles through Amazon.com, Barnes & Noble, Baker & Taylor, and on their website. "We very rarely accept any unsolicited mss, but we accept submissions for the Doris Bakwin Award for Writing by a Woman in Jan-March of even-numbered years."

HOW TO CONTACT Query by mail. "We will accept e-mailed queries—a letter in the body of the e-mail describing your project—but please do not send large attachments."

TERMS Responds in 3 months to queries; 6 months to mss.

TIPS "Best way to get read is to submit to a contest."

CARTWHEEL BOOKS

Imprint of Scholastic Trade Division, 557 Broadway, New York NY 10012. (212)343-6100. **Website:** www.scholastic.com. Estab. 1991. Cartwheel Books publishes innovative books for children, up to age 8. "We are looking for 'novelties' that are books first, play objects second. Even without its gimmick, a Cartwheel Book should stand alone as a valid piece of children's literature." Publishes novelty books, easy readers, board books, hardcover and trade paperback originals. Guidelines available free.

NEEDS Again, the subject should have mass-market appeal for very young children. Humor can be helpful, but not necessary. Mistakes writers make are a reading level that is too difficult, a topic of no interest or too narrow, or mss that are too long.

HOW TO CONTACT *Accepts mss from agents only.*

CAVE HOLLOW PRESS

P.O. Drawer J, Warrensburg MO 64093. **E-mail:** gbcrump@cavehollowpress.com. **Website:** www.cavehollowpress.com. **Contact:** G.B. Crump, editor. Estab. 2001. Publishes trade paperback originals. Book catalog for #10 SASE. Guidelines available free.

NEEDS "Our website is updated frequently to reflect the current type of fiction Cave Hollow Press is seeking."

HOW TO CONTACT Query with SASE.

TERMS Pays 7-12% royalty on wholesale price. Pays negotiable amount in advance. Responds in 1-2 months to queries and proposals; 3-6 months to mss.

TIPS "Our audience varies based on the type of book we are publishing. We specialize in Missouri and Midwest regional fiction. We are interested in talented writers from Missouri and the surrounding Midwest. Check our submission guidelines on the website for what type of fiction we are interested in currently."

CEDAR FORT, INC.

2373 W. 700 S, Springville UT 84663. (801)489-4084. **Fax:** (801)489-1097. **Website:** www.cedarfort.com. Estab. 1986. "Each year we publish well over 100 books, and many of those are by first-time authors. At the same time, we love to see books from established authors. As one of the largest book publishers in Utah, we have the capability and enthusiasm to make your book a success, whether you are a new author or a returning one. We want to publish uplifting and edifying books that help people think about what is important in life, books people enjoy reading to relax and feel better about themselves, and books to help improve lives. Although we do put out several children's books each year, we are extremely selective. Our children's books must have strong religious or moral values, and must contain outstanding writing and an excellent storyline." Publishes hardcover, trade paperback originals and reprints, mass-market paperback and electronic reprints. Catalog and guidelines online.

IMPRINTS Council Press, Sweetwater Books, Bonneville Books, Front Table Books, Hobble Creek Press, CFI, Plain Sight Publishing, Horizon Publishers, Pioneer Plus.

HOW TO CONTACT Submit completed ms.

TERMS Pays 10-12% royalty on wholesale price. Pays $2,000-50,000 advance. Responds in 1 month on queries; 2 months on proposals; 4 months on mss.

TIPS "Our audience is rural, conservative, mainstream. The first page of your ms is very important because we start reading every submission, but good-writing and plot keep us reading."

CHANGELING PRESS LLC

315 N. Centre St., Martinsburg WV 25404. **E-mail:** submissions@changelingpress.com. **Website:** www.changelingpress.com. **Contact:** Margaret Riley, publisher. Novellas only (8,000-25,000 words). Publishes e-books.

NEEDS Accepts unsolicited submissions.

HOW TO CONTACT E-mail submissions only.

TERMS Pays 35% gross royalties monthly. Responds in 1 week to queries.

CHARLESBRIDGE PUBLISHING

85 Main St., Watertown MA 02472. (617)926-0329. **Fax:** (617)926-5720. **E-mail:** tradeeditorial@charlesbridge.com. **Website:** www.charlesbridge.com. Estab. 1980. "Charlesbridge publishes high-quality books for children, with a goal of creating lifelong readers and lifelong learners. Our books encourage reading and discovery in the classroom, library, and home. We believe that books for children should offer accurate information, promote a positive worldview, and embrace a child's innate sense of wonder and fun. To this end, we continually strive to seek new voices, new visions, and new directions in children's literature." Publishes hardcover and trade paperback nonfiction and fiction, children's books for the trade and library markets. Guidelines online.

NEEDS Strong stories with enduring themes. Charlesbridge publishes both picture books and transitional bridge books (books ranging from early readers to middle-grade chapter books). Our fiction titles include lively, plot-driven stories with strong, engaging characters. No alphabet books, board books, coloring books, activity books, or books with audiotapes or CD-ROMs.

HOW TO CONTACT *Exclusive submissions only.* "Charlesbridge accepts unsolicited mss submitted exclusively to us for a period of 3 months. 'Exclusive Submission' should be written on all envelopes and cover letters." Please submit only 1 or 2 mss at a time. For picture books and shorter bridge books, please send a complete ms. For fiction books longer than 30 ms pages, please send a detailed plot synopsis, a chapter outline, and 3 chapters of text.

TERMS Pays royalty. Pays advance. Responds in 3 months.

TIPS "To become acquainted with our publishing program, we encourage you to review our books and visit our website where you will find our catalog."

⊘ CHILDREN'S BRAINS ARE YUMMY (CBAY) BOOKS

P.O. Box 670296, Austin TX 75367. **E-mail:** conflict-submissions@gmail.com; madeline@cbaybooks.com. **Website:** www.cbaybooks.com. **Contact:** Madeline Smoot, publisher. Estab. 2008. "CBAY Books currently focuses on quality fantasy and science fiction books for the middle-grade and teen markets. We are not currently accepting unsolicited submissions." Brochure and guidelines online.

TERMS Pays authors royalty 10%-15% based on wholesale price. Offers advances against royalties. Average amount $500.

◕⊘ CHILD'S PLAY (INTERNATIONAL) LTD.

Child's Play, Ashworth Rd. Bridgemead, Swindon, Wiltshire SN5 7YD United Kingdom. **E-mail:** neil@childs-play.com; office@childs-play.com. **Website:** www.childs-play.com. **Contact:** Sue Baker, Neil Burden, ms acquisitions. Estab. 1972. Specializes in nonfiction, fiction, educational material, multicultural material. Produces 30 picture books/year; 10 young readers/year. "A child's early years are more important than any other. This is when children learn most about the world around them and the language they need to survive and grow. Child's Play aims to create exactly the right material for this all-important time."

◔ "Due to a backlog of submissions, Child's Play is currently no longer able to accept anymore mss."

NEEDS Picture books: adventure, animal, concept, contemporary, folktales, multicultural, nature/environment. Young readers: adventure, animal, anthology, concept, contemporary, folktales, humor, multicultural, nature/environment, poetry. Average word length: picture books—1,500; young readers—2,000.

TIPS "Look at our website to see the kind of work we do before sending. Do not send cartoons. We do not publish novels. We do publish lots of books with pictures of babies/toddlers."

CHRISTIAN BOOKS TODAY LTD

136 Main St., Buckshaw Village Chorley, Lancashire PR7 7BZ United Kingdom. **E-mail:** editme@christian-bookstoday.com. **Website:** www.christianbookstoday.com. **Contact:** Jason Richardson, MD (nonfiction); Lynda McIntosh, editor (fiction). Estab. 2009. Publishes trade paperback originals/reprints and electronic originals/reprints. Catalog and guidelines online.

NEEDS "Please send us your Christian or 'clean read' fiction. Nondenominational Christian romance, suspense, mystery, and contemporary Christian fiction are always welcome."

HOW TO CONTACT Submit chapter-by-chapter outline and 3 sample chapters.

TERMS Pays 10% royalty on Amazon retail price; 15% e-book; 5% wholesale trade. Responds in 1 month to queries; 2 months to proposals and mss.

TIPS "We are looking particularly for Christian romance. Any other genre will likely not find a place with our publishing house at this time. New and unpublished writers are welcome. We appeal to a general Christian readership. We are interested in 'clean read' mss only. No profanity, sexual content, gambling, substance abuse, or graphic violence. Please do not send us conspiracy-type stories."

CHRISTIAN FOCUS PUBLICATIONS

Geanies House, Fearn, Tain Ross-shire Scotland IV20 1TW United Kingdom. (44)1862-871-011. **Fax:** (44)1862-871-699. **E-mail:** submissions@christianfocus.com. **Website:** www.christianfocus.com. **Contact:** Director of Publishing. Estab. 1975. Specializes in Christian material, nonfiction, fiction, educational material.

NEEDS Picture books, young readers, adventure, history, religion. Middle readers: adventure, problem novels, religion. Young adult/teens: adventure, history, problem novels, religion. Average word length: young readers—5,000; middle readers—max 10,000; young adult/teen—max 20,000.

HOW TO CONTACT Query or submit outline/synopsis and 3 sample chapters. Will consider electronic submissions and previously published work.

TERMS Responds to queries in 2 weeks; mss in 3 months.

TIPS "Be aware of the international market as regards writing style/topics as well as illustration styles. Our company sells rights to European as well as Asian countries. Fiction sales are not as good as they were. Christian fiction for youngsters is not a product that is performing well in comparison to nonfiction such as Christian biography/Bible stories/church history, etc."

CHRONICLE BOOKS

680 Second St., San Francisco CA 94107. **E-mail:** submissions@chroniclebooks.com. **Website:** www.chroniclebooks.com. "We publish an exciting range of books, stationery, kits, calendars, and novelty formats. Our list includes children's books and interactive formats; young adult books; cookbooks; fine art, design, and photography; pop culture; craft, fashion, beauty, and home decor; relationships, mind-body-spirit; innovative formats such as interactive journals, kits, decks, and stationery; and much, much more." Book catalog for 9x12 SAE and 8 first-class stamps. Ms guidelines for #10 SASE.

NEEDS Only interested in fiction for children and young adults. No adult fiction.

HOW TO CONTACT Submit complete ms (picture books); submit outline/synopsis and 3 sample chapters (for older readers). Will not respond to submissions unless interested. Will not consider submissions by fax, e-mail or disk. Do not include SASE; do not send original materials. No submissions will be returned.

TERMS Generally pays authors in royalties based on retail price, "though we do occasionally work on a flat fee basis." Advance varies. Illustrators paid royalty based on retail price or flat fee. Responds to queries in 1 month.

CHRONICLE BOOKS FOR CHILDREN

680 Second St., San Francisco CA 94107. (415)537-4200. **Fax:** (415)537-4460. **E-mail:** submissions@chroniclebooks.com. **Website:** www.chroniclekids.com. "Chronicle Books for Children publishes an eclectic mixture of traditional and innovative children's books. Our aim is to publish books that inspire young readers to learn and grow creatively while helping them discover the joy of reading. We're looking for quirky, bold artwork and subject matter." Publishes hardcover and trade paperback originals. Book catalog for 9x12 envelope and 3 first-class stamps. Guidelines online.

NEEDS Does not accept proposals by fax, via e-mail, or on disk. When submitting artwork, either as a part of a project or as samples for review, do not send original art.

TERMS Pays variable advance. Responds in 2-4 weeks to queries; 6 months to mss.

TIPS "We are interested in projects that have a unique bent to them—be it in subject matter, writing style, or illustrative technique. As a small list, we are looking for books that will lend our list a distinctive flavor. Primarily we are interested in fiction and nonfiction picture books for children ages up to 8 years, and nonfiction books for children ages up to 12 years. We publish board, pop-up, and other novelty formats as well as picture books. We are also interested in early chapter books, middle-grade fiction, and young adult projects."

CLARION BOOKS

Houghton Mifflin Co., 215 Park Ave. S., New York NY 10003. **Website:** www.hmhco.com. Estab. 1965. "Clarion Books publishes picture books, nonfiction, and fiction for infants through grade 12. Avoid telling your stories in verse unless you are a professional poet. *We are no longer responding to your unsolicited submission unless we are interested in publishing it. Please do not include a SASE. Submissions will be recycled, and you will not hear from us regarding the status of your submission unless we are interested. We regret that we cannot respond personally to each submission, but we do consider each and every submission we receive.*" Publishes hardcover originals for children. Guidelines online.

NEEDS "Clarion is highly selective in the areas of historical fiction, fantasy, and science fiction. A novel must be superlatively written in order to find a place on the list. Mss that arrive without an SASE of adequate size will *not* be responded to or returned. Accepts fiction translations."

HOW TO CONTACT Submit complete ms. No queries, please. Send to only *1* Clarion editor.

TERMS Pays 5-10% royalty on retail price. Pays minimum of $4,000 advance. Responds in 2 months to queries.

TIPS "Looks for freshness, enthusiasm—in short, life."

CLEIS PRESS

Cleis Press & Viva Editions, 2246 Sixth St., Berkeley CA 94710. (510)845-8000 or (800)780-2279. **Fax:** (510)845-8001. **E-mail:** cleis@cleispress.com. **E-mail:** bknight@cleispress.com. **Website:** www.cleispress. com. **Contact:** Brenda Knight, publisher. Estab. 1980. Cleis Press publishes provocative, intelligent books in the areas of sexuality, gay and lesbian studies, erotica, fiction, gender studies, and human rights. Publishes books that inform, enlighten, and entertain. Areas of interest include gift, inspiration, health, family and childcare, self-help, women's issues, reference, cooking. "We do our best to bring readers quality books

that celebrate life, inspire the mind, revive the spirit, and enhance lives all around. Our authors are practical visionaries; people who offer deep wisdom in a hopeful and helpful manner."

NEEDS "We are looking for high-quality fiction and nonfiction."

HOW TO CONTACT Submit complete ms. Include brief bio, list of publishing credits. Send SASE for return of ms or send a disposable ms and SASE for reply only.

TERMS Pays royalty on retail price. Responds in 2 month to queries.

TIPS "Be familiar with publishers' catalogs; be absolutely aware of your audience; research potential markets; present fresh new ways of looking at your topic; avoid 'PR' language and include publishing history in query letter."

☺ COACH HOUSE BOOKS

80 bpNichol Lane, Toronto ON M5S 3J4 Canada. (416)979-2217. **Fax:** (416)977-1158. **E-mail:** editor@ chbooks.com. **Website:** www.chbooks.com. **Contact:** Alana Wilcox, editorial director. Publishes trade paperback originals by Canadian authors. Guidelines online.

HOW TO CONTACT "Electronic submissions are welcome. Please send your complete ms, along with an introductory letter that describes your work and compares it to at least 2 current Coach House titles, explaining how your book would fit our list, and a literary CV listing your previous publications and relevant experience. If you would like your ms back, please enclose a large enough self-addressed envelope with adequate postage. If you don't want your ms back, a small stamped envelope or e-mail address is fine. We prefer electronic submissions. Please e-mail PDF files to editor@chbooks.com and include the cover letter and CV as a part of the ms. Please send your ms only once. Revised and updated versions will not be read, so make sure you're happy with your text before sending. You can also mail your ms. Please do not send it by ExpressPost or Canada Post courier—regular Canada Post mail is much more likely to arrive here. Be patient. We try to respond promptly, but we do receive hundreds of submissions, so it may take us several months to get back to you. Please do not call or e-mail to check on the status of your submission. We will answer you as promptly as possible."

TERMS Pays 10% royalty on retail price. Responds in 6 months to queries.

TIPS "We are not a general publisher, and publish only Canadian poetry, fiction, artist books and drama. We are interested primarily in innovative or experimental writing."

COFFEE HOUSE PRESS

79 13th NE, Suite 110, Minneapolis MN 55413. (612)338-0125. **Fax:** (612)338-4004. **E-mail:** info@coffeehousepress.org. **Website:** www.coffeehousepress.org. **Contact:** Molly Fuller, production editor. Estab. 1984. This successful nonprofit small press has received numerous grants from various organizations including the NEA, the McKnight Foundation and Target. Books published by Coffee House Press have won numerous honors and awards. Example: The Book of Medicines by Linda Hogan won the Colorado Book Award for Poetry and the Lannan Foundation Literary Fellowship. Publishes hardcover and trade paperback originals. Book catalog and ms guidelines online.

NEEDS Seeks literary novels, short story collections and poetry.

HOW TO CONTACT Query first with outline and samples (20-30 pages) during annual reading periods (March 1-31 and September 1-30).

TERMS Responds in 4-6 weeks to queries; up to 6 months to mss.

TIPS "Look for our books at stores and libraries to get a feel for what we like to publish. No phone calls, e-mails, or faxes."

ⒶⒺ⊘ CONSTABLE & ROBINSON, LTD.

55-56 Russell Square, London WC1B 4HP United Kingdom. (0208)741-3663. **Fax:** (0208)748-7562. **E-mail:** reader@constablerobinson.com. **Website:** constablerobinson.co.uk. Publishes hardcover and trade paperback originals. Book catalog available free.

NEEDS Publishes "crime fiction (mysteries) and historical crime fiction." Length 80,000 words minimum; 130,000 words maximum.

HOW TO CONTACT *Agented submissions only.*

TERMS Pays royalty. Pays advance. Responds in 1-3 months.

⊙ COTEAU BOOKS

Thunder Creek Publishing Co-operative Ltd., 2517 Victoria Ave., Regina SK S4P 0T2 Canada. (306)777-0170. **Fax:** (306)522-5152. **E-mail:** coteau@coteaubooks.com. **Website:** www.coteaubooks.com. **Contact:** Geoffrey Ursell, publisher. Estab. 1975. "Our mission is to publish the finest in Canadian fiction, nonfiction, poetry, drama, and children's literature, with an emphasis on Saskatchewan and prairie writers. De-emphasizing science fiction, picture books." Publishes trade paperback originals and reprints. Book catalog available free. Guidelines online.

NEEDS *Canadian authors only.* No science fiction. No children's picture books.

HOW TO CONTACT Query.

TERMS Pays 10% royalty on retail price. Responds in 3 months.

TIPS "Look at past publications to get an idea of our editorial program. We do not publish romance, horror, or picture books but are interested in juvenile and teen fiction from Canadian authors. Submissions, even queries, must be made in hard copy only. We do not accept simultaneous/multiple submissions. Check our website for new submission timing guidelines."

COVENANT COMMUNICATIONS, INC.

920 E. State Rd., Suite F, P.O. Box 416, American Fork UT 84003. (801)756-9966. **Fax:** (801)756-1049. **E-mail:** submissionsdesk@covenant-lds.com. **Website:** www.covenant-lds.com. **Contact:** Kathryn Gordon, managing editor. Estab. 1958. "Currently emphasizing inspirational, doctrinal, historical, biography, and fiction." Guidelines online.

NEEDS "Mss do not necessarily have to include LDS/Mormon characters or themes, but cannot contain profanity, sexual content, gratuitous violence, witchcraft, vampires, and other such material."

HOW TO CONTACT Submit complete ms.

TERMS Pays 6-15% royalty on retail price. Responds in 1 month on queries; 4-6 months on mss.

TIPS "We are actively looking for new, fresh regency romance authors."

CRAIGMORE CREATIONS

PMB 114, 4110 SE Hawthorne Blvd., Portland OR 97124. (503)477-9562. **E-mail:** info@craigmorecreations.com. **Website:** www.craigmorecreations.com. Estab. 2009.

HOW TO CONTACT Submit proposal package. See website for detailed submission guidelines.

⊕ CRESCENT MOON PUBLISHING

P.O. Box 393, Maidstone Kent ME14 5XU United Kingdom. (44)(162)272-9593. **E-mail:** cresmopub@yahoo.co.uk. **Website:** www.crmoon.com. **Contact:** Jeremy Robinson, director (arts, media, cinema, literature); Cassidy Hushes (visual arts). Estab. 1988. "Our mission is to publish the best in contemporary work, in poetry, fiction, and critical studies, and selections from the great writers. Currently emphasizing nonfiction (media, film, music, painting). De-emphasizing children's books." Publishes hardcover and trade paperback originals. Book catalog and ms guidelines free.

IMPRINTS *Joe's Press, Pagan America Magazine, Passion Magazine.*

NEEDS "We do not publish much fiction at present but will consider high-quality new work."

HOW TO CONTACT Query with SASE. Submit outline, clips, 2 sample chapters, bio.

TERMS Pays royalty. Pays negotiable advance. Responds in 2 months to queries; 4 months to proposals and mss.

TIPS "Our audience is interested in new contemporary writing."

⊘ CRICKET BOOKS

Imprint of Carus Publishing, 70 E. Lake St., Suite 300, Chicago IL 60601. (603)924-7209. **Fax:** (603)924-7380. **Website:** www.cricketmag.com. **Contact:** Submissions Editor. Estab. 1999. Cricket Books publishes picture books, chapter books, and middle-grade novels. Publishes hardcover originals. *Currently not accepting queries or mss. Check website for submissions details and updates.*

TERMS Pays up to 10% royalty on retail price. Average advance: $1,500 and up.

TIPS "Take a look at the recent titles to see what sort of materials we're interested in, especially for nonfiction. Please note that we aren't doing the sort of strictly educational nonfiction that other publishers specialize in."

CRIMSON ROMANCE

Adams Media, a division of F+W Media, Inc., 57 Littlefield St., Avon MA 02322. (508)427-7100. **E-mail:** editorcrimson@gmail.com. **Website:** crimsonromance.com. **Contact:** Jennifer Lawler, editor. "Direct to e-book imprint of Adams Media." Publishes electronic originals.

NEEDS "We're open to romance submissions in 5 popular subgenres: romantic suspense, contemporary, paranormal, historical, and erotic romance. Within those subgenres, we are flexible about what happens. It's romance, so there must be a happily-ever-after, but we're open to how your characters get there. You won't come up against preconceived ideas about what can or can't happen in romance or what kind of characters you can or can't have. Our only rule is everyone has to be a consenting adult. Other than that, we're looking for smart, savvy heroines, fresh voices, and new takes on old favorite themes." Length: 55,000-90,000 words.

HOW TO CONTACT Submit brief description of work–please, no attachments.

Ⓐ ⊘ CROWN PUBLISHING GROUP

Random House, Inc., 1745 Broadway, New York NY 10019. (212)782-9000. **E-mail:** crownosm@randomhouse.com. **Website:** www.randomhouse.com/crown. Estab. 1933. Publishes popular fiction and nonfiction hardcover originals. *Agented submissions only.* See website for more details.

IMPRINTS Amphoto Books; Back Stage Books; Billboard Books; Broadway Books; Clarkson Potter; Crown; Crown Archetype; Crown Business; Crown Forum; Harmony Books; Image Books; Potter Craft; Potter Style; Ten Speed Press; Three Rivers Press; Waterbrook Multnomah; Watson-Guptill.

CRYSTAL SPIRIT PUBLISHING, INC.

P.O. Box 12506, Durham NC 27709. **E-mail:** crystalspiritinc@gmail.com. **E-mail:** submissions@crystalspiritinc.com. **Website:** www.crystalspiritinc.com. **Contact:** Vanessa S. O'Neal, senior editor. Estab. 2004. "Our readers are lovers of high-quality books that are sold as direct sales, in bookstores, gift shops and placed in libraries and schools. They support independent authors and they expect works that will provide them with entertainment, inspiration, romance, and education. Our audience loves to read and will embrace niche authors that love to write." Publishes hardcover, trade paperback, mass-market paperback, and electronic originals. Book catalog and ms guidelines online.

HOW TO CONTACT Submit cover letter, synopsis, and 30 pages by USPS mail or e-mail.

TERMS Pays 20-45% royalty on retail price. Responds in 3-6 months to mss.

TIPS "Submissions are accepted for publication throughout the year. Works should be positive and nonthreatening. Typed pages only. Nontyped entries will not be reviewed or returned. Ensure that all contact information is correct, abide by the submission guidelines and do not send follow-up e-mails or calls."

CUP OF TEA BOOKS

PageSpring Publishing, P.O. Box 21133, Columbus OH 43221. **E-mail:** weditor@pagespringpublishing.com. **Website:** www.cupofteabooks.com. Estab. 2012. "Cup of Tea Books publishes novel-length women's fiction.

We are interested in finely drawn characters, a compelling story, and deft writing. We accept e-mail queries only; see our website for details." Publishes trade paperback and electronic originals. Guidelines online.

HOW TO CONTACT Submit proposal package via e-mail. Include synopsis and the first 30 pages.

TERMS Pays royalty. Responds in 1 month.

DAW BOOKS, INC.

Penguin Group (USA), 375 Hudson St., New York NY 10014-3658. (212)366-2096. **Fax:** (212)366-2090. **E-mail:** daw@us.penguingroup.com. **Website:** www.dawbooks.com. **Contact:** Peter Stampfel, submissions editor. Estab. 1971. DAW Books publishes science fiction and fantasy. Publishes hardcover and paperback originals and reprints. Guidelines online.

NEEDS "Currently seeking modern urban fantasy and paranormals. We like character-driven books with appealing protagonists, engaging plots, and well-constructed worlds. We accept both agented and unagented mss."

HOW TO CONTACT Submit entire ms, cover letter, SASE. "Do not submit your only copy of anything. The average length of the novels we publish varies but is almost never less than 80,000 words."

TERMS Pays in royalties with an advance negotiable on a book-by-book basis. Responds in 3 months.

KATHY DAWSON BOOKS

Penguin Group, 375 Hudson St., New York NY 10014. (212)366-2000. **Website:** kathydawsonbooks.tumblr.com. **Contact:** Kathy Dawson, vice-president and publisher. Estab. 2014. Mission statement: Publish stellar novels with unforgettable characters for children and teens that expand their vision of the world, sneakily explore the meaning of life, celebrate the written word, and last for generations. The imprint strives to publish tomorrow's award contenders: quality books with strong hooks in a variety of genres with universal themes and compelling voices—books that break the modl and the heart. Guidelines online.

HOW TO CONTACT Accepts fiction queries via snail mail only. Include cover sheet with one-sentence elevator pitch, main themes, author version of catalog copy for book, first 10 pages of ms (double-spaced, Times Roman, 12 point type), and publishing history. No SASE needed. Responds only if interested.

TERMS Responds only if interested.

DELACORTE PRESS

Imprint of Random House Publishing Group, 1745 Broadway, New York NY 10019. (212)782-9000. **Web**site: www.randomhouse.com. Publishes middle-grade and young adult fiction in hard cover, trade paperback, mass-market and digest formats. Publishes middle-grade and young adult fiction in hardcover, trade paperback, mass-market and digest formats.

○ All other query letters or ms submissions must be submitted through an agent or at the request of an editor. No e-mail queries.

DEL REY BOOKS

Imprint of Random House Publishing Group, 1745 Broadway, 18th Floor, New York NY 10019. (212)782-9000. **Website:** www.randomhouse.com. Estab. 1977. Del Rey publishes top level fantasy, alternate history, and science fiction. Publishes hardcover, trade paperback, and mass-market originals and mass-market paperback reprints.

IMPRINTS Del Rey/Manga, Del Rey/Lucas Books.

HOW TO CONTACT *Agented submissions only.*

TERMS Pays royalty on retail price. Pays competitive advance.

TIPS "Del Rey is a reader's house. Pay particular attention to plotting, strong characters, and dramatic, satisfactory conclusions. It must be/feel believable. That's what the readers like. In terms of mass market, we basically created the field of fantasy bestsellers. Not that it didn't exist before, but we put the mass into mass market."

DIAL BOOKS FOR YOUNG READERS

Imprint of Penguin Group (USA), 345 Hudson St., New York NY 10014. (212)366-2000. **Website:** www.penguin.com/youngreaders. **Contact:** Lauri Hornik, president/publisher. Estab. 1961. "Dial Books for Young Readers publishes quality picture books for ages 18 months-6 years; lively, believable novels for middle readers and young adults; and occasional nonfiction for middle readers and young adults." Publishes hardcover originals. Book catalog and guidelines online.

NEEDS Especially looking for lively and well-written novels for middle-grade and young adult children involving a convincing plot and believable characters. The subject matter or theme should not already be overworked in previously published books. The approach must not be demeaning to any minority group, nor should the roles of female characters (or others) be stereotyped, though we don't think books should be didactic, or in any way message-y. No topics inappropriate for the juvenile, young adult, and middle-grade audiences. No plays.

HOW TO CONTACT Accepts unsolicited queries and up to 10 pages for longer works and unsolicited mss for picture books. Will only respond if interested.
TERMS Pays royalty. Pays varies advance. Responds in 4-6 months to queries.
TIPS "Our readers are anywhere from preschool age to teenage. Picture books must have strong plots, lots of action, unusual premises, or universal themes treated with freshness and originality. Humor works well in these books. A very well-thought-out and intelligently presented book has the best chance of being taken on. Genre isn't as much of a factor as presentation."

DIVERTIR

P.O. Box 232, North Salem NH 03073. **E-mail:** info@divertirpublishing.com; query@divertirpublishing.com. **Website:** www.divertirpublishing.com. **Contact:** Kenneth Tupper, publisher. Estab. 2009. Publishes trade paperback and electronic originals. Catalog online. Guidelines online.
NEEDS "We are particularly interested in the following: science fiction, fantasy, historical, alternate history, contemporary mythology, mystery and suspense, paranormal, and urban fantasy."
HOW TO CONTACT Electronically submit proposal package, including synopsis and query letter with author's bio.
TERMS Pays 10-15% royalty on wholesale price (for novels and nonfiction). Responds in 1-2 months on queries; 3-4 months on proposals and mss.
TIPS "Please see our Author Info page (online) for more information."

DOWN THE SHORE PUBLISHING

P.O. Box 100, West Creek NJ 08092. **Fax:** (609)597-0422. **E-mail:** info@down-the-shore.com. **Website:** www.down-the-shore.com. "Bear in mind that our market is regional-New Jersey, the Jersey Shore, the mid-Atlantic, and seashore and coastal subjects." Publishes hardcover and trade paperback originals and reprints. Book catalog online. Guidelines online.
HOW TO CONTACT Query with SASE. Submit proposal package, clips, 1-2 sample chapters.
TERMS Pays royalty on wholesale or retail price, or makes outright purchase. Responds in 3 months to queries.
TIPS "Carefully consider whether your proposal is a good fit for our established market."

DUFOUR EDITIONS

P.O. Box 7, 124 Byers Rd., Chester Springs PA 19425. (610)458-5005 or (800)869-5677. **Fax:** (610)458-7103.

Website: www.dufoureditions.com. Estab. 1948. "We publish literary fiction by good writers which is well received and achieves modest sales. De-emphsazing poetry and nonfiction." Publishes hardcover originals, trade paperback originals and reprints. Book catalog available free.
NEEDS "We like books that are slightly off-beat, different and well-written."
HOW TO CONTACT Query with SASE.
TERMS Pays $100-500 advance. Responds in 3-6 months.

ⒶⓄ THOMAS DUNNE BOOKS

Imprint of St. Martin's Press, 175 Fifth Ave., New York NY 10010. (212)674-5151. **Website:** www.thomasdunnebooks.com. Estab. 1986. "Thomas Dunne Books publishes popular trade fiction and nonfiction. With an output of approximately 175 titles each year, his group covers a range of genres including commercial and literary fiction, thrillers, biography, politics, sports, popular science, and more. The list is intentionally eclectic and includes a wide range of fiction and nonfiction, from first books to international bestsellers." Publishes hardcover and trade paperback originals, and reprints. Book catalog and ms guidelines free.
HOW TO CONTACT *Accepts agented submissions only.*

ⒶⓄ DUTTON ADULT TRADE

Imprint of Penguin Group (USA), Inc., 375 Hudson St., New York NY 10014. (212)366-2000. **Website:** us.penguingroup.com. Estab. 1852. "Dutton currently publishes 45 hardcovers a year, roughly half fiction and half nonfiction." Publishes hardcover originals. Book catalog online.
HOW TO CONTACT Agented submissions only. *No unsolicited mss.*
TERMS Pays royalty. Pays negotiable advance.
TIPS "Write the complete ms and submit it to an agent or agents. They will know exactly which editor will be interested in a project."

DUTTON CHILDREN'S BOOKS

Penguin Group (USA), 375 Hudson St., New York NY 10014. **E-mail:** duttonpublicity@us.penguingroup.com. **Website:** www.penguin.com. **Contact:** Julie Strauss-Gabel, vice president and publisher. Estab. 1852. Dutton Children's Books publishes high-quality fiction and nonfiction for readers ranging from preschoolers to young adults on a variety of subjects. Currently emphasizing middle-grade and young adult novels that offer a fresh perspective. De-emphasizing photographic nonfiction and picture books that teach a lesson. Publishes hardcover originals as well as novelty formats.

○ "Cultivating the creative talents of authors and illustrators and publishing books with purpose and heart continue to be the mission and joy at Dutton."

NEEDS Dutton Children's Books has a diverse, general interest list that includes picture books; easy-to-read books; and fiction for all ages, from first chapter books to young adult readers.

HOW TO CONTACT Query. Responds only if interested.

TERMS Pays royalty on retail price. Pays advance.

Ⓐ⦸ THE ECCO PRESS

10 E. 53rd St., New York NY 10022. (212)207-7000. **Fax:** (212)702-2460. **Website:** www.harpercollins.com. **Contact:** Daniel Halpern, editor in chief. Estab. 1970. Publishes hardcover and trade paperback originals and reprints.

NEEDS Literary, short story collections. "We can publish possibly 1 or 2 original novels a year."

HOW TO CONTACT *Does not accept unsolicited mss.*

TERMS Pays royalty. Pays negotiable advance.

TIPS "We are always interested in first novels and feel it's important that they be brought to the attention of the reading public."

○ EDGE SCIENCE FICTION AND FANTASY PUBLISHING/TESSERACT BOOKS

Hades Publications, Box 1714, Calgary AB T2P 2L7 Canada. (403)254-0160. **Fax:** (403)254-0456. **Website:** www.edgewebsite.com. **Contact:** Editorial Manager. Estab. 1996. "We are an independent publisher of science fiction and fantasy novels in hard cover or trade paperback format. We produce high-quality books with lots of attention to detail and lots of marketing effort. We want to encourage, produce and promote thought-provoking and fun-to-read science fiction and fantasy literature by 'bringing the magic alive: one world at a time' (as our motto says) with each new book released." Publishes hardcover and trade paperback originals. Guidelines online.

NEEDS "We are looking for all types of fantasy and science fiction, horror except juvenile/young adlut, erotica, religious fiction, short stories, dark/gruesome fantasy, or poetry." Length: 75,000-100,000/words.

HOW TO CONTACT Submit first 3 chapters and synopsis. Check website for guidelines. Include estimated word count.

TERMS Pays 10% royalty on wholesale price. Negotiable advance. Responds in 4-5 months to mss.

WILLIAM B. EERDMANS PUBLISHING CO.

2140 Oak Industrial Dr. NE, Grand Rapids MI 49505. (616)459-4591. **Fax:** (616)459-6540. **E-mail:** info@eerdmans.com. **Website:** www.eerdmans.com. **Contact:** Jon Pott, editor in chief. Estab. 1911. "The majority of our adult publications are religious and most of these are academic or semi-academic in character (as opposed to inspirational or celebrity books), though we also publish general trade books on the Christian life. Our nonreligious titles, most of them in regional history or on social issues, aim, similarly, at an educated audience." Publishes hardcover and paperback originals and reprints. Book catalog and ms guidelines free.

HOW TO CONTACT Query with SASE.

TERMS Responds in 4 weeks.

ELLORA'S CAVE PUBLISHING, INC.

1056 Home Ave., Akron OH 44310. **E-mail:** submissions@ellorascave.com. **Website:** www.ellorascave.com. Estab. 2000. Publishes electronic originals and reprints; print books. Guidelines online. "Read and follow detailed submission instructions."

NEEDS Erotic romance and erotica fiction of every subgenre, including gay/lesbian, menage and more, and BDSM. All must have abundant, explicit, and graphic erotic content.

HOW TO CONTACT Submit electronically only; cover e-mail as defined in our submission guidelines plus 1 attached .docx file containing full synopsis, first 3 chapters, and last chapter.

TERMS Pays 45% royalty on amount received. Responds in 2-4 months to mss. No queries.

TIPS "Our audience is romance readers who want explicit sexual detail. They come to us because we offer sex with romance, plot, emotion. In addition to erotic romance with happy-ever-after endings, we also publish pure erotica, detailing sexual adventure and experimentation."

FAMILIUS

1254 Commerce Way, Sanger CA 93657. (559)876-2170. **Fax:** (559)876-2180. **E-mail:** bookideas@familius.com. **Website:** familius.com. **Contact:** Michele Robbins, acquisitions editor. Estab. 2011. Familius is all about strengthening families. Collective, the authors and staff have experienced a wide slice of the family-life spectrum. Some come from broken homes. Some are married and in the throes of managing a bursting household. Some are preparing to start families of their own. Together, they publish books, articles, and videos that help families be happy. Publishes hardcover, trade paperback, and electronic originals and reprints. Catalog online. Guidelines online.

NEEDS All fiction must align with Familius values statement listed on the website footer.

HOW TO CONTACT Submit a proposal package, including a synopsis, 3 sample chapters, and your author platform.

TERMS Authors are paid 10-30% royalty on wholesale price. Responds in 1 month to queries and proposals; 2 months to mss.

FANTAGRAPHICS BOOKS, INC.

7563 Lake City Way NE, Seattle WA 98115. (206)524-1967. **Fax:** (206)524-2104. **Website:** www.fantagraphics.com. **Contact:** Submissions Editor. Estab. 1976. Publishes comics for thinking readers. Does not want mainstream genres of superhero, vigilante, horror, fantasy, or science fiction. Publishes original trade paperbacks. Book catalog online. Guidelines online.

NEEDS "Fantagraphics is an independent company with a modus operandi different from larger, factory-like corporate comics publishers. If your talents are limited to a specific area of expertise (i.e. inking, writing, etc.), then you will need to develop your own team before submitting a project to us. We want to see an idea that is fully fleshed-out in your mind, at least, if not on paper. Submit a minimum of 5 fully-inked pages of art, a synopsis, SASE, and a brief note stating approximately how many issues you have in mind."

TERMS Responds in 2-3 months to queries.

TIPS "Take note of the originality and diversity of the themes and approaches to drawing in such Fantagraphics titles as *Love & Rockets* (stories of life in Latin America and Chicano L.A.), *Palestine* (journalistic autobiography in the Middle East), *Eightball* (surrealism mixed with kitsch culture in stories alternately humorous and painfully personal), and *Naughty Bits* (feminist humor and short stories which both attack and commiserate). Try to develop your own, equally individual voice; originality, aesthetic maturity, and graphic storytelling skill are the signs by which Fantagraphics judges whether or not your submission is ripe for publication."

FARRAR, STRAUS & GIROUX

18 W. 18th St., New York NY 10011. (646)307-5151. **Website:** us.macmillan.com. **Contact:** Editorial Department. Estab. 1946. "We publish original and well-written material for all ages." Publishes hardcover originals and trade paperback reprints. Catalog available by request. Guidelines online.

NEEDS Do not query picture books; just send ms. Do not fax or e-mail queries or mss.

HOW TO CONTACT Send cover letter describing submission with first 50 pages.

TERMS Pays 2-6% royalty on retail price for paperbacks, 3-10% for hardcovers. Pays $3,000-25,000 advance. Responds in 2-3 months.

FARRAR, STRAUS & GIROUX
FOR YOUNG READERS

Macmillan Children's Publishing Group, 175 Fifth Ave., New York NY 10010. (212)741-6900. **Fax:** (212)633-2427. **E-mail:** childrens.editorial@fsgbooks.com. **Website:** www.fsgkidsbooks.com. Estab. 1946. Book catalog available by request. Ms guidelines online.

NEEDS All levels: all categories. "Original and well-written material for all ages."

HOW TO CONTACT Submit cover letter, first 50 pages by mail only.

TIPS "Study our catalog before submitting. We will see illustrators' portfolios by appointment. Don't ask for criticism and/or advice—due to the volume of submissions we receive, it's just not possible. Never send originals. Always enclose SASE."

Ⓐⵔ FAWCETT

The Ballantine Publishing Group, A Division of Random House, Inc., 1745 Broadway, New York NY 10019. **Website:** www.randomhouse.com. Estab. 1955. Major publisher of mystery mass-market and trade paperbacks. Publishes paperback originals and reprints.

HOW TO CONTACT Agented submissions only. *All unsolicited mss returned.*

FENCE BOOKS

Science Library 320, Univ. of Albany, 1400 Washington Ave., Albany NY 12222. (518)591-8162. **E-mail:** fencesubmissions@gmail.com. **E-mail:** peter.n.fence@gmail.com. **Website:** www.fenceportal.org. **Contact:** Submissions Manager. Closed to submissions until June 15. Check website for details. Publishes hardcover originals. Guidelines online.

HOW TO CONTACT Submit via contests and occasional open reading periods.

DAVID FICKLING BOOKS

31 Beamont St., Oxford OX1 2NP United Kingdom. (018)65-339000. **Fax:** (018)65-339009. **E-mail:** submissions@davidficklingbooks.com. **Website:** www.davidficklingbooks.co.uk. **Contact:** Simon Mason, managing editor. David Fickling Books is a story house. Guidelines online.

NEEDS Considers all categories.

HOW TO CONTACT Submit cover letter and 3 sample chapters as PDF attachment saved in format "Author Name_Full Title."

TERMS Responds to mss in 3 months, if interested.

TIPS "We adore stories for all ages, in both text and pictures. Quality is our watch word."

FIRST SECOND

Macmillan Children's Publishing Group, 175 5th Ave., New York NY 10010. **E-mail:** mail@firstsecondbooks.com. **Website:** www.firstsecondbooks.com. First Second is a publisher of graphic novels and an imprint of Macmillan Children's Publishing Group. First Second does not accept unsolicited submissions. Catalog online.

TERMS Responds in about 6 weeks.

FLUX

Llewellyn Worldwide, Ltd., Llewellyn Worldwide, Ltd., 2143 Wooddale Dr., Woodbury MN 55125. (651)312-8613. **Fax:** (651)291-1908. **Website:** www.fluxnow.com. Estab. 2005. "Flux seeks to publish authors who see YA as a point of view, not a reading level. We look for books that try to capture a slice of teenage experience, whether in real or imagined worlds." Book catalog and guidelines online.

NEEDS Young Adults: adventure, contemporary, fantasy, history, humor, problem novels, religion, science fiction, sports, suspense. Average word length: 50,000.

HOW TO CONTACT *Accepts agented submissions only.*

TERMS Pays royalties of 10-15% based on wholesale price.

TIPS "Read contemporary teen books. Be aware of what else is out there. If you don't read teen books, you probably shouldn't write them. Know your audience. Write incredibly well. Do not condescend."

FOLDED WORD

79 Tracy Way, Meredith NH 03253. **E-mail:** editors@foldedword.com. **Website:** www.foldedword.com. Estab. 2008. "Folded Word is an independent literary press. Our focus? Connecting new voices to readers. Our goal? To make poetry and fiction accessible for the widest audience possible both on and off the page."

TIPS "We are seeking nonformulaic narratives that have a strong sense of place and/or time, especially the exploration of unfamiliar place/time."

FORWARD MOVEMENT

412 Sycamore St., Cincinnati OH 45202. (513)721-6659; (800)543-1813. **Fax:** (513)721-0729. **E-mail:** rthompson@forwardmovement.org. **Website:** www.forwardmovement.org. **Contact:** Richelle Thompson, managing editor. Estab. 1934. "Forward Movement was established to help reinvigorate the life of the church. Many titles focus on the life of prayer, where our relationship with God is centered, death, marriage, baptism, recovery, joy, the Episcopal Church and more. Currently emphasizing prayer/spirituality." Book catalog free. Guidelines online.

TERMS Responds in 1 month.

TIPS "Audience is primarily Episcopalians and other Christians."

FOUR WAY BOOKS

Box 535, Village Station, New York NY 10014. **E-mail:** editors@fourwaybooks.com. **Website:** www.fourwaybooks.com. **Contact:** Martha Rhodes, director. Estab. 1993. "Four Way Books is a not-for-profit literary press dedicated to publishing poetry and short fiction by emerging and established writers. Each year, Four Way Books publishes the winners of its national poetry competitions, as well as collections accepted through general submission, panel selection, and solicitation by the editors."

NEEDS Open reading period: June 1-30. Book-length story collections and novellas. Submission guidelines will be posted online at end of May. Does not want novels or translations.

FRANCES LINCOLN CHILDREN'S BOOKS

Frances Lincoln, 74-77 White Lion St., Islington, London N1 9PF United Kingdom. (44)(20)7284-4009. **E-mail:** fl@franceslincoln.com. **Website:** www.franceslincoln.com. Estab. 1977. "Our company was founded by Frances Lincoln in 1977. We published our first books 2 years later, and we have been creating illustrated books of the highest quality ever since, with special emphasis on gardening, walking and the outdoors, art, architecture, design and landscape. In 1983, we started to publish illustrated books for children. Since then we have won many awards and prizes with both fiction and nonfiction children's books."

NEEDS Average word length: picture books—1,000; young readers—9,788; middle readers—20,653; young adults—35,407.

HOW TO CONTACT Query by e-mail.

TERMS Responds in 6 weeks to mss.

FREE SPIRIT PUBLISHING, INC.

217 Fifth Ave. N., Suite 200, Minneapolis MN 55401-1299. (612)338-2068. **Fax:** (612)337-5050. **E-mail:** acquisitions@freespirit.com. **Website:** www.freespirit.com. Estab. 1983. "We believe passionately in empowering kids to learn to think for themselves and make their own good choices." Publishes trade paperback originals and reprints. Book catalog and ms guidelines online.

◯ Free Spirit does not accept general fiction, poetry or storybook submissions.

NEEDS "We will consider fiction that relates directly to select areas of focus. Please review catalog and author guidelines (both available online) for details before submitting proposal. If you'd like material returned, enclose a SASE with sufficient postage."

HOW TO CONTACT Accepts queries only—not submissions—by e-mail.

TERMS Pays advance. Responds to proposals in 4-6 months.

TIPS "Our books are issue-oriented, jargon-free, and solution-focused. Our audience is children, teens, teachers, parents and youth counselors. We are especially concerned with kids' social and emotional well-being and look for books with ready-to-use strategies for coping with today's issues at home or in school—written in everyday language. We are not looking for academic or religious materials, or books that analyze problems with the nation's school systems. Instead, we want books that offer practical, positive advice so kids can help themselves, and parents and teachers can help kids succeed."

GERTRUDE PRESS

P.O. Box 83948, Portland OR 97283. (503)515-8252. **E-mail:** edelehoy@fc.edu. **Website:** www.gertrudepress.org. **Contact:** Justus Ballard (all fiction). Estab. 2005. "Gertrude Press is a nonprofit organization developing and showcasing the creative talents of lesbian, gay, bisexual, trans, queer-identified and allied individuals. We publish limited-edition fiction and poetry chapbooks plus the biannual literary journal, *Gertrude*." Reads chapbook mss only through contests.

TIPS Sponsors poetry and fiction chapbook contest. Prize is $50 and 50 contributor's copies. Submission guidelines and fee information on website. "Read the journal and sample published work. We are not impressed by pages of publications; your work should speak for itself."

GIVAL PRESS

Gival Press, LLC, P.O. Box 3812, Arlington VA 22203. (703)351-0079. **E-mail:** givalpress@yahoo.com. **Website:** www.givalpress.com. **Contact:** Robert L. Giron, editor in chief (area of interest: literary). Estab. 1998. Publishes trade paperback, electronic originals, and reprints. Book online. Guidelines online.

HOW TO CONTACT Always query first via e-mail; provide description, author's bio, and supportive material.

TERMS Pays royalty. Responds in 3-5 months.

TIPS "Our audience is those who read literary works with depth to the work. Visit our website—there is much to be read/learned from the numerous pages."

◯ THE GLENCANNON PRESS

P.O. Box 1428, El Cerrito CA 94530. (510)528-4216. **Fax:** (510)528-3194. **E-mail:** merships@yahoo.com. **Website:** www.glencannon.com. **Contact:** Bill Harris (maritime, maritime children's). Estab. 1993. "We publish quality books about ships and the sea." Average print order: 1,000. Member PMA, BAIPA. Distributes titles through Baker & Taylor. Promotes titles through direct mail, magazine advertising and word of mouth. Accepts unsolicited mss. Often comments on rejected mss. Publishes hardcover and paperback originals and hardcover reprints.

IMPRINTS Smyth: perfect binding; illustrations.

HOW TO CONTACT Submit complete ms. Include brief bio, list of publishing credits. Send SASE for return of ms or send a disposable ms and SASE for reply only.

TERMS Pays 10-20% royalty. Responds in 1 month to queries; 2 months to mss.

TIPS "Write a good story in a compelling style."

◯◯ DAVID R. GODINE, PUBLISHER

15 Court Square, Suite 320, Boston MA 02108. (617)451-9600. **Fax:** (617)350-0250. **E-mail:** info@godine.com. **Website:** www.godine.com. Estab. 1970. "We publish books that matter for people who care." This publisher is no longer considering unsolicited mss of any type. Only interested in agented material.

◯◯ GOLDEN BOOKS FOR YOUNG READERS GROUP

1745 Broadway, New York NY 10019. **Website:** www.randomhouse.com. Estab. 1935. "Random House

Books aims to create books that nurture the hearts and minds of children, providing and promoting quality books and a rich variety of media that entertain and educate readers from 6 months to 12 years." *Random House-Golden Books does not accept unsolicited mss, only agented material.* They reserve the right not to return unsolicited material. Book catalog free on request.

TERMS Pays authors in royalties; sometimes buys mss outright.

⊕ GOOSE LANE EDITIONS

500 Beaverbrook Ct., Suite 330, Fredericton NB E3B 5X4 Canada. (506)450-4251. **Fax:** (506)459-4991. **E-mail:** submissions@gooselane.com. **Website:** www.gooselane.com. **Contact:** Angela Williams, publishing assistant. Estab. 1954. "Goose Lane publishes literary fiction and nonfiction from well-read and highly skilled Canadian authors." Publishes hardcover and paperback originals and occasional reprints.

NEEDS Our needs in fiction never change: Substantial, character-centered literary fiction. No children's, YA, mainstream, mass market, genre, mystery, thriller, confessional or science fiction.

HOW TO CONTACT Query with SAE with Canadian stamps or IRCs. No U.S. stamps.

TERMS Pays 8-10% royalty on retail price. Pays $500-3,000, negotiable advance. Responds in 6 months to queries.

TIPS "Writers should send us outlines and samples of books that show a very well-read author with highly developed literary skills. Our books are almost all by Canadians living in Canada; we seldom consider submissions from outside Canada. We consider submissions from outside Canada only when the author is Canadian and the book is of extraordinary interest to Canadian readers. We do not publish books for children or for the young adult market."

🅐🅪 GRAYWOLF PRESS

250 Third Ave. N.,, Suite 600, Minneapolis MN 55401. **E-mail:** wolves@graywolfpress.org. **Website:** www.graywolfpress.org. **Contact:** Lucia Cowles, editorial and administrative assistant. Estab. 1974. "Graywolf Press is an independent, nonprofit publisher dedicated to the creation and promotion of thoughtful and imaginative contemporary literature essential to a vital and diverse culture." Publishes trade cloth and paperback originals. Book catalog free. Guidelines online.

NEEDS "Familiarize yourself with our list first." No genre books (romance, western, science fiction, suspense)

HOW TO CONTACT Agented submissions only.

TERMS Pays royalty on retail price. Pays $1,000-25,000 advance. Responds in 3 months to queries.

🅐🅪 GREENWILLOW BOOKS

HarperCollins Publishers, 10 E. 53rd St., New York NY 10022. (212)207-7000. **Website:** www.greenwillowblog.com. Estab. 1974. *Does not accept unsolicited mss.* "Unsolicited mail will not be opened and will not be returned." Publishes hardcover originals, paperbacks, e-books, and reprints.

HOW TO CONTACT *Agented submissions only.*

TERMS Pays 10% royalty on wholesale price for first-time authors. Offers variable advance.

GREY GECKO PRESS

565 S. Mason Rd., Suite 154, Katy TX 77450. **Phone/Fax:** (866)535-6078. **E-mail:** info@greygeckopress.com. **E-mail:** submissions@greygeckopress.com. **Website:** www.greygeckopress.com. **Contact:** Submissions Coordinator. Estab. 2011. Publishes hardcover, trade paperback, and electronic originals. Guidelines online.

NEEDS "We do not publish extreme horror, erotica, or religious fiction. New and interesting stories by unpublished authors will always get our attention. Innovation is a core value of our company."

HOW TO CONTACT Use online submission page.

TERMS Pays 50-75% royalties on net revenue. Responds in 3-6 months.

TIPS "Be willing to be a part of the Grey Gecko family. Publishing with us is a partnership, not indentured servitude. Authors are expected and encouraged to be proactive and contribute to their book's success."

🅐🅪 GROSSET & DUNLAP PUBLISHERS

Penguin Putnam Inc., 345 Hudson St., New York NY 10014. **Website:** www.penguin.com. **Contact:** Francesco Sedita, vice president/publisher. Estab. 1898. Grosset & Dunlap publishes children's books that show children that reading is fun, with books that speak to their interests, and that are affordable so that children can build a home library of their own. Focus on licensed properties, series and readers. "Grosset & Dunlap publishes high-interest, affordable books for children ages 0-10 years. We focus on original series, licensed properties, readers and novelty books."

Publishes hardcover (few) and mass-market paperback originals.

HOW TO CONTACT *Agented submissions only.*

TERMS Pays royalty. Pays advance.

✪ GROUNDWOOD BOOKS

110 Spadina Ave., Suite 801, Toronto Ontario M5V 2K4 Canada. (416)363-4343. **Fax:** (416)363-1017. **E-mail:** ssutherland@groundwoodbooks.com. **Website:** www.groundwoodbooks.com. Publishes 19 picture books/year; 2 young readers/year; 3 middle readers/year; 3 young adult titles/year, approximately 2 nonfiction titles/year. Visit website for guidelines: www.houseofanansi.com/Groundwoodsubmissions.aspx.

NEEDS Recently published: *Lost Girl Found* by Leah Bassoff and Laura Deluca; *A Simple Case of Angels* by Carolnie Adderson; *This One Summer* by Mariko Tamaki and Jillian Tamaki.

HOW TO CONTACT Submit synopsis and sample chapters via e-mail.

TERMS Offers advances. Responds to mss in 6-8 months.

✪⊘ GROVE/ATLANTIC, INC.

841 Broadway, 4th Floor, New York NY 10003. (212)614-7850. **Fax:** (212)614-7886. **E-mail:** info@groveatlantic.com. **Website:** www.groveatlantic.com. Estab. 1917. "Due to limited resources of time and staffing, Grove/Atlantic cannot accept mss that do not come through a literary agent. In today's publishing world, agents are more important than ever, helping writers shape their work and navigate the main publishing houses to find the most appropriate outlet for a project." Publishes hardcover and trade paperback originals, and reprints. Book catalog available online.

IMPRINTS Black Cat, Atlantic Monthly Press, Grove Press.

HOW TO CONTACT *Agented submissions only.*

TERMS Pays 7.5-12.5% royalty. Makes outright purchase of $5-500,000. Responds in 1 month to queries; 2 months to proposals; 4 months to mss.

⊘✪ GUERNICA EDITIONS

1569 Heritage Way, Oakville Ontario L6M 2Z7 Canada. (905)599-5304. **Fax:** (416)981-7606. **E-mail:** michaelmirolla@guernicaeditions.com. **Website:** www.guernicaeditions.com. **Contact:** Michael Mirolla, editor/publisher (poetry, nonfiction, short stories, novels). Estab. 1978. Guernica Editions is a literary press that produces works of poetry, fiction and nonfiction often by writers who are ignored by the mainstream. Publishes trade paperback originals and reprints. Book catalog available online.

NEEDS "We wish to open up into the fiction world and focus less on poetry. We specialize in European, especially Italian, translations."

HOW TO CONTACT E-mail queries only.

TERMS Pays 8-10% royalty on retail price, or makes outright purchase of $200-5,000. Pays $450-750 advance. Responds in 1 month to queries. Responds in 6 months to proposals. Responds in 1 year to mss

HACHAI PUBLISHING

527 Empire Blvd., Brooklyn NY 11225. (718)633-0100. **Fax:** (718)633-0103. **Website:** www.hachai.com. **Contact:** Devorah Leah Rosenfeld, editor. Estab. 1988. Hachai is dedicated to producing high-quality Jewish children's literature, ages 2-10. Story should promote universal values such as sharing, kindness, etc. Publishes hardcover originals. Book catalog available free. Guidelines online.

○ "All books have spiritual/religious themes, specifically traditional Jewish content. We're seeking books about morals and values; the Jewish experience in current and Biblical times; and Jewish observance, Sabbath and holidays."

NEEDS Picture books and young readers: contemporary, historical fiction, religion. Middle readers: adventure, contemporary, problem novels, religion. Does not want to see fantasy, animal stories, romance, problem novels depicting drug use or violence.

HOW TO CONTACT Submit complete ms.

TERMS Work purchased outright from authors for $800-1,000. Responds in 2 months to mss.

TIPS "We are looking for books that convey the traditional Jewish experience in modern times or long ago; traditional Jewish observance such as Sabbath and holidays and mitzvos such as mezuzah, blessings etc.; positive character traits (middos) such as honesty, charity, respect, sharing, etc. We are also interested in historical fiction for young readers (7-10) written with a traditional Jewish perspective and highlighting the relevance of Torah in making important choices. Please, no animal stories, romance, violence, preachy sermonizing. Write a story that incorporates a moral, not a preachy morality tale. Originality is the key. We feel Hachai publications will appeal to a wider readership as parents become more interested in positive values for their children."

HADLEY RILLE BOOKS

PO Box 25466, Overland Park KS 66225. **E-mail:** subs@hadleyrillebooks.com. **Website:** www.hrbpress. com. **Contact:** Eric T. Reynolds, editor/publisher. Estab. 2005.

Currently closed to submissions. Check website for future reading periods.

TIPS "We aim to produce books that are aligned with current interest in the genres. Anthology markets are somewhat rare in SF these days, we feel there aren't enough good anthologies being published each year and part of our goal is to present the best that we can. We like stories that fit well within the guidelines of the particular anthology for which we are soliciting mss. Aside from that, we want stories with strong characters (not necessarily characters with strong personalities, flawed characters are welcome). We want a sense of wonder and awe. We want to feel the world around the character and so scene description is important (however, this doesn't always require a lot of text, just set the scene well so we don't wonder where the character is). We strongly recommend workshopping the story or having it critiqued in some way by readers familiar with the genre. We prefer clichés be kept to a bare minimum in the prose and avoid re-working old story lines."

HAMPTON ROADS PUBLISHING CO., INC.

665 Third St., Suite 400, San Francisco CA 94107. **E-mail:** submissions@rwwbooks.com. **Website:** www. redwheelweiser.com. **Contact:** Ms. Pat Bryce, Acquisitions Editor. Estab. 1989. "Our reason for being is to impact, uplift, and contribute to positive change in the world. We publish books that will enrich and empower the evolving consciousness of mankind. Though we are not necessarily limited in scope, we are most interested in mss on the following subjects: Body/Mind/Spirit, Health and Healing, Self-Help. Please be advised that at the moment we are not accepting: Fiction or Novelized material that does not pertain to body/mind/spirit, Channeled writing." " Publishes and distributes hardcover and trade paperback originals on subjects including metaphysics, health, complementary medicine, visionary fiction, and other related topics. Guidelines online.

"Please know that we only publish a handful of books every year, and that we pass on many well written, important works, simply because we cannot publish them all. We review each and every proposal very carefully. However, due to the volume of inquiries, we cannot respond to them all individually. Please give us 30 days to review your proposal. If you do not hear back from us within that time, this means we have decided to pursue other book ideas that we feel fit better within our plan."

NEEDS Fiction should have 1 or more of the following themes: spiritual, inspirational, metaphysical, i.e., past-life recall, out-of-body experiences, near-death experience, paranormal.

HOW TO CONTACT Query with SASE. Submit outline, 2 sample chapters, clips. Submit complete ms.

TERMS Pays royalty. Pays $1,000-50,000 advance. Responds in 2-4 months to queries; 1 month to proposals; 6-12 months to mss.

HARCOURT, INC., TRADE DIVISION

Imprint of Houghton Mifflin Harcourt Book Group, 215 Park Ave. S., New York NY 10003. **Website:** www. harcourtbooks.com. Publishes hardcover and trade paperback originals and trade paperback reprints. Book catalog for 9x12 envelope and first-class stamps. Guidelines available online.

HOW TO CONTACT Agented submissions only.

TERMS Pays 6-15% royalty on retail price. Pays $2,000 minimum advance.

HARKEN MEDIA

4308 201st Ave. NE, Sammamish WA 98074-6120. **E-mail:** info@harkenmedia.com. **E-mail:** manuscripts@ harkenmedia.com. **Website:** www.harkenmedia.com. **Contact:** Robert Sappington, editor in chief; Sheila Sappington, editor. Harken Media publishes original, unpublished novels possessing unique insights on compelling themes for young adult, new adult, or adult audiences. Compelling themes explore our humanity and in the process expand awareness and understand. Publishes hardcover originals, trade paperback originals, and electronic originals. Catalog available online at www.harkenmedia.com/p/catalog. html. Guidelines available online at www.harkenmedia.com/p/submmissions.html.

NEEDS "Our notion of entertainment encompasses a broad range of emotional responses from readers. We're as likely to publish a story that makes us cry as laugh. Manipulate our emotions; we like that. A novel's emotional impact is as important as its message. Thus, a successful story for Harken Media both entertains and enlightens."

HOW TO CONTACT Submit a proposal package including a synopsis and a detailed description fo theme(s) and unique insight(s).

TERMS Authors are paid 15-50% royalty on net wholesale price. Responds in 1 month to queries and proposals, 1-3 months to mss.

HARLEQUIN AMERICAN ROMANCE

225 Duncan Mill Rd., Don Mills ON M3B 3K9 Canada. **Website:** www.harlequin.com. **Contact:** Kathleen Scheibling, senior editor. "Upbeat and lively, fast paced and well plotted, American Romance celebrates the pursuit of love in the backyards, big cities and wide-open spaces of America." Publishes paperback originals and reprints. Books: newspaper print paper; web printing; perfect bound. Length: 55,000 words. "American Romance features heartwarming romances with strong family elements. These are stories about the pursuit of love, marriage and family in America today." Guidelines online.

NEEDS Needs "all-American stories with a range of emotional and sensual content that are supported by a sense of community within the plot's framework. In the confident and caring heroine, the tough but tender hero, and their dynamic relationship that is at the center of this series, real-life love is showcased as the best fantasy of all!"

HOW TO CONTACT Submit online.

TERMS Pays royalty. Offers advance.

☺ HARLEQUIN BLAZE

225 Duncan Mill Rd., Don Mills ON M3B 3K9 Canada. (416)445-5860. **Website:** www.harlequin.com. "Harlequin Blaze is a red-hot series. It is a vehicle to build and promote new authors who have a strong sexual edge to their stories. It is also the place to be for seasoned authors who want to create a sexy, sizzling, longer contemporary story." Publishes paperback originals. Guidelines online.

NEEDS "Sensuous, highly romantic, innovative plots that are sexy in premise and execution. The tone of the books can run from fun and flirtatious to dark and sensual. Submissions should have a very contemporary feel—what it's like to be young and single today. We are looking for heroes and heroines in their early 20s and up. There should be a a strong emphasis on the physical relationship between the couples. Fully described love scenes along with a high level of fantasy and playfulness." Length: 55,000-60,000 words.

TIPS "Are you a *Cosmo* girl at heart? A fan of *Sex and the City*? Or maybe you have a sexually adventurous spirit. If so, then Blaze is the series for you!"

HARLEQUIN DESIRE

233 Broadway, Suite 1001, New York NY 10279. (212)553-4200. **Website:** www.harlequin.com. **Contact:** Stacy Boyd, senior editor. Always powerful, passionate, and provocative. "Desire novels are sensual reads and a love scene or scenes are still needed. But there is no set number of pages that needs to be fulfilled. Rather, the level of sensuality must be appropriate to the storyline. Above all, every Silhouette Desire novel must fulfill the promise of a powerful, passionate and provocative read." Publishes paperback originals and reprints. Guidelines online.

NEEDS Looking for novels in which "the conflict is an emotional one, springing naturally from the unique characters you've chosen. The focus is on the developing relationship, set in a believable plot. Sensuality is key, but lovemaking is never taken lightly. Secondary characters and subplots need to blend with the core story. Innovative new directions in storytelling and fresh approaches to classic romantic plots are welcome." Mss must be 50,000-55,000 words.

TERMS Pays royalty. Offers advance.

☺ HARLEQUIN HQN

Imprint of Harlequin, 225 Duncan Mill Rd., Don Mills ON M3B 3K9 Canada. **Website:** harlequin.com. "HQN publishes romance in all subgenres—historical, contemporary, romantic suspense, paranormal—as long as the story's central focus is romance. Prospective authors can familiarize themselves with the wide range of books we publish by reading work by some of our current authors. The imprint is looking for a wide range of authors from known romance stars to first-time authors. At the moment, we are accepting only agented submissions—unagented authors may send a query letter to determine if their project suits our needs. Please send your projects to our New York Editorial Office." Publishes hardcover, trade paperback, and mass-market paperback originals.

HOW TO CONTACT Accepts unagented material. Length: 90,000 words.

TERMS Pays royalty. Pays advance.

☺ HARLEQUIN INTRIGUE

225 Duncan Mill Rd., Don Mills ON M3B 3K9 Canada. **Website:** www.eharlequin.com. Wants crime stories tailored to the series romance market packed with a variety of thrilling suspense and whodunit mystery. Word count: 55,000-60,000. Guidelines online.

HOW TO CONTACT Submit online.

⟳ HARLEQUIN SUPERROMANCE

225 Duncan Mill Rd., Don Mills ON M3B 3K9 Canada. **Website:** www.harlequin.com. **Contact:** Victoria Curran, senior editor. "The Harlequin Superromance line focuses on believable characters triumphing over true-to-life drama and conflict. At the heart of these contemporary stories should be a compelling romance that brings the reader along with the hero and heroine on their journey of overcoming the obstacles in their way and falling in love. Because of the longer length relevant subplots and secondary characters are welcome but not required. This series publishes a variety of story types—family sagas, romantic suspense, Westerns, to name a few—and tones from light to dramatic, emotional to suspenseful. Settings also vary from vibrant urban neighborhoods to charming small towns. The unifying element of Harlequin Superromance stories is the realistic treatment of character and plot. The characters should seem familiar to readers—similar to people they know in their own lives—and the circumstances within the realm of possibility. The stories should be layered and complex in that the conflicts should not be easily resolved. The best way to get an idea of we're looking for is to read what we're currently publishing. The aim of Superromance novels is to produce a contemporary, involving read with a mainstream tone in its situations and characters, using romance as the major theme. To achieve this, emphasis should be placed on individual writing styles and unique and topical ideas." Publishes paperback originals. Guidelines online.

NEEDS "The criteria for Superromance books are flexible. Aside from length (80,000 words), the determining factor for publication will always be quality. Authors should strive to break free of stereotypes, clichés and worn-out plot devices to create strong, believable stories with depth and emotional intensity. Superromance novels are intended to appeal to a wide range of romance readers."

HOW TO CONTACT Submit online.

TERMS Pays royalties. Pays advance.

TIPS "A general familiarity with current Superromance books is advisable to keep abreast of ever-changing trends and overall scope, but we don't want imitations. We look for sincere, heartfelt writing based on true-to-life experiences the reader can identify with. We are interested in innovation."

ⒶⓄ HARLEQUIN TEEN

Harlequin, 233 Broadway, Suite 1001, New York NY 10279. **Website:** www.harlequin.com. **Contact:** Natashya Wilson, executive editor. Harlequin Teen is a single-title program dedicated to building authors and publishing unique, memorable young-adult fiction.

NEEDS Harlequin Teen looks for fresh, authentic fiction featuring extraordinary characters and extraordinary stories set in contemporary, paranormal, fantasy, science-fiction, and historical worlds. Wants commercial, high-concept stories that capture the teen experience and will speak to readers with power and authenticity. All subgenres are welcome, so long as the book delivers a relevant reading experience that will resonate long after the book's covers are closed. Expects that most stories will include a compelling romantic element.

HOW TO CONTACT *Agented submissions only.*

ⒶⓄ HARPERCOLLINS

195 Broadway, New York NY 10007. (212)207-7000. **Website:** www.harpercollins.com. HarperCollins, one of the largest English language publishers in the world, is a broad-based publisher with strengths in academic, business and professional, children's, educational, general interest, and religious and spiritual books, as well as multimedia titles. Publishes hardcover and paperback originals and paperback reprints.

NEEDS "We look for a strong story line and exceptional literary talent."

HOW TO CONTACT Agented submissions only. *All unsolicited mss returned.*

TERMS Pays royalty. Pays negotiable advance.

TIPS "We do not accept any unsolicited material."

Ⓞ⟳ HARPERCOLLINS CANADA, LTD.

2 Bloor St. E., 20th Floor, Toronto ON M4W 1A8 Canada. (416)975-9334. **Fax:** (416)975-5223. **Website:** www.harpercollins.ca. Estab. 1989. *HarperCollins Canada is not accepting unsolicited material at this time.*

Ⓐ HARPERCOLLINS CHILDREN'S BOOKS/HARPERCOLLINS PUBLISHERS

195 Broadway, New York NY 10007. (212)207-7000. **Website:** www.harpercollins.com. **Contact:** Katherine Tegen, vice president and publisher; Anica Mrose Rissi, executive editor; Claudia Gabel, executive editor; Kathleen Duncan, general design assistant; Erica Dechavez, picture book assistant designer. HarperCollins, one of the largest English language publishers in the world, is a broad-based publisher with strengths in academic, business and professional, children's, educational, general interest, and religious

and spiritual books, as well as multimedia titles. Publishes hardcover and paperback originals and paperback reprints. Catalog online.

IMPRINTS HarperCollins Australia/New Zealand: Angus & Robertson, Fourth Estate, HarperBusiness, HarperCollins, HarperPerenniel, HarperReligious, HarperSports, Voyager; **HarperCollins Canada:** HarperFlamingoCanada, PerennialCanada; **HarperCollins Children's Books Group:** Amistad, Julie Andrews Collection, Avon, Joanna Cotler Books, Eos, Laura Geringer Books, Greenwillow Books, HarperAudio, HarperCollins Children's Books, HarperFestival, HarperTempest, HarperTrophy, Rayo, Katherine Tegen Books; **HarperCollins General Books Group:** Access, Amistad, Avon, Caedmon, Ecco, Eos, Fourth Estate, HarperAudio, HarperBusiness, HarperCollins, HarperEntertainment, HarperLargePrint, HarperResource, HarperSanFrancisco, HarperTorch, Harper Design International, Perennial, PerfectBound, Quill, Rayo, ReganBooks, William Morrow, William Morrow Cookbooks; **HarperCollins U.K.:** Collins Bartholomew, Collins, HarperCollins Crime & Thrillers, Collins Freedom to Teach, HarperCollins Children's Books, Thorsons/Element, Voyager Books; **Zondervan:** Inspirio, Vida, Zonderkidz, Zondervan.

NEEDS "We look for a strong story line and exceptional literary talent."

HOW TO CONTACT Agented submissions only. *All unsolicited mss returned.*

TERMS Negotiates payment upon acceptance. Responds in 1 month, will contact only if interested. Does not accept any unsolicted texts.

TIPS "We do not accept any unsolicited material."

Ⓐ HARPERTEEN

195 Broadway, New York NY 10007. (212)207-7000. **Website:** www.harpercollins.com. HarperTeen is a teen imprint that publishes hardcovers, paperback reprints and paperback originals.

Ⓠ *HarperCollins Children's Books is not accepting unsolicited and/or unagented mss or queries. Unfortunately the volume of these submissions is so large that they cannot receive the attention they deserve. Such submissions will not be reviewed or returned.*

Ⓐ⊘ HARPER VOYAGER

Imprint of HarperCollins General Books Group, 195 Broadway, New York NY 10007. (212)207-7000. **Website:** www.eosbooks.com. Estab. 1998. Eos publishes quality science fiction/fantasy with broad appeal. Publishes hardcover originals, trade and mass-market paperback originals, and reprints. Guidelines online.

NEEDS No horror or juvenile.

HOW TO CONTACT Agented submissions only. *All unsolicited mss returned.*

TERMS Pays royalty on retail price. Pays variable advance.

Ⓐ⊘ HARVEST HOUSE PUBLISHERS

990 Owen Loop N., Eugene OR 97402. (541)343-0123. **Fax:** (541)302-0731. **Website:** www.harvesthousepublishers.com. Estab. 1974. Publishes hardcover, trade paperback, and mass-market paperback originals and reprints.

NEEDS *No unsolicited mss, proposals, or artwork.*

HOW TO CONTACT Agented submissions only.

TERMS Pays royalty.

TIPS "For first time/nonpublished authors we suggest building their literary résumé by submitting to magazines, or perhaps accruing book contributions."

HENDRICK-LONG PUBLISHING CO., INC.

10635 Tower Oaks, Suite D, Houston TX 77070. (832)912-READ. **Fax:** (832)912-7353. **E-mail:** hendrick-long@worldnet.att.net. **Website:** hendricklongpublishing.com. **Contact:** Vilma Long. Estab. 1969. "Hendrick-Long publishes historical fiction and nonfiction about Texas and the Southwest for children and young adults." Publishes hardcover and trade paperback originals and hardcover reprints. Book catalog available. Guidelines online.

HOW TO CONTACT Query with SASE. Submit outline, clips, 2 sample chapters.

TERMS Pays royalty on selling price. Pays advance. Responds in 3 months to queries.

HEYDAY BOOKS

c/o Acquisitions Editor, Box 9145, Berkeley CA 94709. **Fax:** (510)549-1889. **E-mail:** heyday@heydaybooks.com. **Website:** www.heydaybooks.com. **Contact:** Gayle Wattawa, acquisitions and editorial director. Estab. 1974. "Heyday Books publishes nonfiction books and literary anthologies with a strong California focus. We publish books about Native Americans, natural history, history, literature, and recreation, with a strong California focus." Publishes hardcover originals, trade paperback originals and reprints. Book catalog online. Guidelines online.

NEEDS Publishes picture books, beginning readers, and young adult literature.

HOW TO CONTACT Submit complete ms for picture books; proposal with sample chapters for longer works. Mark attention: Children's Submission.

TERMS Pays 8% royalty on net price. Responds in 3 months.

HIGHLAND PRESS PUBLISHING

P.O. Box 2292, High Springs FL 32655. **E-mail:** the.highland.press@gmail.com; submissions.hp@gmail.com. **Website:** www.highlandpress.org. **Contact:** Leanne Burroughs, CEO (fiction); she will forward all mss to appropriate editor. Estab. 2005. "With our focus on historical romances, Highland Press Publishing is known as your 'Passport to Romance.' We focus on historical romances and our award-winning anthologies. Our short stories/novellas are heart warming. As for our historicals, we publish historical novels like many of us grew up with and loved. History is a big part of the story and is tactfully woven throughout the romance. We have opened our submissions up to all genres, with the exception of erotica. Our newest lines are inspirational, regency, and young adult." Publishes paperback originals. Catalog and guidelines online.

HOW TO CONTACT Query with outline/synopsis and sample chapters. Accepts queries by snail mail, e-mail. Include estimated word count, target market.

TERMS Pays royalties 7.5-8%. Responds in 3 months to queries; 3-12 months to mss.

TIPS "I don't publish based on industry trends. We buy what we like and what we believe readers are looking for. However, often this proves to be the genres and time-periods larger publishers are not currently interested in. Be professional at all times. Present your ms in the best possible light. Be sure you have run spell check and that the ms has been vetted by at least 1 critique partner, preferably more. Many times we receive mss that have wonderful stories involved, but would take far too much time to edit to make it marketable."

HIPSO MEDIA

8151 E. 29th Ave., Denver CO 80238. **Website:** www.hipsomedia.com. Estab. 2012. Publishes trade and mass-market paperback and electronic originals. Catalog online. Guidelines online.

HOW TO CONTACT Query via online form.

TERMS Authors receive between 15-30% on royalty. Responds in 1 month.

TIPS Describes ideal audience as "hip readers of e-books. We are going digital first, so tell us why someone would want to read your book."

HOLIDAY HOUSE, INC.

425 Madison Ave., New York NY 10017. (212)688-0085. **Fax:** (212)421-6134. **E-mail:** info@holiday-house.com. **Website:** holidayhouse.com. Estab. 1935. "Holiday House publishes children's and young adult books for the school and library markets. We have a commitment to publishing first-time authors and illustrators. We specialize in quality hardcovers from picture books to young adult, both fiction and non-fiction, primarily for the school and library market." Publishes hardcover originals and paperback reprints. Guidelines for #10 SASE.

NEEDS Children's books only.

HOW TO CONTACT Query with SASE. No phone calls, please.

TERMS Pays royalty on list price, range varies. Responds in 4 months.

TIPS "We need mss with strong stories and writing."

Ⓐ⃠ HENRY HOLT

175 Fifth Ave., New York NY 10011. **Website:** www.henryholt.com. *Agented submissions only.*

ⒶⓄ◕Ⓢ HOPEWELL PUBLICATIONS

P.O. Box 11, Titusville NJ 08560. **Website:** www.hopepubs.com. **Contact:** E. Martin, publisher. Estab. 2002. "Hopewell Publications specializes in classic reprints—books with proven sales records that have gone out of print—and the occasional new title of interest. Our catalog spans from 1-60 years of publication history. We print fiction and nonfiction, and we accept agented and unagented materials. Submissions are accepted online only." Format publishes in hardcover, trade paperback, and electronic originals; trade paperback and electronic reprints. Catalog online. Guidelines online.

IMPRINTS Egress Books, Legacy Classics.

HOW TO CONTACT Query online using our online guidelines.

TERMS Pays royalty on retail price. Responds in 3 months to queries; 6 months to proposals; 9 months to mss.

HOUGHTON MIFFLIN HARCOURT BOOKS FOR CHILDREN

Imprint of Houghton Mifflin Trade & Reference Division, 222 Berkeley St., Boston MA 02116. (617)351-5000. **Fax:** (617)351-1111. **Website:** www.houghton-mifflinbooks.com. Houghton Mifflin Harcourt gives shape to ideas that educate, inform, and above all, delight. *Does not respond to or return mss unless interest-*

ed. Publishes hardcover originals and trade paperback originals and reprints. Guidelines online.

HOW TO CONTACT Submit complete ms.

TERMS Pays 5-10% royalty on retail price. Pays variable advance. Responds in 4-6 months to queries.

⊘⊘ HOUGHTON MIFFLIN HARCOURT CO.

222 Berkeley St., Boston MA 02116. (617)351-5000. **Website:** www.hmhco.com. Estab. 1832. "Houghton Mifflin Harcourt gives shape to ideas that educate, inform and delight. In a new era of publishing, our legacy of quality thrives as we combine imagination with technology, bringing you new ways to know." Publishes hardcover originals and trade paperback originals and reprints.

⊘⊘ HOUSE OF ANANSI PRESS

110 Spadina Ave., Suite 801, Toronto ON M5V 2K4 Canada. (416)363-4343. **Fax:** (416)363-1017. **Website:** www.anansi.ca. Estab. 1967. House of Anansi publishes literary fiction and poetry by Canadian and international writers.

NEEDS Publishes literary fiction that has a unique flair, memorable characters, and a strong narrative voice.

HOW TO CONTACT Query with SASE.

TERMS Pays 8-10% royalties. Pays $750 advance and 10 author's copies.

IDEALS CHILDREN'S BOOKS AND CANDYCANE PRESS

2630 Elm Hill Pike, Suite 100, Nashville TN 37214. **Website:** www.idealsbooks.com. **Contact:** Submissions. Estab. 1944.

NEEDS Picture books: animal, concept, history, religion. Board books: animal, history, nature/environment, religion. Ideals publishes for ages 4-8, no longer than 800 words; CandyCane publishes for ages 2-5, no longer than 500 words.

HOW TO CONTACT Submit complete ms.

☺ IDW PUBLISHING

5080 Santa Fe, San Diego CA 92109. **E-mail:** letters@idwpublishing.com. **Website:** www.idwpublishing.com. Estab. 1999. IDW Publishing currently publishes a wide range of comic books and graphic novels including titles based on GI Joe, Star Trek, Terminator: Salvation, and Transformers. Creator-driven titles include Fallen Angel by Peter David and JK Woodward, Locke & Key by Joe Hill and Gabriel Rodriguez, and a variety of titles by writer Steve Niles including Wake the Dead, Epilogue, and Dead, She Said. Publishes hardcover, mass-market and trade paperback originals.

ILIUM PRESS

2407 S. Sonora Dr., Spokane WA 99037. (509)701-8866. **E-mail:** contact@iliumpress.com; submissions@iliumpress.com. **Website:** www.iliumpress.com. **Contact:** John Lemon, owner/editor (literature, epic poetry). Estab. 2010. Publishes trade paperback originals and reprints, electronic originals and reprints. Guidelines online.

NEEDS No epic fantasy or paranormal romance.

TERMS Pays 20-50% royalties on receipts. Responds in 6 months.

☺ IMAGE COMICS

2001 Center St., 6th Floor, Berkeley CA 94704. **E-mail:** submissions@imagecomics.com. **Website:** www.imagecomics.com. **Contact:** Eric Stephenson, publisher. Estab. 1992. Publishes creator-owned comic books, graphic novels. See this company's website for detailed guidelines. Does not accept writing samples without art.

HOW TO CONTACT Query with one-page synopsis and 5 pages or more of samples. "We do not accept writing (that is plots, scripts, whatever) samples! If you're an established pro, we might be able to find somebody willing to work with you but it would be nearly impossible for us to read through every script that might find its way our direction. Do not send your script or your plot unaccompanied by art—it will be discarded, unread."

TIPS "We are not looking for any specific genre or type of comic book. We are looking for comics that are well written and well drawn, by people who are dedicated and can meet deadlines."

IMMEDIUM

P.O. Box 31846, San Francisco CA 94131. (415)452-8546. **Fax:** (360)937-6272. **Website:** www.immedium.com. Estab. 2005. "Immedium focuses on publishing eye-catching children's picture books, Asian American topics, and contemporary arts, popular culture, and multicultural issues." Publishes hardcover and trade paperback originals. Catalog online. Guidelines online.

HOW TO CONTACT Submit complete ms.

TERMS Pays 5% royalty on wholesale price. Pays on publication. Responds in 1-3 months.

TIPS "Our audience is children and parents. Please visit our site."

INNOVATIVE PUBLISHERS INC.

133 Clarendon St., Box 170021, Boston MA 02117. (617)963-0886. **Fax:** (617)861-8533. **E-mail:** admin@innovative-publishers.com. **Website:** www.innovative-publishers.com. Estab. 2000. Publishes hardcover, trade paperback, mass-market, and electronic originals; trade paperback and mass-market reprints. Book catalog for 9x12 SASE with 7 first-class stamps. Guidelines for #10 SASE.

NEEDS "Primarily seeking artists that are immersed in their topic. If you live, eat, and sleep your topic, it will show. Our focus is a wide demographic."

HOW TO CONTACT See submission requirements online.

TERMS Pays 5-17% royalty on retail price. Offers $1,500-125,000 advance. Responds in 3 months to queries; 4-6 months to mss and proposals.

◯ INSOMNIAC PRESS

520 Princess Ave., London ON N6B 2B8 Canada. (416)504-6270. **E-mail:** mike@insomniacpress.com. **Website:** www.insomniacpress.com. **Contact:** Mike O'Connor, publisher. Estab. 1992. Publishes trade paperback originals and reprints, mass-market paperback originals, and electronic originals and reprints. Guidelines online.

NEEDS "We publish a mix of commercial (mysteries) and literary fiction."

HOW TO CONTACT Query via e-mail, submit proposal.

TERMS Pays 10-15% royalty on retail price. Pays $500-1,000 advance.

TIPS "We envision a mixed readership that appreciates up-and-coming literary fiction and poetry as well as solidly researched and provocative nonfiction. Peruse our website and familiarize yourself with what we've published in the past."

INTERLINK PUBLISHING GROUP, INC.

46 Crosby St., Northampton MA 01060. (413)582-7054. **Fax:** (413)582-7057. **E-mail:** info@interlinkbooks.com. **Website:** www.interlinkbooks.com. Estab. 1987. Interlink is an independent publisher of general trade adult fiction and nonfiction with an emphasis on books that have a wide appeal while also meeting high intellectual and literary standards. Publishes hardcover and trade paperback originals. Book catalog and guidelines online.

NEEDS "We are looking for translated works relating to the Middle East, Africa or Latin America." No science fiction, romance, plays, erotica, fantasy, horror.

HOW TO CONTACT Query with SASE. Submit outline, sample chapters.

TERMS Pays 6-8% royalty on retail price. Pays small advance. Responds in 3-6 months to queries.

TIPS "Any submissions that fit well in our publishing program will receive careful attention. A visit to our website, your local bookstore, or library to look at some of our books before you send in your submission is recommended."

INVERTED-A

P.O. Box 267, Licking MO 65542. **E-mail:** amnfn@well.com. **Contact:** Aya Katz, chief editor (poetry, novels, political); Nets Katz, science editor (scientific, academic). Estab. 1985. Books: offset printing. Average print order: POD. Distributes through Baker & Taylor, Amazon, Bowker. Publishes paperback originals. Guidelines for SASE.

HOW TO CONTACT Does not accept unsolicited mss. Query with SASE. Reading period open from January 2-March 15. Accepts queries by e-mail. Include estimated word count.

TERMS Pays 10 author's copies. Responds in 1 month to queries; 3 months to mss.

TIPS "Read our books. Read the *Inverted-A Horn*. We are different. We do not follow industry trends."

ITALICA PRESS

595 Main St., Suite 605, New York NY 10044-0047. (917)371-0563. **E-mail:** inquiries@italicapress.com. **Website:** www.italicapress.com. **Contact:** Ronald G. Musto and Eileen Gardiner, publishers. Estab. 1985. "Italica Press publishes English translations of modern Italian fiction and medieval and Renaissance nonfiction." Publishes hardcover and trade paperback originals. Book catalog and guidelines online.

NEEDS "First-time translators published. We would like to see translations of Italian writers who are well-known in Italy who are not yet translated for an American audience."

HOW TO CONTACT Query via e-mail.

TERMS Pays 7-15% royalty on wholesale price; author's copies. Responds in 1 month to queries; 4 months to mss.

TIPS "We are interested in considering a wide variety of medieval and Renaissance topics (not historical fiction), and for modern works we are only interested in translations from Italian fiction by well-known Italian authors. *Only* fiction that has been previously published in Italian. A *brief* e-mail saves a lot of time. 90% of proposals we receive are completely off base—but we are very interested in things that are right on target."

JEWISH LIGHTS PUBLISHING

LongHill Partners, Inc., Sunset Farm Offices, Rt. 4, P.O. Box 237, Woodstock VT 05091. (802)457-4000. **Fax:** (802)457-4004. **Website:** www.jewishlights.com. **Contact:** Acquisitions Editor. Estab. 1990. "Jewish Lights publishes books for people of all faiths and all backgrounds who yearn for books that attract, engage, educate and spiritually inspire. Our authors are at the forefront of spiritual thought and deal with the quest for the self and for meaning in life by drawing on the Jewish wisdom tradition. Our books cover topics including history, spirituality, life cycle, children, self-help, recovery, theology and philosophy. We do not publish autobiography, biography, fiction, haggadot, poetry or cookbooks. At this point we plan to do only 2 books for children annually, and 1 will be for younger children (ages 4-10)." Publishes hardcover and trade paperback originals, trade paperback reprints. Book catalog and guidelines online.
NEEDS Picture books, young readers, middle readers: spirituality. "We are not interested in anything other than spirituality."
HOW TO CONTACT Query with outline/synopsis and 2 sample chapters; submit complete ms for picture books.
TERMS Pays authors royalty of 10% of revenue received; 15% royalty for subsequent printings. Responds in 3 months to queries.
TIPS "We publish books for all faiths and backgrounds that also reflect the Jewish wisdom tradition. Explain in your cover letter why you're submitting your project to us in particular. Make sure you know what we publish."

JOURNEYFORTH

Imprint of BJU Press, 1700 Wade Hampton Blvd., Greenville SC 29614. (864)242-5100, ext. 4350. **Fax:** (864)298-0268. **E-mail:** journeyforth@bjupress.com. **Website:** www.journeyforth.com. Estab. 1974. "Small independent publisher of trustworthy novels and biographies for readers pre-school through high school from a conservative Christian perspective, Christian living books, and Bible studies for adults." Publishes paperback originals. Book catalog available free. Guidelines online.
NEEDS "Our fiction is all based on a moral and Christian worldview." Does not want short stories.

HOW TO CONTACT Submit 5 sample chapters, synopsis, SASE.
TERMS Pays royalty. Responds in 1 month to queries; 3 months to mss.
TIPS "Study the publisher's guidelines. No picture books and no submissions by e-mail."

⊘ JUPITER GARDENS PRESS

Jupiter Gardens, LLC, PO Box 191, Grimes IA 50111. **Website:** www.jupitergardens.com. **Contact:** Mary Wilson, publisher. Estab. 2007. Format publishes in trade paperback originals and reprints; electronic originals and reprints. Catalog online. Guidelines online.
NEEDS "We only publish romance (all sub-genres), science fiction & fantasy & metaphysical fiction. Our science fiction and fantasy covers a wide variety of topics, such as feminist fantasy, or more hard science fiction and fantasy that looks at the human condition. Our young adult imprint, Jupiter Storm, with thought provoking reads that explore the full range of speculative fiction, includes science fiction or fantasy and metaphysical fiction. These readers would enjoy edgy contemporary works. Our romance readers love seeing a couple, no matter the gender, overcome obstacles and grow in order to find true love. Like our readers, we believe that love can come in many forms."
HOW TO CONTACT Use online submission form. Currently closed to submissions.
TERMS Pays 40% royalty on retail price. Responds in 1 month on proposals; 2 months on mss.
TIPS "No matter which line you're submitting to, know your genre and your readership. We publish a diverse catalog, and we're passionate about our main focus. We want romance that takes your breath away and leaves you with that warm feeling that love does conquer all. Our science fiction takes place i̶ ̶ ̶l̶d̶ and alien worlds, and our fantasy transports r̶ to mythical realms and finds strange worlds our own. And our metaphysical nonfiction w̶ readers gain new skills and awareness for the coming age. We want authors who engage with their readers and who aren't afraid to use social media to connect. Read and follow our submission guidelines."

KAEDEN BOOKS

P.O. Box 16190, Rocky River OH 44116. **Website:** www.kaeden.com. Estab. 1986. "Children's book publisher for education K-3 market: reading stories, fiction/nonfiction, chapter books, science, and social studies materials." Publishes paperback originals. Book catalog and guidelines online.

NEEDS "We are looking for stories with humor, surprise endings, and interesting characters that will appeal to children in kindergarten through third grade." No sentence fragments. Please do not submit: queries, ms summaries, or résumés, mss that stereotype or demean individuals or groups, mss that present violence as acceptable behavior.

HOW TO CONTACT Submit complete ms. "Can be as minimal as 25 words for the earliest reader or as much as 2,000 words for the fluent reader. Beginning chapter books are welcome. Our readers are in kindergarten to third grade, so vocabulary and sentence structure must be appropriate for young readers. Make sure that all language used in the story is of an appropriate level for the students to read independently. Sentences should be complete and grammatically correct."

TERMS Work purchased outright from authors. Pays royalties to previous authors. Responds only if interested.

TIPS "Our audience ranges from kindergarten-third grade school children. We are an educational publisher. We are particularly interested in humorous stories with surprise endings and beginning chapter books."

Ⓐ KANE/MILLER BOOK PUBLISHERS

4901 Morena Blvd., Suite 213, San Diego CA 92117. (858)456-0540. **Fax:** (858)456-9641. **E-mail:** submissions@kanemiller.com. **Website:** www.kanemiller.com. **Contact:** Editorial Department. Estab. 1985. "Kane/Miller Book Publishers is a division of EDC Publishing, specializing in award-winning children's books from around the world. Our books bring the children of the world closer to each other, sharing stories and ideas, while exploring cultural differences and similarities. Although we continue to look for books from other countries, we are now actively seeking works that convey cultures and communities within the U.S. We are looking for picture book fiction and nonfiction on those subjects that may be defined as particularly American: sports such as baseball, historical events, American biographies, American folk tales, etc. We are committed to expanding our early and middlegrade fiction list. We're interested in great stories with engaging characters in all genres (mystery, fantasy, adventure, historical, etc.) and, as with picture books, especially those with particularly American subjects."

NEEDS Picture Books: concept, contemporary, health, humor, multicultural. Young Readers: contemporary, multicultural, suspense. Middle Readers: contemporary, humor, multicultural, suspense.

TERMS Responds in 90 days to queries.

TIPS "We like to think that a child reading a Kane/Miller book will see parallels between his own life and what might be the unfamiliar setting and characters of the story. And that by seeing how a character who is somehow or in some way dissimilar—an outsider—finds a way to fit comfortably into a culture or community or situation while maintaining a healthy sense of self and self-dignity, she might be empowered to do the same."

Ⓢ KAR-BEN PUBLISHING

Lerner Publishing Group, 241 First Ave. N, Minneapolis MN 55401. (612)215-6229. **Fax:** 612-332-7615. **E-mail:** Editorial@Karben.com. **Website:** www.karben.com. Estab. 1974. Publishes hardcover, trade paperback and electronic originals. Book catalog available online; free upon request. Guidelines available online.

NEEDS "We seek picture book mss of about 1,000 words on Jewish-themed topics for children." Picture books: Adventure, concept, folktales, history, humor, multicultural, religion, special needs; must be on a Jewish theme. Average word length: picture books–1,000. Recently published titles: *The Count's Hanukkah Countdown*, *Sammy Spider's First Book of Jewish Holidays*, *The Cats of Ben Yehuda Street*.

HOW TO CONTACT Submit full ms. Picture books only.

TERMS Pays 5% royalty on NET sale. Pays $500-2,500 advance. Responds in 6 weeks.

TIPS "Authors: Do a literature search to make sure similar title doesn't already exist. Illustrators: Look at our online catalog for a sense of what we like—bright colors and lively composition."

KAYA PRESS

USC ASE, 3620 S. Vermont Ave. KAP 462, Los Angeles CA 90089. (213)740-2285. **E-mail:** info@kaya.com. **Website:** www.kaya.com. **Contact:** Sunyoung Lee, editor. Kaya is an independent literary press dedicated to the publication of innovative literature from the Asian diaspora. "We are looking for innovative writers with a commitment to quality literature." Publishes hardcover originals and trade paperback originals and reprints. Book catalog available free. Guidelines online.

HOW TO CONTACT Submit 2-4 sample chapters, clips, SASE.

TERMS Responds in 6 months to mss.

TIPS "Audience is people interested in a high standard of literature and who are interested in breaking down easy approaches to multicultural literature."

KELSEY STREET PRESS

Poetry by Women, 2824 Kelsey St., Berkeley CA 94705. **E-mail:** amber@kelseyst.com. **Website:** www.kelseyst.com. Estab. 1974. "A Berkeley, California press publishing collaborations between women poets and artists. Many of the press's collaborations focus on a central theme or conceit, like the sprawl and spectacle of New York in *Arcade* by Erica Hunt and Alison Saar." Hardcover and trade paperback originals and electronic originals.

KENSINGTON PUBLISHING CORP.

850 Third Ave., 16th Floor, New York NY 10022. (212)407-1500. **Fax:** (212)935-0699. **E-mail:** jscognamiglio@kensingtonbooks.com. **Website:** www.kensingtonbooks.com. **Contact:** John Scognamiglio, editorial director, fiction (historical romance, Regency romance, women's contemporary fiction, gay and lesbian fiction and nonfiction, mysteries, suspense, mainstream fiction); Michaela Hamilton, editor in chief, Citadel Press (thrillers, mysteries, mainstream fiction, true crime, current events); Selena James, executive editor, Dafina Books (African American fiction and nonfiction, inspirational, young adult, romance); Peter Senftleben, assistant editor (mainstream fiction, women's contemporary fiction, gay and lesbian fiction, mysteries, suspense, thrillers, romantic suspense, paranormal romance). Estab. 1975. "Kensington focuses on profitable niches and uses aggressive marketing techniques to support its books." Publishes hardcover and trade paperback originals, mass-market paperback originals and reprints. Book catalog and guidelines online.

NEEDS No science fiction/fantasy, experimental fiction, business texts or children's titles.

HOW TO CONTACT Query.

TERMS Pays 6-15% royalty on retail price. Makes outright purchase. Pays $2,000 and up advance. Responds in 1 month to queries and proposals; 4 months to mss.

TIPS "Agented submissions only, except for submissions to romance lines. For those lines, query with SASE or submit proposal package including 3 sample chapters, synopsis."

KIDS CAN PRESS

25 Dockside Dr., Toronto ON M5A 0B5 Canada. (416)479-7000. **Fax:** (416)960-5437. **Website:** www. kidscanpress.com. **Contact:** Corus Quay, acquisitions. Estab. 1973.

Kids Can Press is currently accepting unsolicited mss from Canadian adult authors only.

NEEDS Picture books, young readers: concepts. "We do not accept young adult fiction or fantasy novels for any age." Adventure, animal, contemporary, folktales, history, humor, multicultural, nature/environment, special needs, sports, suspense/mystery. Average word length: picture books 1,000-2,000; young readers 750-1,500; middle readers 10,000-15,000; young adults over 15,000.

HOW TO CONTACT Submit outline/synopsis and 2-3 sample chapters. For picture books submit complete ms.

TERMS Responds in 6 months only if interested.

DENIS KITCHEN PUBLISHING CO., LLC

P.O. Box 2250, Amherst MA 01004. (413)259-1627. **Fax:** (413)259-1812. **E-mail:** help@deniskitchen.com. **Website:** www.deniskitchen.com. **Contact:** Denis Kitchen, publisher. Publishes hardcover and trade paperback originals and reprints.

This publisher strongly discourages e-mail submissions.

NEEDS "We do not want pure fiction. We seek cartoonists or writer/illustrator teams who can tell compelling stories with a combination of words and pictures." No pure fiction (meaning text only).

HOW TO CONTACT Query with SASE. Submit sample illustrations/comic pages. Submit complete ms.

TERMS Pays 6-10% royalty on retail price. Occasionally makes deals based on percentage of wholesale if idea and/or bulk of work is done in-house. Pays $1-5,000 advance. Responds in 4-6 weeks.

TIPS "Our audience is readers who embrace the graphic novel revolution, who appreciate historical comic strips and books, and those who follow popular and alternative culture. We like to discover new talent. The artist who has a day job but a great idea is encouraged to contact us. The pop culture historian who has a new take on an important figure is likewise encouraged. We have few preconceived notions about mss or ideas, though we are decidedly selective. Historically, we have published many first-time authors and artists, some of whom developed into award-winning creators with substantial followings. Artists or illustrators who do not have confidence in their writing should send us self-promotional postcards (our favorite way of spotting new talent)."

KNOPF

Imprint of Random House, 1745 Broadway, New York NY 10019. **Fax:** (212)940-7390. **Website:** knopfdoubleday.com/imprint/knopf. **Contact:** The editors. Estab. 1915. Publishes hardcover and paperback originals.
NEEDS Publishes book-length fiction of literary merit by known or unknown writers. Length: 40,000-150,000 words.
HOW TO CONTACT Usually only accepts mss submitted by agents. However, writers may submit sample 25-50 pages with SASE.
TERMS Royalties vary. Offers advance. Responds in 2-6 months to queries.

KNOX ROBINSON PUBLISHING

244 Fifth Ave., Suite 1861, New York NY 10001. **E-mail:** subs@knoxrobinsonpublishing.com. **Website:** www.knoxrobinsonpublishing.com. **Contact:** Dana Celeste Robinson, managing director (historical fiction, historical romance, fantasy). Estab. 2010. Knox Robinson Publishing started as an international, independent, specialist publisher of historical fiction, historical romance and fantasy. Now open to well-written literature in all genres. Guidelines online.
NEEDS "We are seeking historical fiction featuring obscure historical figures."
HOW TO CONTACT Submit first 3 chapters and author questionnaire found on website.
TERMS Pays royalty. Responds in 2 months to submissions of first 3 chapters. "We do not accept proposals."

⊘ KREGEL PUBLICATIONS

2450 Oak Industrial Dr. NE, Grand Rapids MI 49505. (616)451-4775. **Fax:** (616)451-9330. **E-mail:** kregelbooks@kregel.com. **Website:** www.kregelpublications.com. **Contact:** Dennis R. Hillman, publisher. Estab. 1949. "Our mission as an evangelical Christian publisher is to provide—with integrity and excellence—trusted, Biblically based resources that challenge and encourage individuals in their Christian lives. Works in theology and Biblical studies should reflect the historic, orthodox Protestant tradition." Publishes hardcover and trade paperback originals and reprints. Guidelines online.
NEEDS Fiction should be geared toward the evangelical Christian market. Wants books with fast-paced, contemporary storylines presenting a strong Christian message in an engaging, entertaining style.
HOW TO CONTACT Finds works through The Writer's Edge and Christian Manuscript Submissions ms screening services.

TERMS Pays royalty on wholesale price. Pays negotiable advance.
TIPS "Our audience consists of conservative, evangelical Christians, including pastors and ministry students."

● KWELA BOOKS

Imprint of NB Publishers, P.O. Box 6525, Roggebaai 8012 South Africa. (27)(21)406-3605. **Fax:** (27)(21)406-3712. **E-mail:** kwela@kwela.com. **Website:** www.kwela.com. Estab. 1994.

LEAPFROG PRESS

Box 505, Fredonia NY 14063. (508)274-2710. **E-mail:** leapfrog@leapfrogpress.com; acquisitions@leapfrogpress.com. **Website:** www.leapfrogpress.com. **Contact:** Sarah Murphy, acquisitions editor. Estab. 1996.
NEEDS "We search for beautifully written literary titles and market them aggressively to national trade and library accounts. We also sell film, translation, foreign, and book club rights." Publishes paperback originals. Books: acid-free paper; sewn binding. Average print order: 3,000. First novel print order: 2,000 (average). Member, Publishers Marketing Association, PEN. Distributes titles through Consortium Book Sales and Distribution, St. Paul, MN. Promotes titles through all national review media, bookstore readings, author tours, website, radio shows, chain store promotions, advertisements, book fairs. "Genres often blur; look for good writing. We are most interested in works that are quirky, that fall outside of any known genre, and of course well written and finely crafted. We are most interested in literary fiction."
HOW TO CONTACT Query by e-mail only. Send letter and first 5 to 10 ms pages within e-mail message. No attachments. Responds in 2-3 weeks to queries by e-mail; 6 months to mss. May consider simultaneous submissions.
TERMS Pays 10% royalty on net receipts. Average advance: negotiable.
TIPS "We like anything that is superbly written and genuinely original. We like the idiosyncratic and the peculiar. We rarely publish nonfiction. Send only your best work, and send only completed work that is ready. That means the completed ms has already been through extensive editing and is ready to be judged. We consider submissions from both previously published and unpublished writers. We are uninterested in an impressive author bio if the work is poor; if the work is excellent, the author bio is equally unimportant."

LEE & LOW BOOKS

95 Madison Ave., #1205, New York NY 10016. (212)779-4400. **E-mail:** general@leeandlow.com. **Website:** www.leeandlow.com. **Contact:** Louise May, vice president/editorial director (multicultural children's fiction/nonfiction). Estab. 1991. "Our goals are to meet a growing need for books that address children of color, and to present literature that all children can identify with. We only consider multicultural children's books. Sponsors a yearly New Voices Award for first-time picture book authors of color. Contest rules online at website or for SASE." Publishes hardcover originals and trade paperback reprints. Book catalog available online. Guidelines available online or by written request with SASE.

NEEDS Picture books, young readers: anthology, contemporary, history, multicultural, poetry. Picture book, middle reader: contemporary, history, multicultural, nature/environment, poetry, sports. Average word length: picture books—1,000-1,500 words. "We do not publish folklore or animal stories."

HOW TO CONTACT Submit complete ms.

TERMS Pays net royalty. Pays authors advances against royalty. Pays illustrators advance against royalty. Photographers paid advance against royalty. Responds in 6 months to mss if interested.

TIPS "Check our website to see the kinds of books we publish. Do not send mss that don't fit our mission."

LERNER PUBLISHING GROUP

1251 Washington Ave. N., Minneapolis MN 55401. (800)452-7236; (612)332-3344. **Fax:** (612)337-7615. **E-mail:** editorial@karben.com. **Website:** www.karben.com; www.lernerbooks.com. Estab. 1957. Lerner Publishing primarily publishes books for children ages 7-18. List includes titles in geography, natural and physical science, current events, ancient and modern history, high interest, sports, world cultures, and numerous biography series. Kar-Ben Publishing, the Jewish-themed imprint of Lerner Publishing Group, primarily publishes books for children ages Pre-K-9. Lerner's list includes titles in geography, natural and physical science, current events, ancient and modern history, high interest, sports, world cultures, and numerous biography series. Kar-Ben's list includes only books on Jewish themes for children and families. Lerner Publishing does not accept unsolicited mss. Kar-Ben does accept unsolicited mss. Illustrators: Please submit samples that show skill in children's book illustration. Digital portfolios preferred. Please do not send original art. Writers: Kar-Ben considers fiction and nonfiction for preschool through middle school, including holiday books, life-cycle stories, Bible tales, folktales, and board books. In particular, Kar-Ben is looking for stories that reflect the cultural diversity of today's Jewish community. Kar-Ben DOES NOT publish games, textbooks, or books in Hebrew. "Your story should be concise, have interesting, believable characters, and action that holds the readers' attention. Good prose is far better than tortured verse." Contact editorial@karben.com.

○ Starting in 2007, Lerner Publishing Group no longer accepts submission in any of their imprints except for Kar-Ben Publishing.

HOW TO CONTACT "We will continue to seek targeted solicitations at specific reading levels and in specific subject areas. The company will list these targeted solicitations on our website and in national newsletters, such as the SCBWI *Bulletin*."

LES ÉDITIONS DU VERMILLON

305 Saint Patrick St., Ottawa ON K1N 5K4 Canada. (613)241-4032. **Fax:** (613)241-3109. **E-mail:** lesedition-sduvermillon@rogers.com. **Website:** www.lesedition-sduvermillon.ca. **Contact:** Jacques Flamand, editorial director. Publishes trade paperback originals. Book catalog available free.

TERMS Pays 10% royalty. Responds in 6 months to mss.

LES FIGUES PRESS

P.O. Box 7736, Los Angeles CA 90007. **E-mail:** info@lesfigues.com. **Website:** www.lesfigues.com. **Contact:** Teresa Carmody and Vanessa Place, co-directors. Les Figues Press is an independent, nonprofit publisher of poetry, prose, visual art, conceptual writing, and translation. With amission is to create aesthetic conversations between readers, writers, and artists, Les Figues Press favors projects which push the boundaries of genre, form, and general acceptability. Submissions are only reviewed through its annual NOS Book Contest.

LETHE PRESS

118 Heritage Ave., Maple Shade NJ 08052. (609)410-7391. **E-mail:** editor@lethepressbooks.com. **Website:** www.lethepressbooks.com. **Contact:** Steve Berman, publisher. Estab. 2001. "Welcomes submissions from authors of any sexual or gender identity." Guidelines online.

NEEDS "Named after the Greek river of memory and forgetfulness (and pronounced Lee-Thee), Lethe Press is a small press devoted to ideas that are often neglected or forgotten by mainstream, profit-oriented publishers." Distributes/promotes titles. Lethe Books are distributed by Ingram Publications and Bookazine, and are available at all major bookstores, as well as the major online retailers.

HOW TO CONTACT Query via e-mail.

ARTHUR A. LEVINE BOOKS

Scholastic, Inc., 557 Broadway, New York NY 10012. (212)343-4436. **Fax:** (212)343-6143. **Website:** www.arthuralevinebooks.com. **Contact:** Arthur A. Levine, VP/publisher. Estab. 1996. Publishes hardcover, paperback, and e-book editions. Guidelines online.

NEEDS "Arthur A. Levine is looking for distinctive literature, for children and young adults, for whatever's extraordinary." Averages 18-20 total titles/year.

HOW TO CONTACT Query.

TERMS Responds in 1 month to queries; 5 months to mss.

LILLENAS PUBLISHING CO.

Imprint of Lillenas Drama Resources, P.O. Box 419527, Kansas City MO 64141. (816)931-1900. **Fax:** (816)412-8390. **E-mail:** drama@lillenas.com. **Website:** www.lillenasdrama.com. "We purchase only original, previously unpublished materials. Also, we require that all scripts be performed at least once before it is submitted for consideration. We do not accept scripts that are sent via fax or e-mail. Direct all mss to the Drama Resources Editor." Publishes mass-market paperback and electronic originals. Guidelines online.

NEEDS "Looking for sketch and monologue collections for all ages—adults, children and youth. For these collections, we request 12-15 scripts to be submitted at one time. Unique treatments of spiritual themes, relevant issues and biblical messages are of interest. Contemporary full-length and one-act plays that have conflict, characterization, and a spiritual context that is neither a sermon nor an apologetic for youth and adults. We also need wholesome so-called secular full-length scripts for dinner theatres and schools." No musicals.

TERMS Pays royalty on net price. Makes outright purchase. Responds in 4-6 months to material.

TIPS "We never receive too many mss."

R.C. LINNELL PUBLISHING

2100 Tyler Ln., Louisville KY 40205. **E-mail:** info@linnellpublishing.com. **Website:** www.linnellpublishing.com. **Contact:** Cheri Powell, owner. Estab. 2010. "We are currently very small and have published a limited number of books. We would review books on other subjects on a case-by-case basis. If a book is well-written and has an audience we would consider it." Publishes print on demand paperbacks. Book catalog and guidelines online.

HOW TO CONTACT Submit complete ms.

TERMS Pays 10-40% royalty on retail price. Responds in 1 month to mss.

TIPS "Visit our website to understand the business model and the relationship with authors. All sales are through the Internet. Author should have a marketing plan in mind. We can help expand the plan but we do not market books. Author should be comfortable with using the Internet and should know their intended readers. We are especially interested in books that inspire, motivate, amuse and challenge readers."

LIQUID SILVER BOOKS

10509 Sedgegrass Dr., Indianapolis IN 46235. **E-mail:** submissions@liquidsilverbooks.com. **Website:** www.lsbooks.com. **Contact:** Terri Schaefer, editorial director. Estab. 1999. Liquid Silver Books is an imprint of Atlantic Bridge Publishing, a royalty paying, full-service ePublisher. Atlantic Bridge has been in business since June 1999. Liquid Silver Books is dedicated to bringing high-quality erotic romance to our readers. Liquid Silver Books, Romance's Silver Lining.

"We are foremost an e-publisher. We believe the market will continue to grow for e-books. It is our prime focus. At this time our print publishing is on hiatus. We will update the submission guidelines if we reinstate this aspect of our publishing."

NEEDS Needs contemporary, gay and lesbian, paranormal, supernatural, sci-fi, fantasy, historical, suspense, and western romances. "We do not accept literary erotica submissions."

HOW TO CONTACT E-mail entire ms as an attachment in .RTF format in Arial 12 pt. "Include in the body of the e-mail: author bio, your thoughts on ePublishing, a blurb of your book, including title and series title if applicable. Ms must include pen name, real name, snail mail and e-mail contact information on the first page, top left corner."

TERMS Responds to mss in 10-15 days.

LITTLE, BROWN AND CO. ADULT TRADE BOOKS

1290 Avenue of the Americas, New York NY 10104. **E-mail:** publicity@littlebrown.com. **Website:** www.

hachettebookgroup.com. Estab. 1837. "The general editorial philosophy for all divisions continues to be broad and flexible, with high quality and the promise of commercial success as always the first considerations." Publishes hardcover originals and paperback originals and reprints. Guidelines online.

HOW TO CONTACT *Agented submissions only.*

TERMS Pays royalty. Offer advance.

ⒶⓄ LITTLE, BROWN BOOKS FOR YOUNG READERS

Hachette Book Group USA, 1290 Avenue of the Americas, New York NY 10104. (212)364-1100. **Fax:** (212)364-0925. **E-mail:** publicity@lbchildrens.com. **Website:** hachettebookgroup.com. Estab. 1837. "Little, Brown and Co. Children's Publishing publishes all formats including board books, picture books, middle-grade fiction, and nonfiction YA titles. We are looking for strong writing and presentation, but no predetermined topics." *Only interested in solicited agented material.*

NEEDS Average word length: picture books—1,000; young readers—6,000; middle readers—15,000-50,000; young adults—50,000 and up.

HOW TO CONTACT *Agented submissions only.*

TERMS Pays authors royalties based on retail price. Pays illustrators and photographers by the project or royalty based on retail price. Sends galleys to authors; dummies to illustrators. Pays negotiable advance. Responds in 1-2 months.

TIPS "In order to break into the field, authors and illustrators should research their competition and try to come up with something outstandingly different."

ⒶⓄ LITTLE SIMON

Imprint of Simon & Schuster, 1230 Avenue of the Americas, New York NY 10020. (212)698-1295. **Fax:** (212)698-2794. **Website:** www.simonsayskids.com. "Our goal is to provide fresh material in an innovative format for preschool to age 8. Our books are often, if not exclusively, format driven." Publishes novelty and branded books only.

NEEDS Novelty books include many things that do not fit in the traditional hardcover or paperback format, such as pop-up, board book, scratch and sniff, glow in the dark, lift the flap, etc. Children's/juvenile. No picture books. Large part of the list is holiday-themed.

HOW TO CONTACT *Currently not accepting unsolicited mss.*

TERMS Offers advance and royalties.

⬤ LITTLE TIGER PRESS

1 The Coda Centre, 189 Munster Rd., London SW6 6AW United Kingdom. (44)(20)7385-6333. **Website:** www.littletigerpress.com. Little Tiger Press is a dynamic and busy independent publisher.

NEEDS Picture books: animal, concept, contemporary, humor. Average word length: picture books—750 words or less.

TIPS "Every reasonable care is taken of the mss and samples we receive, but we cannot accept responsibility for any loss or damage. Try to read or look at as many books on the Little Tiger Press list before sending in your material. Refer to our website for further details."

Ⓞ LIVINGSTON PRESS

University of West Alabama, Station 22, Livingston AL 35470. **E-mail:** jwt@uwa.edu. **Website:** www.livingstonpress.uwa.edu. **Contact:** Joe Taylor, director. Estab. 1974. "Livingston Press, as do all literary presses, looks for authorial excellence in style. Currently emphasizing novels." Reading in June only. Check back for details. Publishes hardcover and trade paperback originals. Book catalog online. Guidelines online.

IMPRINTS Swallow's Tale Press.

NEEDS "We are interested in form and, of course, style."

TERMS Pays 100 contributor's copies, after sales of 1,500, standard royalty. Responds in 2 months to queries; 6-12 months to mss.

TIPS "Our readers are interested in literature, often quirky literature that emphasizes form and style. Please visit our website for current needs."

LOOSE ID

P.O. Box 806, San Francisco CA 94104. **E-mail:** submissions@loose-id.com. **Website:** www.loose-id.com. **Contact:** Treva Harte, editor in chief. Estab. 2004. "Loose Id is love unleashed. We're taking romance to the edge." Publishes e-books and some print books. Distributes/promotes titles. "The company promotes itself through web and print advertising wherever readers of erotic romance may be found, creating a recognizable brand identity as the place to let your id run free and the people who unleash your fantasies. It is currently pursuing licensing agreements for foreign translations, and has a print program of 2 to 5 titles per month." Guidelines online.

○ "Loose Id is actively acquiring stories from both aspiring and established authors."

NEEDS Wants nontraditional erotic romance stories, including gay, lesbian, heroes and heroines, multi-culturalism, cross-genre, fantasy, and science fiction, straight contemporary or historical romances.

HOW TO CONTACT Query with outline/synopsis and 3 sample chapters. Accepts queries by e-mail. Include estimated word count, list of publishing credits, and why your submission is love unleashed. "Before submitting a query or proposal, please read the guidelines on our website. Please don't hesitate to contact us by e-mail for any information you don't see there."

TERMS Pays e-book royalties of 40%. Responds to queries in 1 month.

LUCKY MARBLE BOOKS

PageSpring Publishing, P.O. Box 21133, Columbus OH 43221. **E-mail:** yaeditor@pagespringpublishing.com. **Website:** www.luckymarblebooks.com. Estab. 2012. "Lucky Marble Books publishes novel-length young adult and middle-grade fiction. We are looking for engaging characters and well-crafted plots that keep our readers turning the page. We accept e-mail queries only; see our website for details." Publishes trade paperback and electronic originals. Guidelines online.

NEEDS Does not want picture books.

HOW TO CONTACT Submit proposal package via e-mail. Include synopsis and 30 sample pages.

TERMS Pays royalty. Responds in 3 months.

TIPS "We are particularly interested in books that integrate education content into a great story with vivid characters."

MAGE PUBLISHERS, INC.

(202)342-1642. **Fax:** (202)342-9269. **E-mail:** as@mage.com. **Website:** www.mage.com. Estab. 1985. Mage publishes books relating to Persian/Iranian culture. Publishes hardcover originals and reprints, trade paperback originals. Book catalog available free. Guidelines online.

NEEDS Must relate to Persian/Iranian culture.

HOW TO CONTACT Submit outline, SASE. Query via mail or e-mail.

TERMS Pays royalty. Responds in 1 month to queries.

TIPS "Audience is the Iranian-American community in America and Americans interested in Persian culture."

MAGINATION PRESS

750 First St. NE, Washington DC 20002. (202)336-5618. **Fax:** (202)336-5624. **E-mail:** magination@apa.org. **Website:** www.apa.org. Estab. 1988. Magination Press is an imprint of the American Psychological Association. "We publish books dealing with the psycho/therapeutic resolution of children's problems and psychological issues with a strong self-help component." Submit complete ms. Materials returned only with SASE.

NEEDS All levels: psychological and social issues, self-help, health, parenting concerns and, special needs. Picture books, middle school readers.

TERMS Responds to queries in 1-2 months; mss in 2-6 months.

MANDALA PUBLISHING

Mandala Publishing and Earth Aware Editions, 800 A St., San Rafael CA 94901. **E-mail:** info@mandala-publishing.com. **Website:** www.mandalapublishing.com. Estab. 1989. "In the traditions of the East, wisdom, truth, and beauty go hand in- hand. This is reflected in the great arts, music, yoga, and philosophy of India. Mandala Publishing strives to bring to its readers authentic and accessible renderings of thousands of years of wisdom and philosophy from this unique culture-timeless treasures that are our inspirations and guides. At Mandala, we believe that the arts, health, ecology, and spirituality of the great Vedic traditions are as relevant today as they were in sacred India thousands of years ago. As a distinguished publisher in the world of Vedic literature, lifestyle, and interests today, Mandala strives to provide accessible and meaningful works for the modern reader." Publishes hardcover, trade paperback, and electronic originals. Book catalog online.

HOW TO CONTACT Query with SASE.

TERMS Pays 3-15% royalty on retail price. Responds in 6 months.

☺ MANOR HOUSE PUBLISHING, INC.

452 Cottingham Crescent, Ancaster ON L9G 3V6 Canada. **E-mail:** mbdavie@manor-house.biz. **Website:** www.manor-house.biz. **Contact:** Mike Davie, president (novels, poetry, and nonfiction). Estab. 1998. Publishes hardcover, trade paperback, and mass-market paperback originals reprints. Book catalog online. Guidelines available via e-mail.

NEEDS Stories should have Canadian settings and characters should be Canadian, but content should have universal appeal to wide audience.

HOW TO CONTACT Query via e-mail. Submit proposal package, clips, bio, 3 sample chapters. Submit complete ms.

TERMS Pays 10% royalty on retail price. Queries and mss to be sent by e-mail only. "We will respond in 30 days if interested-if not, there is no response. Do not follow up unless asked to do so."

TIPS "Our audience includes everyone-the general public/mass audience. Self-edit your work first, make sure it is well written with strong Canadian content."

MARINE TECHNIQUES PUBLISHING

126 Western Ave., Suite 266, Augusta ME 04330. (207)622-7984. **E-mail:** info@marinetechpublishing. com. **Website:** www.marinetechpublishing.com. **Contact:** James L. Pelletier, president/owner(commercial maritime); Maritime Associates Globally (commercial maritime). Estab. 1983. "Publishes only books related to the commercial marine/maritime industry." Trade paperback originals and reprints. Book catalog online. Guidelines available by e-mail.

NEEDS Must be commercial maritime/marine related.

HOW TO CONTACT Submit proposal package, including all sample chapters. Submit complete ms.

TERMS Pays 25-55% royalty on wholesale or retail price. Makes outright purchase. Responds in 2 months.

TIPS "Audience consists of commercial marine/maritime firms, persons employed in all aspects of the marine/maritime commercial water-transportation-related industries and recreational fresh and salt water fields, persons interested in seeking employment in the commercial marine industry; firms seeking to sell their products and services to vessel owners, operators, and managers; shipyards, vessel repair yards, recreational and yacht boat building and national and international ports and terminals involved with the commercial marine industry globally worldwide, etc."

MARTIN SISTERS PUBLISHING, LLC

P.O. Box 1154, Barbourville KY 40906-1499. **E-mail:** submissions@martinsisterspublishing.com. **Website:** www.martinsisterspublishing.com. **Contact:** Melissa Newman, Publisher/Editor (Fiction/nonfiction). Estab. 2011. Firm/imprint publishes trade and mass-market paperback originals; electronic originals. Catalog and guidelines online.

IMPRINTS Ivy House Books—literary/mainstream fiction; Rainshower Books—Christian fiction and nonfiction; Skyvine Books—science fiction/fantasy/paranormal; romance; Martin Sisters Books—nonfiction/short story collections/coffee table books/cookbooks; Barefoot Books—young adult. Query Ms. Newman for all imprints listed.

HOW TO CONTACT Send query letter only.

TERMS Pays 7.5% royalty/max on retail price. No advance offered. Responds in 1 month on queries, 2 months on proposals, 3-6 months on mss.

MARVEL COMICS

135 W. 50th St., 7th Floor, New York NY 10020. **Website:** www.marvel.com. Publishes hardcover originals and reprints, trade paperback reprints, mass-market comic book originals, electronic reprints. Guidelines online.

NEEDS Our shared universe needs new heroes and villains; books for younger readers and teens needed.

HOW TO CONTACT Submit inquiry letter, idea submission form (download from website), SASE.

TERMS Pays on a per page work for hire basis or creator-owned which is then contracted. Pays negotiable advance. Responds in 3-5 weeks to queries.

MAVERICK MUSICALS AND PLAYS

89 Bergann Rd., Maleny QLD 4552 Australia. Phone/**Fax:** (61)(7)5494-4007. **E-mail:** gail@maverickmusicals.com. **Website:** www.maverickmusicals.com. Estab. 1978. Guidelines online.

NEEDS "Looking for two-act musicals and one- and two-act plays. See website for more details."

MCBOOKS PRESS

ID Booth Building, 520 N. Meadow St., Ithaca NY 14850. (607)272-2114. **Fax:** (607)273-6068. **E-mail:** mcbooks@mcbooks.com. **Website:** www.mcbooks. com. **Contact:** Alexander G. Skutt, publisher. Estab. 1979. Publishes trade paperback and hardcover originals and reprints. Guidelines online.

"Currently not accepting submissions or queries for fiction or nonfiction."

NEEDS Publishes Julian Stockwin, John Biggins, Colin Sargent, and Douglas W. Jacobson. Distributes titles through Independent Publishers Group.

TIPS "We are currently only publishing authors with whom we have a pre-existing relationship. If this policy changes, we will announce the change on our website."

MCCLELLAND & STEWART, LTD.

The Canadian Publishers, One Toronto St., Unit 300, Toronto ON M5A 2P9 Canada. (416)364-4449. **Fax:** (416)598-7764. **Website:** www.mcclelland.com. Publishes hardcover, trade paperback, and mass-market paperback originals and reprints.

NEEDS "We publish work by established authors, as well as the work of new and developing authors."

HOW TO CONTACT Query. *All unsolicited mss* returned unopened.

TERMS Pays 10-15% royalty on retail price (hardcover rates). Pays advance. Responds in 3 months to proposals.

THE MCDONALD & WOODWARD PUBLISHING CO.

431 E. College St., Granville OH 43023. (740)641-2691. **Fax:** (740)321-1141. **E-mail:** mwpubco@mwpubco. com. **Website:** www.mwpubco.com. **Contact:** Jerry N. McDonald, publisher. Estab. 1986. McDonald & Woodward publishes books in natural history, cultural history, and natural resources. Currently emphasizing travel, natural and cultural history, and natural resource conservation. Publishes hardcover and trade paperback originals. Book catalog online. Guidelines free on request; by e-mail.

HOW TO CONTACT Query with SASE.

TERMS Pays 10% royalty. Responds in less than 1 month.

TIPS "Our books are meant for the curious and educated elements of the general population."

⊘ MARGARET K. MCELDERRY BOOKS

Imprint of Simon & Schuster Children's Publishing Division, 1230 Sixth Ave., New York NY 10020. (212)698-7200. **Website:** www.simonsayskids.com. Estab. 1971. "Margaret K. McElderry Books publishes hardcover and paperback trade books for children from pre-school age through young adult. This list includes picture books, middle-grade and teen fiction, poetry, and fantasy. The style and subject matter of the books we publish is almost unlimited. We do not publish textbooks, coloring and activity books, greeting cards, magazines, pamphlets, or religious publications." Guidelines for #10 SASE.

NEEDS *No unsolicited mss.*

HOW TO CONTACT *Agented submissions only.*

TERMS Pays authors royalty based on retail price. Pays illustrator royalty of by the project. Pays photographers by the project. Original artwork returned at job's completion. Offers $5,000-8,000 advance for new authors.

TIPS "Read! The children's book field is competitive. See what's been done and what's out there before submitting. We look for high quality: an originality of ideas, clarity and felicity of expression, a well-organized plot, and strong character-driven stories. We're looking for strong, original fiction, especially mysteries and middle-grade humor. We are always interested in picture books for the youngest age reader. Study our titles."

MEDALLION MEDIA GROUP

4222 Meridian Pkwy., Aurora IL 60504. (630)513-8316. **E-mail:** emily@medallionmediagroup.com. **E-mail:** submissions@medallionmediagroup.com. **Website:** medallionmediagroup.com. **Contact:** Emily Steele, editorial director. Estab. 2003. "We are an independent, innovative publisher looking for compelling, memorable stories told in distinctive voices." Publishes trade paperback, hardcover, e-book originals, book apps, and TREEbook. Guidelines online.

NEEDS Word count: 40,000-90,000 for YA; 60,000-120,000 for all others. No short stories, anthologies, erotica.

HOW TO CONTACT Submit first 3 consecutive chapters and a synopsis through our online submission form.

TERMS Offers advance. Responds in 2-3 months to mss.

TIPS "We are not affected by trends. We are simply looking for well-crafted, original, compelling works of fiction and nonfiction. Please visit our website for the most current guidelines prior to submitting anything to us."

MELANGE BOOKS, LLC

White Bear Lake MN 55110-5538. **E-mail:** melange-books@melange-books.com. **E-mail:** submissions@ melange-books.com. **Website:** www.melange-books. com. **Contact:** Nancy Schumacher, publisher and acquiring editor for Melange and Satin Romance; Caroline Andrus, acquiring editor for Fire and Ice for Young Adult. Estab. 2011. Melange is a royalty-paying company publishing e-books and print books. Publishes trade paperback originals and electronic originals. Send SASE for book catalog. Guidelines online.

IMPRINTS Imprints include Fire and Ice for Young and New Adults and Satin Romance.

NEEDS Submit a clean mss by following guidelines on website.

HOW TO CONTACT Query electronically by clicking on "submissions" on website. Include a synopsis and 4 chapters.

TERMS Authors receive a minimum of 20% royalty on print sales, 40% on electronic book sales. Does not offer an advance. Responds in 1 month on queries; 2 months on proposals; 4-6 months on mss.

MELICAN PUBLISHING

Unit 4, 36 Devon Rd., Bassendean 6054 Western Australia. (61)0481-369-611. **E-mail:** melican@melicanpublishing.com.au. **E-mail:** submissions@melicanpublishing.com.au. **Website:** www.melicanpublishing.com.au. **Contact:** Alan Malcolm, managing editor; Cicely Binford, literary editor. Estab. 2014. Publishes trade paperback, mass-market paperback, and electronic originals. Catalog available for SASE. Guidelines available online or via e-mail.

HOW TO CONTACT Query with SASE. Submit proposal package with synopsis and 2 sample chapters.

TERMS Pays royalties, according to AWG and Authors Society. Does not offer an advance. Responds in 1 month to queries and proposals.

TIPS "Pay attention to the submission guidelines. Ensure your spelling and punctuation are corrected and the formatting is consistent throughout the document. Do not submit biographical details unless requested."

MERRIAM PRESS

133 Elm St., Suite 3R, Bennington VT 05201. (802)447-0313. **E-mail:** ray@merriam-press.com. **Website:** www.merriam-press.com. Estab. 1988. "Merriam Press specializes in military history, particularly World War II history. We are also branching out into other genres." Publishes hardcover and softcover trade paperback originals and reprints. Book catalog and guidelines online.

NEEDS Especially but not limited to military history.

HOW TO CONTACT Query with SASE or by e-mail first.

TERMS Pays 10% royalty on actual selling price. Responds quickly (e-mail preferred) to queries.

TIPS "Our military history books are geared for military historians, collectors, model kit builders, wargamers, veterans, general enthusiasts. We now publish some historical fiction and poetry and will consider well-written books on a variety of nonmilitary topics."

MESSIANIC JEWISH PUBLISHERS

6120 Day Long Ln., Clarksville MD 21029. (410)531-6644. **E-mail:** editor@messianicjewish.net. **Website:** www.messianicjewish.net. Publishes hardcover and trade paperback originals and reprints. Guidelines via e-mail.

NEEDS "We publish very little fiction. Jewish or Biblical themes are a must. Text must demonstrate keen awareness of Jewish culture and thought."

HOW TO CONTACT Query with SASE. Unsolicited mss are not return.

TERMS Pays 7-15% royalty on wholesale price.

METHUEN PUBLISHING LTD

Editorial Department, 11-12 Buckingham Gate, London SW1E 6LB United Kingdom. (44)(207)798-1600. **Fax:** (44)(207)828-2098. **E-mail:** editorial@metheun.co.uk. **Website:** www.methuen.co.uk. Estab. 1889. Guidelines online.

No unsolicited mss; synopses and ideas welcome. Prefers to be approached via agents or a letter of inquiry. No first novels, cookery books or personal memoirs.

NEEDS No first novels.

HOW TO CONTACT Query with SASE. Submit proposal package, outline, outline/proposal, résumé, publishing history, clips, bio, SASE.

TERMS Pays royalty.

TIPS "We recommend that all prospective authors attempt to find an agent before submitting to publishers and we do not encourage unagented submissions."

MICHIGAN STATE UNIVERSITY PRESS

1405 S. Harrison Rd., Suite 25, East Lansing MI 48823-5202. (517)355-9543. **Fax:** (517)432-2611. **E-mail:** msupress@msu.edu. **Website:** msupress.org. **Contact:** Alex Schwartz and Julie Loehr, acquisitions. Estab. 1947. Michigan State University Press has notably represented both scholarly publishing and the mission of Michigan State University with the publication of numerous award-winning books and scholarly journals. In addition, they publish nonfiction that addresses, in a more contemporary way, social concerns, such as diversity and civil rights. They also publish literary fiction and poetry. Publishes hardcover and softcover originals. Book catalog and ms guidelines online.

NEEDS Publishes literary fiction.

HOW TO CONTACT Submit proposal.

TERMS Pays variable royalty.

MILKWEED EDITIONS

1011 Washington Ave. S., Suite 300, Minneapolis MN 55415. (612)332-3192. **Fax:** (612)215-2550. **Website:** www.milkweed.org. **Contact:** Patrick Thomas, editor and program director. Estab. 1979. "Milkweed Editions publishes with the intention of making a humane impact on society, in the belief that literature is a transformative art uniquely able to convey the essential experiences of the human heart and spirit. To that end, Milkweed Editions publishes distinctive voices of literary merit in handsomely designed, visually dynamic books, exploring the ethical, cultural, and esthetic issues that free societies need continually to address." Publishes hardcover, trade paperback, and electronic originals; trade paperback and electronic reprints. Book catalog online. Guidelines online.

NEEDS Novels for adults and for readers 8-13. High literary quality. For adult readers: literary fiction, nonfiction, poetry, essays. Middle readers: adventure, contemporary, fantasy, multicultural, nature/environment, suspense/mystery. Average length: middle readers—90-200 pages. No romance, mysteries, science fiction.

HOW TO CONTACT Query with SASE, submit completed ms.

TERMS Pays authors variable royalty based on retail price. Offers advance against royalties. Pays varied advance from $500-10,000. Responds in 6 months.

TIPS "We are looking for excellent writing with the intent of making a humane impact on society. Please read submission guidelines before submitting and acquaint yourself with our books in terms of style and quality before submitting. Many factors influence our selection process, so don't get discouraged. Nonfiction is focused on literary writing about the natural world, including living well in urban environments."

MILKWEED FOR YOUNG READERS

Milkweed Editions, Open Book Building, 1011 Washington Ave. S., Suite 300, Minneapolis MN 55415. (612)332-3192. **Fax:** (612)215-2550. **Website:** www.milkweed.org. **Contact:** Patrick Thomas, managing director. Estab. 1984. "We are looking first of all for high-quality literary writing. We publish books with the intention of making a humane impact on society." Publishes hardcover and trade paperback originals. Book catalog for $1.50. Guidelines online.

HOW TO CONTACT "Milkweed Editions now accepts mss online through our Submission Manager. If you're a first-time submitter, you'll need to fill in a simple form and then follow the instructions for selecting and uploading your ms. Please make sure that your ms follows the submission guidelines."

TERMS Pays 7% royalty on retail price. Pays variable advance. Responds in 6 months to queries.

MONDIAL

203 W. 107th St., Suite 6C, New York NY 10025. (212)851-3252. **Fax:** (208)361-2863. **E-mail:** contact@mondialbooks.com. **Website:** www.mondialbooks.

com; www.librejo.com. **Contact:** Andrew Moore, editor. Estab. 1996. Publishes hard cover, trade paperback originals and reprints. Guidelines available online.

HOW TO CONTACT Query through online submission form.

TERMS Pays 10% royalty on wholesale price. Responds to queries in 3 months. Responds only if interested.

MOODY PUBLISHERS

Moody Bible Institute, 820 N. LaSalle Blvd., Chicago IL 60610. (800)678-8812. **Fax:** (312)329-4157. **E-mail:** authors@moody.edu. **Website:** www.moodypublishers.org. Estab. 1894. "The mission of Moody Publishers is to educate and edify the Christian and to evangelize the non-Christian by ethically publishing conservative, evangelical Christian literature and other media for all ages around the world, and to help provide resources for Moody Bible Institute in its training of future Christian leaders." Publishes hardcover, trade, and mass-market paperback originals. Book catalog for 9x12 envelope and 4 first-class stamps. Guidelines online.

HOW TO CONTACT *Agented submissions only.*

TERMS Royalty varies. Responds in 2-3 months to queries.

TIPS "In our fiction list, we're looking for Christian storytellers rather than teachers trying to present a message. Your motivation should be to delight the reader. Using your skills to create beautiful works is glorifying to God."

THE NAUTICAL & AVIATION PUBLISHING CO.

845 A Low Country Blvd., Mt. Pleasant SC 29464. (843)856-0561. **Fax:** (843)856-3164. **E-mail:** nauticalaviationpublishing@comcast.net. **Website:** www.nauticalaviation.bizland.com. Estab. 1979. Publishes hardcover and trade paperback originals and reprints. Book catalog and guidelines available free.

HOW TO CONTACT Submit complete ms with cover letter and brief synopsis.

TERMS Pays royalty.

TIPS "We are primarily a nonfiction publisher, but we will review historical fiction of military interest with strong literary merit."

NBM PUBLISHING

160 Broadway, Suite 700, East Bldg., New York NY 10038. **E-mail:** nbmgn@nbmpub.com. **Website:** nbmpub.com. **Contact:** Terry Nantier, editor/art director.

Estab. 1976. "One of the best regarded quality graphic novel publishers. Our catalog is determined by what will appeal to a wide audience of readers." Publishes hardcover originals, paperback originals. Format: offset printing; perfect binding, e-books. Average print order: 3,000-4,000; average debut writer's print order: 2,000. Publishes 1 debut writers/year. Publishes 20 titles/year. Member: IBPA, CBC. Distributed/promoted by IPG. Imprints: ComicsLit (literary comics), Eurotica (erotic comics). Publishes graphic novels for an audience of YA/adults. Types of books include fiction, mystery and social parodies.

NEEDS literary fiction mostly, children's/juvenile (especially fairy tales, classics), creative nonfiction (especially true crime), erotica, ethnic/multicultural, humor (satire), manga, mystery/suspense, translations, young adult/teen. Does not want superhero or overly violent comics.

HOW TO CONTACT Prefers submissions from writer-artists, creative teams. Send a one-page synopsis of story along with a few pages of comics (copies, NOT originals) and a SASE or submit by e-mail. Attends San Diego Comicon. Agented submissions: 2%. Responds to queries in 1 week; to ms/art packages in 3-4 weeks. Sometimes comments on rejected mss.

TERMS Royalties and advance negotiable. Publishes ms 1 year after acceptance. Writer's guidelines on website. Artist's guidelines on website. Book catalog free upon request.

THOMAS NELSON, INC.

HarperCollins Christian Publishing, Box 141000, Nashville TN 37214-1000. (615)889-9000. **Website:** www. thomasnelson.com. Thomas Nelson publishes Christian lifestyle nonfiction and fiction, and general nonfiction. Publishes hardcover and paperback orginals.

NEEDS Publishes authors of commercial fiction who write for adults from a Christian perspective.

HOW TO CONTACT *Does not accept unsolicited mss.* No phone queries.

TERMS Rates negotiated for each project. Pays advance.

TOMMY NELSON

Imprint of Thomas Nelson, Inc., P.O. Box 141000, Nashville TN 37214-1000. (615)889-9000. **Fax:** (615)902-2219. **Website:** www.tommynelson.com. "Tommy Nelson publishes children's Christian nonfiction and fiction for boys and girls up to age 14. We honor God and serve people through books, videos, software and Bibles for children that improve the lives of our customers." Publishes hardcover and trade paperback originals. Guidelines online.

NEEDS No stereotypical characters.

HOW TO CONTACT *Does not accept unsolicited mss.*

TIPS "Know the Christian Booksellers Association market. Check out the Christian bookstores to see what sells and what is needed."

NEW AMERICAN LIBRARY

Penguin Putnam, Inc., 375 Hudson St., New York NY 10014. (212)366-2000. **Fax:** (212)366-2889. **Website:** www.penguinputnam.com. Estab. 1948. NAL publishes commercial fiction and nonfiction for the popular audience. Publishes mass-market and trade paperback originals and reprints. Book catalog for SASE.

NEEDS All kinds of commercial fiction.

HOW TO CONTACT *Agented submissions only.*

TERMS Pays negotiable royalty. Pays negotiable advance.

NEW DIRECTIONS

80 Eighth Ave., New York NY 10011. **Fax:** (212)255-0231. **E-mail:** editorial@ndbooks.com. **Website:** www.ndpublishing.com. **Contact:** Editorial Assistant. Estab. 1936. "Currently, New Directions focuses primarily on fiction in translation, avant garde American fiction, and experimental poetry by American and foreign authors. If your work does not fall into one of those categories, you would probably do best to submit your work elsewhere." Hardcover and trade paperback originals. Book catalog and guidelines online.

NEEDS No juvenile or young adult, occult or paranormal, genre fiction (formula romances, sci-fi or westerns), arts & crafts, and inspirational poetry.

HOW TO CONTACT Brief query only.

TERMS Responds in 3-4 months to queries.

TIPS "Our books serve the academic community."

NEWEST PUBLISHERS LTD.

201, 8540-109 St., Edmonton AB T6G 1E6 Canada. (780)432-9427. **Fax:** (780)433-3179. **E-mail:** submissions@newestpress.com. **Website:** www.newestpress.com. Estab. 1977. NeWest publishes Western Canadian fiction, nonfiction, poetry, and drama. Publishes trade paperback originals. Book catalog for 9x12 SASE. Guidelines online.

HOW TO CONTACT Submit complete ms.

TERMS Pays 10% royalty. Responds in 6-8 months to queries.

NEW ISSUES POETRY & PROSE

Western Michigan University, 1903 W. Michigan Ave., Kalamazoo MI 49008-5463. (269)387-8185. **Fax:** (269)387-2562. **E-mail:** new-issues@wmich.edu. **Website:** wmich.edu/newissues. **Contact:** Managing Editor. Estab. 1996. Guidelines online.

HOW TO CONTACT Only considers submissions to book contests.

NEW LIBRI PRESS

4230 95th Ave. SE, Mercer Island WA 98040. **E-mail:** query@newlibri.com. **Website:** www.newlibri.com. **Contact:** Michael Muller, editor; Stanislav Fritz, editor. Estab. 2011. Publishes trade paperback, electronic original, electronic reprints. Catalog online. Guidelines online. Electronic submissions only.

NEEDS "Open to most ideas right now; this will change as we mature as a press. As a new press, we are more open than most and time will probably shape the direction. That said, trite as it is, we want good writing that is fun to read. While we currently are not looking for some sub-genres, if it is well written and a bit off the beaten path, submit to us. We are e-book focused. We may not create a paper version if the e-book does not sell, which means some fiction may be less likely to currently sell (e.g. picture books would work only on an iPad or Color Nook as of this writing)."

HOW TO CONTACT Submit proposal package, including synopsis. Prefers complete ms.

TERMS Pays 20-35% royalty on wholesale price. No advance. Responds in 3 months to mss.

TIPS "Our audience is someone who is comfortable reading an e-book, or someone who is tired of the recycled authors of mainstream publishing, but still wants a good, relatively fast, reading experience. The industry is changing, while we accept for the traditional model, we are searching for writers who are interested in sharing the risk and controlling their own destiny. We embrace writers with no agent."

NEW RIVERS PRESS

MSU Moorhead, 1104 Seventh Ave. S., Moorhead MN 56563. **E-mail:** kelleysu@mnstate.edu. **Website:** www. newriverspress.com. **Contact:** Suzzanne Kelley, managing editor. Estab. 1968. New Rivers Press publishes collections of poetry, novels, nonfiction, translations of contemporary literature, and collections of short fiction and nonfiction. "We continue to publish books regularly by new and emerging writers, but we also welcome the opportunity to read work of every char-

acter and to publish the best literature available nationwide. Each fall through the Many Voices Project competition, we choose 2 books: 1 poetry and 1 prose."

NEEDS Sponsors American Fiction Prize to find best unpublished short stories by American writers.

NORTH ATLANTIC BOOKS

2526 MLK Jr. Way, Berkeley CA 94704. **Website:** www.northatlanticbooks.com. **Contact:** Acquisitions Board. Estab. 1974. Publishes hardcover, trade paperback, and electronic originals; trade paperback and electronic reprints. Book catalog free on request (if available). Guidelines online.

IMPRINTS Evolver Editions, Blue Snake Books.

NEEDS "We only publish fiction on rare occasions."

HOW TO CONTACT Submit proposal package including an outline, 3-4 sample chapters, and "a 75-word statement about the book, your qualifications as an author, marketing plan/audience, for the book, and comparable titles."

TERMS Pays royalty percentage on wholesale price. Responds in 3-6 months.

NORTIA PRESS

Santa Ana CA **E-mail:** acquisitions@nortiapress.com. **Website:** www.nortiapress.com. Estab. 2009. Publishes trade paperback and electronic originals.

NEEDS "We focus mainly on nonfiction as well as literary and historical fiction, but are open to other genres. No vampire stories, science fiction, or erotica, please."

HOW TO CONTACT Submit a brief e-mail query. Please include a short bio, approximate word count of book, and expected date of completion (fiction titles should be completed before sending a query, and should contain a sample chapter in the body of the e-mail). All unsolicited snail mail or attachments will be discarded without review.

TERMS Pays negotiable royalties on wholesale price. Responds in 1 month.

TIPS "We specialize in working with experienced authors who seek a more collaborative and fulfilling relationship with their publisher. As such, we are less likely to accept pitches form first-time authors, no matter how good the idea. As with any pitch, please make your e-mail very brief and to the point, so the reader is not forced to skim it. Always include some biographic information. Your life is interesting."

W.W. NORTON & COMPANY, INC.

500 Fifth Ave., New York NY 10110. (212)354-5500. **Fax:** (212)869-0856. **Website:** www.wwnorton.com.

Estab. 1923. "W. W. Norton & Company, the oldest and largest publishing house owned wholly by its employees, strives to carry out the imperative of its founder to 'publish books not for a single season, but for the years' in fiction, nonfiction, poetry, college textbooks, cookbooks, art books and professional books. Due to the workload of our editorial staff and the large volume of materials we receive, *Norton is no longer able to accept unsolicited submissions*. If you are seeking publication, we suggest working with a literary agent who will represent you to the house."

OAK TREE PRESS

1820 W. Lacy Blvd., #220, Hanford CA 93230. **E-mail:** query@oaktreebooks.com. **Website:** www.oaktreebooks.com. **Contact:** Billie Johnson, publisher. Estab. 1998. Oak Tree Press is an independent publisher that celebrates writers, and is dedicated to the many great unknowns who are just waiting for the opportunity to break into print. "We're looking for mainstream, genre fiction, narrative nonfiction, how-to. Sponsors 3 contests annually: Dark Oak Mystery, Timeless Love Romance and CopTales for true crime and other stories of law enforcement professionals." Publishes trade paperback and hardcover books. Catalog and guidelines online.

NEEDS Emphasis on mystery and romance novels. "No science fiction or fantasy novels, or stories set far into the future. Next, novels substantially longer than our stated word count are not considered, regardless of genre. We look for mss of 70-90,000 words. If the story really charms us, we will bend some on either end of the range. No right-wing political or racist agenda, gratuitous sex or violence, especially against women, or depict harm of animals."

HOW TO CONTACT Does not accept or return unsolicited mss. Query with SASE. Accepts queries by e-mail. Include estimated word count, brief bio, list of publishing credits, brief description of ms.

TERMS Royalties based on sales. No advance. Responds in 4-6 weeks.

TIPS "Perhaps my most extreme pet peeve is receiving queries on projects which we've clearly advertised we don't want: science fiction, fantasy, epic tomes, bigoted diatribes and so on. Second to that is a practice I call 'over-taping,' or the use of yards and yards of tape, or worse yet, the filament tape so that it takes forever to open the package. Finding story pitches on my voice mail is also annoying."

OCEANVIEW PUBLISHING

595 Bay Isles Rd., Suite 120-G, Longboat Key FL 34228. **E-mail:** submissions@oceanviewpub.com. **Website:** www.oceanviewpub.com. **Contact:** Robert Gussin, CEO. Estab. 2006. "Independent publisher of nonfiction and fiction, with primary interest in original mystery, thriller and suspense titles. Accepts new and established writers." Publishes hardcover and electronic originals. Catalog and guidelines online.

NEEDS Accepting adult mss with a primary interest in the mystery, thriller and suspense genres—from new and established writers. No children's or YA literature, poetry, cookbooks, technical manuals or short stories.

HOW TO CONTACT Within body of e-mail only, include author's name and brief bio (Indicate if this is an agent submission), ms title and word count, author's mailing address, phone number and e-mail address. Attached to the e-mail should be the following: A synopsis of 750 words or fewer. The first 30 pages of the ms. Please note that we accept only Word documents as attachments to the submission e-mail. Do not send query letters or proposals.

TERMS Responds in 3 months on mss.

ONSTAGE PUBLISHING

190 Lime Quarry Rd., Suite 106-J, Madison AL 35758-8962. (256)461-0661. **E-mail:** onstage123@knology.net. **Website:** www.onstagepublishing.com. **Contact:** Dianne Hamilton, senior editor. Estab. 1999. "At this time, we only produce fiction books for ages 8-18. We have added an e-book only side of the house for mysteries for grades 6-12. See our website for more information. We will not do anthologies of any kind. Query first for nonfiction projects as nonfiction projects must spark our interest. Now accepting e-mail queries and submissions. For submissions: Put the first 3 chapters in the body of the e-mail. Do not use attachments! We will no longer return any mss. Only an SASE envelope is needed. Send complete ms if under 20,000 words, otherwise send synopsis and first 3 chapters."

"To everyone who has submitted a ms, we are currently about 4 months behind. We should get back on track soon. Please feel free to submit your ms to other houses. OnStage Publishing understands that authors work very hard to produce the finished ms and we do not have to have exclusive submission rights. Please let us know if you sell your ms. Meanwhile, keep writing and we'll keep reading for our next acquisitions."

NEEDS Middle readers: adventure, contemporary, fantasy, history, nature/environment, science fiction, suspense/mystery. Young adults: adventure, contemporary, fantasy, history, humor, science fiction, suspense/mystery. Average word length: chapter books—4,000-6,000 words; middle readers—5,000 words and up; young adults—25,000 and up. Recently published *Mission: Shanghai* by Jamie Dodson (an adventure for boys ages 12+); *Birmingham, 1933: Alice* (a chapter book for grades 3-5). "We do not produce picture books."

TERMS Pays authors/illustrators/photographers advance plus royalties.

TIPS "Study our titles and get a sense of the kind of books we publish, so that you know whether your project is likely to be right for us."

☺ OOLICHAN BOOKS

P.O. Box 2278, Lantzville BC V0R 1M0 Canada. (250)390-4839. **Fax:** (866)299-0026. **E-mail:** oolichanbooks@telus.net. **Website:** www.oolichan.com. Estab. 1974. Publishes hardcover and trade paperback originals and reprints. Book catalog online. Guidelines online.

☺ Only publishes Canadian authors.

NEEDS "We try to publish at least 2 literary fiction titles each year. We receive many more deserving submissions than we are able to publish, so we publish only outstanding work. We try to balance our list between emerging and established writers, and have published many first-time writers who have gone on to win or be shortlisted for major literary awards, both nationally and internationally."

HOW TO CONTACT Submit proposal package, publishing history, clips, bio, cover letter, 3 sample chapters, SASE.

TERMS Pays royalty on retail price. Responds in 1-3 months.

TIPS "Our audience is adult readers who love good books and good literature. Our audience is regional and national, as well as international. Follow our submission guidelines. Check out some of our titles at your local library or bookstore to get an idea of what we publish. Don't send us the only copy of your ms. Let us know if your submission is simultaneous, and inform us if it is accepted elsewhere. Above all, keep writing!"

OOLIGAN PRESS

369 Neuberger Hall, 724 SW Harrison St., Portland OR 97201. (503)725-9410. **E-mail:** acquisitions@ooliganpress.pdx.edu. **Website:** ooligan.pdx.edu. Estab. 2001. Publishes trade paperback, and electronic originals and reprints. Book catalog online. Guidelines online.

NEEDS "Ooligan Press is a general trade press at Portland State University. As a teaching press, Ooligan makes as little distinction as possible between the press and the classroom. Under the direction of professional faculty and staff, the work of the press is done by students enrolled in the Book Publishing graduate program at PSU. We are especially interested in works with social, literary, or educational value. Though we place special value on regional authors, we are open to all submissions, including translated works and writings by children and young adults. We do not currently publish picture books, board books, easy readers, or pop-up books or middle-grade readers."

HOW TO CONTACT Query with SASE. *"At this time we cannot accept science fiction or fantasy submissions."*

TERMS Pays negotiable royalty on retail price.

TIPS "For children's books, our audience will be middle grades and young adult, with marketing to general trade, libraries, and schools. Good marketing ideas increase the chances of a ms succeeding."

☺☺ ORCA BOOK PUBLISHERS

P.O. Box 5626, Stn. B, Victoria BC V8R 6S4 Canada. **Fax:** (877)408-1551. **E-mail:** orca@orcabook.com. **Website:** www.orcabook.com. **Contact:** Amy Collins, editor (picture books); Sarah Harvey, editor (young readers); Andrew Wooldridge, editor (juvenile and teen fiction); Bob Tyrrell, publisher (YA, teen); Ruth Linka, associate editor (rapid reads). Estab. 1984. Publishes hardcover and trade paperback originals, and mass-market paperback originals and reprints. Book catalog for 8.5x11 SASE. Guidelines online.

☺ Only publishes Canadian authors.

NEEDS Picture books: animals, contemporary, history, nature/environment. Middle readers: contemporary, history, fantasy, nature/environment, problem novels, graphic novels. Young adults: adventure, contemporary, hi-lo (Orca Soundings), history, multicultural, nature/environment, problem novels, suspense/mystery, graphic novels. Average word length: picture books—500-1,500; middle readers—20,000-35,000;

young adult—25,000-45,000; Orca Soundings—13,000-15,000; Orca Currents—13,000-15,000. No romance, science fiction.

HOW TO CONTACT Query with SASE. Submit proposal package, outline, clips, 2-5 sample chapters, SASE.

TERMS Pays 10% royalty. Responds in 1 month to queries; 2 months to proposals and mss.

TIPS "Our audience is students in grades K-12. Know our books, and know the market."

⚫⚫ ORCHARD BOOKS

557 Broadway, New York NY 10012. **E-mail:** mcroland@scholastic.com. **Website:** www.scholastic.com. **Contact:** Ken Geist, vice president/editorial director; David Saylor, vice president/creative director. *Orchard is not accepting unsolicited mss.*

NEEDS Picture books, early readers, and novelty: animal, contemporary, history, humor, multicultural, poetry.

TERMS Most commonly offers an advance against list royalties.

THE OVERMOUNTAIN PRESS

P.O. Box 1261, Johnson City TN 37605. (423)926-2691. **Fax:** (423)232-1252. **E-mail:** submissions@overmtn. com. **Website:** www.overmtn.com. Estab. 1970. "The Overmountain Press publishes primarily Appalachian history. Audience is people interested in history of Tennessee, Virginia, North Carolina, Kentucky, and all aspects of this region—Revolutionary War, Civil War, county histories, historical biographies, etc." Publishes hardcover and trade paperback originals and reprints. Book catalog available free. Guidelines online.

HOW TO CONTACT Submit complete ms.

TERMS Responds in 3-6 months to mss.

ⓘ RICHARD C. OWEN PUBLISHERS, INC.

P.O. Box 585, Katonah NY 10536. (914)232-3903; (800)262-0787. **E-mail:** richardowen@rcowen.com. **Website:** www.rcowen.com. **Contact:** Richard Owen, publisher. Estab. 1982. "We publish child-focused books, with inherent instructional value, about characters and situations with which 5, 6, and 7-year-old children can identify—books that can be read for meaning, entertainment, enjoyment and information. We include multicultural stories that present minorities in a positive and natural way. Our stories show the diversity in America." Not interested in lesson plans, or books of activities for literature studies or other content areas. Submit complete ms and cover letter. Book catalog available with SASE. Ms guidelines with SASE or online.

⚫ "Due to high volume and long production time, we are currently limiting to nonfiction submissions only."

TERMS Pays authors royalty of 5% based on net price or outright purchase (range: $25-500). Offers no advances. Pays illustrators by the project (range: $100-2,000) or per photo (range: $50-150). Responds to mss in 1 year.

⚫ PETER OWEN PUBLISHERS

20 Holland Park Ave., London W11 3 QU United Kingdom. (44)(208)350-1775. **Fax:** (44)(208)340-9488. **E-mail:** admin@peterowen.com. **Website:** www.peterowen.com. **Contact:** Antonia Owen, editorial director. "We are far more interested in proposals for nonfiction than fiction at the moment. No poetry or short stories." Publishes hardcover originals and trade paperback originals and reprints. Book catalog for SASE, SAE with IRC or on website.

NEEDS "No first novels. Authors should be aware that we publish very little new fiction these days."

HOW TO CONTACT Query with synopsis, sample chapters.

TERMS Pays 7.5-10% royalty. Pays negotiable advance. Responds in 2 months to queries; 3 months to proposals and mss.

⚫ OXFORD UNIVERSITY PRESS: SOUTHERN AFRICA

P.O. Box 12119, NI City Cape Town 7463 South Africa. (27)(21)596-2300. **Fax:** (27)(21)596-1234. **E-mail:** oxford.za@oup.com. **Website:** www.oup.com/za. Academic publisher known for its educational books for southern African schools. Also publishes general and reference titles. Book catalog online. Guidelines online.

HOW TO CONTACT Submit cover letter, synopsis.

PACIFIC PRESS PUBLISHING ASSOCIATION

Trade Book Division, 1350 N. Kings Rd., Nampa ID 83687. (208)465-2500. **Fax:** (208)465-2531. **E-mail:** booksubmissions@pacificpress.com. **Website:** www. pacificpress.com. **Contact:** Scott Cady, acquisitions editor (children's stories, biography, Christian living, spiritual growth); David Jarnes, book editor (theology, doctrine, inspiration). Estab. 1874. "We publish books that fit Seventh-day Adventist beliefs only. All titles are Christian and religious. For guidance, see www.adventist.org/beliefs/index.html. Our books fit into the categories of this retail site: www.adventistbookcenter.com." Publishes hardcover and trade paperback originals and reprints. Guidelines online.

NEEDS "Pacific Press rarely publishes fiction, but we're interested in developing a line of Seventh-day Adventist fiction in the future. Only proposals accepted; no full mss."

TERMS Pays 8-16% royalty on wholesale price. Responds in 3 months to queries.

TIPS "Our primary audience is members of the Seventh-day Adventist denomination. Almost all are written by Seventh-day Adventists. Books that do well for us relate the Biblical message to practical human concerns and focus more on the experiential rather than theoretical aspects of Christianity. We are assigning more titles, using less unsolicited material—although we still publish mss from freelance submissions and proposals."

PAGESPRING PUBLISHING

P.O. Box 2113, Columbus OH 43221. **E-mail:** ps@pagespringpublishing.com. **E-mail:** yaeditor@pagespringpublishing.com; weditor@pagespringpublishing.com. **Website:** www.pagespringpublishing.com. Estab. 2012. "PageSpring Publishing publishes young adult and middle-grade titles under the Lucky Marble Books imprint and women's fiction under the Cup of Tea imprint. See imprint websites for submission details." Publishes trade paperback and electronic originals. Guidelines online.

IMPRINTS Lucky Marble Books, Cup of Tea Books.

HOW TO CONTACT Submit proposal package including synopsis and 3 sample chapters.

TERMS Pays royalty on wholesale price. Responds to queries in 1 month.

PALARI PUBLISHING

107 S. West St., PMB 778, Alexandria VA 22314. (866)570-6724. **Fax:** (866)570-6724. **E-mail:** dave@palaribooks.com. **Website:** www.palaribooks.com. **Contact:** David Smitherman, publisher/editor. Estab. 1998. "Palari provides authoritative, well-written nonfiction that addresses topical consumer needs and fiction with an emphasis on intelligence and quality. We accept solicited and unsolicited mss, however we prefer a query letter and SASE, describing the project briefly and concisely. This letter should include a complete address and telephone number. Palari Publishing accepts queries or any other submissions by e-mail, but prefers queries submitted by U.S. mail. All queries must be submitted by mail according to our guidelines. Promotes titles through book signings, direct mail and the Internet." Publishes hardcover and trade paperback originals. Guidelines online.

Member of Publishers Marketing Association.

NEEDS "Tell why your idea is unique or interesting. Make sure we are interested in your genre before submitting."

HOW TO CONTACT Query with SASE. Submit bio, estimated word count, list of publishing credits. Accepts queries via e-mail (prefer U.S. Mail), fax.

TERMS Pays royalty. Responds in 1 month to queries; 2-3 months to mss.

TIPS "Send a good bio. I'm interested in a writer's experience and unique outlook on life."

PANTHEON BOOKS

Random House, Inc., 1745 Broadway, 3rd Floor, New York NY 10019. **E-mail:** pantheonpublicity@randomhouse.com. **Website:** www.pantheonbooks.com. Estab. 1942. Publishes hardcover and trade paperback originals and trade paperback reprints.

Pantheon Books publishes both Western and non-Western authors of literary fiction and important nonfiction. "We only accept mss submitted by an agent."

HOW TO CONTACT *Does not accept unsolicited mss.* Agented submissions only.

PANTS ON FIRE PRESS

2062 Harbor Cove Way, Winter Garden FL 34787. **E-mail:** editor@pantsonfirepress.com. **E-mail:** submission@pantsonfirepress.com. **Website:** www.pantsonfirepress.com. **Contact:** Becca Goldman, senior editor; Emily Gerety, editor. Estab. 2012. Pants On Fire Press is an award-winning book publisher of picture, middle-grade, young adult, and adult books. They are a digital-first book publisher, striving to follow a high degree of excellence while maintaining quality standards. Publishes hardcover originals and reprints, trade paperback originals and reprints, and electronic originals and reprints. Catalog available on website. Mss guidelines available on website.

NEEDS Publishes big story ideas with high concepts, new worlds, and meaty characters for children, teens, and discerning adults. Always on the lookout for Action, Adventure, Animals, Comedic, Dramatic, Dystopian, Fantasy, Historical, Paranormal, Romance, Sci-Fi, Supernatural, and Suspense stories.

HOW TO CONTACT Submit a proposal package including a synopsis, 3 sample chapters, and a query letter via e-mail.

TERMS Pays 10-50% royalties on wholesale price. Responds in 3 months to queries, proposals, and mss.

PAPERCUTZ

160 Broadway, Suite 700E, New York NY 10038. (646)559-4681. **Fax:** (212)643-1545. **Website:** www.papercutz.com. Estab. 2004. Publisher of graphic novels.

NEEDS "Independent publisher of graphic novels based on popular existing properties aimed at the teen and tween market."

TIPS "Be familiar with our titles—that's the best way to know what we're interested in publishing. If you are somehow attached to a successful tween or teen property and would like to adapt it into a graphic novel, we may be interested."

PARADISE CAY PUBLICATIONS

P.O. Box 29, Arcata CA 95518-0029. (800)736-4509. **Fax:** (707)822-9163. **E-mail:** info@paracay.com; james@paracay.com. **Website:** www.paracay.com. **Contact:** Matt Morehouse, publisher. "Paradise Cay Publications, Inc. is a small independent publisher specializing in nautical books, videos, and art prints. Our primary interest is in mss that deal with the instructional and technical aspects of ocean sailing. We also publish and will consider fiction if it has a strong nautical theme." Publishes hardcover and trade paperback originals and reprints. Book catalog and ms guidelines free on request or online.

IMPRINTS Pardey Books.

NEEDS All fiction must have a nautical theme.

HOW TO CONTACT Query with SASE. Submit proposal package, clips, 2-3 sample chapters.

TERMS Pays 10-15% royalty on wholesale price. Makes outright purchase of $1,000-10,000. Does not normally pay advances to first-time or little-known authors. Responds in 1 month to queries/proposals; 2 months to mss.

TIPS "Audience is recreational sailors. Call Matt Morehouse (publisher)."

PAUL DRY BOOKS

1700 Sansom St., Suite 700, Philadelphia PA 19103. (215)231-9939. **Fax:** (215)231-9942. **E-mail:** pdry@pauldrybooks.com; editor@pauldrybooks.com. **Website:** pauldrybooks.com. "We publish fiction, both novels and short stories, and nonfiction, biography, memoirs, history, and essays, covering subjects from Homer to Chekhov, bird watching to jazz music, New York City to shogunate Japan." Hardcover and trade paperback originals, trade paperback reprints. Book catalog available online. Guidelines available online.

○ "Take a few minutes to familiarize yourself with the books we publish. Then if you think your book would be a good fit in our line, we invite you to submit the following: A one- or two-page summary of the work. Be sure to tell us how many pages or words the full book will be; a sample of 20-30 pages; your bio. A brief description of how you think the book (and you, the author) could be marketed."

HOW TO CONTACT Submit sample chapters, clips, bio.

TIPS "Our aim is to publish lively books 'to awaken, delight, and educate'—to spark conversation. We publish fiction and nonfiction, and essays covering subjects from Homer to Chekhov, bird watching to jazz music, New York City to shogunate Japan."

PAYCOCK PRESS

3819 N. 13th St., Arlington VA 22201. (703)525-9296. **E-mail:** rchrdpeabody9@gmail.com. **Website:** www.gargoylemagazine.com. **Contact:** Richard Peabody. Estab. 1976. "Too academic for the underground, too outlaw for the academic world. We tend to be edgy and look for ultra-literary work." Publishes paperback originals. Books: POD printing. Average print order: 500. Averages 1 total title/year. Member CLMP. Distributes through Amazon and website.

HOW TO CONTACT Accepts unsolicited mss. Accepts queries by e-mail. Include brief bio. Send SASE for return of ms or send a disposable ms and SASE for reply only.

TERMS Responds to queries in 1 month; mss in 4 months.

TIPS "Check out our website. Two of our favorite writers are Paul Bowles and Jeanette Winterson."

❷⊘ PEACE HILL PRESS

Affiliate of W.W. Norton, 18021 The Glebe Ln., Charles City VA 23030. (804)829-5043. **Fax:** (804)829-5704. **E-mail:** info@peacehillpress.com. **Website:** www.peacehillpress.com. Estab. 2001. Publishes hardcover and trade paperback originals.

HOW TO CONTACT Does not take submissions.

TERMS Pays 6-10% royalty on retail price. Pays $500-1,000 advance.

PEACHTREE CHILDREN'S BOOKS

Peachtree Publishers, Ltd., 1700 Chattahoochee Ave., Atlanta GA 30318-2112. (404)876-8761. **Fax:** (404)875-2578. **E-mail:** hello@peachtree-online.com. **Website:** www.peachtree-online.com. **Contact:** Helen Harriss, submissions editor. "We publish a broad range of subjects and perspectives, with emphasis on innovative plots and strong writing." Publishes hardcover and trade paperback originals. Book catalog for 6 first-class stamps. Guidelines online.

NEEDS Looking for very well-written middle-grade and young adult novels. No adult fiction. No collections of poetry or short stories; no romance or science fiction.

HOW TO CONTACT Submit complete ms with SASE.

TERMS Pays royalty on retail price. Responds in 6 months and mss.

PEACHTREE PUBLISHERS, LTD.

1700 Chattahoochee Ave., Atlanta GA 30318. (404)876-8761. **Fax:** (404)875-2578. **E-mail:** hello@peachtree-online.com. **Website:** www.peachtree-online.com. **Contact:** Helen Harriss, acquisitions editor; Loraine Joyner, art director; Melanie McMahon Ives, production manager. Estab. 1977.

NEEDS Picture books, young readers: adventure, animal, concept, history, nature/environment. Middle readers: adventure, animal, history, nature/environment, sports. Young adults: fiction, mystery, adventure. Does not want to see science fiction, romance.

HOW TO CONTACT Submit complete ms or 3 sample chapters by postal mail only.

TERMS Responds in 6-7 months.

◔⊘ PEDLAR PRESS

113 Bond St., St. John's NL A16 1T6 Canada. (709)738-6702. **E-mail:** feralgrl@interlog.com. **Website:** www.pedlarpress.com. **Contact:** Beth Follett, owner/editor. Distributes in Canada through LitDistCo.

NEEDS Experimental, feminist, gay/lesbian, literary, short story collections. Canadian writers only.

HOW TO CONTACT Query with SASE, sample chapter(s), synopsis.

TERMS Pays 10% royalty on retail price. Average advance: $200-400.

TIPS "I select mss according to my taste, which fluctuates. Be familiar with some if not most of Pedlar's recent titles."

PELICAN PUBLISHING COMPANY

1000 Burmaster St., Gretna LA 70053. (504)368-1175. **Fax:** (504)368-1195. **E-mail:** editorial@pelicanpub.com. **Website:** www.pelicanpub.com. Estab. 1926. " "We believe ideas have consequences. One of the consequences is that they lead to a best-selling book. We publish books to improve and uplift the reader. Currently emphasizing business and history titles." Publishes 20 young readers/year; 1 middle reader/year. "Our children's books (illustrated and otherwise) include history, biography, holiday, and regional. Pelican's mission is to publish books of quality and permanence that enrich the lives of those who read them." Publishes hardcover, trade paperback and mass-market paperback originals and reprints. Book catalog and ms guidelines online.

NEEDS We publish no adult fiction. Young readers: history, holiday, science, multicultural and regional. Middle readers: Louisiana History. Multicultural needs include stories about African-Americans, Irish-Americans, Jews, Asian-Americans, and Hispanics. Does not want animal stories, general Christmas stories, "day at school" or "accept yourself" stories. Maximum word length: young readers—1,100; middle readers—40,000. No young adult, romance, science fiction, fantasy, gothic, mystery, erotica, confession, horror, sex, or violence. Also no psychological novels.

HOW TO CONTACT Query with SASE. Submit outline, clips, 2 sample chapters, SASE.

TERMS Pays authors in royalties; buys ms outright "rarely." Illustrators paid by "various arrangements." Advance considered. Responds in 1 month to queries; 3 months to mss.

TIPS "We do extremely well with cookbooks, popular histories, and business. We will continue to build in these areas. The writer must have a clear sense of the market and knowledge of the competition. A query letter should describe the project briefly, give the author's writing and professional credentials, and promotional ideas."

⊜ PENGUIN GROUP: SOUTH AFRICA

P.O. Box 9, Parklands 2121 South Africa. (27)(11)327-3550. **Fax:** (27)(11)327-3660. **E-mail:** publishing@za.penguingroup.com. **Website:** www.penguinbooks.co.za. Seeks adult fiction (literary and mass-market titles) and adult nonfiction (travel, sports, politics, current affairs, business). No children's, young adult, poetry, or short stories.

HOW TO CONTACT Submit intro letter, 3 sample chapters.

TERMS Pays royalty.

PENGUIN GROUP USA

375 Hudson St., New York NY 10014. (212)366-2000. **Website:** www.penguin.com. General interest publisher of both fiction and nonfiction. *No unsolicited mss.* Submit work through a literary agent. DAW Books is the lone exception. Guidelines online.

PENNY-FARTHING PRODUCTIONS

1 Sugar Creek Center Blvd., Suite 820, Sugar Land TX 77478. (713)780-0300 or (800)926-2669. **Fax:** (713)780-4004. **E-mail:** corp@pfpress.com. **Website:** www.pfpress.com. Estab. 1998. "Penny Farthing Productions is not currently accepting submissions and submission messages will not receive a response." Publishes graphic novels. Guidelines online.

THE PERMANENT PRESS

Attn: Judith Shepard, 4170 Noyac Rd., Sag Harbor NY 11963. (631)725-1101. **Fax:** (631)725-8215. **E-mail:** judith@thepermanentpress.com; shepard@thepermanentpress.com. **Website:** www.thepermanentpress.com. **Contact:** Judith and Martin Shepard, acquisitions/co-publishers. Estab. 1978. Mid-size, independent publisher of literary fiction. "We keep titles in print and are active in selling subsidiary rights." Average print order: 1,000-2,500. Averages 16 total titles. Accepts unsolicited mss. Pays 10-15% royalty on wholesale price. Offers $1,000 advance. Publishes hardcover originals.

○ *Will not accept simultaneous submissions.*

NEEDS Promotes titles through reviews. Literary, mainstream/contemporary, mystery. Especially looking for high-line literary fiction, "artful, original and arresting." Accepts any fiction category as long as it is a "well-written, original full-length novel."

TERMS Pays 10-15% royalty on wholesale price. Offers $1,000 advance. Responds in weeks or months.

TIPS "We are looking for good books—be they 10th novels or first ones, it makes little difference. The fiction is more important than the track record. Send us the first 25 pages; it's impossible to judge something that begins on page 302. Also, no outlines—let the writing present itself."

PERSEA BOOKS

277 Broadway, Suite 708, New York NY 10007. (212)260-9256. **Fax:** (212)267-3165. **E-mail:** info@perseabooks.com. **Website:** www.perseabooks.com. Estab. 1975. The aim of Persea is to publish works that endure by meeting high standards of literary merit and relevance. "We have often taken on important books other publishers have overlooked, or have made significant discoveries and rediscoveries, whether of a single work or writer's entire oeuvre. Our books cover a wide range of themes, styles, and genres. We have published poetry, fiction, essays, memoir, biography, titles of Jewish and Middle Eastern interest, women's studies, American Indian folklore, and revived classics, as well as a notable selection of works in translation." Guidelines online.

HOW TO CONTACT Queries should include a cover letter, author background and publication history, a detailed synopsis of the proposed work, and a sample chapter. Please indicate if the work is simultaneously submitted.

TERMS Responds in 8 weeks to proposals; 10 weeks to mss.

PHILOMEL BOOKS

Imprint of Penguin Group (USA), Inc., 375 Hudson St., New York NY 10014. (212)414-3610. **Website:** www.penguin.com. **Contact:** Michael Green, president/publisher. Estab. 1980. "We look for beautifully written, engaging mss for children and young adults." Publishes hardcover originals.

HOW TO CONTACT *No unsolicited mss.*

TERMS Pays authors in royalties. Average advance payment "varies." Illustrators paid by advance and in royalties. Pays negotiable advance.

PIANO PRESS

P.O. Box 85, Del Mar CA 92014. (619)884-1401. **Fax:** (858)755-1104. **E-mail:** pianopress@pianopress.com. **Website:** www.pianopress.com. **Contact:** Elizabeth C. Axford, editor. Estab. 1998. "We publish music-related books, either fiction or nonfiction, coloring books, songbooks, and poetry." Book catalog available for #10 SASE and 2 first-class stamps.

NEEDS Picture books, young readers, middle readers, young adults: folktales, multicultural, poetry, music. Average word length: picture books—1,500-2,000.

TERMS Pays authors, illustrators, and photographers royalty of 5-10% based on retail price. Responds to queries in 3 months; mss in 6 months.

TIPS "We are looking for music-related material only for any juvenile market. Please do not send non-music-related materials. Query first before submitting anything."

PIATKUS BOOKS

Little, Brown Book Group, 100 Victoria Embankment, London WA EC4Y 0DY United Kingdom. (20)7911-

8000. **Fax:** (20)7911-8100. **E-mail:** info@littlebrown. co.uk. **Website:** piatkus.co.uk. Estab. 1979. Publishes hardcover originals, paperback originals, and paperback reprints. Guidelines online.

NEEDS Quality family saga, historical, literary.

HOW TO CONTACT *Agented submissions only.*

⚫⊘ PICADOR USA

MacMillan, 175 Fifth Ave., New York NY 10010. (212)674-5151. **Website:** www.picadorusa.com. Estab. 1994. Picador publishes high-quality literary fiction and nonfiction. "We are open to a broad range of subjects, well written by authoritative authors." Publishes hardcover and trade paperback originals and reprints. Does not accept unsolicited mss. *Agented submissions only.*

TERMS Pays 7-15% on royalty. Advance varies.

PIÑATA BOOKS

Imprint of Arte Publico Press, University of Houston, 4902 Gulf Fwy., Bldg. 19, Room 100, Houston TX 77204-2004. (713)743-2845. **Fax:** (713)743-3080. **E-mail:** submapp@uh.edu. **Website:** www.artepublicopress.com. Estab. 1994. "Piñata Books is dedicated to the publication of children's and young adult literature focusing on U.S. Hispanic culture by U.S. Hispanic authors. Arte Publico's mission is the publication, promotion and dissemination of Latino literature for a variety of national and regional audiences, from early childhood to adult, through the complete gamut of delivery systems, including personal performance as well as print and electronic media." Publishes hardcover and trade paperback originals. Book catalog and guidelines online.

HOW TO CONTACT Submissions made through online submission form.

TERMS Pays 10% royalty on wholesale price. Pays $1,000-3,000 advance. Responds in 2-3 months to queries; 4-6 months to mss.

TIPS "Include cover letter with submission explaining why your ms is unique and important, why we should publish it, who will buy it, etc."

PINEAPPLE PRESS, INC.

P.O. Box 3889, Sarasota FL 34230. (941)706-2507. **Fax:** (800)746-3275. **E-mail:** info@pineapplepress.com. **Website:** www.pineapplepress.com. **Contact:** June Cussen, executive editor. Estab. 1982. "We are seeking quality nonfiction on diverse topics for the library and book trade markets. Our mission is to publish good books about Florida." Publishes hardcover and trade paperback originals. Book catalog for 9x12 SAE with $1.25 postage. Guidelines online.

NEEDS Picture books, young readers, middle readers, young adults: animal, folktales, history, nature/environment.

HOW TO CONTACT Query or submit outline/synopsis and 3 sample chapters.

TERMS Pays authors royalty of 10-15%. Responds in 2 months.

TIPS "Quality first novels will be published, though we usually only do 1-2 novels per year and they must be set in Florida. We regard the author/editor relationship as a trusting relationship with communication open both ways. Learn all you can about the publishing process and about how to promote your book once it is published. A query on a novel without a brief sample seems useless."

🔵 PLAYLAB PRESS

P.O. Box 3701, South Brisbane BC 4101 Australia. **E-mail:** info@playlab.org.au. **Website:** www.playlab.org. au. Estab. 1978. Guidelines online.

HOW TO CONTACT Submit 2 copies of ms, cover letter.

TERMS Responds in 3 months to mss.

TIPS "Playlab Press is committed to the publication of quality writing for and about theatre and performance, which is of significance to Australia's cultural life. It values socially just and diverse publication outcomes and aims to promote these outcomes in local, national, and international contexts."

PLEXUS PUBLISHING, INC.

143 Old Marlton Pike, Medford NJ 08055. (609)654-6500. **Fax:** (609)654-4309. **E-mail:** jbryans@plexuspublishing.com. **Website:** www.plexuspublishing. com. **Contact:** John B. Bryans, editor in chief/publisher. Estab. 1977. Plexus publishes regional-interest (southern New Jersey and the greater Philadelphia area) fiction and nonfiction including mysteries, field guides, nature, travel and history. Publishes hardcover and paperback originals. Book catalog and book proposal guidelines for 10x13 SASE.

NEEDS Mysteries and literary novels with a strong regional (southern New Jersey) angle.

HOW TO CONTACT Query with SASE.

TERMS Pays $500-1,000 advance. Responds in 3 months to proposals.

⚫⊘ POCKET BOOKS

Simon & Schuster, 1230 Avenue of the Americas, New York NY 10020. (212)698-7000. **Website:** www.simonandschuster.com. Estab. 1939. Pocket Books publishes commercial fiction and genre fiction (WWE,

Downtown Press, Star Trek). Publishes paperback originals and reprints, mass-market and trade paperbacks. Book catalog available free. Guidelines online.

HOW TO CONTACT *Agented submissions only.*

○ POCOL PRESS

Box 411, Clifton VA 20124. (703)830-5862. **Website:** www.pocolpress.com. **Contact:** J. Thomas Hetrick, editor. Estab. 1999. "Pocol Press is dedicated to producing high-quality print books and e-books from first-time, nonagented authors. However, all submissions are welcome. We're dedicated to good storytellers and to the written word, specializing in short fiction and baseball. Several of our books have been used as literary texts at universities and in book group discussions around the nation. Pocol Press does not publish children's books, romance novels, or graphic novels." Publishes trade paperback originals. Book catalog and guidelines online.

○ "Our authors are comprised of veteran writers and emerging talents."

NEEDS "We specialize in thematic short fiction collections by a single author and baseball fiction. Expert storytellers welcome."

HOW TO CONTACT Does not accept or return unsolicited mss. Query with SASE or submit 1 sample chapter.

TERMS Pays 10-12% royalty on wholesale price. Responds in 1 month to queries; 2 months to mss.

TIPS "Our audience is aged 18 and over. Pocol Press is unique; we publish good writing and great storytelling. Write the best stories you can. Read them to you friends/peers. Note their reaction. Publishes some of the finest fiction by a small press."

THE POISONED PENCIL

Poisoned Pen Press, 6962 E. 1st Ave., Suite 103, Scottsdale AZ 85251. (480)945-3375. **Fax:** (480)949-1707. **E-mail:** info@thepoisonedpencil.com. **E-mail:** ellen@thepoisonedpencil.com. **Website:** www.thepoisonedpencil.com. **Contact:** Ellen Larson, editor. Estab. 2012. Publishes trade paperback and electronic originals. Guidelines online.

○ *Accepts young adult mysteries only.*

NEEDS "We publish only young adult mystery novels, 45,000 to 90,000 words in length. For our purposes, a young adult book is a book with a protagonist between the ages of 13 and 18. We are looking for both traditional and cross-genre young adult mysteries. We encourage off-beat approaches and narrative choices that reflect the complexity and ambiguity of today's world.

Submissions from teens are very welcome. Avoid serial killers, excessive gore, and vampires (and other heavy supernatural themes). We only consider authors who live in the U.S. or Canada, due to practicalities of marketing promotion. Avoid coincidence in plotting. Avoid having your sleuth leap to conclusions rather than discover and deduce. Pay attention to the resonance between character and plot; between plot and theme; between theme and character. We are looking for clean style, fluid storytelling, and solid structure. Unrealistic dialogue is a real turn-off."

HOW TO CONTACT Submit proposal package including synopsis, complete ms, and cover letter.

TERMS Pays 9-15% for trade paperback; 25-35% for e-books. Pays advance of $1,000. Responds in 6 weeks to mss.

TIPS "Our audience includes young adults and adults who love YA mysteries."

POISONED PEN PRESS

6962 E. 1st Ave., Suite 103, Scottsdale AZ 85251. (480)945-3375. **Fax:** (480)949-1707. **E-mail:** submissions@poisonedpenpress.com. **Website:** www.poisonedpenpress.com. **Contact:** Robert Rosenwald, publisher; Barbara Peters, editor in chief. Estab. 1996. "Our publishing goal is to offer well-written mystery novels of crime and/or detection where the puzzle and its resolution are the main forces that move the story forward." Publishes hardcover originals, and hardcover and trade paperback reprints. Book catalog and guidelines online.

○ *Not currently accepting submissions. Check website.*

IMPRINTS The Poisoned Pencil (Young adult titles. Contact: Ellen Larson).

NEEDS Mss should generally be longer than 65,000 words and shorter than 100,000 words. Member Publishers Marketing Associations, Arizona Book Publishers Associations, Publishers Association of West. Distributes through Ingram, Baker & Taylor, Brodart. Does not want novels centered on serial killers, spousal or child abuse, drugs, or extremist groups, although we do not entirely rule such works out.

HOW TO CONTACT Accepts unsolicited mss. Electronic queries only. "Query with SASE. Submit clips, first 3 pages. We must receive both the synopsis and ms pages electronically as separate attachments to an e-mail message or as a disk or CD which we will not return."

TERMS Pays 9-15% royalty on retail price. Responds in 2-3 months to queries and proposals; 6 months to mss.

TIPS "Audience is adult readers of mystery fiction and young adult readers."

POSSIBILITY PRESS

1 Oakglade Circle, Hummelstown PA 17036. **E-mail:** info@possibilitypress.com. **Website:** www.possibilitypress.com. **Contact:** Mike Markowski, publisher. Estab. 1981. "Our mission is to help the people of the world grow and become the best they can be, through the written and spoken word." Publishes trade paperback originals. Catalog online. Guidelines online.

IMPRINTS Aeronautical Publishers; Possibility Press; Markowski International Publishers.

NEEDS Needs: parables that teach lessons about life and success.

TERMS Royalties vary. Responds in 1 month to queries.

TIPS "Our focus is on co-authoring and publishing short (15,000-40,000 words) bestsellers. We're looking for kind and compassionate authors who are passionate about making a difference in the world, and will champion their mission to do so, especially by public speaking. Our dream author writes well, knows how to promote, will champion their mission, speaks for a living, has a following and a platform, is cooperative and understanding, humbly handles critique and direction, is grateful, intelligent, and has a good sense of humor."

PRESS 53

560 N. Trade St., Suite 103, Winston-Salem NC 27101. **E-mail:** kevin@press53.com. **Website:** www.press53.com. **Contact:** Kevin Morgan Watson, publisher. "Press 53 was founded in October 2005 and quickly began earning a reputation as a quality publishing house of short story and poetry collections." Guidelines online.

NEEDS "We publish roughly 4 short story collections each year by writers who are active and earning recognition through publication and awards, plus the winner of our Press 53 Award for Short Fiction." Collections should include 10-15 short stories with 70% or more of those stories previously published. Does not want novels.

HOW TO CONTACT Finds mss through contest and referrals.

TERMS Responds in 6 months to mss.

TIPS "We are looking for writers who are actively involved in the writing community, writers who are submitting their work to journals, magazines and contests, and who are getting published, building readership, and earning a reputation for their work."

Ⓐ⊘ PRICE STERN SLOAN, INC.

Penguin Group, 375 Hudson St., New York NY 10014. (212)366-2000. **Website:** www.penguin.com. **Contact:** Francesco Sedita, vice-president/publisher. Estab. 1963. "Price Stern Sloan publishes quirky mass-market novelty series for childrens as well as licensed movie tie-in books." Price Stern Sloan only responds to submissions it's interested in publishing. Book catalog online.

NEEDS Publishes picture books and novelty/board books.

HOW TO CONTACT *Agented submissions only.*

TIPS "Price Stern Sloan publishes unique, fun titles."

PRUFROCK PRESS, INC.

P.O. Box 8813, Waco TX 76714. (800)988-2208. **Fax:** (800)240-0333. **E-mail:** info@prufrock.com. **Website:** www.prufrock.com. **Contact:** Joel McIntosh, publisher and marketing director. "Prufrock Press offers award-winning products focused on gifted education, gifted children, advanced learning, and special needs learners. For more than 20 years, Prufrock has supported gifted children and their education and development. The company publishes more than 300 products that enhance the lives of gifted children and the teachers and parents who support them." Book catalog available. Guidelines online.

Accepts simultaneous submissions, but must be notified about it.

NEEDS Prufrock Press "offers award-winning products focused on gifted education, gifted children, advanced learning, and special needs learners. For more than 20 years, Prufrock has supported gifted children and their education and development. The company publishes more than 300 products that enhance the lives of gifted children and the teachers and parents who support them." No picture books.

HOW TO CONTACT "Prufrock Press does not consider unsolicited mss."

Ⓐ⊘ PUFFIN BOOKS

Imprint of Penguin Group (USA), Inc., 375 Hudson St., New York NY 10014. (212)366-2000. **Website:** www.penguin.com. **Contact:** Eileen Bishop Kreit, publisher. "Puffin Books publishes high-end trade paperbacks and paperback reprints for preschool children, beginning and middle readers, and young adults." Publishes trade paperback originals and reprints.

HOW TO CONTACT *No unsolicited mss. Agented submissions only.*

TIPS "Our audience ranges from little children 'first books' to young adult (ages 14-16). An original idea has the best luck."

Ⓐⱺ PUSH

Scholastic, 557 Broadway, New York NY 10012. **E-mail:** dlevithan@scholastic.com. **Website:** www.thisispush. com. Estab. 2002. PUSH publishes new voices in teen literature. PUSH does not accept unsolicited mss or queries, only agented or referred fiction/memoir.

HOW TO CONTACT *Does not accept unsolicited mss.*

Ⓐⱺ G.P. PUTNAM'S SONS HARDCOVER

Imprint of Penguin Group (USA), Inc., 375 Hudson, New York NY 10014. (212)366-2000. **Fax:** (212)366-2664. **Website:** www.penguinputnam.com. **Contact:** Christine Pepe, vice president/executive editor; Kerri Kolen, executive editor. Publishes hardcover originals. Request book catalog through mail order department.

HOW TO CONTACT *Agented submissions only.*

TERMS Pays variable royalties on retail price. Pays varies advance.

Ⓐⱺ RANDOM HOUSE CHILDREN'S BOOKS

1745 Broadway, New York NY 10019. (212)782-9000. **Website:** www.randomhouse.com. Estab. 1925. "Producing books for preschool children through young adult readers, in all formats from board to activity books to picture books and novels, Random House Children's Books brings together world-famous franchise characters, multimillion-copy series and topflight, award-winning authors, and illustrators." Submit mss through a literary agent.

IMPRINTS Kids@Random; Golden Books; Princeton Review; Sylvan Learning.

NEEDS "Random House publishes a select list of first chapter books and novels, with an emphasis on fantasy and historical fiction." Chapter books, middle-grade readers, young adult.

HOW TO CONTACT *Does not accept unsolicited mss.*

TIPS "We look for original, unique stories. Do something that hasn't been done before."

Ⓐ◉ⱺ RANDOM HOUSE CHILDREN'S PUBLISHERS U.K.

61-63 Uxbridge Rd., London En W5 5SA United Kingdom. (44)(208)579-2652. **Fax:** (44)(208)231-6737. **E-mail:** enquiries@randomhouse.co.uk. **Website:** www. kidsatrandomhouse.co.uk. **Contact:** Francesca Dow, managing director.

Ⓞ *Only interested in agented material.*

IMPRINTS Bantam, Doubleday, Corgi, Johnathan Cape, Hutchinson, Bodley Head, Red Fox, Tamarind Books.

NEEDS Picture books: adventure, animal, anthology, contemporary, fantasy, folktales, humor, multicultural, nature/environment, poetry, suspense/mystery. Young readers: adventure, animal, anthology, contemporary, fantasy, folktales, humor, multicultural, nature/environment, poetry, sports, suspense/mystery. Middle readers: adventure, animal, anthology, contemporary, fantasy, folktales, humor, multicultural, nature/environment, problem novels, romance, sports, suspense/mystery. Young adults: adventure, contemporary, fantasy, humor, multicultural, nature/environment, problem novels, romance, science fiction, suspense/mystery. Average word length: picture books—800; young readers—1,500-6,000; middle readers—10,000-15,000; young adults—20,000-45,000.

TERMS Pays authors royalty. Offers advances.

TIPS "Although Random House is a big publisher, each imprint only publishes a small number of books each year. Our lists for the next few years are already full. Any book we take on from a previously unpublished author has to be truly exceptional. Mss should be sent to us via literary agents."

Ⓐⱺ RANDOM HOUSE PUBLISHING GROUP

Division of Random House, Inc., 1745 Broadway, New York NY 10019. (212)782-9000. **Website:** www.randomhouse.com. Estab. 1925. Random House is the world's largest English-language general trade book publisher. It includes an array of prestigious imprints that publish some of the foremost writers of our time. Publishes hardcover and paperback trade books.

IMPRINTS Ballantine Books; Bantam; Delacorte; Dell; Del Rey; Modern Library; One World; Presidio Press; Random House Trade Group; Random House Trade Paperbacks; Spectra; Spiegel & Grau; Triumph Books; Villard.

HOW TO CONTACT *Agented submissions only.*

RAZORBILL

Penguin Young Readers Group, 375 Hudson St., New York NY 10014. (212)414-3600. **Fax:** (212)414-3343. **E-mail:** mgrossman@penguinrandomhouse.com; bschrank@penguinrandomhouse.com. **Website:** www.razorbillbooks.com. **Contact:** Gillian Levinson, editor; Jessica Almon, editor; Elizabeth Tingue, associate editor; Casey McIntyre, associate publisher; Deborah Kaplan, vice president and executive art director. Estab. 2003. "This division of Penguin Young Readers is looking for the best and the most original of commercial contemporary fiction titles for middle-grade and YA readers. A select quantity of nonfiction titles will also be considered."

NEEDS Middle Readers: adventure, contemporary, graphic novels, fantasy, humor, problem novels. Young adults/teens: adventure, contemporary, fantasy, graphic novels, humor, multicultural, suspense, paranormal, science fiction, dystopian, literary, romance. Average word length: middle readers—40,000; young adult—60,000.

HOW TO CONTACT Submit cover letter with up to 30 sample pages.

TERMS Offers advance against royalties. Responds in 1-3 months.

TIPS "New writers will have the best chance of acceptance and publication with original, contemporary material that boasts a distinctive voice and well-articulated world. Check out website to get a better idea of what we're looking for."

REBELIGHT PUBLISHING, INC.

23-845 Dakota St., Suite 314, Winnipeg Manitoba R2M 5M3 Canada. **E-mail:** submit@rebelight.com. **Website:** www.rebelight.com. **Contact:** Editor. Estab. 2014. Rebelight Publishing is interested in mss for middle-grade, young adult and new adult novels. Publishes trade paperback and electronic originals. Catalog available online. Guidelines available online.

Only considers submissions from Canadian writers.

NEEDS All genres are considered, providered they are for a middle-grade, young adult, or new adult audience. "Become familiar with our books. Study our website. Stick within the guidelines. Our tag line is 'crack the spine, blow your mind'—we are looking for well-written, powerful, fresh, fast-paced fiction. Keep us turning the pages. Give us something we just have to spread the word about."

HOW TO CONTACT Submit proposal package, including a synopsis and 3 sample chapters. Read guidelines carefully.

TERMS Pays 12-30% royalties on retail price. Does not offer an advance. Responds in 3 months to queries and mss.

RED DEER PRESS

195 Allstate Pkwy., Markham ON L3R 4TB Canada. (905)477-9700. **Fax:** (905)477-9179. **E-mail:** rdp@reddeerpress.com. **Website:** www.reddeerpress.com. **Contact:** Richard Dionne, publisher. Estab. 1975. Book catalog for 9x12 SASE.

Red Deer Press is an award-winning publisher of children's and young adult literary titles.

NEEDS Publishes young adult, adult science fiction, fantasy, and paperback originals "focusing on books by, about, or of interest to Canadians." Books: offset paper; offset printing; hardcover/perfect-bound. Average print order: 5,000. First novel print order: 2,500. Distributes titles in Canada and the U.S., the U.K., Australia and New Zealand. Young adult (juvenile and early reader), contemporary. No romance or horror.

HOW TO CONTACT Accepts unsolicited mss. Query with SASE. No submissions on disk.

TERMS Pays 8-10% royalty. Responds to queries in 6 months.

TIPS "We're very interested in young adult and children's fiction from Canadian writers with a proven track record (either published books or widely published in established magazines or journals) and for mss with regional themes and/or a distinctive voice. We publish Canadian authors exclusively."

RED HEN PRESS

P.O. Box 40820, Pasadena CA 91114. (818)831-0649. **Fax:** (818)831-6659. **Website:** www.redhen.org. **Contact:** Mark E. Cull, publisher/editor (fiction). Estab. 1993. "At this time, the best opportunity to be published by Red Hen is by entering one of our contests. Please find more information in our award submission guidelines." Publishes trade paperback originals. Book catalog available free. Guidelines online.

HOW TO CONTACT Query with synopsis and either 20-30 sample pages or complete ms using online submission manager.

TERMS Responds in 1-2 months.

TIPS "Audience reads poetry, literary fiction, intelligent nonfiction. If you have an agent, we may be too small since we don't pay advances. Write well. Send queries first. Be willing to help promote your own book."

RED SAGE PUBLISHING, INC.

P.O. Box 4844, Seminole FL 33775. (727)391-3847. **E-mail:** submissions@eredsage.com. **Website:** www.eredsage.com. **Contact:** Alexandria Kendall, publisher; Theresa Stevens, managing editor. Estab. 1995. Publishes books of romance fiction, written for the adventurous woman. Guidelines online.

HOW TO CONTACT Read guidelines.

TERMS Pays advance.

○◑ RED TUQUE BOOKS, INC.

477 Martin St., Unit #6, Penticton BC V2A 5L2 Canada. (778)476-5750. **Fax:** (778)476-5651. **E-mail:** dave@redtuquebooks.ca. **Website:** www.redtuquebooks.ca. **Contact:** David Korinetz, executive editor. Publishes Canadian authors only, other than in the Annual Canadian Tales Anthology, which will accept stories written about Canada or Canadians by non-Canadians. Publication in the anthology is only through submissions to the Canadian Tales writing contest. See website for details.

HOW TO CONTACT Submit a query letter, one-page synopsis, and first 5 pages only. Include total word count. Accepts queries by e-mail and mail. Accepts ms only by mail. SASE for reply only.

TERMS Pays 5-7% royalties on net sales. Pays $250 advance. Responds in 3 weeks.

TIPS "Well-plotted, character-driven stories, preferably with happy endings, will have the best chance of being accepted. Keep in mind that authors who like to begin sentences with 'and, or, and but' are less likely to be considered. Don't send anything gruesome or overly explicit; tell us a good story, but think PG."

RENAISSANCE HOUSE

465 Westview Ave., Englewood NJ 07631. (201)408-4048. **E-mail:** info@renaissancehouse.net. **Website:** www.renaissancehouse.net. "We specialize in the development and management of educational and multicultural materials for young readers, Bilingual and Spanish. Our titles are suitable for the school, library, trade markets and reading programs. Publishes biographies, legends and multicultural with a focus on the Hispanic market. Specializes in multicultural and bilingual titles, Spanish-English." Submit ms; e-mail submissions. Children's, educational, and multicultural. Represents 80 illustrators. 95% of artwork handled is children's book illustration. Currently open to illustrators seeking representation. Open to both new and established illustrators.

TERMS Responds to queries/mss in 2 weeks.

◑⊘ REVELL

Division of Baker Publishing Group, 630 E. Fulton Rd., Ada MI 49301. **Website:** www.bakerbooks.com.

Estab. 1870. "Revell publishes to the heart (rather than to the head). For 125 years, Revell has been publishing evangelical books for the personal enrichment and spiritual growth of general Christian readers." Publishes hardcover, trade paperback and mass-market paperback originals. Book catalog and ms guidelines online.

⚫ *No longer accepts unsolicited mss.*

⊘ RING OF FIRE PUBLISHING LLC

6523 California Ave. SW #409, Seattle WA 98136. **E-mail:** contact@ringoffirebooks.com. **Website:** www.ringoffirebooks.com. Estab. 2011. "We are currently closed to submissions." Check website for updates. Publishes trade paperback and electronic originals. Book catalog and ms guidelines online.

TERMS Pays royalties.

RIPPLE GROVE PRESS

P.O. Box 86740, Portland OR 97286. **E-mail:** submit@ripplegrovepress.com. **Website:** www.ripplegrovepress.com. Estab. 2013. "We started Ripple Grove Press because we have a passion for well-written and beautifully illustrated children's picture books. Each story selected has been read dozens of times, then slept on, then walked away from, then talked about again and again. If the story has the same intrigue and the same interest that it had when we first read it, we move forward." Publishes hardcover originals. Guidelines online.

NEEDS "Our focus is picture books for children age 2-6. We want something unique, sweet, funny, touching, offbeat, colorful, surprising, charming, different, and creative."

HOW TO CONTACT Submit completed ms. Accepts submissions by mail and e-mail. Please submit a cover letter including a summary of your story, the age range of the story, a brief biography of yourself, and contact information.

TERMS Authors receive between 10-12% royalty on net receipt. Responds to queries within 4 months.

TIPS Also targeting the adults reading to the children. "We create books that children and adults want to read over and over again. Our books showcase art as well as stories and tie them together to create a unique and creative product."

RIVER CITY PUBLISHING

1719 Mulberry St., Montgomery AL 36106. **E-mail:** fnorris@rivercitypublishing.com. **Website:** www.rivercitypublishing.com. **Contact:** Fran Norris, editor.

Estab. 1989. Midsize independent publisher. River City publishes literary fiction, regional, short story collections. No poetry, memoir, or children's books. "We are looking mainly for narrative histories, sociological accounts, and travel. Only biographies and memoirs from noted persons will be considered." Publishes hardcover and trade paperback originals.

NEEDS No poetry, memoir, or children's books.

HOW TO CONTACT Send appropriate-sized SASE or IRC, "otherwise, the material will be recycled." Also accepts queries by e-mail. "Please include your electronic query letter as inline text and not an as attachment; we do not open unsolicited attachments of any kind." No multiple submissions. Rarely comments on rejected mss.

TERMS Responds to mss in 9 months.

TIPS "Only send your best work after you have received outside opinions. From approximately 1,000 submissions each year, we publish no more than 8 books and few of those come from unsolicited material. Competition is fierce, so follow the guidelines exactly. All first-time novelists should submit their work to the Fred Bonnie Award contest."

RIVERHEAD BOOKS

Penguin Putnam, 375 Hudson St., New York NY 10014. **Website:** www.penguin.com. **Contact:** Rebecca Saletan, vice president/editorial director.

HOW TO CONTACT *Submit through agent only. No unsolicited mss.*

ROARING BROOK PRESS

Macmillan Children's Publishing Group, 175 Fifth Ave., New York NY 10010. (646)307-5151. **Website:** us.macmillan.com. Estab. 2000. Roaring Brook Press is an imprint of MacMillan, a group of companies that includes Henry Holt and Farrar, Straus & Giroux. *Roaring Brook is not accepting unsolicited mss.*

NEEDS Picture books, young readers, middle readers, young adults: adventure, animal, contemporary, fantasy, history, humor, multicultural, nature/environment, poetry, religion, science fiction, sports, suspense/mystery.

HOW TO CONTACT *Not accepting unsolicited mss or queries.*

TERMS Pays authors royalty based on retail price.

TIPS "You should find a reputable agent and have him/her submit your work."

RONSDALE PRESS

3350 W. 21st Ave., Vancouver BC V6S 1G7 Canada. (604)738-4688. **Fax:** (604)731-4548. **E-mail:** ronsdale@shaw.ca. **Website:** ronsdalepress.com. **Contact:**

Ronald B. Hatch (fiction, poetry, nonfiction, social commentary); Veronica Hatch (YA novels and short stories). Estab. 1988. "Ronsdale Press is a Canadian literary publishing house that publishes 12 books each year, 4 of which are young adult titles. Of particular interest are books involving children exploring and discovering new aspects of Canadian history." Publishes trade paperback originals. Book catalog for #10 SASE. Guidelines online.

NEEDS Young adults: Canadian novels. Average word length: middle readers and young adults—50,000.

HOW TO CONTACT Submit complete ms.

TERMS Pays 10% royalty on retail price. Responds to queries in 2 weeks; mss in 2 months.

TIPS "Ronsdale Press is a literary publishing house, based in Vancouver, and dedicated to publishing books from across Canada, books that give Canadians new insights into themselves and their country. We aim to publish the best Canadian writers."

ST. MARTIN'S PRESS, LLC

Holtzbrinck Publishers, 175 Fifth Ave., New York NY 10010. (212)674-5151. **Fax:** (212)420-9314. **Website:** www.stmartins.com. Estab. 1952. General interest publisher of both fiction and nonfiction. Publishes hardcover, trade paperback and mass-market originals.

HOW TO CONTACT *Agented submissions only. No unsolicited mss.*

TERMS Pays royalty. Pays advance.

SAKURA PUBLISHING & TECHNOLOGIES

P.O. Box 1681, Hermitage PA 16148. (330)360-5131. **E-mail:** skpublishing124@gmail.com. **Website:** www.sakura-publishing.com. **Contact:** Derek Vasconi, talent finder and CEO. Estab. 2007. Mss that don't follow guidelines will not be considered. Publishes hardcover, trade paperback, mass-market paperback and electronic originals and reprints. Book catalog available for #10 SASE. Guidelines online.

HOW TO CONTACT Follow guidelines online.

TERMS Pays royalty of 20-60% on wholesale price or retail price. Responds in 1 week.

TIPS "Please make sure you visit our submissions page at our website and follow all instructions exactly as written. Also, Sakura Publishing has a preference for fiction/nonfiction books specializing in Asian culture."

SALINA BOOKSHELF

3120 N. Caden Ct., Suite 4, Flagstaff AZ 86004. (928)527-0070. **Fax:** (928)526-0386. **Website:** www.

salinabookshelf.com. Publishes trade paperback originals and reprints.

NEEDS Submissions should be in English or Navajo. "All our books relate to the Navajo language and culture."

HOW TO CONTACT Query with SASE.

TERMS Pays varying royalty. Pays advance. Responds in 3 months to queries.

SALVO PRESS

E-mail: info@salvopress.com. **E-mail:** submissions@start-media.com. **Website:** www.salvopress.com. **Contact:** Scott Schmidt, publisher. Estab. 1998. Book catalog and ms guidelines online.

NEEDS "We are a small press specializing in mystery, suspense, espionage and thriller fiction. Our press publishes in trade paperback and most e-book formats."

HOW TO CONTACT Query by e-mail.

TERMS Pays 10% royalty. Responds in 5 minutes to 1 month to queries; 2 months to mss.

SAMHAIN PUBLISHING, LTD

11821 Mason Montgomery Rd., Cincinnati OH 45249. (478)314-5144. **Fax:** (478)314-5148. **E-mail:** horror@samhainpublishing.com; retroromance@samhainpublishing.com. **E-mail:** romance@samhainpublishing.com. **Website:** www.samhainpublishing.com. **Contact:** Christina Brashear, president/publisher. Estab. 2005. "A small, independent publisher, Samhain's motto is 'It's all about the story.' We look for fresh, unique voices who have a story to share with the world. We encourage our authors to let their muse have its way and to create tales that don't always adhere to current trends. One never knows what the next hot genre will be or when it will start, so write what's in your soul. These are the books that, whether the story is based on formula or is an original, when written from the heart will earn you a life-time readership." Publishes e-books and paperback originals. POD/offset printing; line illustrations. Guidelines online.

NEEDS Needs erotica and all genres and all heat levels of romance (contemporary, futuristic/time travel, gothic, historical, paranormal, regency period, romantic suspense, fantasy, action/adventure, etc.), as well as fantasy, urban fantasy or science fiction with strong romantic elements, with word counts between 12,000 and 120,000 words.

HOW TO CONTACT Accepts unsolicited mss. Query with outline/synopsis and either 3 sample chapters or the full ms. Accepts queries by e-mail only. Include estimated word count, brief bio, list of publishing credits, and "how the author is working to improve craft: association, critique groups, etc."

TERMS Pays royalties 30-40% for e-books, average of 8% for trade paper, and author's copies (quantity varies). Responds in 4 months.

TIPS "Because we are an e-publisher first, we do not have to be as concerned with industry trends and can publish less popular genres of fiction if we believe the story and voice are good and will appeal to our customers. Please follow submission guidelines located on our website, include all requested information and proof your query/ms for errors prior to submission."

SARABANDE BOOKS, INC.

2234 Dundee Rd., Suite 200, Louisville KY 40205. (502)458-4028. **Fax:** (502)458-4065. **E-mail:** info@sarabandebooks.org. **Website:** www.sarabandebooks.org. **Contact:** Sarah Gorham, editor in chief. Estab. 1994. "Sarabande Books was founded to publish poetry, short fiction, and creative nonfiction. We look for works of lasting literary value. Please see our titles to get an idea of our taste. Accepts submissions through contests and open submissions." Publishes trade paperback originals. Book catalog available free. Contest guidelines for #10 SASE or on website.

Charges $15 handling fee with alternative option of purchase of book from website (e-mail confirmation of sale must be included with submission).

NEEDS "We consider novels and nonfiction in a wide variety of genres. We do not consider genre fiction such as science fiction, fantasy, or horror. Our target length is 70,000-90,000 words."

HOW TO CONTACT Queries can be sent via e-mail, fax, or regular post.

TERMS Pays royalty. 10% on actual income received. Also pays in author's copies. Pays $500-1,000 advance.

TIPS "Sarabande publishes for a general literary audience. Know your market. Read-and buy-books of literature. Sponsors contests for poetry and fiction. Make sure you're not writing in a vacuum, that you've read and are conscious of contemporary literature. Have someone read your ms, checking it for ordering, coherence. Better a lean, consistently strong ms than one that is long and uneven. We like a story to have good narrative, and we like to be engaged by language."

SASQUATCH BOOKS

1904 Third Ave., Suite 710, Seattle WA 98101. (206)467-4300. **Fax:** (206)467-4301. **E-mail:** custserv@sasquatchbooks.com. **Website:** www.sasquatchbooks.

com. Estab. 1986. "Sasquatch Books publishes books for and from the Pacific Northwest, Alaska, and California is the nation's premier regional press. Sasquatch Books' publishing program is a veritable celebration of regionally written words. Undeterred by political or geographical borders, Sasquatch defines its region as the magnificent area that stretches from the Brooks Range to the Gulf of California and from the Rocky Mountains to the Pacific Ocean. Our top-selling Best Places® travel guides serve the most popular destinations and locations of the West. We also publish widely in the areas of food and wine, gardening, nature, photography, children's books, and regional history, all facets of the literature of place. With more than 200 books brimming with insider information on the West, we offer an energetic eye on the lifestyle, landscape, and worldview of our region. Considers queries and proposals from authors and agents for new projects that fit into our West Coast regional publishing program. We can evaluate query letters, proposals, and complete mss." Publishes regional hardcover and trade paperback originals. Guidelines online.

NEEDS Young readers: adventure, animal, concept, contemporary, humor, nature/environment.

TERMS Pays royalty on cover price. Pays wide range advance. Responds to queries in 3 months.

TIPS "We sell books through a range of channels in addition to the book trade. Our primary audience consists of active, literate residents of the West Coast."

ⓐ SCHOLASTIC PRESS

Imprint of Scholastic, Inc., 557 Broadway, New York NY 10012. (212)343-6100. **Fax:** (212)343-4713. **Website:** www.scholastic.com. Scholastic Press publishes fresh, literary picture book fiction and nonfiction; fresh, literary nonseries or nongenre-oriented middle-grade and young adult fiction. Currently emphasizing subtly handled treatments of key relationships in children's lives; unusual approaches to commonly dry subjects, such as biography, math, history, or science. De-emphasizing fairy tales (or retellings), board books, genre, or series fiction (mystery, fantasy, etc.). Publishes hardcover originals.

NEEDS Looking for strong picture books, young chapter books, appealing middle-grade novels (ages 8-11) and interesting and well-written young adult novels. Wants fresh, exciting picture books and novels—inspiring, new talent.

HOW TO CONTACT *Agented submissions only.*

TERMS Pays royalty on retail price. Pays variable advance. Responds in 3 months to queries; 6-8 months to mss.

TIPS "Read *currently* published children's books. Revise, rewrite, rework and find your own voice, style and subject. We are looking for authors with a strong and unique voice who can tell a great story and have the ability to evoke genuine emotion. Children's publishers are becoming more selective, looking for irresistible talent and fairly broad appeal, yet still very willing to take risks, just to keep the game interesting."

ⓢ SCRIBE PUBLICATIONS

18-20 Edward St., Brunswick VIC 3056 Australia. (61)(3)9388-8780. **Fax:** (61)(3)9388-8787. **E-mail:** info@scribepub.com.au. **Website:** www.scribepublications.com.au. Estab. 1976. Guidelines online.

HOW TO CONTACT Submit synopsis, sample chapters, CV.

TIPS "We are only able to consider unsolicited submissions if you have a demonstrated background of writing and publishing for general readers."

ⓐⓞ SCRIBNER

Imprint of Simon & Schuster Adult Publishing Group, 1230 Avenue of the Americas, 12th Floor, New York NY 10020. (212)698-7000. **Website:** www.simonsays.com. Publishes hardcover originals.

HOW TO CONTACT *Agented submissions only.*

TERMS Pays 7-15% royalty. Pays variable advance. Responds in 3 months to queries

ⓒ SECOND STORY PRESS

20 Maud St., Suite 401, Toronto ON M5V 2M5 Canada. (416)537-7850. **Fax:** (416)537-0588. **E-mail:** info@secondstorypress.ca. **Website:** www.secondstorypress.ca.

NEEDS Considers nonsexist, nonracist, and nonviolent stories, as well as historical fiction, chapter books, picture books.

SEEDLING CONTINENTAL PRESS

520 E. Bainbridge St., Elizabethtown PA 17022. **Website:** www.continentalpress.com. Publishes books for classroom use only for the beginning reader in English. "Natural language and predictable text are requisite. Patterned text is acceptable, but must have a unique story line. Poetry, books in rhyme and full-length picture books are not being accepted. Illustrations are not necessary."

NEEDS young readers: adventure, animal, folktales, humor, multicultural, nature/environment. Does not accept texts longer than 12 pages or over 300 words. Average word length: young readers—100.

HOW TO CONTACT Submit complete ms.

TERMS Work purchased outright from authors. Responds to mss in 6 months.

TIPS "See our website. Follow writers' guidelines carefully and test your story with children and educators."

SERIOUSLY GOOD BOOKS

999 Vanderbilt Beach Rd., Naples FL 34119. **E-mail:** seriouslygoodbks@aol.com. **Website:** www.seriouslygoodbks.net. Estab. 2010. Publishes historial fiction only. Publishes trade paperback and electronic originals. Book catalog and guidelines online.

HOW TO CONTACT Query by e-mail.

TERMS Pays 15% minimum royalties. Responds in 1 month to queries.

TIPS "Looking for historial fiction with substance. We seek well-researched historical fiction in the vein of Rutherfurd, Mary Renault, Maggie Anton, Robert Harris, etc. Please don't query with historical fiction mixed with other genres (romance, time travel, vampires, etc.)."

SEVEN STORIES PRESS

140 Watts St., New York NY 10013. (212)226-8760. **Fax:** (212)226-1411. **E-mail:** info@sevenstories.com. **Website:** www.sevenstories.com. **Contact:** Daniel Simon; Anna Lui. Estab. 1995. Founded in 1995 in New York City, and named for the 7 authors who committed to a home with a fiercely independent spirit, Seven Stories Press publishes works of the imagination and political titles by voices of conscience. While most widely known for its books on politics, human rights, and social and economic justice, Seven Stories continues to champion literature, with a list encompassing both innovative debut novels and National Book Award–winning poetry collections, as well as prose and poetry translations from the French, Spanish, German, Swedish, Italian, Greek, Polish, Korean, Vietnamese, Russian, and Arabic. Publishes hardcover and trade paperback originals. Book catalog and ms guidelines free.

HOW TO CONTACT Submit cover letter with 2 sample chapters.

TERMS Pays 7-15% royalty on retail price. Pays advance. Responds in 1 month.

Ⓐ☺⊘ SEVERN HOUSE PUBLISHERS

Salatin House, 19 Cedar Rd., Sutton, Surrey SM2 5DA United Kingdom. (44)(208)770-3930. **Fax:** (44)

(208)770-3850. **Website:** www.severnhouse.com. Severn House is currently emphasizing suspense, romance, mystery. Large print imprint from existing authors. Publishes hardcover and trade paperback originals and reprints. Book catalog available free.

HOW TO CONTACT *Agented submissions only.*

TERMS Pays 7-15% royalty on retail price. Pays $750-5,000 advance. Responds in 3 months to proposals.

SHAMBHALA PUBLICATIONS, INC.

300 Massachusetts Ave., Boston MA 02115. (617)424-0030. **Fax:** (617)236-1563. **E-mail:** editors@shambhala.com. **Website:** www.shambhala.com. Estab. 1969. Publishes hardcover and trade paperback originals and reprints. Book catalog and ms guidelines free.

IMPRINTS Roost Books; Snow Lion.

HOW TO CONTACT Submit proposal package, outline, résumé, 2 sample chapters, TOC.

TERMS Pays 8% royalty on retail price. Responds in 4 months.

SHIPWRECKT BOOKS PUBLISHING COMPANY LLC

P.O. Box 20, Lanesboro MN 55949. (507)458-8190. **E-mail:** editor@shipwrecktbooks.com. **E-mail:** contact@shipwrecktbooks.com. **Website:** www.shipwrecktbooks.com. **Contact:** Tom Driscoll, managing editor. Publishes trade paperback originals, mass-market paperback originals, and electronic originals. Catalog and guidelines online.

IMPRINTS Rocket Science Press (literary); Up On Big Rock Poetry Series; Lost Lake Folk Art (memoir, biography, essays, and nonfiction).

HOW TO CONTACT E-mail query first. All unsolicited mss returned unopened.

TERMS Authors receive a maximum of 35% royalties. Responds to queries within 2 months.

TIPS "Quality writing. Query first. Development and full editorial services available."

Ⓐ⊘ SIMON & SCHUSTER

1230 Avenue of the Americas, New York NY 10020. (212)698-7000. **Website:** www.simonandschuster.com. *Accepts agented submissions only.*

IMPRINTS Aladdin; Atheneum Books for Young Readers; Atria; Beach Lane Books; Folger Shakespeare Library; Free Press; Gallery Books; Howard Books; Little Simon; Margaret K. McElderry Books; Pocket; Scribner; Simon & Schuster; Simon & Schuster Books for Young Readers; Simon Pulse; Simon Spotlight; Threshold; Touchstone; Paula Wiseman Books.

⚠️⊘ SIMON & SCHUSTER BOOKS FOR YOUNG READERS

Imprint of Simon & Schuster Children's Publishing, 1230 Avenue of the Americas, New York NY 10020. (212)698-7000. **Fax:** (212)698-2796. **Website:** www. simonsayskids.com. "Simon and Schuster Books For Young Readers is the Flagship imprint of the S&S Children's Division. We are committed to publishing a wide range of contemporary, commercial, award-winning fiction and nonfiction that spans every age of children's publishing. BFYR is constantly looking to the future, supporting our foundation authors and franchises, but always with an eye for breaking new ground with every publication. We publish high-quality fiction and nonfiction for a variety of age groups and a variety of markets. Above all, we strive to publish books that we are passionate about." *No unsolicited mss.* All unsolicited mss returned unopened. Publishes hardcover originals. Guidelines online.

HOW TO CONTACT *Agented submissions only.*

TERMS Pays variable royalty on retail price.

TIPS "We're looking for picture books centered on a strong, fully-developed protagonist who grows or changes during the course of the story; YA novels that are challenging and psychologically complex; also imaginative and humorous middle-grade fiction. And we want nonfiction that is as engaging as fiction. Our imprint's slogan is 'Reading You'll Remember.' We aim to publish books that are fresh, accessible and family-oriented; we want them to have an impact on the reader."

SKINNER HOUSE BOOKS

The Unitarian Universalist Association, 24 Farnsworth St., Boston MA 02210. (617)742-2100 ext. 603. **Fax:** (617)948-6466. **E-mail:** bookproposals@ uua.org. **Website:** www.uua.org/publications/skinnerhouse. **Contact:** Betsy Martin. Estab. 1975. "We publish titles in Unitarian Universalist faith, liberal religion, history, biography, worship, and issues of social justice. Most of our children's titles are intended for religious education or worship use. They reflect Unitarian Universalist values. We also publish inspirational titles of poetic prose and meditations. Writers should know that Unitarian Universalism is a liberal religious denomination committed to progressive ideals. Currently emphasizing social justice concerns." Publishes trade paperback originals and reprints. Book catalog for 6x9 SAE with 3 first-class stamps. Guidelines online.

NEEDS Only publishes fiction for children's titles for religious instruction.

HOW TO CONTACT Query.

TERMS Responds to queries in 1 month.

TIPS "From outside our denomination, we are interested in mss that will be of help or interest to liberal churches, Sunday School classes, parents, ministers, and volunteers. Inspirational/spiritual and children's titles must reflect liberal Unitarian Universalist values."

SLEEPING BEAR PRESS

315 E. Eisenhower Pkwy., Suite 200, Ann Arbor MI 48108. (800)487-2323. **Fax:** (734)794-0004. **E-mail:** submissions@sleepingbearpress.com. **Website:** www. sleepingbearpress.com. **Contact:** Manuscript Submissions. Estab. 1998. Book catalog available via e-mail.

NEEDS Picture books: adventure, animal, concept, folktales, history, multicultural, nature/environment, religion, sports. Young readers: adventure, animal, concept, folktales, history, humor, multicultural, nature/environment, religion, sports. Average word length: picture books—1,800.

HOW TO CONTACT Query with sample of work (up to 15 pages) and SASE.

SMALL BEER PRESS

150 Pleasant St., #306, Easthampton MA 01027. (413)203-1636. **Fax:** (413)203-1636. **E-mail:** info@ smallbeerpress.com. **Website:** www.smallbeerpress. com. Estab. 2000. Small Beer Press also publishes the zine *Lady Churchill's Rosebud Wristlet*. "SBP's books have recently received the Tiptree and Crawford Awards."

HOW TO CONTACT Does not accept unsolicited novel or short story collection mss. Send queries with first 10-20 pages and SASE.

TIPS "Please be familiar with our books first to avoid wasting your time and ours, thank you. E-mail queries will be deleted. Really."

SMITH AND KRAUS PUBLISHERS, INC.

177 Lyme Rd., Hanover NH 03755. **E-mail:** editor@ smithandkraus.com. **Website:** smithandkraus.com. Estab. 1990. Publishes hardcover and trade paperback originals. Book catalog available free.

NEEDS Does not return submissions.

HOW TO CONTACT Query with SASE.

TERMS Pays 7% royalty on retail price. Pays $500-2,000 advance. Responds in 1 month to queries; 2 months to proposals; 4 months to mss.

SOFT SKULL PRESS INC.

Counterpoint, 2650 Ninth St., Suite 318, Berkeley CA 94710. (510)704-0230. **Fax:** (510)704-0268. **E-mail:** info@softskull.com. **Website:** www.softskull.com. "Here at Soft Skull we love books that are new, fun, smart, revelatory, quirky, groundbreaking, cage-rattling and/or otherwise unusual." Publishes hardcover and trade paperback originals. Book catalog and guidelines online.

NEEDS Does not consider poetry.

HOW TO CONTACT Soft Skull Press no longer accepts digital submissions. Send a cover letter describing your project in detail and a completed ms. For graphic novels, send a minimum of 5 fully inked pages of art, along with a synopsis of your storyline. "Please do not send original material, as it will not be returned."

TERMS Pays 7-10% royalty. Average advance: $100-15,000. Responds in 2 months to proposals; 3 months to mss.

TIPS "See our website for updated submission guidelines."

SOHO PRESS, INC.

853 Broadway, New York NY 10003. **E-mail:** soho@sohopress.com. **Website:** www.sohopress.com. **Contact:** Bronwen Hruska, publisher; Mark Doten, editor. Estab. 1986. Soho Press publishes primarily fiction, as well as some narrative literary nonfiction and mysteries set abroad. No electronic submissions, only queries by e-mail. Publishes hardcover and trade paperback originals; trade paperback reprints. Guidelines online.

NEEDS Adventure, ethnic, feminist, historical, literary, mainstream/contemporary, mystery (police procedural), suspense, multicultural.

HOW TO CONTACT Submit 3 sample chapters and cover letter with synopsis, author bio, SASE. *No e-mailed submissions.*

TERMS Pays 10-15% royalty on retail price (varies under certain circumstances). Responds in 3 months.

TIPS "Soho Press publishes discerning authors for discriminating readers, finding the strongest possible writers and publishing them. Before submitting, look at our website for an idea of the types of books we publish, and read our submission guidelines."

SOURCEBOOKS CASABLANCA

Sourcebooks, Inc., 232 Madison Ave., Suite 1100, New York NY 10016. **E-mail:** romance@sourcebooks.com. **Website:** www.sourcebooks.com. **Contact:** Deb Werksman. "Our romance imprint, Sourcebooks Casablanca, publishes single title romance in all sub-genres." Guidelines online.

NEEDS "Our editorial criteria call for: a heroine the reader can relate to, a hero she can fall in love with, a world gets created that the reader can escape into, there's a hook that we can sell within 2-3 sentences, and the author is out to build a career with us."

TERMS Responds in 2-3 months.

TIPS "We are actively acquiring single-title and single-title series romance fiction (90,000-100,000 words) for our Casablanca imprint. We are looking for strong writers who are excited about marketing their books and building their community of readers, and whose books have something fresh to offer in the genre of romance."

SOURCEBOOKS LANDMARK

Sourcebooks, Inc., 232 Madison Ave., Suite 1100, New York NY 10016. **E-mail:** editorialsubmissions@sourcebooks.com. **Website:** www.sourcebooks.com. **Contact:** Shana Drehs, Stephanie Bowen, Deb Werksman, Anna Klenke. "Our fiction imprint, Sourcebooks Landmark, publishes a variety of commercial fiction, including specialties in historical fiction and Austenalia. We are interested first and foremost in books that have a story to tell."

NEEDS "We are actively acquiring contemporary, book club, and historical fiction for our Landmark imprint. We are looking for strong writers who are excited about marketing their books and building their community of readers."

HOW TO CONTACT Submit synopsis and full ms preferred. Receipt of e-mail submissions acknowledged within 3 weeks of e-mail.

TERMS Responds in 2-3 months.

STARCHERONE BOOKS

P.O. Box 303, Buffalo NY 14201. (716)885-2726. **E-mail:** starcheroneacquisitions@gmail.com. **Website:** www.starcherone.com. **Contact:** Ed Taylor, managing editor. Estab. 2000. Nonprofit publisher of literary and experimental fiction. Publishes paperback originals and reprints. Submission period at specific time each year. Check website for updates. Catalog and guidelines online.

TERMS Pays 10-12.5% royalty. Responds in 2 months to queries; 6-10 months to mss.

STERLING PUBLISHING CO., INC.

1166 Avenue of the Americas, 17th Floor, New York NY 10036. (212)532-7160. **Fax:** (212)981-0508. **Web-**

site: www.sterlingpublishing.com. "Sterling publishes highly illustrated, accessible, hands-on, practical books for adults and children. Our mission is to publish high-quality books that educate, entertain, and enrich the lives of our readers." Publishes hardcover and paperback originals and reprints. Catalog online. Guidelines online.

NEEDS Publishes fiction for children.

HOW TO CONTACT Submit to attention of "Children's Book Editor."

TERMS Pays royalty or work purchased outright. Offers advances (average amount: $2,000).

TIPS "We are primarily a nonfiction activities-based publisher. We have a picture book list, but we do not publish chapter books or novels. Our list is not trend-driven. We focus on titles that will backlist well. "

STONE ARCH BOOKS

1710 Roe Crest Rd., North Mankato MN 56003. E-mail: author.sub@capstonepub.com. **Website:** www.stonearchbooks.com. Catalog online.

NEEDS Young readers, middle readers, young adults: adventure, contemporary, fantasy, humor, light humor, mystery, science fiction, sports, suspense. Average word length: young readers—1,000-3,000; middle readers and early young adults—5,000-10,000.

HOW TO CONTACT Submit outline/synopsis and 3 sample chapters. Electronic submissions preferred.

TERMS Work purchased outright from authors.

TIPS "A high-interest topic or activity is one that a young person would spend their free time on without adult direction or suggestion."

STONE BRIDGE PRESS

P.O. Box 8208, Berkeley CA 94707. **E-mail:** sbp@stonebridge.com. **Website:** www.stonebridge.com. **Contact:** Peter Goodman, publisher. Estab. 1989. "Independent press focusing on books about Japan and Asia in English (business, language, culture, literature, animation)." Publishes hardcover and trade paperback originals. Books: 60-70 lb. offset paper; web and sheet paper; perfect bound; some illustrations. Distributes titles through Consortium. Promotes titles through Internet announcements, special-interest magazines and niche tie-ins to associations. Book catalog for 2 first-class stamps and SASE. Ms guidelines online.

NEEDS Experimental, gay/lesbian, literary, Japan-themed. "Primarily looking at material relating to Japan. Translations only."

HOW TO CONTACT Does not accept unsolicited mss. Query with SASE. Accepts queries by e-mail, fax.

TERMS Pays royalty on wholesale price. Responds to queries in 4 months; mss in 8 months.

TIPS "Fiction translations only for the time being. No poetry."

STONESLIDE BOOKS

Stoneslide Media LLC, P.O. Box 8331, New Haven CT 06530. **E-mail:** editors@stoneslidecorrective.com. **E-mail:** submissions@stoneslidecorrective.com. **Website:** www.stoneslidecorrective.com. **Contact:** Jonathan Weisberg, editor; Christopher Wachlin, editor. Estab. 2012. Publishes trade paperback and electronic originals. Book catalog and guidelines online.

NEEDS "We will look at any genre. The important factor for us is that the story use plot, characters, emotions, and other elements of storytelling to think and move the mind forward."

HOW TO CONTACT Submit proposal package via online submission form including: synopsis and 3 sample chapters.

TERMS Pays 20-80% royalty. Responds in 1-2 months.

TIPS "Read the Stoneslide Corrective to see if your work fits with our approach."

SUBITO PRESS

University of Colorado at Boulder, Dept. of English, 226 UCB, Boulder CO 80309-0226. **E-mail:** subitopressucb@gmail.com. **Website:** www.subitopress.org. Subito Press is a nonprofit publisher of literary works. Each year Subito publishes 1 work of fiction and 1 work of poetry through its contest. Publishes trade paperback originals. Guidelines online.

HOW TO CONTACT Submit complete ms to contest.

TIPS "We publish 2 books of innovative writing a year through our poetry and fiction contests. All entries are also considered for publication with the press."

SUNBURY PRESS, INC.

P.O. Box 548, Boiling Springs PA 17007. **E-mail:** info@sunburypress.com. **E-mail:** proposals@sunburypress.com. **Website:** www.sunburypress.com. Estab. 2004. "Please use our online submission form." Publishes trade paperback originals and reprints; electronic originals and reprints. Catalog and guidelines online.

NEEDS "We are especially seeking historical fiction regarding the Civil War and books of regional interest."

TERMS Pays 10% royalty on wholesale price. Responds in 2 months.

TIPS "Our books appeal to very diverse audiences. We are building our list in many categories, focusing on many demographics. We are not like traditional publishers—we are digitally adept and very creative. Don't be surprised if we move quicker than you are accustomed to!"

SWAN ISLE PRESS

P.O. Box 408790, Chicago IL 60640. (773)728-3780. **E-mail:** info@swanislepress.com. **Website:** www.swanislepress.com. Estab. 1999. *"We do not accept unsolicited mss."* Publishes hardcover and trade paperback originals. Book catalog online. Guidelines online.

HOW TO CONTACT Query with SASE.

TERMS Pays 7-10% royalty on wholesale price. Responds in 6-12 months.

🌑 TAFELBERG PUBLISHERS

Imprint of NB Publishers, P.O. Box 879, Cape Town 8000 South Africa. (27)(21)406-3033. **Fax:** (27)(21)406-3812. **E-mail:** kristin@nb.co.za. **Website:** www.tafelberg.com. **Contact:** Kristin Paremoer. General publisher best known for Afrikaans fiction, authoritative political works, children's/youth literature, and a variety of illustrated and nonillustrated nonfiction.

NEEDS Picture books, young readers: animal, anthology, contemporary, fantasy, folktales, hi-lo, humor, multicultural, nature/environment, scient fiction, special needs. Middle readers, young adults: animal (middle reader only), contemporary, fantasy, hi-lo, humor, multicultural, nature/environment, problem novels, science fiction, special needs, sports, suspense/mystery. Average word length: picture books—1,500-7,500; young readers—25,000; middle readers—15,000; young adults—40,000.

HOW TO CONTACT Submit complete ms.

TERMS Pays authors royalty of 15-18% based on wholesale price. Responds to queries in 2 weeks; mss in 6 months.

TIPS "Writers: Story needs to have a South African or African style. Illustrators: I'd like to look, but the chances of getting commissioned are slim. The market is small and difficult. Do not expect huge advances. Editorial staff attended or plans to attend the following conferences: IBBY, Frankfurt, SCBWI Bologna."

🅐⊘ NAN A. TALESE

Imprint of Doubleday, Random House, 1745 Broadway, New York NY 10019. (212)782-8918. **Fax:** (212)782-8448. **Website:** www.nanatalese.com. Nan A. Talese publishes nonfiction with a powerful guiding narrative and relevance to larger cultural interests, and literary fiction of the highest quality. Publishes hardcover originals.

NEEDS Well-written narratives with a compelling storyline, good characterization and use of language. We like stories with an edge.

HOW TO CONTACT *Agented submissions only.*

TERMS Pays variable royalty on retail price. Pays varying advance.

TIPS "Audience is highly literate people interested in story, information and insight. We want well-written material submitted by agents only. See our website."

TANTOR MEDIA

2 Business Park Rd., Old Saybrook CT 06475. (860)395-1155. **Fax:** (860)395-1154. **E-mail:** rightsemail@tantor.com. **Website:** www.tantor.com. **Contact:** Ron Formica, director of acquisitions. Estab. 2001. Tantor is a leading independent audiobook publisher, producing more than 90 new titles every month. Publishes hardcover, trade paperback, mass-market paperback, and electronic originals and reprints. Also publishes audiobooks. Catalog online.

HOW TO CONTACT Query with SASE, or submit proposal package including synopsis and 3 sample chapters.

TERMS Pays 5-15% royalty on wholesale price. Responds in 2 months.

TEXAS TECH UNIVERSITY PRESS

3003 15th St., Suite 901, Lubbock TX 79409. (806)834-5821. **Fax:** (806)742-2979. **E-mail:** ttup.editorial@ttu.edu. **Website:** www.ttupress.org. **Contact:** Joanna Conrad, editor in chief. Estab. 1971. Texas Tech University Press, the book publishing office of the university since 1971 and an AAUP member since 1986, publishes nonfiction titles in the areas of natural history and the natural sciences; 18th century and Joseph Conrad studies; studies of modern Southeast Asia, particularly the Vietnam War; costume and textile history; Latin American literature and culture; and all aspects of the Great Plains and the American West, especially history, biography, memoir, sports history, and travel. In addition, the Press publishes several scholarly journals, acclaimed series for young readers, an annual invited poetry collection, and literary fiction of Texas and the West. Guidelines online.

NEEDS Fiction rooted in the American West and Southwest, Jewish literature, Latin American and Latino fiction (in translation or English).

🌐 THISTLEDOWN PRESS LTD.

410 2nd Ave., Saskatoon SK S7K 2C3 Canada. (306)244-1722. **Fax:** (306)244-1762. **E-mail:** edito-

rial@thistledownpress.com. **Website:** www.thistle-downpress.com. **Contact:** Allan Forrie, publisher. "Thistledown originates books by Canadian authors only, although we have co-published titles by authors outside Canada. We do not publish children's picture books." Book catalog free on request.

NEEDS Middle readers, young adults: adventure, anthology, contemporary, fantasy, humor, poetry, romance, science fiction, suspense/mystery, short stories. Average word length: young adults—40,000.

HOW TO CONTACT Submit outline/synopsis and sample chapters. *Does not accept mss.* Do not query by e-mail.

TERMS Pays authors royalty of 10-12% based on net dollar sales. Pays illustrators and photographers by the project (range: $250-750). Responds to queries in 4 months.

TIPS "Send cover letter including publishing history and SASE."

THUNDERSTONE BOOKS

6575 Horse Dr., Las Vegas NV 89131. **E-mail:** info@thunderstonebooks.com. **Website:** www.thunderstonebooks.com. **Contact:** Rachel Noorda, editorial director. Estab. 2014. "At ThunderStone Books, we aim to publish children's books that have an educational aspect. We are not looking for curriculum for learning certain subjects, but rather stories that encourage learning for children, whether that be learning about a new language/culture or learning more about science and math in a fun, fictional format. We want to help children to gain a love for other languages and subjects so that they are curious about the world around them. We are currently accepting fiction and nonfiction submissions." Publishes hardcover, trade paperback, mass-market paperback, and electronic originals. Catalog available for SASE. Guidelines available on website.

NEEDS Interested in multicultural stories with an emphasis on authentic culture and language (these may include mythology).

HOW TO CONTACT Query with SASE.

TERMS Pays 5-15% royalties on retail price. Pays $300-1,000 advance. Responds in 3 months to queries, proposals, and mss.

⬤⬤⬤ TIGHTROPE BOOKS

#207-2 College St., Toronto ON M5G 1K3 Canada. (416)928-6666. **E-mail:** tightropeasst@gmail.com. **Website:** www.tightropebooks.com. **Contact:** Jim

Nason, publisher. Estab. 2005. Publishes hardcover and trade paperback originals. Catalog and guidelines online.

⬤ Accepting submissions for new mystery imprint, Mysterio.

TERMS Pays 5-15% royalty on retail price. Pays advance of $200-300. Responds if interested.

TIPS "Audience is young, urban, literary, educated, unconventional."

⬤ TIN HOUSE BOOKS

2617 NW Thurman St., Portland OR 97210. (503)473-8663. **Fax:** (503)473-8957. **E-mail:** meg@tinhouse.com. **Website:** www.tinhouse.com. **Contact:** Meg Storey, editor; Tony Perez, editor; Masie Cochran, editor. "We are a small independent publisher dedicated to nurturing new, promising talent as well as showcasing the work of established writers." Distributes/promotes titles through Publishers Group West. Publishes hardcover originals, paperback originals, paperback reprints. Guidelines online.

HOW TO CONTACT *Agented mss only.* "We no longer read unsolicited submissions by authors with no representation. We will continue to accept submissions from agents."

TERMS Responds to queries in 2-3 weeks; mss in 2-3 months.

TITAN PRESS

PMB 17897, Encino CA 91416. **E-mail:** titan91416@yahoo.com. **Website:** www.calwriterssfv.com. **Contact:** Stefanya Wilson, editor. Estab. 1981. Publishes hardcover and paperback originals. Ms guidelines for #10 SASE.

HOW TO CONTACT Does not accept unsolicited mss. Query with SASE. Include brief bio, social security number, list of publishing credits.

TERMS Pays 20-40% royalty. Responds to queries in 3 months.

TIPS "Look, act, sound, and *be* professional."

⬤ TOP COW PRODUCTIONS, INC.

3812 Dunn Dr., Culver City CA 90232. **E-mail:** fanmail@topcow.com. **Website:** www.topcow.com. Guidelines online.

HOW TO CONTACT *No unsolicited submissions.* Prefers submissions from artists. See website for details and advice on how to break into the market.

TOP PUBLICATIONS, LTD.

12221 Merit Dr., Suite 950, Dallas TX 75251. (972)628-6414. **Fax:** (972)233-0713. **E-mail:** info@toppub.com.

E-mail: submissions@toppub.com. **Website:** www.
toppub.com. Estab. 1999. Primarily a mainstream fiction publisher. Publishes paperback originals and e-
books. Guidelines online.

○ "It is imperative that our authors realize they
will be required to promote their book extensively for it to be a success. Unless they are willing to make this commitment, they shouldn't
submit to TOP."

TERMS Pays 15% royalty on wholesale price. Pays
$250-$1,000 advance. Acknowledges receipt of queries but only responds if interested in seeing ms. Responds in 6 months to mss.

TIPS "We recommend that our authors write books
that appeal to a large mainstream audience to make
marketing easier and increase the chances of success.
We only publish a few titles a year so the odds at getting published at TOP are slim. If we don't offer you
a contract it doesn't mean we don't like your submission. We have to pass on a lot of good material each
year simply by the limitations of our time and budget."

TOR BOOKS

Tom Doherty Associates, 175 Fifth Ave., New York NY
10010. **Website:** www.tor-forge.com. Tor Books is the
"world's largest publisher of science fiction and fantasy,
with strong category publishing in historical fiction,
mystery, western/Americana, thriller, YA." Book catalog available. Guidelines online.

HOW TO CONTACT Submit first 3 chapters, 3-10
page synopsis, dated cover letter, SASE.

TERMS Pays author royalty. Pays illustrators by the
project.

TORQUERE PRESS

1380 Rio Rancho Blvd., #1319, Rio Rancho NM 87124.
E-mail: editor@torquerepress.com. **E-mail:** submis-
sions@torquerepress.com. **Website:** www.torquere-
press.com. **Contact:** Kristi Boulware, submissions
editor (homoerotica, suspense, gay/lesbian); Lorna
Hinson, senior editor (gay/lesbian romance, historicals). Estab. 2003. "We are a gay and lesbian press
focusing on romance and genres of romance. We
particularly like paranormal and western romance."
Publishes trade paperback originals and electronic
originals and reprints Book catalog online. Guidelines online.

NEEDS All categories gay and lesbian themed.

HOW TO CONTACT Submit proposal package, 3
sample chapters, clips.

TERMS Pays 8-40% royalty. Pays $35-75 for anthol-
ogy stories. Responds in 1 month to queries and proposals; 2-4 months to mss.

TIPS "Our audience is primarily people looking for
a familiar romance setting featuring gay or lesbian
protagonists. Please read guidelines carefully and familiarize yourself with our lines."

TORREY HOUSE PRESS, LLC

2806 Melony Dr., Salt Lake City UT 84124. (801)810-
9THP. **E-mail:** mark@torreyhouse.com. **Website:** tor-
reyhouse.com. **Contact:** Mark Bailey, publisher. Estab.
2010. "Torrey House Press (THP) publishes literary
fiction and creative nonfiction about the world environment with a tilt toward the American West. Want
submissions from experienced and agented authors
only." Publishes hardcover, trade paperback, and electronic originals. Catalog online. Guidelines online.

NEEDS "Torrey House Press publishes literary fiction
and creative nonfiction about the world environment
and the American West."

HOW TO CONTACT Submit proposal package including: synopsis, complete ms, bio.

TERMS Pays 5-15% royalty on retail price. Responds
in 3 months.

TIPS "Include writing experience (none okay)."

○ TOUCHWOOD EDITIONS

The Heritage Group, 103-1075 Pendergast St., Victoria
BC V8V 0A1 Canada. (250)360-0829. **Fax:** (250)386-
0829. **E-mail:** edit@touchwoodeditions.com. **Website:** www.touchwoodeditions.com. **Contact:** Marlyn
Horsdal, editor. Publishes trade paperback originals
and reprints. Book catalog and guidelines online.

HOW TO CONTACT Submit TOC, outline, word count.

TERMS Pays 15% royalty on net price. Responds in 3
months to queries.

TIPS "Our area of interest is Western Canada. We
would like more creative nonfiction and books about
people of note in Canada's history."

○ TRADEWIND BOOKS

202-1807 Maritime Mews, Granville Island, Vancouver BC V6H 3W7 Canada. (604)662-4405. **Website:**
www.tradewindbooks.com. **Contact:** R. David Stephens, senior editor. "Tradewind Books publishes juvenile picture books and young adult novels. Requires
that submissions include evidence that author has
read at least 3 titles published by Tradewind Books."
Publishes hardcover and trade paperback originals.
Book catalog and ms guidelines online.

NEEDS Average word length: 900 words.

HOW TO CONTACT Send complete ms for picture books. *YA novels by Canadian authors only. Chapter books by U.S. authors considered.*

TERMS Pays 7% royalty on retail price. Pays variable advance. Responds to mss in 2 months.

TRISTAN PUBLISHING

2355 Louisiana Ave. N, Golden Valley MN 55427. (763)545-1383. **Fax:** (763)545-1387. **E-mail:** info@tristanpublishing.com; manuscripts@tristanpublishing.com. **Website:** www.tristanpublishing.com. **Contact:** Brett Waldman, publisher. Estab. 2002. Publishes hardcover originals. Catalog and guidelines online.

HOW TO CONTACT Query with SASE; submit completed mss.

TERMS Pays royalty on wholesale or retail price; outright purchase. Responds in 3 months.

TIPS "Our audience is adults and children."

TU BOOKS

Lee & Low Books, 95 Madison Ave., Suite #1205, New York NY 10016. (212)779-4400. **Fax:** (212)683-1894. **Website:** www.leeandlow.com/imprints/3. **Contact:** Stacy Whitman, publisher. The Tu imprint spans many genres: science fiction, fantasy, mystery, and more. "We don't believe in labels or limits, just great stories. Join us at the crossroads where fantasy and real life collide. You'll be glad you did." Guidelines online. Electronic submissions can be submitted here (only): https://tubooks.submittable.com/submit.

NEEDS Focuses on well-told, exciting, adventurous fantasy, science fiction, and mystery novels featuring people of color and/or set in worlds inspired by non-Western folklore or culture. Looking specifically for stories for both middle-grade (ages 8-12) and young adult (ages 12-18) readers.

HOW TO CONTACT Mss should be sent through postal mail only. Mss should be accompanied by a cover letter that includes a brief biography of the author, including publishing history. The letter should also state if the ms is a simultaneous or an exclusive submission. Include a synopsis and the first 3 chapters of the novel. Include full contact information on the cover letter and the first page of the ms.

TERMS Responds only if interested.

TUMBLEHOME LEARNING

P.O. Box 71386, Boston MA 02117. **E-mail:** info@tumblehomelearning.com. **Website:** www.tumblehomelearning.com. **Contact:** Pendred Noyce, editor.

Estab. 2011. Tumblehome Learning helps kids imagine themselves as young scientists or engineers and encourages them to experience science through adventure and discovery. "We do this with exciting mystery and adventure tales as well as experiments carefully designed to engage students from ages 8 and up." Publishes hardcover, trade paperback, and electronic originals. Catalog available online. Guidelines available on request for SASE.

NEEDS "All our fiction has science at its heart. This can include using science to solve a mystery (see *The Walking Fish* by Rachelle Burk or *Something Stinks!* by Gail Hedrick), realistic science fiction, books in our Galactic Academy of Science series, science-based adventure tales, and the occasional picture book with a science theme, such as appreciation of the stars and constellations in *Elizabeth's Constellation Quilt* by Olivia Fu. A graphic novel about science would also be welcome."

HOW TO CONTACT Submit completed ms electronically.

TERMS Pays authors 8-12% royalties on retail price. Pays $500 advance. Responds in 1 month to queries and proposals, and 2 months to mss.

TIPS "Please don't submit to us if your book is not about science. We don't accept generic books about animals or books with glaring scientific errors in the first chapter. That said, the book should be fun to read and the science content can be subtle. We work closely with authors, including first-time authors, to edit and improve their books. As a small publisher, the greatest benefit we can offer is this friendly and respectful partnership with authors."

TUPELO PRESS

P.O. Box 1767, North Adams MA 01247. (413)664-9611. **E-mail:** publisher@tupelopress.org. **E-mail:** www.tupelopress.org/submissions. **Website:** www.tupelopress.org. **Contact:** Jeffrey Levine, publish/editor in chief; Jim Schley, managing editor. Estab. 2001. "We're an independent nonprofit literary press. We accept book-length poetry, poetry collections (48+ pages), short story collections, novellas, literary nonfiction/memoirs and up to 80 pages of a novel." Guidelines online.

NEEDS "For novels—submit no more than 100 pages along with a summary of the entire book. If we're interested we'll ask you to send the rest. We accept very few works of prose (1 or 2 per year)."

HOW TO CONTACT Submit complete ms. **Charges a $45 reading fee.**

☼ TURNSTONE PRESS

Artspace Building, 206-100 Arthur St., Winnipeg MB R3B 1H3 Canada. (204)947-1555. **Fax:** (204)942-1555. **Website:** www.turnstonepress.com. **Contact:** Submissions Assistant. Estab. 1976. "Turnstone Press is a literary publisher, not a general publisher, and therefore we are only interested in literary fiction, literary nonfiction—including literary criticism—and poetry. We do publish literary mysteries, thrillers, and noir under our Ravenstone imprint. We publish only Canadian authors or landed immigrants, we strive to publish a significant number of new writers, to publish in a variety of genres, and to have 50% of each year's list be Manitoba writers and/or books with Manitoba content." Guidelines online.

HOW TO CONTACT "Samples must be 40 to 60 pages, typed/printed in a minimum 12 point serif typeface such as Times, Book Antiqua, or Garamond."

TERMS Responds in 4-7 months.

TIPS "As a Canadian literary press, we have a mandate to publish Canadian writers only. Do some homework before submitting works to make sure your subject matter/genre/writing style falls within the publishers area of interest."

TWILIGHT TIMES BOOKS

P.O. Box 3340, Kingsport TN 37664. **E-mail:** publisher@twilighttimesbooks.com. **Website:** www.twilighttimesbooks.com. **Contact:** Andy M. Scott, managing editor. Estab. 1999. "We publish compelling literary fiction by authors with a distinctive voice." Published 5 debut authors within the last year. Averages 120 total titles; 15 fiction titles/year. Member: AAP, PAS, SPAN, SLF. Guidelines online.

HOW TO CONTACT Accepts unsolicited mss. Do not send complete mss. Queries via e-mail only. Include estimated word count, brief bio, list of publishing credits, marketing plan.

TERMS Pays 8-15% royalty. Responds in 4 weeks to queries; 2 months to mss.

TIPS "The only requirement for consideration at Twilight Times Books is that your novel must be entertaining and professionally written."

TWO DOLLAR RADIO

Website: www.twodollarradio.com. **Contact:** Eric Obenauf, editorial director. Estab. 2005. Two Dollar Radio is a boutique family-run press, publishing bold works of literary merit, each book, individually and collectively, providing a sonic progression that "we believe to be too loud to ignore." Targets readers who admire ambition and creativity. Range of print runs: 2,000-7,500 copies.

HOW TO CONTACT Submit entire, completed ms with a brief cover letter, via Submittable. No previously published work. No proposals. No excerpts. There is a $2 reading fee per submission. Accepts submissions every other month (January, March, May, July, September, November).

TERMS Advance: $500-$1,000.

TIPS "We want writers who show an authority over language and the world that is being created, from the very first sentence on."

ⓐⓞ TYNDALE HOUSE PUBLISHERS, INC.

351 Executive Dr., Carol Stream IL 60188. (800)323-9400. **Fax:** (800)684-0247. **Website:** www.tyndale.com. **Contact:** Katara Washington Patton, acquisitions; Talinda Iverson, art acquisitions. Estab. 1962. "Tyndale House publishes practical, user-friendly Christian books for the home and family." Publishes hardcover and trade paperback originals and mass paperback reprints. Guidelines online.

NEEDS "Christian truths must be woven into the story organically. No short story collections. Youth books: character building stories with Christian perspective. Especially interested in ages 10-14. We primarily publish Christian historical romances, with occasional contemporary, suspense, or standalones."

HOW TO CONTACT *Agented submissions only. No unsolicited mss.*

TERMS Pays negotiable royalty. Pays negotiable advance.

TIPS "All accepted mss will appeal to Evangelical Christian children and parents."

ⓞ TYRUS BOOKS

F+W Media, 1213 N. Sherman Ave., #306, Madison WI 53704. (508)427-7100. **Fax:** (508)427-6790. **E-mail:** submissions@tyrusbooks.com. **Website:** tyrusbooks.com. "We publish crime and literary fiction. We believe in the life changing power of the written word."

HOW TO CONTACT Submissions currently closed; check website for updates.

UNBRIDLED BOOKS

8201 E. Highway WW, Columbia MO 65201. **E-mail:** michalsong@unbridledbooks.com. **Website:** unbridledbooks.com. **Contact:** Greg Michalson. Estab. 2004. "Unbridled Books is a premier publisher of works of rich literary quality that appeal to a broad audience."

HOW TO CONTACT Please query first by e-mail. "Due to the heavy volume of submissions, we regret that at this time we are not able to consider uninvited mss."

TIPS "We try to read each ms that arrives, so please be patient."

⊘ UNITY HOUSE

1901 N.W. Blue Pkwy., Unity Village MO 64065-0001. (816)524-3550. **Fax:** (816)347-5518. **E-mail:** unity@unityonline.org. **E-mail:** sartinson@unityonline.org. **Website:** www.unityonline.org. **Contact:** Sharon Sartin, executive assistant. Estab. 1889. Unity House publishes metaphysical Christian books based on Unity principles, as well as inspirational books on metaphysics and practical spirituality. All mss must reflect a spiritual foundation and express the Unity philosophy, practical Christianity, universal principles, and/or metaphysics. Publishes hardcover, trade paperback, and electronic originals. Catalog and guidelines online.

NEEDS "We are a bridge between traditional Christianity and New Age spirituality. Unity is based on metaphysical Christian principles, spiritual values and the healing power of prayer as a resource for daily living."

HOW TO CONTACT *Not accepting mss for new books at this time.*

TERMS Pays 10-15% royalty on retail price. Pays advance. Responds in 6-8 months.

TIPS "We target an audience of spiritual seekers."

UNIVERSITY OF ALASKA PRESS

P.O. Box 756240, Fairbanks AK 99775-6240. (907)474-5831 or (888)252-6657. **Fax:** (907)474-5502. **E-mail:** james.engelhardt@alaska.edu. **Website:** www.uaf.edu/uapress. **Contact:** James Engelhardt, acquisitions editor. Estab. 1967. "The mission of the University of Alaska Press is to encourage, publish, and disseminate works of scholarship that will enhance the store of knowledge about Alaska and the North Pacific Rim, with a special emphasis on the circumpolar regions." Publishes hardcover originals, trade paperback originals and reprints. Book catalog available free. Guidelines online.

NEEDS Alaska literary series with Peggy Shumaker as series editor. Publishes 1-3 works of fiction/year.

HOW TO CONTACT Submit proposal.

TERMS Responds in 2 months to queries.

TIPS "Writers have the best chance with scholarly nonfiction relating to Alaska, the circumpolar regions

and North Pacific Rim. Our audience is made up of scholars, historians, students, libraries, universities, individuals, and the general Alaskan public."

UNIVERSITY OF GEORGIA PRESS

Main Library, Third Floor, 320 S. Jackson St., Athens GA 30602. (706)369-6130. **Fax:** (706)369-6131. **E-mail:** books@ugapress.uga.edu. **Website:** www.ugapress.org. Estab. 1938. University of Georgia Press is a midsized press that publishes fiction only through the Flannery O'Connor Award for Short Fiction competition. Publishes hardcover originals, trade paperback originals, and reprints. Book catalog and guidelines online.

NEEDS Short story collections published in Flannery O'Connor Award Competition.

TERMS Pays 7-10% royalty on net receipts. Pays rare, varying advance. Responds in 2 months to queries.

TIPS "Please visit our website to view our book catalogs and for all ms submission guidelines."

UNIVERSITY OF IOWA PRESS

100 Kuhl House, 119 W. Park Rd., Iowa City IA 52242. (319)335-2000. **Fax:** (319)335-2055. **E-mail:** james-mccoy@uiowa.edu; elisabeth-chretien@uiowa.edu; cathcampbell@uiowa.edu. **Website:** www.uiowapress.org. **Contact:** James McCoy, director (short fiction, poetry, general trade); Elisabeth Chretien, acquisitions editor (literary criticism, literary and general nonfiction, military and veterans' studies); Catherine Cocks, acquisitions editor (book arts, fan studies, food studies, midwestern history and culture, theatre history and culture). Estab. 1969. "We publish authoritative, original nonfiction that we market mostly by direct mail to groups with special interests in our titles, and by advertising in trade and scholarly publications." Publishes hardcover and paperback originals. Book catalog available free. Guidelines online.

NEEDS Currently publishes the Iowa Short Fiction Award selections.

TERMS Pays 7-10% royalty on net receipts.

UNIVERSITY OF MICHIGAN PRESS

839 Greene St., Ann Arbor MI 48106. **Website:** www.press.umich.edu. "In partnership with our authors and series editors, we publish in a wide range of humanities and social sciences disciplines." Guidelines online.

NEEDS In addition to the annual Michigan Literary Fiction Awards, this publishes literary fiction linked to the Great Lakes region.

HOW TO CONTACT Submit cover letter and first 30 pages.

UNIVERSITY OF NORTH TEXAS PRESS

1155 Union Circle, #311336, Denton TX 76203. (940)565-2142. **Fax:** (940)565-4590. **E-mail:** ronald. chrisman@unt.edu; karen.devinney@unt.edu. **Website:** untpress.unt.edu. **Contact:** Ronald Chrisman, director; Karen De Vinney, assistant director; Lori Belew, administrative assistant. Estab. 1987. "We are dedicated to producing the highest quality scholarly, academic, and general interest books. We are committed to serving all peoples by publishing stories of their cultures and experiences that have been overlooked. Currently emphasizing military history, Texas history, music, Mexican-American studies." Publishes hardcover and trade paperback originals and reprints. Book catalog for 8.5x11 SASE. Guidelines online.

NEEDS "The only fiction we publish is the winner of the Katherine Anne Porter Prize in Short Fiction, an annual, national competition with a $1,000 prize, and publication of the winning ms each Fall."

TERMS Responds in 1 month to queries.

TIPS "We publish series called War and the Southwest; Texas Folklore Society Publications; the Western Life Series; Practical Guide Series; Al-Filo: Mexican-American studies; North Texas Crime and Criminal Justice; Katherine Anne Porter Prize in Short Fiction; and the North Texas Lives of Musicians Series."

UNIVERSITY OF TAMPA PRESS

University of Tampa, 401 W. Kennedy Blvd., Tampa FL 33606. (813)253-6266. **Fax:** (813)258-7593. **E-mail:** utpress@ut.edu. **Website:** www.utpress.ut.edu. **Contact:** Richard Mathews, editor. Publishes hardcover originals and reprints; trade paperback originals and reprints. Book catalog online.

TERMS Responds in 3-4 months to queries.

UNIVERSITY OF WISCONSIN PRESS

1930 Monroe St., 3rd Floor, Madison WI 53711. (608)263-1110. **Fax:** (608)263-1132. **E-mail:** gcwalker@wisc.edu. **E-mail:** kadushin@wisc.edu. **Website:** uwpress.wisc.edu. **Contact:** Raphael Kadushin, senior acquisitions editor; Gwen Walker, acquisitions editor. Estab. 1937. Publishes hardcover originals, paperback originals, and paperback reprints. Guidelines online.

HOW TO CONTACT Query with SASE or submit outline, 1-2 sample chapter(s), synopsis.

TERMS Pays royalty. Responds in 2 weeks to queries; 8 weeks to mss. Rarely comments on rejected mss.

TIPS "Make sure the query letter and sample text are well-written, and read guidelines carefully to make sure we accept the genre you are submitting."

ⓐⓢⓞ ⓞ USBORNE PUBLISHING

83-85 Saffron Hill, London En EC1N 8RT United Kingdom. (44)207430-2800. **Fax:** (44)207430-1562. **E-mail:** mail@usborne.co.uk. **Website:** www.usborne. com. "Usborne Publishing is a multiple-award winning, world-wide children's publishing company publishing almost every type of children's book for every age from baby to young adult."

NEEDS Young readers, middle readers: adventure, contemporary, fantasy, history, humor, multicultural, nature/environment, science fiction, suspense/mystery, strong concept-based or character-led series. Average word length: young readers—5,000-10,000; middle readers—25,000-50,000; young adult—50,000-100,000.

HOW TO CONTACT *Agented submissions only.*

TERMS Pays authors royalty.

TIPS "Do not send any original work and, sorry, but we cannot guarantee a reply."

ⓞ VÉHICULE PRESS

P.O.B. 42094 BP Roy, Montreal QC H2W 2T3 Canada. (514)844-6073. **Fax:** (514)844-7543. **E-mail:** vp@vehiculepress.com. **E-mail:** esplanade@vehiculepress. com. **Website:** www.vehiculepress.com. **Contact:** Simon Dardick, president/publisher. Estab. 1973. "Montreal's Véhicule Press has published the best of Canadian and Quebec literature-fiction, poetry, essays, translations, and social history." Publishes trade paperback originals by Canadian authors mostly. Book catalog for 9x12 SAE with IRCs.

IMPRINTS Signal Editions (poetry); Esplanade Editions (fiction).

NEEDS No romance or formula writing.

HOW TO CONTACT Query with SASE.

TERMS Pays 10-15% royalty on retail price. Pays $200-500 advance. Responds in 4 months to queries.

TIPS "Quality in almost any style is acceptable. We believe in the editing process."

ⓞⓢ VERTIGO

DC Universe, Vertigo-DC Comics, 1700 Broadway, New York NY 10019. **Website:** www.vertigocomics. com. At this time, DC Entertainment does not accept unsolicited artwork or writing submissions.

ⓐⓞ VIKING

Imprint of Penguin Group (USA), Inc., 375 Hudson St., New York NY 10014. (212)366-2000. **Website:** www.penguin.com. Estab. 1925. Viking publishes a mix of academic and popular fiction and nonfiction. Publishes hardcover and originals.

HOW TO CONTACT *Agented submissions only.*

TERMS Pays 10-15% royalty on retail price.

⚫⊘ VIKING CHILDREN'S BOOKS

375 Hudson St., New York NY 10014. **Website:** www. penguin.com. **Contact:** Kenneth Wright, publisher. "Viking Children's Books is known for humorous, quirky picture books, in addition to more traditional fiction. We publish the highest quality fiction, non-fiction, and picture books for pre-schoolers through young adults." *Does not accept unsolicited submissions.* Publishes hardcover originals.

NEEDS All levels: adventure, animal, contemporary, fantasy, history, humor, multicultural, nature/environment, poetry, problem novels, romance, science fiction, sports, suspense/mystery.

HOW TO CONTACT *Accepts agented mss only.*

TERMS Pays 2-10% royalty on retail price or flat fee. Pays negotiable advance. Responds in 6 months.

TIPS "No 'cartoony' or mass-market submissions for picture books."

⚫⊘ VILLARD BOOKS

Imprint of Random House Publishing Group, 1745 Broadway, New York NY 10019. (212)572-2600. **Website:** www.atrandom.com. Estab. 1983. "Villard Books is the publisher of savvy and sometimes quirky, best-selling hardcovers and trade paperbacks."

NEEDS Commercial fiction.

HOW TO CONTACT *Agented submissions only.*

TERMS Pays negotiable royalty. Pays negotiable advance.

⚫⊘ VINTAGE ANCHOR PUBLISHING

Imprint of Random House, 1745 Broadway, New York NY 10019. **Website:** www.randomhouse.com.

HOW TO CONTACT *Agented submissions only.*

TERMS Pays 4-8% royalty on retail price. Average advance: $2,500 and up.

VIVISPHERE PUBLISHING

675 Dutchess Turnpike, Poughkeepsie NY 12603. (845)463-1100, ext. 314. **Fax:** (845)463-0018. **E-mail:** cs@vivisphere.com. **Website:** www.vivisphere.com. **Contact:** Submissions. Estab. 1995. Vivisphere Publishing is now considering new submissions from any genre as follows: game of bridge (cards), nonfiction, history, military, new age, fiction, feminist/gay/lesbian, horror, contemporary, self-help, science fiction

and cookbooks. Publishes trade paperback originals and reprints and e-books. Book catalog and ms guidelines online.

◔ "Cookbooks should have a particular slant or appeal to a certain niche. We also publish out-of-print books."

HOW TO CONTACT Query with SASE.

TERMS Pays royalty. Responds in 6-12 months.

⊘ VIZ MEDIA LLC

P.O. Box 77010, San Francisco CA 94107. (415)546-7073. **Website:** www.viz.com. "VIZ Media, LLC is one of the most comprehensive and innovative companies in the field of manga (graphic novel) publishing, animation and entertainment licensing of Japanese content. Owned by 3 of Japan's largest creators and licensors of manga and animation, Shueisha Inc., Shogakukan Inc., and Shogakukan-Shueisha Productions, Co., Ltd., VIZ Media is a leader in the publishing and distribution of Japanese manga for English speaking audiences in North America, the United Kingdom, Ireland, and South Africa and is a global ex-Asia licensor of Japanese manga and animation. The company offers an integrated product line including magazines such as *Shonen Jump* and *Shojo Beat*, graphic novels, and DVDs, and develops, markets, licenses, and distributes animated entertainment for audiences and consumers of all ages."

HOW TO CONTACT "At the present, all of the manga that appears in our magazines come directly from manga that has been serialized and published in Japan."

WASHINGTON WRITERS' PUBLISHING HOUSE

P.O. Box 15271, Washington DC 20003. **E-mail:** wwphpress@gmail.com. **Website:** www.washingtonwriters.org. **Contact:** Kathleen Wheaton, president. Estab. 1975. Guidelines online.

NEEDS Washington Writers' Publishing House considers book-length mss for publication by fiction writers living within 75 driving miles of the U.S. Capitol, Baltimore area included, through competition only. Mss may include previously published stories and excerpts. "Author should indicate where they heard about WWPH."

HOW TO CONTACT Submit an electronic copy by e-mail (use PDF, .doc, or rich text format) or 2 hard copies by snail mail of a short story collection or novel (no more than 350 pages, double or 1.5" spaced; author's name should not appear on any ms pages). Include separate page of publication acknowledgments plus 2 cover sheets: one with ms title, poet's name, address, telephone number, and e-mail address, the other with ms title only. Include SASE for results only; mss will not be returned (will be recycled). **TERMS** Offers $1,000 and 50 copies of published book plus additional copies for publicity use.

Ⓐⵔ WATERBROOK MULTNOMAH PUBLISHING GROUP

Random House, 12265 Oracle Blvd., Suite 200, Colorado Springs CO 80921. (719)590-4999. **Fax:** (719)590-8977. **E-mail:** info@waterbrookmultnomah.com. **Website:** www.waterbrookmultnomah.com. Estab. 1996. Publishes hardcover and trade paperback originals. Book catalog online.

HOW TO CONTACT *Agented submissions only.*

TERMS Pays royalty. Responds in 2-3 months.

WHITAKER HOUSE

1030 Hunt Valley Circle, New Kensington PA 15068. **E-mail:** publisher@whitakerhouse.com. **Website:** www.whitakerhouse.com. **Contact:** Editorial Department. Estab. 1970. Publishes hardcover, trade paperback, and mass-market originals. Book catalog available online. Guidelines online.

NEEDS All fiction must have a Christian perspective.

HOW TO CONTACT Query with SASE.

TERMS Pays 5-15% royalty on wholesale price. Responds in 3 months.

TIPS "Audience includes those seeking uplifting and inspirational fiction and nonfiction."

ⵔ WHITECAP BOOKS, LTD.

210 - 314 W. Cordova St., Vancouver BC V6B 1 E8 Canada. (604)681-6181. **Fax:** (905)477-9179. **E-mail:** steph@whitecap.ca. **Website:** www.whitecap.ca. "Whitecap Books is a general trade publisher with a focus on food and wine titles. Although we are interested in reviewing unsolicited ms submissions, please note that we only accept submissions that meet the needs of our current publishing program. Please see some of most recent releases to get an idea of the kinds of titles we are interested in." Publishes hardcover and trade paperback originals. Catalog and guidelines online.

NEEDS No children's picture books or adult fiction.

HOW TO CONTACT See guidelines.

TERMS Pays royalty. Pays negotiated advance. Responds in 2-3 months to proposals.

TIPS "We want well-written, well-researched material that presents a fresh approach to a particular topic."

WHITE MANE KIDS

73 W. Burd St., P.O. Box 708, Shippensburg PA 17257. (717)532-2237. **Fax:** (717)532-6110. **E-mail:** marketing@whitemane.com. **Website:** www.whitemane.com. **Contact:** Harold Collier, acquisitions editor. Estab. 1987. Book catalog and writer's guidelines available for SASE.

IMPRINTS White Mane Books, Burd Street Press, White Mane Kids, Ragged Edge Press.

NEEDS Middle readers, young adults: history (primarily American Civil War). Average word length: middle readers—30,000. Does not publish picture books.

HOW TO CONTACT Query.

TERMS Pays authors royalty of 7-10%. Pays illustrators and photographers by the project. Responds to queries in 1 month, mss in 6-9 months.

TIPS "Make your work historically accurate. We are interested in historically accurate fiction for middle and young adult readers. We do *not* publish picture books. Our primary focus is the American Civil War and some America Revolution topics."

WILD CHILD PUBLISHING

P.O. Box 4897, Culver City CA 90231. (310) 721-4461. **E-mail:** mgbaun@wildchildpublishing.com. **Website:** www.wildchildpublishing.com. **Contact:** Marci Baun, editor in chief. Estab. 1999. "We are known for working with newer/unpublished authors and editing to the standards of NYC publishers." Book catalogs on website.

NEEDS Multiple anthologies planned.

HOW TO CONTACT Query with outline/synopsis and 1 sample chapter. Accepts queries by e-mail only. Include estimated word count, brief bio. Often critiques/comments on rejected mss.

TERMS Pays royalties 10-40%. Responds in 1 month to queries and mss.

TIPS "Read our submission guidelines thoroughly. Send in entertaining, well-written stories. Be easy to work with and upbeat."

Ⓐⵔ WILLIAM MORROW

HarperCollins, 195 Broadway, New York NY 10007. (212)207-7000. **Fax:** (212)207-7145. **Website:** www.harpercollins.com. Estab. 1926. "William Morrow publishes a wide range of titles that receive much recognition and prestige—a most selective house." Book catalog available free.

NEEDS Publishes adult fiction. Morrow accepts only the highest quality submissions in adult fiction. *No unsolicited mss or proposals.*

HOW TO CONTACT *Agented submissions only.*
TERMS Pays standard royalty on retail price. Pays varying advance.

WOODBINE HOUSE

6510 Bells Mill Rd., Bethesda MD 20817. (301)897-3570. **Fax:** (301)897-5838. **E-mail:** info@woodbine house.com. **Website:** www.woodbinehouse.com. Estab. 1985. Woodbine House publishes books for or about individuals with disabilities to help those individuals and their families live fulfilling and satisfying lives in their homes, schools, and communities. Publishes trade paperback originals. Guidelines online.

NEEDS Receptive to stories re: developmental and intellectual disabilities, e.g., autism and cerebral palsy.
HOW TO CONTACT Submit complete ms with SASE.
TERMS Pays 10-12% royalty. Responds in 3 months to queries.
TIPS "Do not send us a proposal on the basis of this description. Examine our catalog or website and a couple of our books to make sure you are on the right track. Put some thought into how your book could be marketed (aside from in bookstores). Keep cover letters concise and to the point; if it's a subject that interests us, we'll ask to see more."

○ YELLOW SHOE FICTION SERIES

P.O. Box 25053, Baton Rouge LA 70894. **Website:** www.lsu.edu/lsupress. **Contact:** Michael Griffith, editor. Estab. 2004.

○ "Looking first and foremost for literary excellence, especially good mss that have fallen through the cracks at the big commercial presses. I'll cast a wide net."

HOW TO CONTACT Does not accept unsolicited mss. Accepts queries by mail, Attn: Rand Dotson. No electronic submissions.
TERMS Pays royalty. Offers advance.

YMAA PUBLICATION CENTER

P.O. Box 480, Wolfeboro NH 03894. (603)569-7988. **Fax:** (603)569-1889. **E-mail:** info@ymaa.com. **Contact:** David Ripianzi, director. Estab. 1982. YMAA publishes books on Chinese Chi Kung (Qigong), Taijiquan, (Tai Chi) and Asian martial arts. We are expanding our focus to include books on healing, wellness, meditation and subjects related to Asian culture and Asian medicine. Publishes trade paperback originals and reprints. Publishes 6-8 DVD titles/year. Book catalog online. Guidelines available free.

NEEDS "We are seeking mss that bring the venerated tradition of true Asian martial arts to readers. Your novel length ms should be a thrilling story that conveys insights into true martial techniques and philosophies."
TERMS Responds in 3 months to proposals.
TIPS "If you are submitting health-related material, please refer to an Asian tradition. Learn about author publicity options as your participation is mandatory."

ZEBRA BOOKS

Kensington, 119 W. 40th St., New York NY 10018. (212)407-1500. **E-mail:** esogah@kensingtonbooks. com. **Website:** www.kensingtonbooks.com. **Contact:** Esi Sogah, senior editor. Zebra Books is dedicated to women's fiction, which includes, but is not limited to romance. Publishes hardcover originals, trade paperback and mass-market paperback originals and reprints. Book catalog online.
HOW TO CONTACT Query.

ZUMAYA PUBLICATIONS, LLC

3209 S. Interstate 35, Austin TX 78741. **E-mail:** business@zumayapublications.com. **E-mail:** acquisitions@zumayapublications.com. **Website:** www.zumayapublications.com. **Contact:** Rie Sheridan Rose, acquisitions editor. Estab. 1999. Publishes trade paperback and electronic originals and reprints. Guidelines online.

○ "We accept only electronic queries; all others will be discarded unread. A working knowledge of computers and relevant software is a necessity, as our production process is completely digital."

IMPRINTS Zumaya Arcane (New Age, inspirational fiction & nonfiction), Zumaya Boundless (GLBT); Zumaya Embraces (romance/women's fiction); Zumaya Enigma (mystery/suspense/thriller); Zumaya Thresholds (YA/middle-grade); Zumaya Otherworlds (SF/F/H), Zumaya Yesterdays (memoirs, historical fiction, fiction, western fiction); Zumaya Fabled Ink (graphic and illustrated novels).
NEEDS "We are currently oversupplied with speculative fiction and are reviewing submissions in SF, fantasy and paranormal suspense by invitation only. We are much in need of GLBT and YA/middle-grade, historical and western, New Age/inspirational (no overtly Christian materials, please), noncategory romance, thrillers. As with nonfiction, we encourage people to review what we've already published so as

to avoid sending us more of the same, at least, insofar as the plot is concerned. While we're always looking for good specific mysteries, we want original concepts rather than slightly altered versions of what we've already published."

TERMS Responds in 6 months to queries and proposals; 9 months to mss.

TIPS "We're catering to readers who may have loved last year's best seller but not enough to want to read 10 more just like it. Have something different. If it does not fit standard pigeonholes, that's a plus. On the other hand, it has to have an audience. And if you're not prepared to work with us on promotion and marketing, particularly via social media, it would be better to look elsewhere."

CONTESTS & AWARDS

In addition to honors and, quite often, cash prizes, contests and awards programs offer writers the opportunity to be judged on the basis of quality alone, without the outside factors that sometimes influence publishing decisions. New writers who win contests may be published for the first time, while more experienced writers may gain public recognition for an entire body of work.

Listed here are contests for almost every type of fiction writing. Some focus on form, such as short stories, novels, or novellas, while others feature writing on particular themes or topics. Still others are prestigious prizes or awards for work that must be nominated.

SELECTING AND SUBMITTING TO A CONTEST

Use the same care in submitting to contests as you would sending your manuscript to a publication or book publisher. Deadlines are very important, and, where possible, we've included this information. For some contests, deadlines were only approximate at our press deadline, so be sure to write, call, or look online for complete information.

Follow the rules to the letter. If, for instance, contest rules require your name on a cover sheet only, you will be disqualified if you ignore this and put your name on every page. Find out how many copies to send. If you don't send the correct amount, by the time you are contacted to send more, it may be past the submission deadline. An increasing number of contests invite writers to query by e-mail, and many post contest information on their websites. Check listings for e-mail and website addresses.

One note of caution: Beware of contests that charge entry fees that are disproportionate to the amount of the prize. Contests offering a $10 prize and charging $7 in entry fees are a waste of your time and money.

24-HOUR SHORT STORY CONTEST

WritersWeekly.com, 5726 Cortez Rd. W., #349, Bradenton FL 34210. **E-mail:** writersweekly@writersweekly.com. **Website:** www.writersweekly.com/misc/contest.php. **Contact:** Angela Hoy. Quarterly contest in which registered entrants receive a topic at start time (usually noon Central Time) and have 24 hours to write a story on that topic. All submissions must be returned via e-mail. Each contest is limited to 500 people. Upon entry, entrant will receive guidelines and details on competition, including submission process. Deadline: Quarterly—see website for dates. Prize: First Place: $300; Second Place: $250; Third Place: $200. There are also 20 honorable mentions and 60 door prizes (randomly drawn from all participants). The top 3 winners' entries are posted on WritersWeekly.com (nonexclusive electronic rights only) and receive a Freelance Income Kit. Writers retain all rights to their work. See website for full details on prizes. Judged by Angela Hoy (publisher of WritersWeekly.com and Booklocker.com).

AEON AWARD

Albedo One/Aeon Press, Aeon Award, Albedo One, 2 Post Road, Lusk, Dublin Ireland. +353 1 8730177. **E-mail:** fraslaw@yahoo.co.uk. **Website:** www.albedo1.com. **Contact:** Frank Ludlow, event coordinator. Estab. 2004. Prestigious fiction writing competition for short stories in any speculative fiction genre, such as fantasy, science fiction, horror, or anything in-between or unclassifiable. Deadline: November 30. Contest begins January 1. Prize: Grand Prize: €1,000; Second Prize: €200;, and Third Prize: €100. The top 3 stories are guaranteed publication in *Albedo One*. Judged by Ian Watson, Eileen Gunn, Todd McCaffrey, and Michael Carroll.

AESTHETICA ART PRIZE

P.O. Box 371, York YO23 1WL United Kingdom. **E-mail:** info@aestheticamagazine.com. **E-mail:** artprize@aestheticamagazine.com. **Website:** www.aestheticamagazine.com. The Aesthetica Art Prize is a celebration of excellence in art from across the world and offers artists the opportunity to showcase their work to wider audiences and further their involvement in the international art world. There are 4 categories: Photographic & Digital Art, Three Dimensional Design & Sculpture, Painting & Drawing, Video Installation & Performance. See guidelines at www.aestheticamagazine.com. Deadline: August 31.

Prizes include: £5,000 main prize courtesy of Hiscox, £1,000 Student Prize courtesy of Hiscox, group exhibition and publication in the Aesthetica Art Prize Anthology. Entry is £15 and permits submission of 2 works in 1 category.

AHWA FLASH & SHORT STORY COMPETITION

AHWA (Australian Horror Writers Association), **E-mail:** ahwacomps@australianhorror.com; ahwa@australianhorror.com. **E-mail:** ctrost@hotmail.com. **Website:** www.australianhorror.com. **Contact:** David Carroll, competitions officer. Competition/award for short stories and flash fiction. Looking for horror stories, tales that frighten, yarns that unsettle readers in their comfortable homes. All themes in this genre will be accepted, from the well used (zombies, vampires, ghosts etc) to the highly original, so long as the story is professional and well written. Deadline: May 31. Prize: The authors of the winning Flash Fiction and Short Story entries will each receive paid publication in *Midnight Echo*, The Magazine of the AHWA and an engraved plaque.

MARIE ALEXANDER POETRY SERIES

English Department, 2801 S. University Ave., Little Rock AR 72204. **E-mail:** editor@mariealexanderseries.com. **Website:** mariealexanderseries.com. **Contact:** Nickole Brown. Annual contest for a collection of previously unpublished prose poems or flash fiction by a U.S. writer. Deadline: July 1-31. Prize: $1,000, plus publication.

AMERICAN ASSOCIATION OF UNIVERSITY WOMEN AWARD IN JUVENILE LITERATURE

4610 Mail Service Center, Raleigh NC 27699-4610. (919)807-7290. **E-mail:** michael.hill@ncdcr.gov. **Website:** www.ncdcr.gov. **Contact:** Michael Hill, awards coordinator. Annual award. Book must be published during the year ending June 30. Submissions made by author, author's agent or publisher. SASE for contest rules. Recognizes the year's best work of juvenile literature by a North Carolina resident. Deadline: July 15. Prize: Awards a cup to the winner and winner's name inscribed on a plaque displayed within the North Carolina Office of Archives and History. Judged by three-judge panel.

Competition receives 10-15 submissions per category.

AMERICAN LITERARY REVIEW CONTESTS

American Literary Review, P.O. Box 311307, University of North Texas, Denton TX 76203-1307. (940)565-2755. **E-mail:** americanliteraryreview@gmail.com. **Website:** www.americanliteraryreview.com. Contest to award excellence in short fiction, creative nonfiction, and poetry. Multiple entries are acceptable, but each entry must be accompanied with a reading fee. Do not put any identifying information in the file itself; include the author's name, title(s), address, e-mail address, and phone number in the boxes provided in the online submissions manager. Short fiction: Limit 8,000 words per work. Creative nonfiction: Limit 6,500 words per work. Deadline: October 1. Submission period begins June 1. Prize: $1,000 prize for each category, along with publication in the Spring online issue of the *American Literary Review*.

O AMERICAN MARKETS NEWSLETTER SHORT STORY COMPETITION

1974 46th Ave., San Francisco CA 94116. **E-mail:** sheila.oconnor@juno.com. Award is to give short story writers more exposure. Contest offered biannually. Open to any writer. All kinds of fiction are considered. Especially looking for women's pieces—romance, with a twist in the tale—but all will be considered. Results announced within 3 months of deadlines. Winners notified by mail if they include SASE. Deadline: June 30 and December 31. Prize: First Place: $300; Second Place: $100; Third Place: $50. Judged by a panel of independent judges.

AMERICAN-SCANDINAVIAN FOUNDATION TRANSLATION PRIZE

The American-Scandinavian Foundation, 58 Park Ave., New York NY 10016. (212)779-3587. **E-mail:** grants@amscan.org; info@amscan.org. **Website:** www.amscan.org. **Contact:** Matthew Walters, director of fellowships & grants. The annual ASF translation competition is awarded for the most outstanding translations of poetry, fiction, drama, or literary prose written by a Scandinavian author born after 1800. Deadline: June 1. Prize: The Nadia Christensen Prize includes a $2,500 award, publication of an excerpt in *Scandinavian Review*, and a commemorative bronze medallion; The Leif and Inger Sjöberg Award, given to an individual whose literature translations have not previously been published, includes a $2,000 award, publication of an excerpt in *Scandinavian Review*, and a commemorative bronze medallion.

A MIDSUMMER TALE

E-mail: editors@toasted-cheese.com. **Website:** www.toasted-cheese.com. **Contact:** Theryn Fleming, editor. A Midsummer Tale is open to nongenre fiction and creative nonfiction. There is a different theme each year. Entries must be unpublished. Accepts inquiries by e-mail. Deadline: June 21. Results announced on July 31. Winners notified by e-mail. List of winners on website. Prize: Amazon gift certificates and publication in Toasted Cheese. Entries are blind-judged.

O THE SHERWOOD ANDERSON FOUNDATION FICTION AWARD

12330 Ashton Mill Terrace, Glen Allen VA 23059. **E-mail:** sherwoodandersonfoundation@gmail.com. **Website:** www.sherwoodandersonfoundation.org. **Contact:** Anna McKean, foundation president. Estab. 1988. Contest is to honor, preserve and celebrate the memory and literary work of Sherwood Anderson, American realist for the first half of the 20th century. Annual award supports developing writers of short stories and novels. Deadline: April 1. Prize: $20,000 grant award.

SHERWOOD ANDERSON SHORT FICTION AWARD

Mid-American Review, Mid-American Review, Dept. of English, Box WM, BGSU, Bowling Green OH 43403. (419)372-2725. **Fax:** (419)372-4642. **E-mail:** mar@bgsu.edu. **Website:** www.bgsu.edu/midamericanreview. **Contact:** Abigail Cloud, editor in chief. Offered annually for unpublished mss (6,000 word limit). Contest is open to all writers not associated with a judge or *Mid-American Review*. Deadline: November 1. Prize: $1,000, plus publication in the spring issue of *Mid-American Review*. Four finalists: Notation, possible publication. Judged by editors and a well-known writer, i.e., Aimee Bender or Anthony Doerr.

① THE ATHENAEUM LITERARY AWARD

The Athenaeum of Philadelphia, 219 S. 6th St., Philadelphia PA 19106-3794. (215)925-2688. **Fax:** (215)925-3755. **E-mail:** jilly@PhilaAthenaeum.org. **Website:** www.PhilaAthenaeum.org. **Contact:** Jill Lee, Circulation Librarian. Estab. 1950. The Athenaeum Literary Award was established to recognize and encourage literary achievement among authors who are bona fide residents of Philadelphia or Pennsylvania living within a radius of 30 miles of City Hall at the time their book was written or published. Any volume of general literature is eligible; technical, scientific, and juvenile books are not included. Nominated works are reviewed on the basis of their significance and importance to the general public as well as for literary excellence. Deadline: December 31.

☺ ATLANTIC WRITING COMPETITION FOR UNPUBLISHED MANUSCRIPTS

Writers' Federation of Nova Scotia, 1113 Marginal Rd., Halifax NS B3H 4P7. (902)423-8116. **Fax:** (902)422-0881. **E-mail:** programs@writers.ns.ca. **Website:** www.writers.ns.ca. **Contact:** Robin Spittal, communications and development officer. Estab. 1975. Annual program designed to honor work by unpublished writers in all 4 Atlantic Provinces. Entry is open to writers unpublished in the category of writing they wish to enter. Prizes are presented in the fall of each year. Categories include: novel, writing for children, poetry, short story, juvenile/young adult novel, creative nonfiction, and play. Judges return written comments when competition is concluded. Deadline: February 2. Prizes vary based on categories. See website for details.

AUTUMN HOUSE FICTION PRIZE

Autumn House Press, 87½ Westwood St., Pittsburgh PA 15211. **E-mail:** info@autumnhouse.org. **Website:** autumnhouse.org. Fiction submissions should be approximately 200-300 pages. All fiction sub-genres (short stories, short-shorts, novellas, or novels), or any combination of sub-genres, are eligible. All finalists will be considered for publication. Deadline: June 30. Prize: Winners will receive book publication, $1,000 advance against royalties, and a $1,500 travel grant to participate in the Autumn House Master Authors Series in Pittsburgh. Final judge is Sharon Dilworth.

☺☻ AUTUMN HOUSE POETRY, FICTION, AND NONFICTION PRIZES

P.O. Box 60100, Pittsburgh PA 15211. (412)381-4261. **E-mail:** gcerto@autumnhouse.org; info@autumnhouse.org. **E-mail:** autumnh420@gmail.com. **Website:** autumnhouse.org. **Contact:** Giuliana Certo, managing editor. Estab. 1999. Offers annual prize and publication of book-length ms with national promotion. Submission must be unpublished as a collection, but individual poems, stories, and essays may have been previously published elsewhere. Considers simultaneous submissions. "Autumn House is a nonprofit corporation with the mission of publishing and promoting poetry and other fine literature. We have published books by Gerald Stern, Ruth L. Schwartz,

Ed Ochester, Andrea Hollander Budy, George Bilgere, Jo McDougall, and others." Deadline: June 30. Prize: The winner (in each of 3 categories) will receive book publication, $1,000 advance against royalties, and a $1,500 travel/publicity grant to promote his or her book. Judged by Dorianne Laux (poetry), Sharon Dilworth (fiction), and Dinty W. Moore (nonfiction).

☻ AWP AWARD SERIES

Association of Writers & Writing Programs, George Mason University, 4400 University Drive, MSN 1E3, Fairfax VA 22030. **E-mail:** supriya@awpwriter.org. **Website:** www.awpwriter.org. **Contact:** Supriya Bhatnagar, director of publications. AWP sponsors the Award Series, an annual competition for the publication of excellent new book-length works. The competition is open to all authors writing in English regardless of nationality or residence, and is available to published and unpublished authors alike. Offered annually to foster new literary talent. Deadline: Postmarked between January 1 and February 28. Prize: AWP Prize for the Novel: $2,500 and publication by New Issues Press; Donald Hall Prize for Poetry: $5,500 and publication by the University of Pittsburgh Press; Grace Paley Prize in Short Fiction: $5,500 and publication by the University of Massachusetts Press; and AWP Prize for Creative Nonfiction: $2,500 and publication by the University of Georgia Press.

BALCONES FICTION PRIZE

Austin Commmunity College, Department of Creative Writing, 1212 Rio Grande St., Austin TX 78701. (512)584-5045. **E-mail:** joconne@austincc.edu. **Website:** www.austincc.edu/crw/html/balconescenter.html. **Contact:** Joe O'Connell. Awarded to the best book of literary fiction published the previous year. Books of prose may be submitted by publisher or author. Send 3 copies. Deadline: January 31. Prize: $1,500, winner is flown to Austin for a campus reading.

●☺○☻ THE BALTIMORE REVIEW CONTESTS

The Baltimore Review, 6514 Maplewood Rd., Baltimore MD 21212. **Website:** www.baltimorereview.org. **Contact:** Barbara Westwood Diehl, senior editor. Each summer and winter issue includes a contest theme (see submissions guidelines for theme). Prizes are awarded for First, second, and third place among all categories—poetry, short stories, and creative nonfiction. All entries are considered for publication. Deadline: May 31 and November 30. Prize: First Place:

$500; Second Place: $200; Third Place: $100. All entries are considered for publication. Judged by the editors of *The Baltimore Review* and a guest, final judge.

BARD FICTION PRIZE

Bard College, P.O. Box 5000, Annandale-on-Hudson NY 12504-5000. (845)758-7087. **E-mail:** bfp@bard.edu. **Website:** www.bard.edu/bfp. **Contact:** Irene Zedlacher. Estab. 2001. The Bard Fiction Prize is awarded to a promising, emerging writer who is an American citizen aged 39 years or younger at the time of application. The Bard Fiction Prize is intended to encourage and support young writers of fiction to pursue their creative goals and to provide an opportunity to work in a fertile and intellectual environment. Deadline: June 15. Prize: $30,000 and appointment as writer-in-residence at Bard College for 1 semester. Judged by a committee of 5 judges (authors associated with Bard College).

◑ MILDRED L. BATCHELDER AWARD

50 E. Huron St., Chicago IL 60611-2795. **Website:** www.ala.org/alsc/awardsgrants/bookmedia/batchelderaward. Estab. 1966. The Batchelder Award is given to the most outstanding children's book originally published in a language other than English in a country other than the United States, and subsequently translated into English for publication in the U.S. The purpose of the award, a citation to an American publisher, is to encourage international exchange of quality children's books by recognizing U.S. publishers of such books in translation. Deadline: December 31.

BELLEVUE LITERARY REVIEW GOLDENBERG PRIZE FOR FICTION

Bellevue Literary Review, NYU Dept of Medicine, 550 First Ave., OBV-A612, New York NY 10016. (212)263-3973. **E-mail:** info@blreview.org; stacy@blreview.org. **Website:** www.blreview.org. **Contact:** Stacy Bodziak, managing editor. The BLR prizes award outstanding writing related to themes of health, healing, illness, the mind and the body. Annual competition/award for short stories. Receives about 200-300 entries per category. Send credit card information or make checks payable to Bellevue Literary Review. Guidelines available in February. Accepts inquiries by e-mail, phone, mail. Submissions open in February. Results announced in December and made available to entrants with SASE, by e-mail, on website. Winners notified by mail, by e-mail. Deadline: July 1. Prize: $1,000 and publication in *The Bellevue Literary Re-*

view. BLR editors select semi-finalists to be read by an independent judge who chooses the winner. Previous judges include Nathan Englander, Jane Smiley, Francine Prose, and Andre Dubus III.

◯ GEORGE BENNETT FELLOWSHIP

Phillips Exeter Academy, 20 Main St., Exeter NH 03833. **E-mail:** teaching_opportunities@exeter.edu. **Website:** www.exeter.edu/bennettfellowship. Annual award for fellow and family to provide time and freedom from material considerations to a person seriously contemplating or pursuing a career as a writer. Applicants should have a ms in progress which they intend to complete during the fellowship period. Ms should be fiction, nonfiction, novel, short stories, or poetry. Duties: To be in residency at the Academy for the academic year; to make oneself available informally to students interested in writing. Committee favors writers who have not yet published a book with a major publisher. Deadline for application: November 30. A choice will be made, and all entrants notified in mid-April. Cash stipend (currently $14,933), room and board. Judged by committee of the English department.

◯ BINGHAMTON UNIVERSITY JOHN GARDNER FICTION BOOK AWARD

Creative Writing Program, Binghamton University, Binghamton University, Department of English, General Literature, and Rhetoric, Library North Room 1149, P.O. Box 6000, Binghamton NY 13902-6000. (607)777-2713. **E-mail:** cwpro@binghamton.edu. **Website:** binghamton.edu/english/creative-writing/. **Contact:** Maria Mazziotti Gillan, director. Estab. 2001. Contest offered annually for a novel or collection of fiction published in previous year in a press run of 500 copies or more. Each book submitted must be accompanied by an application form. Publisher may submit more than 1 book for prize consideration. Send 3 copies of each book. Guidelines available on website. Deadline: March 1. Prize: $1,000. Judged by a professional writer not on Binghamton University faculty.

◐◯ JAMES TAIT BLACK MEMORIAL PRIZES

University of Edinburgh, School of Literatures, Languages, and Cultures, 50 George Square, Edinburgh EH8 9JH Scotland. **Website:** www.ed.ac.uk/news/events/tait-black/introduction. Open to any writer. Entries must be previously published. Winners notified by phone, via publisher. Contact department of English Literature for list of winners or check website. Accepts inquiries by e-mail or phone. Deadline: December 1. Prize: Two prizes each of £10,000 are awarded: one for the best work of fiction, one for the best biography or work of that nature, published during the calendar year January 1 to December 31. Judged by professors of English Literature with the assistance of teams of postgraduate readers.

◑◔ THE BLACK RIVER CHAPBOOK COMPETITION

Black Lawrence Press, 326 Bingham St., Pittsburgh PA 15211. **E-mail:** editors@blacklawrencepress.com. **Website:** www.blacklawrencepress.com. Twice each year, Black Lawrence Press runs the Black River Chapbook Competition for an unpublished chapbook of poems or short fiction between 18-36 pages in length. Spring deadline: May 31. Fall deadline: October 31. Prize: $500, publication, and 10 copies. Judged by a revolving panel of judges, in addition to the Chapbook Editor and other members of the BLP editorial staff.

◐◯ THE BOARDMAN TASKER PRIZE FOR MOUNTAIN LITERATURE

The Boardman Tasker Charitable Trust, 8 Bank View Rd., Darley Abbey Derby DE22 1EJ UK. 01332 342246. **E-mail:** steve@people-matter.co.uk. **Website:** www.boardmantasker.com. **Contact:** Steve Dean. Offered annually to reward a work with a mountain theme, whether fiction, nonfiction, drama, or poetry, written in the English language (initially or in translation). Subject must be concerned with a mountain environment. Previous winners have been books on expeditions, climbing experiences, a biography of a mountaineer, novels. Guidelines available in January by e-mail or on website. Entries must be previously published. Open to any writer. The award is to honor Peter Boardman and Joe Tasker, who disappeared on Everest in 1982. Deadline: August 1. Prize: £3,000 Judged by a panel of 3 judges elected by trustees.

BOSTON GLOBE-HORN BOOK AWARDS

The Boston Globe, Horn Book, Inc., 300 The Fenway, Palace Road Building, Suite P-311, Boston MA 02115. (617)628-0225. **Fax:** (617)628-0882. **E-mail:** info@hbook.com; khedeen@hbook.com. **Website:** hbook.com/bghb/. **Contact:** Katrina Hedeen. Estab. 1967. Offered annually for excellence in literature for children and young adults (published June 1-May 31). Categories: picture book, fiction and poetry, nonfiction.

Judges may also name up to 2 honor books in each category. Books must be published in the U.S., but may be written or illustrated by citizens of any country. The Horn Book Magazine publishes speeches given at awards ceremonies. Guidelines for SASE or online. Deadline: May 15. Prize: $500 and an engraved silver bowl; honor book recipients receive an engraved silver plate. Judged by a panel of 3 judges selected each year.

BOULEVARD SHORT FICTION CONTEST FOR EMERGING WRITERS

Boulevard Magazine, 6614 Clayton Rd., PMB #325, Richmond Heights MO 63117. (314)862-2643. **Website:** www.richardburgin.net/boulevard. **Contact:** Jessica Rogen, managing editor. Offered annually for unpublished short fiction to a writer who has not yet published a book of fiction, poetry, or creative nonfiction with a nationally distributed press. Holds first North American rights on anything not previously published. Open to any writer with no previous publication by a nationally known press. Guidelines for SASE or on website. Deadline: December 31. Prize: $1,500, and publication in 1 of the next year's issues.

◑◒ THE BRIAR CLIFF REVIEW FICTION, POETRY, AND CREATIVE NONFICTION COMPETITION

The Briar Cliff Review, Briar Cliff University, 3303 Rebecca St., Sioux City IA 51104-0100. **E-mail:** tricia.currans-sheehan@briarcliff.edu (editor); jeanne.emmons@briarcliff.edu (poetry). **Website:** www.bcreview.org. **Contact:** Tricia Currans-Sheehan, editor. *The Briar Cliff Review* sponsors an annual contest offering $1,000 and publication to each First Prize winner in fiction, poetry, and creative nonfiction. Previous year's winner and former students of editors ineligible. Winning pieces accepted for publication on the basis of first-time rights. Considers simultaneous submissions, "but notify us immediately upon acceptance elsewhere. We guarantee a considerate reading." No mss returned. Award to reward good writers and showcase quality writing. Deadline: November 1. Prize: $1,000 and publication to each First Prize winner in fiction, poetry, and creative nonfiction.

◐◯ THE BRIDPORT PRIZE

P.O. Box 6910, Dorset DT6 9QB United Kingdom. **E-mail:** info@bridportprize.org.uk; kate@bridportprize.org.uk. **Website:** www.bridportprize.org.uk. **Contact:** Kate Wilson, Bridport Prize administrator. Award to promote literary excellence, discover new talent. Categories: Short stories, poetry, flash fiction. Deadline: May 31. Open for submissions starting November 15. Prize: £5,000 ; £1,000 ; £500 ; various runners-up prizes and publication of approximately 13 best stories and 13 best poems in anthology; plus 6 best flash fiction stories. £1,000 First Prize for the best short, short story of under 250 words. Judged by 1 judge for short stories (in 2014, Andrew Miller), 1 judge for poetry (in 2014, Liz Lochhead) and 1 judge for flash fiction (in 2014, Tania Hershman).

BRITISH CZECH AND SLOVAK ASSOCIATION WRITING COMPETITION

24 Ferndale, Tunbridge Wells Kent TN2 3NS England. **E-mail:** prize@bcsa.co.uk. **Website:** www.bcsa.co.uk/specials.html. Estab. 2002. Annual contest for original writing (entries should not exceed 2,000 words) in English on the links between Britain and the Czech/Slovak Republics, or describing society in transition in the Republics since 1989. Entries can be fact or fiction. Topics can include history, politics, the sciences, economics, the arts, or literature. Deadline: June 30. Winners announced in November. First Place: £300; Second Place: £100.

BURNABY WRITERS' SOCIETY CONTEST

E-mail: info@bws.ca. **Website:** www.bws.ca; www.burnabywritersnews.blogspot.com. **Contact:** Contest Committee. Offered annually for unpublished work. Open to all residents of British Columbia. Categories vary from year to year. Send SASE for current rules. For complete guidelines see website or burnabywritersnews.blogspot.com. Purpose is to encourage talented writers in all genres. Deadline: May 31. First Place: $200; Second Place: $100; Third Place: $50 and public reading.

THE CAINE PRIZE FOR AFRICAN WRITING

51 Southwark St., London SE1 1RU United Kingdom. **E-mail:** info@caineprize.com. **Website:** www.caineprize.com. **Contact:** Lizzy Attree. Estab. 2000. Entries must have appeared for the first time in the 5 years prior to the closing date for submissions, which is January 31 each year. Publishers should submit 6 copies of the published original with a brief cover note (no pro forma application). "Please indicate nationality or passport held." The Caine Prize is open to writers from anywhere in Africa for work published in English. Its focus is on the short story, reflecting the con-

temporary development of the African story-telling tradition. Deadline: January 31. Prize: £10,000.

CALIFORNIA BOOK AWARDS

Commonwealth Club of California, 595 Market St., San Francisco CA 94105. (415)597-6700. **Fax:** (415)597-6729. **E-mail:** bookawards@commonwealthclub.org. **Website:** www.commonwealthclub.org/. Estab. 1931. Offered annually to recognize California's best writers and illuminate the wealth and diversity of California-based literature. Award is for published submissions appearing in print during the previous calendar year. Can be nominated by publisher or author. Open to California residents (or residents at time of publication). Deadline: December 31. Prize: Medals and cash prizes to be awarded at publicized event. Judged by 12-15 California professionals with a diverse range of views, backgrounds, and literary experience.

JOHN W. CAMPBELL MEMORIAL AWARD FOR BEST SCIENCE FICTION NOVEL OF THE YEAR

English Department, University of Kansas, Lawrence KS 66045. (785)864-3380. **Fax:** (785)864-1159. **E-mail:** cmckit@ku.edu. **Website:** www.sfcenter.ku.edu/campbell.htm. **Contact:** Chris McKitterick. Estab. 1973. Honors the best science fiction novel of the year. Deadline: Check website. Prize: Campbell Award trophy. Winners receive an expense-paid trip to the university to receive their award. Their names are also engraved on a permanent trophy. Judged by a jury.

CANADIAN AUTHORS ASSOCIATION AWARD FOR FICTION

6 West St. N., Suite 203, Orilla ON L3X 5B8 Canada. **Website:** www.canadianauthors.org. **Contact:** Anita Purcell, executive director. Estab. 1975. Award for full-length, English language literature for adults by a Canadian author. Deadline: January 15. Prize: $2,000 and a silver medal. Judging: Each year a trustee for each award appointed by the Canadian Authors Association selects up to 3 judges. Identities of the trustee and judges are confidential.

CANADIAN AUTHORS ASSOCIATION EMERGING WRITER AWARD

6 West St. N., Suite 203, Orilla ON L3X 5B8 Canada. **Website:** www.canadianauthors.org. **Contact:** Anita Purcell, executive director. Estab. 2006. An-

nual award for a writer under 30 years of age deemed to show exceptional promise in the field of literary creation. Deadline: January 15. Prize: $500. Judging: Each year a trustee for each award appointed by the Canadian Authors Association selects up to 3 judges. Identities of the trustee and judges are confidential.

THE ALEXANDER CAPPON PRIZE FOR FICTION

New Letters, University of Missouri-Kansas City, *New Letters* Awards for Writers, UMKC, University House, 5101 Rockhill Rd., Kansas City MO 64110-2499. (816)235-1168. **Fax:** (816)235-2611. **E-mail:** newletters@umkc.edu. **Website:** www.newletters.org. Offered annually for the best short story to discover and reward new and upcoming writers. Buys first North American serial rights. Open to any writer. Deadline: May 18. Prize: First Place: $1,500 and publication in a volume of *New Letters*. All entries will be given consideration for publication in future issues of *New Letters*.

CASCADE WRITING CONTEST & AWARDS

Oregon Christian Writers, 1075 Willow Lake Road N., Keizer Oregon 97303. **E-mail:** cascade@oregonchristianwriters.org. **Website:** oregonchristianwriters.org/. **Contact:** Marilyn Rhoads and Julie McDonald Zander. The Cascade Awards are presented at the annual Oregon Christian Writers Summer Conference (held at the Red Lion on the River in Portland, Oregon each August) attended by national editors, agents, and professional authors. The contest is open for both published and unpublished works in the following categories: contemporary fiction book, historical fiction book, speculative fiction book, nonfiction book, memoir book, young adult/middle grade fiction book, young adult/middle grade nonfiction book, children's chapter book and picture book (fiction and nonfiction), poetry, devotional, article, column, story, or blog post. Two additional special Cascade Awards are presented each year, the Trailblazer Award to a writer who has distinguished him/herself in the field of Christian writing and a Writer of Promise Award for a writer who demonstrates unusual promise in the field of Christian writing. For a full list of categories, entry rules, and scoring elements, visit website. Annual multi-genre competition to encourage both published and emerging writers in the field of Christian writing. Deadline: March 31. Submissions period begins February 14. Prize: Award certificate

presented at the Cascade Awards ceremony during the Oregon Christian Writers Annual Summer Conference. Finalists are listed in the conference notebook and winners are listed online. Cascade Trophies are awarded to the recipients of the Trailblazer and Writer of Promise Awards. Judged by published authors, editors, librarians, and retail book store owners and employees. Final judging by editors, agents, and published authors from the Christian publishing industry.

JAMIE CAT CALLAN HUMOR PRIZE

Category in the Soul-Making Keats Literary Competition, The Webhallow House, 1544 Sweetwood Dr., Broadmoor Village CA 94015-2029. **E-mail:** SoulKeats@mail.com. **Website:** www.soulmakingcontest.us. **Contact:** Eileen Malone. Deadline: November 30. Prize: First Place: $100; Second Place: $50; Third Place: $25. Judged by Jamie Cat Callan.

KAY CATTARULLA AWARD FOR BEST SHORT STORY

Texas Institute of Letters, P.O. Box 609, Round Rock TX 78680. **E-mail:** tilsecretary@yahoo.com. **Website:** www.texasinstituteofletters.org. Offered annually for work published January 1-December 31 of previous year to recognize the best short story. The story submitted must have appeared in print for the first time to be eligible. Writers must have been born in Texas, must have lived in Texas for at least 2 consecutive years, or the subject matter of the work must be associated with Texas. See website for guidelines. Deadline: January 10. Prize: $1,000.

G. S. SHARAT CHANDRA PRIZE FOR SHORT FICTION

BkMk Press, BkMk Press, University of Missouri-Kansas City, 5100 Rockhill Rd., Kansas City MO 64110-2499. (816)235-2558. **Fax:** (816)235-2611. **E-mail:** bkmk@umkc.edu; newletters@umkc.edu. **Website:** www.newletters.org. Offered annually for the best book-length ms collection (unpublished) of short fiction in English by a living author. Translations are not eligible. Initial judging is done by a network of published writers. Final judging is done by a writer of national reputation. Guidelines for SASE, by e-mail, or on website. Deadline: January 15. Prize: $1,000, plus book publication by BkMk Press.

☙◯ PEGGY CHAPMAN-ANDREWS FIRST NOVEL AWARD

P.O. Box 6910, Dorset DT6 9QB United Kingdom. **E-mail:** info@bridportprize.org.uk. **Website:** www.

bridportprize.org.uk. **Contact:** Frances Everitt, administrator. Award to promote literary excellence and new writers. Enter first chapters of novel, up to 8,000 words (minimum 5,000 words) plus 300 word synopsis. Deadline: May 31. Prize: First Place: £1,000 plus mentoring & possible publication; Runner-Up: £500. Judged by The Literary Consultancy & A.M. Heath Literary Agents.

✪ THE CHARITON REVIEW SHORT FICTION PRIZE

Truman State University Press, 100 East Normal Ave., Kirksville MO 63501-4221. **Website:** tsup.truman. edu. An annual award for the best unpublished short fiction on any theme up to 5,000 words in English. Deadline: September 30. Prize: $500 and publication in *The Chariton Review* for the winner. Two or 3 finalists will also be published and receive $200 each. The final judge will be announced after the finalists have been selected in January.

♻ THE CITY OF VANCOUVER BOOK AWARD

Cultural Services Dept., Woodward's Heritage Building, 111 W. Hastings St., Suite 501, Vancouver BC V6B 1H4 Canada. (604) 829-2007. **Fax:** (604)871-6005. **E-mail:** marnie.rice@vancouver.ca; culture@vancouver. ca. **Website:** https://vancouver.ca/people-programs/city-of-vancouver-book-award.aspx. Estab. 1989. The annual City of Vancouver Book Award recognizes authors of excellence of any genre who contribute to the appreciation and understanding of Vancouver's history, unique character, or the achievements of its residents. The book must exhibit excellence in 1 or more of the following areas: content, illustration, design, format. Deadline: May 14. Prize: $3,000. Judged by an independent jury.

COLORADO BOOK AWARDS

Colorado Humanities & Center for the Book, 7935 E. Prentice Ave., Suite 450, Greenwood Village CO 80111. (303)894-7951, ext. 19. **Fax:** (303)864-9361. **E-mail:** stephanie@coloradohumanities.org. **Website:** www. coloradohumanities.org. **Contact:** Stephanie March. An annual program that celebrates the accomplishments of Colorado's outstanding authors, editors, illustrators, and photographers. Awards are presented in at least 10 categories including anthology/collection, biography, children's, creative nonfiction, fiction, history, nonfiction, pictorial, poetry, and young adult. Deadline: January 2.

COPTALES CONTEST

Sponsored by Oak Tree Press, 140 E. Palmer St., Taylorville IL 62568. **E-mail:** publisher@oaktreebooks. com. **E-mail:** CT-ContestAdmin@oaktreebooks. com. **Website:** www.oaktreebooks.com. **Contact:** Billie Johnson, publisher. Open to novels and true stories that feature a law enforcement main character. Word count should range from 60,000-80,000 words. The goal of the CopTales Contest is to discover and publish new authors, or authors shifting to a new genre. This annual contest is open to writers who have not published in the mystery genre in the past 3 years, as well as completely unpublished authors. Deadline: September 1. Prize: Publishing contract, book published in trade paperback and e-book formats with a professionally designed, 4-color cover. See website for details. Judged by a select panel of editors and professional crime writers.

THE CRUCIBLE POETRY AND FICTION COMPETITION

Crucible, Barton College, College Station, Wilson NC 27893. (800)345-4973 x6450. **E-mail:** crucible@ barton.edu. **Website:** www.barton.edu. **Contact:** Terrence L. Grimes, editor. Open annually to all writers. Entries must be completely original, never published, and in ms form. Does not accept simultaneous submissions. Fiction is limited to 8,000 words; poetry is limited to 5 poems. Guidelines online or by e-mail or for SASE. All submissions should be electronic. Deadline: May 1. Prize: First Place: $150; Second Place: $100 (for both poetry and fiction). Winners are also published in *Crucible*. Judged by in-house editorial board.

THE CUTBANK CHAPBOOK CONTEST

CutBank Literary Magazine, *CutBank*, University of Montana, English Dept., LA 133, Missoula MT 59812. **E-mail:** editor.cutbank@gmail.com. **Website:** www. cutbankonline.org. **Contact:** Allison Linville, editor in chief. This competition is open to original English language mss in the genres of poetry, fiction, and creative nonfiction. While previously published standalone pieces or excerpts may be included in a ms, the ms as a whole must be an unpublished work. Looking for startling, compelling, and beautiful original work. "We're looking for a fresh, powerful ms. Maybe it will overtake us quietly; gracefully defy genres; satisfyingly subvert our expectations; punch us in the mouth page in and page out. We're interested in both prose and poetry—and particularly work that straddles the lines between genres." Deadline: January 15. Submissions period begins November 1. Prize: $1,000 and 25 contributor copies. Judged by a guest judge each year.

DANA AWARDS IN THE NOVEL, SHORT FICTION, AND POETRY

200 Fosseway Dr., Greensboro NC 27445. (336)644-8028. **E-mail:** danaawards@gmail.com. **Website:** www.danaawards.com. **Contact:** Mary Elizabeth Parker, chair. Three awards offered annually for unpublished work written in English. Works previously published online are not eligible. Purpose is monetary award for work that has not been previously published or received monetary award, but will accept work published simply for friends and family. Deadline: October 31 (postmarked). Prizes: $1,000 for each of the 3 awards.

THE DANAHY FICTION PRIZE

University of Tampa, 401 W. Kennedy Blvd., Tampa FL 33606. **E-mail:** utpress@ut.edu. **Website:** www.utpress.ut.edu. Annual award for the best previously unpublished short fiction. Deadline: November 30. Prize: $1,000, plus publication in *The Tampa Review*.

DARK OAK MYSTERY CONTEST

Oak Tree Press, 140 E. Palmer St., Taylorville IL 62568. (217)824-6500. **E-mail:** oaktreepub@aol.com. **E-mail:** DO-ContestAdmin@oaktreebooks.com. **Website:** www.oaktreebooks.com. Offered annually for an unpublished mystery ms (between 60,00-80,000 words) of any sort from police procedurals to amateur sleuth novels. Acquires first North American, audio and film rights to winning entry. Open to authors not published in the past 3 years. Deadline: September 1. Prize: Publishing Agreement, and launch of the title. Judged by a select panel of editors and professional mystery writers.

◑ DEAD OF WINTER

E-mail: editors@toasted-cheese.com. **Website:** www.toasted-cheese.com. **Contact:** Stephanie Lenz, editor. The contest is a winter-themed horror fiction contest with a new topic each year. Topic and word limit announced October 1. The topic is usually geared toward a supernatural theme. Deadline: December 21. Results announced January 31. Winners notified by e-mail. List of winners on website. Prize: Amazon gift certificates and publication in *Toasted Cheese*. Also offers honorable mention. Judged by 2 *Toasted Cheese* editors who blind judge each contest. Each judge uses her own criteria to rate entries.

●◐◉ THE DEBUT DAGGER

Crime Writers' Association, New Writing Competition, P.O. Box 3408, Norwich NR3 3WE England. E-mail: director@thecwa.co.uk. **Website:** www.thecwa.co.uk. **Contact:** Mary Andrea Clarke. Annual competition for unpublished crime writers. Submit the opening 3,000 words of a crime novel, plus a 500- to 1,000-word synopsis of its continuance. Open to any writer who has not had a novel commercially published in any genre. Deadline: January 31. Submission period begins November 1. Prize: First Prize: £700. All shortlisted entrants will receive a professional assessment of their entries. Judged by a panel of top crime editors and agents, and the shortlisted entries are sent to publishers and agents.

◑ DIAGRAM/NEW MICHIGAN PRESS CHAPBOOK CONTEST

New Michigan Press, P.O. Box 210067, English, ML 424, University of Arizona, Tucson AZ 85721. **E-mail:** nmp@thediagram.com. **Website:** www.thediagram.com. **Contact:** Ander Monson, editor. Estab. 1999. The annual *DIAGRAM*/New Michigan Press Chapbook Contest offers $1,000, plus publication and author's copies, with discount on additional copies. Deadline: April 27. Prize: $1,000, plus publication. Finalist chapbooks also considered for publication.

DOBIE PAISANO WRITER'S FELLOWSHIP

The Graduate School, The University of Texas at Austin, Attn: Dobie Paisano Program, 110 Inner Campus Drive Stop G0400, Austin TX 78712-0531. (512)232-3609. **Fax:** (512)471-7620. **E-mail:** gbarton@austin.utexas.edu. **Website:** www.utexas.edu/ogs/Paisano. **Contact:** Gwen Barton. Sponsored by the Graduate School at The University of Texas at Austin and the Texas Institute of Letters, the Dobie Paisano Fellowship Program provides solitude, time, and a comfortable place for Texas writers or writers who have written significantly about Texas through fiction, nonfiction, poetry, plays, or other mediums. The Dobie Paisano Ranch is a very rural and rustic setting, and applicants should read the guidelines closely to insure their ability to reside in this secluded environment. Deadline: January 15. Applications are accepted beginning December 1 and must be post-marked no later than January 15. The Ralph A. Johnston memorial Fellowship is for a period of 4 months with a stipend of $6,250 per month. It is aimed at writers who have already demonstrated some publishing and critical success. The Jesse H. Jones Writing Fellowship is for a period of approximately 6 months with a stipend of $3,000 per month. It is aimed at, but not limited to, writers who are early in their careers.

⑤ JACK DYER FICTION PRIZE

Crab Orchard Review, Department of English, Mail Code 4503, Faner Hall 2380, Southern Illinois University at Carbondale, 1000 Faner Drive, Carbondale IL 62901. **E-mail:** jtribble@siu.edu. **Website:** www.craborchardreview.siu.edu. **Contact:** Jon C. Tribble, managing editor. Offered annually for unpublished short fiction. *Crab Orchard Review* acquires first North American serial rights to all submitted work. One winner and at least 2 finalists will be chosen. Deadline: April 21. Submissions period begins February 21. Prize: $2,000, publication and 1-year subscription to *Crab Orchard Review*. Finalists are offered $500 and publication. Judged by editorial staff (prescreening); winner chosen by genre editor.

MARY KENNEDY EASTHAM FLASH FICTION PRIZE

Category in the Soul-Making Keats Literary Competition, The Webhallow House, 1544 Sweetwood Dr., Broadmoor Village CA 94015-2029. **E-mail:** SoulKeats@gmail.com. **Website:** www.soulmaking-contest.us. **Contact:** Eileen Malone. Keep each story under 500 words. Three stories per entry. One story per page, typed, double-spaced, and unidentified. Deadline: November 30. Prizes: First Place: $100; Second Place: $50; Third Place: $25.

EATON LITERARY AGENCY'S ANNUAL AWARDS PROGRAM

Eaton Literary Agency, P.O. Box 49795, Sarasota FL 34230-6795. (941)366-6589. **Fax:** (941)365-4679. **E-mail:** eatonlit@aol.com. **Website:** www.eatonliterary.com. **Contact:** Richard Lawrence, V.P. Offered biannually for unpublished mss. Entries must be unpublished. Open to any writer. Guidelines available for SASE, by fax, e-mail, or on website. Accepts inquiries by fax, phone and e-mail. Results announced in April and September. Winners notified by mail. For contest results, send SASE, fax, e-mail, or visit website. Deadline: March 31 (short story); August 31 (book-length). Prize: $2,500 (book-length); $500 (short story). Judged by an independent agency in conjunction with some members of Eaton's staff.

THE EMILY CONTEST

18207 Heaton Dr., Houston TX 77084. **E-mail:** emily.contest@whrwa.com. **Website:** www.whrwa.com. Annual award to promote publication of previously unpublished writers of romance. Open to any writer who has not published in a given category within the past 3 years. The mission of The Emily is to professionally support writers and guide them toward a path to publication. Deadline: October 7. Submission period begins September 1. Prize: $100. Final judging done by an editor and an agent.

FABLERS MONTHLY CONTEST

818 Los Arboles Lane, Santa Fe NM 87501. **Website:** www.fablers.net. **Contact:** W.B. Scott. Monthly contest for previously unpublished writers to help develop amateur writers. Guidelines posted online. No entry fee. Open to any writer. Deadline: 14th of each month. Prize: $100. Judged by members of website.

☺ THE FAR HORIZONS AWARD FOR SHORT FICTION

The Malahat Review, University of Victoria, P.O. Box 1700, Stn CSC, Victoria BC V8W 2Y2 Canada. (250)721-8524. **Fax:** (250)472-5051. **E-mail:** malahat@uvic.ca. **E-mail:** horizons@uvic.ca. **Website:** www.malahatreview.ca. **Contact:** John Barton, editor. Open to "emerging short fiction writers from Canada, the U.S., and elsewhere" who have not yet published their fiction in a full-length book (48 pages or more). 2011 winner: Zoey Peterson; 2013 winner: Kerry-Lee Powell. Deadline: May 1 (odd-numbered years). Prize: $1,000 CAD, publication in fall issue of *The Malahat Review* (see separate listing in Magazines/Journals). Announced in fall on website, Facebook page, and in quarterly e-newsletter, *Malahat Lite*.

THE VIRGINIA FAULKNER AWARD FOR EXCELLENCE IN WRITING

Prairie Schooner, 123 Andrews Hall, University of Nebraska-Lincoln, Lincoln NE 68588-0334. (402)472-0911. **Fax:** (402)472-1817. **E-mail:** PrairieSchooner@unl.edu. **Website:** www.prairieschooner.unl.edu. **Contact:** Kwame Dawes. Offered annually for work published in *Prairie Schooner* in the previous year. Categories: short stories, essays, novel excerpts and translations. Prize: $1,000. Judged by Editorial Board.

THE JEAN FELDMAN POETRY PRIZE

Washington Writers' Publishing House, P.O. Box 15271, Washington DC 20003. **E-mail:** wwphpress@gmail.com. **Website:** www.washingtonwriters.org. Poets living within 75 miles of the Capitol are invited to submit a ms of either a novel or a collection of short stories. Ms should be 50-70 pages, single spaced. Deadline: November 1. Submission period begins July 1. Prize: $1,000 and 50 copies of the book.

FINELINE COMPETITION FOR PROSE POEMS, SHORT SHORTS, AND ANYTHING IN BETWEEN

Mid-American Review, Dept. of English, Bowling Green State University, Bowling Green OH 43403. (419)372-2725. **E-mail:** mar@bgsu.edu. **Website:** www.bgsu.edu/midamericanreview. **Contact:** Abigail Cloud, editor in chief. Offered annually for previously unpublished submissions. Contest open to all writers not associated with current judge or *Mid-American Review*. Deadline: June 1. Prize: $1,000, plus publication in fall issue of *Mid-American Review*; 10 finalists receive notation plus possible publication. 2015 judge: Michael Czyzniejewski.

FIRST NOVEL CONTEST

Harrington & Harrington Press, 3400 Yosemite, San Diego CA 92109. **E-mail:** press@harringtonandharrington.com. **Website:** www.harringtonandharrington.com. **Contact:** Laurie Champion, contest/award director. Annual contest for any writer who has not previously published a novel. Entries may be self-published. Accepts full-length works in literary fiction, creative nonfiction, memoir, genre fiction, and short story collections. No poetry. Guidelines available online. Harrington & Harrington Press aims to support writers, and the First Novel Contest will provide many ways to promote authors through networks and connections with writers, artists, and those involved in the technical production of art. Deadline: August 15. Prize: $500 advance royalty and publication by Harrington & Harrington Press. Judged by the Harrington & Harrington staff for the preliminary round. A respected author with numerous publications will act as the final judge.

FIRSTWRITER.COM INTERNATIONAL SHORT STORY CONTEST

firstwriter.com, United Kingdom. **Website:** www.firstwriter.com. **Contact:** J. Paul Dyson, managing editor. Accepts short stories up to 3,000 words on any subject and in any style. Deadline: April 1. Prize: Totals about $300. Ten special commendations will also be awarded and all the winners will be published in *firstwriter* magazine and receive a $36 subscription voucher, allowing an annual subscription to be taken out for free. All submissions are automatically considered for publication in *firstwriter* magazine and may be published there online. Judged by *firstwriter* magazine editors.

☯◑$ FISH POETRY PRIZE

Durrus, Bantry Co. Cork Ireland. **E-mail:** info@fishpublishing.com. **Website:** www.fishpublishing.com. For poems up to 300 words. Age Range: Adult. The best 10 will be published in the Fish Anthology, launched in July at the West Cork Literary Festival. Entries must not have been published before. Enter online or by post. See website for full details of competitions, and information on the Fish Editorial and Critique Services, and the Fish Online Writing Courses. The aim of the competition is to discover and publish new writers. Deadline: March 30. Prize: $1,200. Results announced April 30.

☯◑ FISH PUBLISHING FLASH FICTION COMPETITION

Durrus, Bantry, County Cork Ireland. **E-mail:** info@fishpublishing.com. **Website:** www.fishpublishing.com. Estab. 2004. Annual prize awarding flash fiction. "This is an opportunity to attempt what is one of the most difficult and rewarding tasks—to create, in a tiny fragment, a completely resolved and compelling story in 300 words or less." Deadline: February 28. First Prize: $1,200. The 10 published authors will receive 5 copies of the Anthology and will be invited to read at the launch during the West Cork Literary Festival in July.

☯◑ FISH SHORT STORY PRIZE

Durrus, Bantry Co. Cork Ireland. **E-mail:** info@fishpublishing.com. **Website:** www.fishpublishing.com. Estab. 1994. Annual worldwide competition to recognize the best short stories. Deadline: November 30. Prize: Overall prize fund: $6,000. First Prize: $3,750. Second Prize: 1 week at Anam Cara Writers Retreat in West Cork and $350. Third Prize: $350. Closing date 30th November. The best 10 will be published in the Fish Anthology, launched in July at the West Cork Literary Festival. Winners announced March 17.

FLASHCARD FLASH FICTION CONTEST

Sycamore Review, Department of English, 500 Oval Dr., Purdue University, West Lafayette IN 47907. **E-mail:** sycamore@purdue.edu; sycamorefiction@purdue.edu. **Website:** www.sycamorereview.com/contest/. **Contact:** Kara Krewer, editor in chief. Annual contest for unpublished flash fiction. Deadline: February 1.Submissions period begins January 1. Prize: $100, publication online, and publication on a flashcard to be distributed with *Sycamore Review* at AWP.

FOREWORD'S INDIEFAB AWARDS

ForeWord Magazine, 425 Boardman Ave., Traverse City MI 49684. (231)933-3699. **Fax:** (231)933-3899. **Website:** www.forewordreviews.com. Awards offered annually. In order to be eligible, books must have a current year copyright. *ForeWord*'s Book of the Year Award was established to bring increased attention from librarians and booksellers to the literary achievements of independent publishers and their authors. Deadline: January 15. Prize: $1,500 cash will be awarded to a Best Fiction and Best Nonfiction choice, as determined by the editors of *ForeWord Magazine*. Judged by a jury of librarians, booksellers, and reviewers who are selected to judge the categories for entry and select winners and finalists in 62 categories based on editorial excellence and professional production as well as the originality of the narrative and the value the book adds to its genre.

H.E. FRANCIS SHORT STORY COMPETITION

Ruth Hindman Foundation, University of Alabama in Huntsville, Department of English, Morton Hall Room 222, Huntsville AL 35899. **Website:** www.hefranciscompetition.com. Estab. 1990. Offered annually for unpublished work, not to exceed 5,000 words. Acquires first-time publication rights. Deadline: January 15. Prize: $2,000, publication as an Amazon Kindle Single, an announcement in Poets and Writers, and publication on the website. Judged by a panel of nationally recognized, award-winning authors, directors of creative writing programs, and editors of literary journals.

SOEURETTE DIEHL FRASER AWARD FOR BEST TRANSLATION OF A BOOK

P.O. Box 609, Round Rock TX 78680. **E-mail:** tilsecretary@yahoo.com. **Website:** texasinstituteofletters.org. Offered every 2 years to recognize the best translation of a literary book into English. Translator must have been born in Texas or have lived in the state for at least 2 consecutive years at some time. Deadline: January 10. Prize: $1,000.

☼ FREEFALL SHORT PROSE AND POETRY CONTEST

Freefall Literary Society of Calgary, 922 9th Ave. SE, Calgary AB T2G 0S4 Canada. **E-mail:** editors@freefallmagazine.ca. **Website:** www.freefallmagazine.ca. **Contact:** Ryan Stromquist, managing editor. Offered annually for unpublished work in the categories of poetry (5 poems/entry) and prose (3,000 words or less). Recognizes writers and offers publication credits in a literary magazine format. Contest rules and entry form online. Acquires first Canadian serial rights; ownership reverts to author after one-time publication. Deadline: December 31. Prize: First Place: $500 (CAD); Second Place: $250 (CAD); Third Place: $75; Honorable Mention: $25. All prizes include publication in the spring edition of *FreeFall Magazine*. Winners will also be invited to read at the launch of that issue, if such a launch takes place. Honorable mentions in each category will be published and may be asked to read. Travel expenses not included. Judged by current guest editor for issue (who are also published authors in Canada).

THE FRENCH-AMERICAN AND THE FLORENCE GOULD FOUNDATIONS TRANSLATION PRIZES

28 W. 44th St., Suite 1420, New York NY 10036. (646)588-6781. **E-mail:** tchareton@frenchamerican.org. **Website:** www.frenchamerican.org. **Contact:** Thibault Chareton. Annual contest to promote French literature in the United States by extending its reach beyond the first language and giving translators and their craft greater visibility among publishers and readers alike. The prize also seeks to increase the visibility of the publishers who bring these important French works of literature, in translation of exceptional quality, to the American market by publicizing the titles and giving more visibility to the books they publish. Deadline: January 15. Prize: $10,000 award. Jury committee made up of translators, writers, and scholars in French literature and culture.

THE GHOST STORY SUPERNATURAL FICTION AWARD

The Ghost Story, P.O. Box 601, Union ME 04862. **E-mail:** editor@theghoststory.com. **Website:** www.theghoststory.com. **Contact:** Paul Guernsey. Biannual contest for unpublished fiction. "Ghost stories are welcome, of course—but submissions may involve *any* paranormal or supernatural theme, as well as magic realism. What we're looking for is fine writing, fresh perspectives, and maybe a few surprises in the field of supernatural fiction." Deadline: April 30 and September 30. Prize: $1,000 and publication in *The Ghost Story*. A second writer will receive an Honorable Mention that includes publication and $100. Judged by the editors of *The Ghost Story*.

GIVAL PRESS NOVEL AWARD

Gival Press, LLC, P.O. Box 3812, Arlington VA 22203. (703)351-0079. **E-mail:** givalpress@yahoo.com. **Web-**

site: www.givalpress.com. **Contact:** Robert L. Giron. Offered annually for a previously unpublished original novel (not a translation). Guidelines by phone, on website, via e-mail, or by mail with SASE. Results announced late fall of same year. Winners notified by phone. Results made available to entrants with SASE, by e-mail, on website. Purpose is to award the best literary novel. Deadline: May 30. Prize: $3,000, plus publication of book with a standard contract and author's copies. Final judge is announced after winner is chosen. Entries read anonymously.

O GIVAL PRESS SHORT STORY AWARD

Gival Press, P.O. Box 3812, Arlington VA 22203. (703)351-0079. **E-mail:** givalpress@yahoo.com. **Website:** www.givalpress.com. **Contact:** Robert L. Giron, publisher. Annual literary, short story contest. Entries must be unpublished. Open to anyone who writes original short stories, which are not a chapter of a novel, in English. Receives about 100-150 entries per category. Guidelines available online, via e-mail, or by mail. Results announced in the fall of the same year. Winners notified by phone. Results available with SASE, by e-mail, and on website. Recognizes the best literary short story. Deadline: August 8. Prize: $1,000 and publication on website. Judged anonymously.

GLIMMER TRAIN'S FAMILY MATTERS CONTEST

Glimmer Train, 4763 SW Maplewood Rd., P.O. Box 80430, Portland OR 97280. (503)221-0836. **Fax:** (503)221-0837. **E-mail:** eds@glimmertrain.org. **Website:** www.glimmertrain.org. **Contact:** Susan Burmeister-Brown. This contest is now held twice a year, during the months of May and September. Winners are contacted 2 months after the close of each contest, and results officially announced 1 week later. Submit online at www.glimmertrain.org. Deadline: May 31 and September 30. Prize: First Place: $1,500, publication in *Glimmer Train Stories*, and 20 copies of that issue; Second Place: $500 and consideration for publication; Third Place: $300 and consideration for publication.

O Represented in recent editions of *The Pushcart Prize, New Stories from the Midwest, The PEN/O. Henry Prize Stories, New Stories from the South, Best of the West, Best American Mystery Stories,* and *Best American Short Stories Anthologies.*

GLIMMER TRAIN'S FICTION OPEN

Glimmer Train, Inc., Glimmer Train Press, Inc., 4763 SW Maplewood Rd., P.O. Box 80430, Portland OR

97280. (503)221-0836. **Fax:** (503)221-0837. **E-mail:** eds@glimmertrain.org. **Website:** www.glimmertrain.org. **Contact:** Linda Swanson-Davies. Submissions to this category generally range from 2,000-8,000 words, but up to 20,000 is fine. Held twice a year. Submit online at www.glimmertrain.org. Winners will be called 2 months after the close of the contest. Deadline: June 30 and December 31. Prize: First Place $2,500, publication in *Glimmer Train Stories*, and 20 copies of that issue; Second Place $1,000 and consideration for publication; Third Place: $600 and consideration for publication.

O Represented in recent editions of *The Pushcart Prize, New Stories from the Midwest, The PEN/O. Henry Prize Stories, New Stories from the South, Best of the West, Best American Mystery Stories,* and *Best American Short Stories Anthologies.*

GLIMMER TRAIN'S SHORT-STORY AWARD FOR NEW WRITERS

Glimmer Train Press, Inc., 4763 SW Maplewood Rd., P.O. Box 80430, Portland OR 97280. (503)221-0836. **Fax:** (503)221-0837. **E-mail:** eds@glimmertrain.org. **Website:** www.glimmertrain.org. **Contact:** Linda Swanson-Davies. Offered for any writer whose fiction hasn't appeared in a nationally distributed print publication with a circulation over 5,000. Submissions to this category generally range from 1,500-6,000 words, but up to 12,000 is fine. Held quarterly. Submit online at www.glimmertrain.org. Winners will be called 2 months after the close of the contest. Deadline: February 28, May 31, August 31, and November 30. Prize: First Place: $1,500, publication in *Glimmer Train Stories*, and 20 copies of that issue; Second Place: $500 and consideration for publication; Third Place: $300 and consideration for publication.

O Represented in recent editions of *The Pushcart Prize, New Stories from the Midwest, The PEN/O. Henry Prize Stories, New Stories from the South, Best of the West, Best American Mystery Stories,* and *Best American Short Stories Anthologies.* Pays over $50,000 every year to writers.

GLIMMER TRAIN'S VERY SHORT FICTION CONTEST

Glimmer Train Press, Inc., 4763 SW Maplewood Rd., P.O. Box 80430, Portland OR 97280. (503)221-0836. **Fax:** (503)221-0837. **E-mail:** eds@glimmertrain.org. **Website:** www.glimmertrain.org. **Contact:** Susan Burmeister-Brown. Offered to encourage the art of the very short story. Word count: 3,000 maximum.

Held quarterly. Submit online at www.glimmertrain. org. Results announced 2 months after the close of the contest. Deadline: January 31, April 30, July 31, and October 31. Prize: First Place: $1,500, publication in *Glimmer Train Stories*, and 20 copies of that issue; Second Place: $500 and consideration for publication; Third Place: $300 and consideration for publication.

○ Represented in recent editions of *The Push-cart Prize*, *New Stories from the Midwest*, *The PEN/O. Henry Prize Stories*, *New Stories from the South*, *Best of the West*, *Best American Mystery Stories*, and *Best American Short Stories* Anthologies.

PATRICIA GOEDICKE PRIZE IN POETRY

CutBank Literary Magazine, *CutBank*, University of Montana, English Dept., LA 133, Missoula MT 59812. **E-mail:** editor.cutbank@gmail.com. **Website:** www. cutbankonline.org. **Contact:** Allison Linville, editor in chief. The Patricia Goedicke Prize in Poetry seeks to highlight work that showcases an authentic voice, a boldness of form, and a rejection of functional fixedness. Deadline: January 15. Submissions period begins November 1. Prize: $500 and featured in the magazine. Judged by a guest judge each year.

◎ GOVERNOR GENERAL'S LITERARY AWARDS

Canada Council for the Arts, 150 Elgin St., P.O. Box 1047, Ottawa ON K1P 5V8 Canada. (613)566-4414, ext. 5573. **Website:** www.canadacouncil.ca. Estab. 1937. Established by Parliament, the Canada Council for the Arts provides a wide range of grants and services to professional Canadian artists and art organizations in dance, media arts, music, theater, writing, publishing, and the visual arts. The Governor General's Literary Awards are given annually for the best English-language and French-language work in each of 7 categories, including fiction, nonfiction, poetry, drama, children's literature (text), children's literature (illustration), and translation. Deadline: Depends on the book's publication date. See website for details. Prize: Each GG winner receives $25,000. Nonwinning finalists receive $1,000. Judged by fellow authors, translators, and illustrators. For each category, a jury makes the final selection.

THE GOVER PRIZE

Best New Writing, P.O. Box 11, Titusville NJ 08530. **Fax:** (609)968-1718. **E-mail:** submissions@bestnewwriting.com. **Website:** www.bestnewwriting.com/ BNWgover.html. **Contact:** Christopher Klim, senior editor. The Gover Prize, named after groundbreaking author Robert Gover, awards an annual prize and publication in *Best New Writing* for the best short fiction and creative nonfiction. Deadline: September 15-January 10. Prize: $250 grand prize; publication in *Best New Writing* for finalists (approximately 12), holds 6-month world exclusive rights. Judged by *Best New Writing* editorial staff.

◑ GREAT LAKES COLLEGES ASSOCIATION NEW WRITERS AWARD

535 W. William, Suite 301, Ann Arbor MI 48103. (734)661-2350. **Fax:** (734)661-2349. **E-mail:** wegner@glca.org. **Website:** www.glca.org. **Contact:** Gregory R. Wegner. Estab. 1970. Annual award for a first published volume of poetry, fiction, and creative nonfiction. Deadline: July 25. Prize: Honorarium of at least $500. Each award winner has the opportunity to tour the 13 colleges giving readings, meetings students and faculty, and leading discussions or classes. Judged by professors of literature and writers in residence at GLCA colleges.

THE GRUB STREET NATIONAL BOOK PRIZE

Grub Street, 162 Boylston Street, 5th Floor, Boston MA 02116. (617) 695-0075. **Fax:** (617) 695-0075. **E-mail:** info@grubstreet.org; chris@grubstreet.org. **Website:** grubstreet.org. **Contact:** Christopher Castellani, artistic director. The Grub Street National Book Prize is awarded once annually to an American writer outside New England publishing his or her second, third, fourth (or beyond …) book. First books are not eligible. Writers whose primary residence is Massachusetts, Vermont, Maine, New Hampshire, Connecticut or Rhode Island are also not eligible. Genre of the prize rotates from year to year, between fiction, nonfiction, and poetry. Deadline: October 1. Prize: $5,000.

◓ LYNDALL HADOW/DONALD STUART SHORT STORY COMPETITION

Fellowship of Australian Writers (WA), P.O. Box 6180, Swanbourne WA 6910 Australia. (61)(8)9384-4771. **Fax:** (61)(8)9384-4854. **E-mail:** fellowshipaustralianwriterswa@gmail.com. **Website:** www.fawwa. org. Annual contest for unpublished short stories (maximum 3,000 words). Reserves the right to publish entries in a FAWWA publication or on website. Guidelines online or for SASE. Deadline: June 1. Submissions period begins April 1. Prize: First Place: $400; Second Place; $100; Highly Commended: $50.

HAMMETT PRIZE

International Association of Crime Writers, North American Branch, 243 Fifth Avenue, #537, New York NY 10016. **E-mail:** mfrisque@igc.org. **Website:** www. crimewritersna.org. **Contact:** Mary A. Frisque, executive director, North American Branch. Award for crime novels, story collections, nonfiction by 1 author. "Our reading committee seeks suggestions from publishers and they also ask the membership for recommendations." Nominations announced in January; winners announced in fall. Winners notified by e-mail or mail and recognized at awards ceremony. For contest results, send SASE or e-mail. Award established to honor a work of literary excellence in the field of crime writing by a U.S. or Canadian author. Deadline: December 15. Prize: Trophy. Judged by a committee of members of the organization. The committee chooses 5 nominated books, which are then sent to 3 outside judges for a final selection. Judges are outside the crime writing field.

WILDA HEARNE FLASH FICTION CONTEST

Big Muddy: A Journal of the Mississippi River Valley, WHFF Contest, Southeast Missouri State University Press, One University Plaza, MS 2650, Cape Girardeau MO 63701. **E-mail:** sswartwout@semo.edu. **Website:** www6.semo.edu. **Contact:** Susan Swartwout, publisher. Annual competition for flash fiction, held by Southeast Missouri State University Press. Deadline: October 1. Prize: $500 and publication in *Big Muddy: A Journal of the Mississippi River Valley.* Semi-finalists will be chosen by a regional team of published writers. The final ms will be chosen by Susan Swartwout, publisher of the Southeast Missouri State University Press.

DRUE HEINZ LITERATURE PRIZE

University of Pittsburgh Press, 7500 Thomas Blvd., Pittsburgh PA 15260. (412)383-2492. **Fax:** (412)383-2466. **Website:** www.upress.pitt.edu. Estab. 1981. Offered annually to writers who have published a book-length collection of fiction or a minimum of 3 short stories or novellas in commercial magazines or literary journals of national distribution. Does not return mss. Deadline: Submit May 1- June 30 only. Prize: $15,000. Judged by anonymous nationally known writers such as Robert Penn Warren, Joyce Carol Oates, and Margaret Atwood.

LORIAN HEMINGWAY SHORT STORY COMPETITION

Hemingway Days Festival, P.O. Box 993, Key West FL 33041. **E-mail:** shortstorykeywest@hushmail.com. **Website:** www.shortstorycompetition.com. **Contact:** Eva Eliot, editorial assistant. Estab. 1981. Offered annually for unpublished short stories up to 3,500 words. Guidelines available via mail, e-mail, or online. Award to encourage literary excellence and the efforts of writers whose voices have yet to be heard. Deadline: May 15. Prizes: First Place: $1,500, plus publication of his or her winning story in *Cutthroat: A Journal of the Arts*; Second-Third Place: $500; honorable mentions will also be awarded. Judged by a panel of writers, editors, and literary scholars selected by author Lorian Hemingway. (Lorian Hemingway is the competition's final judge.)

TONY HILLERMAN PRIZE

Wordharvest, 1063 Willow Way, Santa Fe NM 87507. (505)471-1565. **E-mail:** wordharvest@wordharvest. com. **Website:** www.wordharvest.com. **Contact:** Anne Hillerman and Jean Schaumberg, co-organizers. Estab. 2006. Awarded annually, and sponsored by St. Martin's Press, for the best first mystery set in the Southwest. Murder or another serious crime or crimes must be at the heart of the story, with the emphasis on the solution rather than the details of the crime. Honors the contributions made by Tony Hillerman to the art and craft of the mystery. Deadline: June 1. Prize: $10,000 advance and publication by St. Martin's Press. Nominees will be selected by judges chosen by the editorial staff of St. Martin's Press, with the assistance of independent judges selected by organizers of the Tony Hillerman Writers Conference (Wordharvest), and the winner will be chosen by St. Martin's editors.

⊜ THE HODDER FELLOWSHIP

Lewis Center for the Arts, 185 Nassau St., Princeton NJ 08544. (609)258-6926. **E-mail:** ysabelg@princeton.edu. **Website:** arts.princeton.edu. **Contact:** Ysabel Gonzalez, fellowships assistant. The Hodder Fellowship will be given to writers of exceptional promise to pursue independent projects at Princeton University during the current academic year. Typically the fellows are poets, playwrights, novelists, creative nonfiction writers and translators who have published 1 highly acclaimed work and are undertaking a significant new project that might not be possible without the "studious leisure" afforded by the fellowship. Deadline: October 1. Open to applications in July. Prize: $75,000 stipend.

○ TOM HOWARD/JOHN H. REID FICTION & ESSAY CONTEST

c/o Winning Writers, 351 Pleasant St., PMB 222, Northampton MA 01060-3961. (866)946-9748. **Fax:** (413)280-0539. **E-mail:** adam@winningwriters.com. **Website:** www.winningwriters.com. **Contact:** Adam Cohen, President. Estab. 1993. Now in its 23rd year. Open to all writers. Submit any type of short story, essay, or other work of prose. Both published and unpublished works are welcome. In the case of published work, the contestant must own the online publication rights. Contest sponsored by Winning Writers. Nonexclusive rights to publish submissions online, in e-mail newsletters, in e-books, and in press releases. Deadline: April 30. Prizes: 2 First Prizes of $1,000 will be awarded, plus 10 honorable mentions of $100 each. Judged by Arthur Powers.

○ L. RON HUBBARD'S WRITERS OF THE FUTURE CONTEST

P.O. Box 1630, Los Angeles CA 90078. (323)466-3310. **Fax:** (323)466-6474. **E-mail:** contests@authorservicesinc.com. **Website:** www.writersofthefuture.com. **Contact:** Joni Labaqui, contest director. Estab. 1983. Foremost competition for new and amateur writers of unpublished science fiction or fantasy short stories or novelettes. Offered to find, reward and publicize new speculative fiction writers so they may more easily attain professional writing careers. Open to writers who have not professionally published a novel or short novel, more than 1 novelette, or more than 3 short stories. Entries must be unpublished. Limit 1 entry per quarter. Open to any writer. Results announced quarterly in e-newsletter. Winners notified by phone. Contest has 4 quarters. There shall be 3 cash prizes in each quarter. In addition, at the end of the year, the 4 first-place, quarterly winners will have their entries rejudged, and a grand prize winner shall be determined. Deadline: December 31, March 31, June 30, September 30. Prize (awards quarterly): First Place: $1,000; Second Place: $750; and Third Place: $500. Annual grand prize: $5,000. Judged by Dave Wolverton (initial judge), then by a panel of 4 professional authors.

CAROL OTIS HURST CHILDREN'S BOOK PRIZE

Westfield Athenaeum, 6 Elm St., Westfield MA 01085. (413)568-7833. **Website:** www.westath.org. Estab. 2007. The Carol Otis Hurst Children's Book Prize honors outstanding works of fiction and nonfiction, including biography and memoir, written for children and young adults through the age of eighteen that exemplify the highest standards of research, analysis, and authorship in their portrayal of the New England Experience. The prize will be presented annually to an author whose book treats the region's history as broadly conceived to encompass 1 or more of the following elements: political experience, social development, fine and performing artistic expression, domestic life and arts, transportation and communication, changing technology, military experience at home and abroad, schooling, business and manufacturing, workers and the labor movement, agriculture and its transformation, racial and ethnic diversity, religious life and institutions, immigration and adjustment, sports at all levels, and the evolution of popular entertainment. The public presentation of the prize will be accompanied by a reading and/or talk by the recipient at a mutually agreed upon time during the spring immediately following the publication year. Prize: $500.

INDEPENDENT PUBLISHER BOOK AWARDS

Jenkins Group/Independent Publisher Online, 1129 Woodmere Ave., Ste. B, Traverse City MI 49686. (231)933-0445. **Fax:** (231)933-0448. **E-mail:** jimb@bookpublishing.com. **Website:** www.independentpublisher.com. **Contact:** Jim Barnes. Honors the year's best independently published titles from around the world. The IPPY Awards reward those who exhibit the courage, innovation, and creativity to bring about change in the world of publishing. Independent spirit and expertise comes from publishers of all areas and budgets, and they judge books with that in mind. Entries will be accepted in over 75 categories, visit website to see details. Open to any published writer. Deadline: March 16. Price of submission rises after January 25. Prize: Gold, silver and bronze medals for each category; foil seals available to all. Judged by a panel of experts representing the fields of design, writing, bookselling, library, and reviewing.

INDIANA REVIEW K PRIZE

Indiana Review, Ballantine Hall 465, 1020 E. Kirkwood Ave., Indiana University, Bloomington IN 47405-7103. (812)855-3439. **Fax:** (812)855-9535. **E-mail:** inreview@indiana.edu. **Website:** indianareview.org. **Contact:** Katie Moulton, consulting editor.

Offered annually for unpublished work. Maximum story/poem length is 500 words. Guidelines available in March for SASE, by phone, e-mail, on website, or in publication. Deadline: May 31. Submission period begins August 1. Prize: $1,000, plus publication, contributor's copies, and a year's subscription to *Indiana Review*.

O INDIANA REVIEW FICTION CONTEST

Ballantine Hall 465, Indiana University, 1020 E. Kirkwood Ave., Bloomington IN 47405-7103. (812)855-3439. **Fax:** (812)855-4253. **E-mail:** inreview@indiana.edu. **Website:** indianareview.org. **Contact:** Katie Moulton, editor. Contest for fiction in any style and on any subject. Open to any writer. Deadline: October 31. Submission period begins September 1. Prize: $1,000, publication in the *Indiana Review* and contributor's copies. Judged by guest judges.

INDIVIDUAL EXCELLENCE AWARDS

Ohio Arts Council, 30 E. Broad St., 33rd Floor, Columbus OH 43215-2613. (614)466-2613. **E-mail:** olgahelpdesk@oac.state.oh.us. **Website:** www.oac.state.oh.us. The Individual Excellence Awards program recognizes outstanding accomplishments by artists in a variety of disciplines. The awards give the artists who receive them the time and resources to experiment, explore and reflect as they develop their skills and advance their art form. They also provide affirmation and acknowledgment of the excellent work of Ohio artists. Deadline: September 1. Prize: $5,000. Judged by 3-person panel of out-of-state panelists, anonymous review.

INK & INSIGHTS WRITING CONTEST

2408 W. 8th, Amarillo TX 79106. **E-mail:** contest@critiquemynovel.com. **Website:** critiquemynovel.com/ink_insights_2015. **Contact:** Catherine York, contest/award director. This contest is for new and seasoned writers who need to gauge their work in addition to competing for prizes. The focus is on the feedback writers are given for their work, as well as competin for prizes and a guaranteed read with feedback from several literary agents. Three categories: Novels (new writers), Novels (ready to publish), and nonfiction. Deadline: March 1-April 30 (regular entry), May 1-June 30 (late entry). Prize: Prizes vary depending on category. Every novel receives personal feedback from 4 judges. Judges listed on website, including the agents who will be helping choose the top winners this year.

O INTERNATIONAL 3-DAY NOVEL CONTEST

210-111 West Hastings Street, Vancouver BC V6B 1H4 Canada. **E-mail:** info@3daynovel.com. **Website:** www.3daynovel.com. **Contact:** Brittany Huddart, managing editor. Estab. 1977. "Can you produce a masterwork of fiction in 3 short days? The Three-Day Novel Contest is your chance to find out. Each Labour Day weekend, fueled by adrenaline and the desire for literary nirvana, hundreds of writers step up to the challenge. It's a thrill, a grind, a 72-hour kick in the pants and an awesome creative experience. How many crazed plotlines, coffee-stained pages, pangs of doubt and moments of genius will next year's contest bring forth? And what will you think up under pressure?" Entrants write in whatever setting they wish, in whatever genre they wish, anywhere in the world. Entrants may start writing as of midnight on Friday night, and must stop by midnight on Monday night. Then they print entry and mail it in to the contest for judging. Deadline: Friday before Labor Day weekend. Prize: First Place receives publication; Second Place receives $500; Third Place receives $100.

INTERNATIONAL READING ASSOCIATION CHILDREN'S AND YOUNG ADULTS BOOK AWARDS

P.O. Box 8139, 800 Barksdale Rd., Newark DE 19714-8139. (302)731-1600, ext. 221. **E-mail:** kbaughman@reading.org. **E-mail:** committees@reading.org. **Website:** www.reading.org. **Contact:** Kathy Baughman. The IRA Children's and Young Adults Book Awards are intended for newly published authors who show unusual promise in the children's and young adults' book field. Awards are given for fiction and nonfiction in each of 3 categories: primary, intermediate, and young adult. Books from all countries and published in English for the first time during the previous calendar year will be considered. Deadline: October 31. Prize: $1,000.

O THE IOWA REVIEW AWARD IN POETRY, FICTION, AND NONFICTION

308 EPB, University of Iowa, Iowa City IA 52242. **E-mail:** iowa-review@uiowa.edu. **Website:** www.iowareview.org. *The Iowa Review* Award in Poetry, Fiction, and Nonfiction presents $1,500 to each winner in each genre, $750 to runners-up. Winners and runners-up published in *The Iowa Review*. Deadline: Submit January 1-31. Judged by Srikanth Reddy, Kevin Brockmeier, and Wayne Koestenbaum in 2015.

THE IOWA SHORT FICTION AWARD & JOHN SIMMONS SHORT FICTION AWARD

Iowa Writers' Workshop, 507 N. Clinton St., 102 Dey House, Iowa City IA 52242-1000. **Website:** www.uiowapress.org. **Contact:** James McCoy, director. Annual award to give exposure to promising writers who have not yet published a book of prose. Open to any writer. Current University of Iowa students are not eligible. No application forms are necessary. Announcement of winners made early in year following competition. Winners notified by phone. No application forms are necessary. Do not send original ms. Include SASE for return of ms. Deadline: September 30. Submission period begins August 1. Prize: Publication by University of Iowa Press Judged by senior Iowa Writers' Workshop members who screen mss; published fiction author of note makes final selections.

IRA SHORT STORY AWARD

International Reading Association, International Reading Association, 800 Barksdale Rd., PO Box 8139, Newark DE 19714-8139. (302)731-1600. **Fax:** (302)731-1057. **E-mail:** committees@reading.org. **Website:** www.reading.org. Offered to reward author of an original short story published for the first time in a periodical for children. (Periodicals should generally be aimed at readers around age 12.) Write for guidelines or download from website. Award is nonmonetary. Deadline: November 15.

⊕ TILIA KLEBENOV JACOBS RELIGIOUS ESSAY PRIZE CATEGORY

Soul Making Keats Literary Competition, The Webhallow House, 1544 Sweetwood Dr., Broadmoor Village CA 94015-2029. **E-mail:** SoulKeats@mail.com. **Website:** www.soulmakingcontest.us. **Contact:** Eileen Malone. Estab. 2012. Call for thoughtful writings of up to 3,000 words. "No preaching, no proselytizing." Open annually to any writer. Deadline: November 30. Prize: First Place: $100; Second Place: $50; Third Place: $25.

JERRY JAZZ MUSICIAN NEW SHORT FICTION AWARD

Jerry Jazz Musician, 2207 NE Broadway, Portland OR 97232. **E-mail:** jm@jerryjazz.com. **Website:** www.jerryjazzmusician.com. Three times a year, *Jerry Jazz Musician* awards a writer who submits the best original, previously unpublished work of approximately 1,000-5,000 words. The winner will be announced via a mailing of the *Jerry Jazz* newsletter. Publishers, artists, musicians, and interested readers are among those who subscribe to the newsletter. Additionally, the work will be published on the home page of *Jerry Jazz Musician* and featured there for at least 4 weeks. The *Jerry Jazz Musician* reader tends to have interests in music, history, literature, art, film, and theater—particularly that of the counter-culture of mid-20th century America. Guidelines available online. Deadline: September, January, and May. See website for specific dates. Prize: $100. Judged by the editors of *Jerry Jazz Musician*.

JESSE H. JONES AWARD FOR BEST WORK OF FICTION

P.O. Box 609, Round Rock TX 78680. **E-mail:** tilsecretary@yahoo.com. **Website:** texasinstituteofletters.org. Offered annually by Texas Institute of Letters for work published January 1-December 31 of year before award is given to recognize the writer of the best book of fiction entered in the competition. Writers must have been born in Texas, have lived in the state for at least 2 consecutive years at some time, or the subject matter of the work should be associated with the state. Deadline: January 10. Prize: $6,000.

JAMES JONES FIRST NOVEL FELLOWSHIP

Wilkes University, Creative Writing Department, Wilkes University, 84 West South Street, Wilkes-Barre PA 18766. (570)408-4547. **Fax:** (570)408-3333. **E-mail:** jamesjonesfirstnovel@wilkes.edu. **Website:** www.wilkes.edu/. Offered annually for unpublished novels and novellas (must be works-in-progress). This competition is open to all American writers who have not previously published novels. The award is intended to honor the spirit of unblinking honesty, determination, and insight into modern culture exemplified by the late James Jones. Deadline: March 15. Submission period begins October 1. Prize: $10,000; 2 runners-up get $1,000 honorarium.

○ JUNIPER PRIZE FOR FICTION

University of Massachusetts Press, East Experiment Station, 671 North Pleasant St., Amherst MA 01003. (413)545-2217. **Fax:** (413)545-1226. **E-mail:** info@umpress.umass.edu; kfisk@umpress.umass.edu. **E-mail:** fiction@umpress.umass.edu. **Website:** www.umass.edu/umpress. **Contact:** Karen Fisk, competition coordinator. Estab. 2004. Award to honor and publish outstanding works of literary fiction. Deadline: September 30. Submissions period begins August 1. Winners announced online in April on the press website. Prize: $1,500 cash and publication.

E.M. KOEPPEL SHORT FICTION AWARD

P.O. Box 140310, Gainesville FL 32614-0310. **Website:** www.writecorner.com. **Contact:** Mary Sue Koeppel, editor. Annual awards for unpublished fiction in any style and any theme. Send 2 title pages: One with title only and 1 with title, name, address, phone, e-mail, short bio. Place no other identification of the author on the ms that will be used in the judging. Guidelines available for SASE or on website. Accepts inquiries by e-mail and phone. Winning stories published on website. Winners notified by mail, phone in July (or earlier). For results, send SASE or see website. Deadline: April 30. Submission period begins October 1. Prize: first Place: $1,100. Editors' Choice: $100 each. $500 scholarship, in addition, if winner is a student. Judged by award-winning fiction writers.

THE LAWRENCE FOUNDATION AWARD

Prairie Schooner, 123 Andrews Hall, University of Nebraska-Lincoln, Lincoln NE 68588-0334. (402)472-0911. **Fax:** (402)472-9771. **E-mail:** prairieschooner@unl.edu. **Website:** www.prairieschooner.unl.edu. Offered annually for the best short story published in Prairie Schooner in the previous year. Only work published in *Prairie Schooner* in the previous year is considered. Work is nominated by editorial staff. Results announced in the Spring issue. Winners notified by mail in February or March. Prize: $1,000. Judged by editorial staff of *Praire Schooner*.

LAWRENCE FOUNDATION PRIZE

Michigan Quarterly Review, 0576 Rackham Bldg., 915 E. Washington Street, Ann Arbor MI 48109-1070. (734)764-9265. **E-mail:** mqr@umich.edu. **Website:** www.michiganquarterlyreview.com. **Contact:** Vicki Lawrence, managing editor. Estab. 1978. This annual prize is awarded by the *Michigan Quarterly Review* editorial board to the author of the best short story published in *MQR* that year. The prize is sponsored by University of Michigan alumnus and fiction writer Leonard S. Bernstein, a trustee of the Lawrence Foundation of New York. Approximately 20 short stories are published in *MQR* each year. Prize: $1,000. Judged by editorial board.

LEAGUE OF UTAH WRITERS CONTEST

The League of Utah Writers, The League of Utah Writers, P.O. Box 64, Lewiston UT 84320. (435)755-7609. **E-mail:** luwcontest@gmail.com. **Website:** www.luwriters.org. Open to any writer, the LUW Contest provides authors an opportunity to get their work read and critiqued. Multiple categories are offered; see website for details. Entries must be the original and unpublished work of the author. Winners are announced at the Annual Writers Round-Up in September. Those not present will be notified by e-mail. Deadline: June 15. Submissions period begins March 15. Prize: Cash prizes are awarded. Judged by professional authors and editors from outside the League.

LES FIGUES PRESS NOS BOOK CONTEST

P.O. Box 7736, Los Angeles CA 90007. (323)734-4732. **E-mail:** info@lesfigues.com. **Website:** www.lesfigues.com. **Contact:** Teresa Carmody and Vanessa Place, co-directors. Les Figues Press creates aesthetic conversations between writers/artists and readers, especially those interested in innovative/experimental/avant-garde work. The Press intends in the most premeditated fashion to champion the trinity of Beauty, Belief, and Bawdry. Deadline: September 15. Prize: $1,000, plus publication by Les Figues Press. Each entry receives LFP book.

LET'S WRITE LITERARY CONTEST

The Gulf Coast Writers Association, P.O. Box 952, Long Beach MS 39560. **E-mail:** writerpllevin@gmail.com. **Website:** www.gcwriters.org. **Contact:** Philip Levin. The Gulf Coast Writers Association sponsors this nationally recognized contest, which accepts unpublished poems and short stories from authors all around the U.S. This is an annual event that has been held for over 20 years. Deadline: April 10. Prize: first Prize: $100; Second Prize: $60; Third Prize: $25.

FENIA AND YAAKOV LEVIANT MEMORIAL PRIZE IN YIDDISH STUDIES

Modern Language Association of America, 26 Broadway, Third Floor, New York NY 10004-1789. (646)576-5141. **Fax:** (646)458-0030. **E-mail:** awards@mla.org. **Website:** www.mla.org. **Contact:** Coordinator of book prizes. Offered in even-numbered years for an outstanding English translation of a Yiddish literary work or the publication of a scholarly work. Cultural studies, critical biographies, or edited works in the field of Yiddish folklore or linguistic studies are eligible to compete. See website for details on which they are accepting. Deadline: May 1. Prize: A cash prize, and a certificate, to be presented at the Modern Language Association's annual convention in January.

LITERAL LATTÉ FICTION AWARD

Literal Latté, 200 E. 10th St., Suite 240, New York NY 10003. (212)260-5532. **E-mail:** litlatte@aol.com. **Website:** www.literal-latte.com. **Contact:** Edward Estlin, contributing editor. Award to provide talented writers with 3 essential tools for continued success: money, publication, and recognition. Offered annually for unpublished fiction (maximum 10,000 words). Guidelines online. Open to any writer. Deadline: January 15. Prize: First Place: $1,000 and publication in *Literal Latté*; Second Place: $300; Third Place: $200; also up to 7 honorable mentions.

LITERAL LATTE SHORT SHORTS CONTEST

Literal Latté, 200 E. 10th St., Suite 240, New York NY 10003. (212)260-5532. **E-mail:** litlatte@aol.com. **Website:** www.literal-latte.com. **Contact:** Jenine Gordon Bockman, editor. Annual contest. Send unpublished shorts. 2,000 words max. All styles welcome. Name, address, phone number, e-mail address (optional) on cover page only. Include SASE or e-mail address for reply. All entries considered for publication. Deadline: June 30. Prize: $500. Judged by the editors.

THE HUGH J. LUKE AWARD

Prairie Schooner, 123 Andrews Hall, University of Nebraska-Lincoln, Lincoln NE 68588-0334. (402)472-0911. **Fax:** (402)472-1817. **E-mail:** prairieschooner@unl.edu. **Website:** www.prairieschooner.unl.edu. **Contact:** Kwame Dawes. Offered annually for work published in *Prairie Schooner* in the previous year. Results announced in the Spring issue. Winners notified by mail in February or March. Prize: $250. Judged by editorial staff of *Prairie Schooner*.

LUMINA POETRY CONTEST

Sarah Lawrence College, Sarah Lawrence College Slonim House 1 Mead Way, Bronxville NY 10708. **Website:** www.luminajournal.com. Annual poetry competition held by the Sarah Lawrence College's graduate literary journal. Deadline: October 15. Prize: First Place: $500 and publication; Second Place: $250 and publication; Third Place: $100 and online publication.

THE MARY MACKEY SHORT STORY PRIZE CATEGORY

Soul-Making Keats Literary Competition, The Webhallow House, 1544 Sweetwood Dr., Broadmoor Village CA 94015. **E-mail:** SoulKeats@mail.com. **Website:** www.soulmakingcontest.us. **Contact:** Eileen Malone. Open annually to any writer. Deadline: November 30. Prize: Cash prizes.

THE MALAHAT REVIEW NOVELLA PRIZE

The Malahat Review, University of Victoria, P.O. Box 1700 STN CSC, Victoria BC V8W 2Y2 Canada. (250)721-8524. **E-mail:** malahat@uvic.ca. **E-mail:** novella@uvic.ca. **Website:** malahatreview.ca. **Contact:** John Barton, editor. Held in alternate years with the Long Poem Prize. Offered to promote unpublished novellas. Obtains first world rights. After publication rights revert to the author. Open to any writer. Deadline: February 1 (even years). Prize: $1,500 CAD and one-year subscription. Winner published in summer issue of *The Malahat Review* and announced on website, Facebook page, and in quarterly e-newsletter, *Malahat Lite*.

MANITOBA BOOK AWARDS

c/o Manitoba Writers' Guild, 218-100 Arthur St., Winnipeg MB R3B 1H3 Canada. (204)944-8013. **E-mail:** events@mbwriter.mb.ca. **Website:** www.manitobabookawards.com. **Contact:** Anita Daher. Offered annually: The McNally Robinson Book of Year Award (adult); The McNally Robinson Book for Young People Awards (8 and under and 9 and older); The John Hirsch Award for Most Promising Manitoba Writer; The Mary Scorer Award for Best Book by a Manitoba Publisher; The Carol Shields Winnipeg Book Award; The Eileen McTavish Sykes Award for Best First Book; The Margaret Laurence Award for Fiction; The Alexander Kennedy Isbister Award for Nonfiction; The Manuela Dias Book Design of the Year Award; The Best Illustrated Book of the Year Award; the biennial Le Prix Littéraire Rue-Deschambault; The Beatrice Mosionier Aboriginal Writer of the Year Award; and The Chris Johnson Award for Best Play by a Manitoba Playwright. Deadline: October 31 and December 31. See website for specific details on book eligibility at deadlines. Prize: Several prizes up to $5,000 (Canadian).

MARSH AWARD FOR CHILDREN'S LITERATURE IN TRANSLATION

The English-Speaking Union, Dartmouth House, 37 Charles St., London En W1J 5ED United Kingdom. 020 7529 1591. **E-mail:** melanie.aplin@esu.org. **Website:** www.marshchristiantrust.org; www.esu.org. **Contact:** Melanie Aplin, senior education officer. Estab. 1996. The Marsh Award for Children's Literature in Translation, awarded biennially, was founded to celebrate the best translation of a children's book from a foreign language into English and published in the

UK. It aims to spotlight the high quality and diversity of translated fiction for young readers. The Award is administered by the ESU on behalf of the Marsh Christian Trust.

WALTER RUMSEY MARVIN GRANT

274 E. First Ave., Suite 300, Columbus OH 43201. (614)466-3831. **Fax:** (614)728-6974. **E-mail:** ohioana@ohioana.org. **E-mail:** dweaver@ohioana.org. **Website:** www.ohioana.org. **Contact:** David Weaver, executive director. The Marvin Grant, named for the second director of the Ohioana Library, was established by his family to encourage writers 30 years of age or younger who have not published a book. Applicants must be born in Ohio or have lived in Ohio for at least 5 years and must be no older than 30 years of age on January 31 in the year in which the grant is given. Deadline: January 31. Prize: Grant is a $1,000 cash prize and the opportunity to pulish an excerpt from the winning entry in the *Ohioana Quarterly*.

MARY MCCARTHY PRIZE IN SHORT FICTION

Sarabande Books, 2234 Dundee Rd., Suite 200, Louisville KY 40205. (502)458-4028. **Fax:** (502)458-4065. **E-mail:** info@sarabandebooks.org. **Website:** www.sarabandebooks.org. **Contact:** Kirby Gann, managing editor. Annual competition to honor a collection of short stories, novellas, or a short novel. Deadline: February 15. Submission period begins January 1. Prize: $2,000 and publication (standard royalty contract).

⊘ THE MCGINNIS-RITCHIE MEMORIAL AWARD

Southwest Review, P.O. Box 750374, Dallas TX 75275-0374. (214)768-1037. **Fax:** (214)768-1408. **E-mail:** swr@mail.smu.edu. **Website:** www.smu.edu/southwestreview. **Contact:** Jennifer Cranfill, senior editor, and Willard Spiegelman, editor in chief. The McGinnis-Ritchie Memorial Award is given annually to the best works of fiction and nonfiction that appeared in the magazine in the previous year. Mss are submitted for publication, not for the prizes themselves. Guidelines for SASE or online. Prize: $500. Judged by Jennifer Cranfill and Willard Spiegelman.

⦿ MARJORIE GRABER MCINNIS SHORT STORY AWARD

ACT Writers Centre, Gorman House Arts Centre, Ainslie Ave., Braddon ACT 2612 Australia. (61)(2)6262-9191. **Fax:** (61)(2)6262-9191. **E-mail:** admin@actwriters.org.au. **Website:** www.actwriters.org.au.

Open theme for a short story with 1,500-3,000 words. Guidelines available on website. Open only to unpublished emerging writers residing within the ACT or region. Deadline: September 25. Submissions period begins in early September. Prize: $600 and publication. Five runners-up receive book prizes. All winners may be published in the ACT Writers Centre newsletter and on the ACT Writers Centre website.

MEMPHIS MAGAZINE FICTION CONTEST

Memphis Magazine, co-sponsored by booksellers of Laurelwood and Burke's Book Store, Fiction Contest, c/o *Memphis* magazine, P.O. Box 1738, Memphis TN 38101. (901)521-9000, ext. 451. **Fax:** (901)521-0129. **E-mail:** sadler@memphismagazine.com. **Website:** www.memphismagazine.com. **Contact:** Marilyn Sadler. Annual award for authors of short fiction living within 150 miles of Memphis. Deadline: February 15. Prize: $1,000 grand prize, along with being published in the annual Cultural Issue; 2 honorable-mention awards of $500 each will be given if the quality of entries warrants.

DAVID NATHAN MEYERSON PRIZE FOR FICTION

Southwest Review, P.O. Box 750374, Dallas TX 75275-0374. (214)768-1037. **Fax:** (214)768-1408. **E-mail:** swr@smu.edu. **Website:** www.smu.edu/southwestreview. **Contact:** Jennifer Cranfill, senior editor. Annual award given to a writer who has not published a first book of fiction, either a novel or collection of stories. All contest entrants will receive a copy of the issue in which the winning piece appears. Deadline: May 1 (postmarked). Prize: $1,000 and publication in the *Southwest Review*.

⦿ MILKWEED NATIONAL FICTION PRIZE

1011 Washington Ave. S., Suite 300, Minneapolis MN 55415. (612)332-3192. **Fax:** (612)215-2550. **E-mail:** editor@milkweed.org. **Website:** www.milkweed.org. **Contact:** Patrick Thoman, editor and program manager. Annual award for unpublished works. Mss should be one of the following: a novel, a collection of short stories, 1 or more novellas, or a combination of short stories and 1 or more novellas. Deadline: Rolling submissions. Check website for details of when they're accepting mss. Prize: Publication by Milkweed Editions and a cash advance of $5,000 against royalties, agreed upon in the contractual arrangement negotiated at the time of acceptance. Judged by the editors.

MILKWEED PRIZE FOR CHILDREN'S LITERATURE

Milkweed Editions, 1011 Washington Ave. S., Suite 300, Minneapolis MN 55415. (612)332-3192. **Fax:** (612)215-2550. **E-mail:** editor@milkweed.org. **Website:** www.milkweed.org. Milkweed Editions will award the Milkweed Prize for Children's Literature to the best mss for young readers that Milkweed accepts for publication during the calendar year by a writer not previously published by Milkweed. All mss for young readers submitted for publication by Milkweed are automatically entered into the competition. Recognizes an outstanding literary novel for readers ages 8-13 and encourage writers to turn their attention to readers in this age group. Prize: $10,000 cash prize in addition to a publishing contract negotiated at the time of acceptance. Judged by the editors of Milkweed Editions.

MINNESOTA BOOK AWARDS

325 Cedar Street, Suite 555, St. Paul MN 55101. **E-mail:** mnbookawards@thefriends.org; friends@thefriends.org; info@thefriends.org. **Website:** www.thefriends.org. Estab. 1988. A year-round program celebrating and honoring Minnesota's best books, culminating in an annual awards gala. Recognizes and honors achievement by members of Minnesota's book community.

◐ MISSISSIPPI REVIEW PRIZE

Mississippi Review, 118 College Dr., #5144, Hattiesburg MS 39406-0001. (601)266-4321. **Fax:** (601)266-5757. **E-mail:** msreview@usm.edu. **Website:** www.mississippireview.com. Annual contest starting August 1 and running until January 1. Winners and finalists will make up next winter's print issue of the national literary magazine *Mississippi Review*. Each entrant will receive a copy of the prize issue. Deadline: January1. Prize: $1,000 in fiction and poetry.

MONTANA PRIZE IN CREATIVE NONFICTION

CutBank Literary Magazine, *CutBank*, University of Montana, English Dept., LA 133, Missoula MT 59812. **E-mail:** editor.cutbank@gmail.com. **Website:** www.cutbankonline.org. **Contact:** Allison Linville, editor in chief. The Montana Prize in Creative Nonfiction seeks to highlight work that showcases an authentic voice, a boldness of form, and a rejection of functional fixedness. Deadline: January 15. Submissions period

begins November 1. Prize: $500 and featured in the magazine. Judged by a guest judge each year.

MONTANA PRIZE IN FICTION

Cutbank Literary Magazine, *CutBank*, University of Montana, English Dept., LA 133, Missoula MT 59812. **E-mail:** editor.cutbank@gmail.com. **Website:** www.cutbankonline.org. **Contact:** Allison Linville, editor in chief. The Montana Prize in Fiction seeks to highlight work that showcases an authentic voice, a boldness of form, and a rejection of functional fixedness. Deadline: January 15. Submissions period begins November 1. Prize: $500 and featured in the magazine. Judged by a guest judge each year.

THE HOWARD FRANK MOSHER SHORT FICTION PRIZE

Vermont College, 36 College St., Montpelier VT 05602. (802)828-8517. **E-mail:** hungermtn@vcfa.edu. **Website:** www.hungermtn.org. **Contact:** Miciah Bay Gault, editor. Estab. 2002. The Howard Frank Mosher Short Fiction Prize is an annual contest for short fiction. Deadline: June 30. Prize: One first-place winner receives $1,000 and publication. Two honorable mentions receive $100 each, and are considered for publication.

○ NATIONAL BOOK AWARDS

The National Book Foundation, 90 Broad St., Suite 604, New York NY 10004. (212)685-0261. **E-mail:** nationalbook@nationalbook.org; agall@nationalbook.org. **Website:** www.nationalbook.org. **Contact:** Amy Gall. The National Book Foundation and the National Book Awards celebrate the best of American literature, expand its audience, and enhance the cultural value of great writing in America. The contest offers prizes in 4 categories: fiction, nonfiction, poetry, and young people's literature. Books should be published between December 1 and November 30 of the past year. Deadline: Entry form and payment by May 15; a copy of the book by July 1. Prize: $10,000 in each category. Finalists will each receive a prize of $1,000. Judged by a category specific panel of 5 judges for each category.

NATIONAL OUTDOOR BOOK AWARDS

921 S. 8th Ave., Stop 8128, Pocatello ID 83209. (208)282-3912. **E-mail:** wattron@isu.edu. **Website:** www.noba-web.org. **Contact:** Ron Watters. Nine categories: History/biography, outdoor literature, instructional texts, outdoor adventure guides, nature guides, children's books, design/artistic merit, natural history

literature, and nature and the environment. Additionally, a special award, the Outdoor Classic Award, is given annually to books that, over a period of time, have proven to be exceptionally valuable works in the outdoor field. Application forms and eligibility requirements are available online. Applications for the Awards program become available in early June. Deadline: September 1. Prize: Winning books are promoted nationally and are entitled to display the National Outdoor Book Award (NOBA) medallion.

○ NATIONAL WRITERS ASSOCIATION NOVEL WRITING CONTEST

The National Writers Association, 10940 S. Parker Rd. #508, Parker CO 80134. (303)841-0246. **E-mail:** natlwritersassn@hotmail.com. **Website:** www.nationalwriters.com. **Contact:** Sandy Whelchel, director. Open to any genre or category. Contest begins December 1. Open to any writer. Annual contest to help develop creative skills, to recognize and reward outstanding ability, and to increase the opportunity for the marketing and subsequent publication of novel mss. Deadline: April 1. Prize: First Place: $500; Second Place: $250; Third Place: $150. Judged by editors and agents.

NATIONAL WRITERS ASSOCIATION SHORT STORY CONTEST

10940 S. Parker Rd., #508, Parker CO 80134. (303)841-0246. **E-mail:** natlwritersassn@hotmail.com. **Website:** www.nationalwriters.com. Estab. 1971. Opens April 1. The purpose of the National Writers Assn. Short Story Contest is to encourage the development of creative skills, recognize and reward outstanding ability in the area of short story writing. Prize: First Prize: $250; Second Prize: $100; Third Prize: $50; 4th-10th places will receive a book. First-Third Place winners may be asked to grant one-time rights for publication in *Authorship* magazine. Honorable Mentions receive a certificate. Judging will be based on originality, marketability, research, and reader interest. Copies of the judges evaluation sheets will be sent to entrants furnishing an SASE with their entry.

THE NELLIGAN PRIZE FOR SHORT FICTION

Colorado Review/Center for Literary Publishing, 9105 Campus Delivery, Dept. of English, Colorado State University, Ft. Collins CO 80523-9105. (970)491-5449. **E-mail:** creview@colostate.edu. **Website:** nelliganprize.colostate.edu. **Contact:** Stephanie G'Schwind,

editor. Annual competition/award for short stories. Receives approximately 900 stories. All entries are read blind by Colorado Review's editorial staff. Ten to 15 entries are selected to be sent on to a final judge. Stories must be unpublished and under 50 pages. "The Nelligan Prize for Short Fiction was established in memory of Liza Nelligan, a writer, editor, and friend of many in Colorado State University's English Department, where she received her master's degree in literature in 1992. By giving an award to the author of an outstanding short story each year, we hope to honor Liza Nelligan's life, her passion for writing, and her love of fiction." Deadline: March 14. Prize: $2,000 and publication of story in *Colorado Review*.

THE NEUTRINO SHORT-SHORT CONTEST

Passages North, Dept. of English, Northern Michigan University, 1401 Presque Isle Ave., Marquette MI 49855. (906)227-1203. **Fax:** (906)227-1096. **E-mail:** passages@nmu.edu. **Website:** www.passagesnorth. com. **Contact:** Jennifer Howard. Offered every 2 years to publish new voices in literary fiction, nonfiction, hybrid-essays and prose poems (maximum 1,000 words). Guidelines available for SASE or online. Deadline: March 15. Submission period begins January 15. Prize: $1,000, and publication for the winner; 2 honorable mentions also published; all entrants receive a copy of *Passages North*. Judged by Connie Voisine in 2014.

○ NEW LETTERS LITERARY AWARDS

New Letters, UMKC, University House, Room 105, 5101 Rockhill Rd., Kansas City MO 64110-2499. (816)235-1168. **Fax:** (816)235-2611. **Website:** www.newletters.org. Estab. 1986. Award has 3 categories (fiction, poetry, and creative nonfiction) with 1 winner in each. Offered annually for previously unpublished work. For guidelines, send an SASE to *New Letters*, or visit www.newletters.org. Deadline: May 18. First Place: $1,500, plus publication; first runners-up: a copy of a recent book of poetry or fiction courtesy of our affiliate BkMk Press. Judged by regional writers of prominence and experience. Final judging by someone of national repute. Previous judges include Maxine Kumin, Albert Goldbarth, Charles Simic, and Janet Burroway.

NEW MILLENNIUM AWARDS FOR FICTION, POETRY, AND NONFICTION

New Millennium Writings, 4021 Garden Dr., Knoxville TN 37918. (865)254-4880. **Website:** www.newmillenniumwritings.com/awards. No restrictions as to style, content or number of submissions. Previously published pieces acceptable if online or under 5,000 print circulation. Simultaneous and multiple submissions welcome. Deadline: postmarked on or before July 31 for the Summer Awards and January 31 for the Winter Awards. Prize: $1,000 for Best Poem; $1,000 for Best Fiction; $1,000 for Best Nonfiction; $1,000 for Best Short-Short Fiction.

NORTHERN CALIFORNIA BOOK AWARDS

Northern California Book Reviewers Association, c/o Poetry Flash, 1450 Fourth St. #4, Berkeley CA 94710. (510)525-5476. **E-mail:** ncbr@poetryflash.org; editor@poetryflash.org. **Website:** www.poetryflash.org. **Contact:** Joyce Jenkins, executive director. Estab. 1981. Annual Northern California Book Award for outstanding book in literature, open to books published in the current calendar year by Northern California authors. NCBR presents annual awards to Bay Area (northern California) authors annually in fiction, nonfiction, poetry and children's literature. Encourages writers and stimulates interest in books and reading. Deadline: December 28. Prize: $100 honorarium and award certificate. Judging by voting members of the Northern California Book Reviewers.

THE FLANNERY O'CONNOR AWARD FOR SHORT FICTION

The University of Georgia Press, Main Library, Third Floor, 320 S. Jackson St., Athens GA 30602. (706)369-6130. **Fax:** (706)369-6131. **Website:** www.ugapress.org. Estab. 1981. This competition welcomes short story or novella collections. Stories may have been published singly, but should not have appeared in a book-length collection of the author's own work. Length: 40,000-75,000 words. Deadline: April 1-May 31. 2 winners receive $1,000 and book contracts from the University of Georgia Press.

SEAN O'FAOLAIN SHORT STORY COMPETITION

The Munster Literature Centre, Frank O'Connor House, 84 Douglas Street, Cork Ireland. +353-0214319255. **E-mail:** munsterlit@eircom.net. **Website:** www.munsterlit.ie. **Contact:** Patrick Cotter, artistic director. Purpose is to reward writers of outstanding short stories. Deadline: July 31. Prize: First Prize €1500 (approximately U.S. $2,200); Second Prize €500 (approximately $730). Four runners-up prizes of €100 (approximately $146). All 6 stories to be published in *Southword Literary Journal*. First-Prize Winner offered week's residency in Anam Cara Artist's Retreat in Ireland.

OHIOANA BOOK AWARDS

Ohioana Library Association, 274 E. First Ave., Suite 300, Columbus OH 43201-3673. (614)466-3831. **Fax:** (614)728-6974. **E-mail:** ohioana@ohioana.org. **Website:** www.ohioana.org. **Contact:** David Weaver, executive director. Offered annually to bring national attention to Ohio authors and their books, published in the last year. (Books can only be considered once.) Categories: Fiction, nonfiction, juvenile, poetry, and books about Ohio or an Ohioan. Deadline: December 31. Prize: $1,000 cash prize, certificate, and glass sculpture. Judged by a jury selected by librarians, book reviewers, writers and other knowledgeable people.

ON THE PREMISES CONTEST

On The Premises, LLC, 4323 Gingham Court, Alexandria VA 22310. **E-mail:** questions@onthepremises.com. **Website:** www.onthepremises.com. **Contact:** Tarl Roger Kudrick or Bethany Granger, co-publishers. *On the Premises* aims to promote newer and/or relatively unknown writers who can write creative, compelling stories told in effective, uncluttered and evocative prose. Each contest challenges writers to produce a great story based on a broad premise that the editors supply as part of the contest. Deadline: Short story contests held twice a year; smaller mini-contests held 4 times a year; check website for exact dates. Prize: First Prize: $210; Second Prize: $160; Third Prize: $110; Honorable Mentions receive $60. All prize winners are published in *On the Premises* magazine in HTML and PDF format. Judged by a panel of judges with professional editing and writing experience.

OPEN SEASON AWARDS

The Malahat Review, University of Victoria, P.O. Box 1700, Stn CSC, Victoria BC V8V 2Y2 Canada. (250)721-8524. **Fax:** (250)472-5051. **E-mail:** malahat@uvic.ca. **Website:** www.malahatreview.ca. **Contact:** John Barton, editor. The Open Season Awards accepts entries of poetry, fiction, and creative nonfiction. Winners published in spring issue of *Malahat Review* announced in winter on website, Facebook page, and in quarterly e-newsletter, *Malahat lite*. Deadline: November 1. Prize: $1,000 CAD and publication in *The Malahat Review* in each category.

OREGON BOOK AWARDS

925 SW Washington St., Portland OR 97205. (503)227-2583. **Fax:** (503)241-4256. **E-mail:** la@literary-arts.org. **Website:** www.literary-arts.org. **Contact:** Susan Denning, director of programs and events. The annual Oregon Book Awards celebrate Oregon authors in the areas of poetry, fiction, nonfiction, drama and young readers' literature published August 1-July 31 of the previous calendar year. Awards are available for every category. See website for details. Deadline: August 29. Prize: Grant of $2,500. (Grant money could vary.) Judged by writers who are selected from outside Oregon for their expertise in a genre. Past judges include Mark Doty, Colson Whitehead and Kim Barnes.

OREGON LITERARY FELLOWSHIPS

925 S.W. Washington, Portland OR 97205. (503)227-2583. **E-mail:** susan@literary-arts.org. **Website:** www.literary-arts.org. **Contact:** Susan Denning, director of programs and events. Oregon Literary Fellowships are intended to help Oregon writers initiate, develop or complete literary projects in poetry, fiction, literary nonfiction, drama and young readers literature. Writers in the early stages of their career are encouraged to apply. The awards are merit-based. Deadline: Last Friday in June. Prize: $2,500 minimum award, for approximately 10 writers and 2 publishers. Judged by out-of-state writers

KENNETH PATCHEN AWARD FOR THE INNOVATIVE NOVEL

Eckhard Gerdes Publishing, 12 Simpson Street, Apt. D, Geneva IL 60134. **E-mail:** egerdes@experimentalfiction.com. **Website:** www.experimentalfiction.com. **Contact:** Eckhard Gerdes. This award will honor the most innovative novel submitted during the previous calendar year. Kenneth Patchen is celebrated for being among the greatest innovators of American fiction, incorporating strategies of concretism, asemic writing, digression, and verbal juxtaposition into his writing long before such strategies were popularized during the height of American postmodernist experimentation in the 1970s. Deadline: All submissions must be postmarked between January 1 and July 31. Prize: $1,000 and 20 complimentary copies. Judged by novelist James Chapman.

THE PATERSON FICTION PRIZE

The Poetry Center at Passaic Community College, One College Blvd., Paterson NJ 07505. (973)684-6555. **Fax:** (973)523-6085. **E-mail:** mgillan@pccc.edu. **Website:** www.pccc.edu/poetry. **Contact:** Maria Mazziotti Gillan, executive director. Offered annually for a novel or collection of short fiction published the previous calendar year. For more information, visit the website or send SASE. Deadline: April 1. Prize: $1,000.

PEN CENTER USA LITERARY AWARDS

PEN Center USA, P.O. Box 6037, Beverly Hills CA 90212. (323)424-4939. **E-mail:** awards@penusa.org. **E-mail:** pen@penusa.org. **Website:** www.penusa.org. Offered for work published or produced in the previous calendar year. Open to writers living west of the Mississippi River. Award categories: fiction, poetry, research nonfiction, creative nonfiction, translation, children's/young adult, graphic literature, drama, screenplay, teleplay, journalism. Deadline for book categories: 4 copies must be received by December 31. Deadline for nonbook categories: 4 copies must be received by February 28. Prize: $1,000.

PNWA LITERARY CONTEST

Pacifc Northwest Writers Association, PMB 2717, 1420 NW Gilman Blvd., Suite 2, Issaquah WA 98027. (452)673-2665. **Fax:** (452)961-0768. **E-mail:** pnwa@pnwa.org. **Website:** www.pnwa.org. Annual literary contest with 12 different categories. See website for details and specific guidelines. Each entry receives 2 critiques. Winners announced at the PNWA Summer Conference, held annually in mid-July. Deadline: February 20. Prize: First Place: $700; Second Place: $300. Judged by an agent or editor attending the conference.

POCKETS FICTION-WRITING CONTEST

P.O. Box 340004, Nashville TN 37203-0004. (615)340-7333. **Fax:** (615)340-7267. **E-mail:** pockets@upperroom.org. **Website:** www.pockets.upperroom.org. **Contact:** Lynn W. Gilliam, senior editor. Designed for 6- to 12-year-olds, *Pockets* magazine offers wholesome devotional readings that teach about God's love and presence in life. The content includes fiction, scripture stories, puzzles and games, poems, recipes, colorful pictures, activities, and scripture readings. Freelance submissions of stories, poems, recipes, puzzles and games, and activities are welcome. The primary purpose of *Pockets* is to help children grow in their relationship with God and to claim the good news of the gospel of Jesus Christ by applying it to their daily lives. *Pockets* espouses respect for all human beings and for God's creation. It regards a child's faith journey as an integral part of all of life and sees prayer as undergirding that journey. Deadline: August 15. Submission period begins March 15. Prize: $500 and publication in magazine.

EDGAR ALLAN POE AWARD

1140 Broadway, Suite 1507, New York NY 10001. (212)888-8171. **Fax:** (212)888-8107. **E-mail:** mwa@mysterywriters.org. **Website:** www.mysterywriters.org. Estab. 1945. Mystery Writers of America is the leading association for professional crime writers in the United States. Members of MWA include most major writers of crime fiction and nonfiction, as well as screenwriters, dramatists, editors, publishers, and other professionals in the field. Purpose of the award: Honor authors of distinguished works in the mystery field. Previously published submissions only. Submissions made by the author, author's agent; "normally by the publisher." Work must be published/produced the year of the contest. Deadline: November 30. Prize: Awards ceramic bust of "Edgar" for winner; scrolls for all nominees. Judged by professional members of Mystery Writers of America (writers).

THE KATHERINE ANNE PORTER PRIZE FOR FICTION

Nimrod International Journal, The University of Tulsa, 800 S. Tucker Dr., Tulsa OK 74104. (918)631-3080. **Fax:** (918)631-3033. **E-mail:** nimrod@utulsa.edu. **Website:** www.utulsa.edu/nimrod. **Contact:** Eilis O'Neal. Deadline: April 30. Prizes: First Place: $2,000 and publication; Second Place: $1,000 and publication. Judged by the *Nimrod* editors, who select the finalists and a recognized author, who selects the winners.

PRESS 53 AWARD FOR SHORT FICTION

Press 53, 560 N. Trade St., Suite 193, Winston-Salem NC 27101. **E-mail:** kevin@press53.com. **Website:** www.press53.com. **Contact:** Kevin Morgan Watson, publisher. Awarded to an outstanding, unpublished collection of short stories. Deadline: December 31. Submission period begins September 1. Finalists announced March 1. Winner announced on May 3. Publication in October. Prize: Publication of winning short story collection, $1,000 cash advance, travel expenses and lodging for a special reading and book signing in Winston-Salem, NC, attendance as special guest to the Press 53/*Prime Number Magazine* Gathering of Writers, and 10 copies of the book. Judged by publisher Kevin Morgan Watson and fiction editor Christine Norris.

PRIME NUMBER MAGAZINE AWARDS

Press 53, 560 N. Trade St., Suite 103, Winston-Salem NC 27101. **E-mail:** kevin@press53.com. **Website:** www.press53.com. **Contact:** Kevin Morgan Watson, publisher. Awards $1,000 in each of 3 categories: poetry, short fiction, and creative nonfiction. Deadline: March 30. Submission period begins January 1. Finalists announced June 1. Winner announced on August 1. Prize: $1,000 cash. All winners receive publication in Prime Number Magazine online. Judged by industry professionals to be named when the contest begins.

PRISM INTERNATIONAL ANNUAL SHORT FICTION, POETRY, AND CREATIVE NONFICTION CONTESTS

PRISM International, Creative Writing Program, UBC, Buch. E462, 1866 Main Mall, Vancouver BC V6T 1Z1 Canada. **E-mail:** promotions@prismmagazine.ca. **Website:** www.prismmagazine.ca. Offered annually for unpublished work to award the best in contemporary fiction, poetry, drama, translation, and nonfiction. Works of translation are eligible. Guidelines are available on website. Acquires first North American serial rights upon publication, and limited web rights for pieces selected for website. Open to any writer except students and faculty in the Creative Writing Department at UBC, or people who have taken a creative writing course at UBC within 2 years of the contest deadline. Entry includes subscription. Deadlines: Creative Nonfiction: November 21; Fiction and Poetry: January 23. Prize: All grand prizes are $2,000, $300 for first runner up, and $200 for second runner up. Winners are published.

PRISM INTERNATIONAL ANNUAL SHORT FICTION CONTEST

Creative Writing Program, UBC, Buch. E462 - 1866 Main Mall, Vancouver BC V6T 1Z1 Canada. (604)822-2514. **Fax:** (604)822-3616. **Website:** prismmagazine.ca/contests. **Contact:** Clara Kumagai, executive editor, promotions. Offered annually for unpublished work to award the best in contemporary fiction. Works of translation are eligible. Guidelines by SASE, by e-mail, or on website. Acquires first North American serial rights upon publication, and rights to publish online for promotional or archival purposes. Open to any writer except students and faculty in the Creative Writing Department at UBC, or people who have taken a creative writing course at UBC with the 2 years prior to the contest deadline. Deadline: January 23.

Prize: First Place: $2,000; First Runner-up: $300; Second Runner-up: $200; winner is published.

PURPLE DRAGONFLY BOOK AWARDS

4696 W. Tyson St., Chandler AZ 85226-2903. (480)940-8182. **Fax:** (480)940-8787. **E-mail:** cristy@fivestarpublications.com; fivestarpublications@gmail.com. **Website:** www.purpledragonflybookawards.com; www.fivestarpublications.com; www.fivestar-bookawards.com. **Contact:** Cristy Bertini, contest coordinator. Five Star Publications presents the Purple Dragonfly Book Awards, which were conceived and designed with children in mind. "Not only do we want to recognize and honor accomplished authors in the field of children's literature, but we also want to highlight and reward up-and-coming, newly published authors and younger published writers." The Purple Dragonfly Book Awards are divided into 3 distinct subject categories, ranging from books on the environment and cooking to sports and family issues. (Click on the "Categories" tab on the website for a complete list.) The Purple Dragonfly Book Awards are geared toward stories that appeal to children of all ages. Looking for stories that inspire, inform, teach or entertain. "A Purple Dragonfly seal on your book's cover tells parents, grandparents, educators and caregivers they are giving children the very best in reading excellence." Being honored with a Purple Dragonfly Award confers credibility upon the winner, as well as provides positive publicity to further their success. The goal of these awards is to give published authors the recognition they deserve and provide a helping hand to further their careers. Deadline: May 1 (postmarked). Submissions postmarked March 1 or earlier that meet all submission requirements are eligible for the Early Bird reward: A free copy of *The Economical Guide to Self-Publishing* or *Promote Like a Pro: Small Budget, Big Show.* Prize: Grand Prize winner will receive a $300 cash prize, 100 foil award seals (more can be ordered for an extra charge), 1 hour of marketing consultation from Five Star Publications, and $100 worth of Five Star Publications' titles, as well as publicity on Five Star Publications' websites and inclusion in a winners' news release sent to a comprehensive list of media outlets. The Grand Prize winner will also be placed in the Five Star Dragonfly Book Awards virtual bookstore with a thumbnail of the book's cover, price, 1-sentence description and link to Amazon.com for purchasing purposes, if applicable. First

Place: All first-place winners of categories will be put into a drawing for a $100 prize. In addition, each first-place winner in each category receives a certificate commemorating their accomplishment, 25 foil award seals (more can be ordered for an extra charge) and mention on Five Star Publications' websites. Judged by industry experts with specific knowledge about the categories over which they preside.

PUSHCART PRIZE

Pushcart Press, P.O. Box 380, Wainscott NY 11975. (631)324-9300. **Website:** www.pushcartprize.com. **Contact:** Bill Henderson. Estab. 1976. Published every year since 1976, The Pushcart Prize - Best of the Small Presses series "is the most honored literary project in America. Hundreds of presses and thousands of writers of short stories, poetry and essays have been represented in the pages of our annual collections." Little magazine and small book press editors (print or online) may make up to 6 nominations from their year's publications by the deadline. The nominations may be any combination of poetry, short fiction, essays or literary whatnot. Editors may nominate self-contained portions of books—for instance, a chapter from a novel. Deadline: December 1.

DAVID RAFFELOCK AWARD FOR PUBLISHING EXCELLENCE

National Writers Association, 10940 S. Parker Rd., #508, Parker CO 80134. (303)841-0246. **E-mail:** natlwritersassn@hotmail.com. **Website:** www.nationalwriters.com. **Contact:** Sandy Whelchel. Contest is offered annually for books published the previous year. Published works only. Open to any writer. Guidelines for SASE, by e-mail or on website. Winners will be notified by mail or phone. List of winners available for SASE or visit website. Purpose is to assist published authors in marketing their works and to reward outstanding published works. Deadline: May 15. Prize: Publicity tour, including airfare, valued at $5,000.

○ THE RBC BRONWEN WALLACE AWARD FOR EMERGING WRITERS

The Writers' Trust of Canada, 460 Richmond St. W., Suite 600, Toronto ON M5C 1P1 Canada. (416)504-8222. **Fax:** (416)504-9090. **E-mail:** info@writerstrust.com. **Website:** www.writerstrust.com. **Contact:** Amanda Hopkins. Presented annually to a Canadian writer under the age of 35 who is not yet published in book form. The award, which alternates each year between poetry and short fiction, was established in memory of poet Bronwen Wallace. Deadline: Check website, to be announced. Prize: $5,000 and $1,000 to 2 finalists.

🌐 THE RED HOUSE CHILDREN'S BOOK AWARD

Red House Children's Book Award, 123 Frederick Road, Cheam, Sutton, Surrey SM1 2HT United Kingdom. E-mail: info@rhcba.co.uk. Website: www.redhousechildrensbookaward.co.uk. Contact: Sinead Kromer, national coordinator. Estab. 1980. The Red House Children's Book Award is the only national book award that is entirely voted for by children. A shortlist is drawn up from children's nominations and any child can then vote for the winner of the 3 categories: Books for Younger Children, Books for Younger Readers and Books for Older Readers. The book with the most votes is then crowned the winner of the Red House Children's Book Award. Deadline: December 31.

🌐 REGINA BOOK AWARD

Saskatchewan Book Awards, Inc., 315-1102 8th Ave., Regina SK S4R 1C9 Canada. (306)569-1585. E-mail: director@bookawards.sk.ca. Website: www.bookawards.sk.ca. Contact: Courtney Bates-Hardy, administrative director. Estab. 1993. Offered annually. In recognition of the vitality of the literary community in Regina, this award is presented to a Regina author for the best book, judged on the quality of writing. Books from the following categories will be considered: Children's; drama; fiction (short fiction by a single author, novellas, novels); nonfiction (all categories of nonfiction writing except cookbooks, directories, how-to books, or bibliographies of minimal critical content); poetry. Part of a larger group of awards, the Saskatchewan Book Awards. Deadline: November 3. Prize: $2,000 (CAD).

🌐 THE ROGERS WRITERS' TRUST FICTION PRIZE

The Writers' Trust of Canada, 460 Richmond St. W., Suite 600, Toronto ON M5V 1Y1 Canada. (416)504-8222. Fax: (416)504-9090. E-mail: info@writerstrust.com. Website: www.writerstrust.com. Contact: Amanda Hopkins. Awarded annually to the best novel or short story collection published within the previous year. Presented at the Writers' Trust Awards event held in Toronto each fall. Open to Canadian citizens and permanent residents only. Deadline: August. Prize: $25,000 and $2,500 to 4 finalists.

💲 LOIS ROTH AWARD

Modern Language Association, 26 Broadway, Third Floor, New York NY 10004. (646)576-5141. Fax: (646)458-0030. E-mail: awards@mla.org. Website: www.mla.org. Offered in odd-numbered years for an outstanding translation into English of a book-length literary work. Translators need not be members of the MLA. Deadline: April 1. Prize: A cash award and a certificate to be presented at the Modern Language Association's annual convention in January.

ROYAL DRAGONFLY BOOK AWARDS

4696 W. Tyson St., Chandler AZ 85226. (480)940-8182. Fax: (480)940-8787. E-mail: cristy@fivestarpublications.com; fivestarpublications@gmail.com. Website: www.fivestarpublications.com; www.fivestarbookawards.com; www.royaldragonflybookawards.com. Contact: Cristy Bertini. Offered annually for any previously published work to honor authors for writing excellence of all types of literature—fiction and nonfiction—in 52 categories, appealing to a wide range of ages and comprehensive list of genres. Open to any title published in English. Entry forms are downloadable at www.royaldragonflybookawards.com. Deadline: October 1. Prize: Grand Prize winner receives $300, while another entrant will be the lucky winner of a $100 drawing. All first-place winners receive foil award seals and are included in a publicity campaign announcing winners. All first- and second-place winners and honorable mentions receive certificates.

🌐 SASKATCHEWAN FIRST BOOK AWARD

Saskatchewan Book Awards, Inc., 315-1102 8th Ave., Regina SK S4R 1C9 Canada. (306)569-1585. E-mail: director@bookawards.sk.ca. Website: www.bookawards.sk.ca. Contact: Courtney Bates-Hardy, administrative director. Estab. 1993. Offered annually. This award is presented to a Saskatchewan author for the best first book, judged on the quality of writing. Books from the following categories will be considered: Children's; drama; fiction (short fiction by a single author, novellas, novels); nonfiction (all categories of nonfiction writing except cookbooks, directories, how-to books, or bibliographies of minimal critical content); and poetry. Deadline: November 3. Prize: $2,000 (CAD).

ALDO AND JEANNE SCAGLIONE PRIZE FOR A TRANSLATION OF A LITERARY WORK

Modern Language Association, 26 Broadway, Third Floor, New York NY 10004-1789. (646)576-5141. Fax: (646)458-0030. E-mail: awards@mla.org. Website:

www.mla.org. **Contact:** Coordinator of Book Prizes. Offered in even-numbered years for an outstanding translation into English of a book-length literary work. Deadline: April 1. Prize: A cash award and a certificate to be presented at the Modern Language Association's annual convention in January.

○ THE SCARS EDITOR'S CHOICE AWARDS

829 Brian Court, Gurnee IL 60031-3155. **E-mail:** editor@scars.tv. **Website:** scars.tv. **Contact:** Janet Kuypers, editor/publisher (whom all reading fee checks need to be made out to). Award to showcase good writing in an annual book. Deadline: Revolves for appearing in different upcoming books as winners. Prize: Publication of story/essay and 1 copy of the book.

THE MONA SCHREIBER PRIZE FOR HUMOROUS FICTION & NONFICTION

3940 Laurel Canyon Blvd., #566, Studio City CA 91604. **E-mail:** brad.schreiber@att.net. **Website:** www.bradschreiber.com. **Contact:** Brad Schreiber. Estab. 2000. The purpose of the contest is to award the most creative humor writing, in any form less than 750 words, in either fiction or nonfiction, including but not limited to stories, articles, essays, speeches, shopping lists, diary entries, and anything else writers dream up. Complete rules and previous winning entries on website. Deadline: December 1. Prize: First Place: $500; Second Place: $250; Third Place: $100. Judged by Brad Schreiber, author, journalist, consultant, and instructor.

JOANNA CATHERINE SCOTT NOVEL EXCERPT PRIZE CATEGORY

Soul-Making Keats Literary Competition Category, The Webhallow House, 1544 Sweetwood Dr., Broadmoor Village CA 94015-2029. **E-mail:** soulkeats@mail.com. **Website:** www.soulmakingcontest.us. **Contact:** Eileen Malone. Open annually to any writer. Deadline: November 30. Prize: First Place: $100; Second Place: $50; Third Place: $25.

SCREAMINMAMAS MAGICAL FICTION CONTEST

1911 Cleveland St., Hollywood FL 33020. **E-mail:** screaminmamas@gmail.com. **Website:** www.screaminmamas.com/contests. **Contact:** Darlene Pistocchi, editor/managing director. This contest celebrates moms and the magical spirit of the holidays. If you had an opportunity to be anything you wanted to be, what would you be? Transport yourself! Become that character and write a short story around that character. Can be any genre. Length: 800-3,000 words. Open only to moms. Deadline: June 30. Prize: complementary subscription to magazine, plus publication.

SCRIPTAPALOOZA TELEVISION WRITING COMPETITION

7775 Sunset Blvd., Suite #200, Hollywood CA 90046. (310)801-5366. **E-mail:** info@scriptapalooza.com. **Website:** www.scriptapaloozatv.com. Biannual competition accepting entries in 4 categories: Reality shows, sitcoms, original pilots, and 1-hour dramas. There are more than 30 producers, agents, and managers reading the winning scripts. Two past winners won Emmys because of Scriptapalooza and 1 past entrant now writes for Comedy Central. Winners announced February 15 and August 30. For contest results, visit website. Deadline: October 1 and April 15. Prize: First Place: $500; Second Place: $200; Third Place: $100 (in each category); production company consideration.

◌ SKIPPING STONES HONOR (BOOK) AWARDS

P.O. Box 3939, Eugene OR 97403. (541)342-4956. **Fax:** (541)342-4956. **E-mail:** editor@skippingstones.org. **Website:** www.skippingstones.org. **Contact:** Arun N. Toké. Estab. 1994. *Skipping Stones* is a well respected, multicultural literary magazine now in its 27th year. Annual award to promote multicultural and/or nature awareness through creative writings for children and teens and their educators. Seeks authentic, exceptional, child/youth friendly books that promote intercultural, international, intergenerational harmony, or understanding through creative ways. Deadline: February 1. Prize: Honor certificates; gold seals; reviews; press release/publicity. Judged by a multicultural committee of teachers, librarians, parents, students and editors.

◌ SKIPPING STONES YOUTH AWARDS

P.O. Box 3939, Eugene OR 97403-0939. (541)342-4956. **Fax:** (541)342-4956. **E-mail:** editor@skippingstones.org. **Website:** www.skippingstones.org. **Contact:** Arun N. Toké. Annual awards to promote creativity as well as multicultural and nature awareness in youth. Deadline: June 25. Prize: Publication in the autumn issue of *Skipping Stones*, honor certificate, subscription to magazine, plus 5 multicultural and/or nature books.

KAY SNOW WRITING CONTEST

Willamette Writers, Willamette Writers, 2108 Buck St., West Linn OR 97068. (503)305-6729. **Fax:** (503)344-6174. **E-mail:** reg@willamettewriters.com. **Website:** www.willamettewriters.com. Willamette Writers is the largest writers' organization in Oregon and one of the largest writers' organizations in the United States. It is a nonprofit, tax-exempt Oregon corporation led by volunteers. Elected officials and directors administer an active program of monthly meetings, special seminars, workshops and annual writing conference. Continuing with established programs and starting new ones is only made possible by strong volunteer support. The purpose of this annual writing contest, named in honor of Willamette Writer's founder, Kay Snow, is to help writers reach professional goals in writing in a broad array of categories and to encourage student writers. Deadline: April 23. Submission deadline begins January 15. Prize: One first prize of $300, 1 second place prize of $150, and a third place prize of $50 per winning entry in each of the 6 categories.

SOCIETY OF MIDLAND AUTHORS AWARD

Society of Midland Authors, Society of Midland Authors, P.O. Box 10419, Chicago IL 60610-0419. **E-mail:** marlenetbrill@comcast.net. **Website:** www.midlandauthors.com. **Contact:** Marlene Targ Brill, awards chair. Since 1957, the Society has presented annual awards for the best books written by Midwestern authors. The Society of Midland Authors (SMA) Award is presented to 1 title in each of 6 categories: adult nonfiction, adult fiction, adult biography and memoir, children's nonfiction, children's fiction, and poetry. Books and entry forms must be mailed to the 3 judges in each category; for a list of judges and the entry form, visit the website. Do not mail books to the society's P.O. box. Deadline: January 3. Prize: cash prize of $500 and a plaque that is awarded at the SMA banquet in May in Chicago.

STORYSOUTH MILLION WRITERS AWARD

E-mail: terry@storysouth.com. **Website:** www.storysouth.com. **Contact:** Terry Kennedy, editor. Estab. 2003. Annual award to honor and promote the best fiction published in online literary journals and magazines during the previous year. Most literary prizes for short fiction have traditionally ignored web-published fiction. This award aims to show that world-class fiction is being published online and to promote to the larger reading and literary community.

Deadline: August 15. Nominations of stories begins on March 15. Prize: Prize amounts subject to donation. Check website for details.

SYDNEY TAYLOR MANUSCRIPT COMPETITION

Association of Jewish Libraries, Sydney Taylor Manuscript Award Competition, 204 Park St., Montclair NJ 07042-2903. **E-mail:** stmacajl@aol.com. **Website:** www.jewishlibraries.org/main/Awards/SydneyTaylorManuscriptAward.aspx. **Contact:** Aileen Grossberg. Estab. 1985. This competition is for unpublished writers of fiction. Material should be for readers ages 8-13, with universal appeal that will serve to deepen the understanding of Judaism for all children, revealing positive aspects of Jewish life. Deadline: September 30. Prize: $1,000. Judging by qualified judges from within the Association of Jewish Libraries.

THREE CHEERS AND A TIGER

E-mail: editors@toasted-cheese.com. **Website:** www.toasted-cheese.com. **Contact:** Stephanie Lenz, editor. Contestants are to write a short story (following a specific theme) within 48 hours. Contests are held first weekend in spring (mystery) and first weekend in fall (science fiction/fantasy). Word limit announced at the start of the contest. Contest-specific information is announced 48 hours before the contest submission deadline. Results announced in April and October. Winners notified by e-mail. List of winners on website. Prize: Amazon gift certificates and publication. Blind-judged by 2 *Toasted Cheese* editors. Each judge uses his or her own criteria to choose entries.

TIMELESS LOVE/ROMANCE CONTEST

Sponsored by Oak Tree Press, 140 E. Palmer St., Taylorville IL 62568. **E-mail:** tl-contestadmin@oaktreebooks.com. **Website:** www.oaktreebooks.com. Annual contest for unpublished authors or authors shifting to a new genre. Accepts novels of all romance genres, from sweet to supernatural. Guidelines and entry forms are available for SASE. Deadline: July 31. Prize: Publication in both paper and e-book editions. Judged by publishing industry professionals who prescreen entries; publisher makes final selection.

TORONTO BOOK AWARDS

City of Toronto c/o Toronto Arts & Culture, Cultural Partnerships, City Hall, 9E, 100 Queen St. W., Toronto ON M5H 2N2 Canada. **E-mail:** cjones2@toronto.ca. **Website:** www.toronto.ca/book_awards. Estab. 1974.

The Toronto Book Awards honor authors of books of literary or artistic merit that are evocative of Toronto. Deadline: April 30. Prize: Each finalist receives $1,000 and the winning author receives the remaining prize money ($15,000 total in prize money available).

STEVEN TURNER AWARD FOR BEST FIRST WORK OF FICTION

6335 W. Northwest Hwy., #618, Dallas TX 75225. **Website:** www.texasinstituteofletters.org. Offered annually for work published January 1-December 31 for the best first book of fiction. Deadline: normally first week in January; see website for specific date. Prize: $1,000.

WAASNODE SHORT FICTION PRIZE

Passages North, Department of English, Northern Michigan University, 1401 Presque Isle Ave., Marquette MI 49855. (906)227-1203. **Fax:** (906)227-1096. **E-mail:** passages@nmu.edu. **Website:** www.passages-north.com. **Contact:** Jennifer Howard. Offered every 2 years to publish new voices in literary fiction (maximum 10,000 words). Guidelines for SASE or online. Submissions accepted online. Deadline: March 15. Submission period begins January 15. Prize: $1,000 and publication for winner; 2 honorable mentions are also published; all entrants receive a copy of *Passages North*. Judged by Rus Bradburd in 2014.

WABASH PRIZE FOR FICTION

Sycamore Review, Department of English, 500 Oval Dr., Purdue University, West Lafayette IN 47907. **E-mail:** sycamore@purdue.edu; sycamorefiction@purdue.edu. **Website:** www.sycamorereview.com/contest. **Contact:** Kara Krewer, editor in chief. Annual contest for unpublished fiction. Deadline: April 1. Submissions period begins March 1. Prize: $1,000 and publication.

THE WASHINGTON WRITERS' PUBLISHING HOUSE FICTION PRIZE

Washington Writers' Publishing House, P.O. Box 15271, Washington DC 20003. **E-mail:** wwphpress@gmail.com. **Website:** www.washingtonwriters.org. Fiction writers living within 75 miles of the Capitol are invited to submit a ms of either a novel or a collection of short stories (no more than 350 pages, double-spaced). Deadline: November 1. Submission period begins July 1. Prize: $1,000 and 50 copies of the book.

THE ROBERT WATSON LITERARY PRIZE IN FICTION AND POETRY

The Robert Watson Literary Prizes, *The Greensboro Review*, MFA Writing Program, 3302 MHRA Build-

ing, Greensboro NC 27402-6170. (336)334-5459. **E-mail:** jlclark@uncg.edu. **Website:** www.greensbororeview.org. **Contact:** Jim Clark, editor. Offered annually for fiction (up to 25 double-spaced pages) and poetry (up to 10 pages). Entries must be unpublished. No submissions by e-mail. Open to any writer. Deadline: September 15. Prize: $1,000 each for best short story and poem. Judged by editors of *The Greensboro Review*.

WESTERN AUSTRALIAN PREMIER'S BOOK AWARDS

State Library of Western Australia, Perth Cultural Centre, 25 Francis St., Perth WA 6000 Australia. (61)(8)9427-3151. **E-mail:** premiersbookawards@slwa.wa.gov.au. **Website:** pba.slwa.wa.gov.au. **Contact:** Karen de San Miguel. Estab. 1982. Annual competition for Australian citizens or permanent residents of Australia, or writers whose work has Australia as its primary focus. Categories: children's books, digital narrative, fiction, nonfiction, poetry, scripts, writing for young adults, West Australian history, and Western Australian emerging writers. Deadline: January 31. Prize: Awards $25,000 for Premier's Prize; awards $15,000 each for the Children's Books, Digital Narrative, Fiction, and Nonfiction categories; awards $10,000 each for the Poetry, Scripts, Western Australian History, Western Australian Emerging Writers, and Writing for Young Adults; awards $5,000 for People's Choice Award.

WESTERN HERITAGE AWARDS

National Cowboy & Western Heritage Museum, 1700 NE 63rd St., Oklahoma City OK 73111-7997. (405)478-2250. **Fax:** (405)478-4714. **Website:** www.nationalcowboymuseum.org. **Contact:** Jessica Limestall. Estab. 1961. The National Cowboy & Western Heritage Museum Western Heritage Awards were established to honor and encourage the legacy of those whose works in literature, music, film, and television reflect the significant stories of the American West. Accepted categories for literary entries: western novel, nonfiction book, art book, photography book, juvenile book, magazine article, or poetry book. The WHA are presented annually to encourage the accurate and artistic telling of great stories of the West through 16 categories of western literature, television, film and music; including fiction, nonfiction, children's books and poetry. See website for details and category definitions. Deadline: November 30. Prize: Awards a Wrangler bronze sculpture designed by famed western artist, John Free. Judged by a panel of judges selected each year with distinction in various fields of western art and heritage.

WESTERN WRITERS OF AMERICA

271CR 219, Encampment WY 82325. (307)329-8942. **Fax:** (307)327-5465 (call first). **E-mail:** wwa.moulton@gmail.com. **Website:** www.westernwriters.org. **Contact:** Candy Moulton, executive director. Estab. 1953. Seventeen Spur Award categories in various aspects of the American West. The nonprofit Western Writers of America has promoted and honored the best in Western literature with the annual Spur Awards, selected by panels of judges. Awards, for material published last year, are given for works whose inspirations, image and literary excellence best represent the reality and spirit of the American West.

WESTMORELAND POETRY & SHORT STORY CONTEST

Westmoreland Arts & Heritage Festival, 252 Twin Lakes Rd., Latrobe PA 15650-9415. (724)834-7474. **Fax:** (724)850-7474. **E-mail:** info@artsandheritage.com. **Website:** www.artsandheritage.com. **Contact:** Adam Shaffer. Offered annually for unpublished work. Two categories: Poem & Short Story. Short story entries no longer than 4,000 words. Family-oriented festival and contest. Deadline: February 16. Prizes: Award: $200; First Place: $125; Second Place: $100; Third Place: $75.

WILLA LITERARY AWARD

Women Writing the West, 8547 East Arapaho Rd., #J-541, Greenwood Village CO 80112-1436. **E-mail:** cynipid@comcast.net. **Website:** www.womenwritingthewest.org. **Contact:** Cynthia Becker. The WILLA Literary Award honors the year's best in published literature featuring women's or girls' stories set in the West. Women Writing the West (WWW), a nonprofit association of writers and other professionals writing and promoting the Women's West, underwrites and presents the nationally recognized award annually (for work published January 1-December 31). The award is named in honor of Pulitzer Prize winner Willa Cather, one of the country's foremost novelists. The award is given in 7 categories: historical fiction, contemporary fiction, original softcover fiction, creative nonfiction, scholarly nonfiction, poetry, and children's/young adult fiction/nonfiction. Entry forms available on the website. Deadline: November 1-February 1. Prize: $100 and a trophy. Finalist re-

ceives a plaque. Both receive digital and sticker award emblems for book covers. Notice of Winning and Finalist titles mailed to more than 4,000 booksellers, libraries, and others. Award announcement is in early August, and awards are presented to the winners and finalists at the annual WWW Fall Conference. Judged by professional librarians not affiliated with WWW.

THOMAS WOLFE FICTION PRIZE

North Carolina Writers' Network, Thomas Wolfe Fiction Prize, Great Smokies Writing Program, Attn: Nancy Williams, CPO #1860, UNC, Asheville NC 28805. **Website:** www.ncwriters.org. The Thomas Wolfe Fiction Prize honors internationally celebrated North Carolina novelist Thomas Wolfe. The prize is administered by Tommy Hays and the Great Smokies Writing Program at the University of North Carolina at Asheville. Deadline: January 30. Submissions period begins December 1. Prize: $1,000 and potential publication in *The Thomas Wolfe Review*.

TOBIAS WOLFF AWARD FOR FICTION

Bellingham Review, Mail Stop 9053, Western Washington University, Bellingham WA 98225. (360)650-4863. **E-mail:** bellingham.review@wwu.edu. **Website:** www.bhreview.org. **Contact:** Brenda Miller, editor in chief; Kaitlyn Teer, managing editor. Offered annually for unpublished work. Guidelines available on website; online submissions only. Categories: novel excerpts and short stories. Deadline: March 15. Submissions period begins December 1. Prize: $1,000, plus publication and subscription.

WORLD FANTASY AWARDS

P.O. Box 43, Mukilteo WA 98275. **E-mail:** sfexecsec@gmail.com. **Website:** www.worldfantasy.org. **Contact:** Peter Dennis Pautz, president. Offered annually for previously published work in several categories, including life achievement, novel, novella, short story, anthology, collection, artist, special award (pro) and special award (nonpro). Works are recommended by attendees of current and previous 2 years' conventions and a panel of judges. Awards to recognize excellence in fantasy literature worldwide. Deadline: June 1. Prize: Bust of H.P. Lovecraft. Judged by panel.

WORLD'S BEST SHORT-SHORT STORY CONTEST, NARRATIVE NONFICTION CONTEST & SOUTHEAST REVIEW POETRY CONTEST

The Southeast Review, English Department, Florida State University, Tallahassee FL 32306. **E-mail:** southeastreview@gmail.com. **Website:** www.southeastreview.org. **Contact:** Erin Hoover, editor. Estab. 1979. Annual award for unpublished short-short stories (500 words or less), poetry, and narrative nonfiction (6,000 words or less). Visit website for details. Deadline: March 15. Prize: $500 per category. Winners and finalists will be published in *The Southeast Review.*

WOW! WOMEN ON WRITING QUARTERLY FLASH FICTION CONTEST

WOW! Women on Writing, P.O. Box 41104, Long Beach CA 90853. **E-mail:** contestinfo@wow-womenonwriting.com. **Website:** www.wow-womenonwriting.com/contest.php. **Contact:** Angela Mackintosh, editor. Contest offered quarterly. "We are open to all themes and genres, although we do encourage writers to take a close look at our literary agent guest judge for the season if you are serious about winning." Entries must be 250-750 words. Deadline: August 31, November 30, February 28, May 31 Prize: First Place: $350 cash prize, $25 Amazon gift certificate, book from sponsor, story published on WOW! Women On Writing, interview on blog; Second Place: $250 cash prize, $25 Amazon gift certificate, book our sponsor, story published on WOW! Women On Writing, interview on blog; Third Place: $150 cash prize, $25 Amazon gift certificate, book from sponsor, story published on WOW! Women On Writing, interview on blog; 7 runners up: $25 Amazon gift certificate, book from sponsor, story published on WOW! Women on Writing, interview on blog; 10 honorable mentions: $20 gift certificate from Amazon, book our sponsor, story title and name published on WOW!Women On Writing.

WRITER'S DIGEST ANNUAL WRITING COMPETITION

Writer's Digest, a publication of F+W Media, Inc., 10151 Carver Rd., Suite 200, Cincinnati OH 45242. (715)445-4612, ext. 13430. **E-mail:** writing-competition@fwmedia.com. **Website:** www.writersdigest.com. **Contact:** Nicole Howard. Writing contest with 10 categories: Inspirational Writing (spiritual/religious, maximum 2,500 words); Memoir/Personal Essay (maximum 2,000 words); Magazine Feature Article (maximum 2,000 words); Short Story (genre, maximum 4,000 words); Short Story (mainstream/literary, maximum 4,000 words); Rhyming Poetry (maximum 32 lines); Nonrhyming Poetry (maximum 32 lines); Stage Play (first 15 pages and one-page synopsis); TV/Movie Script (first 15 pages and one-page synopsis).

Entries must be original, in English, unpublished/unproduced (except for Magazine Feature Articles), and not accepted by another publisher/producer at the time of submission. *Writer's Digest* retains one-time publication rights to the winning entries in each category. Deadline: May (early bird); June. Grand Prize: $3,000 and a trip to the Writer's Digest Conference to meet with editors and agents; First Place: $1,000 and $100 of Writer's Digest Books; Second Place: $500 and $100 of Writer's Digest Books; Third Place: $250 and $100 of Writer's Digest Books; Fourth Place: $100 and $50 of *Writer's Digest* Books.

○ WRITER'S DIGEST POPULAR FICTION AWARDS

Writer's Digest , 10151 Carver Road, Suite #200, Blue Ash OH 45242. (715)445-4612 ext. 13430. **E-mail:** WritersDigestWritingCompetition@fwmedia.com. **Website:** www.writersdigest.com. **Contact:** Nicole Howard, contest administrator. Annual competition/award for short stories. Categories include romance, crime, science fiction, thriller, horror, and young adult. Length: 4,000 words or fewer. Top Award Winners will be notified by mail by December 31. Winners will be listed in the May/June issue of Writer's Digest, and on writersdigest.com after the issue is published. Early-Bird Deadline: September 16; Final Deadline: October 15. Prizes: Grand Prize: $2,500, a trip to the *Writer's Digest* Conference, $100 off a purchase at writersdigest.com, and the latest edition of *Novel & Short Story Writer's Market*; First Place (1 for each of 6 categories): $500 cash, $100 off a purchase at writersdigest.com, and the latest edition of *Novel & Short Story Writer's Market*; Honorable Mentions (4 in each of 6 categories): will receive promotion at writersdigest.com and the latest edition of *Novel & Short Story Writer's Market*.

WRITER'S DIGEST SELF-PUBLISHED BOOK AWARDS

Writer's Digest, 10151 Carver Road, Suite #200, Blue Ash OH 45242. (715)445-4612, ext. 13430. **E-mail:** WritersDigestSelfPublishingCompetition@fwmedia.com. **Website:** www.writersdigest.com. **Contact:** Nicole Howard. Estab. 1992. Contest open to all English-language, self-published books for which the authors have paid the full cost of publication, or the cost of printing has been paid for by a grant or as part of a prize. Categories include: Mainstream/Literary Fiction, Genre Fiction, Nonfiction, Inspirational (spiritual/new age), Life Stories (biographies/autobiographies/family histories/memoirs), Children's Books, Reference Books (directories/encyclopedias/guide books), Poetry, and Middle-Grade/Young Adult Books. Judges reserve the right to re-categorize entries. Judges reserve the right to withhold prizes in any category. All winners will be notified by October 12. Early bird deadline: April 1; Deadline: May 1. Prizes: Grand Prize: $8,000, a trip to the Writer's Digest Conference, promotion in *Writer's Digest*, 10 copies of the book will be sent to major review houses, and a guaranteed review in *Midwest Book Review*; First Place (9 winners): $1,000 and promotion in *Writer's Digest*; Honorable Mentions: $50 worth of Writer's Digest Books and promotion on writersdigest.com. All entrants will receive a brief commentary from 1 of the judges.

WRITER'S DIGEST SELF-PUBLISHED E-BOOK AWARDS

Writer's Digest, 10151 Carver Road, Suite #200, Blue Ash OH 45242. (715)445-4612, ext. 13430. **E-mail:** WritersDigestSelfPublishingCompetition@fwmedia. com. **Website:** www.writersdigest.com. **Contact:** Nicole Howard. Estab. 2013. Contest open to all English-language, self-published e-books for which the authors have paid the full cost of publication, or the cost of publication has been paid for by a grant or as part of a prize. Categories include: Mainstream/Literary Fiction, Genre Fiction, Nonfiction (includes reference books), Inspirational (spiritual/new age), Life Stories (biographies/autobiographies/family histories/memoirs), Children's Books, Poetry, and Middle-Grade/Young Adult Books. Judges reserve the right to re-categorize entries. Judges reserve the right to withhold prizes in any category. All winners will be notified by December 31. Early bird deadline: August 1; Deadline: September 19. Prizes: Grand Prize: $3,000, promotion in *Writer's Digest*, a full 250-word (minimum) editorial review, $200 worth of Writer's Digest Books, and more; First Place (9 winners): $1,000 and promotion in *Writer's Digest*; Honorable Mentions: $50 worth of Writer's Digest Books and promotion on writersdigest.com. All entrants will receive a brief commentary from 1 of the judges.

WRITER'S DIGEST SHORT SHORT STORY COMPETITION

Writer's Digest, 10151 Carver Road, Suite 200, Blue Ash OH 45242. (715)445-4612; ext. 13430. **E-mail:** WritersDigestShortShortStoryCompetition@fwmedia.com. **Website:** www.writersdigest.com. **Contact:** Nicole Howard. Looking for fiction that's bold, brilliant, and brief. Send your best in 1,500 words or fewer. All entries must be original, unpublished, and not submitted elsewhere at the time of submission. *Writer's Digest* reserves one-time publication rights to the 1st-25th winning entries. Winners will be notified by Feb. 28. Early bird deadline: November 17. Final deadline: December 15. Prize: First Place: $3,000 and a trip to the Writer's Digest Conference; Second Place: $1,500; Third Place: $500; 4th-10th Place: $100; 11th-25th Place: $50 gift certificate for writersdigestshop.com.

WRITERS-EDITORS NETWORK INTERNATIONAL WRITING COMPETITION

CNW Publishing, P.O. Box A, North Stratford NH 03590-0167. **E-mail:** contestentry@writers-editors. com. **E-mail:** info@writers-editors.com. **Website:** www.writers-editors.com. **Contact:** Dana K. Cassell, executive director. Annual award to recognize publishable talent. Categories: Nonfiction (previously published article/essay/column/nonfiction book chapter; unpublished or self-published article/essay/column/nonfiction book chapter); fiction (unpublished or self-published short story or novel chapter); children's literature (unpublished or self-published short story/nonfiction article/book chapter/poem); poetry (unpublished or self-published free verse/traditional). Guidelines available online. Deadline: March 15. Prize: First Place: $100; Second Place: $75; Third Place: $50. All winners and Honorable Mentions will receive certificates as warranted. Judged by editors, librarians, and writers.

○ WRITERS GUILD OF ALBERTA AWARDS

Writers Guild of Alberta, Percy Page Centre, 11759 Groat Rd., Edmonton AB T5M 3K6 Canada. (780)422-8174. **Fax:** (780)422-2663. **E-mail:** mail@writersguild. ab.ca. **Website:** www.writersguild.ab.ca. **Contact:** Executive Director. Offers the following awards: Wilfrid Eggleston Award for Nonfiction; Georges Bugnet Award for Fiction; Howard O'Hagan Award for Short Story; Stephan G. Stephansson Award for Poetry; R. Ross Annett Award for Children's Literature; Gwen Pharis Ringwood Award for Drama; Jon Whyte Memorial Essay Prize; James H. Gray Award for Short

Nonfiction. Deadline: December 31. Prize: Winning authors receive $1,500; essay prize winners receive $700.

WRITERS' LEAGUE OF TEXAS BOOK AWARDS

Writers' League of Texas, 611 S. Congress Ave., Suite 200A-3, Austin TX 78704. (512)499-8914. **Fax:** (512)499-0441. **E-mail:** wlt@writersleague.org. **E-mail:** sara@writersleague.org. **Website:** www.writersleague.org. Open to Texas authors of books published the previous year. Authors are required to show proof of Texas residency, but are not required to be members of the Writers' League of Texas. Deadline: Open to submissions from October 1 to January 15. Prize: $750, a commemorative award, and an appearance at a WLT Third Thursday panel at BookPeople in Austin, TX.

⦿ ZOETROPE SHORT STORY CONTEST

Zoetrope: All Story, Zoetrope: All-Story, Attn: Fiction Editor, 916 Kearny St., San Francisco CA 94133. (415)788-7500. **E-mail:** contests@all-story.com. **Website:** www.all-story.com. Annual short fiction contest. Considers submissions of short stories and one-act plays no longer than 7,000 words. Excerpts from larger works, screenplays, treatments, and poetry will be returned unread. Deadline: October 1. Submissions period begins July 1. Prizes: First Place: $1,000 and publication on website; Second Place: $500; Third Place: $250.

ZONE 3 FICTION AWARD

Zone 3, Austin Peay State University, P.O. Box 4565, Clarksville TN 37044. (931)221-7031. **Fax:** (931)221-7149. **E-mail:** wallacess@apsu.edu. **Website:** www.apsu.edu/zone3/contests. **Contact:** Susan Wallace, managing editor. Annual contest for unpublished fiction. Open to any fiction writer. Deadline: April 1. Prize: $250 and publication.

CONFERENCES & WORKSHOPS

///

Why are conferences so popular? Writers and conference directors alike tell us it's because writing can be such a lonely business—at conferences writers have the opportunity to meet (and commiserate) with fellow writers, as well as meet and network with publishers, editors, and agents. Conferences and workshops provide some of the best opportunities for writers to make publishing contacts and pick up valuable information on the business, as well as the craft, of writing.

The bulk of the listings in this section are for conferences. Most conferences last from one day to one week and offer a combination of workshop-type writing sessions, panel discussions, and a variety of guest speakers. Topics may include all aspects of writing from fiction to poetry to scriptwriting, or they may focus on a specific type of writing, such as those conferences sponsored by the Romance Writers of America (RWA) for writers of romance

or by the Society of Children's Book Writers and Illustrators (SCBWI) for writers of children's books.

Workshops, however, tend to run longer—usually one to two weeks. Designed to operate like writing classes, most require writers to be prepared to work on and discuss their fiction while attending. An important benefit of workshops is the opportunity they provide writers for an intensive critique of their work, often by professional writing teachers and established writers.

Each of the listings here includes information on the specific focus of an event as well as planned panels, guest speakers, and workshop topics. It is important to note, however, some conference directors were still in the planning stages for 2016 when we contacted them. If it was not possible to include 2016 dates, fees, or topics, we provided the most up-to-date information available so you can get an idea of what to expect. For the most current information, it's best to check the conference website or send a self-addressed, stamped envelope to the director in question about three months before the date(s) listed.

FINDING A CONFERENCE

Many writers try to make it to at least one conference a year, but cost and location count as much as subject matter or other considerations when determining which conference to attend. There are conferences in almost every state and province, and even some in Europe open to North Americans.

To make it easier for you to find a conference close to home—or to find one in an exotic locale to fit into your vacation plans—we've divided this section into geographic regions. The conferences appear in alphabetical order under the appropriate regional heading.

Note that conferences appear under the regional heading according to where they will be held, which is sometimes different from the address given as the place to register or send for information. The regions are as follows:

NORTHEAST (PAGE 435): Connecticut, Maine, Massachusetts, New Hampshire, New York, Rhode Island, Vermont

MIDATLANTIC (PAGE 437): Washington DC, Delaware, Maryland, New Jersey, Pennsylvania

MIDSOUTH (PAGE 439): North Carolina, South Carolina, Tennessee, Virginia, West Virginia

SOUTHEAST (PAGE 440): Alabama, Arkansas, Florida, Georgia, Louisiana, Mississippi, Puerto Rico

MIDWEST (PAGE 441): Illinois, Indiana, Kentucky, Michigan, Ohio

NORTH CENTRAL (PAGE 443): Iowa, Minnesota, Nebraska, North Dakota, South Dakota, Wisconsin

SOUTH CENTRAL (PAGE 443): Colorado, Kansas, Missouri, New Mexico, Oklahoma, Texas

WEST (PAGE 445): Arizona, California, Hawaii, Nevada, Utah

NORTHWEST (PAGE 448): Alaska, Idaho, Montana, Oregon, Washington, Wyoming

CANADA (PAGE 450)

INTERNATIONAL (PAGE 450)

LEARNING AND NETWORKING

Besides learning from workshop leaders and panelists in formal sessions, writers at conferences also benefit from conversations with other attendees. Writers on all levels enjoy sharing insights. A conversation over lunch can reveal a new market for your work or let you know which editors are most receptive to the work of new writers. You can find out about recent editor changes and about specific agents. A casual chat could lead to a new contact or resource in your area.

Many editors and agents make visiting conferences a part of their regular search for new writers. A cover letter or query that starts with "I met you at the Green Mountain Writers Conference," or "I found your talk on your company's new romance line at the Moonlight and Magnolias Writers Conference most interesting ..." may give you a small leg up on the competition.

While a few writers have been successful in selling their manuscripts at a conference, the availability of editors and agents does not usually mean these folks will have the time to read your novel or six best short stories (unless, of course, you've scheduled an individual meeting with them in advance). While editors and agents are glad to meet writers and discuss work in general terms, usually they don't have the time (or energy) to give an extensive critique during a conference. In other words, use the conference as a way to make a first, brief contact.

SELECTING A CONFERENCE

Besides the obvious considerations of time, place, and cost, choose your conference based on your writing goals. If, for example, your goal is to improve the quality of your writing, it will be more helpful to choose a hands-on craft workshop rather than a conference offering a series of panels on mar-

keting and promotion. If, on the other hand, you are a science fiction novelist who would like to meet your fans, try one of the many science fiction conferences or "cons" held throughout the country and the world.

Look for panelists and workshop instructors whose work you admire and who seem to be writing in your general area. Check for specific panels or discussions of topics relevant to what you are writing now. Think about the size—would you feel more comfortable with a small workshop of eight people or a large group of one hundred or more attendees?

If your funds are limited, start by looking for conferences close to home, but you may want to explore those that offer contests with cash prizes—and a chance to recoup your expenses. A few conferences and workshops also offer scholarships, but the competition is stiff and writers interested in these should seek out the requirements early. Finally, students may want to look for conferences and workshops that offer college credit. You will find these options included in the listings here. Again, check the conference website or send a self-addressed, stamped envelope for the most current details.

BREAD LOAF IN SICILY WRITERS' CONFERENCE

Middlebury College, Middlebury VT 05753. (802)443-5286. **Fax:** (802)443-2087. **E-mail:** blwc@middlebury.edu. **Website:** www.middlebury.edu/bread-loaf-conferences/blSicily. Estab. 2011.

COSTS The fee (contributor, $2,820) includes the conference program, transfer to and from Palermo Airport, six nights of lodging, three meals daily (except for Wednesday), wine reception at the readings, and an excursion to the ancient ruins of Segesta. The charge for an additional person is $1,575.

ACCOMMODATIONS Accommodations are single rooms with private bath. Breakfast and lunch are served at the hotel and dinner is available at select Erice restaurants. A double room is possible for those who would like to be accompanied by a spouse or significant other.

ADDITIONAL INFORMATION "Application Period: November 1-March 15. Rolling admissions. Space is limited."

BREAD LOAF ORION ENVIRONMENTAL WRITERS' CONFERENCE

Middlebury College, Middlebury VT 05753. (802)443-5286. **Fax:** (802)443-2087. **E-mail:** blwc@middlebury.edu. **Website:** www.middlebury.edu/bread-loaf-conferences/BLOrion. Estab. 2014.

ACCOMMODATIONS Mountain campus of Middlebury College in Vermont.

ADDITIONAL INFORMATION The event is designed to hone the skills of people interested in producing literary writing about the environment and the natural world. The conference is co-sponsored by the Bread Loaf Writers' Conference, Orion magazine, and Middlebury College's Environmental Studies Program.

BREAD LOAF WRITERS' CONFERENCE

Middlebury College, Middlebury College, Middlebury VT 05753. (802)443-5286. **Fax:** (802)443-2087. **E-mail:** blwc@middlebury.edu. **Website:** www.middlebury.edu/bread-loaf-conferences/bl_writers. Estab. 1926.

ACCOMMODATIONS Bread Loaf Campus in Ripton, Vermont.

ADDITIONAL INFORMATION 2015 Conference Dates: August 12-22. Location: mountain campus of Middlebury College in Vermont. Average attendance: 230. The application deadline for the 2015 event is March 1, 2015; there is $15 application fee.

CAPE COD WRITERS CENTER ANNUAL CONFERENCE

P.O. Box 408, Osterville MA 02655. **E-mail:** writers@capecodwriterscenter.org. **Website:** www.capecodwriterscenter.org. **Contact:** Nancy Rubin Stuart, executive director.

COSTS Vary, depending on the number of courses selected.

ACCOMMODATIONS Held at Resort and Conference Center of Hyannis, Hyannis, MA.

GREEN MOUNTAIN WRITERS CONFERENCE

47 Hazel St., Rutland VT 05701. (802)236-6133. **E-mail:** ydaley@sbcglobal.net. **E-mail:** yvonnedaley@me.com. **Website:** vermontwriters.com. **Contact:** Yvonne Daley, director. Estab. 1998.

COSTS $500 before May 1; $550 minimum after May 1. Partial scholarships are available

ACCOMMODATIONS Dramatically reduced rates at The Mountain Top Inn and Resort for attendees. Close to other area hotels, B&Bs in Rutland County, Vermont.

ADDITIONAL INFORMATION Participants' mss can be read and commented on at a cost. Sponsors contests. Conference publishes a literary magazine featuring work of participants. Brochures available on website or e-mail. "We offer the opportunity to learn from some of the nation's best writers at a small, supportive conference in a lakeside setting that allows one-to-one feedback. Participants often continue to correspond and share work after conferences."

IWWG ANNUAL CONFERENCE

International Women's Writing Guild Conference, International Women's Writing Guild, P.O. Box 810, Gracie Station, New York NY 10028. (212)737-7536. **Fax:** (212)737-9469. **E-mail:** iwwgquestions@gmail.com. **Website:** www.iwwg.org.

KINDLING WORDS EAST

VT **Website:** www.kindlingwords.org.

THE MACDOWELL COLONY

100 High St., Peterborough NH 03458. (603)924-3886. **Fax:** (603)924-9142. **E-mail:** admissions@macdowellcolony.org. **Website:** www.macdowellcolony.org. Estab. 1907.

COSTS Travel reimbursement and stipends are available for participants of the residency, based on need. There are no residency fees.

MUSE AND THE MARKETPLACE

Grub Street, 162 Boylston St., 5th Floor, Boston MA 02116. (617)695-0075. **E-mail:** info@grubstreet.org. **Website:** www.grubstreet.org/muse.

The Muse and the Marketplace is a three-day literary conference designed to give aspiring writers a better understanding about the craft of writing fiction and nonfiction, to prepare them for the changing world of publishing and promotion, and to create opportunities for meaningful networking. On all three days, prominent and nationally-recognized established and emerging authors lead sessions on the craft of writing—the "muse" side of things—while editors, literary agents, publicists and other industry professionals lead sessions on the business side—the "marketplace."

ACCOMMODATIONS Boston Park Plaza Hotel.

⊙ ODYSSEY FANTASY WRITING WORKSHOP

P.O. Box 75, Mont Vernon NH 03057. (603)673-6234. **E-mail:** jcavelos@sff.net. **Website:** www.odyssey-workshop.org. Estab. 1996.

COSTS In 2015: $1,995 tuition, $830 housing (double room), $1,660 (single room); $35 application fee, $600 food (approximate), $650 processing fee to receive college credit.

ADDITIONAL INFORMATION Students must apply and include a writing sample. Application deadline: April 8. Students' works are critiqued throughout the 6 weeks. Workshop information available in October. For brochure/guidelines, send SASE, e-mail, visit website, or call. Accepts inquiries by SASE, e-mail, phone.

RT BOOKLOVERS CONVENTION

55 Bergen St., Brooklyn NY 11201. **Website:** rtconvention.com.

COSTS $489 normal registration; $425 for industry professionals (agents, editors). Many other pricing options available. See website.

ACCOMMODATIONS Rooms available nearby.

THE SOUTHAMPTON WRITERS CONFERENCE

239 Montauk Highway, Southampton NY 11968. (631)632-5030. **E-mail:** southamptonarts@stonybrook.edu. **Website:** www.stonybrook.edu/southamp-ton/mfa/summer/cwl_home.html. Estab. 1975. Stony Brook Southampton, 239 Montauk Highway, Southampton NY 11968. (631) 632-5030. **Fax:** (631)632-2578. **E-mail:** southamptonwriters@notes.cc.sunysb.edu. **Website:** www.stonybrook.edu/writers. **Contact:** Christian McLean, conference coordinator. Estab. 1975. Annual. Conference held in July. Conference duration: 12 days. Average attendance: 120. The primary work of the conference is conducted in writing workshops in the novel, short story, poem, play, literary essay and memoir. Site: The seaside campus of Stony Brook Southampton is located in the heart of the Hamptons, a renowned resort area only 70 miles from New York City. During free time, participants can draw inspiration from Atlantic beaches or explore the charming seaside towns. Faculty has included Frank McCourt, Billy Collins, Mark Doty, Roger Rosenblatt, Ursula Hegi, Meg Wolitzer, David Rakoff Alan Alda, and Jules Feiffer, Melissa Bank and Matt Klam.

UNICORN WRITERS CONFERENCE

P.O. Box 176, Redding CT 06876. (203)938-7405. **E-mail:** unicornwritersconference@gmail.com. **Website:** www.unicornwritersconference.com.

ACCOMMODATIONS Held at Reid Castle, Purchase, NY. Directions available on event website.

WESLEYAN WRITERS CONFERENCE

Wesleyan University, 294 High St., Room 207, Middletown CT 06459. (860)685-3604. **Fax:** (860)685-2441. **E-mail:** agreene@wesleyan.edu. **Website:** www.wesleyan.edu/writing/conference. Estab. 1956.

ACCOMMODATIONS Meals are provided on campus. Lodging is available on campus or in town.

ADDITIONAL INFORMATION Ms critiques are available, but not required.

WRITER'S DIGEST CONFERENCES

F+W Media, Inc., 10151 Carver Rd., Suite 200, Blue Ash OH 45242. **E-mail:** jill.ruesch@fwmedia.com. **E-mail:** phil.sexton@fwmedia.com. **Website:** www.writersdigestconference.com. Estab. 1995.

COSTS Cost varies by location and year. There are typically different pricing options for those who wish to stay for the entire event vs. daylong passes.

ACCOMMODATIONS A block of rooms at the event hotel are reserved for guests.

YADDO

The Corporation of Yaddo Residencies, P.O. Box 395, 312 Union Ave., Saratoga Springs NY 12866-0395.

(518)584-0746. **Fax:** (518)584-1312. **E-mail:** chwait@yaddo.org. **Website:** www.yaddo.org. **Contact:** Candace Wait, program director. Estab. 1900. Two seasons: large season is May-August; small season is October-May (stays from 2 weeks to 2 months; average stay is 5 weeks). Accepts 230 artists/year. Accommodates approximately 35 artists in large season. Those qualified for invitations to Yaddo are highly qualified writers, visual artists (including photographers), composers, choreographers, performance artists and film and video artists who are working at the professional level in their fields. Artists who wish to work collaboratively are encouraged to apply. An abiding principle at Yaddo is that applications for residencies are judged on the quality of the artists' work and professional promise. Site includes four small lakes, a rose garden, woodland, swimming pool, tennis courts. Yaddo's nonrefundable application fee is $30, to which is added a fee for media uploads ranging from $5-10 depending on the discipline. Application fees must be paid by credit card. Two letters of recommendation are requested. Applications are considered by the Admissions Committee and invitations are issued by March 15 (deadline: January 1) and October 1 (deadline: August 1). Information available on website.

COSTS No fee is charged; residency includes room, board and studio space. Limited travel expenses are available to artists accepted for residencies at Yaddo.

ACCOMMODATIONS No stipends are offered.

MIDATLANTIC

BALTIMORE COMIC-CON

Baltimore Convention Center, One West Pratt St., Baltimore MD 21201. (410)526-7410. **E-mail:** general@baltimorecomiccon.com. **Website:** www.baltimorecomiccon.com. **Contact:** Marc Nathan. Estab. 1999.

ACCOMMODATIONS Does not offer overnight accommodations. Provides list of area hotels and lodging options.

ADDITIONAL INFORMATION For brochure, visit website.

BALTIMORE WRITERS' CONFERENCE

English Department, Liberal Arts Bldg., Towson University, 8000 York Rd., Towson MD 21252. (410)704-3695. **E-mail:** prwr@towson.edu. **Website:** baltimorewritersconference.org. Estab. 1994.

○ This conference has sold out in the past.

ACCOMMODATIONS Hotels are close by, if required.

ADDITIONAL INFORMATION Writers may register through the BWA website. Send inquiries via e-mail.

BAY TO OCEAN WRITERS CONFERENCE

P.O. Box 1773, Easton MD 21601. (443)786-4536. **E-mail:** info@baytoocean.com. **Website:** www.baytoocean.com. Estab. 1998.

COSTS Adults $115, students $55. A paid ms review is also available—details on website. Includes continental breakfast and networking lunch.

ADDITIONAL INFORMATION Registration is on website. Pre-registration is required; no registration at door. Conference usually sells out one month in advance. Conference is for all levels of writers.

GREATER LEHIGH VALLEY WRITERS GROUP 'THE WRITE STUFF' WRITERS CONFERENCE

3650 Nazareth Pike, PMB #136, Bethlehem PA 18020-1115. **E-mail:** writestuffchair@glvwg.org. **Website:** www.glvwg.org. Estab. 1993.

ADDITIONAL INFORMATION "The Writer's Flash contest is judged by conference participants. Write 100 words or less in fiction, creative nonfiction, or poetry. Brochures available in January by SASE, or by phone, e-mail, or on website. Accepts inquiries by SASE, e-mail or phone. Agents and editors attend conference. For updated info refer to the website. Greater Lehigh Valley Writers Group hosts a friendly conference and gives you the most for your money. Breakout rooms offer craft topics, business of publishing, editor and agent panels. Book fair with book signing by published authors and presenters."

HIGHLIGHTS FOUNDATION FOUNDERS WORKSHOPS

814 Court St., Honesdale PA 18431. (570)253-1122. **Fax:** (570)253-0179. **E-mail:** klbrown@highlightsfoundation.org. **E-mail:** jo.lloy@highlightsfoundation.org. **Website:** highlightsfoundation.org. **Contact:** Kent L. Brown, Jr. Estab. 2000.

COSTS Prices vary based on workshop. Check website for details.

ACCOMMODATIONS Coordinates pickup at local airport. Offers overnight accommodations. Participants stay in guest cabins on the wooded grounds surrounding Highlights Founders' home adjacent to the house/conference center.

ADDITIONAL INFORMATION Some workshops require pre-workshop assignment. Brochure available for SASE, by e-mail, on website, by phone, by fax. Accepts inquiries by phone, fax, e-mail, SASE. Editors attend conference. "Applications will be reviewed and accepted on a first-come, first-served basis, applicants must demonstrate specific experience in writing area of workshop they are applying for—writing samples are required for many of the workshops."

MONTROSE CHRISTIAN WRITERS' CONFERENCE

218 Locust St., Montrose PA 18801. (570)278-1001 or (800)598-5030. **Fax:** (570)278-3061. **E-mail:** mbc@montrosebible.org. **Website:** montrosebible.org. Estab. 1990.

COSTS Tuition is $180.

ACCOMMODATIONS Will meet planes in Binghamton, NY and Scranton, PA. On-site accommodations: room and board $340-475/conference, including food (2015 rates). RV court available.

ADDITIONAL INFORMATION "Writers can send work ahead of time and have it critiqued for a small fee." The attendees are usually church related. The writing has a Christian emphasis. Conference information available in April. For brochure, visit website, e-mail or call. Accepts inquiries by phone or e-mail.

JENNY MCKEAN MOORE COMMUNITY WORKSHOPS

English Department, George Washington University, 801 22nd St. NW, Rome Hall, Suite 760, Washington DC 20052. (202)994-6180. **Fax:** (202)994-7915. **E-mail:** lpageinc@gwu.edu. **Website:** www.gwu.edu/~english/creative_jennymckeanmoore.html. **Contact:** Lisa Page, acting director of creative writing. Estab. 1976.

ADDITIONAL INFORMATION Admission is competitive and by decided by the quality of a submitted ms.

NEW JERSEY ROMANCE WRITERS PUT YOUR HEART IN A BOOK CONFERENCE

P.O. Box 513, Plainsboro NJ 08536. **Website:** www.njromancewriters.org/conference.html. Estab. 1984.

PENNWRITERS CONFERENCE

5706 Sonoma Ridge, Missouri City TX 77459. **E-mail:** conferenceco@pennwriters.org. **Website:** www.pennwriters.org/prod. **Contact:** Carol A. Silvis, conference coordinator. Estab. 1987.

As the official writing organization of Pennsylvania, Pennwriters has 8 different areas that have smaller writing groups that meet. Each of these areas sometimes has their own, smaller

event during the year in addition to the annual writing conference.

ACCOMMODATIONS $289 for members, $324 for nonmembers.

ADDITIONAL INFORMATION Sponsors contest. Published authors judge fiction in various categories. Agent/editor appointments are available on a first-come, first serve basis.

PHILADELPHIA WRITERS' CONFERENCE

P.O. Box 7171, Elkins Park PA 19027-0171. (215) 619-7422. **E-mail:** info@pwcwriters.org. **E-mail:** info@pwcwriters.org. **Website:** pwcwriters.org. Estab. 1949.

"A 3-day conference that offers from 14 workshops, usually four seminars, several 'ms rap' sessions, a Friday Roundtable Forum Buffet with speaker, and the Saturday Annual Awards Banquet with speaker. The 150 to 200 conferees may submit mss in advance for criticism by the workshop leaders, and are eligible to submit entries in about a dozen contest categories. Cash prizes and certificates are given to first and second place winners, plus full tuition for the following year's conference to first place winners."

ACCOMMODATIONS Wyndham Hotel (formerly the Holiday Inn), Independence Mall, Fourth and Arch Streets, Philadelphia, PA 19106-2170. Hotel offers discount for early registration.

ADDITIONAL INFORMATION Accepts inquiries by e-mail. Agents and editors attend the conference. Many questions are answered online.

SCBWI—NEW JERSEY; ANNUAL SUMMER CONFERENCE

SCBWI-New Jersey: Society of Children's Book Writers & Illustrators, New Jersey NJ **Website:** njscbwi.com. **Contact:** Leeza Hernandez, regional advisor.

WINTER POETRY & PROSE GETAWAY

18 N. Richards Ave., Ventnor NJ 08406. (888)887-2105. **E-mail:** info@wintergetaway.com; amanda@murphywriting.com. **Website:** www.wintergetaway.com. **Contact:** Peter Murphy. Estab. 1994.

ACCOMMODATIONS See website or call for current fee information.

ADDITIONAL INFORMATION Previous faculty has included Julianna Baggott, Christian Bauman, Laure-Anne Bosselaar, Kurt Brown, Mark Doty (National Book Award winner), Stephen Dunn (Pulitzer Prize winner), Dorianne Laux, Carol Plum-Ucci, James Richardson, Mimi Schwartz, Terese Svoboda, and more.

MIDSOUTH

AMERICAN CHRISTIAN WRITERS CONFERENCES

P.O. Box 110390, Nashville TN 37222-0390. (800)219-7483. **Fax:** (615)834-7736. **E-mail:** acwriters@aol.com. **Website:** www.acwriters.com. **Contact:** Reg Forder, director. Estab. 1981.

COSTS Costs vary based on conference. Prices also depend on whether it is a conference or a mentoring retreat.

ACCOMMODATIONS Special rates are available at the host hotel (usually a major chain like Holiday Inn).

ADDITIONAL INFORMATION Send a SASE for conference brochures/guidelines.

ASSOCIATION OF WRITERS & WRITING PROGRAMS ANNUAL CONFERENCE

Association of Writers & Writing Programs, George Mason University, 4400 University Drive, MSN 1E3, Fairfax VA 22030-4444. (703)993-4317. **Fax:** (703)993-4302. **E-mail:** conference@awpwriter.org; events@awpwriter.org. **Website:** www.awpwriter.org/awp_conference. Estab. 1992.

ADDITIONAL INFORMATION Upcoming conference locations include Minneapolis (2015), Los Angeles (March 30-April 2, 2016), and Washington, D.C. (February 8-11, 2017).

CELEBRATION OF SOUTHERN LITERATURE

Southern Lit Alliance, 3069 S. Broad St., Suite 2, Chattanooga TN 37408-3056. (423)267-1218. **Fax:** (866)483-6831. **E-mail:** srobinson@southernlitalliance.org. **Website:** www.southernlitalliance.org. **Contact:** Susan Robinson.

This event happens every other year in odd-numbered years.

CHRISTOPHER NEWPORT UNIVERSITY WRITERS' CONFERENCE & WRITING CONTEST

(757)269-4368. **E-mail:** eleanor.taylor@cnu.edu. **Website:** cnu.edu/lifelonglearning/conferences/. Estab. 1981.

ACCOMMODATIONS Provides list of area hotels.

ADDITIONAL INFORMATION 2015 conference dates are set for February 27-28.

HAMPTON ROADS WRITERS CONFERENCE

P.O. Box 56228, Virginia Beach VA 23456. **E-mail:** hrwriters@cox.net. **Website:** hamptonroadswriters.org.

COSTS Maximum of $255. Costs vary. There are discounts for members, for early bird registration, for students and more

HIGHLAND SUMMER CONFERENCE

Box 7014, Radford University, Radford VA 24142-7014. **E-mail:** tburriss@radford.edu; rbderrick@radford.edu. **Website:** tinyurl.com/q8z8ej9. **Contact:** Dr. Theresa Burriss, Ruth Derrick. Estab. 1978.

JAMES RIVER WRITERS CONFERENCE

2319 East Broad St., Richmond VA 23223. (804)433-3790. **Fax:** (804)291-1466. **E-mail:** info@jamesriverwriters.com; fallconference@jamesriverwriters.com. **Website:** www.jamesriverwriters.com. Estab. 2003.

COSTS $240-290.

ACCOMMODATIONS Hilton Garden Inn, 501 E. Broad St.

⊙ KILLER NASHVILLE

P.O. Box 680759, Franklin TN 37068-0686. (615)599-4032. **E-mail:** contact@killernashville.com. **Website:** www.killernashville.com. **Contact:** Maria Giordano. Estab. 2006.

COSTS Early Bird Registration: $210 (February 15); Advanced Registration: $230 (April 30); $230 for three day full registration.

ACCOMMODATIONS The Omni Nashville Hotel has all rooms available for the Killer Nashville Writers' Conference.

ADDITIONAL INFORMATION Additional information about registration is provided online.

NORTH CAROLINA WRITERS' NETWORK FALL CONFERENCE

P.O. Box 21591, Winston-Salem NC 27120. (336)293-8844. **E-mail:** mail@ncwriters.org. **Website:** www.ncwriters.org. Estab. 1985.

COSTS Approximately $250 (includes 4 meals).

ACCOMMODATIONS Special rates are usually available at the conference hotel, but conferees must make their own reservations.

ADDITIONAL INFORMATION Available at www.ncwriters.org.

SEWANEE WRITERS' CONFERENCE

735 University Ave., 119 Gailor Hall, Stamler Center, Sewanee TN 37383-1000. (931)598-1654. **E-mail:** allatham@sewanee.edu. **Website:** www.sewaneewriters.org. **Contact:** Adam Latham. Estab. 1990.

COSTS $1,000 for tuition and $800 for room, board, and activity costs

ACCOMMODATIONS Participants are housed in single rooms in university dormitories. Bathrooms are shared by small groups.

SOUTH CAROLINA WRITERS WORKSHOP

4840 Forest Drive, Suite 6B: PMB 189, Columbia SC 29206. **E-mail:** scwwliaison@gmail.com; scww2013@gmail.com. **Website:** www.myscww.org. Estab. 1991.

WILDACRES WRITERS WORKSHOP

233 S. Elm St., Greensboro NC 27401. (336)255-8210. **E-mail:** judihill@aol.com. **Website:** www.wildacreswriters.com. **Contact:** Judi Hill, Director. Estab. 1985. **COSTS** The current price is $790. Check the website for more info.

ADDITIONAL INFORMATION Include a one-page writing sample with your registration. See the website for information.

SOUTHEAST

ARKANSAS WRITERS' CONFERENCE

6817 Gingerbread Lane, Little Rock AR 72204. (501)833-2756. **E-mail:** breannacone1@yahoo.com. **Website:** www.arkansaswritersconference.org.

ATLANTA WRITERS CONFERENCE

E-mail: awconference@gmail.com. **E-mail:** gjweinstein@yahoo.com. **Website:** www.atlantawritersconference.com. **Contact:** George Weinstein.

ACCOMMODATIONS Westin Airport Atlanta Hotel

ADDITIONAL INFORMATION There is a free shuttle that runs between the airport and the hotel.

WRITERS IN PARADISE

Eckerd College, 4200 54th Ave. South, St. Petersburg FL 33711. (727) 864-7994. **Fax:** (727) 864-7575. **E-mail:** wip@eckerd.edu. **Website:** writersinparadise.eckerd.edu/. Estab. 2005.

ADDITIONAL INFORMATION Application (December deadline) materials are required of all attendees.

FLORIDA CHRISTIAN WRITERS CONFERENCE

530 Lake Kathryn Circle, Casselberry FL 32707. (386)295-3902. **E-mail:** FloridaCWC@aol.com. **Website:** floridacwc.net. **Contact:** Eva Marie Everson & Mark T. Hancock. Estab. 1988.

FLORIDA ROMANCE WRIITERS FUN IN THE SUN CONFERENCE

Florida Romance Writers, P.O. Box 550562, Fort Lauderdale FL 33355. **E-mail:** FRWfuninthesun@yahoo.com. **Website:** frwfuninthesunmain.blogspot.com. Estab. 1986.

GULF COAST WRITERS CONFERENCE

P.O. Box 35038, Panama City FL 32412. (800)628-6028. **E-mail:** PulpwoodPress@gmail.com. **Website:** www.gulfcoastwritersconference.com. Estab. 1999.

Although the conference is free, there are affordable add-on features, such as a ms critique, editor/agent appointments, keynote luncheons, and more.

KACHEMAK BAY WRITERS' CONFERENCE

Kenai Peninsula College - Kachemak Bay Campus, 533 East Pioneer Ave., Homer AK 99603. (907)235-7743. **E-mail:** iyconf@uaa.alaska.edu. **Website:** writersconference.uaa.alaska.edu.

Previous keynote speakers have included Dave Barry, Amy Tan, Jeffrey Eugenides, and Anne Lamott.

COSTS See the website. Some scholarships available.

ACCOMMODATIONS Homer is 225 miles south of Anchorage, Alaska on the southern tip of the Kenai Peninsula and the shores of Kachemak Bay. There are multiple hotels in the area.

MONTEVALLO LITERARY FESTIVAL

Sta. 6420, University of Montevallo, Montevallo AL 35115. (205)665-6420. **Fax:** (205)665-6422. **E-mail:** murphyj@montevallo.edu. **Website:** www.montevallo.edu/arts-sciences/college-of-arts-sciences/departments/english-foreign-languages/student-organizations/montevallo-literary-festival/. **Contact:** Dr. Jim Murphy, director. Estab. 2003.

MOONLIGHT AND MAGNOLIAS WRITER'S CONFERENCE

Georgia Romance Writers, 3741 Casteel Park Dr., Marietta GA 30064. **Website:** www.georgiaromancewriters.org/mm-conference/. Estab. 1982.

OZARK CREATIVE WRITERS, INC. CONFERENCE

P.O. Box 9076, Fayetteville AR 72703. **E-mail:** ozarkcreativewriters1@gmail.com. **Website:** www.ozarkcreativewriters.org.

A full list of sessions and speakers is online. The conference usually has agents and/or editors in attendance to meet with writers.

SLEUTHFEST

MWA Florida Chapter, **E-mail:** Sleuthfestinfo@yahoo.com. **Website:** sleuthfest.com.

ACCOMMODATIONS Doubletree by Hilton in Deerfield Beach

SOUTHEASTERN WRITERS ASSOCIATION–ANNUAL WRITERS WORKSHOP

161 Woodstone, Athens GA 30605. **E-mail:** purple@southeasternwriters.org. **Website:** www.southeasternwriters.com. Estab. 1975.

ACCOMMODATIONS Multiple hotels available in St. Simon's Island, GA.

MIDWEST

ANTIOCH WRITERS' WORKSHOP

c/o Antioch University Midwest, 900 Dayton St., Yellow Springs OH 45387. (937)769-1803. **E-mail:** info@antiochwritersworkshop.com. **Website:** www.antiochwritersworkshop.com. **Contact:** Sharon Short, director. Estab. 1986.

ACCOMMODATIONS Accommodations are available at local hotels and bed & breakfasts.

ADDITIONAL INFORMATION The easiest way to contact this event is through the online website contact form.

BOOKS-IN-PROGRESS CONFERENCE

Carnegie Center for Literacy and Learning, 251 West Second Street, Lexington KY 40507. (859)254-4175. **E-mail:** lwhitaker@carnegiecenterlex.org. **Website:** carnegiecenterlex.org/. **Contact:** Laura Whitaker. Estab. 2010.

Note: Personal meetings with faculty (agents and editors) are only available to full conference participants. Limited slots available. Please choose only one agent – only one pitching session per participant.

ACCOMMODATIONS Several area hotels are nearby.

BUSINESS OF WRITING INTERNATIONAL SUMMIT

P.O. Box 768, Simpsonville KY 40204. (502)303-7926. **E-mail:** larry@tbowt.com. **Website:** www.businessofwritingsummit.com. **Contact:** Larry DeKay or Peggy DeKay. Estab. 2012.

COSTS $200-300 range

ACCOMMODATIONS An official hotel is designated each year for attendees that offers a special money-saving room rate and is within close proximity of the event. Details available online.

ADDITIONAL INFORMATION This is a fun, exciting and energy-filled event which allows unprecedented access to speakers and exhibitors. Event organizers Larry and Peggy DeKay pride themselves on creating a warm and hospitable environment where attendees feel welcome and have the opportunity to make new and lasting friendships and business relationships.

CAPON SPRINGS WRITERS' WORKSHOP

2836 Westbrook Dr., Cincinnati OH 45211-7617. (513)481-9884. **E-mail:** whbeckman@gmail.com. **Website:** wendyonwriting.com. Estab. 2000.

COSTS Check in 2015.

ACCOMMODATIONS Facility has swimming, hiking, fishing, tennis, badminton, volleyball, basketball, ping pong, etc. A 9-hole golf course is available for an additional fee.

ADDITIONAL INFORMATION Brochures available for SASE. Inquire via e-mail.

CENTRAL OHIO FICTION WRITERS ANNUAL CONFERENCE

A chapter of the Romance Writers of America, P.O. Box 4213, Newark OH 43058. **E-mail:** susan_gee_heino@yahoo.com; msgigimorgan@gmail.com. **Website:** www.cofw.org. **Contact:** Susan Gee Heino, current president; Gigi Morgan, conference chair. Estab. 1990.

COSTS Costs will be decided as the next event draws near.

CHICAGO WRITERS CONFERENCE

E-mail: contact@chicagowritersconference.org. **Website:** chicagowritersconference.org. **Contact:** Mare Swallow. Estab. 2011.

DETROIT WORKING WRITERS ANNUAL WRITERS CONFERENCE

Detroit Working Writers, Box 82395, Rochester MI 48308. **E-mail:** conference@detworkingwriters.org. **Website:** dww-writers-conference.org. Estab. 1961.

COSTS Costs $65-155, depending on early bird registration and membership status within the organization

INDIANA UNIVERSITY WRITERS' CONFERENCE

464 Ballantine Hall, 1020 E. Kirkwood Ave., Bloomington IN 47405-7103. (812)855-1877. **Fax:** (812)855-9535. **E-mail:** writecon@indiana.edu. **Website:** www.indiana.edu/~writecon. Estab. 1940.

ACCOMMODATIONS Information on accommodations available on website.

ADDITIONAL INFORMATION Connect on Twitter at @iuwritecon.

KENTUCKY WOMEN WRITERS CONFERENCE

University of Kentucky College of Arts & Sciences, 232 E. Maxwell St., Lexington KY 40506. (859)257-2874. **E-mail:** kentuckywomenwriters@gmail.com. **Website:** kentuckywomenwriters.org. **Contact:** Julie Wrinn, director. Estab. 1979.

COSTS $175 early bird discount, $200 thereafter; $125 without workshop; $30 for students; includes boxed lunch on Friday; $20 for writers' reception. Other meals and accommodations are not included.

ADDITIONAL INFORMATION Sponsors prizes in poetry ($200), fiction ($200), nonfiction ($200), playwriting ($500), and spoken word ($500). Winners also invited to read during the conference. Pre-registration opens May 1.

KENTUCKY WRITERS CONFERENCE

Southern Kentucky Book Fest, Knicely Conference Center, 2355 Nashville Road, Bowling Green KY 42101. (270)745-4502. **E-mail:** kristie.lowry@wku. edu. **Website:** www.sokybookfest.org/KYWriter-sConf. **Contact:** Kristie Lowry.

◯ Since the event is free, interested attendees are asked to register in advance. information on how to do so is on the website.

KENYON REVIEW WRITERS WORKSHOP

Kenyon College, Gambier OH 43022. (740)427-5207. **Fax:** (740)427-5417. **E-mail:** kenyonreview@kenyon. edu; writers@kenyonreview.org. **Website:** www.kenyonreview.org. **Contact:** Anna Duke Reach, director. Estab. 1990.

COSTS $1,995; includes tuition, room and board.

ACCOMMODATIONS The workshop operates a shuttle to and from Gambier and the airport in Columbus, Ohio. Offers overnight accommodations. Participants are housed in Kenyon College student housing. The cost is covered in the tuition.

ADDITIONAL INFORMATION Application includes a writing sample. Admission decisions are made on a rolling basis. Workshop information is available online at www.kenyonreview.org/workshops in November. For brochure send e-mail, visit website, call, or fax. Accepts inquiries by SASE, e-mail, phone, fax.

MIDWEST WRITERS WORKSHOP

Ball State University, Department of Journalism, Muncie IN 47306. (765)282-1055. **E-mail:** midwestwriters@yahoo.com. **Website:** www.midwestwriters. org. **Contact:** Jama Kehoe Bigger, director.

COSTS $185-395. Most meals included.

ADDITIONAL INFORMATION Offers scholarships. See website for more information. Keep in touch with the MWW at facebook.com/MidwestWriters and twitter.com/MidwestWriters.

OHIO KENTUCKY INDIANA CHILDREN'S LITERATURE CONFERENCE

Northern Kentucky University, 405 Steely Library, Highland Heights KY 41099. (859)572-6620. **Fax:** (859)572-5390. **E-mail:** smithjen@nku.edu. **Website:** oki.nku.edu. **Contact:** Jennifer Smith.

COSTS $75; includes registration/attendance at all workshop sessions, *Tri-state Authors and Illustrators of Childrens Books Directory*, continental breakfast, lunch, author/illustrator signings. Manuscript critiques are available for an additional cost. E-mail or call for more information.

☺◯ SPACE (SMALL PRESS AND ALTERNATIVE COMICS EXPO)

Back Porch Comics, P.O. Box 20550, Columbus OH 43220. **E-mail:** bpc13@earthlink.net. **Website:** www. backporchcomics.com/space.htm.

COSTS Admission: $5 per day or $8 for weekend.

ADDITIONAL INFORMATION For brochure, visit website. Editors participate in conference.

WESTERN RESERVE WRITERS & FREELANCE CONFERENCE

7700 Clocktower Dr., Kirtland OH 44094. (440)525-7812. **E-mail:** deencr@aol.com. **Website:** www.deannaadams.com. **Contact:** Deanna Adams, director/conference coordinator. Estab. 1983.

COSTS Fall all-day conference includes lunch: $105. Spring half-day conference, no lunch: $69.

ADDITIONAL INFORMATION Brochures for the conferences are available by January (for spring conference) and July (for fall). Also accepts inquiries by e-mail and phone. Check Deanna Adams' website for all updates. Editors always attend the conferences. Private editing consultations are available, as well.

WOMEN WRITERS WINTER RETREAT

Homestead House B&B, 38111 West Spaulding, Willoughby OH 44094. (440)946-1902. **E-mail:** deencr@ aol.com. **Website:** www.deannaadams.com. Estab. 2007.

COSTS Single room: $315; shared room: $235 (includes complete weekend package, with B&B stay and all meals and workshops); weekend commute: $165; Saturday only: $125 (prices.include lunch and dinner).

ADDITIONAL INFORMATION Brochures for the writers retreat are available by December. Accepts inquiries and reservations by e-mail or phone. See Deanna's website for additional information and updates.

WRITE-TO-PUBLISH CONFERENCE
WordPro Communication Services, 9118 W. Elmwood Dr., Suite 1G, Niles IL 60714-5820. (847)296-3964. **Fax:** (847)296-0754. **E-mail:** lin@writetopublish.com. **Website:** www.writetopublish.com. **Contact:** Lin Johnson, director. Estab. 1971.

COSTS $475; includes conference and banquet.

ACCOMMODATIONS Attendees stay in campus residence halls. Cost is $280-360.

ADDITIONAL INFORMATION Optional ms evaluation available. College credit available. Conference information available in January. For details, visit website, or e-mail brochure@writetopublish.com. Accepts inquiries by e-mail, fax, phone.

NORTH CENTRAL

① ART WORKSHOPS IN GUATEMALA
4758 Lyndale Ave. S., Minneapolis MN 55419-5304. (612)825-0747. **E-mail:** info@artguat.org. **Website:** www.artguat.org. **Contact:** Liza Fourre, director. Estab. 1995.

COSTS See website. Includes tuition, lodging, breakfast, ground transportation.

ACCOMMODATIONS All transportation and accommodations included in price of conference.

ADDITIONAL INFORMATION Conference information available now. For brochure/guidelines visit website, e-mail or call. Accepts inquiries by e-mail, phone.

INTERNATIONAL MUSIC CAMP CREATIVE WRITING WORKSHOP
111 11th Ave. SW, Minot ND 58701. (701)838-8472. **Fax:** (701)838-1351. **E-mail:** info@internationalmusiccamp.com. **Website:** www.internationalmusiccamp.com. **Contact:** Christine Baumann and Tim Baumann, camp directors. Estab. 1956.

COSTS $395, includes tuition, room and board. Early bird registration (postmarked by May 1) is $380

ACCOMMODATIONS Airline and depot shuttles are available upon request. Housing is included in the fee.

ADDITIONAL INFORMATION Conference information is available on the website. Welcomes questions via e-mail.

IOWA SUMMER WRITING FESTIVAL
The University of Iowa, C215 Seashore Hall, University of Iowa, Iowa City IA 52242. (319)335-4160. **Fax:** (319)335-4743. **E-mail:** iswfestival@uiowa.edu. **Website:** uiowa.edu/~iswfest. Estab. 1987.

ACCOMMODATIONS Accommodations available at area hotels. Information on overnight accommodations available by phone or on website.

ADDITIONAL INFORMATION Brochures are available in February. Inquire via e-mail or on website.

UNIVERSITY OF WISCONSIN AT MADISON WRITERS INSTITUTE
21 N. Park St., Madison WI 53715-1218. (608)262-3447. **Website:** https://uwwritersinstitute.wisc.edu/. Estab. 1990.

COSTS $125-260, depending on discounts and if you attend one day or multiple days.

ACCOMMODATIONS The 2015 location is at the Madison Concourse Hotel.

UW-MADISON WRITERS' INSTITUTE
21 North Park St., Room 7331, Madison WI 53715. (608)265-3972. **Fax:** (608)265-2475. **E-mail:** lscheer@dcs.wisc.edu. **Website:** www.uwwritersinstitute.org. **Contact:** Laurie Scheer. Estab. 1989.

COSTS $260-310; includes materials, breaks

ACCOMMODATIONS Provides a list of area hotels or lodging options.

ADDITIONAL INFORMATION Sponsors contest.

WISCONSIN BOOK FESTIVAL
Madison Public Library, 201 W. Mifflin St., Madison WI 53703. (608)266-6300. **E-mail:** bookfest@mplfoundation.org. **Website:** www.wisconsinbookfestival.org. Estab. 2002.

COSTS All festival events are free.

SOUTH CENTRAL

ASPEN SUMMER WORDS LITERARY FESTIVAL & WRITING RETREAT
Aspen Words, 110 E. Hallam St., #116, Aspen CO 81611. (970)925-3122. **Fax:** (970)925-5700. **E-mail:** aspenwords@aspeninstitute.org. **Website:** www.aspenwords.org. **Contact:** Caroline Tory, programs coordinator. Estab. 1976.

CRESTED BUTTE WRITERS CONFERENCE
P.O. Box 1361, Crested Butte CO 81224. **E-mail:** coordinator@conf.crestedbuttewriters.org. **Website:** www.crestedbuttewriters.org/conf.php. **Contact:**

Barbara Crawford or Theresa Rizzo, co-coordinators. Estab. 2006.

COSTS $330 nonmembers; $300 members; $297 Early Bird; The Sandy Writing Contest Finalist $280; and groups of 5 or more $280.

ACCOMMODATIONS The conference is held at The Elevation Hotel, located at the Crested Butte Mountain Resort at the base of the ski mountain. The quaint historic town lies nestled in a stunning mountain valley 3 short miles from the resort area of Mt. Crested Butte. A free bus runs frequently between the 2 towns. The closest airport is 30 miles away, in Gunnison. The conference website lists 3 lodging options besides rooms at the event facility. All condos, motels, and hotel options offer special conference rates. No special travel arrangements are made through the conference; however, information for car rental from Gunnison airport or the Alpine Express shuttle is listed on the online conference FAQ page.

ADDITIONAL INFORMATION "Our conference workshops address a wide variety of writing craft and business. Our most popular workshop is Our First Pages Readings—with a twist. Agents and editors read opening pages volunteered by attendees-with a few best selling authors' openings mixed in. Think the A/E can identify the bestsellers? Not so much. Each year one of our attendees has been mistaken for a bestseller and obviously garnered requests from some on the panel. Writers may request additional information by e-mail."

EAST TEXAS CHRISTIAN WRITERS CONFERENCE

The School of Humanities, Dr. Jerry L. Summers, Dean, Scarborough Hall, East Texas Baptist University, 1 Tiger Dr., Marshall TX 75670. (903)923-2083. **E-mail:** jhopkins@etbu.edu; contest@etbu.edu. **Website:** www.etbu.edu/News/CWC. **Contact:** Elizabeth Hoyer, humanities secretary. Estab. 2002.

ACCOMMODATIONS Visit website for a list of local hotels offering a discounted rate.

KINDLING WORDS WEST

Breckenridge CO **Website:** www.KindlingWords.org.

MISSOURI WRITERS' GUILD CONFERENCE

St. Louis MO **E-mail:** mwgconferenceinfo@gmail.com. **Website:** www.missouriwritersguild.org. **Contact:** Tricia Sanders, vice president/conference chairman.

ADDITIONAL INFORMATION The primary contact individual changes every year, because the conference chair changes every year. See the website for contact info.

NIMROD ANNUAL WRITERS' WORKSHOP

800 S. Tucker Dr., Tulsa OK 74104. (918)631-3080. **E-mail:** nimrod@utulsa.edu. **Website:** www.utulsa.edu/nimrod. **Contact:** Eilis O'Neal, editor in chief. Estab. 1978.

COSTS Approximately $50. Lunch provided. Scholarships available for students.

ADDITIONAL INFORMATION *Nimrod International Journal* sponsors literary awards: The Katherine Anne Porter Prize for fiction and The Pablo Neruda Prize for poetry. Poetry and fiction prizes: $2,000 each and publication (top prize); $1,000 each and publication (other winners). Deadline: must be postmarked no later than April 30.

NORTHERN COLORADO WRITERS CONFERENCE

2107 Thunderstone Court, Fort Collins CO 80525. (970)556-0908. **E-mail:** kerrie@northerncoloradowriters.com. **Website:** www.northerncoloradowriters.com. Estab. 2006.

COSTS $255-541, depending on what package the attendee selects, whether you're a member or nonmember, and whether you're renewing your NCW membership.

ACCOMMODATIONS The conference is hosted at the Fort Collins Hilton, where rooms are available at a special rate.

PIKES PEAK WRITERS CONFERENCE

Pikes Peak Writers, PO Box 64273, Colorado Springs CO 80962. (719)244-6220. **Website:** www.pikespeakwriters.com/ppwc/. Estab. 1993.

COSTS $300-500 (includes all meals).

ACCOMMODATIONS Marriott Colorado Springs holds a block of rooms at a special rate for attendees until late March.

ADDITIONAL INFORMATION Readings with critiques are available on Friday afternoon. Also offers a contest for unpublished mss; entrants need not attend the conference. Deadline: November 1. Registration and contest entry forms are online; brochures are available in January. Send inquiries via e-mail.

ROCKY MOUNTAIN FICTION WRITERS COLORADO GOLD

Rocky Mountain Fiction Writers, P.O. Box 735, Conifer CO 80433. **E-mail:** conference@rmfw.org. **Website:** www.rmfw.org. Estab. 1982.

COSTS Available online.

ACCOMMODATIONS Special rates will be available at conference hotel.

ADDITIONAL INFORMATION Editor-conducted critiques are limited to 8 participants, with auditing available. Pitch appointments available at no charge. Friday morning master classes available. Pitch coaching is available. Special critiques are available. Craft workshops include beginner through professional levels.

ROMANCE WRITERS OF AMERICA NATIONAL CONFERENCE

14615 Benfer Road, Houston TX 77069. (832)717-5200. **Fax:** (832)717-5201. **E-mail:** info@rwa.org. **Website:** www.rwa.org/conference. Estab. 1981.

COSTS $450-675 depending on your membership status as well as when you register.

ADDITIONAL INFORMATION Annual RTA awards are presented for romance authors. Annual Golden Heart awards are presented for unpublished writers. Numerous literary agents are in attendance to meet with writers and hear book pitches.

SUMMER WRITING PROGRAM

Naropa University, 2130 Arapahoe Ave., Boulder CO 80302. (303)245-4862. **Fax:** (303)546-5287. **E-mail:** swpr@naropa.edu. **Website:** www.naropa.edu/swp. **Contact:** Kyle Pivarnik, special projects manager. Estab. 1974.

ADDITIONAL INFORMATION Writers can elect to take the Summer Writing Program for noncredit, graduate, or undergraduate credit. The registration procedure varies, so consider whether or not you'll be taking the SWP for academic credit. All participants can elect to take any combination of the first, second, third, and/or fourth weeks. To request a catalog of upcoming program or to find additional information, visit naropa.edu/swp. Naropa University also welcomes participants with disabilities.

TAOS SUMMER WRITERS' CONFERENCE

Department of English Language and Literature, MSC 03 2170, 1 University of New Mexico, Albuquerque NM 87131-0001. **E-mail:** swarner@unm.edu. **Website:** taosconf.unm.edu. **Contact:** Sharon Oard Warner. Estab. 1999.

COSTS Week-long workshop registration $700, weekend workshop registration $400, master classes between $1,350 and $1,625, publishing consultations are $175.

TEXAS CHRISTIAN WRITERS' CONFERENCE

1108 Valerie, Pasadena TX 77502. **E-mail:** patav@aol.com. **Website:** tcwhouston.blogspot.com. **Contact:** Pat Vance, conference registration. Estab. 1990.

TONY HILLERMAN WRITERS CONFERENCE

1063 Willow Way, Santa FE NM 87505. (505)471-1565. **E-mail:** wordharvest@wordharvest.com. **Website:** www.wordharvest.com. **Contact:** Anne Hillerman and Jean Schaumberg, co-founders. Estab. 2004.

COSTS A full registration is $695, but there are many options in terms of lower prices if the attendee only comes 1-2 days. All information available on website.

ACCOMMODATIONS Hilton Santa Fe Historic Plaza.

WRITERS' LEAGUE OF TEXAS AGENTS CONFERENCE

Writers' League of Texas, 611 S. Congress Ave., Suite 200 A-3, Austin TX 78704. (512)499-8914. **Fax:** (512)499-0441. **E-mail:** conference@writersleague.org. **E-mail:** jennifer@writersleague.org. **Website:** www.writersleague.org. Estab. 1982.

COSTS Rates vary based on membership and the date of registration. The starting rate (registration through January 15) is $349 for members. Rate increases by through later dates by members and no-members. See website for updates.

ADDITIONAL INFORMATION 2015 dates: June 26-28. Contests and awards programs are offered separately. Brochures are available upon request.

WRITING FOR THE SOUL

Jerry B. Jenkins Christian Writers Guild, P.O. Box 88288, Black Forest CO 80908. (866)495-7551. **Fax:** (719)494-1299. **E-mail:** Jerry@JerryJenkins.com. **Website:** www.Jerry-Jenkins.com.

THE HELENE WURLITZER FOUNDATION

P.O. Box 1891, Taos NM 87571. (575)758-2413. **Fax:** (575)758-2559. **E-mail:** hwf@taosnet.com. **Website:** www.wurlitzerfoundation.org. **Contact:** Michael A. Knight, executive director. Estab. 1954. Residence duration: 3 months.

ACCOMMODATIONS "Provides individual housing in fully furnished studio/houses (casitas), rent and utility free. Artists are responsible for transportation to and from Taos, their meals, and materials for their work. Bicycles are provided upon request."

WEST

ABROAD WRITERS CONFERENCES

17363 Sutter Creek Rd., Sutter Creek CA 95685. (209)296-4050. **E-mail:** abroadwriters@yahoo.com; nancy@abroadwritersconference.com. **Website:** abroadwritersconference.com.

> See the complete schedule online. Recent events include Italy, Spain and England in 2014-2015.

COSTS See website for pricing details.

ADDITIONAL INFORMATION Agents participate in conference. Application is online at website.

BLOCKBUSTER PLOT INTENSIVE WRITING WORKSHOPS (SANTA CRUZ)

Santa Cruz CA **E-mail:** contact@blockbusterplots. com. **Website:** www.blockbusterplots.com. **Contact:** Martha Alderson (also known as the Plot Whisperer), instructor. Estab. 2000.

COSTS Costs vary based on the time frame of the retreat/workshop.

ACCOMMODATIONS Updated website provides list of area hotels and lodging options.

ADDITIONAL INFORMATION Accepts inquiries by e-mail.

CALIFORNIA CRIME WRITERS CONFERENCE

Co-sponsored by Sisters in Crime/Los Angeles and the Southern California Chapter of Mystery Writers of America, **E-mail:** sistersincrimela@gmail.com. **Website:** www.ccwconference.org. Estab. 1995.

ADDITIONAL INFORMATION Conference information is available at www.ccwconference.org.

DESERT DREAMS CONFERENCE: REALIZING THE DREAM

P.O. Box 27407, Tempe AZ 85285. **E-mail:** desert-dreams@desertroserwa.org; desertdreamsconference@gmail.com. **Website:** www.desertroserwa.org. **Contact:** Conference coordinator. Estab. 1986.

ADDITIONAL INFORMATION Agents and editors participate in conference.

LAS VEGAS WRITERS CONFERENCE

Henderson Writers' Group, PO Box 92032, Henderson NV 89009. (702)564-2488; or, toll-free, (866)869-7842. **E-mail:** lasvegaswritersconference@gmail.com. **Website:** www.lasvegaswritersconference.com.

COSTS 2015 prices: $400 until January 31, 2015; $450 starting February 1, 2015; $500 at door; $300 for one day.

ADDITIONAL INFORMATION Sponsors contest. Agents and editors participate in conference.

LEAGUE OF UTAH WRITERS' ANNUAL WRITER'S CONFERENCE

Dianne Hardy, League of Utah Writers, 420 W. 750 N., Logan UT 84321. **E-mail:** Luwriters@gmail.com. **Website:** www.luwriters.org/index.html. **Contact:** Tim Keller.

MENDOCINO COAST WRITERS CONFERENCE

1211 Del Mar Dr., second address is P.O. Box 2087, Fort Bragg CA 95437. (707)485-4032. **E-mail:** info@mcwc.org. **Website:** www.mcwc.org. Estab. 1988.

COSTS $525 (minimum) includes morning intensives, afternoon panels and seminars, social events, and most meals. Scholarships available. Early application advised.

ADDITIONAL INFORMATION Emphasis is on encouragement, expertise and inspiration in a literary community where authors are also fantastic teachers. Registration opens March 15.

☉ MOUNT HERMON CHRISTIAN WRITERS CONFERENCE

PO Box 413, Mount Hermon CA 95041. **E-mail:** info@mounthermon.org. **Website:** writers.mounthermon. org. Estab. 1970.

NAPA VALLEY WRITERS' CONFERENCE

Napa Valley College, 1088 College Ave., St. Helena CA 94574. (707)967-2900. **E-mail:** writecon@napavalley. edu. **Website:** www.napawritersconference.org. **Contact:** Andrea Bewick, managing director. Estab. 1981.

> On Twitter as @napawriters and on Facebook as facebook.com/napawriters.

COSTS $975; $25 application fee.

PACIFIC COAST CHILDREN'S WRITERS WHOLE-NOVEL WORKSHOP: FOR ADULTS AND TEENS

P.O. Box 244, Aptos CA 95001. **Website:** www.childrenswritersworkshop.com. Estab. 2003.

PIMA WRITERS' WORKSHOP

Pima College, 2202 W. Anklam Rd., Tucson AZ 85709. (520)206-6084. **Fax:** (520)206-6020. **E-mail:** mfiles@pima.edu. **Contact:** Meg Files, director.

SAN DIEGO STATE UNIVERSITY WRITERS' CONFERENCE

SDSU College of Extended Studies, 5250 Campanile Dr., San Diego State University, San Diego CA 92182-

1920. (619)594-3946. **Fax:** (619)594-8566. **E-mail:** sd-suwritersconference@mail.sdsu.edu. **Website:** ces. sdsu.edu/writers. Estab. 1984.

COSTS Approximately $399-435. Parking is available for $8/day.

ACCOMMODATIONS Attendees must make their own travel arrangements. A conference rate for attendees is available at the event hotel (Marriott Mission Valley Hotel).

SAN FRANCISCO WRITERS CONFERENCE

1029 Jones St., San Francisco CA 94109. (415)673-0939. **E-mail:** Barbara@sfwriters.org. **Website:** sfwriters. org. **Contact:** Barbara Santos, marketing director. Estab. 2003.

COSTS Check the website for pricing on later dates. 2015 pricing was $650-795 depending on when you signed up and early bird registration, etc.

ACCOMMODATIONS The Intercontinental Mark Hopkins Hotel is a historic landmark at the top of Nob Hill in San Francisco. The hotel is located so that everyone arriving at the Oakland or San Francisco airport can take BART to either the Embarcadero or Powell Street exits, then walk or take a cable car or taxi directly to the hotel.

ADDITIONAL INFORMATION "Present yourself in a professional manner and the contacts you will make will be invaluable to your writing career. Fliers, details and registration information are online."

SANTA BARBARA WRITERS CONFERENCE

27 W. Anapamu St., Suite 305, Santa Barbara CA 93101. (805)568-1516. **E-mail:** info@sbwriters.com. **Website:** www.sbwriters.com. Estab. 1972.

COSTS Early conference registration is $575, and regular registration is $650.

ACCOMMODATIONS Hyatt Santa Barbara.

ADDITIONAL INFORMATION Register online or contact for brochure and registration forms.

SCBWI WINTER CONFERENCE ON WRITING AND ILLUSTRATING FOR CHILDREN

8271 Beverly Blvd., Los Angeles CA 90048. (323)782-1010. **Fax:** (323)782-1892. **E-mail:** scbwi@scbwi.org. **Website:** www.scbwi.org. **Contact:** Stephen Mooser. Estab. 2000.

COSTS See website for current cost and conference information

ADDITIONAL INFORMATION SCBWI also holds an annual summer conference in August in Los Angeles.

SQUAW VALLEY COMMUNITY OF WRITERS

P.O. Box 1416, Nevada City CA 95959-1416. (530)470-8440. **E-mail:** info@squawvalleywriters.org. **Website:** www.squawvalleywriters.org. **Contact:** Brett Hall Jones, executive director. Estab. 1969.

Annual conference held in July. Conference duration: 7 days. Average attendance: 124. "Writers workshops in fiction, nonfiction, and memoir assist talented writers by exploring the art and craft as well as the business of writing." Offerings include daily morning workshops led by writer-teachers, editors, or agents of the staff, limited to 12-13 participants; seminars; panel discussions of editing and publishing; craft colloquies; lectures; and staff readings. Past themes and panels included "Personal History in Fiction, Narrative Structure, Promise and Premise: Recognizing Subject"; "The Nation of Narrative Prose: Telling the Truth in Memoir and Personal Essay"; and "Anatomy of a Short Story." The workshops are held in a ski lodge at the foot of this ski area. Literary agent speakers have recently included Michael Carlisle, Henry Dunow, Susan Golomb, Joy Harris, B.J. Robbins, Janet Silver, and Peter Steinberg. Agents will be speaking and available for meetings with attendees. Agents and editors attend/participate in conferences.

COSTS Tuition is $1,075, which includes 6 dinners. Limited financial aid is available.

ACCOMMODATIONS The Community of Writers rents houses and condominiums in the Valley for participants to live in during the week of the conference. Single room (1 participant): $700/week. Double room (twin beds, room shared by conference participant of the same sex): $465/week. Multiple room (bunk beds, room shared with 2 or more participants of the same sex): $295/week. All rooms subject to availability; early requests are recommended. Can arrange airport shuttle pick-ups for a fee.

ADDITIONAL INFORMATION Online submittal process, see squawvalleywriters.org/writers_ws.htm#APPLY for instructions and application form. Send inquiries via e-mail to info@squawvalleywriters.org.

THRILLERFEST

P.O. Box 311, Eureka CA 95502. **E-mail:** infocentral@thrillerwriters.org. **Website:** www.thrillerfest.com.

Contact: Kimberley Howe, executive director. Estab. 2006.

COSTS Price will vary from $330-1,100, depending on which events are selected. Various package deals are available offering savings, and Early Bird pricing is offered beginning September of each year.

ACCOMMODATIONS Grand Hyatt in Manhattan.

TMCC WRITERS' CONFERENCE

Truckee Meadows Community College, 7000 Dandini Blvd., Reno NV 89512. (775)673-7111. **E-mail:** wdce@tmcc.edu. **Website:** wdce.tmcc.edu. Estab. 1991.

COSTS $119 for a full-day seminar; $32 for a 10-minute one-on-one appointment with an agent or editor; $12 for lunch.

ACCOMMODATIONS Contact the conference manager to learn about accommodation discounts.

ADDITIONAL INFORMATION "The conference is open to all writers, regardless of their level of experience. Brochures are available online and mailed in January. Send inquiries via e-mail."

WRITING AND ILLUSTRATING FOR YOUNG READERS CONFERENCE

1480 East 9400 South, Sandy UT 84093. **E-mail:** staff@wifyr.com. **Website:** www.wifyr.com. Estab. 2000. BYU, conferences and workshops, 348 HCEB, BYU, Provo UT 84602-1532. (801)422-2568. **Fax:** (801)422-0745. **E-mail:** cw348@byu.edu. **Website:** wifyr.byu.edu. **Contact:** Conferences & Workshops. Estab. 2000. Annual. 5-day workshop held in June of each year. The workshop is designed for people who want to write or illustrate for children or teenagers. Participants focus on a single market during daily four-hour morning writing workshops led by published authors or illustrators. Afternoon workshop sessions include a mingle with the authors, editors and agents. Workshop focuses on fiction for young readers: picture books, book-length fiction, fantasy/science fiction, nonfiction, mystery, illustration and general writing. Site: Conference Center at Brigham Young University in the foothills of the Wasatch Mountain range.

○ Guidelines and registration are on the website.

COSTS Costs available online.

ACCOMMODATIONS A block of rooms are available at the Best Western Cotton Tree Inn in Sandy, UT at a discounted rate. This rate is good as long as there are available rooms.

ADDITIONAL INFORMATION There is an online form to contact this event.

NORTHWEST

ALASKA WRITERS CONFERENCE

Alaska Writers Guild, PO Box 670014, Chugiak AK 99567. **E-mail:** alaskawritersguild.awg@gmail.com. **Website:** alaskawritersguild.com.

○ Ms critiques available. Note also that the AWG has many events and meetings each year, not just the annual conference.

FLATHEAD RIVER WRITERS CONFERENCE

P.O. Box 7711, Kalispell MT 59904-7711. (406)881-4066. **E-mail:** answers@authorsoftheflathead.org. **Website:** www.authorsoftheflathead.org/conference.asp. Estab. 1990.

COSTS Check the website for updated cost information.

ACCOMMODATIONS Rooms are available at a discounted rate.

ADDITIONAL INFORMATION Watch website for additional speakers and other details. Register early as seating is limited.

IDAHO WRITERS LEAGUE WRITERS' CONFERENCE

601 W. 75 S., Blackfoot ID 83221-6153. (208)684-4200. **Website:** www.idahowritersleague.com. Estab. 1940.

COSTS A minimum of $145, depending on early bird pricing and membership. Check the website for updates on cost.

JACKSON HOLE WRITERS CONFERENCE

PO Box 1974, Jackson WY 83001. (307)413-3332. **E-mail:** nicole@jacksonholewritersconference.com. **Website:** jacksonholewritersconference.com. Estab. 1991.

COSTS $365 if registered by May 12. Accompanying teen writer: $175. Pre-Conference Writing Workshop: $150.

ADDITIONAL INFORMATION Held at the Center for the Arts in Jackson, Wyoming and online.

NORWESCON

100 Andover Park W. PMB 150-165, Tukwila WA 98188-2828. (425)243-4692. **Fax:** (520)244-0142. **E-mail:** info@norwescon.org. **Website:** www.norwescon.org. Estab. 1978.

ACCOMMODATIONS Conference is held at the Doubletree Hotel Seattle Airport.

ADDITIONAL INFORMATION Brochures are available online or for a SASE. Send inquiries via e-mail.

OREGON CHRISTIAN WRITERS SUMMER CONFERENCE

Red Lion Hotel on the River, 909 N. Hayden Island Dr., Portland OR 97217-8118. **E-mail:** summerconf@oregonchristianwriters.org. **Website:** www.oregonchristianwriters.org. **Contact:** Lindy Jacobs, OCW Summer Conference Director. Estab. 1989.

COSTS $500 for OCW members, $535 for nonmembers. Registration fee includes all classes, workshops, and 2 lunches and 3 dinners. Lodging additional. Full-time registered registrants may also pre-submit three proposals for review by an editor (or agent) through the conference, plus sign up for a half-hour mentoring appointment with an author.

ACCOMMODATIONS Conference is held at the Red Lion on the River Hotel. Conferees wishing to stay at the hotel must make a reservation through the hotel. A block of rooms has been reserved at the hotel at a special rate for conferees and held until mid-July. The hotel reservation link will be posted on the website in late spring. Shuttle bus transportation will be provided by the hotel for conferees from Portland Airport (PDX) to the hotel, which is 20 minutes away.

ADDITIONAL INFORMATION Conference details will be posted online beginning in January. All conferees are welcome to attend the Cascade Awards ceremony, which takes place Wednesday evening during the conference. For more information about the Cascade Writing Contest, please check the website.

OUTDOOR WRITERS ASSOCIATION OF AMERICA ANNUAL CONFERENCE

615 Oak St., Suite 201, Missoula MT 59801. (406)728-7434. **E-mail:** info@owaa.org. **Website:** owaa.org. **Contact:** Jessica Seitz, conference and membership coordinator.

COSTS $425-449.

PNWA SUMMER WRITERS CONFERENCE

317 NW Gilman Blvd., Suite 8, Issaquah WA 98027. (425)673-2665. **E-mail:** pnwa@pnwa.org. **Website:** www.pnwa.org. Estab. 1955.

ACCOMMODATIONS SeaTac Hilton Hotel and Conference Center.

SOUTH COAST WRITERS CONFERENCE

Southwestern Oregon Community College, P.O. Box 590, 29392 Ellensburg Ave., Gold Beach OR 97444. (541)247-2741. **Fax:** (541)247-6247. **E-mail:** scwc@socc.edu. **Website:** www.socc.edu/scwriters. Estab. 1996.

ADDITIONAL INFORMATION See website for cost and additional details.

TIN HOUSE SUMMER WRITERS WORKSHOP

P.O. Box 10500, Portland OR 97296. (503)219-0622. **Website:** www.tinhouse.com/blog/workshop. Estab. 2003.

COSTS $40 application fee; $1,200 for program + room and board (breakfast and one dinner).

ACCOMMODATIONS Sylvia Beach Hotel.

ADDITIONAL INFORMATION Attendees must apply; all information available online. "A board composed of Tin House editorial staff members decides upon applications. Acceptance is based on the strength and promise of the submitted writing sample, as well as how much the board feels an applicant might benefit from the Winter Workshop. We will notify applicants of acceptance or rejection within 4 weeks of the application's receipt. Once accepted, enrollment into the program is granted on a first-come, first-serve basis (meaning you need to register in order to guarantee your spot). We encourage you to apply early, as workshops can fill quickly."

WHIDBEY ISLAND WRITERS' CONFERENCE

P.O. Box 1289, Langley WA 98260. (360)331-0307. **E-mail:** writeonwhidbey.org. **Website:** writeonwhidbey.org.

COSTS Cost: $395; early bird and member discounts available

WILLAMETTE WRITERS CONFERENCE

2108 Buck St., West Linn OR 97068. (503)305-6729. **Fax:** (503)344-6174. **Website:** willamettewriters.com/wwcon/. Estab. 1981.

Over 50 literary agents and editors, plus Hollywood film managers, agents and producers, will be on hand in 2013 to listen to pitches.

COSTS Pricing schedule available online.

ACCOMMODATIONS If necessary, arrangements can be made on an individual basis through the conference hotel. Special rates may be available. 2015 location is the Lloyd Center DoubleTree Hotel.

ADDITIONAL INFORMATION Brochure/guidelines are available for a catalog-sized SASE.

WRITE ON THE SOUND WRITERS' CONFERENCE

Edmonds Arts Commission, Frances Anderson Center, 700 Main St., Edmonds WA 98020. (425)771-0228.

Fax: (425)771-0253. **E-mail:** wots@edmondswa.gov.
Website: www.writeonthesound.com. Estab. 1985.
COSTS See website for more information on applying to view costs.
ADDITIONAL INFORMATION Brochures are available in July. Accepts inquiries via phone, e-mail, and
fax.

WRITERS WEEKEND AT THE BEACH

P.O. Box 877, Ocean Park WA 98640. (360)665-4367.
E-mail: director@opretreat.org. **Contact:** Brandon
Scheer; Tracie Heskett. Estab. 1992.
COSTS $200 for full registration before Feb. 15 and
$215 after Feb. 15.
ACCOMMODATIONS Offers on-site overnight lodg-
ing.

CANADA

⊘ SASKATCHEWAN FESTIVAL OF WORDS

217 Main St. N., Moose Jaw SK S6J 0W1 Canada. **Website:** www.festivalofwords.com. Estab. 1997.
ACCOMMODATIONS Information available at
www.templegardens.sk.ca, campgrounds, and bed
and breakfast establishments. Complete information
about festival presenters, events, costs, and schedule
also available on website.

⊘ THE SCHOOL FOR WRITERS FALL WORKSHOP

The Humber School for Writers, Humber Institute of
Technology & Advanced Learning, 3199 Lake Shore
Blvd. W., Toronto ON M8V 1K8 Canada. (416)675-
6622. **E-mail:** antanas.sileika@humber.ca; hilary.hig-
gins@humber.ca. **Website:** www.humber.ca/scapa/
programs/school-writers.
COSTS around $850 (in 2014). Some limited scholar-
ships are available.
ADDITIONAL INFORMATION Accepts inquiries by
e-mail, phone, and fax.

INTERNATIONAL

◐◉ INTERNATIONAL WOMEN'S FICTION FESTIVAL

Via Cappuccini 8E, Matera 75100 Italy. (39)0835-
312044. **Fax:** (39)0835-312093. **E-mail:** e.jennings@
womensfictionfestival.com. **Website:** www.wom-
ensfictionfestival.com. **Contact:** Elizabeth Jennings.
Estab. 2004.
COSTS 220 euros.
ACCOMMODATIONS Le Monacelle, a restored 17th
century convent. Conference travel agency will find
reasonably priced accommodation. A paid shuttle is
available from the Bari Airport to the hotel in Matera.

◉ SALT CAY WRITERS RETREAT

Salt Cay Bahamas. (732)267-6449. **E-mail:** admin@
saltcaywritersretreat.com. **Website:** www.saltcaywrit-
ersretreat.com. **Contact:** Karen Dionne and Christopher Graham.
Individualized instruction from bestselling authors, top editors, and literary agents; dolphin
swim; built-in scheduled writing time; evening
gatherings with student and author readings;
closing festivities including authentic Bahami-
an feast. All sleeping rooms at the retreat hotel
are suites; free or deeply discounted activities for
families, including water park, water bikes, kay-
aks, dolphin and sea lion encounters, snorkeling,
scuba-diving, and much more. Complimentary
guest access to Atlantis Resort & Casino.
COSTS $2,450 through May 1; $2,950 after.
ACCOMMODATIONS Comfort Suites, Paradise Island, Nassau, Bahamas.

◓ THE UNIVERSITY OF WINCHESTER WRITERS' FESTIVAL

University of Winchester, Winchester Hampshire
WA S022 4NR United Kingdom. 44(0)1962-827238.
E-mail: judith.heneghan@winchester.ac.uk. **Website:**
www.writersfestival.co.uk.

PUBLISHERS & THEIR IMPRINTS

The publishing world is in constant transition. With all the buying, selling, reorganizing, consolidating, and dissolving, it's hard to keep publishers and their imprints straight. To help make sense of these changes, here's a breakdown of major publishers (and their divisions)—who owns whom and which imprints are under each company umbrella. Keep in mind that this information changes frequently. The website of each publisher is provided to help you keep an eye on this ever-evolving business.

HACHETTE BOOK GROUP USA

www.hachettebookgroup.com

CENTER STREET

FAITHWORDS

Jericho Books

GRAND CENTRAL PUBLISHING

5 Spot

Business Plus

Forever

Forever Yours

Grand Central Life & Style

Twelve

Vision

HACHETTE DIGITAL MEDIA

HACHETTE AUDIO

HYPERION

LITTLE, BROWN AND COMPANY

Back Bay Books

Mulholland Books

Reagan Arthur Books

LITTLE, BROWN BOOKS FOR YOUNG READERS

LB Kids

Poppy

ORBIT

Redhook

YEN PRESS

HARLEQUIN ENTERPRISES

www.harlequin.com

CARINA PRESS

HARLEQUIN

Harlequin American Romance

Harlequin Blaze

Harlequin Desire

Harlequin Heartwarming

Harlequin Historical

Harlequin Intrigue

Harlequin Kimani Romance

Harlequin KISS

Harlequin Medical Romance

Harlequin Nocturne

Harlequin Presents

Harlequin Romance

Harlequin Romantic Suspense

Harlequin Special Edition

Harlequin Superromance

Love Inspired

Love Inspired Historical

Love Inspired Suspense

HARLEQUIN HQN

Spice

HARLEQUIN KIMANI ARABESQUE

HARLEQUIN KIMANI TRU

HARLEQUIN KIMANI PRESS

HARLEQUIN TEEN

HARLEQUIN LUNA

HARLEQUIN MIRA

SILHOUETTE SPECIAL RELEASES

Silhouette Desire

Silhouette Romantic Suspense

Silhouette Special Edition

WORLDWIDE LIBRARY ROGUE ANGEL

WORLDWIDE LIBRARY
WORLDWIDE MYSTERY

HARLEQUIN U.K.

Mills & Boon

Mira Ink

HARPERCOLLINS

www.harpercollins.com

HARPERCOLLINS GENERAL BOOKS GROUP

Amistad

Avon

Avon Impulse

Avon Red

Ecco

Fourth Estate

Harper

Harper Business

Harper Design

Harper Luxe

Harper Paperbacks

Harper Perennial

Harper Perennial Modern Classics

Harper Voyager

HarperAudio

HarperOne

ItBooks

William Morrow

William Morrow Trade Paperbacks

HARPERCOLLINS CHILDREN'S BOOKS

Amistad Press

Balzer & Bray

Collins

Greenwillow Books

HarperChildren's Audio

HarperCollins Children's Books

HarperCollins e-books

HarperFestival

HarperTeen

Katherine Tegen Books

Rayo

TOKYOPOP

Walden Pond Press

HARPERCOLLINS CHRISTIAN PUBLISHING

Zondervan

Thomas Nelson

HARPERCOLLINS U.K.

Avon

Blue Door

Collins Education

Collins Geo

Collins Language

Fourth Estate

Harper

Harper NonFiction

HarperAudio

HarperCollins Children's Books

HarperImpulse

The Friday Project

Voyager

William Collins

HARPERCOLLINS CANADA

Amistad

Avon Impulse

Avon Romance

Broadside Books

Ecco

Greenwillow

Harper Business

Harper Design

Harper Perennial

Harper Voyager

HarperAudio

HarperCollins Children's

HarperOne

It Books

Katherine Tegen Books

Morrow Cookbooks

Walden Pond Press

William Morrow Paperbacks

HARPERCOLLINS AUSTRALIA/NEW ZEALAND

HARPERCOLLINS INDIA

MACMILLAN US (HOLTZBRINCK)

us.macmillan.com

FARRAR, STRAUS AND GIROUX

North Point Press

Hill and Wang

Faber and Faber, Inc.

FSG Books for Young Readers

Sarah Crichton Books

FSG Originals

Scientific American

FIRST SECOND

FLATIRON BOOKS

HENRY HOLT & CO.

Henry Holt Books for Young Readers

Holt Paperbacks

Metropolitan Books

Times

MACMILLAN AUDIO

MACMILLAN CHILDREN'S

FSG Books for Young Readers

Feiwel & Friends

Holt Books for Young Readers

Kingfisher

Roaring Brook

Priddy Books

Starscape/Tor Teen

Square Fish

Young Listeners

Macmillan Children's Publishing Group

PICADOR

QUICK AND DIRTY TIPS

ST. MARTIN'S PRESS

Griffin

Minotaur

St. Martin's Press Paperbacks

Let's Go

Thomas Dunne Books

Truman Talley Books

TOR/FORGE BOOKS

Starscape

Tor Teen

PENGUIN GROUP (USA), INC.

www.penguingroup.com

PENGUIN ADULT DIVISION

Ace Books

Alpha Books

Amy Einhorn Books/Putnam

Avery

Berkley Books

Blue Rider Press

C.A. Press

Current

Dutton Books

Gotham Books

G.P. Putnam's Sons

HP Books

Hudson Street Press

Jeremy P. Tarcher

Jove

NAL

Pamela Dorman Books

Penguin

Penguin Press

Perigree

Plume

Portfolio

Prentice Hall Press

Riverhead

Sentinel

The Viking Press

YOUNG READERS DIVISION

Dial Books for Young Readers

Dutton Children's Books

Firebird

Frederick Warne

G.P. Putnam's Sons Books for Young Readers

Grosset & Dunlap

Nancy Paulsen Books

Philomel

Price Stern Sloan

Puffin Books

Razorbill

Speak

Viking Books for Young Readers

RANDOM HOUSE, INC. (BERTELSMANN)

www.randomhouse.com

CROWN PUBLISHING GROUP

Amphoto Books

Back Stage Books

Billboard Books

Broadway Books

Clarkson Potter

Crown

Crown Archetype

Crown Business

Crown Forum

Doubleday Religion

Harmony Books

Image Books

Potter Craft

Potter Style

Ten Speed Press

Three Rivers Press

Waterbrook Multnomah

Watson-Guptill

KNOPF DOUBLEDAY PUBLISHING GROUP

Alfred A. Knopf

Anchor Books

Doubleday

Everyman's Library

Nan A. Talese

Pantheon Books

Schocken Books

Vintage Books

RANDOM HOUSE PUBLISHING GROUP

Ballantine Books

Bantam

Del Rey/Lucas Books

Del Rey/Manga

Delacorte

Dell

The Dial Press

The Modern Library

One World

Presidio Press

Random House Trade Group

Random House Trade Paperbacks

Spectra

Spiegel and Grau

Triumph Books

Villard Books

RANDOM HOUSE CHILDREN'S BOOKS

Kids@Random (RH Children's Books)

Golden Books

Princeton Review

Sylvan Learning

RANDOM HOUSE DIGITAL PUBLISHING GROUP

Books on Tape

Fodor's Travel

Living Language

Listening Library

Random House Audio

RH Large Print

RANDOM HOUSE INTERNATIONAL

Random House Australia

Random House of Canada

The Random House Group (UK)

Random House India

Random House Mondadori (Argentina)

Random House Mondadori (Chile)

Random House Mondadori (Colombia)

Random House Mondadori (Mexico)

Random House Mondadori (Spain)

Random House Mondadori (Uruguay)

Random House Mondadori (Venezuela)

Random House New Zealand

Random House Struik (South Africa)

Transworld Ireland

Verlagsgruppe Random House

SIMON & SCHUSTER

www.simonandschuster.com

SIMON & SCHUSTER ADULT PUBLISHING

Atria Books

Beyond Words

Folger Shakespeare Library

Free Press

Gallery Books

Howard Books

Pocket Books

Scribner

Simon & Schuster

Threshold Editions

Touchstone

SIMON & SCHUSTER CHILDREN'S PUBLISHING

Aladdin

Atheneum Books for Young Readers

Bench Lane Books

Little Simon

Margaret K. McElderry Books

Paula Wiseman Books

Simon & Schuster Books for Young Readers

Simon Pulse

Simon Spotlight

SIMON & SCHUSTER AUDIO

Simon & Schuster Audio

Pimsleur

SIMON & SCHUSTER INTERNATIONAL

Simon & Schuster Australia

Simon & Schuster Canada

Simon & Schuster UK

GLOSSARY

ADVANCE. Payment by a publisher to an author prior to the publication of a book, to be deducted from the author's future royalties.

ADVENTURE STORY. A genre of fiction in which action is the key element, overshadowing characters, theme, and setting. The conflict in an adventure story is often man against nature. A secondary plot that reinforces this kind of conflict is sometimes included.

ALL RIGHTS. The rights contracted to a publisher permitting a manuscript's use anywhere and in any form, including movie and book club sales, without additional payment to the writer.

AMATEUR SLEUTH. The character in a mystery, usually the protagonist, who does the detection but is not a professional private investigator or police detective.

ANTHOLOGY. A collection of selected writings by various authors.

ASSOCIATION OF AUTHORS' REPRESENTATIVES (AAR). An organization for literary agents committed to maintaining excellence in literary representation.

AUCTION. Publishers sometimes bid against each other for the acquisition of a manuscript that has excellent sales prospects.

BACKLIST. A publisher's books not published during the current season but still in print.

BIOGRAPHICAL NOVEL. A life story documented in history and transformed into fiction through the insight and imagination of the writer. This type of novel melds the elements of biographical research and historical truth into the framework of a novel, complete with dialogue, drama, and mood. A biographical novel resembles historical fiction, save for one aspect: Characters in a historical novel may be fabricated and then placed into an authentic setting; characters in a biographical novel have actually lived.

BOOK PRODUCER/PACKAGER. An organization that may develop a book for a publisher based upon the publisher's idea or may plan all elements of a book, from its initial concept to writing and marketing strategies, and then sell the package to a book publisher and/or movie producer.

CLIFFHANGER. Fictional event in which the reader is left in suspense at the end of a chapter or episode, so that interest in the story's outcome will be sustained.

CLIP. Sample, usually from a newspaper or magazine, of a writer's published work.

CLOAK-AND-DAGGER. A melodramatic, romantic type of fiction dealing with espionage and intrigue.

COMMERCIAL. Publishers whose concern is salability, profit, and success with a large readership.

CONTEMPORARY. Material dealing with popular current trends, themes, or topics.

CONTRIBUTOR'S COPY. Copy of an issue of a magazine or published book sent to an author whose work is included.

CO-PUBLISHING. An arrangement in which the author and publisher share costs and profits.

COPYEDITING. Editing a manuscript for writing style, grammar, punctuation and factual accuracy.

COPYRIGHT. The legal right to exclusive publication, sale, or distribution of a literary work.

COVER LETTER. A brief letter sent with a complete manuscript submitted to an editor.

"COZY" (OR "TEACUP") MYSTERY. Mystery usually set in a small British town, in a by-gone era, featuring a somewhat genteel, intellectual protagonist.

ELECTRONIC RIGHTS. The right to publish material electronically, either in book or short story form.

ELECTRONIC SUBMISSION. A submission of material by e-mail or on computer disk.

ETHNIC FICTION. Stories whose central characters are black, Native American, Italian-American, Jewish, Appalachian, or members of some other specific cultural group.

EXPERIMENTAL FICTION. Fiction that is innovative in subject matter and style; avant-garde, non-formulaic, usually literary material.

EXPOSITION. The portion of the story line, usually the beginning, where background information about character and setting is related.

E-ZINE. A magazine that is published electronically.

FAIR USE. A provision in the copyright law that says short passages from copyrighted material may be used without infringing on the owner's rights.

FANTASY (TRADITIONAL). Fantasy with an emphasis on magic, using characters with the ability to practice magic, such as wizards, witches, dragons, elves, and unicorns.

FANZINE. A noncommercial, small-circulation magazine usually dealing with fantasy, horror or science-fiction literature and art.

FIRST NORTH AMERICAN SERIAL RIGHTS. The right to publish material in a periodical before it appears in book form, for the first time, in the United States or Canada.

FLASH FICTION. *See* short short stories.

GALLEY PROOF. The first typeset version of a manuscript that has not yet been divided into pages.

GENRE. A formulaic type of fiction such as romance, western, or horror.

GOTHIC. This type of category fiction dates back to the late eighteenth and early nineteenth centuries. Contemporary gothic novels are characterized by atmospheric, historical settings and feature young, beautiful women who win the favor of handsome, brooding heroes—simultaneously dealing successfully with some life-threatening menace, either natural or supernatural. Gothics rely on mystery, peril, romantic relationships, and a sense of foreboding for their strong, emotional effect on the reader. A classic early gothic novel is Emily Brontë's *Wuthering Heights*.

GRAPHIC NOVEL. A book (original or adapted) that takes the form of a long comic strip or heavily illustrated story of forty pages or more, produced in paperback. Though called a novel, these can also be works of nonfiction.

HARD-BOILED DETECTIVE NOVEL. Mystery novel featuring a private eye or police detective as the protagonist; usually involves a murder. The emphasis is on the details of the crime, and the tough, unsentimental protagonist usually takes a matter-of-fact attitude toward violence.

HARD SCIENCE FICTION. Science fiction with an emphasis on science and technology.

HIGH FANTASY. Fantasy with a medieval setting and a heavy emphasis on chivalry and the quest.

HISTORICAL FICTION. A fictional story set in a recognizable period of history. As well as telling the stories of ordinary people's lives, historical fiction may involve political or social events of the time.

HORROR. Howard Phillips (H.P.) Lovecraft, generally acknowledged to be the master of the horror tale in the twentieth century and the most important American writer of this genre since Edgar Allan Poe, distinguishes horror literature from fiction based entirely on physical fear and the merely gruesome. It is that atmosphere—the creation of a particular sensation or emotional level—that, according to Lovecraft, is the most important element in the creation of horror literature. Contemporary writers enjoying considerable success in horror fiction include Stephen King, Robert Bloch, Peter Straub, and Dean Koontz.

HYPERTEXT FICTION. A fictional form, read electronically, which incorporates traditional elements of storytelling with a non-linear plot line, in which the reader determines the direction of the story by opting for one of many author-supplied links.

IMPRINT. Name applied to a publisher's specific line (e.g. Owl, an imprint of Henry Holt).

INTERACTIVE FICTION. Fiction in book or computer-software format where the reader determines the path the story will take by choosing from several alternatives at the end of each chapter or episode.

INTERNATIONAL REPLY COUPON (IRC). A form purchased at a post office and enclosed with a letter or manuscript to an international publisher, to cover return postage costs.

JUVENILES, WRITING FOR. This includes works intended for an audience usually between the ages of two and eighteen. Categories of children's books are usually divided in this way: (1) picture books and storybooks (ages two to eight); (2) young readers or easy-to-read books (ages five to eight); (3) middle readers or middle grade (ages nine to eleven); (4) young adult books (ages twelve and up).

LIBEL. Written or printed words that defame, malign, or damagingly misrepresent a living person.

LITERARY AGENT. A person who acts for an author in finding a publisher or arranging contract terms on a literary project.

LITERARY FICTION. The general category of fiction that employs more sophisticated technique, driven as much or more by character evolution than action in the plot.

MAINSTREAM FICTION. Fiction that appeals to a more general reading audience, versus literary or genre fiction. Mainstream is more plot-driven than literary fiction and less formulaic than genre fiction.

MALICE DOMESTIC NOVEL. A mystery featuring a murder among family members, such as the murder of a spouse or a parent.

MANUSCRIPT. The author's unpublished copy of a work, usually typewritten, used as the basis for typesetting.

MASS MARKET PAPERBACK. Softcover book on a popular subject, usually around 4" × 7", directed to a general audience and sold in drugstores and groceries as well as in bookstores.

MIDDLE READER. Also called *middle grade*. Juvenile fiction for readers aged nine to eleven.

MS(S). Abbreviation for *manuscript(s)*.

MULTIPLE SUBMISSION. Submission of more than one short story at a time to the same editor. Do not make a multiple submission unless requested.

MYSTERY. A form of narration in which one or more elements remain unknown or unexplained until the end of the story. The modern mystery story contains elements of the mainstream novel: a convincing account of a character's struggle with various physical and psychological obstacles in an effort to achieve his goal, good characterization, and sound motivation.

NARRATION. The account of events in a story's plot as related by the speaker or the voice of the author.

NARRATOR. The person who tells the story, either someone involved in the action or the voice of the writer.

NEW AGE. A term including categories such as astrology, psychic phenomena, spiritual healing, UFOs, mysticism, and other aspects of the occult.

NOIR. A style of mystery involving hard-boiled detectives and bleak settings.

NOM DE PLUME. French for "pen name"; a pseudonym.

NONFICTION NOVEL. A work in which real events and people are written [about] in novel form, but are not camouflaged, as they are in the roman à clef. In the nonfiction novel, reality is presented imaginatively; the writer imposes a novelistic structure on the actual events, keying sections of narrative around moments that are seen (in retrospect) as symbolic. In this way, he creates a coherence that the actual story might not have had. *The Executioner's Song*, by Norman Mailer, and *In Cold Blood*, by Truman Capote, are notable examples of the nonfiction novel.

NOVELLA (ALSO NOVELETTE). A short novel or long story, approximately 20,000–50,000 words.

#10 ENVELOPE. 4" × 9½" envelope, used for queries and other business letters.

OFFPRINT. Copy of a story taken from a magazine before it is bound.

ONETIME RIGHTS. Permission to publish a story in periodical or book form one time only.

OUTLINE. A summary of a book's contents, often in the form of chapter headings with a few sentences outlining the action of the story under each one; sometimes part of a book proposal.

OVER THE TRANSOM. A phrase referring to unsolicited manuscripts, or those that come in "over the transom."

PAYMENT ON ACCEPTANCE. Payment from the magazine or publishing house as soon as the decision to print a manuscript is made.

PAYMENT ON PUBLICATION. Payment from the publisher after a manuscript is printed.

PEN NAME. A pseudonym used to conceal a writer's real name.

PERIODICAL. A magazine or journal published at regular intervals.

PLOT. The carefully devised series of events through which the characters progress in a work of fiction.

POPULAR FICTION. Generally, a synonym for category or genre fiction; i.e., fiction intended to appeal to audiences for certain kinds of novels. Popular, or category, fiction is defined as such primarily for the convenience of publishers, editors, reviewers, and booksellers who must identify novels of different areas of interest for potential readers.

PRINT ON DEMAND (POD). Novels produced digitally one at a time, as ordered. Self-publishing through print on demand technology typically involves some fees for the author. Some authors use POD to create a manuscript in book form to send to prospective traditional publishers.

PROOFREADING. Close reading and correction of a manuscript's typographical errors.

PROOFS. A typeset version of a manuscript used for correcting errors and making changes, often a photocopy of the galleys.

PROPOSAL. An offer to write a specific work, usually consisting of an outline of the work and one or two completed chapters.

PROTAGONIST. The principal or leading character in a literary work.

PSYCHOLOGICAL NOVEL. A narrative that emphasizes the mental and emotional aspects of its characters, focusing on motivations and mental activities rather than on exterior events. The psychological novelist is less concerned about relating what happened than about exploring why it happened. The term is most often used to describe twentieth-century works that employ techniques such as interior monologue and stream of consciousness. Two examples of contemporary psychological novels are Judith Guest's *Ordinary People* and Mary Gordon's *The Company of Women*.

PUBLIC DOMAIN. Material that either was never copyrighted or whose copyright term has expired.

PULP MAGAZINE. A periodical printed on inexpensive paper, usually containing lurid, sensational stories or articles.

QUERY. A letter written to an editor to elicit interest in a story the writer wants to submit.

READER. A person hired by a publisher to read unsolicited manuscripts.

READING FEE. An arbitrary amount of money charged by some agents and publishers to read a submitted manuscript.

REGENCY ROMANCE. A subgenre of romance, usually set in England between 1811 and 1820.

REMAINDERS. Leftover copies of an out-of-print book, sold by the publisher at a reduced price.

REPORTING TIME. The number of weeks or months it takes an editor to report back on an author's query or manuscript.

REPRINT RIGHTS. Permission to print an already published work whose rights have been sold to another magazine or book publisher.

ROMAN À CLEF. French "novel with a key." A novel that represents actual living or historical characters and events in fictionalized form.

ROMANCE NOVEL. A type of category fiction in which the love relationship between a man and a woman pervades the plot. The story is often told from the viewpoint of the heroine, who meets a man (the hero), falls in love with him, encounters a conflict that hinders their relationship, then resolves the conflict. Romance is the overriding element in this kind of story: The couple's relationship determines the plot and tone of the book.

ROYALTIES. A percentage of the retail price paid to an author for each copy of the book that is sold.

SAE. Self-addressed envelope.

SASE. Self-addressed stamped envelope.

SCIENCE FICTION (VS. FANTASY). It is generally accepted that, to be science fiction, a story must have elements of science in either the conflict or setting (usually both). Fantasy, on the other hand, rarely utilizes science, relying instead on magic, mythological and neomythological beings, and devices and outright invention for conflict and setting.

SECOND SERIAL (REPRINT) RIGHTS. Permission for the reprinting of a work in another periodical after its first publication in book or magazine form.

SELF-PUBLISHING. In this arrangement, the author keeps all income derived from the book, but he pays for its manufacturing, production, and marketing.

SERIAL RIGHTS. The rights given by an author to a publisher to print a piece in one or more periodicals.

SERIALIZED NOVEL. A book-length work of fiction published in sequential issues of a periodical.

SETTING. The environment and time period during which the action of a story takes place.

SHORT SHORT STORY. A condensed piece of fiction, usually under 1,000 words.

SIMULTANEOUS SUBMISSION. The practice of sending copies of the same manuscript to several editors or publishers at the same time. Some editors refuse to consider such submissions.

SLANT. A story's particular approach or style, designed to appeal to the readers of a specific magazine.

SLICE OF LIFE. A presentation of characters in a seemingly mundane situation that offers the reader a flash of illumination about the characters or their situation.

SLUSH PILE. A stack of unsolicited manuscripts in the editorial offices of a publisher.

SOCIAL FICTION. Fiction written with the purpose of bringing positive changes in society.

SOFT/SOCIOLOGICAL SCIENCE FICTION. Science fiction with an emphasis on society and culture versus scientific accuracy.

SPACE OPERA. Epic science fiction with an emphasis on good guys versus bad guys.

SPECULATION (OR SPEC). An editor's agreement to look at an author's manuscript with no promise to purchase.

SPECULATIVE FICTION (SPECFIC). The all-inclusive term for science fiction, fantasy, and horror.

SUBSIDIARY. An incorporated branch of a company or conglomerate (e.g. Alfred Knopf, Inc., a subsidiary of Random House, Inc.).

SUBSIDIARY RIGHTS. All rights other than book publishing rights included in a book contract, such as paperback, book club, and movie rights.

SUBSIDY PUBLISHER. A book publisher who charges the author for the cost of typesetting, printing, and promoting a book. Also called a *vanity publisher*.

SUBTERFICIAL FICTION. Innovative, challenging, nonconventional fiction in which what seems to be happening is the result of things not so easily perceived.

SUSPENSE. A genre of fiction where the plot's primary function is to build a feeling of anticipation and fear in the reader over its possible outcome.

SYNOPSIS. A brief summary of a story, novel or play. As part of a book proposal, it is a comprehensive summary condensed in a page or page and a half.

TABLOID. Publication printed on paper about half the size of a regular newspaper page (e.g. the *National Enquirer*).

TEARSHEET. Page from a magazine containing a published story.

THEME. The dominant or central idea in a literary work; its message, moral, or main thread.

THRILLER. A novel intended to arouse feelings of excitement or suspense. Works in this genre are highly sensational, usually focusing on illegal activities, international espionage, sex, and violence. A thriller is often a detective story in which the forces of good are pitted against the forces of evil in a kill-or-be-killed situation.

TRADE PAPERBACK. A softbound volume, usually around 5" × 8", published and designed for the general public, available mainly in bookstores.

UNSOLICITED MANUSCRIPT. A story or novel manuscript that an editor did not specifically ask to see.

URBAN FANTASY. Fantasy that takes magical characters, such as elves, fairies, vampires, or wizards, and places them in modern-day settings, often in the inner city.

VANITY PUBLISHER. See subsidy publisher.

VIEWPOINT. The position or attitude of the first- or third-person narrator or multiple narrators, which determines how a story's action is seen and evaluated.

WESTERN. Genre with a setting in the West, usually between 1860 and 1890, with a formula plot about cowboys or other aspects of frontier life.

WHODUNIT. Genre dealing with murder, suspense, and the detection of criminals.

WORK-FOR-HIRE. Work that another party commissions you to do, generally for a flat fee. The creator does not own the copyright and therefore cannot sell any rights.

YOUNG ADULT (YA). The general classification of books written for readers twelve and up.

ZINE. A small, noncommercial magazine, often one- or two-person operations run from the home of the publisher/editor. Themes tend to be specialized, personal, experimental, and often controversial.

GENRE GLOSSARY

Definitions of Fiction Subcategories

The following were provided courtesy of The Extended Novel Writing Workshop, created by the staff of Writers Online Workshops (www.writersonlineworkshops.com).

MYSTERY SUBCATEGORIES

The major mystery subcategories are listed below, each followed by a brief description and the names of representative authors, so you can sample each type of work. Note that we have loosely classified "suspense/thriller" as a mystery category. While these stories do not necessarily follow a traditional "whodunit" plot pattern, they share many elements with other mystery categories.

AMATEUR DETECTIVE. As the name implies, the detective is not a professional detective (private or otherwise), but is almost always a professional something. This professional association routinely involves the protagonist in criminal cases (in a support capacity), gives him or her a special advantage in a specific case, or provides the contacts and skills necessary to solve a particular crime.

(Jonathan Kellerman, Patricia Cornwell, Jan Burke)

CLASSIC MYSTERY (WHODUNIT). A crime (almost always a murder) is solved. The detective is the viewpoint character; the reader never knows any more or less about the crime than the detective, and all the clues to solving the crime are available to the reader.

COURTROOM DRAMA. The action takes place primarily in the courtroom; protagonist is generally a defense attorney out to prove the innocence of his or her client by finding the real culprit.

COZY. A special class of the amateur detective category that frequently features a female protagonist. (Agatha Christie's Miss Marple stories are the classic example.) There is less onstage violence than in other categories, and the plot is often wrapped up in a final scene where the detective identifies the murderer and explains how the crime was solved. In contemporary stories, the protagonist can be anyone from a chronically curious housewife to a mystery-buff clergyman to a college professor, but he or she is usually quirky, even eccentric. (Susan Isaacs, Andrew Greeley, Lillian Jackson Braun)

ESPIONAGE. The international spy novel is less popular since the end of the Cold War, but stories can still revolve around political intrigue in unstable regions. (John le Carré, Ken Follett)

HEISTS AND CAPERS. The crime itself is the focus. Its planning and execution are seen in detail, and the participants are fully drawn characters that may even be portrayed sympathetically. One character is the obvious leader of the group (the "brains"); the other members are often brought together by the leader specifically for this job and may or may not have a previous association. In a heist, no matter how clever or daring the characters are, they are still portrayed as criminals, and the expectation is that they will be caught and punished (but not always). A caper is more lighthearted, even comedic. The participants may have a noble goal (something other than personal gain) and often get away with the crime. (Eric Ambler, Tony Kenrick, Leslie Hollander)

HISTORICAL. May be any category or subcategory of mystery, but with an emphasis on setting, the details of which must be diligently researched. But beyond the historical details (which must never overshadow the story), the plot develops along the lines of its contemporary counterpart. (Candace Robb, Caleb Carr, Anne Perry)

JUVENILE/YOUNG ADULT. Written for the 8–12 age group (middle grade) or the 12 and up age group (young adult), the crime in these stories may or may not be murder, but it is serious. The protagonist is a kid (or group of kids) in the same age range as the targeted reader. There is no graphic violence depicted, but the stories are scary and the villains are realistic. (Mary Downing Hahn, Wendy Corsi Staub, Cameron Dokey, Norma Fox Mazer)

MEDICAL THRILLER. The plot can involve a legitimate medical threat (such as the outbreak of a virulent plague) or the illegal or immoral use of medical technology. In the former scenario, the protagonist is likely to be the doctor (or team) who identifies the virus and procures the antidote; in the latter he or she could be a patient (or the relative of a victim) who uncovers the plot and brings down the villain. (Robin Cook, Michael Palmer, Michael Crichton, Stanley Pottinger)

POLICE PROCEDURALS. The most realistic category, these stories require the most meticulous research. A police procedural may have more than one protagonist since cops rarely work alone. Conflict between partners, or between the detective and his or her superiors, is a common theme. But cops are portrayed positively as a group, even though there may be a couple of bad or ineffective law enforcement characters for contrast and conflict. Jurisdictional disputes are still popular sources of conflict as well. (Lawrence Treat, Joseph Wambaugh, Ridley Pearson, Julie Smith)

PRIVATE DETECTIVE. When described as "hard-boiled," this category takes a tough stance. Violence is more prominent, characters are darker, the detective—while almost always licensed by the state—operates on the fringes of the law, and there is often open resentment between the detective and law enforcement. More "enlightened" male detectives and a crop of contemporary females have brought about new trends in this category. (For female P.I.s: Sue Grafton, Sara Paretsky; for male P.I.s: John D. MacDonald, Lawrence Sanders)

SUSPENSE/THRILLER. Where a classic mystery is always a whodunit, a suspense/thriller novel may deal more with the intricacies of the crime, what motivated it, and how the villain (whose identity may be revealed to the reader early on) is caught and brought to justice. Novels in this category frequently employ multiple points of view and have broader scopes than more traditional murder mysteries. The crime may not even involve murder—it may be a threat to global economy or regional ecology; it may be technology run amok or abused at the hands of an unscrupulous scientist; it may involve innocent citizens victimized for personal or corporate gain. Its perpetrators are kidnappers, stalkers, serial killers, rapists, pedophiles, computer hackers, or just about anyone with an evil intention and the means to carry it out. The protagonist may be a private detective or law enforcement official, but is just as likely to be a doctor, lawyer, military officer, or other individual in a unique position to identify the villain and bring him or her to justice. (James Patterson, John J. Nance)

TECHNO-THRILLER. These are replacing the traditional espionage novel and feature technology as an integral part of not just the setting but the plot as well.

WOMAN IN JEOPARDY. A murder or other crime may be committed, but the focus is on the woman (and/or her children) currently at risk, her struggle to understand the nature of the danger, and her eventual victory over her tormentor. The protagonist makes up for her lack of physical prowess with intellect or special skills and solves the problem on her own or with the help of her family (but she runs the show). Closely related to this category is romantic suspense. But, while the heroine in a romantic suspense is certainly a "woman in jeopardy,'" the mystery or suspense element is subordinate to the romance. (Mary Higgins Clark, Mary Stewart, Jessica Mann)

ROMANCE SUBCATEGORIES

These categories and subcategories of romance fiction have been culled from the *Romance Writer's Sourcebook* (Writer's Digest Books) and Phyllis Taylor Pianka's *How to Write Romances* (Writer's Digest Books). We've arranged the "major" categories below, with the subcategories beneath them, each followed by a brief description and the names of authors who write in each category, so you can sample representative works.

CATEGORY OR SERIES. These are published in "lines" by individual publishing houses (such as Harlequin); each line has its own requirements as to word length, story content, and amount of sex. (Debbie Macomber, Nora Roberts, Glenda Sanders)

CHRISTIAN. With an inspirational Christian message centering on the spiritual dynamic of the romantic relationship and faith in God as the foundation for that relationship; sensuality is played down. (Janelle Burnham, Ann Bell, Linda Chaikin, Catherine Palmer, Dee Henderson, Lisa Tawn Bergen)

GLITZ. So called because they feature generally wealthy characters with high-powered positions in careers that are considered glamorous—high finance, modeling/acting, publishing, fashion—and are set in exciting or exotic (often metropolitan) locales, such as Monte Carlo, Hollywood, London, or New York. (Jackie Collins, Judith Krantz)

HISTORICAL. Can cover just about any historical (or even prehistorical) period. Setting in the historical is especially significant, and details must be thoroughly researched and accurately presented. For a sampling of a variety of historical styles, try Laura Kinsell (*Flowers from the Storm*), Mary Jo Putney (*The Rake and the Reformer*), and Judy Cuevas (*Bliss*). Some currently popular periods/themes in historicals are:

- **GOTHIC:** Historical with a strong element of suspense and a feeling of supernatural events, although these events frequently have a natural explanation. Setting plays an important role in establishing a dark, moody, suspenseful atmosphere. (Phyllis Whitney, Victoria Holt)
- **HISTORICAL FANTASY:** With traditional fantasy elements of magic and magical beings, frequently set in a medieval society. (Amanda Glass, Jayne Ann Krentz, Kathleen Morgan, Jessica Bryan, Taylor Quinn Evans, Carla Simpson, Karyn Monk)
- **EARLY AMERICAN:** Usually Revolution to Civil War, set in New England or the South, but "frontier" stories set in the American West are quite popular as well. (Robin Lee Hatcher, Ann Maxwell, Heather Graham)
- **NATIVE AMERICAN:** Where one or both of the characters are Native Americans; the conflict between cultures is a popular theme. (Carol Finch, Elizabeth Grayson, Karen Kay, Kathleen Harrington, Genell Dellim, Candace McCarthy)
- **REGENCY:** Set in England during the Regency period from 1811 to 1820. (Carol Finch, Elizabeth Elliott, Georgette Heyer, Joan Johnston, Lynn Collum)

MULTICULTURAL. Most currently feature African-American or Hispanic couples, but editors are looking for other ethnic stories as well. Multiculturals can be contemporary or historical and fall into any subcategory. (Rochelle Alers, Monica Jackson, Bette Ford, Sandra Kitt, Brenda Jackson)

PARANORMAL. Containing elements of the supernatural or science fiction/fantasy. There are numerous subcategories (many stories combine elements of more than one) including:

- **TIME TRAVEL:** One or more of the characters travels to another time—usually the past—to find love. (Jude Deveraux, Linda Lael Miller, Diana Gabaldon, Constance O'Day-Flannery)
- **SCIENCE FICTION/FUTURISTIC:** S/F elements are used for the story's setting: imaginary worlds, parallel universes, Earth in the near or distant future. (Marilyn Campbell, Jayne Ann Krentz, J.D. Robb [Nora Roberts], Anne Avery)
- **CONTEMPORARY FANTASY:** From modern ghost and vampire stories to "New Age" themes such as extraterrestrials and reincarnation. (Linda Lael Miller, Anne Stuart, Antoinette Stockenberg, Christine Feehan)

ROMANTIC COMEDY. Has a fairly strong comic premise and/or a comic perspective in the author's voice or the voices of the characters (especially the heroine). (Jennifer Crusie, Susan Elizabeth Phillips)

ROMANTIC SUSPENSE. With a mystery or psychological thriller subplot in addition to the romance plot. (Mary Stewart, Barbara Michaels, Tami Hoag, Nora Roberts, Linda Howard, Catherine Coulter)

SINGLE TITLE. Longer contemporaries that do not necessarily conform to the requirements of a specific romance line and therefore feature more complex plots and nontraditional characters. (Mary Ruth Myers, Nora Roberts, Kathleen Gilles Seidel, Kathleen Korbel)

YOUNG ADULT (YA). Focus is on first love with very little, if any, sex. These can have bittersweet endings, as opposed to the traditional romance happy ending, since first loves are often lost loves. (YA historical: Nancy Covert Smith, Louise Vernon; YA contemporary: Kathryn Makris)

SCIENCE FICTION SUBCATEGORIES

Peter Heck, in his article "Doors to Other Worlds: Trends in Science Fiction and Fantasy," which appears in the 1996 edition of *Science Fiction and Fantasy Writer's Sourcebook* (Writer's Digest Books), identifies some science fiction trends that have distinct enough characteristics to be defined as categories. These distinctions are frequently the result of marketing decisions as much as literary ones, so understanding them is important in deciding where your novel idea belongs. We've supplied a brief description and the names of authors who write in each category. In those instances where the author writes in more than one category, we've included titles of appropriate representative works.

ALTERNATE HISTORY. Fantasy, sometimes with science fiction elements, that changes the accepted account of actual historical events or people to suggest an alternate view of history. (Ted Mooney, *Traffic and Laughter*; Ward Moore, *Bring the Jubilee*; Philip K. Dick, *The Man in the High Castle*)

CYBERPUNK. Characters in these stories are tough outsiders in a high-tech, generally near-future society where computers have produced major changes in the way society functions. (William Gibson, Bruce Sterling, Pat Cadigan, Wilhelmina Baird)

HARD SCIENCE FICTION. Based on the logical extrapolation of real science to the future. In these stories the scientific background (setting) may be as, or more, important than the characters. (Larry Niven)

MILITARY SCIENCE FICTION. Stories about war that feature traditional military organization and tactics extrapolated into the future. (Jerry Pournelle, David Drake, Elizabeth Moon)

NEW AGE. A category of speculative fiction that deals with subjects such as astrology, psychic phenomena, spiritual healing, UFOs, mysticism, and other aspects of the occult. (Walter Mosley, *Blue Light*; Neil Gaiman)

SCIENCE FANTASY. Blend of traditional fantasy elements with scientific or pseudo-scientific support (genetic engineering, for example, to "explain" a traditional fantasy creature like the dragon). These stories are traditionally more character driven than hard science fiction. (Anne McCaffrey, Mercedes Lackey, Marion Zimmer Bradley)

SCIENCE FICTION MYSTERY. A cross-genre blending that can either be a more-or-less traditional science fiction story with a mystery as a key plot element, or a more-or-less traditional whodunit with science fiction elements. (Philip K. Dick, Lynn S. Hightower)

SCIENCE FICTION ROMANCE. Another genre blend that may be a romance with science fic-

tion elements (in which case it is more accurately placed as a subcategory within the romance genre) or a science fiction story with a strong romantic subplot. (Anne McCaffrey, Melanie Rawn, Kate Elliott)

SOCIAL SCIENCE FICTION. The focus is on how the characters react to their environments. This category includes social satire. (George Orwell's *1984* is a classic example.) (Margaret Atwood, *The Handmaid's Tale*; Ursula K. Le Guin, *The Left Hand of Darkness*; Marge Piercy, *Woman on the Edge of Time*)

SPACE OPERA. From the term "horse opera," describing a traditional good-guys-versus-bad-guys western, these stories put the emphasis on sweeping action and larger-than-life characters. The focus on action makes these stories especially appealing for film treatment. (The Star Wars series is one of the best examples; also Samuel R. Delany.)

STEAMPUNK. A specific type of alternate-history science fiction set in Victorian England in which characters have access to 20th-century technology. (William Gibson; Bruce Sterling, *The Difference Engine*)

YOUNG ADULT. Any subcategory of science fiction geared to a YA audience (12–18), but these are usually shorter novels with characters in the central roles who are the same age as (or slightly older than) the targeted reader. (Jane Yolen, Andre Norton)

FANTASY SUBCATEGORIES

Before we take a look at the individual fantasy categories, it should be noted that, for purposes of these supplements, we've treated fantasy as a genre distinct from science fiction. While these two are closely related, there are significant enough differences to warrant their separation for study purposes. We have included here those science fiction categories that have strong fantasy elements, or that have a significant amount of crossover (these categories appear in both the science fiction and the fantasy supplements), but "pure" science fiction categories are not included below. If you're not sure whether your novel is fantasy or science fiction, consider this definition by Orson Scott Card in *How to Write Science Fiction and Fantasy* (Writer's Digest Books): "Here's a good, simple, semi-accurate rule of thumb: If the story is set in a universe that follows the same rules as ours, it's science fiction. If it's set in a universe that doesn't follow our rules, it's fantasy. Or in other words, science fiction is about what could be but isn't; fantasy is about what couldn't be."

But even Card admits this rule is only "semi-accurate." He goes on to say that the real boundary between science fiction and fantasy is defined by how the impossible is achieved: "If you have people do some magic, impossible thing [like time travel] by stroking a talisman or praying to a tree, it's fantasy; if they do the same thing by pressing a button or climbing inside a machine, it's science fiction."

Peter Heck, in his article "Doors to Other Worlds: Trends in Science Fiction and Fantasy," which appears in the 1996 edition of the *Science Fiction and Fantasy Writer's Sourcebook* (Writer's Digest Books),

does note some trends that have distinct enough characteristics to be defined as separate categories. These categories are frequently the result of marketing decisions as much as literary ones, so understanding them is important in deciding where your novel idea belongs. We've supplied a brief description and the names of authors who write in each category, so you can sample representative works.

ARTHURIAN. Reworking of the legend of King Arthur and the Knights of the Round Table. (T.H. White, *The Once and Future King*; Marion Zimmer Bradley, *The Mists of Avalon*)

CONTEMPORARY (ALSO CALLED "URBAN") FANTASY. Traditional fantasy elements (such as elves and magic) are incorporated into an otherwise recognizable modern setting. (Emma Bull, *War for the Oaks*; Mercedes Lackey, *The SERRAted Edge*; Terry Brooks, the Word & Void series)

DARK FANTASY. Closely related to horror but generally not as graphic. Characters in these stories are the "darker" fantasy types: vampires, witches, werewolves, demons, etc. (Anne Rice; Clive Barker, *Weaveworld*, *Imajica*; Fred Chappell)

FANTASTIC ALTERNATE HISTORY. Set in an alternate historical period (in which magic would not have been a common belief) where magic works, these stories frequently feature actual historical figures. (Orson Scott Card, *Alvin Maker*)

GAME-RELATED FANTASY. Plots and characters are similar to high fantasy, but are based on a particular role-playing game. (Dungeons and Dragons; Magic: The Gathering; World of Warcraft)

HEROIC FANTASY. The fantasy equivalent to military science fiction, these are stories of war and its heroes and heroines. (Robert E. Howard, the Conan the Barbarian series; Elizabeth Moon, *Deed of Paksenarrion*; Michael Moorcock, the Elric series)

HIGH FANTASY. Emphasis is on the fate of an entire race or nation, threatened by an ultimate evil. J.R.R. Tolkien's Lord of the Rings trilogy is a classic example. (Terry Brooks, David Eddings, Margaret Weis, Tracy Hickman)

HISTORICAL FANTASY. The setting can be almost any era in which the belief in magic was strong; these are essentially historical novels where magic is a key element of the plot and/or setting. (Susan Schwartz, *Silk Roads and Shadows*; Margaret Ball, *No Earthly Sunne*; Tim Powers, *The Anubis Gates*)

JUVENILE/YOUNG ADULT. Can be any type of fantasy, but geared to a juvenile (8–12) or YA audience (12–18); these are shorter novels with younger characters in central roles. (J.K. Rowling, Christopher Paolini, C.S. Lewis)

SCIENCE FANTASY. A blend of traditional fantasy elements with scientific or pseudo-scientific support (genetic engineering, for example, to "explain" a traditional fantasy creature like the dragon). These stories are traditionally more character driven than

hard science fiction. (Anne McCaffrey, Mercedes Lackey, Marion Zimmer Bradley)

HORROR SUBCATEGORIES

Subcategories in horror are less well defined than in other genres and are frequently the result of marketing decisions as much as literary ones. But being familiar with the terms used to describe different horror styles can be important in understanding how your own novel might be best presented to an agent or editor. What follows is a brief description of the most commonly used terms, along with names of authors and, where necessary, representative works.

DARK FANTASY. Sometimes used as a euphemistic term for horror in general, but also refers to a specific type of fantasy, usually less graphic than other horror subcategories, that features more "traditional" supernatural or mythical beings (vampires, werewolves, zombies, etc.) in either contemporary or historical settings. (Contemporary: Stephen King, *Salem's Lot*; Thomas Tessier, *The Nightwalker*. Historical: Brian Stableford, *The Empire of Fear* and *Werewolves of London*)

HAUNTINGS. "Classic" stories of ghosts, poltergeists, and spiritual possessions. The level of violence portrayed varies, but many writers in this category exploit the reader's natural fear of the unknown by hinting at the horror and letting the reader's imagination supply the details. (Peter Straub, *Ghost Story*; Richard Matheson, *Hell House*)

JUVENILE/YOUNG ADULT. Can be any horror style, but with a protagonist who is the same age as, or slightly older than, the targeted reader. Stories for middle grades (8–12 years old) are scary, with monsters and violent acts that might best be described as "gross," but stories for young adults (12–18) may be more graphic. (R.L. Stine, Christopher Pike, Carol Gorman)

PSYCHOLOGICAL HORROR. Features a human monster with horrific, but not necessarily supernatural, aspects. (Thomas Harris, *The Silence of the Lambs*, *Hannibal*; Dean Koontz, *Whispers*)

SPLATTERPUNK. Very graphic depiction of violence—often gratuitous—popularized in the 1980s, especially in film. (*Friday the 13th*, *Halloween*, *Nightmare on Elm Street*, etc.)

SUPERNATURAL/OCCULT. Similar to the dark fantasy, but may be more graphic in its depiction of violence. Stories feature satanic worship, demonic possession, or ultimate evil incarnate in an entity or supernatural being that may or may not have its roots in traditional mythology or folklore. (Ramsey Campbell; Robert McCammon; Ira Levin, *Rosemary's Baby*; William Peter Blatty, *The Exorcist*; Stephen King, *Pet Sematary*)

TECHNOLOGICAL HORROR. "Monsters" in these stories are the result of science run amok or technology turned to purposes of evil. (Dean Koontz, *Watchers*; Michael Crichton, *Jurassic Park*)

PROFESSIONAL ORGANIZATIONS

AGENTS' ORGANIZATIONS

ASSOCIATION OF AUTHORS' AGENTS (AAA) Johnson & Alcock Ltd. Clerkenwell House, 45-47 Clerkenwell Green, London EC1R0HT. (020)7251-0125. E-mail: ed@johnsonandalcock.co.uk. Website: www.agentsassoc.co.uk.

ASSOCIATION OF AUTHORS' REPRESENTATIVES (AAR) 676-A Ninth Ave., Suite 312, New York, NY 10036. E-mail: administrator@aaronline.org. Website: www.aar-online.org.

ASSOCIATION OF TALENT AGENTS (ATA) 9255 Sunset Blvd., Suite 930, Los Angeles, CA 90069. (310)274-0628. Fax: (310)274-5063. E-mail: rnoval@agentassociation.com. Website: www.agentassociation.com.

WRITERS' ORGANIZATIONS

ACADEMY OF AMERICAN POETS 75 Maiden Lane, Suite 901, New York, NY 10038. (212)274-0343. Fax: (212)274-9427. E-mail: academy@poets.org. Website: www.poets.org.

AMERICAN CRIME WRITERS LEAGUE (ACWL) 17367 Hilltop Ridge Dr., Eureka, MO 63205. **Email:** shirley@shirleykennett.com. Website: www.acwl.org.

AMERICAN MEDICAL WRITERS ASSOCIATION (AMWA) 30 W. Gude Drive, Suite 525, Rockville, MD 20850-4347. (240)238-0940. Fax: (301)294-9006. E-mail: amwa@amwa.org. Website: www.amwa.org.

AMERICAN SCREENWRITERS ASSOCIATION (ASA) E-mail: info@americanscreenwriters.com. Website: www.americanscreenwriters.com.

AMERICAN TRANSLATORS ASSOCIATION (ATA) 225 Reinekers Lane, Suite 590, Alexandria, VA 22314. (703)683-6100. Fax: (703)683-6122. E-mail: ata@atanet.org. Website: www.atanet.org.

EDUCATION WRITERS ASSOCIATION (EWA) 3516 Connecticut Avenue NW, Washington, DC 20008. (202)452-9830. Fax: (202)452-9837. E-mail: ewa@ewa.org. Website: www.ewa.org.

GARDEN WRITERS ASSOCIATION (GWA)
7809 FM 179, Shallowater, TX 79363.
(806)832.1870. Fax: (806)832.5244. E-mail:
info@gardenwriters.org. Website: www.gar
denwriters.org.

HORROR WRITERS ASSOCIATION (HWA) 244
Fifth Ave., Suite 2767, New York, NY 10001.
(917)720-6959. E-mail: hwa@horror.org.
Website: www.horror.org.

**THE INTERNATIONAL WOMEN'S WRITING
GUILD (IWWG)** 317 Madison Avenue, Suite
1704, New York, NY 10017. Website: www.
iwwg.com.

MYSTERY WRITERS OF AMERICA (MWA) 1140
Broadway, Suite 1507, New York, NY 10001.
(212)888-8171. Fax: (212)888-8107. E-mail:
mwa@mysterywriters.org. Website: www
.mysterywriters.org.

**NATIONAL ASSOCIATION OF SCIENCE WRIT-
ERS (NASW)** P.O. Box 7905, Berkeley, CA
94707. (510)647-9500. E-mail: editor@nasw
.org. Website: www.nasw.org.

**ORGANIZATION OF BLACK SCREENWRIT-
ERS (OBS)** 3010 Wilshire Blvd., #269, Los
Angeles, CA 90010. (323)735-2050. Web-
site: www.obswriter.com.

**OUTDOOR WRITERS ASSOCIATION OF
AMERICA (OWAA)** 615 Oak St., Ste. 201, Missoula, MT 59801. (406)728-7434. E-mail:
info@owaa.org. Website: www.owaa.org.

POETRY SOCIETY OF AMERICA (PSA) 15
Gramercy Park, New York, NY 10003.
(212)254-9628. Fax: (212)673-2352. Website: www.poetrysociety.org.

POETS & WRITERS 90 Broad St., Suite 2100,
New York, NY 10004. (212)226-3586. Fax:
(212)226-3963. Website: www.pw.org.

ROMANCE WRITERS OF AMERICA (RWA)
14615 Benfer Road, Houston, TX 77069.
(832)717-5200. E-mail: info@rwa.org. Website: www.rwa.org.

**SCIENCE FICTION AND FANTASY WRITERS
OF AMERICA (SFWA)** P.O. Box 3238, Enfield,
CT 06083-3238. Website: www.sfwa.org.

**SOCIETY OF AMERICAN BUSINESS EDITORS
& WRITERS (SABEW)** Walter Cronkite School
of Journalism and Mass Communication,
Arizona State University, 555 N. Central Ave.,
Suite 416, Phoenix, AZ 85004-1248 (602)
496-7862. Fax: (602)496-7041. E-mail: sa
bew@sabew.org. Website: www.sabew.org.

**SOCIETY OF AMERICAN TRAVEL WRITERS
(SATW)** 11950 W. Lake Park Drive, Suite 320,
Milwaukee, WI 53224-3049. (414)359-1625.
Fax: (414)359-1671. E-mail: info@satw.org.
Website: www.satw.org.

**SOCIETY OF CHILDREN'S BOOK WRITERS &
ILLUSTRATORS (SCBWI)** 8271 Beverly Blvd.,
Los Angeles, CA 90048. (323)782-1010. Fax:
(323)782-1892. E-mail: scbwi@scbwi.org.
Website: www.scbwi.org.

WESTERN WRITERS OF AMERICA (WWA) E-
mail: wwa.moulton@gmail.com. Website:
www.westernwriters.org.

INDUSTRY ORGANIZATIONS

**AMERICAN BOOKSELLERS ASSOCIATION
(ABA)** 333 Westchester Avenue, Suite S202,
White Plains, NY 10604. (914)406-7500.

Fax: (914)417-4013. E-mail: info@bookweb. org. Website: www.bookweb.org.

AMERICAN SOCIETY OF JOURNALISTS & AUTHORS (ASJA) Times Square, 1501 Broadway, Suite 403, New York, NY 10036. (212)997-0947. Website: www.asja.org.

ASSOCIATION FOR WOMEN IN COMMUNI- CATIONS (AWC) 3337 Duke St., Alexandria VA 22314. (703)370-7436. Fax: (703)342- 4311. E-mail: info@womcom.org. Website: www.womcom.org.

ASSOCIATION OF AMERICAN PUBLISHERS (AAP) 71 Fifth Ave., 2nd Floor, New York NY 10003. (212)255-0200. Fax: (212)255- 7007. Or: 455 Massachusetts Ave. NW, Suite 700, Washington, DC 20001. (202)347-3375. Fax: (202)347-3690. Website: www.publish- ers.org.

THE ASSOCIATION OF WRITERS & WRITING PROGRAMS (AWP) George Mason Universi- ty, 4400 University Drive, MSN 1E3, Fairfax, VA 22030. (703)993-4301. Fax: (703)993- 4302. E-mail: awp@awpwriter.org. Web- site: www.awpwriter.org.

THE AUTHORS GUILD, INC., 31 E. Thirty- second St., 7th Floor, New York, NY 10016. (212)563-5904. Fax: (212)564-5363. E-mail: staff@authorsguild.org. Website: www .authorsguild.org.

CANADIAN AUTHORS ASSOCIATION (CAA) 6 W St. N, Suite 203, Orilla, ON L3V 5B8 Canada. (705)325-3926. E-mail: admin@ canadianauthors.org. Website: www.cana dianauthors.org.

CHRISTIAN BOOKSELLERS ASSOCIATION (CBA) 9240 Explorer Drive, Suite 200, Col-

orado Springs, CO 80920. (800)252-1950. Fax: (719)272-3508. E-mail: info@cbaon- line.org. Website: www.cbaonline.org.

THE DRAMATISTS GUILD OF AMERICA 1501 Broadway, Suite 701, New York, NY 10036. (212)398-9366. Fax: (212)944-0420. Web- site: www.dramatistsguild.com.

NATIONAL LEAGUE OF AMERICAN PEN WOMEN (NLAPW) Pen Arts Building, 1300 17th St. NW, Washington DC 20036-1973. (202)785-1997. Fax: (202)452-8868. E-mail: contact@nlapw.org. Website: www.nlapw.org.

NATIONAL WRITERS ASSOCIATION (NWA) 10940 S. Parker Rd., #508, Parker, CO 80134. (303)841-0246. E-mail: natlwritersassn@ho tmail.com. Website: www.nationalwriters. com

NATIONAL WRITERS UNION (NWU) 256 W. Thirty-eigth St., Suite 703, New York, NY 10018. (212)254-0279. Fax: (212)254-0673. E-mail: nwu@nwu.org. Website: www.nwu. org.

PEN AMERICAN CENTER 588 Broad- way, Suite 303, New York, NY 10012-3225. (212)334-1660. Fax: (212)334-2181. E-mail: info@pen.org. Website: www.pen.org.

THE PLAYWRIGHTS GUILD OF CANADA (PGC) 401 Richmond Street W., Suite 350, Toronto, Ontario M5V 3A8 Canada. (416)703-0201. Fax: (416)703-0059. E-mail: info@play- wrightsguild.ca. Website: http://www.play wrightsguild.ca.

VOLUNTEER LAWYERS FOR THE ARTS (VLA) 1 E. Fifty-third St., Sixth Floor, New York, NY 10022. (212)319-2787, ext.1. Fax:

(212)752-6575. E-mail: vlany@vlany.org. Website: www.vlany.org.

WOMEN IN FILM (WIF) 6100 Wilshire Blvd., Suite 710, Los Angeles, CA 90048. (323)935-2211. Fax: (323)935-2212. E-mail: info@wif.org. Website: www.wif.org.

WOMEN'S NATIONAL BOOK ASSOCIATION (WNBA) P.O. Box 237, FDR Station, New York NY 10150. (212)208-4629. Fax: (212)208-4629. E-mail: info@wnba-books.org. Website: www.wnba-books.org.

WRITERS GUILD OF ALBERTA (WGA) Percy Page Centre, 11759 Groat Rd., Edmonton AB T5M 3K6 Canada. (780)422-8174. Fax: (780)422-2663 (attn: WGA). E-mail: mail@writersguild.ab.ca. Website: writersguild.ab.ca.

WRITERS GUILD OF AMERICA-EAST (WGA) 250 Hudson Street, Suite 700, New York, NY 10013. (212)767-7800. Fax: (212)582-1909. E-mail: gbynoe@wgaeast.org. Website: www.wgaeast.org.

WRITERS GUILD OF AMERICA-WEST (WGA) 7000 W. Third St., Los Angeles CA 90048. (323)951-4000. Fax: (323)782-4800. Website: www.wga.org.

WRITERS UNION OF CANADA (TWUC) 600-400 Richmond St. W., Toronto, ON M5V 1Y1 Canada. (416)703-8982. Fax: (416)504-9090. E-mail: info@writersunion.ca. Website: www.writersunion.ca.

LITERARY AGENTS SPECIALTIES INDEX

CATEGORY INDEX

GENERAL INDEX